D1614058

ENCYCLOPEDIA OF
Espionage, Intelligence, and Security

ENCYCLOPEDIA OF
Espionage, Intelligence, and Security

K. LEE LERNER AND BRENDA WILMOTH LERNER, EDITORS

volume
| 2 |
F–Q

GALE®

THOMSON

GALE

Detroit • New York • San Diego • San Francisco • Cleveland • New Haven, Conn. • Waterville, Maine • London • Munich

Encyclopedia of Espionage, Intelligence, and Security

K. Lee Lerner and Brenda Wilmoth Lerner, editors

Project Editor
Stephen Cusack

Editorial
Erin Bealmear, Joann Cerrito, Jim Craddock, Miranda Ferrara, Kristin Hart, Melissa Hill, Carol Schwartz, Christine Tomassini, Michael J. Tyrkus, Peter Gareffa

Permissions
Lori Hines

Imaging and Multimedia
Dean Dauphinais, Leitha Etheridge-Sims, Mary K. Grimes, Lezlie Light, Luke Rademacher

Product Design
Kate Scheible

Manufacturing
Rhonda Williams

Cover Photos

Volume 1: Ethel and Julius Rosenberg following arraignment on charges of espionage, August 23, 1950. ©Bettmann/Corbis

Volume 2: SR-71 Blackbird, c. 1991. ©Corbis

Volume 3: Clean-up crews scour the American Media Inc. building in Boca Raton, Florida, after the discovery of anthrax spores, October 9, 2001. AP/Wide World Photos.

While every effort has been made to ensure the reliability of the information presented in this publication, The Gale Group, Inc. does not guarantee the accuracy of the data contained herein. The Gale Group, Inc. accepts no payment for listing; and inclusion in the publication of any organization, agency, institution, publication, service, or individual does not imply endorsement of the editors or publisher. Errors brought to the attention of the publisher and verified to the satisfaction of the publisher will be corrected in future editions.

Library of Congress Cataloging-in-Publication Data

Encyclopedia of espionage, intelligence, and security / K. Lee Lerner and Brenda Wilmoth Lerner, editors.
    p. cm.
Includes bibliographical references and index.
    ISBN 0-7876-7546-6 (set : hardcover : alk. paper) — ISBN 0-7876-7686-1 (v. 1) — ISBN 0-7876-7687-X (v. 2) — ISBN 0-7876-7688-8 (v. 3)
    1. Espionage—Encyclopedias. 2. Intelligence service—Encyclopedias. 3. Security systems—Encyclopedias. I. Lerner, K. Lee. II. Lerner, Brenda Wilmoth.
JF1525.I6E63 2004
327.12'03—dc21

2003011097

This title is available as an e-book.
ISBN 0-7876-7762-0

Contact your Gale sales representative for ordering information.

Printed in the United States of America
10 9 8 7 6 5 4 3 2 1

Contents

INTRODUCTION ~~~~~~~~~~~~~~~~~~~~~~~~~~~~~~~~~~~~ VII

ADVISORS AND CONTRIBUTORS ~~~~~~~~~~~~~~~~~~~~~~~ XI

LIST OF ENTRIES ~~~~~~~~~~~~~~~~~~~~~~~~~~~~~~~~~ XIII

The Encyclopedia of Espionage,
Intelligence, and Security ~~~~~~~~~~~~~~~~~~~~~~ 1

GLOSSARY ~~~~~~ 289

CHRONOLOGY ~~~~~~~~~~~~~~~~~~~~~~~~~~~~~~~~~~~~~~ 317

SOURCES ~~~~~~ 353

INDEX ~~~~~~ 403

▌▐▐▌▌ Introduction ▌▐▐▌▌

In composing *The Encyclopedia of Espionage, Intelligence, and Security (EEIS)*, our goal was to shape a modern encyclopedia offering immediate value to our intended readers by emphasizing matters of espionage, intelligence, and security most frequently in the news.

EEIS is not intended as a classical "spy book," filled with tales of daring operations. Instead, within a framework of historical overviews, *EEIS* emphasizes the scientific foundations, applications of technology, and organizational structure of modern espionage, intelligence, and security. High school and early undergraduate students can use this book to expand upon their developing awareness of the fundamentals of science, mathematics, and government as they begin the serious study of contemporary issues.

EEIS is also intended to serve more advanced readers as a valuable quick reference and as a foundation for advanced study of current events.

EEIS devotes an extensive number of articles to agencies and strategies involved in emerging concepts of homeland security in the United States. Faced with a daunting amount of information provided by agencies, organizations, and institutes seeking to put their best foot forward, we have attempted to allocate space to the topics comprising *EEIS* based upon their relevance to some unique facet of espionage, intelligence, or security—especially with regard to science and technology issues—as opposed to awarding space related to power of the agency or availability of material.

A fundamental understanding of science allows citizens to discern hype and disregard hysteria, especially with regard to privacy issues. Spy satellites powerful enough to read the details of license plates do so at peril of missing events a few steps away. With regard to electronic intercepts, the capability to identify what to carefully examine—often a decision driven by mathematical analysis—has become as essential as the capacity to gather the intelligence itself. Somewhere between the scrutiny of

Big Brother and the deliberately blind eye lie the shadows into which terrorists often slip.

With an emphasis on the realistic possibilities and limitations of science, we hope that *EEIS* finds a useful and unique place on the reference shelf.

It seems inevitable that within the first half of the twenty-first century, biological weapons may eclipse nuclear and chemical weapons in terms of potential threats to civilization. Because informed and reasoned public policy debates on issues of biological warfare and bioterrorism can only take place when there is a fundamental understanding of the science underpinning competing arguments, *EEIS* places special emphasis on the multifaceted influence and applications of the biological sciences and emerging biometric technologies. Future generations of effective intelligence and law enforcement officers seeking to thwart the threats posed by tyrants, terrorists, and the technologies of mass destruction might be required to be as knowledgeable in the terminology of epidemiology as they are with the tradecraft of espionage.

Knowledge is power. In a time where news can overwhelm and in fact, too easily mingle with opinion, it is our hope that *EEIS* will provide readers with greater insight to measure vulnerability and risks, and correspondingly, an increased ability to make informed judgments concerning the potential benefits and costs of espionage, intelligence, and security matters.

■ K. LEE LERNER & BRENDA WILMOTH LERNER, EDITORS
CORNWALL, U.K.
MAY, 2003

How to Use the Book

The *Encyclopedia of Espionage, Intelligence, and Security* was not intended to contain a compendium of weapons systems. Although *EEIS* carries brief overviews of specifically selected systems commonly used in modern intelligence operations, readers interested in detailed information regarding weapons systems are recommended to *Jane's Strategic Weapon Systems*, or *Jane's Defense Equipment Library*.

Although *EEIS* contains overview of significant historical periods and events, for those readers interested in additional information regarding the history of espionage operations and biographies of intelligence personnel, the editors recommend Jeffrey T. Richelson's *A Century of Spies : Intelligence in the Twentieth Century* (Oxford University Press, 1995), Vincent Buranelli and Nan Buranelli's *Spy/Counterspy: An Encyclopedia of Espionage* (New York: McGraw-Hill, 1982), and Allen Dulles', *The Craft of Intelligence* (New York: Harper & Row, 1963).

The articles in *EEIS* are meant to be understandable by anyone with a curiosity about topics in espionage, intelligence, and security matters, and this first edition of the book has been designed with ready reference in mind:

- Entries are arranged alphabetically. In an effort to facilitate easy use of this encyclopedia, and to attempt order in a chaotic universe of names and acronyms the editors have adopted a "common use" approach. Where an agency, organization, or program is known best by its acronym, the entry related to that organization will be listed by the acronym (e.g. FEMA is used instead of Federal Emergency Management Agency). To facilitate use, the editors have included a number of "jumps" or cross-referenced titles that will guide readers to desired entries.

- To avoid a log jam of terms starting with "Federal" and "United States," titles were broken to most accurately reflect the content emphasized or subject of agency authority.

- **"See Also" references** at the end of entries alert the readers to related entries not specifically mentioned in the body of the text that may provide additional or interesting resource material.

- An extensive **Glossary** of terms and acronyms is included to help the reader navigate the technical information found in *EEIS*.

- The **Chronology** includes significant events related to the content of the encyclopedia. Often accompanied by brief explanations, the most current entries date represent events that occurred just as *EEIS* went to press.

- A **Sources** section lists the most worthwhile print material and web sites we encountered in the compilation of this volume. It is there for the inspired reader who wants more information on the people and discoveries covered in this volume.

- A comprehensive general **Index** guides the reader to topics and persons mentioned in the book. Bolded page references refer the reader to the term's full entry.

- The editors and authors have attempted to explain scientific concepts clearly and simply, without sacrificing fundamental accuracy. Accordingly, an advanced understanding of physics, chemistry, or biochemistry is not assumed or required. Students and other readers should not, for example, be intimidated or deterred by the complex names of biochemical

molecules—where necessary for complete understanding, sufficient information regarding scientific terms is provided.

- To the greatest extent possible we have attempted to use Arabic names instead of their Latinized versions. Where required for clarity we have included Latinized names in parentheses after the Arabic version. Alas, we could not retain some diacritical marks (e.g. bars over vowels, dots under consonants). Because there is no generally accepted rule or consensus regarding the format of translated Arabic names, we have adopted the straightforward, and we hope sensitive, policy of using names as they are used or cited in their region of origin.

- EEIS relies on open source material and no classified or potentially dangerous information is included. Articles have been specifically edited to remove potential "how to" information. All articles have been prepared and reviewed by experts who were tasked with ensuring accuracy, appropriateness, and accessibility of language.

- With regard to entries regarding terrorist organizations, *EEIS* faced a serious dilemma. For obvious reasons, it was difficult to obtain balanced, impartial, and independently verifiable information regarding these organizations, nor could *EEIS* swell to incorporate lengthy scholarly analysis and counter-analysis of these organizations without losing focus on science and technology issues. As a compromise intended to serve students and readers seeking initial reference materials related to organizations often in the news, *EEIS* incorporates a series of supplemental articles to convey the information contained in the U.S. Department of State annual report to Congress titled, *Patterns of Global Terrorism, 2001*. These articles contain the language, assertions of fact, and views of the U.S. Department of State. Readers are encouraged to seek additional information from current U.S. Department of State resources and independent non-governmental scholarly publications that deal with the myriad of issues surrounding the nature and activities of alleged terrorist organizations. A number of governmental and non-governmental publications that deal with these issues are cited in the bibliographic sources section located near the index.

Key *EEIS* articles are signed by their authors. Brief entries were compiled by experienced researchers and reviewed by experts. In the spirit of numerous independent scientific watchdog groups, during the preparation of *EEIS* no contributors held a declared affiliation with any intelligence or security organization. This editorial policy not only allowed a positive vetting of contributors, but also assured an independence of perspective and an emphasis on the fundamentals of science as opposed to unconfirmable "insider" information.

When the only verifiable or attributable source of information for an entry comes from documents or information provided by a governmental organization (e.g., the U.S. Department of State), the editors endeavored to carefully note when the language used and perspective offered was that of the governmental organization.

Although some research contributors requested anonymity, no pseudonyms are used herein.

Acknowledgments

The editors wish to thank Herbert Romerstein, former USIA Soviet Disinformation Officer and Coordinator of Programs to Counter Soviet Active Measures, United States Information Agency, for his assistance in compiling selected articles.

The editors wish to thank Lee Wilmoth Lerner for his assistance in compiling technical engineering data for inclusion in EEIS.

The editors acknowledge the assistance of the members of the Federation of American Scientists for the provision of reports and materials used in the preparation of selected articles.

Although certainly not on the scale of the challenge to provide security for a nation with approximately 85 deep-draft ports, 600,000 bridges, 55,000 independent water treatment systems, 100 nuclear power plants, and countless miles of tunnels, pipelines, and electrical and communications infrastructure, the task of incorporating changes brought on by creation of the Department of Homeland Security—and the most massive reorganization of the United States government since World War II—as this book went to press provided a unique challenge to EEIS writers and advisors. The editors appreciate their dedication and willingness to scrap copy, roll up their sleeves, and tackle anew the smorgasbord of name and terminology changes.

As publishing deadlines loomed, EEIS was also well served by a research staff dedicated to incorporating the latest relevant events—especially information related to the search for weapons of mass destruction—that took place during war in Iraq in March and April of 2003.

EEIS advisors, researchers, and writers tenaciously attempted to incorporate the most current information available as EEIS went to press. The editors pass any credit or marks for success in that effort, and reserve for themselves full responsibility for omissions.

The editors gratefully acknowledge the assistance of many at St. James Press for their help in preparing The Encyclopedia of Espionage, Intelligence, and Security. The editors extend thanks to Mr. Peter Gareffa and Ms. Meggin Condino for their faith in this project. Most directly, the editors wish to acknowledge and thank the project editor, Mr. Stephen Cusack, for his talented oversight and for his tireless quest for secure engaging pictures for EEIS.

The editors lovingly dedicate this book to the memory of Wallace Schaffer, Jr., HM3, USNR, who died on January 8, 1968, in Thua Thien (Hue) Province, Vietnam.

"A small rock holds back a great wave."—Homer, The Odyssey.

▌▐▌▌▌ Advisors and Contributors ▌▐▌▌▌

Julie Berwald, Ph.D.
*Geophysicist, writer on marine science,
    environmental biology, and issues in geophysics.*
Austin, Texas

Robert G. Best, Ph.D.
*Clinical cytogeneticist and medical geneticist who
    has written on a range of bioscience issues*
Director, Division of Genetics
University of South Carolina School of Medicine

Tim Borden, Ph.D.
*Doctorate in History from Indiana University, and is
    an inspector with the U.S. Bureau of Customs
    and Border Protection*
Toledo, Ohio

Brian Cobb, Ph.D.
Bioscience writer, researcher
Institute for Molecular and Human Genetics
Georgetown University, Washington, D.C.

Cecilia Colomé, Ph.D.
Astrophysicist, translator, and science writer
Austin, Texas

Laurie Duncan, Ph.D.
Geologist, science writer, and researcher
Austin, Texas

William J. Engle, P.E.
*Writer on contemporary geophysics issues and the
    impacts of science and technology on history*
Exxon-Mobil Oil Corporation (Rt.) New Orleans,
    Louisiana

Antonio Farina, M.D., Ph.D.
*Physician, researcher, and writer on medical
    science issues*
Assistant Professor, University of Bologna, Italy

Christopher T. Fisher, Ph.D.
*Assistant Professor, Department of African
    American Studies and the Department of History*
The College of New Jersey, Ewing, New Jersey

Larry Gilman, Ph.D.
Electrical engineer and science writer
Sharon, Vermont

William Haneberg, Ph.D.
*Former research scientist and professor, now an
    independent consulting geologist and science
    writer*
Portland, Oregon

Brian D. Hoyle, Ph.D.
*Science writer and Chief Microbiologist,
    Government of New Brunswick from 1993 to
    1997*
Nova Scotia, Canada

Joseph Patterson Hyder
*Writer on the historical impacts of science and
    technology*
University of Tennessee College of Law, Knoxville,
    Tennessee

Alexandr Ioffe, Ph.D.
*Writer on the history of science and researcher
    with the Geological Institute of Russian Academy
    of Sciences in Moscow*
Russian Academy of Sciences, Moscow

Judson Knight
Science writer, researcher, and editor
Knight Agency Research Services, Atlanta, Georgia

Michael Lambert, Ph.D.
*Researcher at the Great Plains/Rocky Mountain
    Hazardous Substance Research Center and at the
    U.S. Naval Research Laboratory*
Manhattan, Kansas

Adrienne Wilmoth Lerner
*Writer of various articles on the history of science,
    archaeology, and the evolution of security-
    related law*
University of Tennessee College of Law, Knoxville,
    Tennessee

Agnes Lichanska, Ph.D.
Science writer who has conducted research at the Department of Medical Genetics and Ophthalmology at Queen's University of Belfast (Northern Ireland)
University of Queensland, Brisbane, Australia

Eric v.d. Luft, Ph.D., M.L.S.
Writer on cultural, scientific, and intellectual history, and philosophy
Curator of Historical Collections
SUNY Upstate Medical University, Syracuse, New York

Martin Manning
Served on the Economic Security Team, Office of International Information Programs, U.S. Department of State
Bureau of Public Diplomacy
U.S. Department of State, Washington, D.C.

Kelli Miller
Served as news writer and producer for Inside Science TV News *at the American Institute of Physics (AIP) and as executive producer of* Discoveries & Breakthroughs Inside Science
Atlanta, Georgia

Caryn E. Neumann
Instructor and doctoral candidate in the Department of History at Ohio State University
Columbus, Ohio

Mike O'Neal, Ph.D.
Independent scholar and writer
Moscow, Idaho

Belinda M. Rowland, Ph.D.
Science and medical writer
Voorheesville, New York

Judyth Sassoon, Ph.D., ARCS
Science writer with research experience in NMR and X-ray crystallography techniques
Department of Biology & Biochemistry
University of Bath, United Kingdom

Morgan Simpson
Aerospace Engineer
National Aeronautical and Space Administration (NASA)
Kennedy Space Center, Cape Canaveral, Florida

Constance K. Stein, Ph.D.
Writer on medical and bioscience issues related to modern genetics
Director of Cytogenetics, Assistant Director of Molecular Diagnostics
SUNY Upstate Medical University, Syracuse, New York

Tabitha Sparks, Ph.D.
Marion L. Brittain fellow, Georgia Institute of Technology and Fellow, Center for Humanistic Inquiry, Emory University
Atlanta, Georgia

David Tulloch
Science and technology writer
Wellington, New Zealand

Michael T. Van Dyke, Ph.D.
Served as visiting assistant professor, Department of American Thought & Language
Michigan State University, East Lansing, Michigan

Stephanie Watson
Science writer specializing in the social impacts of science and technology
Smyrna, Georgia

Simon Wendt, Ph.D.
Ph.D. candidate in Modern History and History instructor
John F. Kennedy Institute for North American Studies, Free University of Berlin, Germany

List of Entries

| A |

Abu Nidal Organization (ANO)
Abu Sayyaf Group (ASG)
Abwehr
ADFGX Cipher
Aflatoxin
Africa, Modern U.S. Security Policy and
    Interventions
Agent Orange
Air and Water Purification, Security Issues
Air Force Intelligence, United States
Air Force Office of Special Investigations, United
    States
Air Marshals, United States
Air Plume and Chemical Analysis
Aircraft Carrier
Airline Security
Al-Aqsa Martyrs Brigade
Alex Boncayao Brigade (ABB)
Al-Gama'a al-Islamiyya (Islamic Group, IG)
Al-Ittihad al-Islami (AIAI)
Al-Jama'a al-Islamiyyah al-Muqatilah bi-Libya
Al-Jihad
Allied Democratic Forces (ADF)
Al-Qaeda (also known as Al-Qaida)
Americas, Modern U.S. Security Policy and
    Interventions
Ames (Aldrich H.) Espionage Case
Anthrax
Anthrax, Terrorist Use as a Biological Weapon
Anthrax Vaccine
Anthrax Weaponization
Antiballistic Missile Treaty
Antibiotics
Anti-Imperialist Territorial Nuclei (NTA)
APIS (Advance Passenger Information System)
Archeology and Artifacts, Protection of during War
Architecture and Structural Security
Area 51 (Groom Lake, Nevada)
Argentina, Intelligence and Security
Argonne National Laboratory
Armed Islamic Group (GIA)
Arms Control, United States Bureau

Army for the Liberation of Rwanda (ALIR)
Army Security Agency
'Asbat al-Ansar
Asilomar Conference
Assassination
Assassination Weapons, Mechanical
Asymmetric Warfare
ATF (United States Bureau of Alcohol, Tobacco,
    and Firearms)
Atmospheric Release Advisory Capability (ARAC)
Audio Amplifiers
Aum Supreme Truth (Aum)
Australia, Intelligence and Security
Austria, Intelligence and Security
Aviation Intelligence, History
Aviation Security Screeners, United States

| B |

B-2 Bomber
B-52
Bacterial Biology
Ballistic Fingerprints
Ballistic Missile Defense Organization, United
    States
Ballistic Missiles
Balloon Reconnaissance, History
Basque Fatherland and Liberty (ETA)
Bathymetric Maps
Bay of Pigs
Belgium, Intelligence and Security Agencies
Belly Buster Hand Drill
Berlin Airlift
Berlin Tunnel
Berlin Wall
Biochemical Assassination Weapons
Biocontainment Laboratories
Biodetectors
Bio-Engineered Tissue Constructs
Bio-Flips
Biological and Biomimetic Systems
Biological and Toxin Weapons Convention
Biological Input/Output Systems (BIOS)

Biological Warfare
Biological Warfare, Advanced Diagnostics
Biological Weapons, Genetic Identification
Bio-Magnetics
Biomedical Technologies
Biometrics
Bio-Optic Synthetic Systems (BOSS)
Biosensor Technologies
BioShield Project
Bioterrorism
Bioterrorism, Protective Measures
Black Chamber
Black Ops
Black Tom Explosion
Bletchley Park
Bolivia, Intelligence and Security
Bomb Damage, Forensic Assessment
Bomb Detection Devices
Bombe
Bosnia and Herzegovina, Intelligence and Security
Botulinum Toxin
Brain-Machine Interfaces
Brain Wave Scanners
Brazil, Intelligence and Security
British Terrorism Act
Brookhaven National Laboratory
Bubonic Plague
Bugs (Microphones) and Bug Detectors
Bush Administration (1989–1993), United States
   National Security Policy
Bush Administration (2001–), United States
   National Security Policy

| C |

Cambodian Freedom Fighters (CFF)
Cambridge University Spy Ring
Cameras
Cameras, Miniature
Canada, Counter-Terrorism Policy
Canada, Intelligence and Security
Canine Substance Detection
Carter Adminstration (1977–1981), United States
   National Security Policy
CDC (United States Centers for Disease Control
   and Prevention)
CERN
Chechen-Russian Conflict
Chemical and Biological Defense Information
   Analysis Center (CBIAC)
Chemical and Biological Detection Technologies
Chemical Biological Incident Response Force,
   United States
Chemical Safety and Hazard Investigation Board
   (USCSB), United States
Chemical Safety: Emergency Responses
Chemical Warfare
Chemistry: Applications in Espionage, Intelligence,
   and Security Issues
Chernobyl Nuclear Power Plant Accident, Detection
   and Monitoring
Chile, Intelligence and Security
China, Intelligence and Security

Chinese Espionage against the United States
Church Committee
CIA (United States Central Intelligence Agency)
CIA (CSI), Center for the Study of Intelligence
CIA Directorate of Science and Technology (DS&T)
CIA, Foreign Broadcast Information Service
CIA, Formation and History
CIA, Legal Restriction
Cipher Disk
Cipher Key
Cipher Machines
Cipher Pad
Civil Aviation Security, United States
Civil War, Espionage and Intelligence
Classified Information
Clinton Administration (1993–2001), United States
   National Security Policy
Clipper Chip
Closed-Circuit Television (CCTV)
Coast Guard (USCG), United States
Coast Guard National Response Center
Code Name
Code Word
Codes and Ciphers
Codes, Fast and Scalable Scientific Computation
COINTELPRO
Cold War (1945–1950), The Start of the Atomic Age
Cold War (1950–1972)
Cold War (1972–1989): The Collapse of the Soviet
   Union
Colombia, Intelligence and Security
Colossus I
COMINT (Communications Intelligence)
Commerce Department Intelligence and Security
   Responsibilities, United States
Commission on Civil Rights, United States
Communicable Diseases, Isolation, and Quarantine
Communications System, United States National
Comprehensive Test Ban Treaty (CTBT)
Computer and Electronic Data Destruction
Computer Fraud and Abuse Act of 1986
Computer Hackers
Computer Hardware Security
Computer Keystroke Recorder
Computer Modeling
Computer Security Act (1987)
Computer Software Security
Computer Virus
Concealment Devices
Consumer Product Safety Commission (CPSC),
   United States
Continuity Irish Republican Army (CIRA)
Continuity of Government, United States
Continuous Assisted Performance (CAP)
Coordinator for Counterterrorism, United States
   Office
Copyright Security
Counterfeit Currency, Technology and the
   Manufacture
Counter-Intelligence
Counter-Terrorism Rewards Program
Covert Operations
Crib
Crime Prevention, Intelligence Agencies

Critical Infrastructure
Critical Infrastructure Assurance Office (CIAO), United States
Croatia, Intelligence and Security
Cruise Missile
Cryptology and Number Theory
Cryptology, History
Cryptonym
Cuba, Intelligence and Security
Cuban Missile Crisis
Customs Service, United States
Cyanide
Cyber Security
Cyber Security Warning Network
Czech Republic, Intelligence and Security

| D |

D Notice
DARPA (Defense Advanced Research Projects Agency)
Data Mining
DCI (Director of the Central Intelligence Agency)
DEA (Drug Enforcement Administration)
Dead Drop Spike
Dead-Letter Box
Decontamination Methods
Decryption
Defense Information Systems Agency, United States
Defense Nuclear Facilities Safety Board, United States
Defense Security Service, United States
Delta Force
Department of State Bureau of Intelligence and Research, United States
Department of State, United States
DIA (Defense Intelligence Agency)
Dial Tone Decoder
Diplomatic Security (DS), United States Bureau
Dirty Tricks
Disinformation
DNA
DNA Fingerprinting
DNA Recognition Instruments
DNA Sequences, Unique
Document Destruction
Document Forgery
DOD (United States Department of Defense)
DOE (United States Department of Energy)
Domestic Emergency Support Team, United States
Domestic Intelligence
Domestic Preparedness Office (NDPO), United States National
Doo Transmitter
Dosimetry
Double Agents
Drop
Drug Control Policy, United States Office of National
Drug Intelligence Estimates
Dual Use Technology

| E |

E-2C
Ebola Virus
E-Bomb
Echelon
Economic Espionage
Economic Intelligence
Egypt, Intelligence and Security
Eichmann, Adolf: Israeli Capture
Eisenhower Administration (1953–1961), United States National Security Policy
El Salvador, Intelligence and Security
Electromagnetic Pulse
Electromagnetic Spectrum
Electromagnetic Weapons, Biochemical Effects
Electronic Communication Intercepts, Legal Issues
Electronic Countermeasures
Electronic Warfare
Electro-Optical Intelligence
Electrophoresis
EM Wave Scanners
Emergency Response Teams
Encryption of Data
Enduring Freedom, Operation
Energy Directed Weapons
Energy Regulatory Commission, United States Federal
Energy Technologies
Engraving and Printing, United States Bureau
Engulf, Operation
Enigma
Entry-Exit Registration System, United States National Security
Environmental Issues Impact on Security
Environmental Measurements Laboratory
EPA (Environmental Protection Agency)
Epidemiology
Espionage
Espionage Act of 1917
Espionage and Intelligence, Early Historical Foundations
Estonia, Intelligence and Security
European Union
Executive Orders and Presidential Directives
Explosive Coal

| F |

F-117A Stealth Fighter
FAA (United States Federal Aviation Administration)
Facility Security
FBI (United States Federal Bureau of Investigation)
FCC (United States Federal Communications Commission)
FDA (United States Food and Drug Administration)
Federal Protective Service, United States
Federal Reserve System, United States
FEMA (United States Federal Emergency Management Agency)
FEST (United States Foreign Emergency Support Team)

Fingerprint Analysis
Finland, Intelligence and Security
First of October Anti-fascist Resistance Group
	(GRAPO)
FISH (German *Geheimschreiber* Cipher Machine)
Fission
Flame Analysis
Flight Data Recorders
FM Transmitters
FOIA (Freedom of Information Act)
Food Supply, Counter-Terrorism
Ford Administration (1974–1977), United States
	National Security Policy
Foreign Assets Control (OFAC), United States
	Office
Foreign Intelligence Surveillance Act
Foreign Intelligence Surveillance Court of Review
Forensic Geology in Military or Intelligence
	Operations
Forensic Science
Forensic Voice and Tape Analysis
France, Counter-Terrorism Policy
France, Intelligence and Security
French Underground during World War II,
	Communication and Codes
Fusion

| G |

G–2
GAO (General Accounting Office, United States)
Gas Chromatograph-Mass Spectrometer
General Services Administration, United States
Genetic Code
Genetic Information: Ethics, Privacy and Security
	Issues
Genetic Technology
Genomics
Geologic and Topographical Influences on Military
	and Intelligence Operations
Geospatial Imagery
Germany, Counter-Terrorism Policy
Germany, Intelligence and Security
Gestapo
GIS
Global Communications, United States Office
Glomar Explorer
Government Ethics (USOGE), United States Office
GPS
Great Game
Greece, Intelligence and Security
GSM Encryption
Guatemala, Intelligence and Security
Guerilla Warfare

| H |

HAMAS (Islamic Resistance Movement)
Hanssen (Robert) Espionage Case
Harakat ul-Jihad-I-Islami (HUJI) (Movement of
	Islamic Holy War)

Harakat ul-Jihad-I-Islami/Bangladesh (HUJI-B)
	(Movement of Islamic Holy War)
Harakat ul-Mujahidin (HUM) (Movement of Holy
	Warriors)
Hardening
Health and Human Services Department, United
	States
Heavy Water Technology
Hemorrhagic Fevers and Diseases
Hizballah (Party of God)
Homeland Security, United States Department of
HUMINT (Human Intelligence)
Hungary, Intelligence and Security
Hypersonic Aircraft

| I |

IBIS (Interagency Border Inspection System)
IDENT (Automated Biometric Identification System)
Identity Theft
IFF (Identification Friend or Foe)
IMF (International Monetary Fund)
IMINT (Imagery Intelligence)
India, Intelligence and Security
Indonesia, Intelligence and Security
Infectious Disease, Threats to Security
Information Security
Information Security (OIS), United States Office of
Information Warfare
Infrared Detection Devices
Infrastructure Protection Center (NIPC), United
	States National
INS (United States Immigration and Naturalization
	Service)
INSCOM (United States Army Intelligence and
	Security Command)
INSPASS (Immigration and Naturalization Service
	Passenger Accelerated Service System)
Inspector General (OIG), Office of the
Intelligence
Intelligence Agent
Intelligence and Counterespionage Careers
Intelligence and Democracy: Issues and Conflicts
Intelligence and International Law
Intelligence and Law Enforcement Agencies
Intelligence & Research (INR), United States
	Bureau of
Intelligence Authorization Acts, United States
	Congress
Intelligence Community
Intelligence Literature
Intelligence Officer
Intelligence Policy and Review (OIPR), United
	States Office of
Intelligence Support, United States Office of
Intelligence, United States Congressional
	Oversight of
Interagency Security Committee, United States
Internal Revenue Service, United States
International Atomic Energy Agency (IAEA)
International Narcotics and Law Enforcement
	Affairs (INL), United States Bureau of

Internet
Internet: Dynamic and Static Addresses
Internet Spam and Fraud
Internet Spider
Internet Surveillance
Internet Tracking and Tracing
INTERPOL (International Criminal Police
    Organization)
Interpol, United States National Central Bureau
Interrogation
Interrogation: Torture Techniques and
    Technologies
Iran-Contra Affair
Iran, Intelligence and Security
Iranian Hostage Crisis
Iranian Nuclear Programs
Iraq, Intelligence and Security Agencies in
Iraq War: Prelude to War (The International Debate
    Over the Use and Effectiveness of Weapons
    Inspections)
Iraq War (Immediate Aftermath)
Iraqi Freedom, Operation (2003 War Against Iraq)
Ireland, Intelligence and Security
Irish Republican Army (IRA)
Islamic Army of Aden (IAA)
Islamic Movement of Uzbekistan (IMU)
Isotopic Analysis
Israel, Counter-Terrorism Policy
Israel, Intelligence and Security
Italy, Intelligence and Security

| J |

Jaish-e-Mohammed (JEM) (Army of Mohammed)
Japan, Intelligence and Security
Japanese Red Army (JRA)
JDAM (Joint Direct Attack Munition)
Jemaah Islamiya (JI)
Johnson Administration (1963–1969), United States
    National Security Policy
Joint Chiefs of Staff, United States
Jordan, Intelligence and Security
J-STARS
Justice Department, United States

| K |

Kahane Chai (Kach)
Kennedy Administration (1961–1963), United States
    National Security Policy
Kenya, Bombing of United States Embassy
KGB (Komitet Gosudarstvennoi Bezopasnosti,
    USSR Committee of State Security)
Khobar Towers Bombing Incident
Knives
Korean War
Kosovo, NATO Intervention
Kumpulan Mujahidin Malaysia (KMM)
Kurdistan Workers' Party (PKK)
Kuwait Oil Fires, Persian Gulf War

| L |

Language Training and Skills
Laser
Laser Listening Devices
Lashkar-e-Tayyiba (LT) (Army of the Righteous)
Law Enforcement, Responses to Terrorism
Law Enforcement Training Center (FLETC), United
    States Federal
Lawrence Berkeley National Laboratory (LBL)
Lawrence Livermore National Laboratory (LLNL)
League of Nations
Lebanon, Bombing of U.S. Embassy and Marine
    Barracks
Less-Lethal Weapons Technology
L-Gel Decontamination Reagent
Liberation Tigers of Tamil Eelam (LTTE)
Libraries and Information Science (NCLIS), United
    States National Commission on
Libya, Intelligence and Security
Libya, U.S. Attack (1986)
LIDAR (Light Detection and Ranging)
Lock-Picking
Locks and Keys
Looking Glass
Lord Haw-Haw
Lord's Resistance Army (LRA)
Los Alamos National Laboratory
Loyalist Volunteer Force (LVF)

| M |

Mail Sanitization
Malicious Data
Manhattan Project
Mapping Technology
Marine Mammal Program
McCarthyism
Measurement and Signatures Intelligence
    (MASINT)
Metal Detectors
Meteorology and Weather Alteration
Mexico, Intelligence and Security
MI5 (British Security Service)
MI6 (British Secret Intelligence Service)
Microbiology: Applications to Espionage,
    Intelligence, and Security
Microchip
Microfilms
Microphones
Microscopes
Microwave Weaponry, High Power (HPM)
Middle East, Modern U.S. Security Policy and
    Interventions
Military Police, United States
MOAB (Massive Ordnance Air Burst Bomb)
Molecular Biology: Applications to Espionage,
    Intelligence, and Security
Moles
Monroe Doctrine
Morocco, Intelligence and Security
Mossad
Motion Sensors

Mount Weather
Movies, Espionage and Intelligence Portrayals
Mujahedin-e Khalq Organization (MEK or MKO)
Mustard Gas

| N |

NAILS (National Automated Immigration Lookout
   System)
Nanotechnology
Napoleonic Wars, Espionage during
NASA (National Air and Space Administration)
National Archives and Records Administration
   (NARA),Unites States
National Command Authority
National Drug Threat Assessment
National Information Infrastructure Protection Act,
   United States
National Intelligence Estimate
National Interagency Civil-Military Institute (NICI),
   United States
National Liberation Army (ELN)—Colombia
National Military Joint Intelligence Center
National Preparedness Strategy, United States
National Response Team, United States
National Security Act (1947)
National Security Advisor, United States
National Security Strategy, United States
National Security Telecommunications Advisory
   Committee
National Telecommunications Information
   Administration, and Security for the Radio
   Frequency Spectrum, United States
NATO (North Atlantic Treaty Organization)
Natural Resources and National Security
Navy Criminal Investigative Service (NCIS)
NCIX (National Counterintelligence Executive),
   United States Office of the
NDIC (Department of Justice National Drug
   Intelligence Center)
Near Space Environment
Nerve Gas
Netherlands, Intelligence and Security
New People's Army (NPA)
New Zealand, Intelligence and Security
NFIB (United States National Foreign Intelligence
   Board)
NIC (National Intelligence Council)
Nicaragua, Intelligence and Security
Nigeria, Intelligence and Security
Night Vision Scopes
NIH (National Institutes of Health)
NIJ (National Institute of Justice)
NIMA (National Imagery and Mapping Agency)
NIMH (National Institute of Mental Health)
NIST (National Institute of Standards and
   Technology), United States
NIST Computer Security Division, United States
Nixon Administration (1969–1974), United States
   National Security Policy
NMIC (National Maritime Intelligence Center)
NNSA (United States National Nuclear Security
   Administration)

NOAA (National Oceanic & Atmospheric
   Administration)
Noise Generators
Nongovernmental Global Intelligence and Security
Non-Proliferation and National Security, United
   States
NORAD
North Korea, Intelligence and Security
North Korean Nuclear Weapons Programs
Norway, Intelligence and Security
NRO (National Reconnaissance Office)
NSA (United States National Security Agency)
NSC (National Security Council)
NSC (National Security Council), History
NSF (National Science Foundation)
NTSB (National Transportation Safety Board)
Nuclear Detection Devices
Nuclear Emergency Support Team, United States
Nuclear Power Plants, Security
Nuclear Reactors
Nuclear Regulatory Commission (NRC), United
   States
Nuclear Spectroscopy
Nuclear Weapons
Nuclear Winter
Nucleic Acid Analyzer (HANAA)

| O |

Oak Ridge National Laboratory (ORNL)
Official Secrets Act, United Kingdom
OPEC (Organization of Petroleum Exporting
   Countries)
Operation Liberty Shield
Operation Magic
Operation Mongoose
Operation Shamrock
Orange Volunteers (OV)
OSS (United States Office of Strategic Services)

| P |

P-3 Orion Anti-Submarine Maritime
   Reconnaissance Aircraft
Pacific Northwest National Laboratory
Pakistan, Intelligence and Security
Palestine Islamic Jihad (PIJ)
Palestine Liberation Front (PLF)
Palestinian Authority, Intelligence and Security
PanAm 103, (Trial of Libyan Intelligence Agents)
Panama Canal
Parabolic Microphones
Pathogen Genomic Sequencing
Pathogen Transmission
Pathogens
Patriot Act Terrorist Exclusion List
Patriot Act, United States
Patriot Missile System
Pearl Harbor, Japanese Attack on
People Against Gangsterism and Drugs (PAGAD)
Persian Gulf War
Peru, Intelligence and Security

Petroleum Reserves, Determination
PFIAB (President's Foreign Intelligence Advisory Board)
Phoenix Program
Photo Alteration
Photographic Interpretation Center (NPIC), United States National
Photographic Resolution
Photography, High-Altitude
Playfair Cipher
Plum Island Animal Disease Center
Poland, Intelligence and Security
Politics: The Briefings of United States Presidential Candidates
Pollard Espionage Case
Polygraphs
Polymerase Chain Reaction (PCR)
Popular Front for the Liberation of Palestine (PFLP)
Popular Front for the Liberation of Palestine-General Command (PFLP-GC)
Port Security
PORTPASS (Port Passenger Accelerated Service System)
Portugal, Intelligence and Security
Postal Security
Postal Service (USPS), United States
Potassium Iodide
President of the United States (Executive Command and Control of Intelligence Agencies)
Pretty Good Privacy (PGP)
Privacy: Legal and Ethical Issues
Profiling
Propaganda, Uses and Psychology
Pseudoscience Intelligence Studies
Psychotropic Drugs
Public Health Service (PHS), United States
Pueblo Incident
Purple Machine

| Q |

Quantum Physics: Applications to Espionage, Intelligence, and Security Issues

| R |

RADAR
RADAR, Synthetic Aperture
Radiation, Biological Damage
Radio Direction Finding Equipment
Radio Frequency (RF) Weapons
Radioactive Waste Storage
Radiological Emergency Response Plan, United States Federal
Reagan Administration (1981–1989), United States National Security Policy
Real IRA (RIRA)
Reconnaissance
Red Code
Red Hand Defenders (RHD)
Red Orchestra
Remote Sensing

Retina and Iris Scans
Revolutionary Armed Forces of Colombia (FARC)
Revolutionary Nuclei
Revolutionary Organization 17 November (17 November)
Revolutionary People's Liberation Party/Front (DHKP/C)
Revolutionary Proletarian Initiative Nuclei (NIPR)
Revolutionary United Front (RUF)
Revolutionary War, Espionage and Intelligence
RF Detection
Ricin
Robotic Vehicles
Romania, Intelligence and Security
Room 40
Rosenberg (Ethel and Julius) Espionage Case
Russia, Intelligence and Security
Russian Nuclear Materials, Security Issues

| S |

Sabotage
Salafist Group for Call and Combat (GSPC)
Salmonella and Salmonella Food Poisoning
Sandia National Laboratories
Sarin Gas
Satellite Technology Exports to the People's Republic of China (PRC)
Satellites, Non-Governmental High Resolution
Satellites, Spy
Saudi Arabia, Intelligence and Security
Scanning Technologies
SEAL Teams
Secret Service, United States
Secret Writing
Security Clearance Investigations
Security, Infrastructure Protection, and Counterterrorism, United States National Coordinator
Security Policy Board, United States
Seismograph
Seismology for Monitoring Explosions
Senate Select Committee on Intelligence, United States
Sendero Luminoso (Shining Path, or SL)
SENTRI (Secure Electronic Network for Travelers' Rapid Inspection)
September 11 Terrorist Attacks on the United States
Sequencing
Serbia, Intelligence and Security
Sex-for-Secrets Scandal
Ships Designed for Intelligence Collection
"Shoe Bomber"
Shoe Transmitter
Short-Wave Transmitters
SIGINT (Signals Intelligence)
Silencers
Skunk Works
Slovakia, Intelligence and Security
Slovenia, Intelligence and Security
Smallpox
Smallpox Vaccine

SOE (Special Operations Executive)
Soldier and Biological Chemical Command
    (SBCCOM), United States Army
Solid-Phase Microextraction Techniques
Soman
SONAR
SOSUS (Sound Surveillance System)
South Africa, Intelligence and Security
South Korea, Intelligence and Security
Soviet Union (USSR), Intelligence and Security
Space Shuttle
Spain, Intelligence and Security
Spanish-American War
Special Collection Service, United States
Special Counsel and Security Related
    "Whistleblower" Protection Issues, United States
    Office
Special Operations Command, United States
Special Relationship: Technology Sharing between
    the Intelligence Agencies of the United States
    and United Kingdom
Spectroscopy
Spores
SR-71 Blackbird
START I Treaty
START II
STASI
Stealth Technology
Steganography
Strategic Defense Initiative and National Missile
    Defense
Strategic Petroleum Reserve, United States
Sudan, Intelligence and Security
Suez Canal
Supercomputers
Surgeon General and Nuclear, Biological, and
    Chemical Defense, United States Office
Sweden, Intelligence and Security
Switzerland, Intelligence and Security
Syria, Intelligence and Security

| T |

Tabun
Taiwan, Intelligence and Security
Taser
Technical Intelligence
Technology Transfer Center (NTTC), Emergency
    Response Technology Program
Telemetry
Telephone Caller Identification (Caller ID)
Telephone Recording Laws
Telephone Recording System
Telephone Scrambler
Telephone Tap Detector
Terror Alert System, United States
Terrorism, Domestic (United States)
Terrorism, Intelligence Based Threat and Risk
    Assessments
Terrorism, Philosophical and Ideological Origins
Terrorism Risk Insurance
Terrorist and Para-State Organizations
Terrorist Organization List, United States

Terrorist Organizations, Freezing of Assets
Terrorist Threat Integration Center
Thin Layer Chromatography
TIA (Terrorism Information Awareness)
Tissue-Based Biosensors
Tokyo Rose
Toxicology
Toxins
Tradecraft
Transportation Department, United States
Treasury Department, United States
Truman Administration (1945–1953), United States
    National Security Policy
Truth Serum
Tularemia
Tunisian Combatant Group (TCG)
Tupac Amaru Revolutionary Movement (MRTA)
Turkey, Intelligence and Security
Turkish Hizballah
Typex

| U |

U-2 Incident
U-2 Spy Plane
Ukraine, Intelligence and Security
Ulster Defense Association/Ulster Freedom Fighters
    (UDA/UVF)
Ultra, Operation
Underground Facilities, Geologic and Structural
    Considerations in the Construction
Undersea Espionage: Nuclear vs. Fast Attack Subs
Unexploded Ordnance and Mines
United Kingdom, Counter-Terrorism Policy
United Kingdom, Intelligence and Security
United Nations Security Council
United Self-Defense Forces/Group of Colombia
    (AUC Autodefensas Unidas de Colombia)
United States, Counter-Terrorism Policy
United States, Intelligence and Security
United States Intelligence, History
Unmanned Aerial Vehicles (UAVs)
Uranium
Uranium Depletion Weapons
USAMRICD (United States Army Medical Research
    Institute of Chemical Defense)
USAMRIID (United States Army Medical Research
    Institute of Infectious Diseases)
USS Cole
USS Liberty
USSTRATCOM (United States Strategic Command)

| V |

Vaccination
Vaccines
Variola Virus
Venezuela, Intelligence and Security
Venona
Vietnam War
Viral Biology

Viral Exposure Therapy, Antiviral Drug
    Development
Voice Alteration, Electronic
Voice of America (VOA), United States
Vozrozhdeniye Island, Soviet and Russian
    Biochemical Facility
Vulnerability Assessments
VX Agent

| W |

Walker Family Spy Ring
War of 1812
Water Supply: Counter-Terrorism
Watergate
Weapon-Grade Plutonium and Uranium, Tracking
Weapons of Mass Destruction

Weapons of Mass Destruction, Detection
Windtalkers
World Health Organization (WHO)
World Trade Center, 1993 Terrorist Attack
World Trade Center, 2001 Terrorist Attack
World War I
World War I: Loss of the German Codebook
World War II
World War II: Allied Invasion of Sicily and "The
    Man Who Never Was"
World War II, The Surrender of the Italian Army
World War II, United States Breaking of Japanese
    Naval Codes

| Z |

Zoonoses

F-117A Stealth Fighter

Striking and unusual in appearance, the birdlike F-117A Nighthawk is the world's first aircraft designed to make full use of stealth technology. Conceived and designed in just 31 months at the Lockheed Advanced Development Projects "Skunk Works" in Burbank, California, the Nighthawk was built for the United States Air Force between 1982 and 1990. The single-seat, twin-engine F-117 was the only U.S. or coalition aircraft to strike targets in downtown Baghdad during the Persian Gulf War.

Both the air force and Lockheed are understandably reticent regarding the specific stealth technologies that make the Nighthawk virtually invisible to radar. However, it appears that the plane's distinctive shape serves to deflect radar waves, and that the materials used in building the craft absorb electromagnetic energy.

As befits an extraordinary aircraft, even the story of its birth is something of a saga: from the initial production decision in 1978 to the first test flight on June 18, 1981 was less than three years, lightning-quick for an undertaking of such magnitude. The speed of production has been credited not only to the engineers at the "Skunk Works," but also to the management team at the Aeronautical Systems Center at Wright-Patterson Air Force Base in Ohio.

The F-117A was not an aircraft the United States was inclined to share, even with allies, and therefore the only F-117A unit in the world is the 49th Fighter Wing (formerly the 4450th Tactical Group) at Holloman Air Force Base in New Mexico. Designed to deliver laser-guided weapons against critical targets, the F-117A has quadruple redundant fly-by-wire controls, and is equipped with a variety of sophisticated navigation and attack systems integrated into its digital avionics suite.

Capable of being refueled in the air, the F-117A flew 18.5 hours nonstop from Holloman to Kuwait during Operation Desert Storm in 1991, setting a record for single-seat fighters. The aircraft was also deployed in Operation Allied Force in 1999, when it led the first North Atlantic Treaty Organization (NATO) strike against Yugoslavia on March 24. Additionally, the Nighthawk was selected to strike targets in downtown Baghdad in Operation Iraqi Freedom in 2003, not only because its invisibility to radar made it the safest craft to use, but also because its extraordinary accuracy made it capable of performing its job with minimal harm to innocent bystanders.

■ FURTHER READING:

BOOKS:

Aronstein, David C., and Albert C. Piccirillo. *Have Blue and the F-117A: Evolution of the "Stealth Fighter"*. Reston, VA: American Institute of Aeronautics and Astronautics, 1997.

Lake, Jon. *Jane's How to Fly and Fight in the F-117A Stealth Fighter*. London: HarperCollins Publishers, 1997.

Macy, Robert, and Melinda Macy. *Destination Baghdad: The Story of the F-117A Stealth Fighter, the Plane Credited with Ripping out the Eyes and the Heart of the Iraqi War Machine, as Told by the Pilots who Flew the Most Dangerous Missions of Operation Desert Storm*. Las Vegas, NV: M&M Graphics, 1991.

ELECTRONIC:

F-117A Nighthawk. United States Air Force. <http://www.af.mil/news/factsheets/F_117A_Nighthawk.html> (March 8, 2003).

SEE ALSO

Persian Gulf War
Skunk Works
Stealth Technology

An F-117A Nighthawk Stealth fighter flies over the New Mexico desert during a training mission. AP/WIDE WORLD PHOTOS.

FAA (United States Federal Aviation Administration)

∎ STEPHANIE WATSON

The Federal Aviation Administration (FAA) is the government agency charged with ensuring the safety of air travel in America, developing new aviation technologies, and overseeing air traffic control for both passenger and military aircraft.

The FAA takes flight. As air travel began to take off at the beginning of the 20th century, the government realized that a special agency was needed to regulate the fledgling airline industry. In 1926, Congress passed the Air Commerce Act, putting the U.S. Department of Commerce in charge of air travel and commerce. Under its wing emerged the earliest predecessor of the FAA, called the Aeronautics Branch. A former lawyer, William P. MacCracken, Jr., was chosen to head up the new agency. On April 6, 1927, MacCracken received the very first pilot's license. Three

months later, the agency issued the first aircraft mechanic's license.

In 1934, the Aeronautics Branch was renamed the Bureau of Air Commerce. Four years later, the oversight of civil aviation passed into the hands of an independent government agency, called the Civil Aeronautics Authority. President Franklin D. Roosevelt eventually split the authority into two agencies, the Civil Aeronautics Administration (CAA) and the Civil Aeronautics Board (CAB). The CAA issued pilot and aircraft certification, enforced safety regulations, and developed new air routes, while the CAB enacted safety rules, investigated crashes, and regulated the economic aspects of the airline industry.

America entered the jet age in the 1950s, with faster, more powerful airplanes that allowed the public to travel more easily and affordably. As more Americans took to the skies, the number of airplane crashes rose, and the government recognized the need for new aviation security measures. In 1958, Congress passed the Federal Aviation Act, creating the Federal Aviation Agency, which took over safety and air traffic control responsibilities from the CAA and CAB. When the organization became part of the new Department of Transportation in 1967, the word agency in the FAA's title was changed to administration.

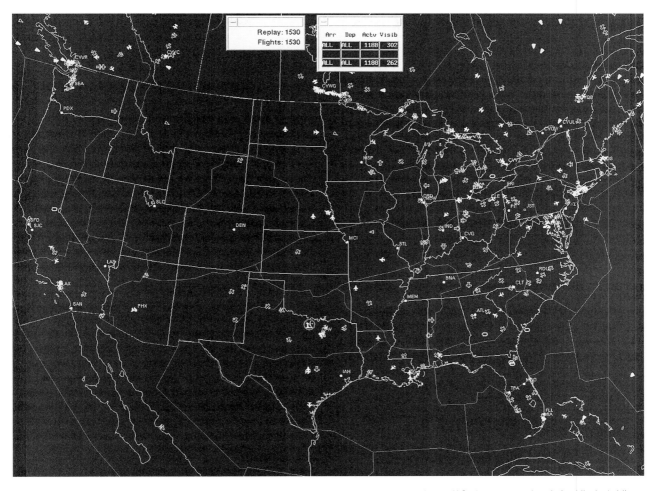

Very light air traffic is shown at 11:30 a.m. on September 11, 2001, in this Federal Aviation Administration image. U.S. airspace was closed after hijacked airliners crashed into the World Trade Center towers and the Pentagon. AP/WIDE WORLD PHOTOS.

As the aviation industry and the world itself changed in the latter part of the 20th century, the role of the FAA evolved and expanded. A wave of hijackings in the 1960s gave a greater urgency to the need for more stringent passenger security standards. Concerns over the environment led to aircraft noise standards in 1968. Increasing air traffic led to the National Airspace System (NAS), a 1982 plan that modernized ground-to-air surveillance and communications systems.

Following the terrorist attacks on September 11, 2001, the FAA enacted tougher airport security measures, including background checks for all airport employees with access to secure areas, new rules prohibiting passengers from carrying-on knives and other potential weapons, and more widespread use of explosive-detection machines for examining checked baggage. The agency also replaced privately owned airport security companies with federally employed screeners.

In April, 2003, the FAA announced that hardened cockpit doors had been retrofitted in over 10,000 foreign and domestic aircraft. The new doors are meant to deter and stop small arms fire or forced entry, and can only be opened by the pilots from inside the cockpit.

The FAA today. The FAA is headquartered in Washington, D.C., with nine branches scattered across the country. Heading the agency is the administrator, who is assisted by a deputy administrator and six associate administrators. First and foremost, their job is to keep the skies over America safe. To that end, no aircraft can fly without first meeting the FAA's stringent safety standards, and no pilot can earn his or her wings without first receiving FAA certification. Mechanics, dispatchers, and flight instructors must be similarly certified. The agency also researches and develops new technologies to improve the quality of airplanes, navigation systems, and air traffic control communications systems and equipment. The FAA oversees a national network of some 450 airport towers, 21 air traffic control centers, and 61 flight service stations in the United States, and maintains close contact with international aviation agencies to ensure the safety of American passengers abroad.

■ FURTHER READING:

BOOKS:

Preston, Edmund. *FAA Historical Chronology: Civil Aviation and the Federal Government, 1926–1996.* Washington: DOT/FAA, 1998.

Thompson, Scott A. *Flight Check! The Story of FAA Flight Inspection.* Washington: DOT/FAA, Office of Aviation System Standards, 1993.

ELECTRONIC:

Federal Aviation Administration <http://www1.faa.gov/> (January, 20, 2003).

SEE ALSO

Air Marshals, United States
Airline Security
Aviation Security Screeners, United States
Civil Aviation Security, United States
September 11 Terrorist Attacks on the United States
Transportation Department, United States

Face Recognition Vendor Test (FRVT).

SEE *Biometrics.*

Facility Security

Facility security is the protection, and the measures taken toward the protection, of a building or other physical location. Among the components of facility security are access control, or the protection against entry by unauthorized persons, fire detection and suppression, and emergency-response planning. Facility security planning involves both the use of personnel and technology, but though both are important, the quality, training, and trustworthiness of personnel is of greater significance ultimately than the sophistication of the equipment used to protect a facility.

Personnel. Facility security is the business both of government agencies and of private firms. The skills required for facility security work in the public and private sectors are essentially the same, and personnel with experience in one area are usually able to move easily into the other. Not all facility security personnel are the same: the more sensitive the area being guarded, and the more valuable or potentially dangerous its contents, the greater the skills required of the individuals who ensure its security.

One of the thorniest issues of personnel policy in facility security is pay, a factor that involves greater subtlety than initially meets the eye. Although there is not a direct correspondence or correlation between pay and honesty, in general. the higher the pay, the greater the amount of qualifications an employer can demand.

After the September 11, 2001, terrorist attacks, as the federal government began to reconsider the security screening process at airports, many observers questioned the reliability of security personnel.

Qualifications. An effective facility security officer must be of unquestionable honesty and trustworthiness, such that no amount of money or other inducements would be a temptation to betray an employer. The potential officer should expect to undergo background checks, which would typically be intensive on a level commensurate with the sensitivity of the job. These checks may include examination of the individual's financial and credit history; family and domestic history; arrest and police record, as well as other government records on the individual.

Whereas American citizens have a legal expectation of privacy, if not a constitutionally specified "right to privacy," such is not the case for an individual who offers his or her services to guard valuable or sensitive materials.

Beyond these considerations, a facility security officer should be resourceful, and capable of thinking in a non-linear fashion. He or she should be able to consider the possibility that a given action will have more than one possible result, and that a given event may have more than one possible cause. In testing the abilities of facility security personnel for highly sensitive roles, it is not enough that the officer be able to protect his or her facility from invasion: he or she should be capable of penetrating other facilities. Some private firms advertise the fact that their operatives have been able to penetrate supposedly secure buildings.

In a test of post-September 11 building security, government investigators were able to enter four federal buildings in Atlanta using false law enforcement identification equipment—a clear indication that those facilities were not properly protected by the personnel in place. As noted at the time in *Security Management,* the General Services Administration, which provided security for those federal buildings, was notorious for its low pay and minimal benefits, and this made it difficult to attract highly qualified personnel.

Procedure and equipment. Though the importance of personnel to facility security can hardly be overstated, people are not the only dimension. There are also procedure and equipment, though these can only be used to a degree of effectiveness commensurate with the capabilities of the security staff.

In the realm of procedure, there are necessary steps to be taken when securing areas containing valuable or potentially dangerous materials. It may be deemed wise, for instance, to keep sensitive areas and items as separated as possible, so as to maximize the amount of time and work necessary for an intruder to obtain the goods sought. On the other hand, a facility security plan may call for centralization of sensitive areas so as to maintain a closer watch on those areas.

Equipment may be necessary for access control, surveillance, detection, communication, and incident response. Access control can be as simple as a lock, or as high-tech as biometric scanning devices that read handprints or the iris of an individual's eye. Surveillance equipment usually involves cameras, and may be augmented by motion sensors, alarms, and other forms of equipment for detection.

Personnel must be equipped with devices for communicating with one another, and with a central monitoring station. In the event of a serious security breach or other incident, they should also be able to contact outside services. Communications equipment also aids in incident response, for which a facility security can also prepare with fire suppression items (handheld extinguishers and/or sprinklers installed on site), as well as first aid kits. Incident response, depending on the nature of the facility and the qualifications of the persons guarding it, may also require that personnel be equipped with weapons or defensive equipment such as tear gas.

■ FURTHER READING:

BOOKS:

Kozlow, Christopher, and John P. Sullivan. *Jane's Facility Security Handbook.* Alexandria, VA: Jane's Information Group, 2000.

PERIODICALS:

Gips, Michael A. "Options Reviewed for Federal Building Security." *Security Management* 46, no. 7 (July 2002): 14.

Thompson, Cheryl W. "Lawmaker Faults Nuclear Facility Security Policies." *Washington Post.* (March 25, 2002): A17.

Wolkowitz, Dave. "Facility Security—Playing It Safe." *Area Development Site and Facility Planning* 37, no. 9 (September 2002): 72.

SEE ALSO

Architecture and Structural Security
Biological and Biomimetic Systems
General Services Administration, United States
Security Clearance Investigations

Fast Breeder Reactor.

SEE *Nuclear Reactors.*

WARNING from the FBI

The war against spies and saboteurs demands the aid of every American.

When you see evidence of sabotage, notify the Federal Bureau of Investigation at once.

When you suspect the presence of enemy agents, tell it to the FBI.

Beware of those who spread enemy propaganda! Don't repeat vicious rumors or vicious whispers.

Tell it to the FBI!

J. Edgar Hoover, *Director*
Federal Bureau of Investigation

The nearest Federal Bureau of Investigation office is listed on page one of your telephone directory.

An FBI poster signed by J. Edgar Hoover warns civilians against saboteurs and spies. ©CORBIS.

FBI (United States Federal Bureau of Investigation)

■ ADRIENNE WILMOTH LERNER

The United States Federal Bureau of Investigation (FBI) is the nation's primary federal investigative service. The mission of the FBI is to uphold and enforce federal criminal laws, aid international, state, and local police and investigative services when appropriate, and to protect the United States against terrorism and threats to national interests.

The FBI employs nearly 30,000 men and women, including 12,000 special agents. The organization, headquartered in Washington, D.C., is field-oriented, maintaining a network of 56 domestic field offices, 45 foreign posts, and 400 satellite offices (resident agencies). The agency relies on both foreign and domestic intelligence information, to aid its anti-terror operations. As a law enforcement authority, the FBI only has jurisdiction in interstate, or federal, crimes.

Origins and Formation of the FBI

In the nineteenth century, municipal and state governments shouldered the responsibility of law enforcement. State legislatures defined crimes, and criminals were prosecuted in local courts. The development of railroads and automobiles, coupled with advancements in communication technology, introduced a new type of crime that contemporary legal and law enforcement system was unequipped to handle. Criminals were able to evade the law by fleeing over state lines. To combat the growing trend of interstate crime, President Theodore Roosevelt proposed the creation of a federal investigative and law enforcement agency.

In 1908, Roosevelt and his attorney general, Charles Bonaparte, created a force of Special Agents within the Department of Justice. They sought the expertise of accountants, lawyers, Secret Service agents, and detectives to staff the ranks of the new investigative service. The new recruits reported for examination and training on July 26, 1908. This first corps of federal agents was the forerunner of the modern FBI.

When the federal bureau began operations, there were few federal crimes in the legal statutes. Federal agents investigated railroad scams, banking crimes, labor violations, and antitrust cases. The findings of their investigations, however, were usually disclosed to local or state law enforcement officials and courts for prosecution. In 1910, the federal government passed the Mann Act, expanding the jurisdiction of the investigation bureau by outlawing the transport of women over state lines for the purpose of prostitution. Granting federal agents the right to investigate, arrest, and prosecute persons in violation of the Mann Act solidified the interstate authority of federal investigative services.

The Special Agents force also aided border guards, investigating smuggling cases and immigration violations. At the outbreak of the Mexican revolution, bureau agents conducted limited espionage operations, gathering intelligence for the military and the government.

World War I and the Interwar Years

When World War I erupted in Europe, the United States government, under President Woodrow Wilson, proclaimed American neutrality in the conflict. Despite the official declaration of neutrality, the United States increasingly aided Allied nations such as Britain and France with sales of weapons and supplies for the war effort. As a result, rival Germany sent saboteurs and spies into the United States to conduct espionage against United States military instillations and ammunition factories. Several incidents, including an explosion near New York City, at Black Tom Pier, fanned public fear of German spies and saboteurs infiltrating the United States. Federal investigators were charged with investigating acts of terrorism and sabotage, as well as ferreting out potential spies. For this job, Special Agents worked closely with military intelligence, gaining new law enforcement and espionage tradecraft skills.

With the entry of the United States into the European conflict, federal investigators gained jurisdiction over the enforcement of the Espionage, Sabotage, and Selective Service Acts. The bureau investigated alien enemies, and arrested men who dodged conscription.

After World War I ended in 1918, the force of Special Agents became the Bureau of Investigation. The agency gained considerable autonomy from Department of Justice oversight. During the 1920s, federal agents investigated several regional and national crime syndicates. Prohibition, the ban on sale and consumption of alcoholic beverages, prompted a rise in the illegal manufacture, trade, and sale of alcohol. Since the Department of the Treasury had jurisdiction over Prohibition violations, federal investigators worked closely with Treasury agents.

The interwar era was also marked by increased gangsterism. Gangsters posed a unique challenge to the Bureau of Investigation's narrow interstate jurisdiction. Many of the most notorious crime bosses were eventually arrested on charges of racketeering, tax evasion, or war profiteering. With no other means available, within their legal bounds, to bring down the resurgence of the often violent and well-armed Ku Klux Klan (KKK), the Bureau of Investigation targeted the leader of the Louisiana Klan for violations of the Mann Act.

The onset of the Great Depression helped escalate crime rates. The sour economy gave rise to increased labor violations, corruption, swindling, and murder. Two events, however, strengthened and expanded the Bureau of Investigation's jurisdiction. The kidnapping of the Lindbergh baby in 1932 prompted Congress to pass federal kidnapping statutes. Two years later, Congress passed legislation prohibiting the escape of criminals across state lines, providing for interstate extradition of criminals, and granting federal agents the right to investigate and arrest criminals who fled or operated across state lines. Further reforms of federal law enforcement services permitted agents to carry guns.

The structure of the agency changed dramatically in the 1920s and 1930s. J. Edgar Hoover assumed the directorship of the Bureau of Investigation. Hoover expanded the field office network from nine offices to over 30 offices within ten years. Agency personnel policy changed, requiring new agents to complete a rigorous , centralized training course. Promotions within the organization were secured through merit and consistency of service, not seniority. The agency still sought agent-recruits with training in accountancy and law, but expanded their search to include linguists, mathematicians, physicists, chemists, forensics specialists, and medical practitioners.

Technical advancements also changed agency operations. Basic forensic investigation began to be employed in FBI crime scene investigations. The bureau established a fingerprint identification and index system in 1924. The national index assumed fingerprint records from state and local law enforcement agencies, as well as an older Department of Justice fingerprint registry dating back to 1905. The agency opened its first technical laboratory in 1932. The facility quickly expanded to cover a variety of forensic research, aiding investigators by comparing bullets, guns, tire tracks, watermarks, counterfeiting techniques, handwriting samples, and pathology reports.

World War II and the Interwar Years

In 1935, the special task force of agents who formerly worked to combat Prohibition were separated from the agency, and the organization was renamed the Federal Bureau of Investigation (FBI). When war again broke out in Europe, FBI agents performed many of the same duties as they had during World War I. Before the United States entered the war in 1941, the FBI concentrated its efforts on locating, infiltrating, and dismantling political organizations sympathetic to German and Italian Fascism, and Soviet Communism, despite the latter nation's wartime alliance with Britain and France. President Franklin D. Roosevelt, and Secretary of State Cordell Hull, pushed for increased power for the FBI to investigate perceived subversives, even if these people were ordinary American citizens. A 1939 presidential directive, followed by the Smith Act of 1940, outlawed public advocacy of overthrowing the government.

When the United States entered the war after the bombing of Pearl Harbor, FBI agents aided national defense efforts by placing trained agents at key military and defense industry sites. Wartime agents received more intense training in counterintelligence measures, and the FBI established special counterintelligence units for covert operations at the government's discretion. FBI agents thwarted German and Japanese attempts at sabotaging national interests, including fuel reserves.

World War II also marked one of the darkest chapters of FBI operations. Despite opposition from FBI director Hoover, government officials declared all Japanese immigrants, and American citizens of Japanese descent, enemy aliens. The Japanese-American population on the West Coast was evicted from their homes and sent to internment camps for the duration of the war. Many lost homes and businesses that they were forced to leave behind. Since internment camps and enemy alien laws fell under federal jurisdiction, the FBI imposed curfews, administered deportations, and arrested those in violation of internment laws.

Conversely, FBI agents were the first federal authority since Reconstruction to enforce desegregation laws. Though segregation remained legal practice during the 1940s, the president appointed the Fair Employment Practices Commission (FEPC) to address concerns of African-American workers. FEPC possessed no enforcement authority, but FBI agents arrested several employers found in violation of the FEPC on the grounds of impeding the war effort.

The FBI during the Cold War

The early Cold War years.
When World War II ended in August 1945, increasingly hostile relations between the United States and the Soviet Union led to the Cold War, a diplomatic and military standoff that lasted over four decades. In the early Cold War years, the American government, and many members of the public, worried about the presence of Communist organizations and spies within the United States. The discovery of Soviet agents operating within government agencies, and the trial of individuals accused of stealing atomic secrets, and the test detonation of the first Soviet atomic bomb in 1949, fanned public anti-Communist hysteria. While the newly formed Central Intelligence Agency (CIA) worked to stop the expansion of the Soviet Union abroad, the FBI gained the past-war responsibility of defeating Communist organizations at home.

In the first fifteen years of the Cold War, the FBI investigations contributed to the McCarthy hearings, as well as high-profile spy cases like that of Julius and Ethel Rosenberg. The FBI gained the authority to conduct background checks on potential government employees, and investigate federal employees suspected of disloyal acts or espionage. The 1946 Atomic Energy Act gave the FBI jurisdiction over the secrecy and protection of atomic secrets. Legislation throughout the 1950s expanded the FBI's role to cover the security of atomic facilities, and defense industry sites.

In more routine law enforcement duties, the FBI continued to pursue interstate and federal criminals. In 1950, the agency published its first "Ten Most Wanted List."

The early 1960s and the Civil Rights Movement.
Although the Cold War continued, the anti-Communist hysteria faded away in the late 1950s. FBI investigations of anti-government organizations and "subversive individuals" shifted with the political mood of the 1960s. The decade witnessed the assassination of President John F. Kennedy, the Vietnam War, and ushered in the Civil Rights Movement, both events signaled new duties and an expanded legal jurisdiction for the FBI.

When President Kennedy was assassinated in Dallas, Texas in 1963, the crime was legally a local homicide. No special legal provisions existed for the investigation of the assassination of a government official or the president. President Lyndon B. Johnson called in FBI agents to investigate the murder, setting the precedent for future legislation that designated assassination as a federal crime, and granted the agency jurisdiction in assassination cases.

The FBI was responsible for federal enforcement of the Civil Rights Act of 1964, and aiding desegregation efforts by investigating pro-segregation organizations and individuals. The FBI's charge to enforce civil rights legislation often put federal agents in conflict with local law enforcement officials, especially in the South and Midwest. Though the FBI routinely investigated violations of civil rights laws, they did not win the authority to prosecute violators through federal law until after 1966.

The FBI investigated, and helped prosecute criminals, in several high profile civil rights cases. Field agents in Louisiana and Mississippi investigated the murder of three voter registration workers in Philadelphia, Mississippi, before turning the case over to FBI headquarters in Washington, D.C. FBI agents conducted crime scene, forensics, and extended investigations of the assassinations of civil rights leaders Martin Luther King, Jr., and Medger Evers. They eventually arrested, aided the prosecution of, and gained convictions for the assassins, although Byron De La Beckwith, who shot Medger Evers, was not found guilty until 1994.

The Vietnam and Watergate era.

The United States, in an attempt to stem Soviet influence in Asia, entered the Vietnam War. The war was controversial, with many young people opposing U.S. military intervention in the conflict. The re-institution of the draft further angered anti-war sympathizers. Government officials grew increasingly suspicious of anti-war organizations and the large demonstrations they organized. Though the vast majority of anti-war demonstrators and organizations advocated peaceful protest and civil disobedience, a few militant and extremist groups resorted to acts of violence and sabotage. The actions of these groups prompted the FBI to conduct widespread surveillance of the anti-war movement. Utilizing counterintelligence techniques, the FBI used a myriad of intrusive surveillance, known as "Cointelpro," methods to thwart terrorist action by radicals. However, some criticized the organization of conducting domestic espionage, especially on the peaceful majority of anti-war supporters. Hoover, still director of the FBI, responded by promoting passage of the Omnibus Crime Control Act, which limited the use of wiretaps, listening devices, clandestine photographs, and other surveillance methods. The act defined new operational procedures for FBI agents, and was the first legal compromise between intelligence and privacy interests.

In 1972, public attention shifted from the Vietnam conflict, to the actions of the Nixon administration. On June 17, 1972, five men were arrested while breaking into the Watergate apartment complex that housed the headquarters for the Democratic Party. Subsequent investigations by a special team of federal agents connected the men, most whom were former CIA and FBI agents, to the Office of the President. Despite the implication of a few FBI agents in the extensive cover-up operation that followed the break-in, FBI investigators cooperated with a specially appointed Senate investigatory committee, surrendering all information pertaining to Watergate. The ensuing scandal, known as Watergate, not only forced the resignation of Nixon and most of his administration, but also damaged public faith in the government and its intelligence and security agencies.

The end of the Cold War.

A period of Cold War détente in the 1980s allowed the FBI to concentrate on agency reforms and expansion of its domestic intelligence capabilities. In 1982, following a outburst of international terrorism, the director of the FBI, William Webster, made counterintelligence and anti-terrorism operations an agency priority. He established the National Center for the Analysis of Violent Crime, a facility that would conduct sophisticated forensic analysis on crimes. The renewed agency attention to counterintelligence discovered over 30 cases of espionage against the United States government in 1985.

Combating the rise of white-collar financial crimes and the drug trade were other priorities of the FBI during the 1980s. FBI investigations implicated high-ranking government officials in financial fraud and abuse of power scandals, including members of the Congress (ABSCAM), defense industry (ILL WIND), and judiciary (GREYLORD). Federal agents also investigated fraud cases during the savings and loan crisis.

The Rise of Terrorism and the FBI Today

In 1991, the Soviet Union collapsed. Its formal dissolution on December 25, 1991, marked the end of the Cold War. In the decade that followed, the international political map drastically altered, changing the global balance of power and permitting the rise of new threats to United States national security. In response to the changing international environment, the FBI shifted the priority of its operations. Several key events, including the 1993 bombing of the World Trade Center by Islamist, foreign terrorists, and the 1995 bombing of a federal building in Oklahoma City by a domestic terrorist, prompted the FBI to restructure its counterintelligence and counter-terrorism operations.

To aid its current operations, the FBI embraced the use of several new technologies in its operations. The advent of personal computers and the Internet aided research and processing of investigation information. Searchable databases store information on suspects, crime statistics, fingerprints, and DNA samples. However, their use also created security risks that necessitated the creation of specialized information systems protection task forces. The agency created Computer Analysis and Response Teams (CART) to aid field investigators with the recovery of data from damaged or sabotaged electronic sources. In 1998, the establishment of the National Infrastructure Protection Center (NIPC) permitted the FBI to monitor the dissemination of computer viruses and worms.

Forensic use of DNA radically altered both the legal process and forensic research of FBI investigations. DNA analysis allows specialists to positively identify victims and perpetrators of crimes by comparing particular patterns in individual DNA. FBI forensic specialists created a national DNA databank in 1998 to aid ongoing investigations.

After the September 11, 2001, terrorist attacks on the United States, and subsequent anthrax attacks on national post offices and media outlets, the FBI expanded its counterintelligence and counter-terrorism operations to include anti-bioterror task forces. The FBI, working in conjunction for the Centers for Disease Control (CDC), employs agents to aid in the investigation and identification of bioterror agents, and law enforcement in the event of a bioterror attack. FBI analysis and research divisions have compiled massive databases on known biological agents, stockpiles of weapons, and terrorist groups who may possess biological weapons. FBI analysts develop profiles of terrorist groups to better understand their mindsets and possible future actions.

The FBI's focus on the prevention of terrorism failed to thwart the September 11, 2001, terrorist attacks on the World Trade Center and the Pentagon. However, FBI investigations successfully found and prosecuted the perpetrators of the Oklahoma City bombing and the 1993 attack on the World Trade Center. In its ongoing investigation of the events of September 11, FBI agents have found and arrested several persons suspected of having connections to the al-Qaeda terrorist network and the recent terrorist attacks. The FBI is also designated as the primary agency of enforcement for the Patriot Act.

Although no major FBI operations were assumed into the Department of Homeland Security (DHS), the establishment of pending DHS committees to govern intelligence agency cooperation and information sharing will alter the manner in which the FBI relays information to the President and other government officials. Proponents of the DHS hope the agency will streamline communication among intelligence and security agencies. Critics of proposed DHS intelligence reforms charge that agencies, such as the FBI, will lose investigative and operational autonomy. Despite the changing future of the structure of the United States intelligence community, the FBI will undoubtedly play a central role.

■ FURTHER READING:

BOOKS:

Kessler, Ronald. *The Bureau: The Secret History of the FBI.* New York: St. Martin's Press, 2002.

ELECTRONIC:

United States Federal Bureau of Investigation. <http://www.fbi.gov> (May 2003).

SEE ALSO

Anthrax, Terrorist Use as a Biological Weapon
Black Tom Explosion
CIA (CSI), Center for the Study of Intelligence
COINTELPRO
Cold War (1945–1950), The Start of the Atomic Age
Cold War (1950–1972)
Cold War (1972–1989): The Collapse of the Soviet Union
Commission on Civil Rights, United States
Counter-Intelligence
Counter-terrorism Policy, United States
Infrastructure Protection Center (NIPC), United States National
Justice Department, United States
McCarthyism
Pearl Harbor, Japanese Attack on
Privacy: Legal and Ethical Issues
September 11 Terrorist Attacks on the United States

FCC (United States Federal Communications Commission)

■ STEPHANIE WATSON

The Federal Communications Commission (FCC), an independent government agency, oversees the media and communications industries in the United States. Included under the FCC's jurisdiction are radio, television, cable, telephone, satellite, and wireless (cellular phones and pagers) providers. As part of their regulatory responsibilities, FCC commissioners review and grant broadcasting licenses, approve corporate mergers and acquisitions, and protect consumers by responding to complaints and investigating claims of unfair rates and fraudulent business practices.

In the wake of the September 11, 2001 terrorist attacks, the FCC tightened its focus on security, and began looking at new ways to protect the nation's communications infrastructure. In March of the following year, it announced the creation of a new Media Security and Reliability Council. The federal advisory committee, comprised of media company executives, public service representatives, trade association members, and manufacturers, meets regularly to evaluate the security of national communications networks, and to strategize measures to protect against future attacks.

The FCC is governed by five commissioners, who are appointed by the president with the Senate's approval. Rules governing the FCC stipulate that no more than three commissioners can be from the same political party. Each commissioner serves for a five-year period. The agency is funded by and reports to the United States Congress. The FCC chairman directs the organization's activities and is responsible for hiring its bureau chiefs and department heads.

The FCC is divided into six bureaus, each of which has been designated to provide a specific function. The Media

Bureau regulates and licenses broadcast television and radio stations, cable and satellite providers; the Wireless Telecommunications Bureau oversees cellular phones, pagers, and two-way radios; the Consumer and Governmental Affairs Bureau educates the public and coordinates with other government agencies to protect consumer interests; the Enforcement Bureau carries out the rules set forth under the Communications Act; the International Bureau directs communications activities outside the United States; and the Wireline Competition Bureau regulates telephone companies that provide interstate and intrastate wire-based service. Ten staff offices have been set up to support these bureaus.

The birth of the FCC. The FCC was set up under the 1934 Communications Act to regulate radio and telephone communications. It combined functions originally designated to the Federal Radio Commission, Interstate Commerce Commission, and Postmaster General. As the television, cable and wireless industries emerged in subsequent years, the FCC's reach was extended and its responsibilities increased. New regulations were enacted to govern each new industry, for example the Communications Satellite Act of 1962 and the Cable Act of 1992.

Each industry under the FCC's jurisdiction was originally designated a separate entity, and prohibited by the government from crossing over into each other's territory. That is, until Congress signed the landmark 1996 Telecommunications Act. The act relaxed the rules governing corporate ownership within the telephone, television, and computer industries; allowing, for example, local phone companies to offer long-distance service and cable companies to offer Internet access. The move allowed greater competition among companies, and more choice and protection against monopolistic pricing practices for consumers. It also set the stage for a host of media mergers and acquisitions, most notably: America Online/Time Warner/Turner Broadcasting system, and ABC/Walt Disney Co., and MCI/Worldcom.

Over the years, the FCC has directed a number of important initiatives. In the early 1960s, when then-chairman Newton Minnow called television "a vast wasteland," television stations were spurred to raise programming standards. In 1990, the Children's Television Act limited advertising in programs geared to children and made children's programming a stipulation for license renewal. The FCC has also had to deal with First Amendment issues, for example obscenity cases relating to the music industry and radio broadcasts by so-called "shock jocks."

■ FURTHER READING:

BOOKS:

Fleissner, Jennifer *The Federal Communications Commission.* New York: Chelsea House Publishers, 1992.

Hilliard, Robert L. *The Federal Communications Commission: A Primer.* Boston: Focal Press 1991.

Paglin, Max D., ed. *A Legislative History of the Communications Act of 1934.* New York: Oxford University Press, 1990.

PERIODICALS:

Hickey, Neil. "So Big: The Telecommunications Act at Year One." *Columbia Journalism Review* Jan/Feb. 1997: 23–28.

ELECTRONIC:

The Federal Communications Commission <http://www.fcc.gov/> (January 30, 2003).

SEE ALSO

Communications System, United States National
Electronic Communication Intercepts, Legal Issues
National Telecommunications Information Administration, and Security for the Radio Frequency Spectrum, United States
Telephone Recording Laws

FDA (United States Food and Drug Administration)

The Food and Drug Administration (FDA), a Department of Health and Human Services agency, regulates the development, sale, and distribution of food products, prescription and over-the-counter drugs, cosmetics, and medical equipment. The FDA's reach is so extensive that one-fifth of all consumer dollars spent in the U.S. purchase a product regulated by the FDA. The goal of the FDA is to protect consumers by ensuring the safety of food and drug products sold in the U.S.

The FDA traces its history to 1862, when President Abraham Lincoln created a chemistry division under the Department of Agriculture. Congress created the modern FDA in 1906 with the passage of the Food and Drugs Act. The 1906 law gave limited power to the FDA to monitor the safety of food and drug products. In 1938, Congress expanded the power of the FDA by passing the Food, Drug, and Cosmetic Act. This act granted the FDA the power to test drugs and determine their safety and efficacy before allowing companies to sell the new drugs. The act also granted the FDA authority to regulate cosmetics.

While the FDA's primary task is to ensure food and drug safety, in recent years the agency has taken on an increased role in the fight against bioterrorism. The FDA is leading efforts to develop and produce vaccines and treatments plans to prevent or stop the spread of a bioterror attack. In this quest, the FDA must quickly test vaccines, so private companies can produce and stockpile vaccines.

The variety of possible pathogens (disease-causing microorganisms) that might be used in bioterrorism has tested the limits of the FDA. The administration must simultaneously assess the effectiveness of vaccines and treatments for anthrax, smallpox, botulism, plague, hemorrhagic fevers, and other potential bioweapons. Additionally, the FDA, in conjunction with the Centers for Disease Control, must take into account that terrorists might genetically alter existing pathogens to reduce the efficacy of current vaccines and treatments. The FDA plans to thwart potential terrorist attacks by expediting its approval process for new vaccines and drugs that could reduce the severity of a bioterror attack.

■ FURTHER READING:

ELECTRONIC:

Department of Health and Human Services. "United States Food and Drug Administration." <http://www.fda.gov> (May 2003).

SEE ALSO

Bioterrorism, Protective Measures
Food Supply, Counter-Terrorism
Salmonella and Salmonella Food Poisoning
Vaccination

Federal Protective Service, United States

■ CARYN E. NEUMANN

The United States Federal Protective Service (FPS) is the security arm of the General Services Administration (GSA) and it is responsible for the protection of most of the civilian workspace owned or leased by the federal government, as well as the safety of the workers and visitors who use these sites. Headquartered in Washington, D.C. since its 1949 founding, FPS guards more than 8000 sites and one million federal workers and visitors on a daily basis. It promotes safety by employing law enforcement, physical security, and investigative personnel as well as contract guards, electronic surveillance, entry control devices, and a crime prevention awareness campaign. The agency serves as a centralized communication provider by networking with federal, state, and local law enforcement agencies.

The mission of FPS is to permit the conduct of government business by ensuring a safe environment that is open and inviting in a professional and cost effective manner. The agency traces its origins to the Federal Property and Administrative Services Act of 1949, which consolidated real property functions within the newly created GSA and brought the U.S. Special Police under the protection division of the GSA's Public Building Service. In 1971, GSA established the Federal Protective Force, which later became FPS, in response to the growing number of demonstrations occurring at federal facilities. FPS covers buildings housing most federal agencies, committees, and commissions; U.S. District and Appellate Courts; and U.S. senators and congressional representatives. It bears responsibility for the protection of U.S. Border Patrol Stations, including the San Ysidro Border Station, which separates Tijuana, Mexico from San Diego, California and is considered to be the busiest land port in the world.

Over the years, FPS has shifted its emphasis from the fixed guardpost concept of security to a mobile police force that promotes physical security and crime prevention. The agency has recently adopted community policing, which means that it has moved its officers out of vehicles to allow them to spend more time in and around the buildings leased and operated by GSA. FPS coordinates regional activities with control centers in New York, Boston, Philadelphia, Atlanta, Denver, Chicago, San Francisco, Seattle, Fort Worth, Kansas City, and Washington, D.C. as well as branches in the Far East and Caribbean. It has additional offices in all fifty states plus Puerto Rico and the Virgin Islands.

To meet its responsibilities, FPS performs both security and law enforcement functions with uniformed and plainclothes personnel and regularly coordinates its activities with the Federal Emergency Management Agency (FEMA). Security, increasingly performed by contract guards as well as physical security specialists, includes such activities as the placement of security equipment and technology. FPS security personnel participate in the modification and repair of existing buildings as well as the construction of new ones to ensure that these sites have specially tailored security measures, equipment, and technology in place. FPS also routinely conducts building assessments of all GSA-controlled facilities to identify security weaknesses. Law enforcement security officers (LESOs), who hold the core FPS position, conduct preliminary investigations of accidents, incidents, and criminal complaints occurring on GSA-controlled property. LESOs do not investigate criminal offenses involving GSA employees but they are responsible for gathering protective intelligence information pertaining to demonstrations, bomb threats, and other criminal activities. FPS law enforcement personnel carry guns and are trained at the Federal Law Enforcement Training Center in Glynco, Georgia.

Until the 1995 bombing of the Alfred P. Murrah Federal Building in Oklahoma City, FPS had suffered from repeated budgetary and personnel cuts that compromised its ability to guarantee the safety of federal workers and visitors. After the attack, the GSA bolstered all of its security systems including FPS. As long as fear of terrorism remains strong, FPS will likely play a significant role in homeland security.

■ FURTHER READING:

BOOKS:

United States Congress. Committee on Environment and Public Works. Subcommittee on Transportation and Infrastructure. *Federal Protective Service Reform Act of 2000: Hearing Before the Subcommittee on Transportation and Infrastructure on the Committee on Environment and Public Works, U.S. Senate, 106 Congress, second session, September 28, 2000 on H.R. 809, a Bill to Amend the Act of June 1, 1948 to Provide for the Reform of the Federal Protective Service.* Washington, D.C.: Government Printing Office, 2000.

United States General Services Administration. Office of Federal Protective Service. *Careers in Security and Law Enforcement.* Washington, D.C.: Government Printing Office, 2002.

———. Public Buildings Service. Law Enforcement Division. *The Federal Protective Service* Washington, D.C.: Government Printing Office, 1998.

SEE ALSO

FEMA (United States Federal Emergency Management Agency)
General Services Administration, United States
Intelligence and Counter-Espionage Careers

Federal Reserve System, United States

■ JUDSON KNIGHT

Created by the passage of the Federal Reserve Act in 1913, the Federal Reserve System serves as the central bank of the United States. Commonly known as the Fed, it conducts monetary policy for the nation by exerting direct influence on the money supply, interest rates, and the purchase of government securities. It is the means by which federally issued currency and coinage reaches financial institutions, which receive these through the 12 Federal Reserve district banks located in various major cities throughout the United States. The Fed also sets the interest rate at which it loans money to member financial institutions, thus establishing a baseline for the rates of interest at which money is borrowed and lent throughout the United States.

Conducting Monetary Policy

The initial mandate granted to the Federal Reserve System by Congress was to provide and ensure stability, safety, and flexibility in the national monetary and financial system. Since 1913, the responsibilities and powers accorded to the Fed have grown considerably.

Today the Federal Reserve shapes, directs, and conducts U.S. monetary policy. Its overall concern is the well being of the national economy, which it seeks to achieve through a number of measurable goals, including price stability and full employment. These goals it achieves, in turn, through three principal means at its disposal: the control of the money supply by the issuance of currency to member financial institutions, the setting of interest rates at which it loans funds to those institutions, and the open market purchase of government securities.

Controlling the money supply. Under the Legal Tender Act of 1862, the United States began issuing currency notes, known as U.S. notes, through the Treasury Department, and continued to do so until January 21, 1971. At the time it passed the act, Congress set a limit of $300 million on the value of U.S. notes that could be in circulation at any one time. Significant by the standards of the Civil War era, this sum represents a tiny portion of the funds in circulation today, which are known as Federal Reserve notes.

Whereas U.S. notes represented obligations of the federal government alone, Federal Reserve notes, authorized under the 1913 act that created the Fed itself, represent an obligation both of the federal government and the Federal Reserve system. The original Legal Tender Act was accordingly amended to include Federal Reserve notes as legal tender, meaning that they legally satisfy debts equal to the face value of the note tendered.

It is technically illegal to refuse legal tender (which today is synonymous with Federal Reserve notes) for services already rendered, though it is not illegal to refuse it for services not yet rendered. Therefore, a business that accepts only checks or credit must post a notice indicating this, so that the customer is aware of the fact prior to tendering payment.

Setting interest rates. In addition to controlling the money supply through the issuance of legal tender, the Federal Reserve directly affects monetary policy by a second and perhaps even more significant means: the setting of interest rates. This is accomplished by determining the discount rate, or the rate it charges member institutions for loans. These institutions, in turn, charge other depository institutions a certain rate for overnight loans of funds that are immediately available at the Federal Reserve Bank. The rate at which Fed member banks charge money to depository institutions, known as the federal funds rate, will always be slightly higher than the discount rate, but varies from institution to institution, and from day to day.

In order to turn a profit, banks that borrow money at the federal funds rate, in turn, charge borrowers—both

Guided by tradition, Federal Reserve Chairman Alan Greenspan assembles members of the Federal Open Market Committee around this 27-foot magohany table eight times a year to set interest rates. AP/WIDE WORLD PHOTOS.

businesses and individuals—slightly higher rates. By this chain of relationships, the Fed exerts an all but direct influence on consumer credit costs ranging from the annual percentage rate on a credit card to the rate charged on a 30-year housing loan.

Open market operations. In addition to setting interest rates and controlling the money supply, the Fed conducts monetary policy through a third instrument, open market operations, or the buying and selling on the open market of securities issued by the U.S. Treasury and federal agencies. These securities include bonds of various types, as well as other government certificates. In each case, the value of the bond or certificate ultimately rests in the fiscal strength of the federal government.

Historically, the Federal Reserve has tied its objectives for open market operations either to a certain quantity of reserves, or a certain price. Prior to the administration of Federal Reserve Chairman Alan Greenspan, who was appointed by President Ronald Reagan in 1987, the Fed tended to focus on seeking a desired quantity of securities as reserves. Since that time, however, the Fed has sought to attain desirable levels in the price of securities, which are the federal funds rate. From 1995, it began

announcing target levels for the federal funds rate, which rose in the healthy economic climate of 1999 and 2000, but fell in the recessionary economies of 2001 and 2002.

Maintaining Financial Stability

The open market operations of the Federal Reserve System are a clear means by which the Fed helps to maintain both financial and ultimately, political stability in the nation. Although it continually pursues its objective of ensuring stability through the three significant means at its disposal, the actions of the Federal Reserve become particularly evident during periods of financial upheaval.

The stock market crash of October, 1987, the Asian financial crisis and its aftermath in late 1998, and the terrorist attacks of September, 2001 each presented an occasion in which the U.S. financial system faced challenges, and when consumer faith in the national economy wavered. In each such situation, as well as in less significant crises, the Federal Reserve has gone into action, ensuring monetary liquidity through large balances of available cash; keeping interest rates manageable by extending discount loans to depository institutions; and setting the example of faith in U.S. institutions by purchasing government securities on the open market.

Even in times when the affairs of the nation are running more smoothly, the Fed continues to influence monetary policy. Americans are less likely to take note of the Federal Reserve in those situations, yet it is the Fed itself that deserves much of the credit for the stability in such times. The most visible means by which the Fed affects the economy is through the discount rate, which serves, in effect, like a gas pedal for economic growth. When rates are low, economic activity increases, and the economy grows. If the economy grows too fast, the Fed may raise interest rates as a means of ensuring price stability and protecting against inflation.

Structure of the Federal Reserve

The chairman of the Federal Reserve leads a seven-member Board of Governors, all of whom are appointed by U.S. presidents. The president also appoints the chairman and vice-chairman from among the board members, appointments that must be confirmed by the U.S. Senate.

Alongside the board is another entity that arguably exerts as much power, the Federal Open Market Committee (FOMC), which oversees open market operations. The FOMC sets the objective for open market operations, meaning that it sets the federal funds rate. If the Fed purchases securities, thus adding to reserves, then depository institutions will tend to take on new loans and investments, which has the effect of lowering interest rates.

Of the seats on the FOMC, seven are filled by the members of the Board of Governors, and an eighth by the president of the New York Federal Reserve Bank. The other four are divided among the 11 other Federal Reserve banks, which fall into four groups (Boston, Philadelphia, and Richmond; Chicago and Cleveland; Atlanta, St. Louis, and Dallas; Minneapolis, Kansas City, and San Francisco), with presidents from each city in a group serving rotating one-year terms.

Banks. Although there are only 12 Federal Reserve banks, each has branches in other cities. For example, the Federal Reserve Bank of San Francisco has branches in Los Angeles, Portland, Seattle, and Salt Lake City. The 12 district banks release currency, and every banknote issued in the United States bears the seal of one of the district banks to the left of the portrait on the observe side.

Federal Reserve banks sell stock to member institutions, which include national and state-chartered banks, as well as trust companies. All national banks, which are chartered by the Office of the Comptroller of the Currency in the Treasury Department, automatically belong to the Fed, while state banks and trust companies have to meet requirements set by the Board of Governors. All members are required to purchase from their regional Federal Reserve banks stock equal to six percent of their capital, of which half is paid in, while the other half can be called in by the Board of Governors.

Relationship with the federal government. The Federal Reserve System is a part of the government in the sense that it was created by Congress, and is subject to congressional oversight. Furthermore, its leadership is appointed by presidents, although board members' 14-year terms extend far beyond the term of the chief executive who appointed them. Unlike most bureaus of the federal government, however, the Fed is independent of any cabinet-level department. Its decisions do not require the approval of the president, Congress, or any other member or body of the executive or legislative branches.

Nor does it depend on funding appropriated by Congress. Almost alone among government institutions, the Fed actually pays for itself through the interest it receives on its holdings of federal securities, and through the fees it charges depository institutions for such services as processing and clearing checks. As a non-profit institution, it turns its net earnings over to the Treasury each year. These earnings are far from inconsiderable: in 2001, the Federal Reserve paid $27.14 billion to the federal government.

■ **FURTHER READING:**

BOOKS:

Greider, William. *Secrets of the Temple: How the Federal Reserve Runs the Country.* New York: Simon and Schuster, 1987.

Mayer, Martin. *The Fed: The Inside Story of How the World's Most Powerful Financial Institution Drives the Market.* New York: Free Press, 2001.

Woodward, Bob. *Maestro: Greenspan's Fed and the American Boom.* New York: Simon and Schuster, 2000.

ELECTRONIC:

Federal Reserve Board. <http://www.federalreserve.gov/> (February 5, 2003).

SEE ALSO

Counterfeit Currency, Technology and the Manufacture
IMF (International Monetary Fund)
Treasury Department, United States

FEMA (United States Federal Emergency Management Agency)

Although today a component of the Department of Homeland Security (DHS), the Federal Emergency Management Agency (FEMA) is a formerly independent agency of

"Cowboy," a search and rescue canine for the Federal Emergency Management Agency (FEMA), pauses during his work searching the World Trade Center site in New York in September, 2001. AP/WIDE WORLD PHOTOS.

the U.S. federal government tasked with responding to all aspects of natural and manmade disasters. This excludes specialized response capabilities such as those of radiological teams—although FEMA works with these—but includes all phases of disaster response, mitigation, and prevention. Created by a 1979 executive order, FEMA employs some 2,600 people at its headquarters in Washington, D.C., and at sites across the nation.

Early history. Federal efforts at disaster relief had their beginnings surprisingly early, in an 1803 congressional act authorizing assistance to a New Hampshire town ravaged by fire. Over the next century and a quarter, more than a hundred pieces of ad hoc legislation were passed in response to floods, hurricanes, earthquakes and other disasters.

The establishment of the Reconstruction Finance Program (RFP) under the New Deal of President Franklin D.

Roosevelt in the 1930s finally gave shape to federal disaster-relief efforts. The RFP, which made loans for repair and reconstruction in the wake of disasters, was soon augmented by the Bureau of Public Roads, which provided funding for the replacement of roads and bridges, and by the Flood Control Act, designed to enable the U.S. Army Corps of Engineers to implement flood control projects.

During the 1960s, a series of hurricanes lashed the United States, prompting the establishment of the Federal Disaster Assistance Administration within the Department of Housing and Urban Development. In 1968, Congress passed the National Flood Insurance Act, which increased the flood protection afforded to homeowners. The Disaster Relief Act of 1974 established the principle and process of disaster declarations on the part of the president, whose executive powers were sufficient to direct resources toward relief.

With more than 100 federal agencies involved in some aspect of disaster relief, the need for a coordinating agency became apparent, and in 1979 President James E. Carter issued an executive order creating FEMA. The new agency absorbed a number of entities, among them the Federal Preparedness Agency of the General Services Administration, HUD's Federal Disaster Assistance Administration, and the Defense Civil Preparedness Agency of the Department of Defense.

FEMA today. In its first quarter-century of existence, FEMA dealt with a vast array of natural and human disasters, including the nuclear accident at Three Mile Island in Pennsylvania in 1979, the Cuban refugee crisis in 1980, the San Francisco earthquake in 1989, Hurricane Andrew in 1992, floods in the Midwest and West in 1993, and the terrorist attacks of September 11, 2001.

The appointment of James L. Witt by President William J. Clinton in 1993 put FEMA for the first time under the leadership of a director with experience as a state emergency manager. Witt undertook wide-scale reforms that streamlined relief measures. Thanks to the end of the Cold War, he was also able to direct resources from civil defense toward disaster relief, as well as recovery and mitigation programs.

In the post-September 2001 era, a new type of "civil defense" emerged: homeland security. FEMA became part of DHS when the latter was formally established on March 1, 2003.

Organization and mission. In addition to its 2,600 full-time employees, FEMA has between 4,000 and 5,000 reservists. Its force operates out of FEMA headquarters; the FEMA training center at Emmitsburg, Maryland; the Mount Weather Emergency Operations Center in Virginia; and other facilities. FEMA often works in partnership with other groups, including some 27 federal agencies, state and local emergency management agencies, and the American Red Cross.

The mission and activities of FEMA relate to what the agency's own literature describes as the "life cycle of disaster." Starting with the disaster itself, there is the response phase, followed by recovery, mitigation, risk reduction, prevention, and preparedness—all of which makes the nation and its communities more equipped to deal with future catastrophes.

Among the specific activities FEMA undertakes are assisting with flood-plain management and implementation of building codes; teaching local communities how to survive a disaster; and equipping state and local emergency teams to prepare them for a disaster situation. In the event of a calamity, FEMA helps coordinate the federal response, and makes disaster assistance available to states, communities, businesses, and individuals. It also trains emergency managers, supports fire services nationwide, and administers national flood and crime insurance programs.

■ **FURTHER READING:**

BOOKS:

Gore, Albert. *Federal Emergency Management Agency: Accompanying Report of the National Performance Review.* Washington, D.C.: Office of the Vice President, 1994.

Landesman, Linda Young. *Public Health Management of Disasters: The Practical Guide.* Washington, D.C.: American Public Health Association, 2001.

Therese, McAllister, and Gene Corley. *World Trade Center Building Performance Study: Data Collection, Preliminary Observations, and Recommendations.* Washington, D.C.: Federal Emergency Management Agency, 2002.

PERIODICALS:

Adams, Shawn. "A Beginner's Guide to Learning Emergency Management." *Risk Management* 49, no. 5 (May 2002): 24–28.

"Reports Shed Light on World Trade Center Collapses, Look to Safer Structures in the Future." *JOM* 54, no. 6 (June 2002): 6.

Rubin, Debra K. "FEMA and Corps Plan New Guide for Terrorism Catastrophes." *ENR* 249, no. 15 (October 7, 2002): 14.

ELECTRONIC:

Federal Emergency Management Agency. <http://www.fema.gov> (March 26, 2003).

SEE ALSO

Architecture and Structural Security
Chemical Safety: Emergency Responses
Homeland Security, United States Department
Radiological Emergency Response Plan, United States Federal

FEST (United States Foreign Emergency Support Team)

The United States Foreign Emergency Support Team (FEST) is a rapid-response unit designed to respond to terrorist attacks against U.S. interests overseas. Created in 1985, it is directed by the Department of State, but constitutes an interagency force. Its most famous deployment occurred in 1998, when operatives of Osama bin Laden's al-Qaeda network bombed U.S. embassies in Kenya and Tanzania.

FEST was created to provide coordination and assistance to U.S. personnel and host nations in the event of an attack against American personnel and/or property overseas. Whenever deployed, it is directed by the chief of mission, who is the leading representative of the U.S.

president in a host nation (usually, but not always, this is an ambassador). Its efforts are coordinated by the Department of State, working through the Office of the Coordinator for Counterterrorism.

In crisis situations, FEST has the mission of advising, assisting, assessing, and coordinating. It provides the chief of mission, incident managers, and leaders of the host government with direction concerning Washington's response to a terrorist attack. FEST personnel are prepared to work around the clock in crisis and consequence management, communication augmentation, and other specialized tasks as directed. During the 1998 bombings in Africa, teams focused on restoring communications, ensuring security, and coordinating the flow of assistance to the embassies and personnel.

■ FURTHER READING:

PERIODICALS:

Marcus, David L. "Horror at U.S. Embassies." *Boston Globe.* (August 8, 1998): A1.

Reiss, Tom. "Now Will We Heed the Biological Threat?" *New York Times.* (February 21, 1998): 11.

ELECTRONIC:

Foreign Emergency Support Team. U.S. Department of State. <http://www.state.gov/s/ct/rls/fs/2002/13045.htm> (February 23, 2003).

SEE ALSO

Coordinator for Counterterrorism, United States Office
Department of State, United States
Domestic Emergency Support Team, United States
Kenya, Bombing of United States Embassy

Fibaloy.

SEE *Stealth Technology.*

Field Sieves Algorithms.

SEE *Cryptology and Number Theory.*

Fingerprint Analysis

■ AGNIESZKA LICHANSKA

Fingerprints are the patterns on the inside and the tips of fingers. The ridges of skin, also known as friction ridges, together with the valleys between them form unique patterns on the fingers. Fingerprint analysis is a biometric technique comparing scanned image of prints with a database of fingerprints. Uniqueness of prints, and the fact that they do not change during a person's life, form the basis for fingerprint analysis. The uniqueness of the prints is determined by the minute changes in local environment during fetal development; therefore, the identical twins undistinguishable by DNA analysis can be differentiated with fingerprint analysis. Although the fingerprint pattern remains the same, growth accounts for an enlargement of the patterns. Additionally, accidents or some diseases may alter fingerprint patterns

History of fingerprint use. Notes about the ridges, loops, and spirals of fingerprints were first made in 1686 by Marcello Malpighi. However, it was not until 1880 that fingerprints were recognized as a means of personal identification by Henry Faulds, who also identified a first ever fingerprint. The first book about fingerprints was published in 1888 by Sir Francis Galton, and was titled simply *Fingerprints.* Galton established the first classification system for fingerprints and was the first to assert that no two prints are the same, or that the odds of two prints being identical were about 1 in 64 billion. Later, the Henry Classification System was developed in 1901 by Sir Edward Henry, and today forms the basis for print recognition in most English speaking countries. This system categorized the ridge patterns into three groups: loops, whorls, and arches.

Fingerprinting was soon introduced in prisons, army and widely used for identification by law enforcement. The Federal Bureau of Investigation collection has millions of fingerprint cards and consists of approximately 70 million fingerprints. Although the main use of prints remains in forensic science and law enforcement, new uses of fingerprints have been developed.

Detection of fingerprints. Presence of pores on the surface of the ridges of the fingers results in the accumulation of perspiration on the fingertips. This moisture remains on the surface of the object a person touches, leaving prints. Depending on the surface touched, prints can be visible to the naked eye (e.g. metal, glass or plastic) or invisible (paper, cardboard or timber). Prints left on non-porous surfaces such as metal can be visualized with powders and lifted with tape. In contrast, the prints on porous objects require special lighting, such as lasers or x rays.

There are two major methods of the identification of fingerprints—comparison of lifted prints and live scanning. The first method is mainly used in forensics, while the second is used for authentication purposes (in security applications) and is also slowly becoming a method for identification at some police stations.

A fingerprint is seen on the back of a wireless device called an ''IBIS.'' It can record a fingerprint in the field, then send the fingerprint via a wireless connection to be checked against a database. AP/WIDE WORLD PHOTOS.

Analysis and classification of fingerprints. Ridges present on the fingers are classified based on the patterns they form. The most important features are ridge endings and bifurcations (separation of a ridge into two). These features are called minutiae and form the basis for further classification and identification. Based on the forms created by the minutiae (loops, whorls, etc.) fingerprints are further sub-classified into many more distinct patterns.

Modern fingerprint analysis uses computer algorithms to determine the similarity between a print and images stored in a database. Analysis is usually performed on multiple levels. First, the algorithms are compared to the prints on the coarse level to identify a type of a print, and then subsequently to identify more and more details until a match is found. The computer analysis of prints compares ridges, bifurcations and their relative location. Fingerprint analysis software and scanners identify a set number of similarity points, this number being determined by the software used, typically up to 90 points are compared. After identification of a set number of features, a template of the scanned print is formed and this is subsequently compared to the templates stored in the computer to determine if the print has a match. Although limiting the characteristics to be compared speeds up the matching process, it can also affect the accuracy if inadequate numbers are compared. Accuracy also depends on the application for which the fingerprint analysis is used.

Scanners have comparison algorithms and a number of recognizable characteristics programmed in, together with the prints of the users (enrolment) to provide the templates for comparison. The FBI fingerprint system is over 98% accurate, while the authentication systems accept only 97% of authorized users. Among some of the reasons for the rejection are: scars, calluses, cracks, dirt, or excess fingernail length.

Fingerprint analysis tools. Two types of fingerprint scanners are normally used, optical scanners and capacitance scanners. Optical scanners identify the print using light; depending on the brightness of the reflected light, optical scanners depict ridges as dark and valleys as light. Capacitance scanners determine the print by using an electrical current. Valleys and ridges on the fingers produce different voltage output, allowing for discrimination between them.

As sophisticated they are, the existing scanners are not totally immune to fraud. Optical scanners can be fooled by a picture, whereas the capacitance scanners can be fooled by a mold of a finger. Some scanners also have temperature and pulse sensors, but they are still vulnerable to molds placed over real fingers.

A number of portable fingerprint scanners were developed mainly by computer companies to provide a secure access for the users. In 1998, Compaq was the first to have a print reader attached to the computer. Currently, there are multiple systems for use with desktop and laptop computers in the form of PC cards and biometric mice. A portable print reader used for computer security employs a tiny digital camera to take a picture of a print and convert it into a map that is subsequently stored in the computer and cannot be duplicated.

Commercial fingerprint identification systems were introduced over 15 years ago. They are now used in security applications to gain access to a building or areas within the building, or computers or network access. Some companies, police offices, and high-security government buildings require fingerprint identification for access to the building or its selected parts.

In order to protect sensitive data, some businesses and the military often use scanners that are attached to computers (the U-Match mouse, for example) or installed in keyboards. These provide either immediate identification for access to the terminal or remote identification for access to secure documents or archives. NATO facilities in Turkey, and the U.S. Office of Legislative Council uses similar technology. New scanner trials are on the way to provide the same protection for e-commerce and Internet banking in order to secure transactions.

In order to combat cell phone thefts, the industry is considering equipping phones with fingerprint readers. Fingerprint protection is also offered for a new generation of safes, such as those provided by Biometrics Marketing. Finally, the scanners are being used to replace timecards in companies and to integrate payroll systems. Five U.S. airports, including Chicago's O'Hare have installed fingerprint scanners to check employees' backgrounds. Some banks use fingerprint scans before a check is cashed. Similarly, government agencies sometimes utilize fingerprint scans to ensure that payments are given to the proper recipients.

Today, fingerprint analysis technology is the most wide-spread biometric method of identification and authentication for forensic and security purposes.

■ **FURTHER READING:**

BOOKS:

Ashbourn, Julian. *Advanced Identity Verification: The Complete Guide.* London: Springer Verlag, 2000.

Nanavati, Samir, Michael Thieme, and Raj Nanavati. *Biometrics: Identity Verification in a Networked World.* New York: Wiley and Sons, 2002.

ELECTRONIC:

Find Biometrics. <http://www.findbiometrics.com/index.html> (14 December 2002).

NCSC. "Individual biometrics." <http://ctl.ncsc.dni.us/biomet%20web/BMFingerprint.html> (14 December 2002).

SEE ALSO

FBI (United States Federal Bureau of Investigation)
Forensic Science
Identity Theft

Finland, Intelligence and Security

Finland's geographic location made the nation one of the key strategic intelligence points during the twentieth century. Its position on the Baltic Sea, and proximity to both Russia and Western Europe, influenced the development of its national political character and intelligence community.

During World War II, as the Nazis planned their invasion of the Soviet Union and sought to stop operations of the Soviet Navy in the Baltic region, the Finnish government feared invasion. With the aid of the United States Office of Strategic Services, the forerunner of the Central

Intelligence Agency (CIA), members of Finland's intelligence community were smuggled into neighboring Sweden. The operation was known as Stella Polaris. There, agents sold the United States information on both Nazi Germany and the Soviet Union. However, Finnish intelligence also sold the same information to several other nations.

During the Cold War, Finland again was a key espionage and intelligence outpost. Both American and Soviet agents operated in Finland. Finland did not join the North Atlantic Treaty Organization (NATO), but provided western European and United States intelligence forces with crucial information on Soviet operations. As well, many Soviet defectors were smuggled through Finland.

Today, Finland maintains a few strategic intelligence services. Finnish intelligence's specialty is electronic and remote intelligence systems. As Finland is a member of the European Union (EU), its intelligence community is aiding the development of EU military intelligence.

In Finland, all intelligence services operate under the direction of the ministry of defense or the ministry of the interior. The national intelligence community makes the traditional distinction between internal and external intelligence, and divides its military and civilian agencies accordingly. Finnish military intelligence service is the General Staff Intelligence Division (PT). The agency is responsible for boarder control and foreign intelligence surveillance. Signals intelligence is gathered and processed at the agency's Communications Expertise Facility (VKL).

The civilian intelligence service, charged with domestic intelligence and internal security, is the Security Police (SUPO). The agency maintains extensive counter-espionage and counterintelligence units and aids development of security structures within the other national intelligence organizations. The agency maintains three operational divisions, the Unit of Development and Supportive activities, the Security Unit, and the Counter-espionage Unit.

In 2001, Finnish intelligence services began a two-year project to upgrade their existing electronic and remote surveillance equipment. Within the international community, Finnish intelligence pledged the use of this equipment to aid in global anti-terrorism efforts.

First of October Anti-fascist Resistance Group (GRAPO)

The First of October Anti-fascist Resistance Group (GRAPO, or *Grupo de Resistencia Anti-Fascista Primero de Octubre*)

was formed in 1975 as the armed wing of the illegal Communist Party of Spain during the Franco era. Advocating the overthrow of the Spanish Government and replacement with a Marxist-Leninist regime, GRAPO is vehemently anti-U.S., calls for the removal of all U.S. military forces from Spanish territory, and has conducted and attempted several attacks against U.S. targets since 1977. The group issued a communiqué following the 11 September attacks in the United States, expressing its satisfaction that "symbols of imperialist power" were decimated and affirming that "the war" has only just begun. GRAPO has killed more than 90 persons and injured more than 200. The group's operations traditionally have been designed to cause material damage and gain publicity rather than inflict casualties, but the terrorists have conducted lethal bombings and close-range assassinations. In May, 2000, the group killed two security guards during a botched armed robbery attempt of an armored truck carrying an estimated $2 million, and in November, 2000, members assassinated a Spanish policeman in a possible reprisal for the arrest that month of several GRAPO leaders in France. The group also has bombed business and official sites of the Madrid headquarters of the ruling Popular Party, including the Barcelona office of the national daily El Mundo in October 2000, when two police officers were injured.

Operating in Spain, GRAPO's exact strength is unknown, but likely has fewer than a dozen dedicated activists. Spanish and French officials have made periodic large-scale arrests of GRAPO members, crippling the organization and forcing it into lengthy rebuilding periods. The French and Spanish arrested several key leaders in 2001.

■ **FURTHER READING:**

ELECTRONIC:

CDI (Center for Defense Information), Terrorism Project. CDI Fact Sheet: Current List of Designated Foreign Terrorist Organizations. March 27, 2003. <http://www.cdi.org/terrorism/terrorist.cfm> (April 17, 2003).

Central Intelligence Agency. World Factbook, 2002. <http://www.cia.gov/cia/publications/factbook/> (April 16, 2003).

Taylor, Francis X. U.S. Department of State. "Patterns of Global Terrorism 2001," Annual Report: On the Record Briefing. May 21, 2002 <http://www.state.gov/s/ct/rls/rm/10367.htm> (April 17,2003).

U.S. Department of State. Annual Reports. <http://www.state.gov/www/global/terrorism/annual_reports.html> (April 16, 2003).

SEE ALSO

Terrorism, Philosophical and Ideological Origins
Terrorist and Para-State Organizations
Terrorist Organization List, United States
Terrorist Organizations, Freezing of Assets

FISH (German *Geheimschreiber* Cipher Machine)

■ ADRIENNE WILMOTH LERNER

As late as the World War I era, cryptology depended on highly trained people at both ends of a communication to cipher and decipher a message. Codes were often kept in books that were vulnerable to enemy capture. The capturing of German code books by British military intelligence in World War I gave the Allies a significant tactical advantage. Soon after the war, technological advances in communication were applied to the sending and receiving of complexly coded text. Skilled cipherers and and codebooks were replaced by cipher machines. Modern cryptographers, therefore, not only had to break enemy codes, but also determine how foreign cipher machines operated and generated codes. Cipher machines produced more mathematically intricate and random codes that were difficult to break. Because many cipher machine codes were dependent upon both the sender and the receiver machines, the caputre of coded teleprinters did not dictate that a code could be broken.

In the 1930s, the German government comissioned the Seimans Company to create a cipher machine teleprinter that could produce, send, and receive plain and coded text. The idea behind the teleprinter was to randomize codes to make them more difficult to break, and to increase code information security. Seimans developed their first cipher teleprinter, the *Geheimschreiber*, with two encription features, overlaying of code and transposition of pulses. Long pre-dating digital technology, both the basic encription functions and the receipt of transpositioned pulses depended on mechanical circuts, namely various code wheels for text and charged capacators and their corresponding relays for the pulse. The machine's ten code wheels had periods corresponding with prime numbers between 47 and 73. Thus, the wheels combined to form 893,622,318,929,520,960 permutations, or steps. Eight basic patterns with over two billion variations were possible in regards to pulse transposition. These combined encryption mechanisms led the German government to assume that the *Geheimschreiber* was nearly random and unbreakable; however, the mathematical patterns used by the machines proved to be more systematic than they perceived.

Teleprinters utilized the 32-character Baudot code. The code output consisted of five channels, represented as holes or no holes in varying orders, to produce each character. The German cipher machines relied on the Vernam cipher system, a mathematical code based on the principle of binary addition. That is, two coded characters were added together to produce the ciphered text. Code breakers knew of both the Baudot code and Vernam system, but the obscuring factors of the German *Geheimschreiber* made deciphering the code difficult.

The German cipher machines were supposed to change starting positions with every message, notifying the receiving end of a given transmission in plain text of the starting steps on the code wheels. Thus, the obscuring sequence of each code was supposedly unique. Code breakers in Sweden worked to break the *Geheimschreiber* code mathematically, and did so with measurable success in 1942. However, the work was tedious and by the time they had produced several decoding machines, the highest levels of the German command had begun to use the newer Lorenz cipher machine. Swedish cryptologists were unable to decipher any wire traffic after February, 1944.

British intelligence cryptologists at Bletchley Park thought the best hope of readily deciphering German teleprinters was to intercept a depth, or two messages that utilized the same starting position. While codebreakers had some success mathmatically decoding Fish ciphered German transmissions, on August 30, 1941, British intelligence intercepted a 4,000-character-long depth. The Lorenz code was broken soon afterward by John Tiltman and Bill Tutte. Working out long code sequences by hand, the two uncovered the logical structure of the German cipher. With this knowledge, several "Tunny," now the code name for Lorenz transmissions, machines were constructed to facilitate decoding of intercepts. However, the start position settings of each message still had to be discovered by hand.

In 1943, British mathematician Max Newman and British engineer Tommy Flowers designed and built Colossus, a machine that not only simplified the process of deciphering German teleprinter intercepts, but that could be used with *Geheimschreiber*, Lorenz, and radio transmissions. Colossus' greatest contribution to codebreaking however was its ability to electronically decode the start position of each ciphered intercept, eliminating the need for painstaking hand calculations. The system was instrumental in the planning and execution of the allied D-Day invasion.

■ FURTHER READING:

BOOKS:

Goldreich, Oded. *Foundations of Cryptography: Basic Tools.* Cambridge: Cambridge University Press, 2001.

Hinsley, F. H. *British Intelligence in the Second World War.* Cambridge: Cambridge University Press, 1988.

Hinsley, F. H. and Alan Stripp, eds. *Codebreakers: The Inside Story of Bletchley Park.* Oxford: Oxford University Press, 2001.

Stinson, Douglas. *Cryptography: Theory and Practice*, second edition. Chapman and Hall, 2002.

SEE ALSO

Bletchley Park
Cipher Machines
Colossus I

Fission

Nuclear fission is a process in which the nucleus of an atom splits, usually into two daughter nuclei, with the transformation of tremendous levels of nuclear energy into heat and light.

The fission reaction was discovered when a target of uranium was bombarded by neutrons. Fission fragments were shown to fly apart with a large release of energy. The fission reaction was the basis of the atomic bomb first developed by the United States during World War II. After the war, controlled energy release from fission was applied to the development of nuclear reactors. Reactors are utilized for production of electricity at nuclear power plants, for propulsion of ships and submarines, and for the creation of radioactive isotopes used in medicine and industry.

Long before the internal construction of the atom was well understood in terms of protons, neutrons, electrons, nuclear transformations that resulted in observable radioactivity were observed as early as 1896 by Henri French physicist Henri Becquerel (1852–1908). The fission reaction was first articualted by two German scientists, Otto Hahn (1879–1968) and Fritz Strassmann (1902–1980). In 1938, Hahn and Strassmann conducted a series of experiments in which they used neutrons to bombard various elements. Bombardment of copper, for example, produced a radioactive form of copper. Other elements became radioactive in the same way. When uranium was bombarded with neutrons, however, an entirely different reaction occurred. The uranium nucleus apparently underwent a major disruption. Accordingly, the initial evidence for the fission process came from chemical analysis. Hahn and Strassmann published a scientific paper showing that small amounts of barium (element 56) were produced when uranium (element 92) was bombarded with neutrons. Hahn and Strassmann questioned how a single neutron could transform element 92 into element 56.

Lise Meitner (1878–1968), a long-time colleague of Hahn who had left Germany due to Nazi persecution, suggested a helpful model for such a reaction. One can visualize the uranium nucleus to be like a liquid drop containing protons and neutrons. When an extra neutron enters, the drop begins to vibrate. If the vibration is violent enough, the drop can break into two pieces. Meitner named this process "fission" because it is similar to the process of cell division in biology. Moreover, it takes only a relatively small amount of energy to initiate nuclear instability.

Scientists in the United States and elsewhere quickly confirmed the idea of uranium fission, using other experimental procedures. For example, a cloud chamber is a device in which vapor trails of moving nuclear particles can be seen and photographed. In one experiment, a thin sheet of uranium was placed inside a cloud chamber. When it was irradiated by neutrons, photographs showed a pair of tracks going in opposite directions from a common starting point in the uranium. Clearly, a nucleus had been photographed in the act of fission.

Another experimental procedure used a Geiger counter, which is a small, cylindrical tube that produces electrical pulses when a radioactive particle passes through it. For this experiment, the inside of a modified Geiger tube was lined with a thin layer of uranium. When a neutron source was brought near it, large voltage pulses were observed, much larger than from ordinary radioactivity. When the neutron source was taken away, the large pulses stopped. A Geiger tube without the uranium lining did not generate large pulses. Evidently, the large pulses were due to uranium fission fragments. The size of the pulses showed that the fragments had a very large amount of energy.

To understand the high energy released in uranium fission, scientists made some theoretical calculations based on German-American physicist Albert Einstein's (1879–1955) famous equation $E=mc^2$. The Einstein equation states that mass m can be converted into energy E (and, conversely that energy can create mass). The conversion factor becomes c, the velocity of light squared. One can calculate that the total mass of the fission products remaining at the end of the reaction is slightly less than the mass of the uranium atom plus the neutron at the start. This decrease of mass, multiplied by c, shows numerically why the fission fragments are so energetic.

Through fission, neutrons of low energy can trigger a very large energy release. With the imminent threat of war in 1939, a number of scientists began to consider the possibility that a new and very powerful "atomic bomb" could be built from uranium. Also, they speculated that uranium perhaps could be harnessed to replace coal or oil as a fuel for industrial power plants.

Nuclear reactions in general are much more powerful than chemical reactions. A chemical change such as burning coal or even exploding TNT affects only the outer electrons of an atom. A nuclear process, on the other hand, causes changes among the protons and neutrons inside the nucleus. The energy of attraction between protons and neutrons is about a million times greater than the chemical binding energy between atoms. Therefore, a single fission bomb, using nuclear energy, might destroy a whole city. Alternatively, nuclear electric power plants theoretically could run for a whole year on just a few tons of fuel.

In order to release a substantial amount of energy, many millions of uranium nuclei must split apart. The fission process itself provides a mechanism for creating a so-called chain reaction. In addition to the two main fragments, each fission event produces two or three extra neutrons. Some of these can enter nearby uranium nuclei and cause them in turn to fission, releasing more neutrons, which causes more fission, and so forth. In a bomb explosion, neutrons have to increase very rapidly, in a fraction of a second. In a controlled reactor, however, the neutron population has to be kept in a steady state. Excess neutrons must be removed by some type of absorber material (e.g., neutron absorbing control rods).

In 1942, the first nuclear reactor with a self-sustaining chain reaction was built in the United States. The principal designer was Enrico Fermi (1901–1954), an Italian physicist and the 1938 Nobel Prize winner in physics. Fermi emigrated to the United States to escape Benito Mussolini's fascism. Fermi's reactor design had three main components: lumps of uranium (the fuel), blocks of carbon (the moderator, which slows down the neutrons), and control rods made of cadmium (an excellent neutron absorber). Fermi and other scientists constructed the first nuclear reactor pile at the University of Chicago. When the pile of uranium and carbon blocks was about 10 ft (3 m) high and the cadmium control rods were pulled out far enough, Geiger counters showed that a steady-state chain reaction had been successfully accomplished. The power output was only about 200 watts, but it was enough to verify the basic principle of reactor operation. The power level of the chain reaction could be varied by moving the control rods in or out.

General Leslie R. Groves was put in charge of the project to convert the chain reaction experiment into a usable military weapon. Three major laboratories were built under wartime conditions of urgency and secrecy. Oak Ridge, Tennessee, became the site for purifying and separating uranium into bomb-grade material. At Hanford, Washington, four large reactors were built to produce another possible bomb material, plutonium. At Los Alamos, New Mexico, the actual work of bomb design was started in 1943 under the leadership of the physicist J. Robert Oppenheimer (1904–1967).

The fissionable uranium isotope, uranium-235, constitutes only about 1% of natural uranium, while the non-fissionable neutron absorber, uranium-238, makes up the other 99%. To produce bomb-grade, fissionable uranium-235, it was necessary to build a large isotope separation facility. Since the plant would require much electricity, the site was chosen to be in the region of the Tennessee Valley Authority (TVA). The technology of large-scale isotope separation involved solving many difficult, unprecedented problems. By early 1945, the Oak Ridge Laboratory was able to produce kilogram amounts of uranium-235 purified to better than 95%.

An alternate possible fuel for a fission bomb is plutonium-239. Plutonium does not exist in nature but results from radioactive decay of uranium-239. Fermi's chain reaction experiment had shown that uranium-239 could be made in a reactor. However, to produce several hundred kilograms of plutonium required a large increase from the power level of Fermi's original experiment. Plutonium production reactors were constructed at Hanford, Washington, located near the Columbia River to provide needed cooling water. A difficult technical problem was how to separate plutonium from the highly radioactive fuel rods after irradiation. This was accomplished by means of remote handling apparatus that was manipulated by technicians working behind thick protective glass windows.

With uranium-235 separation started at Oak Ridge and plutonium-239 production under way at Hanford, a third laboratory was set up at Los Alamos, New Mexico, to work on bomb design. In order to create an explosion, many nuclei would have to fission almost simultaneously. The key concept was to bring together several pieces of fissionable material into a so-called critical mass. In one design, two pieces of uranium-235 were shot toward each other from opposite ends of a cylindrical tube. A second design used a spherical shell of plutonium-239, to be detonated by an "implosion" toward the center of the sphere.

The first atomic bomb was tested at an isolated desert location in New Mexico on July 16, 1945. President Truman then issued an ultimatum to Japan that a powerful new weapon could soon be used against them. On August 8, a single U.S. atomic bomb destroyed the city of Hiroshima with over 80,000 casualties. On August 11, a second bomb was dropped on Nagasaki with a similar result. Japan surrendered three days later to end WWII.

The possibility of a terrorist group or a dictator hostile to Western democracies obtaining nuclear weapons is a continuing threat to world peace. In late 2001, in the aftermath of the terrorist attacks on the World Trade Center in New York, intelligence agencies released evidence of terrorist attempts to acquire weapons grade uranium and the other technology related to bomb production.

The first nuclear reactor designed for producing electricity was put into operation in 1957 at Shippingsport, Pennsylvania. From 1960 to 1990, more than 100 nuclear power plants were built in the United States. These plants now generate about 20% of the nation's electric power. World-wide, there are over 400 nuclear power stations.

The most common reactor type is the pressurized water reactor (abbreviated PWR). The system operates like a coal-burning power plant, except that the firebox of the coal plant is replaced by a reactor. Nuclear energy from uranium is released in the two fission fragments. The fuel rod becomes very hot because of the cumulative energy of fissioning nuclei. A typical reactor core contains hundreds of these fuel rods. Water is circulated through the core to remove the heat. The hot water is prevented from boiling by keeping the system under pressure (i.e., creating superheated steam).

The pressurized hot water goes to a heat exchanger where steam is produced. The steam then goes to a turbine, which has a series of fan blades that rotate rapidly when hit by the steam. The turbine is connected to the rotor of an electric generator. Its output goes to cross-country transmission lines that supply the electrical users in the region. The steam that made the turbine rotate is condensed back into water and is recycled to the heat exchanger.

Safety features at a nuclear power plant include automatic shutdown of the fission process by insertion of control rods, emergency water-cooling for the core in case of pipeline breakage, and a concrete containment shell. It is impossible for a reactor to have a nuclear explosion because the fuel enrichment in a reactor is intentionally limited to about 3% uranium-235, while almost 100% pure uranium-235 is required for a bomb. Regardless, nuclear power plants remain potential targets for terrorists who would seek to cause massive and lethal release of radioactivity by compromising the containment shell.

The fuel in the reactor core consists of several tons of uranium. As the reactor is operated, the uranium content gradually decreases because of fission, and the radioactive waste products (the fission fragments) build up. After about a year of operation, the reactor must be shut down for refueling. The old fuel rods are pulled out and replaced. These fuel rods, which are very radioactive, are stored under water at the power plant site. After five to ten years, much of their radioactivity has decayed. Only those materials with a long radioactive lifetime remain, and eventually they must be stored in a suitable underground depository.

There are vehement arguments for and against nuclear power. As with other forms of electricity production, nuclear power generation can have serious and unintended environmental impacts. The main objections to nuclear power plants are the fear of possible accidents, the unresolved problem of nuclear waste storage, and the possibility of plutonium diversion for weapons production by a terrorist group. The issue of waste storage becomes particularly emotional because leakage from a waste depository could contaminate ground water. Opponents of nuclear power often cite accidents at the Three Mile Island nuclear poser plant in United States and the massive leak at the Chernobyl nuclear plant in the USSR (now the Ukraine) as evidence that engineering or technical failures can have long lasting and devastating environmental and public health consequences

The main advantage of nuclear power plants is that they do not cause atmospheric pollution. No smokestacks are needed because nothing is being burned. France initiated a large-scale nuclear program after the Arab oil embargo in 1973 and has been able to reduce its acid rain and carbon dioxide emissions by more than 40%. Nuclear power plants do not contribute to potential global warming. Shipments of fuel are minimal and so the hazards of coal transportation and oil spills are avoided.

■ FURTHER READING:

BOOKS:

Cottingham, W. Noel and Derek A. Greenwood. *An Introduction to the Standard Model of Particle Physics.* New York: Cambridge Univeristy Press, 1999.

Sagan, Scott D. and Kenneth N. Waltz. *The Spread of Nuclear Weapons: A Debate Renewed,* Second Edition. New York: W W Norton & Co., 2003.

Whiting, Jim. *Otto Hahn and the Story of Nuclear Fission.* Childs. MD: Mitchell Lane Publishers, Inc. 2003.

PERIODICALS:

Ladika, Susan. "Tracing the Shadowy Origins of Nuclear Contraband." *Science* no. 5522 (2001): 1634.

ELECTRONIC:

United States Department of Energy. "Guide to the Nuclear Wallchart: Energy From Nuclear Science" (August 2000) <http://www-nsd.lbl.gov/abc/wallchart/chapters/14/0.html> (March 20, 2003).

SEE ALSO

Fusion
Heavy Water Technology
Manhattan Project
Nuclear Detection Devices
Nuclear Emergency Support Team, United States
Nuclear Power Plants, Security
Nuclear Reactors
Nuclear Regulatory Commission (NRC), United States
Nuclear Spectroscopy
Nuclear Weapons
Oak Ridge National Laboratory (ORNL)
Weapon-Grade Plutonium and Uranium, Tracking

Flame Analysis

Flame tests are useful means of determining the composition of substances. The colors produced by the flame test are compared to known standards. And the presence of certain elements in the sample can be confirmed. The color of the flame and its spectrum (component colors) is unique for each element.

Flame analysis or atomic emission spectroscopy (AES) is based on the physical and chemical principle that atoms—after being heated by flame—return to their normal energy state by giving off the excess energy in the form of light. The frequencies of the light given off are characteristic for each element.

Flame analysis is a qualitative test and not a quantitative test. A qualitative chemical analysis is designed to identify the components of a substance or mixture. Quantitative tests measure the amounts or proportions of the components in a reaction or substance.

The unknown to be subjected to flame analysis is either sprayed into the flame or placed on a thin wire that is then put into the flame. Volatile elements (chlorides) produce intense colors. The yellow color of sodium, for example, can be so intense that it overwhelms other colors. To prevent this the wire to be coated with the unknown sample is usually dipped in hydrochloric acid and subjected to flame to remove the volatile impurities and sodium.

The flame test does not work on all elements. Those that produce a measurable spectrum when subjected to flame include, but are not limited to, lithium, sodium, potassium, rubidium, cesium, magnesium, calcium, strontium, barium, zinc, and cadmium. Other elements may need hotter flames to produce measurable spectra.

Special techniques are required to properly interpret the results of flame analysis. The colors produced by a potassium flame (pale violet) can usually be observed only with the assistance of glass that can filter out interfering colors. Some colors are similar enough that line spectrum must be examined to make a complete and accurate identification of the unknown substance, or the presence of an identifiable substance in the unknown.

Flame analysis can also be used to determine the presence of metal elements in water by measuring the spectrum produced by the metals exposed to flame. The water is vaporized and then the emissions of the vaporized metals can be analyzed.

■ FURTHER READING:

BOOKS:

Broekaert, José. C. *Analytic Atomic Spectrometry with Flames and Plasmas.* New York: Wiley-VCH Publishing, 2001.

ELECTRONIC:

Helmenstein, Anne Marie. "What You Need To Know About Chemistry-Quantitative Flame Analysis" About, Inc, <http://chemistry.about.com/library/weekly/aa110401a.htm> (March 29, 2003).

SEE ALSO

Air and Water Purification, Security Issues
Chemical and Biological Detection Technologies
Isotopic Analysis
Spectroscopy
Water Supply: Counter-Terrorism

Flash X-Ray Facility.

SEE *Lawrence Livermore National Laboratory (LLNL).*

Flight Data Recorders

■ KELLI A. MILLER

In the earliest days of air transportation, plane crashes yielded few clues for safety investigators. Investigators

The charred casing of the flight data recorder recovered from the crash of American Airlines flight 587 is displayed at the National Transportation Safety Board in 2001, along with a normal, undamaged flight recorder (at rear). AP/WIDE WORLD PHOTOS.

would struggle to figure out what happened immediately preceding the accident but often fail to come to any definite conclusions regarding the cause of the crash. In June 1960, a Fokker F27 plane crashed while landing in Queensland, Australia, killing 29 people. Despite intensive investigations, the underlying cause for the accident was never determined. The mystery prompted the Australia board of inquiry to recommend that all airplanes be fitted with a flight data recorder (FDR) that would detail the flight crew's conversation.

Efforts to make the FDR a mandatory part of civil aircraft date back to the early 1940s. The idea, however, was wrought with one enormous technological challenge. Design specifications required that the unit survive the forces of an aircraft crash, as well as any resulting fire exposure.

In 1953, at a time when flight engineers were attempting to understand why a number of airliners had inexplicably crashed, Australian aviation scientist David Warren of the Aeronautical Research Laboratories in Melbourne invented a fully automatic "Flight Memory Unit." His prototype could record cockpit noise and instrument readings and remain in tact following a crash or fire. Much to Warren's surprise, Australian aviation experts and pilots originally rejected the idea, on the premise of privacy issues. Warren took the concept to the United Kingdom, where it was well received by aviation officials. By 1957, the FDR was in production. Australia was among the first countries to require the device on commercial aircraft.

The phrase "black box," however, is a misnomer. Flight data recorders are actually painted a bright red or orange for easier location after a crash. The FDR is encased in heavy steel and surrounded by multiple layers of insulation to provide protection against a crash, fire, and extreme climatic conditions. The device records actual flight conditions, including altitude, airspeed, heading, vertical acceleration and aircraft pitch. A second device, the cockpit voice recorder (CVR), keeps tabs on cockpit conversations and engine noise. Both are installed in the rear of the aircraft.

In the 1970s, FDR technology was combined with a flight-data acquisition unit (FDAU), located at the front of the aircraft. The unit acts as the relay for the entire data-recording process. Sensors run from various areas on the plane to the FDAU, which in turn sends the information to the FDR.

In the early days, data were embossed onto a type of magnetic foil known as Incanol Steel. The foil proved to be destructible and FDR manufacturers began using a more reliable form of magnetic tape. Electromagnetic technology remained the data-recording medium of choice until the late 1990s, when solid-state electronics began to show promise. Solid-state recorders rely on stacked arrays of non-moveable memory chips. The technology is considered more reliable than magnetic tape, as the lack of moving parts provides a reduced chance of breakage during a crash.

Solid-state recorders also track a much greater number of parameters; 700 are tracked compared to the magnetic tape parameter recording potential of 100. Faster data flow allows the solid-state devices to record up to 25 hours of flight data. In 1997, the United States Federal Aviation Administration (FAA) issued a requirement that all aircraft manufactured after August 19, 2002 record at least 88 parameters. The action came in the wake of two B-737 airplane crashes in which insufficient data was available for determining the cause of the accidents.

In addition to the five above-mentioned parameters recorded by the earliest data recorders, today's devices also track time, control-column position, rudder-pedal position, control-wheel position, horizontal stabilizer, and fuel flow.

Since its inception, the FDR has played a vital role in establishing the probable cause of a crash or other unusual occurrences and has allowed safety regulators to implement corrective actions. The value of flight data recorders was clearly evident in the investigation of the ATR-72 accident in Roselawn, Indiana in October 1994. The FDR captured information on 115 parameters. Analysis of the data revealed a telltale, rapid wing movement that prompted the National Transportation and Safety Board to immediately issue urgent safety recommendations to improve flying in icing conditions.

■ **FURTHER READING:**

ELECTRONIC:

"The Black Box: An Australian Contribution to Air Safety," March 21, 2002 <http://www.dsto.defence.gov.au/corporate/history/jubilee/blackbox.html>(December 08, 2002).

"Black Boxes," February 22, 2002 <http://www.atsb.gov.au/aviation/editorial/flrec/index.cfm>(December 08, 2002).

"A History of the Black Box," <http://www.millennium.scps.k12.fl.us/istfbbhistory.html>(December 08, 2002).

"How Things Work: Black Boxes," <http://www.howstuffworks.com/black-box1.htm>(December 08, 2002).

L-3 Communications Corp., "Aviation Recorders," 2002, <http://www.l-3ar.com/html/history.html> (December11, 2002).

National Transportation and Safety Board, " Data Collection and Improved Technologies," May 20, 1998 <http://www.ntsb.gov/speeches/s980520.htm> (December 08, 2002).

SEE ALSO

FAA (United States Federal Aviation Administration)
NTSB (National Transportation Safety Board)
Shoe Transmitter
Short-Wave Transmitters

FM Transmitters

FM (frequency modulation) transmitters can yield a number of results, depending on their power and range. Extremely low-power transmitters can be used in very small locales, for purposes such as eavesdropping. At the high end, radio transmitters are sometimes used for propaganda and psychological warfare through broadcasting. Between these extremes are the low-power radio transmitters, capable of making every user a broadcaster, that have long been an issue of concern for the Federal Communications Commission (FCC).

Mini transmitters, which have a range of about 50 feet (15.2 m), are available commercially to serve purposes such as that of a baby monitor, but are easily adapted for eavesdropping as well. Although they are capable of operating anywhere on the FM dial, from 88 to 108 MHz, the recommended range for most of these is 88 to 95 MHz, where there is least likely to be interference. Low-power FM transmitters, with a range of 100 to 400 feet (30.5–122 m), make it possible to transmit voices over a greater distance, and are applied commercially for purposes such as listening to compact discs (CDs) in a car that does not have a CD player.

Both mini and low-power FM transmitters have such limited power—less than 1 watt—that they pose no concern to communications regulators. On the other hand, high-power or professional FM transmitters that are commercially available—some with as many as 35 watts of power—theoretically have the capacity to make anyone a radio broadcaster. This could pose serious concerns with regard to interference and communication jamming, and by 1998, the availability of FM transmitters forced the FCC to at least consider the idea of legalizing low-power transmission. The concept has been under consideration for some time, but many would-be broadcasters are as likely to choose the Internet as a simpler, non-interfering environment in which to operate a radio site.

In the realm of very high-power radio stations, there are many such facilities overseas operated by the federal government for the purposes of winning over local populations. In February, 2002, a year before the administration of President George W. Bush launched Operation Iraqi Freedom, it provided assistance to the opposition Iraqi National Congress as it began transmitting from the Kurdish-dominated north of Iraq on the FM dial. The United States already broadcast on short-wave radio into Iraq, but FM is both more popular and harder to jam than short-wave or AM (ampere modulation).

■ FURTHER READING:

PERIODICALS:

Braga, Newton C. "Experimenting with Small FM Transmitters." *Poptronics* 2, no. 9 (September 2001): 41–46.

Gordon, Michael R. "Radio Transmitter to Oppose Hussein Wins U.S. Support." *New York Times.* (February 28, 2002): A1.

"Low-Power FM Transmitters." *Electronics Now* 70, no. 8 (August 1999): 37–40.

Schneider, Howard. "A Little U.S. Pop-aganda for Arabs." *Washington Post.* (July 26, 2002): A24.

Schweber, Bill. "FM Transmitter/Receiver Provides 433-MHz Link." *EDN* 47, no. 9 (April 18, 2002): 22.

SEE ALSO

FCC (United States Federal Communications Commission)
Iraqi Freedom, Operation (2003 War Against Iraq)
National Telecommunications Information Administration, and Security for the Radio Frequency Spectrum, United States
Shoe Transmitter
Short-Wave Transmitters

FOIA (Freedom of Information Act)

The Freedom of Information Act (FOIA) limits the ability of United States federal government agencies to withhold

Kate Martin, shown in her office at the Center for National Security Studies of George Washington University's Gelman Library. She was a lead attorney in a Freedom of Information Act case seeking the disclosure of the identities of hundreds of individuals who were arrested and jailed after the September 11 terrorist attacks. AP/WIDE WORLD PHOTOS.

information from the public by classifying that information as secret. Passed by Congress in 1967, it applies to the agencies of the executive branch, and not to the legislative or judicial branches, or to state or local governments, although every state has its own privacy and public access laws. FOIA did not become a significant aspect of American public life until the early to mid-1970s, when several events, including the Watergate scandal, the passage of the Privacy Act in 1974, and amendments in 1975, helped give it much greater importance.

Historical Background

When Congress first passed FOIA, the law did not apply to investigatory files compiled for the purposes of law enforcement. This exempted files collected by the Justice Department and its agencies, most notably the Federal Bureau of Investigation (FBI), from the FOIA. Within a few years of the law's passage, however, the fabric of American public life would change dramatically, bringing with it changes in many of the nation's laws, including FOIA.

Whereas ordinary citizens had long been accustomed to trusting their government and to respecting organizations such as the FBI and Central Intelligence Agency (CIA), revelations of spying and other "dirty tricks" committed by the Nixon administration before and during the Watergate years helped influence a sense of distrust of Washington. Prior to the early 1970s, suspicion of the federal government was limited primarily to those on the political fringes of right and left, but thereafter, the belief that the government was spying on its citizens became an increasingly prevalent attitude.

The Privacy Act and changes to the FOIA. By the mid-1970s, this change in attitude would be reflected in Washington by efforts to increase the openness of the federal government to its citizens. Nixon himself issued an executive order limiting the number of agencies that could classify information as top secret, and thus exempt it from FOIA provisions. He also required officials in such situations to explain why information had been classified as top secret in the first place.

The scandal surrounding Watergate, and the looming possibility of an impeachment, forced Nixon's resignation in 1974, the same year Congress passed the Privacy Act. The latter greatly restricted the authority of agencies to collect information on individuals, and to disclose that information to persons other than the individual. At the same time, it required the agencies to furnish the individual with any information on him or her that the agency had in its files. The Privacy Act, along with 1975 amendments to FOIA, greatly broadened access to federal files—including those of law-enforcement, intelligence, and security agencies—that had formerly been under severe restriction.

FOIA procedure today. In addition to restricting the purview of federal agencies with regard to documents, what came to be known as the Freedom of Information-Privacy Acts (FOIPA) placed an enormous onus on those agencies to respond to all requests for information. For example, in the quarter-century after 1975, the FBI handled some 300,000 requests involving the release of more than 6 million pages of documents. Not every part of every request is granted, however: FOIPA does allow exemptions for sensitive material.

In some situations, the requester has to pay for fulfillment of the request. Answers to questions regarding payment and any number of other specifics may be found with the Department of Justice, which in 2003 maintained an FOIA section at its Web site. There it listed FOIA contacts at various government agencies, as well as other information relating to FOIPA.

By the early twenty-first century, every federal department, agency, office, and bureau had its own FOIA contact. For most entities of any size, there was at least one individual tasked full-time with processing, responding to, and fulfilling these requests. In some cases, there were multiple individuals or even an entire office devoted to this purpose.

At the FBI, for instance, requests are received, logged into computers, and assigned a tracking number. The agency then formally acknowledges the request, and conducts an indices search to determine whether it even has the records requested. Once an apparent match is located, it is reviewed to determine whether it is the exact file requested.

Assuming the file exactly matches the request, it is photocopied, and an analyst reviews the work copy to determine if there is any material that meets any one of nine exemptions and three exclusions covered in FOIPA. If any such material exists in the file, the analyst uses a colored marker to delete it, and in the margins cites the appropriate exemption. The pages are then re-copied using a photocopier with a special filter so that there is no chance anyone can detect the deleted material. At that point, the copies are mailed to the requester.

During the early twenty-first century, the FBI and other agencies were developing automated document processing systems that would replace many of these steps. These systems would also remove the need for a marker pen, and would allow for documents to be released in electronic format.

■ **FURTHER READING:**

BOOKS:

Henderson, Harry. *Privacy in the Information Age.* New York: Facts on File, 1999.

Sherick, L. G. *How to Use the Freedom of Information Act (FOIA).* New York: Arco, 1978.

Theoharis, Athan G. *A Culture of Secrecy: The Government Versus the People's Right to Know.* Lawrence: University of Kansas Press, 1998.

Ullmann, John, and Steve Honeyman. *The Reporter's Handbook: An Investigator's Guide to Documents and Techniques.* New York: St. Martin's Press, 1983.

ELECTRONIC:

Freedom of Information Act (FOIA). U.S. Department of Justice. <http://www.usdoj.gov/04foia/> (March 16, 2003).

SEE ALSO

CIA, Legal Restriction
Classified Information
FBI (United States Federal Bureau of Investigation)
Intelligence, United States Congressional Oversight
Justice Department, United States
Nixon Administration (1969–1974), United States National Security Policy
Privacy: Legal and Ethical Issues
Security Clearance Investigations
Watergate

Food Supply, Counter-Terrorism

■ BRIAN HOYLE

The 1995 release of Sarin gas in the Tokyo subway system, and the events of September 11, 2001 in the United States illustrate society's vulnerability to terrorist attack in the course of everyday activities. Much of the infrastructure of public life (i.e., buildings, subways, airports) was not initially designed to thwart malicious activity. Food supplies are an additional component of the infrastructure, and as such, are also vulnerable to terrorism. Crops in the field are relatively unprotected. Food that is processed is monitored, not to detect the deliberate addition of a poison or an infectious agent, but to verify that the product is free from a small number of bacterial contaminants. Finally, on the supermarket shelf, products can be altered.

Terrorist attacks on a nation's food supply could not only cause illness, but also can cripple an economy. For example, the agricultural sector in the U.S. accounts for 13% of the country's gross domestic product and provides jobs for about 40 million Americans.

A disease outbreak carries the potential to cripple an economy. One example is the 1997 outbreak of Foot and Mouth disease among herds of pork in Taiwan. Battling the outbreak cost $7 billion. A similar outbreak in Britain in 2001 drained well over $4 billion from the economy.

The threats to food supplies. Obtaining a strain of bacteria or virus that causes plant or animal diseases is much easier than obtaining a highly infectious human pathogen. Agricultural pathogens can even be obtained from the environment. For example, scraping the surface of infected leaves is sufficient to recover some disease-causing viruses. Both the former Soviet Union and Iraq are known to have experimented with agricultural pathogens. Thus, a terrorist group having some microbiological expertise could acquire the microorganisms needed for their attacks.

Microorganisms can also be purchased from supply laboratories. An organization with convincing paperwork would be able to acquire microbes that are not considered to be highly infectious.

The advent of recombinant DNA technology in the 1970s—where a segment of genetic material coding for a protein of interest (i.e., a toxin) can be isolated and spliced into the DNA of a target microbe—holds the potential for the genetic modification of bacteria or viruses that are common in the environment. These genetic versions could spread quickly through the natural world.

Counter-terrorism measures. Following the September 11, 2001 terrorist attacks, the U.S. government moved to strengthen the country's defense against bioterrorism. This initiative culminated in the signing into law, on June 12, 2002, of the Public Health Security and Bioterrorism Preparedness and Response Act of 2002 (the Bioterrorism Act). The act authorized the secretary of Health and Human Services to protect the nation's food supply. The U.S. Food and Drug Administration (FDA) is the lead agency in initiating the protective measures.

The U.S. measures are aimed at providing a system of accountability. For example, all businesses or growers who sell food for consumption in the U.S. must register with the government. As well, these firms will be required to maintain records of their food handling and processing activities. In the event of a deliberate contamination, this information would allow the source of the contamination to be traced.

The surveillance of food also must include inspection of food entering the country. This involves the manual inspection of foods arriving by air, sea, rail, and surface routes. As of 2003, these inspections typically consist of the visual examination of foods, although the use of portable devices that detect microorganisms or their products is being used experimentally. Other such devices are in the laboratory stage of testing, and have produced accurate results in laboratory settings.

Because protection of a nation's food supply cannot be absolute, a system of early warning of a bioterrorist attack is important. If widespread alerts are recognized soon enough, relatively few people will have consumed the contaminated food. Consumer vigilance is an additional important counter-terrorism measure. For example, even if raw produce has been doused with a poison or an infectious microorganism, careful washing will usually remove the threat. Canned foods that are damaged or swollen should be identified and discarded.

■ FURTHER READING:

BOOKS:

Layton, Peggy Diane. *Emergency Food Storage & Survival Handbook: Everything You Need to Know to Keep Your Family Safe in a Crisis.* Roseville, CA: Prima Publishing, 2002.

Pottier, John. *Anthropology of Food: The Social Dynamics of Food Security.* Oxford: Polity Pr., 1999.

PERIODICALS:

Turco, R.P., A.B. Toon, T.P. Ackerman, et al."Nuclear Winter: Global Consequences of Multiple Nuclear Explosions." *Science* no. 222 (1983): 1283–1297.

ELECTRONIC:

Purdue University. "Agoterrorism." Purdue Extension Backgrounder. September 24, 2001. <http://www.ces.purdue.edu/eden/disasters/agro/Agroterrorism.doc>(24 January 2003).

United States Food and Drug Administration. "Frequently Asked Consumer Questions About Food Safety and

Terrorism." Center for Food Safety and Applied Nutrition. January16, 2002. <http://vm.cfsan.fda.gov/~dms/fsterrqu.html>(23 January 2003).

———. "Protecting the Food Supply: FDA Actions on New Bioterrorism Legislation." Center for Food Safety and Applied Nutrition. November 18, 2002. <http://www.cfsan.fda.gov/~dms/fsbtact3.html>(24 January 2003).

SEE ALSO

Biosensor Technologies
Microbiology: Applications to Espionage, Intelligence and Security
Polymerase Chain Reaction (PCR)
Salmonella and Salmonella Food Poisoning

Ford Administration (1974–1977), United States National Security Policy

■ CARYN E. NEUMANN

When Gerald Ford assumed the presidency of the United States upon the 1974 resignation of Richard Nixon, he chose to continue most of Nixon's national security policy. Secretary of State Henry Kissinger remained in office as the principal manager of national security matters while détente with the Soviet Union continued as a chief U.S. goal. The two administrations differed in that Ford never enjoyed Nixon's foreign policy successes. The Ford administration's accomplishments in arms control were overshadowed by the loss of South Vietnam to the Communists as well as doubts about the enforceability of the Vladivostok arms agreement.

A cautious mainstream Republican from Michigan who had served for many years as the minority leader in the U.S. House of Representatives, the amiable Ford came to the White House at an inauspicious time. Some Americans had lost faith in political leaders, largely as a result of the Watergate scandal, and this change made it difficult for Ford to marshal public support for his policies. With little experience in foreign affairs, Ford relied almost exclusively on Kissinger to pursue Nixon's aims of stability in the Middle East, rapprochement with China, and an easing of tensions with the Soviet Union.

Ford did make a change at the top of the National Security Council (NSC). Kissinger served as both national security adviser and secretary of state. During 1975, strong public and congressional disapproval developed over the accretion of so much power over foreign policy in the hands of one man. Watergate had discredited Nixon's system of a White House-centered system operating largely independently of the various security agencies. Accordingly, as part of a cabinet shakeup on November 3, 1975, Ford replaced Kissinger as national security adviser with Lieutenant General Brent Scowcroft, who had been Kissinger's deputy at the NSC. This personnel shift produced little real change as Kissinger continued to dominate as the presidential advisor. Scowcroft acted in a low-key, low profile capacity while overseeing the flow of interdepartmental proposals and analyses of decisions.

Kissinger had two notable achievements under Ford. He managed to reduce Middle East tensions by persuading Egypt and Israel to rely on negotiations rather than force to settle future disagreements. He also presided over the Vladivostok treaty, signed by Ford and Soviet General Secretary Leonid Brezhnev in 1974. This pact, a continuation of the Strategic Arms Limitation Treaty (SALT) talks, was designed to serve as a basis for SALT II. It allowed each side to retain 2,400 strategic vehicles. This latter term was defined to include intercontinental ballistic missiles (ICBMs), submarine-launched ballistic missiles (SLBMs) such as the nuclear-powered Polaris, and, for the first time, intercontinental bombers. The land-based ICBMs are anti-missile missiles while the less-accurate SLBMs offer more security and are therefore regarded as a main deterrent force. Both the U.S. and U.S.S.R. were permitted to possess a limit of 1,320 multiple, independently targetable, reentry vehicles (MIRVs) on their ICBMs. It is essentially impossible to monitor the number of warheads within any missile without on-site inspections and, for this reason, MIRVs and other forms of multiple warhead systems had been omitted from consideration in the 1972 SALT agreement. Any anti-ballistic missile system is likely to be overwhelmed if the attack against it is from missiles with multiple warheads. On the other hand, a nation can withstand the loss of many retaliatory missiles and still have a formidable second-strike capability if the surviving ones are of the MIRV type.

Vladivostok raised concerns because neither the U.S. nor the Soviet Union possessed 2,400 strategic vehicles. The agreement seemed to many to be more of an arms expansion accord than an arms limitation one. The treaty also did nothing to address the existing inequity in large missiles, a category in which the Soviets were vastly superior.

While Ford faced attacks from Congress and the American public over Vladivostok, Cambodian Communists captured the American merchant ship *Mayaguez* in May, 1975. Ford sent the marines to rescue the crew, but initial public approval of this forceful act diminished when it was disclosed that the Cambodians had already agreed to release the Americans. Forty-one seamen died in the rescue. In that same month, South Vietnam fell to communist-controlled North Vietnam. Ford's tottering presidency received yet another blow when he stated, in televised debate with 1976 presidential opponent Jimmy Carter, that Eastern Europe was free of Soviet domination. Ford's defeat in the election meant that the Carter administration would negotiate the SALT II agreement.

■ FURTHER READING:

BOOKS:

Boll, Michael M. *National Security Planning Roosevelt through Reagan.* Lexington: University Press of Kentucky, 1988.

Brodie, Bernard and Fawn M. Brodie. *From Crossbow to H-Bomb: The Evolution of the Weapons and Tactics of Warfare.* Bloomington: Indiana University Press, 1973.

Carroll, Peter N. *It Seemed like Nothing Happened: America in the 1970s.* New Brunswick: Rutgers University Press, 1990.

Crabb, Cecil V. and Kevin V. Mulcahy. *American National Security: A Presidential Perspective.* Pacific Grove, CA: Brooks/Cole, 1991.

SEE ALSO

Ballistic Missiles
Cold War (1972–1989): The Collapse of the Soviet Union
Middle East, Modern U.S. Security Policy and Interventions
National Security Advisor, United States
National Security Strategy, United States
Nixon Administration (1969–1974), United States National Security Policy
NSC (National Security Council)
NSC (National Security Council), History
Nuclear Weapons

Foreign Assets Control (OFAC), United States Office

The Office of Foreign Assets Control (OFAC) enforces economic and trade sanctions against foreign nations, drug traffickers, and terrorist organizations. The OFAC is part of the Department of the Treasury and acts under the authority of legislative controls and the wartime and national emergency power acts. Under these measures the OFAC has authority to trace and freeze foreign assets of those deemed to be a threat to national security.

The OFAC has its roots in the American Civil War. During this period, the Treasury Department sought and seized money and goods being traded or sold by the Confederacy under the Trading with the Enemy Act. During World War I, Congress updated the Treasury Department's authority under the revised Trading with the Enemy Act of 1917. In 1940 Congress sought to prevent the Nazis from using assets seized from the countries that Germany occupied by creating the Office of Foreign Funds Control (OFFC). After the United States entered World War II, the OFFC froze Axis assets and enforced the prohibition on trading with Axis nations.

President Truman established the current Office of Foreign Assets Control (OFAC) in 1950 as a reaction to Chinese involvement in the Korean War. The OFAC was charged with freezing and blocking all asset transfers by China and North Korea. Although modified several times, American economic sanctions against North Korea have continued under The Foreign Assets Control Regulations since 1950.

Recently, the OFAC has been primarily concerned with tracing and freezing the assets of drug traffickers and terrorist organizations. The OFAC has played a key role in American efforts to cut funding to terrorist organizations since the September 11, 2001, terrorist attacks on the United States. Executive Order 13224 "Blocking Property and Prohibiting Transactions with Persons who Commit, Threaten to Commit, or Support Terrorism" granted the OFAC wide powers in administering and enforcing economic sanctions against suspected terrorist. This order also allowed the OFAC, in conjunction with the secretary of state and attorney general, to determine those responsible for funding terrorism and take appropriate action.

■ FURTHER READING:

ELECTRONIC:

United States Department of Foreign Assets Control. <http://www.ofac.gov/>(05 January 2003).

SEE ALSO

Terrorist Organizations, Freezing of Assets

Foreign Intelligence Surveillance Act

The Foreign Intelligence Surveillance Act (FISA) was passed by the United States Congress in 1978 following an intensive investigation of the activities of U.S. intelligence and law enforcement agencies by the Church Committee.

The Church Committee (chaired by Sen. Frank Church) uncovered evidence of illegal wiretaps and illegal entry by the Federal Bureau of Investigation (FBI) as part of FBI efforts during the 1960s and early 1970s to conduct domestic surveillance on Vietnam War protesters and civil rights advocates.

FISA was also inspired by a ruling by the United States Supreme Court in 1972 (*United States v. U.S. District Court*), 407 U.S. 297, where the Supreme Court stated: "Given these potential distinctions between [Wiretap statute] criminal surveillances and those involving the domestic security, Congress may wish to consider protective standards for the latter which differ from those already prescribed for specified crimes [under the Wiretap statute]. Different standards may be compatible with the Fourth Amendment if they are reasonable both in relation to the legitimate need of Government for intelligence information and the protected rights of our citizens."

FISA established the United States Foreign Intelligence Surveillance Court and authorized the Court to conduct judicial oversight in matters of electronic surveillance related to intelligence and counterintelligence operation. The Court was composed of U.S. federal district court judges, appointed by the Chief Justice, who rotate membership on the court.

Because of the secret nature of the Court, and in order not to violate the Fourth Amendment of the Constitution (specifying the need for probable cause) warrants for surveillance were to be restricted to the gathering of information not intended to be used in criminal prosecution.

The Court reviews Justice Department applications for electronic surveillance. The Court meets two days each month and the proceedings are non-adversarial. Akin to grand jury procedures, the Court only considers arguments for surveillance brought by the Department of Justice Office of Intelligence Policy and Review.

FISA also broadly interpreted associations with "foreign power" so that individuals associated with foreign organizations designated as terrorist organizations by either the Court or Department of State are not entitled to the same Constitutional protections as individuals accuse of other crimes. FISA permits domestic surveillance if there is a judicial finding of probable cause that the individual or organization to be scrutinized acts for a foreign power. The acts constituting probable cause do not need to be criminal; they may, for example, fall into the realm civil economic activities. If the surveillance target is a U.S. citizen FISA requires that, in order to grant permission for surveillance based upon FISA, there must exist a probable cause to argue that the target's acts involve espionage or other criminal conduct. FISA places a heavy reliance on "acts" so that U.S. citizens cannot be designated as agents of a foreign power "solely upon the basis of activities protected by the first amendment to the Constitution of the United States" (i.e. free speech rights).

Although initially limited to setting conditions for electronic surveillance, during the 1990s Congress expanded FISA to include provisions allowing physical searches.

It is estimated that FISA conditions applied to approximately 750 cases a year prior to the September 11, 2001, terrorist attacks on the U.S.

The Patriot Act, passed following the terrorist attacks on the United States on September 11, 2001, extended the government's surveillance authority under FISA. New powers included roving wiretap authority (the surveillance of communications related to an individual or organization without regard to particular telephone line, computer station, or other mode of communication to be monitored. Other extensions included a more liberalized allowed use of pen register, trap and trace devices (removing the need to assert that the surveillance target is "an agent of a foreign power"). The lower Foreign Intelligence Surveillance Court specifically rejected Justice Department attempts at "information screening" and "minimization"

procedures are intended to allow the use of material gathered under Foreign Intelligence Surveillance Court authorization to criminal proceedings.

■ FURTHER READING:

ELECTRONIC:

Electronic Privacy Information Center. Foreign Intelligence Surveillance Act (FISA) November 22, 2002. <http://www.epic.org/privacy/terrorism/fisa/#Overview> (April 15, 2003).

SEE ALSO

COINTELPRO
Foreign Intelligence Surveillance Court of Review

Foreign Intelligence Surveillance Court of Review

The United States Foreign Intelligence Surveillance Court of Review is an appellate court for the review of matters related to espionage and counterintelligence.

Although the Court was established by the Foreign Intelligence Surveillance Act (FISA) passed by the United States Congress in 1978, the Court has had no record of meeting prior to its review of Justice Department electronic surveillance in September, 2002.

Following the terrorist attacks on the United States on September 11, 2001, the Justice Department's use of domestic wiretaps increased and the department began to operate under broad new powers that Attorney General John Ashcroft asserted were granted to law enforcement agencies under the 2001 Patriot Act. A lower court, the Foreign Intelligence Surveillance Court—also authorized by FISA—ruled aspects of the Justice Department interpretation of those new powers to be unconstitutional. The Justice Department then appealed to the Foreign Intelligence Surveillance Court of Review, the first known appeal of a Foreign Intelligence Surveillance Court ruling.

The Court of Review operates as a three-judge panel composed of federal appellate judges—or retired appellate judges—appointed on a rotating basis by Chief Justice of the United States Supreme Court.

Court deliberations were conducted in secret and took place in an electronically secure room at the Justice Department. No public notice was given prior to the Court's session and the Court issued no ruling or public statements following the session.

Congressional officials including Senate Intelligence and Judiciary Committee staff were denied requests to attend the appellate court's initial hearing, according to

Justice Department officials, because the hearing contained detailed discussions of sources and methods used in intelligence gathering. Following congressional protests, the Court of Review, agreed to provide Senate Judiciary Committee members with an unclassified transcript of its proceedings and an unclassified copy of its rulings.

■ FURTHER READING:

ELECTRONIC:

Electronic Privacy Information Center. November 22, 2002. <http://www.epic.org/privacy/terrorism/fisa/#Overview> (April 15, 2003).

SEE ALSO

Church Committee
COINTELPRO
Patriot Act, United States
Senate Select Committee on Intelligence, United States

Forensic Geology in Military or Intelligence Operations

■ WILLIAM C. HANEBERG

Forensic geology is strictly defined as the use of geologic principles and techniques to establish facts or provide evidence used in a court of law. A broader working definition includes the use of the same principles and techniques to establish facts or sequences of events regardless of whether they are used in court. Thus, the gathering and interpretation of geologic data for intelligence, espionage, and national security purposes can fall under the second definition of forensic geology. Forensic geology overlaps with the field of forensic soil science. In many cases, the work performed by practitioners in the two fields is very similar and the only distinction lies in the details of their academic training and professional experience. Also related is the field of forensic geophysics, in which geophysical instruments such as seismographs can be used as the basis for inferences about activities in remote or otherwise inaccessible areas.

Origin of forensic geology. The first written description of forensic geology is generally attributed to the fictional detective Sherlock Holmes, who was created by Arthur Conan Doyle (British, 1859–1930). In A Study in Scarlet, published in 1887, Holmes was endowed with the ability to easily distinguish soils of different types and infer from mud on their shoes and clothes the places to which people had traveled. He was also described by Dr. Watson, his

fictional colleague, as having a "practical, but limited" knowledge of geology.

The first real use of forensic geology to solve a crime does not appear to have occurred until 1904, when a German chemist named Georg Popp used geologic evidence to help identify a murder suspect from a handkerchief containing traces of snuff, coal dust, and the mineral hornblende. The prime suspect used snuff, and divided his labors between a coal gasification plant and a quarry in which the rocks were rich in the hornblende. (Coal gasification was then a common process in which coal was transformed into natural gas.) Soil in the suspect's pant cuffs also was matched to soil at the crime scene and outside of the victim's home. Taken together, the evidence convinced the suspect to confess. Four years later, Popp was able to show that one layer of soil on the shoes of a murder suspect matched the soil and distinctly green goose droppings around the suspect's home. A second layer contained red sandstone fragments identical to those in the soil where the body was found. The third, and outermost, layer contained coal, brick, and cement dust identical to that found at the location where the murder weapon was found. The suspect claimed that he was walking in the fields near his home and therefore could not have committed the murder. Popp was able to show that, in addition to all of the geologic evidence that was preserved on the shoes, there was no sign of the distinctive milky white quartz particles that were characteristic of soil from those fields.

Methods of forensic geology. The methods used by forensic geologists are adaptations of the methods used by geologists engaged in academic research, mineral exploration, and other activities. For example, it is a fundamental principle of stratigraphy (the study of sequences of sedimentary rocks) that a layer of sedimentary rock is in most cases younger than the layers below it and older than the layers above it. This principle is known as the law of superposition. The implications for forensic geology are that a layer of mud deposited on shoes or an automobile is younger than the layers beneath it. Understanding the sequence of mud, sediment, or dirt layers can therefore allow forensic geologists to reconstruct a chain of events such as visits to several locations characterized by different soil or bedrock types.

Other techniques employed by forensic geologists are derived from the disciplines of petrography and petrology, which are concerned with the description and interpretation of rock types. Soils and rocks can be distinguished on the basis of their particle size distributions as well as the sphericity, angularity, and mineralogy of individual particles. Two samples of sand, for example, may be composed of grains that appear significantly different to an experienced geologist. Forensically important distinctions can sometimes be made with the unaided eye or a small magnifying lens. In other cases, binocular microscopes can be used to view grains using reflected light. A more elaborate method is the examination of thin sections using transmitted polarized light. Thin sections are made by gluing a soil or rock to a glass slide and then grinding it to a standardized thickness of 30 microns. Most minerals are transparent in thin section (although a few metallic minerals remain opaque) and can be identified by their crystal shape and the degree to which they distort light passing through polarizing filters placed above and below the thin section. Fragments of macrofossils and intact microfossils, as well as pollen, in a soil or rock can likewise be identified by microscopy.

Particles smaller than sand grains can be difficult to identify using optical microscopes, but their shape and surface texture can be examined using instruments such as electron microscopes. Another class of instruments known as electron microprobes can perform non-destructive chemical analyses, including mapping variations in chemical composition across grains much less than a millimeter in diameter. Electron microprobe maps of oxygen content, for example, might be used to determine whether two metallic mineral grains have experienced similar degrees of oxidation.

The origin and history of a soil or rock particle is known as its provenance. Geologists in general and forensic geologists in particular can infer whether the source of sand grains is likely to have been an igneous or sedimentary rock, whether the grains were likely to have been transported by running water or exposed in an arid environment, and the climate in which a soil was formed. The presence of rare minerals or distinctive microfossils may allow them to further limit the possible sources to a small geographic area, perhaps a single watershed or rock body described in a published map or report. Thus, establishing the provenance of sand or mud recovered as forensic evidence can place a suspect at a crime scene or confirm an alibi.

Forensic geology case histories. There have been several publicly known cases in which forensic geology has played an important role in espionage, intelligence, security, and military operations.

During the second half of World War II, the Japanese military developed a plan to attack the United States with unmanned balloons carrying explosive and incendiary bombs. Using meteorological observations and calculations, they were able to design balloons that could be launched from Japanese beaches and carried by the jet stream to the western United States. The balloons were designed to be self-regulating, releasing sandbags in order to gain elevation during cold nights and releasing hydrogen to loose elevation during warm days. It is believed that 9000 balloons were launched, of which an estimated 1000 reached North America. Two balloons drifted as far east as Michigan. Although they ignited a few small fires and killed only six people (five children and a minister's wife who came across an unexploded bomb while on a fishing trip in Oregon), their origin was of concern. It was not known whether the balloons were

being launched from Japanese submarines, by shore parties that had landed on American beaches, from German prisoner of war camps, or from the internment camps to which many Japanese-American citizens had been forcibly relocated. Geologists in the military geology unit of the U.S. Geological Survey were asked to determine the launching point of the balloons from the provenance of sand that had been used for ballast and which had been recovered from many balloon crash sites. Because sand has a low economic value and is expensive to transport, it was likely that the source of the sand was at or near the launching areas. The geologists first eliminated North American sources for the sand, which contained an unusual combination of minerals, fossil and recent diatoms (single celled algae that secrete siliceous cell walls), foraminifera (single celled organisms with calcareous shells), mollusk shell fragments, and no coral. The absence of coral was important because coral grows only in warm water, meaning that the sand most likely came from a northern area. By comparing the sand to geologic maps and reports that had been published before the war, one as early as 1889, the geologists suggested two possible launching sites along the northern coast of Japan. In reality, balloons were being launched from three sites. One of them was a site identified by the geologists and the other two, separated by approximately 15 km, were close to the second site identified by the geologists.

Forensic geology has also been used to investigate politically motivated murders and terrorist attacks. Grains of sand and microfossils found on the body of Italian Prime Minister Aldo Moro, who was kidnapped and murdered by Red Brigade terrorists in 1978, led investigators to conclude that he had been held at least part of the time along an 11 km long stretch of beach north of Rome. The total mass of sand collected from Moro's clothing and the car in which his body was discovered was approximately 1 gram. The presence of bitumen (a tar-like substance in this case derived from oil spills dispersed by waves) and resins used in boat building further supported the beach hypothesis. Because of the high profile and political sensitivity of the case, collection of sand samples for comparison with the grains found on Moro's body occurred in secret. The geologist working on the case was accompanied by his wife, who posed as a tourist picking plants and observing the scenery while her husband surreptitiously collected sand samples.

The Federal Bureau of Investigation (FBI) relied heavily on geologic evidence to learn how the Mexico Federal Judicial Police (MFJP) attempted to cover up the murder of Drug Enforcement Agency (DEA) agent Enrique Salazar and pilot Alfredo Avelar, who assisted Salazar on clandestine missions for the United States government. Salazar had been kidnapped at gunpoint from the streets of Guadalajara, Mexico and his body was discovered, along with that of Avelar, after a shootout between the MFJP and family engaged in the drug trade. The entire family was killed in the shootout, and the implication was that Salazar had been kidnapped and killed by the family. Traces of soil on the bodies of Salazar and Avelar, however, did not match the soil at the ranch where the shootout occurred and caused suspicion to be cast on the explanation offered by the Mexican government. Detailed studies by an FBI geologist posing as a DEA agent (FBI agents were not allowed to work in Mexico, but DEA agents were) revealed an extremely uncommon assemblage of mineral grains and shards of pink volcanic glass. This geologic evidence led the investigators to a state park in mountainous terrain where, based on detailed examination of individual soil particles, the site at which Salazar and Avelar had originally been buried was discovered. Other forensic evidence showed that the MFJP had been involved in the kidnapping, torture, and burial of Salazar and Avelar.

Geologic interpretation of photographs and videotapes can also shed light on the location in which a photograph or a recording was made. A notable example of this kind of forensic geology occurred shortly after the September 11, 2001 terrorist attacks on the World Trade Center in New York City and the Pentagon in Washington, D.C. American geologists who had worked in Afghanistan were able to identify rocks in the background of a videotaped message from the terrorist leader Osama bin Laden, and therefore the region of the country in which the message was taped. The use of geologic knowledge to infer location was widely publicized, however, and subsequent messages were recorded against a cloth background in order to prevent the location of the taping from being discerned.

Knowledge of the principles of forensic geology can be used to obscure evidence or mislead investigators. Double agent Kim Philby (British, 1912–1988), who spied for the Soviet Union while at the same time working in the British intelligence service during the Cold War years, once used a small trowel to bury a camera in a wooded area near the Potomac River in Virginia. He then returned to his home and used the trowel to dig in his garden in order obscure any soil particles that might be used to identify the location of the camera. This incident would never have been known if Philby had not described it in his autobiography. Terrorists arrested in conjunction with the Aldo Moro case insisted that forensic evidence had been planted in order to steer authorities away from the true location of their activities, which might have led to the arrest of additional suspects. It appears, though, that the forensic evidence was authentic and reliable.

Forensic seismology. The use of geophysical methods, especially those derived from seismological studies of the Earth, can also provide information about remote events. Analysis of seismograms produced by the explosion of the Russian submarine Kursk in 2000, for example, have shown that a small initial explosion was followed by a much larger explosion that produced vibrations equivalent to those from a magnitude 4.1 earthquake. This information was used to infer that the size of the explosion was equivalent to that which would have been produced by 4000 to 6000 kilograms of TNT. Seismologists were also able to analyze information about the oscillations of a bubble of hot gas that rose through the sea after the explosion, and infer that the main explosion took place at a depth of approximately 100 meters. Bathymetric data suggest that the seafloor is about 100 meters deep at the explosion site, so it is likely that the second explosion occurred when the sinking submarine struck the seafloor.

Seismological data have also been used to help infer the details of 1995 bombing of the Murrah Federal Building in Oklahoma City, the 2001 World Trade Center attack, and the 2001 Pentagon attack. Analysis of seismograms associated with the collapse of the World Trade Center towers, for example, suggests that the actual structural collapse occurred over a period of about three seconds. The same principles can be used to obtain evidence of clandestine conventional or nuclear explosions, and in particular to verify that nuclear test ban treaties are not being violated.

Seismological data may provide information about the February 2003 disintegration of the space shuttle Columbia. The sonic boom produced as a shuttle descends is normally recorded on seismographs, but the seismogram produced by the final Columbia reentry does not contain evidence of a sonic boom. Although the reasons for this were unclear at the time this article was written, the seismic data provided enough information to allow the location of the disintegration to be calculated and compared against other observations.

■ FURTHER READING:

BOOKS:

Mikesh, Robert C. *Japan's World War II Balloon Bomb Attacks on North America.* Washington, D.C.: Farrar, Smithsonian Institution Press. 1990.

Murray, R. C. and J. C. Tedrow. *Forensic Geology.* Englewood Cliffs, New Jersey: Prentice Hall, 1998.

PERIODICALS:

Buck, S. "Searching for Graves Using Geophysical Technology: Field Tests with Ground Penetrating Radar, Magnetometry, and Electrical Resistivity." *Journal of Forensic Sciences,* vol. 48, no. 1 (2003): 5–11.

Holzer, T. L., J. B. Fletcher, G. S. Fuis, T. Ryberg, T. M. Brocher, and C. M. Dietel. " Seismograms Offer Insight into Oklahoma City Bombing." *Eos, Transactions American Geophysical Union,* vol. 77, no. 41 (October 8, 1996): 393, 396–397.

Koper, K. D., T. C. Wallace, S. R. Taylor, and H. E. Hartse. "Forensic Seismology and the Sinking of the Kursk." *Eos, Transactions, American Geophysical Union,* vol. 82, no. 4 (2001): 37.

Lombardi, Gianni. "The Contribution of Forensic Geology and Other Trace Evidence Analysis to the Investigation of the Killing of Italian Prime Minister Aldo Moro." *Journal of Forensic Sciences,* v. 44, no. 3 (1999): 634–642.

McPhee, John. "Annals of Crime—The Gravel Page." *The New Yorker.* (January 29, 1996): 44–69.

ELECTRONIC:

American Society of Forensic Geologists." American Society of Forensic Geologists." 2002. <http://www.forensicgeology.org/>(13 March 2003).

Levine, Alissa. "Secrets Hidden in Soil." September 5, 2001. <http://ltpwww.gsfc.nasa.gov/globe/forengeo/secret.htm>(13 March 2003).

Murray, Raymond. "Devil in the Details, the Science of Forensic Geology." January 29, 2003. <http://www.forensicgeology.net/science.htm>(13 March 2003).

Pinsker, Lisa M. "Geology Adventures in Afghanistan." Geotimes Web Feature. February 2002. <http://www.agiweb.org/geotimes/feb02/Feature_Shroderside.html>(13 March 2003).

SEE ALSO

Geologic and Topographical Influences on Military and Intelligence Operations
Geospatial Imagery
GPS
Mapping Technology
Seismograph
Seismology for Monitoring Explosions
Weapons of Mass Destruction, Detection

Forensic Science

■ AGNIESZKA LICHANSKA

Forensic science is a multidisciplinary subject used for examining crime scenes and gathering evidence to be used in prosecution of offenders in a court of law. Forensic science techniques are also used to examine compliance with international agreements regarding weapons of mass destruction.

The main areas used in forensic science are biology, chemistry, and medicine, although the science also includes the use of physics, computer science, geology, and psychology. Forensic scientists examine objects, substances (including blood or drug samples), chemicals (paints, explosives, toxins), tissue traces (hair, skin), or impressions (fingerprints or tidemarks) left at the crime scene. The majority of forensic scientists specialize in one area of science.

Evidence and Trace Examination

The analysis of the scene of crime or accident involves obtaining a permanent record of the scene (forensic photography) and collection of evidence for further examination and comparison. Collected samples include biological (tissue samples such as skin, blood, semen, or hair), physical (fingerprints, shells, fragments of instruments or equipment, fibers, recorded voice messages, or computer discs) and chemical (samples of paint, cosmetics, solvents, or soil).

Most commonly, the evidence collected at the scene is subsequently processed in a forensic laboratory by scientists specializing in a particular area. Scientists identify, for example, fingerprints, chemical residues, fibers, hair, or DNA left behind. However, miniaturization of equipment and the ability to perform most forensic analysis at the scene of crime results in more specialists being present in the field. Presence of more people at the scene of crime introduces a greater likelihood of introduction of contamination into the evidence. Moreover, multi-handling of a piece of evidence (for example a murder weapon being analyzed by many specialists) is also likely to introduce traces of tissue or DNA not originating from the scene of a crime. All this results in strict quality controls imposed on collection, handling, and analysis of evidence to ensure lack of contamination. For example, in DNA analysis it is essential that samples are stored at the correct temperature and that there is no contamination from a person handling a sample by wearing clean gloves and performing analysis in a clean laboratory.

Ability to properly collect and process forensic samples can affect the ability of the prosecution to prove their case during a trial. The presence of chemical traces or DNA on a piece of debris is also crucial in establishing the chain of events leading to a crime or accident.

A growing area of forensic analysis is monitoring non-proliferation of weapons of mass destruction, analysis of possible terrorist attacks or breaches of security. The nature of samples analyzed is wide, but slightly different to a criminal investigation. In addition to the already described samples, forensic scientists who gather evidence of mass destruction collect swabs from objects, water, and plant material to test for the presence of radioactive isotopes, toxins, or poisons, as well as chemicals that can be used in production of chemical weapons. The main difference from the more common forensic investigation is the amount of chemicals present in a sample. Samples taken from the scene of suspected chemical or biological weapons often contain minute amounts of chemicals and require very sensitive and accurate instruments for analysis.

Biological traces. Biological traces are collected not only from the scene of crime and a deceased person, but also from surviving victims and suspects. Most common samples obtained are blood, hair, and semen. DNA can be extracted from any of these samples and used for comparative analysis.

DNA is the main method of identifying people. Victims of crashes or fires are often unrecognizable, but adequate DNA can be isolated and a person can be positively identified if a sample of their DNA or their family's

A member of the International Commission on Missing Persons in Bosnia, inspects human remains found by forensics experts in a mass grave at the village of Kamenica, an area of Serbian-controlled Bosnia, in 2002. AP/WIDE WORLD PHOTOS.

DNA is taken for comparison. Such methods are being used in the identification of the remains in Yugoslav war victims, the World Trade Center terrorist attack victims, and the 2002 Bali bombing victims.

Biological traces, investigated by forensic scientists come from bloodstains, saliva samples (from cigarette buts or chewing gum) and tissue samples, such as skin, nails, or hair. Samples are processed to isolate the DNA and establish the origin of the samples. Samples must first be identified as human, animal, or plant before further investigation proceeds. For some applications, such as customs and quarantine, traces of animal and plant tissue have to be identified to the level of the species, as transport of some species is prohibited. A presence of a particular species can also prove that a suspect or victim visited a particular area. In cases of national security, samples are tested for the presence of pathogens and toxins, and the latter are also analyzed chemically.

Chemical traces. Forensic chemistry performs qualitative and quantitative analysis of chemicals found on people, various objects, or in solutions. The chemical analysis is the most varied from all the forensic disciplines. Chemists analyze drugs as well as paints, remnants of explosives,

fire debris, gun shot residues, fibers, and soil samples. They can also test for a presence of radioactive substances (nuclear weapons), toxic chemicals (chemical weapons) and biological toxins (biological weapons). Forensic chemists can also be called on in a case of environmental pollution to test the compounds and trace their origin. The samples are obtained from a variety of objects and often contain only minute amounts of chemicals.

The identification of fire accelerants such as kerosene or gasoline is of great importance for determining the cause of a fire. Debris collected from a fire must be packed in tight, secure containers, as the compounds to be analyzed are often volatile. An improper transport of such debris would result in no detection of important traces. One of the methods used for this analysis involves the use of charcoal strips. The chemicals from the debris are absorbed onto the strip and subsequently dissolved in a solvent before analysis. This analysis allows scientists to determine the hydrocarbon content of the samples and identify the type of fire accelerator used.

Physical evidence. Physical evidence usually involves objects found at the scene of a crime. Physical evidence may include all sorts of prints such as fingerprints, footprints, handprints, tidemarks, cut marks, tool marks, etc. Analysis of some physical evidence is conducted by making impressions in plaster, taking images of marks, or lifting the fingerprints from objects encountered. These serve later as a comparison to identify, for example, a vehicle that was parked at the scene, a person that was present, a type of manufacturing method used to create a tool, or a method used to break in a building or harm a victim.

An examination of documents found at the scene or related to the crime is often an integral part of forensic analysis. Such examination is often able to establish not only the author, but more importantly identify any alterations that have taken place. Specialists are also able to recover text from documents damaged by accident or on purpose.

Identification. The identification of people can be performed by fingerprint analysis or DNA analysis. When none of these methods can be used, the facial reconstruction can be used instead to generate a person's image. TV and newspapers then circulate the image for identification.

Other Forensic Scientists

Pathologists and forensic anthropologists play a very important part in forensic examination. They are able to determine the cause of death by examining marks on the bone(s), skin (gunshot wounds), and other body surfaces for external trauma. They can also determine a cause of death by toxicological analysis of blood and tissues.

A number of analytical methods are used by forensic laboratories to analyze evidence from a crime scene. Methods vary, depending on the type of evidence analyzed and information that needs to be extracted from the traces found. If a type of evidence is encountered for the first time, a new method is developed.

Biological samples are most commonly analyzed by polymerase chain reaction (PCR). The results of PCR are then visualized by gel electrophoresis. Forensic scientists tracing the source of a biological attack could use the new hybridization or PCR-based methods of DNA analysis. Biological and chemical analysis of samples can identify toxins found.

Imaging used by forensic scientists can be as simple as a light microscope, or can involve an electron microscope, absorption in ultraviolet to visible range, color analysis or fluorescence analysis. Image analysis is used not only in cases of biological samples, but also for analysis of paints, fibers, hair, gunshot residue, or other chemicals. Image analysis is often essential for an interpretation of physical evidence. Specialists often enhance photographs to visualize small details essential in forensic analysis. Image analysis is also used to identify details from surveillance cameras.

The examination of chemical traces often requires very sensitive chromatographic techniques or mass spectrometric analysis. Four major types of chromatographic methods used are: thin layer chromatography (TLC) to separate inks and other chemicals, atomic absorption chromatography for analysis of heavy metals, gas chromatography (GC), and liquid chromatography (HPLC). GC is most widely used in identification of explosives, accelerators, propellants, and drugs or chemicals involved in chemical weapon production, while liquid chromatography (HPLC) is used for detection of minute amounts of compounds in complex mixtures. These methods rely on separation of the molecules based on their ability to travel in a solvent (TLC) or to adhere to adsorbent filling the chromatography column. The least strongly absorbed compounds are eluted first and the most tightly bound last. By collecting all of the fractions and comparing the observed pattern to standards, scientists are able to identify the composition of even the most complex mixtures.

New laboratory instruments are able to identify nearly every element present in a sample. Because the composition of alloys used in production of steel instruments, wires or bullet casings is different between various producers, it is possible to identify a source of the product.

In some cases chromatography alone is not an adequate method for identification. It is then combined with another method to separate the compounds even further and results in greater sensitivity. One such method is mass spectrometry (MS). A mass spectrometer uses high voltage to produce charged ions. Gaseous ions or isotopes are then separated in a magnetic field according to their masses. A combined GC-MS instrument has a very high sensitivity and can analyze samples present at concentrations of one part-per-billion.

As some samples are difficult to analyze with MS alone, a laser vaporization method (imaging laser-ablation mass spectroscopy) was developed to produce small amounts of chemicals from solid materials (fabrics, hair, fibers, soil, glass) for MS analysis. Such analysis can examine hair samples for presence of drugs or chemicals. Due to its high sensitivity, the method is of particular use in monitoring areas and people suspected of production of chemical, biological or nuclear weapons, or narcotics producers.

While charcoal sticks are still in use for fire investigations, a new technology of solid-phase microextraction (SPME) was developed to collect even more chemicals and does not require any solvent for further analysis. The method relies on the use of sticks similar to charcoal, but coated with various polymers for collecting different chemicals (chemical warfare agents, explosives, or drugs). Collected samples are analyzed immediately in the field in by GC.

A number of instruments used are smaller than ever before, allowing them to be used directly in the field with rapid results. For example, a combined GC-MS analysis device can analyze a sample within 15 minutes directly in the field. The standard laboratory instrument is large with a weight over 100 kilograms, while the portable version is only 28 kilograms. A number of government agencies (for example the FBI) are now armed with the portable instruments and can perform rapid forensic analysis in the field in a time shorter than it would take to transport samples to a forensic laboratory. United States troops are equipped with similar instruments on board some tanks and trucks, in order to quickly determine the presence of chemical or biological weapons on the battlefield

Applications of forensic science. The main use of forensic science is for purposes of law enforcement to investigate crimes such as murder, theft, or fraud. Forensic scientists are also involved in investigating accidents such as train or plane crashes to establish if they were accidental or a result of foul play. The techniques developed by forensic science are also used by the army to analyze the possibility of the presence of chemical weapons, high explosives or to test for propellant stabilizers. Gasoline products often evaporate rapidly and their presence cannot be confirmed, but residues of chemicals, such as propellant stabilizers, are present for much longer indicating that an engine or missile was used.

■ **FURTHER READING:**

Houde, John. *Crime Lab: A guide for Nonscientists.* Rolling Bay: Calico Press, 1998.

Kelly, John F., and Phillip K, Wearne. *Tainting Evidence: Inside the Scandals at the FBI Crime Lab.* New York: Free Press, 1998.

Saferstein, Richard. *Criminalistics: An Introduction to Forensic Science.* New York: Prentice-Hall, 2000.

ELECTRONIC:

American Academy of Forensic Science <http://www.aafs.org.> (7 February 2003).

Consulting and Ducation in Forensic Science. "Forensic Science Timeline." Norah Rudin. <http://www.forensicdna.com/Timeline.htm.>(7 February 2003).

Forensic Science Center, University of California Lawrence Livermore National Laboratory, 7000 East Ave., Livermore, CA 94550–9234. (925) 423–1189. <http://www.llnl.gov/IPandC/op96/10/10h-for.html.> (7 February 2003).

Forensic Science Web Pages. 7 February 1997. <http://home.earthlink.net/~thekeither/Forensic/forsone.htm.>(7 February 2003).

National Center for Forensic Science, University of Central Florida 12354 Research Parkway Orlando, FL 32826. (407) 823–6469. <http://ncfs.ucf.edu/navbar.html.> (7 February 2003).

SEE ALSO

Chemistry: Applications in Espionage, Intelligence, and Security Issues

DNA Recognition Instruments
Document Forgery
Gas Chromatograph-Mass Spectrometer
Isotopic analysis
Polymerase Chain Reaction (PCR)
Thin Layer Chromatography

Forensic Voice and Tape Analysis

Methods of forensic voice and tape analysis first entered the limelight during the Watergate scandal in the early 1970s, and the basic methodology—if not the tools and precision with which the techniques are practiced—has changed little since. Much of this field is concerned with identification or elimination using voice-stress analysis, but controversy over techniques and their admissibility as evidence remains. This disagreement, even among specialists, came to the forefront as forensic scientists on both sides of the Atlantic studied tapes allegedly released by terrorist mastermind Osama bin Laden in the fall of 2002.

Early history. Spectrographic analysis and related techniques make it possible to match a suspect to an incriminating sample of his or her speech—a threatening phone call, for instance, or a taped admission of guilt. Voice and tape analysis can also be used to clear a suspect. In this field, a scientifically verified match between a suspect (or another individual) and a voice sample is known as an identification, while scientific proof, by means of voice analysis, that a suspect and a voice sample do not match is called an elimination.

The U.S. Federal Bureau of Investigation (FBI) used spectrographic or voice identification analysis as early as the 1950s, but the technique did not gain scientific acceptance until a 1962 study by Lawrence Kersta, a researcher working with a 1940s-model Bell Laboratory sound spectrograph. Kersta maintained that "voiceprints," a term he coined, provide a unique means of identifying individuals. He went on to establish a professional association, the International Association of Voice Identification, which in 1980, became part of the more general International Association for Identification.

The 1970s. The word "voiceprint" would later be discarded, due to the false association with fingerprinting, which is a much more exact science. Nevertheless, spectrographic techniques continued to gain respect in forensic and law enforcement circles, thanks in part to a 1972 study at

Michigan State University. The study found an error rate of two percent for false identification (instances in which the examiner chose the wrong match, or found a match when none existed), and five percent for false elimination, in which the examiner failed to recognize that a match existed. In the years immediately following this study, spectrographic techniques came to widespread public attention during the examination of tapes made by President Richard M. Nixon in the White House.

In 1979, a National Research Council committee presented the FBI with the results of a study on spectrographic voice identification under forensic conditions, involving some 2,000 forensic comparisons made by FBI personnel. The researchers' findings confirmed the impression that, while it was not an exact science, voice analysis could be useful. According to the study, error rates varied as a function of the properties of the voice studied, the conditions and techniques used, and the examiners' skills and knowledge.

Voice analysis today. The period since the 1970s has seen considerable evolution in spectrographic analysis and the related methods and tools, which include evidence handling, critical listening, magnetic development, waveform analysis, spectrum analysis, tape enhancement, and speed correction. The core methodology, however, remains the same; from machine readings of stress and other patterns in a subject's voice, a graphic representation is made so as to illustrate patterns of frequency, intensity, pitch, and inflection. Analysts use a two-step process, first the aural or listening stage, then the visual stage, which involves looking over the spectrograms or readouts.

Spectrographic analysis remains controversial. It is permissible as evidence in 35 of 50 states, and has a status—both in the eyes of the law and of professionals—akin to that of polygraphy or lie detection; although not perfectly reliable, it can be a helpful tool for screening suspects. Controversy over spectrographic analysis came to the forefront in November, 2002, when the Arabic news station al Jazeera released a recording of an alleged telephone call from bin Laden.

Analysts working for the U.S. Central Intelligence and National Security agencies studied, and verified the authenticity of, the tape, in which the voice spoke of recent terrorist actions and promised to unleash more attacks. At the Institute for Perceptual Artificial Intelligence in Switzerland, however, researchers were not as certain. Using biometric software, they judged it a 55%–60% likelihood that the tape was not genuine.

■ FURTHER READING:

BOOKS:

Gardner, Robert. *Crime Lab 101: Experimenting with Crime Detection.* New York: Walker, 1992.

Ross, David F., and J. Don Read. *Adult Eyewitness Testimony: Current Trends and Developments.* New York: Press Syndicate of the University of Cambridge, 1994.

Saferstein, Richard. *Criminalistics: An Introduction to Forensic Science.* NJ: Prentice Hall, 1998.

PERIODICALS:

Romanko, J. R. "Truth Extraction." *New York Times Magazine.* (November 19, 2000): 54.

ELECTRONIC:

Sachs, Jessica Snyder. Graphing the Voice of Terror. Popular Science. <http://www.popsci.com/popsci/science/article/0,12543,426271,00.html> (April 13, 2003).

SEE ALSO

Forensic Science
Polygraphs
Voice Alteration, Electronic

France, Counter-Terrorism Policy

Counter-terrorism is the use of military, law enforcement, intelligence, and other resources to identify, circumvent, and neutralize terrorist groups within a country. Like all western European nations, France has been forced by events since the 1960s to develop a response to terrorism. The most attention-getting aspect of French counter-terrorism is GIGN, the Group d'Intervention de la Gendarmerie Nationale (National Police Intervention Group), but this small, elite counter-terrorism action team is only a small component of counter-terrorism activities and policy in France.

Overseeing and coordinating antiterrorist activity in France is the Interministerial Liaison Committee against Terrorism, or Comité Interministériel de Lutte Anti-Terroriste. The committee, which includes the prime minister and the ministers of the Interior, Defense, Justice, and Foreign Affairs, develops and directs counter-terrorism policy. Below the committee in rank is the Anti-Terrorism Coordination Unit (Unité de Coordination de la Lutte Anti-Terroriste), which includes agencies from the Interior and Defense ministries, and which coordinates operations.

Unlike in the United States, where the Department of the Interior manages natural resources, France's Ministry of the Interior (Ministère de L'Intérieur) is a security and law-enforcement department. The ministry, which oversees the Anti-Terrorism Coordination Unit, includes the National

Police, the Central Headquarters for Surveillance of the Territory, and the General Intelligence Central Service. All of these services are responsible for law enforcement and/or monitoring of suspicious activities in French territories.

Enforcement agencies.

The National Police, or Direction Générale de la Police Nationale, is the principal civilian national police force in large urban areas. Within the National Police are specialized groups with functions such as border security and the protection of dignitaries. In addition to the National Police, which falls under the Ministry of the Interior, there is the National Gendarmerie, or Direction Générale de Gendarmerie Nationale, directed by the Ministry of Defense. The National Gendarmerie oversees law enforcement in small towns and rural areas.

Also under the Ministry of Defense is GIGN, which, like its German counterpart, GSG-9, was formed in the aftermath of the terrorist incident at the 1972 Munich Olympics. GIGN, though highly effective in special circumstances, is a small force, consisting of fewer than a hundred full-time personnel at the end of the twentieth century. Its activities are, therefore, rather limited compared to those of larger police forces.

Intelligence agencies.

The Central Headquarters for Surveillance of the Territory (Direction de la Surveillance du Territoire), an arm of the National Police, gathers intelligence regarding potential threats from external organizations. Overseeing potential threats by internal organizations is the General Intelligence Central Service (Direction Centrale des Renseignenments Généreaux).

Outside of France, intelligence gathering is the job of the General Headquarters for Security Overseas (Direction Générale de la Sécurité Exterieure), which is under the Ministry of Defense. The Central Headquarters Military Intelligence (Direction Reseignments Militaire), also under the Ministry of Defense, gathers and interprets military intelligence.

■ FURTHER READING:

BOOKS:

Bourret, Jean Claude. *GIGN, Vingt Ans d'Actions: 1974–1994.* Paris: M. Lafon, 1995.

Linde, Erik J. G. van de. *Quick Scan of Post 9/11 National Counter-terrorism Policymaking and Implementation in Selected European Countries: Research Project for the Netherlands Ministry of Justice.* Santa Monica, CA: RAND Europe, 2002.

PERIODICALS:

Hoffman, Bruce. "Is Europe Soft on Terrorism?" *Foreign Policy* no. 115 (summer 1999): 62–76.

SEE ALSO

European Union
France, Intelligence and Security
Germany, Counter-Terrorism Policy

France, Intelligence and Security

■ ADRIENNE WILMOTH LERNER

Although France has employed espionage agents since the Middle Ages, the modern intelligence community emerged in the nineteenth century. As France expanded its boundaries during the Napoleonic era and Age of Empire, military intelligence was equally crucial to the success of battlefield operations and the security of territorial government outposts. At the outbreak of World War I in 1914, France maintained one of the most skilled and well-organized intelligence forces in the world. Modern domestic intelligence can trace its roots to the revolution, but it was most acutely influenced by the formation and operation of underground Resistance groups during the World War II Nazi Occupation. Vichy France and French officials who collaborated with the Nazis left a legacy of mistrust of and within the government in the years following the war. These tensions were heightened by the onset of the Cold War. When France began the process of recreating its intelligence systems, it placed special emphasis on domestic and political intelligence.

The French intelligence community is divided between military and civilian agencies, all of which report to the executive branch. The civilian intelligence system emphasizes counter-intelligence and domestic security. This requires not only the substantial national intelligence and security structure, but also the assistance and continued cooperation of provincial security and law enforcement agencies. External intelligence is almost exclusively dominated by the military. This separation of powers gives military and civilian intelligence organizations their own *de facto* jurisdictions in the intelligence community.

French military intelligence is administered by the individual military branches (Army, Navy, and Air Force) and the Ministry of Defense. The National Defense General Secretariat (SDGN) coordinates intelligence and security operations within the various intelligence community agencies. Military intelligence, as well as strategic information and counter-espionage operations, is directed by the General Directorate for External Security (DSGE). The agency employs analysts as well as active field operatives, and is the primary foreign intelligence agency. The Directorate of Military intelligence performs many of the same plenary and investigative functions as the DSGE, but does not have an active field operations branch.

Military counterintelligence is charged to two agencies, the Directorate for the Defense Protection and Security (DPSD) and the Intelligence and Electronic Warfare Brigade (BRGE). The DPSD is the primary military counterintelligence agency, planning and coordinating most military security operations. The agency also conducts political surveillance of the armed forces and national military police, the Gendarmerie. The BRGE works closely with the DPSD, and is charged with monitoring sensitive communications and securing military computer information systems.

Civilian intelligence agencies operate under the directorship of the Ministry of the Interior. The General Information Service (RG) is the main domestic intelligence agency in the French government. The director of the RG reports to the minister of the Interior and briefs the president on domestic national security issues. Charged with the protection of internal security and domestic counterintelligence, the RG works in close conjunction with provincial governments and prefectures of the national police to protect national interests within France.

In French territories, the Directorate of Territorial Security (DST) performs the functions of the RG. The DST works closely with military intelligence units to protect French interests throughout the world. In twenty-first century anti-terrorist intelligence operations, the DST and RG have infiltrated and arrested several persons with alleged connections terrorist groups smuggling money and weapons via French territories. The DST also focuses on protecting French scientific, research, and economic interests abroad.

In recent years, French intelligence and security forces have grappled with increasing terrorist threats, mostly from members of North African, Islamist militant groups. After the September 11, 2001, attacks on the United States, France joined an international intelligence coalition to find and dismantle terrorist organizations and their operative cells.

■ FURTHER READING:

BOOKS:

Porch, Douglas. *The French Secret Services: From the Dreyfus Affair to the Gulf War*. New York: Farrar, Straus & Giroux, 1995.

PERIODICALS:

Porch, Douglas. "French Intelligence Culture: A Historical and Political Perspective." *Intelligence and National Security* 10, no. 3 (Jul. 1995): 486–511.

SEE ALSO

European Union

French Underground during World War II, Communication and Codes

■ ADRIENNE WILMOTH LERNER

By 1940, Nazi Germany had invaded several Eastern European nations and turned its attention to gaining control of Western Europe. With strategic planning reminiscent of World War I, the Nazis planned to forcefully invade France, Belgium, and Holland. However, when Marshal Henri-Philippe Petain rose to power in France, he negotiated an armistice with the Germans. On June 22, France was divided into two parts: the northern three-fifths and the Atlantic coast to be directly controlled by Nazi Germany, and the remaining parts of the south to be ruled by a French puppet government. The southern region was known as Vichy. The armistice also disbanded the French army, sending many French soldiers who could escape into exile in England. The settlement angered many French citizens, many of whom wished to continue the war against Germany.

As soon the occupation began, partisan groups arose to sabotage the Nazi government. These groups called themselves by many names (maquis, partisans, resistance, and freedom fighters) and the individual groups remained separate entities until the Allied invasion of France in 1944. These underground bands of French and foreign men and women who fought against the German occupation government became known collectively as the French Resistance.

The German secret police, the Gestapo, and intelligence agency, Abwehr, were powerful opponents to the resistance. In the early war period, German agents easily infiltrated resistance groups. In response, resistance groups developed codes, complex communications networks, and security structures to protect members and information.

Many of the earliest resistance groups were formed by political parties that the Nazi government had earlier banned. Communists and Socialists were persecuted under the Nazi regime. Partisan groups with political ties, such as the Socialist *Comité d'Action Socialiste* and the Communist *Front National* used their extensive media and member network to produce and distribute anti-Nazi propaganda. As resistance groups began to arm themselves and carry out acts of sabotage, the papers published coded messages that communicated instructions to members. During the course of the war, underground newspapers supplied information to over a million readers.

The resistance relied on coded messages to communicate with members and plan operations. Members were called by code names, and operational units had their own cryptonym or symbols. Underground newspaper published coded articles and drawings. Poetry was even used as a means of sending coded messages or identifying oneself as a member of a resistance group to other members.

The most famous, and perhaps ingenious security device of resistance groups was the use of a pyramid command structure. The pyramid structure ensured that no member of a partisan group even interacted or conducted operations with more than two other members of the organization. No records of membership were kept, and messages were sent only by word-of-mouth. Each resistance member knew one commanding member and one other partner member. Members kept strict confidentiality, and rarely met in groups larger than their operational units. This structure insured that enemy infiltrators and captured partisans could positively identify no more than two resistance operatives, leaving the rest of the organization unscathed. The strategy worked with some success, until Gestapo agents began to infiltrate the command echelons of various partisan groups.

The pyramid structure also added an operational advantage as well as security. Ambushes and assassinations of German officers were carried out by a group of three men. One man served as a decoy, the other carried the weapon and shot the victim at close range, while the third member took the weapon after the shooting and walked away from the scene. Often the actual assailants would remain at or near the scene until authorities arrived. As they possessed no weapons, they were cleared of suspicion. Because resistance members in most urban areas did not keep their own weapons as a security measure, weapons used in attacks were returned to their stockpile via courier, often a child, who would seldom arouse the suspicion of Gestapo agents.

French Resistance groups also developed an "underground railroad" system to smuggle downed Allied airmen back to Britain or the front lines. Using standardized coded messages, Allied servicemen were shuttled to various safe houses on route to their destination. Toward the end of the war, these same networks were used by Allied forces to send messages to various resistance groups throughout the countryside. Allied "Jedburg" teams, soldiers trained to aid the resistance, sabotage German supply lines, and unify the command of partisan groups, parachuted into France behind German lines. Individual Jedburg soldiers used the underground network to reach the towns or groups in which they were to operate. The two-way traffic of Allied servicemen in the "underground railroad" system facilitated communication not only with diverse resistance groups, but also with Allied command.

Jedburg groups also coordinated the procurement and allocation of radios to facilitate communication. While radios carried an increased risk of detection by occupation forces, they made mass communication over longer distance possible. Coded messages were transmitted nightly, both to Allied command and to various area partisans. Messages identified their recipients with a cryptonym and gave necessary instructions in coded messages. The codes were agreed upon in person, and then used in broadcasts to activate plans. When intercepted, the messages were easily identifiable as partisan transmissions, but their meanings were indecipherable. British radio, and the European underground radio, often rebroadcast Jedburg and other resistance messages. While this coding method was primitive, it required German forces to use spies instead of technology as primary means of breaking resistance group communications. Such missions were a costly drain on human intelligence resources, and carried a high level of risk.

In 1944, many of the largest French underground groups united to form the *Conseil National de la resistance*. The organization stockpiled weapons and worked with Allied intelligence operatives to prepare for the Allied invasion of France. During the D-Day invasion in June, 1944, the resistance cut German supply lines and aided Allied forces as they marched through France. Urban partisan members in Paris took to the streets in open warfare against the Germans, engaging forces until the liberation of Paris. With the Allied invasion, exiled members of the French Army, under the command of Charles de Gaulle, returned to France. Many resistance members then joined the army, fighting enemy forces throughout Europe.

Over the course of the war, the French Resistance scored key victories against the German occupations forces. Resistance members tracked and ferreted-out French collaborators, assassinated many ranking Nazi officials, tapped the phones of the Abwehr's Paris headquarters, and destroyed trains, convoys, and ships used by the German army. The resistance provided Allied forces with invaluable human intelligence resources and aided Allied troops who fell behind enemy lines. Resistance groups shielded political dissidents, refugees, and Jews escaping the Holocaust.

These numerous accomplishments carried a heavy price. German agents often infiltrated partisan groups, despite security precautions. When they captured a maquis, Gestapo agents employed torture as means of extracting the names of other resistance members. The Gestapo occasionally carried out bloody reprisals on innocent civilians after partisan sabotage operations. As many as 25,000 French men and women, members of the resistance and those suspected of aiding their cause, were sent to German concentration camps. Another 25,000 were executed in France by Gestapo agents, including the population of an entire Northern French village.

■ FURTHER READING:

BOOKS:

Aubrac, Lucie. Konrad Bieber and Betsy Wing (trans.). *Outwitting the Gestapo.* Lincoln: University of Nebraska Press, 1994.

Aubrac, Raymond, and Lucie Aubrac. *The French Resistance: 1940–1944.* Paris: Hazan Editeur, 1997.

Ottis, Sherri Greene. *Silent Heroes: Downed Airmen and the French Underground.* Lexington, KY: University of Kentucky Press, 2001.

Ousby, Ian. *Occupation.* Lanham, MD: Cooper Square Press, 2000.

Weitz, Margaret Collins. *Sisters in the Resistance : How Women Fought to Free France, 1940–1945.* New York: John Wiley & Sons., 1998.

SEE ALSO

France, Intelligence and Security
OSS (United States Office of Strategic Services)

Fusion

Nuclear fusion is the process by which two light atomic nuclei combine to form one heavier atomic nucleus. As an example, a proton (the nucleus of a hydrogen atom) and a neutron will, under the proper circumstances, combine to form a deuteron (the nucleus of an atom of "heavy" hydrogen). In general, the mass of the heavier product nucleus is less than the total mass of the two lighter nuclei. Nuclear fusion is the initial driving process of nucelosynthesis.

The practical problems of building a fusion power plant are formidable, and the technology to construct a suitable containment vessel or field in which controlled fusion reactions could take place does not yet exist. Currently the only fusion reactions that take place on Earth are uncontrolled fusion reaction in nuclear weapons (e.g., H-bombs).

In April, 2003, Sandia scientists reported that they had achieved controlled thermonuclear fusion in a pulsed power source. If ultimately reproduced and verified, the process, and other competing approaches to controlled fusion, holds the promise of nearly unlimited clean power generation. Unlike fission reactions, fusion based energy technology would not produce long-lived radioactive waste.

Instead of using magnetic containment to compress hydrogen and thereby achieve temperatures hot enough for fusion to occur, Sandia scientists used pulsed releases of current to achieve a rapid series of limited micro fusion reactions. Using an improved and more powerful Z accelerator, high current is induced in a tungsten wire cage surrounding a 2 mm plastic capsule containing deuterium (an heavier isotope of hydrogen). The tungsten cage is vaporized, but the short-lived current impulse generated in the wires creates a powerful magnetic pulse and shockwave of superheated tungsten that creates an intense x-ray source that, along with the shockwave compresses and heats the hydrogen to more than 20 million degrees Fahrenheit (more than 11 million degrees Celsius) to induce fusion.

The Sandia reaction process contrasts with another promising approach undertaken at the Lawrence Livermore National Laboratory (LLNL) that seeks to initiate fusion reactions by shining high energy lasers on hydrogen globules. The LLNL approach will be further explored at the National Ignition Facility.

Scientists who worked on the first fission (atomic) bomb during World War II were aware of the potential for building an even more powerful bomb that operated on fusion principles. A fusion bomb uses a fission bomb as a trigger (a source of heat and pressure to create a fusion chain reaction. In the microseconds following a fission explosion fusion begins to occur within the casing surrounding the fission bomb. Protons, deuterons, and tritons begin fusing with each other, releasing more energy, and initiating other fusion reactions among other hydrogen isotopes.

The fusion sequence. When a proton and neutron combine, the mass of the resulting deuteron is 0.00239 atomic mass units (amu) less than the total mass of the proton and neutron combined. This "loss" of mass is expressed in the form of 2.23 MeV (million electron volts) of kinetic energy of the deuteron and other particles and as other forms of energy produced during the reaction. Nuclear fusion reactions are like nuclear fission reactions, therefore, in that some quantity of mass is transformed into energy. This is the reason stars "shine" (i.e., radiate tremendous amounts of electromagnetic energy into space).

The particles most commonly involved in nuclear fusion reactions include the proton, neutron, deuteron, a triton (a proton combined with two neutrons), a helium-3 nucleus (two protons combined with a neutron), and a helium-4 nucleus (two protons combined with two neutrons). Except for the neutron, all of these particles carry at least one positive electrical charge. That means that fusion reactions always require very large amounts of energy in order to overcome the force of repulsion between two like-charged particles. For example, in order to fuse two protons, enough energy must be provided to overcome the force of repulsion between the two positively charged particles.

As early as the 1930s, a number of physicists considered the possibility that nuclear fusion reactions might be the mechanism by which energy is generated in the stars. No familiar type of chemical reaction, such as combustion or oxidation, could possibly explain the vast amounts of energy released by even the smallest star. In 1939, the German-American physicist Hans Bethe worked out the mathematics of energy generation in which a proton first fuses with a carbon atom to form a nitrogen atom. The reaction then continues through a series of five more steps, the net result of which is that four protons are consumed in the generation of one helium atom.

Bethe chose this sequence of reactions because it requires less energy than does the direct fusion of four protons and, thus, is more likely to take place in a star.

Bethe was able to show that the total amount of energy released by this sequence of reactions was comparable to that which is actually observed in stars.

The Bethe carbon-cycle is by no means the only nuclear fusion reaction. A more direct approach, for example, would be one in which two protons fuse to form a deuteron. That deuteron could then fuse with a third proton to form a helium-3 nucleus. Finally, the helium-3 nucleus could fuse with a fourth proton to form a helium-4 nucleus. The net result of this sequence of reactions would be the combining of four protons (hydrogen nuclei) to form a single helium-4 nucleus. The only net difference between this reaction and Bethe's carbon cycle is the amount of energy involved in the overall set of reactions.

Other fusion reactions include D-D and D-T reactions. The former stands for deuterium-deuterium and involves the combination of two deuterium nuclei to form a helium-3 nucleus and a free neutron. The second reaction stands for deuterium-tritium and involves the combination of a deuterium nucleus and a tritium nucleus to produce a helium-4 nucleus and a free neutron.

The term "less energy" used to describe Bethe's choice of nuclear reactions is relative; however, since huge amounts of energy must be provided in order to bring about any kind of fusion reaction. In fact, the reason that fusion reactions can occur in stars is that the temperatures in their interiors are great enough to provide the energy needed to bring about fusion. Because those temperatures generally amount to a few million degrees, fusion reactions are also known as thermonuclear (thermo = heat) reactions. The heat to drive a thermonuclear reaction is created during the conversion of mass to energy during other thermonuclear reaction.

Fusion bombs. From a military standpoint, the fusion bomb had one powerful advantage over the fission bomb. For technical reasons, there is a limit to the size one can make a fission bomb. However, there is no technical limit on the size of a fusion bomb. One simply makes the casing surrounding the fission bomb larger. On August 20, 1953, the Soviet Union announced the detonation of the world's first fusion bomb. It was about 1,000 times more powerful than was the fission bomb that was dropped on Hiroshima less than a decade earlier. Since that date, both the Soviet Union (now Russia) and the United States have stockpiled thousands of fusion bombs and fusion missile warheads. The manufacture, maintenance, and destruction of these weapons remain a source of scientific and geopolitical debate.

Possible peaceful uses for fusion. As research on fusion weapons continued, attempts were also being made to develop peaceful uses for nuclear fusion. The containment vessel problems remain daunting because at the temperatures at which fusion occurs, known materials vaporize instantly. Traditionally, two general approaches hold promise of possibly solving this problem: magnetic and inertial containment.

One way to control hot plasma is with a magnetic field. One can design such a field so that a swirling hot mass of plasma within it can be held in a specified shape. Other proposed methods of control include the use of suspended microballoons that are then bombarded by the laser, electron, or atomic beam to cause implosion. During implosion, enough energy is produced to initiate fusion.

The production of useful nuclear fusion energy depends on three factors: temperature, containment time, and energy release. That is, it is first necessary to raise the temperature of the fuel (the hydrogen isotopes) to a temperature of about 100 million degrees. Then, it is necessary to keep the fuel suspended at that temperature long enough for fusion to begin. Finally, some method must be found for tapping off the energy produced by fusion.

In late twentieth century, scientists began to explore approaches to fusion power that departed from magnetic and inertial confinement concepts. One such approach was called the PBFA process. In this machine, electric charge is allowed to accumulate in capacitors and then discharged in 40-nanosecond micropulses. Lithium ions are accelerated by means of these pulses and forced to collide with deuterium and tritium targets. Fusion among the lithium and hydrogen nuclei takes place, and energy is released. However, the PBFA approach to nuclear fusion has been no more successful than has that of more traditional methods.

In March of 1989, two University of Utah electrochemists, Stanley Pons and Martin Fleischmann, reported that they had obtained evidence for the occurrence of nuclear fusion at room temperatures (i.e., cold fusion). During the electrolysis of heavy water (deuterium oxide), it appeared that the fusion of deuterons was made possible by the presence of palladium electrodes used in the reaction. If such an observation could have been confirmed by other scientists, it would have been truly revolutionary. It would have meant that energy could be obtained from fusion reactions at moderate temperatures. The Pons-Fleischmann discovery was the subject of immediate and intense scrutiny by scientists around the world. It soon became apparent, however, that evidence for cold fusion could not consistently be obtained by other researchers. A number of alternative explanations were developed by scientists for the apparent fusion results that Pons and Fleischmann believed they had obtained and most researchers now assert that Pons and Fleischmann's report of "cold fusion" was an error and that the results reported were due to other chemical reactions that take place during the electrolysis of the heavy water.

In January 2003, the United States rejoined the International Fusion Program, an international effort to construct an experimental fusion reactor. Recent progress in controlling plasmas and developing technologies for burning plasma reactors may eventually provide a workable containment system.

■ FURTHER READING:

BOOKS:

Boyd, T. J. M. and J. J. Anderson *The Physics of Plasma.* Cambridge, UK: Cambridge University Press, 2003.

ELECTRONIC:

United Kingdom Atomic Energy Authority. "Focus on Fusion." <http://www.fusion.org.uk/focus/index.htm> (March 29, 2003).

United States Department of Energy, Office of Fusion Energy Sciences. "Welcome to the U.S. Fusion Energy Sciences Program." <http://wwwofe.er.doe.gov/> (March 30, 2003).

SEE ALSO

Nuclear Detection Devices
Nuclear Weapons
Radioactive Waste Storage

G

G-2

The term *G-2* refers to the intelligence staff of a unit in the United States Army. It is contrasted with G-1 (personnel), G-3 (operations), and G-4 (supply). In the navy, these sections have their counterparts, each with an *N-* designation, while at the level of the Joint Staff, the sections use the prefix *J-*.

The *G-*system, as well as the basic structure of military intelligence and even the concept of an army general staff, are surprisingly modern creations. Although George Washington proved shrewd at gathering and using intelligence in the American Revolution, it was only in 1885 that the army formally instituted its Division of Military Information under the Adjutant General's Office.

European armies had meanwhile adopted the G-designations, which originated in France. In 1903, the U.S. Army implemented the concept of a permanent general staff, and with it the four sections pioneered in Europe. The Division of Military Information thus became G-2.

Interest in military intelligence grew during World War I, which saw the formation of an intelligence division under the War Department General Staff. The army also instituted the use of staffs that included intelligence officers all the way down to the battalion level. This emphasis on military intelligence, however, subsided after the armistice.

The army treated the work of G-2 as a function that any officer could fill, hence there was no need for any permanent military intelligence organization. In 1950, General Dwight D. Eisenhower commented in an address to the War College, "I think that officers of ability in all our services shied away from the intelligence branch in the fear that they would be forming dimples in their knees by holding teacups in Buenos Aires or Timbuctoo."

Although the army had developed a Military Intelligence Division (MID) at the end of World War I, its resources were limited, even during World War II. At the same time, the war finally saw the transfer of signals intelligence from the signal corps to G-2. In a 1946 reorganization of the army, MID was placed over the Army Security Agency (ASA) and the Counter Intelligence Corps (CIC), but in contrast to this emphasis on signals intelligence, there was no command concerned with human and imagery intelligence.

Those demands would be met in the postwar era, which saw an explosion in the growth of G-2 functions. Today, military intelligence is as critical a component of army operations as logistics, and it may seem difficult to imagine a time when commanders did not recognize that fact.

■ FURTHER READING:

BOOKS:

Berkowitz, Bruce D., and Allan E. Goodman. *Strategic Intelligence for American National Security.* Princeton, NJ: Princeton University Press, 1989.

Finnegan, John Patrick, and Romana Danysh. *Military Intelligence.* Washington, D.C.: Center of Military History, United States Army, 1998.

Miller, Nathan. *Spying for America: The Hidden History of U.S. Intelligence.* New York: Paragon House, 1989.

Suvorov, Viktor. *Inside Soviet Military Intelligence.* New York: Macmillan, 1984.

SEE ALSO
Army Security Agency
INSCOM (United States Army Intelligence and Security Command)
Joint Chiefs of Staff, United States

Gamma Radition Detectors.

SEE *Environmental Measurements Laboratory.*

GAO (General Accounting Office, United States)

The United States General Accounting Office, or GAO, is an independent agency charged with investigating expenditures by the federal government, as well as activities associated with those expenditures. The GAO issues some 1,000 reports a year, and since September 2001, its evaluation of security measures undertaken by the federal government have provided a key means for assessing the degree to which various agencies and departments are prepared, or not prepared, for terrorist threats. The GAO, which reports directly to Congress, is known as the "congressional watchdog" for its role in overseeing federal spending of taxpayer dollars.

The early GAO. In the aftermath of World War I, government accounting and financial management was in a state of disarray. The war had brought unprecedented costs on the federal government, which had expanded considerably to accommodate its new role on the world stage, and Congress lacked adequate means of reviewing budgets and spending. To address the problem, in 1921, it passed the Budget and Accounting Act, which created GAO as an auditor independent of the executive branch.

The next major phase of government expansion attended the implementation of President Franklin D. Roosevelt's New Deal during the 1930s, and GAO grew apace. Its workforce, including 1,700 employees in 1921, grew to 5,000 by 1940. With the coming of World War II, the size of government ballooned to proportions not seen even in World War I or the Great Depression, and the growth of GAO to 14,000 employees by 1945 reflected this. At the same time, GAO administrators found themselves unable to keep up with the ever-burgeoning paperwork, and this forced a reconsideration of GAO practices at war's end.

Reassessing its mission. Prior to the end of World War II, the GAO had dutifully tracked every expenditure undertaken by the federal government, but by 1945 it had become clear that this practice was not working. GAO was awash in a sea of paper, and the minutiae of regular accounting had begun to obscure the larger picture of government finances. The agency therefore set about transferring some of its accounting functions, such as the checking of vouchers, to the executive branch of the federal government. Thereafter, its accounting role became more strategic than tactical. Instead of reviewing every expense sheet, the GAO began to oversee the financial control and management of federal agencies. In the late 1940s, it began to work with the Department of the Treasury and the Bureau of the Budget (which later became the Office of Management and Budget), assisting the agencies of the executive branch in improving their own accounting systems and

controls. It thus, delegated the more detailed tasks, and turned its attention to comprehensive auditing.

This reassessment of the GAO mission was reflected in reduction of its payroll to fewer than 7,000. The GAO, in fact, is one of the rare government agencies that actually decreased in size with the passage of time. Today its employees number about 3,300, including experts in program evaluation, law, accounting, economics, and other areas.

The modern GAO. Despite the reduction in its numbers, the GAO in the second half of the twentieth century expanded its operations commensurate with the growth of government that attended the early Cold War, the Great Society and War on Poverty, Vietnam, and later developments. The number of GAO offices around the country and around the world has expanded, as has the range of specialties among its employees. During the 1970s, GAO added scientists, actuaries, and specialists in fields such as health care, information systems, and public policy. In 1986, GAO developed its own team of professional investigators, many of whom have backgrounds in law enforcement.

Security and intelligence-related work has become increasingly important to the GAO mission, particularly in the atmosphere of heightened alert since the September 11, 2001 terrorist attacks upon the United States. The GAO has evaluated plans for the Department of Homeland Security and other measures undertaken in the wake of the terrorist attack, and has identified areas for improvement in many aspects of security at the local, state, or federal levels. In the fall 2002, for instance, the GAO reported that 13 of the hijackers involved in the September 11 incidents had not been interviewed by U.S. consular officials prior to the granting of visas. The GAO also evaluated the measures taken by 24 of the largest federal departments and agencies to protect their computers from fraud, misuse, or cyberterrorism, and found that 14 of these had failed to undertake appropriate measures for the protection of their information systems.

■ FURTHER READING:

BOOKS:

Alexander, Yonah, and Michael S. Swetnam. *Cyber Terrorism* . Ardsley, NY: Transnational, 2001.

Trask, Roger R. *Defender of the Public Interest: The General Accounting Office, 1921–1996*. Washington, D.C.: General Accounting Office, 1996.

PERIODICALS:

Eggen, Dan. "Hijackers Got Visas with Little Scrutiny, GAO Reports." *Washington Post*. (October 22, 2002): A7.

ELECTRONIC:

Lee, Christopher. "Agencies Fail Cyber Test; Report Notes 'Significant Weaknesses' in Computer Security." *Washington Post*. (November 20, 2002): A23.

General Accounting Office. <http://www.gao.gov/> (February 23, 2003).

SEE ALSO

Counter-Intelligence
Critical Infrastructure Assurance Office (CIAO), United States
Cyber Security
Intelligence, United States Congressional Oversight
United States, Counter-Terrorism Policy

Gas Chromatograph-Mass Spectrometer

■ LAURIE DUNCAN

The gas chromatograph-mass spectrometer (GC/MS) is an instrument used to analyze the molecular and ionic composition of chemical compounds. GC/MS technology combines two widely used laboratory techniques: gas chromatography (GC), which separates and identifies compounds in complex mixtures, and mass spectrometry (MS), which determines the molecular weight and ionic components of individual compounds. The combination of these two powerful tools into a single instrument—the chemical separates produced by the gas chromatograph become the input for the mass spectrometer—allows for quick, precise analyses of solid, liquid and gaseous chemical compounds.

Scientists from a wide range of fields currently use GC/MS to identify and analyze inorganic, organic, and bio-organic chemicals. Academic researchers have long used either gas chromatography or mass spectrometry to assess experimental outcomes, analyze biochemical reactions, and age-date geological samples; many of these theoretical and experimental scientists have adopted the newer, more precise, and faster GC/MS technology to replace the two separate instruments. Industrial applications of GC/MS include pharmaceutical drug discovery and testing, process monitoring in the petroleum, chemical, and pharmaceutical industries, and identification of unknown chemicals in applied forensic, military, and environmental sciences.

Gas chromatography is a technique for separating closely-related compounds (solutes) from a liquid or gaseous mixture. (Solids must be vaporized or liquefied before analysis.) GC is most commonly used to separate and detect volatile and semi-volatile organic compounds (VOCs and SVOCs) with molecular weights less than 500 atomic mass units (amu). Although chemists have probably used rudimentary chromatography to separate mixtures since the Middle Ages, the modern chromatograph was not developed until 1941 when British biochemists Archer Martin and Richard Synge invented a chromatographic method that allowed for precise partitioning and detection. Martin and Synge were awarded the 1952 Nobel Prize in chemistry for their efforts.

The GC component of a GC/MS system includes a carrier gas supply, a sample introduction inlet, a capillary column coated with a stationary liquid or solid, and an outlet to the detection system, in this case a mass spectrometer. To begin analysis, a GC/MS technician vaporizes the sample, or analyte, and introduces it into the chromatograph by syringe injection through a rubber septum. A flow of inert carrier gas like helium, argon, or nitrogen moves the analyte into the separation column. Partitioning occurs as the gaseous components of the original analyte assume different velocities when confronted with the column's liquid or solid coating. Partitioning behavior is temperature-dependent, and precise temperature control is an important part of the GC process. A filter removes the separated compounds from the carrier gas at the end of the column before they are fed into the mass spectrometer for individual analysis.

Mass spectrometry is a method of determining the molecular weights of a chemical compound's component ions. (Ions are electrically charged atoms or groups of atoms, and sub-particles of molecules.) The MS instrument, known as the "smallest scale in the world", provides a graph, or mass spectrum, with peaks that indicate the relative amount of each type of ion within a compound. Today's MS systems are based on Sir J. J. Thomson's research at the Cavendish Laboratory at the University of Cambridge. Thomson discovered the electron in 1897, and went on to observe that the parabolic paths of ions traveling through electrical and magnetic fields vary according to the ions' mass-to-charge (m/z) ratios. His experimental instruments were the first mass spectrometers, and he was awarded the 1906 Nobel Prize in physics for his discoveries.

MS instrumentation has become increasingly accurate and complex since Thomson's time, but the principles of the technique and its basic components have remained the same. The MS component of a GC/MS system includes a sample inlet into a vacuum-sealed chamber that houses an ionization source, a mass analyzer, and an ion detector. In a GC/MS system the input sample is always a chemically homogenous gas produced by the GC component that can be introduced directly to the ionizer. Once ionized, the partitioned compound moves into the mass analyzer where the ions travel through an electrical or magnetic field that sorts them according to their m/z ratios. The detector measures the beam of now-separated ions arriving at the end of the analyzer, and converts changes in its intensity to produce the mass spectrum. A sample's mass spectrum is then displayed, catalogued, and compared to a library of known mass spectra by a computer data

A researcher at the Environmental Technology Group at Pennsylvania State University holds a Suma canister, a device used to collect air samples, in front of a cryogenic concentrator and gas chromatograph that is used to analyze the sample. AP/WIDE WORLD PHOTOS.

system. For many applications, environmental monitoring or drug testing at sporting events, for examples, an unknown sample can be identified using a fairly short list of possible spectra. Other applications, like theoretical chemistry, organic chemistry, or planetary exploration may require an enormous library of possible molecules for identification, and may even produce previously unknown molecules.

Improvements in the individual GC and MS components, electronic automation, and computer data analysis and storage have led to machines that can analyze ever more complex, fragile, and tiny chemical components; GC/MS can now be used to quickly analyze proteins, DNA, and even viruses, and has become a common technique in molecular biology and medical science. GC/MS instruments are also becoming smaller and less expensive, and field laboratory and even portable, suitcase-sized systems that can be used to analyze forensic samples, environmental contaminants, and unknown agents of chemical and biological warfare on site now exist. Remotely operated GC/MS systems are planned components of future space exploration expeditions that hope to characterize the chemical makeup of extra-terrestrial environments, and to search for organic material elsewhere in our solar system.

■ FURTHER READING:

ELECTRONIC:

Massachusetts Institute of Technology. "Present Life: Spectroscopic Analysis Gas Chromatography/Mass Spectrometry (GC/MS)." Mars Mission 2004, student final presentation. December 10, 2000. <http://web.mit.edu/12.000/www/finalpresentation/experiments/index.html>(January 5, 2003).

Scripps Center for Mass Spectrometry (BC-007), 10550 North Torrey Pines Rd., La Jolla, CA 92037. (858) 784–9596. Gary Suizdak, director. <http://masspec.scripps.edu/information/intro/index.html.> (January 5, 2003).

Signature Science, LLC8329 North Mopac Blvd Austin, TX 78759. (512) 533–2022. Cassandra Hutson, staff chemist. <http://www.signaturescience.com.> (January 8, 2003).

United States Environmental Protection Agency. "Technology: Gas Chromatography." January 2001. <http://fate.clu-in.org/gc.asp?techtypeid=44> (January 9, 2003).

SEE ALSO

Air Plume and Chemical Analysis
Biological Warfare
Isotopic Analysis
Microbiology: Applications to Espionage, Intelligence and Security

General Services Administration, United States

The General Services Administration (GSA) is one of the three central management agencies of the federal government, along with the Office of Personnel Management and the Office of Management and Budget. It affects almost $66 billion in federal spending, or about a quarter of total procurement dollars at the government's disposal, and manages assets collectively valued at almost $500 billion. Its mission is to support federal employees by securing the buildings, equipment, and property they need.

Early roles. GSA was the result of a study conducted in the 1940s by a commission under the direction of President Herbert Hoover. Charged with developing a means to enhance the effectiveness of administrative services provided by the federal government, the Hoover Commission recommended that the government disband four small agencies and consolidate them into a single large office. The result was GSA, created by the Federal Property and Administrative Services Act, which President Harry S. Truman signed into law on July 1, 1949.

The functions of the early GSA included many retained by the agency today, as well as others that have either fallen by the wayside or been transferred to other parts of the federal government. It oversaw emergency management functions that were transferred to the Federal Emergency Management Agency in 1979; kept national archives that were moved to the National Archives and Records Administration in 1985; and stockpiled strategic materials that would be in short supply during wartime, a function given over to the Department of Defense in 1988.

GSA and government infrastructure. GSA in the early years also had a number of exotic roles, including management of hemp plantations in South America. On the other hand, the first two decades of GSA's life also saw the introduction of operations that would become integral to its mission over the years that followed. In 1954, GSA established the first federal motor pool, and in 1959 created the Federal Procurement Regulation System. In the early 1960s GSA—which in 1957 had been the first federal agency to use the term "telecommunication system"—initiated the federal intercity telecommunications system.

In 1962, a GSA committee recommended to President John F. Kennedy that a number of government buildings in Washington, D.C., needed to be updated or replaced, and thus began a massive federal construction program. Ten years later, in 1972, GSA established the Federal Buildings Fund to pay for the maintenance, operation, renovation, and construction of federal buildings through the rental income paid to GSA by federal tenants.

One of the most visible aspects of GSA as it relates to the public appeared in 1970, with the establishment of the Consumer Information Center, whose many pamphlets and television commercials made its Pueblo, Colorado, distribution center famous around the country. In 1972, the agency created its Automated Data and Telecommunications Service, today known as the Federal Technology Service. GSA in 1984 began issuing its own credit cards, which federal employees use for small work-related purchases, as well as travel expenses. GSA opened its first child care center in 1987, and by the beginning of the twenty-first century managed some 111 centers in which 7,600 children of government employees were cared for while their parents worked—often in the same building.

Beginning with the creation of the Office of Federal Management Policy in 1973, GSA acquired a number of policymaking functions, which in 1995 were consolidated in the Office of Government-wide Policy. GSA in the 1990s was a leading proponent of new technology and practices, encouraging the use of telecommuting and introducing government employees to both the Internet and intranets.

GSA today. Among the most important of GSA's functions is its role in new government construction, which gained an added security dimension in the wake of the 1995 Oklahoma City bombings. As a result, GSA undertook a series of studies directed toward ensuring increased security for buildings. By the time of the 2001 terrorist incidents, GSA had begun to put some of these recommendations into place. For example, the portion of the Pentagon damaged by terrorists on September 11, 2001 had been recently remodeled with new measures in mind, a factor that probably saved a number of lives.

In its Design Excellence Program, GSA has worked with a number of leading architects from the private sector on public buildings ranging from courthouses—it has built or renovated court facilities in some 160 locations since the mid-1990s—to the Ronald Reagan Building and the International Trade Center. GSA also manages security in many of the more than 8,300 government-owned or -leased buildings it manages.

Today GSA controls a fleet of some 170,000 vehicles, and manages information technology products ranging from laptop computers to vast computer systems. The majority of its operating funds come from rental of the products, services, and properties it provides, and only one percent of its budget comes through congressional appropriations.

■ FURTHER READING:

BOOKS:

U.S. Government Printing Office. *Portals and Related Matters: Evidence Warranting Further Action by Federal*

Enforcement Authorities. Washington, D.C.: U.S. Government Printing Office, 1999.

PERIODICALS:

Ballard, Tanya N. "Horror, then a Helping Hand." *Government Executive* 33, no. 13 (October 2001): 12–14.

Grant, Peter. "Plots & Ploys." *Wall Street Journal.* (December 26, 2001): B4.

"RAMPART Assesses Threats." *Signal* 56, no. 1 (September 2001): 7.

Williams, Krissah. "U.S. Seeks to Build Secure Online Network." *Washington Post.* (October 11, 2001): A10.

ELECTRONIC:

General Services Administration. <http://www.gsa.gov/> (February 23, 2003).

SEE ALSO

Architecture and Structural Security
Critical Infrastructure
Facility Security

Genetic Code

Although the genetic code is not a "code" in the sense normally used in intelligence and espionage terminology, a fundamental understanding of the genetic code is essential to understanding the molecular basis of advanced DNA and genetic tests that are increasingly important in forensic science and identification technology.

The genetic information that is passed on from parent to offspring is carried by the DNA of a cell. The genes on the DNA code for specific proteins that determine appearance, different facets of personality, health etc. In order for the genes to produce the proteins, it must first be transcribed from DNA to RNA in a process known as transcription. Thus, transcription is defined as the transfer of genetic information from the DNA to the RNA. Translation is the process in which genetic information, carried by messenger RNA (mRNA), directs the synthesis of proteins from amino acids, whereby the primary structure of the protein is determined by the nucleotide sequence in the mRNA.

The genetic code is the set of correspondences between the nucleotide sequences of nucleic acids such as deoxyribonucleic acid (DNA), and the amino acid sequences of proteins (polypeptides). These correspondences enable the information encoded in the chemical components of DNA to be transferred to the ribonucleic acid messenger (mRNA) and then used to establish the correct sequence of amino acids in the polypeptide. The elements of the encoding system, the nucleotides, differ by only four different bases. These are known as adenine (A), guanine, (G), thymine (T) and cytosine (C), in DNA or uracil (U) in RNA. Thus RNA contains U in the place of C and the nucleotide sequence of DNA acts as a template for the synthesis of a complementary sequence of RNA, a process known as transcription. For historical reasons, the term genetic code in fact refers specifically to the sequence of nucleotides in mRNA, although today it is sometimes used interchangeably with the coded information in DNA.

Proteins found in nature consist of 20 naturally occurring amino acids. One important question is, how can four nucleotides code for 20 amino acids? This question was raised by scientists in the 1950s soon after the discovery that the DNA comprised the hereditary material of living organisms. It was reasoned that if a single nucleotide coded for one amino acid, then only four amino acids could be provided for. Alternatively, if two nucleotides specified one amino acid, then there could be a maximum number of 16 (4^2) possible arrangements. If, however, three nucleotides coded for one amino acid, then there would be 64 (4^3) possible permutations, more than enough to account for all the 20 naturally occurring amino acids. The latter suggestion was proposed by the Russian born physicist, George Gamow (1904–1968) and was later proved to be correct. It is now well known that every amino acid is coded by at least one nucleotide triplet or codon, and that some triplet combinations function as instructions for the termination or initiation of translation. Three combinations in tRNA, UAA, UGA and UAG, are termination codons, while AUG is a translation start codon.

The genetic code was solved between 1961 and 1963. The American scientist Marshall Nirenberg (1927–), working with his colleague Heinrich Matthaei, made the first breakthrough when they discovered how to make synthetic mRNA. They found that if the nucleotides of RNA carrying the four bases A, G, C and U, were mixed in the presence of the enzyme polynucleotide phosphorylase, a single stranded RNA was formed in the reaction, with the nucleotides being incorporated at random. This offered the possibility of creating specific mRNA sequences and then seeing which amino acids they would specify. The first synthetic mRNA polymer obtained contained only uracil (U) and when mixed *in vitro* with the protein synthesizing machinery of *Escherichia coli* it produced a polyphenylalanine—a string of phenylalanine. From this it was concluded that the triplet UUU coded for phenylalanine. Similarly, a pure cytosine (C) RNA polymer produced only the amino acid proline, so the corresponding codon for cytosine had to be CCC. This type of analysis was refined when nucleotides were mixed in different proportions in the synthetic mRNA and a statistical analysis was used to determine the amino acids produced. It was quickly found that a particular amino acid could be specified by more than one codon. Thus, the amino acid serine could be produced from any one of the combinations UCU, UCC, UCA, or UCG. In this way the genetic code is said to be degenerate, meaning that each of the 64 possible triplets

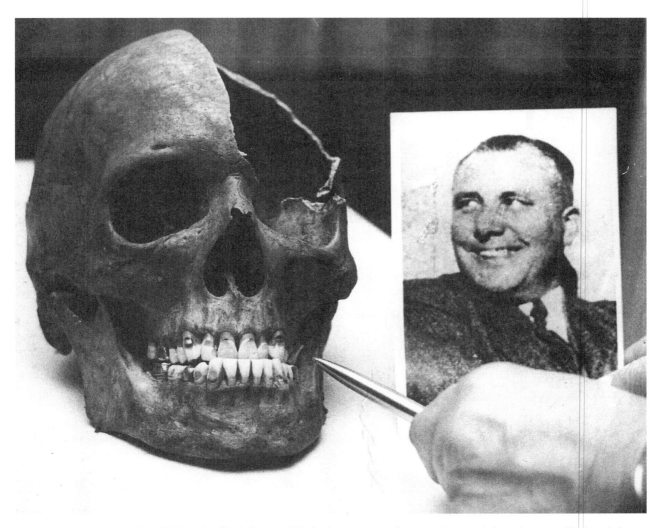

Genetic testing showed that this skull belonged to Martin Bormann, Hitler's private secretary. Bormann, who was missing and sentenced in absentia for war crimes at the Nuremberg trials of 1946, is shown in the photo at right. AP/WIDE WORLD PHOTOS.

have some meaning within the code and that several codons may encode a single amino acid.

This work confirmed the ideas of the British scientists Francis Crick (1916–) and Sydney Brenner (1927–). Brenner and Crick were working with mutations in the bacterial virus bacteriophage T4 and found that the deletion of a single nucleotide could abolish the function of a specific gene. However, a second mutation in which a nucleotide was inserted at a different, but nearby position, restored the function of that gene. These two mutations are said to be suppressors of each other, meaning that they cancel each other's mutant properties. It was concluded from this that the genetic code was read in a sequential manner starting from a fixed point in the gene. The insertion or deletion of a nucleotide shifted the reading frame in which succeeding nucleotides were read as codons, and was thus termed a frameshift mutation. It was also found that whereas two closely spaced deletions, or two closely

spaced insertions, could not suppress each other, three closely spaced deletions or insertions could do so. Consequently, these observations established the triplet nature of the genetic code. The reading frame of a sequence is the way in which the sequence is divided into the triplets and is determined by the precise point at which translation is initiated. For example, the sequence CATCATCAT can be read CAT CAT CAT or C ATC ATC AT or CA TCA TCA T in the three possible reading frames. Sometimes, as in particular bacterial viruses, genes have been found that are contained within other genes. These are translated in different reading frames so the amino acid sequences of the proteins encoded by them are different. Such economy of genetic material is, however, quite rare.

The same genetic code appears to operate in all living things, but exceptions to this universality are known. In human mitochondrial mRNA, AGA and AGG are termination or stop codons. Other differences also exist in the correspondences between certain codon sequences and amino acids.

■ **FURTHER READING:**

BOOKS:

Brenner, Sydney. *My Life in Science.* London: BioMed Central, Ltd., 2001.

Davies, Kevin. *Cracking The Genome: Inside The Race To Unlock Human DNA.* New York: Free Press, 2001.

Watson, James D. *The Double Helix: A Personal Account of the Discovery of the Structure of DNA.* Westport, CT: Touchstone Books, 2001.

———. *DNA: The Secret of Life.* New York: Knopf, 2003.

SEE ALSO

DNA Fingerprinting
Forensic Science
Genetic Information: Ethics, Privacy, and Security Issues
Genetic Technology
Genomics

Genetic Fingerprinting.

SEE *DNA Fingerprinting.*

Genetic Identification.

SEE *Sequencing.*

Genetic Imagery Exploitation (GENIE).

SEE *Los Alamos National Laboratory.*

Genetic Information: Ethics, Privacy, and Security Issues

■ CONSTANCE K. STEIN

Genetic information refers to all of the known genetic data for all organisms, but it can also refer to the genetic make-up of one individual or one family. Initially, genetics was highly statistical and relied on the expression of particular characters in various family members to determine a pattern of inheritance and estimate risks of recurrence. However, the field has become much more complicated

with the accumulation of data on over 10,000 genes that have been associated with human disease or phenotypic variation. It is now possible to identify individuals using genetic markers (DNA fingerprinting) and to predict with relative confidence that certain persons will have particular genetic diseases or features while others will be disease free. The data collected have improved diagnosis and treatment of some diseases, but this has also led to a series of ethical, privacy and security issues including concerns about what types of genetic testing are necessary, who should have access to the information after the testing is complete, and how that information should be used.

One of the great benefits of genetics has been the ability to uniquely identify individuals. In criminal cases, it is now possible to examine a crime scene specimen and directly connect it to a suspect. Molecular genetic technologies have also proven useful in the identification of human remains from plane crashes, the World Trade Center disaster, and a set of bones from the Tomb of the Unknown Soldier. Genetic identification has proven so robust that the United States Armed Forces now routinely maintains genetic profiles on all service personnel to facilitate identification. In addition, some metropolitan police units are offering DNA identity testing for children if the parents wish to have profiles of their children placed in a database in case of a future tragedy.

Whenever such genetic information is collected and stored, the issue of security becomes paramount. Databases must be very secure, and only authorized individuals should access the data, and then only with subject consent and when it's absolutely necessary. Password protection, restricted access, and encryption of data may be employed to assure confidentiality. It is also possible to set up a coding system whereby an individual's name is assigned a code, and the genetic results are only linked to the code number. The code and the key list must then be filed in separate secure locations.

Ethical considerations have also multiplied with the increase in genetics knowledge. Although it is now often possible to tell an individual that he or she will have a genetic disease, that person may not want to know that information. The primary concerns regarding genetic testing are both social and financial. Many people are frightened that a positive finding on a genetic test will result in discrimination and ostracism because they will be considered abnormal. There is also a very real concern that genetic test information may result in loss of or inability to get insurance or a job. Another issue is quality of life. If a test is done on a 20 year old who is then told that he or she will have a debilitating disease starting about the age of 45, how will that affect him or her psychologically? Regarding personal autonomy, should children be tested for late onset diseases or should testing be delayed until an individual is old enough to make his or her own decision about it? Because genetic diseases are typically inherited, identification of a disease causing mutation in one person may mean that other family members are at risk for the disease. Should genetic information be shared within families, and, if so, how should that be accomplished keeping an individual's autonomy in mind? Should prenatal genetic testing be done, and if a mutation for a deleterious disease is found, how should that pregnancy be handled? For serious diseases, should population-screening tests be mandated so that affected individuals are recognized and appropriate treatment can be rendered? Should population screening be done for all identifiable diseases or only those for which treatment is available?

At the present time, there is no one answer to any of these very difficult ethical questions. Each person must approach the problem in his or her own way. Most experts agree that a person's genetic information should be private, and that, following counseling to explain the reason for and consequences of the test in question, individuals should be allowed to chose when and which tests are done and with whom the results are shared. Only tests of proven reliability and significance should be performed, and results should be interpreted and utilized by trained personnel. Tests for late onset diseases are usually restricted to persons old enough to understand the ramifications of the assay and the disease. The number and type of population screening tests currently being done is limited and only involves those diseases for which some type of treatment is available. These principles continue to be tested as new genes are identified, and the use of genetic information becomes increasing important in diagnosis.

The next challenge is to keep all of the information collected confidential. A standard "release of medical information" will include the results of genetic tests as one element of the total package. Insurance companies frequently review a person's medical records before issuing a policy, but individuals with documented genetic disorders are considered high risks, and, so could be refused coverage. Employers may also decline to hire someone with a genetic "defect", fearing the employee may not be able to do the job. Alternatively, a genetic disease that does not affect a person's performance may still be a liability by increasing the health insurance premiums for everyone in the group policy. Recent new legislation has provided some protection against wholesale release of medical information, but this is not foolproof, and it is still possible for genetic data to get into the wrong hands. It has been suggested that some form of socialized medicine in the United States may be needed to give everyone equal protection and reduce the negative impact of a genetic diagnosis.

One final area of concern is research. Although the Human Genome Project has been completed, researchers are now attempting to isolate all of the genes present, determine their function, and identify mutations that lead to disease. Currently, individuals with rare diseases are recruited to participate in studies aimed at finding their disease gene, developing drugs to treat that disease, and testing those drugs for efficacy. In order to protect against the unauthorized use of patient samples or the release of sensitive genetic information, the United States Code of Federal Regulations has established guidelines that are overseen by the Office for Human Research Protection. All participants must sign an informed consent, and specimens must be either anonymized or a coding system must be set up so that subjects and their genetic results cannot be easily connected. As a result, research protocols tend to have a very high level of security for their data.

Education may be the single most helpful tool in alleviating the concerns that surround the storage and use of genetic information. As the public becomes more aware of genetic principles, misunderstandings and misuse are lessening. Genetic counseling and access to the Internet are proving to be extremely valuable methods of providing the needed pieces of information.

■ FURTHER READING:

BOOKS:

Nussbaum, R. L., R. R. McInnes, and H. F. Willard. *Thompson and Thompson Genetics in Medicine,* Sixth Edition. Philadelphia: Saunders, 2001.

PERIODICALS:

Collins, F. S., and V. A. McKusick. "Implemication of the Human Genome Project for Medical Science." *Journal of the American Medical Association* no. 285 (7) (2001): 540–544.

Gerard, S., M. Hayes, and M. A. Rothstein. "On the Edge of Tomorrow: Fitting Genomics Into Public Health Policy." *Journal of Law, Medicine and Ethics* no. 30 (3 Suppl) (2002): 173–176.

Jeffers, B. R. "Human Biological Materials in Research: Ethical Issues and the Role of Stewardship in Minimizing Research Risks." *Advances in Nursing Science* no. 24 (2) (2001): 32–46.

Khoury, M. J., L. L. McCabe, and E. R. B. McCabe. "Genomic Medicine: Population Screening in the Age of Genomic Medicine." *The New England Journal of Medicine* no. 348 (1) (2003): 50–58.

Nowlan, W. "A Rational View of Insurance and Genetic Discrimination." *Science* no. 297 (5579) (2002): 195–196.

Rothenberg, K. H., S. F. Terry. "Before It's Too Late—Addressing Fear of Genetic Information." *Science.* no. 297(5579) (2002): 196–197.

ELECTRONIC:

The Office of Human Research Protection. U.S. Department of Health and Human Services. April 14, 2003 <http://ohrp.osophs.dhhs.gov.> (April 18, 2003).

Online Mendelian Inheritance in Man, OMIM (TM). McKusick-Nathans Institute for Genetic Medicine, Johns Hopkins University (Baltimore, MD) and National Center for Biotechnology Information, National Library of Medicine (Bethesda, MD), 2000. <http://www.ncbi.nlm.nih.gov/omim/> (April 18, 2003).

SEE ALSO

DNA Fingerprinting

DNA Sequences, Unique
Forensic Science
Genomics
Health and Human Services Department, United States
Molecular Biology: Applications to Espionage, Intelligence
  and Security

Genetic Technology

■ BRYAN COBB

Deoxyribonucleic acid (DNA), or an organism's genetic material—inherited from one generation to the next—holds many clues that have unlocked some of the mysteries behind human behavior, disease, evolution, and aging. As technological advances lead to a better understanding of DNA, new DNA-based genetic technologies will emerge. Recent advances in genetic and DNA technology, including cloning, PCR, recombinant DNA technology, DNA fingerprinting, gene therapy, DNA microarray technology, and DNA profiling, have already begun to shape medicine, forensic sciences, environmental sciences, and national security.

In 1956, the structure and composition of DNA was elucidated and confirmed previous studies more than a decade earlier demonstrating DNA is the genetic material that is passed down from one generation to the next. A novel tool called PCR (polymerase chain reaction) was developed not long after DNA was descovered. PCR represents one of the most significant discoveries or inventions in DNA technology and it led to a 1993 Nobel Prize award for American born Kary Mullis (1949–).

PCR is the amplification of a specific sequence of DNA so that it can be analyzed by scientists. Amplification is important, particularly when it is necessary to analyze a small sequence of DNA in quantities that are large enough to perform other molecular analyses such as DNA sequencing. Not long after PCR technology was developed, genetic engineering of DNA through recombinant DNA technology quickly became possible. Recombinant DNA is DNA that has been altered using bacterial derived enzymes called restriction endonucleases that act like scissors to cut DNA. The pattern that is cut can be matched to a pattern cut by the same enzymes from a different DNA sequence. The sticky ends that are created bind to each other and a DNA sequence can therefore be inserted into another DNA sequence.

Restriction endonucleases are also important in genetic fingerprinting. In this case, enzymes that recognize specific DNA sequences can produce fragments of DNA by cutting different parts of a long strand of DNA. If there are differences in the sequence due to inherited variation—meaning that there are extra DNA or specific sequences altered such that the restriction enzymes no longer recognize the site, variable patterns can be produced. If these patterns are used to compare two different people, they will have a different fragment pattern or fingerprint. Genetic fingerprinting can be used to test for paternity. In forensics, genetic fingerprinting can be used to identify a criminal based on whether the person's unique DNA sequence matches to DNA extracted from a crime scene. This technology can also allow researchers to produce genetic maps of chromosomes based on these restriction enzyme fingerprints. Becasue there are many different enzymes, many different fingerprints can be ascertained.

Recombinant DNA technology can also be applied to splicing genes into molecular devices that can transport these genes to various cellular destinations. This technique, also called gene therapy, has been used to deliver corrected genes into individuals who have defective genes that cause disease. Gene splicing has also been applied to the environment as well. Various bacteria have been genetically modified to produce proteins that break down harmful chemical contaminants such as DDT. Currently, scientists are investigating the application of this technology to produce genetically engineered plants and crops that can produce substances that kill insects. Similarly, fruits can be engineered to have genes that produce proteins that slow the ripening process in an effort to extend their shelf life.

DNA microarray technology, also known as the DNA chip, is the latest in nanotechnology that allows researchers to study the genome in a high throughput manner. It can be used for gene expression profiling which gives scientists insights into what genes are being up or down-regulated. Various genetic profiles can be determined in order to estimate cancer risk or to identify markers that may be associated with disease. It has the ability only to detect changes in gene expression that are large enough to be detected above a baseline level. Therefore, it does not detect subtle changes in gene expression that might cause disease or play a role in the development of disease. It can also be used for genotyping, although clinical diagnostic genotyping using microarray technology is still being investigated.

Genes from other species can also be used to add new traits to a particular organism. For example, bacteria, mice, and plants have all had luminescent (light glowing) genes from jelly fish added to their genomes. Another reason for adding genes to a foreign organism is to manufacture various nutritional or pharmaceutical products. Some cows have been modified so that they can produce human insulin or vitamins in their milk in bulk. Pigs have been modified to overcome a number of transplantation problems so that some limited transplantation of organs can be carried out from pigs to humans, also called xenotransplantation.

DNA technology is a relatively new area of research with enormous controversy. It will likely continue to be a large part of public debate and have an impact on every aspect of medical diagnostics, therapeutics, forensics, genetic profiling, and potential weapons development.

■ FURTHER READING:

BOOKS:

Nussbaum, Robert L., Roderick R. McInnes, and Huntington F. Willard. *Genetics in Medicine.* Philadelphia: Saunders, 2001.

Rimoin, David L. *Emery and Rimoin's Principles and Practice of Medical Genetics.* London; New York: Churchill Livingstone, 2002.

SEE ALSO

Biological Weapons, Genetic Identification
DNA Recognition Instruments
DNA Sequences, Unique
Genomics

Genetrix Balloons.

SEE *U-2 Spy Plane.*

GENIE (Genetic Imagery Exploitation).

SEE *Los Alamos National Laboratory.*

Genomics

■ JULI BERWALD

Genomics is the study of genes and their function in relation to the environment. In contrast to genetics, which focuses on genes and inheritance, the goal of genomics is to understand genes, their products and how, when, and why these products are synthesized.

The genome of every organism is the collection of the genetic information contained in the DNA (deoxyribonucleic acid). DNA is a molecule consisting of long strands of four different molecules called nucleotides: adenine, cytosine, guanine and thymine or A, C, G and T, as they appear in published sequences. The strands of DNA are paired so that A on one strand always corresponds to T on the opposite strand and similarly, C always corresponds to G. These paired strands of DNA are further twisted into the conformation of a double helix. A functional unit of DNA is called a gene. In a gene, the sequence of A, C, G, and T on a strand of DNA specifies the sequence of amino acids that make up a protein. In order for a specific protein to be synthesized, the DNA in a gene is first transcribed to messenger RNA (ribonucleic acid), which is similar to DNA, but single stranded. The messenger RNA is then translated into a sequence of amino acids. In this process, three nucleotides of DNA, for example CGT, are transcribed into three nucleotides of messenger RNA, in this case GCA, which code for one amino acid, in this case alanine. Proteins and products of proteins are fundamentally responsible for all cellular behavior. Protein function is altered by changes in the sequence of amino acids. Genomics investigates how variations in genes affect protein structure and function throughout the life of a cell.

The field of genomics. Although it is a young and evolving field, genomics generally includes at least three key research areas: bioinformatics, proteomics and structural genomics. Masses of DNA sequence data have accumulated though projects like the Human Genome Project, the Mouse Genome Project and over 40 microbial genomes have been sequenced. Not all DNA is made up of genes. In humans, for example, only about 3% of the DNA is actually genes. Some of this non-coding DNA is used by enzymes as markers indicating the beginning and ends of genes. Some of it, the so-called junk DNA, may not have any function at all. Using statistical tools and data-mining techniques, the field of bioinformatics attempts to identify genes in the DNA and to determine the relationships among genes in different individuals. Although the DNA in organisms is essentially constant throughout their lives, the kinds and amounts of proteins that are synthesized at any instant are subject to much variation. The field of proteomics investigates which proteins are expressed at what stages in an organism's life and exactly how and why these proteins are expressed. Translating a sequence of DNA to its corresponding amino acid sequence is only the beginning of understanding the function of a protein. Many amino acid chains are modified after they are synthesized and protein structure changes depending on environmental conditions, e.g. heat, pH or association with other molecules. The study of structural genomics attempts to unravel the molecular structures that result from a sequence of DNA.

Applications of genomics. One of the most promising applications of genomics is improving the ability to fight diseases. Many diseases, such as sickle cell anemia, cystic fibrosis and Huntington's disease, are caused by abnormalities in the sequence of DNA that codes for a specific protein or proteins. Genomics will be able to help in both the diagnosis of these diseases and the treatment of these conditions. It is estimated that only about 500 molecules are actually targeted by drugs currently available. Genomics will hopefully lead to an increase in the number of drug targets used in pharmaceuticals. It may also provide information on the genetic basis for side effects and the effectiveness of treatments that can be used to tailor prescriptions for individuals. Two specific types of gene therapies have been advanced. Somatic cell therapy involves the insertion of therapeutic genes into specific cells in the body. This will hopefully allow those cells to synthesize proteins that they are unable to produce or to turn off genes that are overexpressed. Germ line therapy involves the insertion of normal genes into an egg cell, with the hope that the normal gene will be incorporated in to the genome of the offspring and that a genetic disease will not be inherited.

In addition to their importance in medicine, bacteria, viruses and fungi play key roles in agriculture. Because their genomes are small, the genomes of at least 40 species of microorganisms have been sequenced. Understanding the genomics of these organisms has the potential to improve crop yields, decrease damage done by pest species and increase the nutritional value of food. As part of their metabolism, some microorganisms have the ability to break down harmful products and to produce energy as a product. Understanding the gene products involved in these transformations may lead to industrial uses, with the potential for solving different types of environmental problems and providing new energy sources.

Military uses of genomics. Identifying the genes and gene products in the organisms that lead to disease in humans will lead to the development of treatments for these diseases. Characterizing genes responsible for diseases will likely lead to the development of new antibiotics and other drugs used to treat diseases caused by biological warfare. It can also reveal methods for combating drug resistance and preventing the use of this phenomenon by opponents. Genomics should also provide new techniques for identifying biological agents on the battlefield. One of the most promising technologies is the biochip or DNA chip, which is a microarray of molecular probes on a silicon chip that specifically bind to the DNA of biological threats. Once bound, the DNA is then detected using a fluorescent signal. These arrays identify genes that are active in cells, and indicate if a particular immune response is occurring. In the case of a biological attack, this can provide quick, detailed information about the course of the infection to medical personnel.

■ FURHER READING:

ELECTRONIC:

American Medical Association. "Proteomics."<http://www. ama-assn.org/ama/pub/category/3668.html#3> (April 3, 2003).

Human Genome Project. "From the Genome to the Proteome." <http://www.ornl.gov/TechResources/ Human_Genome/project/info.html> (March 14, 2003).

Pharmaceutical Researchers and Manufacturers of America. "Genomics: A Global Resource." <http://genomics. phrma.org/> (April 3, 2003).

U.S. Department of Energy Joint Genome Institute. "An Introduction to Genomics." <http://www.jgi.doe.gov/edu-cation/genomics_1.html> (April 3, 2003).

Weizmann Institute of Science Genome and Informatics. <http://bip.weizmann.ac.il/mb/functional_genomics. html> (April 3, 2003).

SEE ALSO
Pathogen Genomic Sequencing

Geologic and Topographical Influences on Military and Intelligence Operations

■ WILLIAM C. HANEBERG

Geology and topography have placed important constraints on military operations since the beginning of organized warfare. The movement of troops on foot, on horseback, or in motorized vehicles can be hindered by topography and soil conditions. Bedrock type and strength are important factors in the construction of fortifications, the availability of groundwater supplies can control the location of military installations, and mountainous terrain can offer cover to guerilla forces or small groups of operatives. The collection and analysis of geologic information relevant to military operations falls into the discipline of military geology, and military geologic information is often referred to as terrain intelligence.

Two people with knowledge of geology are reported to have participated in Napoleon's invasion of Egypt in 1798. The first military operation guided by terrain analysis, however, was the defeat of Napoleon's troops near the Katzback River in Silesia by the Prussian general von Blucher in 1813. In 1823, the United States Military Academy became one of the first institutions of higher learning to offer instruction in geology. Geologic and topographic considerations continued to play an important role in military operations throughout the nineteenth century, for example at the Battle of Gettysburg in 1863. Union soldiers occupied boulder covered terrain underlain by a hard igneous rock known as diabase, which provided protection from Confederate soldiers advancing unprotected through flat fields underlain by softer shale and sandstone. The first extensive use of geology in military operations was probably during the Russo-Japanese War (1904–1905), when the Russian Army used geologists to provide advice on the construction of fortifications. The use of geologic information became commonplace during World War I and World War II, and included the creation of a military geology branch within the United States Geological Survey. The United States Army Topographic Engineering Center and the National Imagery and Mapping Agency (NIMA) currently provide a variety of products and services directly related to terrain intelligence.

One of the principal concerns of military geologists is trafficability, or the ease with which a landscape can be traversed by troops. An assessment of trafficability requires knowledge of soil types (which are in turn controlled by the underlying bedrock type); the physical, chemical, and biological soil forming processes at work in an area; and meteorological conditions. Arctic areas underlain by permafrost, for example, may be trafficable in winter but impassible in summer when the upper portion melts. Likewise, desert lakebeds known as playas may be trafficable when dry but impassible after a short rainstorm. Trafficability can in some cases be assessed using published topographic maps, geologic reports, and soil surveys. In other cases, reconnaissance forces can use specialized trafficability instrument kits to conduct soil tests and obtain detailed information along potential routes.

Satellite or aircraft-based remote sensing technology can provide the information for terrain analysis and trafficability studies in denied or otherwise inaccessible areas. For example, multispectral satellite imagery can be used to remotely map soil and rock types based on the spectral reflectance of minerals. High-resolution satellite imagery can also be used to visually interpret geologic and topographic conditions. The Shuttle Radar Topography Mission, flown in February 2000, used synthetic aperture radar to produce an elevation data set covering 80% of Earth's land surface. The elevation data can be used to create topographic maps or three dimensional images of inaccessible areas for use in terrain analysis, virtual reality based training, flight simulators, and other military applications.

Manual terrain analysis is time consuming and requires the expertize of a trained specialist. The result is typically a map on which terrain is classified into three categories based upon trafficability: go, slow-go, and no-go. Current research is aimed at the creation of computer expert systems that will be able to combine map layers showing roads, soil types, topography, rivers, vegetation, and land use to produce probabilistic estimates of trafficability for specific vehicle types and weather conditions. These results will include estimates of the reliability of calculated trafficability values.

Geology also plays an important role in the survivability or penetrability of fortifications and facilities, particularly those constructed underground. Information about geology, particularly the strength of different rock types, is used in the design of underground structures that must resist conventional attack. Likewise, information about the geologic setting of an enemy facility can be used to select weapons and methods of attack that are most likely to be successful.

■ FURTHER READING:

BOOKS:

Underwood, James R., Jr. and Peter L. Guth. *Military Geology in War and Peace.* Boulder, CO: Geological Society of America, 1998.

Zen, E-An and A.S. Walker. *Rocks and War: Geology and the Civil War Campaign of Second Manassas.* Shippensburg, PA: White Mane Publishing, 2000.

ELECTRONIC:

Leith, William. "Military Geology in a Changing World." Geotimes. February, 2002. <http://www.agiweb.org/geotimes/feb02/feature_military.html> (11 February 2003).

Surdu, J.R., C. Gates, J. Sullivan, M. Rudak, N. Colvin, and K. Slocum. "Trafficability Analysis Engine." 23rd Army Science Conference. December 2–5, 2002. <http://www.asc2002.com/summaries/e/EP-17.pdf> (11 February 2003).

U.S. Army Corps of Engineers Topographic Engineering Center. "TEC Web Site." 2002. <http://www.tec.army.mil/> (11 February 2003).

SEE ALSO

Geospatial Imagery
GPS
Mapping Technology
Natural Resources and National Security
NIMA (National Imagery and Mapping Agency)
Photography, High-Altitude
RADAR, Synthetic Aperture
Remote Sensing

Geospatial Imagery

■ WILLIAM C. HANEBERG

Geospatial imagery encompasses a wide range of graphical products that convey information about natural phenomena and human activities occurring on Earth's surface. The term can include color and panchromatic (black and white) aerial photographs, multispectral or hyperspectral digital imagery (including portions of the electromagnetic spectrum that lie beyond the range of human vision), and products such as shaded relief maps or three-dimensional images produced from digital elevation models. A related term, geospatial intelligence, describes the use of geospatial imagery for intelligence, security, or defense purposes.

The earliest form of geospatial imagery was aerial photography, which consists of photographs taken from an airborne or spaceborne camera. Aerial photographs can be taken either vertically, which is preferred if the photographs are to be used to prepare maps of an area, or obliquely. Overlapping vertical aerial photographs can be viewed stereoscopically to obtain a three-dimensional effect that can be useful for topographic or geologic analysis, and also used to create topographic maps. Another common form of geospatial imagery is the multispectral or hyperspectral image, which can resemble a color photograph. Instead of being created by the interaction of visible spectrum light with chemicals, however, modern multispectral and hyperspectral images are created by measuring the response of an electronic sensor to a particular portion, or band, or the electromagnetic spectrum. The bands sampled by a sensor can extend far beyond the portion of the spectrum visible to the human eye; hence multispectral and hyperspectral imagery has the potential to convey much more information than a traditional photograph. Whereas multispectral images may consist of several bands, (perhaps representing infrared, red, green, and blue light), hyperspectral images can include information from more than 200 bands. Multispectral and hyperspectral bands that fall outside the range of human vision must be assigned colors if they are to be seen by humans. The resulting images are known as false color images because their chosen colors represent the intensity of the sensor response to invisible wavelengths, not wavelengths corresponding to the colors on the printed image. Synthetic aperture radar (SAR) images consist of information obtained by instrument that actively emits a radio signal rather than passively sensing naturally reflected radiation. SAR technology can be used to generate detailed topographic maps of Earth's surface from space, even in areas covered by clouds.

The resolution of geospatial imagery has increased over time. Keyhole intelligence satellites, which have been launched by the United States since the early 1960s, currently have a resolution on the order of 2 cm (although no images of this resolution have been released to the public). The resolution of geospatial imagery currently available to the public is far less than that of classified intelligence imagery. The Landsat 1 satellite, launched in 1972, had a resolution of 80 m. Landsat 7, launched in 1999, has resolutions of 15 m for panchromatic images, 30 m for six multispectral bands, and 60 m for its thermal band. The French SPOT 5 satellite obtains images ranging in resolution from 5 m for panchromatic to 20 m for infrared. The commercial Quickbird satellite, which was launched in 2001, provides commercially available imagery with 61 cm panchromatic and 2.44 m multispectral resolution. The commercial IKONOS satellite, launched in 1999, can produce 1 m resolution color images.

Within the United States, the National Imagery and Mapping Agency (NIMA) is the single agency that the federal government relies upon to manage the acquisition, interpretation, and dissemination of geospatial information and imagery. Although it is primarily a combat support agency within the Department of Defense, NIMA also provides support to federal policy makers and government agencies. NIMA was formed in 1996 by consolidating the Defense Mapping Agency, the Central Imagery Office, the Defense Dissemination Program Office, the National Photographic Interpretation Center along with some parts of the Defense Intelligence Agency, the National Reconnaissance Office, the Defense Airborne Reconnaissance Office, and the Central Intelligence Agency.

The collection and application of geospatial imagery in support of defense and intelligence operations is heavily dependent upon computer technology. Image processing software can be used to identify features on multispectral images according their spectral signatures. The response of a multispectral sensor to grass or trees, for example, will be different than its response to a concrete road or steel building. Other applications include the use of sharpening filters to enhance images. Geographic information system (GIS) software can be used to combine different types of imagery, for example by superimposing a multispectral image and road network map on a shaded topographic relief map.

■ FURTHER READING:

BOOKS:

Bossler, John D., John R. Jensen, Chris McMaster, and Chris Rizos (editors). *Manual of Geospatial Science and Technology.* Mount Laurel, NJ: Taylor & Francis, 2001.

Campbell, James B. *Introduction to Remote Sensing,* 3rd edition. New York: Guilford Press, 2002.

U.S. Department of Defense. *21st Century Complete Guide to the National Imagery and Mapping Agency (NIMA): Geospatial Intelligence for National Security, Geodesy for the Layman, Combat Support, Terrain Visualization.* Mount Laurel, NJ: Progressive Management, 2003.

ELECTRONIC:

International Society for Photogrammetry and Remote Sensing, c/o Ian Dowman, Department of Geomatic Engineering, University College London, Gower Street, London WC1E 6BT, United Kingdom. <http://www.isprs.org/.>.

National Imagery and Mapping Agency. "NIMA HOME." <http://www.nima.mil> (7 March 2003).

Short, Nicholas M., Sr. "The Remote Sensing Tutorial." NASA. October 22, 2002. <http://rst.gsfc.nasa.gov/> (7 March 2003).

Skorve, Johnny E. "Using Satellite Imagery to Map Military Bases of the Former Soviet Union." Earth Observation Magazine. April 2002. <http://www.eomonline.com/Common/currentissues/Apr02/skorve.htm> (7 March 2003).

U.S. Geological Survey "Ask USGS: Satellite Imagery." August 19, 2002. <http://ask.usgs.gov/satimage.html> (7 March 2003).

SEE ALSO

Bomb Damage, Forensic Assessment
Cameras
Cuban Missile Crisis
Electromagnetic Spectrum
Electro-Optical Intelligence
Geospatial Imagery
LIDAR (Light Detection and Ranging)
Photographic Resolution
Photography, High-Altitude
RADAR, Synthetic Aperture
Remote Sensing
U-2 Spy Plane
Unmanned Aerial Vehicles (UAVs)

Germany, Counter-Terrorism Policy

JUDSON KNIGHT

Since the 1972 Olympics in Munich, counter-terrorism—the use of military, law enforcement, intelligence, and other resources to identify, circumvent, and neutralize terrorist groups within a country—has been among the principal security concerns in Germany. This priority has changed little with the reunification of the country in 1990; rather, the states of eastern Germany have been integrated into the federal system, which provides the framework for response to terrorist threats.

The Lessons of 1972

When the West German city of Munich hosted the Olympic Games in 1972, it was the first time in 36 years that Germany had hosted the Olympic Games. Whereas Hitler had used the 1936 Olympics as a showcase for Nazi power, the West Germans of 1972 were eager to show that theirs was an open, peaceful, and democratic society. For that reason, the Germans took few measures to protect the athletes at the Olympic Village in Munich. Nor did it seem, in 1972, that such measures were necessary; at that time, the world had little exposure to modern terrorism, with its hijacking, hostage-taking, and other acts of crime under cover of political action.

All of that would change on September 5, 1972, when eight Palestinian terrorists entered an apartment building that housed the Israeli delegation to the Olympics. By the time the day was over, after more than 18 hours in which police surrounded the Olympic Village and the terrorists negotiated with authorities, nine Israeli athletes and one German policeman lay dead. In the aftermath of the Olympic terror, security became a priority not only for the Olympic Games, whose athletes' compounds were heavily secured thereafter, but for nations facing the threat of terrorism. German counter-terrorist policy thus emerged from the painful lessons of Munich.

The German Counter-Terrorist Structure

Directing counter-terrorism in Germany is the coordinator for Intelligence, or Koordinierung der Nachrichtendienste des Bundes, who has the ear of the chancellor—the nation's head of government—and who coordinates state efforts under a general national policy. Actual day-to-day implementation of counter-terrorist activities is the work of the Federal Ministry of the Interior, under whose auspices are police, intelligence agencies, and border police. In line with the federal model on which the German political system is built, each state has its own ministry of the interior, which also has police, intelligence, and emergency preparedness responsibilities for local situations.

Many aspects of the German counter-terrorism structure are similar to those of France. However, the French—despite their heavily centralized government—permit a regional political appointee, or *préfet,* to assume control in the event of a local incident. The *préfet* oversees police and emergency activities on the scene. By contrast, in Germany the federal police, when directed to do so by the federal prosecutor or state authorities, take control in terrorist situations. They are usually assisted by state police, which are likely to be the first responders in the event of a local incident.

The Federal Criminal Police (Bundeskriminalamt), an office of the Ministry of the Interior, provides protection for dignitaries, and investigate acts of terrorism. Intelligence is gathered by a number of agencies, including the German Intelligence Service, or Bundesnachrichtendienst. Within the states, the State Criminal Police (Ländeskriminalamt) conduct criminal investigations.

BGS and GSG 9. The Federal Border Guard (BGS or Bundesgrenzschutz), although they act in a federal capacity, are directed by the states' ministries of the interior. It is the responsibility of the BGS to secure borders, transportation sites, and other sensitive federally controlled areas. Within the BGS is an elite counter-terrorist organization, analogous to the U.S. Delta Force, the British SAS, or the French GIGN. This is GSG 9, or Grenzschutzgruppe 9. A direct outgrowth of the Munich massacre, GSG has taken part in over 1,300 operations since its inception. One of the most notable of these—and one of only a handful of times when GSG 9 has been required to use firearms—was the rescue of passengers aboard a Lufthansa flight hijacked by Arab terrorists in October 1977.

The terrorists, who were working with Germany's notorious Red Army Faction (sometimes known as the Baader Meinhof Gang), seized control of the plane on its way from the Balearic Islands to Germany. Denied landing in a number of locations, the plane finally made its way to Mogadishu, Somalia. There, after Somali troops distracted the hijackers by lighting a bonfire in front of the aircraft, two GSG 9 groups, assisted by SAS personnel, stormed the plane. All of the more than 80 passengers survived, and all but one of the terrorists died in the assault.

FURTHER READING:

BOOKS:

Combatting Terrorism: How Five Foreign Countries Are Organized to Combat Terrorism. Washington, D.C.: General Accounting Office, 2000.

Linde, Erik J. G. van de. *Quick Scan of Post 9/11 National Counter-terrorism Policymaking and Implementation in Selected European Countries: Research Project for the*

Netherlands Ministry of Justice. Santa Monica, CA: RAND Europe, 2002.

Tophoven, Rolf. *GSG 9, German Response to Terrorism.* Koblenz, Germany: Bernard & Graefe Verlag, 1984.

PERIODICALS:

Hoffman, Bruce. "Is Europe Soft on Terrorism?" *Foreign Policy* no. 115 (summer 1999): 62–76.

ELECTRONIC:

Calahan, Alexander B. "Countering Terrorism: The Israeli Response to the 1972 Munich Olympic Massacre and the Development of Independent Cover Action Teams." Federation of American Scientists. <http://www.fas.org/irp/eprint/calahan.htm> (February 22, 2003).

SEE ALSO

European Union
France, Counter-Terrorism Policy
Germany, Intelligence and Security

Germany, Intelligence and Security

Germany is an active, key participant in the North Atlantic Treaty Organization (NATO) and the European Union (EU), working closely with neighboring European nations and the United States on international economic, intelligence, and security issues. However, Germany weathered a turbulent and sometimes violent past century. Germany is currently one the world's leading democratic governments, but for the nation's intelligence and security agencies, overcoming the legacy of their role in two world wars, the Nazi government, the Holocaust, and Soviet-dominated East Germany, has proved a formidable challenge.

During the late nineteenth century and through World War I, the German Abwehr was one of the world's leading, most sophisticated, and successful intelligence agencies. The Abwehr maintained one of the largest spy networks and made tremendous advances in the technology of espionage, cryptology, and signals intelligence. During World War II, the Abwehr was again successful in many operations, especially in the recruitment of double agents who infiltrated Allied military instillations. Some of the Abwehr's leading officers opposed Nazi rule, and organized a failed attempt to assassinate Nazi leader Adolf Hitler. The organization was dissolved before the fall of the Third Reich.

While the Abwehr was operated much like any other modern intelligence agency, some German intelligence agencies of the era were more sinister. In 1941, Hitler issued a directive known as the "Night and Fog Decree." This decree elevated Nazi intelligence and security agencies such as the Gestapo above the law, granting them sweeping powers of arrest, detainment, torture, and imprisonment of persons suspected of anti-government offenses. The decree was expanded to cover the arrest, detainment, and deportation to concentration camps of Jews, gypsies, prisoners of war, and political dissidents.

After the war, Germany was partitioned into two separate nations. Soviet influenced East Germany employed a powerful secret police and intelligence force, known as the STASI. The East German government charged the STASI with spying on citizens to ferret-out political dissidents. The force gained an oppressive and brutal reputation much like that of its Nazi predecessors. In 1989, the fall of Communist East Germany and the Berlin Wall began Germany's reunification process. After endeavoring for decades to heal the wounds of Nazism, the German government had to address the oppressive legacy of former East German government agencies. After the formal reunification of Germany, government leaders set forth a highly publicized campaign to restructure and reform the re-emergent nation's intelligence and security agencies. Today's German intelligence community has actively sought to distance itself from its predecessors.

Germany's primary intelligence agency is the *Bundesnachrichtendienst* (BND), the Federal Intelligence Service. The BND handles both internal and external intelligence and is part of the Federal Chancellor's Office, the German government's executive office. The BND manages a substantial network of human intelligence worldwide and conducts extensive radio and signals surveillance in Germany and throughout Europe. Working in cooperation with other security agencies, especially the Federal Criminal Police, the BND collects information relevant to the location and prosecution of terrorist groups, illegal narcotics traffickers, money launderers, and arms dealers. In accordance with international law, the BND conducts intelligence operations aimed at preventing the proliferation of nuclear technology and materials.

Aside from the BND, the German intelligence community makes the traditional distinction between internal and external intelligence and divides their military and civilian intelligence agencies accordingly. Military intelligence is coordinated by individual branches of the armed forces and the Defense Ministry. The primary military intelligence agency is the *Amt füpr Nachrichtenwesen der Bundeswehr* (ANBw), or the Office of Federal Armed Forces Intelligence. ANBw coordinates the operations of various branches of military intelligence and facilitates the sharing of vital intelligence information with civilian agencies in the German intelligence community. ANBw primarily assesses the military strength, operations, and political position of foreign militaries.

The *Militaerischer Abschirmdienst* (MAD), Military Security Service, is responsible for counterintelligence operations. One of the federal intelligence offices, MAD collects intelligence on foreign intelligence operations, and assesses security systems intended to guard classified materials and maintain military secrecy when needed. MAD advises the armed forces and German government on security issues. The counterintelligence agency relies on the cooperative efforts of the *Amt für Fernmeldewesen Bundeswehr* (AFMBw), the Office for Radio Monitoring of the Federal Armed Forces, when conducting surveillance operations.

The Interior Ministry administers Germany's civilian intelligence agencies. Charged with collecting and analyzing internal intelligence and security information, the nation's main civilian agencies are the *Bundesamt für Sicherheit in der Informationstechnik* (BSI), Federal Office for Information Technology Security, and the *Bundesamt für Verfassungsschutz* (BfV), Federal Office for the Protection of the Constitution. The BSI is responsible for the security of all government information technology. The office assesses potential security threats, and develops protective measures to guard sensitive and classified materials. While mainly concerned with government information systems, the BSI has also conducted operations to assess the security of the nation's banking computer systems. The office publishes a yearly manual on information technology security, and distributes it to German corporations. The BSI also conducts of surveillance of Internet and information systems crimes, such as fraud.

The Federal Office for the Protection of the Constitution (BfV) assesses risks posed by various extremist groups. The agency conducts surveillance operations and infiltrates extremist groups to gather information about their organization, financial resources, weapons, and plans for action. The BfV is not a censorship organization, and does not conduct espionage against law-abiding citizens. The BfV's mission is to monitor extremists and paramilitary groups that pose a potential threat to national interests. Extensive intelligence resources are devoted to monitoring and destroying Neo-Nazi groups that are banned under German law.

In its most important capacity, the BfV interprets and processes all information regarding espionage cases. When necessary, the agency shares this information with Federal Police, justice officials, and defense lawyers.

Germany participates in many international intelligence operations, including global anti-terrorism measures. In recent years, the German intelligence community has become one of the main sources of information on extremist political organizations and subversive groups throughout Europe.

BOOKS:

Browder, George C. *Hitler's Enforcers: The Gestapo and SS Security Service in the Nazi Revolution.* Oxford: Oxford University Press, 1996.

Childs, David and Richard Popplewell. *The Stasi: The East German Intelligence and Security Service.* New York: New York University Press, 1996.

Schiel, Katy. *Inside Germany's BND: The Federal Intelligence Service (Inside the World's Most Famous Intelligence Agencies).* New York: Rosen Publishing Group, 2003.

SEE ALSO

European Union
Germany, Counter-Terrorism Policy

Gestapo

▌ ADRIENNE WILMOTH LERNER

The *Geheime Staatspolizei*, or Gestapo, a German secret police force, was created in 1933 after Adolf Hitler became chancellor of Germany. The Gestapo was created to help solidify Nazi control by identifying and arresting anti-Nazi agents in Germany. The agency was restructured several times during its twelve year history and was instrumental in perpetrating the Nazi deportation and destruction of European Jews during the Holocaust.

Hitler named Herman Göring the director of the Gestapo soon after its founding. Göring encouraged his officers to root out and arrest leftist sympathizers, especially communists, whom he considered a threat to the Nazi government. He also oversaw the Gestapo's enforcement of the anti-Semitic Nuremberg Laws. In 1936, Heinrich Himmler, head of Hilter's special forces unit, the *Schutzstaffel* (SS), was given command of the Gestapo and the *Kriminalpolizei*, or Kripo.

In 1939, in the months prior to the beginning of the second world war, Hitler reorganized the German armies. The Gestapo was integrated, with the rest of the Nazi police and intelligence organizations, into the *Reichssicherheitshauptamt* (RHSA) under the direction of Reinhard Heydrich. Though officially part of the Reich Security Central Office, the organization remained popularly known as the Gestapo.

At the outbreak of the Second World War in 1939, there were approximately 40,000 Gestapo agents in Germany. As the war progressed and the Nazis gained territory throughout Europe, the Gestapo swelled to employ over 150,000 informants, agents, and accessory personnel. Gestapo agents were charged with rooting out foreign agents and resistance fighters, but they also expanded their role as an internal police force. Gestapo agents and informants concentrated on finding suspected political dissidents of the Third Reich. Spying on citizens became pervasive, and the Gestapo encouraged people to turn in "suspect persons" to local authorities. While victims of the Gestapo were subject to both civil and criminal prosecution, the secret police themselves operated above the law. On February 10, 1936, the Nazi government officially decreed that the organization was not subject to judicial review. There were no legal restraints on detention of suspects, evidence collection, or police violence. This lack of legal restraint, paired with the Gestapo's tendency to attract and employ Nazi extremists and former criminals

leader Adolf Hitler, liquidated the Abwehr intelligence service. Canaris and his followers were executed. The discovery of the July Plot to assassinate Hitler, and Canaris' spy ring was a key counter-intelligence victory for the Gestapo, SD, and RHSA.

The Gestapo, as well as its parent organization, the SS, aided the *Einsatzgruppen*, or mobile killing units, responsible for the massacre of nearly one million Jews during the Holocaust. Gestapo and SS members also tracked down refugees in hiding and policed ghettos and concentration camps. After the war at the Nuremberg trials of Nazi war criminals, the Gestapo was named as one of the chief institutional perpetrators of the Holocaust.

The Gestapo was dissolved with the fall of the Third Reich in 1945.

■ FURTHER READING:

BOOKS:

Browder, George C. *Hitler's Enforcers: The Gestapo and SS Security Service in the Nazi Revolution.* Oxford: Oxford University Press, 1996.

Gellately, Robert. *The Gestapo and German Society.* Oxford: Oxford University Press, 1991.

SEE ALSO

French Underground during World War II, Communication and Codes
Germany, Intelligence and Security
World War II

Heinrich Himmler, chief of the Gestapo, the German secret police, poses in his military uniform in 1938. AP/WIDE WORLD PHOTOS.

in its ranks, permitted the brutality for which the force became infamous.

The Gestapo also aided intelligence work during the war, but the department was secondary to the *Sicherheitsdienst* (SD), or Security Service. The department employed counter-intelligence agents, ciphers, and oversaw a vast network of informants in Allied countries. In the occupied territories, the Gestapo infiltrated partisan resistance groups. The organization also aided the massive Nazi propaganda campaign both before and during the war.

Intelligence, security, and police forces often overlapped in jurisdiction during the Nazi regime. Several departments performed the same functions, and were often in conflict with each other. The Abwehr, the intelligence service under the direction of spymaster Wilhelm Canaris, negotiated an agreement with the SD about their respective roles. Despite the agreement, both organizations maintained their own network of spies and informants, and did not often coordinate their international operations. In 1943, Canaris and several other key members of the Abwehr joined the Resistance movement against the Nazi government. Canaris used the Abwehr intelligence network to leak secrets and troop positions to the Allies. The Gestapo investigated Canaris and the Abwehr, and in 1944, after a failed attempt to assassinate Nazi

GIS

■ K. LEE LERNER

GIS is the common abbreviation for Geographic Information Systems, a powerful and widely used computer database and software program that allows scientists to link geographically referenced information related to any number of variables to a map of a geographical area. GIS allows its users to analyze and display data using digitized maps. In addition, GIS can generate maps and tables useful to a wide-range of applications involving planning and decision-making. GIS programs allow the rapid storage, manipulation, and correlation of geographically referenced data (i.e., data tied to a particular point or latitude and longitude intersection on a map).

In addition to scientific studies, by 2003, GIS programs were in wide use in a number of emergency support agencies and systems (e.g., the Federal Emergency Management Agency (FEMA)).

Members of the investigating team inspect part of the left wing from the Space Shuttle *Columbia* wreckage in the hangar where it is reconstructed at the Kennedy Space Center in Cape Canaveral, Florida. NASA engineers used GIS mapping technology to map debris field patterns that helped narrow the areas to be searched. AP/WIDE WORLD PHOTOS.

GIS programs allow scientists to layer information so that different combinations of data plots can be assigned to the same defined area. GIS also allows users to manipulate data plots to predict changes or to interpret the evolution of historical data.

GIS maps are able to convey the same information as conventional maps, including the locations of rivers, roads, topographical features, and geopolitical information (e.g., location of cites, political boundaries, etc.). In addition, to conventional map features, GIS offers geologists, geographers, and other scholars the opportunity to selectively overlay data tied to geographic position. By overlaying different sets of data, scientists can look for points or patterns of correspondence. For example, rainfall data can be layered over another data layer describing terrain features. Over these layers, another layer data representing soil contamination data might be used to identify sources of pollution. In many cases, the identification of data correspondence spurs additional study for potential causal relationships.

GIS software data plots (e.g., sets of data describing roads, elevations, stream beds, etc.) are arranged in layers that can be selectively turned on or turned off.

NASA engineers and teams of other scientists—including researchers and undergraduates from Stephen F. Austin University in Nacogdoches, Texas—employed GIS mapping to map remains found after the break up of the space shuttle Columbia in January 2003. Debris field maps helped narrow search patterns and—by linking the location of debris—allowed engineers and investigators to reconstruct critical elements of the disaster sequence. GPS data were used to construct the debris maps and to provide accurate representations of the retrogressive pattern of debris impacts.

GIS technology can also aid epidemiologists in tracking diseases and would be instrumental in the early identification of patterns of disease that could reveal a bioterrorist attack.

■ FURTHER READING:

BOOKS:

Rigaux, P. et al. *Spatial Databases: With Application to GIS.* Morgan Kaufmann, 2001.

Steede-Terry, K. *Integrating GIS and the Global Positioning System.* ESRI Press, 2000.

SEE ALSO

Forensic Geology in Military or Intelligence Operations
Geologic and Topographical Influences on Military and
  Intelligence Operations
Geospatial Imagery

Global Communications, United States Office

President George W. Bush created the Office of Global Communication (OGC) through executive order in January, 2003. The OGC, a White House office, is headed by the deputy assistant to the president for Global Communications. The OGC's mission is to shape and disseminate news and information about the United States in areas of the world with high anti-American sentiments.

In the aftermath of the September 11, 2001 terrorist attacks on the World Trade Center and the Pentagon, American observers noted that anti-American sentiment was widespread in the Middle East, Southeast Asia, North Africa, and other parts of the world. The Bush administration established the OGC to decrease the fervor and prevalence of these sentiments by thoroughly and clearly explaining the foreign policy and values of the United States. The OGC not only endeavors to explain the positions of the United States, it will also seek to actively encourage open dialogue between the United States and its detractors. The Bush White House established the OGC to provide a united voice for spreading America's message.

The OGC replaced and expanded the operations of the Coalition Information Center (CIC), which distributed information to the press in Afghanistan during Operation Enduring Freedom. Unlike the CIC, the OGC focuses on more than military operations. In many respects, the OGC is an office to market all facets of American policies and life to the world. The OGC's does not focus solely on countries that have a negative image of the United States. The Bush administration also uses the OGC to coordinate the formulation and dissemination of positive information on U.S foreign policy to American allies in Europe.

The OGC accomplishes its objectives through several means, including sending out daily talking points to reporters around the world. The OGC also arranges interviews for American representatives on foreign language television networks. In 2003, before and during the war in Iraq, the OGC placed American officials including Secretary of Defense Donald Rumsfeld on Al-Jazeera and other Arabic language networks to advocate America's stance against Iraq.

Critics argue that the OGC's spin is not well received in parts of the world already hostile to the United States. The Bush administration, however, argues that the OGC

will continue to play an important role in the administration's efforts to reduce anti-American sentiment, even though such a project may take years to produce substantial results.

■ FURTHER READING:

ELECTRONIC:

United States Office of Global Communications. <http://www.whitehouse.gov/ogs> (May 9, 2003).

Glomar Explorer

■ ADRIENNE WILMOTH LERNER

The Hughes *Glomar Explorer* was a salvage ship built for a clandestine Central Intelligence Agency mission to retrieve a sunken Soviet submarine. The United States government approached billionaire Howard Hughes in the late 1960s with a proposal to build the vessel under the guise of a business venture to mine manganese nodules off the ocean floor. The building of *Glomar Explorer*, or Hughes Mining Barge 1, and the submarine recovery effort were code named Project Jennifer.

On April 11, 1968, Naval Intelligence at Pearl Harbor intercepted distress messages from a Soviet submarine. The submarine, located in waters approximately 750 miles northwest of Hawaii, reported an onboard explosion while near the surface and then quickly sank. Hoping to find the wreckage of the submarine and recover the ballistic missiles on board, the Soviet fleet launched a search party. After two months of searching, the Soviets failed to locate their downed ship.

The Golf-class diesel submarine was one of the older vessels in the Soviet fleet, but nonetheless, the prospect of retrieving Soviet technology, nuclear weapons, and codebooks was enticing to American intelligence agencies. Because it could not send marked American Naval vessels to recover the sunken submarine without arousing suspicion from the Soviets, Naval intelligence enlisted the help of billionaire Howard Hughes to construct the specialized equipment and ship necessary for the salvage project. The six-year venture to build the ship and raise the Soviet submarine operated under the guise of a deep-sea mining operation.

Recovery efforts began on June 20, 1974. The 63,000-ton *Glomar Explorer* located the wreckage on the seabed at a depth of 17,000 feet (5,200 m) and scouted the downed vessel. *Glomar Explorer* had been fitted with a giant claw mechanism, nicknamed Clementine. A series of tethers stabilized the claw during underwater maneuvers. As the salvage effort began, the *Glomar Explorer* crew lowered Clementine to the wreck site. When the claw was nearly into position, an operator error at the controls sent the

The Hughes *Glomar Explorer*, a 618-foot-long ship used in the partial recovery of a sunken Soviet submarine in the Pacific Ocean, northwest of Hawaii. AP/WIDE WORLD PHOTOS.

claw careening into the sea floor. The salvage effort continued, however, and the claw was positioned around the ship. When the wreckage of the Soviet submarine was about a mile (1.6 k) from the water's surface, three of the mechanical claw's tine malfunctioned, apparently damaged in the crash into the ocean floor. Unable to sustain its own weight, the wrecked Soviet submarine tore apart. The crew aboard *Glomar Explorer* tensely waited for the broken part of the wreckage to hit the sea floor, fearing detonation of weapons on board the submarine.

While the crew of *Glomar Explorer* remained safe, the salvage effort suffered a substantial loss. Only the forward section of the ship was ultimately recovered. The CIA recovered Soviet communications apparatus, a few ballistic missiles, and various codebooks. A majority of the desired items and information, including most of the nuclear weapons and the Soviet crypto keys, remained on the sea floor in the wreckage.

The remains of six Soviet sailors were found in the recovered section of the submarine. The crew of the *Glomar Explorer* gave the sailors a ceremonial burial at sea, conducted in Russian.

In 1975, reporters from the *Los Angeles Times* broke the story of the *Glomar Explorer*. In the following months, various articles linked the *Glomar Explorer*, and its cover as deep-sea mining operation, to the CIA and the submarine salvage effort. After reporters appealed to the government for information on Project Jennifer, CIA officials refused to acknowledge the existence of any records pertaining to the operation. Since then, the terms "Glomar response" and "Glomarization" have been applied to situations when the existence of government documents is neither confirmed nor denied. Most of the records concerning Project Jennifer were declassified in 1995.

Although the submarine salvage effort did not meet expectations, and the *Glomar Explorer* was retired to dry dock for over fifteen years, the ship was completely overhauled in 1996 and converted for use in commercial exploration and deep-sea drilling.

■ FURTHER READING:

BOOKS:

Burleson, Clyde W. *The Jennifer Project.* College Station: Texas A&M University Press, 1997.

Varner, Roy D. *Matter of Risk: The Incredible Inside Story of the CIA's Hughes Glomar Explorer Mission to Raise a Russian Submarine.* New York: Random House, 1979.

Government Ethics (USOGE), United States Office

The United States Office of Government Ethics (OGE) is charged with setting standards intended to regulate and ensure ethical conduct of personnel within the executive branch. The office's mission is to prevent personnel from using their position in the federal government for personal gain (monetary or otherwise), and to prevent fraud and abuses of power. Acting as an impartial review committee, the OGE also assesses cases of conflict of interest and ensures the veracity of financial and personal information provided by executive branch officials. The overall purpose of the OGE is to maintain a high standard of ethics in the practice of government and to build and maintain public trust.

The OGE is an independent agency within the executive branch. The director of the office, who is appointed by the president, oversees four divisions, each of which is responsible for different duties. The office of the director is charged with the verification and analysis of personal financial records of high-level members of the executive branch for conflicts of interest and violations of campaign finance, donation, and personal gain regulations. The director of the OGE also certifies similar disclosures for presidential appointments before sending the records to Senate for discussion of confirmation.

The Office of General Counsel and Legal Policy maintains the policy and legal structure of ethical practice and review in the executive branch. The committee advises necessary offices of changes laws and regulations, and recommends new policy to strengthen existing programs. General Counsel is also responsible for media relations for the OGE.

The Office of Government Relations and Special Projects (OGRSP) is responsible for advising Congress, the Office of Management and Budget, and the president on ethical implications of monetary, economic, and corporate policy. In recent years, the committee has addressed, in the wake of the Enron scandal, domestic corporate fraud and international anti-corruption measures.

The Office of Agency Programs (OAP) manages personnel education programs on ethics issues. The office coordinates ethics regulations and enforcement of ethical conduct with ethical review boards in the individual agencies of the executive branch.

■ FURTHER READING:

ELECTRONIC:

United States Department of Government Ethics. <http://www.usoge.gov>(December 1, 2002).

GPS

Global Positioning System (GPS) is a navigation system consisting of a constellation of 24 navigational satellites orbiting Earth, launched and maintained by the U.S. military. GPS satellites orbit at approximately 11,000 mi (17,700 km) above Earth, with orbit periods of approximately 10 hours. The final satellite was placed in orbit in 1993. Because each satellite houses cesium and rubidium atomic clocks that are periodically updated and synchronized with a ground station in Colorado, GPS receivers can decode signals from the satellites to calculate location and exact time.

To overcome shortcomings in earlier navigation systems, United States developed another system: Navstar (Navigation Satellite for Time and Ranging) Global Positioning System. This system consists of 24 operational satellites equally divided into six different orbital planes (each containing four satellites) spaced at 60° intervals. The new system can measure to within 33 ft, (10 m), whereas earlier systems (e.g. Transit) were accurate only to 0.1 mi (0.16 km). Military users have access to systems with still greater accuracy.

Ground users commonly rely on GPS receivers. The receivers are small, hand-held devices that receive and decode GOS satellite signals. Small differences in the time lapse between signal receptions from three orbiting satellite signals (allowing triangulation of signals) are mathematically converted to latitude, longitude, and altitude. Sophisticated hand-held units are capable of determining latitude and longitude to a thousandth of an arc minute; these units show changes in reading as vehicles move very short distances).

With GPS, two types of systems are available with different frequencies and levels of accuracy. The Standard Positioning System (SPS) is used primarily by civilians and commercial agencies. As of midnight, May 1, 2000, the SPS system became 30 times more accurate when President William Jefferson Clinton ordered that the Selective Availability (SA) component of SPS be discontinued. SA was the deliberate decrease of accurate positioning information available for commercial or civilian use. The SPS obtains information from a frequency labeled GPS L1. The United States military has access to GPS L1 and a second frequency, L2. The use of L1 and L2 permits the transfer of data with a higher level of security. In addition to heightened security, the United States military also has access to much more accurate positioning by using the Precise Positioning System (PPS). Use of the PPS is usually limited to the U.S. military and other domestic government agencies.

Long before the space age, people used the heavens for navigation. Besides relying on the sun, moon, and stars, the early travelers invented the magnetic compass, the sextant, and the seagoing chronometer. Eventually,

A United States Customs official, right, receives instruction on LoJack, a technology that utilizes GPS, intended to help recover stolen cars before they are smuggled out of the United States. AP/WIDE WORLD PHOTOS.

radio navigation in which a position could be determined by receiving radio signals broadcast from multiple transmitters came into existence. Improved high frequency signals gave greater accuracy of position, but were sometimes blocked by high terrain and could not bend over the horizon. This limitation was overcome by moving the transmitters into space on Earth-orbiting satellites, where high frequency signals could accurately cover wide areas.

The principle of early satellite navigation was relatively simple. When a transmitter moves toward an observer, the Doppler shifted radio waves have a higher frequency, just like a train's horn sounds higher as it approaches a listener. A transmitter's signal will have a lower frequency when it moves away from an observer. If measurements of the amount of shift in frequency of a satellite radiating a fixed frequency signal with an accurately known orbit are carefully made, the observer can determine a correct position on Earth.

The United States Navy developed such a system, named Transit, in the late 1960s and early 1970s. Transit helped submarines update their on-board inertial navigation systems. After nearly ten years of perfecting the system, the Navy released it for civilian use. However, a major drawback to Transit was that it was not accurate enough; a user had to wait until the satellite passed overhead, position fixes required some time to be determined, and an accurate fix was difficult to obtain on a moving platform.

Both Transit and Navstar use instantaneous satellite position data to help users traveling from one place to another. But another satellite system uses positioning data to report where users have been. This system, called Argos, is a little more complicated: an object on the ground sends a signal to a satellite, which then retransmits the signal to the ground. Argos can locate the object to within 0.5 mi (0.8 km). It is used primarily for environmental studies. Ships and buoys can collect and send data on weather, currents, winds, and waves. Land-based stations can send weather information, as well as information about hydrologic, volcanic, and seismic activity. Argos

A Brazilian federal police officer uses GPS technology in anti-drug operations near Brazil's border with Colombia in 2000. AP/WIDE WORLD PHOTOS.

can be used with balloons to study weather and the physical and chemical properties of the atmosphere. In addition, the system is being perfected to track animals, including marine life.

In addition to GPS use in weapons systems and for navigation, use of the GPS system in everyday life is becoming more frequent. Equipment providing and utilizing GPS is shrinking both in size and cost, while it increases in reliability. The number of people able to use the systems is also increasing. GPS devices are being installed in cars to provide directional, tracking, and emergency information. Emergency personnel can respond more quickly to 911 calls using to tracking signal devices in their vehicles and in the cell phones of the person making the call. As technology continues to advance the accuracy of navigational satellite and without the impedance of Selective Availability, the uses for GPS will continue to develop.

■ FURTHER READING:

BOOKS:

Balazs, G. H. "Homeward bound: satellite tracking of Hawaiian green turtles from nesting beaches to foraging pastures." *Proceedings of the Thirteenth Annual Symposium on Sea Turtle Biology and Conservation.* U.S. Dep. Commer., NOAA Tech. Memo. NOAA-TM-NMFS-SEFSC-341, (1994):205–208.

El-Rabbany, Ahmed. *Inroduction to GPS: The Global Positioning System* Norwood, MA: Artech Publishing, 2002.

ELECTRONIC:

Dana, Peter H. "Global Positioning Overview" The Geographer's Craft Project. May 1, 2000. University of Colorado. <http://www.colorado.edu/geography/gcraft/notes/gps/gps_f.html> (March 29, 2003).

SEE ALSO

Mapping Technology

Great Game

■ ERIC v.d. LUFT

In intelligence history, the "Great Game" described a complex rivalry—characterized by wars, assassinations, and espionage conspiracies—between Britain and Russia for control of Central Asia and the Near East.

In many critical facets, the mentality of the Great Game foreshadowed that of the Cold War and remains an important factor in world geopolitics at the dawn of the twenty-first century. The Soviet Union's incursion into Afghanistan in 1979 prompted the United States to support the Mujahedin throughout the 1980s. Ultimately, during the coursings of shifting political priorities, the United States formed and then broke ties with a number of factions—including Mujahedin elements that eventually found their way into the Taliban regime (deposed by the United States in 2002) and the al-Qaeda terrorist organization.

The deep suspicion and resentment that many of the Islamic peoples of Iran, Chechnya, Afghanistan, Pakistan, and neighboring regions now harbor against Russia, Britain, and more recently the United States, may in part be explained by the region's experience with—and resistance to—the imperialism of the Great Game.

The "Tournament of Shadows."

The main friction points were the Black Sea, the Baltic regions, Persia, Afghanistan, Kashmir, the Punjab, and the steppes and deserts between the Caspian Sea and China. The Russians called this extended intrigue the "Tournament of Shadows," a term coined by Count Karl Robert Nesselrode (1780–1862), but in the West it was known as the "Great Game," apparently the coinage of Arthur Conolly (1807–1842), a British military diplomat and spy against Russia in Persia, the Caucasus, and the Himalayas from 1829 until Nasrullah Khan, emir of Bokhara (reigned 18261–1860), beheaded him in 1842.

In the mid-nineteenth century the two greatest world powers were Britain under Queen Victoria (1819–1901) and Russia under Czars Nicholas I (1796–1855), Alexander II (1818–1881), and Alexander III (1845–1894). This was true despite the acknowledged naval superiority of France over Russia. Russia was jealous of Britain's conquest of India and ascendancy over France since the end of the Napoleonic Wars. Russia was especially worried that British expansion along the northwest frontier of India would eventually threaten its own borders and thwart its longstanding quest for the warm-water port it needed to enhance both its navy and its merchant fleet.

From 1804 to 1864 the czars gained territory between the Black and Caspian Seas and from 1824 to 1895 they vigorously expanded west of the Caspian Sea into Kazakhstan, Turkmenistan, Uzbekistan, Kyrgyzstan, and Tajikistan, threatening China as well as the Ottoman Empire, Persia, Afghanistan, and India. This rapid and steady expansion of the Russian Empire into Central Asia alarmed the British, but there was little they could do about it. They soon began sending spies among native populations to learn of Russian intentions and to forge alliances against possible Russian incursions.

The earliest sortie of the Great Game was the expedition of Henry Eldred Pottinger (1789–1856) and Charles Christie (d. 1812) from Bombay through Baluchistan to Herat in 1810. Their mission was to spy out possible overland routes by which Russia might invade India. Meanwhile John Malcolm (1769–1833) was negotiating with Persia to prevent any such attack. John Macdonald Kinneir (1782–1830) analyzed these routes and published his results in *A Geographical Memoir of the Persian Empire* (1813). Similar probes by both the Russians and British, such as the journey of Nikolai Nikolaevich Muraviev (1794?–1866) to Khiva in 1819 and that of William Moorcroft (1767–1825) to Bokhara in 1820, soon became common.

The exploits of General Alexis Yermolov (1772–1861), the Russo-Persian War (1827–1828), and the Russo-Turkish War (1828–1829) all further aroused British suspicion that Russia might have designs on India via Persia. Colonel George de Lacy Evans (1787–1870) galvanized these nascent fears with two pamphlets, *On the Designs of Russia* (1828) and *On the Practicability of an Invasion of India* (1829). British spies and military advisers actively helped Persian Prince Abbas Mirza (1783–1833) against Russia in the 1820s.

Evidence is strong, but proof remains absent, that Russian spies fomented unrest among the various native populations of the Indian subcontinent and surrounding lands so that they would arise against the British. Chief among these conflicts were the two Anglo-Afghan Wars (1839–1842 and 1878–1880), the two Anglo-Sikh Wars (1845–1846 and 1848–1849), and the Indian Mutiny (1857–1858).

The Royal Geographical Society was founded in 1830 and the Imperial Russian Geographical Society in 1845. By mid-century both were fronts for spying expeditions in Asia. Among the earliest of these missions were the journeys of Alexander Burnes (1805–1841) to the Punjab in 1831 and to Bokhara in 1832. John McNeill (1795–1883), a British diplomat in Tehran, published anonymously in 1836 *The Progress and Present Position of Russia in the East*, which bolstered British rationale for keeping a sizeable network of spies in Central Asia.

In the 1830s Conolly was one of the busiest of these "explorers." He was a religious zealot who believed it was Britain's duty to civilize Islamic Central Asia by converting its natives to Christianity. As such, he was a typical hero of Victorian imperialism and "muscular Christianity." The emir of Bokhara would have none of that, and tortured him and Charles Stoddart (1806–1842) in a pit for several months before executing them. The more successful British operatives, such as Burnes, had greater respect for native culture.

On the northwest frontier of India, the British had a staunch ally in Sikh ruler Ranjit Singh (1780–1839), against whom Dost Mohammed (1791–1863), emir of Afghanistan, sought help from Russia. Afghanistan in the 1830s became a diplomatic nightmare for Britain, as the colonial government in Calcutta sought to widen the buffer between India and Russia in this crucial region. Soldiers of fortune complicated the mix, such as the Italian adventurer Paolo di Avitabile (1791–1850), who ruled Peshawar for the British from 1835 to 1843. In 1837 Henry Rawlinson (1810–1895), en route from Tehran to Herat, happened upon a Russian delegation led by Yan Vitkevitch (d. 1838), headed toward Kabul. The rivals uneasily backed off from each other. Subsequently Vitkevitch was partially successful in sowing anti-British feelings among Dost Mohammed and several other Afghan leaders.

Burnes became the British envoy to Afghanistan in 1836, headquartered in Kabul. Eldred Pottinger (1811–1843) helped the Afghans defend Herat against Russia and Persia in 1837. These two skilled operatives might have been more successful if Burnes had not been placed under the command of Conolly's cousin, William Macnaghten (1793–1841), whose critics described him as "ignorant and tactless." Increasingly distrustful of Dost Mohammed, the British plotted to install Shah Shujah (1780–1842) as puppet ruler of Afghanistan. Macnaghten's bungling prompted the Afghans to rise up and murder Burnes. Macnaghten himself, perhaps the victim of an elaborate plot of entrapment, was murdered by Mohammed Akbar Khan (1818–1847), son of Dost Mohammed, as summary justice for being caught in the act of double dealing with Afghan tribal leaders. The incompetent General William Elphinstone (1782–1842) allowed nearly his entire command to be massacred while retreating from Kabul to Jalalabad.

Besides Kabul, Bokhara, and Herat, several other cities attracted both Russian and British interest, notably Khiva, Khokand, Kashgar, Merv, and Kandahar. James Abbott (1807–1896) journeyed from Herat to Khiva in 1839 and 1840. In 1840 Richmond Campbell Shakespear (1812–1861) persuaded Allah Quli (d. 1842), Khan of Khiva, to free his Russian slaves, probably as much to incite insurrection and destablize the region as to make a diplomatic or humanitarian gesture.

Count Nikolai Pavlovich Ignatiev (1832–1908) was the leading Russian spymaster in the Great Game. After a series of successful diplomatic missions to China, he served as ambassador to the Ottoman Empire from 1864 to 1877. Utterly ruthless and with keen intuitions about military strategy, he sparked clandestine anti-British operations in India before the mutiny and throughout Central Asia for most of the rest of his career.

In the 1850s France and Britain were both anxious to bolster the sagging Ottoman Empire and thus prevent Russia from gaining unrestricted access to the Mediterranean Sea through the Dardanelles, the Sea of Marmara, and the Bosporus. Britain knew that Russia's main objective was Constantinople, not Calcutta, but conducted its foreign policy as if Russia desired both. Thus the Crimean War could be seen as part of the Great Game, because it served to divert Russia's attention from India for a while.

Meanwhile the British worked hard, especially in the wake of the Indian Mutiny, to rebuild alliances with native Asian leaders. These efforts were mostly successful, even though the native rank and file scarcely trusted the British again. Because Persia was allied with Russia, Britain applauded when Dost Mohammed recaptured Herat from the Persians in 1863. Sher Ali (1825–1879), another son of Dost Mohammed, was emir of Afghanistan from 1863 until his death. At first he favored the British, but his gradual shift toward Russia prompted the Second Anglo-Afghan War. The British replaced him with his nephew, Abdur Rahman (1844–1901).

By 1865, Yakub Beg (1820–1877) in Kashgar was the main potentate between China and Russia. Robert Barkley Shaw (1839–1879) and George J. W. Hayward (1840?–1870) made separate trips to Kashgar in 1868, ostensibly to "survey," but really to try to create a British alliance with Yakub Beg. The Russians made similar overtures, but also sent troops to the region under Konstantin Kaufman (1818–1882). Francis Younghusband (1863–1942) led several expeditions through western China, finally entering Lhasa, Tibet, in 1904, ahead of the Russians.

The British grew bolder. Frederick Gustavus Burnaby (1842–1885) dared to travel from St. Petersburg itself to Khiva in 1876. James Thomas Walker (1826–1896), surveyor general of India, ordered more spying expeditions, as did the Russians. By the late 1880s, Britain clearly had the diplomatic advantage in the regions of Central Asia that Russia had not already annexed.

Russian power declined under Czar Nicholas II (1868–1918) in the first decade of the twentieth century. In August, 1907, the Anglo-Russian Convention in St. Petersburg formally ended the Great Game, although the posturing and espionage continued.

■ FURTHER READING:

BOOKS:

Edwardes, Michael. *Playing the Great Game: A Victorian Cold War.* London: Hamish Hamilton, 1975.

Hopkirk, Peter. *The Great Game: The Struggle for Empire in Central Asia.* New York: Kodansha International, 1994.

Ingram, Edward. *The Beginning of the Great Game in Asia: 1828–1834.* Oxford: Clarendon, 1979.

James, Lawrence. *Raj: The Making and Unmaking of British India.* New York: St. Martin's Griffin, 1997.

Khan, Munawwar. *Anglo-Afghan Relations, 1798–1878: A Chapter in the Great Game in Central Asia.* Khyber Bazar-Peshawar: University Book Agency, 1963.

Meyer, Karl Ernest, and Shareen Blair Brysac. *Tournament of Shadows: The Great Game and the Race for Empire in Central Asia.* Washington, D.C.: Counterpoint, 1999.

SEE ALSO

Assassination
Geologic and Topographical Influences on Military and Intelligence Operations

Greece, Intelligence and Security

Agents of espionage have been employed in the area corresponding to the modern nation of Greece for thousands of years. Spies are mentioned in the works the philosophers and playwrights of ancient Greece, giving the Grecian intelligence community one of the longest lineages and traditions in the world. However, scant comparisons can be drawn between ancient Greece and modern Greece, and their individual employment of intelligence services. Today, Greece maintains a sophisticated civilian intelligence force that utilizes human, signals, communications, and electronic intelligence gathering techniques.

Greece's main intelligence agency is the Hellenic National Intelligence Service (NIS). A recent government reform and restructuring of the Grecian intelligence community expanded the role of the NIS to include both domestic and foreign intelligence operations, and added a counter-terrorism unit to the agency's permanent staff. The NIS is charged with the collection, analysis, and dissemination of intelligence information necessary for the protection of national security. In addition, routine counterintelligence operations, including testing the security of the national communications infrastructure, fall under the jurisdiction of the NIS.

Although the National Intelligence Service is a civilian organization, Greece also maintains limited military intelligence forces, embedded within operational units of the military.

Greece is a member of the North Atlantic Treaty Organization (NATO) and the European Union (EU). Diplomatic negotiations with Turkey over extensive maritime and territorial border disputes are ongoing, but have yielded little consensus between the two nations over national water boundaries in the Aegean Sea. The two nations continue to disagree over the partitioning of neighboring Cyprus.

■ FURTHER READING:

ELECTRONIC:

Central Intelligence Agency. The World Factbook, 2002. "Greece" <http://www.cia.gov/cia/publications/factbook/geos/gr.html> (March 30, 2003).

SEE ALSO

NATO (North Atlantic Treaty Organization)
Turkey, Intelligence and Security

GSM Encryption

GSM stands for either "group special mobile" or "general system for mobile communications," a protocol or standard for digital cellular communications. GSM encryption is the means by which phone conversations on networks using GSM are scrambled, such that they cannot be descrambled and intercepted by others. Due to their potential uses by terrorist and hostile nations, intelligence agencies in the West are concerned about the dangers inherent in exporting such codes.

In 1982, the European Conference of Post and Telecommunications Administrations adopted the GSM standard, which 18 nations formalized in 1987 with the signing of the GSM Memorandum of Understanding. The first GSM networks began operations in 1991. By the end of the 1990s, some 230 million users worldwide—approximately 65% of the digital wireless market—used digital GSM phones made by companies that included Motorola, Ericsson, and Siemens.

Among the key features of GSM is its security technology, the methods of which reportedly make it the most secure cellular telecommunications standard in the world. Vital to this security is the use of sophisticated encryption algorithms. Conversations are encrypted using a temporary and randomly generated ciphering key, and for added security, the subscriber is identified by a temporary identity, which may change periodically.

Despite these and other advanced security measures, authorities have raised concerns about the safety of GSM codes, and these concerns have been justified by attempts to reveal or break into GSM codes. United States, British, French, and Dutch intelligence and law-enforcement agencies have called for restrictions on the export of encryption technology, which could be used by aggressor nations or terrorists. For example, if terrorists gained encryption codes for cellular telephone communications, they might be able to impede the abilities of law-enforcement authorities to track them and other criminals.

A 1993 compromise permitted the export of the strong A 5/1 encryption algorithm only to secure, fully industrialized countries, mostly in western Europe. The weaker A 5/2 algorithm would be exported to central and eastern Europe, while Russia and some other countries would have no encryption technology.

In April 1998, a group of what *Time* magazine described as "Silicon Valley cypherpunks" hacked into GSM encryption technology, and bragged that they could tap into calls and "clone" other users' cellular phones. A year and a half later, in December 1999, Israeli researchers Alex Biryukov and Adi Shamir announced that they had successfully attacked the A 5/1 algorithm, and claimed that with a modest-sized personal computer, they could penetrate an allegedly secure phone call or data transmission within less than a second. However, an official with the

GSM Association noted that no hardware would allow a hacker to intercept calls on the GSM network.

■ FURTHER READING:

PERIODICALS:

Carlson, Caron. "No Threat from GSM Hackers." *Wireless Week* 5, no. 50 (December 13, 1999): 3.

"Firms Are Lining up to See." *Electronic Times* (October 16, 2000): 40.

ELECTRONIC:

GSM Association. <http://www.gsmworld.com> (March 5, 2003).

SEE ALSO

Computer Hackers
Encryption of Data
Telephone Scrambler

Guatemala, Intelligence and Security

Guatemala gained its independence from Spain in 1821. After colonial rule, the region was politically dominated by rival large-land owners. In the latter half of the twentieth century, the government suffered endemic turmoil. Various military coups devastated the national infrastructure, co-opting the nation's small intelligence and security community into political and secret police operations. A 36-year civil war further devastated Guatemala, leaving 100,000 people dead and some one million refugees displaced from their homes.

In 1996, the government issued a peace agreement, formally ending the conflict, but sporadic fighting remains a problem. In peacetime, Guatemala has begun the task of rebuilding its political infrastructure, including its intelligence and security services. New agencies seek to distance themselves from those that operated during the era of political upheaval, but lingering fears of rebel insurgency has prompted the continued use of political espionage against dissidents.

Guatemala's largest intelligence agency is under the direction of the military. The Military Intelligence Wing, D-2, conducts both domestic and foreign intelligence operations. Though D-2 conducts a variety of surveillance missions, a large focus of their operations is the identification and infiltration of paramilitary groups. D-2 also monitors and attempts to stem the trafficking of contraband weapons across national borders.

Guatemala's civilian intelligence community is administered by the Ministry of the Interior and the National Police. The Ministry of the Interior maintains a sizable investigations and security-intelligence force to combat organized crime, government corruption, and counterfeiting. The National Police are the nation's main law enforcement agency, and maintain their own, specialized intelligence and investigative units.

In recent years, Guatemala has become a major staging area for the trafficking of illegal drugs. The government has joined with others in the region, and the United Nations, to combat the problem, but with varying degrees of success. Government corruption also remain endemic in Guatemala, stifling attempts to rebuild the nation's economy.

■ FURTHER READING:

ELECTRONIC:

Central Intelligence Agency. "Guatemala" CIA World Factbook <http://wwhttp://www.cia.gov/cia/publications/factbook/geos/gt.html> (April 8, 2003).

Guerilla Warfare

■ MARÍA LÓPEZ

In the modern era, guerilla warfare refers to armed resistance by paramilitary or irregular groups toward an occupying force. Guerilla warfare also describes a set of tactics employed by smaller forces against larger, better equipped, and better supplied forces. Guerilla warfare tactics often rely on isolating smaller units of the larger occupying force so as to attack parts of the larger force by ambush. Guerilla forces often practice espionage, industrial sabotage, and wage propaganda campaigns by portraying themselves as a popular but suppressed political movement. In many areas of the world, guerilla warfare is practiced by local groups against government forces, and is especially effective in areas with a rugged natural topography or areas of dense vegetation (e.g., forest or jungle) that provide natural hiding places from which to stage guerilla operations.

Derived from the Spanish term for "little war," guerilla warfare has a long history. Although the term was not used until Spanish partisans resisted the intrusions of Napoleon during the Peninsular War in the early nineteenth century, American colonist revolutionaries practiced guerilla warfare tactics against British forces to win independence from what was arguably the finest military power in the world at the time. During the twentieth century, communist guerilla forces fought succedfullly against French and then American forces in Vietnam.

Confederate raiders—including Quantrill's raiders (led by William C. Quantrill) and Mosby's raiders (led by John S. Mosby) practiced guerilla warfare against Union forces

A blindfolded Palestinian boy assembles an AK-47 assault rifle, demonstrating skills that he learned at one of the two-week warfare summer camps run by the Palestinian Authority across the West Bank and Gaza in 2000. AP/WIDE WORLD PHOTOS.

during the American Civil War. Following the aquisition of the Philippines after the Spanish-American War, U.S. President Theodore Roosevelt's administration and U.S. forces struggled to suppress Filipino guerilla forces led by Emilio Aguinaldo.

Although usually confined to mountainous or forested terrain, Arab forces inspired by T. E. Lawrence (Lawrence of Arabia) and led by King Faisal al-Husayn used the harsh environment of the desert to fight a successful guerilla war against superior Turkish forces during World War I.

During World War II guerilla forces (also termed "partisan" or "underground" forces) in France and other countries fiercely resisted Nazi occupation.

Well known modern guerilla wars that resulted in permanent changes in government occurred in China, Vietnam, and Cuba. Chinese communist guerillas led by Mao Zedong, prevailed against a number of opponents to eventually take power after WWII. Communist Viet Minh forces led by Ho Chi Minh and later Viet Cong guerilla forces outlasted French and then American forces in Vietnam. In Cuba, Fidel Castro and Ernesto (Che) Guevara fought a three year long guerilla war from 1956 to 1959 that eventually ousted the launched a guerilla war in Cuba against the government of Fulgencio Batista.

Guevara's writings became politically influential for a number of guerilla groups that organized across Central and South America. Guevara wrote that "popular forces can win a war against (an) army" and that "it (was) not necessary to wait until all conditions for making revolution exist; the insurrection can create them."

Other nationalist movements sprung from guerilla movement roots in Algeria (against the French in 1954); Cyprus (Greek nationalists against the British in the late 1950s).

Although often portraying themselves as a popular front, guerilla forces seizing power often engage in bloody "cleansing" and destruction of local populations once loyal to the former government. After seizing power in Cambodia, the Khmer Rouge led by Pol Pot (also known as Soloth Sar) killed an estimated two million Cambodians.

Although sometimes only a matter of semantics, there is often considerable debate concerning the overlap of guerilla tactics with tactics employed by terrorists (e.g., hijacking, kidnapping). There are no easily agreed upon definitional lines to distinguish the two groups. In general, most historians hinge such distinctions not necessarily upon tactics employed, but rather on relations between the opposing parties and the targets selected. Although there are many historical exceptions, terrorists generally represent minority or extreme viewpoints and target civilian, military, or government targets. Guerilla forces generally represent broader popular movements and generally attack occupying military or government forces. A key element in defining guerilla forces as opposed to other types of forces or movements involves the general principle that guerilla forces are generally accepted—in fact often supported and sheltered—by local populations. In accord with international law, in stark contrast to the legal treatment of terrorist groups, guerilla forces are to be treated as combatants in accord with the rules of the Geneva Convention if the forces operate in uniform or carry as distinctive emblem (e.g., patch, red scarf, etc.).

In many cases, whether to declare a particular group a group of freedom fighters, a guerilla force, or a terrorist organization is often a matter of political or geographical perspective.

Cyberspace opens new opportunities and perils for what may come to be considered a new form of guerilla warfare in the twenty-first century as activists (also known as "hacktivists") use Internet technology to combat electronic monitoring and Internet censorship by governments in many parts of the world.

SEE ALSO

Terrorist and Para-State Organizations

H

Hackers.

SEE *Computer Hackers.*

HAMAS (Islamic Resistance Movement)

HAMAS was formed in late 1987 as an outgrowth of the Palestinian branch of the Muslim Brotherhood. Various HAMAS elements have used both political and violent means, including terrorism, to pursue the goal of establishing an Islamic Palestinian state in place of Israel. HAMAS is loosely structured, with some elements working clandestinely and others working openly through mosques and social service institutions (including charities organized by HAMAS) to recruit members, raise money, organize activities, and distribute propaganda. HAMAS' strength is concentrated in the Gaza Strip and a few areas of the West Bank. HAMAS also has engaged in political activity, such as running candidates in West Bank Chamber of Commerce elections.

Organization activities. HAMAS is a large organization with tens of thousands of supporters and sympathizers. HAMAS activists, especially those in the Izz el-Din al-Qassam Brigades, have conducted many attacks—including large-scale suicide bombings—against Israeli civilian and military targets. In the early 1990s, HAMAS also targeted Fatah rivals and began a continuing practice of targeting suspected Palestinian collaborators. HAMAS increased operational activity in 2001 during the Intifadah, claiming numerous attacks against Israeli interests. HAMAS has not directly targeted U.S. interests and continues to confine its attacks to Israelis inside Israel and the territories.

HAMAS operates primarily in the West Bank, Gaza Strip, and Israel. In August 1999, Jordanian authorities closed the group's Political Bureau offices in Amman, arrested its leaders, and prohibited the group from operating on Jordanian territory. HAMAS leaders are also present in other parts of the Middle East, including Syria, Lebanon, and Iran.

HAMAS receives funding from Palestinian expatriates, Iran, and private benefactors in Saudi Arabia and other moderate Arab states. Some fundraising and propaganda activity take place in Western Europe and North America.

■ **FURTHER READING:**

ELECTRONIC:

Central Intelligence Agency. World Factbook, 2002. <http://www.cia.gov/cia/publications/factbook/> (April 16, 2003).

Taylor, Francis X. U.S. Department of State. Patterns of Global Terrorism 2001, Annual Report: On the Record Briefing. May 21, 2002 <http://www.state.gov/s/ct/rls/rm/10367.htm> (April 17, 2003).

U.S. Department of State. Annual Reports. <http://www.state.gov/www/global/terrorism/annual_reports.html> (April 16, 2003).

SEE ALSO

Terrorism, Philosophical and Ideological Origins
Terrorist and Para-State Organizations
Terrorist Organization List, United States
Terrorist Organizations, Freezing of Assets

Hanssen (Robert) Espionage Case

■ ADRIENNE WILMOTH LERNER

Robert Phillip Hanssen, a 25-year FBI veteran, was one of the most successful double agents to ever steal secrets

Photo released by the FBI February 20, 2001, showing FBI agent Robert Philip Hanssen, who was arrested under the accusation of spying for Russia. ©AFP/CORBIS.

from the United States government. Hanssen used his position in the FBI to sell classified information to the Soviet KGB and later Russian Intelligence. A complex and often contradictory portrait emerged in the 109-page federal affidavit that detailed Hanssen's activities. The FBI alleged that Hanssen intentionally stole secret documents and sold them for private financial gain to the KGB over a period of 15 years. Like most double agents, a different social portrait of the man emerged. Friends, neighbors, and family described Hanssen as quiet, frugal, and devout.

Born in April 1944, Hanssen was the only child of Vivian and Howard Hanssen, a Chicago police lieutenant. He studied Russian and earned degrees in chemistry. After flirting with various career interests, Hanssen joined the Chicago Police Department in October, 1972. His first post was in a new undercover unit called C-5, which sought out corrupt police officers.

Hanssen's intelligence and ability stood out even in the elite C-5 group. A colleague suggested he join the FBI. On January 12, 1976, he joined the FBI, working in Indiana and New York City before being transferred to the Washington, D.C., headquarters in 1981. He initially tracked white-collar crime and monitored foreign officials assigned to the United States. Hanssen also spent two years as a member of a high-level analytical unit that monitored Soviet intelligence. While working as an analyst, Hanssen

gathered and copied classified materials and began making contact with the Soviet KGB.

In 1985, Hanssen transferred to the FBI's Manhattan bureau to head a foreign counterintelligence squad. At that post, Hanssen could more readily funnel information to his Soviet handlers. Though his motives remained unclear, within nine days of joining the New York office Hanssen allegedly mailed a letter to the KGB offering stolen classified documents in exchange for $100,000. Over the next 15 years, with varying frequency, Hanssen sold information to rival foreign intelligence services.

In February 2000, Hanssen was arrested on espionage charges at a "dead drop" at a park near his home. The FBI accused him of receiving more than $600,000 in cash and diamonds for delivering 6,000 pages of documents and 26 computer discs to his Russian handlers. It was also alleged that $800,000 more was waiting for him in a Moscow bank. The FBI built its case against Hanssen by collecting, from unidentified sources, packages that bore Hanssen's fingerprints, and the apparent KGB file on Hanssen, which detailed his drops and letters to the Russian intelligence agency. Upon further investigation, the FBI compiled evidence of Hanssen's decades-long career as a double agent.

On May 10, 2002, Hanssen was sentenced to life in prison without the possibility of parole. In his trial, he plead guilty to all counts of espionage and conspiracy that were levied against him.

■ FURTHER READING:

ELECTRONIC:

The Center for Counterintelligence and Security Studies. <http://www.cicentre.com/Documents/DOC_Hanssen_1.htm> (April 2003).

United States Federal Bureau of Investigation. <http://www.fbi.gov/libref/historic/famcases/hanssen/hanssen.htm#anchor26782> (April 2003).

SEE ALSO

Ames (Aldrich H.) Espionage Case
Dead Drop Spike
Dead-Letter Box
FBI (United States Federal Bureau of Investigation)
KGB (Komitet Gosudarstvennoi Bezopasnosti, USSR Committee of State Security)
Russia, Intelligence and Security

Harakat ul-Jihad-I-Islami (HUJI) (Movement of Islamic Holy War)

Harakat ul-Jihad-I-Islami (HUJI)—Movement of Islamic Holy War—is a Sunni extremist group that follows the

Deobandi tradition of Islam, and was founded in 1980 in Afghanistan to fight in the Jihad against the Soviets. It is also affiliated with the Jamiat Ulema-I-Islam Fazlur Rehman faction (JUI-F) and the Deobandi school of Sunni Islam. The group, led by chief commander Amin Rabbani, is made up primarily of Pakistanis and foreign Islamists who are fighting for the liberation of Kashmir and its accession to Pakistan. HUJI has conducted a number of operations against Indian military targets in Kashmir, and are linked to the Kashmiri militant group al-Faran that kidnapped five Western tourists in Kashmir in July 1995; one was killed in August 1995 and the other four reportedly were killed in December of the same year.

HUJI strength is unknown, but intelligence services estimate that there may be several hundred members operating in Pakistan and Kashmir. HUJI trained members in Afghanistan until Operation Enduring Freedom began in the fall of 2001.

■ FURTHER READING:

ELECTRONIC:

CDI (Center for Defense Information), Terrorism Project. CDI Fact Sheet: Current List of Designated Foreign Terrorist Organizations. March 27, 2003. <http://www.cdi. org/terrorism/terrorist.cfm> (April 17, 2003).

Central Intelligence Agency. World Factbook, 2002. <http:// www.cia.gov/cia/publications/factbook/> (April 16, 2003).

Taylor, Francis X. U.S. Department of State. "Patterns of Global Terrorism 2001," Annual Report: On the Record Briefing. May 21, 2002 <http://www.state.gov/s/ct/rls/ rm/10367.htm> (April 17, 2003).

U.S. Department of State. Annual Reports. <http://www. state.gov/www/global/terrorism/annual_reports.html> (April 16, 2003).

SEE ALSO

Terrorism, Philosophical and Ideological Origins
Terrorist and Para-State Organizations
Terrorist Organization List, United States
Terrorist Organizations, Freezing of Assets

Harakat ul-Jihad-I-Islami/ Bangladesh (HUJI-B) (Movement of Islamic Holy War)

The mission of Harakat ul-Jihad-I-Islami/Bangladesh (HUJI-B) (Movement of Islamic Holy War), led by Shauqat Osman, is to establish Islamic rule in Bangladesh. HUJI-B has

connections to the Pakistani militant groups Harakat ul-Jihad-I-Islami (HUJI) and Harakat ul-Mujahidin (HUM), who advocate similar objectives in Pakistan and Kashmir. HUJI-B was accused of stabbing a senior Bangladeshi journalist in November, 2000, for making a documentary on the plight of Hindus in Bangladesh. HUJI-B was suspected in the July 2000, assassination attempt of Bangladeshi Prime Minister Sheikh Hasina.

HUJI-B has an estimated cadre strength of several thousand members and operates and trains members in Bangladesh, where it maintains at least six camps. Funding of the HUJI-B comes primarily from madrassas in Bangladesh. The group also has ties to militants in Pakistan that may provide another funding source.

■ FURTHER READING:

ELECTRONIC:

CDI (Center for Defense Information), Terrorism Project. CDI Fact Sheet: Current List of Designated Foreign Terrorist Organizations. March 27, 2003. <http://www.cdi. org/terrorism/terrorist.cfm> (April 17, 2003).

Central Intelligence Agency. World Factbook, 2002. <http:// www.cia.gov/cia/publications/factbook/> (April 16, 2003).

Taylor, Francis X. U.S. Department of State. "Patterns of Global Terrorism 2001," Annual Report: On the Record Briefing. May 21, 2002 <http://www.state.gov/s/ct/rls/ rm/10367.htm> (April 17, 2003).

U.S. Department of State. Annual Reports. <http://www. state.gov/www/global/terrorism/annual_reports.html> (April 16, 2003).

SEE ALSO

Terrorism, Philosophical and Ideological Origins
Terrorist and Para-State Organizations
Terrorist Organization List, United States
Terrorist Organizations, Freezing of Assets

Harakat ul-Mujahidin (HUM) (Movement of Holy Warriors)

The Harakat ul-Mujahidin is an Islamic militant group based in Pakistan that operates primarily in Kashmir. It is politically aligned with the radical political party, Jamiat Ulema-I Islam Fazlur Rehman faction (JUI-F). Long-time leader of the group, Fazlur Rehman Khalil, in mid-February 2000 stepped down as HUM emir, turning the reins over to the popular Kashmiri commander and his second-in-command, Farooq Kashmiri. Khalil, who has been linked to Osama Bin Ladin and signed his fatwa in February 1998 calling for attacks on United States and Western interests, assumed the position of HUM Secretary General.

HUM operated terrorist training camps in eastern Afghanistan until Coalition airstrikes destroyed them during the Fall of 2001.

Organization activities.

HUM has conducted a number of operations against Indian troops and civilian targets in Kashmir. HUM also has been linked to the Kashmiri militant group al-Faran that kidnapped five Western tourists in Kashmir in July 1995—one was killed in August 1995 and the other four reportedly were killed in December of the same year. The HUM is responsible for the hijacking of an Indian airliner on December 24, 1999, that resulted in the release of Masood Azhar—an important leader in the former Harakat ul-Ansar imprisoned by the Indians in 1994—and Ahmad Omar Sheikh, who was arrested for the abduction and murder in January-February 2001 of U.S. journalist Daniel Pearl.

HUM is based in Muzaffarabad, Rawalpindi, and several other towns in Pakistan, but members conduct insurgent and terrorist activities primarily in Kashmir. The HUM trained its militants in Afghanistan and Pakistan. They have several thousand armed supporters located in Azad Kashmir, Pakistan, and India's southern Kashmir and Doda regions. Supporters are mostly Pakistanis and Kashmiris and also include Afghans and Arab veterans of the Afghan war. HUM uses light and heavy machine guns, assault rifles, mortars, explosives, and rockets. HUM lost a significant share of its membership in defections to the Jaish-e-Mohammed (JEM) in 2000.

HUM collects donations from Saudi Arabia and other Gulf and Islamic states and from Pakistanis and Kashmiris. The HUM's financial collection methods also include soliciting donations through magazine ads and pamphlets. The sources and amount of HUM's military funding are unknown. In anticipation of asset seizures by the Pakistani Government, the HUM withdrew funds from bank accounts and invested in legal businesses, such as commodity trading, real estate, and production of consumer goods. Its fundraising in Pakistan has been constrained since the government clampdown on extremist groups and freezing of terrorist assets.

■ FURTHER READING:

ELECTRONIC:

Central Intelligence Agency. World Factbook, 2002. <http://www.cia.gov/cia/publications/factbook/> (April 16, 2003).

Taylor, Francis X. U.S. Department of State. Patterns of Global Terrorism 2001, Annual Report: On the Record Briefing. May 21, 2002 <http://www.state.gov/s/ct/rls/rm/10367.htm> (April 17, 2003).

U.S. Department of State. Annual reports. <http://www.state.gov/www/global/terrorism/annual_Reports.html> (April 16, 2003).

SEE ALSO

Terrorism, Philosophical and Ideological Origins

Terrorist and Para-State Organizations
Terrorist Organization List, United States
Terrorist Organizations, Freezing of Assets

Hardening

In a general sense, hardening is the process of securing a computer. More specifically, hardening is the removal or disabling of all components in a computer system that are not necessary to its principal function or functions. By reducing the purposes for which a computer is used, the computer is rendered less vulnerable to outside attack by hackers or other intruders.

General hardening steps include limiting the number of users allowed to access a computer, tightening password and access control, and installing basic intrusion-detection software. The more specific variety of hardening requires the involvement of a highly trained computer technician. Once the user has defined the principal purpose or purposes for which the computer is to be used, then the technician can disable or remove all components that are not necessary to those purposes.

An example of a computer that needs to be hardened is a server, a computer, or device on a network (a group of linked computers) that manages network resources. The server should be equipped with high-quality firewall software to prevent outside intrusion. Often, such software may not provide enough security, in which case hardening is necessary. If the server is properly hardened, this narrows the avenues of access for intruders hoping to get past the server to other computers on the local network.

During the hardening process, a computer should be disconnected from any network. Once it is hardened, the computer will no longer be a general-purpose machine, but will be usable only for the very specific purposes for which it has been designated. The more specific that purpose, and the fewer general-purpose features on the computer, the more difficult it will be for a would-be intruder to access the computer, or to use it effectively once it has been accessed.

■ FURTHER READING:

BOOKS:

Akin, Thomas. Hardening Cisco Routers. Sebastopol, CA: O'Reilly, 2002.

PERIODICALS:

Connolly, P. J. "Fight DDoS Attacks with Intelligence." InfoWorld 23, no. 39 (September 24, 2001): 58.

Levine, Bernard. "What's Next for Electronics?" Electronic News 47, no. 40 (October 1, 2001): 1.

Wang, Wallace. "Hardening Your System." *Boardwatch* 15, no. 8 (June 2001): 44–46.

SEE ALSO

Computer Hackers
Computer Hardware Security
Computer Software Security

Health and Human Services Department, United States

The United States Department of Health and Human Services (HHS) is responsible for overseeing government departments and programs devoted to public health. The HHS manages federal health insurance programs Medicare and Medicaid for certain citizens. Other operational departments within the HHS have a direct impact on general matters of national security, public safety, and counter-terrorism.

The HHS currently oversees over 300 various programs and has an annual operating budget of around 460 billion dollars. The department was founded in the 1930s as part of the New Deal, but has since grown in scope to cover everything from preschool programs to medical research.

Two main branches of the HHS are especially important to the preservation of national security. The Food and Drug Administration (FDA) is responsible for pharmaceutical research and the approval of medicines for sale and distribution in the United States. The FDA also regulates some aspects of agriculture and insures the safety of food products for consumers. Working with the Environmental Protection Agency, the FDA helped to establish guidelines for drinking water treatment and regulation. Food safety, water purity, and drug research and approval have increased in importance in recent years since America has come under terrorist threat. The FDA sponsors research into protecting food and water systems from bioterrorism attacks. Other research funding supports the development and testing of vaccines and drugs to fight diseases that are most likely to be used in such an attack.

Perhaps the most important organizational branch of the HHS in terms of national security, as well as public health, is the Centers for Disease Control and Prevention (CDC). The CDC, located in Atlanta, Georgia, is the primary disease research facility in the world and monitors the spread of epidemic diseases whether natural or the result of bioterrorism. The CDC has introduced several new initiatives to investigate, plan for, and combat bioterrorism and radiological attacks. Constant research on disease virulence, transmission, and treatments insures that most diseases are readily identifiable. Several instances in the past, including the September 11th terrorist attacks on the Unites States, have prompted the CDC to issue advisories to doctors on symptoms of diseases that can be the result of bioterrorism. The CDC stressed that some of these diseases could be difficult to diagnose because they had been eradicated from the United States for decades. Also, the organization released information to the general public regarding the best ways to prepare for and survive a biological or radiological attack.

The HHS, with the aid of the CDC, also administers general and emergency vaccination and inoculation programs, including advising the military on possible health threats that could be encountered abroad. Individual state bioterrorism readiness plans must also be approved by the HHS.

■ FURTHER READING:

ELECTRONIC:

Centers for Disease Control "Bioterrorism Preparedness." <http://www.bt.cdc.gov/> (November 28, 2002).

SEE ALSO

CDC (United States Centers for Disease Control and Prevention)

Heavy Water Technology

■ LARRY GILMAN

Heavy water is water (H_2O) in which oxygen is bound to atoms of the hydrogen isotope deuterium (^2H). Heavy water is so named because it is significantly more dense (>1.1 g/cm^3) than ordinary ("light") water, ^1H_2O (1 gm/cm^3). Heavy water is not radioactive and has the same chemical properties as light water; a person could drink a glass of heavy water without harm. However, heavy water is better than light water at moderating (slowing) neutrons, which makes it useful in some nuclear reactor cores. Its scarcity during World War II, partly assured by bombing raids and daring Allied commando missions to destroy heavy-water production facilities, interfered critically with the German and Japanese nuclear programs.

Deuterium and tritium. All hydrogen atoms have atomic number 1, that is, one proton in the nucleus; common or light hydrogen also has mass number 1, that is, its nucleus consists solely of a lone proton. Deuterium (^2H) has atomic number 1 and mass number 2, because its nucleus contains one proton plus one neutron. The presence of the neutrons in the deuterium atoms of heavy water is what makes it "heavy" (i.e., more dense than common water). Tritium (^3H) is an isotope of hydrogen whose nuclei contain one proton plus two neutrons. Tritium can also combine with oxygen to form heavy water, but tritium is much rarer than deuterium, so virtually all heavy water consists of ^2H_2O (deuterium oxide). Tritium heavy water is radioactive and has been used as a tracer in certain biological experiments.

About .015% of the hydrogen atoms in natural water are deuterium atoms. Heavy water is produced by using electricity to break up water molecules, releasing its hydrogen as gas. (This process is known as electrolysis.) Deuterium oxide molecules are more resistant to electrolysis than light-water molecules, so electrolysis of a volume of water tends to increase its concentration of heavy water. By repeated concentration steps, almost pure heavy water can be obtained. Heavy water can also be extracted from natural water by repeated evaporation steps, as its heavier molecules are less volatile than those of light water (i.e., less likely to gain enough kinetic energy in random molecular collisions to leave the surface of a liquid mass). The electrolysis method was important during World War II, but evaporation methods are used today because they are less expensive.

Neutron moderation.

The utility of heavy water in nuclear reactors arises from its ability to slow down or moderate neutrons. Slow or thermal neutrons are more likely to cause unstable nuclei (e.g., of uranium) to fission upon impact; however, neutrons emitted by fissioning nuclei generally have high velocities. To make a nuclear chain reaction sustainable, therefore, it is often desirable to slow down or moderate neutrons released by fissioning nuclei. Slowed-down neutrons are termed thermal neutrons, and reactors that employ a moderator to produce thermal neutrons are termed thermal reactors. (Other reactor designs are also possible.) Interposing a neutron-slowing substance or moderator between thin rods filled with nuclear fuel is a common feature of thermal reactor cores. Most of the neutrons released by fissioning nuclei in the fuel rods escape quickly from the thin rods and collide with atoms in the moderator before passing into other fuel rods; these collisions impart some of the neutrons' kinetic energy to atoms in the moderator. This heats the moderator, and some of the slowed neutrons go on to enter fuel rods and to cause nuclei to fission in them.

Several substances have been used as moderators in nuclear reactors, especially carbon (in the form of graphite), light water, heavy water, and beryllium. Heavy water is a desirable moderator for several reasons. It has excellent moderation properties and, being a liquid, can act simultaneously as a coolant to transfer heat out of the core to a power-generation loop.

Today, most power-generating reactors in the world utilize light water as a moderator. Light water has less desirable moderation properties than heavy water, but the fact that it is essentially free, while heavy water is expensive, gives it an advantage. However, one class of modern reactor—the Canadian CANDU (CANada Deuterium Uranium) reactor type—uses heavy water as a moderator. A CANDU reactor core consists of a stack of horizontal fuel-rod assemblies immersed in a large holding tank full of heavy water that serves to reduce stray radiation in the vicinity of the unit. Hot heavy water circulates through tubes stacked between the fuel-rod assemblies, acting both to moderate neutrons in the core and to carry away heat energy. The circulating heavy water is under high pressure to keep it from flashing to steam. After being heated in the reactor core, it is passed through a heat exchanger, a device which allows hot water to circulate on one side of a thin metal barrier and relatively cool water to circulate on the other; heat is conducted through the metal from the hotter to the cooler water, which is then pumped away and allowed to expand into steam to drive turbines. The turbines, in turn, drive generators that make electricity.

Heavy water during World War II.

During the early days of nuclear fission, in the 1930s and early 1940s, scientists struggled with what is today a routine task: the production of a sustained, controlled nuclear chain reaction in a reactor core. It took intense research to discover that a moderator was required at all. Graphite was known to be a good moderator, and some of the earliest nuclear reactors consisted of large piles of graphite blocks riddled with pellets of nuclear fuel. However, heavy water was easier to handle and had superior moderation properties; rapid progress in nuclear fission, given the state of knowledge at that time, required heavy water.

However, heavy water was rare. The only commercial producer of heavy water in the world in the late 1930s was Norsk Hydro, the state-owned Norwegian hydroelectric company. In 1940, the Germans invaded and occupied Norway, seizing the heavy-water production facility at Rjukan-Vemork, Norway. By 1942, U.S. intelligence was aware that the German nuclear research program was using heavy water produced using the electrolysis method at Rjukan-Vemork. In November 1942, British commandos (special forces trained to operate in small numbers behind enemy lines) attempted to land in Norway and destroy essential machinery at Rjukan-Vemork; they were all killed in crashes or captured and executed by the Germans. (Hitler had ordered that all captured commandos were to be shot.) In February 1943, a second commando raid was attempted. This raid succeeded in putting the Rjukan-Vemork heavy-water plant temporarily out of commission. All commandos involved escaped, and the German fission program was delayed by some months. However, the facility was repaired and put back into operation. In November 1943, a force of 460 U.S. bombers was dispatched from England to bomb the Norwegian plant. Not all essential heavy-water machinery at the site was destroyed, but the German government decided to move what was left, including whatever stocks of heavy water had been accumulated, to Germany, where they could be better defended. However, Norwegian resistance personnel succeeded in sinking the ferry that was to carry the precious barrels of heavy water across a lake on its way to Germany, further impeding German nuclear efforts. In the months remaining before the Germans were defeated they could not produce sufficient quantities of heavy water, and their nuclear program (which was mostly devoted to the goal of producing electricity, rather than a nuclear bomb) did not succeed. The extreme scarcity of heavy water in Japan was also a factor in that country's decision not to pursue development of nuclear explosives during World War II.

■ FURTHER READING:

BOOKS:

Dahl, Per F. *Heavy Water and the Wartime Race for Nuclear Energy.* Bath, UK: Institute of Physics Publishing, 1999.

Glasston, Samuel, and Alexander Sesonske. *Nuclear Reactor Engineering: Vol. 1, Reactor Design Basics.* New York: Chapman & Hall, 1994.

SEE ALSO

Chemistry: Applications in Espionage, Intelligence, and Security Issues
Manhattan Project
Nuclear Power Plants, Security
Nuclear Reactors
Nuclear Weapons

Hemorrhagic Fevers and Diseases

■ BRIAN D. HOYLE

Hemorrhagic diseases are caused by infection with viruses or bacteria. As the name implies, a hallmark of a hemorrhagic disease is copious bleeding. The onset of a hemorrhagic fever or disease can lead to relatively mild symptoms that clear up within a short time. However, hemorrhagic diseases are most recognized because of the ferocity and lethality of their symptoms as well as the speed at which they render a person extremely ill.

High rates of infection, easy transmission, and high levels of morbidity (illness) and mortality (death) mean that some hemorrhagic viruses hold the potential for use as biological weapons. Viruses including, but not limited, Ebola, Marburg, Lassa fever, and New World arenaviruses, offer characteristics desirable in potential bioweapon agents.

Four groups of hemorrhagic viruses. The viruses that cause hemorrhagic diseases are members of four groups. These are the arenaviruses, filoviruses, bunyaviruses, and the flaviviruses. Arenaviruses are the cause of Argentine hemorrhagic fever, Bolivian hemorrhagic fever, Sabia-associated hemorrhagic fever, Lassa fever, Lymphocytic choriomeningitis, and Venezuelan hemorrhagic fever. The bunyavirus group causes Crimean-Congo hemorrhagic fever, Rift Valley fever, and Hantavirus pulmonary syndrome. Filoviruses are the cause of Ebola hemorrhagic fever and Marburg hemorrhagic fever. Lastly, the flaviviruses cause tick-borne encephalitis, yellow fever, Dengue hemorrhagic fever, Kyasanur Forest disease, and Omsk hemorrhagic fever.

Virtually all the hemorrhagic diseases of microbiological origin that arise with any frequency are caused by viruses. The various viral diseases are also known as viral hemorrhagic fevers. Bacterial infections that lead to hemorrhagic fever are rare. One example is a bacterium known as scrub typhus.

None of the known viral hemorrhagic diseases are indigenous to the United States (i.e., none occur naturally). Accordingly, a primary risk factor of viral hemorrhagic diseases includes travel to areas where the virus is indigenous (e.g., portions of Africa, Asia, the Middle East, and South America).

Work with these viruses must only be conducted in high containment (BSL-4) laboratories. There are two such labs in the U.S.; one is located at the Centers for Disease Control and Prevention (CDC), and the other at the United States Army Medical Research Institute of Infectious Diseases (USAMRIID). All personnel at these laboratories must wear protective clothing (e.g., double-gloves, biohazard suits, shoe coverings, face shields, respirators, etc.) and often work in negative pressure rooms.

Although Ribavirin, an antiviral medication, has shown some effectiveness against arenaviridae and bunyaviridae viruses, there are currently no antiviral medications effective against filoviridae and flaviviridae viruses. A vaccine exists for only yellow fever. Insect vectors are controlled by a concerted campaign of spraying and observance of precautionary measures (e.g., use of insect repellent, proper clothing, insect netting over sleeping areas, etc.).

Molecular biology and modes of transmission. While the viruses in the groups display differences in structure and severity of the symptoms they can cause, there are some features that are shared by all the viruses. For instance, all the hemorrhagic viruses contain ribonucleic acid as their genetic material. The nucleic acid is contained within a so-called envelope that is typically made of lipids. Additionally, all the viruses require a host in which to live. The animal or insect that serves as the host is also called the natural reservoir of the particular virus. This natural reservoir does not include humans. Infection of humans occurs only incidentally upon contact with the natural reservoir.

Symptoms of hemorrhagic diseases can progress from mild to catastrophic in only hours. As a result, an outbreak of hemorrhagic disease tends to be self-limiting in a short time. In some cases, this is because the high death rate of those who are infected literally leaves the virus with no host to infect. Often the outbreak fades away as quickly as it appeared.

Hemorrhagic-fever-related illnesses appear in a geographical area where the natural reservoir and humans are both present. If the contact between the two species is close enough, then the disease-causing microorganism may be able to pass from the species that is the natural reservoir to the human.

Although little is clear about the state of the microbes in their natural hosts, it is reasonably clear now that the viruses do not damage these hosts as much as they do a human who acquires the microorganisms. Clarifying the reasons for the resistance of the natural host to the infections would be helpful in finding an effective treatment for human hemorrhagic diseases.

The speed at which hemorrhagic fevers appear and end in human populations, combined with their frequent occurrence in relatively isolated areas of the globe has made detailed study difficult. Even though some of the diseases, such as Argentine hemorrhagic fever, have been known for almost 50 years, knowledge of the molecular basis of the disease is lacking. For example, while it is apparent that some hemorrhagic viruses can be transmitted through the air as aerosols, the pathway of infection once the microorganism has been inhaled is still largely unknown.

The transmission of hemorrhagic viruses from the animal reservoir to humans makes the viruses the quintessential zoonotic disease. For some of the viruses, the host has been determined. Hosts include the cotton rat, deer mouse, house mouse, arthropod ticks, and mosqitoes. However, for other viruses, such as the Ebola and Marburg viruses, the natural host still remains undetermined. Outbreaks with the Ebola and Marburg viruses have involved transfer of the virus to humans via primates. Whether the primate is the natural host or acquired the virus as the result of contact with the true natural host is not clear.

Another fairly common feature of hemorrhagic diseases is that once humans are infected with the agent of the disease, human-to-human transmission can occur. Often this transmission is via body fluids that accidentally contact a person who is offering care to the afflicted person.

Hemorrhagic diseases typically begin with a fever, a feeling of tiredness, and aching muscles. These symptoms may not progress further, and recovery may occur within a short time. However, damage that is more serious often is characterized by copious bleeding, especially from orifices such as the mouth, eyes, and ears. More seriously, internal bleeding also occurs as organs are attacked by the infection. Death can result, though usually not from direct loss of blood, but from nervous system failure, coma, or seizures.

■ FURTHER READING:

BOOKS:

Andreoli, Thomas E., et al. *Cecil Essentials of Medicine.* Philadelphia: W. B. Saunders, 1993.

Cormican, M. G., and M. A. Pfaller. "Molecular Pathology of Infectious Diseases," in *Clinical Diagnosis and Management by Laboratory Methods.* 20th ed. Philadelphia: W. B. Saunders, 2001.

PERIODICALS:

Dutton, Gail. "Biotechnology Counters Bioterrorism." *Genetic Engineering News* no. 21 (December 2000): 1–22ff.

Peters, C. J., and J. W. LeDuc. "An Introduction to Ebola: The Virus and the Disease." *The Journal of Infectious Diseases* no. 179 (Supplement 1, February 1999): ix–xvi.

ELECTRONIC:

Centers for Disease Control. "Ebola Hemorrhagic Fever." 2001. <http://www.cdc.gov/ncidod/dvrd/spb/mnpages/dispages/ebola.htm> (March 12, 2003).

Centers for Disease Control. "Viral Hemorrhagic Fevers." 2000. <http://www.cdc.gov/ncidod/dvrd/spb/mnpages/dispages/vhf.htm> (March 12, 2003).

Centers for Disease Control. "Yellow Fever: Disease and Vaccine." 2001. <http://www.cdc.gov/ncidod/dvbid/yellowfever/index.htm> (March 12, 2003).

SEE ALSO

Biological Warfare
Biological Weapons, Genetic Identification
Bioshield Project
Bioterrorism
Bioterrorism, Protective Measures
CDC (United States Centers for Disease Control and Prevention)
Chemical and Biological Detection Technologies

Hizballah (Party of God)

Hizballah (Party of God) (also operates as, or is known as: Islamic Jihad, Revolutionary Justice Organization, Organization of the Oppressed on Earth, and Islamic Jihad for the Liberation of Palestine) was formed in 1982 in response to the Israeli invasion of Lebanon. This Lebanon-based radical Shi'a group takes its ideological inspiration from the Iranian revolution and the teachings of the Ayatollah Khomeini. The Majlis al-Shura, or Consultative Council, is the group's highest governing body and is led by Secretary General Hassan Nasrallah. Hizballah formally advocates ultimate establishment of Islamic rule in Lebanon and liberating all occupied Arab lands, including Jerusalem. Hizballah has expressed as a goal the elimination of Israel. Hizballah has also expressed its unwillingness to work within the confines of Lebanon's established political system; however, this stance changed with the party's decision in 1992 to participate in parliamentary elections. Although closely allied with and often directed by Iran, the group may have conducted operations that were not approved by Tehran. While Hizballah does not share the Syrian regime's secular orientation, the group has been a strong tactical ally in helping Syria advance its political objectives in the region.

Organization activities. Hizballah is known or suspected to have been involved in numerous anti-U.S. terrorist attacks, including the suicide truck bombings of the U.S. Embassy in Beirut in April 1983, the U.S. Marine barracks in Beirut in October 1983, and the U.S. Embassy annex in Beirut in September 1984. Three members of Hizballah, 'Imad Mughniyah, Hasan Izz-al-Din, and Ali Atwa, have been on the FBI's list of the 22 most wanted terrorists for the hijacking in 1985 of TWA Flight 847 during which a U.S. Navy diver was murdered. Elements of Hizballah were responsible for the kidnapping and detention of U.S. and other Western hostages in Lebanon. The group also attacked the Israeli Embassy in Argentina in 1992 and is a suspect in the 1994 bombing of the Israeli cultural center in Buenos Aires. In fall 2000, it captured three Israeli soldiers in the Shabaa Farms and kidnapped an Israeli noncombatant whom it may have lured to Lebanon under false pretenses.

Hizballah is known to have several thousand supporters and a few hundred terrorist operatives operating in the Bekaa Valley, Hermil, the southern suburbs of Beirut, and southern Lebanon. They have established cells in Europe, Africa, South America, North America, and Asia.

Hizballah receives substantial amounts of financial, training, weapons, explosives, political, diplomatic, and organizational aid from Iran and received diplomatic, political, and logistical support from Syria.

■ FURTHER READING:

ELECTRONIC:

Central Intelligence Agency. World Factbook, 2002. <http://www.cia.gov/cia/publications/factbook/> (April 16, 2003).

Taylor, Francis X. U.S. Department of State. Patterns of Global Terrorism 2001, Annual Report: On the Record Briefing. May 21, 2002 <http://www.state.gov/s/ct/rls/rm/10367.htm> (April 17, 2003).

U.S. Department of State. Annual Reports. <http://www.state.gov/www/global/terrorism/annual_reports.html> (April 16, 2003).

SEE ALSO

Terrorism, Philosophical and Ideological Origins
Terrorist and Para-State Organizations
Terrorist Organization List, United States
Terrorist Organizations, Freezing of Assets

Holocaust Art Theft.

SEE *Archeology and Artifacts, Protection of during War.*

Homeland Security, United States Department of

■ JUDSON KNIGHT

The Department of Homeland Security (DHS) is a direct outgrowth of the terrorist attacks on September 11, 2001, which highlighted America's vulnerability to terrorism. Initiated by President George W. Bush as the Office of Homeland Security, the DHS became fully operational in 2003. The DHS incorporates several dozen offices and agencies, many of them previously assigned to other departments and some entirely new. They include the U.S. Coast Guard (USCG), U.S. Secret Service (USSS), Federal Emergency Management Agency (FEMA), Immigration and Naturalization Service (INS), and the newly created Transportation Security Administration (TSA). These and many other bureaus would be placed under, or work in tandem with, one of the five DHS directorates—Border and Transportation Security, Emergency Preparedness and Response, Science and Technology, Information Analysis and Infrastructure Protection, and Management—to fulfill the greater DHS mission of preventing, mitigating, and protecting against terrorism on U.S. soil.

Civil Defense and Homeland Security

Prior to September 11, 2001, what Americans now refer to as "homeland security"—protection of the nation, its people, its land, and its resources from attack—bore a different name: civil defense. The civil defense concept had its origins in World War II, when Americans organized local groups to prepare for and protect against the threat of Axis attack on American shores. This concept carried over into the Cold War, with a few changes; the enemy was now the Soviet Union, and the threat had the dimensions of nuclear annihilation.

In the early 1960s, the heyday of Cold War civil defense efforts, some American families built bomb shelters, and students practiced "duck and cover" maneuvers that would supposedly protect them in the event of a nuclear attack. A decade later, however, with the Cuban Missile

Homeland Security Director Tom Ridge addresses the Homeland Security Tech Expo at the Armory in Washington, D.C., in September 2002. Congress later approved President Bush's plan for a cabinet-level Department of Homeland Security to fight terrorism. AP/WIDE WORLD PHOTOS.

Crisis relegated to history and a new era of U.S.-Soviet détente emerging, use of these measures declined.

The end of the Cold War brought with it new dangers. The enemy was no longer the Soviet Union, a superpower with fairly predictable aims not entirely different from those of the United States. Instead, America faced terrorists whose motives were based upon political and religious zealotry with little regard for international laws, and were therefore more difficult to predict. The reality of the twenty-first century security environment manifested itself on the morning of September 11, 2001.

On October 8, less than four weeks after the attacks, President Bush issued Executive Order (E.O.) 13228 creating the Office of Homeland Security, along with the Homeland Security Council (whose members included the President, Vice President, and several Cabinet-level officials) as an advisory board. The order gave the office's director the title of Assistant to the President for Homeland Security, nomenclature that harkened to the official title of the National Security Advisor—thus highlighting the importance of the homeland security chief.

For the new position, Bush chose former Pennsylvania governor Tom Ridge, who was approved by the Senate in January 2003. Meanwhile, in November 2002, Congress passed the Homeland Security Act, legislation creating a permanent Cabinet-level department. On January 24, 2003, DHS began operation at its new headquarters at a former U.S. Navy facility, the Nebraska Avenue Center in Washington, D.C. Most agencies scheduled for transfer to the new department were officially moved in a special March 1, 2003, ceremony attended by the President.

In his initial proposal for the creation of DHS, President Bush noted that at that time, there were some 100 government agencies involved in emergency response. DHS would greatly streamline those activities; but before that could happen, a great deal of restructuring would have to occur. The initial appropriation request from the president to Congress was for nearly $40 billion, and many pundits judged that with the task before it, the new department would need every penny. The creation of DHS was the most fundamental change in the structure of government since the passage of the National Security Act, which created the Department of Defense in 1947.

DHS was scheduled to absorb 22 agencies from nine different departments (Agriculture, Commerce, Defense, Energy, Health and Human Services, Justice, State, Transportation, and Treasury) and two independent offices (FEMA and the General Services Administration, or GSA). With these would come 170,000 government employees, ranging from the men and women of the Coast Guard and Secret Service, to plant and animal health inspectors and computer security specialists.

DHS Framework

DHS has a threefold mission: to prevent terrorist attacks within the United States, to reduce America's vulnerability to terrorism, and to minimize the danger from potential attacks and natural disasters. In pursuing this mission, DHS works through its five directorates. In order to create these directorates, DHS established some new offices, but much of its framework came from existing ones, listed by the department from which they came:

Agriculture: Animal and Plant Health Inspection Service; Plum Island Animal Disease Center.

Commerce: Computer Security Division of the National Institute of Standards & Technology; Critical Infrastructure Assurance Office; National Hazard Information Strategy of the National Oceanic & Atmospheric Administration.

Defense: National Bio-Weapons Defense Center; National Communications System.

Energy: Environmental Measurements Laboratory; Lawrence Livermore National Laboratory; National Infrastructure Simulation & Analysis Center; National Nuclear Security Administration; Nuclear Incident Response; Oak Ridge National Laboratory; Office of Biological & Environmental Research; Office of Energy Assurance; Office of Security.

Health and Human Services: Metropolitan Medical Response System; National Pharmaceutical Stockpile Program; National Disaster Medical System/Office of Emergency Preparedness; Office of Health and Safety Information System.

Justice: Domestic Emergency Support Team; Executive Office for Immigration Review; INS; National Infrastructure Protection Center (except for the Computer Investigations and Operations Section, which would remain with the Federal Bureau of Investigation); National Domestic Preparedness Office; and Office of Domestic Preparedness.

State: Visa Services.

Transportation: USCG; TSA.

Treasury: Federal Law Enforcement Training Center (FLETC); USSS; Customs.

Additionally, DHS incorporated FEMA in its entirety, along with two GSA offices, the Computer Incident Response Center and the Office of Federal Protective Service.

The directorates. By far the largest component of DHS is the Directorate of Border and Transportation Security (BTS), which is responsible for maintaining the security of the nation's borders and transportation systems. BTS accounts for about 58% of DHS employees, along with nearly half of its operating budget, and includes what was formerly TSA, Customs, the border security functions of INS, the Animal and Plant Health Inspection Service, and FLETC. Like the other directorates of DHS, it is overseen by an undersecretary of homeland security.

Second in size is the Directorate of Emergency Preparedness and Response (EPR), which includes FEMA and numerous smaller agencies. EPR is charged with ensuring that the nation is prepared for and able to recover from both terrorist attacks and natural disasters. The Directorate of Science and Technology (S&T) is DHS's principal research and development arm. Among the areas of focus for S&T is the range of technology needed to prepare for and respond to terrorist threats involving weapons of mass destruction.

Information Analysis and Infrastructure Protection (IAIP) is the directorate concerned with the nation's critical infrastructure, particularly the computer systems that serve as the brain center for a modern industrialized superpower. IAIP brings together a number of specialists capable of identifying and assessing current and future threats to the homeland. Finally, the smallest and least visible directorate is Management, which is concerned with DHS internal affairs, including budget and personnel issues.

Independent agencies. In addition to the directorates, DHS includes a number of agencies that, while in some cases associated with specific directorates, nevertheless have an independent existence. Among these is the Coast Guard, which has a clear function in relation to border security but which, upon declaration of war or specific orders from the president, operates as an element of the Department of Defense. Secret Service is also an independent agency within DHS.

Other independent agencies include ones that did not exist as such prior to the establishment of DHS. These include the Bureau of Citizenship and Immigration Services, which assists the BTS directorate by easing the transition of immigrants to U.S. citizenship; the Office of State and Local Government Coordination; the Office of Private Sector Liaison, which works to foster dialogue between DHS and the business community; and the Office of Inspector General, an independent body responsible for inspection, auditing, and investigating charges of fraud, abuse, mismanagement, and waste.

DHS in action. Americans are likely to be most familiar with the DHS advisory system, whereby colors are equated with levels of threat. Green indicates low threat, and blue a "guarded condition" in which there is a general risk of terrorist attacks.

From the time the system was instituted through the spring of 2003, as the United States waged its military campaign in Iraq, the alert level never dipped below yellow, for "elevated condition," indicating a significant risk of terrorist attacks. On a few occasions it went above yellow and into orange, indicating a high threat of terrorist attacks. During that period, the threat level did not spike above orange to the most severe of conditions, red, though that color would have been used if the color-coded system had been in place at the time of the September 11 terrorist attacks.

On February 7, 2003, concerns about terrorist threats associated with an Islamic holiday caused a raise of the threat level to orange. Ridge encouraged Americans to stock up on food and water, as well as plastic sheeting and duct tape for sealing doors and windows. Ridge was criticized for what some observers described as scare mongering. On February 27, the threat level indicator again returned to yellow. When Ridge hiked it to orange again on March 18, 2003, at the beginning of the war with Iraq, such specific recommendations were not included with the warning; instead it was simply noted for Americans to be vigilant for multiple attempted attacks.

Mayors and governors commented on the fact that, while the DHS called upon cities and states to take extra preparedness measures, it did not provide adequate additional federal funding for such measures. In early April 2003, DHS announced that seven major cities would receive a total of $100 million to increase anti-terror security efforts.

■ **FURTHER READING:**

PERIODICALS:

Houston, Betsy. "Science and Technology Is Prominent in the Department of Homeland Security." *JOM* 55, no. 1 (January 2003): 9.

Hughes, David. "Homeland Security Dept.: So Many Details, So Little Time." *Aviation Week & Space Technology* 157, no. 23 (December 2, 2002): 71.

———. "Homeland Security Dept.: Is $36.2 Billion Enough?" *Aviation Week & Space Technology* 158, no. 7 (February 17, 2003): 57–58.

Huleatt, Richard S. "Computer Supersnoop: The New Department of Homeland Security." *Information Intelligence Online Newsletter* 23, no. 12 (December 2002): 2–4.

Inchniowski, Tom. "Ridge Will Face Big Challenges as Homeland Security Leader." *ENR* 250, no. 3 (January 27, 2003): 9.

Miller, Bill. "National Alert System Defines Five Shades of Terrorist Threat." *Washington Post.* (March 13, 2002): A15.

"The New Department of Homeland Security." *Chemical Engineering Progress* 99, no. 2 (February 2003): 25.

"U.S. Homeland Security: Behind the Curve in Funding and Commitment." *Aviation Week & Space Technology* 158, no. 9 (March 3, 2003): 66.

Waugh, William L., Jr., and Richard T. Sykes. "Organizing the War on Terrorism." *Public Administration Review* 62, special issue (September 2002): 145–153.

ELECTRONIC:

The American Civil Defense Association. <http://www.tacda.org/> (April 11, 2003).

Department of Homeland Security Reorganization. C-SPAN. <http://www.c-span.org/homelandsecurity/chart.asp> (April 11, 2003).

U.S. Department of Homeland Security. <http://www.dhs.gov/dhspublic/> (April 10, 2003).

SEE ALSO

Air Marshals, United States
Aviation Security Screeners, United States
Bush Administration (2001–), United States National Security Policy
Civil Aviation Security, United States
Coast Guard (USCG), United States
Communications System, United States National
Critical Infrastructure Assurance Office (CIAO), United States
DOE (United States Department of Energy)
Domestic Emergency Support Team, United States
Domestic Preparedness Office (NDPO), United States National
Federal Protective Service, United States
FEMA (United States Federal Emergency Management Agency)
General Services Administration, United States
Health and Human Services Department, United States
Infrastructure Protection Center (NIPC), United States National
INS (United States Immigration and Naturalization Service)
Law Enforcement Training Center (FLETC), United States Federal
Lawrence Livermore National Laboratory (LLNL)
NNSA (United States National Nuclear Security Administration)
NOAA (National Oceanic & Atmospheric Administration)
NSC (National Security Council)
NIST Computer Security Division, United States
Oak Ridge National Laboratory (ORNL)
Plum Island Animal Disease Center
Secret Service, United States
September 11 Terrorist Attacks on the United States
Transportation Department, United States

HUMINT (Human Intelligence)

Human intelligence, or HUMINT, is the gathering of information through human contact. It is, along with signals intelligence and imagery intelligence (SIGINT and IMINT respectively), one of the three traditional means of intelligence gathering. After the September 11, 2001, terrorist attacks, many observers in the United States decried previous cutbacks in HUMINT that had helped create an environment in which U.S. intelligence was largely unaware of the impending attacks.

The value of HUMINT. Whereas SIGINT, IMINT, and non-traditional measurement and signature intelligence (MASINT) are high-tech enterprises, HUMINT is decidedly low-tech. It is a matter, ultimately, of personal interaction, and practitioners of HUMINT are "spies" in the purest sense of the word. The more closely an operative functions in the community, the more his or her information comes from word of mouth, and the more he or she is practicing true HUMINT.

Simple though it may seem in comparison to the sophisticated electronic systems used in the other intelligence-gathering fields, HUMINT is a difficult method that requires precision. Humans are a far more difficult source from which to coax information than are electronic listening devices or cameras. Yet, the information that can come from human sources can be the most useful and up-to-date.

A hypothetical infiltrator. Terrorist groups may train in open-air camps whose activities are visible by satellite, but their most important work takes place beyond the reach of satellite photographic equipment. The visual and electronic evidence obtained from the Afghan training camps of the al-Qaeda terror network—the widely aired videotapes of training activities and speeches by leader Osama bin Laden—offered little in the way of concrete clues as to the group's plans for the devastation of September 11, 2001. Such information would likely have come only by close contact with al-Qaeda operatives on the part of personnel in contact with U.S. authorities.

Most likely, that undercover individual would have been an Arab national. Even though al-Qaeda and their Taliban hosts drew recruits from all over the world, including the United States, even an American of Arab descent would have most likely been under so much scrutiny that his job would have been impossible. Even if the United States had contact with an undercover operative in al-Qaeda circles prior to September 11, that person would probably have come from the same circles as other al-Qaeda members—a world of religious fundamentalists, terrorists, opium smugglers, and arms dealers. In other words, anyone the United States worked with in that situation was likely to be what most Americans would judge an unsavory character.

An example of such a figure is Ali Mohamed, a former Egyptian army officer who joined the U.S. Army in the 1980s, and trained U.S. Special Forces at Fort Bragg, North Carolina, on Islamic terrorism. Mohamed also served in an undercover capacity, infiltrating the al-Kifah Refugee Center in Brooklyn, New York, where he associated with terrorists. Mohamed later switched alliances, joining Osama bin Laden. Captured and arrested by U.S. authorities, Mohamed told them about al-Qaeda's plans to bomb two U.S. embassies in Africa—but he only divulged this information in 1999, a year after the bombings occurred.

Disgust with figures such as Ali Mohamed had led the administration of President William J. Clinton to adopt rules of human intelligence that many later blamed for the breaches that made attacks such as those of September 11, 2001, possible. On the heels of revelations that agents of the Central Intelligence Agency (CIA) in Guatemala had committed human rights violations, CIA general counsel Jeffrey H. Smith in 1995 drew up a set of guidelines intended to rid the agency of its association with disreputable characters. The rules prohibited the hiring of agents with records of human-rights violations, barred agents from posing as priests or journalists, and required local CIA recruiters to divulge the identities of recruits to agency headquarters.

Unintended consequences. Well-meaning though they may have been, these guidelines further eroded the intelligence-gathering capabilities of an agency whose roster of spies had already been badly reduced two decades earlier by the purges that followed the Church Committee hearings of the mid-1970s. The Iran-Contra scandal of the 1980s had further eroded support for CIA dealings with questionable figures overseas. In subsequent years, the agency had largely sought its intelligence as much as possible through photographic or electronic means.

■ **FURTHER READING:**

PERIODICALS:

Fialka, John J. "Aftermath of Terror: Rules for Hiring Agents Are Criticized as Hampering Spy Agencies' Recruiting." *Wall Street Journal.* (September 13, 2001): A13.

Jones, Jerry W. "CI and HUMINT or HUMINT and CI or CI/HUMINT or TAC HUMINT (Confusing, Isn't It?)" *Military Intelligence Professional Bulletin* 28, no. 2 (April-June 2002): 28–33.

Thomas, Evan. "The Road to September 11." *Newsweek.* (October 1, 2001): 38–49.

SEE ALSO

Church Committee
CIA, Formation and History
Iran-Contra Affair
Measurement and Signatures Intelligence (MASINT)

NIMA (National Imagery and Mapping Agency)
September 11 Terrorist Attacks on the United States
SIGINT (Signals Intelligence)

Hungary, Intelligence and Security

Part of the Empire of Austria-Hungary preceding World War I, Hungary gained its independence following the collapse of the imperial government in 1918. After World War II, the nation fell under the Soviet sphere of influence as a reluctant satellite nation. The Hungarian government endeavored to dissolve their participation in the Warsaw Pact and break ties with the Soviet Union in 1956. The action was met with Soviet military intervention in the region, and the establishment of a Soviet-influenced government.

During the Cold War, the Hungarian government maintained secret police forces and used intelligence services to conduct political espionage. Like other Soviet satellites, Hungary maintained a censorship state, but media and political controls were less strict than in many other communist nations. During the détente years of the 1980s, Hungary began to ease communist regulations, embarking on a program of democratic reforms before most other Warsaw Pact nations. With the collapse of the Soviet Union in 1991, Hungary expedited its ambitious reform plan. One of the first government functionaries to be reformed in post-communist Hungary was the nation's intelligence community.

The primary civilian intelligence organization in Hungary is the National Security Office (NBH). The NBH coordinated most intelligence operations in Hungary, including the gathering and processing of both domestic and foreign intelligence information. The NBH works closely with the National Security Services (NBSzSz) to protect national interests within Hungary's borders, and provide security services for Hungarian government personnel and diplomats at home and abroad. Civilian intelligence has recently focused on the identification and eradication of organized crime syndicates. Political espionage is expressly forbidden, and actions of security forces, including national police, are subject to government review as means of restoring citizen trust in national intelligence and security forces.

In addition to civilian organizations, Hungary maintains military intelligence forces, such as the Military Security Agency (KBH) and the Military Detection Agency (KFH). Though the daily operations of these agencies are classified, the mission of Hungarian military intelligence is identification and neutralization of foreign threats to national security. Military intelligence also conducts anti-terrorism and counterintelligence operations.

Hungary joined the North Atlantic Treaty Organization (NATO) in 1999. The country has petitioned to join the European Union (EU). Having already participated in European anti-terrorism, non-proliferation, and joint-intelligence operations, the Hungarian intelligence community continues to increase its technological and operational capabilities to better aid international, cooperative intelligence efforts.

■ FURTHER READING:

ELECTRONIC:

Central Intelligence Agency. The World Factbook, 2002. "Hungary."<http://www.cia.gov/cia/publications/factbook/geos/hu.html> (March 30, 2003).

SEE ALSO

Cold War (1945–1950): The Start of the Atomic Age
Cold War (1950–1972)
Cold War (1972–1989): The Collapse of the Soviet Union
European Union

Hydrophones.

SEE SOSUS (Sound Surveillance System).

Hypersonic Aircraft

A supersonic aircraft flies faster than Mach 1, or the speed of sound, whereas a hypersonic aircraft is a plane capable of flying at Mach 5, or five times the speed of sound. At sea-level atmospheric pressure, with air temperatures of 59°F (15°C), the speed of sound is about 760 miles per hour (1,225 kph). Hypersonic flight has been possible since the late 1950s, but before it can become practical, designers will have to address some of the physical challenges associated with ultra-high-speed flight.

The X-15. On October 14, 1947, Major Charles E. "Chuck" Yeager broke the sound barrier in a Bell XS–1 rocket-powered research plane. Five years later, in 1952, officials at the National Advisory Committee for Aeronautics (NACA) set out to develop a craft capable of hypersonic flight. That craft was the X–15, designed by North American Aviation. The X–15 debuted on October 15, 1958, and between June 8, 1959, and October 24, 1968, more than a dozen pilots in three X–15s flew 199 missions, successively passing Mach 3 (1960), Mach 4 and 5 (1961), and Mach 6 (1963).

Had the X–15 program continued, it might have provided the model, not only for hypersonic flight on Earth, but also for space flight. However, a number of circumstances brought an end to the program. One was a change in leadership as NACA, founded in 1917, gave way in 1958 to the National Aeronautics and Space Administration (NASA). Another change was the urgent political goal of beating the Soviets in the space race after the surprise launch of the *Sputnik* satellite in 1958. Desirous of putting the first man on the Moon, U.S. leaders bypassed the X–15 flight model in favor of rockets.

The X–15 was also challenged by the physical constraints of hypersonic flight. On October 3, 1967, pilot Peter Knight reached Mach 6.7, and nearly incinerated the tail of his craft. Six weeks later, on November 15, the inflight breakup of the third X–15 claimed the life of pilot Mike Adams. The X–15 made its final flight on October 24, 1968.

Other hypersonic studies. By the time the X–15 ceased operation, the United States had already developed two other extraordinary aircraft, the U2 and the SR–71. The latter, introduced in December 1964, was capable of attaining Mach 3—a speed that, while fast, was not hypersonic. During the early 1990s, the SR–71 was taken off-line for a few years due to the high cost of keeping it aloft, and this hiatus fanned reports that the U.S. Air Force (USAF) and Department of Defense (DOD) were developing a replacement.

Since 1979, there had been talk of this putative SR–71 successor, identified as "Aurora" by a code name accidentally included in a 1985 Pentagon budget request. However, the USAF and DOD repeatedly denied that they were developing a replacement for the SR–71, which went back into commission in 1995.

Research on hypersonic flight has continued, however. Aerospace engineers have promoted the concept of the HyperSoar hypersonic Global Range Recce/Strike Aircraft, which could attain speeds up to Mach 10 and carry a payload nearly twice as large as that of a subsonic craft. Flying at an altitude of approximately 130,000 feet (39,624 m), it would skip across the top layer of Earth's atmosphere like a rock skipping across the surface of water.

In June 2001, NASA tested the X–43A, a hypersonic craft with a special engine called a scramjet, which brought together features of both a conventional turbojet and a

An artist's rendition from the Institute of Future Space Transport at the University of Florida showing one concept for a future space vehicle that would take off and land like an airplane, yet travel at hypersonic speeds. AP/WIDE WORLD PHOTOS.

rocket. It was to be launched by a Pegasus rocket, but unfortunately the rocket failed during the test flight. NASA has continued to work on hypersonic craft, but before such planes can be made operational, engineers will have to develop a means of controlling temperatures so as to keep the craft from bursting into flame as it reenters the atmosphere.

■ FURTHER READING:

BOOKS:

Godwin, Robert. *X-15: The NASA Mission Reports, Incorporating Files from the USAF.* Burlington, Ontario: Apogee Books, 2000.

Henne, P. A. *Applied Computational Aerodynamics.* Washington, D.C.: American Institute of Aeronautics and Astronautics, 1990.

Noor, Ahmed Khairy, and Samuel L. Venneri. *Future Aeronautical and Space Systems.* Reston, VA: American Institute of Aeronautics and Astronautics, 1997.

PERIODICALS:

Grier, Peter. "Hypersonic Aircraft Test Fails." *Air Force Magazine* 84, no. 8 (August 2001): 17.

Leary, Warren E. "Test of Revolutionary Jet Promises to Transform Flight." *New York Times.* (May 22, 2001): F4.

ELECTRONIC:

Aurora/Senior Citizen. Federation of American Scientists. <http://www.fas.org/irp/mystery/aurora.htm> (March 4, 2003).

HyperSoar Hypersonic Global Range Recce/Strike Aircraft. Federation of American Scientists. <http://www.fas.org/man/dod-101/sys/ac/hypersoar.htm> (March 4, 2003).

X–15—Hypersonic Research at the Edge of Space. National Aeronautics and Space Administration. <http://www.hq.nasa.gov/office/pao/History/x15/cover.html> (March 4, 2003).

SEE ALSO

Photography, High-Altitude
U-2 Spy Plane

IBIS (Interagency Border Inspection System)

∎ K. LEE LERNER

The Interagency Border Inspection System (IBIS) is a database of names and other identifying information used to deter and apprehend suspects—including suspected terrorists—as they attempt to pass through international border crossing checkpoints.

IBIS provides a rapid means to link names with other identifying information such as passport or credit card numbers. IBIS data is intended for easy crosschecking with other databases such as the FBI's National Crime Information Center (NCIC) database and state-level National Law Enforcement Telecommunications Systems (NLETS) databases.

The IBIS database is also used by more than twenty federal investigative agencies and, following the terrorist attacks on the United States in September 2001, elements of IBIS name-recognition technology are finding increased usage by the FAA and private security companies (principally companies serving airlines and insurance agencies) wishing to identify suspected terrorists. For example, all airlines operating within United States airspace must crosscheck passenger and crew lists against IBIS.

As of March 1, 2003, the newly created United States Department of Homeland Security (DHS) absorbed the former Immigration and Naturalization Service (INS). All INS border patrol agents and investigators—along with agents from the U.S. Customs Service and the Transportation Security Administration—were placed under the direction of the DHS Directorate of Border and Transportation Security (BTS). Responsibility for U.S. border security and the enforcement of immigration laws was transferred to BTS.

BTS is scheduled to incorporate the United States Customs Service (previously part of the Department of Treasury), the enforcement division of the Immigration and Naturalization Service (previously part of the Department of Justice), the Animal and Plant Health Inspection Service (previously part of the Department of Agriculture), the Federal Law Enforcement Training Center (previously part of the Department of Treasury), Transportation Security Administration (previously part of the Department of Transportation) and the Federal Protective Service (previously part of the General Services Administration).

Former INS immigration service functions are scheduled to be placed under the direction of the DHS Bureau of Citizenship and Immigration Services. Under the reorganization the INS and other absorbed agencies will formally cease to exist on the date the last of their functions are transferred.

Although the IBIS database is scheduled to continue, in an effort to facilitate border security, BTS plans call for higher levels of coordination between formerly separate agencies and databases. As of April 2003, the specific coordination and future of the IBIS program was uncertain with regard to name changes, database custody, and policy changes.

Prior to integration of INS and Customs service functions into DHS, IBIS was used and maintained principally by those two agencies. Other United States law enforcement and regulatory bodies that utilize IBIS data and technology include the CIA, NSA, FBI, Secret Service, and Coast Guard. International agencies such as Interpol also contribute to and use the IBIS database. Regular updates to lists of names of persons prohibited from entering the United States, criminal suspects, or individuals sought for questioning are provided from a global network of Consular Officers at U.S. embassies and consulates managed by the Department of State.

In addition to attempting to identify terrorists, IBIS is also a key component in attempts by the DEA to deter drug trafficking and ATF attempts to regulate arms shipments. A number of other agencies such as the Internal Revenue

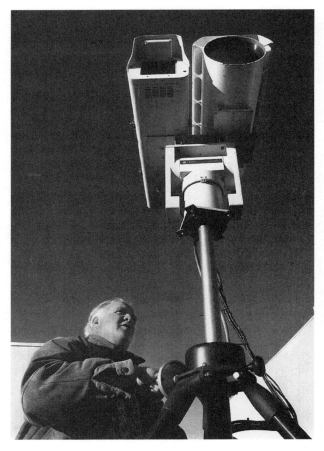

An electronics technician for the U.S. Border Patrol uses a crank to manually turn two surveillance cameras, a thermo imager, right, and a daytime camera, left. AP/WIDE WORLD PHOTOS.

Service (IRS) and Animal Plant Health Inspection Service utilize IBIS to identify individuals suspected of offenses within their respective agency jurisdictions. IBIS is also designed to facilitate identification of vehicles, aircraft, and vessels.

Proponents of the IBIS system argue that the system allows the majority of individuals seeking to cross the border for legitimate purposes to do so in a rapid, uncomplicated manner. Rather than subjecting every individual to what would be a lengthy wait while lists of names from various agencies are checked, IBIS permits a simpler, quicker, and more secure clearance procedure.

In an effort to enhance accuracy, IBIS technology incorporates language analysis software (e.g., name recognition software) and specialized search tools. One goal of name recognition software is to provide a mechanism to correct faulty transliteration of names (e.g. the erroneous translation of an Arabic name into English). Errors common to transliteration—especially oral to written transliterations—include faulty phonetic assignment of letters to unfamiliar ethnic sounds, faulty fusion of syllables (e.g., a fusion of parts of a name such as a given name

with a family name), and faulty assignment of parts of names to specified fields in the input sequence of analysis programs. For example, in some European based languages "van" or "von" is most often a surname prefix but in some Asiatic languages "Van" is most often a surname. Some Arabic names, for example, may be commonly translated into more than thirty different English spellings or variations from the single form found in Arabic.

In standard database searches, if a name entered does not match the spelling or form of a name originally entered in a database, matching the names may be impossible. Standard database search techniques such as key-searches that attempt to match character strings (e.g., specific combinations of letters) often provide erroneous results based upon input errors that occur either during the checking procedure or when a name was originally loaded into the database. More complex search protocols utilize so-called fuzzy logic subroutines that look for similarities and patterns in character strings while allowing for some degree of variation. Fuzzy logic based database search programs allow search protocols to check for common errors, and provide enhanced accuracy to search routines.

The great number of languages and ethnic variations of spellings, however, requires specialized name recognition software. As of 2003, a company under contract to the U.S. government , Virginia based Language Analysis Systems, was developing programs with search components designed to facilitate the identification of the cultural origins of names and terms. Other techniques include protocols that analyze data for specific errors. Other companies have developed programs that apply multiple prefixes and suffixes to input names, use multiple phonetic spellings, translate spellings into various foreign alphabets, and employ result-ranking schemes to enhance search results.

Such name recognition software will play a critical role in linking often dissimilar databases maintained by separate agencies and such "smart" search protocols will be essential in achieving efficiency and accuracy in the new Department of Homeland Security. For example, IBIS combined with the INS Advance Passenger Information System (APIS), allows immigration and customs inspectors to use a single input screen to make a joint search. Other systems targeted for database interface include the FAA Computer Assisted Passenger Screening System (CAPS).

■ FURTHER READING:

ELECTRONIC:

Bureau of Citizenship and Immigration Services. INSPASS. March 1, 2003. <http://www.immigration.gov/graphics/howdoi/inspassloc.htm> (April 14, 2003).

Department of Homeland Security. April 2, 2003. <http://www.dhs.gov/dhspublic/index.jsp> (April 11, 2003).

United States Department of Homeland Security. Bureau of Citizenship and Immigration Services, PORTPASS. March 11, 2003. <http://www.immigration.gov/graphics/howdoi/portpass.htm> (April 9, 2003).

United States Department of Homeland Security. Immigration Information, INSPASS. March 4, 2003. <http://www.immigration.gov/graphics/shared/howdoi/inspass.htm> (April 9, 2003).

SEE ALSO

APIS (Advance Passenger Information System)
IDENT (Automated Biometric Identification System)
INSPASS (Immigration and Naturalization Service Passenger Accelerated Service System)
NAILS (National Automated Immigration Lookout System)
PORTPASS (Port Passenger Accelerated Service System)
SENTRI (Secure Electronic Network for Travelers' Rapid Inspection)

IDENT (Automated Biometric Identification System)

The Automated Biometric Identification System (IDENT) is a database system using automated fingerprint identification systems (AFIS) technology as part of programs supervised by the U.S. Department of Homeland Security that intend to thwart illegal entry into the United States by criminal aliens.

IDENT was implemented on a trial basis in 1994 and put into wide use by 1998. In August 1998, INS IDENT mangers established standardized policies on the use of IDENT but for financial reasons decided not to include historical data in the IDENT database. Accordingly, IDENT queries were limited to returns of data acquired since IDENT implementation. By 1999, approximately 1.8 million biometrics were keyed into the IDENT "recidivist" (repeat offender) database.

The IDENT system biometrics includes photos and the two index finger fingerprints (entered via a portable TouchView fingerprint reader) of individuals previously apprehended by border and immigration agents. That data is augmented by available data on the individual's criminal history. With this data IDENT provides access to both a recidivist database and a "lookout" database for criminal offenders.

IDENT fingerprint searches of the two databases normally takes only a few minutes. IDENT fingerprint matching is based upon a numerical score derived from degrees of relationship in standard fingerprint characteristics. An IDENT terminal then provides agents with photographs and fingerprint displays of individuals under examination alongside photographs and fingerprints of potential matches. This final visual matching is key because, especially under field conditions, fingerprint analysis is often hampered by dirt on the alien's fingers or the scanner.

Records are ultimately linked to a unique fingerprint identification number (FIN) for each alien. The IDENT fingerprinting technology does not require ink, but uses a machine that scans and digitizes prints before transferring them to a standard ten-print card and storing them in the electronic database.

Use of the IDENT system is critical because studies have shown that apprehended illegal aliens often attempt to falsify their identity by providing a fictitious name and/or a birthdate. As of March 2003, the IDENT database contained records on more than 400,000 aliens who had a history of attempted illegal entry and a criminal history that precluded their entry into the U.S. Prior to DHS reorganization, INS and Border Patrol agents had detained more than 75,000 individuals based on IDENT data.

The IDENT system can also provide basic identification information that allows access to several other security and law enforcement databases including, but not limited to, the Central Index System (CIS), National Automated Immigration Lookout System II (NAILS), Deportable Alien Control System (DACS), National Crime Information Center (NCIC) database, and the Treasury Enforcement Communication System (TECS). Under pending security proposals the IDENT database and system may be fused with the Integrated Automated Fingerprint Identification System (IAFIS) used by the FBI.

As of March 1, 2003, the newly created United States Department of Homeland Security (DHS) absorbed the former Immigration and Naturalization Service (INS). All INS border patrol agents and investigators—along with agents from the U.S. Customs Service and Transportation Security Administration—were placed under the direction of the DHS Directorate of Border and Transportation Security (BTS). Responsibility for U.S. border security and the enforcement of immigration laws was transferred to BTS.

BTS is scheduled to incorporate the United States Customs Service (previously part of the Department of Treasury), and the enforcement division of the Immigration and Naturalization Service (previously part of the Department of Justice). Former INS immigration service functions are scheduled to be placed under the direction of the DHS Bureau of Citizenship and Immigration Services. Under the reorganization the INS formally ceases to exist on the date the last of its functions are transferred.

Although the technologies involved in the IDENT entry security program remained stable, in an effort to facilitate border security, BTS plans to establish higher levels of coordination between formerly separate agencies and databases. As of April 2003, the specific coordination and future of the IDENT program was uncertain with regard to name changes, program administration, and policy changes.

■ FURTHER READING:

ELECTRONIC:

Department of Homeland Security. April 2, 2003. <http://www.dhs.gov/dhspublic/index.jsp> (April 11, 2003).

Department of Homeland Security, Bureau of Citizenship and Immigration Services. Law Enforcement: The National Border Patrol Strategy. <http://www.immigration.gov/graphics/publicaffairs/statements/igstate.htm> (April 12, 2003).

SEE ALSO

APIS (Advance Passenger Information System)
IBIS (Interagency Border Inspection System)
INSPASS (Immigration and Naturalization Service Passenger Accelerated Service System)
NAILS (National Automated Immigration Lookout System)
PORTPASS (Port Passenger Accelerated Service System)
SENTRI (Secure Electronic Network for Travelers' Rapid Inspection)

Identity Theft

■ KELLI A. MILLER

Identity theft is among the fastest growing crimes in America. A thief typically steals someone's identity, opens checking and credit card accounts in that person's name, then goes on a spending spree. The rate of identity theft or identity fraud had so escalated in the late 1990s that the Social Security Administration declared it a national crisis.

Identity theft is the most popular—and most profitable—form of consumer fraud. It encompasses all types of crime in which someone illegally obtains and fraudulently uses another person's confidential information, most often for financial gain. A person's Social Security number is valuable to an identity thief. Armed with the Social Security number, a criminal can open a bank account or credit card account, apply for a loan, and remove funds from varying financial accounts. In some cases, criminals have assumed the victim's identity altogether, amassing debt and committing crimes that become a part of the victim's criminal record.

The identity trail. Advanced computer and telecommunication technologies have armed thieves with new ways to obtain large amounts of personal data from afar. Hackers can spy on e-mail and Internet users, silently stealing passwords or banking information. Old-fashioned concepts such as "dumpster diving" still prevail. Thieves sort through garbage for telltale signs of identity such as

Associated Press reporter Nedra Pickler displays the unauthorized credit card bills charged to her name in 2002 after she became the victim of identity theft, a growing crime. In a matter of a week, thieves charged $30,000 worth of merchandise on credit cards obtained using her identity. AP/WIDE WORLD PHOTOS.

cleared checks, bank statements, even junk mail, such as "preapproved" credit cards.

Other criminal tactics include "shoulder surfing" and "skimming." A "shoulder surfing" criminal spies on someone as they type in a Pin number or password at an automatic teller machine (ATM). "Skimming," one of the newest schemes, occurs when a cashier receives a credit card for a purchase, then unknown to the victim, swipes it through a portable device that records the card information.

Consumer advocates estimate that 750,000 people will become victims of identity fraud every year. The statistic is a startling difference from numbers logged just a decade ago. In 1992, the credit reporting agency TransUnion logged about 35,000 identity theft complaints. A decade later, the company received more than a million calls.

Measures can be taken to minimize the risk of identity theft. Security experts recommend carrying a limited number of ID cards and credit cards, signing all new credit cards immediately with permanent ink, steering clear from unsecured Internet sites, and never writing a PIN, password, or Social Security number on credit cards or in briefcases or wallets. Cashiers should be observed as they process an order and personal or account information should not be revealed to anyone without first verifying their identity. Other tips include creating passwords that are not obvious (i.e., do not use birth dates) and checking credit reports periodically for accuracy.

Identity theft affidavit. In many cases, the victim may not realize their identity has been stolen until a negative situation arises. When the crime is finally discovered, the victim must provide proof that they did not create the debt themselves. This involves a laborious process of contacting each and every company where accounts were fraudulently opened. Persons whose identities have been stolen can spend months, even years, remedying the problem. To reduce the burden, the government established the ID Theft Affidavit, a single form that alerts all participating companies about the crime. A number of financial organizations, including the top three credit reporting agencies, endorse the ID Theft Affidavit.

According to the U.S. Federal Trade Commission (FTC) and U.S. General Accounting Office (GAO), the average victim spends anywhere from $1,000 to over $10,000 per incident of identity theft or fraud to reclaim and reestablish identity and credit. Victims of identity fraud should notify all three national credit reporting agencies (Equifax, Experian, TransUnion) immediately and request that their files be flagged with a fraud alert. The crime should also be reported to the police and the FTC, and in some cases, the Social Security Administration, Department of Motor Vehicles, and the U.S. Post Office.

Identity Theft and Assumption Deterrence Act. The threat to privacy has prompted a number of new laws governing fraud. In 1998, Congress passed the Identity Theft and Assumption Deterrence Act. The legislation created a new offense of identity theft, making it a separate crime against the person whose identity was stolen. Prior to this legislation, identity theft was considered a crime only against the company the victim defrauded. Under the Federal identity theft act, it is a crime for any person to "knowingly transfer[ring] or use[ing], without lawful authority, a means of identification of another person with the intent to commit, or to aid or abet, any unlawful activity that constitutes a violation of Federal law, or that constitutes a felony under any applicable State or local law." Violators face a maximum term of 15 years in prison, a fine, and criminal forfeiture of any personal property used or intended to be used to commit the offense.

ID thieves are often charged with other violations, including credit card fraud, computer fraud, and mail fraud. These felonies can carry substantial penalties and up to 30 years' imprisonment. The Federal Bureau of Investigation (FBI), the United States Secret Service, and the United States Postal Inspection Service help prosecute identity theft cases. Many states have also enacted legislation regarding identity theft. Arizona led the way with a specific identity theft statute passed in 1996. As the crime's serious threat became evident, more states followed suit. In 1999, 22 states passed identity theft legislation. According to a GAO 2002 report, identity theft can be a felony offense in 45 of the 49 states that have laws to address the problem. Two years after the passage of the federal identity theft act, the Justice Department testified that it had used the statute in 92 cases, according to a GAO report.

The Identity Theft and Assumption Deterrence Act required the FTC to "log and acknowledge the receipt of complaints by individuals who certify that they have a reasonable belief" that someone stole their identity. The act enabled the creation of the Identity Theft Data Clearinghouse, a federal database for tracking complaints. Consumers call a toll-free hotline (1–877-ID-THEFT) to enter their complaint, and have the option to do so anonymously. When established in 1999, the FTC logged about 260 calls per week. In December 2001, the hotline was receiving more than 3,000 contacts a week.

Identity fraud complaints and related information are shared electronically between the FTC and other law enforcement agencies nationwide via the Consumer Sentinel Network, a secure, encrypted website. The network was initially set up in 1997 as a way of tracking telemarketing scams. As of May 2002, 46 federal law enforcement agencies and over 18,000 state and local departments had enrolled in the FTC's Consumer Sentinel Network collaboration. Accessing the Network allows police to analyze identity theft cases and determine if there is a larger pattern of crime. At this time, comprehensive results involving the number of cases prosecuted under the federal identity theft act and state statutes are not available.

■ FURTHER READING:

ELECTRONIC:

Federal Trade Commission. "ID Theft: When Bad Things Happen to Good People." September 2002. <http://www.ftc.gov/bcp/conline/pubs/credit/idtheft.htm#occurs> (December 11, 2002).

Federal Trade Commission. "Identity Theft." August 7, 2002. <http://www.consumer.gov/idtheft/>(December 01, 2002).

Georgia Stop Identity Theft. "What is Identity Theft?" 2002. <http://www.stopidentitytheft.org/prevention.html#what>(December 01, 2002).

ID Theft Resource Center. "ID Theft." October 28, 2002. <http://www.idtheftcenter.org/.> (December 01, 2002).

SEE ALSO

Computer Fraud and Abuse Act of 1986
FBI (United States Federal Bureau of Investigation)
Justice Department, United States

Postal Security
Postal Service (USPS), United States
Secret Service, United States

IFF (Identification Friend or Foe)

Identification friend or foe (IFF) systems are methods of identifying aircraft using electronic means. Applied by both military and civilian entities, IFF—which in its civilian form is more properly known as the air traffic control radar beacon system, or ATCRBS—uses radar to identify aircraft, which are assigned unique identifier codes. There are various modes of operation for IFF, depending on the level of security desired.

Challenge and response. In World War II, as radar was emerging, Allied aviators and ground controllers soon became aware of a shortcoming in the existing electronic identification system; radar could only recognize that a plane was in the sky, but could not differentiate friendly planes from those of the Axis. The Germans were the first to develop a crude IFF system, which required pilots to roll their planes in midflight as a means of creating a distinctive radar blip that would identify them as Luftwaffe craft to radar operators. The Allies developed their own active systems: first Mk I in 1940, and later the much more effective Mk III, which greatly enhanced identification technology by adding a separate transmitter that tuned through radar bands even as the receiver in the air did the same. Mk III also was made to respond to as many as six different codes.

From the beginning, IFF was a system of challenge and response, operating on much the same principal as a guard demanding a password before allowing entrance. In the case of IFF, the radar on the ground (the interrogator) transmits on one frequency, and receives a coded signal from the plane's transponder on another frequency. In the United States, these transmissions typically take place at 1030 megahertz (MHz) for challenges, and 1090 MHz for replies.

Security and modes of operation. There are several modes of operation, as well as an important submode, relating to levels of security in military IFF operation. Mode 1, for instance, is a nonsecure, low-cost mode used by ships to track aircraft and other ships, while Mode 2 is used by aircraft making carrier-controlled approaches to ships during times of inclement weather.

Commercial aircraft chiefly use Mode 3, the standard system by which they relay positions to ground controllers across the globe. The Federal Aviation Administration (FAA) requires that all aircraft, military or civilian, that fly at 10,000 feet or higher must be equipped with working IFF transponder systems capable of reporting altitude. To do so requires Mode C, a submode that automatically includes an altitude report.

At the highest security level is Mode 4, the only true IFF system, as opposed to a mere means of differentiating obviously friendly aircraft in order to enable greater control of traffic from the ground. This mode, used on warfighting planes, utilizes sophisticated encryption that includes a long challenge word with a preamble to inform the transponder that it is about to receive a secure message. If the plane's transponder is incapable of deciphering the challenge, it effectively identifies the aircraft as something other than a friend. Key codes are periodically changed and reentered into transponders and interrogators so as to ensure the continued security of codes.

■ **FURTHER READING:**

BOOKS:

Launius, Roger D. *Innovation and the Development of Flight.* College Station: Texas A&M University Press, 1999.

Murray, Williamson, and Allan Reed Millett. *Military Innovation in the Interwar Period.* New York: Cambridge University Press, 1996.

Rihaczek, August W., and Stephen J. Hershkowitz. *Theory and Practice of Radar Target Identification.* Boston: Artech House, 2000.

ELECTRONIC:

Identification Friend or Foe (IFF) Systems. 551st and 552nd AEW&C Wings, U.S. Air Force. <http://www.dean-boys.com/extras/iff/iffqa.html> (March 16, 2003).

SEE ALSO

Codes and Ciphers
Electromagnetic Spectrum
FAA (United States Federal Aviation Administration)
RADAR
Radio, Direction Finding Equipment

Imbedding.

SEE *Steganography.*

IMF (International Monetary Fund)

■ STEPHANIE WATSON

The International Monetary Fund (IMF) is an economic organization that promotes financial cooperation, economic stability, and fair trade among its 184 member nations and provides temporary monetary assistance to countries in need.

In its role as global economic watchdog, the IMF must continually keep an eye out for illegal activities. Following the events of September 11, 2001, that role took on an even greater urgency. Since then, the organization has launched a global effort to combat money laundering and to cut off funding to terrorist groups.

The need for a new world economic order. In the early 1940s, the world was still reeling from the financial turmoil of the Great Depression. As markets in the United States and around the world collapsed, countries sought to protect their weakened economies by closing their doors to foreign imports and restricting their citizens from making purchases abroad. The result was catastrophic; world trade nearly ground to a halt. In order to protect the world economy from suffering another similar blow, and to hasten financial recovery among war-torn nations, leaders from forty-five countries came together during the summer of 1944; their historic meeting in Bretton Woods, New Hampshire, established a new international system of economic collaboration called the IMF. The Bretton Woods Conference also launched the IMF's sister organization, the International Bank for Reconstruction and Development (IBRD), or World Bank. On December 27, 1945, representatives from twenty-nine member nations signed the Articles of Agreement, formally bringing the IMF into existence. The initial goals of the organization were to expand international trade, and to protect the stability of international currencies and exchange rates.

The IMF today. The IMF currently has three main responsibilities: surveillance, financial assistance, and technical assistance. The IMF keeps a watchful eye over its member nations throughout the year, monitoring each country's exchange rate and economic policies to protect the stability of the world economy. All member countries are entitled to financial assistance to help them recover from an economic crisis or to pay off foreign debt. By 2003, the IMF had about $88 billion in outstanding loans to eighty-eight nations. Because strategies of the IMF hold that one of the keys to worldwide economic stability is financial self-sufficiency, it has programs in place to teach countries how to plan and implement their own monetary, tax, and exchange rate policies.

With the increasing trend toward globalization (the merging of international markets), the IMF has turned its focus to emerging markets such as Asia and Latin America. By supporting economic growth and fostering the development of stable financial systems in these nations, the IMF hopes to avert an international financial crisis such as the worldwide depression of the late 1920s and 1930s, and to further strengthen the world economy.

Today, the IMF is headquartered in Washington, D.C., and staffed by a team of more than 2,500 people from

nearly 140 countries. At the helm is the Board of Governors, composed of banking leaders and ministers of finance from each member country. The Board of Governors comes together once a year at the IMF-World Bank meeting, but much of the substantial operations are carried out by the twenty-four Executive Directors of the Executive Board. The Managing Director of the IMF serves as Chairman of the Executive Board. Corresponding to each Executive Director is one Governor from the International Monetary and Financial Committee (IMFC). This committee meets twice a year to advise the IMF on issues related to the international monetary system.

A country's voting power is based on the size of its economy and on the amount of the quota (subscription fee) it pays when it joins the IMF, however most decisions are based on a member consensus, rather than on a vote. The United States has the largest quota, contributing nearly 18% of the IMF's total funding.

■ **FURTHER READING:**

BOOKS:

Danaher, Kevin, ed. *Fifty Years is Enough: The Case Against the World Bank and the International Monetary Fund.* Cambridge, MA: South End Press, 1994.
Harper, Richard H.R. *Inside the IMF.* San Diego, CA: Academic Press, 1998.
Stiglitz, Joseph E. *Globalization and its Discontents.* New York: W.W. Norton & Co., 2002.

PERIODICALS:

Garritsen De Vries, Margaret. "The IMF Fifty Years Later." *Finance & Development* June 1995: 43—47.

ELECTRONIC:

The International Monetary Fund. <http://www.imf.org> (January 31, 2003).

SEE ALSO

Federal Reserve System, United States
National Telecommunications Information Administration, and Security for the Radio Frequency Spectrum, United States
Terrorist Organizations, Freezing of Assets

IMINT (Imagery Intelligence)

IMINT, or imagery intelligence, is one of the four major branches of intelligence, along with HUMINT, MASINT, and SIGINT (human, measurement and signatures, and signals intelligence respectively). Formerly known as photographic intelligence, or PHOTINT, IMINT is derived from photography, infrared sensors, synthetic aperture radar, and other forms of imaging technology. It was this wealth of imagery sources and techniques that influenced the shift in terminology from PHOTINT to IMINT during the 1970s.

Collection platforms for IMINT have ranged from surveillance balloons, employed from the time of the French Revolution onward, to satellites such as those of the KH or KEYHOLE series. In addition to KEYHOLE, CORONA, and other satellite systems employed by U.S. intelligence, there are satellites that are not obviously tasked for intelligence gathering. Aircraft, both manned and unmanned, have long served in the mission of gathering IMINT. These range from the B-17 Flying Fortress of World War II to the U-2, in use since the 1950s, to Pioneer Unmanned Aerial Vehicles used in the Persian Gulf War.

Once gathered, imagery has to be transmitted to processing centers, most of which are in Washington, D.C. Technicians at the National Photographic Interpretation Center (NPIC), the National Imagery and Mapping Agency (NIMA), and other such units are highly skilled at studying photographs taken from high altitudes or from space. From these images, many of which would be extremely difficult for the layperson to interpret in even the most basic sense, imagery technicians can discern information on the movement of troops and materiel, or other enemy activities.

■ FURTHER READING:

BOOKS:

Imagery Intelligence. Washington, D.C.: Department of the Army, 1996.

Krepon, Michael. Commercial Observation Satellites and International Security. New York: St. Martin's, 1990.

Richelson, Jeffrey T. The U.S. Intelligence Community, fourth edition. Boulder, CO: Westview Press, 1999.

ELECTRONIC:

Imagery Intelligence. Federation of American Scientists. <http://www.fas.org/irp/imint/> (April 3, 2003).

SEE ALSO

Balloon Reconnaissance, History
Geospatial Imagery
NIMA (National Imagery and Mapping Agency)
Persian Gulf War
Photographic Interpretation Center (NPIC), United States National
Photography, High-Altitude
Satellites, Spy
U-2 Spy Plane
Vietnam War

India, Intelligence and Security

Espionage and intelligence appears in the recorded history of the Indus Valley as early as the fifth century.

The modern nation of India gained its independence from Britain in 1947. The withdrawal of the British colonial government left India with little governmental infrastructure, and the nation embarked on an ambitious plan to create a new national government. Indian independence, however, also sparked resistance from ethnic groups on the Indian Subcontinent, such as the large Muslim community. As a result of the developing conflict, India quickly established military and intelligence forces.

India's intelligence community is divided into a traditional structure that separates military and civilian, and foreign and domestic intelligence. Though each agency is charged with its own mission, the government has provided a means to facilitate the sharing of information between members of the intelligence community. The Joint Intelligence Committee (JIC) processes and analyzes data gathered by both civilian and military intelligence agencies and coordinates joint operations. The National Security Council acts as liaison between the government's executive branch and the intelligence services, advising leadership on intelligence and security issues.

The main civilian intelligence agency in India is the Intelligence Bureau (IB). The IB focuses on domestic intelligence, but the exact structure and operations of the agency are largely unknown. Political espionage is illegal in India, and police gathered wiretapping information is inadmissible as evidence in court proceedings. However, the IB conducts regular electronic monitoring of telephone communications, and mail surveillance, despite occasional admonitions from Parliament. The Central Bureau of Investigations handles most criminal investigations, often acting on initial information provided by one of the IB's many departments. Increasing political tensions with neighboring Pakistan altered the focus of IB operations in recent years, with increasing attention paid to the protection and surveillance of national borders.

The Research and Analysis Wing (RAW) is India's primary agency responsible for foreign intelligence. RAW operations are largely focused on espionage against Pakistan. With the addition of both India and Pakistan to the growing cadre of the world's nuclear powers, India's RAW conducts counter-intelligence operations, as well as technological and remote espionage, against Pakistani defense and military interests. The RAW is not subject to Parliamentary review, and its actions are highly secret. The Indian government also used RAW resources to aid predominantly-Hindu Bangladesh's 1971 quest for independence from Muslim Pakistan. Most recently, the RAW aided international antiterrorism efforts by providing the United States and British governments information on the al-Qaeda terrorist network and its strongholds in Pakistan and Afghanistan.

Military intelligence is conducted by the Army Directorate of Military Intelligence. The agency is the weakest of India's intelligence community, but often aids civilian intelligence operations. The Army also maintains the Joint Cipher Bureau, the main code breaking department of Indian intelligence.

Three blindfolded men accused of working for India's intelligence agency and plotting to sabotage Pakistan's 2002 parliamentary elections are presented to the press in Rawalpindi, Pakistan. AP/WIDE WORLD PHOTOS.

To the northwest, the independent Muslim nation of Pakistan claims the Kashmir region of India. The two nations have never resolved the border dispute, and tensions recently reached a climax when both nations declared themselves nuclear powers and began testing weapons of mass destruction. The nuclear programs of India and Pakistan raise interesting questions about the efficacy of current non-proliferation measures and the increasing global prevalence of industrial and scientific espionage. The increasing instability of the region has aroused the concern of the international community and the United Nations Security Council.

■ FURTHER READING:

PERIODICALS:

Ramana, M.V., et al. "India, Pakistan, and the Bomb." *Scientific American.* December 2001.

SEE ALSO

Great Game

Indonesia, Intelligence and Security

Once the Netherlands's colonial stronghold in the Asian Pacific region, Indonesia gained its independence in 1949. The nation fell under military-influenced authoritarian rule for four decades, but began the transition to demilitarized, popular government in 1985. Since that time, the archipelago nation has strived to flourish despite persistent problems such as growing poverty, tribal and ethnic tensions, territorial disputes, government corruption, and political turmoil. Despite these issues, the government has taken crucial steps to reform and rebuild the nation's intelligence and security communities.

The Indonesian president and the commander of the armed forces administer the Council for the Enforcement of Security and the Law (DPKN) . The council is composed of representatives from the nation's government ministries and five main religious councils. DPKN coordinates intelligence and security force responses to national security threats, utilizing the resources of both military and civilian agencies.

Indonesia has several small civilian intelligence agencies responsible for specific security functions, such as counterintelligence, antiterrorism efforts, government protective services, and media relations. These operational divisions are largely autonomous, but work under the limited direction and coordination of the largest civilian agency, the State Intelligence Coordinating Agency (BAKIN). BAKIN focuses mainly on domestic intelligence information, especially information regarding national defenses.

Another government agency, the Coordinating Agency for National Stability (BAKORSTANAS), combines intelligence and law enforcement activities. The agency is tasked with ferreting out anti-government organizations in Indonesia. However, BAKORSTANAS has few legal limitations on its operations, often detaining and interrogating political dissidents. The agency is under suspicion of human rights violations from several international humanitarian organizations. International criticism prompted the Indonesian government to reform some of the sub-departments of the agency. BAKORSTANAS gained the ability to intervene in social conflicts such as strikes and worker's disputes, but reforms also limited its powers to control action forces without government consent.

Indonesia maintains a three-branch military, including an army, navy, and air force. Each branch of service employs its own strategic intelligence forces within its operations units. BAIS is the nation's main military intelligence agency, and as such oversees and coordinates the efforts of various military intelligence forces. Indonesian military intelligence focuses on foreign intelligence information, especially that garnered from communications surveillance. In recent years, the Indonesian government has made the actions of military intelligence agencies more directly responsible to the DPKN in order to gauge political sentiment within the military and prevent the rise of insurgent groups.

One of the most pressing political and security problems plaguing the Indonesian government was resolved in 2002. In August 1999, the Timor region approved a referendum for independence. After garnering international criticism for their policies and actions regarding Timor, the Indonesian government agreed to the region's appeal for sovereignty. On May 20, 2002, the international community recognized the region, now called East Timor, as an independent state.

Reforms continue to address international concerns of past human rights violations by Indonesia's military and former regime. The nation also embarked on ambitious banking and finance reforms to meet International Monetary Fund (IMF) standards. Despite progress in changing the nation's infrastructure to increase Indonesian participation in the international organizations, political extremist and terrorist groups operating within Indonesia's

national borders undermine the nation's status in the international community.

■ FURTHER READING:

ELECTRONIC:

Central Intelligence Agency. CIA World Factbook. <http://www.cia.gov/cia/publications/factbook/geos/id.html> (April 18, 2003).

Industrial Espionage.

SEE Economic Espionage.

Infectious Disease, Threats to Security

■ BRIAN HOYLE

Infectious diseases are those diseases that are caused by microorganisms such as bacteria and viruses, many of which are spread from person to person. An intermittent host, or vector, aids the spread of some infectious diseases. One example is the transmission of the viral agent of Yellow Fever to humans via the bite of a mosquito. Other infectious diseases are spread directly from one person to another via infected body fluids or contaminated droplets in the air, as from a sneeze. Examples include influenza (aerosolized droplets) and hemorrhagic fevers such as Ebola (body fluids).

The scope of infectious diseases. Of the estimated 54 million deaths that occurred worldwide in 1998, approximately one-fourth to one-third (i.e., 13.5 to 18 million) were the result of an infectious disease. The bulk of these deaths occurred in the developing world and many involved children.

Infectious diseases have been part of human history for thousands of years. For example, descriptions of a disease with symptoms like those of anthrax, which is caused by the bacterium *Bacillus anthracis*, appear in the Old Testament Book of Exodus; anthrax is also thought to be the "burning wind of plague" mentioned in Homer's epic poem *Iliad*. Another example of an ancient infectious disease is bubonic plague. A huge epidemic of bubonic plague during the Middle Ages was called the Black Death, because of the characteristic skin discoloration produced by the bacterial infection.

The increasing ease of global travel and prevalence of antimicrobial treatments (i.e., antibiotics) in the twentieth

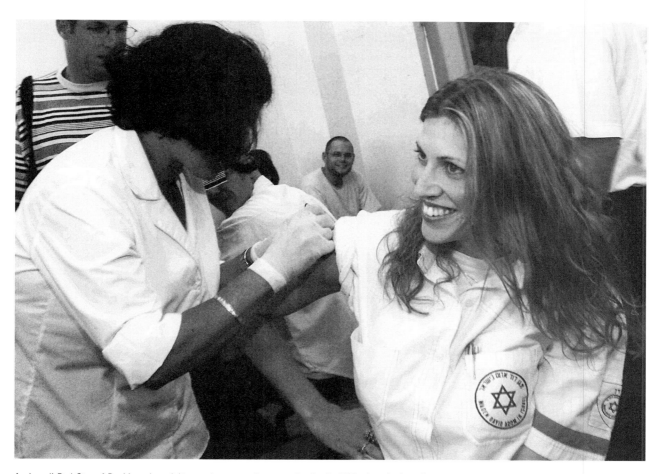

An Israeli Red Star of David worker, right, receives a smallpox vaccination in 2002, after the Israeli government decided to innoculate 15,000 emergency workers who in turn could vaccinate the rest of the population of Israel within four days in the event of a bioterrorist attack. AP/WIDE WORLD PHOTOS.

century produced an increase in the spread of infectious diseases, as well as the emergence of new or newly recognized diseases. One example is Acquired Immuno-deficiency Syndrome (AIDS). Recognized in the 1980s, AIDS is now a world-wide epidemic affecting millions of people. Tuberculosis, which is caused by the bacterium *Mycobacterium tuberculosis* has reemerged as a health threat. More than 30 new infectious diseases have emerged since 1975.

Infectious disease and security: Disease as a weapon.
Throughout most of recorded history, the suffering and huge loss of life produced by infectious diseases like anthrax and bubonic plague has mostly been accidental. Nonetheless, biological warfare is also ancient. For example, hundreds of years ago, the bodies of cattle were dumped into wells to poison the drinking water, and the bodies of human victims of anthrax were catapulted into fortified cities to spread the disease to the enemy.

In the twentieth century, the use of infectious disease as a weapon and security threat became an accepted strategy of war. Anthrax weaponry was researched in

World Wars I and II. During World War II, Britain produced millions of anthrax packages that were planned for air dropping in Germany to infect the population as well as the food chain. The ancient infections of anthrax and plague, along with smallpox, were explored as biological weapons by the former Soviet Union. Soviet scientists considered these microbes as strategic weapons, potentially capable of destroying entire populations.

In the last few decades of the twentieth century, the use of infectious disease became part of the arsenal of terrorist organizations. For example the Japanese cult Aum Shinrikyo, which released poison gas into the Tokyo subway system in 1995, killing 12 people and hospitalizing thousands, was also developing weapons to disperse the Ebola virus and anthrax spores.

The mass illness and death caused by the deliberate release of an infectious microorganism is a threat to the security of a country. The microorganisms can be easily disguised and transported virtually anywhere people can travel. As well, various microbes can be spread by insects, the wind, and in water. Thus, traditional security measures that have secured borders from other threats are ineffective against the deliberate use of microorganisms.

The consequences of the deliberate use of infectious agents are potentially catastrophic. For example, it has been estimated that the release of 100 kilograms of powdered anthrax upwind of a city as compact and populated as Washington, D.C. could kill up to 300,000 people and cripple the operation of the city.

Part of the appeal of the use of infectious disease as a weapon is the economic hardship that can be caused. A 1997 report from the United States Centers for Disease Control and Prevention conservatively estimated that the costs of dealing with the aftermath of an anthrax outbreak in a major urban center would be approximately $26.2 billion (U.S.) per 100,000 people. In a city such as New York, the tally could be in the thousands of billions of dollars. Several such attacks might bankrupt a country.

This economic drain would be on top of the already excessive economic burden that countries face in dealing with natural disease outbreaks. The cost of dealing with a long-lasting disease such as tuberculosis can be thousands of dollars per person. And, hospitalization is frequently required, which strains a nation's health care infrastructure.

Infectious disease and security: The spread of infection.
The main security threat from infectious diseases remains the spread of a disease through the population. For example, in 2000, 1,128 cases of malaria were imported into the United Kingdom by arriving travelers. Once in a country, an infection can spread rapidly. This has happened in the United States and Canada with West Nile fever. From a handful of cases in New York City in 1999, the virus has spread to most of the continental U.S. and Canada, and has sickened or killed thousands of people.

This ease of disease spread has produced unexpected outbreaks of disease all over the world. A few examples include legionellosis and leptospirosis in Australia, yellow fever and Creutzfeld-Jacob disease in Europe, and West Nile fever, hantavirus pulmonary syndrome, cryptococcosis and *Escherichia coli* O157:H7 in North America.

Another aspect of infectious disease that is a threat to security is the emergence of bacteria that have acquired resistance to the treatments used against them. A well-known example is the increasing resistance of bacteria to antibiotics. The microorganisms that cause infectious diseases such as AIDS, tuberculosis, malaria, and hospital-acquired infections are becoming more prevalent.

The development of resistance is a natural process, as a microbe seeks to adapt to the stress imposed by the antimicrobial agent. However, the refinement of genetic engineering technologies has made possible the tailoring of bacteria and viruses so as to be more lethal.

Current security issues.
In June 1996, U.S. President Bill Clinton initiated a process to develop a national policy concerning infectious diseases. A part of this policy concerned the influence of infectious diseases on the country's internal and international security. A report issued in 2000 by the National Security Council warned that the economic downturn and political destabilization caused by epidemics of infectious disease, primarily in underdeveloped countries, could constitute a security threat to the United States in the twenty-first century. In the underdeveloped world, the majority of deaths due to infectious diseases involve children. Thus, the next generation of some countries has been decimated. U.S. reliance on the natural resources of the affected countries, and the hostility towards the West that could develop in the underdeveloped world, could put the U.S. and other developed nations at risk.

In 2002, the principal government-sponsored security threat for biological weapon use came from Iraq. The government of Saddam Hussein had previously sanctioned a biological weapons development program. The Iraqi government acknowledged past production and testing of thousands of liters of anthrax-contaminated material for use as weapons. This threat was one of the primary reasons for the 2003 war that toppled the Hussein government.

As more states and groups develop the capacity for biological warfare or terrorism, the security threat against military and civilian personnel grows. For example, in the aftermath of the September 11, 2001 terrorist attacks in the U.S., several incidents of deliberate dispersal of anthrax bacterial spores occurred. These incidents highlighted the ease by which the biological agents could be delivered to their target in something as nondescript as a letter.

■ FURTHER READING:

BOOKS:

Inglesby, Thomas V. "Bioterrorist Threats: What the Infectious Disease Community Should Know about Anthrax and Plague," in *Emerging Infections 5*. Washington, DC: American Society for Microbiology Press, 2001.

PERIODICALS:

Kaufmann, A.F., M.I. Meltzer, and G.P. Schmid. "The Economic Impact of a Bioterrorist Attack: Are Prevention and Postattack Intervention Program Justifiable?" *Emerging Infectious Diseases* no. 3 (1997): 83–94.

ELECTRONIC:

Central Intelligence Agency. "The Global Infectious Disease Threat and Its Implications for the United States." January 2000 <http://www.cia.gov/cia/publications/nie/report/nie99–17d.html> (22 November 2002).

World Health Organization. "Strengthening Global Preparedness for Defense against Infectious Disease Threats." Statement to the United States Senate Committee on Foreign Relations—Hearing on The Threat of Bioterrorism and the Spread of Infectious Diseases. 5

September 2001 <http://www.who.int/emc/pdfs/Senate_hearing.pdf>(24 November 2002).

SEE ALSO

Anthrax, Terrorist Use as a Biological Weapon
USAMRIID (United States Army Medical Research Institute of Infectious Diseases

Infinite Justice, Operation.

SEE *Enduring Freedom, Operation.*

Information Security

∎ LARRY GILMAN

Information security, often compressed to "infosec," is the preservation of secrecy and integrity in the storage and transmission of information. Whenever information of any sort is obtained by an unauthorized party, information security has been breached. Breaches of information security can be grouped into five basic classes: (1) interception of messages; (2) theft of stored data; (3) information sabotage (i.e., alteration or destruction of data belonging to another party); (4) spoofing (i.e., using stolen information to pose as somebody else); and (5) denial of service (i.e., deliberate shutdown of cash machines, electric-supply grids, air-traffic control networks, or the like). Individual computer experts ("hackers"), intelligence agencies, criminals, rival businesses, disgruntled employees, and other parties may all seek to breach information security. All these parties, plus law-abiding private individuals who wish to guard their privacy and protect themselves from identity theft, also have an interest in preserving information security.

Messages and secrets have been subject to interception and theft ever since the invention of writing, but the modern situation is especially challenging. Electronic storage, processing, and transmission of information are now ubiquitous in the developed world, creating novel vulnerabilities. People are authorized to withdraw cash or purchase products on the basis of a piece of information (password or credit card number); trade secrets and business plans are electronically transmitted around the globe. In the U.S., over 95% of military and intelligence communications pass through network facilities owned by private carriers (e.g., the telephone system). Private speech may be broadcast locally by a mobile or cellular telephone or transmitted digitally over a network that can be tapped in numerous locations; databases full of confidential data reside in computers that can be accessed, perhaps illegally, by other computers communicating through networks; and so on. Information security—or insecurity—is a pervasive fact of modern life.

Consequently, breaching information security has become a common practice. For example, credit-card fraud costs approximately $20 per card per year. In 1994, an international criminal group used the Internet to penetrate Citicorp's computer system and shift $12 million from legitimate users' accounts to its own. Two ex-directors of the French intelligence agency DGSE (Direction Generale de la Sécurité Extérieure) have confirmed that one of the agency's highest priorities is to spy on non-French corporations and business-related government agencies. United States government agencies such as the Office of the U.S. Trade Representative and high-tech companies such as Boeing, General Dynamics, Hughes Aircraft, and others have been specifically targeted by French espionage—and probably also by other organizations that happen to be less frank (or more prudent) in their public statements.

There are many tools for increasing information security, including software that scans for computer viruses or prevents unauthorized intrusions into computer systems from the networks; password systems of all sorts; physical access security for computers, discs, passcards, credit cards, and other objects containing sensitive information; and encryption of messages and of databases. While all these tools are important to the conduct of business by a large business or government department, passwords and encryption are probably the most important.

Passwords have the advantage of being simple to use. They are not, however, capable by themselves of providing a high level security for large numbers of users. First, most users are asked to supply passwords for many different systems: banking, shopping, e-mail, and so forth. This tempts users to choose short passwords (which are easier to remember but also easier to guess, therefore weaker) and to use the same password for more than one system (causing a domino effect if a password is guessed).

Cryptography—the process by which raw message information (*plaintext*) is mapped or *encrypted* to a scrambled form (*ciphertext*) before transmission or storage, then mapped back to its original form again (*decrypted*) when an authorized party wishes to read the plaintext—is arguably the ultimate tool of information security. High-quality cryptographic systems that are breachable (if at all) only by resource-rich groups like the U.S. National Security Agency are widely available to businesses, governments, and private individuals. Appropriate cryptography can virtually guarantee the security of messages in transit and of information in databases; it can also, through "authentication," act as a super-password system whereby the identity of a would-be user (or information service supplier) can be positively confirmed. Cryptography has the disadvantages of added complexity, higher cost, and system slowdown.

Cryptography is also politically controversial, despite—or rather, because of—its technical power. Governments, corporations, private individuals, and private groups all have both legitimate and, occasionally, illegitimate motives for information security. Law-abiding persons and groups, or those rebelling against repressive laws, wish to be secure from surveillance by governments; criminals, terrorists, and the like also wish to be secure from surveillance by governments; government agents who are committing crimes wish to avoid public exposure; and so forth. It is generally advantageous to *all* parties, whether their activities are legitimate or illegitimate in whatever sense, to advocate maximum privacy for their own activities; it is generally advantageous to *governments* to advocate, in addition, maximum transparency for everyone else. Thus, for example, the U.S. government has sought (with little success) to prevent the spread of high-quality encryption algorithms, such as Pretty Good Privacy, outside the U.S., and inside the country has sought to establish voluntary compliance with "escrowed" cryptography systems. In such systems a government agency stores copies of cryptographic keys that enable it to decrypt communications between private parties using the system. In theory, these escrowed keys would be released to police or other government agents only when the court system had determined that there was a legitimate law-enforcement or national-security need to do so. Because such systems allow for third-party access to encrypted information by design, they are intrinsically less secure than a non-escrowed cryptography system, and therefore predictably unpopular with the private sector.

■ **FURTHER READING:**

BOOKS:

Dam, Kenneth W., and Herbert S. Lin, eds. *Cryptography's Role in Securing the Information Society.* Washington, DC: National Academy Press, 1996.

Hoffman, Lance J., ed. *Building in Big Brother: The Croptographic Policy Debate.* New York: Springer-Verlag, 1995.

ELECTRONIC:

Information Systems Security Association: The Global Voice of the Information Security Profession. 2003. <http://www.issa.org/> (February 21, 2003).

SEE ALSO

Computer Hardware Security
Computer Software Security
DNA sequences, Unique
Encryption of Data
Information Security (OIS), United States Office
Pretty Good Privacy (PGP)

Information Security (OIS), United States Office of

The Office of Information Security (OIS) is a unit within the General Service Administration (GSA) charged with the protection of computer data for the federal government. It employs a team of skilled technicians and specialists to manage, store, process, and most importantly provide security for electronic information systems. Under the umbrella of the GSA Federal Technology Service (FTS), OIS is part of the critical infrastructure protection system of the federal government.

The mission of OIS is to provide technology security systems to federal agencies to reduce risks and exposure of critical and sensitive information, and to do so in a cost-effective manner. To fulfill this mission, OIS has on staff an experienced group of technical specialists trained in protection and security methods for electronic data. In addition, it is capable of deploying engineers and technicians from the private sector as needed to federal or allied facilities anywhere in the world to meet transmission, storage, and processing requirements.

Among the solutions at the disposal of OIS are firewalls, or systems to prevent unauthorized access of hardware or software to or from a private network. Other techniques and principles applied by OIS include intrusion detection, security planning, risk management, data encryption, contingency planning, configuration management, and network mapping.

In accordance with President Decision Directive (PDD) 63, issued by President William J. Clinton in May 1998, OIS has worked to protect federal critical infrastructure from attacks by computer hackers. In 1999, it began working with firms in the private sector to provide infrastructure security consulting to federal agencies.

Beginning in October 2000, OIS divided its functions between its Information Security Services Center and its new Office of Information Assurance and Critical Infrastructure Protection. FTS took control of the first of these, through which OIS had met customer-service needs with offerings such as the Safeguard Program and the Access Certifications for Electronic Services Program. Meanwhile, the OIS concentrated its efforts in the critical infrastructure protection area, serving the imperatives of PDD–63 by providing cyber attack incident warnings and response services through the Federal Computer Incident Response Capability.

■ **FURTHER READING:**

PERIODICALS:

Frank, Diane. "GSA Preps Security Pacts." *Federal Computer Week* 13, no. 6 (March 15, 1999): 1.

ELECTRONIC:

Office of Information Security. General Service Administration Federal Technology Service. <http://www.fts.gsa.gov/infosec/> (March 4, 2003).

SEE ALSO

Computer Hardware Security
Computer Software Security

*Critical Infrastructure
Information Security*

Information Warfare

▮ JUDSON KNIGHT

The term "information warfare" refers not to a single idea or phenomenon, but to a variety of tools and techniques all centered around the concept that military success is as much a matter of information and ideas as of weapons and tactics. According to the National Defense University's Martin C. Libicki, seven distinct areas of information warfare exist. These include command and control, intelligence-based, electronic, psychological, and economic information warfare, as well as cyberwarfare and computer hacking. Examples of information warfare in practice include a number of techniques applied by the United States in Western Hemisphere conflicts and the Persian Gulf War of 1991, as well as the overall campaign of "shock and awe" waged as part of the 2003 Operation Iraqi Freedom.

Libicki's Definition and Critique

According to Libicki, the seven components of information warfare include command-and-control warfare, designed to strike at the enemy's command systems, leadership, and infrastructure; intelligence-based warfare; electronic warfare, including cryptographic and radio-electronic techniques; psychological warfare, involving the use of information to influence the views of allies, enemies, and neutrals; "hacker warfare," or attacks on enemy computer systems; economic information warfare, the control of information in pursuit of economic dominance; and cyberwarfare, which Libicki describes as "a grab bag of futuristic scenarios" involving computer technology.

Libicki has cautioned, not only that "information warfare" is not a single, monolithic entity, but that its value in some cases has been overestimated. He has sought to distinguish between historically useful forms of information warfare, and others that he dismisses as "fantastic," or "involv[ing] assumptions about societies and organizations that are not necessarily true."

Even though information systems are becoming increasingly more important to defensive forces, Libicki has maintained it is not necessarily the case that attacks on information systems yield increasing returns, the reason being that these systems have increasingly become distributed and compartmentalized. Above all, it is Libicki's contention that, outside of specific applications such as electronic jamming, information should not be regarded as a medium of warfare to any greater degree than other aspects of combat support such as logistics.

Shock and Awe, Rapid Dominance, and Decisive Force

Notwithstanding these cautionary statements, the quick U.S. victory in Operation Iraqi Freedom revealed the success of information warfare as articulated by Harlan K. Ullman, James P. Wade, and others in *Shock and Awe: Achieving Rapid Dominance.* The book, published in 1996 by the Center for Advanced Concepts and Technology, provided a strategic blueprint for the methods applied seven years later in Iraq.

"Shock and awe" defines two principal components of combat, "rapid dominance" and "decisive force." These can be equated to threats and intimidation (rapid dominance), coupled with the ability to back up those threats (decisive force). The analogy is not a perfect one, however, because rapid dominance also involves the use of force, albeit in a more limited and targeted fashion.

The objective of rapid dominance is to control the perceptions, understanding, and even the will of the adversary, whereas that of decisive force is military victory. Rapid dominance uses military force in support of its objective, so as to make the enemy impotent—or convinced that he is impotent, which amounts to much the same thing. Use of military capabilities within the framework of decisive force is more straightforward, and once again supports its objective.

Accordingly, forces employed for rapid dominance may be much smaller than those of the opposition, as long as they possess the advantage in training and technology. In the case of decisive force, the technological edge is likewise critical, but so is sheer volume of numbers. It follows that casualties may be high in the case of decisive force, while they could be relatively low in the realm of rapid dominance. Speed of action, desirable for decisive force, is essential to rapid dominance, whose scope is all-encompassing rather than a matter of one fighting group against another.

Information Warfare in Action

Long before "shock and awe," or even more general modern concepts of information warfare, military forces practiced basic principles of psychological warfare. Ancient Biblical texts describe several instances in which the armies of the Israelites used psychological tactics in one form or another against their enemies, including banging loud cymbals and shouting as a means of convincing the inhabitants of their numbers and aggressive intentions.

Assyrian armies employed "shock and awe"-style techniques apparently designed to influence by intimidation as much as by sheer military force. It has been noted by military historians that the Nazis' blitzkrieg style of warfare—which again was as effective psychologically as it was militarily—was influenced by the Assyrians' high-speed chariot warfare tactics. The Nazis also seem to

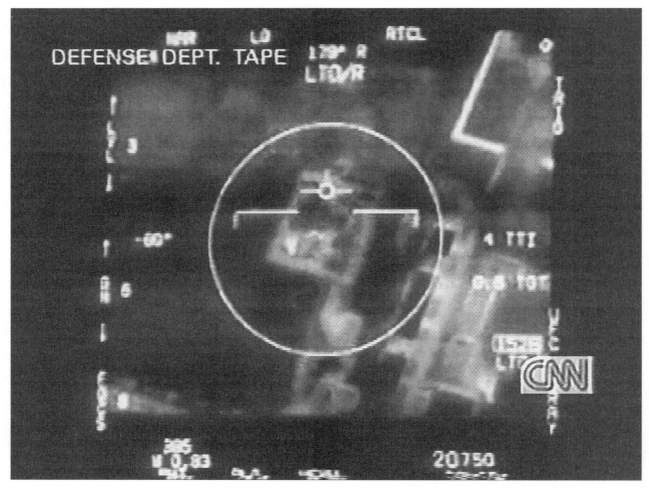

CNN broadcasted this 1998 Defense Department video of an Iraqi radio relay facility moments before its destruction by a 1600-pound laser-guided bomb during airstrikes by U.S. and British forces. AP/WIDE WORLD PHOTOS.

have appropriated aspects of the iconography and military regalia used by the Assyrian empire to impress and psychologically dominate their foes.

Certainly German leaders made use of Roman symbols such as the war eagle, which may have been influenced by Assyrian models. The Romans themselves, of course, were ancient masters at psychological warfare, from their impressive uniforms and the legions' imposing battle standards to the triumphal parades, in which defeated kings and their treasures were paraded through the streets of the capital city.

Aided by propaganda minister Josef Goebbels, as well as architect Albert Speer and others, Adolf Hitler made his forces into an intimidating spectacle for all the senses. Every aspect of Nazi regalia, beginning with the bold red flag and its intimidating black swastika on a white field, was intended to present an image of overwhelming power. The swastika was an ancient Buddhist symbol for life, but when the Nazis adopted it for their own purposes, they made two critical changes. Turning the symbol to the

right, along with a 45-degree shift of its axis, the symbol resembled a wheel rolling forward against all adversaries.

As powerful as the dextrogyrate (rightward-turning) swastika were the uniforms of the German forces, particularly the SS. These have been repeatedly imitated, and even parodied in movies, but they are unparalleled in the care with which they were designed. The black SS uniform, with its black boots, jodhpurs, and swastika armband, could make even a slight, bespectacled figure such as SS director Heinrich Himmler—a chicken farmer before he joined the Nazi regime—appear intimidating. After the war, when the Nazis who had not committed suicide or escaped were placed on trial at the World Court in The Hague, they looked small indeed in civilian clothes, a testament to the terror inspired by their uniforms.

Nazi psychological warfare with visual images also included their wide use of film for propaganda purposes. They even flirted with television, then in its developmental stages. Nor did they ignore the aural sense: for example, they equipped their Stuka dive-bombers with sirens for no purpose other than to strike fear into their victims. Late in the war, Hitler fired his V2 rockets toward London, and though they had limited success militarily, these too served a strong psychological warfare purpose.

American forces were latecomers to the idea of psychological warfare, though they did wage a number of successful propaganda campaigns in World War II through the use of leaflets and radio broadcasts. Attempts to win "hearts and minds" in the Vietnam War proved much less successful, however, in part because the United States lacked a clear strategic plan in that war.

In contrast to lack of U.S. success in strategic psychological warfare were a number of achievements in tactical psychological operations, or psyops. In the late 1940s, for instance, operatives with knowledge of rural Filipino folklore used sounds and imagery to convince local Philippine communist insurgents that they were being chased by ghosts.

Operation Just Cause and Commander Solo.
During Operation Just Cause, the campaign against Panama's General Manuel Noriega in 1989, psychological warfare experts accompanied U.S. Army Rangers on airborne missions. They broadcast U.S. propaganda from loudspeakers, and bombarded the Vatican embassy, where Noriega had taken refuge, with loud rock music.

Aiding U.S. psychological and propaganda techniques is an array of technology, an example of which is the EC-130F aircraft flown on "Commander Solo" missions. These carry equipment for broadcasting on the AM, FM, television, and military communications bands, with missions flying at the highest possible altitude to ensure maximum coverage.

Commander Solo operated in Just Cause, during which it broadcast propaganda against the Noriega regime. During Operation Uphold Democracy in 1994, it was used for radio and television broadcasts to the people of Haiti, and its frequent relays of messages from President Jean-Bertrand Aristide contributed significantly to the orderly transition from military to civilian rule. In 1991, during Operation Desert Storm, or the Persian Gulf War, Commander Solo aircraft deploying from bases in Saudi Arabia and Turkey broadcast a program called *Voice of the Gulf,* along with other programs designed to convince Iraqi soldiers to lay down their arms.

The Persian Gulf War.
U.S. psyops tactics in the 1991 Persian Gulf War revealed considerable sophistication. While U.S. forces jammed local radio signals, they broadcast on their own channels, and even dropped portable radios into Iraqi units so as to ensure that opposition forces would hear U.S. broadcasts. Members of the 13th Psychological Operations Battalion operated among prisoners of war in camps, playing "good cop" to the "bad cop" of the military police.

Whereas the latter carried weapons and enforced order, psyops personnel presented themselves as the prisoners' friends. They provided them with prayer mats and signs indicating the direction of the Moslem holy city of Mecca, and passed out cigarettes, extra food, and candy to those who cooperated. Each night, they showed the prisoners movies for entertainment, but uncooperative detainees were not allowed to attend. Recalled one member of the 13th Psyops, "We had some Iraqi movies that were [made] according to strict Muslim laws, but they didn't want to see those. They wanted to see *Superman.*"

The Iraqis made their own attempts at psychological warfare in at least one regard. Using a tactic applied by Axis radio broadcaster Tokyo Rose against Allied forces in the Pacific during World War II, and by Hanoi radio against American GIs in Vietnam, they attempted to convince enemy soldiers that their wives and girlfriends were cheating on them back home. One leaflet that was intended to inform the American soldier that his wife was being unfaithful at home referred to a figure the Iraqis apparently mistook for a film star: Bart Simpson, actually a cartoon character.

Operation Iraqi Freedom.
Both in Operation Desert Storm and Operation Iraqi Freedom 12 years later, U.S. forces made extensive use of propaganda leaflets. In Operation Desert Storm alone, 14 million leaflets were dropped over Iraq. These were designed to be as simple as possible, keeping in mind the fact that many Iraqi soldiers had only enough education to enable them to read the Koran. Therefore, leaflets relied on images such as a picture of Americans making an amphibious landing—a ruse designed to divert Iraqi defenses for an attack that never occurred.

In early March 2003, just before the launch of Operation Iraqi Freedom, coalition aircraft operating from Turkey undertook Operation Northern Watch, in which they dropped leaflets over Kurdish areas in northern Iraq. The leaflet campaign continued and expanded as hostilities began, and forces bombarded Iraq with messages designed to win over the populace, and to convince the Iraqi military that resistance was futile. An example of the latter was a leaflet that stated, "Attention Iraqi air defense. Any hostile action by Iraqi air defenses toward coalition aircraft will be answered by immediate retaliation. Iraqi air defense positions which fire on coalition aircraft or activate air defense radar will be attacked and destroyed."

Other psychological tactics employed in Operation Iraqi Freedom included announcements by U.S. leadership that Iraqi leaders were prepared to surrender at the outset of the war. Coalition forces used amplified sound to convince Iraqi forces that tanks were operating outside the city of Basra, and continually broadcast to the populace over radio and television.

Coalition aircraft dropped millions of leaflets over Iraq even after the fighting ended, with the purpose of convincing the Iraqi populace that the invaders had come not to conquer, but to turn the country over to its people. The coalition also released a set of playing cards depicting key personnel from the regime of dictator Saddam Hussein who had yet to be caught or otherwise neutralized. Hussein himself was the ace of spades.

■ FURTHER READING:

BOOKS:

Alexander, John B. *Future War: Non-Lethal Weapons in Twenty-First Century Warfare.* New York: St. Martin's Press, 1999.

Lesser, Ian O. *Countering the New Terrorism.* Santa Monica, CA: RAND, 1999.

Libicki, Martin C. *What Is Information Warfare?* Washington, D.C.: National Defense University, 1995.

Schwartau, Winn. *Information Warfare: Chaos on the Electronic Superhighway.* New York: Thunder's Mouth Press, 1994.

Ullman, Harlan, James P. Wade, et al. *Shock and Awe: Achieving Rapid Dominance.* Washington, D.C.: Center for Advanced Concepts and Technology, 1996.

ELECTRONIC:

Information Warfare and Information Security on the Web. Federation of American Scientists. <http://www.fas.org/irp/wwwinfo.html> (April 14, 2003).

The Information Warfare Site. <http://www.iwar.org.uk/> (April 14, 2003).

Institute for the Advanced Study of Information Warfare. <http://www.psycom.net/iwar.1.html> (April 14, 2003).

SEE ALSO

Americas, Modern U.S. Security Policy and Interventions
FM Transmitters
Iraqi Freedom, Operation (2003 War Against Iraq)
Persian Gulf War
Propaganda, Uses and Psychology
Short-Wave Transmitters
World War II

A U.S. Navy aviation systems warfare operator searches for and tracks surface contacts using radar and the Infrared Detection System during a flight mission in support of Operation Enduring freedom in October 2001. AP/WIDE WORLD PHOTOS.

Infrared Detection Devices

■ LARRY GILMAN

Infrared detection devices are sensors that detect radiation in the infrared portion of the electromagnetic spectrum (>10^{12} to 5×10^{14} Hz). Often, such devices form the information they gather into visible-light images for the benefit of human users; alternatively, they may communicate directly with an automatic system, such as the guidance system of a missile.

Because all objects above absolute zero emit radiation in the infrared part of the electromagnetic spectrum, infrared detection provides a means of "seeing in the dark"—that is, forming images when light in the visible portion of the spectrum (>4.3×10^{14} to 7.5×10^{14} Hz) is scarce or absent. Because the warmer an object is, the more infrared radiation it emits, infrared imaging is also useful for the detection of outstanding heat sources that may be invisible or hard to detect even when there is ample visible light (e.g., exhaust heat from ships, tanks, jets, or rockets). Many devices used by police, security, and military organizations, including user-wearable, gun-mounted, vehicle-mounted, missile-mounted, and orbital systems, exploit some form of infrared detection technology.

Principles of infrared detection. Infrared—"below-red"—light consists of electromagnetic radiation that is too low in frequency (i.e., too long in wavelength) to be perceived by the human eye, yet is still too high in frequency to be classed as microwave radio. Infrared (IR) light that is just beyond the human visual limit (>1.0×10^{14} to 4.0×10^{14} Hz) is termed near IR, while light farther from the visible spectrum is divided into middle IR, far IR, and extreme IR. Military and security systems utilize mostly near IR and a narrow band in the far IR centered on 3.0×10^{13} Hz, because the Earth's atmosphere happens to be transparent to IR radiation primarily in these two "windows."

All objects above absolute zero glow in the far IR, so no source of illumination is needed to image scenes using such radiation; to image scenes in near IR, illumination from a light-emitting diode or filtered light bulb must be supplied. Near-IR imagers, however, are still cheaper than passive, far-IR imagers.

There are two basic designs for electronic IR imagers. The first is the scanner. In this design, light from a tiny portion of the scene to be imaged is focused by an optical and mechanical system on a small circuit element that is sensitive to photons in the desired IR frequency range. The intensity of the signal from the IR detector element is recorded, then the mechanico-optical system shifts its focus to a different fragment of the scene. The response of the IR detector element is again recorded, the view shifts again, and so forth, systematically covering the scene. Many scene-covering geometries have been employed by scanning imagers; the scanner may record horizontal or vertical lines (rasters), spiral outward from a central point, cover a series of radii, and so on.

The second basic type of IR imaging system is the "starer." Such a system is said to "stare" because its optics do not move like a scanner's, scanning the scene a little bit at a time; instead, they focus the image onto an extended focal plane. Located in this plane is a flat (planar) array of tiny sensors, each equivalent to the single IR sensor employed in a scanning system. By measuring the IR response of all the elements in the flat array simultaneously (or rapidly), the system can record an entire image at once. Image resolution in a staring scanner is limited by the number of elements in the array, whereas in a scanning system it is limited by the size of the scanning dot.

Hybrid designs, in which partial or entire scan-lines are sensed simultaneously by rows of sensors, have also been developed. Chemical films have also proved useful for IR imaging, but these are rarely used today.

The earliest IR imagers, built in the 1940s, 1950s, and 1960s, were scanners. Starers were not technologically feasible until the early 1970s, when large-scale circuit integration made possible the manufacture of focal-plane arrays with good resolution. As integrated-circuit technology has been refined, focal-plane arrays have become cheaper. Starers have many advantages, including greater reliability due to the absence of moving parts, quicker image acquisition, and freedom from internally-produced mechanical vibration.

Formerly, both scanners and starers needed to be cooled by liquid nitrogen in order to keep the sensor from blinding itself with its own IR radiation. In recent years, however, uncooled IR imagers, both scanners and starers, have been increasing in quality and decreasing in price.

Military applications. Aircraft, ground vehicles, surface ships, human beings, industrial facilities, rockets, and warheads entering the atmosphere are some of the objects of military interest that emit IR radiation in telltale patterns. To exploit these patterns, a wide array of military IR systems have been developed. For example, "heat-seeking" missiles that home in on the IR-bright gasses emitted by jet-aircraft engines have been commonplace since the 1950s. Heat-seeking missiles have also been developed for use against surface vehicles and ships. Also, starting in the early 1960s, military IR-imaging satellites have been observing the Earth to detect the IR emissions of rocket and missile launches, and modern proposals for ballistic-missile defense depend heavily on space- and ground-based IR detectors that will track missiles and warheads as they arc through space. The U.S. military is currently designing a new system of satellites dedicated to tracking missiles using IR imaging, the Space Based Infrared System. According to the United States Air Force, this system will have a "unique capability to track missiles throughout their trajectory—not just during the 'hot' boost phase [when IR emissions from the missile are most intense]—allow[ing] the system to effectively cue missile defense systems with accurate targeting data."

Various IR camera systems for "seeing in the dark" are also commonplace. These may be mounted on vehicles or at stationary locations to allow nighttime surveillance of a fixed area. Night-vision systems worn on helmets and mounted on portable weapons usually do *not* operate by sensing IR; instead, they amplify the visible light already present in a dark scene. Hence they are sometimes called "starlight" vision systems.

IR imaging is being investigated for use in the detection of landmines. Antipersonnel mines are typically buried only a few centimeters below the surface, so the heat radiation (IR) pattern of an area can, under some conditions reveal their presence.

Police and security applications. The security of a building or area of land from intruders is often enhanced by cameras that image the perimeter of the secure area and can be monitored by personnel in a central office. At night, such systems must either be supplied with illumination or must be capable of IR imaging. Visible-light camera systems are cheaper and easier for human users to interpret; however, because excess illumination of an area by visible light ("light pollution") is sometimes a concern, and because security forces may wish to keep an area under surveillance without making their presence known, IR systems are widely used for perimeter security and other surveillance tasks.

IR imaging has many other uses in police and security work besides surveillance. Aerial IR imaging can track vehicles, show which vehicles in a parking lot have arrived most recently, distinguish heated buildings, and locate buried structures (e.g., clandestine chemical laboratories) emitting heat through vents. IR images can be used to precisely determine the time of death of a person deceased for less than 15 hours or to detect document forgery by revealing subtle mechanical and chemical disturbances of the original paper and ink. The power consumption in a building can be estimated in real time by observing the IR radiation emitted by the power transformer on the pole outside; modifications to walls or automobiles are often obvious in IR images; and IR images can reveal such visually inconspicuous features of crime scenes as use of cleaning solvents to remove blood, drag-marks across carpets, fresh paint, and explosives residues.

Countermeasures. IR imaging, like all surveillance and targeting technologies, has given risen to a thriving countermeasures field. IR countermeasures fall into three broad categories: blinding, decoys, and concealment. Blinding refers to the use of IR lasers to overload an enemy's imaging detectors, as for example those of an approaching missile. Decoys are heat sources released in the vicinity of a target heat source (e.g., aircraft or ship) in order to reduce the chances that an approaching missile will home in on the true target. For example, a system named the AN/ALQ-156(V)2 Missile Approach Detector is standard on several U.S. military aircraft. This system uses radar to scan for approaching heat-seeking missiles. When one is detected, the AN/ALQ-156(V)2 automatically activates the M-130 General Purpose Dispenser System, which releases a flare from the aircraft. The flare emits more IR radiation than the aircraft itself, hopefully distracting the missile from the aircraft.

Since most proposals for ballistic missile defense include interceptor missiles that home in on the heat signature of ballistic warheads approaching from space (and thus IR-bright against a cool background), thought has also been given to the question of "infrared stealth" measures for ballistic-missile warheads. One possibility is "shrouding," which would involve the placement of a close-fitting cap over the cone-shaped warhead. The cap would consist, essentially, of a hollow aluminum shell filled with liquid nitrogen and kept aloof from the warhead itself by insulated supports. The liquid nitrogen would cool the exterior of the warhead, reducing its IR emissions to low levels and making it difficult or impossible for the heat-seeking system of an interceptor missile to locate. The exterior coating of the warhead could be made of a radar-absorbing material, making the warhead radar-stealthy as well.

■ **FURTHER READING:**

BOOKS:

Schlessinger, Monroe. *Infrared Technology Fundamentals.* New York: Marcel Dekker, Inc., 1995.

PERIODICALS:

Carter, L. J., et al. "Thermal Imaging for Landmine Detection," in proceedings from Second International Conference on the Detection of Abandoned Land Mines, *IEEE* 110–114, 1998.

Maki, M. C., and M. C. Dickie. "New Options in Using Infrared for Detection, Assessment and Surveillance," in proceedings from the International Carnahan Conference on Security Technology, *IEEE* 12–18, 1996.

Riedel, R. B., J. S. Coffin, and F. J. Prokoski. "Forensic Uses of Infrared Video," in proceedings from the International Carnahan Conference on Security Technology, *IEEE* 108–112, 1992.

SEE ALSO

Night Vision Scopes
Strategic Defense Initiative and National Missile Defense

Infrastructure Protection Center (NIPC), United States National

Formerly a unit of the Federal Bureau of Investigation (FBI), the National Infrastructure Protection Center (NIPC) moved to the Department of Homeland Security (DHS) when the latter began its functions in March 2003. NIPC is charged with assessing threats to critical infrastructure—particularly computer systems—and providing warnings concerning threats and vulnerabilities. It also conducts investigations and provides a response to computer attacks.

NIPC's mission. Although infrastructure, or critical infrastructure, includes vital systems ranging from roads to banking, the tasks of NIPC are directed toward those computer and information systems that provide much of the control mechanism over other components of the national infrastructure. The mission of NIPC is manifold, though its many components all relate in some way to computers. The NIPC is tasked with detecting, averting, assessing, warning against, responding to, and investigating unlawful acts that target or threaten critical infrastructures in general, and computer and information technologies in particular. It manages investigations of computer intrusion, and supports the response of law enforcement to cyber crimes and computer intrusion.

When incidents of intrusion go beyond the level of crime to that of terrorism or acts of warfare, NIPC works with counterintelligence, counterterrorism, and national security authorities in responding to attacks on interests of the United States. It also coordinates the training of computer investigators and other protectors of infrastructure both in the public and private sectors.

NIPC at work. An example of NIPC at work occurred in May 2000, when the "Love Bug" computer worm (a virus-like program) propagated itself across world computer networks. Within 24 hours, investigators at the New York FBI field office, assisted by NIPC, tracked the virus to Onel de Guzman in the Philippines. Due to the lack of cyber crime statutes in the Philippines, Guzman was not charged, but the incident led to Philippine approval of the international E-Commerce Act, which provides for criminal prosecution of cyber crimes. NIPC has conducted a number of other major investigations against cyber criminals.

The NIPC issues three levels of infrastructure warnings: assessments, which provide general information about non-specific threats; advisories, which address particular dangers that call for preparedness or a change in posture; and alerts, which warn of major and specific threats. In September 2002, for instance, it issued an assessment warning against possible "hacktivism" (the use of computer hacking in the service of political activism) connected with upcoming meetings of the International Monetary Fund and World Bank. As of February 2003, NIPC advisory addressed the dangers of global hacking associated with escalating tensions between the United States and Iraq. In August, 2002, NIPC issued an alert based on "credible but nonspecific information" concerning possible cyber attacks originating from Europe. That no problems were reported may be evidence that there was no actual threat—or that NIPC was successful in its job.

■ FURTHER READING:

BOOKS:

Improving Our Ability to Fight Cybercrime: Oversight of the National Infrastructure Protection Center: Hearing Before the Subcommittee on Technology, Terrorism, and Government Information of the Committee on the Judiciary, United States Senate, One Hundred Seventh Congress, First Session, July 25, 2001. Washington, D.C.: U.S. Government Printing Office, 2002.

National Infrastructure Protection Center (NIPC): A Public-Private Partnership to Protect America's Critical Infrastructures. Washington, D.C.: U.S. Department of Justice, 2002.

PERIODICALS:

Amon, Michael. "Agencies Working to Boost Security." *Washington Post.* (February 23, 2003): T1.

Johnston, David. "F.B.I. Warns Local Agencies to Be Aware." *New York Times.* (September 10, 2002): A17.

Verton, Dan. "NIPC Warns of Attacks, But No Impact Felt." *Computerworld* 36, no. 33 (August 12, 2002): 17.

———. "NIPC Loses One of Its Own to 'Beltway' Sniper." *Computerworld* 36, no. 43 (October 21, 2002): 6.

ELECTRONIC:

National Infrastructure Protection Center. <http://www. nipc.gov> (March 4, 2003).

SEE ALSO

Computer Hackers
Computer Hardware Security
Computer Software Security
Critical Infrastructure
Critical Infrastructure Assurance Office (CIAO), United States

INS (United States Immigration and Naturalization Service)

■ ADRIENNE WILMOTH LERNER

The United States Immigration and Naturalization Service (INS) was a subsidiary of the Department of Justice. Immigration services are now part of the new Department of Homeland Security. The agency was charged with enforcing laws regulating the immigration of foreign-born individuals, the admission of refugees into the United States, and the naturalization of qualified foreigners wishing to become U.S. citizens. The INS granted tourist, student, and extended stay visas for foreign citizens wishing to visit the United States. Now restructured into the Department of Homeland Security, immigration services are essential in the enforcement of antiterrorism laws and the promotion of national security.

The first federal immigration agency in the United States was established in 1864. At that time, the office was directed to encourage immigration to the United States. Over time, the office evolved as immigration policy changed. By 1890, the government abandoned the "open door policy" and adopted laws restricting the flow of immigrants into the country. The first laws prohibited the entry of people convicted of serious crimes, suffering from contagious diseases, polygamists, and severely mentally ill persons. Later legislation barred immigrants from certain nations and established quotas for immigrants from various regions or countries. As social and political policy changed, so too did the federal immigration agency.

The modern Immigration and Naturalization Service was established in 1933 by Executive Order 6166. The order combined existing separate agencies of immigration and naturalization services. The INS was then part of the Department of Labor. In 1940, the organization was restructured under the President's Reorganization Plan Number V. With the advent of World War II, immigration shifted from being an economic to a security issue. Accordingly, the INS was moved under control of the Department of Justice. The move gave INS more power to adjudicate cases in violation of immigration laws. Furthermore, the INS managed the U.S. border patrol. Border patrol agents apprehended illegal immigrants and regulated the entry of people into the United States from border crossings and other ports-of-entry.

After the September 11, 2001, attacks on the United States, the INS took a lead role in the strengthening of national security and antiterrorism policy. The agency enacted new guidelines for the issuance of visas, making the general criteria for prolonged entry into the U.S. more stringent. Efforts to satisfy 1996 legislation that mandated the creation of tracking systems to monitor entries and exits from land points of entry have been increased. The controversial Coordinating Interagency Partnership Regulating International Students (CIPRIS), a database that tracks student visa holders, remains largely opposed by the university community, but gained the support of the government as a key means of controlling access to sensitive technology and information.

The INS also gained increased powers of detention and questioning of illegal aliens and visa holders suspected of being connected to terrorist organizations. The period of detention without formal charges was augmented from 24 hours to any reasonable length of time necessary to gather information regarding the case. Mobilization Against Terrorism Act (MATA) granted the INS the power to remove, deport, or prosecute foreign nationals connected to terrorist groups, or who harbor persons connected to such organizations. MATA further applied to foreign nationals granted permanent resident status. Permanent residents also could be detained or deported if certified to be connected with a terrorist group.

Despite these changes to INS operations, the agency was radically restructured under the Homeland Security Act. Former INS duties of border security and immigration services were separated and tasked to separate operational departments under the Department of Homeland Security. The Bureau of Citizenship and Immigration Services (CIS) administers the citizenship program and the granting of visas. Border security is now tasked to the Directorate of Border and Transportation Security (BTS). Screening measures of persons wishing to enter the United States have become more rigorous, as has the enforcement of immigration laws, since the CIS and BTS assumed the powers of the former INS.

U.S. immigration policy is currently based on a preference system that favors skilled workers, professionals, and prospective immigrants from underrepresented nations. Accordingly, one of the main tasks of CIS is to manage the visa selection process efficiently. Refugees fleeing from war or political oppression are handled separately, in conjunction with United Nations and the U.S. Department of Health and Human Services.

The various operational departments of the Department of Homeland Security are also responsible for the apprehension, adjudication, and deportation of criminal aliens. These can be foreign nationals wanted for crimes in their home countries or who have been convicted of a crime in the United States. In addition, foreign nationals who remain in the United States after their visas expire are considered criminal or illegal aliens, depending on the circumstances of their activities in the U.S. In 2001, immigration services removed nearly 180,000 criminal and illegal aliens, most of whom were apprehended on visa-related violations.

■ FURTHER READING:

ELECTRONIC:

Bureau of Citizenship and Immigration Services. INSPASS. March 1, 2003. <http://www.immigration.gov/graphics/howdoi/inspassloc.htm> (April 14, 2003).

United States Department of Homeland Security. Bureau of Citizenship and Immigration Services, PORTPASS. March 11, 2003. <http://www.immigration.gov/graphics/howdoi/portpass.htm> (April 9, 2003).

United States Department of Homeland Security. Immigration Information, INSPASS. March 4, 2003. <http://www.immigration.gov/graphics/shared/howdoi/inspass.htm> (April 9, 2003).

SEE ALSO

United States, Counter-terrorism Policy

INSCOM (United States Army Intelligence and Security Command)

Headquartered at Fort Belvoir, Virginia, the United States Army Intelligence and Security Command (INSCOM) plans and conducts intelligence, security, and information operations for the U.S. Army and its military commanders, as well for the president and other national decisionmakers. Since the time of its establishment in the years immediately after the war in Vietnam, as geopolitical conditions have realigned, INSCOM has been forced to adjust its mission numerous times.

INSCOM's first quarter-century. Formed from the old Army Security Agency, INSCOM began its life on January 1, 1977, at Arlington Hall Station in Virginia. This was a time of downsizing for the U.S. military, as America entered a period of relative isolationism, but the crises in Afghanistan and Iran during the late 1970s brought about a resurgence in military growth. In its first seven years, INSCOM grew in strength from 10,400 to 15,000 personnel.

By the mid-1980s, the departure of the Defense Intelligence Agency (DIA) from the Arlington Hall facilities allowed INSCOM to consolidate its headquarters, part of which had been at Fort Meade, Maryland. INSCOM reorganized its five multidiscipline intelligence groups as brigades, and placed a greater emphasis on training its personnel to be warfighters rather than information-gatherers alone. INSCOM relocated to Fort Belvoir in 1989.

After the Cold War. That year also saw the beginning of the end of the Cold War, and the decade that followed (1990s) brought considerable change for INSCOM. It was downsized, along with much of the military, and after absorbing the Army Intelligence Agency in 1991, it returned to its earlier emphasis on intelligence-gathering. At mid-decade, it transferred all of its human intelligence operations to DIA.

In the 1990s, INSCOM, like much of the military, found itself tasked with humanitarian operations rather than warfighting. Other unaccustomed activities in the mid-1990s, according to information posted at the INSCOM Web site in 2003, included "supporting treaty verification, conducting counterdrug operations, and protecting the army against an espionage threat posed by nations not traditionally our adversaries."

INSCOM today. September 11, 2001, brought about another phase in the history of INSCOM and the military as a whole. It would be faced with new challenges in a world once again polarized as in the Cold War, but this time with a more enigmatic enemy.

INSCOM had not remained idle during the 1990s; among the new systems it had helped develop were the Sandcrab jammer, the Trackwolf high-frequency direction-finding system, the Trojan Spirit deployable intelligence communications system, the airborne reconnaissance low platform, and the army portion of the Joint Surveillance and Target Acquisition Radar System (J-STARS).

INSCOM consists of four brigades, as well as eight other groups or activities worldwide tasked to specific intelligence disciplines or functions. In all, members of its 14 major subordinate commands and numerous smaller units are in some 180 locations across the globe.

■ **FURTHER READING:**

BOOKS:

Richelson, Jeffrey T. *The U.S. Intelligence Community,* third edition. Boulder, CO: Westview Press, 1995.

PERIODICALS:

Girardeau, John H. "Doctrine Corner: INSCOM Intelligence Support to the Tactical Commander." *Military*

Intelligence Professional Bulletin 28, no. 2 (April-June 2002): 56–57.

ELECTRONIC:

United States Army Intelligence and Security Command. <http://www.inscom.army.mil> (February 2, 2003).

SEE ALSO

Army Security Agency
G–2

INSPASS (Immigration and Naturalization Service Passenger Accelerated Service System)

INSPASS (Immigration and Naturalization Service Passenger Accelerated Service System) is a component of the Port Passenger Accelerated Service System (PORTPASS) in use at selected airports to facilitate passage through entry checkpoints. INSPASS and other expedited U.S. national entry systems are designed to identify preapproved low-risk international travelers using a combination of biometric measurements. Automated entry systems are designed to allow inspectors additional time to focus on high-risk entrants.

As of March 1, 2003, the newly created United States Department of Homeland Security (DHS) absorbed the former Immigration and Naturalization Service (INS). All INS border patrol agents and investigators—along with agents from the U.S. Customs Service and Transportation Security Administration—were placed under the direction of the DHS Directorate of Border and Transportation Security (BTS). Responsibility for U.S. border security and the enforcement of immigration laws was transferred to BTS.

BTS is scheduled to incorporate the United States Customs Service (previously part of the Department of Treasury), the enforcement division of the Immigration and Naturalization Service (previously part of the Department of Justice), the Animal and Plant Health Inspection Service (previously part of the Department of Agriculture), the Federal Law Enforcement Training Center (previously part of the Department of Treasury), Transportation Security Administration (previously part of the Department of Transportation) and the Federal Protective Service (previously part of the General Services Administration).

Former INS immigration service functions are scheduled to be placed under the direction of the DHS Bureau of

Citizenship and Immigration Services. Under the reorganization the INS formally ceases to exist on the date the last of its functions are transferred.

Although the description of the technologies involved in the INSPASS entry security program remains stable, in an effort to facilitate border security BTS plans envision higher levels of coordination between formerly separate agencies and databases. As of April 2003, the specific coordination and future of the INSPASS program was uncertain with regard to name changes, program administration, and policy changes.

INSPASS systems utilize hand geometry biometrics. Hand geometry measurements include biometric registration of hand length, thickness and translucency.

At entry points an INSPASS station compares hand geometry biometric images to a database of preregistered travelers. The INSPASS system is integrated in such a way that data obtained can generate entry records that can be utilized by other monitoring programs. The ability to cross reference databases is a key component in the Department of Homeland Security's emerging strategy to eliminate gaps and spot suspicious activity in entry security systems.

INSPASS also allows travelers to save time. The INSPASS imaging process generally takes less than a minute but still allows positive identification for inspectors. After the prospective entrant's identity is validated, automatic doors or gates open to allow passage. If a file is flagged, more than one person attempts entry, or there is a question of identity, a warning message appears on inspectors' monitors to alert them to a need to conduct a personal interview.

As with other automated entry systems, INSPASS utilizes a "one-to-one" search protocol to verify identity. Instead of comparing gathered biometrics across a broad database, an identification number allows direct comparison with the biometric measurements on file for that identification number. In essence, the automated systems only verify that the person is the same person initially associated with the biometric measurements on file in the database. Unlike fingerprint search protocols used by the FBI, the entry search protocols are, as of March 2003, unable to take biometrics and conduct a broad search to identify a subject's identity. In theory, the same biometric measurements could be registered to two different identities.

As of March 2003, the airport INSPASS was available at airports in New York, Newark, San Francisco, Los Angeles, Miami, and some Canadian sites.

INSPASS is available to citizens and lawful permanent residents of the United States, citizens of Canada or Bermuda, and landed immigrants of Canada who are citizens of British Commonwealth countries. Citizens of Visa Waiver Pilot Program countries are also eligible. Applicants for the airport INSPASS must travel to the United States on business at least three times per year. In addition to other restrictions, INSPASS is not available to travelers who have a criminal record.

The legal basis of all entry inspections derives from the Immigration and Nationality Act (INA) and the Code of Federal Regulations [CFR].

Other countries have similar automated immigration systems. For example, Canada uses the CANPASS system (Canadian Passenger Accelerated Service System).

■ FURTHER READING:

ELECTRONIC:

Bureau of Citizenship and Immigration Services. INSPASS. March 1, 2003. <http://www.immigration.gov/graphics/howdoi/inspassloc.htm> (April 14, 2003).

Department of Homeland Security. April 2, 2003. <http://www.dhs.gov/dhspublic/index.jsp> (April 11, 2003).

United States Department of Homeland Security. Bureau of Citizenship and Immigration Services, PORTPASS. March 11, 2003. <http://www.immigration.gov/graphics/howdoi/portpass.htm> (April 9, 2003).

———. Immigration Information, INSPASS. March 4, 2003. <http://www.immigration.gov/graphics/shared/howdoi/inspass.htm> (April 9, 2003).

SEE ALSO

APIS (Advance Passenger Information System)
IBIS (Interagency Border Inspection System)
IDENT (Automated Biometric Identification System)
NAILS (National Automated Immigration Lookout System)
PORTPASS (Port Passenger Accelerated Service System)
SENTRI (Secure Electronic Network for Travelers' Rapid Inspection)

Inspector General (OIG), Office of the

The Office of the Inspector General (OIG) is part of the United States Department of State and serves as a reviewer of department operations. The office also handles claims of government fraud, waste, and abuse, whether reported by department personnel or outside sources. The inspector general is responsible for briefing the executive branch and Congress on oversight issues, as well as coordinating investigations undertaken by the inspection offices of other Federal departments.

One of the main subsidiaries of the OIG is the Office of Security and Intelligence Oversight. The oversight committee routinely examines the administration of intelligence and security programs. The inspections serve the overall Department of State responsibility of providing international security for U.S. personnel, information, economic interests, and property. More recently, special attention has been paid to the assessment of terrorism threats and counter-terrorism readiness plans in U.S. offices abroad.

The OIG also investigates general forms of government malpractice, such as embezzlement, theft of government property, abuse of power or position, and misconduct. If sufficient case evidence is found during an OIG investigation, the case can be recommended to legislative oversight committees or the Federal Bureau of Investigation (FBI) if necessary.

Other government departments have their own internal offices of Inspector General. Like that of the Department of State, some of these serve important functions in the greater intelligence community. The Inspector General of the Department of Energy aids the National Nuclear Security Administration, the commission responsible for assessing the current age, state, and safety of the U.S. nuclear arsenal. In 2002, the Inspector General of the Treasury aided congressional investigations of large-scale corporate fraud and carried out a major review of the security structure protecting credit information and electronic funds transfers.

Many duties of the Office of the Inspector General coincide with those of the Department of Homeland Security. As the new department is established and grows, the umbrella structure surrounding the OIG will likely change.

SEE ALSO

Homeland Security, United States Department of

Intelligence

Intelligence is information concerning a foreign entity, usually (although not always) an adversary, as well as agencies concerned with collection of such information. It is intimately tied with the intelligence cycle, a process whereby raw information is acquired, converted into intelligence, and disseminated to the appropriate consumers.

The intelligence cycle, as defined in the United States Senate hearings of the Church Committee during the mid-1970s, consists of four or five steps. In the first of these, called either *planning, direction,* or *planning and direction,* intelligence requirements are determined, a plan for the collection is developed, and agencies are assigned to specific collection tasks. Throughout the intelligence cycle, this first step recurs in the form of continued checking on the productivity of collecting agencies.

The second step, *collection,* is probably the one that most readily comes to mind when the average person thinks of intelligence. Collection involves actions the layperson would call "spying." Collection includes the gathering of information through means such as surveillance of various types, as well as the cultivation of human contacts. Through these and other means, information sources are exploited, and this information is delivered to the appropriate processing unit.

The third and fourth steps, *processing* and *production,* are sometimes viewed as a single step. In the processing phase, raw data is converted into a more usable form; then that information is evaluated, analyzed, integrated, and interpreted to produce what is no longer mere information, but true intelligence. Suppose numerical data on a factory's output is collected; in the processing phase, these numbers may be put into the form of a graph, while in the production phase, an analyst determines overall patterns and what they mean.

Finally, there is *dissemination,* the step in which processed intelligence is distributed to the appropriate consumers, which are usually government or military officials.

■ FURTHER READING:

BOOKS:

Martin, David C. *Wilderness of Mirrors.* New York: Harper & Row, 1980.

Polmar, Norman, and Thomas B. Allen. *Spy Book: The Encyclopedia of Espionage.* New York: Random House, 1998.

Richelson, Jeffrey T. *The U.S. Intelligence Community,* fourth edition. Boulder, CO: Westview Press, 1999.

Wright, Peter. *Spycatcher: The Candid Autobiography of a Senior Intelligence Officer.* New York: Viking, 1987.

SEE ALSO

Espionage
HUMINT (Human Intelligence)
Intelligence Agent
Intelligence and Counter-Espionage Careers
Intelligence Community
Intelligence Officer
Measurement and Signatures Intelligence (MASINT)
SIGINT (Signals Intelligence)

Intelligence Agent

■ JUDSON KNIGHT

In general terms, an agent is one authorized to act in place of, or on behalf of, another. An intelligence agent, however, is not simply an agent of or for an intelligence agency. Whereas members of the agency are called intelligence officers, operatives, or special agents, an agent is someone hired or recruited from outside. There are numerous other variations in the informal taxonomy of agents, including secret or undercover agents, agents provocateur, agents-in-place, double agents, and agents of influence.

The distinction between agents and operatives.

Intelligence agency employees who work in the field do not call themselves agents; an agent is someone hired or recruited by an intelligence agency to do its bidding. The person to whom the agent reports—the actual agency employee—is known as an operative.

The distinction goes back to World War II and the origins of modern intelligence agencies. At that time, Office of Strategic Services (OSS) manuals defined an operative as "an individual employed by and responsible to the OSS and assigned under special programs to field activity." An agent, on the other hand, was defined by OSS as "an individual recruited in the field who is employed or directed by an OSS operative." The Central Intelligence Agency (CIA), successor to OSS, calls its operatives CIA officers.

There are numerous variations on the term "agent." In the Federal Bureau of Investigation (FBI) under J. Edgar Hoover, operatives called themselves "special agents." By this designation, Hoover meant to distinguish FBI agents from ordinary police officers.

Secret agents, double agents, and agents-in-place.

A *secret agent* or *undercover agent* is, simply enough, an agent who works in a clandestine capacity, such that the relationship with the intelligence agency is not obvious to those around him or her. These terms are more likely to show up in the vocabulary of laypeople than of intelligence operatives. In fact, such terminology is somewhat redundant, inasmuch as most agents must be secret or undercover in order to function effectively.

More useful are terms such as *double agent* or *agent-in-place*. A double agent is someone who seems to serve one intelligence agency, but actually works on behalf of another. Usually these agencies represent enemy governments, and the double agent provides information to one agency about the other or others. If, instead of two agencies, an agent serves three, the term *triple agent* is used. The double or triple agent may even be providing information to each service about the others, but usually there is only one entity that the double agent truly or ultimately serves.

A double agent whose perfidy has been discovered by the agency against which he or she is spying, and who is then used in that agency's service against the other, is a *redoubled agent*. An agent may be forced against his or her will to become a double agent. The same is true of a

redoubled agent, a role an agent can assume without even knowing that he or she is doing so—for example, by being given inaccurate or deliberately deceptive material to pass on as genuine intelligence.

An agent-in-place is similar to a double agent, with the difference that, whereas a double agent is usually called upon by agency to take that role, the agent-in-place usually volunteers for the position. Suppose a person works for Agency A, then is sent to work for agency B so as to report information to Agency A without anyone at Agency B knowing. That is a double agent. On the other hand, an agent-in-place would be someone working for Agency B who, of his or her own initiative, offered services to Agency A. The agent would continue to work for Agency B, and feed information to Agency A.

An agent-in-place is extremely valuable to the employing agency, but his or her role has great risks. For agents in place working on behalf of America's enemies— for example, Robert Hanssen, the FBI special agent who sold secrets to the Soviets and later the Russians—discovery led to imprisonment. For agents-in-place working on behalf of America in the Soviet camp, the penalty for discovery was far worse. According to an anecdote reported by Henry Becket, when KGB officers discovered that one of their own was serving the Americans as an agent-in-place, he was thrown feet first into a roaring furnace while his colleagues watched.

Sleepers, provocateurs, and agents of influence.

Several other interesting variations on the concept of an agent are sleeper agents, agents provocateur, and agents of influence. A *sleeper agent* is one placed in an undercover situation and told to await further instructions before beginning to actively engage in espionage activities. A sleeper may remain inactive for months or years, or even the rest of his or her life.

An *agent provocateur* is someone who infiltrates a group or organization with the purpose of inciting its members to unlawful acts that would bring them to the attention of—and most likely cause them to receive punishment from—authorities. Agents provocateur in labor organizations of the late nineteenth or early twentieth centuries, for instance, instigated mob violence that brought police action against workers' groups.

Finally, an *agent of influence* is someone who does not directly work for an intelligence agency, but is willing to act on its behalf. For example, right-leaning American intellectuals during the mid-twentieth century who worked for the Congress of Cultural Freedom, a CIA-sponsored group intended to influence western European opinion during the Cold War, often knowingly acted as agents of influence for U.S. intelligence. At the same time, many left-leaning Western intellectuals who were fed Soviet propaganda or disinformation, and who disseminated that material as truth, unwittingly acted as agents of influence for the KGB.

■ FURTHER READING:

BOOKS:

Bennett, Richard M. *Espionage: An Encyclopedia of Spies and Secrets.* London: Virgin Books, 2002.

Nash, Jay Robert. *Spies: A Narrative Encyclopedia of Dirty Deeds and Double Dealing from Biblical Times to Today.* New York: M. Evans, 1997.

Richelson, Jeffrey T. *The U.S. Intelligence Community,* fourth edition. Boulder, CO: Westview Press, 1999.

SEE ALSO

CIA, Formation and History
Hanssen (Robert) Espionage Case
Intelligence
Intelligence Officer
KGB (Komitet Gosudarstvennoi Bezopasnosti, USSR Committee of State Security)
OSS (United States Office of Strategic Services

Intelligence and Counterespionage Careers

■ JUDSON KNIGHT

There is no single template for a career in intelligence and espionage. Three of the nation's leading intelligence organizations—the Central Intelligence Agency (CIA), Federal Bureau of Investigation (FBI), and National Security Agency (NSA)—hold a wide array of opportunities in areas ranging from science, engineering, and mathematics, to linguistics, cartography, and foreign analysis. For each agency, career choices are naturally geared for the tasks at hand, with the NSA, for instance, concentrating on mathematics and cryptography, and the FBI focused on law enforcement. Nevertheless, opportunities are varied, though requirements, which call for extensive background checks, are high.

The CIA

Intelligence agencies have always been, by their nature, secretive. During the Cold War, this secrecy extended to their personnel requirements and practices. Today, however, while computerized encryption and other forms of technology maintain a higher level of secrecy than ever, where vital intelligence information is concerned, the CIA and other agencies are remarkably open about matters such as hiring.

The CIA, which regularly publishes declassified studies of past operations (some of them highly critical of CIA

activities), has been a leader in establishing a tradition of openness among intelligence agencies. In 1998, it even took out newspaper advertisements to recruit talented personnel for what the ads called "the ultimate international career for the extraordinary individual." Since that time, Israel's Mossad has also undertaken a recruiting effort.

Despite the scaling back of CIA resources following the end of the Cold War, director of recruitment Gil Medeiros told the media in 1998, "We found no lessening of tasking to the agency. We had to face the fact that it takes people in the field to do human sourcing intelligence." Soon the CIA also had in place job listings at its Web site, where it listed dozens of possible professions within the organization. Many of these fit under one of several categories: analytical positions; language positions; scientists, engineers, and technologists; and "clandestine service."

CIA jobs and the intelligence cycle. Most jobs in intelligence relate to some particular point in the intelligence cycle, a process whereby raw information is acquired, converted into intelligence, analyzed, and disseminated to the appropriate consumers. The acquisition in the field may be most familiar to civilians, but a much greater amount of activity is involved in the conversion of raw data into intelligence.

Among the areas of specialty the CIA uses in the processing and production phases of the intelligence cycle are various language and analytical skills. Within language skill areas, demands in 2003 were highest for Arabic and Korean, a reflection of the efforts against terrorism in the Middle East and weapons proliferation in North Korea at that time. The CIA also called for instructors and foreign media analysts with abilities in a variety of languages. Among the analytical positions advertised in 2003 were statisticians, as well as analysts specializing in China, the Middle East, the military, counterintelligence threats, and counterterrorism.

In acquiring, processing, and disseminating information, the CIA calls on the skills of scientists, engineers, and technologists. Advertised positions in 2003 ranged from mechanical, civil, electrical, and materials engineers to software specialists, signals intelligence officers, and even textile specialists.

The CIA also advertised opportunities in what it referred to as "clandestine service," including the positions of operations officer and language officer. Additionally, it has an ongoing need for a range of other professional personnel, including architects, attorneys, cost estimators, geographers, graphic designers, human resource consultants, medical officers, nurses, paralegals, physicians, psychiatrists, psychologists, video production specialists, and many others.

The agency offers a number of opportunities for college students, including a generous scholarship program (up to $15,000 yearly in 2003) for qualifying applicants

Students at the FBI Academy in Quantico, Virginia, learn techniques for subduing suspects. ©ANNA CLOPET/CORBIS.

majoring in electrical engineering or computer science. Requirements include U.S. citizenship, an SAT (Scholastic Aptitude Test) score of 1000 or above, a grade point average of 3.0 or better, and demonstrated financial need. Internships are also available, as are student trainee and graduate studies programs, all of which require at least temporary relocation to the Washington, D.C., area.

NSA

Although it is a much more secretive organization than the CIA in many regards, the NSA has a number of available positions, and is known as both the largest employer in Maryland and the largest employer of mathematicians in the United States. Its areas of specialty as of 2003 included language and intelligence analysts, electronic and computer engineers, and systems analysts and computer scientists, mathematicians, and cryptanalysts.

Prospective employees in any sensitive government position must expect a fairly extensive process of background checks, and nowhere is this more apparent than with NSA. Employment of any kind with NSA requires that an individual obtain a high-level security clearance. Applicants should expect to undergo medical screening, a polygraph interview, and a background investigation that

will open up past financial dealings and other details that a private citizen would consider personal business.

NSA employees do not enjoy the same privacy rights as ordinary citizens: overseas travel, plans to marry a non-U.S. citizen, even one's choice of a doctor or dentist, must be submitted for approval. (In the case of the doctor or dentist, this is because the employee might reveal secrets while under anaesthesia.) In addition, NSA employees, like many others in government positions, must submit to random drug testing. On the other hand, NSA is willing to consider persons with dual citizenship, though dual citizenship raises potential issues that must be addressed on an individual basis. All NSA new-hires must relocate to NSA headquarters at Fort Meade, Maryland.

The FBI

Within the FBI, the most visible position is that of special agent, but the bureau also offers an array of professional, administrative, technical, and clerical positions. Among the specific positions for which the bureau has a continuing need are attorneys, intelligence research specialists, and secretaries. Other examples of professional support personnel with the FBI include financial analysts, program analysts, computer specialists, nurses, auditors, language specialists, and photographers.

All applicants for professional support personnel positions must be U.S. citizens, with at least a high school diploma, as well as college or graduate degrees appropriate to particular areas of specialty. They must undergo a background investigation with a duration of between one and four months, during which time investigators will contact former and current employers, personal references, friends, neighbors, and family members. FBI personnel will also review school, credit, arrest, medical, and military records of prospective employees.

Special-agent applicants must be U.S. citizens, at least 23 years of age, but younger than 37. They must possess a four-year degree from an accredited college or university, as well as a valid driver's license, and must pass polygraph, drug, and color vision tests. Uncorrected vision must not be worse than 20/200 in one eye, and 20/40 in the other. If accepted for employment, they will undergo 16 weeks of intensive training at the FBI Academy in Quantico, Virginia, where they will receive 708 instructional hours in areas that include academics, firearms, physical training, defensive tactics, and practical exercises. Following graduation, special agents will undergo a two-year probationary period.

Once hired, an employee can expect to spend four years in the first office of assignment. For a special agent who has spent 10 years at the same office, a non-voluntary rotational transfer to a second field office will most likely take place. Some professional support positions, such as that of language specialist or investigative specialist, may call for temporary duty or short-term transfers.

■ FURTHER READING:

BOOKS:

Phillips, David Atlee. *Careers in Secret Operations: How to Be a Federal Intelligence Officer.* Frederick, MD: University Publications of America, 1984.

PERIODICALS:

Boyle, Matthew. "The Prying Game." *Fortune.* (September 17, 2001): 235.

Lang, John. "CIA Ads Tout Career in Espionage." *Dallas Morning News.* (November 1, 1998): 15A.

ELECTRONIC:

Careers in Intelligence. Association of Former Intelligence Officers. <http://www.afio.com/sections/careers/> (April 30, 2003).

CIA Careers. Central Intelligence Agency. <http://www.cia.gov/employment/> (April 30, 2003).

Employment. Federal Bureau of Investigation. <http://www.fbi.gov/employment/employ.htm> (April 30, 2003).

NSA Career Center. National Security Agency. <http://www.nsa.gov/programs/employ/homepage.html> (April 30, 2003).

Online Career Center. Intelligence Careers. <http://www.intelligencecareers.com/_homeroom/index.cfm> (April 30, 2003).

SEE ALSO

CIA (United States Central Intelligence Agency)
Classified Information
Crime Prevention, Intelligence Agencies
FBI (United States Federal Bureau of Investigation)
Intelligence Community
Law Enforcement Training Center (FLETC), United States Federal
Mossad
NSA (United States National Security Agency)
Privacy: Legal and Ethical Issues
Security Clearance Investigations
United States, Intelligence and Security

Intelligence and Democracy: Issues and Conflicts

■ TIMOTHY G. BORDEN

There have always been conflicts between individual rights and national security interests in democracies. Limits on civil liberties during wartime, including restrictions on free speech, public assembly, and mass detentions, have been the most serious threats to individual freedom. Even in peacetime, counter-terrorist measures including profiling, detention, and exclusion, along with the use of national identification cards, have raised concerns about racism, constitutional violations, and the loss of privacy. With the passage of new anti-terrorist laws after September 11, 2001, these tensions have increased. Supporters of broader governmental powers insist that they are part of the increased security measures necessary to safeguard national security. In contrast, many civil rights groups fear that the infringement upon individual rights is another step in the erosion of democratic civil society.

Wartime measures. The severest restrictions on civil liberties have occurred in times of war. In September 1862, during the American Civil War, President Abraham Lincoln (1809–1865) suspended the right of *habeas corpus* in order to allow federal authorities to arrest and detain suspected Confederate sympathizers without arrest warrants or speedy trials. Well aware of the drastic nature of such a step, Lincoln justified it as a necessary wartime measure. After the United States Supreme Court found Lincoln's abrogation of *habeas corpus* an unconstitutional intrusion on Congressional authority, Congress itself ratified the measure by passing the *Habeas Corpus* Act in September 1863. Through 1864, about 14,000 people were arrested under the act; about one in seven were detained at length in federal prisons, most on allegations of offering aid to the Confederacy but others on corruption and fraud charges.

Generations of historians have debated whether the suspension of a basic constitutional right such as *habeas corpus* was indeed justified, even though Article 1, Section 9, of the Constitution allowed *habeas corpus* to be suspended "in cases of rebellion or invasion" in the name of public safety. The controversy continued through the Reconstruction Era (1866–1876) and the passage of the Ku Klux Klan Act of 1871, which reiterated the use of federal military intervention and suspension of *habeas corpus* to force state officials to secure voting rights, jury service, and equal protection under the law for all citizens regardless of race. When Reconstruction ended in 1876, the law quickly fell into disuse.

Another major conflict between individual rights and national security and intelligence interests occurred during World War I. Although President Woodrow Wilson (1856–1924) had campaigned in 1916 on a platform of keeping the United States out of the conflict that raged in Europe, public sentiment against the Central Powers, led by Germany and Austria-Hungary, grew after sensational reports surfaced of German atrocities against civilians and a plot to inveigle Mexico to join the war against the United States. Wilson responded by instituting a peacetime military draft in July 1917, and persuading Congress to pass the Espionage Act that same year. Amended by the Sedition Act of 1918, the Espionage and Sedition Acts broadened the arrest powers granted to federal agents in apprehending and detaining individuals suspected of treason or antiwar activity. About 1,500 people were arrested under the acts for refusing to comply with the draft, publicly criticizing American foreign policy, and voicing opposition to America's involvement in the war. The Industrial Workers of the World union and Socialist Party came under particular scrutiny, given their antiwar platforms; the Socialist Party even had its newspapers banned from the U.S. mail because of their antiwar editorials and reports. Socialist Party leader Eugene V. Debs (1855–1926) was also convicted and sentenced to a ten-year prison term under the Espionage Act for an antiwar speech he gave in Canton, Ohio, in June 1918. Debs was later pardoned by President Warren G. Harding (1872–1936) in December 1921.

After the conclusion of World War I in November 1918, the federal government continued to use the Espionage and Sedition Acts as the basis for mass arrests and intelligence gathering. The Russian Revolution of 1917 and the brief takeover of the Hungarian government in 1919 by communists, as well as the presence of an estimated 40,000 Communist Party members in the United States, fueled concerns by authorities over the potential threat of communist-inspired unrest. The fears increased after anarchist groups targeted several government and business leaders with bombs in April and May of 1919, a terrorist wave that culminated in a series of bombings in eight American cities on June 2, 1919. Under the orders of Attorney General A. Mitchell Palmer, federal agents began rounding up suspected communists and anarchists in November 1919. The Palmer Raids, as they became known,

lasted until March 1920, and resulted in the arrest of 6,000 suspects. Palmer then announced that he had uncovered an anarchist-organized plot to stage a wave of violence on May Day, 1920. The day passed without incident and America's first "Red Scare" faded away, only to reappear later under McCarthyism.

The largest detainment of American citizens in the name of national security occurred with the internment of 110,000 Japanese-Americans during World War II. In the two months after the Japanese attack on Pearl Harbor on December 7, 1941, the U.S. Department of Justice ordered the detention of about 2,200 Japanese; 1,400 German; and 269 Italian nationals. After considering a large-scale roundup of all alien residents from the Axis Powers, the government decided to place Italian nationals under travel restrictions and prohibited them from using short-wave radios and owning guns. The restrictions on resident aliens from Italy were abandoned by the end of 1942. Fewer limits were placed on German resident aliens, although 254 of them were banned from specific military areas for security reasons.

In contrast, the 47,000 Issei living in the United States, Japanese-born residents who were barred under federal law from gaining American citizenship, and 80,000 of their American-born family members, called Nissei, were subjected to internment under Executive Order 9066, signed by President Franklin D. Roosevelt (1882–1945) in February 1942. The Roosevelt administration cited national security and sabotage risks for the decision, but exempted almost all of the ethnic Japanese living in Hawaii, whose freedom was vital to the island's economic survival. The mass detention was upheld by a U.S. Supreme Court ruling and was not lifted until December 1944. In 1988, Congressman Norman Y. Mineta, a former detainee, sponsored the Civil Liberties Act, which granted a payment of $20,000 to each detainee. Most contemporary scholars agree that the Japanese internment camps were not justified by intelligence or security demands, but were motivated by wartime hysteria, racism, and political lobbying by California farmers, who resented the success that some Japanese immigrants had as growers and gardeners in the region.

Peacetime measures: The FBI and CIA. Although the United States and Soviet Union were nominally allies during World War II, a resumption of anticommunist sentiment characterized the American political scene after the war. The Taft-Hartley Act of 1947 banned members of the Communist Party from holding leadership positions in American labor unions, and the continuing investigations by the U.S. House Un-American Activities Committee (HUAC) regularly made headlines. The 1950 McCarran Act required all Communist Party members to register with the U.S. Attorney General and allowed the U.S. Justice Department to arrest and detain resident aliens who were subject to deportation hearings. The Federal Bureau of Investigation (FBI) participated in the growing Red Scare by conducting another roundup of suspected Communist agents, using the powers it retained under the 1940 Smith Act, which permitted the arrest of any individual inciting the overthrow of the government.

The leading anticommunist crusader was Wisconsin Senator Joseph McCarthy (1908–1957), who accused the U.S. State Department of being infiltrated with communist spies in a speech before a West Virginia audience in February 1950. McCarthy's charges stunned the nation, even though it was later proved that he had fabricated them. Under McCarthyism, as the period came to be known, hundreds of government workers were fired as a result of so-called loyalty investigations. In the Senate's Army-McCarthy Hearings in 1954, it was revealed that McCarthy had launched an investigation of the Army after it had rejected one of his aides for a commissioned post, and the Senator's public support diminished. Later censured by the Senate, McCarthy died in 1957 as a symbol of the worst excesses of America's anticommunist hysteria.

Despite the controversies engendered by the role of the FBI and Central Intelligence Agency (CIA) during the McCarthy era, it was not until the 1960s that the agencies came under intense scrutiny for their practices. The FBI was widely praised for its investigation of crimes against civil-rights activists during the decade, yet its infiltration of students' and antiwar groups, particularly those opposed to America's involvement in the Vietnam War, raised suspicions that it routinely violated the constitutional rights of American citizens. The CIA, officially established in 1947, also came under criticism for its involvement in overthrowing foreign governments that were perceived as being hostile to the United States, especially if they were aligned with the Soviet Union. The failed Bay of Pigs invasion of Cuba in 1961 with a group of CIA-trained Cuban exiles was a major embarrassment to the Kennedy administration and was later cited as an example of the disregard of American intelligence agencies for international law. Reforms in the 1970s put stricter limits on the activities of both the FBI and CIA, including narrower prerogatives for collecting intelligence, conducting operations, and initiating covert activities.

Intelligence and democracy conflicts around the world.

Democratic countries other than the United States have also faced the conflict between maintaining the individual rights of their citizens and conducting vital intelligence and security operations. While the United States government moved to reassure the public that its civil liberties would be safeguarded, however, some nations have responded somewhat differently in the face of imminent terrorist threats.

The threat of terrorist attacks by its neighbors had been a constant presence in Israeli life, particularly since the first bombings by the Palestine Liberation Organization (PLO) in 1965. The PLO's terrorist campaign against Israel became acute during its Intifada (or "shaking off") of Israeli authority in the Occupied Territories in 1987 and again in 2001. Ranking the threat of terrorism as one of the

state's most pressing concerns, Israeli law allowed the indefinite detention of suspected terrorists without trial and forbid public shows of support for terrorist groups. Although the measures were condemned by some in the international community as selectively applied against non-Israelis, the country's leaders consistently defended the practices as a necessity for survival in the face of imminent and ongoing terrorist threats.

The United Kingdom has also faced international criticism for its actions against the Irish Republican Army's violence in protest of the British presence in Northern Ireland. Under the Prevention of Terrorism Act of 1974, British authorities could arrest suspected terrorists without a warrant and detain them for a week without bringing charges against them. While being interned, detainees were subjected to a range of harsh practices that included "hooding"—being isolated and forced to wear a hood over their heads—noise bombardment, and sleep and food deprivation.

Post-September 11 developments.
After the terrorist attacks of September 11, 2001, on the United States, the government moved to enact stricter counter-terrorist measures that once again raised concerns about the sanctity of individual civil liberties. On October 26, 2001, President George W. Bush signed the Patriot Act into law, giving the FBI and CIA broader investigatory powers and allowing them to share confidential information about suspected terrorists with one another. Under the act, both agencies could conduct residential searches without a warrant and without the presence of the suspect and could seize personal records on the spot. The provisions were not limited to investigating suspected terrorists, but were allowed in any criminal investigation. The Patriot Act also granted the FBI and CIA greater latitude in using computer tracking devices such as the Carnivore (DCS1000) to gain access to Internet and phone records.

The United Kingdom also passed a new counter-terrorist bill in December 2001, the Anti-Terrorism, Crime, and Security Act. The act allowed authorities to detain suspected terrorists for up to six months before reviewing their cases and for additional six-month periods after that. As in the United States, watchdogs in the United Kingdom criticized the new law for potentially infringing upon a basic civil liberty, in this case the right to avoid unlawful detention and gain access to a speedy trial.

The controversy over post-September 11, 2001, measures also extended to the screening of passengers on commercial airlines. The Computer Assisted Passenger Prescreening System (CAPPS), which had been selectively used before September 11, now came into wider usage in American airports. CAPPS looked at numerous factors to determine whether a passenger represented an elevated risk of being a terrorist, including how the plane ticket was bought, whether it was a round-trip or one-way ticket, and where the flight originated, and a 2001 U.S.

Department of Justice review ruled that it was not discriminatory. Despite this reassurance, some Arab rights groups maintained that CAPPS unfairly singled out individuals of Arab descent based on racial profiling.

■ FURTHER READING:

BOOKS:

Conroy, John. *Unspeakable Acts: The Dynamics of Torture.* New York: Alfred A. Knopf, 2000.

Hewitt, Christopher. *Understanding Terrorism in America.* New York: Routledge, 2002.

Heymann, Philip B. *Terrorism and America: A Commonsense Strategy for a Democratic Society.* Cambridge, MA: MIT Press, 1998.

Michel, Lou, and Dan Herbeck. *American Terrorist: Timothy McVeigh and the Oklahoma City Bombing.* New York: Regan Books, 2001.

Rehnquist, William H. *All the Laws But One: Civil Liberties in Wartime.* New York: Alfred A. Knopf, 1998.

Schrecker, Ellen. *Many Are the Crimes: McCarthyism in America.* Boston: Little, Brown and Company, 1998.

SEE ALSO

Airline Security
Assassination
Biological and Toxin Weapons Convention
Biological Warfare
Bioterrorism
Bioterrorism, Protective Measures
Bugs (microphones) and Bug Detectors
Church Committee
CIA (United States Central Intelligence Agency)
CIA, Legal Restriction
Classified Information
Cold War (1945–1950): The Start of the Atomic Age
Cold War (1950–1972)
Cold War (1972–1989): The Collapse of the Soviet Union
Commission on Civil Rights, United States
Continuity of Government, United States
Covert Operations
Dirty Tricks
Espionage Act of 1917
FBI (United States Federal Bureau of Investigation)
FOIA (Freedom of Information Act)
Foreign Intelligence Surveillance Court of Review
Intelligence, United States Congressional Oversight
Internet Spider
Internet Tracking and Tracing
Interrogation
Interrogation: Torture Techniques and Technologies
Iran-Contra Affair
Israel, Counter-terrorism Policy
Israel, Intelligence and Security
Justice Department, United States
McCarthyism
Official Secrets Act, United Kingdom
Patriot Act Terrorist Exclusion List
Patriot Act, United States
Politics: The Briefings of United States Presidential Candidates
President of the United States (Executive Command and Control of Intelligence Agencies)
Privacy: Legal and Ethical Issues
Profiling
Telephone Recording Laws
United Kingdom, Counter-terrorism Policy
United States, Counter-terrorism Policy
United States, Intelligence and Security
Watergate

Intelligence and International Law

■ JUDSON KNIGHT

The principal statutes of international law guiding intelligence operations are the laws of war established by the conferences at The Hague in The Netherlands in 1899 and 1907, and by a series of conventions in Geneva, Switzerland, between 1864 and 1975. Particularly significant are the 1907 Hague Land Warfare Regulations and the third and fourth Geneva Conventions of 1949, which address treatment of prisoners of war (POWs), spies, and mercenaries. U.S. actions to combat terrorism and terror-supporting entities following the September 11, 2001, attacks prompted a national and international debate over the application of international law.

The Framework of International Law

The term "international law" is somewhat misleading, inasmuch as *law* usually implies a system to which its subjects are required to submit, whether they agree to it or not. International law, on the other hand, rests almost entirely on the consent of nations to abide by that law, and the willingness of signatories to enforce it through sanctions, military actions, or other means. International law governs rules of peace, war, and neutrality. Laws of peace address matters such as the recognition of one nation by another, as well as guarantees of territorial sovereignty and the extent of territorial waters. Laws of neutrality prevent combatants in a war from moving troops or material across neutral territory, while laws of war govern treatment of combatants, civilians, medical personnel, and POWs in wartime.

Geneva 1864 and the Hague conferences. The concept of international law dates back to the writings of seventeenth-century Dutch statesman Hugo Grotius, who established the principle that nations should abide by conventions of conduct. The first significant attempt to establish a body of international law occurred when 12 nations met in Geneva in 1864. The first Geneva Convention, which addressed "the amelioration of the condition of the wounded on the field of battle," resulted in principles for protecting noncombatant personnel caring for the wounded, and established the International Red Cross.

During two conferences held at The Hague in 1899 and 1907, a much larger body of nations—44 in the case of the 1907 Hague Peace Conference—signed a total of 14 conventions governing laws of war, peace, and neutrality. The 1899 Hague Convention established a Permanent Court of Arbitration, which became the Permanent Court of International Justice under the League of Nations following World War I. The United Nations, established after World War II, changed its name to the International Criminal Court, but it is known popularly as the World Court.

Laws on treatment of POWs.

During the period from 1928 and 1975, a series of Geneva Conventions addressed a number of issues relating to warfare, including the use of chemical and bacteriological weapons, as well as the treatment of POWs. These, along with the earlier Hague agreements, established the principles whereby intelligence could and could not be gathered from combatants. Particularly significant in this regard were the third and fourth Geneva Conventions of 1949, often referred to as Geneva Conventions III and IV.

According to Article 17 of Geneva Convention III, POWs are required to provide interrogators only with surname, first name, rank, date of birth, identification number, or equivalent information. The same article states that "No physical or mental torture, nor any other form of coercion, may be inflicted on prisoners of war to secure from them information of any kind whatever." Article 31 of Geneva Convention IV prohibits the use of torture against civilians "in particular to obtain information from them or from third parties."

On the other hand, Article 24 of the 1907 Hague Land Warfare Regulations notes that "measures necessary for obtaining information about the enemy and the country are considered permissible"—a recognition of the fact that nations will conduct intelligence operations in wartime. Protocol I, Article 46 states that military personnel gathering intelligence while in uniform are to be accorded the treatment due other combatants, but expressly withholds these protections from undercover operatives or agents captured while in the act of conducting espionage. Article 47 similarly exempts mercenaries—those who fail to meet standards of lawful combatants established by Article 44 of 1907 Conference—from the rights of POWs. A similar provision exists in Geneva Convention III.

International law and the war on terrorism.

After the September 11 attacks, the United States launched a war on Afghanistan, whose Taliban regime was harboring and abetting operatives of the al-Qaeda terror network. The United States transported large numbers of Taliban and al-Qaeda personnel to holding centers at Guantanamo Bay, U.S.-controlled territory on the island of Cuba. U.S.

authorities accorded Taliban members, because they represented a national government, the rights of POWs, but regarded al-Qaeda personnel as mercenaries according to international law.

In practice, this distinction resulted in more aggressive questioning, and less concern for the physical comfort, of al-Qaeda operatives. Nevertheless, al-Qaeda personnel were provided with basic necessities, allowed to practice their religion, and otherwise treated in a manner no different from their Taliban cohorts. However, many groups in Europe and America regarded the distinction between al-Qaeda and Taliban as unlawful, and the American Bar Association passed a resolution calling for the granting of legal counsel to al-Qaeda detainees. Many critics of American policy cited "Protocol One," a 1977 addition to the Geneva Conventions designed to provide rights to personnel previously regarded as "unlawful combatants." President Ronald Reagan had rejected "Protocol One" in 1987 on the grounds that it was designed to protect the rights of terrorists.

American actions against terrorists also elicited criticism when senior al-Qaeda operative Khaled Sheikh Mohammed, captured in Pakistan in 2003, was detained in an undisclosed location while U.S. personnel—in the words of a Department of Defense statement—applied "all appropriate pressure" to extract intelligence from him. Government officials maintained repeatedly that Mohammed was not being tortured, and several noted that, aside from all moral or legal implications, torture is not usually an effective means of obtaining reliable information.

■ **FURTHER READING**:

BOOKS:

Kish, John, and David Turns. *International Law and Espionage.* Boston: M. Nijhoff Publishers, 1995.

Reisman, W. Michael, and James E. Baker. *Regulating Covert Action: Practices, Contexts, and Policies of Covert Coercion Abroad in International and American Law.* New Haven, CT: Yale University Press, 1992.

PERIODICALS:

Bonner, Raymond, et al. "Questioning Terror Suspects in a Dark and Surreal World." *New York Times.* (March 9, 2003): 1.

Bowman, M. E. "Intelligence and International Law." *International Journal of Intelligence and Counterintelligence* 8, no. 3 (fall 1995): 321–335.

Khor, Jennifer. "Information Gathering, the Law of War, and Peacekeeping." *Peacekeeping & International Relations* 24, no. 6 (November 1995): 16.

McManus, Doyle. "A U.S. License to Kill." *Los Angeles Times.* (January 11, 2003): A1.

Rivkin, David B., Jr. "The Laws of War." *Wall Street Journal.* (March 4, 2003): A14.

SEE ALSO

CIA, Legal Restriction

Electronic Communication Intercepts, Legal Issues
Interpol (International Criminal Police Organization)
Interrogation: Torture Techniques and Technologies
Privacy: Legal and Ethical Issues
Telephone Recording Laws

Intelligence and Law Enforcement Agencies

■ JUDSON KNIGHT

Despite the obvious relationship between intelligence and law enforcement, historically a number of barriers have separated the two. One of the most important of those barriers in the American experience has been the law itself, which has sought to prevent the development of an internal security apparatus more suited to an authoritarian or totalitarian nation than a liberal democracy. The end of the Cold War and the subsequent war on terrorism, however, presented the nation with threats that seemed to require blurring the lines between intelligence and law enforcement. These changes have in turn forced a rethinking of the relationship between national security, internal security, and the rights of citizens under the rule of law.

"Posse Comitatus" law.

Few ideas are as antithetical to American sensibilities as the notion of a government free to enforce its will with armed troops, or invisible spies, moving among the citizenry. Only once in American history has martial law prevailed over a large geographic region for an extensive period. That period was the Reconstruction (1865–77), in which the former states of the Confederacy were ruled by federal troops. In the aftermath of the Reconstruction, Congress passed the Posse Comitatus Act of 1878. The title of the act harkened to an ancient institution of English law whereby the local lord could raise a citizen militia to maintain public order, but the purpose of the 1878 law was to protect the citizenry from encroachments by government.

Although the Posse Comitatus Act made it illegal to use the U.S. military to enforce domestic law, a few occasions in the years since have necessitated adjustments. Such was the case in 1957, for instance, when President Dwight D. Eisenhower federalized the Arkansas National Guard and used it, along with the 101st Airborne Division, to integrate the high schools of Little Rock, Arkansas. Again in the 1980s, President Ronald Reagan used the military for the domestic "war on drugs."

Restrictions on the intelligence community.

The National Security Act of 1947, which created the Central Intelligence Agency (CIA), explicitly forbade it from operating in a law-enforcement or internal security capacity. With World War II recently concluded, America's leaders had a negative example in the form of the Nazis' Gestapo, not to mention the Soviet internal security apparatus that would become the KGB in the 1950s. Additionally, the National Security Act reinforced a division of labor between the nascent intelligence community (represented during the war by the Office of Strategic Services, or OSS) and the highest law-enforcement agency in the land, the Federal Bureau of Investigation (FBI). Though the FBI had been engaged in intelligence-gathering operations in Latin America, for the most part it had maintained its focus on internal affairs while OSS concentrated on external ones.

In today's U.S. intelligence community, which consists of more than a dozen agencies, most are members of the Department of Defense (DOD), which is effectively prevented by posse comitatus law from playing a role in internal security. Another factor that discourages the blurring of law enforcement and intelligence is the strong sentiment against domestic intelligence and surveillance operations such as those conducted by the FBI under the leadership of J. Edgar Hoover in the 1950s and 1960s. Such activities, when they came to light, served to reinforce a growing attitude of suspicion toward the federal government.

New threats and the blurring of lines.

Countering popular concerns for civil liberties and the rule of law are growing threats to national and internal security whose response almost seems to necessitate a blurring between intelligence and law enforcement duties. This has been particularly the case with the end of the Cold War and the rise of terrorist organizations. Not only do the latter threaten national security, but they are also involved in a number of activities usually dealt with by law enforcement: drug trafficking, counterfeiting, money laundering, and so on.

Additionally, the 1990s saw the rise of internal terrorism such as that perpetrated by the Oklahoma City bombers and the Unabomber. These actions required a response by domestic law-enforcement agencies, including the FBI and the Bureau of Alcohol, Tobacco, and Firearms. In a move that resembled actions of the CIA or National Security Agency, the FBI reportedly used satellites to conduct surveillance on Theodore Kaczynski, the Unabomber.

This new environment of combined law enforcement and intelligence efforts was reflected by the rise of state and local organizations devoted to providing intelligence to law enforcement agencies. An example was the Intelligence Network of the Iowa Department of Safety, established in 1984 to support multi-jurisdictory operations within the state. Law enforcement agencies in the Washington, D.C., and Baltimore area formed the Washington-Baltimore High Intensity Drug Trafficking Area Information Center, designed to serve as a hub for intelligence on drug and weapons trafficking, as well as money laundering, in the two cities.

As early as March, 1993, an awareness of the potential problems to be faced by the increased merging of law enforcement and intelligence operations spurred the formation of a federal study panel. In August, 1994, the Joint Task Force on Intelligence and Law Enforcement released a series of recommendations, including the creation of "focal points," or coordinating offices, that would provide an interface between the Justice Department and CIA. A decade later, the FBI and CIA engaged in a turf battle over new domestic intelligence responsibilities that arose from the war on terror. The administration of President George W. Bush chose to make CIA the lead agency in those efforts.

■ FURTHER READING:

BOOKS:

Best, Richard A., Jr. *Intelligence and Law Enforcement: Countering Transnational Threats to the U.S.* Washington, D.C.: Congressional Research Service, 2001.

PERIODICALS:

Eggen, Dan. "FBI Seeks Data on Foreign Students; College Calls Request Illegal." *Washington Post.* (December 25, 2002): A1.

Phillips, Edward H. "It Wasn't Us." *Aviation Week & Space Technology* 144, no. 15 (April 8, 1996): 19.

ELECTRONIC:

Information Center. Washington-Baltimore High Intensity Drug Trafficking Area. <http://www.hidta.org/programs/info_center.asp> (April 4, 2003).

Iowa Law Enforcement Intelligence Network. <http://www.state.ia.us/government/dps/intell/support.htm> (April 4, 2003).

SEE ALSO

CIA, Legal Restriction
Crime Prevention, Intelligence Agencies
DEA (Drug Enforcement Administration)
Domestic Intelligence
Drug Intelligence Estimates
Intelligence Community
Law Enforcement, Responses to Terrorism

Intelligence & Research (INR), United States Bureau of

The Bureau of Intelligence & Research (INR) is a unit of the U.S. State Department tasked with providing intelligence to department policymakers. As the major State Department component of the U.S. intelligence community, it holds a unique position, as most intelligence organizations are affiliated, either directly or by association, with the Department of Defense (DOD). In addition to its intelligence work, INR is involved in a number of geographic issues, from studying boundaries to encouraging geographic learning among U.S. students.

Established in 1946, INR assists the Secretary of State with timely assessments of international events through value-added independent analysis. It is the job of INR to ensure that intelligence activities support not only national security purposes (traditionally the topmost priority of DOD) but also foreign policy, a much greater concern for State. Although its principal customer is the State Department, INR also supplies its services to the White House, National Security Council, DOD, and other agencies within the intelligence community.

The 19 offices of INR are a reflection of the geographic and functional bureaus within the Department of State. INR employs some 300 persons, of whom about 75 percent are members of the civil service, with the remainder from the Foreign Service. These personnel speak and/or read a total of 36 languages, and 71 percent have postgraduate degrees. The average INR analyst has spent 13 years studying the country in which he or she is tasked. In addition to monitoring incoming traffic, INR analysts continually work to integrate data and insights into their ongoing analysis of overseas situations.

Additionally, INR has specialists concerned with analyzing international boundary issues and disputes. With its emphasis on geographic learning, INR has been a leading proponent of geography education for American students. On the Internet, it maintains its Geographic Learning Site for students from kindergarten through high school.

■ FURTHER READING:

BOOKS:

Global Trends 2015: A Dialogue about the Future with Nongovernment Experts. Langley, CA: National Intelligence Council, 2000.

INR, Intelligence and Research in the Department of State. Washington, D.C.: Bureau of Intelligence and Research, 1983.

PERIODICALS:

Barnes, Scottie. "State Department Hosts Forum on Geographic Information." *Geospatial Solutions* 12, no. 9 (September 2002): 18.

Meyer, Josh. "At Least 70,000 Terrorist Suspects on Watch List." *Los Angeles Times.* (September 22, 2002): A1.

ELECTRONIC:

Bureau of Intelligence and Research. U.S. Department of State. <http://www.state.gov/s/inr/> (April 7, 2003).

Department of State. U.S. Intelligence Community. <http://www.intelligence.gov/1-members_state.shtml> (April 7, 2003).

SEE ALSO

Department of State, United States
Intelligence Community
Terrorist Organization List, United States

Intelligence Authorization Acts, United States Congress

Intelligence authorization acts are annual legislative Acts of Congress whereby current intelligence issues are addressed and appropriations made for intelligence activities in the coming year. These date to 1979, although the first true intelligence authorization act was signed by President Ronald Reagan in 1981. The intelligence authorization acts are an example of the increased legislative oversight of intelligence activities that originated in the mid-1970s.

As a result of the Watergate scandal and its implication of the Central Intelligence Agency (CIA) as a participant in some part, combined with numerous revelations of clandestine CIA activities, Congress enacted a number of measures to exert greater legislative control over intelligence activities. Among these was the practice of passing yearly intelligence authorization acts.

The first of these was the Intelligence and Intelligence-Related Activities Authorization Act of 1979. The Act for 1980 had the same title, and only in 1981 was it titled the Intelligence Authorization Act. The 1981 Act was particularly important inasmuch as it established the process whereby the CIA notifies the leadership of the House and Senate intelligence committees of covert actions it intends to undertake.

Intelligence authorization acts have been passed in each fiscal year since 1981. They are far from a "rubber stamp" of the CIA or the administration. For instance, President William J. Clinton vetoed the original Intelligence Authorization Act for Fiscal Year 2001 (H.R. 5630) because of what he called "the badly flawed provision that would have made a felony of unauthorized disclosure of classified information."

■ FURTHER READING:

Bush, George W. "Remarks on Signing the Intelligence Authorization Act for Fiscal Year 2003." Weekly Compilation of Presidential Documents 38, no. 48 (December 2, 2002): 2101–2102.

———. "Statement on Signing the Intelligence Authorization Act for Fiscal Year 2002." Weekly Compilation of Presidential Documents 37, no. 52 (December 31, 2001): 1834.

Cannon, Carl M. "Central Intelligence Agency." National Journal 33, no. 25 (June 23, 2001): 1903–1904.

Clinton, William J. "Statement on Signing the Intelligence Authorization Act for Fiscal Year 2001." Weekly Compilation of Presidential Documents 36, no. 52 (January 1, 2001): 3184–3185.

SEE ALSO

Bush Administration (1989–1993), United States National Security Policy
Bush Administration (2001–), United States National Security Policy
CIA, Legal Restriction
Clinton Administration (1993–2001), United States National Security Policy
Intelligence, United States Congressional Oversight
President of the United States (Executive Command and Control of Intelligence Agencies)
Reagan Administration (1981–1989), United States National Security Policy

Intelligence Community

The United States Intelligence Community (IC) is a group of 14 agencies and organizations responsible for conducting intelligence activities necessary to the national security of the United States and the success of its foreign relations. Headed by the Director of Central Intelligence (DCI), its members include the Central Intelligence Agency (CIA), a number of Department of Defense (DOD) agencies and organizations, and intelligence-gathering agencies within the departments of State, Energy, Justice, the Treasury, and Homeland Security.

Defining the Intelligence Community

In contrast to the generic term "intelligence community," the United States has a formal Intelligence Community established as a result of Executive Order 12333, signed by President Ronald Reagan on December 4, 1981. The order directs, in part, that the United States intelligence effort shall provide the president and the National Security Council with the necessary information on which to base decisions concerning the conduct and development of foreign, defense, and economic policy, and the protection of United States national interests from foreign security threats. All departments and agencies shall cooperate fully to fulfill this goal.

In addition to the CIA, the IC includes 13 other agencies and organizations. Those from DOD include the Defense Intelligence Agency (DIA), National Security Agency (NSA), National Reconnaissance Office (NRO),

(l to r) Former U.S. Attorney Mary Jo White, former Senator Warren Rudman, former FBI director Louis Freeh, and CIA National Intelligence Officer Paul Pillar are sworn in during intelligence hearings, 2002. AP/WIDE WORLD PHOTOS.

National Imagery and Mapping Agency (NIMA), and the intelligence agencies of the Army, Navy, Air Force, and Marine Corps. Non-DOD members include the Federal Bureau of Investigation (a part of the Justice Department), the United States Coast Guard (part of the Department of Homeland Security as of 2003), the State Department's Bureau of Intelligence and Research, and the intelligence agencies of the Energy and Treasury departments.

Tasks

The 14 members of the IC work separately and together in fulfillment of a number of functions. They collect information required by the president, the National Security Council (NSC), the secretaries of state and defense, and other officials of the executive branch. In meeting the needs of these and other customers, they produce and disseminate a variety of intelligence gathered through the four traditional methods of intelligence collection: human, signals, imagery, and measurement and signatures intelligence (HUMINT, SIGINT, IMINT, and MASINT respectively).

Intelligence collection is directed toward information on international terrorist and narcotics trafficking activities, as well as other hostile activities against the United States by foreign powers, organizations, persons, and/or their agents. Members of the IC are also involved in the

conduct of special activities, which can and do involve covert action against entities deemed a threat to national security.

Leadership and oversight. The DCI serves a triple function as head of the CIA, principal intelligence advisor to the president, and director of the IC. He reports to the president, directly and through the national security advisor and/or the NSC. Each year, DCI presents the president with the annual IC budget, known as the National Foreign Intelligence Program (NFIP).

As head of the IC, the DCI is responsible for directing and coordinating national foreign intelligence activities, though he only exercises direct authority over CIA, as well as staff organizations outside the CIA. The latter include the National Intelligence Council (NIC), responsible for preparing national intelligence estimates, and the Community Management Staff, which assists DCI in his IC executive functions.

Advisory boards. DCI also chairs two advisory boards, the National Foreign Intelligence Board (NFIB) and the Intelligence Community Executive Committee (IC/EXCOM). Membership of both is made up of representatives from IC agencies. The NFIB exercises authority over approving national intelligence estimates, coordination of interagency intelligence exchanges as well as exchanges with the intelligence and security agencies of friendly foreign nations, and development of policy for the protection of intelligence sources and methods.

The IC/EXCOM advises DCI on national intelligence policy and resource issues, including matters relating to the IC budget, the establishment of needs and priorities, evaluation of intelligence activities, and formulation and implementation of intelligence policy. Its members include, in addition to DCI, the Deputy Secretary of Defense and undersecretaries whose roles relate to intelligence; the Vice Chairman of the Joint Chiefs of Staff; the directors of NSA, NRO, NIMA, and DIA; the Assistant Secretary of State for Intelligence and Research; the NIC chairman; and the executive directors for IC affairs and CIA.

Internal and external oversight.

A number of mechanisms exist for providing oversight and accountability to the IC. These include entities within its membership, as well as from both the executive and legislative branches of government. Within the IC is the CIA Inspector General, appointed by the President and confirmed by the Senate, who is responsible for investigating allegations of impropriety and mismanagement within CIA. DOD has its own inspector general, a position created by statute, while DOD elements of the IC have non-statutory inspectors general appointed by the directors of the respective agencies. Independent inspectors general exert oversight for non-DOD member organizations.

At the executive level, the Intelligence Oversight Board of the President's Foreign Intelligence Advisory Board provides oversight, and reviews the functions of IC oversight mechanisms. In the area of budgeting, controlled ultimately by the President, the Office of Management and Budget ensures that IC activities comport with the President's overall program. Within the executive branch, Congress provides checks and balances through the Senate Select Committee on Intelligence, the House Permanent Select Committee on Intelligence, and other committees concerned with activities relating to national security.

■ FURTHER READING:

BOOKS:

Fain, Tyrus G., and Katharine C. Plant. *The Intelligence Community: History, Organization, and Issues.* New York: R. R. Bowker, 1977.

Gore, Albert. *The Intelligence Community: Accompanying Report of the National Performance Review, Office of the Vice President.* Washington, D.C.: U.S. Government Printing Office, 1993.

Hopple, Gerald W., and Bruce W. Watson. *The Military Intelligence Community.* Boulder, CO: Westview Press, 1986.

Kirkpatrick, Lyman B. *The U.S. Intelligence Community: Foreign Policy and Domestic Activities.* New York: Hill and Wang, 1973.

Richelson, Jeffrey T. *The U.S. Intelligence Community,* fourth edition. Boulder, CO: Westview Press, 1999.

Smist, Frank John. *Congress Oversees the United States Intelligence Community, 1947–1989.* Knoxville: University of Tennessee Press, 1990.

ELECTRONIC:

Intelligence Agency Profiles. Federation of American Scientists. <http://www.fas.org/irp/agency/> (April 14, 2003).

U.S. Intelligence Community. <http://www.intelligence.gov/> (April 14, 2003).

SEE ALSO

Air Force Intelligence, United States
CIA (United States Central Intelligence Agency)
Coast Guard (USCG), United States
DCI (Director of the Central Intelligence Agency)
DIA (Defense Intelligence Agency)
DOD (United States Department of Defense)
DOE (United States Department of Energy)
FBI (United States Federal Bureau of Investigation)
INSCOM (United States Army Intelligence and Security Command)
Intelligence & Research (INR), United States Bureau
Intelligence, United States Congressional Oversight
NIC (National Intelligence Council)
NSC (National Security Council)
NFIB (United States National Foreign Intelligence Board)
NIMA (National Imagery and Mapping Agency)
NMIC (National Maritime Intelligence Center)
NRO (National Reconnaissance Office)
NSA (United States National Security Agency)
PFIAB (President's Foreign Intelligence Advisory Board)
President of the United States (Executive Command and Control of Intelligence Agencies)
Treasury Department, United States

Intelligence Literature

■ TABITHA SPARKS

The emergence of the "spy thriller" in the twentieth century reflects the modern era's technological advancements, and the institutionalization of intelligence services that works to monitor these advancements and their attendant risks on the global stage. Political conflicts between nations are the staple feature of the literature of espionage or intelligence, which also usually figures a heroic spy at the center of the international crisis. While spy novels for most of the twentieth century were dominantly a British invention, American novelists in the last decades have contended for the audience of this hugely popular genre.

The genre of the British spy novel that exploded in the early twentieth century has many nineteenth century influences. The global expansion of the British Empire in the second half of the nineteenth century introduced into

Alexander Litvinenko, former KGB spy and author of the book *Blowing Up Russia: Terror from Within,* photographed at his home in London in 2002. While serving in Russia's main security agency, Litvinenko's job was to try to infiltrate and topple terrorist networks. AP/WIDE WORLD PHOTOS.

British culture a range of foreign interests, languages, and customs. British power faltered as the nation expanded into colonies, inciting fears about the loss of British identity in the face of rapid foreign expansion. Many late-Victorian novels pit blameless Englishmen and women against evil foreigners in a black-and-white interpretation of the threats to "home" from abroad. The heightened sense of xenophobia was one precursor to the spy genre that rested upon the security of national borders.

Early British novels that feature the threat of imperial invasion and/or power include Bram Stoker's *Dracula* (1898) and Rudyard Kipling's *Kim* (1901). While not formally a spy novel, *Dracula* contains a detailed international plot whereby the title character, a vampire, is finally ensnared by a band of heroic Englishmen. Kipling's novel takes place in India, with an Anglo-Indian boy using his ambiguous racial identity as a cover for colonial espionage, or the "Great Game" between European and Asian factions.

Alongside a growing awareness of an increasingly pluralistic world was a rise of technology that made national security and police work a modern science. Fascination with detective work and forensics at the end of the

nineteenth century is exemplified by popular interest in the Jack-the-Ripper murders in London (the 1880s and 90s), and Arthur Conan-Doyle's series of detective novels featuring Sherlock Holmes. Both murder case and detective series detailed the new technologies of modern police work, including fingerprinting, handwriting analysis, and instruments of surveillance such as the camera and the telescope.

Joseph Conrad's critically acclaimed novels include several tales of espionage. *The Secret Agent* (1907) and *Under Western Eyes* (1911) critique the autocratic and revolutionary regimes in a stunning anticipation of World War I and the Bolshevik Revolution of 1917. The psychological complexity of Conrad's novels set them apart from the new wave "spy thrillers" written during this period, which predominantly depend on action and suspense rather than interior character development.

The spy novel in the early twentieth century was inspired most specifically by the advent of organized intelligence agencies in the period prior to World War I. The expansion of the London publishing industry in the late 1800s and early 1900s also contributed to the growing market for "pot boilers"—novels including spy thrillers with popular appeal but little critical value. These books are formulaic, usually with simplistically drawn good and evil characters, but appealed for their seemingly topical reflection of current politics.

Erskine Childers's *The Riddle of the Sands* (1903), for instance, concerns two Englishmen uncovering a German plot to launch a naval attack on Great Britain. The novel was so convincing in its analysis of naval security that the British Naval Intelligence Division was moved to investigate Childers himself for possible underground associations.

Among the many anti-German spy novels in English during this period are best-selling author William LeQueux's *Spies of Kaiser* (1909), which includes exhaustive descriptions of technological gadgetry of the new age of espionage, and E. Phillips Oppenheim's *The Kingdom of the Blind* (1916). Oppenheim's novel built upon the anti-German sentiment following the German sinking of the British ship The Lusitania in 1915, and includes a plot to sink a passenger ship. Also enormously popular was John Buchan's *The Thirty-Nine Steps* (1915), which details the urgent necessity for counterespionage in a typical German plot against the English navy.

Following World War I and the cynicism it fostered, the next phase of espionage literature reflects a perspective increasingly critical of official state authority. The spies in works by authors including Eric Ambler, Somerset Maugham, and especially, Graham Greene, often are lonely individuals on the outskirts of a power-hungry or opportunistic state government. Maugham and Greene built their reputations in part upon their own experience in espionage. During the Russian Revolution of 1917, Maugham went under cover as a reporter in order to communicate information to British Intelligence. While his novels and stories do not exclusively focus on espionage, he is credited with writing the first modern spy story with literary merit. This work is *Ashenden; or the British Agent* (1928), inspired by his own experience in Russia, and more famously known through Alfred Hitchcock's film interpretation, *The Secret Agent*.

Greene worked with the British Secret Intelligence Service in Sierra Leone (1941), a job he found perfunctory. His critique of the Intelligence Service emerges in left-wing novels, from *The Quiet American* (1952) and *A Burnt-out Case* (1961), to *The Human Factor* (1978).

Writing spy fiction at the same time as Greene, but in a very different style was Ian Fleming, the creator of Britain's most famous fictional spy, James Bond. Fleming, like Greene, had also worked as a spy, but his far-fetched and spectacular plots (which depend heavily on fantastic gadgetry and amazing escapes) appeal to an audience more interested in sensation than realism. Some of Fleming's most famous tales (many of which have been made into movies) include *Dr. No* (1958) and *Goldfinger* (1959), which figure Chinese and Russian threats to Western capitalism.

Challenging Bond's flashy exploits are the fictional spies created by British authors John le Carré and Len Deighton. These writers stress the moral conflicts inherent in espionage and geopolitical conflict, particularly during the Cold War. For instance, in le Carré's *The Spy Who Came in from the Cold* (1963), the hero himself ultimately dies on the Berlin Wall, after infiltrating East German intelligence. Le Carré's *The Tailor of Panama* (1966) and Deighton's *The Ipcress File* (1962) concern internal corruption of the intelligence service; their spies face crimes from both inside and outside their governments and bureaucracies.

British dominance in espionage literature waned somewhat during the last quarter of the twentieth century. Since the 1980s, American novelists including Robert Ludlow and Tom Clancy have rivaled their British counterparts in writing best-selling spy fiction. Clancy's hero Jack Ryan foils Cold War plots in novels including *The Hunt for Red October* (1984) and *Patriot Games* (1987), from a pro-government, relatively conservative vantage point. These stories have become popular films, with their emphasis on technology and gadgetry translating easily to the visual medium.

A somewhat ambivalent treatment of the security services, such as those offered by the nuanced works of le Carré and Deighton, perhaps anticipates the future of the literature of intelligence. The world of international politics is no longer viewed as Western-centric or bipolar (divided into adversarial nation states) as it was throughout much of the twentieth century. As international secret services turn to current crises like drug trafficking and bioterrorism, the shrinking world stage will likely be reflected on the pages of the literature of intelligence in the coming generations.

■ FURTHER READING:

BOOKS:

Cawalti, John G., and Bruse A. Rosenberg. *The Spy Story.* Chicago: University of Chicago Press, 1987.

Panek, LeRoy L. *The Special Branch: The British Spy Novel, 1890–1980.* Bowling Green, Ohio: Bowling Green University Popular Press, 1981.

Smith, Myron J., Jr., and Terry White. *Cloak and Dagger Fiction: An Annotated Guide to Spy Thrillers,* 3rd ed. New York: Greenwood Press, 1995.

Winks, Robin W. (ed. and introd.); Maureen Corrigan (ed.) *The Literature of Crime, Detection, and Espionage, I–II.* New York: Charles Scribners, 1998.

PERIODICALS:

Price, Thomas J. "Spy Stories: Espionage and the Public in the Twentieth Century." *Journal of Popular Culture* no. 30 (1996): 81–89.

SEE ALSO

Cold War (1945–1950): The Start of the Atomic Age

Cold War (1950–1972)
Cold War (1972–1989): The Collapse of the Soviet Union
Great Game

Intelligence Officer

An intelligence officer is a professional employed by an intelligence service. Members of the intelligence community make sharp distinctions between intelligence officers and intelligence agents, who are outsiders employed by the intelligence agency. Intelligence officers, on the other hand, are operatives of the agency itself, but their professional role—and the fact that many are military officers and/or intelligence specialists—gives them particular distinction.

The distinction goes back to World War II and the origins of modern intelligence agencies. At that time, Office of Strategic Services (OSS) manuals defined an operative as "an individual employed by and responsible to the OSS and assigned under special programs to field activity." An agent, on the other hand, was defined by OSS as "an individual recruited in the field who is employed or directed by an OSS operative." The Central Intelligence Agency (CIA), successor to OSS, calls its operatives CIA officers.

Intelligence officers often work with agents in the role of case officer. A case officer is an intelligence officer whose job it is to supervise agents working on a case, a term referring to an entire intelligence operation. The case officer provides direction to the agent, and if the case officer works on a one-on-one basis with the agent, then he or she is known as the agent's handler. An intelligence officer may assign one agent to perform the role of surrogate handler, working directly with other agents and reporting to the intelligence officer. In that case, the surrogate handler is known as a principal agent.

■ FURTHER READING:

BOOKS:

Phillips, David Atlee. *Careers in Secret Operations: How to Be a Federal Intelligence Officer.* Frederick, MD: University Publications of America, 1984.

Roosevelt, Archibald. *For Lust of Knowing: Memoirs of an Intelligence Officer.* Boston: Little, Brown, 1988.

Wright, Peter. *Spycatcher: The Candid Autobiography of a Senior Intelligence Officer.* New York: Viking, 1987.

Zacharias, Ellis M. *Secret Missions: The Story of an Intelligence Officer.* New York: G. P. Putnam's Sons, 1946.

SEE ALSO

Intelligence
Intelligence Agent
Intelligence and Counter-Espionage Careers

Intelligence Policy and Review (OIPR), United States Office of

The Office of Intelligence Policy and Review (OIPR) advises the United States attorney general regarding matters relating to U.S. national security activities. In accordance with the Foreign Intelligence Surveillance Act of 1978, OIPR prepares and files all applications for authorization to conduct electronic surveillance and physical searches. It also acts as legal adviser, not only to the attorney general and the Department of Justice as a whole, but also to the Central Intelligence Agency (CIA), Federal Bureau of Investigation (FBI), Department of Defense, Department of State, and other federal agencies. Additionally, OIPR acts as the Department of Justice representative on several interagency committees.

Acting under the direction of the Counsel for Intelligence Policy, the attorney general's legal adviser in intelligence matters, OIPR helps keep the attorney general—as the chief law-enforcement executive in the United States—abreast of all relevant national security activities. Under the provisions of the Foreign Intelligence and Surveillance Act, OIPR also prepares applications for surveillance and searches, and presents these to the U.S. Foreign Intelligence Surveillance Court.

Both for the attorney general and for various intelligence agencies such as the CIA, OIPR provides formal and informal legal counsel on matters relating to U.S. intelligence activities and procedures. For example, in the 1980s, OIPR helped bring an end to an FBI probe of the Committee in Support of the People of El Salvador (CISPES). That group supported the overthrow of the Salvadoran government by Marxist guerrillas, but based on OIPR's analysis, did not appear to be a communist front organization, and OIPR advised FBI leadership in 1985 that the probe threatened CISPES's First Amendment rights.

More than a decade later, OIPR was involved in the scandals surrounding Chinese nuclear spying in the United States during the administration of President William J. Clinton. OIPR twice received applications to wiretap scientist Wen Ho Lee at the Los Alamos National Laboratory, and twice rejected these applications on the basis that there was not sufficient evidence against him. The FBI disagreed, and in 1999, Attorney General Janet Reno blamed the burgeoning scandal in part on the two agencies for not bringing their disagreement before her.

OIPR serves as a sounding board for other agencies' opinions on matters involving proposed legislation regarding intelligence-related matters. It also represents the attorney general on a variety of interagency task forces and committees concerned with issues of national security and nonproliferation, as well as scientific exchanges, administration of exports, information security, personnel security, and foreign overflights of U.S. territory. Serving the Department of Justice as a whole, OIPR represents the department on interagency committees, including the National Foreign Intelligence Council.

Within the Justice Department, OIPR heads the Department Review Committee, which carries out department policy on security classifications and makes decisions regarding Privacy Act and Freedom of Information Act appeals. On the Intelligence-Law Enforcement Policy Board, OIPR co-chairs a variety of groups whose purpose is to facilitate better working relationships between components of the intelligence, security, and law-enforcement communities.

■ FURTHER READING:

PERIODICALS:

Jackson, Robert L. "Sessions Concedes FBI Erred in Central American Activist Probe." *Los Angeles Times*. (February 3, 1988): 16.

Safire, William. "Whitewash at Justice." *New York Times*. (July 16, 1999): A19.

ELECTRONIC:

Office of Intelligence Policy and Review. Department of Justice. <http://www.usdoj.gov/oipr/> (March 15, 2003).

Office of Intelligence Policy and Review. Federation of American Scientists. <http://www.fas.org/irp/agency/doj/oipr/> (March 15, 2003).

SEE ALSO

Chinese Espionage Against the United States
Clinton Administration (1993–2001), United States National Security Policy
Counter-intelligence
FBI (United States Federal Bureau of Investigation)
Foreign Intelligence Surveillance Act
Foreign Intelligence Surveillance Court of Review
Justice Department, United States
Reagan Administration (1981–1989), United States National Security Policy

Intelligence Support, United States Office of

The Office of Intelligence Support (OIS) is the sole United States Treasury Department office that also belongs to the national Intelligence Community. Established in 1977 to replace the Office of National Security, it assists the Secretary of the Treasury, who serves as the president's chief economic and financial adviser as well as the head of the second largest federal law-enforcement department. The OIS also participates in the preparation of National Intelligence Estimates.

In 1961, Treasury Secretary Douglas Dillon established the Office of National Security (ONS) to act as an interface, liaison, and coordinator between Treasury and the National Security Council. Ten years later, in 1971, a presidential memorandum clearly established the ONS as a member of the U.S. Intelligence Community. In response to the report of the Murphy Commission to Congress, which placed an emphasis on links between the Intelligence Community and the nation's economic policy leadership, Treasury was added to the National Foreign Intelligence Board in 1972.

In 1977, Treasury Secretary Michael Blumenthal changed ONS to OIS to emphasize its role in support of the Intelligence Community. Executive Order 12333 ("United States Intelligence Activities"), issued by President Ronald Reagan on December 4, 1981, explicitly spelled out the intelligence role of Treasury alongside that of other agencies and departments more obviously connected with intelligence gathering. The Special Assistant to the Secretary (National Security) is a senior officer in the Intelligence Community, as noted in E.O. 12333. On December 19, 2002, Treasury Secretary Paul H. O'Neill issued Treasury Order 113–01, defining the duties and responsibilities both of the Special Assistant and the office he or she directs, OIS.

The Special Assistant, along with his or her staff, supports the Secretary of the Treasury, whose critical functions include his or her role as chief economic and financial adviser to the president; director of the second-largest department in the federal government (after Justice) with law-enforcement authority; and chief official responsible for the integrity of U.S. currency. The Special Assistant is charged by 113–01 with providing day-to-day intelligence support to the Secretary and other officials, representing Treasury on committees of the Intelligence Community, and maintaining continuous liaison between Treasury and members of that community.

There are three principal components to the mission of OIS. First, it is responsible for alerting the Secretary and other officials of fast-breaking events, both foreign and domestic, of which it becomes aware as chief intelligence officer of the treasury. Second, it provides Treasury officials with intelligence reports and products, usually obtained from Intelligence Community collectors and producers of intelligence. Finally, it is charged with overseeing the relationship between Treasury's offices and bureaus and the members of the Intelligence Community, as well as the Community as a whole.

Additionally, OIS assists in the preparation of National Intelligence Estimates. It also assists other members of the Intelligence Community in the production of intelligence by contributing information to which Treasury is privy. OIS officers act as Treasury representatives of national intelligence committees and subcommittees within the Intelligence Community.

■ FURTHER READING:

ELECTRONIC:

Office of Intelligence Support. Federation of American Scientists. <http://www.fa.org/irp/agency/ustreas/tdois.htm> (March 17, 2003).

U.S. Department of the Treasury. <http://www.ustreas.gov> (March 17, 2003).

SEE ALSO

Intelligence Community
National Intelligence Estimate
NFIB (United States National Foreign Intelligence Board)
Treasury Department, United States

Intelligence, United States Congressional Oversight of

■ JUDSON KNIGHT

Although the United States Congress served as facilitator to the establishment of the U.S. intelligence community by passing the National Security Act of 1947, during the next quarter-century it exerted little oversight in matters of intelligence. Then, in the 1970s, as distrust of the executive branch grew in the wake of the Watergate scandal and the Vietnam War, Congress began to take a more activist stance. The result was the formation of the Church Committee in the Senate and the Pike Committee in the House of Representatives, both precursors to permanent committees exerting legislative oversight for intelligence activities. From 1981 onward, presidents have been required to sign Intelligence Authorization Acts, annual requests for funds and authority to undertake broadly defined actions.

For the first quarter-century after it passed the National Security Act, which, among other things, created the Central Intelligence Agency (CIA), Congress had little to say about the activities of the nascent intelligence community. Among significant legislation during this time were the 1949 revisions to the 1947 Act, whereby the structure of the National Security Council was altered; the State Department Basic Authorities Act of 1956; and the National Security Agency Act of 1959. The second of these acts provided rewards leading to the arrest of foreign saboteurs (it was amended to increase the rewards after the September, 2001, terrorist attacks), while the third act formalized aspects of the National Security Agency (NSA)

created in a secret 1952 memorandum by President Harry S. Truman.

The new era of congressional oversight began in 1974, with the passage of the Hughes-Ryan Act amending the Foreign Service Act. Passed in the wake of covert activities that helped bring down the Marxist regime of Salvador Allende in Chile, the Hughes-Ryan Act required the President to submit plans for covert actions to the relevant congressional committees.

The mid-1970s also saw new legislation designed to protect private citizens from government snooping. Congress had passed the Freedom of Information Act (FOIA) in 1967, but strengthened it in 1975 with new provisions that gave U.S. citizens access to files on them kept by federal law-enforcement agencies. In the meantime, the Privacy Act of 1974 greatly restricted the authority of agencies to collect information on individuals, and to disclose that information to persons other than the individual.

The Church and Pike committees. In the meantime, the Church Committee (officially known as the Senate Select Committee to Study Governmental Operations with Respect to Intelligence Activities) had begun meeting in 1975. Its principal focus was domestic intelligence activities, but after interviewing NSA witnesses, it broadened its efforts. Chaired by Frank Church (D-ID), the committee revealed so much about U.S. covert operations that President Gerald R. Ford finally called Church and asked him, in the name of national security, to stop the release of sensitive information.

The Church Committee issued its final report on April 26, 1976, but its effect would extend over several decades. Less well known than the Church Committee was its House counterpart, the Pike Committee. Chaired by Otis Pike (D-NY), it also operated from 1975 to 1976, and likewise focused on the NSA. When Pike demanded a copy of the "charter" establishing NSA, he was rebuffed, as the so-called charter was actually Truman's secret memorandum. Although the committee subpoenaed the directive, the NSA, with help from the Justice Department and the Pentagon, successfully blocked them from seeing it. Aside from a very small portion (revealed only for the purpose of showing that NSA was exempt from certain legal restrictions on the use of communications intelligence), the NSA "charter" remains one of the most deeply buried secrets of the federal government.

Notwithstanding Church's and Pike's partisanship and desire to grandstand, their committees did introduce checks upon the perceived adventurism of the CIA, NSA, and other agencies. These efforts continued into the early 1980s. In 1980, Congress passed the Classified Information Act, which gives guidelines for the use of classified information by both government and defendant in a legal case. A year later, it introduced the Intelligence Authorization Act, whereby the President makes a yearly accounting of the intelligence community's current and planned operations.

Despite corrective measures that might have established a framework for positive interactions between executive and legislative branches where intelligence was concerned, the 1980s saw a deepening rift between the conservative Republican administration of President Ronald Reagan and the Democrat-dominated Congress. The situation reached its nadir with the Iran-Contra affair, in which the administration and the CIA went around Congress to fund anticommunist fighters in Nicaragua and free American hostages in the Middle East by selling arms to the regime in Iran. Although the Iran-Contra fallout did not result in significant new legislation reaffirming Congressional authority over intelligence activities, the lengthy hearings that followed served to reassert congressional authority.

Congressional oversight today. Today, numerous sections of the U.S. Code address intelligence activities, among them Title 5 (Government Organization and Employees), Title 10 (Armed Forces), Title 18 (Crimes and Criminal Procedure), Title 22 (Foreign Relations and Intercourse), and Title 50 (War and National Defense). An annual Intelligence Authorization Act reinforces congressional oversight in the realm of intelligence, as do two standing committees that resulted from the Church and Pike hearings: the Senate Select Committee on Intelligence, and the House Permanent Select Committee on Intelligence.

Congressional authority over intelligence is high, as reflective of a legislative republican democracy under the rule of law. Certainly it will never be high enough for those who subscribe to the conspiratorial view of U.S. intelligence activities; likewise it will always be too high for their counterparts at the other extreme. After the end of Iran-Contra, however, the relationship between Congress, the President, and the intelligence community has been, though far from collegial, usually less than adversarial.

The aftermath of the September, 2001, terrorist attacks, in fact, revealed that national leaders are capable of setting aside differences in the interests of the nation as a whole. In the heightened atmosphere of security that followed those attacks, a growing majority supported a freer rein on intelligence activities. Covert action, minimized as the result of the 1970s and 1980s scandals, would again be on the rise in the fight against terrorism.

■ **FURTHER READING:**

BOOKS:

Legislative Oversight of Intelligence Activities: The U.S. Experience: Report. Washington, D.C.: U.S. Government Printing Office, 1994.

Roberts, Brad. *U.S. Foreign Policy After the Cold War.* Cambridge, MA: MIT Press, 1992.

Smist, Frank John. *Congress Oversees the United States Intelligence Community, 1947–1994.* Knoxville: University of Tennessee Press, 1994.

Wittkopf, Eugene R., and James M. McCormick. *The Domestic Sources of American Foreign Policy: Insights and Evidence.* Lanham, MD: Rowman and Littefield Publishers, 1999.

ELECTRONIC:

Intelligence Laws and Regulations. Federation of American Scientists. <http://www.fas.org/irp/offdocs/laws.htm> (March 26, 2003).

Intelligence Oversight. <http://intellinet.muskingum.edu/oversight_folder/oversighttoc.html> (March 26, 2003).

Sturtevant, Mary. Congressional Oversight of Intelligence: One Perspective. Federation of American Scientists. <http://www.fas.org/irp/eprint/sturtevant.html> (March 26, 2003).

SEE ALSO

Church Committee
CIA, Legal Restriction
Classified Information
Electronic Communication Intercepts, Legal Issues
FOIA (Freedom of Information Act)
Intelligence Authorization Acts, United States Congress
Iran-Contra Affair
National Security Act (1947)
President of the United States (Executive Command and Control of Intelligence Agencies)
Privacy: Legal and Ethical Issues
Security Clearance Investigations
Senate Select Committee on Intelligence, United States

Interagency Security Committee, United States

The United States Interagency Security Committee was created on October 19, 1995, by executive order of President Bill Clinton. The order provided for increased security measures for non-military federal buildings. The committee operates within the executive branch of the government and consists of the President and heads of nearly 20 major departments and agencies of the United States government.

After the bombing of the Alfred P. Murrah Federal Building in Oklahoma City, Oklahoma, and the first bombing of the World Trade Center in 1993, several government officials lobbied for increased security in and around various federal offices around the nation. While many of the buildings hired private security personnel, or reached agreements with local law enforcement about providing security services, many locations were not adequately staffed. In addition, some facilities were not built to adequately survive a terrorist attack. The Interagency Security Committee was charged with inspecting each federal facility for structural stability and for needed security measures. The committee further discussed implementation of metal detectors, security cameras, and other security technologies. These measures were intended to create a safer place for people to work.

Other sensitive security needs also fall into the committee's jurisdiction. When the Interagency Security Committee was first assembled, a central database of all federal facilities did not exist. A database was created that not only listed properties, but also building function and condition, security systems, and even employees. This database stores information about the general infrastructure of the extended federal government.

In addition, the creation of the Interagency Security Committee provided increased data protection measures. A number of mishaps involving the loss or mishandling of sensitive information stored on computers prompted the need for centralized discussion of how best to protect federal data. Since the committee's inception, two additional laws have been passed to strengthen computer privacy and data protection not only on the federal, but also on the corporate and private level.

Questions of the overall effectiveness of the committee came into question following the most recent attacks on the World Trade Center and the Pentagon in 2001. Critics claim the database remains incomplete, federal computer privacy systems are dated and ineffective, and overall security in federal facilities has not significantly improved. Others expect the committee to be replaced by or subsumed into the Department of Homeland Security. Many supporters maintain that the committee has not had enough time or resources to finish their task, but have made progress toward their goals.

SEE ALSO

Homeland Security, United States Department of

Interception Capabilities.

SEE *ECHELON.*

Internal Revenue Service, United States

Among the most visible arms of the U.S. federal government is the Internal Revenue Service (IRS). As most Americans know, the IRS is an office in the Treasury Department responsible for collecting all individual and corporate taxes. Although dealings with the IRS are sometimes dreaded by taxpayers, it is nevertheless a necessary component of operating the world's only superpower, and the money it collects—more than $2 billion in 2001—serves to fund operations ranging from the war on terrorism to research into the development of non-petroleum-burning engines. Among the most important components of the IRS is its Criminal Investigation (CI) division, which tracks down tax evaders and helps the federal government in its war on drug trafficking, money laundering, and terrorism.

History

The history of American taxation is inexorably tied with the history of American military activity. For the better part of a century, the federal government funded its operations through customs tariffs, but in 1862, President Abraham Lincoln created the Office of Internal Revenue to pay expenses associated with the Civil War. A decade later, the income tax was repealed, but it reappeared a half-century later in the beginnings of its modern form, with the ratification of the Sixteenth Amendment to the Constitution in 1913.

The amendment gave Congress the power to levy an income tax, which was collected by the Bureau of Internal Revenue (BIR). The latter had been created in 1877 to collect the few types of taxes that existed at the time, and as America entered World War I, its level of activity increased dramatically. In 1918, the top income tax rate reached a staggering 77 percent, but dropped again to 24 percent in 1929, only to rise again during the Great Depression. The coming of the Second World War brought with it the system of payroll withholding still in place today.

Formation and Operations. In 1952, the BIR became the IRS. Up to that time, the agency was staffed by appointees associated with the current presidential administration. Thenceforth, only the IRS commissioner and chief counsel were selected by the President and confirmed by the Senate, with the rest of the IRS run by professionals. Half a century later, the IRS went through a massive program of reform spurred by taxpayer dissatisfaction with the agency, which gained a voice in Washington after Republicans won a majority in Congress in 1994. The result was the IRS Restructuring and Reform Act of 1998, which created provisions to protect taxpayers' rights.

By 2003, the IRS had some 100,000 employees and a budget of $9.9 billion. It consisted of four major operating divisions: wage and investment, which dealt with 116 million taxpayers who filed individual and joint tax returns; small business and self-employment, which involved some 45 million small businesses and self-employed taxpayers; large and mid-sized business, concerned with corporations possessing assets of more than $10 million; and tax exempt and government entities, which also served employee benefit plans. Other areas included the appeals, chief counsel, communications and liaison, and criminal investigation divisions.

Criminal investigation.

The roots of CI go back to the BIR's Intelligence Unit, created in 1919 and staffed by six U.S. Post Office inspectors. In the 1930s, the unit succeeded in securing the conviction of gangster Al Capone, and assisted in solving the kidnapping of the Lindbergh baby. In July 1978, it assumed its present name. Over the course of its history, CI has had a conviction rate of 90 percent or better, a record unmatched among federal law enforcement agencies.

Staffed by some 2,900 special agents, CI enforces tax and money laundering laws, as well as the Bank Secrecy Act. Its agents are trained in accounting and forensic computer technology, necessary for recovering financial data that may have been encrypted or otherwise hidden by electronic means. In addition to its investigative work, CI serves as an information clearinghouse regarding taxpayer obligations, as well as tax scams. For example, an IRS advisory released in January 2002, warned of slavery reparation scams whereby unscrupulous companies charge African Americans fees to learn how they can receive tax exemption for their ancestors' enslavement. (There is no such exemption.)

The top investigative priorities of CI are legal tax crimes (that is, evasion of taxes on legal income), illegal source financial crimes, and narcotics-related financial crimes. IRS efforts against terrorists fall under the last of these categories, and include operations alongside other federal agencies in a number of multiagency programs such as the Joint Terrorism Task Force and Operation Green Quest. The Strategic Information Operations Center at Federal Bureau of Investigation headquarters in Washington, D.C., coordinates all these efforts.

■ FURTHER READING:

BOOKS:

Burnham, David. *A Law unto Itself: Power, Politics, and the IRS.* New York: Random House, 1989.

Davis, Shelley L. *Unbridled Power: Inside the Secret Culture of the IRS.* New York: HarperBusiness, 1997.

PERIODICALS:

Leader, Stefan. "Cash for Carnage: Funding the Modern Terrorist." *Jane's Intelligence Review.* (May 1, 1998): 36.

"Victory in the War on Terrorism Will Not Be Won on the Defensive." *New York Times.* (September 10, 2002): A19.

ELECTRONIC:

Internal Revenue Service. <http://www.irs.gov/> (April 4, 2003).

SEE ALSO

ATF (United States Bureau of Alcohol, Tobacco, and Firearms)
Treasury Department, United States

International Atomic Energy Agency (IAEA)

Established in 1957, the International Atomic Energy Agency (IAEA) is an independent intergovernmental organization tasked by the United Nations to monitor nuclear technology related matters. In 1979 the U.N. assigned the IAEA the task of Non-Proliferation Treaty (NPT) monitoring and for developing nuclear safeguards. In addition to monitoring activities, IAEA attempts to facilitate the safe and peaceful use of nuclear power for the generation of electricity and to assist health agencies in developing standards that protect against detrimental ionizing radiation. IAEA scientists and engineers offer specific advice regarding the safe operation of nuclear power stations and the disposal of radioactive waste.

With a staff of nearly 3000, including more than 600 field inspectors, IAEA currently serves 134 member states and maintains its headquarters in Vienna, Austria. As of May 2003, Mohamed El Baradei was serving as director-general of IAEA.

Nuclear detection technologies (many developed by the United States national laboratory system) allow IAEA inspectors to attempt to enhance security of nuclear materials and to deter the unintentional transfer of nuclear materials and nuclear technology to terrorists or nations seeking to develop nuclear weapons.

Limitations of the IAEA.

The IAEA has no enforcement authority and compliance with IAEA inspections is voluntary; enforcement actions must be mandated by the United Nations Security Council.

Scientists also criticize the fact that IAEA leadership is composed of former civil servants or diplomats rather than scientists. Despite an expert staff of scientists, political forces have sometimes thwarted IAEA inspectors. The IAEA has suffered notable failures, including the discovery of Iraqi nuclear weapons development facilities in the early 1990s after declarations by the then IAEA chief, Hans Blix, that Iraq had no viable nuclear weapons program.

IAEA monitors selected industrial processes, namely enrichment plants, fuel-fabrication facilities, and reprocessing facilities; but military nuclear materials are not tracked by the IAEA. Accordingly, the civil inventories of the largest nuclear-power states (i.e., the United States,

United Kingdom, China, France, and Russia) are not subject to IAEA safeguards. Approximately 24 tons of weapon-grade plutonium and uranium—less than 1% of the world stock—is safeguarded by IAEA. Although a small percentage, this material is critical because it could produce hundreds of nuclear weapons. Moreover, intelligence experts consider the IAEA monitored sites to be among those sites most vulnerable to potential diversion of nuclear materials.

IAEA actions. Following the 1986 Chernobyl disaster in the former Soviet Union (now Ukraine) IAEA inspectors and technical teams helped stabilize the damaged reactor. IAEA continued its role at Chernobyl to include the ongoing decommissioning of the facility.

IAEA inspectors took a lead role in controversial inspections programs in Iraq, North Korea, and Iran.

In 1991, IAEA's Iraq Action Team began inspecting suspect sites in Iraq under U.N. Security Council mandate. IAEA's mandate in Iraq was two-fold: uncover and dismantle Iraq's clandestine nuclear program, and manage an ongoing monitoring and verification plan (OMV). Prior to the invasion of Iraq by U.S.-led Coalition forces in March 2003, El Baradei, reported to the U.N. that Iraq had apparently been unable to successfully reconstitute its nuclear weapons program following its destruction and dismantling in the early 1990s.

IAEA inspectors have been consistently frustrated in their attempts to deal with North Korea. In 1999, IAEA officials reported to the United Nations Security Council that "critical parts" of the North Korean reactor at Yongbyon had been unaccounted for since 1994. Missing parts included those needed to control nuclear reactions and/or those that would be needed to construct another nuclear reactor. Special requests for inspections continued to be rejected by North Korea and in April 1993, the IAEA reissued its early 1990s ruling that North Korea was in "non-compliance" with its agreements regarding nuclear inspection and safeguards. IAEA inspectors further concluded that their limited inspections could not provide "meaningful assurance" that North Korea was using its nuclear facilities for peaceful purposes (e.g., only for energy generation or authorized research).

Concerned that Iran was attempting to accelerate its nuclear programs in such a way as to facilitate nuclear weapon development, in late 2002, IAEA inspectors requested additional access to inspect Iranian facilities. IAEA requests were initially denied. In February 2003, however, IAEA inspectors, including IAEA chief inspector Mohamed El Baradei were permitted to visit several new nuclear sites in Iran.

Since 1993, the IAEA has reported more than 400 cases of trafficking in nuclear materials. While 18 cases involved plutonium or weapons-grade uranium, most cases involved low-level medical and industrial radioactive waste, the kind used in dirty bombs.

■ FURTHER READING:

ELECTRONIC:

IAEA News Update on IAEA and North Korea. IAEA. <http://www.iaea.org/worldatom/Press/Focus/IaeaDprk/> (March 10, 2003).

International Atomic Energy Agency (IAEA). 2003. <http://www.iaea.org/worldatom/> (April 2, 2003).

Lu, Ming-Shih. "The IAEA Strengthened International Safeguards System." Brookhaven National Laboratory. 1998. <http://www.nautilus.org/library/security/papers/LuISODARCO.PDF> (April 2, 2003).

SEE ALSO

Iranian Nuclear Programs
Iraq War: Prelude to War (The International Debate Over the Use and Effectiveness of Weapons Inspections)
Los Alamos National Laboratory
Nonproliferation and National Security, United States
North Korean Nuclear Weapons Programs
Nuclear Power Plants, Security
Nuclear Regulatory Commission (NRC), United States
Russian Nuclear Materials, Security Issues
Weapon-Grade Plutonium and Uranium, Tracking

International Narcotics and Law Enforcement Affairs (INL), United States Bureau of

The Bureau for International Narcotics and Law Enforcement Affairs (INL) is an office of the U.S. State Department that advises the president, the secretary of state and other bureaus within the State Department, and other departments and agencies of the federal government on U.S. programs to combat international drug trafficking and other crimes. Its efforts support two strategic goals of the State Department: to reduce the flow of illegal drugs into the United States, and to minimize the impact of international crime within the country and among American citizens. As such, since the time of its founding in 1978, it has experienced a shift of focus from efforts against the drug trade to a larger anti-crime mission.

Recognizing the increased internationalization of drug-related crime, the State Department in 1978 created the Bureau of International Narcotics Matters (INM). Its efforts were directed toward support of police activities against the drug trade in far-flung corners of the world. Then, in November 1993, President William J. Clinton expanded its mission in Presidential Decision Directive (PDD) 14. Thereafter INM would also undertake military and economic/security assistance for drug control. The name was changed to the INL in 1995.

Today INL is known by the nickname "drugs and thugs." The nickname was the result of a broadened mandate pursuant to PDD 14, which saw an expansion of INM's focus in the period 1993–94. In addition to drugs, INM would thenceforth be concerned also with money laundering, international traffic in stolen vehicles, sales of arms and other contraband, smuggling of illegal aliens, and other varieties of crime at a transnational level. Accordingly, INM's name was changed early in 1995 to reflect the breadth of its new mission.

Working with domestic drug law-enforcement and regulatory agencies, INL acts as a U.S. representative on international bodies concerned with the drug trade. It promotes those aspects of U.S. foreign relations that can be used to stop the production of illegal drugs, and their smuggling into the United States. It advises the Secretary of State and other federal bureaus on issues of international drug control, and prepares the annual *International Narcotics Control Strategy Report* on drug production, traffic, and abuse worldwide. Additionally, it manages a drug control certification process mandated in a 1986 law.

A large portion of INL's budget, which in 1997 was $195 million (with an additional $20 million for criminal justice programs), is directed toward drug control assistance in some 85 countries. A great deal of these funds go to the Drug Enforcement Administration, Coast Guard, U.S. Customs Service, and other agencies that train foreign law-enforcement personnel in drug interdiction techniques. Particular attention and effort is directed toward those countries that loom large as sites for the production or transit of drugs, an array that ranges from the Bahamas to Pakistan, and from Colombia to Thailand. These and many other nations have INL narcotics affairs sections, which may consist of a single individual, or (in the case of Bolivia, Colombia, and Peru) may include dozens of foreign service officers, contractors, and Department of Defense pilots.

Efforts against international crime. In accordance with its expanded mission since the mid-1990s, INL has been involved in numerous efforts, not just against drugs, but against "thugs" as well. It has issued warnings against advance fee business scams, many of which originate from Nigeria and other parts of west Africa, and which typically involve a fax or e-mail requesting assistance in transferring a large amount of money. In the end, after the perpetrator has gotten hold of the target's bank account numbers or other sensitive information, the only transfer of funds is to the perpetrator. INL, in an advisory on the subject, indicated that persons receiving such a proposition should refer it to law enforcement officials. In another advisory, INL counseled Americans traveling abroad never to get involved in drug smuggling, because the best that the U.S. consul can do for a jailed American is to ensure that he or she will be treated in accordance with local law that in many cases is far more severe and restrictive of individual rights than U.S. law.

INL does more than advise: as with drugs, it has been involved in efforts against those who smuggle in aliens from China and other countries to become virtual slaves as payment for their tickets. It also works to counter international insurance fraud, such as that involving international car-theft rings operating in the United States. Often the cars stolen are leased vehicles, and the "owner," rather than turn in the car and pay a large fee for driving it too many miles, arranges to have it stolen, and collects the insurance money along with a fee from the car-theft ring. Such insurance fraud costs the U.S. consumer hundreds of dollars a year in increased premiums and indirect costs.

In an effort to enhance crime-fighting efforts internationally, INL in the 1990s cooperated with other U.S. law enforcement agencies to establish several International Law Enforcement Academies (ILEAs) overseas. Among the ILEAs established are facilities in Budapest, Hungary (1995); Bangkok, Thailand (1998); and Gabarone, Botswana (2001). In 2001, INL also opened an ILEA in Roswell, New Mexico.

■ **FURTHER READING:**

ELECTRONIC:

Bureau for International Narcotics and Law Enforcement Affairs. <http://www.state.gov/g/inl/> (March 19, 2003).

SEE ALSO

DEA (Drug Enforcement Administration)
Department of State, United States
Drug Control Policy, United States Office of National
Interpol (International Criminal Police Organization)
Law Enforcement, Responses to Terrorism
NDIC (Department of Justice National Drug Intelligence Center)

Internet

■ JUDSON KNIGHT

The Internet is a vast worldwide conglomeration of linked computer networks. Its roots lie in the mid-twentieth century, with a number of projects by the United States government and the private sector, most notable of which was the computer network created by the Advanced Research Projects Agency (ARPA) of the Department of Defense (DOD) in 1969. Until the early 1990s, the Internet remained largely the province of specialists, including defense personnel and scientists. The creation of browsers, or software that provided a convenient graphical interface between user and machine, revolutionized the medium, and spawned rapid economic growth throughout the 1990s. In addition to the World Wide Web and e-mail, the parts of the Internet most familiar to casual users, the Internet

A U.S. college student is arrested by FBI agents in Los Angeles, California, for the perpetration of an Internet hoax in 2000, in which he made over $241,000 and lost a Southern California high-tech company billions of dollars in market value. ©AFP/CORBIS.

contains a frontier that offers both great promise and great challenges to law and security.

Birth of the Internet

The basis of the Internet is the network, a group of computers linked by communication lines. The distant ancestors of today's networks were highly specialized systems used either by DOD, or by private companies (for example, airlines, which tracked reservations on the SABRE system) during the late 1950s and early 1960s. The development of semiconductor technology in the 1960s enabled the growth of computer activity in general, and networking in particular. Universities and research centers participated in time-sharing, whereby multiple users accessed the same system.

ARPANET, which connected time-sharing facilities at research centers, is generally regarded as the first true computer network. It provided a testing-ground for technologies that are still used today: simple mail transfer protocol (SMTP), the system that makes e-mail possible, and file transfer protocol (FTP), for transmitting large messages. To maximize effectiveness, ARPANET broke messages into small pieces, or packets, that could easily be transmitted and reassembled. The technique, known as

packet switching, enhanced communication between computers.

The 1970s: TCP/IP. During the 1970s, ARPA (now known as the Defense Advanced Research Projects Agency, or DARPA) continued its efforts to connect its users, but it eventually ran into a dead-end posed by the primitive systems of networking used at the time. Faced with this roadblock, DARPA turned to two computer scientists, Vinton Cerf and Robert Kahn, who developed a design that revolutionized networks.

This was the transmission control protocol (TCP), which, coupled with the related Internet Protocol (IP), provided a mechanism for addressing messages and routing them to their destinations using an open architecture that connected standardized networks. In 1980, DOD adopted TCP/IP as its standard, and required all participants to adopt the protocol as of January 1, 1983. Some observers regard this event as the true birth of the Internet.

The 1980s: civilian agencies get involved. The 1980s saw use of computer networks expand to include civilian agencies. Among these was the National Science Foundation (NSF), which worked with five supercomputing centers spread across the country to create NSFNET, a "backbone" system intended to connect the entire nation. NSF succeeded in linking small local and regional networks to NSFNET. Other civilian participants in computer networks, which began to increasingly overlap with one another, included the Department of Energy and the National Aeronautics and Space Administration (NASA), as well as a number of private companies.

Also during this period, several independent consortiums took on themselves the task of organizing and policing the rapidly growing Internet. Among these were the Internet Engineering Task Force and the Internet Society, both of which are concerned with Internet standards, as well as the Internet Corporation for Assigned Names and Numbers (ICANN). The latter controls policy with regard to the assignment of domain names, including top-level domains such as .com for commercial enterprises, .gov for government offices, .edu for schools, and so on.

The Internet Explosion

The mid-1980s saw the birth of the first commercial computer networks, including Prodigy, Compuserve, and Quantum Computer Services. The first two would eventually recede in significance as larger companies took over the Internet, but the third—founded in 1985 and renamed America Online (AOL) in 1989—would eventually merge with publishing and entertainment conglomerate Time Warner to control a wide span of media. All of that lay far in the future, however, during the mid-1980s, as the few commercial participants developed their first subscriber bases and linked up to NSFNET through the Commercial Internet Exchange (CIX).

A number of technological innovations in the 1980s and early 1990s portended the explosive growth of the Internet that would take place in the next decade. Among these was the development of the personal computer or PC, as well as local area networks (LANs), which linked computers within a single business or location. NSFNET, working with the Corporation for National Research Initiatives, sponsored the first commercial use of e-mail on the Internet. Then, in 1993, new legislation at the federal level permitted the full opening of the NSFNET to commercial users.

The result was much like the opening of lands in the western United States to homesteaders, only the "land" in this case existed in virtual or cyberspace, and instead of wagons, the new settlers used browsers. The first important browser was Mosaic, developed at the University of Illinois using standards created at the European Organization for Nuclear Research (CERN) by Tim Berners-Lee. Thus was born the World Wide Web, which uses hypertext transfer protocol, or HTTP. In this environment, Mosaic—known as Netscape Navigator after the formation of the Netscape Communications Corporation in 1994—and Microsoft's competing Internet Explorer would prove the most useful navigating tools.

Users of the Internet today can still travel to regions beyond the World Wide Web, where they can see what the Internet was like prior to 1993. The most significant surviving portion of this older section is Usenet, a worldwide bulletin board system containing some 14,000 forums or newsgroups. In addition to the Web and Usenet, the Internet includes e-mail (electronic mail), FTP sites (used for transferring pictures and other large files), instant messaging, and other components. At the edges of the Internet are proprietary services such as those accessible only to AOL users, as well as other pay sites. Additionally, company and government intranets (private networks accessible only through a password) lie beyond the periphery of the Internet, though a browser may be used to access both.

By 1988, the size of the Internet was doubling every year, and the advent of browsers made possible an enormous consumer influx. The mid- to late 1990s saw the formation of thousands of Internet service providers (ISPs), through which users gained access to the Internet in exchange for a monthly fee. As competition increased, fees decreased, forcing consolidation of providers. By the beginning of the twenty-first century, major companies such as AOL, AT&T, and Earthlink, along with a few second-tier ISPs, controlled most of the market.

The explosive growth of the Internet itself, coupled with the expanded opportunities for commerce it provided, fueled one of the greatest periods of economic growth in U.S. history, from 1996 to 2000. The economic downturn that began in April, 2000, and continued throughout the early 2000s, however, served as an indicator that the Internet—while it had certainly transformed communications—would not solve all problems.

There were several problems associated with the Internet itself, and simplest among these were the technological challenges involved in moving ever larger amounts of data. By the beginning of the twenty-first century, it became possible to access video and complex graphics using powerful data streams, and computer scientists envisioned technology that would make possible the use of high-resolution video or multiple streams on networks capable of processing 100 gigabits of data a second. To expand the number of available addresses, hitherto limited by the 32-bit IP address standard, the Internet Engineering Task Force in 1998 approved a new 128-bit standard. This made possible so many addresses that every electronic device in the world could have its own unique location in an ever-expanding Internet.

Less simple were some of the challenges associated with human activities. There were cybercrimes, such as hacking or the dissemination of viruses, either of which could be used simply as a form of information-age vandalism, or for extortion. Hacking of financial service sites also offered the opportunity to commit robbery without picking locks, and for this reason many companies adopted secure, encrypted sites. (The latter were designated by the prefix https://, in contrast to the ordinary http://.)

Just as the Internet could be used for education, commerce, and a host of other purposes, it also provided a forum for activities that tested the limits of free speech; extremist political parties and hate groups could operate a Web site. On the other hand, use of the Web to distribute drugs, weapons, or child pornography carried stiff penalties. At the same time, government attempts to restrict or control aspects of the Internet raised concerns over the abrogation of First Amendment rights. The Internet itself was worldwide, beyond the reach of even the U.S. Constitution or any law, and although China's totalitarian regime attempted to restrict citizens' access to it, the network continued to work its way deeper and deeper into the fabric of modern life.

■ FURTHER READING:

BOOKS:

Gillies, James, and R. Cailliau. *How the Web Was Born: The Story of the World Wide Web*. New York: Oxford University Press, 2000.

Hafner, Katie, and Matthew Lyon. *Where Wizards Stay Up Late: The Origins of the Internet*. New York: Simon & Schuster, 1996.

Young, Gray, ed. *The Internet*. New York: H. W. Wilson, 1998.

ELECTRONIC:

Defense Advanced Research Projects Agency. <http://www.darpa.mil/> (April 14, 2003).

Internet Society. <http://www.isoc.org/> (April 14, 2003).

Webopedia: Online Dictionary for Computer and Internet Terms. <http://www.webopedia.com/> (April 14, 2003).

SEE ALSO

CERN
Computer Hackers
Computer Software Security
Computer Virus
DARPA (Defense Advanced Research Projects Agency)
Internet: Dynamic and Static Addresses
Internet Spam and Fraud
Internet Spider
Internet Surveillance
Internet Tracking and Tracing
NSF (National Science Foundation)

Internet: Dynamic and Static Addresses

Every computer operating on the Internet has a unique IP, or Internet protocol, address. Because the Internet's original design did not take into account the vast size it would assume from the mid-1990s onward, as more and more people went online, the architecture did not account for an infinite number of IP addresses. To conserve these, an Internet service provider (ISP) has a limited number of permanent IP addresses, and issues temporary IP addresses for customers to use while online. The permanent and temporary IP locations are known as static and dynamic addresses, respectively.

An IP address takes the form of a dot address, or a dotted quad, that looks something like this: 123.456.789.000. Each of the three-digit numbers represents 8 bits of information, forming a 32-bit address that defines the Internet protocol. Because the Internet is really a network connecting various smaller computer networks, the IP address begins with data indicating the particular network to which a computer belongs. For very large networks, a great portion of the IP number gives the local address, whereas for extremely small networks, the majority of the address identifies the network, with only the last few numbers serving as a unique identifier.

In cases of computer crime or espionage, an IP address—sometimes described as a "social security number"—can be used to pinpoint the computer used. Naturally, a dynamic address is more desirable for concealment, just as a person who does not want a telephone call traced to his or her home may place the call from a payphone. Even so, the dynamic IP address can usually be traced to a network. In any case, dynamic addresses are likely to disappear from the scene, due to the adoption of a 128-bit Internet protocol, IPv6. Together with allocation technology known as supernetting or CIDR (Classless Inter-Domain Routing), IPv6 will make it possible to assign every computer a static IP address.

■ FURTHER READING:

BOOKS:

Gelman, Robert B., and Stanton McCandlish. *Protecting Yourself Online: The Definitive Resource on Safety, Freedom, and Privacy in Cyberspace*. New York: HarperEdge, 1998.

Schneier, Bruce. *Secrets and Lies: Digital Security in a Networked World*. New York: John Wiley, 2000.

Schwartau, Winn. *Cybershock: Surviving Hackers, Phreakers, Identity Thieves, Internet Terrorists, and Weapons of Mass Disruption*. New York: Thunder's Mouth Press, 2000.

PERIODICALS:

Cholewka, Kathleen. "Address Management Made Easier?" *Telephony* 234, no. 1 (January 5, 1998): 39.

Ng Ken Boon. "Enabling Net Connection Sharing." *InternetWeek* no. 872 (August 6, 2001): 1.

Prince, Paul. "Static Electricity." *Tele.com* 6, no. 17 (September 3, 2001): 28.

SEE ALSO

Computer Hackers
Cyber Security
Internet Spam and Fraud
Internet Spider

Internet Surveillance
Internet Tracking and Tracing

Internet Spam and Fraud

■ K. LEE LERNER

An increasingly costly and vexing economic security issue involves the high traffic in unsolicited commercial email (termed "spam") and the use of internet communication to commit fraud.

Nearly one-half of the estimated 50 billion email messages sent each day are spam mail that contain usually misleading or fraudulent representations for products or services ranging from health and well-being products to pornography. Internet experts assert that nearly 90 percent of the spam mail sent is sent by a network of less than 200 individuals or direct marketing companies that use spam. Spam is costly to Internet service providers (ISP) and to consumers in terms of money, time, and bandwidth. Spam can also disrupt the normal operation of many network systems. Current efforts to curb spam involve legal restrictions and technical measures to block the transfer of such messages.

Spam technology commonly exploits openings in the program structure of computers (e.g. open proxies, etc.) attached to the Internet that are then designated to act as relays for sending spam. Spammers use special programs to identify vulnerable computers. Messages relayed from these computers often carry only the "innocent" relaying computer's identification. Special internet spiders can also be used by spammers to extract email addresses from websites.

In late April 2003, the state of Virginia enacted tough anti-spam laws and congressional leaders promised action on similar measures at the federal level. One legislative initiative, the "Can Spam Act," would include civil fines for senders of commercial e-mail with fraudulent or otherwise invalid return email addresses. Virginia's law potentially subjects repeat or "serial" spammers to felony penalties. That tough legislation was first passed in Virginia is significant because Virginia hosts a number of major Internet hubs and providers, including the United States' largest ISP, America Online.

The first anti-spam bill was passed by Nevada in 1997, and about half of all states have such laws. Some simply require that bulk email senders offer email recipients a method to prevent further mailings from a particular sender. Other laws prohibit false identifiers, misleading subject headings or require unsolicited e-mail to be identified with "ADV" in the subject line. Messages with a characteristic label or portion of text in their subject line are more easily filtered from email traffic. Conventional filters can also scan email for characteristic strings of text such as "no

prescription required" that often accompany fraudulent email related to drugs normally available only by prescription. Other Congressional proposals include the potential creation of a national registry of addresses who do not want to receive spam.

Within the United States, the Federal Trade Commission (FTC) is responsible for internet commercial regulation and has acted to stop spamming by use of anti-fraud laws.

■ FURTHER READING:

BOOKS:

Mulligan, Geoff. *Removing the Spam: Email Processing and Filtering.* Boston: Addison-Wesley Publishing, 1999.

PERIODICALS:

Frank, Diane. "Cybersecurity Center Takes Shape." *Federal Computer Week* 16, no. 4 (February 18, 2002): 10.

SEE ALSO

Computer and Electronic Data, Destruction
Computer Fraud and Abuse Act of 1986
Computer Hackers
Computer Keystroke Recorder
Computer Software Security
Computer Virus
Internet: Dynamic and Static Addresses
Internet Spider
Internet Surveillance
Internet Tracking and Tracing

Internet Spider

An Internet spider is a program designed to "crawl" over the World Wide Web, the portion of the Internet most familiar to general users, and retrieve locations of Web pages. It is sometimes referred to as a webcrawler. Many search engines use webcrawlers to obtain links, which are filed away in an index. When a user asks for information on a particular subject, the search engine pulls up pages retrieved by the Internet spider. Without spiders, the vast richness of the Web would be all but inaccessible to most users, rather as the Library of Congress would be if the books were not organized.

Some search engines are human-based, meaning that they rely on humans to submit links and other information, which the search engine categorizes, catalogues, and indexes. Most search engines today use a combination of human and crawler input. Crawler-based engines send out spiders, which are actually computer programs that have sometimes been likened to viruses because of their ability to move between, and insert themselves into, other areas in cyberspace.

Spiders visit Web sites, record the information there, read the meta tags that identify a site according to subjects, and follow the site's links to other pages. Because of the many links between pages, a spider can start at almost any point on the Web and keep moving. Eventually it returns the data gathered on its journey to the search engine's central depository of information, where it is organized and stored. Periodically the crawler will revisit the sites to check for changed information, but until it does so, the material in the search engine's index remains the same. It is for this reason that a search at any time may yield "dead" Web pages, or ones that can no longer be found.

No two search engines are exactly the same, the reason being (among other things) a difference in the choice of algorithm by which the indices are searched. Algorithms can be adjusted to scan for the frequency of certain keywords, and even to circumvent attempts at keyword stuffing or "spamdexing," the insertion of irrelevant search terms intended simply to draw traffic to a site.

■ FURTHER READING:

BOOKS:

Fah-Chun Cheong. *Internet Agents: Spiders, Wanderers, Brokers, and 'Bots.* Indianapolis, IN: New Riders, 1996.

Sherman, Chris, and Gary Price. *The Invisible Web: Uncovering Information Sources Search Engines Can't See.* Medford, NJ: CyberAge Books, 2001.

Young, Gray. *The Internet.* New York: H. W. Wilson, 1998.

SEE ALSO

Computer Virus
Internet: Dynamic and Static Addresses
Internet Spam and Fraud
Internet Surveillance
Internet Tracking and Tracing

Internet Surveillance

■ LARRY GILMAN

Internet surveillance is the monitoring of Internet data traffic for information useful to government authorities.

Targeted content may be illegal (e.g., child pornography), politically suspect (e.g., human-rights websites accessed by citizens living under authoritarian regimes), or evidential (e.g., e-mails or voice messages exchanged by suspects). Because the volume of information passing through the Internet is large, Internet surveillance generally requires a software component that scans for selected patterns of text, speech, addressing, or usage, and which flags items of interest for inspection by a human operator. Countermeasures against Internet surveillance include

avoidance of the Internet as a means of communication, the establishment of Internet aliases that conceal users' identities, and encryption.

Levels of Internet surveillance. Internet surveillance may target individuals, local networks, or Internet traffic in bulk. Surveillance of individual users (or, rather, of individual electronic addresses, which may actually have more than one user) is analogous to traditional telephone wiretapping: a law-enforcement agency, intelligence agency, or other surveillant first gains physical access to one or more computers through which the Internet traffic of a suspect party passes. Using specialized hardware and software, the surveillant then scans all data traffic passing to and from the targeted party. Some or all of that traffic may be recorded by the surveillant for later use. All transmissions, recorded or not, are allowed to continue on to their intended destinations so that the surveillance remains secret.

Surveillance systems have been proposed recently that would scan Internet content and usage patterns in bulk, not user-by-user. For example, in December 2002 the President's Critical Infrastructure Protection Board released a report entitled "The National Strategy to Secure Cyberspace" (http://www.whitehouse.gov/pcipb/). This report urged the creation of a centralized computer system to monitor the Internet. Such monitoring might, the paper said, be restricted to the analysis of network usage patterns (e.g., a wave of e-mails possibly indicating the spread of a new computer virus via the Internet), rather than being empowered to examine message content. Non-content information that might be gleaned by such a surveillance system includes the source and destination addresses of e-mails, the electronic addresses of websites visited by various persons, or the electronic addresses of persons visiting various websites. However, it would probably be impractical to build a high-level monitoring system that did not provide, at least potentially, access to individual users' information.

Uses and abuses. Many governments are interested in Internet surveillance, whether to fight crime and terrorism, monitor the political speech of their citizens, or both. For example, immediately after the terrorist attacks of September 11, 2001, the British government asked British Internet service providers (ISPs) to temporarily record all their users' Internet traffic, hoping that clues to the attacks might be preserved. Various authoritarian governments block access to certain websites or spy on users to enforce political conformity, including the governments of Laos, Myanmar, Saudi Arabia, Syria, the United Arab Emirates, and Yemen. China monitors public Internet use for political keywords such as "June 4" (the date of the 1989 pro-democracy protests in Tiananmen Square, which the Chinese government violently suppressed), and maintains "public security bureaus" around the country to monitor Internet traffic. As of February 2003, China has jailed at least 33 people for forbidden Internet use of a political nature, including downloading of articles from foreign pro-democracy websites. In the U.S. and many other countries it is illegal for the government to spy on citizens' nonviolent political activities, whether via Internet surveillance or by other means; however, there is evidence that these laws have been tested in the past and, some experts argue, might be broken even more readily using powerful, impossible-to-detect Internet surveillance tools such as are already in use or technically feasible. The topic of Internet surveillance is thus fraught with political controversy.

In 2002, for example, the U.S. Defense Advanced Research Projects Agency (DARPA)—the same branch of the Pentagon that created the beginnings of the Internet—proposed an ambitious Internet surveillance system termed Total Information Awareness (TIA). TIA would, according to DARPA, not only allow access to the content of virtually the whole Internet, but would enable the government to integrate that information with data gained by virtually any other means: wiretaps, criminal and other public records, on-line shopping habits, credit-card use, automated tollbooth data, cell-phone calling records, and so on. TIA bids for information omniscience.

However, the TIA proposal met instant protest from across the political spectrum, and in January 2003 the U.S. Senate voted restrictions on its development and deployment. Development of TIA cannot, the Senate has said, continue unless the president certifies that halting it "would endanger the national security of the United States." (As of this writing, the president has not yet made any such certification.) The political future of TIA is therefore doubtful; there is, however, little doubt about its technical feasibility.

In a similar vein, the U.S. National Security Agency (NSA), whose official mission is eavesdropping on communications outside the U.S. and across its borders and which has a bigger budget than the Central Intelligence Agency, is thought by some analysts to already have a system ("Echelon") that can scan Internet message traffic for nonencrypted keywords. Since other governments certainly possess such software, there cannot be any technical obstacles to its development by the NSA; however, as of February 2003 the existence of Echelon remains unconfirmed.

In the meantime, the U.S. Federal Bureau of Investigation (FBI) routinely employs the Carnivore program for Internet surveillance of individuals. Carnivore, whose use has been publicly acknowledged by the FBI since June 2000, is classified as a "high-speed packet sniffer" (a term explained below). It is part of a larger surveillance toolbox called the Dragonware Suite. Dragonware is comprised of three software tools: Carnivore, Packeteer, and Coolminer. No public information about Packeteer and Coolminer is available, but some experts assert that these programs organize the information collected by Carnivore and analyze it for various patterns (probably under the guidance of human users).

What "Carnivore" does. Binary information streaming over the Internet is organized into "packets." Each packet is a collection of bits containing both message content and information about where it has come from and where it is going to. Data to be transmitted over the Internet are thus not sent as a continuous stream of 1s and 0s over dedicated channels, but as a blizzard of tiny, independent messages (packets) that may follow different paths to their final destination. They are reassembled at the receiving party's ISP before final transmission to the user over a dedicated line (e.g., a telephone line). A packet sniffer examines ("sniffs") every packet being handled by an ISP to see if its source or destination are on a target list of electronic addresses. The packet sniffer may be set either to simply record all packets meeting these criteria or to further examine each packet to see if its content matches court-mandated search guidelines (e.g., mention of bombs, drugs, insider trading). If a packet's content does not match search-order guidelines, it is not recorded. Alternatively, the packet sniffer may ignore content altogether, recording only routing information (source and destination addresses).

Use of Carnivore is governed by the Electronic Communications Privacy Act of 1994 (ECPA) and by the federal law governing wiretaps, the Wire and Electronic Communications Interception and Interception of Oral Communications Act (also known as Title III). These laws state that officials need to obtain a search warrant from a court in order to look at stored digital data such as e-mails held in memory by an ISP or the contents of a user's hard drive. They also state that a court order must be obtained before a program such as Carnivore can be used to monitor communications in real time (e-mails in transit, for example). There are several kinds of court orders authorizing Internet surveillance, each allowing different information to be collected: (1) a *content wiretap* allows the recording of all information in packets that meet certain criteria (e.g., mention of a specific activity or person); (2) a *trap-and-trace* wiretap allows the FBI only to record information about destinations and websites visited, not content; (3) a *pen register* wiretap, like a trap-and-trace in reverse, determines where e-mail received by the suspect party has come from, what the electronic addresses are of parties that access the suspect's website, and so forth. Again, a pen register wiretap is not authorized to record content.

Controversy. Like almost any technical tool, Internet surveillance can be used for both legitimate and illegitimate purposes. Unfortunately, all official organizations, in all countries, declare that they are legitimate and that the individuals they surveil are dangerous criminals. In the U.S., the FBI and DARPA defend Internet surveillance tools like Carnivore and TIA by pointing out that they are only supposed to be used as authorized by a federal court (in the case of Carnivore) or to preserve national security (in the case of the proposed TIA program). According to the FBI, "The ability of law enforcement agencies to conduct lawful electronic surveillance of the communications of its criminal subjects represents one of the most important capabilities for acquiring evidence to prevent serious criminal behavior." John Poindexter, head of the Information Awareness Office (part of DARPA), which is developing TIA, says that the U.S. needs TIA because "[w]e must be able to detect, classify, identify, and track terrorists so that we may understand their plans and act to prevent them from being executed."

Critics such as the American Civil Liberties Union argue that what the FBI and the intelligence agencies are supposed to do is not always the same as what they have done; there is a long public record of potentially illegal political surveillance of U.S. citizens by U.S. police and government organizations. Therefore, critics argue, certain tools—especially those that would make it possible to filter the Internet transactions of thousands or millions of people simultaneously—should not even be developed, whereas those with lesser capabilities, such as Carnivore, should operate under more severe restrictions than they presently do.

■ FURTHER READING:

PERIODICALS:

Lee, Jennifer. "Guerilla Warfare, Waged with Code." *New York Times.* October 10, 2002.

Markoff, John, and John Schwartz. "Bush Administration to Propose System for Monitoring Internet." *New York Times.* December 20, 2002.

McCullagh, Declan. "FBI Agents Soon May Be Able to Spy on Internet Users Legally Without a Court Order." *New York Times.* September 14, 2001.

ELECTRONIC:

Poindexter, John. "Overview of the Information Awareness Office." Defense Advanced Research Projects Agency. August 2, 2002. <http://www.fas.org/irp/agency/dod/poindexter.html> (Jan. 28, 2003).

SEE ALSO

Cyber Security

Internet Tracking and Tracing

■ BRIAN HOYLE

Electronic passage through the Internet leaves a trail that can be traced. Tracing is a process that follows the Internet activity backwards, from the recipient to the user. As well, a user's Internet activity on web sites can also be tracked on the recipient site (i.e., what sites are visited and how often). Sometimes this tracking and tracing ability is used to generate email to the user promoting a product that is related to the sites visited. User information, however, can also be gathered covertly.

Techniques of Internet tracking and tracing can also enable authorities to pursue and identify those responsible for malicious Internet activity. For example, on February 8, 2000, a number of key commercial Internet sites such as Yahoo, Ebay, and Amazon were jammed with incoming information and rendered inoperable. Through tracing and tracking techniques, law enforcement authorities established that the attacks had arisen from the computer of a 15-year-old boy in Montreal, Canada. The youth, whose Internet identity was "Mafiaboy," was arrested within months of the incidents.

Law enforcement use of Internet tracking is extensive. For example, the U.S. Federal Bureau of Investigation has a tracking program designated Carnivore. The program is capable of scanning thousands of emails to identify those that meet the search criteria.

Tracking Tools

Cookies. Cookies are computer files that are stored on a user's computer during a visit to a web site. When the user electronically enters the web site, the host computer automatically loads the file(s) to the user's computer.

The cookie is a tracking device, which records the electronic movements made by the user at the site, as well as identifiers such as a username and password. Commercial web sites make use of cookies to allow a user to establish an account on the first visit to the site and so to avoid having to enter account information (i.e., address, credit card number, financial activity) on subsequent visits. User information can also be collected unbeknownst to the user and subsequently used for whatever purpose the host intends.

Cookies are files, and so can be transferred from the host computer to another computer. This can occur legally (i.e., selling of a subscriber mailing list) or illegally (i.e., "hacking in" to a host computer and copying the file). Also, cookies can be acquired as part of a law enforcement investigation.

Stealing a cookie requires knowledge of the file name. Unfortunately, this information is not difficult to obtain. A survey, conducted by a U.S. Internet security company in 2002, on 109, 212 web sites that used cookies found that almost 55 percent of them used the same cookie name. Cookies may be disabled by the user, however, this calls for programming knowledge that many users do not have or do not wish to acquire.

Bugs or Beacons. A bug or a beacon is an image that can be installed on a web page or in an email. Unlike cookies, bugs cannot be disabled. They can be prominent or surreptitious. As examples of the latter, graphics that are transparent to the user can be present, as can graphics that are only 1x1 pixels in size (corresponding to a dot on a computer monitor). When a user clicks onto the graphic in an attempt to view, or even to close the image, information is relayed to the host computer.

Information that can be gathered by bugs or beacons includes:

- the user's IP address (the Internet address of the computer)
- the email address of the user
- the user computer's operating system (which can be used to target viruses to specific operating systems
- the URL (Uniform Record Locator), or address, of the web page that the user was visiting when the bug or beacon was activated
- the browser that was used (i.e., Netscape, Explorer)

When used as a marketing tool or means for an entrepreneur to acquire information about the consumer, bugs or beacons can be merely an annoyance. However, the acquisition of IP addresses and other user information can be used maliciously. For example, information on active email addresses can be used to send "spam" email or virus-laden email to the user. And, like cookies, the information provided by the bug or beacon can be useful to law enforcement officers who are tracking down the source of an Internet intrusion.

Active X, JavaScript.
These computer-scripting languages are automatically activated when a site is visited. The mini-programs can operate within the larger program, so as to create the "pop-up" advertiser windows that appear with increasing frequency on web sites. When the pop-up graphic is visited, user information such as described in the above sections can be gathered.

Tracing email.
Email transmissions have several features that make it possible to trace their passage from the sender to the recipient computers. For example, every email contains a section of information that is dubbed the header. Information concerning the origin time, date, and location of the message is present, as is the Internet address (IP) of the sender's computer.

If an alias has been used to send the message, the IP number can be used to trace the true origin of the transmission. When the message source is a personally owned computer, this tracing can often lead directly to the sender. However, if the sending computer serves a large community—such as a university, and through which malicious transmissions are often routed—then identifying the sender can remain daunting.

Depending on the email program in use, even a communal facility can have information concerning the account of the sender.

The information in the header also details the route that the message took from the sending computer to the recipient computer. This can be useful in unearthing the identity of the sender. For example, in the case of Mafiaboy, examination of the transmissions led to a computer at the University of California at Santa Barbara that had been commandeered for the prank. Examination of the log files

allowed authorities to trace the transmission path back to the sender's personal computer.

Chat rooms.
Chat rooms are electronic forums where users can visit and exchange views and opinions about a variety of issues. By piecing together the electronic transcripts of the chat room conversations, enforcement officers can track down the source of malicious activity.

Returning to the example of Mafiaboy, enforcement officers were able to find transmissions at certain chat rooms where the upcoming malicious activity was described. The source of the transmissions was determined to be the youth's personal computer. Matching the times of the chat room transmissions to the malicious events provided strong evidence of the youth's involvement.

Tracking, tracing, and privacy.
While Internet tracking serves a useful purpose in law enforcement, its commercial use is increasingly being examined from the standpoint of personal privacy. The 1984 Cable Act in the United States permits the collection of such information if the information is deemed to aid future commercial developments. User consent is required, however, if the information that is capable of being collected can exceed that needed for commerce.

■ FURTHER READING:

BOOKS:

Bosworth, Seymour, and Michel E. Kabay, eds. *Computer Security Handbook*. New York: John Wiley & Sons, 2002.

National Research Council, Computer Science and Telecommunications Board. *Cyber Security Today and Tommorow: Pay Now or Pay Later.* Washington, DC: The National Academies Press, 2002.

Northcutt, Stephen, Lenny Zeltser, Scott Winters, et al. *Inside Network Perimeter Security: The Definitive Guide to Firewalls, Virtual Private Networks (VPNs), Routers, and Intrusion Detection Systems.* Indianapolis: New Riders Publishing, 2002.

SEE ALSO

Computer Hackers
Computer Keystroke Recorder
Information Security

Interpol (International Criminal Police Organization)

■ CARYN E. NEUMANN

Interpol is an international organization based in Lyon, France, that fosters global police cooperation by sharing

Ronald Noble, secretary of the International Police Agency, Interpol, at a press conference in 2002, when the agency hoped to recruit three Asian countries—Afghanistan, Yajikistan, and Turkmenistan—as members to help fight international crimes and apprehend fugitives. Soon afterward, Afghanistan joined the Interpol ranks. AP/WIDE WORLD PHOTOS.

intelligence about cross-border criminal activities among its 181 member nations. Despite popular misconception, the organization maintains no police force of its own. Each member nation maintains and staffs a National Central Bureau to direct Interpol intelligence, while local authorities investigate and prosecute criminals according to national laws. Interpol's actions are limited to receiving requests for assistance; analyzing criminal activities that are not of a political, military, religious, or racial character; and disseminating notices published in four languages (English, French, Spanish, and Arabic) to its members. It currently focuses upon public safety and terrorism, organized crime, illegal drug production and smuggling, weapons dealing, trafficking in human beings, money laundering, and financial and high technology wrongdoing.

Begun in 1923, Interpol is an international effort to halt crime that has occurred or is projected to occur in multiple countries. Although headquartered in France, no country dominates the group and its funding is provided by a sliding scale membership fee that is based upon each country's gross national product (GNP). The organization's policies are set by a vote of its member countries while the governors on its executive committee are required to be drawn from different continents. The secretary general, elected every five years by two-thirds of the

members attending the annual General Assembly, is Interpol's chief executive and senior full-time official. Daily activities are conducted at the General Secretariat in Lyon with a staff of 384 who represent 54 different countries. National Central Bureaus (NCB) in member countries ferry Interpol information to appropriate local authorities who bear responsibility for apprehending and extraditing suspected criminals. Five NCBs also act as Regional Stations with Lyon covering Europe, North America, and the Middle East: Nairobi, Kenya, responsible for East Africa; Abidjan, Ivory Coast, focusing on West Africa; Buenos Aires, Argentina, addressing South America; Tokyo, Japan, transmitting to Asia; and Puerto Rico, assisting the Caribbean and Central America.

No nation is required to respond to an Interpol request. Some countries, notably the United States in the years leading up to World War II, have declined to fully cooperate with Interpol for fear that its files may be misused for the prosecution of political criminals. In 1956, the organization agreed to forbid any activities of a political, military, religious, or racial character, but concerns remain that some countries may potentially ignore these guidelines. The chief fear of many member countries is that classified information may fall into the hands of terrorists since the distribution of intelligence cannot be restricted once it enters the Interpol system. Although this worry has reduced the amount of classified information flowing through Interpol, the organization has experienced a steady increase in information traffic. In 2000, Interpol transmitted 2.5 million messages, placed 15,116 notices of criminal activity in circulation, and projected that 1400 people would be arrested or located as the result of Interpol intelligence. Interpol notices are coded into ten different colors that represent different purposes. The red wanted notices are the most common and this type of communication requests the arrest of subjects for whom an arrest warrant has been issued and extradition will be sought. The other notices are: seeking the identity and location of subjects who have committed or witnessed criminal offenses (blue); providing warning about career criminals who have committed offenses in several countries (green); seeking missing or lost people, especially children abducted by parents (yellow); seeking the identification of corpses (black); warning of unusual modus operandi (purple); sharing knowledge of organized crime groups (gray); and advising of criminal activity with international ramifications that does not involve a specific person or group (orange). Stolen property notices are also distributed but are not coded.

As the second largest international organization behind the United Nations, Interpol has a record of proven success. It continues to grow as new nations join and the organization betters its communications system. The increasing global movement of people and the concomitant jump in international crime likely means that Interpol will remain a popular crime-fighting tool well into the twenty-first century.

■ FURTHER READING:

BOOKS:

Anderson, Malcolm. *Policing the World: Interpol and the Politics of International Police Co-operation.* Oxford: Clarendon Press, 1989.

Bresler, Fenton. *Interpol.* London: Sinclair-Stevenson, 1992.

United States Department of Justice and United States Department of the Treasury. *Interpol: The International Criminal Police Organization.* Washington, D.C.: Government Printing Office, 2002.

ELECTRONIC:

Interpol. "Interpol Information." <http://www.interpol.int/Public/Icpo/default.asp> (January 17, 2003).

SEE ALSO

Classified Information
Interpol (International Criminal Police Organization)

Interpol, United States National Central Bureau

■ CARYN E. NEUMANN

As the United States branch of Interpol, an international police organization, the National Central Bureau (NCB) in Washington, D.C., serves as a communications clearinghouse for police seeking assistance in criminal investigations that cross international boundaries. Directed by the U.S. Attorney General and representing sixteen law enforcement agencies under the Department of Justice in conjunction with the Department of the Treasury, the USNCB focuses on fugitives, financial fraud, drug violations, terrorism, and violent crimes. It can refuse to respond to any of the 200,000 annual inquiries from other nations and, as required by Interpol bylaws, does not assist in the capture of people sought for political, racial, or ethnic reasons.

Although Interpol dates back to 1923, the USNCB did not come into existence until the 1960s because of a lukewarm American attitude toward the organization. Hesitant about the benefits of international policework, the Federal Bureau of Investigation (FBI) in the Department of Justice did not post wanted notices with Interpol until 1936. When J. Edgar Hoover (1895–1972), head of the FBI from 1924 to 1972, observed Interpol's success in apprehending criminals, his subsequent support of the police force prompted Congress to order the Attorney General to accept Interpol membership in 1938. Hoover became the permanent American representative to Interpol with only the FBI authorized to do business with the group. In 1950, Hoover pulled the FBI out of Interpol for reasons that remain unclear. The Treasury, however, continued to maintain informal contact with the organization and became the official U.S. representative in 1958. When the U.S. decided to establish an NCB in 1962 as part of Attorney General Robert F. Kennedy's fight against organized crime, the history of American involvement dictated a sharing of power between the two agencies, with Justice as the dominant partner.

The NCB became operational in 1969 with a staff of three and an annual caseload of 300. Agents are complemented by computer specialists, analysts, translators, and administrative and clerical support personnel drawn largely from the ranks of the Department of Justice. The agents operate in divisions dedicated to specific investigative areas while the analysts review case information to identify patterns and links. The law enforcement agencies represented at the USNCB include the Bureau of Alcohol, Tobacco, and Firearms; the Drug Enforcement Administration (DEA); the Environmental Protection Agency; the FBI; the Financial Crimes Enforcement Network; the Fish and Wildlife Service; the Immigration and Naturalization Service (INS); Internal Revenue Service; U.S. Customs Service; the Department of Agriculture; the Department of Justice, Criminal Division; the Department of State; the U.S. Marshals Service; the U.S. Mint; the U.S. Postal Inspection Service; and the U.S. Secret Service. Additionally, each state, the District of Columbia, and New York City have established points of contact to receive international criminal reports from the NCB.

The USNCB operates by linking the Treasury Enforcement Computer System, the FBI's National Crime Information Center, the INS files, and the DEA records to Interpol. The international organization then funnels information from country to country. Classified information, including the vast majority of international terrorism cases, is not placed by the U.S. into Interpol channels because the flow of intelligence cannot be controlled and there are concerns that terrorists may tap into Interpol's intelligence system to plan strikes against the U.S. However, Interpol is utilized as a weapon against potential terrorists. The U.S. began accepting counter-terrorism cases in 1985. In 1990, the U.S. and Canadian governments established an Interpol Interface between the USNCB and the Canadian NCB in Ottawa. This link allows police to tap into law enforcement networks across the border to verify driver registrations and vehicle ownership.

The USNCB has grown considerably since its founding, responding to the increasing internationalization of crime as well as a jump in the numbers of foreign nationals entering the country. As these trends are likely to continue, the USNCB will likely see its crime fighting role increase in the future.

■ FURTHER READING:

BOOKS:

Anderson, Malcolm. *Policing the World: Interpol and the Politics of International Police Co-operation.* Oxford: Clarendon Press, 1989.

Bresler, Fenton. *Interpol.* London: Sinclair-Stevenson, 1992.

United States Department of Justice and United States Department of the Treasury. *Interpol: The International Criminal Police Organization.* Washington, D.C.: Government Printing Office, 2002.

SEE ALSO

Classified Information
FBI (United States Federal Bureau of Investigation)
DEA (Drug Enforcement Administration)
Department of State, United States
INS (United States Immigration and Naturalization Service)
Internal Revenue Service, United States
Interpol (International Criminal Police Organization)
Justice Department, United States
Law Enforcement, Responses to Terrorism
Secret Service, United States
Treasury Department, United States

Interrogation

■ BRIAN HOYLE

Interrogation is a conversational process of information gathering. The intent of interrogation is to control an individual so that he or she will either willingly supply the requested information or, if someone is an unwilling participant in the process, to make the person submit to the demands for information. The latter can involve techniques of humiliation, intimidation, and fear. In more extreme cases in some countries, physical pain is inflicted.

Every interrogation is intended to strip away the subject's defenses and resilience. If the process is successful, the subject will eventually "give in" and supply the interrogator with the information being sought.

The interrogators hold much power in the interrogation process. By various techniques that are intended to manipulate the subject psychologically, the interrogator's aim is to dominate the subject. For example, an interrogator can display a great knowledge of the subject's background and actions. Whether or not the interrogator actually knows much about the subject is irrelevant. The point is to convince the subject that what the interrogator says is true, and so that resistance is pointless.

The surroundings are also an important part of the interrogation process. Often, as in a police station, jail, or clandestine hideaway, the conditions are foreign, Spartan, and even uncomfortable to the subject. This throws

A captured Viet Cong suspect found with a hidden automatic weapon during a "search and seal" operation is interrogated, South Vietnam, 1967. AP/WIDE WORLD PHOTOS.

the subject off balance. If the conditions are abruptly changed, as for example, being brought out of solitary confinement to be given a hot shower and a tasty meal, a subject's mood may change abruptly from despair to relief. Then, information may be offered to the interrogator out of gratitude.

During the early stages of an interrogation process, an interrogator will "get to know" the subject. It is important to find out whether a subject is, for example, zealously dedicated to a cause, to the point of becoming a martyr, or whether the subject needs little persuasion to become compliant.

A skilled interrogator will also observe a subject's physical posture and listen carefully to the tone of his or her voice, especially if behavior changes in response to some aspect of the conversation. For example, many people who are nervous or under stress will unconsciously and protectively draw their elbows in to their sides. As another example, when many people are talking about something they either know a lot about or are passionate about, their rate of speaking increases. But, if a subject area is uncomfortable, many people pause and speak slowly. Knowing what topics a subject is sensitive to, and observing visual cues, can be used later as levers.

If a subject is reluctant to offer information, an interrogator will often begin to probe the topics that make the subject uncomfortable. By turns an interrogator can be calm or bluntly insistent. Both the topics discussed and the interrogator's manner are intended to keep the subject tense and off-balance, and to indicate to the interrogator how hard he or she may need to press to gain the information that is sought. A subject can become hostile during this phase of an interrogation, or may be compliant.

In the next phase of an interrogation process, the interrogator attempts to elicit the sought-after detailed information. The interrogator is firm and to the point at this stage, never allowing the conversation to stray off topic. The interrogator also will want to establish whether the subject's information is reliable. The interrogator can employ a variety of tactics, including leaving the subject alone for some time, making the subject think that he or she has no allies, using threats, talking about the subject's family, and even adopting a warm tone.

An interrogation is sometimes accomplished by a pair of interrogators, often with very different personalities. One person will be domineering, crass, profane, and loud. The other interrogator will be friendly, sympathetic, and quiet. This contrast, which is reinforced by a rehearsed routine, can work to the interrogator's advantage, particularly with women, teenagers, and shy people, who usually will respond to the quiet interrogator.

An interrogation can take place over days, with periods of solitary confinement in between. These solitary periods serve to build up tension in the subject and, especially if the surroundings are loud or uncomfortable, to make the subject exhausted.

As of late 2002, Amnesty International estimates that torture is part of interrogation in over 100 countries worldwide if a subject is especially uncooperative or displays great resiliency. Interrogation with torture may utilize drugs, hypnosis, threats of violence, and physical pain and injury to extract information.

■ FURTHER READING:

BOOKS:

Elliston, Jon. *InTERRORgation: The CIA's Secret Manual on Coercive Questioning, 2nd ed.* San Francisco: AK Press, 1999.

Gordon, Nathan J., William L. Fleisher, and C. Donald Weinberg. *Effective Interviewing and Interrogation Techniques.* New York: Academic Press, 2001.

SEE ALSO

Interrogation: Torture Techniques and Technologies
Language Training and Skills

Interrogation: Torture Techniques and Technologies

■ BRIAN HOYLE

Interrogation seeks to acquire information from a person. Since the person being interrogated is often not comfortable with the process or even willing to divulge information, the interrogation process is different from a conversation. Conversationally, information is freely exchanged and offered. However, interrogation is a less compliant process. Interrogation can take different forms, but these all have a similar aim: to control the subject in such a way that he or she yields to pressure and provides the information being asked for.

Information can be obtained by the use of pain. Torture is centuries old. In medieval times, as a few examples, victims were stretched on a rack, burned with hot branding irons, stoned, or uncomfortably shackled. But over the past century, techniques and technologies of physical and psychological torture have been "refined." Information can now be obtained without leaving a physical trace of the trauma of torture.

Newer methods of torture have been driven by the need for speed in obtaining the information, and, in the case of governments, in disguising the torture from organizations like Amnesty International that can hinder the information-gathering process.

Torture Components

The techniques and technologies of torture can be grouped into three categories: hardware, software, and liveware. The term "hardware" refers to the equipment used; software refers to the techniques of torture that are taught to interrogators. Torture liveware refers to the human element of torture, typically the interrogator.

Torture hardware. Examples of torture hardware include shackles for the arms, legs, and even thumbs, whips, canes, beating devices (i.e., clubs, rubber hoses), water, electrical generators to administer electroshocks, and devices that suspend someone painfully above the ground. In fact, the list of physical harm that can be inflicted is long. Any possible route to inflict pain that can be conceived of has been used.

Machines that generate intolerable noise ("white noise") or bright pulses of ultraviolet light are sometimes used. Hardware can also have a chemical nature. Some drugs can cause physical discomfort, pain, and disruptions to the body's biochemistry. Examples include curare,

A British soldier stands in a room used for torture and interrogation in the Serbian military police headquarters in Pristina, 1999. Later, United Nations investigators examined the knives, wooden bats, brass knuckles, and drugs found in the building as part of a war crimes investigation. AP/WIDE WORLD PHOTOS.

insulin, and apomorphine. Drugs such as these differ from psychoactive drugs that alter thought processes or biochemical activity in the brain. Food and water deprivation, or maintaining an uncomfortable position for a long time, can also induce biochemical changes.

Electromagnetic radiation can also be a means of torture. Studies in animals have shown that electromagnetic waves of certain wavelengths can destroy lung and brain cells. While not necessarily lethal, these effects are debilitating and can be painful. Electromagnetic stimulation can have other nonlethal effects on humans. Extreme emotions of rage, lust, and fatigue can be caused. A 1950s research program called "Operation Knockout," which was funded by the United States Central Intelligence Agency, discovered that electroshock treatments could be used to cause amnesia. Memories could be erased, and the subjects reprogrammed. This "psychic driving" is a form of torture.

The most widely used torture hardware is electroshock. Pulses of energy, which are therapeutically useful in some medical treatments, have been adapted as a torture technique. The application of electricity stimulates muscle activity to such an extent that involuntary and painful muscular contractions occur. Longer pulses of electricity produce successively greater debilitation. For example, a five-second discharge from a cattle prod can completely immobilize someone for up to 15 minutes

Torture software. The use of intimidation, threats, harsh and comforting language, and even silence are all techniques that, when combined with the hardware of torture, can extract information from a victim.

Such interrogation techniques have become standard operating procedures for interrogators. Indeed, manuals have been written for interrogators. One example is the *Human Resource Exploitation Training Manual,* which was written by the U.S. Central Intelligence Agency, and whose existence became known in 1997 as part of a Freedom of Information Request. A second example is the School of the Americas at Fort Benning, Georgia, which trained interrogators until 1991. The U.S. is by no means unique in providing such training.

Technical and technological orchestration of torture. Interrogation techniques are intended to "soften up" the victim,

A man cleans, numbers, and stacks skulls near a mass grave at the Cheung Ek torture camp run by the Khmer Rouge in Cambodia, where Pol Pot tortured and murdered between one and two million people to eliminate perceived oppposition in the 1970s. AP/WIDE WORLD PHOTOS.

depleting the physical and mental resources that can be used to resist the pressure to reveal information. This is also known as breaking of the spirit. Depriving someone of sleep and sensory stimulation (by keeping them in a dark and soundless environment, akin to solitary confinement) can cause extreme anxiety, intense fear, and paranoia.

The behavior of the interrogator is an important part of the process. For example, a comforting word or supplying water and food can make a victim grateful enough to yield to a request for information. Conversely, degrading or demeaning behavior can cause the victim to give up.

Torture as practiced by terrorist organizations, military and paramilitary forces, and by other government agencies is seldom a haphazard affair. The task of breaking someone's spirit involves the coordination of activities, and the use of certain techniques and technologies at certain times.

The torture process can begin at the moment of arrest or kidnapping. Taking someone by surprise is more jarring than if someone has time to physically and mentally prepare himself or herself for arrest. The majority of people are at their lowest ebb both physiologically and

psychologically in the early morning or near bedtime. A surprise detainment at those times is especially jarring.

The feeling of disorientation and fear can be heightened during transport to wherever the victim is to be detained. For example, the use of a blindfold or a hood deprives someone of visual cues that can help them maintain a sense of control.

The next phase is usually detention. Time spent alone in unfamiliar surroundings, deprived of familiar and comfortable clothing, wondering about what is to come can be disorienting and terrifying. Also the detainee is forced to rely on his or her own mental resources, which can lead to self-doubt and fear.

Removing the stimuli for senses like sight and sound can be used during this and other phases of torture. Human physiology and behavior is largely governed by the input of information. If sensory stimulation is lacking, physical and mental deterioration often occurs. For example, a study was done where subjects were immersed in body-temperature water up to their necks. Their heads were hooded to blind them. After just a few hours, sensations of tension gave way to hallucinations.

Conversely, stimulating senses such as smell—by, for example, the lack of toilet facilities—can prove overwhelming.

The threat of torture can be as effective as the actual pain in destroying resistance. This is because many people are able to tolerate pain more so than they believe they can. Once the reality occurs, victims may even draw strength from their ability to withstand the torture. Once physical torture has begun, the threat of death can also help the victim. Indeed, death can be a welcome relief from the pain. If however, the torture is perceived as unending, information can be volunteered in the hopes of ending the suffering.

Pain is an inherent part of torture. Because people have different tolerances to pain, or are more sensitive to some forms of pain than to others, torture can be tailored to exploit the sensitivities of the victim.

The techniques and technologies of torture are pervasive and widespread. As newer technologies are developed for other humane purposes, it is likely that these will be adapted for the inhumane purpose of torture.

■ FURTHER READING:

BOOKS:

Elliston, Jon. *InTERRORgation: The CIA's Secret Manual on Coercive Questioning, 2nd ed.* San Francisco: AK Press, 1999.

Gordon, Nathan J., William L. Fleisher, and C. Donald Weinberg. *Effective Interviewing and Interrogation Techniques.* San Diego: Academic Press, 2001.

SEE ALSO

Noise Generators
Psychotropic Drugs
Truth Serum

Iran-Contra Affair

■ LARRY GILMAN

In October and November of 1986, it was discovered that for several years, agents of the United States government had been running an illegal operation to sell weapons to Iran and funnel the profits to the Contras, a military organization dedicated to overthrowing the leftist government of Nicaragua. In December, 1986, Lawrence E. Walsh was appointed independent counsel by the U.S. Court of Appeals for the District of Columbia Circuit. (An independent counsel is a prosecutor appointed by the Court of Appeals at the request of the Attorney General of the United States to investigate suspected crimes by members of the executive branch of government.) During the early phases of the investigation, a cover-up was attempted

Lt. Col. Oliver North holds up a National Security Council intelligence document marked "TOP SECRET" during testimony before the House-Senate investigating committee at the Iran-Contra hearings in Washington, D.C., 1987. AP/WIDE WORLD PHOTOS.

by the Reagan administration. In the words of Walsh's final report, "following the revelation of [the Iran-Contra] operations in October and November 1986, Reagan Administration officials deliberately deceived the Congress and the public about the level and extent of official knowledge of and support for these operations."

The Iran-Contra investigation lasted from 1986 to 1994. During this period, Walsh charged 14 Reagan Administration officials with criminal acts. He obtained convictions and guilty pleas in 11 cases. Two convictions were overturned on a technicality, and several officials, including Secretary of Defense Caspar Weinberger, were issued pre-trial pardons by President George H. W. Bush during the "lame duck" period following his electoral defeat in 1992. Walsh's investigation concluded that "the sales of arms to Iran contravened United States Government policy and may have violated the Arms Export Control Act," that "the provision and coordination of support to the Contras violated the Boland Amendment ban on aid to military activities in Nicaragua" (passed by Congress in 1984), and that "the Iran operations were carried out with the knowledge of, among others, President Ronald Reagan, Vice President George H. W. Bush, Secretary of

State George P. Schultz, Secretary of Defense Caspar W. Weinberg, and Director of Central Intelligence William J. Casey." Walsh did not did not have legal power to bring charges against President Reagan or Vice President George H. Bush, as the Boland Amendment was not a criminal statute containing specific enforcement provisions. Congress did not exercise its power to impeach.

Historical background.

In 1979, the Somoza dictatorship in Nicaragua was overthrown by a left-wing revolutionary group calling itself the Sandinistas (after Nicaragua revolutionary leader Augusto Cesár Sandino, 1893–1934). Soon after taking office in 1981, President Ronald Reagan ordered the Central Intelligence Agency (CIA) to secretly fund and equip the Contras, mostly former members of the Somoza military who sought the overthrow of the Sandinista government, and who were operating from bases in Honduras and Costa Rica (to the north and south of Nicaragua, respectively). On December 8, 1982, a bill was passed by the U.S. House of Representatives forbidding U.S. covert actions "for the purpose of overthrowing the government of Nicaragua;" some funding for the Contras was still allowed. Some of the Congressional reluctance to give U.S. support to the Contras arose from their unsavory tactics. As General John Galvin, commander of the U.S. Southern Command, testified to Congress, the Contras were directed by the CIA to "[go] after soft [i.e., undefended] targets . . . not to try to duke it out with the Sandinistas directly." In practice, this meant attacking medical clinics, schools, farmer's cooperatives, and other undefended elements of the civil infrastructure, causing almost exclusively civilian casualties.

In May, 1984, Congress discovered that its 1982 restrictions had been disregarded by the Reagan administration. CIA agents, acting at the behest of National Security Council member Oliver North, had been placing mines in Nicaraguan harbors despite the Congressional ban on such activities. Consequently, Congress cut off all funding for the Contras and passed the Boland Amendment, a statute prohibiting any U.S. agency involved in "intelligence activities" from "supporting, directly or indirectly, military or paramilitary operations in Nicaragua by any nation, group, organization or individual."

The "Enterprise."

Direct and indirect support for the Contras continued in spite of the Boland Amendment, coordinated by Oliver North through a complex network he termed the "Enterprise." North's agents solicited money and arms for the Contras from three primary sources: (1) countries dependent on U.S. support, including South Africa, Brunei, Saudi Arabia, South Korea, and Israel; (2) wealthy Americans sympathetic to President Reagan's policies; and (3) weapons sales to Iran. The Reagan administration was secretly selling arms to Iran (in probable violation of the Arms Export Control Act of 1976, according to independent counsel Walsh); North's organization diverted money from these sales to the Contras. The

Contras also raised money by allegedly selling large quantities of crack cocaine in the United States with CIA complicity. All these activities violated the Boland Amendment's ban on aid to military activities in Nicaragua, as well as other laws.

Administration support of the Contras became public knowledge when a Contra military supply plane was shot down over Nicaragua on October 5, 1986. An American crew member, Eugene Hasenfus, was taken prisoner and revealed that he was a CIA agent. A month later, a Lebanese newspaper exposed the Reagan administration's secret sales of arms to Iran. On November 25, 1986, Justice Department officials went public with the information that these two news items were linked: proceeds from the Iranian arms sales has been diverted to the Contras.

At this stage, what independent counsel Walsh characterized in his official report as "a new round of illegality" began: "Senior Reagan administration officials engaged in a concerted effort to deceive Congress and the public about their knowledge of and support for the operations."

Outcome of the investigation.

Fourteen officials were charged with criminal violations as a result of the Iran-Contra investigation. All individuals tried were convicted; one CIA official's case was dismissed because the government refused to declassify information needed for his defense; and two convictions were overturned on technicalities. A few of the most prominent persons charged, as described in the final report of the independent counsel, are listed below:

(1) Elliott Abrams (Assistant Secretary of State for Inter-American Affairs): plead guilty to withholding information from Congress.

(2) Robert C. McFarlane (National Security Advisor): plead guilty to four counts of withholding information from Congress.

(3) Oliver L. North (Lieutenant Colonel, U.S. Marine Corps and Assistant Deputy Director for Political-Military Affairs of the National Security Council, 1981–1986): convicted of altering and destroying documents, accepting an illegal gratuity, and aiding and abetting in the obstruction of Congress.

(4) John M. Poindexter (National Security Advisor): convicted of conspiracy, false statements, falsification, destruction and removal of records, and obstruction of Congress. Poindexter's conviction on all counts was overturned on appeal on the grounds that although he lied to Congress, he did so while speaking under a guarantee of immunity. Independent counsel Walsh noted in his final report that North's and Poindexter's convictions were "reversed on appeal on constitutional grounds that in no way cast doubt on the factual guilt of the men convicted."

(5) Secretary of Defense Caspar W. Weinberger was charged with four counts of false statements and perjury. He was pardoned before trial by President George H. W. Bush, who also pardoned

Elliot Abrams, Robert McFarlane, and two other men at the same time.

Aftermath. The Iran-Contra affair, like the CIA-organized invasion of the Bay of Pigs in Cuba in 1961, struck a global blow to American credibility. Officials at the highest level had been detected organizing international terrorism (i.e., the Contras), violating U.S. law, and lying under oath. However, like that of the Bay of Pigs before it, the long-term impact of the Iran-Contra affair on U.S. politics and foreign policy was slight, and the central figures in the controversy later enjoyed high-profile careers in both the public and private sectors.

■ **FURTHER READING:**

BOOKS:

Busby, Robert. *Reagan and the Iran-Contra Affair.* Chippenham, Wiltshire, Great Britain: Macmillan, 1999.

Marshall, Jonathan, Peter Scott, and Jane Hunter. *The Iran-Contra Connection.* Boston: South End Press, 1987.

ELECTRONIC:

Walsh, Lawrence E. "Final Report of the Independent Counsel for Iran-Contra Matters: Volume I: Investigations and Prosecutions." United States Court of Appeals for the District of Columbia, Division for the Purpose of Appointing Independent Counsel. August 4, 1993. <http://www.fas.org/irp/offdocs/walsh/> (December 10, 2002).

Webb, Gary. "Dark Alliance: The CIA, the Contras, and the Crack Cocaine Explosion." 2002. Originally published in San Jose Mercury News, 1996. <http://home.attbi.com/~gary.webb/wsb/html/view.cgi-home.html-.html> (December 10, 2002).

Iran, Intelligence and Security

Iran has a number of intelligence and security organizations that include the Ministry of Intelligence and Security (known as VEVAK for its initials in Farsi), as well as the group called the Pasdaran, or Guardians of the Islamic Revolution. Up to 1978, Iran was controlled by Shah Mohammed Reza Pahlevi, who maintained power through a state security organization, SAVAK. His overthrow led to the establishment, in 1979, of the world's first major Islamic theocracy under the Ayatollah Ruhollah Khomeini. Thus was born a new form of police state in contrast to the Soviet, Nazi, or nationalist models—a state in which security forces are often directed toward the enforcement of religious law.

In accordance with the theocratic nature of government in a country officially known as "the Islamic Republic of Iran," the nation's "supreme leader" is a religious authority: first Khomeini and then, after Khomeini's death in 1989, Ayatollah Sayyed Ali Khamenei. The "supreme leader" sits on the Joint Committee for Special Operations, an Iranian organizational equivalent of the U.S. National Security Council.

Other members of the Joint Committee include the nation's president (its top secular official), and representatives of the Pasdaran, the Ministry of Foreign Affairs, and the Ministry of Security and Intelligence. The Joint Committee coordinates international activities of Iranian operatives, which include intelligence-gathering, attempts to obtain special weapons technology by clandestine means, and efforts to control the community of Iranian exiles—as well as alleged enemies of the revolution—overseas.

VEVAK. Iranian leaders' legendary hatred of the United States is rooted in history. The Central Intelligence Agency helped overthrow the government of Mohammad Mossadeqh in 1953, and provided support to his replacement, the Shah. U.S. and Israeli intelligence helped train the hated SAVAK, which included some 15,000 operatives and practiced torture using electric shock and other brutal methods. Ironically, when the new regime established its replacement for SAVAK—initially known as SAVAMA, and later retitled VEVAK—it needed experienced intelligence operatives, so it brought in former low-ranking officers of SAVAK and the Shah's military.

VEVAK operatives overseas use a number of covers, posing as bankers, students, laborers, or employees of Iran Air. These operatives help oversee an international terror network that claimed well over 1,000 lives in more than 200 terrorist attacks during the first two decades after the revolution. At times their work is assassination, as when they conducted a worldwide manhunt for author Salman Rushdie after the publication of his allegedly blasphemous 1989 novel *The Satanic Verses.*

In 1997, a German court convicted four assassins linked with Iran for the slaying of three Kurdish dissidents and their translator at a restaurant in Berlin in 1992. Much of the Iranians' operations in Germany took place through their diplomatic mission, from which they monitored some 100,000 Iranian expatriates throughout the country. Iran also used its diplomatic mission as cover for efforts to procure nuclear, chemical, and biological weapons technology.

Iranian and Iranian-sponsored terrorists have been involved in an array of worldwide terrorist activities including: the bombing of the U.S. Marine barracks in Beirut, Lebanon, in 1983; bombings in Paris in 1986; at the Israeli embassy and a Jewish community center in Buenos Aires in 1992 and 1994; and at Dhahran, Saudi Arabia, in June 1995. Following the terrorist attacks of September 11, 2001, President George W. Bush labeled Iran, Iraq, and North Korean "Axis of Evil" in his 2002 State of the Union speech.

The Pasdaran. Western analysts argue that sponsorship of terror in the name of Islam is one of the few things Iran has in common with Iraq, against which it fought what became the longest and bloodiest war anywhere in the world since WWII. Among the notable aspects of the grisly 1980–88 Iran-Iraq war were the *Bajeef* (volunteers), young men without military training who volunteered to go to the front on suicide missions. After the war, they were incorporated in a larger force that had existed since May 1979, when Khomeini established it by decree: the Pasdaran.

Former Bajeef members, and other Pasdaran with lower levels of training, were detailed to perform the functions of a theocratic police force—harassing or arresting women who wore makeup or inappropriate attire, and seizing forbidden items such as videotapes, photographs, pork products, and alcohol. At the more sophisticated end of Pasdaran operations are its activities overseas, including those of the Qods or Jerusalem Force, which in the mid-1990s allegedly trained terrorists in Sudan and elsewhere.

Exporting the revolution. Iran sought to export its revolution through support of Sh'ia Muslim factions such as Hizballah in Lebanon, but its leadership did not necessarily resist alliances with Muslims of the larger Sunni sect. Hence, during the mid-1990s Iran sought to build ties with Bosnia—ironically, a country known in the West for the relative moderation of its Muslims. Still, Iran succeeded in placing several hundred agents in Bosnia, where they even penetrated U.S. efforts to train the Bosnian army.

Another branch of the Pasdaran consisted of some 12,000 Arabic-speaking operatives of many nationalities working with Hizballah, Kurdish groups, and other armies in central Asia. In a particularly stunning example of the continued international flavor of terrorism, the Pasdaran "Operation of Liberation Movements" attended a coordination meeting in Beirut in April 1995 with representatives of Hizballah, the Iraqi Da'Wah Party, the Islamic Front for the Liberation of Bahrain, the Kurdistan Workers' Party, the Armenian Secret Army, and the Japanese Red Army.

■ **FURTHER READING:**

BOOKS:

Daughtery, William J. *In the Shadow of the Ayatollah: A CIA Hostage in Iran.* Annapolis, MD: Naval Institute Press, 2001.

Roosevelt, Kermit. *Countercoup, the Struggle for the Control of Iran.* New York: McGraw-Hill, 1979.

PERIODICALS:

Karmon, Ely. "Counterterrorism Policy: Why Tehran Stops and Starts Terrorism." *Middle East Quarterly* V, no. 4 (December 1998).

Samii, Abbas William. "The Shah's Lebanon Policy: The Role of SAVAK." *Middle Eastern Studies* 33, no. 1 (January 1997): 66–91.

ELECTRONIC:

Iran—A Country Study. Library of Congress. <http://lcweb2.loc.gov/frd/cs/irtoc.html> (March 26, 2003).

Iran-e-Azad: Supporters of the National Council of Resistance of Iran. <http://www.iran-e-azad.org/english/index.html> (March 26, 2003).

Iranian Intelligence Agencies. Federation of American Scientists. <http://www.fas.org/irp/world/iran/index.html> (March 26, 2003).

SEE ALSO

ADFGX Cipher
European Union
Iran-Contra Affair
Iranian Nuclear Programs
Iraq, Intelligence and Security Agencies
Khobar Towers Bombing Incident

Iranian Hostage Crisis

■ STEPHANIE WATSON

On November 4, 1979, a group of Iranian militants stormed the American embassy in Tehran, Iran, and captured dozens of embassy and military personnel. For 444 days, fifty-two Americans remained captive in Iran, while their nation waited, hoped, and hung yellow ribbons. The outcome of the hostage crisis would ultimately change the course of a presidency, and malign relations between two powerful nations.

The origins of anti-American fervor. In the early 1970s, America and Iran enjoyed mutually satisfying relations. At the time, the country was ruled by Shah Mohammad Reza Pahlavi, a man the American government had supported for more than twenty-five years. Pahlavi had risen to power thanks to British and Soviet forces, which jointly installed Pahlavi on the throne in 1941 to gain valuable influence over the country's oil. Two years later, the United States and Great Britain made a formal declaration to promote Iran's independence, primarily to prevent the communists from gaining a strong foothold in the country.

In the early 1950s, the Iranian prime minister, Mohammad Mossadegh, began gaining power and public support, and vehemently opposed the western influence in Iran. In 1952, Mossadegh's party won the national elections, and he demanded control over Iran's armed forces, which Pahlavi denied. In 1953, the United States Central

Blindfolded and with his hands bound, an American hostage is led by young militants in front of the United States Embassy in Tehran, November 8, 1979. AP/WIDE WORLD PHOTOS.

A portrait of Iranian leader Ayatollah Khomeini hangs from the roof inside the compound of the United States Embassy in Tehran. AP/WIDE WORLD PHOTOS.

Intelligence Agency (CIA) secretly helped to overthrow Mossadegh and restore Pahlavi to power. Pahlavi remained a friend to the United States, but endured harsh criticism by his countrymen for ruling with an iron fist, and living opulently off the spoils of his country's oil production while the majority of his people lived in poverty. During the next two decades, the Shah attempted to bring further Western influence to Iran, a practice that was an anathema to the growing numbers of fundamentalist Islamic groups in the country. Those who dared oppose the Shah's rule faced the risk of torture or death at the hands of his secret police.

In 1978, Iranian opposition leaders organized strikes, demonstrations, and riots in protest of the Shah's policies. In Paris, exiled Islamic leader Ayatolla Ruhollah Khomeini (Pahlavi had sent Khomeini from the country amid riots in the early 1960s) slowly began to gain popularity among the Iranian people. In December, 1978, Khomeini issued a proclamation calling for Iranians to "unite, arise, and sacrifice your blood," urging them to defy the Shah's order prohibiting public demonstrations. Khomeini's words

inspired his followers to fill the streets, chanting religious slogans and calling for revolution. The Shah was left with two choices: surrender or clamp down on his people militarily to restore order. On January 16, 1979, the Shah stepped down from power and fled to Morocco.

Khomeini returned to Iran on February 1, 1979, where he was greeted by millions of his followers. Less than two weeks later, Khomeini assumed power, announcing the creation of a new fundamentalist Islamic state. Khomeini labeled the United States "The Great Satan." Hatred grew when U.S. President Jimmy Carter allowed the deposed Shah to travel to America later that year for cancer treatment. Furious students gathered in the streets, raising their fists and shouting, "Death to America," assuming the United States was again trying to secretly restore the Shah to power.

On the morning of November 4, 1979, Iranian fervor reached a boiling point. A crowd gathered around the U.S. embassy, shouting anti-American slogans. At 10:30 A.M. about three thousand people jumped the ten-foot wall surrounding the embassy and swarmed the grounds, forcing their way into the basement and first floor of the chancery building. The guards launched tear gas, but they were unable to control the mob. The Islamic militants rounded up 66 embassy workers, military officials, and Marine guards. The hostages were blindfolded, bound, and shoved into windowless rooms. Fifty-three people were held captive in the embassy compound. It was unclear what role, if any, Khomeini played in orchestrating the hostage crisis, but it was clear that he did little to stop it. When Khomeini noted how popular the hostage situation had become among his people, he allowed it to continue, despite continuous pressure from the United States government.

Americans watched the events of the crisis played out on television. Yellow ribbons were tied around tree trunks throughout the country in commemoration of the hostages. President Carter responded by freezing billions of dollars in Iranian assets, both in the United States and abroad, and by instituting an embargo on Iranian oil. Still, the Iranians refused to release the hostages, demanding the Shah's extradition to Iran.

A rescue attempt. While President Carter was trying to negotiate the hostages' release, behind-the-scenes a daring rescue plan was taking shape. The proposal was to swoop in and land eight American military helicopters in the embassy compound, extract the hostages, and escape to six planes waiting on an airstrip in the Iranian desert. On April 24, 1980, the plan was launched. The mission, however, was fraught with mistakes and bad luck. Three of the helicopters malfunctioned; the pilot of a fourth, blinded by a dust storm, crashed into a refueling aircraft. Eight U.S. servicemen were killed in the unsuccessful operation.

The hostage-takers responded to the failed rescue attempt by moving their captives to several secret locations in different cities. On July 11, one ill captive was released. Meanwhile, the ongoing hostage crisis was costing President Carter the support of his people and some of his advisors, including Secretary of State Cyrus Vance, who had opposed the rescue. Carter later lost his re-election bid to former California governor Ronald Reagan in a landslide.

The siege ends. In the fall of 1980, the exiled Shah died of cancer complications. In September, Iran agreed to begin negotiations for the hostages' release. In exchange for their release, the United States agreed to turn over $8 billion of Iran's frozen assets, and to refrain from interfering politically or militarily in Iran's internal affairs. The United States and Iran signed the agreement on January 19, 1981, but in a final embarrassment to Carter, the militants did not release the hostages until January 20, the day President Reagan was inaugurated. Just minutes after Reagan took office, a plane carrying the fifty-two remaining hostages left Tehran for a U.S. Army base in Germany. From his home in Georgia, former president Carter announced that the plane carrying the hostages had cleared Iranian airspace, and that every one of the hostages "was alive, was well, and free."

■ **FURTHER READING:**

BOOKS:

Rivers, Gayle, and James Hudson. *The Teheran Contract.* Garden City, New York: Doubleday & Company, Inc., 1981.

Sick, Gary. *All Fall Down: America's Tragic Encounter with Iran.* New York: Random House, Inc., 1985.

Wells, Tim. *Four Hundred and Forty-Four Days: The Hostages Remember.* Orlando, Florida: Harcourt Brace Jovanovich Publishers, 1985 .

PERIODICALS:

Schaumburg, Ron. "Americans Held Hostage." *New York Times Upfront.* (January 15, 2001):23.

Olson, Tod. "America Held Hostage: The Iranian Hostage Crisis Would Torment America—and Topple a President." *Scholastic Update.* (May 11, 1998):20–22.

SEE ALSO

Carter Adminstration (1977–1981), United States National Security Policy
Iran, Intelligence and Security

Iranian Nuclear Programs

■ K. LEE LERNER

In his 2002 State of the Union speech, United States President George W. Bush labeled Iran, Iraq, and North Korea as rogue nations that constituted an "axis of evil" seeking to develop weapons of mass destruction (i.e., nuclear, chemical, or biological weapons).

Late in 2002, reports began to circulate in the press that Iran had taken steps to accelerate an already active nuclear program that could develop nuclear weapons. As a signatory to the Non-Proliferation Treaty, Iran has a right to pursue nuclear technology for peaceful purposes, subject to oversight by the International Atomic Energy Agency (IAEA). A development of nuclear weapons by Iran, however, would violate nuclear non-proliferation treaties.

Initial reports of Iranian nuclear program development by the National Council of Resistance of Iran, a private group that paid for their own intelligence estimates—including satellite imagery—gained influence because of the group's track record about supplying verifiable and reliable information regarding Iran's nuclear program. Western intelligence agencies soon confirmed the validity of the physical evidence of activity at Iranian nuclear facilities.

In December, U.S. State Department spokesman Richard Boucher argued that satellite imagery depicting the covering of buildings at the Natanz site indicated that Iran was building "a secret underground site where it could produce fissile material."

Iran quickly denied any attempt to develop nuclear weapons of mass destruction. Iranian officials asserted that the building programs underway at the suspected facilities were designed to expand Iran's ability to produce electrical energy. In particular, Iranian officials denied that its first nuclear plant—a reactor facility under construction at Bushehr, an Iranian town near the Persian Gulf Coast— would be equipped to produce weapons grade uranium. Iran's development of the facility at Bushehr (allegedly a 1,000-megawatt reactor) was supported by equipment and technical assistance from Russia.

In January, 2003, Iran announced its intention to develop a nuclear fuel program. Iran announced the mining of uranium and the adaptation of facilities, including the Natanz nuclear facility under construction, so that they could process ore into fissionable fuel for nuclear power plants. Iranian opposition groups and Western intelligence services argue that the nuclear fuel program could easily be extended to produce weapons grade fuel. The Iranian decision to produce its own fuels was chilling to Western intelligence services because it would eliminate the protections afforded by Russian demands to return spent fuel initially supplied for Iranian reactors.

Although Russian sales and support of nuclear materials and reactor equipment to Iran was well known, evidence of additional international interests in the Iranian program surfaced when the National Council of Resistance of Iran provided evidence that Chinese nuclear scientists and engineers were sighted at a uranium mine near Saghand. Chinese and North Korean scientists and engineers were reportedly involved in the development of uranium enrichment capability at a site near Isfahan. There were also allegations of centrifuge facility construction near Tehran.

The events in Iran signaled a change in the pace of Iranian nuclear program development that might allow Iran to construct an operational nuclear weapon by 2004 or 2005.

Concerned that Iran was attempting to accelerate its nuclear programs in such a way as to facilitate nuclear weapon development—especially while world attention was focused on events in Iraq and North Korea—IAEA inspectors requested additional access to inspect Iranian facilities. IAEA requests were initially denied. Iranian officials also initially declined to elaborate the intended uses of a facility in Kashan.

In February, 2003, IAEA inspectors, including IAEA chief inspector Mohamed El Baradei, were permitted to visit several new Iranian nuclear sites suspected of being able to enrich uranium for potential weapons use. Inspectors were also to make inquiries regarding the status of processing equipment located at Natanz and Arak (a heavy-water production facility) and to ask Iranian officials to accept regular monitoring of Iranian nuclear programs.

Satellite imagery indicated buried facilities near Natanz, and ground-based reports indicated the assembly of more than 150 centrifuges near the Natanz facility

nearing operational capability to process uranium gas into nuclear fuel capable of undergoing fission. Parts for additional facilities were also reportedly near the Natanz site. Iran admitted to IAEA officials the construction of a plant to convert uranium into UF6 (uranium hexafluoride)— a gaseous form of uranium used in centrifuges.

Western intelligence scientists and analysts predicted that if Iran built its projected 5000 centrifuges, it could produce enough fuel each year for several nuclear weapons. United States officials briefed on IAEA reports from Iran expressed surprise at the advanced state of Iranian nuclear development. Several officials described Iran as being years ahead of prior projections and much closer to having nuclear weapons capability than previously estimated.

The United States has imposed sanctions against Russian companies and attempted to exert diplomatic pressure on Russia, Ukraine, and China, in an effort to prevent Iranian acquisition of sensitive nuclear technologies and equipment. Despite these efforts, intelligence sources predict that Iran's current nuclear program infrastructure will soon support the development of uranium-based weapons.

■ **FURTHER READING**:

PERIODICALS:

Dareini, Ali A. "U.N. Nuclear Chief Arrives in Iran to Visit Nuclear Facilities." *The Washington Post.* February 21, 2003.

Kessler, Glenn. "Group Alleges New Nuclear Site in Iran." *Washington Post.* February 20, 2003.

Warrick, J., and G. Kessler. "Iran's Nuclear Program Speeds Ahead 'Startling' Progress at Complex Poses Challenge to Bush Administration at Delicate Time." *Washington Post.* March 10, 2003.

SEE ALSO

Air Plume and Chemical Analysis
Iran, Intelligence and Security
Nuclear Detection Devices
Nuclear Reactors
Nuclear Weapons

Iraq, Intelligence and Security Agencies in

■ K. LEE LERNER

Prior to Operation Iraqi Freedom, under the rule of Saddam Hussein, the intelligence and security agencies of Iraq, commonly referred to as the *Mukhabarat*, included the General Intelligence Directorate (GID), Amn al Amm, Special Security Service (SSS), Fedayeen Saddam (named after the Iraqi dictator, Saddam Hussein), Murafaqin, and Al Hadi.

The GID was tasked to collect and analyze foreign and domestic intelligence. The GID operated under state security officers and utilized a staff of nearly 4,500 intelligence officers and operatives. Following the Persian Gulf War, until weapons inspectors were expelled by Iraq in 1998, GID personnel often acted as "minders" for United Nations weapons inspectors and were tasked with both developing intelligence regarding inspector activities and with carrying out disinformation events designed to thwart inspector's efforts to identify prohibited weapons.

In 1993, American forces launched an attack using Tomahawk cruise missiles that destroyed GID headquarters in retaliation for a failed Iraqi attempt to assassinate former United States president George H. W. Bush during his visit to liberated Kuwait.

The Amn al Amm (also known as the General Security Service) functioned as a secret police force under the control of the Iraqi Security Directorate. Amn al Amm personnel were tasked with spying on Iraqi citizens to ensure loyalty to Hussein's regime—and to prevent anti-government rebellions from organizing. Amn al Amm officers were integrated into local police units throughout Iraq. A good deal of Amn al Amm's operations were devoted to developing and maintaining extensive files on Iraqi citizens.

The Amn al Khas (also known as the Special Security Service or Presidential Affairs Service) was under the direct control of one of Hussein's sons, Qusay Hussein. Under the close and brutal control of Qusay, Amn al Khas contained highly motivated Ba'thist party members who were intensely loyal to the Hussein family and served as Hussein family bodyguards. Following the Persian Gulf War, Qusay directed Amn al Khas troops in the hiding of biological and chemical weapons of mass destruction. U.N. weapons inspectors were continually thwarted by Amn al Khas personnel to the extent that the U.N. weapons inspectors failed to find evidence of Iraq's extensive biological weapons program (e.g., anthrax production) until they received information following the 1995 defection of Hussein Kamil, Saddam's son-in-law. Kamil was later lured back to Iraq by promises of leniency, and, despite the pleas of Saddam's daughter, who was married to Kamil, he was tortured and executed.

Qusay Hussein reportedly directed Amn al Khas personnel in the vicious suppression of a rebellion by Shi'a groups in southern Iraq who led a failed rebellion against the Hussein regime following the Persian Gulf War. Qusay's troops also directly controlled Iraq's chemical weapons program and arsenal.

The Fedayeen Saddam (translated as Men of Sacrifice) was a group of zealous paramilitary thugs and criminals under the control of Saddam's son Uday Hussein. Qusay was also known to exercise control over the Fedayeen during some operations. Numbering nearly 40,000 troops, the irregular Fedayeen forces carried out harassment operations against U.S. led coalition forces and supply lines during Operation Iraqi Freedom.

Murafaqin (Companions of Saddam) security personnel were composed of Hussein's al Bu Nasir tribal kinsmen. They acted as a protective secret service for the Hussein family—and often contributed guards assigned to physically protect Hussein family members.

The Al Hadi, also known and Department 858 or Project 858, functioned as Iraq's signals intelligence (SIGINT) and electronic intelligence (ELINT) service under Hussein's rule.

Qusay Hussein and his brother Uday were killed in a firefight with U.S forces on July 22, 2003.

■ FURTHER READING:

PERIODICALS:

Marashi Ibrahim al-. "Iraq's Security and Intelligence Network: A Guide and Analysis," *Middle East Review of International Affairs* 6, no.3 (September, 2002).

Iraq War: Prelude to War (The International Debate Over the Use and Effectiveness of Weapons Inspections)

■ K. LEE LERNER

In the aftermath of the September 11, 2001, terrorist attacks on the United States and the subsequent war against the Taleban and al-Qaeda in Afghanistan, United States leaders turned their attention to an old enemy, Iraq, and specifically its dictatorial leader, Saddam Hussein.

Although Iraq was not as powerful a military threat as during the Persian Gulf War of 1990–1991, U.S. officials asserted that Iraq's proven development and use of weapons of mass destruction made Iraq a potential source of those weapons for terrorists who could then use them against U.S. or other Western targets. Hussein ordered the use of chemical weapons against Iranian forces during the 1980s Iran-Iraq War, and additionally used chemical weapons against civilians in rebellious area of Iraq.

After Iraqi forces were expelled by U.S.-led Western coalition forces during the Persian Gulf War, and as a part of the agreements that prevented the occupation of Iraq and allowed Hussein to remain in power, Hussein agreed to destroy all weapons of mass destruction and forsake

In their trademark blue caps, United Nations weapons inspectors take notes during a visit to a veterinary research center in Baghdad, January 9, 2003. ©AFP/CORBIS.

the future development of nuclear, biological, and chemical weapons. During the next decade, however, 17 specific United Nations Security Council resolutions, weapons inspection programs, and economic sanctions against Iraq failed to secure Hussein's full compliance and assure disarmament of such weapons.

U.S. officials offered prior UN weapons-inspector declarations of Iraqi compliance as proof that Hussein was able to deceive inspectors. Discovery of Iraqi nuclear weapons development facilities in the early 1990s invalidated declarations by IAEA chief Hans Blix that Iraq had no viable nuclear weapons program. After dismantling the Iraqi nuclear program, weapons inspectors had also failed to uncover Iraqi biological and chemical weapons facilities until information supplied to Western intelligence sources by the defection of a son-in-law of Hussein (later executed by Hussein when he returned to Iraq) provided evidence of biological and chemical weapons programs.

Although many weapons were subsequently discovered and destroyed by inspection teams, Iraqi defiance of UN resolutions continued throughout the 1990s. The United

Nations Monitoring, Verification and Inspection Commission (UNMOVIC) was created by the UN Security Council (resolution 1284) in December, 1999. UNMOVIC was chartered to replace the former UN Special Commission (UNSCOM) and continue the mandate to disarm Iraq of its weapons of mass destruction and monitor compliance with other UN stipulations (e.g., that Iraq not possess missiles with a range of more than 150 km). Blix was named the commission's executive chairman. UNMOVIC staff included weapons specialists, scientific analysts, engineers and operational planners. In 1998 Iraq expelled the weapons inspectors and no meaningful inspections took place between 1998 and 2002.

Some Pentagon and administration officials urged immediate and direct action be taken by the United States to disarm Iraq. There were also more controversial calls for a "regime change" in Baghdad as the only means to assure Iraqi disarmament. United States President George W. Bush decided instead to seek international cooperation to disarm Iraq. In September 2002, Bush addressed the United Nations and called for a strong resolution that, backed by the threat of the use of military force, would assure that Iraq possessed no weapons of mass destruction. In October 2002, the U. S. Congress voted Bush the authority to use military force to enforce UN resolutions.

In November 2002, the United Nations Security Council unanimously passed resolution 1441 that reiterated Iraq's obligations to disarm in accordance with prior treaty and resolution obligations and further recognized the threat that "Iraq's non-compliance with Council resolutions and proliferation of weapons of mass destruction and long-range missiles poses to international peace and security." Resolution 1441 went on to restate Security Council intentions to "restore international peace and security in the area."

Resolution 1441 specifically stated that Iraq "has not provided an accurate, full, final, and complete disclosure...of all aspects of its program to develop weapons of mass destruction and ballistic missiles with a range greater than one hundred and fifty kilometers, and of all holdings of such weapons, their components and production facilities and locations, as well as all other nuclear programs, including any which it claims are for purposes not related to nuclear-weapons-usable material."

Resolution 1441 additionally stated that Iraq had "repeatedly obstructed immediate, unconditional, and unrestricted access to sites designated by the United Nations Special Commission (UNSCOM) and the International Atomic Energy Agency (IAEA), [and had] failed to cooperate fully and unconditionally with UNSCOM and IAEA weapons inspectors...." The resolution deplores "the absence, since December 1998, in Iraq of international monitoring, inspection, and verification, as required by relevant resolutions, of weapons of mass destruction and ballistic missiles, in spite of the Council's repeated demands that Iraq provide immediate, unconditional, and unrestricted access to the United Nations Monitoring, Verification, and Inspection Commission (UNMOVIC), established in resolution 1284 (1999) as the successor organization to UNSCOM, and the IAEA...."

Important to U.S. concerns regarding potential links between Iraq and terrorist organizations, resolution 1441 recognized that Iraq had "failed to comply with its commitments pursuant to resolution 687 (1991) with regard to terrorism, pursuant to resolution 688 (1991) to end repression of its civilian population and to provide access by international humanitarian organizations to all those in need of assistance in Iraq...." Important to questions of legitimacy regarding potential military action against Iraq, resolution 1441 recalled "that in its resolution 687 (1991) the Council declared that a ceasefire [of the Persian Gulf War] would be based on acceptance by Iraq of the provisions of that resolution, including the obligations on Iraq contained therein."

Resolution 1441 declared Iraq to be in material breach (a violation of an important or substantial issue, not just a violation of a technicality or legal process issue) of prior resolutions and set out specific demands for Iraq including resumption of inspections in Iraq by UNMOVIC and the IAEA based upon a full and truthful declaration of prohibited weapons (e.g., chemical weapons, biological weapons, nuclear weapons, nuclear programs, ballistic missiles, and prohibited weapons delivery systems).

Resolution 1441 specifically warned Iraq that future false statements or omissions in the declarations submitted by Iraq would constitute "a further material breach of Iraq's obligations" and reiterated the Security Council's warnings that "Iraq will face serious consequences as a result of its continued violations of its obligations."

In December, 2002, Iraq produced a 12,000-page document on its weapons programs. U.S. and U.K. officials declared the declaration false, and subsequently, UN weapons inspection teams argued that the document contained little in the way of new information and that it failed to signal Iraq's willingness to cooperate with the international community. Weapons inspectors from UNMOVIC and IAEA returned to Iraq in December 2002.

In late January, Blix, now the chief UNMOVIC weapons inspector, delivered what many observers concluded was a negative report on Iraq's cooperation with the latest in a twelve-year string of UN resolutions to disarm. Blix's report to the Security Council stated, "Iraq appears not to have come to genuine acceptance—not even today—of the disarmament which was demanded of it and which it needs to carry out to win the confidence of the world and live in peace." Blix went on to specifically cite Iraqi failures to eliminate prohibited chemical and biological arms programs.

Mohamed El Baradei, the IAEA chief inspector for atomic weapons, reported that Iraq had apparently been unable to successfully reconstitute its nuclear weapons program. Although there was disputed evidence that Iraq continued to try to obtain elements of nuclear weapons, it became apparent to inspectors that the destruction or dismantling of Iraq's nuclear program in the early 1990s had prevented Iraq from successfully developing nuclear weapons. Prior to the first Gulf War and the subsequent dismantling of equipment by UN forces, Western intelligence analysts estimated that without intervention, Iraq had been within two years of developing operational nuclear weapons. Based upon El Baradei's report, attention quickly focused on Iraq's chemical and biological weapons program.

Iraq rejected all of the inspectors' negative comments and the Iraqi ambassador, Mohammed A. Aldouri, insisted that Iraq had "fully complied with all its obligations" with regard to UN resolution 1441, which required disclosure of weapons and disarmament by Iraq.

Repeating a stand carefully articulated prior to the passage of UN 1441, President Bush reiterated U.S. resolve to disarm Iraq by force if necessary—even without support by other United Nations Security Council members with veto power (France, Russia, China). The other country with veto power, the United Kingdom, sided with the United States. At peril to their political futures, U.K.

Prime Minister Tony Blair and Home Secretary Jack Straw (their own Labour party remained deeply divided over the use of force to disarm Iraq) carefully articulated both the strategic need to prevent Iraq from becoming a conduit through which terrorists could obtain weapons of mass destruction, and also of the humanitarian need to liberate the Iraqi people from the despotic rule of Saddam Hussein. Veto-bearing Security Council members (i.e., France, Russia and China)—joined by members Germany and Syria—contended that the inspections process was yielding results and that additional time should be allowed for Iraq's disarmament.

In statements and reports, Blix's inspection team reported that despite Iraq's denials, there were indications that Iraq had created weapons of mass destruction, including VX agent, a weapon that Blix described as "one of the most toxic [nerve agents] ever developed." Blix's report also contained evidence that Iraq had provided contradictory information about its VX stocks in a 12,000-page declaration regarding Iraq's weapons programs that Iraq supplied to the Security Council in December 2002. The United States and United Kingdom contended that Iraq's false declaration to the Security Council was clear and convincing evidence of Iraq's continued unwillingness to comply with United Nations resolutions and to peacefully disarm.

UN inspection reports provided evidence to the Security Council that Iraq had failed to account for 6,500 chemical bombs, thousand of tons of known chemical agents, empty chemical warheads (including an empty Sakr-18 chemical warhead) discovered subsequent to Iraq's declaration, and stocks of thiodiglycol (a precursor of mustard gas).

Iraq admitted to producing—in violation of international law—8,500 liters of anthrax bacteria capable of use in biological warfare. Iraq claimed that production stopped before the first Persian Gulf War and that it destroyed the anthrax. UN inspection reports stated, "Iraq has provided little evidence for this production and no convincing evidence for its destruction." In addition, UN inspectors concluded that there were strong indications that Iraq had manufactured far greater stores of anthrax.

Blix also reported that Iraq had manufactured a missile, the Samoud 2, that violated United Nations range restrictions limiting missiles to a range of 90 miles (150 kilometers). Inspectors also provided evidence to the Security Council that Iraq rebuilt a missile plant that had previously been destroyed by earlier inspection teams and that it continued to illegally import chemicals used in formulating missile fuels and prohibited weapons. Blix ordered Iraq to begin destruction of the prohibited missiles by March 1, 2003, and to cease production of the missiles. Blix also insisted that Iraq begin to allow U-2 reconnaissance aircraft overflights demanded by inspectors.

U.S. secretary of state Colin Powell presented additional evidence to the Security Council of Baghdad's alleged non-compliance with UN disarmament resolutions.

Powell, accompanied to the Security Council meeting by CIA Director George Tenet, also articulated United States assertions of links between al-Qaeda and Iraq. Powell asserted Western intelligence sources had evidence that Osama bin Laden met with senior Iraqi intelligence officials and that al-Qaeda operatives enjoyed safe haven in Iraq.

Powell also contended that Iraq possessed mobile laboratories to make biological weapons. Powell played intercepts of Iraqi officers apparently ordering concealment of prohibited weapons and displayed satellite pictures of alleged chemical weapons facilities. Powell questioned Iraq's development of unmanned drone airplanes capable of delivering chemical or biological weapons, and claimed that up to 500 tons of chemical weapons agents remained unaccounted for by Iraq.

Powell stressed that the United States and it's coalition partners had "limited patience" for continued Iraqi noncompliance with United Nations resolutions. President Bush and other United States officials insisted that Iraq was in "material breech" of UN resolutions and that military action could be undertaken to disarm Iraq under the terms of existing resolutions.

Other Security Council members disagreed with U.S. and U.K. contentions and, led by France, appealed for more time to seek a peaceful resolution to the crisis. Politics—including political struggles with the European Union and NATO—intermingled with diplomacy as nations sought to position themselves with regard to a need for military action to enforce UN resolutions. France seized on the politically motivated pacifist stance of German Prime Minister Gerhard Schroder to form a unified anti-war alliance fronted by France, Germany, and Russia. Schroder, in deep political trouble regarding domestic economic problems that plagued his 2002 election campaign, ultimately secured a narrow election victory by promising socialist, Green, and anti-American elements of the German electorate that he would never allow German forces to support military action against Iraq. In addition to their anti-war stance, France, Germany, and Russia all maintained important economic interests in Iraq.

Support for France's anti-war position reached its highest point on February 14, 2003, when French foreign minister Dominique de Villepin delivered an impassioned speech that appealed to the noblest aspirations of the United Nations. In a breech of protocol, sympathetic members applauded both de Villepin's and the Russian foreign minister Igor Ivanov's appeals for additional time to allow Iraq to disarm under a stricter inspections program.

The next day, February 15, 2003, saw the largest civil demonstrations for peace in the history of the world. Millions of demonstrators at sites around the globe protested potential U.S.-led military action against Iraq.

Events moved to a diplomatic breaking point in early March. France, Germany, Russia, and China staunchly opposed military enforcement of UN resolution 1441 and threatened veto of any resolution that might—even indirectly—authorize the United States and United Kingdom to lead forces to disarm Iraq. The United States, United Kingdom, and Spain put forth a resolution that simply declared Iraq in material breech of 17 prior UN resolutions. President Bush openly declared that he would force countries to "show their cards" with regard to Iraq. In a press conference on March 6, President Bush asserted that Saddam Hussein posed a direct and immediate danger to the security of the United States and, with regard to the United Nations and pending debate and resolutions, asserted that "diplomacy has failed" and that "we really don't need anybody's permission" to defend the United States.

At a meeting of the Security Council the next morning, weapons inspectors Blix and El Baradei reported cooperation had improved, but that Iraqi cooperation was less than complete. Blix issued a report to the Council specifying a number of questions that remained unsolved since the passage of resolution 1441 (and previous resolutions). The UN weapons inspector's report specifically stated that Iraq had not accounted for up to 10,000 liters of anthrax, Scud missile warheads (missiles Iraq fired at Israel and coalition forces in the Persian Gulf War and that could be armed chemical or biological agents), and drone aircraft that could fly past UN-allowed limits and that also could be fitted with spray units that could deliver chemical or biological weapons.

With war seemingly imminent, the United States, United Kingdom, and Spain amended a final resolution that set March 17, 2003, as a final deadline for the council to certify Iraqi compliance with prior resolutions. The resolution stated "...that Iraq will have failed to take the final opportunity afforded by resolution 1441 (2002) unless, on or before 17 March 2003 the council concludes that Iraq has demonstrated full, unconditional, immediate and active cooperation in accordance with its disarmament obligations under resolution 1441 (2002) and previous relevant resolutions, and is yielding possession to UNMOVIC and the IAEA of all weapons, weapon delivery and support systems and structures, prohibited by resolution 687 (1991) and all subsequent relevant resolutions, and all information regarding prior destruction of such items."

Although a threat of force was not contained within the resolution, there was little doubt that should Iraq fail to meet the deadline, the United States and United Kingdom would lead a multinational coalition to militarily disarm Iraq. The United States also sought and promised to depose Saddam Hussein and allow the Iraqi people a chance for democratic government.

France vehemently opposed the new resolution setting specific deadlines and actively lobbied against it. The trans-Atlantic alliance between NATO allies was strained more severely than ever in its history. There were terse exchanges between diplomats and angry and severe rhetoric exchanged in the media of France and America. American press reports detailed how French intelligence officials had passed false documents to British intelligence

regarding potential Iraqi purchases of uranium. French contracts with the Iraqi dictatorship called French motives into question, and U.S. press and Western intelligence reports claimed evidence of possible sales by France to Iraq of military hardware in violation of prior UN prohibitions.

France and Russia threatened to veto the deadline resolution, and intense diplomatic efforts to sway the votes of the non-permanent members to the Security Council followed. Although the United States and United Kingdom anticipated a French veto, Prime Minister Blair promised his own government that he would seek this final resolution. With France, Russia, China, Germany, and Syria on record in opposition to the resolution, and the U.S., U.K., Spain, and Bulgaria on record in favor of the resolution, the decision rested with the remaining six temporary member states (Angola, Cameroon, Chile, Guinea, Mexico, and Pakistan). Nine votes and no veto were required to pass the resolution. Although a chance at outright passage remained slim, the U.S. and U.K. pressed for a vote before commencing military action against Iraq.

American and British diplomats claimed that the diplomatic efforts and intransigence of France ultimately "poisoned the diplomatic process." In spite of British attempts to make amendments to pending resolutions and set specific tasks for Iraq to perform to indicate willingness to comply with UN resolutions, France promised to veto the pending resolution—in some cases before Iraq could itself reject the U.K. proposals. On March 15, President Bush, Prime Minister Blair and Spain's President Jose Maria Anzar convened an emergency summit in the Azores where they reaffirmed the trans-Atlantic alliance and stated that March 17 would be the final date for the UN to agree on a diplomatic solution to enforce resolution 1441.

With the UN Security Council deadlocked, the probable votes of the nonpermanent members hotly disputed, and the deadline at hand, the U.S., U.K. and Spain allowed their new proposal to die without a vote. Although he had once promised to call for a vote, President Bush stated that France "had shown their cards" and administration officials declared the "diplomatic window closed." Although France, Russia, and China declared that any U.S.- and U.K.-led coalition action against Iraq would be illegitimate and in violation of the UN charter, U.S. and U.K. officials rested on existing UN resolutions (one reason some experts claimed that another vote was not sought), Iraq's violation of the treaty that ended the Persian Gulf War, and assertions of the right of self defense to legitimize military action.

On the evening of March 17 (Washington time), President Bush, in a televised address that was carried around the world by major news organizations, issued Saddam Hussein and his sons (both high ranking Iraqi officials) a 48-hour deadline to leave Iraq or face war.

UN weapons inspectors were withdrawn from Iraq and most countries withdrew diplomats and other personnel in anticipation of imminent war. France called for a ministerial-level meeting of the UN Security Council, and a meeting of heads of state. The U.S. and U.K. ignored further French efforts and insisted that Hussein could only avoid war by exile.

Hussein ignored the deadline and U.S.- and U.K.-led forces launched aerial attacks against Iraq on the evening of March 19, 2002 (March 20, 2002, in Europe and Iraq).

FURTHER READING:

PERIODICALS:

DeYoung, K., and Colum Lynch. "Britain Races To Rework Resolution: U.S. Insists on Limiting Concessions for Iraq." *Washington Post.* March 11, 2003.

Evans, D. and D. Charter. "Iraq Strikes Back with Suspected Banned Missiles." *The Times.* March 21, 2003.

Fisher, I. "Chief Weapons Inspectors See No Big Breakthrough after Talks in Baghdad." *New York Times.* February 10, 2003.

Gellman, B. "U.S. Reaps New Data on Weapons." *Washington Post.* March 20, 2003.

Sanger, D., and F. Barringer. "President Readies U.S. for Prospect of Imminent War." *New York Times.* March 7, 2003.

Tagliabue, J. "France and Russia Ready To Use Veto Against Iraq War." *New York Times.* March 6, 2003.

ELECTRONIC:

United Nations. Security Council Resolution 1441. November 7, 2002. <http://www.un.int/usa/sres-iraq.htm> (March 23, 2003).

SEE ALSO

Iraq, Intelligence and Security Agencies
Iraqi Freedom, Operation (2003 War Against Iraq)

Iraq War
(Immediate Aftermath)

K. LEE LERNER

On May 1, 2003, United States President George W. Bush announced an end to major military combat operations related to Operation Iraqi Freedom.

Although evidence of Saddam Hussein's reign of terror was rapidly forthcoming—including the discovery of numerous mass gravesites of those brutally executed for resisting Hussein's rule—the anticipated discovery of large caches of Iraqi weapons of mass destruction (WMD)

proved elusive. By the end of May 2003, both British and American intelligence agencies began to downplay the possibility of finding large stores of such weapons. Although both U.S. and British officials continued to assert prior claims about the extent of Iraq's arsenal, questions remained as to whether the weapons had been removed, destroyed, or whether intelligence reports regarding the weapons had been mishandled, exaggerated, or falsified.

Although some seized on the growing controversy regarding the lack of WMD finds as a partisan political issue, all Western intelligence agencies, including those of war dissenter nations France and Germany, agreed before the war that Hussein's regime possessed weapons of mass destruction.

Attention in America and Europe focused on to what degree claims regarding Iraqi WMD programs might have been exaggerated, or as the British Broadcasting Corporation (BBC) reported, "sexed up" by both the Bush and Blair administrations to gain support for the war.

At the core of the controversy lay the handling of critical reports compiled by British intelligence regarding Hussein's possession and potential use of weapons of mass destruction. One report, publicly released by the British in 2002, asserted that Hussein's "military planning allows for some weapons of mass destruction to be ready within 45 minutes of an order to use them." This statement was used by Coalition governments to stress the urgency of war. Another report, also compiled by British intelligence and released just weeks before the start of military operations, allegedly had new intelligence information, but was subsequently exposed to contain material plagiarized from a previously published academic source.

A BBC report in late May 2003, alleged that a senior British official involved in the preparation of the Fall, 2002 report (containing claims regarding Iraq's ability to rapidly assemble and use biological and chemical weapons) claimed that the report was rewritten on the instructions of officials in the administration of British Prime Minister Tony Blair to make it "sexier" (i.e., to stress the urgency of war). The BBC described their source as one of a number of senior British officials in charge of drawing up the report.

Officials in the Blair government, including John Scarlett, head of the Joint Intelligence Committee, countered that the report was entirely the work product of the intelligence community and that no pressure had been exerted to change its contents. Blair administration officials demanded a retraction and apology from the BBC. The BBC refused and stood by its story. Other British government officials initially characterized the BBC sources as "rogue elements within the intelligence services" who were against the government.

The British House of Commons foreign affairs committee began a series of hearings into the controversy and took statements from government officials and journalists regarding the BBC report. As of July 2003, the committee's initial conclusion was there was insufficient evidence of "improper influence," but that there was sufficient evidence to conclude that parts of the reports regarding Iraqi weapons readiness were given unwarranted emphasis. The committee specifically concluded that Alastair Campbell, the Blair administration's director of communications—specifically identified in BBC reports as one administration official who tried to influence report content—was not responsible for attempting to influence the contents of the report.

Another inquiry was led by the British Intelligence and Security Committee. During their hearings, testimony was provided by David Kelly, a government weapons expert. Although the BBC initially protected the identity of its source, following Kelly's death the BBC acknowledged that Kelly was the "principal source" for its claim that the report had been "sexed-up."

After the BBC aired its story in late May 2003, other news organizations sought the source of the BBC information and Kelly's name became publicly identified as the potential source of the BBC story. In July 2003, Kelly initially confirmed meeting with a BBC reporter, but denied he was the main source for the BBC report. Intense scrutiny along with and criticism of Kelly and his potential role in the story circulated in both press and government circles. Kelly blamed U.K. Ministry of Defense officials and others in the Blair government for leaking his name to the press. Kelly claimed that he was put under "intolerable" pressure by the disclosure of his association with the potential intelligence scandal.

Kelly went missing on July 17, 2003, and the next day his body was discovered near his Oxfordshire home with a knife and a packet of painkillers close to his body. Police confirmed that subsequent forensic examination concluded that Kelly committed suicide and bled to death from cuts to his wrist. Prime Minister Blair confirmed that there would be a judicial inquiry dealing with the events surrounding Kelly's death.

In July, 2003, U.S. Director of Central Intelligence, George Tenet accepted the blame for allowing subsequently discredited information from British Intelligence—that Hussein's government "recently sought significant quantities of uranium from Africa"—to remain in the text of President Bush's January 2003 State of the Union speech. Tenet acknowledged that the CIA had doubted the validity of the reports and that the evidence did not rise to the "level of certainty" normally required for insertion into presidential speeches.

At the end of July 2003, several inquires were underway into the formulation and use by Coalition governments of intelligence related to Iraqi possession and development of weapons of mass destruction.

The hunt for Hussein's regime. Against steady sniper and terrorist attacks, Coalition forces continued the hunt for former officials of Saddam Hussein's regime.

In July 2003, U.S. Army soldiers and Task Force 20 personnel (a special unit tasked with capturing or killing former Iraqi leaders) surrounded and killed Qusay and Uday Hussein, Saddam Hussein's sons and top officials of the former Iraqi regime. Following their discovery in Mosul, the former Iraqi leaders refused to surrender and an intense firefight ended in their deaths. U.S. officials debated and then released photos of the bodies, in part, to alleviate Iraqi fears that the two might still be alive and attempt a return to power. U.S. officials also hoped that the confirmation of the deaths of Qusay and Uday would encourage Iraqis to come forward with intelligence related to capturing Saddam.

As of July 30, 2003, Coalition forces and Task Force 20 had killed or captured almost 40 former Iraqi leaders depicted in a famous deck of playing cards sometimes dubbed the "deck of death," circulated to Coalition forces to assist them in spotting wanted former Iraqi leaders.

At the end of July, 2003, U.S. Central Command confirmed the deaths of 90 American service personnel killed in Iraq since President Bush's May 1 declaration of an end to major combat operations. At least 49 of those soldiers were killed in combat.

■ **FURTHER READING:**

PERIODICALS:

Schmitt, E. and B. Weinraub. "Pentagon Asserts the Main Fighting Is Finished in Iraq." *New York Times.* April 15, 2003.

Sanger D., and J. Risen. "C.I.A. Chief Takes Blame in Assertion on Iraqi uranium." *New York Times.* July 12, 2003.

ELECTRONIC:

BBC News: "CIA Takes Blame for Iraq Claims." July 12, 2003. <http://news.bbc.co.uk/1/hi/world/americas/3060615.stm> (July 30, 2003).

BBC News. Timeline: "US losses in Iraq." Updated July 30, 2003. <http://news.bbc.co.uk/2/hi/middle_east/3019552.stm> (July 30, 2003).

United Kingdom Parliament. Oral evidence Taken before the Foreign Affairs Committee on Tuesday, July 15, 2003. <http://www.publications.parliament.uk/pa/cm200203/cmselect/cmfaff/uc1025-i/uc102502.htm>. July 30, 2003.

SEE ALSO

Iraq, Intelligence and Security Agencies
Iraq War: Prelude to War (The International Debate Over the Use and Effectiveness of Weapons Inspections.)
Iraqi Freedom, Operation (2003 War Against Iraq)

A British soldier returns fire on enemy Iraqi positions to give protection to civilians fleeing the city of Basra, southern Iraq. AP/WIDE WORLD PHOTOS.

Iraqi Freedom, Operation (2003 War Against Iraq)

■ K. LEE LERNER

After failed efforts to persuade the United Nations Security Council to endorse the use of force to disarm Iraq and oust the regime of Saddam Hussein, the United States, United Kingdom, and a coalition of countries resolved to achieve those aims through military action. Although regime change—the forced elimination of the Iraqi dictator Saddam Hussein and his sons from power—was initially only a stated goal of the United States, it became a *de facto* goal of all coalition forces.

Although Iraq's military power was not as great—and the cause not as directly apparent as the need to expel Iraqi forces following their brutal invasion and occupation of Kuwait that led to the Persian Gulf War of 1990–1991—U.S. officials asserted that Iraq's proven development and use of weapons of mass destruction in the past made Iraq a potential source of those weapons for terrorists who could then use them against U.S. or other Western targets.

In 2002, some Pentagon and administration officials urged immediate and direct action be taken by the United States to disarm Iraq. There were also more controversial calls for a regime change in Baghdad as the only means to assure Iraqi disarmament. United States President George W. Bush decided instead to seek international cooperation to disarm Iraq. In September 2002, Bush addressed the United Nations and called for a strong resolution that, backed by the ultimate threat of the use of military force to disarm Iraq, would assure that Iraq possessed no weapons of mass destruction and assure that Iraq's capability to develop such weapons was destroyed.

In October 2002, the United States Congress voted Bush the authority to use military force to enforce UN resolutions.

In November 2002, the United Nations Security Council unanimously passed resolution 1441 that reiterated Iraq's obligations to disarm in accordance with prior treaty and resolution obligations and further recognized the threat that "Iraq's non-compliance with Council resolutions and proliferation of weapons of mass destruction and long-range missiles poses to international peace and security." Resolution 1441 proceeded to restate Security Council intentions to "restore international peace and security in the area."

U.S. secretary of state Colin Powell stressed that the United States and its coalition partners had "limited patience" for continued Iraqi noncompliance with United Nations resolutions. President Bush and other United States officials insisted that Iraq was in "material breech" of UN resolutions and that military action could be undertaken to disarm Iraq under the terms of existing resolutions.

In February and March of 2003, it became apparent that the United States, United Kingdom, and supporting countries on the United Nations Security Council could not reach a consensus with other permanent members France, Russia, and China, on the need to use immediate

On their march toward Baghdad during Operation Iraqi Freedom, U.S. Army soldiers, under fire from Iraqi troops and irregular forces guarding a key bridge over the Euphrates River at Al Hindiyah, struggle to reach an injured woman caught in the crossfire. The woman, kneeling by a civilian casualty, was ultimately rescued and carried to safety. AP/WIDE WORLD PHOTOS.

military force to enforce UN resolutions. As the diplomatic efforts stalled, war became more likely.

In late February 2003, a series of political and tactical setbacks seemingly delayed American action. Although a measure to support American bases in Turkey was supported by Turkey's president and military leaders, the Turkish parliament failed to muster a sufficient majority to pass a resolution allowing United States forces to use Turkish soil as a base for a northern front against Iraq. The resolution would have allowed Pentagon planners to place 62,000 American troops and heavy tanks along the northern Iraqi border with Turkey. It was not until after hostilities eventually started that Turkey allowed coalition forces limited use of Turkey's airspace to strike Iraq.

In the final weeks before the war, British and American air forces that had been patrolling the southern no-fly zone since the end of the Gulf War began a psychological campaign to discourage Iraqi resistance. Aircraft began dropping massive numbers of leaflets near military sites that encouraged Iraqi soldiers not to resist the overwhelming attack to come, and specifically warned Iraqi military leaders that they would be held accountable as war criminals for any use of biological or chemical weapons. In addition to radio broadcasts, psychological operations

(PSYOPS) also included targeting Iraqi officials with e-mails and phone calls designed to discourage their resistance or warn them of the consequences of war crimes.

Despite the logistical setbacks and delays, by March 5, U.S. secretary of defense Donald H. Rumsfeld and U.S. general Tommy R. Franks announced that U.S. military forces were ready to execute an attack against Iraq upon President Bush's order.

Diplomatic efforts continued to secure Turkish cooperation, but military planners set out a number of options and alternatives for war against Iraq without the immediate use of the U.S. infantry divisions and airborne forces moving southward from Turkey. One focus of the planning involved the threat of a sudden and massive first strike (termed "shock and awe" warfare) that would immediately overwhelm Iraqi defense forces. Planners worried that a gradual or escalating series of attacks would risk allowing Saddam Hussein to strike preemptively at Israel and thus potentially widen the war.

Counting army, navy, marine corps, air force and special operations forces, U.S. General Tommy Franks commanded a force of approximately 225,000 American and 25,000 British soldiers from the Central Command

A key element of the U.S.-led coalition strategy during Operation Iraqi Freedom in 2003 was the bombing of communications centers to disrupt Iraqi intelligence as well as Iraqi command and control infrastructure. Intense bombing with precision weapons destroyed the function of this Iraqi communication building without extensive damage to surrounding buildings. AP/WIDE WORLD PHOTOS.

post in Qatar. As with the Gulf War, the United States utilized a special reserve of commercial aircraft chartered specifically to transport forces to the region. An estimated 110,000 army and marine corps troops were located in Kuwait. Although the force was large, ground forces were approximately half the numbers used in the Gulf War.

Naval forces in the coalition centered upon five U.S. naval aircraft carriers located either in the Persian Gulf or eastern Mediterranean that remained within striking range of targets in Iraq. The carriers hosted air wings capable of delivering ordnance or in maintaining air superiority. In addition to the carriers, fleet forces consisted of more than two dozen missile ships and submarines—most capable of firing Tomahawk cruise missiles.

In addition to the naval air forces, more than 500 combat aircraft—including B–52s stationed in England, F117 stealth fighters, and B–2 stealth bombers—formed a powerful coalition air arsenal. For the first time in United States military history, some B–2 bombers were "forward deployed" to a base in Diego Garcia in the Indian Ocean. Special climate controlled protective hangers were constructed to maintain the sophisticated stealth capabilities of the bombers.

Without a northern front with supply bases in Turkey, U.S. tactical plans called for the launching of a massive attack from Kuwait, with the insertion of lighter forces (e.g., airborne paratroopers) into northern Iraq to secure the oil fields and other critical infrastructure in that region. Without the support of the heavy artillery of the U.S. Fourth Infantry Division, which was stalled offshore near Iraq, the lighter forces would need to take on the well-equipped and entrenched Iraqi Republican Guard units defending the northern approaches to Baghdad. U.S. leaders were also concerned that troops prevent rival Kurdish groups located in the north from starting a civil war or launching raids against Turkish forces that would further destabilize the region.

Options to open a second front without Turkish cooperation included the use of forces from the 82nd Airborne Division in Kuwait, the 173rd Airborne brigade in Italy, Army Ranger units, and elements of the 101st Airborne Division assembling in the region.

U.S. and British air strikes against Iraqi targets in the northern and southern no-fly zones increased and expanded from simple retaliation against Iraqi air defense installations that routinely fired upon U.S. and British

More than 80 percent of bombs dropped in Operation Iraqi Freedom were precision-guided ordnance. Here, smoke billows from a building in Baghdad hit by U.S.-led coalition forces during an air raid on March 31, 2003. AP/WIDE WORLD PHOTOS.

aircraft to include Iraqi ground-to-ground missile launchers (e.g., Iraqi Astros-2 rockets, a Brazilian-made multiple-rocket launcher routinely transported via truck).

Events moved to a diplomatic breaking point in early March. France, Germany, Russia, and China staunchly opposed military enforcement of UN resolution 1441 and threatened veto of any United Nations resolution that might—even indirectly—authorize the United States and United Kingdom to lead forces to disarm Iraq. The United States, United Kingdom, and Spain put forth a resolution that simply declared Iraq in material breech of 17 prior UN resolutions. President Bush openly declared that he would force countries to "show their cards" with regard to Iraq. In a press conference on March 6, President Bush asserted that Saddam Hussein posed a direct and immediate danger to the security of the United States and, with regard to the United Nations and pending debate and resolutions, asserted that "diplomacy has failed" and that the "we really don't need anybody's permission" to defend the United States.

With war seemingly imminent, the United States, United Kingdom, and Spain amended a final resolution that set March 17, 2003, as a final deadline for the council to certify Iraqi compliance with prior resolutions. Although a threat of force was not contained within the resolution, there was little doubt that should Iraq fail to meet the deadline, the United States and United Kingdom would lead a multinational coalition to militarily disarm Iraq. The United States also sought and promised to depose Saddam Hussein and allow the Iraqi people a chance for democratic government.

With the UN Security Council deadlocked, the probable votes of the nonpermanent members hotly disputed, and the deadline at hand, the U.S., U.K. and Spain allowed their new proposal to die without a vote. Although he had once promised to call for a vote, President Bush stated that France "had shown their cards" and administration officials declared the "diplomatic window closed." Although France, Russia, and China declared that any U.S.- and U.K.-led coalition action against Iraq would be illegitimate and in violation of the UN charter, U.S. and U.K. officials rested on existing UN resolutions (one reason some experts claimed that another vote was not sought), Iraq's violation of the treaty that ended the Persian Gulf War, and assertions of the right of self defense to legitimize military action.

On the evening of March 17 (Washington time) President Bush, in a televised address carried around the world by major news organizations, issued Saddam Hussein and his sons (both high ranking Iraqi officials) a 48-hour deadline to leave Iraq or face war.

Bush urged Iraqi forces not to destroy infrastructure or natural resources (e.g., oil wells), and warned Iraqi military officials that the use of chemical or biological weapons would be treated as a war crime.

After citing potential threats to American security, Bush stated, "The United States did nothing to deserve or invite this threat, but we will do everything to defeat it. Instead of drifting along toward tragedy, we will set a course toward safety." "The danger is clear," Bush said. "Using chemical, biological or, one day, nuclear weapons obtained with the help of Iraq, the terrorists could fulfill their stated ambitions and kill thousands or hundreds of thousands of innocent people in our country...." President Bush also issued a message to the Iraqi people stating, "the day of your liberation is near" and promised that "the tyrant [Hussein] will soon be gone."

Citing the increased "possibility" (indeed, some administration officials used the term "probability") of retaliatory terrorist strikes against U.S. interests, Bush raised the terror alert level to "high" (color code orange). As of May, 2003, no such attacks occurred.

Iraq immediately denounced the ultimatum and promised defiance. UN weapons inspectors were withdrawn from Iraq and most countries withdrew diplomats and other personnel. France called for a ministerial level meeting of the UN Security Council, and a meeting of heads of state. The U.S. and U.K. ignored further French efforts and insisted that Hussein could only avoid war by exile. The British Parliament voted support of the use of U.K. forces in a military invasion of Iraq.

Sporadic fighting flared as the deadline approached. Hussein ignored the March 19 deadline, and approximately 90 minutes later—near dawn in Baghdad—U.S. jets made a strike using precision guided bunker buster bombs on a target near Baghdad believed to contain senior Iraqi officials, including Hussein. Pentagon officials subsequently said F–117 Nighthawk stealth fighter-bombers dropped 2000-pound (900-kilogram) satellite-guided bombs on a site where CIA officers developed information that Hussein might be in conference with other Iraqi leaders. For several weeks, the fate of Hussein would be debated, with Iraqi television showing images of Hussein that did not verify his survival.

Weeks later, a similar strike on an Iraqi leadership target occurred as U.S. forces were preparing to enter Baghdad. Once again, the fate of Hussein and other leaders remained uncertain.

Coalition intelligence services and special operations units played an important role in identifying and in some cases physically "painting" targets. Target painting refers to the process of identifying a target with a laser or an electronic signature device that allows weapons platforms (e.g. airplanes, tanks, etc.) to identify targets. Coalition special forces and intelligence units—including CIA units—operated inside Iraq for weeks prior to the initial attack. In addition to identifying targets, intelligence and psychological operations (PSYOPS) teams dropped tens of thousands of leaflets, and made radio broadcasts designed to discourage Iraqi resistance and possibly spark a coup against Hussein. Special efforts were made to psychologically separate regular Iraqi units, better trained Iraqi Republican Guard units, and Hussein's inner circle to facilitate the surrender of as many Iraqi forces as possible.

Bush made a further television address to announce the start of hostilities. Across Iraq, U.S. forces launched probing attacks, along with attacks to destroy Iraqi command and control facilities. Anti-aircraft radar and missile facilities were the targets of Tomahawk cruise missiles launched by U.S. naval vessels, and U.S. aircraft dropped precision-guided bombs against targets.

Hours after the U.S. strikes, Iraq fired at least four missiles into northern Kuwait. According to American officials, Patriot missiles intercepted at least two missiles. Fear of chemical attacks by Iraq forced coalition forces and residents of northern Kuwait to repeatedly put on protective clothing and gas masks. Subsequent analysis of missile remains—and others eventually launched into Kuwait—indicated that the missiles carried conventional, not chemical, warheads.

Fear of the use of weapons of mass destruction was based upon Hussein's use of chemical weapons against Iranian forces during the 1980s Iran-Iraq War, and his prior use of chemical weapons against civilians in rebellious areas of Iraq.

In an attempt to prove that Hussein had survived the initial attack and thus forestall possible Iraqi defections, Iraqi television broadcast a speech allegedly by Hussein. Western intelligence sources could not immediately verify that the speech was actually made by Hussein. Intelligence officials had long known that Hussein had a number of body doubles—some surgically altered to bear a closer resemblance to the Iraqi leader.

On March 20, U.S.-led forces intensified attacks and forces breached Iraqi defensive positions and barriers along the Kuwait border. Tank and mechanized infantry units penetrated nearly 100 miles (160km) into Iraq by the end of the first day. Embedded journalists relayed back video of tank units racing across the Iraqi desert toward Baghdad. British forces raced to surround and isolate the port city of Basra. U.S. forces began the mechanized march to Baghdad.

A brief lull in the aerial attacks on Baghdad by coalition forces, along with statements by U.S. officials regarding the potential surrender of significant portions of Iraq's Republican Guard units, provided additional evidence of special forces and intelligence unit contact with Hussein's inner circle. The lull in attacks against Baghdad also fueled speculation about whether Hussein was still alive, or in complete control of his forces.

In a Pentagon press briefing, Rumsfeld said, "We are in communication with still more people who are officials of the military at various levels, the regular army, the Republican Guard, the Special Republican Guard...." Offering surrender, Rumsfeld added, "We continue to feel that there's no need for a broader conflict if the Iraqi leaders act to save themselves and to prevent such further conflict." Although there were significant defections and surrenders of Iraqi forces, nothing approached the mass surrenders anticipated by optimistic U.S. officials.

On March 21, U.S.-led coalition forces launched a massive aerial bombardment of Baghdad and other targets throughout Iraq. GPS precision guided bombs and an estimated 300 cruise missiles targeted Iraqi command and control facilities. Within an hour of the start of the attack on Baghdad, coalition forces destroyed more than 25 major buildings that housed Iraqi governmental offices. Hussein's presidential palaces in and around Baghdad were also destroyed.

The March 21 assault, designated by Pentagon planners as "A-Day" (aerial attack day), was the start of the "shock and awe" pattern of precise, but massive attacks designed to stun the Iraqis into submission.

At a Pentagon press briefing Rumsfeld made a special effort to address comparisons of the coalition "A-Day" attacks to similar massive attacks during WWII (e.g. the firebombing of Dresden). Rumsfeld dismissed the comparisons as invalid because of the use of precision weapons against military and government targets as opposed to the deliberate use of "dumb bombs against broad areas."

Over the next three weeks, coalition forces moved farther and faster than any army in history. British forces surrounded Basra and Umm Qasr, and systematically took control of the cities with minimal losses. Within days the entire coastline of Iraq was under coalition control, although terrorist actions and pockets of resistance worked to slow the promised quick delivery of humanitarian assistance to Iraqis falling under U.S. control.

Special forces helped secure airfields designated H2 and H3 in the western region of Iraq. These forces also help control the "Scud box" area from which Iraq had launched missiles against Israel during the Gulf War.

On the road to Baghdad, U.S. troops fought battles in Najaf, Kut, and waged a pitched battle in Nasiriya before capturing a key bridge over the Euphrates River. U.S. forces fought Iraqi troops, terrorist guerrillas known as Martyrs of Saddam who engaged in suicide bombings, and fedayeen militia conducting suicide attacks. This was often complicated by Iraqi use of civilian human shields. However, the biggest delays in the U.S. advance were caused by a major sandstorm that precluded helicopter operations and the need to secure rapidly extending supply lines from rearguard attacks by troops and guerilla forces bypassed on the lightening thrust toward the Iraqi capital. U.S. forces also encountered fierce fighting in Karbala.

Coalition forces were also slowed by the need to wear clothing and equipment designed to protect them against chemical or biological weapons, although such protection ultimately proved unnecessary.

For a few days, American forces conducted operations about 100 miles south of Baghdad before resuming their push toward the city.

The war was the most intensely covered news event in history. Journalists embedded with coalition forces provided live pictures from the battlefield. In terms of both quantity and quality of coverage, the war was a profound event in media history. In many cases, the same facts were reported with vastly differing emphasis depending on the reporter's perspective or political/editorial orientation of the news agency. At other times, there were wide discrepancies in the amount of airtime or print space offered to particular stories. For the first time, several Arab television news channels, including Al-Jazeera, provided continuous coverage that competed with U.S.-based news organizations, the BBC, and European based news organizations.

While coalition forces were lauded by reporters and commentators from some news organizations for the use of precision weapons that reduced civilian casualties, other organizations continually emphasized graphic pictures of civilian and military casualties. Al-Jazeera, criticized before the war by many Western media editors for airing biased, inaccurate, and inflammatory anti-Western reports, drew intense criticism from U.S. officials for showing controversial video of coalition POWs held or executed by Iraqis.

Although considered an almost comical media sideshow by Western news agencies, the farcical interviews and briefings conducted by Iraq's minister of information, Said Sahaf, were reported more seriously by Arab news channels. Even as U.S. troops raced toward Baghdad, Sahaf continued to insist that U.S. troops had been "slaughtered," and "driven out of the country." When U.S. troops were literally within blocks of his Baghdad location, Sahaf confidently told reporters that American troops were not within 100 miles of Baghdad. Belief in Sahaf's assurances and boasts about the power of the Iraqi army (once the third largest ground force in the world) engendered shock and surprise among some viewers of Al-Jazeera and other Arab news outlets when the Iraqi government abruptly collapsed soon afterward.

Although coalition forces ultimately managed a quick and decisive military victory, the effects of the differing perspectives in news coverage may take years to fully determine.

Given the demanding pace of round-the-clock media coverage, operational pauses for rest or logistical resupply by coalition forces often led to open speculation as to whether coalition forces were "bogged down." Delays caused by duststorms, and deaths caused by suicide bombers attacking checkpoints caused some commentators to openly speculate that America was getting involved in "another Vietnam-like quagmire" or that the war could stretch on for many months, perhaps years.

The use of fewer troops than used in the Gulf War also drew criticism. The war plan was a test of a new policy of smaller force deployments. Advocates of the lighter force concept argued that mobility, precision weapons, and real-time integration of intelligence information acted as "force multipliers." Pentagon or war plan critics contended that the U.S. had not deployed adequate ground troops to ensure maximum safety for both military personnel and Iraqi civilian populations.

Despite criticisms, within three weeks, coalition forces toppled the Hussein regime. The speed of attack also allowed coalition forces to accomplish major goals. Iraqi command and control was virtually eliminated within hours of the start of military operations. The Iraqis could offer little organized resistance. U.S., British, and Australian forces secured both southern, and then northern, oil fields before Hussein's forces could set significant fires or cause significant environmental damage as they did during the Gulf war. The Iraqi air force was totally destroyed or immobilized and launched no sorties against coalition forces. In the north, a major terrorist facility was overrun and destroyed.

In a battle on April 2, army and marine troops routed the elite Iraqi Republican Guard units about 20 miles of south of Baghdad and a two-pronged assault on the capital began. On April 4, U.S. troops seized Baghdad's main airport located just 10 miles from the center of the city.

After brief preliminary incursions, on April 9, U.S. forces advanced into central Baghdad and Saddam Hussein's government was symbolically toppled. Carried live by global television networks, Iraqis celebrating liberation—with the technical assistance of U.S. troops—pulled down a large statue of Saddam Hussein located in central Baghdad. Kurdish fighters and U.S forces secured the northern cities of Kirkuk and Mosul during the next three days.

On April 15, U.S. marines captured Tikrit, the ancestral home of Saddam Hussein. After an intense bombardment, U.S. forces encountered only sporadic resistance as they captured what was thought to be Hussein's last military stronghold. Pentagon officials stated that the main military fight in Iraq was finished.

The speed of the American advance and coalition determination not to be seen as oppressive occupying powers unfortunately resulted in a lack of policing activities and resultant looting. Iraqi looters and criminals from other countries stole freely and openly, in some cases taking valuable artifacts and cultural treasures. The looting, and perceived slowness in restoration of water and electricity, sparked anti-American protests in newly liberated Iraq. Religious fundamentalists also took the opportunity afforded by liberation to begin to organize anti-Western protests.

Nine weeks after the start of military action against Iraq, the United Nations Security Council—including France, Russia, and China—overwhelmingly approved a resolution lifting economic sanctions against Iraq and gave its backing to U.S.-led administration by coalition forces until the situation in Iraq stabilized.

The lack of success in finding massive stockpiles of biological or chemical weapons spurred charges that the CIA and other Western intelligence agencies had exaggerated reports of Iraqi capabilities in this area. Even the French government, one of the harshest critics of U.S. war plans, had openly accepted that large stockpiles of chemical and biological agents existed in Iraq prior to the war.

Although French intelligence reports disagreed with American and British assessments of ongoing links between Iraq and al-Qaeda, French Foreign Minister Dominique de Villepin stated that his sources nevertheless confirmed much of the information regarding biological and chemical weapons stockpiles reported by U.S. and U.K. intelligence services. De Villepin, however, dismissed CIA and MI-6 information as common knowledge among Western intelligence services and therefore not a cause for immediate war.

As of May 2003, coalition teams were continuing to explore for sites containing weapons of mass destruction. Although there were many preliminary findings of illegal equipment that might have been used to manufacture such weapons, none had yet withstood careful scientific scrutiny. U.S. officials invited international inspectors to examine specific finds (e.g., suspected mobile biological weapons laboratories.)

UN chief weapons inspector Hans Blix subsequently concluded that Iraq may not have had weapons of mass destruction—or at least not on the scale previously anticipated, and that Saddam Hussein's evasive behavior with inspectors may have resulted from his dictatorial need to control information. U.S. officials openly speculated about the possible diversion of weapons to Syria and accused Syria of harboring deposed Iraqi leaders and of attempting to develop and test chemical weapons. Syria denied the U.S. allegations.

Leading administration officials claimed that inspection efforts would take many months and that the best hope of finding weapons stockpiles would come from the interrogation of captured Iraqi leaders and scientists. Intelligence reports leaked to the press also indicated that there was evidence of massive smuggling of materials (including possible weapons shipments) into Syria. There was also mounting evidence that during the diplomatic infighting prior to the war the French and Russian governments had provided assistance to Iraqi leaders as they attempted to conceal the extent of their support of the Hussein regime. British press reporters discovered documents with Bin Laden's name covered with correction fluid that, if ultimately proved genuine, would provide evidence of formal communications and cooperation between the Hussein regime and al-Qaeda.

Unarguable evidence concerning the brutality of Hussein's regime was provided with the discovery of mass gravesites at Abul Kasib, Basra, Najaf, al-Mahawil, Babylon, Muhammad Sakran, and Kirkuk. Many of the graves contained men, women, and children apparently executed after failed uprisings against Saddam Hussein. South of Baghdad, many graves contained those executed following the attempted Shia rebellion that followed the Gulf War. Northern mass graves contained the remains of political prisoners and Kurds executed during Hussein's policy of ethnic cleansing.

As of May 2003 the whereabouts or fate of Hussein and other top Iraqi leaders remained uncertain. The U.S.

abolished the Baath Party and security institutions of Saddam Hussein's former regime. With Iraq occupied and administered by coalition forces, the U.S. removed Iraq from the list of countries not cooperating with the fight against terrorism.

Coalition goals and plans for the postwar stabilization of Iraq asserted that coalition forces would maintain physical civil security, while U.S.-administered government departments regulate infrastructure and aid. Under Coalition guidance, Iraqi citizens and returning expatriates would be encouraged to form a broad-based, multi-ethnic interim Iraqi administration that would eventually become a self-governing Iraqi government recognized by the international community.

■ FURTHER READING:

PERIODICALS:

Gordon, M. "The Test for Rumsfeld: Will Strategy Work?" *New York Times.* April 1, 2003.

Sanger, D., and F. Barringer. "President Readies U.S. for Prospect of Imminent War." *New York Times.* March 7, 2003.

Schmitt, E., and T. Shanker. "U.S. Reports Talks Urging Surrender of Elite Troops." *New York Times.* March 21, 2003.

Schmitt, E. and B. Weintraub. "Pentagon Asserts the Main Fighting Is Finished in Iraq." *New York Times.* April 15, 2003.

Tyler, Patrick E. "Hussein Statue Is Toppled—Rumsfeld Urges Caution." *New York Times.* April 10, 2003.

ELECTRONIC:

BBC News. Iraq War. Key Maps. <http://news.bbc.co.uk/1/shared/spl/hi/middle_east/03/v3_iraq_key_maps/html/graves/link1.stm> (May 12, 2003).

Central Intelligence Agency. "Iraq." *CIA World Factbook* <http://www.cia.gov/cia/publications/factbook/geos/iz.html>(May 25, 2003).

U.S. Department of Defense. Operation Iraqi Freedom Special Report. "President Bush Outlines Progress in Operation Iraqi Freedom." <http://www.whitehouse.gov/news/releases/2003/04/iraq/20030416–9.html> (April 16, 2003).

SEE ALSO

International Atomic Energy Agency (IAEA)
Iraq, Intelligence and Security Agencies in
Iraq War: Prelude to War (The International Debate Over the Use and Effectiveness of Weapons Inspections.)

Ireland, Intelligence and Security

The failed Easter Rebellion of 1916 sparked decades of guerilla warfare and terrorist attacks in Ireland. Ireland finally gained its independence from Britain in 1921, but the accord that granted the establishment of the Irish Republic also divided the island. Six northern counties, now Northern Ireland, remained in British possession. The partitioning of Ireland brought relative peace to the Irish Republic, but initiated decades of violent conflict between Irish loyalists and British unionists in the north. After remaining officially neutral during World War II, Ireland withdrew from the British Commonwealth in 1948 in protest over continued English rule in Northern Ireland.

Despite earlier conflict, Ireland and Britain have worked closely to stem terrorism and political conflict in Northern Ireland and throughout the British Isles. Today, Ireland is enjoying relative calm in the Northern Ireland conflict. A series of peace accords and disarmament treaties between rival factions in the region have yielded limited successes. In 2001, Irish intelligence and security forces joined a European coalition to fight global terrorism. While not a member of the North Atlantic Treaty Organization (NATO), the Irish republic is an influential member of the European Union.

Ireland maintains a stated policy of neutrality, however the nation has a sizable military. The *Óglaigh na h-Éireann*, or Irish Defense Forces, have two dedicated intelligence and security divisions. The G-2 military intelligence branch collects and analyzes both foreign and domestic intelligence. The agency often aids other European nations and the United States in international intelligence operations. G-2 provides intelligence information on terrorist organizations associated with the Northern Ireland conflict, often cooperating with British intelligence at MI5. G-2 is one of Europe's most sophisticated intelligence agencies, conducting remote, computer systems, signals, and human surveillance.

The Irish Defense Forces also possess a highly specialized action unit known as the *Sciathán Fianóglach an Airm*, or Army Ranger Wing. Recognizing the need for a special deployment force to respond to terrorist threats and hostage situations, the Irish government arranged for the training of an elite force of Irish Defense soldiers at the United States Army Ranger School at Ft. Benning, Georgia. The specially trained unit returned to Ireland to train other military personnel. In 1980, the official Army Ranger Wing was formed. The Army Rangers conduct counterterrorism operations, and are trained in hostage rescue and urban street fighting.

In addition to military forces, Ireland's largest civilian security force is the *An Garda Siochana*, known commonly as the Garda. The Garda is the Republic of Ireland's national police force. The main charge of the agency is the protection of citizens and domestic national interests. In conjunction with the Army Ranger Wing, the security and intelligence unit of the Garda conducts regular counterintelligence surveillance. The Special Branch C3 Section is the Garda's elite counterterrorism unit.

Ireland is one of Europe's leading sites of technological and computer systems. The growth of Ireland's technology industry has increased the need for corporate and economic security. The Garda and other Irish government agencies have increased efforts to thwart corporate espionage, money laundering, and the illegal trafficking of technology and funds to suspected terrorist organizations.

While terrorism related to the conflict in Northern Ireland has substantially subsided in recent years, the Irish intelligence community continues extensive counterterrorism operations. Irish Defense Forces have trained counterterrorism forces from other European nations. In response to increasing global terrorism threats, the Irish Defense Forces and Garda are preparing heightened defense structures and tightening domestic security measures in preparation for the Irish Presidency of the European Union in 2004.

SEE ALSO

European Union
United Kingdom, Counter-terrorism Policy

Irish Republican Army (IRA)

The Irish Republican Army (IRA) also operates as, or is known as, the Provisional Irish Republican Army (PIRA or "Provos").

The IRA formally became a terrorist group in 1969 as the clandestine armed wing of Sinn Fein, a legal political movement dedicated to removing British forces from Northern Ireland and unifying Ireland. The IRA originated with a Marxist orientation and was organized into small, tightly knit cells under the leadership of the Army Council. The IRA has been observing a cease-fire since 1997 and in October 2001, took the historic step of putting an unspecified amount of arms and ammunition "completely beyond use." The International Commission on Decommissioning characterized the step as a significant act of decommissioning. The IRA retains the ability to conduct operations. Its traditional activities have included bombings, assassinations, kidnappings, punishment beatings, extortion, smuggling, and robberies. Bombing campaigns were conducted against train and subway stations and shopping areas on mainland Britain. Targets included senior British government officials, civilians, police, and British military targets in Northern Ireland.

The IRA has, at a minimum, several hundred members, plus several thousand sympathizers—despite the possible defection of some members to the Real IRA (RIRA). The IRA operates in Northern Ireland, the Republic of Ireland, Great Britain, and Europe. During its history, the IRA has received aid from a variety of groups and countries and considerable training and arms from Libya and the Palestinian Liberation Organization. The IRA is suspected of receiving funds, arms, and other terrorist related materiel from sympathizers in the United States.

■ FURTHER READING:

ELECTRONIC:

CDI (Center for Defense Information) Terrorism Project. CDI Fact Sheet: Current List of Designated Foreign Terrorist Organizations. March 27, 2003. <http://www.cdi.org/terrorism/terrorist.cfm> (April 17, 2003).

Central Intelligence Agency. World Factbook, 2002. <http://www.cia.gov/cia/publications/factbook/> (April 16, 2003).

Taylor, Francis X. U.S. Department of State. "Patterns of Global Terrorism 2001." Annual Report: On the Record Briefing. May 21, 2002 <http://www.state.gov/s/ct/rls/rm/10367.htm> (April 17, 2003).

U.S. Department of State. Annual reports. <http://www.state.gov/www/global/terrorism/annual_reports.html> (April 16, 2003).

SEE ALSO

Terrorism, Philosophical and Ideological Origins
Terrorist and Para-State Organizations
Terrorist Organization List, United States
Terrorist Organizations, Freezing of Assets

Islamic Army of Aden (IAA)

Islamic Army of Aden (IAA) also operates as, or is known as, the Aden-Abyan Islamic Army (AAIA).

The IAA emerged publicly in mid-1998 when the group released a series of communiqués that expressed support for Osama Bin Laden (also spelled Usama Bin Ladin) appealed for the overthrow of the Yemeni government and the commencement of operations against U.S. and other Western interests in Yemen. The IAA engages in bombings and kidnappings to promote its goals. IAA members kidnapped 16 British, Australian, and U.S. tourists in late December 1998 near Mudiyah in southern Yemen. Since the capture and trial of the Mudiyah kidnappers and the execution in October 1999 of the group's leader, Zein al-Abidine al-Mihdar (a.k.a. Abu Hassan), individuals associated with the IAA have remained involved in terrorist activities. In 2001, the Yemeni government convicted an IAA member and three associates for their roles in the October 2000 bombing of the British Embassy.

IAA operates in the southern governorates of Yemen—primarily Aden and Abyan.

■ FURTHER READING:

ELECTRONIC:

CDI (Center for Defense Information) Terrorism Project. CDI Fact Sheet: Current List of Designated Foreign Terrorist Organizations. March 27, 2003. <http://www.cdi.org/terrorism/terrorist.cfm> (April 17, 2003).

Central Intelligence Agency. World Factbook, 2002. <http://www.cia.gov/cia/publications/factbook/> (April 16, 2003).

Taylor, Francis X. U.S. Department of State. "Patterns of Global Terrorism 2001." Annual Report: On the Record Briefing. May 21, 2002. <http://www.state.gov/s/ct/rls/rm/10367.htm> (April 17, 2003).

U.S. Department of State. Annual reports. <http://www.state.gov/www/global/terrorism/annual_reports.html> (April 16, 2003).

SEE ALSO

Terrorism, Philosophical and Ideological Origins
Terrorist and Para-State Organizations
Terrorist Organization List, United States
Terrorist Organizations, Freezing of Assets

Islamic Movement of Uzbekistan (IMU)

Islamic Movement of Uzbekistan (IMU) is a coalition of Islamic militants from Uzbekistan and other Central Asian states opposed to Uzbekistani President Islom Karimov's secular regime. Before the counterterrorism coalition began operations in Afghanistan in October 2001, the IMU's primary goal was the establishment of an Islamic state in Uzbekistan. If IMU political and ideological leader Tohir Yoldashev survives the counterterrorism campaign and can regroup the organization, however, he might widen the IMU's targets to include all those he perceives as fighting Islam. The group's propaganda has always included anti-Western and anti-Israeli rhetoric.

Organization activities. The IMU primarily targeted Uzbekistani interests before October 2001 and is believed to have been responsible for five car bombs in Tashkent in February 1999. IMU militants also took foreigners hostage in 1999 and 2000, including four U.S. citizens who were mountain climbing in August 2000, and four Japanese geologists and eight Kyrgyzstani soldiers in August 1999. Since October 2001, the coalition has captured, killed, and dispersed many of the militants who remained in Afghanistan to fight with the Taliban and al-Qaida, severely degrading the IMU's ability to attack Uzbekistani or coalition interests in the near term. IMU military leader Juma Namangani apparently was killed during an air strike. As of May 2002, Yoldashev remained at large.

Islamic Movement of Uzbekistan militants probably number under 2000 and are scattered throughout South Asia and Tajikistan. Areas of operations for the IMU include Afghanistan, Iran, Kyrgyzstan, Pakistan, Tajikistan, and Uzbekistan. Receiving support from other Islamic extremist groups and patrons in the Middle East and Central and South Asia, the IMU leadership also broadcasts statements over Iranian radio.

■ FURTHER READING:

ELECTRONIC:

Central Intelligence Agency. World Factbook, 2002. <http://www.cia.gov/cia/publications/factbook/> (April 16, 2003).

Taylor, Francis X. U.S. Department of State. Patterns of Global Terrorism 2001. Annual Report: On the Record Briefing. May 21, 2002. <http://www.state.gov/s/ct/rls/rm/10367.htm> (April 17,2003).

U.S. Department of State. Annual reports. <http://www.state.gov/www/global/terrorism/annual_reports.html> (April 16, 2003).

SEE ALSO

Terrorism, Philosophical and Ideological Origins
Terrorist and Para-State Organizations
Terrorist Organization List, United States
Terrorist Organizations, Freezing of Assets

Isotopic Analysis

■ ALEXANDR IOFFE

Varieties of the same chemical element, but with different atomic weights, are called isotopes. Isotopic analysis (IA) is the analysis of the isotope composition of a sample. Samples in IA can contain almost anything: different objects of everyday life, pieces of rocks, pieces of wood, samples of tissue taken from a human body, chemical compounds, and so on. In general, and with some degree of simplification, isotopic analysis is used for identification of a sample and for the determination of its age. Isotopic analysis is based upon the use of mass spectrometers or radioactive radiation counters. A mass spectrometer is a device that determines the quantity and composition of different isotopes (of the same chemical element as well as various elements) in the sample.

The Oak Ridge National Laboratory in 2001 designed a portable mass spectrometer that is capable of detecting chemical and biological agents of war in the air, and can also detect chemical warfare agents on the ground. Called the chemical-biological mass spectrometer (CBMS), the device works by collecting an air sample or chemical sample via a chemical probe and classifying it first according to its size, then according to its unique ion products. The system can detect a wide range of chemical and biological weapons on the battlefield, such as anthrax spores, nerve gas, viruses, and toxins. The CMBS is scheduled to be manufactured in sufficient numbers to be operational in the field by 2004.

Another new mass spectrometry device, similar to the walk-through scanners used in airports, may soon be able to detect microscopic amounts of explosives or narcotic substances hidden in clothing or on a person. When passing through the scanner, a jet of air puffs clothing and air samples immediately surrounding the person are concentrated and analyzed using ion mobility spectrometry. Minute amounts of explosives, chemical weapons, and illegal drugs that cling to the skin or clothing can be easily found. The highly sensitive nature of the scanner can also be a drawback, as targeted substances may be found on persons unaware of their presence. For example, the scanner could detect a narcotic residue on coins randomly received at an airport vending machine by an unsuspecting person. The likelihood for false positive results, along with the high cost of the machine and the seven-second period necessary to scan each individual, may inhibit its widespread use in airports. Some airports do use similar technology to screen checked baggage.

The isotope composition of many objects is unique (relative to the composition itself as well as to the isotope concentrations), and because of this, isotopic analysis offers the possibility for identification of a sample. Isotopic analysis is also utilized in varying disciplines, including chemistry, medicine, biology, geology, archeology, and criminal forensics. Recently, isotopic analysis has seen use in the diagnosis of some diseases through analysis of air exhaled by the patient. Often, isotopic analysis permits the scientist to distinguish the genuine product from its imitation. For example, the technology is used to distinguish expensive types of wine and liquor from their imitations. When archaeologists investigate various fragments of ancient objects, they sometimes use isotopic analysis to determine where these objects were made, or to elucidate the source of the raw material for their production.

Isotopes can be both stable and radioactive. Isotopic analysis of radioactive isotopes permits scientists to determine the age of the investigated sample. Often the isotope C^{14} is used for this purpose. This isotope itself is unstable and decays with time, and in the decay process, other stable isotopes are created. In nature, the concentration of C^{14} is maintained because of cosmic radiation. While a tree lives, for example, the concentration of C^{14} in its wood is equal to the C^{14} concentration in the environment, because atoms of radioactive carbon penetrate the wood from the atmosphere with CO^2 molecules due to photosynthesis, and also through the tree root system. But when the tree dies, these exchange processes cease, and the C^{14} concentration in the tree begins to decrease. The law of radioactive carbon concentration alteration in the sample is known, hence if its concentration is measured in the sample and compared with the concentration of the isotope in nature, the age of the tree itself can be determined (or more precisely, the time since the tree died). When the decay period of the radioisotope is considered, the age of the sample can be determined within an accuracy of several decades. For this analysis, a sample weight of only several milligrams (mg) is often sufficient. For example, a mammoth calf whose body was recently found in Siberia in the frozen ground was determined to have lived about 27,000 years ago, and only 4 mg of the mammoth muscle tissue was needed for the analysis.

■ FURTHER READING:

ELECTRONIC:

Lawrence Livermore National Laboratory. "National Resource for Biomedical Accelerator Mass Spectrometry." <http://www.llnl.gov/bioams/index.html> (January, 4, 2003).

"New Airport Security Measures." I-mass.com. <http://i-mass.com/airp1100.html> (January, 4, 2003).

Oak Ridge National Laboratory. "Chemical Biological Mass Spectrometer." <http://infosrv1.ctd.ornl.gov/ORNLReview/measure/analy/direct/chem-bio.htm> (January, 4, 2003).

SEE ALSO

Air Plume and Chemical Analysis
Biological Warfare
Gas Chromatograph-Mass Spectrometer
Microbiology: Applications to Espionage, Intelligence, and Security

Israel, Counter-Terrorism Policy

■ TIMOTHY G. BORDEN

Since it was founded in 1948, the nation of Israel has implemented some of the most rigorous counter-terrorist measures of any country in the world. It suffered its first attacks by the Palestine Liberation Organization (PLO) in 1965 and was subject to PLO Intifadas, or uprisings, in 1987 and again in 2001, which produced dozens of terrorist bombings with hundred of casualties. Israel's zeal to contain and prevent terrorist attacks against its citizens has at times prompted international criticism, particularly regarding its state-sponsored assassinations of known terrorists in other countries and use of coercive interrogation to gather information on terrorist activites.

Israel has perhaps the greatest experience with counter-terrorist measures than any other modern nation. Facing hostility from its Arab neighbors, the Jewish state enacted the Prevention of Terrorism Ordinance upon its establishment in 1948. The law defined terrorism to include direct acts of violence as well as threats of violence against an individual, and broadly categorized membership in a terrorist organization to include those who had given money or resources to such a group in addition to those who directly participated in it. The 1948 ordinance also gave authorities such as Shin Bet, the country's intelligence agency, broad prosecutorial powers to detain individuals and shut down suspected terrorist centers. Later amendments to the 1948 ordinance made it illegal to sympathize with terrorist organizations by flying their flags or displaying their symbols and criminalized most contacts made abroad with terrorists (a stipulation repealed in 1993).

Although Israel's counter-terrorist policies were sometimes criticized as being too harsh, its citizens came to expect a high degree of government vigilance over their daily lives. Much of the counter-terrorist effort was resource-intensive, not technologically sophisticated. Searches of individuals and their belongings were routine in public places, and scrutiny at border crossings and the country's main international airport was intense. The government rigorously screened all employees manning security checkpoints at airports and borders and travelers at borders were asked extensively about their travel plans, sources of income, contacts in Israel, and other personal issues.

Although the scrutiny with which Israel conducted such inquiries provoked accusations of anti-Arabic racial profiling, it was largely responsible for producing a near-perfect record of safety on the government-owned airline, El Al. The only incident of hijacking on El Al occurred in July 1968, when three members of the Popular Front for the Liberation of Palestine took control of a plane on its way from Rome to Tel Aviv. The hijackers held the plane's passengers hostage for forty days until Israel acceded to their demands for the release of a group of Palestinian terrorists.

The Israeli government stiffened its resolve to follow a zero-tolerance policy in negotiating with terrorists in June 1976, when a group of Palestinian and German terrorists abducted an Air France plane and held its passengers hostage at an airport in Entebbe, Uganda. After the hijackers demanded the release of fifty-three jailed Palestinian terrorists during an eight-day standoff, an Israeli commando squad stormed the plane and ended the siege. All of the hijackers were killed in the raid. The lives of 98 hostages were saved; four hostages were killed in the raid.

Despite the continuing emphasis on counter-terrorism in Israel, an Intifada, or uprising, sponsored by the PLO from 1987 onward against the Israeli presence in the Occupied Territories resulted in at least 20,000 casualties on both sides. Although tensions subsided after the withdrawal of Israeli troops from much of the Occupied Territories under a series of accords from 1993 to 1997, Israeli citizens continued to face terrorist threats on a daily basis.

In 2001, a renewed wave of Intifada actions resulted in dozens of bombings on Israeli soil, which occurred at the rate of two every month. Given the ongoing threat, about 10 percent of the Israeli gross national product is annually spent on defense.

■ FURTHER READING:

BOOKS:

Heller, Mark A. *Continuity and Change in Israeli Security Policy.* New York: Oxford University Press, 2000.

Inbar, Efraim. *Rabin and Israel's National Security.* Baltimore: Johns Hopkins University Press, 1999.

James, Ron. *Frontiers and Ghettos: State Violence in Serbia and Israel.* Berkeley: University of California Press, 2003.

Katz, Samuel M. *The Hunt for the Engineer: How Israeli Agents Tracked the Hamas Master Bomber.* New York: Fromm International, 1999.

Thomas, Gordon. *Gideon's Spies: The Secret History of the Moussad.* New York: St. Martin's Press, 2000.

PERIODICALS:

Gladwell, Martin. "Safety in the Skies." *New Yorker.* October 1, 2002.

Morris, Jim. "Israel Offers Lessons in Aviation Security." *Dallas Morning News.* November 8, 2001.

Schwarts, Nelson. "Learning from Israel." *Fortune.* (January 21, 2002).

SEE ALSO

Airline Security
Egypt, Intelligence and Security
Eichmann, Adolf: Israeli capture
Intelligence and Democracy: Issues and Conflicts
Mossad
Palestinian Authority, Intelligence and Security
Pollard Espionage Case
Syria, Intelligence and Security
Terrorism, Philosophical and Ideological Origins
Terrorist and Para-State Organizations

Israel, Intelligence and Security

Israel gained its independence following World War II after Britain ended its colonial mandate of Palestine. Jewish refugees and victims of the Holocaust immigrated to Palestine in order to create the Jewish homeland promised in the British Balfour Declaration. The influx of immigrants created tension in the Arab dominated region. The United Nations intervened, creating the Jewish state of Israel in the south, and Arab Palestine in the north. To ease hostility between the two factions, the city of Jerusalem, holy to Jews, Muslims, and Christians, was declared an international city. A series of wars between Israel and its Arab neighbors led to an expansion of Israeli territory, including gaining control of Jerusalem, and heightened animosity between Jews and Arabs in the region.

The Israeli Intelligence Community

Israel built its intelligence and security communities to ensure the survival of the precarious state. Israel's first intelligence forces were groups of special agents whose task was to locate Nazi war criminals and either assassinate them, or bring them to justice. The government then trained agents to spy on rival governments and militaries in the Middle East. By the 1960s, the Israeli intelligence service was one of the most well-trained, sophisticated, and effective intelligence services in the world.

Today, four primary agencies comprise the Israeli intelligence community. Israeli intelligence services are divided along traditional lines, but all Israeli intelligence officers receive military training due to the nation's policy of compulsory service.

The Center for Political Research. The Ministry of Foreign Affairs creates and implements Israel's foreign policy. The ministry supports and oversees the Center for Political Research, which monitors the political climate of the Middle East. The Center's mission is to collect and analyze information about political organizations, public political attitudes, and rival governments. Research analysts use openly available sources, as well as intelligence information, to advise the Minister of Foreign Affairs and the Office of the Prime Minister. The Center for Political Research also aids Israeli missions overseas, and advises allied foreign intelligence services on Middle East issues.

Mossad. The Institute for Intelligence and Special Tasks, more commonly known as the Mossad, is Israel's primary intelligence agency. Mossad is responsible for human intelligence and covert actions. Formed in 1951 to hunt for fugitive Nazi war criminals, the agency began as a collection of special forces units. To a lesser extent, Mossad maintains that organizational tradition today, and contains several small forces tasked with specific responsibilities and covert operations. Mossad task force agents assist with the movement of Jewish refugees out of hostile territories, attempt to infiltrate and sabotage Palestinian nationalist groups, and conduct counterintelligence operations.

In addition to numerous specialized forces, the Mossad maintains eight operational divisions. The Collections Department, Mossad's largest, administers Israel's extensive human intelligence network. The department focuses

Israeli nuclear spy Moredechai Vanunu, right, sits next to his lawyer during his trial in Beer Sheva in 1998 for revealing Israel's secrets. AP/WIDE WORLD PHOTOS.

on foreign intelligence operations, conducting espionage under a variety of diplomatic and industrial covers.

The Political Action and Liaison Department coordinates Mossad activities and shares information with allied nations. These agents are usually stationed in Israel's foreign embassies.

Mossad's third largest division, the Research Department, processes all intelligence material collected by Mossad field agents. Researchers also produce detailed reports, using openly available sources, for use by Mossad agents, the military, and other government agencies. The Research Department is subdivided into fifteen desks, each overseeing information regarding a specific geographic location. A specially dedicated desk monitors nuclear issues, such as weapons proliferation and development.

Mossad employs propaganda and deception operations with the aid of the Lohamah Psichologit (LAP). Agents trained in computers and engineering staff the Technology Department. The department extracts data from stolen, damaged, or foreign information systems, while ensuring the security of Mossad systems.

Little is known publicly about Mossad's final department, the Special Operations Division, also known as Metsada. The group has the tacit permission to carry out

assassinations and acts of sabotage against confirmed threats to Isreal.

Shabak. Shin Bet, or Shabak, conducts counterintelligence and internal security operations for the Israeli intelligence community. The agency focuses on domestic and regional intelligence operations, but maintains a network of personnel worldwide.

Three internal departments aid Shabak operations. The Arab Affairs Department maintains information on Arab terrorist networks, and conducts anti-terrorism operations. The Non-Arab Affairs department concerns itself with other nations, with special attention paid to Russia and Eastern Europe. Both agencies operate within Israel and abroad. The third Shabak department, Protective Security, is responsible for the protection of Israeli diplomatic missions abroad, as well as internal security at military, government, industrial, and scientific installations within Israel's borders.

Shabak is also a political espionage agency. The agency monitors extremist political groups. Scrutiny and surveillance of the political associations of foreigners living within Israel is an additional routine Shabak activity. The agency also possesses the authority to arrest and detain persons suspected of anti-government activity. The government attempted to keep the actions of Shabak from public view, but increased incidents of suspected brutality drew attention to agency operations in the 1980s. Despite a series of highly-publicized investigations that brought to light suspected Shabak practices (such as coercion, torture, and lying to the courts) the agency maintains the tacit consent of the Israeli government to employ special measures, including physical intimidation, to elicit information deemed urgently needed to protect Israeli security.

Aman. Israel's military intelligence community consists of numerous tactical intelligence units maintained by the individual branches of the Israeli Defense Force. A central agency collates, processes, and disseminates military intelligence information, as well as coordinates interagency operations. The Aman is an independent service, a peer of the army, navy, and air force. The agency produces reports for military and government use, acts as liaison between the military and government, coordinates the flow of information between civilian and military intelligence agencies, and assesses the threat of war.

Two sub-departments within the Aman assist agency operations. The Foreign Relations Department is the agency liaison with foreign military commanders and military intelligence services. The Sayeret Maktal, or Deep Reconnaissance Unit, conducts counter-terrorism operations.

Israeli State Security Today

Israel and its Arab neighbors entered into extensive peace negotiations in the 1990s. The U.S. president and secretary of state moderated peace talks between the Israelis and the Palestinians. On October 26, 1994, long-standing territorial disputes between Israel and Jordan were settled with the signing of the Israeli-Jordanian Treaty of Peace. The following year, an Israeli right-wing extremist who opposed peace negotiations with Arab states, assassinated Israeli Prime Minister Yitzhak Rabin, a driving force in the Israeli peace movement.

Limited progress continues to be made, with Israel withdrawing from Lebanon in 2000. Growing nationalism in Israel and Palestine, however, thwarted further negotiations. A resurgence of violence between the Palestinian Muslims and Israeli Jews in 2001 marked the beginning of the second Intifada.

The Israeli government and Palestinian Authority were set to attempt a new round of peace talks in 2003, but the outbreak of war in Iraq further polarized the two governments and postponed negotiations. In May, 2003, U.S. Secretary of State Colin Powell traveled to the Middle East to call upon the new Palestinian Prime Minister Mahmoud Abbas to disarm the militant factions that have attacked Israel. Powell also urged the Israeli government to ease its crippling blockade on Palestinian cities. Both measures are deemed vital to U.S. President George W. Bush's

peace plan that calls for an end to Palestinian-Israeli violence, and the creation of a Palestinian state by the year 2005.

■ FURTHER READING:

BOOKS:

Sacher, Howard. *A History of Israel: From Zionism to Our Time.* 2nd ed. New York: Knopf, 1996.

Thomas, Gordon. *Gideon's Spies: The Secret History of the Mossad.* New York: Griffin, 2000.

SEE ALSO

Eichmann, Adolf: Israeli capture
Middle East, Modern U.S. Security Policy and Interventions
Palestinian Authority, Intelligence and Security

Italy, Intelligence and Security

Although the Italian city-states were among the most prosperous and influential political organizations during the Middle Ages and the Renaissance, the modern nation-state of Italy did not emerge until the nineteenth century. King Victor Emmanuel united the city-states and kingdoms on the Italian peninsula, and the neighboring island provinces of Sicily and Sardinia in 1861. Italy was ruled by a monarchy and parliamentary government until the 1920s when Benito Mussolini established a fascist dictatorship. Through his fascist reforms, Mussolini hoped to make Italy's more agrarian south as prosperous as its industrialized north, but his alliance with Nazi Germany thrust Italy into World War II. Italian nationalists, sympathetic to the Allies, formed partisan groups that fought the Germans and fascist secret police forces behind enemy lines until the Allies successfully invaded the Italian peninsula. After Italy's defeat, the fascist regime was replaced by a democratic government.

The Executive Committee for the Intelligence and Security Services (CESIS) maintains the Office of the Secretary General, which filters and disseminates information collected by the various branches of the Italian intelligence and security committee. The main mission of the office is to act as a liaison between the intelligence services and the government, briefing government officials on intelligence matters and threats to national security when necessary. Representatives from the Office of the Secretary General routinely brief the President of the Council of Ministers regarding intelligence policy and operations. The office also coordinates inter-agency intelligence operations and established protocol regulations for intelligence personnel.

The Service for Information and Democratic Security (SISDE), administered by the Ministry of the Interior, is Italy's main domestic intelligence agency. The organization carries out all forms of surveillance and intelligence gathering operations, using some of the most sophisticated technologies in the European intelligence community. The SISDE contains several specialized operational departments, including anti-terrorism, counterintelligence, and anti-industrial espionage forces. The SISDE is also responsible for analysis of its own intelligence information, submitting completed reports or time-critical information to the CESIS.

Italy maintains specialized, strategic intelligence units within all branches of its military. However, the military and the government also administer the Intelligence and Military Security Service (SISMI). The Ministry of Defense oversees SISMI, whose responsibilities include the collection of military-related intelligence, counterespionage, and information analysis. The organization focuses on assessing threats to military and national security, whether from foreign or domestic entities.

Law enforcement in Italy is two-tiered. The military trains and administers the national police force, the Carabinieri, which has jurisdiction throughout Italy. The military police work closely with intelligence agencies, protecting national interests and investigating federal crimes. Provinces and municipalities maintain their own civil police.

Today, Italy is part of the expanding European Union (EU). The nation participates in the European Monetary Union, North Atlantic Treaty Organization (NATO), the United Nations (UN), and several other international organizations. In 2002, Italian representatives to the EU successfully lobbied for a proposal to create EU-managed, pan-European defense and intelligence forces.

Italy is closely allied with the United States and in 2003 supported U.S. efforts in Iraq. The Italian intelligence community aids international anti-terrorist efforts, devoting considerable resources to the ferreting-out of terrorist cells operating or distributing finances within Italy's national borders.

◼ FURTHER READING:

BOOKS:

Richelson, Jeffrey T. *Foreign Intelligence Organizations,* 2nd ed. Cambridge, MA: Ballinger Publishing, 1994.

Willan, Philip. *Puppet Masters: The Political Use of Terrorism in Italy.* London: Constable, 1991.

J

Jaish-e-Mohammed (JEM) (Army of Mohammed)

The Jaish-e-Mohammed (JEM) is an Islamic extremist group based in Pakistan that was formed by Masood Azhar upon his release from prison in India in early 2000. The group's aim is to unite Kashmir with Pakistan. It is politically aligned with the radical political party, Jamiat-i Ulema-i Islam Fazlur Rehman faction (JUI-F). The United States added JEM to the Foreign Terrorist Organization list as well as the list kept by the U.S. Treasury Department's Office of Foreign Asset Control (OFAC), which includes organizations that are believed to support terrorist groups and have assets in U.S. jurisdiction that can be frozen or controlled. The group was banned and its assets were frozen by the Pakistani government in January 2002.

Organization activities. The JEM's leader, Masood Azhar, was released from Indian imprisonment in December 1999, in exchange for 155 hijacked Indian Airlines hostages. The 1994 HUA kidnappings by Omar Sheikh of U.S. and British nationals in New Delhi and the July 1995 HUA/Al Faran kidnappings of Westerners in Kashmir were two of several previous HUA efforts to free Azhar. On October 1, 2001, the JEM claimed responsibility for a suicide attack on the Jammu and Kashmir legislative assembly building in Srinagar that killed at least 31 persons, but later denied the claim. The Indian government has publicly implicated the JEM, along with Lashkar-e-Tayyiba for an attack on the Indian Parliament that killed nine and injured 18.

JEM is based in Peshawar and Muzaffarabad, but members conduct terrorist activities primarily in Kashmir. They have several hundred armed supporters located in Azad Kashmir, Pakistan, and in India's southern Kashmir and Doda regions, including a large cadre of former Harakat ul-Mujahidin (HUM) (Movement of Holy Warriors) members. Supporters are mostly Pakistanis and Kashmiris and also include Afghans and Arab veterans of the Afghan war. JEM uses light and heavy machine guns, assault rifles, mortars, improvised explosive devices, and rocket grenades. The JEM maintained training camps in Afghanistan until the fall of 2001.

Most of the JEM's cadre and material resources have been drawn from the militant groups Harakat ul-Jihad al-Islami (HUJI) and the HUM. The JEM had close ties to Afghan Arabs and the Taliban. Osama Bin Ladin (also known as Usama Bin Ladin) is suspected of giving funding to the JEM. The JEM also collects funds through donation requests in magazines and pamphlets. In anticipation of asset seizures by the Pakistani government, the JEM withdrew funds from bank accounts and invested in legal businesses, such as commodity trading, real estate, and production of consumer goods.

ELECTRONIC:

Central Intelligence Agency. World Factbook, 2002. <http://www.cia.gov/cia/publications/factbook/> (April 16, 2003).

Taylor, Francis X. U.S. Department of State. Patterns of Global Terrorism 2001. Annual Report: On the Record Briefing. May 21, 2002. <http://www.state.gov/s/ct/rls/rm/10367.htm> (April 17,2003).

U.S. Department of State. Annual reports. <http://www.state.gov/www/global/terrorism/annual_reports.html> (April 16, 2003).

SEE ALSO

Terrorism, Philosophical and Ideological Origins
Terrorist and Para-State Organizations
Terrorist Organization List, United States
Terrorist Organizations, Freezing of Assets

Jamming.

SEE *Electronic Countermeasures.*

Japan, Intelligence and Security

Japan is one of the oldest nations in Asia. Over the past two hundred years, the nation has struggled with its desire to retain its national culture while absorbing Western technology and economics. United by a strong imperial government, Japan waged war against its Asian neighbors for the first half of the twentieth century. The nation's defeat by Allied forces during World War II led to a period of United States occupation, rebuilding, and complete demilitarization. After decades of recovery, Japan re-emerged on the international stage as a democratized and economically robust nation.

In 1997, the Japanese government unveiled a plan for wide-scale centralization and reform of the nation's intelligence community. Hoping to consolidate the myriad of small intelligence agencies and bureaus, the plan called for the creation of super-agencies that combined military and civilian, foreign and domestic intelligence operations. Most of Japan's intelligence services are now controlled by the nation's Japanese Self-Defense Force, the Office of the Prime Minister, and the Ministry of Foreign Affairs.

Japan's central intelligence agency is the Naicho, or Cabinet Research Office. Only 100 personnel, all members of the Office of the Prime Minister, staff the agency. Naicho operations focus on the collection and analysis of foreign intelligence information, including that which is gathered by other national civilian and military intelligence forces. The agency coordinates inter-agency intelligence operations and acts as liaison between the intelligence community and the government, reporting to the prime minister and legislature when necessary.

The Bureau of Defense Policy, the government ministry which drafts Japan's defense policy and coordinates defense efforts, maintains the Jouhou Honbu, Defense Intelligence Office (DIO). The DIO is divided into two operational sections, the First and Second Intelligence Divisions. The First Intelligence Division, now known simply as the Intelligence Division, conducts domestic intelligence and security operations. Its general mission is to procure and process information relating to threats to Japan's national security. The division employs its own counterintelligence and anti-terrorism experts. The Second Intelligence Division is responsible for foreign intelligence information, and is now known as the International Planning Division.

Intelligence community reforms in the 1990s concentrated their centralization efforts on the former Defense Administration (DA). The old agency divided intelligence operations among several internal bureaus, each of which maintained their own action forces and military support teams. The Defense Intelligence Headquarters (DIH) serves as nerve center for the new intelligence agencies that were formerly DA intelligence bureaus. The DIH conducts both foreign and domestic intelligence operations and manages various specialized sources, including human, signals, communications, and remote intelligence. The DIH also employs both civilian and military agents, and maintains its own analytics, logistics, and research force to process intelligence information.

Despite consolidation, centralization, and reform efforts, Japan's intelligence community has not yet completed its structural transformation. Many small bureaus continue to operate, and there is substantial overlap of the duties of various agencies.

Japan's economic success has made extensive counterintelligence and anti-industrial espionage measures a primary concern of the nation's domestic intelligence community. The nation's proximity to more volatile states in Southern Asia, and occasional terrorist attacks in Tokyo, prompted Japan's intelligence services to extensively cooperate with international and foreign intelligence and security organizations. Currently, Japan participates in the international initiative to combat global terrorism, and helps to monitor the proliferation of weapons in Asia.

■ FURTHER READING:

BOOKS:

McClain, James. *Japan: A Modern History.* New York: W. W. Norton, 2002.

Mercado, Stephen C. *The Shadow Warriors of Nakano: A History of the Imperial Japanese Army's Elite Intelligence School.* Washington, D.C.: Brasseys, 2002.

Japanese Red Army (JRA)

The Japanese Red Army (JRA) also operates as, or is known as, the Anti-Imperialist International Brigade (AIIB).

The JRA is an international terrorist group formed around 1970 after breaking away from the Japanese Communist League-Red Army Faction. Fusako Shigenobu led the JRA until her arrest in Japan in November, 2000. The JRA's historical goal has been to overthrow the Japanese government and monarchy and to help foment world revolution. After her arrest, Shigenobu announced she intended to pursue her goals using a legitimate political party rather than revolutionary violence, and the group announced it would disband in April, 2001. JRA may control or at least have ties to the Anti-Imperialist International Brigade (AIIB) and also may have links to the Antiwar Democratic Front—an overt leftist political organization—inside Japan. Details released following Shigenobu's arrest indicate that the JRA was organizing cells in Asian cities, such as Manila and Singapore. The group had a history of close relations with Palestinian terrorist groups—based and operating outside Japan—since its inception, primarily through Shigenobu. The current status of the connections is unknown. During the 1970s, JRA carried out a series of attacks around the world, including the massacre in 1972 at Lod Airport in Israel, two Japanese airliner hijackings, and an attempted takeover of the U.S. Embassy in Kuala Lumpur. In April, 1988, JRA operative Yu Kikumura was arrested with explosives on the New Jersey Turnpike, apparently planning an attack to coincide with the bombing of a USO club in Naples, a suspected JRA operation that killed five, including a U.S. servicewoman. Kikumura was convicted and is serving a lengthy prison sentence in the United States. Tsutomu Shirosaki, captured in 1996, is also jailed in the United States. In 2000, Lebanon deported to Japan four members arrested there in 1997, but granted a fifth operative, Kozo Okamoto, political asylum. Longtime leader Shigenobu was arrested in November 2000 on charges of terrorism and passport fraud.

The JRA has about six dedicated members and an undetermined number of sympathizers. At its peak, the group claimed to have 30 to 40 members. The exact location of JRA is unknown, but intelligence estimates indicate that it possibly operates in Asia and/or Syrian-controlled areas of Lebanon.

■ FURTHER READING:

ELECTRONIC:

CDI (Center for Defense Information), Terrorism Project. CDI Fact Sheet: Current List of Designated Foreign Terrorist Organizations. March 27, 2003. <http://www.cdi.org/terrorism/terrorist.cfm> (April 17, 2003).

Central Intelligence Agency. World Factbook, 2002. <http://www.cia.gov/cia/publications/factbook/> (April 16, 2003).

Taylor, Francis X. U.S. Department of State. "Patterns of Global Terrorism 2001." Annual Report: On the Record Briefing. May 21, 2002. <http://www.state.gov/s/ct/rls/rm/10367.htm> (April 17,2003).

U.S. Department of State. Annual reports. <http://www.state.gov/www/global/terrorism/annual_reports.html> (April 16, 2003).

SEE ALSO

Terrorism, Philosophical and Ideological Origins
Terrorist and Para-State Organizations
Terrorist Organization List, United States
Terrorist Organizations, Freezing of Assets

JDAM (Joint Direct Attack Munition)

The Joint Direct Attack Munition (JDAM) is a satellite-guided "smart" bomb capable of accurate and high-precision strikes in any weather. JDAM munitions have found increasing use in military missions and the use of precision bombs exceeded 80 percent in the U.S.-led Operation Iraqi Freedom conducted in 2003. Because of their high degree of accuracy, JDAM munitions can also be used to selectively strike at intelligence-related targets, and in the Iraq campaign, they were used to strike at military and intelligence (e.g. leadership targets) that Saddam Hussein's forces had placed or attempted to conceal in or near civilian areas.

JDAM munitions also found wide use in the NATO air campaign against the Federal Republic of Yugoslavia in 1999 and in the 2001 U.S.-led Operation Enduring Freedom against the Taliban regime and al-Qaeda forces hiding in Afghanistan. As of April 2003, U.S. B-1, B-2, B-52, F-16 and F/A-18 bombers and fighter/strike aircraft were capable of carrying JDAM munitions.

JDAM munitions are intended to provide accurate delivery of general purpose bombs in adverse weather conditions. Although not quite as accurate as laser-guided munitions, JDAM offer high precision—but at a far lower cost than laser-guided munitions. JDAMs are dumb bombs converted to smart bombs by the supplemental addition of fixed aerodynamic surfaces (mid-body strakes and tail fins) and a guidance package that allows inertial navigational guidance of the bomb following release. Targeting is maintained via continuously updated global positioning satellite (GPS) data that steers the bomb to the target. Under normal conditions, JDAMs can determine location and strike within 10 yards of an intended target. Because they rely on GPS signals, JDAMs can be used even under cloudy conditions, or when the sky is obscured by smoke.

Jamming equipment that can scramble or block GPS signals has limited effectiveness against JDAM munitions because the tracking sequence is progressive (i.e., the jamming is not effective until the bomb is almost on target) and software corrections allow the bombs to revert to inertial navigation if the GPS signal is blocked or obscured. In general, Iraqi forces using Russian-made jamming equipment found little success in reducing JDAM precision. Although detailed assessments were not yet complete as of May 2003, Iraqi attempts at jamming JDAMs—intended for precision strikes at military targets hidden near civilian areas—may have accounted for some unintended civilian casualties.

Other significant JDAM misses include the accidental bombing of the Chinese embassy by a JDAM released by a U.S. B-2 bomber over Belgrade in May 1999. The bombing killed three Chinese citizens. That targeting error was not a result of jamming but was attributed to a software error that relied on outdated maps.

■ **FURTHER READING:**

ELECTRONIC:

Federation of American Scientists. Military Analysis Network. Joint Direct Attack Munition (JDAM) GBU-29, GBU-30, GBU-31, GBU-32. September 18, 2002. <http://www.fas.org/man/dod-101/sys/smart/jdam.htm> (April 15, 2003).

SEE ALSO

Iraqi Freedom, Operation (2003 War Against Iraq)

Jemaah Islamiya (JI)

Jemaah Islamiya (JI) is an Islamic extremist group with cells operating throughout Southeast Asia. Members arrested in Singapore, Malaysia, and the Philippines have revealed links with al-Qaeda. The JI's stated goal is to create an Islamic state comprising Malaysia, Singapore, Indonesia, and the southern Philippines. Three Indonesian extremists, one of whom is in custody in Malaysia, are the reported leaders of the organization. JI began developing plans in 1997 to target U.S. interests in Singapore and, in 1999, conducted videotaped casings of potential U.S. targets in preparation for multiple attacks in Singapore. A cell in Singapore acquired four tons of ammonium nitrate, which has not yet been found. In December 2001, Singapore authorities arrested 15 Jemaah Islamiya members—some of whom had trained in al-Qaeda camps in Afghanistan—who planned to attack the U.S. and Israeli embassies and British and Australian diplomatic buildings in Singapore. Additionally, the Singapore police discovered forged immigration stamps, bomb-making materials, and al-Qaeda-related material in several suspects' homes.

The exact numbers of JI are unknown but press reports approximate that the Malaysian cells may comprise 200 members. The JI has cells in Singapore and Malaysia; press reports indicate the JI is also present in Indonesia and possibly the Philippines.

In October 2002, a bomb destroyed a nightclub in Bali, Indonesia , killing 202 people. In August 2003, an Indonesian court convicted and sentenced to death a member of the Islamist militant group Jemaah Islamiyah for helping plan the attack. Although one-half of the people killed in the Bali attack were vacationing Australians, the convicted

terrorist claimed subsequently through his lawyer that "the targets were the Americans and the Jews."

■ **FURTHER READING:**

ELECTRONIC:

CDI (Center for Defense Information), Terrorism Project. CDI Fact Sheet: Current List of Designated Foreign Terrorist Organizations. March 27, 2003. <http://www.cdi.org/terrorism/terrorist.cfm> (April 17, 2003).

Central Intelligence Agency. World Factbook, 2002. <http://www.cia.gov/cia/publications/factbook/> (April 16, 2003).

Taylor, Francis X. U.S. Department of State. "Patterns of Global Terrorism 2001." Annual Report: On the Record Briefing. May 21, 2002. <http://www.state.gov/s/ct/rls/rm/10367.htm> (April 17,2003).

U.S. Department of State. Annual reports. <http://www.state.gov/www/global/terrorism/annual_reports.html> (April 16, 2003).

SEE ALSO

Terrorism, Philosophical and Ideological Origins
Terrorist and Para-State Organizations
Terrorist Organization List, United States
Terrorist Organizations, Freezing of Assets

Johnson Administration (1963–1969), United States National Security Policy

■ CARYN E. NEUMANN

President Lyndon B. Johnson continued the longstanding commitment of the United States to Southeast Asian security by providing increasing amounts of support to anti-communist South Vietnam. A former congressman from Texas and vice-president since 1960, Johnson took office in 1963 upon the assassination of President John F. Kennedy. In light of the circumstances, Johnson considered it his obligation to the electorate to continue Kennedy's polices. He stated his determination to resist Soviet expansionism and reiterated the nation's support of South Vietnam.

Johnson also moved national security policy in the direction that Kennedy had indicated. Kennedy allowed the structure of the National Security Council to atrophy and Johnson continued to this process. Congress had established the NSC as a means of encouraging the president to consider political and military advice, but the men in the Oval Office did not always cooperate with the plans of the legislative branch. Both leaders sought greater direct presidential control over foreign relations.

Johnson generally operated outside the formal advisory structure of the NSC. He saw the council as too large and unwieldy to serve as a forum for policy formulation. Perhaps more significantly, the Johnson NSC also established a reputation as a major source of leaks to the news media and to Capitol Hill. With the president holding the NSC at arm's length and treating it as only a symbolic mechanism, the frequency of its meetings declined during his administration. The president generally used the council as a means of informing subordinates about the future direction of policy.

For national security advice, the Johnson administration depended chiefly upon the national security advisor (NSA). This role was filled by McGeorge Bundy, Kennedy's NSA who remained in office through February 1966, and Bundy's successor, economist Walt Rostow, who served to the end of the administration. The NSA staff, various ad hoc groups, and trusted friends also offered assistance. In 1966, Johnson officially turned over responsibility for the supervision and coordination of interdepartmental activities overseas to Secretary of State Dean Rusk. Kennedy's Secretary of Defense Robert McNamara continued to fill that role under Johnson.

While serving under Kennedy, McNamara began to develop a doctrine of mutual assured destruction (MAD) that he honed under Johnson. According to MAD, deterrence depended upon the confidence of each superpower in the ability of its own nuclear forces to survive a first attack and retaliate. Mutual fear of massive deaths among the populace served as an incentive to avoid making that first strike.

As MAD indicates, potential nuclear conflict dominated the administration's treatment of the Soviet Union. Warnings by McNamara about the suicidal arms race that both nations were running helped persuade Johnson to agree to a nuclear nonproliferation treaty. In 1968, each power pledged to halt the distribution of nuclear weapons. While 59 other nations also signed the treaty, not every country agreed; China, France, and India refused to participate.

Johnson sought to de-escalate Cold War rhetoric, but continued to see the Russians as a threat that had to be contained and this objective would lead to the escalation of involvement in Vietnam. As did the presidents before him, Johnson struggled to find a means to save South Vietnam from communist aggression. A brief and confusing episode between North Vietnamese and American naval forces in the Tonkin Gulf in 1964 gave Johnson his opportunity. He used the incident to secure a resolution from Congress giving him authority to employ armed forces to defend American personnel in South Vietnam and stop further attacks.

Johnson used the resolution as his authority to wage war in Southeast Asia. A supporter of the domino theory, Johnson held that if South Vietnam fell to communism, then the other free governments in the region would also topple, thereby costing the U.S. its valuable Asian allies. Under Johnson, the American military commitment to Vietnam rose rapidly to a force that peaked at 543,000 in 1969.

Protests against the war grew slowly. In 1966, Senator J. William Fulbright, head of the Senate Foreign Relations Committee began nationally televised hearings on American national security policy. Fulbright, a powerful Arkansas Democrat, argued that by escalating the war, Johnson had exceeded the limits of the authority granted to him by Congress in the Tonkin Gulf Resolution. Witness George Kennan, a top State Department expert on Russia who had helped shape Truman's doctrine of containment, challenged testimony by Secretary of State Rusk that the U.S. had to fight in Vietnam to prevent Soviet expansion. Kennan argued that the conflict in Vietnam had so preoccupied the government that areas of more important strategic significance had been stripped of forces sufficient to deter a possible Soviet attack. The hearings indicated deep divisions over foreign policy.

During 1966, increasing numbers of members of the Johnson administration spoke out against the Vietnam War. Unable to brook dissent, Johnson did not tolerate attacks on his policy. His intolerance of criticism persuaded some of his most trusted national security counselors, including NSA Bundy and George Ball of the State Department, to leave government service. Whereas Bundy had informed Johnson of the full range of senior opinions about national security, Rostow gave hawkish advice. Increasingly isolated from contrary opinions, Johnson had established an administration with little dissenting opinion.

Throughout 1967, doubts about the Vietnam War consumed additional members of the government. Both Secretary of Defense McNamara and the Central Intelligence Agency challenged the judgment of the military. While the Joint Chiefs sought intensified bombing of North Vietnam, McNamara had concluded that massive bombing only boosted patriotism in that country instead of destroying the will of its people to fight. After McNamara categorized administration policy as dangerous, expensive, and failed, Johnson decided to replace him, and McNamara left in 1967. His successor, Clark Clifford, a longtime Democratic party stalwart who had helped establish the NSC, finally managed to persuade Johnson that Vietnam could not be won. Johnson did not run for re-election.

The Johnson administration's national security policy strained the resources of the U.S. and made it difficult for succeeding presidents to mobilize support for military security efforts. Besides eroding American military effectiveness, Johnson's failed effort in Vietnam raised doubts about the nation's willingness to use military power to support its foreign policy of deterring the spread of communist governments abroad.

■ FURTHER READING:

BOOKS:

Boll, Michael M. *National Security Planning: Roosevelt Through Reagan.* Lexington: University Press of Kentucky, 1988.

Crabb, Cecil V., and Kevin V. Mulcahy. *American National Security: A Presidential Perspective.* Pacific Grove, CA: Brooks/Cole, 1991.

Hunt, Michael H. *Lyndon Johnson's War: America's Cold War Crusade in Vietnam, 1945–1968.* New York: Hill and Wang, 1996.

ELECTRONIC:

White House. "History of the National Security Council, 1947–1997." <http://www.whitehouse.gov/nsc/history.html> (April 25, 2003).

SEE ALSO

CIA (United States Central Intelligence Agency)
Cold War (1950–1972)
Joint Chiefs of Staff, United States
National Security Advisor, United States
NSC (National Security Council)
NSC (National Security Council), History
National Security Strategy, United States
Nonproliferation and National Security, United States
Vietnam War

Joint Chiefs of Staff, United States

■ JOSEPH PATTERSON HYDER

The Joint Chiefs of Staff (JCS) of the United States is a six-member committee that advises the president, the secretary of defense, and the National Security Council on military affairs. A chairman, vice-chairman, and the chiefs of each of the four branches of the military form the Joint Chiefs of Staff. The chief of each military branch also serves as manager of his military branch, although these management duties typically fall to the vice-chief. The chairman conducts meetings of the JCS and serves as the primary military advisor to the President.

The Joint Chiefs of Staff was formed following the Arcadia Conference in 1942, during which President Franklin D. Roosevelt and United Kingdom Prime Minister Winston Churchill formed the Combined Chiefs of Staff to conduct the war effort on behalf of the United States and Britain. The Combined Chiefs of Staff consisted of senior members of the American and British armed forces. While the British established a Joint Chief of Staff Committee in 1924 in order to advise the Prime Minister and War Cabinet, the United States did not have a central military command in place to contribute a coordinated military plan to the Combined Chiefs. U.S. Admiral William Leahy led an effort to establish an American unified high command. The result of Admiral Leahy's efforts was the formation of the Joint Chiefs of Staff, of which he was named Chief of Staff to the Commander in Chief of the Army and Navy.

During World War II, Roosevelt granted great latitude to the actions of the Joint Chiefs of Staff. During the war, the Joint Chiefs acted as executive commanders of troops in the field, answering only to the President. The National Security Act of 1947 formally established the Joint Chiefs of Staff and defined the roles of the chiefs as that of advisers to the President and not as commanders with executive authority.

Despite the statute prohibiting the chiefs from commanding forces, the chief of each armed service branch continued to act with executive authority in originating contact with combat commanders, thus violating the spirit of the National Security Act of 1947. Congress amended the National Security Act in 1953 to prevent such contact with field commanders.

The Goldwater-Nichols Department of Defense Reorganization Act of 1986 further redefined the function of the Joint Chiefs of Staff. This act went beyond the National Security Act in terms of expressly stating the role of the executive authority in relation to the Joint Chiefs of Staff. The Goldwater-Nichols Act mandated that the chain of command run from the President to the Secretary of Defense to the combatant commanders. The chairman of the Joint Chiefs of Staff may transmit orders to commanders from either the President or the Secretary of Defense, but the Chairman may not exert executive authority or command troops.

The act also defined other functions that the chairman may perform. The chairman may consult with the other chiefs and with commanders in the field but may not commit or command forces. He must then present the advice that he receives to the president, secretary of defense, or National Security Council. All members of the Joint Chiefs of Staff are presidential advisers and may submit their opinions to the president through the chairman.

The Goldwater-Nichols Act also established the position of vice-chairman. The vice-chairman conducts meetings of the Joint Chiefs in the absence of the chairman and carries out duties as stipulated by the chairman. Originally the vice-chairman was not a full, voting member of the Joint Chiefs of Staff. The National Defense Authorization Act of 1992 granted the vice-chairman full status, increasing the Joint Chiefs of Staff to six members.

■ FURTHER READING:

ELECTRONIC:

United States Department of Defense. "JCS Link, The Joint Chiefs of Staff." <http://www.dtic.mil/jcs/> (May 5, 2003).

The Joint Chiefs of Staff pose together in an official photograph in the Joint Chiefs of Staff Gold Room at the Pentagon, January 11, 2000. ©REUTERS NEWMEDIA INC./CORBIS.

SEE ALSO

DOD (United States Department of Defense)
NSC (National Security Council)

Jordan, Intelligence and Security

The primary Jordanian intelligence agency is the *Dairat al Mukhabarat,* or General Intelligence Department (GID). The GID is charged with the collection and analysis of intelligence information. GID officials brief the government on matters of national security and coordinate efforts with the military and national law enforcement agencies. The focus of GID operations is the collection of intelligence pertaining to security issues within the Middle East, including surveillance of paramilitary groups and guarding borders to prevent an influx of refugees from the neighboring area of Palestine. The GID also provides the government with regular reports of the political climate of the nation and the surrounding region, though the means by which this information is gathered remains secret.

Because the Jordanian intelligence community is consolidated into one major agency, the GID maintains several special task forces devoted to specialized areas of intelligence, including counter-intelligence and communications surveillance. An anti-terrorism task force conducts operations to gather information on organizations working in Jordan and throughout the Middle East. The Jordanian government has aided international anti-terrorism efforts following the September 11 terrorist attacks on the United States. The government also employs GID staff

The car belonging to the wife of a senior anti-terrorism official in Jordan was destroyed in a February 2002, explosion in response to Jordan's support for the U.S.-led campaign against terrorism. AP/WIDE WORLD PHOTOS.

to monitor the security of government information systems and personnel. Security surveillance of the government also includes an anti-corruption department to root-out incidences of government abuse. Economic, industrial, scientific, and limited political espionage is also conducted by GID forces.

During the Persian Gulf War in 1991, Jordan was the only Arab country that did not openly condemn the Iraqi invasion of Kuwait. However, the Jordanian government did not provide aid to the Iraqi government during the war and tried to maintain diplomatic relations with both Israel and the United States. Jordan opposed coalition military involvement in Iraq again in 2003, but permitted United States and British forces to use Jordan's airspace and bases for some operations. Jordan's monarchy and government continues to walk a tightrope in Middle East politics, signing a formal peace treaty with Israel in 1994 and fostering favorable diplomatic relations with the West, even though the majority of the nation's Arab population opposes both policies.

FURTHER READING:

ELECTRONIC:

Intelligence Services of Jordan. <http://www.gid.gov.jo/> (March 28, 2003).

SEE ALSO

Iraqi Freedom, Operation (2003 War Against Iraq)
Persian Gulf War

J-STARS

J-STARS (Joint Surveillance and Target Acquisition Radar System) is the name for a type of surveillance aircraft developed jointly by the U.S. Army and Air Force. Adapted from the Boeing 707–320, the aircraft itself—on which both Boeing and Grumman worked as contractors—is designated the E–8. Its capabilities include sophisticated radar systems that allow it to conduct extensive ground surveillance.

For the better part of two decades, the air force had sought to develop an aircraft with improved radar capabilities, and in 1985 it began these efforts in earnest by joining forces with the army to create such a plane. The result was J-STARS, whose most notable feature is the pod or radome under the forward fuselage measuring some 24 feet (7.3 m) and shaped like a canoe; it contains a radar system capable of detecting targets the size of a truck over an area of 200 square miles (518 sq km).

Whereas aircraft have long had radar systems to track other planes and stationary objects, the uniqueness of J-STARS lay not only in the fact that its radar monitored activity on the ground, but that it did so with unparalleled precision. J-STARS made it possible to monitor literally hundreds of stations at the same time, using high-resolution imaging.

Two E-8A prototype J-STARS made their initial flight on April 1, 1988, and these two later saw service in Operation Desert Storm during January 1991. Flown on 49 combat sorties for a total of 500 combat hours, the aircraft displayed almost flawless effectiveness in tracking mobile Iraqi ground forces, tanks, and Scud missiles.

J-STARS again saw service during Operation Joint Endeavor, a North Atlantic Treaty Organization (NATO) action in Bosnia to monitor compliance with the Dayton Peace Treaty agreements in December 1995. The E-8A test craft, as well as the pre-production E-8C model, logged more than 1,000 flight hours on 98 sorties, with a 98 percent effectiveness rate. J-STARS have also been used in NATO's Operation Allied Force in March to June 1999 over Kosovo, and in the U.S. Operation Enduring Freedom in Afghanistan in October 2001.

■ FURTHER READING:

BOOKS:

Polmar, Norman, and Thomas B. Allen. *Spy Book: The Encyclopedia of Espionage.* New York: Random House, 1998.

PERIODICALS:

Babbin, Jed. "Some Things Can't Wait: Speedy Approval of New Military Technologies Will Save Lives." *Washington Times.* (June 27, 2002): A23.

ELECTRONIC:

Grumman/Boeing E-8 J-STARS. <http://www.zap16.com/mil%20fact/e-8%20j-stars.htm> (January 22, 2003).

SEE ALSO

Persian Gulf War
RADAR

Justice Department, United States

■ JUDSON KNIGHT

The U.S. Department of Justice is responsible for enforcing federal law, preventing and controlling crime, and protecting the interests of the nation in legal matters. Created in 1870, it is directed by the attorney general, the nation's chief law enforcement officer, whose office long predates the department itself. Under the aegis of the Justice Department are a number of prominent law enforcement bureaus and agencies, including the Federal Bureau of Investigation (FBI), Drug Enforcement Administration (DEA), United States Marshal Service (USMS), and many others. Another prominent Justice agency, the Immigration and Naturalization Service (INS), became part of the Department of Homeland Security in 2003. In the twenty-first century, key areas of concern for Justice are terrorism, worldwide drug trafficking, community violence, white collar crime, substance abuse, and hate crimes.

History. In 1789, the first Congress passed the Judiciary Act, which established the federal justice system and created the Office of the Attorney General. A member of the cabinet without his own executive department, the attorney general advised the president on legal matters and represented the federal government before the Supreme Court. Among the prominent attorneys general of those early years were Roger B. Taney (1831–33), who later became one of the most notable chief justices of the Supreme Court, and Edwin M. Stanton (1860–61), who became Secretary of War under President Abraham Lincoln.

In 1870, Congress created the Department of Justice, and placed all existing federal law enforcement agencies—for example, USMS, also created by the 1789 Judiciary Act—under the new department. Its head would be the attorney general, and its second-highest office would be that of solicitor general, whose job it is to supervise and conduct government litigation before the Supreme Court. Prominent solicitors general included future president William Howard Taft (1890–92); future Supreme Court justices Charles Evans Hughes, Jr. (1929–30) and Thurgood Marshall (1965–67), who was also the first African American solicitor general; Archibald Cox (1961–65), Robert Bork (1973–77), and Kenneth Starr (1989–93).

Among the notable attorneys general since 1870 were A. Mitchell Palmer (1919–21), a leading figure in the post-World War I "Red Scare"; future Supreme Court Chief Justice Harlan Fiske Stone (1924–25); Robert F. Kennedy (1961–64); Ramsey Clark (1967–69), noted for his later involvement in protest movements and highly publicized court cases; John N. Mitchell (1969–72) and a host of other attorneys general associated in some way with the Watergate scandal; and Janet Reno (1993–2001), first female attorney general.

Mission, agencies, and activities. The mission of the Department of Justice is to enforce the law and defend the interests of the United States according to law; to provide federal leadership in preventing and controlling crime; to seek just punishment for those found guilty of unlawful acts; to administer and enforce the nation's immigration

Attorney General John Ashcroft briefs reporters at a press conference at the Justice Department in Washington, D.C., on October 29, 2001, as the FBI issued a new terrorism warning asking Americans and law enforcement to be on the highest alert for possible attacks in the United States and abroad. AP/WIDE WORLD PHOTOS.

laws fairly and effectively; and to ensure fair and impartial administration of justice for all Americans.

The Justice Department accomplishes that mission through a vast array of activities. In addition to the FBI and DEA, prominent agencies include the Bureau of Alcohol, Tobacco, Firearms, and Explosives (part of the Treasury Department until 2002); the Federal Bureau of Prisons and its National Institute of Corrections, which are responsible for the incarceration of sentenced offenders; the U.S. National Central Bureau of Interpol; and USMS, which is responsible for protecting federal courts and ensuring the effective operation of the judicial system. Long celebrated in story and legend, U.S. marshals pursue 55 percent of all federal fugitives, more than all other federal agencies combined.

The Justice Department conducts legal actions against violations of federal antitrust laws through its Antitrust Division, and violations of civil rights laws through its Civil Rights Division. Its Civil Division represents federal interests in civil litigation, while the Criminal Division develops, supervises the application of, and even enforces

federal criminal statutes not covered by other agencies. The Asset Forfeiture Program handles money and other goods involved in criminal activities.

Through sections such as the Community Oriented Policing Services (COPS) and the Office of Justice Programs (which includes numerous bureaus such as the American Indian and Alaska Native Affairs Desk), the Department of Justice maintains state, municipal, and community outreach activities designed to reduce crime and crime-related behaviors, and encourage citizen involvement in crime prevention. It maintains databases on criminal activity through the Bureau of Justice Statistics and the National Drug Intelligence Center. The National Institute of Justice develops and disseminates studies on issues related to crime and justice.

The Justice Department *Strategic Plan,* released late in 2001, discussed the challenges and opportunities faced by the department at the beginning of the twenty-first century. Whereas crime rates had gone down from the 1930s to the 1960s, in the latter decade they had begun to climb, and continued to do so until the mid-1990s. The period after the mid-1990s, however, saw a steady reduction in criminal activity nationwide.

The report credited more coordinated national policing efforts in the wake of the congressional passage of the Safe Streets Act in 1968. This had led to increased financial assistance for law enforcement at the federal, state, and local levels, resulting in the development of agencies that were better prepared to meet the challenges of their environments.

Additionally, since the late 1980s, criminal and juvenile justice agencies had increasingly partnered with community-based organizations such as schools, churches, businesses, social services, and victim advocacy groups. In 1984, the Victims of Crime Act established an Office for Victims of Crime in the Justice Department, even as numerous national and community-based organizations were formed to provide support to victims of rape, spousal abuse, drunk driving, and other crimes.

The Justice Department was given broader authority to enforce federal law against criminal organizations, including gangs, criminal syndicates, and terrorists. During the mid-1990s, the Brady Handgun Violence Prevention Act and the establishment of a National Instant Criminal Background Check System had helped bring about a steady decrease in gun-related crimes. The Sentencing Reform Act of 1984 greatly stiffened prison sentences, requiring mandatory terms for certain crimes and abolishing federal parole. These changes, along with more aggressive enforcement measures, led to an increase in the number of incarcerated persons, which reached an all-time high of 1.8 million detainees in 1999.

From the present to the future Among the notable aspects of the early twenty-first century law enforcement environment noted in the report were globalization and advances in science and technology. The terrorist attacks of September, 2001, had dramatically illustrated the international scope of criminal activity, but the Justice Department had also increasingly taken a multinational approach, working with Interpol and other groups overseas.

Similarly, advances in information technology made possible new opportunities for crimes involving fraud, theft of intellectual property, and child pornography, while scientific advances in the use of DNA evidence and other forensic technology provided a boost to law-enforcement activities. Other technologies noted in the Justice Department report were advances in biotechnology and bioengineering (most notably the decoding of the human genome), and nanotechnology, or the ability to manipulate matter at the molecular or even atomic levels.

Leading the list of key concerns for the coming years, of course, was terrorism, followed by its close cousin, worldwide drug trafficking. Other significant criminal areas include white collar and economic crimes such as health-care fraud, as well as hate crimes and crimes involving infringement of victims' civil rights.

■ FURTHER READING:

BOOKS:

200th Anniversary of the Office of the Attorney General, 1789–1989. Washington, D.C.: Department of Justice, 1991.

The Department of Justice Manual. Gaithersburg, MD: Aspen Law & Business, 2000.

Moriarty, Laura J., and David L. Carter. *Criminal Justice Technology in the 21st Century.* Springfield, IL: Charles C. Thomas, 1998.

Riley, Kevin Jack, and Bruce Hoffman. *Domestic Terrorism: A National Assessment of State and Local Preparedness.* Santa Monica, CA: RAND Corporation, 1995.

ELECTRONIC:

U.S. Department of Justice. <http://www.usdoj.gov/> (April 14, 2003).

SEE ALSO

ATF (United States Bureau of Alcohol, Tobacco, and Firearms)
Commission on Civil Rights, United States
DEA (Drug Enforcement Administration)
Domestic Preparedness Office (NDPO), United States National
FBI (United States Federal Bureau of Investigation)
INS (United States Immigration and Naturalization Service)
Interpol (International Criminal Police Organization)
NDIC (Department of Justice National Drug Intelligence Center)
NIJ (National Institute of Justice)
Terrorist Organizations, Freezing of Assets

Kahane Chai (Kach)

Kahane Chai's (Kach) stated goal is to restore the biblical state of Israel. Kach (founded by radical Israeli-American rabbi Meir Kahane) and its offshoot Kahane Chai, which means "Kahane Lives" (founded by Meir Kahane's son Binyamin following his father's assassination in the United States), were declared to be terrorist organizations in March 1994, by the Israeli Cabinet under the 1948 Terrorism Law. This followed the groups' statements in support of Dr. Baruch Goldstein's attack in February 1994 on the al-Ibrahimi mosque. Goldstein was affiliated with Kach and their verbal attacks on the Israeli government. Palestinian gunmen killed Binyamin Kahane and his wife in a drive-by shooting in December 2000 in the West Bank.

Kach organizes protests against the Israeli government, harasses and threatens Palestinians in Hebron and the West Bank. Members have threatened to attack Arabs, Palestinians, and Israeli government officials. Additionally, Kach members have vowed revenge for the death of Binyamin Kahane and his wife.

The size of Kach is unknown. They operate in Israel and West Bank settlements, particularly Qiryat Arba' in Hebron, and the group receives support from sympathizers mostly in the United States and Europe.

■ **FURTHER READING:**

ELECTRONIC:

Central Intelligence Agency. World Factbook, 2002. <http://www.cia.gov/cia/publications/factbook/> (April 16, 2003).

Taylor, Francis X. U.S. Department of State. Patterns of Global Terrorism 2001. Annual Report: On the Record Briefing. May 21, 2002. <http://www.state.gov/s/ct/rls/rm/10367.htm> (April 17,2003).

U.S. Department of State. Annual reports. <http://www.state.gov/www/global/terrorism/annual_reports.html> (April 16, 2003).

SEE ALSO

Terrorism, Philosophical and Ideological Origins
Terrorist and Para-State Organizations
Terrorist Organization List, United States
Terrorist Organizations, Freezing of Assets

Kennedy Administration (1961–1963), United States National Security Policy

■ CARYN E. NEUMANN

President John F. Kennedy entered the White House with confidence that instability in the developing world posed the greatest risk to the national security of the United States. Kennedy planned to resist Soviet expansionism in Latin America, Asia, and Africa by abandoning Eisenhower's policy of massive retaliation in favor of a flexible response, combining economic support with military assistance.

Aggressive and eager to prove himself, Kennedy viewed the Cold War as a struggle of good against evil that required tough action. Through his experiences of World War II, Kennedy held that democracies tended to move too slowly to oppose totalitarianism. He also took note of the narrow margin of victory that had brought him to power and allowed it to shape his security policy. Kennedy tended to defer to military and intelligence experts who favored military action rather than pursue negotiations that would be harder to sell to the American public.

During the Cuban Missile Crisis in October 1962, President John F. Kennedy meets with his cabinet and advisors at the White House. ©BETTMANN/CORBIS.

Kennedy's confrontational style did not mesh with the quiet negotiating habits of diplomats in the State Department, and the agency subsequently lost some influence in the White House. The National Security Council (NSC) under adviser McGeorge Bundy increasingly served as an alternate source of policy development and advice at the expense of the State Department under Dean Rusk. This NSC was a far different construct than the one that had served Eisenhower, but it remained focused almost exclusively on foreign policy matters.

While Kennedy would probably have eventually dismantled the elaborate Eisenhower-era NSC in favor of a more open system, the Senate gave him a push. In 1960, the Senate Subcommittee on National Policy Machinery, popularly known as the Jackson Subcommittee for its chairman Senator Henry Jackson, charged that the NSC had been rendered virtually useless by ponderous, bureaucratic machinery. The formality of the NSC system forced the continuation of established policies rather than the generation of new ideas. Heavily influenced by this

report, Kennedy deliberately snuffed out the distinction between planning and operation that had governed Eisenhower's NSC, holding that security policy is much more affected by day-to-day events than by any long term planning effort. Kennedy adopted a collegial style of decision-making in which information flows to the president from several competing sources rather than through one bureaucratic process.

The first serious security problem that confronted Kennedy involved intelligence about a purported missile gap between the U.S. and the Soviet Union. The missile gap controversy, which dominated the national security debates of the late 1950s and early 1960s, arose from the fear that the Soviets would possess a commanding superiority in intercontinental ballistic missiles (ICBMs) in just a few years. Both Soviet braggadocio and the American military services encouraged this idea of a missile gap. Two centuries of America's near imperviousness to direct attack appeared at an end. When Kennedy entered office, he discovered the gap was a myth. In order to avoid future self-serving use of intelligence estimates by the military, Secretary of Defense Robert McNamara set up the Defense Intelligence Agency to centralize intelligence.

During Kennedy's three years in office, he would work closely with McNamara to supervise the largest and most rapid buildup of military forces in the peacetime history of the U.S. Designed to serve as a deterrent, the buildup provided the nation with an arsenal of both conventional and nuclear armaments. Weaponry included ICBMs and bombers in numbers that dwarfed Soviet forces. This modernization and expansion of the missile system confronted any potential aggressors with the impossibility of a strategic victory and the certainty of total destruction. It also established a direct connection between national security policy and strategic forces procurement.

The Kennedy administration security strategy, called "flexible response" because it expanded the options for fighting the communist threat, rested on three cornerstones. Along with a dramatic increase in the nation's military, Kennedy increased economic and military assistance to the developing world. The Agency for International Development coordinated foreign aid, while the Alliance for Progress acted as a blueprint for Latin America by promoting massive modernization and development. The most celebrated economic aid program offered by the administration was the Peace Corps, established by executive order in 1961. This volunteer group, consisting mostly of young adults, went into developing nations as teachers, agricultural advisers, and technicians. The Peace Corps involved the implicit assumption that technical expertise rather than anti-communist ideology and military dominance would be the best way to win support in the developing world. The last aspect of flexible response aimed to deter aggression by training Latin American paramilitary forces. The Pentagon established the Jungle Warfare School, which taught Latin American police officers how to infiltrate leftist groups.

Kennedy's desire to assist democracy in Latin America led to a serious blunder. As president-elect, Kennedy learned of a secret CIA plan for the invasion of Cuba by anti-communist refugees who had fled the nation when Fidel Castro took power. A few aides expressed doubts about the viability of the plan, but Kennedy was determined to strike against communism in Cuba. The decision to abandon the bureaucratic NSC may have contributed to the resulting debacle. The NSC, which rarely met, did not handle the decision to invade Cuba. The attack, in April 1961, failed within three days. The exposure of U.S. involvement led to widespread international condemnation and a humiliating loss of prestige in Latin America.

In late 1961, an American U-2 spy plane photographed intermediate-range nuclear missile sites in Cuba. Military officials warned Kennedy that the missiles would soon be operational and could strike cities along the East Coast of the United States. If Kennedy declined to respond to the presence of Soviet missiles in the Western Hemisphere, Soviet prestige in the Third World would be bolstered and the communists would gain an important bargaining chip for future negotiations on other issues. After rejecting an air strike to destroy the missiles because the Soviets were likely to respond in a manner that would trigger a general nuclear war, Kennedy imposed a naval blockade of Cuba. The Soviets eventually backed down and removed the missiles, but not before the U.S. and the U.S.S.R. came close to war.

The possibility of nuclear war, brought home by the Cuban missile crisis, led to a softening of Cold War attitudes and a new emphasis on cooperation. The White House and Kremlin agreed to the installation of a "hot line" to establish instantaneous communication between the two superpowers. In 1963, the thaw in relations led to the signing of the Nuclear Test Ban Treaty, which halted atmospheric and underwater nuclear testing.

The Kennedy administration came into office with a determination to continue the aggressive Cold War policies of the past. Although it focused on aid to the developing world, little changed in regard to basic national security policy until 1962. The Cuban missile crisis brought the U.S. to the brink of a possible nuclear war and forced a reexamination of American attitudes toward the Soviet Union and the Cold War.

■ FURTHER READING:

BOOKS:

Ball, Desmond. *Politics and Force Levels: The Strategic Missile Program of the Kennedy Administration.* Lexington: University Press of Kentucky, 1988.

Boll, Michael M. *National Security Planning Roosevelt Through Reagan.* Lexington: University Press of Kentucky, 1988.

Crabb, Cecil V., and Kevin V. Mulcahy. *American National Security: A Presidential Perspective.* Pacific Grove, CA: Brooks/Cole, 1991.

ELECTRONIC:

White House. "History of the National Security Council, 1947–1997." <http://www.whitehouse.gov/nsc/history.html> (April 25, 2003).

SEE ALSO

Ballistic Missiles
Bay of Pigs
Berlin Wall
Cold War (1950–1972)
Cuban Missile Crisis
DIA (Defense Intelligence Agency)
Executive Orders and Presidential Directives
National Security Strategy, United States
NSC (National Security Council)
NSC (National Security Council), History
U-2 Spy Plane

Rescue workers pull an injured man from the ruins of a neighboring building after a powerful blast detonated next to the U.S. Embassy in Nairobi, Kenya, in 1998. Islamist al-Qaeda members were blamed for the explosion, which killed over 200 people and injured over 1,600. AP/WIDE WORLD PHOTOS.

Kenya, Bombing of United States Embassy

■ MICHAEL VAN DYKE

At approximately 10:30 on the morning of August 7, 1998, a yellow van approached the United States Embassy in Nairobi, Kenya. When the vehicle stopped, one of the passengers exited and threw a grenade-like device at the gate-guard. The guard fled while the van went through the gate and proceeded to the underground parking garage. Moments later, an explosion ripped through the embassy, also demolishing the nearby Ufundi Coop House and the 17-story Cooperative Bank. A secretarial college was also severely damaged. Two hundred and fourteen persons were killed in the bombing, including twelve American citizens, and more than four thousand were injured. A near-simultaneous bombing of the U.S. Embassy in Dar es Salaam, Tanzania, killed eleven more people.

Within days, the man who had thrown the grenade-like device was captured and identified as Mohamed Rashed Daoud al-Owhali. Al-Owhali had been injured in the grenade explosion and had gone to a local hospital for treatment. Under questioning, al-Owhali revealed that the operation was linked to the Arab-Afghan al-Qaeda organization run by Saudi financier Osama bin Laden. Al-Owhali claimed to have been trained in several al-Qaeda terrorist camps in Afghanistan, where he had received instruction in explosives, highjacking, and kidnapping. He had also attended conferences where Bin Laden was present, and was aware of a 1996 fatwa (religious ruling), signed by Bin Laden, that urged the killing of Americans worldwide. Al-Owhali also stated that the bombing was supposed to have been a "martyrdom operation," and that he hadn't expected to survive it. Soon thereafter, a second suspect was captured and identified as Mohamed Saddiq Odeh. Odeh, a 34-year-old Palestinian engineer, admitted that he had provided technical and logistical support to the bombers. Further investigation showed that Odeh had been a member of al-Qaeda since 1992, and had lived in Kenya since 1996, where he had been in frequent communication with top al-Qaeda commanders. He also was aware of Bin Laden's 1996 fatwa. Al-Owhali, the first suspect, was a Yemeni national who agreed to speak to authorities if he was guaranteed trial in the United States ("because America is my enemy and Kenya is not"). In his testimony, al-Owhali claimed that the Nairobi embassy had been targeted because it was a lightly guarded, "easy target." In regard to the timing of the bombing, al-Owhali testified that it had been planned for late Friday morning because observant Muslims would be going to mosques for prayer services at that time.

Within weeks of the bombing, the United States responded with SCUD missile attacks on likely Bin Laden base camps in Afghanistan. Satellites had observed the dispersion of people away from these camps in the days immediately following the August 7 embassy bombings. Combined with the testimony of al-Ohwali and Odeh, these observed movements gave the United States evidence to consider al-Qaeda and Osama bin Laden fully responsible for the deadly attacks. By the fourth anniversary of the bombing, the United States had given $42 million in assistance to Kenya and four of the perpetrators had been convicted and sentenced to life in prison.

■ **FURTHER READING:**

BOOKS:

Benjamin, Daniel, and Steven Simon. *The Age of Sacred Terror.* New York: Random House, 2002.

Gunaratna, Rohan. *Inside Al Qaeda: Global Network of Terror.* New York: Columbia University Press, 2002.

Kushner, Harvey W., ed. *Essential Readings on Political Terrorism: Analyses of Problems and Prospects for the 21st Century.* Lincoln, Nebraska: Gordian Knot Books, University of Nebraska Press, 2002.

ELECTRONIC:

The Avalon Project at Yale Law School. "Documents on Terrorism: Criminal Complaint Against Kenya Bombing Suspect Al-Owhali." August 26, 1998. <http://www.yale.edu/lawweb/avalon/terrorism/t_0024.htm> (December 13, 2002).

SEE ALSO

Clinton Administration (1993–2001), United States National Security Policy
Enduring Freedom, Operation
Interrogation
Satellites, Spy
September 11 Terrorist Attacks on the United States
Terrorist and Para-State Organizations
Terrorist Organization List, United States
United States, Counter-terrorism Policy

Keyhole Satellites.

SEE *Satellites, Spy.*

KGB (Komitet Gosudarstvennoi Bezopasnosti, USSR Committee of State Security)

■ K. LEE LERNER

The KGB (*Komitet Gosudarstvennoi Bezopasnosti* or Committee of State Security) was the preeminent Soviet intelligence agency and Soviet equivalent of the American CIA.

The KGB was the primary organization for intelligence and counterintelligence matters during the later Soviet period. Although the NKVD was tasked with internal security, the KBG role in political security and counterintelligence was so broad that its operations often touched on internal security matters. For example, in 1957, Soviet border guards were placed under KGB supervision.

The KGB and Western intelligence services played a continual deadly game of "cat and mouse" (both as pursuers and the pursued) throughout the Cold War, with some of the most intense activity centered on Berlin (e.g., Operation Gold and the Berlin tunnel episode). In 1967, Yuri Andropov, then head of KGB and later Soviet premier, described the role of the KGB and other state security bodies as "a bitter and stubborn battle on all fronts, economic, political, and ideological."

Origin and formation of the KGB. The first Soviet state security organization, the Cheka (aka, Vecheka or All-Russian Extraordinary Commission for Combating Counter-revolution and Sabotage) was created by the new Soviet leaders almost immediately following the November revolution in 1917. In 1922, the State Political Directorate (GPU) succeeded the Cheka and was then placed under the control of the NKVD (People's Commissariat of Internal Affairs).

When the Union of Soviet Socialist Republics was formally created the next year, the GPU became the OGPU (Unified State Political Directorate) and was made an independent directorate (disassociated from the NKVD) of the Soviet Council of People's Commissars. In the political infighting and turmoil of the early 1930s in the Soviet Union, the OGPU was renamed the GUGB (Chief Directorate of State Security) and simultaneously placed under the control of the also reformed All-Union NKVD.

This fusion of state security and intelligence functions produced powerful influence embodied in a string of leaders that included G. G. Yagoda, N. I. Yezhov (1936), and Lavrentii Beria (1938).

In 1941, during World War II, the GUGB was split from the NKVD and granted equal status as the NKGB. The first NKGB director, V. N. Merkulov, had worked directly with Beria and followed similar brutal methodologies. The NKGB was tasked with conducting both external espionage and counter-espionage activities as well as guaranteeing Communist Party rule by suppressing counter-revolutionary organizations.

As the Nazi invasion pushed deeper into Russia, the NKGB was once again briefly fused with NKVD under its old title as the GUGB to streamline efforts to coordinate an effective defense against the Nazi forces. As the front stabilized and the Soviets began to push the Germans back, the GUGB was once again given independent status as the NKGB.

Derived from special sections of the NKVD Army (NKO) and Navy (NKVMF), a powerful new element,

Russians step on the head of the statue of the founder of the KGB, Felix Edmundovich Dzerzhinsky. The statue, which had long stood in front of KGB headquarters in Moscow, was toppled in 1991 as thousands of Muscovites watched. AP/WIDE WORLD PHOTOS.

SMERSH (*SMERrt SHpionam* or "Death to Spies") became a forerunner to KGB assassination teams. In 1940, Leon Trotsky was assassinated in Mexico City by SMERSH. Trotsky had long been a rival of Soviet dictator Josef Stalin, who recognized that Trotsy's role in launching the Bolshevik takeover of Russia alongside V. I. Lenin gave him much greater revolutionary legitimacy. SMERSH agents tracked Trotsky for more than a decade before the assassination.

Following World War II, the Soviet government renamed the People's Commissariats as ministries and the NKVD became the MVD and the NKGB became the MGB. In March, 1953, the day after Stalin died, Beria united the MGB and MVD into one organization (retaining the title MVD). After Beri's trial and execution in 1954, espionage activities were assigned to a reconstituted unit designated as the KGB and placed under the direction of the Soviet Council of Ministers. In 1978, the KGB chairman was assured a place on the Soviet Council of Ministers.

As part of his attempted reforms of the Soviet Union (e.g., *glasnost*), the last Soviet premier, Mikhail Gorbachev also attempted to reform the KGB before it was dissolved in 1991 but these attempts were met with resistance within the KGB hierarchy and eventually created tension significant to the collapse of the Soviet Union. The fate of

the KGB was sealed when its leader, Colonel General Vladimir Kryuchkov, ordered KGB agents to participate in the failed August, 1991, coup attempt against Mikhail Gorbachev. KGB-directed forces surrounded Gorbachev's Crimean dacha (house) for three tense days before the coup collapsed.

The Soviet Union collapsed and splintered in 1991. The KGB was dissolved and the *Federal'naya Sluzhba Bezopasnosti*, or Federal Security Service (FSB), Russian Federal Counterintelligence Service (FSK), and Foreign Intelligence Service (SVR) were formed (from resources that included some former KGB elements) to serve the intelligence needs of the new Russian Federation.

KGB tactics. KGB operatives were masters at tactics ranging from disinformation (in Russian, *dezinformatsiya*) to assassination. As did their Western counterparts, KGB operatives also employed technology specifically designed for espionage operations. KGB agents employed a range of weapons, including exotic devices like poison pens that fired hydrocyanic acid gas or pellets of ricin. Another celebrated example involved the KGB development of the lipstick pistol, or "kiss of death." Created by KGB scientists, the lipstick pistol contained a 4.5-mm single-shot pistol encased in rubber and disguised as a tube of lipstick.

The deadly poison ricin came to widespread public attention in 1978, when it was used during the KGB assassination of Bulgarian dissenter Georgi Markov in the United Kingdom. Markov, a BBC broadcaster, died several days after being jabbed by an umbrella at a bridge in London. The poison-tipped umbrella injector was designed by KGB scientists.

KGB operatives used disinformation not only directly against Western governments, but also against governments not following pro-Soviet policies. For example, KGB operatives used disinformation tactics in attempts to destabilize Egyptian president Anwar Sadat for his increasingly pro-Western policies by issuing false statements and writing attributed to Islamist fundamentalists. The disinformation not only contributed to the assassination of Sadat, but also helped fuel Islamist terrorism.

To avoid direct conflict with the U.S., the KGB funded subversive groups and domestic terrorists within the United States (e.g., the Weathermen, a 1960s radical group) through intermediaries such as Cuba.

Spy vs. spy. As did their Western intelligence counterparts, KBG officers continually attempted to recruit agents and plant moles in Western intelligence organizations. The KGB's success in this effort was unparalleled, the most infamous success coming with the compromise of British intelligence by the Cambridge University spy ring and mole Kim Philby.

KGB methods of suppression of moles and traitors could be brutal. According to one eyewitness account, when KGB officers discovered a fellow officer had provided information to the CIA, he was thrown feet first into a roaring furnace while his colleagues watched.

The most well known mole for Western intelligence operating within the KGB was Colonel Oleg Penkovsky. Penkovsky initially served the Soviet regime faithfully, but when he became disillusioned with communism and the Soviet leadership, Penkovsky ultimately offered his services to British intelligence. United States President John F. Kennedy used information provided by Penkovsky during the Cuban Missile Crisis. The KGB subsequently arrested Penkovsky. After being convicted of treason, Penkovsky was executed.

The Legacy of the KGB. Since the fall of the Soviet Union and the dissolution of the KGB, access to secret archives and testimony of former KGB officers and agents has exposed several double agents. The extent of the Walker family espionage activities became apparent, and specific sensitive U.S. Navy and National Security Agency documents were discovered in the KGB archives.

In 1994, long-time CIA veteran Aldrich Ames was discovered to be a KGB mole. The information he sold to the KGB included the names of Russian double agents and operatives working for the U.S. within the Soviet intelligence community, ultimately leading to their capture, imprisonment, or execution by Soviet authorities.

In 2001, FBI agent Robert Philip Hanssen was arrested for conspiracy to commit espionage. Hanssen eventually pled guilty to charges that he had spied for the KGB.

Although the predominant sentiment in contemporary Russia is one of relief from fear of the KGB, some express the sentiment that the once omnipresent intelligence-gathering entity was so powerful and invasive that it minimized the commission of ordinary crimes, which now plague Russia.

Some of the bizarre disinformation created by the KGB has become a source of urban legends occasionally regurgitated by ill-informed or profoundly anti-U.S. critics. For example, documents in the KGB archives provide evidence that operatives mounted a disinformation campaign laden with pseudo-scientific "proofs" that the United States had deliberately created the AIDS virus in the laboratory to use as a biological weapon.

The KGB mounted a major disinformation campaign during the Korean War that resulted in lasting influences on North Korean and Western relations. KGB operatives disseminated information that accused U.S.-led United Nations forces of using biological and chemical warfare against North Korean civilians, information that is still propagated by the North Korean government and so continues to poison public opinion against the U.S. and other Western powers.

■ **FURTHER READING:**

BOOKS:

Bittmann, Ladislav. *The KGB and Soviet Disinformation.* Washington: Pergamon-Brassey's International Defense Publishers, 1985.

Kessler, Ronald. *Moscow Station: How the KGB Penetrated the American Embassy.* New York: Scribner's, 1989.

Mitrokhin, Vasily, ed. *KGB Lexicon: The Soviet Intelligence Officer's Handbook.* London: Frank Cass, 2002.

PERIODICALS:

Gordievsky, Oleg. "The KGB Archives." *Intelligence and National Security* 6, no. 1 (Jan. 1991): 7–14.

Waller, Michael J. "State within a State: The KGB and its Successors" *Perspective* IV, no. 4 (1994).

OTHER:

Romerstein, Herbert. "Disinformation as a KGB Weapon in the Cold War." Prepared for a Conference on Germany and Intelligence Organizations: The Last Fifty Years in Review, sponsored by Akademie fur Politische Bildung Tutzing, June 18–20, 1999.

SEE ALSO

Ames (Aldrich H.) Espionage Case

Assassination
Assassination Weapons, Mechanical
Berlin Tunnel
Biochemical Assassination Weapons
Cambridge University Spy Ring
Cameras
Cameras, Miniature
CIA (United States Central Intelligence Agency)
CIA, Formation and History
Cold War (1945–1950), The Start of the Atomic Age
Cold War (1950–1972)
Cold War (1972–1989): The Collapse of the Soviet Union
Concealment Devices
Crime Prevention, Intelligence Agencies
Cuba, Intelligence and Security
Czech Republic, Intelligence and Security
Dirty Tricks
Disinformation
Document Forgery
Double Agents
Hanssen (Robert) Espionage Case
Intelligence Agent
MI5 (British Security Service)
MI6 (British Secret Intelligence Service)
Propaganda, Uses and Psychology
Rosenberg (Ethel and Julius) Espionage Case
Soviet Union (USSR), Intelligence and security
Stasi
Ukraine, Intelligence and Security
Venona
Walker Family Spy Ring

Khobar Towers Bombing Incident

■ STEPHANIE WATSON

On June 25, 1996, a truck laden with explosives ignited in front of the Khobar Towers apartment building in Dhahran, Saudi Arabia. The resulting explosion killed 19 American servicemen and wounded hundreds more. It was the second terrorist attack in that country within a year.

In the early 1990s, a fundamentalist Islamist movement was gaining fervor in Saudi Arabia, and its leaders were enraged over the expansion of American and Western influence in that country. Much of their anger was directed at United States military personnel who had established a presence in Saudi Arabia following the 1991 Persian Gulf War. In November 1995, a group of radical Sunni Muslims expressed their rage by setting off a bomb at a Saudi Arabian National Guard facility in the capital city of Riyadh, killing five Americans. The Saudi government in May of the next year executed four of the men involved in the bombing. Following the attack, U.S. intelligence officials uncovered additional threats against American military personnel in Saudi Arabia, but no specific information that would lead them to believe another attack was imminent.

In 1996 more than 3,000 U.S. service personnel were living in the Khobar Towers apartment complex in the port city of Dhahran. On the night of June 25, guards on the roof of the complex were alerted when they noticed two men running from a truck parked near one of the buildings. They acted quickly, but could do nothing to stop the massive explosion that followed. The truck, which was loaded with at least 5,000 pounds of plastic explosives, (larger than the bomb that destroyed the Alfred P. Murrah Federal building in Oklahoma City the previous year) set off an explosion that tore off the northeast side of Building 131, killing 19 Americans and wounding approximately 500 Americans and Saudis.

After the attack, President William J. Clinton announced a "declaration on terrorism," and called upon other world leaders to join in the fight against international terrorists. The Secretary of Defense appointed a task force to investigate the incident, and began implementing measures to protect against future attacks.

The investigation. Soon after the attack, a local wing of the Lebanon-based militant group Hezbollah claimed responsibility. Terrorism experts extrapolated that Iran also played a role in the bombing, in part because it backs the Hezbollah. Iranian officials denied playing a role in the attack, and claimed that the terrorists were not in their country. Saudi officials asserted that the bombing was the work of Saudi dissidents who were aided by Iran. Although the Saudis rounded up several suspects, they were reluctant to share information with the CIA and FBI, and were unwilling to provide the Americans with access to the detainees. In March 1997, a Saudi citizen named Hani Abdel Rahim Hussein Al-Sayegh was arrested in Canada. American authorities later claimed he gave the signal for the bombing.

Following a nearly five-year investigation, on June 21, 2001, a federal grand jury in Virginia indicted thirteen Saudis and a Lebanese man on charges of murder and conspiracy in the Khobar Towers bombing. Nine of the men were charged with forty-six criminal counts, ranging from conspiracy to kill Americans and employees of the United States, to bombing and murder. The other five men were charged with five counts each. According to the indictment, all fourteen men were members of Hezbollah, working on orders from Iranian government officials to disrupt the American military presence in Saudi Arabia. According to the Saudi government, many of the named individuals were already in custody at the time of the indictment.

■ FURTHER READING:

BOOKS:

Ferguson, Amanda, and Nancy L. Stair. *The Attack on U.S. Servicemen at Khobar Towers in Saudi Arabia on June 25, 1996.* New York: Rosen Publishing Group, 2003.

A crater 35 feet deep and 85 feet wide was made by a truck bomb exploded at the Khobar Towers in Dhahran, Saudi Arabia. The bomb killed 19 American servicemen and wounded hundreds more. AP/WIDE WORLD PHOTOS.

PERIODICALS:

Duffy, Brian. "Terror in the Gulf: Bombs in the Desert" *U.S. News & World Report*. July 8, 1996: 28–32.

SEE ALSO

Clinton Administration (1993–2001), United States National Security Policy
DOD (United States Department of Defense)
FBI (United States Federal Bureau of Investigation)
Iran, Intelligence and Security
Persian Gulf War
Saudi Arabia, Intelligence and Security
Terrorist Threat Integration Center
USS Cole

Kinetic Weapons.

SEE *Strategic Defense Initiative and National Missile Defense.*

Kiss of Death.

SEE *Assassination Weapons, Mechanical.*

Knives

■ JUDSON KNIGHT

Knives come in all shapes and sizes, but for many of the purposes for which an undercover operative might need one, small is preferred; hence, the plethora of diminutive edge weapons available to persons working covert operations for a well-supplied organization such as the Central Intelligence Agency (CIA). Knives may be used for escape and related applications such as lock-picking, or—more infamously—to inflict personal harm. For the latter application, where assassination is the intent, concealment is key, and small daggers (a smaller instrument, made purely for stabbing) are favored. Other knives are made for close combat, in which case a longer blade offers an advantage.

Small knives for concealment. At the extremely small end are thumb knives, lapel daggers, coin knives, and the like. Developed by the British in World War II, the coin knife looks like an ordinary piece of pocket change, which makes it easy for a prisoner to keep it on his person, even after being searched. The blade itself is crescent-shaped, and attaches to the back by a small hasp so that it can

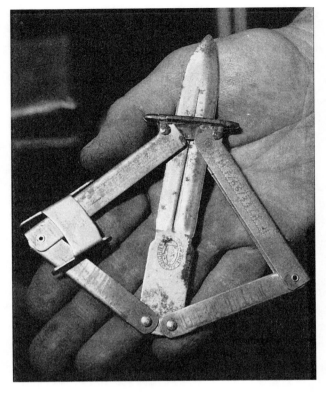

A butterfly knife carried by German pilots in World War II helped downed pilots and paratroopers cut through parachute lines. AP/WIDE WORLD PHOTOS.

rotate outward. It is too blunt to be used for inflicting bodily harm, but can be useful in escape. The inside of the blade is much sharper, after the manner of a cigar cutter, and was sometimes used to slice through the tire stems on German vehicles during the war. The British favored their one-pence piece, though any large coin would serve the purpose.

A similar concept is the ring knife, whose blade is much sharper than that of the coin knife, and not retractable. To conceal its purpose, users hide the curved blade on the inside of the hand until it is needed, at which point the ring can be turned around and used. Lapel daggers, also used widely by the Allies and Resistance in World War II, resemble thumb knives. (The latter are discussed elsewhere, in the context of assassination weapons.) Very sharp and short, the lapel dagger often had a hole at one end, through which passed a loop to attach it to the forefinger so as to ensure greater control when using it. Originally these weapons really were concealed in lapels, but after the Germans became aware of this practice, agents found other places to hide them, including in the lining of their clothes. Some hid them in their socks after the style of the kilted Scottish warriors, whose *shen du* had been the model for the lapel dagger.

Long knives for power. Knives and daggers have been concealed in belts (that is, on the inside of the belt and

parallel to it), in belt buckles, and even in the plastic arms of eyeglasses. But when the user is going into a situation of open combat, and concealment is not necessary, a large knife is desirable. An example is the throwing knife, which looks like an elongated spear point (though with the flanges rounded off) along with about six inches of the "spear" itself as a grip. It is very thin, which makes it easy to throw, but in order to be effective, it must be thrown with both accuracy and power, and throwing must be followed by one or more thrusts at close quarters.

Most formidable-looking of all is the Fairbairn-Sykes fighting knife, developed in World War II by two British officers, W. E. Fairbairn and E. A. Sykes. Based on knowledge gained from their experience in close combat while serving with the Shanghai police, the knife would quickly dispatch a victim by striking at his vital organs. Its blade was long, but the handle was nearly as lengthy, so as to ensure great control on the part of the user. First produced in 1941, it was readily adopted by the Allies. British commandoes carried it on raids into Norway, and the United States Office of Strategic Services (OSS), which employed Fairbairn as an instructor, developed its own version. Revised over the years, the knife remained in production through the 1990s.

■ **FURTHER READING:**

BOOKS:

De Riaz, Yvan A. *The Book of Knives*. New York: Crown, 1981.

Melton, H. Keith. *The Ultimate Spy Book*. New York: DK Publishing, 1996.

Minnery, John. *CIA Catalog of Clandestine Weapons, Tools, and Gadgets*. Boulder, CO: Paladin Press, 1990.

Stephens, Frederick John, and Michael Boxall. *Fighting Knives: An Illustrated Guide to Fighting Knives and Military Survival Weapons of the World*. New York: Arco, 1980.

SEE ALSO

Assassination Weapons, Mechanical

Korean War

■ JUDSON KNIGHT

Although it is often described as the "forgotten war," the conflict in Korea cost some 3 million lives over the course of three years, and helped set the tone for the larger Cold War. Both an international and a national conflict, the Korean War demonstrated the strengths and limitations of the United Nations (UN), and established the framework for the policy of containment that would lead the United States into the much longer conflict in Vietnam. Korea also solidified American attitudes toward communism, and

Korean war spy John T. Downey, freed after 20 years in Chinese prison, when asked in 1973 if he had revealed any secret information answered, "I can say, yes. I revealed about every information I had." ©BETTMANN/CORBIS.

reaction to events there served to influence both the rise of Senator Joseph McCarthy and the fear of communist "brainwashing." As much a war of intelligence as of arms, Korea saw the birth of the modern U.S. signals intelligence framework as the Armed Forces Security Agency (AFSA) gave way to the National Security Agency (NSA). In the end, an allied force of South Korean, American, British, Australian, and Turkish troops frustrated the aspirations of the North Korean Communist government, aided by the People's Republic of China, to control the Korean peninsula. The truce in 1953 established an uneasy framework—not quite war, not quite peace—that nevertheless remains in place half a century later.

Background

The roots of the Korean War, like those of the Vietnam conflict, lay in World War II. Soon after 1945, the British

and American alliance with the Soviet Union broke down in Europe, and the Korean hostilities brought the end of this partnership in Asia as well. The Soviets had fought World War II entirely on their western front, and only entered the Pacific war on a last minute bid for territory. Years earlier, the little-known tank battle between Soviet and Japanese forces at Nomonhan in August 1939, had discouraged Japan from any hope that a war with the Soviets would yield easy victory. Therefore, when Adolf Hitler invaded the Soviet Union in June 1941, his Japanese allies did not join him in making war on Russia.

Soviet dictator Josef Stalin's lack of participation in the Pacific theatre did not preclude his plans to extend the reach of Soviet Communism into that area. He was aided by an agreement with the United States that the Japanese would surrender to Soviet forces north of the 38th parallel on the Korean peninsula, which enabled him to establish a Communist government in Pyongyang under the leadership of Kim Il Sung. (Despite North Korean state hagiographers' later attempt to recast their "Great Leader" as a war hero, in fact he had spent the entire war under Stalin's protection, behind Soviet lines.)

By 1947, it had become apparent that Korea, in Japanese hands since 1910, would not easily be reunited under a non-Communist government. Soon another event served to further raise the specter of Communist expansionism in Asia. In October 1949, the victory of Mao Zedong's forces placed the world's largest population under the Communist rule of the People's Republic of China (PRC). Meanwhile, the United States had withdrawn its troops from Korea, and it now petitioned the UN to ensure free elections in Korea. The Soviets had withdrawn their troops as well, but refused to agree to these elections. On June 25, 1950, Kim's armies swept southward to unite the country by force.

An emergency meeting of the UN Security Council resulted in a resolution to stop the North Korean assault. Though the Soviet Union was one of the five permanent Security Council members—along with the United States, United Kingdom, France, and the Republic of China—it had boycotted the meeting in protest of the U.S. effort to block the admission of the PRC. Because of their failure to show up at the Security Council meeting (a mistake they would not again repeat), the Soviets were unable to exercise their veto power against the American call for a "police action" on the Korean peninsula.

Although the Korean conflict is rightly called a war, there was no accompanying declaration by the U.S. Congress; instead, President Harry S. Truman ordered U.S. troops into battle as part of a UN peacekeeping force on June 27, 1950. Four U.S. divisions landed on the Korean peninsula to join the South Korean forces there, but the North Koreans soon drove them all the way to Pusan, at the extreme southeastern end of the peninsula. Soon afterward, however, General Douglas MacArthur abruptly shifted the tide of the war by landing a massive force at Inchon, some 100 miles (160 km) south of the 38th parallel and well behind North Korean lines. He thus, cut the North Korean army in two, and began moving northward, toward what now looked like an easy victory.

As the UN forces moved toward the Yalu River, which separated North Korea from China, Beijing issued a stern warning that it would not look lightly on the presence of a hostile force just across the border. MacArthur, however, remained confident, and at Thanksgiving 1950 promised Americans that their sons would be home for Christmas. This was not to be, as on November 25 the Chinese People's Liberation Army swept across the border with a force of some 180,000 soldiers. By December 15, the allied forces had fallen back below the 38th parallel, and two weeks later, on the last day of 1950, a Chinese-North Korean force numbering half a million troops pushed into South Korea again.

Thanks to relentless bombing by allied forces, the Communist force did not manage to move any further into South Korean territory, and thus began a lengthy stalemate that would characterize the remainder of the war. American leaders were sharply divided as to the means of resolving the conflict. MacArthur favored an extremely aggressive policy toward China, and proposed a naval blockade combined with bombing of Chinese bases in Manchuria. Truman, however, recognized the danger of such action, which he believed would bring a swift response from the Soviet Union. In the sharply polarized world climate, the price of aggression in Korea would almost certainly be armed conflict with the Soviets, and since they had managed to acquire atomic secrets through spies in the West, the result could very well be nuclear war.

The difference of opinion between MacArthur and Truman characterized that which would come to prevail between hard-line anti-Communists on the one hand, and pragmatists on the other. Overstepping the bounds of his authority as a military leader, MacArthur called on the American people to support his war plans, and for this act of insubordination, Truman relieved him of duty on April 11, 1951. Replaced by General Matthew B. Ridgway, MacArthur returned to the United States a hero, as much for his determination to defeat Communism as for his leadership against the Japanese in World War II. He would become a powerful symbol for the most extreme anti-Communist elements, who soon gained a voice in the Senate under the leadership of McCarthy. Thus began a sort of cold war within the Cold War, a division of the American public that would culminate with the bitter disagreements over the Vietnam War that emerged nearly two decades later.

Eisenhower and the War's End

Meanwhile, on July 10, 1951, the allied forces began a lengthy series of talks with the Communists. The situation remained unresolved during the 1952 presidential elections, and helped pave the way to victory for Republican presidential candidate Dwight D. Eisenhower. One of the most misunderstood of modern American leaders, Eisenhower was neither a fool nor a hard-liner, and precisely because he had led U.S. forces in Europe during World War II, he recognized the dangers of military adventurism, and tended to be even more of a pragmatist in military matters than Truman had been. Eisenhower, who years later would coin the phrase "military-industrial complex" as he warned against its rise in his farewell presidential address, opposed the Korean War, and vowed to end it.

Winning the presidency with the promise "I shall go to Korea," Eisenhower soon made good on his vow. His policy was the embodiment of Theodore Roosevelt's famous dictum about walking softly and carrying a big stick: though mild on the surface, in private discussions with Chinese leaders he made it clear that he would take aggressive steps, up to and including the use of nuclear weapons, if the talks were not soon brought to resolution. Though fighting resumed briefly in June 1953, in the end Eisenhower's gambit won out, and on July 27, the two sides signed an armistice. Although the South gained possession of some eastern mountains north of the 38th parallel, the line virtually served as the boundary between North and South Korea.

In keeping with the emerging modern face of warfare, the Korean conflict was as much a battle of propaganda and intelligence as it was one of military forces. Both sides took large numbers of prisoners of war (POWs), which they exchanged at the end of the fighting, and the Communists in particular made heavy use of the propaganda value to be gained from POWs. Eight different POW camps dotted a stretch along the Yalu River, and in these facilities the Communists sought to demoralize their captives by segregating them according to rank, nationality, and even race. They bombarded the POWs on a daily basis with lessons on the superiority of Communism over capitalism, but the purpose of these activities seems to have been harassment rather than an actual effort to win converts.

The experience added a new term to the English language: brainwashing. The term referred to a variety of psychological and sometimes physical techniques intended to obliterate an individual's beliefs and replace them with new ones. Despite fears of brainwashing that spread through American society in the war's aftermath, there was never any conclusive psychological proof that brainwashing as such actually occurred. Some servicemen did make statements favorable to their captors, and others collaborated with the Communists, but these actions were the result either of fatigue under captivity, or of a simple desire for self-preservation.

Allied signals intelligence. In the behind-the-scenes dimension of the Korean War, the success of allied efforts in signals intelligence (SIGINT) was much more firmly established than that of the Communists in brainwashing. Continuing their record of achievements established in World War II, British and American cryptanalysts proved highly adept at breaking Chinese ciphers. Of particular significance was the breaking of Chinese one-time pad ciphers, which had been supposedly unbreakable, by American cryptanalysts. This was especially noteworthy in light of criticisms that U.S. intelligence had failed to predict the coming of the war itself.

In fact, the modern U.S. intelligence community had only barely come into existence at the war's outset, and Korea marked a turning point. Before the war, budgets for intelligence operations had been lean, but after the outbreak of hostilities, Washington made a much firmer commitment to its intelligence community. Only three years before the war began, the National Security Act of 1947 had established the Central Intelligence Agency, and NSA had yet to be born. Instead, AFSA coordinated all cryptographic activities, though the leading SIGINT agency for the U.S. forces was the Army Security Agency (ASA).

Whereas AFSA is remembered as an administrative failure, and was further tainted by the discovery that one

of its personnel, William Weisband, had been working for the Soviets since 1934, ASA had a number of notable successes. It cultivated a program of Korean linguists, and used a signal intercept technique from World War I to great effect. This was the ground-return intercept, which used the principle of electric induction to pick up Chinese and North Korean telephone traffic. Also significant was the work of the Air Force Security Service (AFSS), which regularly intercepted information on planned bombing runs and helped allied forces protect their facilities. As for the AFSA, it had been formed to coordinate the SIGINT activities of the military services, but by 1952 Washington had recognized its lack of success in doing so, and in that year a secret memo from Truman established the NSA.

The Legacy of Korea

Some 37,000 Americans died in Korea, along with smaller casualties among the British, Australian, and Turkish forces. The North Koreans lost half a million soldiers, and the Chinese sustained losses of one million. By far the worst casualties belonged to the South Koreans, who lost 1.3 million civilian and military personnel. Though the war resulted in a stalemate, it preserved South Korean independence, and resulted in the establishment of boundaries that remained in place 50 years later.

The war helped draw sharp lines between the Communist world and the West, and in its immediate aftermath, Americans were confronted with the specter of not one but two Communist superpowers allied against them. The Soviet-Chinese alliance would not hold, however, and by 1969 the two nations had become more hostile toward one another than either was toward the United States.

By gaining what could be construed as a victory in Korea, American leaders came away with the mistaken impression that large commitments of troops was a viable means of containing Communist expansion in small Asian nations. Thus, within a year of the Korean War's end, U.S. forces would become involved in another effort to roll back the Communist tide on the Asian continent, this time much further south, in Vietnam.

As for the two countries whose conflict had drawn the world's attention, the war only solidified the division between them. For many years, South Korea would maintain a strict authoritarian regime that, while liberal in comparison to that of North Korea, was hardly so by modern standards. In the 1980s, however, it would emerge as an economic powerhouse, and as its populace prospered, they began to demand greater political options. In time, their nation would become an example of the relationship between economic and political liberalization.

By contrast, North Korea would serve to exemplify the disastrous consequences of strict totalitarian control in practice. An Orwellian state, it was the virtual kingdom of Kim, which he would pass on—along with the gruesome cult of personality that developed around him—to his son Kim Jong II upon his death in 1994. Plagued by famine, unable to sustain even the most basic needs of its populace, North Korea survived on the remittances sent home by citizens living in Japan, and by arms sales to other rogue dictatorships. Its development of missile technology, which it exported to extremist regimes of the Islamic world, would earn it a place, along with Iran and Iraq, on the "axis of evil" described by President George W. Bush in 2002.

■ **FURTHER READING:**

BOOKS:

Blair, Clay. *The Forgotten War: America in Korea, 1950–1953.* New York: Times Books, 1987.

Goulden, Joseph C. *Korea, the Untold Story of the War.* New York: Times Books, 1982.

Hastings, Max. *The Korean War.* New York: Simon and Schuster, 1987.

Ridgway, Matthew B. *The Korean War: How We Met the Challenge; How All-Out Asian War Was Averted; Why MacArthur Was Dismissed; Why Today's War Objectives Must Be Limited.* Garden City, NY: Doubleday, 1967.

Stokesbury, James L. *A Short History of the Korean War.* New York: W. Morrow, 1988.

Toland, John. *In Mortal Combat, Korea, 1950–1953.* New York: Morrow, 1991.

Tomedi, Rudy. *No Bugles, No Drums: An Oral History of the Korean War.* New York: Wiley, 1993.

Weintraub, Stanley. *MacArthur's War: Korea and the Undoing of an American Hero.* New York: Free Press, 2000.

ELECTRONIC:

Korean War 50th Anniversary Commemoration. U.S. Department of Defense. <http://korea50.army.mil/> (April 12, 2003).

NSA Korean War 1950–1953 Commemoration. National Security Agency. <http://www.nsa.gov/korea/> (April 12, 2003).

SEE ALSO

Army Security Agency
COMINT (Communications Intelligence)
McCarthyism
North Korea, Intelligence and Security
North Korean Nuclear Weapons Programs
NSA (United States National Security Agency)
SIGINT (Signals Intelligence)
South Korea, Intelligence and Security
United Nations Security Council
Vietnam War
World War II

Kosovo, NATO Intervention

■ JUDSON KNIGHT

Operation Allied Force, the NATO (North Atlantic Treaty Organization) action in the Yugoslav province of Kosovo in 1999, marked the first time the organization actually undertook a large-scale troop mobilization. Sparked by genocidal acts on the part of the Serb-dominated Yugoslavian government against ethnic Albanians, the 78-day operation was launched on March 24, 1999. It proved a success, restoring peace to Kosovo and helping to set in motion events that brought about the downfall of Yugoslavia's president, Slobodan Milosevic, 16 months later. Of perhaps even greater significance, it illustrated NATO's capability to fulfill the peacekeeping mission for which it had been established 50 years earlier.

Prelude to war. The symbolic significance of Kosovo loomed large in the worldview of Serbian nationalism. It was there, on June 28, 1389, that Serbian armies had lost to the Ottoman Turks, an event lodged in the Serbian consciousness comparable to Pearl Harbor in that of Americans. When Serbian student Gavrilo Princip shot the visiting Austrian archduke Francis Ferdinand in the Bosnian town of Sarajevo on June 28, 1914—the event that launched Europe into World War I—the choice of date was no accident.

Exactly 75 years later, June 28, 1989, marked a key date in the transition from Yugoslav communism to Serbian nationalism. On the 600th anniversary of the battle, Milosevic—a Communist party leader in the Yugoslav federation—spoke at commemoration ceremonies, where he announced that "After six centuries, we are again engaged in battles and quarrels. They are not armed battles, but this cannot be excluded yet." This met with a roar of approval from the mostly Serbian crowd.

Milosevic's wars. In 1991, Milosevic became president of Serbia, and over the following years conducted campaigns of "ethnic cleansing" (elimination, through killing or forced deportation, of non-Serb populations) against Bosnia and Croatia. These led to the first airstrikes in NATO history, in April 1994, against Bosnian Serbs. Further airstrikes, combined with Croat and Bosnian ground offenses, finally brought Milosevic to the bargaining table, and on November 21, 1995, the Dayton Accords ended the war in Bosnia.

Then, in 1996, the Serb army engaged in its first battles with the newly formed Kosovo Liberation Army (KLA), and over the next three years, hostilities continued to escalate. In retaliation for KLA attacks on four policemen, Serb forces on January 15, 1999, killed 45 ethnic Albanians in the town of Racak. The weeks that followed saw repeated attempts at negotiation by officials of the Clinton administration, as well as NATO, the United Nations, and the international Kosovo Verification Mission. All attempts to settle the crisis failed.

NATO attack begins. During this time, U.S. attention was primarily focused on the impeachment trial of President William J. Clinton, but when the Senate acquitted him on February 12, Clinton turned his attention to Kosovo and announced plans to deploy 4,000 U.S. peacekeepers. By mid-March, peace talks in Paris had failed, and on March 20, Westerners began to evacuate the Yugoslav capital of Belgrade.

The air war began on March 24, even as Serb forces continued to wage a ground war against ethnic Albanians. On the first night of bombing, NATO warplanes destroyed some 40 targets. In the wake of the attacks and the Serb reprisals that followed, some 800,000 Kosovar Albanians fled the region.

Operation Allied Force.

In the weeks that followed, the United States faced a number of diplomatic battles with Russia and China, both of which supported Serbia. Initially, Russian president Boris Yeltsin took a hard-line stance with the West, but a change of special envoys to the Balkans in mid-April signaled an attempt to mend relations. The war spread into Albania with the deployment of 24 Apache attack helicopters and 2,000 troops there on April 4. Two days later, NATO missiles misfired, and hit a neighborhood in the mining town of Aleksinac.

Ironically, it was during the Kosovo war that NATO celebrated its 50th anniversary, in Washington, D.C., on April 22. Meanwhile, the war—both of words and armaments—continued. On May 5, NATO experienced its first casualties when two U.S. soldiers were killed in a non-combat helicopter accident, and on May 8, NATO forces accidentally bombed the Chinese embassy in Belgrade, killing three Chinese personnel. Though the Chinese claimed that the attack was no accident, after several tense days they accepted an apology.

Conclusion and aftermath.

On May 27, the United Nations war crimes tribunal in The Hague, Netherlands, announced an indictment against Milosevic and four other Yugoslav leaders for war crimes in Kosovo. NATO bombers continued to pound Kosovo, and on June 10, 1999, UN secretary-general Javier Solana announced an end to hostilities. Two days later, in a move that surprised Western forces, Russian troops entered Kosovo to take control of the airport at Pristina.

As the Albanians returned in the wake of the NATO victory, some 200,000 Serbs fled. Though outbreaks of ethnic violence continued—most of them reprisals by empowered Albanian nationalists against Serbs—the presence of NATO troops ensured order. Many members of the UCK, the Albanian insurgent army, joined the official Kosovo Protection Force as U.S.-funded efforts began to rebuild houses for some 300,000 people rendered homeless by the bombing. Kosovo-wide elections in October 2000 placed the moderate Democratic League, led by Ibrahim Rugova, in power.

The Serbs evicted from Kosovo descended on Serbia, where they proved a thorn in Milosevic's side. Joined by frustrated soldiers and their families, they conducted a series of protests against the president, and Milosevic responded by calling for early elections—an act that would

prove his undoing. When he changed the election laws to benefit himself and attempted to falsify the outcome, this proved too much for the Yugoslav people, who ousted him. The newly elected government transferred him to The Hague to stand trial for war crimes in June 2001.

■ FURTHER READING:

BOOKS:

Clark, Wesley K. *Waging Modern War: Bosnia, Kosovo, and the Future of Combat.* New York: Public Affairs, 2001.

Judah, Tim. *Kosovo: War and Revenge.* New Haven, CT: Yale University Press, 2000.

Malcolm, Noel. *Kosovo: A Short History.* New York: New York University Press, 1998.

Power, Samantha. *A Problem from Hell: America in the Age of Genocide.* New York: Basic Books, 2002.

ELECTRONIC:

A Kosovo Chronology. Frontline: War in Europe. Public Broadcasting System. <http://www.pbs.org/wgbh/pages/frontline/shows/kosovo/etc/cron.html> (April 7, 2003).

Focus on Kosovo. Cable News Network. <http://www.cnn.com/SPECIALS/1998/10/kosovo/> (April 7, 2003).

NATO and Yugoslavia. Radio Free Europe/Radio Liberty. <http://www.rferl.org/nca/special/nato-kosovo/> (April 7, 2003).

SEE ALSO

Clinton Administration (1993–2001), United States National Security Policy
Cold War (1972–1989): The Collapse of the Soviet Union
European Union
NATO (North Atlantic Treaty Organization)
Serbia, Intelligence and Security
United Nations Security Council

Kumpulan Mujahidin Malaysia (KMM)

Kumpulan Mujahidin Malaysia (KMM) favors the overthrow of the Mahathir government and the creation of an Islamic state comprising Malaysia, Indonesia, and the southern Philippines. Malaysian authorities believe that smaller, more violent, extremist groups have split from KMM. Zainon Ismail, a former mujahid in Afghanistan, established KMM in 1995. Nik Adli Nik Abdul Aziz, currently detained under Malaysia's Internal Security Act (ISA), assumed leadership in 1999. Malaysian police assert that three Indonesian extremists, one of whom is in custody, have disseminated militant ideology to the KMM. Malaysia is currently holding alleged members of the KMM and its more extremist wing under the ISA for activities deemed threatening to Malaysia's national security, including planning to wage a jihad, possession of weaponry, bombings and robberies, the murder of a former state assemblyman, and planning attacks on foreigners, including U.S. citizens. Several of the arrested militants have reportedly undergone military training in Afghanistan, and some fought with the Afghan mujahidin during the war against the former Soviet Union. Others are alleged to have ties to Islamic extremist organizations in Indonesia and the Philippines.

Malaysian police assess the KMM to have 70 to 80 members. The Malaysian press reports that police are currently tracking 200 suspected Muslim militants. KMM is reported to have networks in the Malaysian states of Perak, Johor, Kedah, Selangor, Terengganu, and Kelantan. They also operate in Wilayah Persukutuan, the federal territory comprising Kuala Lumpur. According to press reports, the KMM has ties to radical Indonesian Islamic groups and has sent members to Ambon, Indonesia, to fight against Christians.

■ **FURTHER READING:**

ELECTRONIC:

CDI (Center for Defense Information), Terrorism Project. CDI Fact Sheet: Current List of Designated Foreign Terrorist Organizations. March 27, 2003. <http://www.cdi.org/terrorism/terrorist.cfm> (April 17, 2003).

Central Intelligence Agency. World Factbook, 2002. <http://www.cia.gov/cia/publications/factbook/> (April 16, 2003).

Taylor, Francis X. U.S. Department of State. "Patterns of Global Terrorism 2001." Annual Report: On the Record Briefing. May 21, 2002 <http://www.state.gov/s/ct/rls/rm/10367.htm> (April 17,2003).

U.S. Department of State. Annual reports. <http://www.state.gov/www/global/terrorism/annual_reports.html> (April 16, 2003).

SEE ALSO

Terrorism, Philosophical and Ideological Origins
Terrorist and Para-State Organizations
Terrorist Organization List, United States
Terrorist Organizations, Freezing of Assets

Kurdistan Workers' Party (PKK)

Kurdistan Workers' Party (PKK) was founded in 1974 as a Marxist-Leninist insurgent group primarily composed of Turkish Kurds. The group's goal has been to establish an independent Kurdish state in southeastern Turkey, where the population is predominantly Kurdish. In the early 1990s, the PKK moved beyond rural-based insurgent activities to include urban terrorism. Turkish authorities

captured Chairman Abdullah Ocalan in Kenya in early 1999; the Turkish State Security Court subsequently sentenced him to death. In August 1999, Ocalan announced a "peace initiative," ordering members to refrain from violence and requesting dialogue with Ankara on Kurdish issues. At a PKK Congress in January 2000, members supported Ocalan's initiative and claimed the group now would use only political means to achieve its new goal, improved rights for Kurds in Turkey.

Primary targets have been government security forces in Turkey. The PKK also conducted attacks on Turkish diplomatic and commercial facilities in dozens of Western European cities in 1993 and again in 1995. In an attempt to damage Turkey's tourist industry, the PKK bombed tourist sites and hotels and kidnapped foreign tourists in the early to mid-1990s.

PKK strength is estimated at approximately 4,000 to 5,000 members, most of whom currently are located in northern Iraq. The PKK has thousands of sympathizers in Turkey and Europe. PKK operates in Turkey, Europe, and the Middle East, and they receive safe haven and modest aid from Syria, Iraq, and Iran. Damascus generally upheld its September 2000 antiterror agreement with Ankara, pledging not to support the PKK.

■ **FURTHER READING:**

ELECTRONIC:

Central Intelligence Agency. World Factbook, 2002. <http://www.cia.gov/cia/publications/factbook/> (April 16, 2003).

Taylor, Francis X. U.S. Department of State. "Patterns of Global Terrorism 2001." Annual Report: On the Record Briefing. May 21, 2002. <http://www.state.gov/s/ct/rls/rm/10367.htm> (April 17,2003).

U.S. Department of State. Annual reports. <http://www.state.gov/www/global/terrorism/annual_reports.html> (April 16, 2003).

SEE ALSO

Terrorism, Philosophical and Ideological Origins
Terrorist and Para-State Organizations
Terrorist Organization List, United States
Terrorist Organizations, Freezing of Assets

Kuwait Oil Fires, Persian Gulf War

■ LAURIE DUNCAN

When Iraqi troops withdrew from Kuwait at the end of the Persian Gulf War in early 1991, they set fire to more than 600 oil wells and pools of spilled oil in Kuwait, a parting shot that exacted a significant economic toll on the country's lucrative petroleum industry. Connecticut-sized Kuwait

An Iraqi tank rests near a series of oil well fires in northern Kuwait during the 1991 Persian Gulf War. Hundreds of fires burned out of control, casting a pall of toxic smoke over Kuwait before firefighting companies, mostly from the United States, extinguished the last fire months later. AP/WIDE WORLD PHOTOS.

contains about 9 percent of the world's total proven oil reserves, and petroleum revenues account for 95 percent of its export earnings. Ignition of oil well fires also created a serious threat to environmental and human health in the Persian Gulf region. The Kuwait oil fires burned for more than eight months, consuming an estimated five to six million barrels of crude oil and 70 to 100 million cubic meters of natural gas per day. Between late February, when the first fires were ignited, and November 6, when the last fire was extinguished, smoke plumes containing a hazardous mixture of gaseous emissions and particulate matter engulfed a downwind area as large as 150 by 1000 kilometers.

The geography and climate of the Persian Gulf region affected the distribution of the oil well plumes, as well as the severity of their effect on human populations and natural ecosystems. Though Saudi Arabia and Iraq border Kuwait's petroleum fields, the region's strong prevailing northerly winds ensured that relatively tiny Kuwait bore the majority of the fires' ill effects. Uneven heating of the land and sea surfaces created local atmospheric inversions during the summer months that trapped smoke in the lower atmosphere, and occasionally caused the plumes to blanket the Kuwaiti land surface. Violent sandstorms, driven by intense summer winds, mixed sand and dust with the smoke plumes.

Kuwait's most productive petroleum reservoir, the greater Al Burqan field, accounted for the majority of the smoke, and for the greatest amount of incinerated oil. Saddam Hussein's Republican Guard set 365 of Al Burqan's approximately 700 wells on fire, and high subsurface pressures kept the fires burning despite heroic firefighting efforts. The Al Burqan fires also presented the greatest risk to human health because of the field's proximity to Kuwait City and the coastal towns where most of Kuwait's approximately two million inhabitants reside.

In general, smoke produced by burning unrefined petroleum contains a mixture of gases and particulate matter including carbon dioxide (CO_2), carbon monoxide (CO), sulfur dioxide (SO_2), nitrogen oxides (NO_x), volatile organics (VOCs), polycyclic aromatic hydrocarbons (PAHs), hydrogen sulfide (H_2S), acidic aerosols, and soot. (Soot is composed of solid particles embedded in tar.) Non-toxic carbon dioxide accounted for approximately 96 percent of the relatively clean-burning Kuwaiti crude oil smoke. The other chemical elements and compounds in oil well smoke, however, can be toxic, carcinogenic (cancer-causing), and otherwise hazardous to human health, as well as ecologically and climatically disruptive in relatively small concentrations. Airborne measurements above the Al Burqan fires in May and June 1991 found that particulate matter and gases made up equal parts of the fires' non-carbonaceous emissions. The Al Burqan wells tap Mesozoic-age limestone, dolomite, and sandstone layers containing high-grade crude oil and salt deposits, geologic factors that account for the fairly low concentrations of toxic emissions, and for the presence of salt crystals in the smoke plumes.

Considering the dramatic appearance and scale of the Kuwait oil fires—satellite and space shuttle images showed the plumes extending across the Arabian Peninsula and Persian Gulf, and the smoke blocked the sunlight from large areas for weeks at time—the environmental and human health effects of the fires were much less significant than expected. The largest and longest-burning fires, like those at the Al Burqan field, burned crude oil with low concentrations of potentially harmful impurities, and the "dirtiest" fires, typically pools of crude oil at the surface, were quickly extinguished. Atmospheric inversions kept the plumes close to the land surface where rain droplets and wind-blown dust particles could quickly cleanse harmful particulate matter, organic compounds, and heavy metals from the atmosphere. In fact, numerous studies found that concentrations of most harmful airborne chemicals like VOCs, PAHs, and heavy metals were lower in Kuwait City and at American military bases just miles from the fires than in major cities in the United States. Concentrations were also below levels recommended by American health and industrial regulators. The smoke did contain high levels of particulate matter that may have caused some of the respiratory problems that Kuwaiti residents and Gulf War soldiers reported as symptoms of so-called "Gulf War syndrome." Fears that the plumes would inject soot and sulfur dioxide into the upper atmosphere and cause global cooling or widespread acid rain also did not materialize.

Kuwait has largely recovered from the socio-economic, environmental, and public health effects of the 1991 oil fires. However, the fires did leave a legacy of more subtle impacts, including long-term environmental damage and chronic human disease. Damaged wells have leaked large amounts of oil into pools on the land surface that threaten fragile desert ecosystems and present a human safety hazard. Furthermore, the Iraqi army set a precedent during the 1991 Gulf War by introducing oil fire ignition as a military tactic. Military forces and threatened nations may face the specter of oil well fires in future armed conflicts in the Middle East and other petroleum-rich regions.

■ FURTHER READING:

ELECTRONIC:

Energy Information Administration, U.S. Department of Energy. "Country Analysis Briefs: Kuwait." August 17, 2002. <http://www.eia.doe.gov/emeu/cabs/kuwait.html>(January 4, 2003).

National Defense Research Institute. "A Review of the Scientific Literature as it Pertains to Gulf War Illnesses. Volume 6. Oil Well Fires." Dalia M. Spektor, Editor. Rand. 1998. <http://www.gulflink.osd.mil/library/rowl/#contents>(January 4, 2003).

Public Broadcasting Service. "Last Battle of the Gulf War: Oil-Well Fire Smoke." Frontline online. 1998. <http://www.pbs.org/wgbh/pages/frontline/shows/syndrome/analysis/oilwell.html> (January 4, 2003).

Rove.To. "457 Shuttle Images of Kuwait." Images from NASA. 1998. <http://rove.to/kuwait/>(January 4, 2003).

SEE ALSO

Air Plume and Chemical Analysis
Environmental Issues Impact on Security
Natural Resources and National Security

L

Language Training and Skills

JUDSON KNIGHT

Language skills are critical to the performance of intelligence, diplomatic, and military duties of many types, both inside the United States and overseas. In this regard, the historic world dominance of English-speaking nations—first the British Empire in the nineteenth century, then the United States in the twentieth and twenty-first centuries—has proven a mixed blessing. On the one hand, the fact that much of the world speaks English offers many advantages, but on the other hand, this fact has kept Americans from learning foreign languages to the extent to which Europeans or other foreign nationals have accomplished the task.

The need for foreign language skills. Foreign language skills play a significant role in work for the State Department or its international information programs. These are also vital to HUMINT and SIGINT (human and signals intelligence respectively) work ranging from undercover operations to analysis of raw data captured by eavesdropping. Likewise, military organizations—particularly elite groups such as Delta Force or the Navy SEALs—often look for personnel with a good working knowledge of a language or languages.

In many cases, particularly military or intelligence work, knowledge of obscure languages is likely to be in demand. A diplomat stationed in a West African country, for instance, may speak French to most contacts in the capital city, but intelligence or military operations are likely to take personnel deep into the hinterlands or the underbelly of urban society, where only local languages or dialects are spoken. For example, during the U.S. military effort in Afghanistan in 2001 and thereafter, proficiency in Pashto, Dari, Tajik, and Farsi, the dominant languages in that country, was greatly in demand.

High demand, small supply. Coupled with heavy demand is a slim supply of available workers trained in multiple languages. Whereas students in many other countries are required to study English from elementary school onward, few American students are compelled to take more than a few years' worth of a language in high school or college.

Of the languages offered to American students, almost all are Western European tongues. French and Spanish dominate the foreign-language programs in U.S. high schools, and at least these are good starting places for students who hope to work overseas; the vast colonial reach of the Spanish in the sixteenth century, and of the French thereafter, created a world in which millions of Latin Americans speak Spanish, while French is spoken throughout much of Africa, Asia, the Pacific, and selected parts of the New World.

The other languages offered in high schools are not as likely to prove useful to intelligence or military personnel. German, despite its great significance in intellectual history, is seldom useful as an international *lingua franca* because Germany united too late (1870) to develop a significant colonial empire. Only in Central and Eastern Europe is German widely spoken. Latin, the other major language offered in most high schools, is useful as a key to studying the Romance languages (Italian, French, Spanish, Portuguese) derived from it—but there have not been any indigenous Latin-speaking populations for many centuries.

Colleges offer a somewhat broader program, with the other Romance languages, as well as perhaps Russian and even a language or two outside the Indo-European family—Japanese, for instance. The higher a language is on the scale of obscurity, however, the lower (by a great degree) the number of students engaged in its study. According to a 1998 Modern Language Association study, a relatively high number of American college students—25,000—were studying Russian. But Farsi, which is an Indo-European language widely spoken throughout Iran and central Asia, had only 600 students nationwide. As for Tajik, common to many forces of the Northern Alliance in Afghanistan, fewer than 10 American students every year were studying it.

The federal language education system.

The federal government has two major language facilities: the Defense Language Institute Foreign Language Center in Monterey, California, and the Foreign Service Institute School for Language Studies in Arlington, Virginia. Additionally, the Defense Language Institute, or DLI, maintains an English Language Center in San Antonio, Texas, for foreign military and government personnel studying English in the United States.

Languages are tested through the Defense Language Aptitude Battery (DLAB) or the Defense Language Proficiency Test (DLPT). Whereas the latter tests proficiency in a particular language, the first test is for job candidates who do not already know the language in question, or perhaps any language other than English. It simply tests language-learning potential, and the only way to prepare for such a test is to master English grammar and syntax, so as to have a good basis for learning an unfamiliar tongue.

Depending on one's score for the DLAB, a candidate may be allowed to progress to a particular course of study at DLI. Below are examples of languages, categorized according to degree of learning difficulty for a native English-speaker, and the score required in order to qualify for that language program:

Category I (Dutch, French, Italian, Spanish, Portuguese): 85

Category II (German): 90

Category III (Greek, Hebrew, Persian, Polish, Russian, Serbo-Croatian, Slovak, Tagalog, Thai, Turkish, Vietnamese): 95

Category IV (Arabic, Chinese, Japanese, Korean): 100

Another system of grading, used by both the government and the educational system in the United States, grades proficiency on a scale from zero to five. Level two is referred to as minimal working proficiency, allowing an individual to function in daily life. Level three, working proficiency, would qualify a person to work as a doctor, professor, or engineer within a foreign culture. Level five is extremely rare in non-native speakers of a language, and indicates full ability to function on a level equivalent to that of a native speaker.

■ FURTHER READING:

PERIODICALS:

Molloy, Thomas. "Why Some In-Country English Language Programs Do Not Work." *DISAM Journal of International Security Assistance Management* 24, no. 4 (summer 2002): 125–130.

Peters, Katherine McIntire. "Lost in Translation." *Government Executive* 34, no. 5 (May 2002): 39–45.

Reppert, Barton. "Training the Tongue-Tied." *Government Executive* 34, no. 4 (April 2002): 66.

ELECTRONIC:

Defense Language Institute English Language Center. <http://www.dlielc.org/> (April 4, 2003).

Defense Language Institute Foreign Language Center. <http://pom-www.army.mil/> (April 4, 2003).

Foreign Service Institute. <http://www.state.gov/m/fsi/> (April 4, 2003).

National Foreign Language Center. University of Maryland. <http://www.nflc.org/> (April 4, 2003).

SEE ALSO

Delta Force
Department of State, United States
DOD (United States Department of Defense)
Enduring Freedom, Operation
Intelligence Community

Laser

■ LARRY GILMAN

"Laser" is an acronym for lightwave amplification by stimulated emission of radiation. Lasers exploit the fact that electrons in atoms' outer orbitals can move between energy levels. Like a marble being shifted up and down a set of stairs, an electron can be raised to a higher energy level by giving it the right amount of energy or can give up a fixed amount of energy when it drops to a lower level. The energy given up when an electron drops to a lower level is emitted as a photon (minimal unit of light); the greater the energy lost by the electron, the shorter the wavelength of the emitted light. If the electrons in a material happen to be undergoing energy shifts corresponding to wavelengths that our eyes can see, the material is seen to "glow."

Laser light is a special type of glow. In some materials, a photon passing near an atom with an outer-orbital electron in a high-energy state can, without being absorbed or deflected, stimulate that electron to drop to a lower energy state. The electron gives up its energy in the form of a photon that is of the same wavelength as the impinging photon, in phase with it, and traveling in the same direction. (To say that two photons are "in phase" means that, if they are considered as waves extended through space, their peaks and troughs are aligned; peak matches peak and trough matches trough.) Such light is termed "coherent." Coherent light is rare in nature because atoms in most light sources (e.g., the Sun) are and so on. The result is that most of the energy locked up in the excited electrons of the laser's working substance is turned quickly into a burst of coherent light. A substance undergoing this process is said to "lase." The resulting light pulse, which is aligned with the long axis of the sample of lasing substance, can be very intense. Lasers that beam continuously, rather than pulsing, can also be built; the trick is to devise a means of continually re-exciting the electrons in the lasing substance as their energy drains away as laser light.

Laser light has several important characteristics: (1) It forms a tight beam, that is, a beam that spreads only slightly with distance. (2) It can be very bright: it is commonplace for a laser to be brighter than the surface of the sun. (3) As all the photons in a given laser beam are produced by identical electron-orbital changes, they are all of the same frequency. That is, a laser beam is of an extremely pure color. (4) Because laser light is coherent, slight shifts in the frequency of laser light, such as those caused by the Doppler effect, are easy to detect. Also, light from a single laser source can be used to interfere with itself after following different paths to a common destination, allowing the extremely precise measurement of distances by the technique termed interferometry.

Since their invention in the 1950s, lasers have found thousands of applications in manufacturing, communications, medicine, astronomy and the other sciences, and weaponry. A few outstanding military applications of laser technology are as follows:

- *Laser-guided weapons.* The distinctive character of laser light—its coherence, brilliance, and purity of color—enables it to stand out from its surroundings, even during broad daylight. Thus, it is easy for a missile to home in on a target (e.g., tank or building) that has been "painted" or illuminated temporarily by a laser beam. Munitions that guide themselves to laser-painted targets are termed laser-guided weapons. Most of the precision-guided munitions in the U.S. arsenal today are laser-guided.

- *Missile-defense lasers.* Beginning with the Star Wars program proposed by President Ronald Reagan in the early 1980s, several schemes have been proposed for using large lasers to shoot down ballistic missiles. The Stars Wars program proposed orbital laser stations or x-ray lasers pumped by nuclear bombs to shoot down ballistic missiles; these ideas were abandoned as too expensive and, possibly, too susceptible to countermeasures. However, development of less-ambitious laser-defense schemes continues. In 2003 or 2004, the U.S. Air Force hopes to perform the first missile-shootdown tests of its YAL-1A Airborne Laser system, a powerful laser mounted on a modified Boeing 747 jetliner.

- *LIDAR.* LIDAR (light detection and ranging) is analogous to radar (radio detection and ranging), but has capabilities that radar does not. In its simplest form, it measures the distance from a laser transmitter to a

U.S. ordnance handlers haul a rack of GBU12 laser guided bombs along the deck of the USS *Theodore Roosevelt* in the Arabian Sea in 2001. AP/WIDE WORLD PHOTOS.

emitting photons at random moments and in random directions, independently of each other. In a laser, however, a chain reaction or domino effect occurs.

The electrons in a sample of some substance, for example, a cylinder of gas or a cylindrical crystal of artificial sapphire, are first fed energy—"pumped" to high energy levels. (Pumping was accomplished in all early lasers by illuminating the laser's working substance with intense light, hence "*lightwave* amplification" in the acronym.) If enough of the atoms in the substance are in the excited state to begin with, a domino effect can begin when one atom emits a photon. This photon impinges on a nearby atom, causing it to release a photon having the same frequency, direction, and phase. These two photons go on to stimulate other atoms, which stimulate others, reflective object by measuring how much time it takes for a laser pulse to make the round trip. Doppler LIDAR, like doppler radar, deduces the velocity of the target by measuring the frequency shift of the echo. LIDAR can also measure the *composition* of distant reflectors by sending paired laser beams having differing frequencies; differing absorption by the substance reflecting the beams (e.g., smoke particles) reveals information about the chemical composition of the target. LIDAR is used by low-flying stealth aircraft to track terrain ahead of them; unlike conventional radar, LIDAR illuminates a very small area of terrain and so is difficult to detect.

■ *Virtual retinal displays.* A virtual retinal display shines low-powered lasers mounted on a headset directly onto the retina of the human eye. The display lasers—one for each primary color—are directed at scanning mirrors that rapidly scan the lasers over the user's retina. (The eyes' own movements are tracked in real time and compensated for by a computer.) The scanning occurs so rapidly that the user perceives a solid image, not a moving dot of light. Virtual retinal displays have the advantage that they allow the user to see normally at the same time; the image produced by the virtual retinal display is *superimposed* over whatever else the user happens to be looking at. This can be a boon to pilots, allowing them to receive information from electronic sources without having to look away from their flight environment.

■ FURTHER READING:

ELECTRONIC:

"Lasers: Spontaneous and Stimulated Emission." Kottan Labs. 2001. <http://www.kottan-labs.bgsu.edu/teaching/workshop2001/chapter4a.pdf> (April 18, 2003).

"Virtual Retinal Display Technology." Naval Postgraduate School, Department of Computer Science. September 15, 1999. <http://www.cs.nps.navy.mil/people/faculty/capps/4473/projects/fiambolis/vrd/vrd_full.html#VRDworks> (April 18, 2003).

SEE ALSO
Laser Listening Devices

space. As the window-glass is made to move to and fro by the alternating pressure of incident sound waves, some component of its motion will be toward and away from an observer viewing the glass at any angle except 90° to the direction of vibration. Laser light reflected from the glass toward the operator of the laser listening device will, therefore, be Doppler shifted by a continuously changing amount. By detecting this Doppler shift, the vibrations of the reflecting surface, and thus, of the adjacent air, can be detected. Doppler shift occurs when light (or any other moving wave) is reflected from a moving surface or radiated by a moving source. Laser light reflected when the window is vibrating toward the laser listening device is shifted upward in frequency, while light reflected when the window is vibrating away is shifted downward. Laser listening devices have the drawback that they require line-of-sight access to an appropriate reflector; they have the advantage that they can record conversations from a considerable distance and without access to the monitored space itself ever being needed.

Infrared laser light is used in this application both because (a) infrared laser light is invisible, making naked-eye detection of the eavesdropping device unlikely, and (b) because a laser's light is all emitted at one frequency, measurement of Doppler shift of the reflected beam is straightforward.

Effective laser listening devices are available from commercial suppliers; more sophisticated versions have long been used by various national security agencies. Embassies and other locations wishing to be secure against laser listening devices can deploy such countermeasures as multi-paned windows, exterior meshes to break up laser light, infrared laser detectors, and noise generators that add random vibrations to those caused by conversation.

■ FURTHER READING:

ELECTRONIC:

"Spy Suspect Hanssen Betrayed U.S. Countermeasures." NewsMax.com. March 6, 2001. <http://www.newsmax.com/archives/articles/2001/3/5/201418.shtml> (April 16, 2003).

Laser Listening Devices

Laser listening devices—sometimes termed laser-bounce listening devices—are remote-eavesdropping systems that do not require the placement of a microphone or bug in the space to be monitored. Instead, they measure changes in light reflected from some surface (usually a window) that is made to vibrate by sound waves in the monitored

Lashkar-e-Tayyiba (LT) (Army of the Righteous)

The Lashkar-e-Tayyiba (LT) (Army of the Righteous) is the armed wing of the Pakistan-based religious organization, Markaz-ud-Dawa-wal-Irshad (MDI), a Sunni anti-U.S. missionary organization formed in 1989. The LT is led by Abdul Wahid Kashmiri and is one of the three largest and best-trained groups fighting in Kashmir against India. The LT is not connected to a political party. The United States added the group to the list kept by the Treasury Department's Office of Foreign Asset Control (OFAC), which includes organizations that are believed to support terrorist groups and have assets in U.S. jurisdiction that can be frozen or controlled. The group was banned and its assets were frozen by the Pakistani government in January 2002.

The LT has conducted a number of operations against Indian troops and civilian targets in Kashmir since 1993. The LT claimed responsibility for numerous attacks in 2001, including a January attack on Srinagar airport that killed five Indians along with six militants; an attack on a police station in Srinagar that killed at least eight officers and wounded several others; and an attack in April against Indian border security forces that left at least four dead. The Indian government publicly implicated the LT along with the Jaish-e-Mohammed (JEM) (Army of Mohammed) for an attack on the Indian parliament building.

LT has several hundred members in Azad Kashmir, Pakistan, and in India's southern Kashmir and Doda regions. Almost all LT cadres are non-Kashmiris mostly Pakistanis from madrassas across the country and Afghan veterans of the Afghan wars. During attacks, LT uses assault rifles, light and heavy machine guns, mortars, explosives, and rocket propelled grenades. Based in Muridke (near Lahore) and Muzaffarabad, LT trains its militants in mobile camps across Pakistan-administered Kashmir; prior to the fall of 2001, it also conducted training in Afghanistan.

LT collects donations from the Pakistani community in the Persian Gulf and United Kingdom, Islamic NGOs, and Pakistani and Kashmiri businessmen. They also maintain a website (under the name of its parent organization, Jamaat ud-Daawa), through which it solicits funds and provides information on the group's activities. The amount of LT funding is unknown. The LT maintains ties to religious military groups around the world, from the Philippines to the Middle East and Chechnya, through the MDI fraternal network. In anticipation of asset seizures by the Pakistani government, the LT withdrew funds from bank accounts and invested in legal businesses, such as commodity trading, real estate, and production of consumer goods.

■ FURTHER READING:

ELECTRONIC:

Central Intelligence Agency. World Factbook, 2002. <http://www.cia.gov/cia/publications/factbook/> (April 16, 2003).

Taylor, Francis X. U.S. Department of State. Patterns of Global Terrorism 2001. Annual Report: On the Record Briefing. May 21, 2002. <http://www.state.gov/s/ct/rls/rm/10367.htm> (April 17, 2003).

U.S. Department of State. Annual reports. <http://www.state.gov/www/global/terrorism/annual_reports.html> (April 16, 2003).

SEE ALSO

Terrorism, Philosophical and Ideological Origins
Terrorist and Para-State Organizations
Terrorist Organization List, United States
Terrorist Organizations, Freezing of Assets

Law Enforcement, Responses to Terrorism

The terrorist attacks of September 11, 2001, constituted a watershed event in American history, particularly for law enforcement. In the aftermath of that event, the nation's principal law enforcement officer, the attorney general, introduced new measures designed to prevent and combat terrorism, while the leading U.S. law enforcement agency, the Federal Bureau of Investigation (FBI), increasingly turned its intention toward terrorism. Through its Community Oriented Policing Services (COPS) program, which provides assistance and coordination to first responders at the local level, the Justice Department has helped state, county, and municipal forces respond to terrorism. The agencies have in turn developed a myriad of programs to improve intelligence collection and processing, increase the capacity to address terrorist acts, communicate with other public safety agencies, and respond to citizen fear while assisting victims.

The Patriot Act

Following the attacks, Attorney General John Ashcroft drafted legislation known as the U.S. Patriot Act, which President George W. Bush signed into law on October 26, 2001. Controversial among civil libertarians, who regarded it as an erosion of freedoms, the 342-page bill contained changes to some 15 different statutes. Collectively, these changes gave the Justice Department and its agencies a number of new powers in intelligence gathering and criminal procedure against drug trafficking, immigration violations, organized criminal activity, money laundering, and terrorism and terrorism-related acts themselves.

Among its specific provisions, the Patriot Act gave increased authority to intercept communications related to an expanded list of terrorism-related crimes; allowed investigators to aggressively pursue terrorists on the Internet; provided new subpoena power to obtain financial

A 17-pound miniature helicopter created by a group of researchers at the Massachusette Institute of Technology in 2002 could have future uses for civilian or military surveillance, shooting aerial camera footage, or scouting disaster areas and other dangerous terrain. AP/WIDE WORLD PHOTOS.

information; reduced bureaucracy by allowing investigators to use a single court order for tracing a communication nationwide; and encouraged sharing of information between local law enforcement and the intelligence community.

Prior to the Patriot Act, federal law had sharply limited the ability of prosecutors and law-enforcement officials to share investigative information with other federal officials, let alone local ones. Thanks to the Patriot Act, sharing would increase between intelligence organizations such as the Central Intelligence Agency (CIA), whose purview is international; the FBI, whose area of focus is domestic; and first responders, whose focus is the community. Such information sharing, it was hoped, would prevent information from falling through the cracks.

The FBI

Allegations made by several special agents against their employer, the FBI, provided an example of the problems that occurred prior to the implementation of such information sharing. In July, 2001, Special Agent Kenneth Williams of the Phoenix FBI office sent his superiors a memo warning that Arab males with possible links to terrorist leader Osama bin Laden were training at an Arizona flight school. The bureau rejected his pleas for an investigation.

Around the same time, Special Agent Colleen Rowley of the Minneapolis office requested a warrant to conduct wiretaps and a computer search against an Arab trainee at a local flight school who had aroused suspicions when he told instructors that he only wanted to learn how to fly a plane, not how to land it. He was arrested for immigration violations in August, but still the bureau took little interest in Zacarias Moussaoui. Only after the September 11 attacks did authorities search the computer of the so-called "20th hijacker," at which time they found phone numbers that might have led them to Moussaoui's alleged co-conspirators.

A new focus on counterterrorism. The problem with the FBI was not incompetence or ignorance; rather, prior to September 2001, its mission had been strictly that of a law-enforcement agency. Its job was primarily to solve crimes that had already occurred, not to collect intelligence concerning terrorist attacks and other crimes that had yet to take place. Nor did it work closely with the CIA, because their missions were different, the one concerned with domestic affairs and the other focused on international concerns.

In the wake of September 11, Ashcroft and FBI Director Robert S. Mueller III refocused the bureau's efforts toward counterterrorism. In December, 2001, Mueller announced plans to reorganize headquarters by creating new counterterrorism, cybercrimes, and counterintelligence divisions; by modernizing information systems; and by emphasizing relationships with local first responders.

Criticized for not taking enough measures to direct the bureau toward its new mission, Mueller in the spring of 2002 announced a number of new reforms. These included the hiring of more analysts; the re-tasking of special agents to counterterrorism; the creation of an intelligence office; development of terrorism expert support teams to work with the bureau's 56 field officers; recruitment of Arabic speakers and others fluent in Middle Eastern and South Asian languages; creation of a joint terrorism task force to coordinate with the CIA and other federal agencies; and the improvement of financial analysis and other forms of strategic analysis directed toward terrorist groups.

COPS, Local Law Enforcement, and Community Policing

Even as the nation's law enforcement leadership worked to refocus efforts toward combatting terrorism, the Justice Department had already put in place a program that greatly assisted local law enforcement in responding to terrorist acts and threats. This was COPS, which was already in place in September, 2001. COPS has helped local forces to strengthen their response to terrorism by improving data and intelligence collection and processing, capitalizing on technology advancements, encouraging communication with other public safety agencies, and helping local agencies to respond to citizen fear and prepare to assist potential victims.

As noted in a 2002 report on COPS programs, "Of course, these approaches are only one piece of the equation. A successful response to terrorism involves an array of activities, many of which are reliant on human intelligence gathering activities and productive partnerships between local law enforcement and other agencies." Still, COPS and similar federal programs have served to greatly improve the abilities of local forces to respond to situations. While each community force remains distinct, federal involvement increases the degree of coordination in activities.

Local forces have at their disposal a number of tools for managing data and intelligence, including in-field laptop computers, computer aided dispatch systems, enhanced records management systems, geographical information systems (GIS), and 311 phone systems. The last of these is aptly characterized by the tagline used to promote it in Chicago—the city's "*other* help line." In contrast to 911, the number set aside purely for emergencies, 311 is for non-emergency calls to police, and for answering citizens' questions.

An example of an integrated information management system at the local level is the crime analysis workstation developed in Seattle through a 1997 COPS grant. Included in the station is crime-mapping software that can be used for traditional crime analysis (e.g., to detect patterns of burglary in a neighborhood), or adapted for emergency mobilization as in a terrorist situation. Under such conditions, peace officers might consult it to locate critical facilities such as fire stations and hospitals, or to provide emergency mobilization maps to all officers on patrol.

Crime mapping and information management can also be used to protect against terrorism, often by integrating law enforcement data (e.g., arrests, citations, and accidents) with non-law enforcement data such as financial and credit records, census information, tax and license registrations to businesses, and so on. Also included among varieties of non-law enforcement information is geographic data such as aerial photographs, floor plans, three-dimensional images of buildings, zoning and parcel information, and sewer and water systems.

By using such materials, authorities might, for instance, obtain information on companies such as plant nurseries or farm supply stores that serve as potential repositories for ammonium nitrate fertilizer, an ingredient used in many explosive devices. If a burglary were to occur at one of these facilities, this law enforcement information could be combined with the non-law enforcement information obtained earlier to track the possible use of ammonium nitrate for terrorist purposes. Similarly, if officials tracked a sharp increase in sales of flu medicine at drug stores, this might indicate that a biological attack had taken place.

GIS and Crisis Management

Use of GIS applies geography, not so much to track criminal activity as to minimize and manage crises. Geographic information can be used to predict risks, and decrease loss of life and property, in the wake of a terrorist attack. It can also be used to develop target inventories and specific incident response scenarios, as well as to map out potential citizen evacuation routes. Use of GIS in integrated systems can enhance the coordination of law enforcement responses to crises.

In 1998, COPS provided a grant to Broward County, Florida, which used the funding to develop a means of information-sharing between local authorities and non-law enforcement first responders, such as firefighters and hospital emergency response teams, as well as law enforcement officials outside the local area. The Broward program included in-car mobile data computers and a county-wide computerized dispatch system. Encompassed within this larger initiative was Operation Safe Schools, a software package provided to all first responders, which made possible the quick retrieval of floor plans, interior photographs, contact names and phone numbers, and evacuation routes for local schools.

In July, 2002, Representative Jim Saxton of New Jersey introduced the Law Enforcement Partnership to Combat Terrorism Act, designed to designate 25 percent of COPS funding toward intelligence programs. The move was another sign of the growing responsibilities placed on law enforcement in the post-September 11 world.

Since September, 2001, law enforcement has been encouraged, on the one hand, to be on the lookout for terrorists, but on the other hand, it is tasked with upholding the civil rights of persons unfairly targeted with suspicion. In the wake of the terrorist attacks, some civilians took it upon themselves to threaten, harass, or cause harm to persons of Middle Eastern descent or the Muslim faith. Along with these were other persons from south Asia who had no connection either to Islam or the Middle East. It is the role of police to prevent such hate crimes, and to enforce laws against them.

Similarly, law enforcement officers play a role in maintaining public calm, restoring order, providing a visible law enforcement presence, and answering requests for information and assistance. For the latter purpose, COPS in 2000 funded the National Center for Victims of Crime (NCVC), which operates a help line and distributes information cards. After September 11, the NCVC distributed half a million trauma information cards.

Not just the NCVC, but the entire system of incident response in the United States has been retasked since September 11, 2001. More than ever, first responders—law enforcement, firefighters, hospital emergency personnel, and others—will work together, as will agencies at the federal, state, and local levels. This integration of efforts will also see increased cooperation involving agencies whose role in upholding public security is not widely recognized by the general populace. Among these are the Environmental Protection Agency and the Nuclear Regulatory Commission, which, along with the Federal Emergency Management Agency and the Coast Guard, are involved in situations involving chemical, biological, and/or nuclear hazards.

■ FURTHER READING:

BOOKS:

Campbell, Kurt M., and Michele A. Flournoy. *To Prevail: An American Strategy for the Campaign Against Terrorism.* Washington, D.C.: CSIS Press, 2001.

Chapman, Robert, et. al. *COPS Innovations: A Closer Look: Local Law Enforcement Responds to Terrorism: Lessons in Prevention and Preparedness.* Washington, D.C.:

U.S. Department of Justice Office of Community Oriented Policing Services, 2002.

PERIODICALS:

Eggen, Dan, and Jim McGee. "FBI Rushes to Remake Its Mission: Counterterrorism Focus Replaces Crime Solving." *Washington Post.* (November 12, 2001): A1.

ELECTRONIC:

Introduction of the Law Enforcement Partnership to Combat Terrorism. Federation of American Scientists. <http://www.fas.org/irp/congress/2002_cr/h072902.html> (April 29, 2003).

Resources for Law Enforcement. Anti-Defamation League. <http://www.adl.org/learn/additional_resources/default.asp> (April 29, 2003).

SEE ALSO

Coordinator for Counterterrorism, United States Office
FBI (United States Federal Bureau of Investigation)
Food Supply, Counter-Terrorism
Intelligence and Law Enforcement Agencies
Justice Department, United States
Law Enforcement Training Center (FLETC), United States Federal
September 11 Terrorist Attacks on the United States
United States, Counter-terrorism Policy

Law Enforcement Training Center (FLETC), United States Federal

The Federal Law Enforcement Training Center (FLETC) is an organization, rather than a single facility, dedicated to training personnel from some 75 federal law-enforcement agencies. In addition, it provides training to personnel from state, local, and international agencies, and to those from federal agencies not immediately tasked with law enforcement duties. In addition to its headquarters, at Glynco, Georgia, FLETC has a facility in Artesia, New Mexico, a temporary training center in Charleston, South Carolina, and a facility in development in Cheltenham, Maryland. Founded in 1970, FLETC is today part of the Department of Homeland Security.

Studies of federal law enforcement training during the 1960s showed the need for a uniform system of training. Not only would this standardize the training process across the many law-enforcement branches of the federal government, but also it would prove most cost-effective. This would in turn make it possible to develop a center

An instructor, background, teaches two Park Service Rangers the finer points of arresting a combative subject at the Federal Law Enforcement Training Center. AP/WIDE WORLD PHOTOS.

where a talented and educated cadre of instructors could provide comprehensive training using modern facilities and a course content that would ensure the highest possible level of proficiency among students. The result was the establishment, in 1970, of the Consolidated Federal Law Enforcement Training Center (CFLETC) as a bureau of the Department of the Treasury.

Originally the headquarters of CFLETC, today known simply as FLETC, was to be in the Washington, D.C., area. After three years of construction delays, however, Congress requested a survey of surplus federal installations, and this resulted in planners reviewing the former Glynco Naval Air Station outside Brunswick, Georgia. In May 1975, Glynco was chosen as FLETC headquarters.

The Glynco campus, located between Savannah, Georgia, and Jacksonville, Florida, is similar to a town, and in fact it has its own zip code (31524). Included on the site are a practical exercise complex comprised of 34 buildings; enclosed firing ranges; a driver-training complex; numerous physical training areas; classroom buildings, which include laboratories and other specialized facilities; a computer resource learning center and library; and a television studio with the capability of broadcasting to field units throughout the United States and the world.

Glynco has a dining room where 4,000 meals are served each day. Included on the campuses are residence halls, administrative buildings, and a wide array of recreational facilities for basketball, volleyball, tennis, soccer, billiards, ping pong, running, and swimming. There are also television lounges and a convenience complex that includes a barber shop, post office, laundry and dry cleaner, credit union, and convenience store. During the early 1990s, the center undertook a $144 million expansion program.

FLETC added a second major facility in 1989, when the former Artesia Christian College campus in Artesia, New Mexico, became the FLETC Artesia Center. Artesia remains the principal advanced training facility for the Immigration and Naturalization Service (INS), U.S. Border Patrol, Bureau of Prisons, and other organizations with headquarters or large concentrations of personnel in the western United States. Artesia is similar to Glynco in the range of facilities offered, but it is smaller and houses fewer students at a time.

As a result of significant increases in the size of the INS and Border Patrol, mandated by Congress in 1995, FLETC needed a facility for training these officers. Planners chose the former Charleston Navy Base and Naval Weapons Station in Charleston. Renovation of the base began in January 1996 with the intention of developing a facility that would mirror Glynco. Training would continue at that facility for as long as the build-up of INS and Border Patrol officers continued.

Finally, in June 2001, FLETC chose a new site at the former Naval Communications Detachment facility in Cheltenham, Maryland. The 247-acre complex would become an area for firearms and vehicle operations requalification, and accordingly would contain facilities for simulations and exercises involving related skills. Construction began in late 2002, with completion scheduled for a year later.

The principal basic programs at FLETC are the Criminal Investigator Training Program; the Land Management Training Program, designed primarily for officers of agencies with a land management mission, such as the U.S. Forest Service or the National Park Service; and the Mixed Basic Police Training Program, which was created for uniformed services with a security or police mission, examples being the U.S. Secret Service Uniformed Division or the U.S. Capitol Police.

These and other programs at FLETC provide a combination of classroom instruction on hands-on practical exercises. Areas of study include firearms, driver training, physical techniques, legal, behavioral science, marine operations, enforcement operations and techniques, and security specialties. There are also advanced courses in specialized areas ranging from law enforcement photography to seized computers and evidence recovery.

In addition to training for federal, state, and local agencies—in some cases through specially designed agency-specific courses—FLETC offers training to foreign agencies. This training focuses on three main areas: the Law and Democracy Program of the U.S. government; the Antiterrorism Assistance Program; and the International Law Enforcement Academy sponsored by the Bureau for International Narcotics and Law Enforcement Affairs.

■ FURTHER READING:

BOOKS:

Calhoun, Frederick S. *The Trainers: The Federal Law Enforcement Training Center and the Professionalization of Federal Law Enforcement.* Washington, D.C.: U.S. Government Printing Office, 1996.

PERIODICALS:

Johnson, Kevin. "Recruits Flood Federal 'Boot Camp'." *USA Today.* (September 23, 2002): A3.

"September 11 Leaves Facility Pushed to Its Maximum." *Augusta Chronicle* (Augusta, GA). September 2, 2002: B5.

ELECTRONIC:

Federal Law Enforcement Training Center. <http://www.fletc.gov> (March 19, 2003).

SEE ALSO

Homeland Security, United States Department
United States, Intelligence and Security

Lawrence Berkeley National Laboratory (LBL)

■ K. LEE LERNER

The Lawrence Berkeley National Laboratory (LBL), located near the University of California Berkeley campus, is operated by the University of California for the United States Department of Energy (DOE).

Founded in 1931 by Nobel Prize-winning physicist Ernest Orlando Lawrence, LBL was designed to be a model for use of the interdisciplinary approach to scientific research. Initially dedicated to World War II military projects, in 1942, LBL became the first in a string of federal laboratories. Research at LBL brings scientists from a variety of disciplines to work on military and non-military funded projects. LBL scientists have developed a number of technologies related to national security interests, technology advancement, and environmental research.

LBL researchers developed a hand-held radiation detector that was able to distinguish between radioactive isotopes intended for biomedical research or clinical medical applications, and the form of isotopes most likely to be used by terrorists to construct a "dirty bomb" (a bomb that spreads radioactive materials by a non-nuclear explosion). The Cryo3 detector, developed in collaboration with researchers at Lawrence Livermore National Laboratory, employs radiation spectrometry to identify radioactive materials. The battery-powered unit utilizes a high purity germanium crystal that absorbs photons emanating from isotopes. By comparing differences in charge characteristics, the detector can further characterize both quantitative and qualitative attributes of a radioactive source. The development of new generations of detectors useful in identifying radioactive, chemical, and biological weapons detection remains a research interest. LBL researchers also developed a highly portable device capable of detecting explosives.

Although LBL's early work was heavily devoted to weapons research, in addition to making direct contributions to the technology of security, LBL scientists now engage in—and as an institution emphasize—a variety of research projects that advance both basic science and industry related projects to improve the quality of life.

The scientific divisions at LBL provide evidence of the emphasis on both physical and biological sciences. As of March 2003, LBL maintained divisions in Accelerator and Fusion Research; Advanced Light Sources; Chemical Sciences; Computational Research; Computing Sciences; Earth Sciences; Engineering; Environment, Health and Safety; Environmental Energy Technologies; Genomics; Information Technologies and Services; Life Sciences; Materials

Sciences; NERSC (National Energy Research Scientific Computing Center), Nuclear Sciences; Physical Biosciences; and Physics.

LBL scientists contributions to medical science and biotechnology include development of radiation therapies for treating cancer and research into HDL and LDL cholesterol physiology. LBL projects have also allowed a more complete understanding of how radon exposure increases cancer risk. Radon (usually in the form of the Radon-222 isotope) is a colorless and odorless radioactive gas formed from radioactive decay. The most common geologic source of radon derives from the decay of uranium. Radon is commonly found at low levels in widely dispersed crustal formations, soil, and water samples. Produced underground, radon moves toward the surface and eventually diffuses into the atmosphere or in groundwater. To some extent, radon can be detected throughout the United States. Specific geologic formations, however, frequently present elevated concentration of radon that may pose a significant health risk.

Scientists at LBL, Lawrence Livermore National Laboratory (LLNL), and Sandia National Laboratories California have also collaborated on the development of environmental remediation technologies useful in the cleanup of military disposal sites (e.g., the nearby Alameda Naval Air Station). LBL scientists also support the National Energy Research Scientific Computing Center (NERSC) (hosting the most powerful computer in the U.S. used for unclassified research) and an 88-inch cyclotron used to advance basic nuclear science.

■ FURTHER READING:

ELECTRONIC:

Berkeley Lab. 88" Organization. 88-inch cyclotron. <http://www-nsd.lbl.gov/LBL-Programs/nsd/user88/> (March 23, 2003).

Berkeley Lab Research News. "DOE's NERSC Center deploys 10 teraflops per second IBM supercomputer." March 10, 2003. <http://www.lbl.gov/Science-Articles/Archive/NERSC-10-teraflop-IBM.html.> (March 23, 2003).

United States Department of Energy, Office of Science. National Laboratories and User Facilities. <http://www.sc.doe.gov/Sub/Organization/Map/national_labs_and_userfacilities.htm> (March 23, 2003).

United States Department of Homeland Security. Research & Technology. <http://www.dhs.gov/dhspublic/display?theme=27&content=374> (March 23, 2003).

University of California. Department of Energy National Laboratories. <http://www.universityofcalifornia.edu/labs/>(March 22, 2003).

SEE ALSO

Argonne National Laboratory
Brookhaven National Laboratory
DOE (United States Department of Energy)
Environmental Measurements Laboratory
Lawrence Livermore National Laboratory (LLNL)
Los Alamos National Laboratory
NNSA (United States National Nuclear Security Administration)
Oak Ridge National Laboratory (ORNL)
Pacific Northwest National Laboratory
Plum Island Animal Disease Center
Sandia National Laboratories

Lawrence Livermore National Laboratory (LLNL)

■ K. LEE LERNER

The Lawrence Livermore National Laboratory (LLNL), located near the University of California Berkeley campus, is operated by the University of California for the United States Department of Energy (DOE).

Founded in 1952, LLNL initially served as a nuclear weapons research and development facility. Research eventually expanded to serve a wider scope of science and engineering projects. Although LLNL's primary mission is to develop technologies that safeguard U.S. nuclear weapons, LLNL applications are also used to prevent proliferation of nuclear weapons technology and to verify existing treaties regarding nuclear weapons development and testing. In addition, LLNL research projects serve biomedical research and environmental interests.

LLNL responsibilities for nuclear weapons safety also include ensuring that the stockpile of U.S. weapons remains reliable. This role became especially important after the U.S. committed to a comprehensive nuclear test ban in 1995. As part of its Stockpile Stewardship and Management Program (SSMP), LLNL must certify the reliability of nuclear weapons without detonation testing. SSMP programs also involve scientists and engineers from Los Alamos National Laboratory (LANL), Sandia National Laboratories, and production facilities at Pantex, Savannah River, Kansas City, and Oak Ridge.

LLNL personnel maintain a special interest in predicting the impact of aging on the nuclear stockpile. Weapons-grade uranium, plutonium, and subcritical elements change over time and preventing weapon degradation is a critical concern in ensuring weapon reliability. LLNL developed ultrashort-pulse laser technology, which provides for more efficient use of weapons-grade materials used to refurbish weapons. Certification of the nuclear stockpile requires separate and independent inspections by at least two SSMP component laboratories. The dual certification approach enhances inspection confidence.

LLNL scientists and engineers are also responsible for weapons design, subcritical testing (nonexplosive testing) at the Nevada Test Site (a nuclear weapons test site adjacent to the Nellis Air Force range complex located approximately 65 miles from Las Vegas), and the development of sensors that can be utilized in noninvasive and nondestructive weapons surveillance tests. Highly sensitive standoff sensors allow the accurate measurement from a safe distance of trace amounts of airborne contaminants emanating from a suspected weapons facility. In addition, low-level radiation sensors help identify potential nuclear threats. LLNL hydrodynamic experiments allow scientists to evaluate explosive detonation and implosion phases in the nuclear detonation sequence.

Other LLNL facilities include a High Explosives Applications Facility, Nova Laser Facility, Flash X-Ray Facility, and the National Ignition Facility (NIF) that hosts the largest laser in the world. High-speed supercomputer facilities that are a part of the Accelerated Strategic Computing Initiative (ASCI) allow improved modeling and database assembly.

To facilitate the identification of biological weapons, LLNL scientists developed a mini-PCR (polymerase chain reaction) test that can be used for *in situ* analysis. Polymerase chain reaction is a technique in which cycles of denaturation, annealing with primer, and extension with DNA polymerase, are used to amplify the number of copies of a target DNA sequence by hundreds of times in just a few hours.

Environmental safety is enhanced by LLNL initiatives in plutonium disposal.

In addition to developing technologies utilized in monitoring the Comprehensive Test Ban Treaty, LLNL programs also develop technologies used to monitor the Chemical Weapons Convention. LLNL scientists are actively involved in securing the former Soviet Union nuclear stockpile now held by the Russian Federation.

■ FURTHER READING:

ELECTRONIC:

Lawrence Livermore National Laboratory. March 24, 2003. <http://www.llnl.gov/> (March 24, 2003).

United States Department of Energy, Office of Science. National Laboratories and User Facilities. <http://www.sc.doe.gov/Sub/Organization/Map/national_labs_and_userfacilities.htm> (March 23, 2003).

United States Department of Homeland Security. Research & Technology. <http://www.dhs.gov/dhspublic/display?theme=27&content=374> (March 23, 2003).

SEE ALSO

Argonne National Laboratory
Brookhaven National Laboratory
DOE (United States Department of Energy)
Environmental Measurements Laboratory
Lawrence Berkeley National Laboratory
Los Alamos National Laboratory
NNSA (United States National Nuclear Security Administration)
Oak Ridge National Laboratory (ORNL)
Pacific Northwest National Laboratory
Plum Island Animal Disease Center
Sandia National Laboratories

League of Nations

■ ADRIENNE WILMOTH LERNER

When the United States entered World War I in 1917, President Woodrow Wilson declared that the nation's intention was to fight in the final war to ensure the survival and strength of democracy in the Western world. After the war, Wilson encouraged the victorious Allied powers to establish an international organization that would mediate conflict through diplomacy and promote peace. Wilson's idea led to the creation of the League of Nations, and earned him the Nobel Peace Prize in 1919. The League of Nations was short lived, and plagued with problems from its inception. The organization did, however, lay the foundations for international cooperative efforts in the latter half of the twentieth century.

Despite Wilson's efforts to gain public support for the League of Nations, the United States government failed to ratify the Treaty of Versailles, the final agreement of the ending of World War I, and therefore, did not join the League. The lack of United States participation and financial backing forever plagued the League, hampering its efficacy and political influence. United States abstention from the League drew ire from some nations, and made others suspicious of the organization itself. Britain expressed dissatisfaction with the League, but ratified the treaty with the League of Nations provisions simply to avoid extended negotiation on reforming the already delayed peace settlement. Despite U.S. reservations, over 30 other nations joined the League in 1920 when the Treaty of Versailles went into effect on January 10: Australia, Belgium, Bolivia, Brazil, Britain, Canada, China, Cuba, Czechoslovakia, Ecuador, France, Greece, Guatemala, Haiti, Hejaz, Honduras, Italy, India, Japan, Liberia, New Zealand, Nicaragua, Panama, Peru, Poland, Portugal, Romania, Serb-Croat-Sloven State (later, Yugoslavia), Siam, South Africa, and Uruguay.

The League was headquartered in Geneva, Switzerland, because of the nations long-standing policy of declared neutrality. Though the Treaty of Versailles provided for the establishment of the diplomatic entity, it did not outline its organization. Its eventual structure took shape over the first two years of representative meetings of member nations. Eventually, the League came to be composed of three principal organs and several technical organizations.

The main body of the League of Nations was the assembly. Composed of representatives from each member states, the assembly met annually. Each resolution, or legal advisory, passed by the assembly was subsequently published.

The council was a smaller body of representatives separate from, but still accountable to, the assembly. Membership on the council varied, and included a mixture of permanent and non-permanent seats. The mission of the council was to mediate and settle international disputes. The League of Nations charter stipulated that the council meet every four years, or as needed in the event of a crisis. In the League of Nation's 20-year history, the council met 107 times.

The secretary-general directed the League of Nations, serving as its chief negotiator and the leader of the assembly. The office of the secretary-general, the secretariat, carried out the routine office work of the league.

In addition to the principal organs of the league, several technical committees advised the assembly and council on international policy and special concerns. The league maintained a health organization, an economic and financial organization, the Opium Advisory Committee, and the Permanent Mandates Commission, in addition to several other temporary groups.

In its two-decade tenure, the League of Nations produced the first truly international laws and cooperative initiatives. The League Health Organization promoted safe hospital practices, vaccination campaigns, and public health information campaigns to curb the spread of venereal disease and tuberculosis. In response to the horrors of poison gas on the World War I battlefield, member nations negotiated bans on chemical weaponry. The rules of engagement for war were modified and codified for the modern era in the terms of the Geneva Convention. The league prompted member states to adhere to its terms, but to avoid war if possible.

In the mid-1930s, the league became increasingly ineffective. Though several nations attempted to halt the spread of Nazism, Fascism, and Communism through diplomacy, their efforts failed to prevent the outbreak of World War II in 1939. The league met for the last time during the war, and was dissolved by its member states on April 18, 1946.

Despite its limitations, the League of Nations established modern, international diplomatic protocol and fostered increasing cooperation between large and small nations on both sides of the Atlantic. Participation in the league drew some nations out of isolationism and propelled others onto the international economic and political stage. After the dissolution of the League of Nations, another international and legal entity, the United Nations, emerged. The atrocities of the Holocaust and a rise in war crimes prompted the international community to establish a body that could define and administer international law. The United States joined the United Nations as a charter member, officially ending its remnant isolationist policies. The United Nations assumed the duties of the former League of Nations and continues to expand its role in international diplomacy.

■ FURTHER READING:

BOOKS:

Knock, Thomas A. *To End All Wars,* reprint ed. Princeton, N.J.: Princeton University Press, 1995.

SEE ALSO

United Nations Security Council
World War I

Lebanon, Bombing of U.S. Embassy and Marine Barracks

On two occasions in 1983, terrorists bombed United States targets in Beirut, Lebanon. The first target, on April 18, was the U.S. embassy, where 63 people, including 17 Americans, were killed. Half a year later, on October 23, the terrorists struck again, this time at barracks that housed members of an international peacekeeping force sent to help restore order in the war-torn nation. Killed in this second attack were 242 U.S. Marines, along with 58 French troops. Until September 11, 2001, the October 1983 assault would remain the most devastating terrorist attack on American citizens, and it remains the bloodiest terrorist assault on Americans outside of the United States. The group Islamic Jihad, affiliated with Hezbollah and ultimately Iran, claimed responsibility for both attacks.

The April attack, along with the simultaneous assaults on U.S. and French barracks in October, were all suicide bombings using vehicles laden with explosives. In the first bombing, the vehicle was a van that had reportedly been stolen from the embassy in June of the preceding year. At lunchtime on April 18, it slammed into the side of the seven-story building, and the driver detonated 2,000 pounds of explosives. The blast tore away the front portion of the building, leaving a site that looked much as the

U.S. Marines and an Italian soldier, right, dig through the debris at battalion headquarters in Beirut after the bombing. AP/WIDE WORLD PHOTOS.

Alfred P. Murrah Federal Building in Oklahoma City would after the attack there 12 years later. Among the dead were the entire U.S. Central Intelligence Agency Middle East contingent, several State department officials (including three USAID employees), several U.S. Army trainers and a Marine embassy guard, and journalist Janet Lee Stevens.

In the October 23 attacks, the terrorists struck two targets simultaneously, a maneuver that would be replicated by al Qaeda in the bombing of U.S. embassies in Africa 15 years later. The attack occurred on a Sunday morning at 6:22 a.m. local time, when a large Mercedes truck burst through the barrier surrounding the Marine compound and slammed into the first floor of the four-story concrete building. The driver then detonated his 12,000-pound bomb. At almost the same moment, a 400-pound bomb carried by a pickup truck exploded outside the nine-story French barracks.

The attack occurred just as the United States launched its first significant military operation since the end of the Vietnam War 10 years earlier: the assault on Grenada, a Caribbean island that had fallen under the control of a Marxist regime. Perhaps because of divided attention, combined with the sensitive nature of relationships in Lebanon, at that time a veritable no-man's land of warring factions, the United States took no significant overt re-taliatory action against Islamic Jihad.

■ FURTHER READING:

BOOKS:

Frank, Benis M. *U.S. Marines in Lebanon, 1982–1984.* Washington, D.C.: U.S. Marine Corps, 1987.

Hammel, Eric M. *The Root: The Marines in Beirut, August 1982-February 1984.* San Diego: Harcourt Brace Jovanovich, 1985.

Jenkins, Brian Michael. *The Lessons of Beirut: Testimony Before the Long Commission.* Santa Monica, CA: Rand Corporation, 1984.

Petit, Michael. *Peacekeepers at War: A Marine's Account of the Beirut Catastrophe.* Boston: Faber and Faber, 1986.

ELECTRONIC:

Beirut Memorial Online. <http://www.beirut-memorial.org/history/> (April 7, 2003).

SEE ALSO

Cold War (1972–1989): The Collapse of the Soviet Union
Iran, Intelligence and Security
Israel, Intelligence and Security
Kenya, Bombing of United States Embassy
Libya, U.S. Attack (1986)
Middle East, Modern U.S. Security Policy and Interventions

Reagan Administration (1981–1989), United States National
  Security Policy
Syria, Intelligence and Security

Less-Lethal
Weapons Technology

I JUDSON KNIGHT

Less-lethal weapons are tools and techniques designed
for riot control and other security functions with the intention of neutralizing hostile activity without killing or causing permanent bodily harm. Varieties of less-lethal weapons technology range from batons and beanbag rounds
(non-lethal bullets fired from an ordinary or modified rifle
or shotgun) to electric Tasers, pepper spray and tear gas,
and equipment that emits loud noises, bright lights, or
even bad smells. Supporters of less-lethal weapons technology maintain that it constitutes a humane means of
controlling disturbances, but detractors hold that these
weapons are more harmful than authorities claim.

A Survey of Less Lethal Weapons

The array of technologies under the heading of "less-
lethal weapons" is vast. As early as 1972, a report by the
U.S. National Science Foundation identified no less than
34 varieties of less-lethal weapons technology then in the
research or developmental stages. Among these were
electrified water jets; stroboscopic light and pulsed sound
weapons; infrasound weapons which would use low-fre-
quency noises inaudible to the human ear; guns for firing drug-filled rounds; "stench darts," which would emit
a powerful and unpleasant smell; and a device called
an "instant banana peel," designed to make pavement
slippery. A later weapon in development at the beginning of the twenty-first century used sticky foam which,
when fired at an attacker, made it impossible for the
attacker to move.

Among the most well known of devices is the M26
Advanced Taser, which can be used to neutralize an individual by means of electric shock. Similarly, electronic riot
shields and electroshock batons also use voltage to neutralize attackers. Manufactured since the mid-1980s, electrified riot shields make use of special plates fitted with
metal strips. In the handle of the shield is a button which,
when pushed, can send as much as 100,000 volts—twice
the capacity of an ordinary Taser—through the metal, an
act accompanied by the emission of loud noises and
bright sparks.

Numerous varieties of less-lethal devices are fired
from an ordinary rifle or shotgun, or one that has been
modified for that purpose. This technology originated
with British colonial forces in Hong Kong, who used wooden

rounds. Varieties of less-lethal ammunition include baton
rounds or plastic bullets; wooden bullets; rubber balls;
and nylon bags filled with lead pellets known as "beanbag" rounds.

Sounds, smells, and light. Numerous varieties of less lethal
weapons technology make use of sounds, smells, or light.
The basic idea behind such techniques is not new; biblical
texts report that prior to attacking the city of Jericho, the
Israelites marched around it seven times, shouting and
smashing cymbals to intimidate the inhabitants. In World
War II, the U.S. Office of Strategic Services (OSS) issued to
its operatives in Asia a "psychological harassing agent"
called "Who, Me?" According to an OSS manual, the gas
"is to be squirted directly upon the body or clothing of a
person a few feet away. The odor is that of Occidental
feces, which is extremely offensive..."

In the late twentieth century, a British government
research project was tasked with developing means of
using noxious odors for crowd control in Northern Ireland.
Among the items in development, according to a *Financial
Times* report, were chemical compounds intended to produce "transient symptoms of nausea and gagging." The
principal is not different from that of tear gas and pepper
spray (itself a variety of tear or CS gas), chemicals long
used to quell riots or neutralize attackers.

Researchers at U.S. national laboratories are also
reportedly in the process of developing various means for
using sound and light as weapons. For example, ultrasound generators, as well as microwave and acoustic
disabling systems, may be used to disturb the inner ear,
throwing an individual off balance. Another item of future
technology is a radiator shell that would use superheated
gaseous plasma, or ionized gas, to produce bursts of light.

Controversy

In discussing less-lethal weapons technology, there is
little middle ground. On the one hand, law enforcement
agencies and supporters present these materials and techniques as humane alternatives to more violent means of
crowd control. On the other hand, opponents view them
as methods by which a police state can potentially exert
greater power over its subjects.

The antipathy toward less-lethal weapons technology by environmental, socialist, and anarchist groups is
not surprising, given the fact that protesters associated
with these movements have most often been the target of
less-lethal weapons. They have been used, for instance, to
quell anti-globalization demonstrations in recent years, as
well as antiwar protests in the United States during the
2003 war in Iraq.

Unfortunately, discussion of less-lethal weapons technology, pro or con, is limited beyond the ranks of extremist groups. Reports in law enforcement journals tend to be
confined largely to scientific evaluation of the weapons'

An executive with American Technology Corporation displays a type of sound-gun device that can beam sound to a person so that it appears to be coming from a wall or other inanimate object. Soldiers may someday have similar non-lethal weapons in their arsenals. AP/WIDE WORLD PHOTOS.

effectiveness, rather than to questions of whether they meet designers' putative aim of providing more humane control systems.

A 2002 *Law & Order* review of less-lethal weapons did, however, note that "while they do greatly reduce the risk that a subject will be killed, the risk is still unfortunately present." For this reason, the National Tactical Officers Association had undertaken a study to assess the causes of deaths from less lethal weapons, and to develop means of reducing the dangers. "In the interim," the report noted, "one of the best things that departments can do is [to] restrict the use of these projectiles to the upper end of the force spectrum."

■ FURTHER READING:

PERIODICALS:

Eaglesham, Jean. "'Bad Smells' Could Be Used to Disperse Crowds." *Financial Times.* (October 31, 2002): 3.

"IACP's Less Lethal Force Options Course." *Law & Order* 49, no. 9 (September 2001): 95–99.

Oldham, Scott. "Less-Lethal Munitions." *Law & Order* 50, no. 2 (September 2002): 54–56.

Rappert, Brian. "Assessing Technologies of Political Control." *Journal of Peace Research* 36, no. 6 (November 1999): 741–750.

Rosenbarger, Matt. "Less-Lethal Improvements: Federal and ALS Work Together." *Law & Order* 49, no. 11 (November 2001): 84–86.

ELECTRONIC:

An Appraisal of Technologies of Political Control. <http://cryptome.org/stoa-atpc.htm> (April 15, 2003).

L-Gel Decontamination Reagent

■ BRIAN HOYLE

L-Gel is a coating that was developed at Lawrence Livermore National Laboratory (LLNL) in Berkeley, California.

An old baton round, left, and one of the new baton rounds, right, also known as plastic bullets. The plastic bullets expand upon contact and release most of their destructive energy before penetrating vital organs. AP/WIDE WORLD PHOTOS.

The coating is effective at decontaminating areas exposed to both chemical and biological agents.

The need to decontaminate spills of a liquid or powdered poison or infectious organism is potentially urgent. In order to prevent injury from chemical or biological warfare agents, for example, the source agent must be contained before anyone touches the material, or before the agents become dispersed in air currents. For example, a spill of powdered anthrax spores can become airborne if not contained quickly, and could travel throughout a building's ventilation system.

The development of L-Gel began in the 1990s. Among those striving to develop a nonhazardous, portable, and inexpensive decontamination reagent were LLNL researchers. Their L-Gel formulation incorporates a chemical compound called potassium peroxymonosulfate into a material called silica.

Potassium peroxymonosulfate is an oxidant. That is, it contributes an electron to the chemical bonds of the target compound, which disrupts the bonds that hold the target together or make it active. Bleach is another oxidant. However, bleach produces noxious fumes, making its use in confined settings dangerous. Bleach is also corrosive, and could damage equipment that is being decontaminated.

The acidic nature of the peroxymonosulfate oxidant proved effective against a variety of biological agents, including anthrax spores. Spores such as those of anthrax have several hard coats that are very resistant to chemicals and physical stresses such as heat, ultraviolet light, and temperature. Acidic oxidants, however, can break apart the proteins that make up the outer coats. The oxidizer can then enter the core of the spore, which houses the genetic material, and can destroy the nucleic acid that is vital for the germination of the spore into a growing and infectious bacterium.

The oxidant is incorporated into a gel. The thick gel is able to cling to surfaces better than water, and remains where it has been applied. A water-based solution will spread out and could even run down an inclined surface, which could further disperse the poison or infectious microbe. Another advantage of a gel is that the oxidant is kept in contact with the target longer than would be possible if the oxidant was dissolved in water.

L-Gel is effective at killing over 99% of populations of bacteria including *Bacillus anthracis* (the bacterium that causes anthrax) and *Yersinia pestis* (the bacterium that causes plague). Surfaces as varied as carpet, wood, and stainless steel are all efficiently decontaminated with L-Gel.

During the fall of 2001, letters containing anthrax spores were sent to a number of locations in the eastern United States. L-Gel was successfully used to decontaminate offices of Congress and at the American Broadcasting Company's (ABC) newsrooms.

Research is underway to produce L-Gel capsules that could be blown into ventilation ducts, where clean up of chemical and biological agents is especially difficult.

■ FURTHER READING:

PERIODICALS:

Raber, E. "L-Gel Decontaminates Better Than Bleach." *Science and Technology Review.* (March 2002): 10–16.

SEE ALSO

Biocontainment Laboratories
Decontamination Methods
Pathogens

Liberation Tigers of Tamil Eelam (LTTE)

The Liberation Tigers of Tamil Eelam (LTTE), also known as the World Tamil Association (WTA), World Tamil Movement (WTM), the Federation of Associations of Canadian Tamils (FACT), the Ellalan Force, and the Sangilian Force, was founded in 1976. LTTE is the most powerful Tamil group in Sri Lanka and uses overt and illegal methods to raise funds, acquire weapons, and publicize its cause of establishing an independent Tamil state. The LTTE began its armed conflict with the Sri Lankan government in 1983 and relies on a guerrilla strategy that includes the use of terrorist tactics.

Other names

The Tigers have integrated a battlefield insurgent strategy with a terrorist program that targets not only key personnel in the countryside, but also senior Sri Lankan political and military leaders in Colombo and other urban centers. The Tigers are most notorious for their cadre of suicide bombers, the Black Tigers. Political assassinations and bombings are commonplace. The LTTE has refrained from targeting foreign diplomatic and commercial establishments but maintains an active media effort.

The exact strength of LTTE is unknown, but it is estimated to have 8,000 to 10,000 armed combatants in Sri Lanka, with a core of trained fighters of approximately 3,000 to 6,000. The LTTE also has a significant overseas support structure for fundraising, weapons procurement, and propaganda activities.

The Tigers control most of the northern and eastern coastal areas of Sri Lanka but have conducted operations throughout the island. Headquartered in northern Sri Lanka, LTTE leader Velupillai Prabhakaran has established an extensive network of checkpoints and informants to keep track of any outsiders who enter the group's area of control.

The LTTE's overt organizations support Tamil separatism by lobbying foreign governments and the United Nations. The LTTE also uses its international contacts to procure weapons, communications, and any other equipment and supplies it needs. The LTTE exploits large Tamil communities in North America, Europe, and Asia to obtain funds and supplies for its fighters in Sri Lanka, often through false claims or even extortion.

■ FURTHER READING:

ELECTRONIC:

Central Intelligence Agency. World Factbook, 2002. <http://www.cia.gov/cia/publications/factbook/> (April 16, 2003).

Taylor, Francis X. U.S. Department of State. Patterns of Global Terrorism 2001. Annual Report: On the Record Briefing. May 21, 2002 <http://www.state.gov/s/ct/rls/rm/10367.htm> (April 17,2003).

U.S. Department of State. Annual reports. <http://www.state.gov/www/global/terrorism/annual_reports.html> (April 16, 2003).

SEE ALSO

Terrorism, Philosophical and Ideological Origins
Terrorist and Para-State Organizations
Terrorist Organization List, United States
Terrorist Organizations, Freezing of Assets

Libraries and Information Science (NCLIS), United States National Commission on

The membership of the commission consists of the Librarian of Congress and fourteen other members who serve five-year terms. Five members of the commission are required to be professional librarians or information science specialists. Other members can be non-professionals, but must have distinguished themselves as having a special dedication to literacy causes, library technology, or information services. Several well-known authors and celebrity champions of literacy have served on the commission. Three committee members are designated to oversee policy addressing information access and literacy issues of the handicapped, elderly, and children. All members are appointed to the position by the President, and approved by the legislature.

During the 1990s, the commission focused on formulating policies and guidelines for the use of technology in library systems. The advent of the internet created new opportunities for the creation of electronic information storage and dissemination. As individual libraries, including the Library of Congress, converted their own directory systems from paper to electronic indices, NCLIS issued advisory guidelines addressing equal access concerns for the vision and hearing impaired. Internet access and electronic databases of government information within library systems was the focus of a 1995 committee study, with special attention paid to numerous security issues. The committee endeavors to make public-domain government information readily available through the library system, but also advises on security measures to adequately curate more sensitive information.

In 2001, the NCLIS undertook a study of the distribution and dissemination of government archives and information in national, state, local, and school library systems. After the September 11 terrorist attacks, the NCLIS drafted a policy on the availability and dissemination of terrorism readiness and prevention information.

■ FURTHER READING:

ELECTRONIC:

United States National Commission on Libraries and Information Science. <http://www.nclis.gov/about/about.cfm>(1 December 2002).

Libya, Intelligence and Security

Libya, under the leadership of Colonel Muamar Abu Minyar al-Qadhafi, espouses a political theory that combines elements of socialism and fundamentalist Islamic law. Qadafi promoted his political system, which he dubbed the Third International, by a series of military incursions into neighboring Chad and sponsoring anti-capitalist terrorist organizations. Throughout the 1980s, Libya garnered international scorn for its policy of state-sponsored terrorism. In 1992, the United Nations imposed strict sanctions on the nation, including a ban on all its international air traffic.

Under Qadhafi's rule, Libya's intelligence community was reorganized into a militarized force. Intelligence and police forces engage in political espionage, ferreting out dissident groups. Libyan intelligence was also accused by members of the international community for training terrorist operatives and paramilitary agents.

The main agency of Libyan intelligence is the Military Intelligence Force. Military intelligence collects both foreign and domestic intelligence information. Most intelligence forces operate as strategic, special units, whose daily operations remain largely unknown.

The Secretariat of the Interior administers intelligence services responsible for the preservation of national security, and protection of government buildings and officials. A variety of specialized police forces, including the People's Security Force and the National Police, combine intelligence and law enforcement duties. However, elite elements of these Special Branch Units also operate as secret police forces, arresting and detaining any individuals suspected of anti-government activity.

Tensions between Libya and Western nations escalated throughout the 1980s and 1990s. In April, 1986, The U.S. launched a series of air strikes upon military targets in Libya, destroying command centers and military bases that were directly linked through intelligence sources to terrorist training and operations. The strikes, codenamed El Dorado Canyon, were carried out ten days after a bomb exploded in a discotheque frequented by American military personnel, where one American died and 63 others were among the over 200 injured. American intelligence officials had previously intercepted a message from Qadhafi ordering the attack.

Libya withdrew its military forces from Chad in the late 1980s, but then attempted to sabotage Western-Arab relations by interfering with ongoing peace negotiations between Israel and the Palestinian Authority. The Libyan government called upon Arab nations to stall the Middle East peace process through acts of terrorism and the repatriation of Palestinian refugees. In return, the United States government enacted strict laws prohibiting U.S.

companies from doing business in Libya or with Libyan companies.

Under the yoke of sanctions, Libya extradited two suspected terrorists for trial in the Netherlands. The act prompted the UN to ease, and then suspend sanctions. In July of 2000, Libya resumed air travel to Morocco and Egypt. Following the September 11, 2001, terrorist attacks on the United States, however, Libya's state-sponsorship of Islamist terrorist organizations, and their resumed relations with Iraq, drew sharp criticism from the United States and British governments.

■ FURTHER READING:

ELECTRONIC:

CIA World Factbook. "Libya."<http://www.cia.gov/cia/publications/factbook/geos/ly.html> (April 28,2003).

Libya, U.S. Attack (1986)

The United States air assault on Libya in April 1986 marked the first major American military response to modern terrorism. The immediate cause was a terrorist bombing in West Berlin ten days earlier, an incident to which U.S. intelligence sources linked Libyan strongman Muammar Qadhafi. The response of President Ronald Reagan was a massive bombing raid on facilities in Tripoli and Benghazi, the country's two major cities. Although the 1986 attacks did not bring an end to Qaddafi's state-sponsored terrorism—the 1988 bombing of Pan Am flight 103 over Lockerbie, Scotland, occurred less than two years later—it marked the first step on a long road toward open confrontation with terrorism and terror-sponsoring states.

Early provocations. Qadhafi seized power in 1969, and during the 1970s and 1980s used his oil wealth to sponsor terrorist movements in 50 or more countries from Northern Ireland to the Philippines. He also undertook other aggressive moves, such as his declaration in 1973 that the Gulf of Sidra between Tripoli and Benghazi belonged to Libya.

The United States refused to recognize this claim, and in August 1981—on orders from Reagan—the U.S. Sixth Fleet conducted exercises in the gulf. The result was a skirmish between two U.S. F-14 Tomcat fighters and two Soviet-made Su-22 fighter-bombers. The Americans shot down both Libyan planes, whose pilots ejected and were rescued by their own forces; the incident proved the superiority of Sidewinder missiles over Soviet Atoll air-to-air missiles.

Operation El Dorado Canyon.

Over the course of the next five years, tensions grew between the Reagan administration and the Qadhafi regime, which increased its sponsorship of and direct involvement in terrorism. On March 24, 1986, Libya launched six SA-5 missiles against the U.S. Sixth Fleet, which was conducting maneuvers nearby in the Mediterranean. The attacks failed, and in subsequent strikes and counterstrikes, the Americans sunk two Libyan vessels. On April 5, 1986, a bomb exploded in Berlin's La Belle discotheque, killing a U.S. soldier and a Turkish civilian, and injuring some 200 others, including 63 U.S. soldiers.

Ten days later, late in the evening of April 15, the United States prepared for air strikes against Libyan ground targets in five areas: the Aziziya barracks, known as a command and control post for terrorist activities; the military facilities at the Tripoli international airport; the Side Bilal base, said to be a facility for training terrorists in underwater sabotage; the Jamahariya military barracks in Benghazi, another terrorist command post; and the Benina air base southeast of Benghazi.

The attack, known as Operation El Dorado Canyon, involved more than 100 U.S. aircraft. The principal strike force was in the form of Navy A-6s from the aircraft carriers USS*America* and USS*Coral Sea,* and Air Force F-111s from airbases in the United Kingdom. The refusal of the French government to grant authority for an American overflight of their country greatly complicated matters, and necessitated refueling of the aircraft in a much longer flight around the Iberian peninsula.

Despite this obstacle, the U.S. force was able to launch its attack at 2:00 a.m. local time on April 16. Over the course of 12 minutes, U.S. forces dropped 60 tons (61 tonnes) of munitions and encountered negligible resistance from the Libyans, who failed to get a single aircraft airborne to challenge the attackers.

Aftermath.

Qadhafi's agents later took part in the Lockerbie bombing, but for the most part his interest in international terrorism cooled after April 1986. After a protracted battle of words, in March 1999 he agreed to turn over two suspects in the Lockerbie bombing but claimed that the Americans who carried out the 1986 bombing raids should be charged for killing 31 people and wounding 226 others.

In May 2001, Qadhafi admitted to a German newspaper that Libya had been behind the discotheque bombing 15 years earlier, an apparent act of retaliation for the U.S. sinking of the two vessels in March 1986. In the La Belle bombing, he had received help from the East German Stasi intelligence service, but according to Stasi files retrieved after the end of the Cold War, the East Germans actively discouraged Middle-Eastern terrorism in Germany following the April 1986 U.S. retaliation against Libya. The La Belle bombing case, which could not have been possible prior to German reunification, finally went to trial in 2001, and in November, a German court found four people guilty of the attacks. They included a German woman and

three men: a Palestinian, a Lebanese-born German, and a Libyan.

■ FURTHER READING:

BOOKS:

Davis, Brian L. *Qaddafi, Terrorism, and the Origins of the U.S. Attack on Libya.* New York: Praeger, 1990.

Venkus, Robert E. *Raid on Qaddafi: The Untold Story of History's Longest Fighter Mission by the Pilot Who Directed It.* New York: St. Martin's Press, 1992.

PERIODICALS:

Greenberger, Robert S. "Dictating Terms: Sept. 11 Aids Gadhafi in Effort to Get Libya off U.S. Terrorist List." *Wall Street Journal.* (January 14, 2002): A1.

Herschensohn, Bruce. "What Proof? Terrorism Alone Is Cause for Action." *Los Angeles Times.* (October 5, 2001): B15.

Weinberger, Caspar, and Peter Schweizer. "...But We've Defeated Terrorists Before." *USA Today.* (September 24, 2001): A15.

Williamson, Hugh. "Libya Blamed for 1986 Berlin Disco Bombing." *Financial Times.* (November 14, 2001): 12.

ELECTRONIC:

Operation El Dorado Canyon. Federation of American Scientists. <http://www.fas.org/man/dod-101/ops/el_dorado_canyon.htm> (April 7, 2003).

SEE ALSO

Aircraft Carrier
Cold War (1972–1989): The Collapse of the Soviet Union
Enduring Freedom, Operation
Iraqi Freedom, Operation (2003 War Against Iraq)
Libya, Intelligence and Security
Pan Am 103 (Trial of Libyan Intelligence Agents)
Reagan Administration (1981–1989), United States National Security Policy

LIDAR (Light Detection and Ranging)

LIDAR is an active remote sensing system that allows exceptionally accurate and rapid determination of terrain and structural features (e.g. height). LIDAR produces highly accurate three-dimensional data measurements that can then be utilized by mapping, guidance, and navigation systems. For example, LIDAR data utilized by Geographic Information Systems (GIS) software, and coordinated with differential Global Positioning System (GPS) data can produce extremely accurate terrain maps that be integrated with other tactical data (e.g. location of targets, etc).

LIDAR technology measures distance by calculating the time delay between the emission and reception of a pulse of infrared light. The infra red light returns after reflecting off the surface of the target (e.g. in terrain feature mapping, the light reflects off the Earth's surface). LIDAR can operate in either profiling or scanning mode to illuminate the terrain under study.

LIDAR, in combination with GPS and Inertial Navigational System (INS) data, allows for highly accurate determination of altitude and position for aircraft, missiles, and other weapons and reconnaissance systems.

In addition to military and intelligence applications, LIDAR has been used to map ice flows and monitor storm erosion damage to beaches.

■ FURTHER READING:

PERIODICALS:

Harney, R. C. "Physics and Technology of Coherent Infrared Radar." *Proceedings of the SPIE* Vol. 300 (1981).

Wertner, C., and Bilbro, J. "Coherent Laser Radar: Technology and Applications." *Proceedings of the SPIE* Vol. 1181 (1989).

SEE ALSO

Mapping Technology
Unmanned Aerial Vehicles (UAVs)

Lipstick Pistol.

SEE *Assassination weapons, Mechanical.*

Lock-Picking

Lock-picking is an ability possessed primarily by locksmiths and by persons involved in intelligence or detective work for which secrecy is a necessity. Requiring a high degree of reasoning power and mechanical dexterity, lock-picking even has its amateur enthusiasts who simply enjoy the challenge. The tools of the trade can involve an amazing array of devices, but most are variations on a simple pick mechanism that a skilled and patient practitioner can replicate even with a paper clip.

Basic technique. One of the simplest types of lock to pick is known as a pin-and-tumbler design. This lock uses a row of pins, divided into pairs, which rest in a row of shafts running perpendicular to the lock's main cylinder plug and its housing mechanism. Insertion of the right key forces

the top and bottom pins apart at just the right distance so that all of the upper pins rest in the outer housing and all of the lower pins rest in the plug. At that point, no pins bind the plug to the housing, meaning that the cylinder can be turned freely, releasing the bolt that holds the locking mechanism in place.

To open such a lock without a key, one needs a long, thin piece of metal with a curved end (a pick), which can be inserted carefully inside the lock as one would a key. Moving with finesse, it is possible to adjust all the pins into place so that the cylinder can be turned as though the key had been used. Or one can apply a sloppier variation, known as raking, in which a pick is inserted and pulled out quickly while the cylinder is turned with a tension wrench such as a flathead screwdriver.

Tools. Experienced lock-pickers use a wide array of tools. They are likely to go to work using an entire tool kit with picks, "rakes" (picks for raking a lock), and tension wrenches, all of which are small enough that a basic lock-picking kit could fit into a pocket. To be equipped for a greater range of eventualities, a lock-picker may use a kit that includes other tools, such as a burglar alarm evasion kit, a key-impression kit (for making a key based on impressions that a lock makes on a key blank), a key-pattern device (for copying old-fashioned warded keys, made to fit into lever locks), files, and other items.

Even more sophisticated is an electric lock-opening device, which is used in tandem with a pick to move the pins into the proper position. Additionally, a lockpick gun can be used to open most pin-tumbler mechanisms. By squeezing the trigger, one strikes the pins with the pick, after which a tension wrench is applied to turn the lock cylinder.

There are other varieties of techniques and tools, just as there are variations in lock design, such as the wafer-tumbler lock, in which tumblers in the shape of wafers take the place of pins. Most aspects of lock-picking are simple in concept, but far from easy in application. Good locksmiths are almost always good lock-pickers, and the reverse is almost as true: a talented lock-picker, for instance, should be able to reconfigure a lock to fit a particular key, a skill that would obviously be of enormous advantage to an intelligence officer in a covert operation.

■ FURTHER READING:

BOOKS:

Macaulay, David, with Neil Ardley. *The New Way Things Work.* Boston: Houghton Mifflin, 1998.

Melton, H. Keith. *The Ultimate Spy Book.* New York: DK Publishing, 1996.

Phillips, Bill. *The Complete Book of Locks and Locksmithing.* New York: McGraw-Hill, 1995.

Roper, C. A. *The Complete Book of Locks and Locksmithing.* Blue Ridge Summit, PA: Tab Books, 1983.

Sloane, Eugene A. *The Complete Book of Locks, Keys, Burglar and Smoke Alarms, and Other Security Devices.* New York: Morrow, 1977.

ELECTRONIC:

Harris, Tom, and Marshall Brain. How Lock Picking Works. Howstuffworks.com. <http://home.howstuffworks.com/lock-picking.htm> (April 5, 2003).

SEE ALSO

Black Ops
Covert Operations
Locks and Keys
Watergate

Locks and Keys

Locks can be either mechanical or electronic, the latter being a modern variation for which a specific numeric code is required to release the locking mechanism. Much more common is a mechanical lock, opened by purely physical means. Locks do not have an independent existence; they must lock something or someone in or out, and they must have a key. The key is based on principles that go back to ancient times, using one of the most rudimentary types of machine known to humankind: the inclined plane.

Historical background. In the history of physics and technology, there are three simple machines: the lever, the inclined plane, and the hydraulic press. The last of these only came into existence during the 1600s, but the first two date to a time before the dawn of civilization. The simplest form of inclined plane is a ramp, which makes it possible to move an object across a vertical distance with a smaller amount of exertion than would be required to lift it straight upward. Other modifications of the inclined plane are wedges, knives, axes, screws, corkscrews, and a key and lock mechanism.

The earliest locks date back to ancient Egypt, and even the more modern variations on lock design that developed in the wake of industrialization still harken back to the design used in the pharaohs' palaces. For example, American locksmith and inventor Linus Yale, Jr., whose name remains an important one in the lock and key industry, based his cylinder lock in the 1860s on the Egyptian design. The latter consisted of a wooden housing containing wooden pegs of varying length, fitted into holes bored into the top of a wooden bolt. Only when a long wooden key with pegs of specific lengths was inserted into the bolt could it be opened.

Basic workings of a lock. Modern locks and keys are made of steel rather than wood, but otherwise the design is not remarkably different from that used to lock doors thousands of years ago. Inside a modern mechanical lock is a row of pins, usually five in number. Each pin has its own cylinder, and when the lock is locked, they hold together two pieces of metal rather as the "teeth" of a belt hold together two sections of a piece of leather. The pins are of varying length, meaning that in order to open the lock, it is necessary to raise them all together so that the bottoms are in alignment.

The solution to this problem is, quite literally, a key, whose serrated edge is actually a row of inclined planes fitted to the configuration of pins inside the lock. The notches on the key are made to push the pins upward just the right amount for each pin, so as to force them all into their respective cylinders and separate the two blocks from one another. The shape of the notches is such that the key can be withdrawn from the lock after use, at which point springs push the pins back downward into their original place.

Mechanical and electronic variations. A variation on this model is Yale's cylinder lock. In this design, the pins are lined up along a larger metal cylinder, which they hold in place inside a cylindrical housing. Inserting the proper key raises the pins and frees the cylinder so that, when it is turned, it rotates and draws back a cam that holds a bolt in place. The bolt is spring-loaded, such that when the key is withdrawn, the spring pushes the bolt back into place, turning the cylinder back to its original position and making it possible to withdraw the key.

There are other variations on the mechanical lock, most notably the old-fashioned lever lock, but the basic principle is the same. By contrast, an electronic lock requires the use of a keypad and a numeric code. The user enters a code, which the machine interprets as a series of binary (on-off) electric pulses. These pulses are bits in a number sequence, which are read by a computer chip. Assuming the sequence matches the one encoded on the chip, the latter sends out an electric signal that opens a mechanical bolt holding the lock in place.

■ **FURTHER READING:**

BOOKS:

Macaulay, David, with Neil Ardley. *The New Way Things Work.* Boston: Houghton Mifflin, 1998.

Phillips, Bill. *The Complete Book of Locks and Locksmithing.* New York: McGraw-Hill, 1995.

Roper, C. A. *The Complete Book of Locks and Locksmithing.* Blue Ridge Summit, PA: Tab Books, 1983.

Sloane, Eugene A. *The Complete Book of Locks, Keys, Burglar and Smoke Alarms, and Other Security Devices.* New York: Morrow, 1977.

SEE ALSO

Black Ops
Covert Operations
Lock-Picking

Looking Glass

Looking Glass is the nickname for the Airborne Command Post, which was implemented by the U.S. Strategic Air Command (SAC) during the Cold War to ensure that operations would continue in the event that the primary strategic command centers were rendered unusable. The name "Looking Glass" derives from the fact that the aircraft used are equipped to fulfill, or "mirror" all functions normally performed on the ground. In the initial phase of the mission, anticipating possible military aggression by the Soviet Union, SAC had an EC-135 aircraft aloft 24 hours a day, seven days a week. After 1990, as that threat seemed to subside, the continuous flights were discontinued. However, the Looking Glass mission continues with a fleet of highly sophisticated aircraft that may be launched as needed.

The birth of Looking Glass. Whereas many people in the second half of the twentieth century envisioned scenarios of global annihilation through nuclear warfare, the U.S. military believed that a nuclear war would actually be more limited and that the Soviets would seek first to neutralize American defensive power. Most command and control centers had been placed, therefore, far from large population centers; few were as important as SAC, located in Offutt, Nebraska.

If the Soviets did decide to attack the United States, wisdom suggested they would send their bombers over the North Pole, giving the U.S. leadership just one hour's notice. With the development of intercontinental ballistic missiles, or ICBMs, in the late 1950s, lead-time was reduced to just 15 minutes. In that span of time, a Soviet ICBM could eliminate the ground center at SAC. It was clear that some response to such a scenario must be developed.

Looking Glass at work. This mirror operation of SAC ground control went into service on February 3, 1961, aboard an EC-135, which had the frame of a Boeing 707 loaded with state-of-the-art communications equipment. Each member of the 24-man crew, composed of personnel from all branches of the armed services, had a specific role. Among these were the positions of airborne launch control officer, emergency actions non-commissioned officer, and force status non-commissioned officer. At the lead was a commander, assisted by an integrated operations plan advisor, who advised the commander regarding the war plans available to the president.

Over the years that followed, Looking Glass pursued its mission, one as grim—based as it was on a doomsday scenario—as it was necessary. During that time, one Looking Glass craft was always in the air, night and day, while at least one more waited on the ground, fully manned and prepared to take over. Over the course of 29 years of nonstop flying, Looking Glass crews accumulated more than 281,000 accident-free hours aloft.

Post Cold-War changes. On July 24, 1990, with the Berlin Wall a memory and the Soviet Union fast receding from the world stage, Looking Glass ended its continuous airborne alert mission. Thenceforth, the system would make use of fewer planes, which operated on an alert status—ready to fly at a moment's notice, but not necessarily aloft at all times.

Further changes followed. In 1992, SAC was disestablished and replaced by the United States Strategic Command (USSTRATCOM), and Looking Glass became a joint military operation. Then in 1998 EC-135 planes were retired and replaced by the newer E-6B, known as the "Take Charge and Move Out" (TACAMO) aircraft. Also based on the 707 airframe, the E-6B accommodated a crew of 15 or more.

■ FURTHER READING:

PERIODICALS:

Healy, Melissa. "Doomsday Plane's Round-the-Clock Flights Called Off." *Los Angeles Times.* (July 28, 1990): 2.

"Looking Glass Gets a Rest at Last." *Chicago Tribune.* (July 29, 1990): 2.

ELECTRONIC:

E-6B Airborne Command Post (ABNCP). U.S. Strategic Command. <http://www.stratcom.af.mil/factsheetshtml/ABNCP.htm> (April 3, 2003).

EC-135, Looking Glass. Federation of American Scientists. <http://www.fas.org/nuke/guide/usa/c31i/ec-135.htm> (April 3, 2003).

Looking Glass. Nebraska Studies.org. <http://www.nebraskastudies.org/0900/stories/0901_0124.html> (April 3, 2003).

SEE ALSO

Cold War (1950–1972)

The last of the EC-135 planes used for the Looking Glass mission from 1961 to 1998 taxies to its retirement ceremony at Offutt Air Force Base in Nebraska. In 1998, the Looking Glass mission began using the newer E-6B plane. AP/WIDE WORLD PHOTOS.

Nuclear Weapons
USSTRATCOM (United States Strategic Command)

"Loose Nukes."

SEE *Russian Nuclear Materials, Security Issues.*

Lord Haw-Haw

▌ ADRIENNE WILMOTH LERNER

Lord Haw-Haw was the nickname of Nazi propagandist and broadcaster William Joyce. During World War II, Joyce broadcast a well-known English-language propaganda show from Berlin, often taunting Allied forces. Though never calling himself Lord Haw-Haw on air, he became infamous among Allied combat troops and British citizens.

Joyce was born in Brooklyn, New York, the son of an Irish father and English mother. His family returned to England when he was an infant. As an adult, Joyce joined several radical political organizations, including the British Fascisti. He wrote a series of articles for several extremist newspapers and gained a reputation as a skilled propagandist. In 1934, he served as the Director of Propaganda for the British Union of Fascists. While serving the political organization, Joyce donned full Blackshirt uniform and engaged in a number of street fights with protestors, earning his trade mark facial scar in one scuffle.

As Joyce gained power in the organization, he became more radical. He used his position as a platform for his deeply anti-Semitic views, blaming most of the era's political and social ills on "Jewish communists." He formed his own political party, the British National Socialist League, in 1937. The party proclaimed brotherhood with the Nazi party in Germany and championed similar causes.

Before the war, Joyce did not attempt to disguise his admiration for Adolph Hitler and Nazi policies. On August 26, 1939, Joyce fled to Berlin. He narrowly escaped arrest in Britain under a law that mandated the detention of Nazi sympathizers and political activists. Shortly after arriving in Berlin, Joyce formally joined the Nazi Party. He took a job working on an anti-Allied propagandist radio show.

British journalists were quick to dismiss Joyce's broadcasts and portrayed him a mere stooge. He was dubbed "Lord Haw-Haw" because of his distinct nasal drawl. Listening to Lord Haw-Haw's show was technically prohibited in Britain under a ban on enemy radio, but the show was popular on the British home front. The program drew strong denunciation, but many simply laughed at its absurdity and obviously propagandistic content. On a few occasions, the program managed to frighten listeners with discussions of German saboteurs in Britain and with accurate details of British towns, such as descriptions of belfries and landmarks.

At the war's end, Joyce fled Berlin and broadcast his final shows from Hamburg. When allied forces moved to occupy the city, Joyce retreated to nearby Flensburg and was captured. He was shot in the leg in the process of trying to escape into a patch of woods. Joyce was turned over to British authorities and detained until he was flown back to Britain as a prisoner.

The British government passed a new Treason Act of 1945 in order to prosecute citizens who seriously impeded or compromised the British war effort. The media attention surrounding Joyce's radio program and capture, as well as their portrayal of Joyce as a possible spy, encouraged the government to charge Joyce with treason under the new act. Although the courts could not substantiate charges of espionage, they did convict Joyce of treason based on his broadcasts and voluntary association and cooperation with Nazi officials. Joyce was sentenced to death by gallows and executed on January 3, 1946.

■ FURTHER READING:

BOOKS:

Martland, Peter. *Lord Haw-Haw: The English Voice of Nazi Germany.* Barnsley, South Yorkshire: Pen & Sword Books, 2003.

SEE ALSO

Tokyo Rose
Propaganda, Uses and Psychology

Lord's Resistance Army (LRA)

Founded in 1989, the Lord's Resistance Army (LRA) was the successor to the Holy Spirit Movement. The LRA seeks to overthrow the incumbent Ugandan government and replace it with a regime that will implement the group's brand of Christianity. The LRA frequently kidnaps and kills local Ugandan civilians in order to discourage foreign investment and precipitate a crisis in Uganda.

The LRA is estimated to have 2,000 members who operate in northern Uganda and southern Sudan. The LRA has been supported by the government of Sudan.

■ FURTHER READING:

ELECTRONIC:

CDI (Center for Defense Information), Terrorism Project. CDI Fact Sheet: Current List of Designated Foreign Terrorist Organizations. March 27, 2003. <http://www.cdi.org/terrorism/terrorist.cfm> (April 17, 2003).

Central Intelligence Agency. World Factbook, 2002. <http://www.cia.gov/cia/publications/factbook/> (April 16, 2003).

Taylor, Francis X. U.S. Department of State. "Patterns of Global Terrorism 2001." Annual Report: On the Record Briefing. May 21, 2002 <http://www.state.gov/s/ct/rls/rm/10367.htm> (April 17,2003).

U.S. Department of State. Annual reports. <http://www.state.gov/www/global/terrorism/annual_reports.html> (April 16, 2003).

SEE ALSO

Terrorism, Philosophical and Ideological Origins
Terrorist and Para-State Organizations
Terrorist Organization List, United States
Terrorist Organizations, Freezing of Assets

Los Alamos National Laboratory

■ K. LEE LERNER

Los Alamos National Laboratory (LANL), located near Sante Fe, New Mexico, is operated by the University of California for the National Nuclear Security Administration (NNSA, a component of the United States Department of Energy).

Founded in 1942, LANL was initially staffed by a team of physicists under the direction of J. Robert Oppenheimer to work on the development of an atomic bomb as part of the Manhattan Project. LANL is now a major research facility with approximately 50 operational laboratories. LANL also hosts supercomputing facilities that support both on-site and off-site research programs. Research at LANL brings scientists from a variety of disciplines to work on military and non-military related projects. LANL scientists have developed a number of technologies related to national security interests.

Research at LANL has broadened from its initial emphasis on physics and engineering into biotechnology related projects. LANL scientists participated in the development of the human genome map. Research programs also develop and improve an array of detection devices—including bio-detectors—that are used by intelligence and law enforcement agencies to detect the presence of nuclear, biological, or chemical weapons, or weapons related materials. LANL engineers develop and provide handheld radiation and isotope identifiers. LANL also provides other agencies technical advice and training in detector use.

LANL personnel directly and indirectly support DOE Nuclear Emergency Support Team (NEST) operations that

A program director of the nuclear weapons computing department at Los Alamos National Laboratory stands among the many components of a supercomputer called Blue Mountain at the lab in Los Alamos, New Mexico. AP/WIDE WORLD PHOTOS.

are designed to provide rapid response to accidents or terrorist use of radiological materials. NEST teams would be a critical part of first response operations in the event of a "dirty bomb" attack (i.e., and attack using a non-nuclear explosion to disperse radioactive materials).

Nuclear detection technologies developed as a part of NNSA's Materials Protection, Control and Accounting (MPC&A) program are used by International Atomic Energy Agency (IAEA) inspectors and some foreign countries (e.g., the Russian Federation) to enhance security of nuclear materials and to deter the unintentional transfer of nuclear materials and nuclear technology to terrorists or nations seeking to develop nuclear weapons.

Bio-detector technologies include the Biological Aerosol Sentry and Information System (BASIS), designed to warn of airborne biological weapons attacks; Swept Frequency Acoustic Interferometer (SFAI) technologies allow detection of chemicals that may be components of chemical weapons. BASIS detectors were used at the 2002 Winter Olympics in Utah. SFAI detectors, termed "standoff acoustic identification" detectors provide inspection teams with remote sensing capabilities that enhance safe inspection of packages because traces of chemical elements can often be detected without unsealing containers or opening packages.

LANL's powerful supercomputers allow epidemiologists and biohazard specialists to develop detailed modeling programs to forecast dispersal patterns of airborne toxins.

Not all research programs have direct security applications; some hold the potential for broad engineering applications in industry. For example, LANL scientists have developed tape capable of conducting electricity with very low resistance, and computer specialists have developed software capable of improving regulation of engine ignition systems to promote greater fuel efficiency. LANL personnel often work in conjunction with industry contractors in industrial partnership programs. Other LANL programs support medical research; for example, laboratory teams have assembled a vast virus database that is used around the world to facilitate research into a potential AIDS vaccine.

As one of three NNSA national laboratories, LANL scientists have contributed to a number of research projects designed to supported arms control and counterterrorism technologies. Following the September 11, 2001, terrorist attacks on the United States, LANL's Center for Homeland Security assumed the role of coordinating work on homeland security and counterterrorism technologies.

In conjunction with Sandia National Laboratory scientists, LANL engineers developed the National Infrastructure Simulation and Analysis Center (NISAC) that allows officials to create and test response strategies. Threat analysis and warning technologies provide intelligence and law enforcement agencies enhanced capabilities to deter smuggling and other terrorist-related activities. LANL research programs are also attempting to improve INS (Immigration & Naturalization Service) regulation of border activity by improving automated entry/exit systems. One such program—GENetic Imagery Exploitation (GENIE)—is designed to improve biometric and feature-extraction analysis.

■ **FURTHER READING:**

ELECTRONIC:

Los Alamos National Laboratory. <http://www.lanl.gov/worldview/> (March 23, 2003).

United States Department of Energy, Office of Science. National Laboratories and User Facilities. <http://www.sc.doe.gov/Sub/Organization/Map/national_labs_and_userfacilities.htm> (March 23, 2003).

United States Department of Homeland Security. Research & Technology. <http://www.dhs.gov/dhspublic/display?theme=27&content=374> (March 23, 2003).

University of California. Department of Energy National Laboratories. <http://www.universityofcalifornia.edu/labs/>(March 22, 2003).

SEE ALSO

Argonne National Laboratory
Brookhaven National Laboratory
DOE (United States Department of Energy)
Environmental Measurements Laboratory
Lawrence Berkeley National Laboratory
Lawrence Livermore National Laboratory (LLNL)
NNSA (United States National Nuclear Security Administration)
Oak Ridge National Laboratory (ORNL)
Pacific Northwest National Laboratory
Plum Island Animal Disease Center
Sandia National Laboratories

Loyalist Volunteer Force (LVF)

The Loyalist Volunteer Force (LVF) is an extreme loyalist group formed in 1996 as a faction of the mainstream loyalist Ulster Volunteer Force (UVF), though it did not emerge publicly until February, 1997. The LVF is composed largely of UVF hardliners who have sought to prevent a political settlement with Irish nationalists in Northern Ireland by attacking Catholic politicians, civilians, and Protestant politicians who endorse the Northern Ireland peace process. In October, 2001, the British Government ruled that the LVF had broken the cease-fire it declared in 1998. The LVF decommissioned a small but significant amount of weapons in December, 1998, but it has not repeated this gesture as of May, 2002. LVF participates in bombings, kidnappings, and close-quarter shooting attacks. LVF bombs often have contained Powergel commercial explosives, typical of many loyalist groups. LVF attacks have been particularly vicious: The group has murdered numerous Catholic civilians with no political or terrorist affiliations, including, in July 1997, an 18-year-old Catholic girl who had a Protestant boyfriend. The terrorists also have conducted successful attacks against Irish targets in Irish border towns. In 2000 and 2001, the LVF also engaged in a violent feud with other loyalists in which several individuals were killed.

LVF has approximately 150 activists who operate in Northern Ireland and Ireland.

■ **FURTHER READING:**

ELECTRONIC:

CDI (Center for Defense Information), Terrorism Project. CDI Fact Sheet: Current List of Designated Foreign Terrorist Organizations. March 27, 2003. <http://www.cdi.org/terrorism/terrorist.cfm> (April 17, 2003).

Central Intelligence Agency. World Factbook, 2002. <http://www.cia.gov/cia/publications/factbook/> (April 16, 2003).

Taylor, Francis X. U.S. Department of State. "Patterns of Global Terrorism 2001." Annual Report: On the Record Briefing. May 21, 2002 <http://www.state.gov/s/ct/rls/rm/10367.htm> (April 17,2003).

U.S. Department of State. Annual reports. <http://www.state.gov/www/global/terrorism/annual_reports.html> (April 16, 2003).

SEE ALSO

Terrorism, Philosophical and Ideological Origins
Terrorist and Para-State Organizations
Terrorist Organization List, United States
Terrorist Organizations, Freezing of Assets

MAD (Mutually Assured Destruction).

SEE *Strategic Defense Initiative and National Missile Defense.*

Mad Man Theory.

SEE *Cold War (1950–1972).*

Magic Chips (Micro Array of Gel-Immobilized Compounds).

SEE *Argonne National Laboratory.*

Mail Sanitization

■ BELINDA ROWLAND

Mail sanitization is the process in which mail is decontaminated by exposure to radiation, high pressure, or gases. Microorganisms, such as the bacterium that causes anthrax, cannot survive these conditions. The process of mail sanitization can be applied as a precautionary measure to kill microorganisms that may be contained in the mail or to sterilize mail that is known to be contaminated.

Shortly after the September 11, 2001, terrorist attacks, the United States Postal Service (USPS) was the vehicle for bioterrorism attacks on the American people. Mail containing the anthrax bacterium was detected. Five persons who were infected by the anthrax bacterium died from the disease. As a direct result of this, the USPS developed an Emergency Preparedness Plan with the goal of protecting USPS employees and customers from future bioterrorism attacks. The plan is composed of six initiatives:

■ Prevention—reducing the risk that the mail could be used as a vehicle for bioterrorism

■ Protection and health-risk reduction—reducing the risk that USPS employees and customers could be exposed to biological weapons and preventing contaminated mail from contaminating other mail

■ Detection and identification—detection and identification of biological weapons as early in the mail stream as possible

■ Intervention—routine decontamination of mail as a precautionary measure

■ Decontamination—elimination of known biological weapons in the mail

■ Investigation—enhancement of criminal investigation methods

Mail sanitization applies to the intervention and decontamination initiatives. Achieving mail safety is no small undertaking when one considers the complexity of the USPS system and volume of mail that is processed. The postal service handles nearly 680 million pieces of mail each day. This mail is primarily letters, "flats" such as catalogs and magazines, and packages. Mail enters the USPS system in many different ways including street collection boxes, post offices, personal mailboxes, and business mail entry units. The USPS has about 300 processing and distribution centers that manage outgoing mail. The computer-controlled sorting equipment and data processing systems located at these centers distribute mail to its destination. Mail is moved from processing and distribution centers to final destination processing centers by ground, rail, or air transportation. Once at a final destination processing center, mail is then sorted and distributed to the recipients.

Methods to Sanitize Mail

The USPS is studying several different methods of decontamination to find one (or more) that can effectively sanitize mail. To be useful in mail sanitization, the decontamination method must thoroughly penetrate letters, flats, and packages but not damage the mail in any way. As of late 2002, irradiation was the only acceptable method for decontaminating mail. The addition of a sanitization step to the USPS mail system may slow down the mail delivery rate.

Ionizing radiation. Ionizing radiation kills bacteria. The energy from ionizing radiation is absorbed by molecules, breaking chemical bonds and thus destroying chemical structures. Reactive chemicals (ions and free radicals) that are produced by this process cause even further damage. This results in significant damage to the DNA and proteins of bacteria and causes them to die.

The USPS is considering three sources of ionizing radiation as candidates for mail sanitization: x rays, gamma rays, and electron beams. All three are used to sterilize medical equipment and to kill microorganisms in food to prevent spoilage. They each can kill the anthrax bacteria. Radiation can easily penetrate and sanitize most types of mail, however, it may damage film, electronics, and live objects such as seeds.

X rays are a type of high-energy electromagnetic radiation. X-ray particles, or photons, are generated when electron-dense materials are bombarded by high-energy electrons. X rays have a high-energy content and can penetrate most objects.

Gamma rays are another type of high-energy electromagnetic radiation. Gamma rays are released by decaying radioactive compounds such as cesium 137 or cobalt 60.

An electron beam, or e-beam, is a stream of electrons that is propelled by an high accelerating voltage. The energy content of the e-beam is determined by the accelerating voltage and is lower than both x rays and gamma rays.

Of the three ionizing radiation sources, e-beam technology is the safest and most readily adaptable system for mail sanitization. In 2001, the USPS bought eight e-beam machines and planned to install them in Washington D.C. and the New York and New Jersey area. The e-beam machine requires high power and chilled water and must be contained by a structure with 10 to 15 foot-thick concrete walls and a six foot-thick concrete ceiling. As of late 2002, e-beam technology has been used to sanitize incoming federal government mail only.

Non-ionizing radiation. Types of non-ionizing radiation that have been used for sterilization are ultraviolet (UV) light and microwaves. Both are effective at killing microorganisms, but in different ways.

UV light radiation damages DNA by causing DNA strand breaks and binding DNA bases together (thymine dimers). Bacteria with damaged DNA cannot reproduce or survive. UV light radiation cannot penetrate objects and is used to sterilize surfaces and air only. In addition, some microorganisms are resistant to the effects of UV radiation. Therefore, UV radiation is an unacceptable method to sanitize mail.

Microwave radiation is a low energy non-ionizing radiation. The energy in microwaves is transferred to water molecules in microorganisms. The water molecules heat up and the heat is transferred to surrounding molecules, thereby damaging and ultimately killing the microorganism. Microwave radiation sanitization has shortcomings. Most importantly, it is difficult to control the heating effects and it is common to have "hot spots" and "cold spots." Also, the water content of dormant bacterial cells (spores) is low, so microwave radiation may not destroy them. Microwave radiation would be ineffective for mail sanitization.

Ultra-high-pressure sterilization. Ultra-high-pressure (UHP) sterilization is accomplished by applying a pressure of almost 100,000 psi, which causes physical changes to DNA and proteins. The resulting cellular damage kills the microorganisms. Without added heat, UHP sterilization techniques may be less effective against bacterial spores than against growing bacterial cells.

UHP sterilization is being developed for the food industry and has been shown to be effective on both solid and liquid foods. The UHP sterilization cycle time can be less than 30 minutes and the process is non-destructive to the object being sterilized. This method could be applied to mail as a sanitization method, however, a UHP sterilization system for mail will not be available for several years.

Gaseous treatment. Certain gases have anti-microbial properties and are used for disinfection and sterilization. The USPS has identified chlorine dioxide, ethylene oxide, methyl bromide, and ozone as candidates for gaseous sanitization.

- Chlorine dioxide: an oxidizer that disrupts proteins and protein synthesis. It was used to disinfect an office building that was contaminated with anthrax spores.
- Ethylene oxide: an alkylating agent that damages proteins, leading to bacterial or viral death. It is used to sterilize medical equipment.
- Methyl bromide: a toxic pesticide that has been used to fumigate large buildings. It is an ozone-depleting chemical and will not be used after 2006.
- Ozone: an oxidizing agent used to disinfect water and decontaminate unoccupied spaces. Its effect on spores is variable depending upon the specific bacterial strain.

Large amounts of gas would be needed to sterilize mail and it is not evident that gases can kill microorganisms within sealed letters, flats, and packages. Gaseous sterilization of mail is not currently a viable option for mail sanitization.

■ FURTHER READING:

PERIODICALS:

"Months After Anthrax Scare, Mail-Safety Goals are Unmet." *USA Today.* (August 29, 2002): 12a.

"USPS Builds to Sterilize Mail." *Engineering News-Record* no. 247 (November 26, 2001): 11.

ELECTRONIC:

United States Postal Service. <http://www.usps.com/welcome.htm.>(December 14, 2002).

SEE ALSO

Anthrax, Terrorist Use as a Biological Weapon
Bioterrorism, Protective Measures
Decontamination Methods
Postal Security
Postal Service (USPS), United States
Radiation, Biological Damage
September 11 Terrorist Attacks on the United States

Malicious Data

Malicious data is data that, when introduced to a computer—usually by an operator unaware that he or she is doing so—will cause the computer to perform actions undesirable to the computer's owner. It often takes the form of input to a computer application such as a word-processing or spreadsheet program. It is thus distinguished from a malicious program such as a computer virus, compared to which malicious data is perhaps even more stealthy.

An example of malicious data at work is the Melissa "virus," which spread through the e-mail systems of the world on March 26, 1999. Though the media called Melissa a virus, this was a misnomer; rather, it was a case of malicious data wedded to a macro virus, or a virus that works by setting in motion an automatic sequence of actions within a software application. Melissa did not damage computers themselves, yet it produced a result undesirable to anyone but its creator. By taking advantage of a feature built into the Microsoft Word program, it sent itself to the first 50 addresses in the user's Outlook Express, an e-mail program also produced by Microsoft. Melissa, for which computer programmer David L. Smith was eventually charged, caused $80 million worth of damage, primarily in the form of lost productivity resulting from the shutdown of overloaded mailboxes.

In practice, malicious data is much like a malicious program, yet it is difficult to protect against malicious data using the methods typically used to circumvent malicious programs, such as file access control, firewalls, and the like. Malicious data has been used not simply for pranks such as Smith's, but to transfer funds out of the operator's financial accounts, and into those of the perpetrator. In this crime, the operator him- or herself is a participant, albeit an unwitting and unwilling one.

■ FURTHER READING:

BOOKS:

Gelman, Robert B., and Stanton McCandlish. *Protecting Yourself Online: The Definitive Resource on Safety, Freedom, and Privacy in Cyberspace.* New York: HarperEdge, 1998.

Schneier, Bruce. *Secrets and Lies: Digital Security in a Networked World.* New York: John Wiley, 2000.

Schwartau, Winn. *Cybershock: Surviving Hackers, Phreakers, Identity Thieves, Internet Terrorists, and Weapons of Mass Disruption.* New York: Thunder's Mouth Press, 2000.

PERIODICALS:

Mitchell, Russ, Richard Folkers, and Susan Gregory. "Why Melissa Is So Scary." *U.S. News & World Report.* (April 12, 1999): 34–36.

ELECTRONIC:

Sibert, W. Olin. Malicious Data and Computer Security. <http://home.earthlink.net/~wolfboy/ARCHIVE/GenSecure/maldata.htm> (April 3, 2003).

SEE ALSO

Computer Hackers
Computer Software security
Computer Virus
Infrastructure Protection Center (NIPC), United States National

Manhattan Project

■ BRENDA WILMOTH LERNER

The Manhattan Project was an epic, secret, wartime effort to design and build the world's first nuclear weapon. Commanding the efforts of the world's greatest physicists and mathematicians during World War II, the $20 billion project resulted in the production of the first uranium and plutonium bombs. The American quest for nuclear explosives was driven by the fear that Hitler's Germany would invent them first and thereby gain a decisive military advantage. The monumental project took less than four years, and encompassed construction of vast facilities in Oak Ridge, Tennessee, and Hanford, Washington, that

Brigadier General Leslie Groves (second from left), shown in conversation with Manhattan project scientists Sir James Chadwick (left), Dr. Richard Tolman (second from right), and Dr. H. D. Smyth. ©HULTON-DEUTSCH COLLECTION/CORBIS.

were used for the purpose of obtaining sufficient quantities of the isotopes uranium-235 and plutonium-239, necessary to produce the fission chain reaction, which released the bombs' destructive energy. After a successful test in Alamogordo, New Mexico, the United States exploded a nuclear bomb on the Japanese city of Hiroshima on August 6, 1945. Three days later another bomb was dropped on the Japanese city of Nagasaki, and spurred the Japanese surrender that ended World War II.

In the 1930s and early 1940s, fundamental discoveries regarding the neutron and atomic physics allowed for the possibility of induced nuclear chain reactions. Danish physicist Neils Bohr's (1885–1962) compound nucleus theory, for example, laid the foundation for the theoretical exploration of fission, the process whereby the central part of an atom, the nucleus, absorbs a neutron, then breaks into two equal fragments. In certain elements, such as plutonium-239, the fragments release other neutrons which quickly break up more atoms, creating a chain reaction that releases large amounts of heat and radiation.

Hungarian physicist Leo Szilard (1898–1964) conceived the idea of the nuclear chain reaction in 1933, and immediately became concerned that, if practical, nuclear energy could be used to make weapons of war. Szilard, who fled Nazi persecution first in his native Hungary, then again in

Germany, conveyed his concerns to his friend and contemporary, noted physicist Albert Einstein (1879–1955). In 1939, the two scientists drafted a letter (addressed from Einstein) warning United States President Franklin D. Roosevelt of the plausibility of nuclear weapons, and of German experimentation with uranium and fission. In December, 1941, after the Japanese attack at Pearl Harbor and the United States' entry into the war, Roosevelt ordered a secret United States project to investigate the potential development of atomic weapons. The Army Corps of Engineers took over and in 1942 consolidated various atomic research projects into the intentionally misnamed Manhattan Engineering District (now commonly known as the Manhattan Project), which was placed under the command of Army Brigadier General Leslie Richard Groves.

Groves recruited American physicist Robert Oppenheimer (1904–1967) to be the scientific director for the Manhattan Project. Security concerns required the development of a central laboratory for physics weapon research in Los Alamos, New Mexico. Oppenheimer's leadership attracted many top young scientists, including American physicist Richard Feynman (1918–1988), who joined the Manhattan Project while still a graduate student. Feynman and his mentor Hans Bethe (1906–) calculated the critical mass fissionable material necessary to begin a chain reaction.

Fuel for the nuclear reaction was a primary concern. At the outset, the only materials seemingly satisfactory for sustaining an explosive chain reaction were either U-235 (derived from U-238) or P-239 (an isotope of the yet unsynthesized element plutonium). Additional requirements included an abundant supply of heavy water (e.g., deuterium and tritium). At Oak Ridge, the process of gaseous diffusion was used to extract the U-235 isotope from uranium ore. At Hanford, production of P-239 was eventually made possible by leaving plutonium-238 in a nuclear reactor for an extended period of time.

In 1942, Italian physicist Enrico Fermi (1901–1954) supervised the first controlled sustained chain reaction at the University of Chicago. Underneath the university football stadium, in modified squash courts, Fermi and his team assembled a lattice of 57 layers of uranium metal and uranium oxide embedded in graphite blocks to create the first reactor pile.

The Manhattan Project eventually produced four bombs. Little Boy, the code name for the uranium bomb, utilized explosives to crash pieces of uranium together to begin an explosive chain reaction. Fat Man, the code name for the plutonium bomb, was more difficult to design. It required a neutron-emitting source to initiate a chain reaction within a series of concentric nested spheres. The outermost shell was an explosive lens system surrounding a pusher/neutron absorber shell designed to reduce the effect of Taylor waves, the rapid drop in pressure that occurs behind a detonation front and could interfere with an implosion. The next nested sphere was a uranium tamper/reflector shell containing a plutonium pit and beryllium neutron initiator. The spheres were designed to implode, causing the plutonium to fuse, reach critical mass, then start the reaction

The simple design of the uranium bomb left scientists confident of its success, but the complicated implosion trigger required by the plutonium bomb raised engineering concerns about reliability. On July 16, 1945, a plutonium test bomb code named Gadget was detonated in a remote area near Alamogordo, New Mexico. Observed by scientists wearing only welder's glasses and suntan lotion for protection, the test blast (code named Trinity) was more powerful than originally thought, roughly equivalent to 20,000 tons of TNT, and caused total destruction up to one mile from the blast center.

Protecting the secrecy of the Manhattan Project was one of the most complex intelligence and security operations during the war. At the Los Alamos facility, all residents were confined to the project area and surrounding town. Though several leading scientists knew the nature and scope of the entire project, most lab facilities were compartmentalized with various teams working on different project elements. Those who worked in the lab were forbidden to discuss any aspect of the project with friends or relatives. Military security personnel guarded the grounds and monitored communications between research teams. Official communications outside of Los Alamos, especially to the other Manhattan Project sites, were coded

and enciphered. Mail was permitted, but heavily censored. Since the actual location of the Los Alamos facility was secret, all residents used the clandestine address "Box 1663, Santa Fe, New Mexico," for correspondence.

Communities were created around other project sites as well. The government created the towns of Oak Ridge and Hanford, relocating thousands of area residents before beginning construction. The towns, thus secured for facility personnel and their families, placed severe restrictions on civilian activities. In some areas, private telephones and radios were prohibited. Residents were encouraged to use simple pseudonyms outside of the lab. Children did not use their full names in school in Oak Ridge, Tennessee.

Managing several different facilities, spaced nearly two thousand miles apart, raised some significant security challenges. Communication was limited, and incoming and outgoing traffic from facility areas was closely monitored. Security of key documents was a constant concern. The isolated locations of the sites helped to insulate them from enemy espionage. However, the separate locations were also a key security strategy. Breaking the Manhattan Project into various smaller operations prevented jeopardizing the entire project in the event of a nuclear accident. The compartmentalization of such projects remains a common practice.

On August 6, 1945, an American B-29 "Flying Fortress," the *Enola Gay,* dropped the uranium bomb over Hiroshima. Sixty thousand people were killed instantly, and another 200,000 subsequently died as a result of burn and radiation injuries. Three days later, a plutonium bomb was dropped over Nagasaki. Although it missed its actual target by over a mile, the more powerful plutonium bomb killed or injured more than 65,000 people and destroyed half of the city. Ironically, ground zero, the point under the bomb explosion, turned out to be the Mitsubishi Arms Manufacturing Plant, at one time the major military target in Nagasaki. The fourth bomb remained unused.

Many Manhattan Project scientists eventually became advocates of the peaceful use of nuclear power and advocates for nuclear weapons control.

■ FURTHER READING:

BOOKS:

Fermi, Rachel, and Esther Samra. *Picturing the Bomb: Photographs from the Secret World of the Manhattan Project.* New York: H. N. Abrams, 1995.

Norris, Richard. *Racing For the Bomb: General Leslie R. Groves, the Manhattan Project's Indispensable Man.* South Royalton, VT: Steerforth Press, 2002.

Rhodes, Richard. *The Making of the Atomic Bomb.* New York: Touchstone, 1995 (reprint).

ELECTRONIC:

Los Alamos National Laboratory. Manhattan Project History. "The Italian Navigator Has Landed in the New

World. Secret Race Won with Chicago's Chain Reaction"<http://www.lanl.gov/worldview/welcome/history.shtml> (February, 24, 2003).

National Atomic Museum, Albuquerque, New Mexico. "The Manhattan Project." <http://www.atomicmuseum.com/tour/manhattanproject.cfm>(February 24, 2003).

SEE ALSO

Heavy Water Technology
Los Alamos National Laboratory
Nuclear Detection Devices
Nuclear Reactors
Nuclear Regulatory Commission (NRC), United States
Nuclear Weapons
Oak Ridge National Laboratory (ORNL)
Quantum Physics: Applications to Espionage, Intelligence, and Security Issues
Weapons of Mass Destruction

Mapping Technology

■ WILLIAM C. HANEBERG

Mapping technology is a broad term that describes the equipment and techniques used to prepare, analyze, and distribute maps of all kinds. This can include satellites used to obtain high resolution and multispectral data; software to enhance or classify digital images; global positioning system (GPS) satellites; and geographic information systems (GIS).

Intelligence-related mapping within the United States is largely the responsibility of the National Imagery and Mapping Agency. It was formed in 1996 by consolidating the capabilities of several federal agencies involved with the acquisition and analysis of imagery and other forms of geospatial intelligence. The U.S. Geological Survey, a civilian agency within the Department of the Interior, produces detailed topographic and geologic maps of areas within the United States.

One of the primary uses of mapping technology is to gather data from which maps can be made. Classified images from intelligence satellites and sub-meter resolution images from both government and commercial satellites can be used to obtain information about the civil and military infrastructure of foreign powers without having to set foot in dangerous or restricted areas. Technologies such as interferometric synthetic aperture radar (InSAR) can be used to create digital elevation models (DEMs) depicting the elevation of the Earth's surface and serve as the basis for detailed topographic maps. The Shuttle Radar Topography Mission, flown in February 2000, used specialized InSAR technology to map the elevation of Earth's land surface between 60 degrees north and 56 degrees south latitude. Elevations were measured every arc-second of latitude and longitude, which is equivalent to a spacing of about 30 m. Detailed topographic information such as that collected by the Shuttle Radar Topography Mission can be used to create topographic maps that are essential to military operations or to depict realistic landscapes in combat training simulators.

Multispectral imagery is created using sensors that respond to different bands within the visible and invisible portions of the electromagnetic spectrum. An image that appears to be a color photograph may actually be a color composite composed of, at minimum, red, blue, and green bands. Hyperspectral images are those in which the spectrum is divided into many narrow bands instead of several broad bands. Multispectral or hyperspectral image processing can be used to make inferences about soil or bedrock type, soil moisture, crop growth, chemical pollution, and other properties. Military or intelligence applications can include the determination of the ground conditions to be encountered by an invasion force or estimation of an enemy's crop production. Domestic applications include monitoring elements of a nation's infrastructure, for example unguarded energy transmission lines that are vital to national security and may present targets to terrorist networks.

The global positioning system (GPS) is a network of 24 satellites orbiting Earth at an altitude of 20,200 m (12.55 mi). Launched and maintained by the United States military, the satellites issue signals that can be decoded by GPS receivers to determine the location of the receiver and the time within several hundred nanoseconds. While it is principally a navigational system, GPS is also an important piece of mapping technology. Scientists, geographers, land surveyors, and others can use GPS to determine with great accuracy the locations of objects to be shown on maps. GPS receivers installed on moving vehicles, for example trucks carrying nuclear materials, allow them to be continuously tracked and maps of their locations updated in real time.

Geographic information system (GIS) software allows users to digitally store, retrieve, analyze, and display maps of all kinds. Maps created using different scales or projections can be adjusted and combined to form new composite maps that answer specific questions. For example, a GIS user can combine a computer model of air pollution dispersion with meteorological and troop location data to simulate the effects of possible chemical weapons attacks in different locations. GIS is likewise useful for homeland security projects such as constructing maps of critical infrastructure, developing emergency response plans, and evaluating the consequences of terrorist attacks.

■ FURTHER READING:

BOOKS:

Burrough, P. A., and R. A. McDonnell. *Principles of Geographic Information Systems,* 2nd ed. Oxford: University Press,1998.

Wilford, G. N. *The Mapmakers.* New York: Knopf, 2000.

ELECTRONIC:

National Imagery and Mapping Agency. "NIMA Home." <http://www.nima.mil/>(December 9, 2002).

National Imagery and Mapping Agency. "Shuttle Radar Topography Mission Navigation Page." October 11, 2002. <http://www.nima.mil/srtm/navigation.html> (December 9, 2002).

Dana, Peter H. "The Global Positioning System." May 1, 2000. <http://www.colorado.Edu/geography/gcraft/notes/gps/gps_f.html> (December 9, 2002).

Lawrence Livermore National Laboratory. "GIS Group Home Page." August 24, 2000. <http://gis.llnl.gov/indexm.html>(December 9, 2002).

SEE ALSO

Geospatial Imagery
NIMA (National Imagery and Mapping Agency)
Photographic Interpretation Center (NPIC), United States National
Photography, High-Altitude
RADAR, Synthetic Aperture
Satellites, Non-Governmental High Resolution

Marine Mammal Program

■ JULI BERWALD

The U.S. Navy has used marine mammals, or cetaceans, for military purposes since the late 1950s. Atlantic bottlenose dolphins, Pacific white-sided dolphins, and California sea lions are currently used in military operations, and training has also been conducted with belugas, killer whales, and pilot whales. Because dolphins have superior sonar that is currently unmatched by technology and sea lions have an excellent sense of directional hearing along with sensitive low light vision, these marine mammals are extremely well suited for search and rescue and swimmer defense operations.

History of marine mammals in the military.

In the 1959, the United States Navy established a marine mammal program at Marineland near Los Angeles, California. Naval researchers were initially interested in studying the hydrodynamics of dolphin swimming in order to better understand boat and submarine design. Dolphins can attain high swimming speeds and can maintain those speeds for long periods of time. Marine scientists found that the dolphin's keen sense of echolocation was ideal for finding lost equipment on the sea floor and for locating enemy mines and torpedoes. In addition, dolphins are extremely intelligent and trainable. One of the first dolphins involved with the program was a Pacific white-sided dolphin named Notty.

In 1962, the marine mammal program was moved to Point Magu, California. Three years later, the Point Magu program established an underwater laboratory called Sea Lab II, which was 200 feet below the surface of the ocean. There a dolphin named Tuffy was trained to work with divers in experiments designed to see if the use of dolphins might help circumvent the dangers to humans inherent in deepwater diving. Tuffy's work also showed that dolphins could easily be trained to work without tethers in the open ocean. The successes of Sea Lab II led to the establishment of the Advanced Marine Biological Systems (AMBS) program, which currently funds military marine mammal programs.

In 1967, the marine mammal program was moved from Point Magu to Point Loma in San Diego, and a separate marine mammal training facility was opened in the Marine Corps Air Station in Kaneohe Bay, Hawaii. Both of these programs investigated the physiology and behavior of cetaceans, developed techniques for medical diagnosis and treatment, and worked to understand the communicative noises made by dolphins. In Hawaii, research was also conducted on the reproductive physiology of dolphins. In addition, investigators studied the cost and safety benefits of using marine mammals. In 1993, the facility at Kaneohe Bay was closed and most of the marine mammals were relocated to Point Loma.

During the Cold War, the Soviet Union also developed a marine mammal program. Dolphins were trained to search for underwater explosives and were used to guard coastal waters from attack. After the dissolution of the Soviet Union, the dolphins became part of the Ukrainian navy. In 1997, the Ukrainian navy donated the dolphins to a program that uses the animals in therapy for disabled children.

Training and maintenance.

The U.S. Navy maintains the marine mammals in their training and operational programs in open-mesh enclosures in bays and harbors in the ocean. This allows the dolphins to experience their natural echolocation and social environments. During training, the animals are untethered in the open ocean. All operational training is based on positive reinforcement, using food for rewards. Animals are not punished for failure to perform tasks by withholding food. Survival rates for the marine mammals maintained by the navy are between 95 and 100 percent. During thousands of training exercises in the open ocean over a 30-year period, only seven animals have not returned to their enclosures.

Several groups have criticized the navy's marine mammal program, citing undue stress to and mistreatment of animals used for military purposes. In the 1980s, the Progressive Animal Welfare Society (PAWS) successfully sued the navy to halt its marine mammal program in Washington State. However, a committee appointed by the president reviewed the program in 1988 and 1990 and gave satisfactory or outstanding ratings to all aspects of the program. The National Marine Fisheries (NMFs) reported that survival rates of dolphins in the program were the highest of all organizations maintaining large numbers of cetaceans.

U.S. Navy Sergeant Andrew Garrett with K-Dog, a bottle-nose dolphin who was being trained for mine-clearing operations in support of Operation Iraqi Freedom, 2003. AP/WIDE WORLD PHOTOS.

Marine Mammal Systems. The navy currently operates four Marine Mammal Systems (MMS) as part of its fleet. An operational MMS consists of four to eight marine mammals, an officer-in-charge, and several enlisted personnel. Before a MMS is approved for operations, it undergoes the same type of rigorous testing as other operational naval systems. It must prove effective and reliable as well as cost effective. Marine Mammal Systems are highly transportable and can be airlifted to any operational site. SPAWAR (Space and Naval Systems Center, San Diego) supports a deployed MMS, replenishing animals and providing training, documentation, and personnel.

The four operational MMS include both dolphin and sea lion systems. Mk4 and Mk7 are dolphin mine detection and location systems. They can be deployed from a ship in order to search for and mark mines that are tethered to the ocean floor. Mk5 is a sea lion mine detection system, which can detect mines to a depth of 1000 feet. The sea lions are trained to attach a grabber device to a mine so that naval personnel can recover it. Mk6 is a dolphin swimmer defense system. Dolphins are trained to locate an intruder trying to come ashore via the ocean.

Although dolphins and sea lions are the only marine mammals currently used in military operations, pilot whales, killer whales and beluga whales have also been involved with object search and recovery. These cetaceans have the ability to dive to extreme depths, much beyond those attainable by human divers. A project called Deep Ops studied the abilities of pilot whales and killer whales to recover objects from deep depths. The pilot whale was able to successfully recover a dummy torpedo from a depth of 1,654 feet using a gas-inflated recovery device. The killer whales recovered objects from 500 and 850 feet. Belugas were able to dive to 2,100 feet and were able to recover dummy torpedoes from 1,300 feet.

Marine mammal deployments. The military first used the dolphin swimmer detection system in the Vietnam War in 1970. This successful operation, which involved dolphins patrolling the waters near warships, brought an end to underwater sabotage in Cam Ranh Bay.

In 1987 and 1988, the navy used dolphins for mine surveillance in waters off Bahrain in the Persian Gulf. The animals patrolled the waters for mines and escorted Kuwaiti tankers through areas where the Iranian military was attempting to disrupt oil shipments.

Marine mammal systems were in operation during the Republican Party Convention in 1996. Both dolphin mine detection and location systems and sea lion swimmer defense systems were used to protect the waters off of San Diego from terrorist attack.

After British forces took control of the southern Iraq port city of Umm Qasr in 2003, the U.S. Navy brought in Atlantic bottlenose dolphins to search the bay for mines and mark them for destruction by human divers. Sea lions were also deployed around ships in Bahrain to detect and defend against armed swimmers. These sea lions were trained to attach floater devices to intruders so that security officers could apprehend them.

■ **FURTHER READING:**

ELECTRONIC:

Bulletin of Atomic Scientists. "U.S., Ukraine at cross porpoises." <http://www.bullatomsci.org/issues/1997/nd97/nd97bulletins.html> (April 22, 2003).

Dolphins of War. <http://www.angelfire.com/nj4/navy dolphins/> (April 22, 2003).

MSNBC News. "Dolphins go to front lines in Iraq war." <http://www.msnbc.com/news/890520.asp> (March 25, 2003).

Public Broadcasting System. "The Story of Navy Dolphins." <http://www.pbs.org/wgbh/pages/frontline/shows/whales/etc/navycron.html> (April 22, 2003).

U.S. Navy Marine Mammal Program. <http://www.spawar.navy.mil/sandiego/technology/mammals/> (April 22, 2003).

SEE ALSO

Unexploded Ordnance and Mines

McCarthyism

■ JOSEPH PATTERSON HYDER

In the early 1950s, Joseph McCarthy, a U.S. Senator from Wisconsin, conducted highly publicized congressional hearings to uncover subversive elements within American culture, government, and military. For over three years, McCarthy used questionable means to uncover information about suspects. The McCarthy era represents the height of the post-war "Red scare" and demonstrates the degree to which paranoia about subversive communist activities had gripped America.

The wartime Alien Registration Act of 1940 laid the foundation for McCarthyism. This act required that all aliens over the age of 14 residing in the United States register with the American government. Each resident alien had to file a report detailing his or her political beliefs and work status. The act also made it illegal for anyone to plan to overthrow the government of the United States.

The Alien Registration Act had a twofold purpose. First, with American involvement in World War II likely, Congress hoped the act would help identify potential wartime saboteurs. The government wanted to avoid a repeat of the situation in World War I, when German-supported saboteurs and German sympathizers targeted

Dalton Trumbo, left, and John Howard Lawson, two screenwriters of the Hollywood Ten, smile and wave from inside a U.S. Marshal's van after receiving prison sentences for refusing to testify before the House Un-American Activities Committee. AP/WIDE WORLD PHOTOS.

American industry and shipping that aided the European war effort. By acquiring a detailed work history of aliens, the government sought to identify potential problems before they occurred. The second and primary objective of the Alien Registration Act was to identify elements of the American Communist Party or other socialist organizations.

It was subsequently determined that the existing House Un-American Activities Committee (HUAC) would serve as the body that would seek out subversive elements. In 1947, HUAC began a campaign to rid Hollywood of all leftist elements. In a series of highly publicized congressional hearings, some individuals in the entertainment industry identified their peers as belonging to questionable leftist organizations, including the American Communist Party.

In an effort to avoid further embarrassing hearings and to regain public trust, Hollywood studios drew up a blacklist of individuals suspected of belonging to or having an interest in subversive organizations. These individuals found it difficult to work in Hollywood until they

had cleared their names before HUAC. The blacklist included many well-known celebrities, including Charlie Chaplain, Burl Ives, Leonard Bernstein, Aaron Copeland, and Arthur Miller.

The Hollywood blacklist and the HUAC hearings fed the atmosphere of suspicion that gripped American society. To the public, the threat of a complex communist plot to infiltrate American society and government seemed tangible. The high-profile HUAC hearings, combined with the well-publicized Rosenberg and Alger Hiss trials, served to reinforce this sentiment. In the fall of 1949, the government began a crackdown, arresting most of the leadership of the American Communist Party and charging them under the Alien Registration Act.

In February 1950, Joseph McCarthy became involved in the search for subversive elements within the government. McCarthy claimed to have a list containing the names of State Department employees belonging to the American Communist Party. McCarthy's list did not contain any arcane knowledge, having been compiled by the

State Department several years earlier following an internal investigation. Additionally, most of the names were on the list for other questionable behaviors. Few members on the list had any current or previous ties to the Communist Party.

McCarthy took to the pulpit when he became chairman of the Government Committee on Operations of the Senate. Using his position, McCarthy began investigating possible Communist infiltration of various government agencies. McCarthy worked closely with the Federal Bureau of Investigation and his close friend, J. Edgar Hoover. The FBI supplied McCarthy with the information that he needed to keep his committee hearings effective. Government employees found to have ties to the Communist Party or other left-wing groups were removed from office and forced to divulge the names of other individuals affiliated with leftist organizations.

McCarthy's committee also targeted the Overseas Library Program. The Government Committee on Operations of the Senate identified and banned over 30,000 books thought to have been written by communist sympathizers or to contain procommunist themes. Many public libraries across the United States removed these books from their shelves.

McCarthy's operations further expanded into the realm of American politics. His committee conducted disinformation campaigns to thwart the reelection bids of politicians that opposed him. McCarthy even targeted the Truman administration, including President Harry S. Truman himself and cabinet member George Marshall, the renowned architect of the postwar Marshall Plan, for supporting the New Deal and for being perceived as soft on communism in Korea. McCarthy supported Dwight D. Eisenhower's presidential campaign in 1952, and in return, Eisenhower allowed McCarthy to continue his anti-Communist hearings.

In October 1953, after nearly three years of targeting civilian agencies, McCarthy set his sights on identifying and removing subversive elements within the United States Army. Eisenhower, a former army general, decided to stop him. Vice-president Richard M. Nixon spoke out, asserting that McCarthy was motivated not by concern for his country but by a desire for personal aggrandizement. It was revealed that McCarthy had tried to prevent the army from drafting one of his staff members, G. David Schine. After failing in that attempt, McCarthy and his chief counsel, Roy Cohn, had petitioned Stevens to grant special privileges to Schine. The Schine affair prompted McCarthy to target Secretary Stevens: when Stevens refused his request, McCarthy claimed that the army was holding Schine hostage in order to prevent his committee from uncovering communist elements within their ranks.

McCarthy determined that Congress should investigate the matter. He also sealed his fate by allowing television cameras to air the Army-McCarthy hearings. During the hearings, McCarthy and Cohn sought to characterize the army as an organization riddled with subversive elements. Throughout the hearings, McCarthy appeared rude to an attentive television audience. On the other hand, a personable attorney, Joseph Welch, represented the army. It was Welch who ultimately destroyed McCarthy's credibility with his retort to McCarthy, "Have you no sense of decency, sir, at long last? Have you left no sense of decency?" A bewildered McCarthy did not realize that the power that he once wielded had been crushed before a national television audience. In December 1954, Congress censured Joseph McCarthy by a vote of 67–22.

■ FURTHER READING:

BOOKS:

Fried, Albert. *McCarthyism: The Great American Red Scare: A Documentary History.* Oxford: Oxford University Press, 1996.

Reeves, Thomas C. *The Life and Times of Joe McCarthy: A Biography.* Madison, WI: Madison Books, 1997.

Schrecker, Ellen. *The Age of McCarthyism.* New York: St. Martin's, 1994.

SEE ALSO

Cold War (1945–1950), The Start of the Atomic Age
KGB (Komitet Gosudarstvennoi Bezopasnosti, USSR Committee of State Security)
Rosenberg (Ethel and Julius) Espionage Case
Venona

Measurement and Signatures Intelligence (MASINT)

Measurement and signature intelligence (MASINT) is the term for forms of information gathered by analysis of signals (SIGINT), imagery (IMINT), or data acquired through human contact (HUMINT). In the United States, MASINT operations are directed by the Central Measurement and Signatures Office, usually designated as Central MASINT Office or CMO, which is an office of the Defense Intelligence Agency (DIA).

Under the heading of MASINT are the following subcategories: acoustic intelligence (ACINT), infrared intelligence (IRINT), laser intelligence (LASINT), nuclear intelligence (NUCINT), optical intelligence (OPINT), and unintentional radiation intelligence (RINT).

Components of MASINT. ACINT, as its name implies, involves the collection and analysis of data derived from sound waves. Most notable among these are the acoustic markings or "signatures" of military vessels and the weapons they carry, which can be detected by sonar (SOund NAvigation and Ranging) devices underwater. There is some overlap with LASINT, which can be used for audio monitoring. A laser is an extremely narrow, powerful, and focused beam of light. In the LASINT context, a laser beam directed at a closed room can be used to detect the vibrations produced by sound waves.

The term OPINT encompasses all intelligence derived across the spectrum of visible light, as well as light that has been made visible. It is contrasted with IMINT, which is concerned specifically with electronically generated images. Some of the visible material that falls under the purview of OPINT may have been obtained by special equipment that captures light from the infrared portion of the electromagnetic spectrum, and thus once again there may be some overlap, in this case with IRINT.

Infrared waves (lower in frequency than the red, or lowest-frequency, end of the visible spectrum) may also provide a means for radio communication. For instance, in the 1960s, West Germany developed a device that sent and received audible messages, using the infrared range as a medium of transmission. (By contrast, ordinary radio and television transmission occurs at frequencies much lower than that of infrared light.)

Unintentional radiation intelligence (RINT) also involves monitoring of the electromagnetic spectrum, although in this case, for non-information-bearing elements of intelligence. For example, highly radioactive material of the type that might be used in a sophisticated nuclear device, may emit gamma rays, which occupy the highest energy level in the electromagnetic spectrum. Once more, there may be overlap with nuclear intelligence or NUCINT, which is defined as information derived from the collection and analysis of radiation from radioactive sources.

The U.S. Central MASINT Office.

The office responsible for MASINT is the Defense Intelligence Agency's CMO. By 1986, the U.S. intelligence community had come to recognize the need for a MASINT office, and in that year formed the Intelligence Community Staff MASINT Committee to oversee all relevant activities. As part of the 1992 reorganization of the intelligence community, the secretary of defense and the director of the CIA gave the director of DIA responsibility over national and defense MASINT. A year later, DIA established CMO, which reports to the director of DIA.

CMO consists of four divisions, designated as CMO–1, 2, 3, and 4. The first of these is responsible for developing national and defense policy, including long-term plans, and for establishing the interface between MASINT and other intelligence-gathering disciplines. CMO-2 is responsible for resource management, or the management of MASINT assets nationally and worldwide. CMO–3 oversees

MASINT collection operations, and is responsible for time-sensitive and short-turnaround jobs. CMO–4, the Advanced Concepts Division, manages research, development, testing, and evaluation.

■ FURTHER READING:

BOOKS:

Richelson, Jeffrey T. *The U.S. Intelligence Community*, third edition. Boulder, CO: Westview Press, 1995.

Scanlon, Charles Francis. *In Defense of the Nation: DIA at Forty Years.* Washington, D.C.: Defense Intelligence Agency, 2002.

ELECTRONIC:

Evaluation Report on Measurement and Signature Intelligence. <http://www.fas.org/irp/program/masint_evaluation_rep.htm> (January 17, 2003).

SEE ALSO

Lasers
Nuclear Detection Devices

Metal Detectors

■ LARRY GILMAN

Metal detectors use electromagnetic fields to detect the presence of metallic objects. They exist in a variety of walk-through, hand-held, and vehicle-mounted models and are used to search personnel for hidden metallic objects at entrances to airports, public schools, courthouses, and other guarded spaces; to hunt for landmines, archaeological artifacts, and miscellaneous valuables; and for the detection of hidden or unwanted metallic objects in industry and construction. Metal detectors detect metallic objects, but do not image them. An x-ray baggage scanner, for example, is not classed as a metal detector because it images metallic objects rather than merely detecting their presence.

Metal detectors use electromagnetism in two fundamentally different ways, active and passive. (1) Active detection methods illuminate some detection space—the opening of a walk-through portal, for example, or the space directly in front of a hand-held unit—with a time-varying electromagnetic field. Energy reflected from or passing through the detection space is affected by the presence of conductive material in that space; the detector detects metal by measuring these effects. (2) Passive detection methods do not illuminate the detection space, but take advantage of the fact that every unshielded detection space is already permeated by the Earth's natural

FBI agents use metal detectors to search for evidence in a series of sniper attacks that occurred in the Washington, D.C., area in 2002. AP/WIDE WORLD PHOTOS.

magnetic field. Ferromagnetic objects moving through the detection space cause temporary, but detectable changes in this natural field. (Ferromagnetic objects are made of metals, such as iron, that are capable of being magnetized; many metals, such as aluminum, are conducting but not ferromagnetic, and cannot be detected by passive means.)

Walk-through metal detectors. Walk-through or portal detectors are common in airports, public buildings, and military installations. Their portals are bracketed with two large coils or loop-type antennae, one a source and the other a detector. Electromagnetic waves (in this case, low-frequency radio waves) are emitted by the source coil into the detection space. When the electromagnetic field of the transmitted wave impinges on a conducting object, it induces transient currents on the surface of the object; these currents, in turn, radiate electromagnetic waves. These secondary waves are sensed by the detector coil.

Hand-carried metal detectors. Metal detectors small enough to be hand-held are often used at security checkpoints to localize metal objects whose presence has been detected by a walk-through system. Some units are designed to be carried by a pedestrian scanning for metal objects in the ground (e.g., nails, loose change, landmines). All such

devices operate on variations of the same physical principle as the walk-through metal detector, that is, they emit time-varying electromagnetic fields and listen for waves coming back from conducting objects. Some ground-search models further analyze the returned fields to distinguish various common metals from each other. Hand-carried metal detectors have long been used to search for landmines; however, modern land mines are often made largely of plastic to avoid this cheap and obvious countermeasure. New technologies, especially neutron activation analysis and ground-penetrating radar, are being developed to search for nonmetallic landmines.

Gradiometer metal detectors. Gradiometer metal detectors are passive systems that exploit the effect of moving ferromagnetic objects on the earth's magnetic field. A gradiometer is an instrument that measures a gradient—the difference in magnitude between two points—in a magnetic field. When a ferromagnetic object moves through a gradiometer metal detector's detection space, it causes a temporary disturbance in the earth's magnetic field, and this disturbance (if large enough) is detected. Gradiometer metal detectors are usually walk-through devices, but can also be mounted on a vehicle such as a police car, with the intent of detecting ferromagnetic weapons (e.g., guns) borne by persons approaching the vehicle. Gradiometer metal detectors are limited to the detection of ferromagnetic objects and so are not suitable for security situations

where a would-be evader of the system is likely to have access to nonferromagnetic weapons.

Magnetic imaging portals.

The magnetic imaging portal is a relatively new technology. Like traditional walk-through metal detectors, it illuminates its detection space with radio-frequency electromagnetic waves; however, it does so using a number of small antennas arranged ringlike around its portal, pointing inward. Each of these antennas transmits in turn to the antennas on the far side of the array; each antenna acts as a receiver whenever it is not transmitting. A complete scan of the detection space can take place in the time it takes a person to walk through the portal. Using computational techniques adapted from computed axial tomography (CAT) scanning, a crude image of the person (or other object) inside the portal is calculated and displayed. The magnetic imaging portal may for some purposes be classed as a metal detector rather than as an imaging system because it does not produce a detailed image of the metal object detected, but only reveals its location and approximate size.

■ FURTHER READING:

ELECTRONIC:

"Guide to the Technologies of Concealed Weapon and Contraband Imaging and Detection (NIJ Guide 602–00)." Institute of Justice, US Department of Justice. February 2001. <http://www.ojp.usdoj.gov/nij/pubs-sum/184432. htm> (April 23, 2003).

Meteorology and Weather Alteration

■ AGNES GALAMBOSI

Up to 40 percent of the estimated $10 trillion U.S. economy is affected by weather and climate each year. The National Aeronautics and Space Administration (NASA) and the National Oceanic and Atmospheric Administration (NOAA) are the two U.S. agencies with primary responsibility for developing technology related to earth observation (e.g., the design and operation of weather satellites) and meteorological monitoring.

Meteorology is a science that studies the processes and phenomena of the atmosphere. Meteorology consists of many areas: physical meteorology, dealing with physical aspects of the atmosphere such as rain or cloud formation; synoptic meteorology, the analysis and forecast of large-scale weather systems; dynamic meteorology, which is based on the laws of theoretical physics; climatology,

the study of the climate of an area; aviation meteorology, researching weather information for aviation; atmospheric chemistry, examining the chemical composition and processes in the atmosphere; atmospheric optics, analyzing the optical phenomena of the atmosphere such as halos or rainbows; or agricultural meteorology, studying the relationship between weather and vegetation.

In his book *Meteorologica,* written c. 340 B.C., Greek philosopher and scientist Aristotle (384 – 322 B.C.) was the first to record the use of the term meteorology. Aristotle's work summarized the knowledge of the day concerning atmospheric phenomena. He speculatively wrote about clouds, rain, snow, wind, and climatic changes, and although many of his findings later proved to be incorrect, many of them were insightful.

The fourteenth-century invention of weather measuring instruments made scientific study of atmospheric phenomena possible, but it was the seventeenth century inventions of the thermometer, barometer (a device used to measure atmospheric pressure), and anemometer (a device used for measuring wind speed) that laid the foundation for modern meteorological observation. In 1802, the first cloud classification system was formulated, and in 1805, a wind scale was first introduced. These measuring instruments and new ideas made possible the gathering of actual data from the atmosphere that, in turn, provided the basis for the advancement of scientific theories involving atmospheric structure, properties (pressure, temperature, humidity, etc.), and governing physical laws.

In the early 1840s, the first weather forecasting services started with ability to transmit observational data via telegraph. At that time, meteorology was still in the descriptive phase, still on an empirical basis with few scientific theories.

Meteorological science was spurred by World War I military demands. Norwegian physicist Vilhelm Bjerknes (1862–1951) introduced a modern meteorological theory stating that weather patterns in the temperate middle latitudes are the results of the interaction between warm and cold air masses. His description of atmospheric phenomena and forecasting techniques were based on the laws of physics and provided a template for modern dynamic meteorological modeling. By assuming a given set of atmospheric conditions to which were applied governing physical laws, meteorologists could make predictions about future weather and climatic conditions.

By the 1940s, upper-level measurements of pressure, temperature, wind, and humidity provided detailed insight into the vertical properties of the atmosphere. In the 1940s, Englishman R. C. Sutcliffe and Swede S. Peterssen developed three-dimensional analysis and forecasting methods. American military pilots flying above the Pacific during World War II discovered a strong stream of air rapidly flowing from west to east, which became known as the jet stream—an important factor in the movement of air masses. Weather radar first came into use in the United

The Norman Doppler Radar stands beneath ominous-looking clouds at the National Severe Storms Laboratory in Norman, Oklahoma. AP/WIDE WORLD PHOTOS.

States in 1949 with the efforts of Horace Byers (1906–1998) and R. R. Braham. Conventional weather radar shows precipitation location and intensity. Ultimately, the development of radar, rockets, and satellites greatly improved data collection and weather forecasting.

In 1946, the process of cloud seeding made possible early weather modification experiments. In the 1950s, radar became important for detecting precipitation of a remote area. Also in the 1950s, with the invention of the computer, weather forecasting became not only quicker but also more reliable, because the computers could more rapidly solve the mathematical equations of atmospheric models. In 1960, the first meteorological satellite was launched.

Satellites now give three-dimensional data to high-speed computers for faster and more precise weather predictions. Modern computers are capable of plotting observational data, and performing both short term and long term modeling analysis ranging from next day weather forecasting to decades long climatic models. Even so, the computers still have their capacity limits, the models still have many uncertainties, and the effects of the atmosphere on our complex society and environment can be serious. Many complicated issues remain at the forefront of meteorology, including air pollution, global warming, El Niño events, climate change, ozone hole or acid rain,

making meteorology a scientific area still fraught with challenges and unanswered questions.

Weather forecasting. Weather forecasting is the attempt by meteorologists to predict the state of the atmosphere at a near future time and the weather conditions that may be expected. Many military planners consider weather to be a "force multiplier" (i.e., forces prepared to operate effectively in adverse conditions can fare substantially better than unprepared forces). Accurate weather forecasts are especially critical to the tactical operation of aviation and naval forces.

In the United States, weather forecasting is the responsibility of the National Weather Service (NWS), a division of the National Oceanic and Atmospheric Administration (NOAA) of the Department of Commerce. NWS maintains more than 400 field offices and observatories in all 50 states and overseas. The future modernized structure of the NWS will include 116 weather forecast offices (WFO) and 13 river forecast centers, all collocated with WFOs. WFOs also collect data from ships at sea all over the world and from meteorological satellites. Each year the NWS collects nearly four million pieces of information about atmospheric conditions from these sources.

The information collected by WFOs is used in the weather forecasting work of NWS. The data is processed by nine National Centers for Environmental Prediction (NCEP). Each center has a specific weather-related responsibility: seven of the centers focus on weather prediction—the Aviation Weather Center, the Climate Prediction Center, the Hydrometeorological Prediction Center, the Marine Prediction Center, the Space Environment Center, the Storm Prediction Center, and the Tropical Prediction Center. The other two centers—the Environmental Prediction Center and NCEP Central Operations—develop and run complex computer models of the atmosphere and provide support to the other centers. Severe weather systems such as thunderstorms, tornadoes, and hurricanes are monitored at the National Storm Prediction Center in Norman, Oklahoma, and the National Hurricane Center in Miami, Florida. Hurricane watches and warnings are issued by the National Hurricane Center's Tropical Prediction Center in Miami serving the Atlantic, Caribbean, Gulf of Mexico, and eastern Pacific Ocean) and by the Forecast Office in Honolulu (serving the central Pacific). WFOs, other government agencies, and private meteorological services rely on NCEP's information, and many of the weather forecasts in the paper and on radio and television originate at NCEP.

Global weather data are collected at more than 1,000 observation points around the world and then sent to central stations maintained by the World Meteorological Organization, a division of the United Nations. Global data also is sent to NWS's NCEPs for analysis and publication.

According to steady-state or trend models, weather conditions are strongly influenced by the movement of air masses that often can be charted quite accurately. A weather map might show that a cold front is moving across the great plains of the United States from west to east with an average speed of 10 mph (16 kph). It might be reasonable to predict that the front would reach a place 100 mi (1,609 km) to the east in a matter of 10 hours. Since characteristic types of weather often are associated with cold fronts it then might be reasonable to predict the weather at locations east of the front with some degree of confidence.

A similar approach to forecasting is called the analogue method because it uses analogies between existing weather maps and similar maps from the past. For example, suppose a weather map for December 10, 2003, is found to be almost identical with a weather map for January 8, 1996. Because the weather for the earlier date is already known it might be reasonable to predict similar weather patterns for the later date.

Another form of weather forecasting makes use of statistical probability. In some locations on Earth's surface, one can safely predict the weather because a consistent pattern has already been established. In parts of Peru, it rains no more than a few inches per century. A weather forecaster in this region might feel confident that he or she could predict clear skies for tomorrow with a 99.9% chance of being correct.

The complexity of atmospheric conditions is reflected in the fact that none of the forecasting methods outlined above is dependable for more than a few days, at best. This reality does not prevent meteorologists from attempting to make long-term forecasts, but accuracy declines as the forecast interval increases.

The basis for long-range forecasting is a statistical analysis of weather conditions over an area in the past. For example, a forecaster might determine that the average snow fall in December in Grand Rapids, Michigan, over the past 30 years had been 15.8 in (40.1 cm). A reasonable way to try estimating next year's snowfall in Grand Rapids would be to assume that it might be close to 15.8 inches (40.1 cm). This kind of statistical data is augmented by studies of global conditions such as winds in the upper atmosphere and ocean temperatures. If a forecaster knows that the jet stream over Canada has been diverted southward from its normal flow for a period of months, that change might alter precipitation patterns over Grand Rapids over the next few months.

The term numerical weather prediction is something of a misnomer because all forms of forecasting make use of numerical data such as temperature, atmospheric pressure, and humidity. More precisely, numerical weather prediction refers to forecasts that are obtained by using complex mathematical calculations carried out with high-speed computers.

Numerical weather prediction is based on mathematical models of the atmosphere. A mathematical model is a system of equations that attempts to describe the properties of the atmosphere and changes that may take place within it. These equations can be written because the gases that comprise the atmosphere obey the same physical and chemical laws that gases on earth's surface follow. For example, Charles' Law says that when a gas is heated it tends to expand. This law applies to gases in the atmosphere as it does to gases in a laboratory.

The technical problem that meteorologists face is that atmospheric gases are influenced by many different physical and chemical factors at the same time. A gas that expands according to Charles' Law may also be decomposing because of chemical forces acting on it. Meteorologists select a group of equations that describe the conditions of the atmosphere as completely as possible for any one location at any one time. This set of equations can never be complete because even a computer is limited as to the number of calculations it can complete in a reasonable time. Thus, meteorologists must select the factors they predict will be the most important in influencing the development of atmospheric conditions.

The accuracy of numerical weather predictions depends primarily on two factors. First, the more data that is available to a computer the more accurate its results. Second, the faster the speed of the computer the more calculations it can perform and the more accurate its report will be. In the period from 1955 (when computers were first used in weather forecasting) to the current time, the percent skill of forecasts has improved from about 30 percent to more than 60 percent. The percent skill measure was invented to describe the likelihood that a weather forecast will be better than pure chance.

Today, an accurate next-day forecast often is possible. For periods of less than a day, a forecast covering an area of 100 sq mi (259 sq km) is likely to be quite dependable.

In the 1990s, the more advanced Doppler radar, which can continuously measure wind speed in addition to precipitation location and intensity, came into wide use. Using mathematical models to automatically analyze data, calculators and computers gave meteorologists the ability to process large amounts of data and make complex calculations quickly. Today the integration of communications, remote sensing, and computer systems makes it possible to predict the weather almost simultaneously. Weather satellites, the first launched in 1960, can now produce sequence photography showing cloud and frontal movements, water-vapor concentrations, and temperature changes.

In addition to directly impacting operational effectiveness of military and other security forces. Emergency planners rely on accurate forecast maps to predict the dissemination patterns of nuclear, chemical, and biological materials.

Cloud seeding.
Starting in the 1940s, researchers experimented with modifying precipitation patterns.

After about three years of investigative work at the General Electric Research Laboratory in Schenectady, New York, researchers Irving Langmuir and his assistant, Vincent Joseph Schaefer, created the first human-made rainfall. Their work had originated as war-influenced research on airplane wing icing. On November 13, 1946, Schaefer sprinkled several pounds of dry ice (frozen carbon dioxide) from an airplane into a supercooled cloud, a cloud in which the water droplets remain liquid in sub-zero temperatures. He then flew under the cloud to experience a self-induced snowfall. The snow changed to rain by the time it reached Langmuir, who was observing the experiment on the ground.

Langmuir and Schaefer selected dry ice as cloud "seed" for its quick cooling ability. As the dry ice travels through the cloud, the water vapor behind it condenses into rain-producing crystals. As the crystals gain weight, they begin to fall and grow larger as they collide with other droplets.

Another General Electric scientist who had worked with Langmuir and Schaefer, Bernard Vonnegut, developed a different cloud-seeding strategy. The formation of water droplets requires microscopic nuclei. Under natural conditions, these nuclei can consist of dust, smoke, or sea salt particles. Instead of using dry ice as a catalyst, Vonnegut decided to use substitute nuclei around which the water droplets in the cloud could condense. He chose silver iodide as this substitute because the shape of its crystals

resembled the shape of the ice crystals he was attempting to create.

The silver iodide was not only successful, it had practical advantages over dry ice. It could be distributed from the ground through the use of cannons, smoke generators, and natural cumulonimbus cloud updrafts. Also, it could be stored indefinitely at room temperature.

A nucleation event is the process of condensation or aggregation (gathering) that results in the formation of larger drops or crystals around a material that acts as a structural nucleus around which such condensation or aggregation proceeds. Moreover, the introduction of such structural nuclei can often induce the processes of condensation or crystal growth. Accordingly, nucleation is one of the ways that a phase transition can take place in a material.

In addition to their importance in explaining a wide variety of geophysical and geochemical phenomena—including crystal formation—the principles of nucleation were used in cloud seeding weather modification experiments where nuclei of inert materials were dispersed into clouds with the hopes of inducing condensation and rainfall.

During a phase transition, a material changes from one form to another. For example, ice melts to form liquid water, or a liquid boils to form a gas. Phase transitions occur due to changes in temperature. Certain transitions occur smoothly throughout the whole material, while others happen suddenly at different points in the material. When the transitions occur suddenly, a bubble forms at the point where the transition began, with the new phase inside the bubble and the old phase outside. The bubble expands, converting more and more of the material into the new phase. The creation of a bubble is called a nucleation event.

Phase transitions are grouped into two categories, known as first order transitions and second order transitions. Nucleation events happen in first order transitions. In this kind of transition, there is an obstacle to the transition occurring smoothly. A prime example is condensation of water vapor to form liquid water. Condensation requires that many water molecules collide and stick together almost simultaneously. This requirement for simultaneous collisions presents a temporary but measurable barrier to the formation of a bubble of liquid phase. Following formation, the bubble expands as more water molecules strike the surface of the bubble and are absorbed into the liquid phase. Because of the obstacle to the phase transition, a liquid may exist in its gaseous state even though the temperature is well below the boiling point.

A liquid in this state is said to be supercooled. Accordingly, in order for a liquid to be supercooled, it must be pure, because dust or other impurities act as nucleation centers. If the liquid is very pure, however, it may remain supercooled for a long time. A supercooled state is termed metastable due to its relatively long lifetime.

The other type of phase transition is called second order, and it proceeds simultaneously throughout the whole material. An example of a second order transition is the melting of a solid. As the temperature rises, the magnitude of the thermal vibrations of molecules causes the solid to break apart into a liquid form. As long as the solid is in thermal equilibrium and the melting occurs slowly, the transition takes place at the same time everywhere in the solid, rather than taking place through nucleation events at isolated points.

There is general disagreement over the success and practicality of cloud seeding. Opponents of cloud seeding contend that there is no real proof that the precipitation experienced by the seeders is actually of their own making. Proponents, on the other hand, declare that the effect of seeding may be more than local.

Regardless, until the 1990s, when efforts were generally abandoned for lack of scientific proof of their effectiveness, cloud seeding was an accepted part of the strategy to combat drought. During the Vietnam War, the U.S. attempted to deny use of roads and trails to the North Vietnamese by seeding clouds and inducing localized rainfall. The effectiveness of those attempts remains questionable.

■ FURTHER READING:

BOOKS:

Hamblin, W. K., and E. H. Christiansen. *Earth's Dynamic Systems,* 9th ed. Upper Saddle River, NJ: Prentice Hall, 2001.

Hancock, P. L., and B. J. Skinner, eds. *The Oxford Companion to the Earth.* New York: Oxford University Press, 2000.

Lutgens, Frederick, K., et al. *The Atmosphere: A Introduction to Meteorology,* 8th ed. Upper Saddle River, NJ: Prentice Hall, 2001.

ELECTRONIC:

National Weather Service. "Internet Weather Source." <http://weather.noaa.gov/> (March 29, 2003).

National Oceanic and Atmospheric Administration. <http://www.noaa.gov/> (March 29, 2003).

SEE ALSO

FEMA (United States Federal Emergency Management Agency)
NOAA (National Oceanic & Atmospheric Administration)

Mexico, Intelligence and Security

The seat of complex ancient civilizations, espionage and intelligence work has long been practiced in Mexico. Mayan societies and great city-states employed spies to seek information about political rivals and assess the strength of opposing armies. During the age of Spanish colonialism, Indian and Spanish leaders both employed intelligence personnel and diplomats to smuggle weapons, secure peace treaties, act as interpreters, and conduct espionage. After gaining independence from Spanish rule in 1910, Mexico established its own modern intelligence community. However, the nation weathered periodic political and economic turmoil.

Mexico maintains both civilian and military intelligence services, as well as a national police force. The Mexican intelligence community is organized according to the traditional distinctions between domestic and foreign intelligence, though many agencies utilize a multiplicity of intelligence gathering technologies and operational strategies.

The main civilian intelligence organization in Mexico is the *Centro de Información de Seguridad Nacional* (CISEN), or Center for Research on National Security. A government restructuring of the intelligence community established CISEN in 1989. The agency focuses on domestic intelligence and the assessment of threats to national security. The dramatic rise in illegal immigration, organized crime, and illicit drug trafficking have influenced intelligence policy, with increasing CISEN and law enforcement resources being devoted to combat these problems in recent years. CISEN employs human intelligence, as well as technological surveillance, and advises the government on security systems to guard sensitive communications and computer systems.

The *Secretaría de la Defensa Nacional* (SEDENA), Secretariat of National Defense, administers Mexican military intelligence. Though each branch of the Mexican military employs embedded intelligence units, the main military intelligence agency is the S-2 Second Section. S-2 coordinates joint intelligence efforts and processes information gathered by military intelligence operations. Military intelligence focuses on the collection and analysis of foreign intelligence, especially that which pertains to the strength and deployment operations of foreign militaries. Both CISEN and S-2 conduct regular counter-intelligence operations, and both have contributed to international anti-trafficking and anti-terrorism efforts.

■ FURTHER READING:

ELECTRONIC:

Central Intelligence Agency. The World Factbook, 2002. "Mexico." <http://www.cia.gov/cia/publications/factbook/geos/mx.html> (March 30, 2003).

MI5 (British Security Service)

■ K. LEE LERNER/JUDSON KNIGHT

Best known by its designation MI5, the Security Service is the leading counter-espionage agency working in the

United Kingdom. Its functions are somewhat akin to those of the United States Federal Bureau of Investigation, but MI5 places a much greater emphasis on intelligence, and its operatives have no arrest powers. Formed in 1916, MI5 devoted itself to intelligence operations against the Germans in both world wars, and against Communists in the interwar and postwar periods. During the early Cold War, MI5 suffered a number of embarrassments involving Soviet moles in its midst. From the 1970s onward, it devoted increasing attention to terrorist activities, and in the 1990s, attempted to balance its sensitive security functions with an increased concern for openness with the British public.

Wartime successes (1909–45).

MI5 grew out of the Secret Service Bureau, created in 1909 to protect the British realm against German infiltrators. At the beginning of World War I, the Home Section of the bureau came under the control of the War Office, which designated it MI5 (the "MI" refers to military intelligence) in 1916. Over the course of the war, MI5 assisted in the arrest of several dozen German operatives in Britain.

Under the direction of Captain Vernon Kell, who served as director-general until 1940, MI5 in the immediate postwar years directed its efforts toward spies associated with the new Communist regime in Russia. It uncovered a major Soviet front operation in 1927, but by the 1930s had begun to focus once again on German infiltration. MI5, led by Sir David Petrie in the war years, apprehended numerous German spies, who were subsequently executed. Also important, it succeeded in turning a number of other Axis operatives, such that the Nazis remained convinced they had an extensive spy network in Britain—although in fact the spies were working against them.

Soviet infiltration (1946–79).

The postwar years saw some successes, including Operation Engulf, a program of communications interception directed against the Soviets, French, and Egyptians during the Suez Crisis in 1956. MI5 also captured several Soviet operatives, but its achievements were overshadowed by the uncovering of the Cambridge spy ring, whose members served as Soviet moles while working for the British government. Although neither Donald Maclean nor Kim Philby actually worked for MI5, both were under investigation by the agency when they escaped to the other side of the iron curtain in 1949 and 1963, respectively.

Worse revelations were to come. In 1963 it was discovered that Anthony Blunt, who had worked for MI5 in the war years, was also a Soviet agent. Eventually it became apparent that the Soviets had been infiltrating MI5 for most of the postwar period. The list of suspected Soviet agents included some extremely high officials: director-general Sir Roger Hollis (1956–65) and future director-general Sir Michael Hanley (1972–79). These revelations did little to inspire the trust of American intelligence agencies, which cooperated little with MI5 until after the end of Hanley's tenure.

Focus on terrorism (1979–present).

By the 1960s, MI5 had become increasingly concerned with terrorism, both by Palestinian and Northern Irish groups. Revelations of Soviet infiltration continued even into the 1980s, when former MI5 operative Michael Bettaney was convicted of espionage on behalf of the KGB. The spy scandals eventually ended, although not so much because of measures MI5 took to counter infiltration, but because of the Soviet Union's collapse.

During the mid-1980s, MI5 came under intense government scrutiny in the form of an investigation by Britain's Security Commission. The result of this was the appointment of Sir Anthony Duff to the director-general's position, and in 1988 Duff took measures to reform the agency. The Security Service Act of 1989 for the first time conferred legal status on MI5, which in December 1991 signaled a new era of openness by announcing the appointment of Stella Rimington as director-general. Rimington became not only its first female director, but the first MI5 chief named in the media.

In 1993, MI5 further demonstrated its openness by publishing a booklet titled *The Security Service,* which described MI5's six branches of operation: counter-terrorism, counterespionage, counter-subversion, protective security, security intelligence, and record keeping. Meanwhile, in 1992, MI5 was given chief responsibility for British intelligence efforts against Irish terrorism, and over the next seven years it helped bring about 21 convictions for crimes related to terrorism. An emphasis on counter-terrorism continued under the leadership of Stephen Lander, appointed director-general in 1996.

■ **FURTHER READING:**

BOOKS:

Andrew, Christopher M. *Her Majesty's Secret Service: The Making of the British Intelligence Community.* New York: Viking, 1986.

Bar-Joseph, Uri. *Intelligence Intervention in the Politics of Democratic States: The United States, Israel, and Britain.* University Park: Pennsylvania State University Press, 1995.

The Security Service: MI5. London: HMSO, 1993.

West, Nigel. *Molehunt: Searching for Soviet Spies in MI5.* New York: W. Morrow, 1989.

ELECTRONIC:

MI5: The Security Service. <http://www.mi5.gov.uk/> (April 11, 2003).

United Kingdom Intelligence Agencies. Federation of American Scientists. <http://www.fas.org/irp/world/uk/index.html> (April 11, 2003).

SEE ALSO

Cambridge University Spy Ring
Engulf, Operation

Moles
United Kingdom, Intelligence and Security

MI6 (British Secret Intelligence Service)

■ K. LEE LERNER/JUDSON KNIGHT

Officially known as the Secret Intelligence Service (SIS), MI6 is the chief British foreign intelligence organization, analogous to the United States Central Intelligence Agency. The organization is even more secretive than either its American counterpart, or another well-known member of the British intelligence community, the Security Service, or MI5. Although their functions are quite separate, the MI6 and MI5 share origins, and much of their history in the world wars and Cold War era ran along parallel lines. Yet, whereas MI5 has established a tone of openness with the British public since the early 1990s, MI6 remains guarded concerning the details of its activities.

World War I and the interwar era. In 1909, a parliamentary study found evidence of widespread German infiltration, and noted that there was "no organization...for accurately identifying its extent and objectives." As a result, the British government established the Secret Service Bureau. The bureau was divided into a Home Section under Captain Mansfield Cumming, and a Foreign Section directed by Captain Vernon Kell. The two came to be known, respectively, as "C" and "K." After World War I broke out, the Foreign Section became MI1(c), and in 1921 the Secret Intelligence Service (SIS), or MI6. Directors of SIS have thenceforth been known by the designation "C" after Cumming, who remained the head of SIS/MI6 until 1923. (The "K" designation, on the other hand, seems to have ended with Kell, first director-general of MI5.)

During World War I, MI6 conducted intelligence operations involving both Germany and Russia, and its operatives and agents included both the author W. Somerset Maugham and the legendary spy Sidney Reilly. In 1919, MI6 took charge of the Government Code & Cypher School (GC&CS), formed from the remains of the British Admiralty's Room 40, along with a smaller War Office program. GC&CS soon proved successful at breaking ciphers used by the new Bolshevik government. MI6 efforts against both Russia and Germany in the 1930s uncovered evidence of Nazi-Soviet cooperation in the development of weapons technology, but during this era, MI6 also suffered a number of failures, leaving the British government unprepared for such moves as Hitler's reoccupation of the Rhineland in 1935.

World War II and the early Cold War. A new era began for MI6 in November 1939 when, just three months after the outbreak of war, Colonel Stewart Menzies became the new "C." In that same month, MI6 suffered a major setback when the Germans captured two of its officers in Holland, and obtained considerable information from them under interrogation. Yet, MI6 excelled in its cryptanalytic efforts against the Germans through GC&CS, which in 1942 became the Government Communications Headquarters (GCHQ). Operating from Bletchley Park outside London, GCHQ successfully broke German ciphers on the Enigma machine—the single greatest cryptanalytic success of the war.

Despite the spirit of wartime cooperation with Josef Stalin's Russia, Menzies in 1944 wisely established a section devoted to Soviet espionage and subversion. Less felicitous was his choice of a section head, Harold (Kim) Philby. In what proved to be a classic case of the fox guarding the chicken coop, Philby would later be exposed as a Soviet spy, and he was not alone; among the many Soviet moles exposed in the two decades after the war were John Cairncross and Charles H. Ellis, both with MI6. Further misfortunes followed as MI6 attempted unsuccessfully to gain intelligence on a Soviet ship docked at Portsmouth, an effort that cost the life of a former navy diver named Lionel Crabb. Yet, MI6 was not without successes in the immediate postwar years; it cultivated a relationship with Soviet intelligence officer Oleg Penkovsky, who would prove a valuable asset to both British and U.S. intelligence.

From the late Cold War to the present. By the 1970s, MI6 had turned its attention toward a number of areas other than the Soviet bloc. These included economic espionage, as well as efforts against terrorist groups in Northern Ireland. In the latter capacity, the agency found itself in a turf war with MI5, which was already working on the problems in Northern Ireland. MI6 proved an invaluable asset in the conflict, establishing key links with top Irish Republican Army (IRA) and Sinn Fein figures. Unfortunately, MI6 suffered another embarrassment when two brothers claiming to be MI6 operatives conducted a number of bank robberies in Northern Ireland and claimed that they had been directed to assassinate IRA leaders.

During the 1980s and 1990s, MI6 recovered its standing through successful operations in the Falklands War, Persian Gulf War, and Balkan wars. It gained new statutory grounding with the 1994 passage of the Intelligence Services Act, which defined its responsibilities and functions, as well as those of its chief. The act also set in place a framework of government oversight for MI6 activities. In 1993, Sir Colin McColl became the first MI6 director to be publicly identified. He was replaced in 1994 by Sir David Spedding, and in 1999, Spedding was replaced by Sir Richard B. Dearlove.

The headquarters of the British intelligence services MI6 in London, seen from across the River Thames on the night of September 20, 2000, after an anti-tank rocket was fired at the building. No injuries resulted from the attack, thought to have been perpetrated by the Real IRA. AP/WIDE WORLD PHOTOS.

■ FURTHER READING:

BOOKS:

Andrew, Christopher M. *Her Majesty's Secret Service: The Making of the British Intelligence Community.* New York: Viking, 1986.

Dorril, Stephen. *MI6: Inside the Cover World of Her Majesty's Secret Intelligence Service.* New York: Free Press, 2000.

ELECTRONIC:

United Kingdom Intelligence Agencies. Federation of American Scientists. <http://www.fas.org/irp/world/uk/index.html> (April 11, 2003).

SEE ALSO

Bletchley Park
Cambridge University Spy Ring
Enigma
Room 40
Ultra, Operation
United Kingdom, Intelligence and Security

Microbiology: Applications to Espionage, Intelligence, and Security

■ BRIAN HOYLE

Microbiology is concerned with the study of microorganisms such as bacteria, viruses, fungi, protozoa, and algae. There are many facets to the science, ranging from basic studies of organism structure and genetic arrangement, to the development of methods or treatments against those microorganisms that cause diseases in humans, animals, and other living things. A classic example of a strategy against a pathogen (disease-causing organism) is the development of a vaccine. The stimulation of the immune system by the exposure to a component of the particular bacterial or viral strain, or to a weakened, but living version of the virus can confer protection against subsequent exposure to the disease causing bacterium or virus. Microorganisms can also be used for offensive purposes (i.e., biological weapons). The use of recombinant DNA technology—where a gene that specifies the protein of interest can be removed from the genetic material of one organism and added to the genetic material of the target organism—has enabled the design of biological weapons of frightening potency. For example, the former Soviet Union investigated the insertion of the gene for cobra venom into the genetic material of the influenza virus. The combination of the poison and an easily transmitted virus could have caused swift, catastrophic effects upon its intended population. The science of microbiology contributes in fundamentally important ways to national security, and even influences the gathering of intelligence and espionage activities.

Microorganisms and Security

The most urgent threat posed by microorganisms to national security is the development of an epidemic. An epidemic is an infection that, because of its ease of transmission from person to person (directly or via an intermediate) affects a large number of people within a very short period of time. The human toll and strain on the health care infrastructure due to naturally occurring epidemics such as influenzae are well known. In the past few decades, the emergence of diseases such as Acquired Immunodeficiency Syndrome (AIDS) and the re-emergence of tuberculosis has further strained the economies of even nations as wealthy as the United States.

The specter of the deliberate use of microorganisms as a weapon—biological warfare—while historically ancient, has taken on new importance in recent years. In the United States, the terrorists attacks of September 11, 2001, were followed by a spate of incidents involving the deliberate release of spores of *Bacillus anthracis*, the bacterium that causes anthrax. While the consequences of these biological attacks were minimized due to a rapid response to track and contain the source, five people died from anthrax, and the incident illustrated the vulnerability of a population to infection.

Even more ominously, evidence indicates that the terrorists responsible for the September 11, 2001, attacks made serious enquiries about the piloting and rental of crop dusting planes. Scenarios envisioning the aerial dispersal of anthrax spores over a major urban center via such a plane indicate that even 100 kilograms of spores carry the potential to kill hundreds of thousands or even millions of people within a few days.

The security threat posed by biological warfare is also ancient. Centuries ago, the decaying bodies of cattle that had died of infections were dumped into wells to poison the drinking water. Even deceased people provided the seed for the spread of infection to an enemy encampment, when the bodies of human victims of anthrax were catapulted over the walls of fortified communities. This military use of microorganisms became frighteningly refined in the twentieth century. Both sides of the conflicts of World Wars I and II researched the development of weapons that would deliver anthrax spores. During World War

II Britain produced millions of anthrax "cakes" that were to be parachuted into Germany. The intent was to decimate the population as well as the food chain.

Other microorganisms, equally as ancient as anthrax, continue to be security threats because of their natural potential to cause massive disease outbreaks, and because of their potential as biological weapons. One example is the disease known as plague, caused by the bacterium *Yersinia pestis*. Another example is smallpox, a disease that is caused by a virus.

The tremendous infectivity of anthrax, plague, and smallpox have caused millions of deaths throughout history. This destructive potential did not escape the attention of governments, such as that of the former Soviet Union, which were interested in developing weapons. Indeed, the microorganisms that cause anthrax, plague, and smallpox have been included in the list of weapons that are strategic weapons. Strategic weapons are those weapons that are capable of destroying entire populations. This puts these microorganisms on the same lethal level as nuclear weapons.

The security threat posed by microorganisms took on an added urgency in the last two decades of the twentieth century, when their potential as a terrorist weapon was recognized. In contrast to bombs and other such munitions, the manufacture of lethal payloads of microorganisms does not require huge manufacturing facilities or large numbers of people. Moreover, the scientific and manufacturing expertise for the development of biological weapons is not beyond the typical microbiologist.

Likewise, the transport of infectious microorganisms can be disguised. Microorganisms can be transported anywhere people can travel. A quantity of anthrax spores that would circulate through the ventilation system of an office building can be contained in a vial carried in someone's pocket. The ease by which microorganisms can be transported and released (i.e., by a small aircraft) is redefining the nature of security. Methods that are successful in detecting missile silos and troop movements are useless against the deliberate use of microorganisms by a few individuals.

The refinement of genetic engineering technologies has made possible the tailoring of bacteria and viruses to make them more lethal. Microorganisms can normally be rapidly detected using antibodies that recognize a surface antigen. Redesigning a pathogen via genetic engineering so that the surface antigen is different and therefore no longer recognizable to the antibody thwarts the test.

Natural infections. A variety of contemporary examples have shown how vulnerable even developed countries are to the spread of infections. From only a few cases in New York City in 1999, the virus that causes West Nile fever has spread through the U.S. and Canada. Thousands of people have contracted West Nile, and the infection shows no signs of abating. Other examples of naturally-occurring infections are legionellosis in Australia, yellow fever and

Creutzfeld-Jacob disease in Europe, and hantavirus pulmonary syndrome and cryptococcosis in North America.

Modern technology has unexpectedly aided the spread of disease. The classic example is the development of resistance by bacteria to antibiotics. Antibiotics were considered to be "wonder drugs" as recently as the 1960s. However, they have proved to only provide selective pressure for the development of bacteria that are even hardier and more capable of causing disease.

A report issued in 2000 by the U.S. National Security Council warned of the security threat posed to the U.S. in the twenty-first century by epidemics of natural infections in underdeveloped, politically volatile countries. The decimation of the next generation of these countries could exacerbate feelings of hostility towards the wealthy nations of the West, putting the U.S. and other developed nations at risk. In 2003, U.S. President George W. Bush pledged 15 billion dollars worth of American aid for the delivery of antiretroviral drugs to African citizens in the effort to halt the spread of AIDS, a naturally occurring infection that affects up to one half of some African populations.

Microbiological Techniques Relevant to National Security and Intelligence

Various microbiological techniques have long assumed a security role, principally in the detection of infectious microorganisms or toxic components. The ability to rapidly and accurately sequence genetic material came about in the 1990s, largely because of the demands of the Human Genome Project. So did the development (which continues) of software capable of processing the vast amount of genetic data into information that can be used to derive the composition and three-dimensional structure of proteins (i.e., the disciplines of bioinformatics and proteomics). The modeling of protein structures, for example, is important in the development of vaccines that act by blocking the action of some vital bacterial or viral protein.

The lessons learned from the Human Genome Project have been applied to security issues. For example, genetic material can be rapidly isolated from complex samples such as soil and even air (after the air has been filtered to trap the microorganisms on a solid support), and the identity of the microorganism can be determined by the sequencing of the material. The identification is so sensitive that one type (or strain) of bacterium can be distinguished from another. Such analyses were used to show that the strain of *Bacillus anthracis* used in some of the anthrax terrorist attacks of 2001 in the U.S. originated from the government's Army Medical Institute of Infectious Disease (USAMRIID).

Other technologies permit the rapid detection of bacteria or viruses. For example, the binding of an antibody to the specific antigen it recognizes can trigger a color development reaction, which is used in test kits to test for the presence of a particular microorganism. Also, genetic amplification techniques like the polymerase chain reaction, or the detection of microorganisms based on target genetic sequences (i.e., amplified fragment length polymorphism analysis, single nucleotide polymorphism analysis) can detect the presence of target sequences of genetic material in samples. The Joint Genome Institute at the Lawrence Berkeley National Laboratory, for example, has catalogued characteristic genetic sequences from a variety of bacterial pathogens.

Other U.S. government laboratories are also developing techniques aimed at thwarting the use of biological weapons. For example, the Los Alamos National Laboratory has developed the Biological Aerosol Sentry and Information System (BASIS), which is intended to provide an early warning of biological incidents. BASIS consists of a series of sampling sites clustered around another site that has been identified as a potential target of sabotage or terrorist/military action. Regular sampling from the sites and analysis of the samples will reveal the presence of a microorganism. The intent is not to prevent the deliberate release of microbes. Rather, the prompt detection of an incident, and subsequent response and mobilization of medical resources is intended to help alleviate the spread of an infection.

Microorganisms and intelligence. The national security concerns of microbiology influence intelligence gathering. This influence is two-pronged. First, the need to understand the nature of microbial behavior for the development of defensive strategies such as vaccines requires an open exchange of information and unrestricted research opportunities. However, the sensitive nature of some information, particularly if used by an enemy, can limit the exchange.

The heightened security climate in the U.S. since the terrorist attacks of 2001 has produced a call for limits to information exchange. In March 2002, the chief of staff warned against the open exchange of information concerning scientific advancements that could be utilized in the development of weapons of mass destruction. This issue is contentious, as it goes to the heart of the openness of inquiry that is the hallmark of research science.

Microbiology can also contribute to intelligence by being a direct source of information. It has been successfully demonstrated that messages can be programmed into deoxyribonucleic acid (DNA)—the genetic material that provides the information blueprint for many living organisms—through the arrangement of the components of the DNA. By assigning letters or grammatical symbols to triplets of the components, a section of DNA can be artificially constructed that contains a sequence that, when decoded, yields a message. The artificial sequence can be "spliced" into the DNA sequence of an organism, or even simply blotted onto a pre-determined region of a letter.

The recipient who knew the location of the DNA, could retrieve it and decipher the message.

Microorganisms and espionage. The ability to covertly transmit information via genetic sequences also has implications for espionage. Unless someone has knowledge of the means being used to transmit the information, and the technical means to acquire the genetic material and decipher the message, the message will remain secret. Microorganisms also have more traditional uses in espionage; for example, food and water can be deliberately contaminated to make someone ill, so as to compromise a project or a mission.

■ FURTHER READING:

BOOKS:

Preston, Richard. *The Demon in the Freezer: A True Story.* New York: Random House, 2002.

PERIODICALS:

Atlas, R. N. "National Security and the Biological Research Community." *Science.* no. 298 (2002): 753–754.

Walter, K. "A Two-Pronged Attack on Bioterrorism." *Science & Technology.* (June 2002): 4–11.

ELECTRONIC:

Central Intelligence Agency. "The Global Infectious Disease Threat and Its Implications for the United States." January 2000.<http://www.cia.gov/cia/publications/nie/report/nie99–17d.html> (November 22, 2002).

SEE ALSO

Anthrax Weaponization
Biological and Biomimetic Systems
Biological and Toxin Weapons Convention
Biological Warfare
Biological Warfare, Advanced Diagnostics
Biological Weapons, Genetic Identification
Bioterrorism
Bioterrorism, Protective Measures
CDC (United States Centers for Disease Control and Prevention)
Infectious Disease, Threats to Security
Pathogens

Microchip

■ LARRY GILMAN

Microchips, also termed "integrated circuits" or "chips," are small, thin rectangles of a crystalline semiconductor, usually silicon, that have been inlaid and overlaid with microscopically patterned substances so as to produce transistors and other electronic components on its surface. It is the components on the chip, not the chip itself, that are micro or too small see with the naked eye. The microchip has made it possible to miniaturize digital computers, communications circuits, controllers, and many other devices. Since 1971, whole computer CPUs (central processing units) have been placed on some microchips; these devices are termed microprocessors.

Manufacture of a microchip begins with the growing of a pure, single crystal of silicon or other semiconducting element. A semiconductor is a substance whose resistance to electrical current is between that of a conductive metal and that of an insulating material such as glass (silicon dioxide, SiO_2). This large, single crystal is then sawed into thin, disc-shaped wafers 4–12 inches (10–30 cm) across and only .01–.024 inches (.025–.06 cm) thick. One side of each wafer is polished to high precision, then processed to produce on it a number of identical microchips. These are cut apart later, placed in tiny protective boxes or packages, and connected electrically to the outside world by metal pins protruding from the packages.

Producing a microchip requires industrial facilities that cost billions of dollars and must be retooled every few years as technology advances. The basics of the microchip fabrication process, however, remain the same: by bombarding the surface of the wafer with atoms of various elements, impurities or "dopants" can be introduced into its crystalline structure. These atoms have different electron-binding properties from the silicon atoms around them and so populate the crystal either with extra electrons or with holes, gaps that behave much like positively charged electrons. Holes and extra electrons confer specific electrical properties on the regions of the crystal where they reside. By arranging the doped regions containing holes or extra electrons and covering them with multiple, interleaved layers of SiO_2, polycrystalline silicon (silicon comprised of small, jumbled crystals), and metal strips to conduct current from one place to another, each microchip can be endowed with thousands or millions of microscopic devices. Such chips are termed integrated because the electronic components in them are integral parts of a single, solid object; this both decreases their size and increases their reliability.

The microchip was conceived simultaneously in 1958 by U.S. engineers Jack Kilby and Robert Noyce (1927–1990). In 1962, microchips were used in the guidance computer of the U.S. Minuteman missile (a nuclear-tipped intercontinental ballistic missile based in holes or silos in the American Midwest); the U.S. government also funded early microchip mass-production facilities as part of its Apollo program, for which it requires lightweight digital computers. The Apollo command and lunar modules each had microchip-based computers with 32-kilobyte memories.

For some 40 years, the number of electronic components on an individual microchip has doubled every few years; this trend has been described as Moore's Law ever since 1965, when U.S. engineer Gordon Moore described the beginning of the trend. Engineers continually strive to fit more electronic components on each microchip; however, this is becoming steadily more difficult as device dimensions decrease toward the atomic scale, where quantum uncertainty renders traditional electronics unreliable. Microchip engineers predict that by about 2020, the exponential increases of the last few decades will cease.

Since their advent, microchips have transformed much of human society. They permit the manufacture of small electronic devices containing many millions of components; they are essential to computers, missiles, "smart" bombs, satellites, communications devices, televisions, aircraft, spacecraft, and motor vehicles. Without microchips the personal computer, cell phone, calculator, Global Positioning System, and many other familiar technologies, both military and civil, would be impossible. As chip complexity increases and cost decreases thanks to improvements in manufacturing technique, new applications are continually being found.

■ FURTHER READING:

ELECTRONIC:

Moore, Gordon. "No Exponential is Forever…but We Can Delay 'Forever'." International Solid State Circuits Conference, February 10, 2003. <ftp://download.intel.com/research/silicon/Gordon_Moore_ISSCC_021003.pdf> (April 3, 2003).

SEE ALSO

Nanotechnology

Microfilms

■ AGNIESZKA LICHANSKA

Microfilms are miniature films used for photographing objects and documents. The images on these films cannot be seen without an optical aid, either in the form of a magnifying glass or a projector. The main advantages of microfilm include relatively low cost, good image quality, long life and lack of necessity for expensive viewing hardware. Although the images are not visible with a naked eye, only a magnifying glass is needed for reading the microfilms.

Technology behind microfilms. The first mini-photographs (8x11mm) were taken using a portable Daguerrean camera produced in 1839. Much later, during the Cold War, the mini-photographs were developed into microdots, tiny photographs of 1mm or less in diameter, looking like a period in a typewritten letter.

The microfilm itself was invented in 1839 by John Dancer. He replaced a slide on the microscope stage with a photographic film and reversed the normal process of microscopy. As a result, instead of seeing a large version of a biological specimen, he was able to produce a miniature image of a large object.

Early microfilms were based on cellulose acetate and over the decades they broke down into acetic acid (vinegar syndrome) and records were destroyed. Currently, there are three types of microfilm: silver halide, diazo, and vesicular. Silver halide films are similar to the traditional film. They consist of the polyester base and silver nitrate emulsion, and are used in cameras for producing the original microfilms. Silver halide films produce the highest resolution and are available as positive and negative image films. If properly stored, their life is estimated to be at least 500 years. Diazo and vesicular films are less stable. Images on diazo films are formed from diazonium salts exposed to ultraviolet light in the presence of ammonium; these images fade with time. The vesicular films produce images by little bubbles inside the film that are sensitive to pressure and can also be destroyed by heat.

Not only did the films (down to 8mm wide) and images become smaller, but cameras were reduced in size and often disguised as everyday items such as watches, cigarette packs, books, and matchboxes. In fact, Kodak produced a camera known as Camera X or Matchbox camera. This camera was used during the Second World War by allied resistance groups. A second camera that was developed just before the war was the Riga Minox camera designed by Walter Zapp in 1936. Initially the minicameras were marketed for the public, but they were very quickly adopted for espionage purposes by intelligence and government agencies.

Microfilms in espionage. Microfilms were first used for espionage in 1859, and were later used to transport messages during the Franco-Prussian war of 1870 by carrier pigeon. However, they came to much more prominence in the 1920s for keeping copies of bank records and development of Recordak by Kodak. It was, however, during the Second World War when the microfilms flourished. They were used in regular military mail by the American forces to reduce the cost of shipping tons of mail. Microfilms were also the main way to photograph military installations and documents, as well as types and rates of weapons production. They were also used to transfer coded messages between the army and the intelligence agents behind enemy lines. Transport of the microfilms was not difficult due to their small size. Microfilms were, and still are, easily concealed in hollowed-out pencils, pens, cans, coins or other instruments smuggled by couriers across borders, and in many cases they remain a method of choice for espionage.

Microdots can be concealed even more easily than microfilms by being placed in a regular letter, under a stamp or in a dental filling. Microdots have also become

An American coin showing hidden microfilm. ©JEFFREY L. ROTMAN/CORBIS.

an anti-theft device: a Stoptheft microdot can be used to mark property.

FURTHER READING:

BOOKS:

Pritchard, Michael, and Douglas St. Denny. *Spy Camera: A Century of Detective and Subminiature Cameras.* London: Classic Collections, 1993.

White, William. *The Microdot: History and Application.* Williamstown: Phillips Publications, 1992.

ELECTRONIC:

Minoxography Community. D. Scott Young and Ferry Ansgar. "A Brief History of Minox." <http://www.minoxography.org/history.html> (10 March 2003).

University of California. Southern Regional Library Facility. The history of microfilm: 1839 to present. December 3, 2002. <http://www.srlf.ucla.edu/exhibit/text/BriefHistory.htm> (10 March 2003).

SEE ALSO

DNA Sequences, Unique

Photographic Resolution
Rosenberg (Ethel and Julius) Espionage Case

Microphones

■ AGNIESZKA LICHANSKA

A microphone is a transducer that converts sound waves into electrical signals proportional to the strength of the sound. The microphone output can be recorded or transmitted.

Although there are various types of microphones, the operating principal is the same. A diaphragm, either metal or plastic, vibrates in response to a sound wave and transmits the movement to an electrical component causing an induction of an electrical current. Microphones can be classified according to the way the diaphragm transmits sound or the way they pick up the sounds.

Based on the way the sound is transmitted, there are five groups of microphones: carbon, dynamic, ribbon, condenser and crystal. Each of these microphones can be

U.S. Ambassador to the United Nations Henry Cabot Lodge, left, complains to the United Nations Security Council in 1960 about a wooden carving of the Great Seal of the Unites States in the office of the U.S. Ambassador in Moscow (shown) that had been implanted with a miniature listening device by the Soviets. AP/ WIDE WORLD PHOTOS.

made to pick up sounds from various directions. There are omnidirectional, bidirectional, cardioid, hypercardioid, supercardioid and parabolic microphones. Omnidirectional microphones pick up sounds from the entire surrounding area (360°). In contrast, bidirectional devices have only a 90° pickup arc. The various cardioid microphones pick up sounds from a 105–131° arc. Parabolic microphones are the most unidirectional microphones, therefore, they have to be pointed directly at the source of sound. Their name comes from the fact the microphone itself (for example, omnidirectional) is surrounded by a parabolic dish. This dish gathers sounds and, by directing it to the microphone, also amplifies it.

None of the different types of microphones is superior to the other. They are all suited for different purposes. Important factors in selecting a microphone include the

sensitivity, quality of sound, overload characteristics, and, especially for surveillance and intelligence purposes, the size of the microphone.

The sensitivity of the microphone is measured by an amount of current produced. The currents produced by the microphones are very small and a signal has to be amplified before it can be used. However, amplification is not selective. Not only are the sounds amplified, but also any noise that was produced by an instrument itself. Sounds that are too loud or bad placement of a microphone can lead to distortion of the diaphragm known as an overload.

In any surveillance operation, placement of the microphone is crucial, not just for the quality of sound, but also for remaining inconspicuous. Microphones can also be carried by people to provide continuous surveillance or rapid identification and response. Such microphones are often combined with a transmitter or a recorder to send or record conversations.

Applications of microphones. The most obvious application in security, surveillance, and espionage is to listen in on conversations. Microphones are combined with an amplifier to provide good sound quality. These sounds can be recorded or transmitted, depending on the situation or application of the microphone. They are used by individuals, police, security agencies, intelligence and counterintelligence agents. The purpose is to monitor and identify the suspects, and obtain intelligence as to their plans and contacts.

The type of microphone used depends on the intended use. Parabolic microphones are used for distance surveillance as the best ones can pick up sounds from as far as 300 yards. However, most of these microphones can be easily blocked by an obstacle in the form of an object or person, causing poor sound quality or loss of sound reception. A solid wall or door would be impenetrable if it was not for a contact microphone that can intercept any audio signal through a solid material. The choices among microphones to be placed in a room or to be carried by a person are immense. A number of microphones built into pens are available. There are also microphones as small as a tiepin, allowing inconspicuous surveillance and spying.

Microphones are used as security devices alone or in combination with other instruments such as fingerprint scanners, retinal scanners or passwords, to secure access to high security areas or computers.

■ **FURTHER READING:**

BOOKS:

White, Paul, ed. *Basic Microphones.* London: Sanctuary Press, 2000.

ELECTRONIC:

How Stuff Works. "How do microphones work, and why are there so many different types?" <http://electronics. howstuffworks.com/question309.htm> (6 March 2003).

Nave, C. R. Georgia State University (2000). <http:// hyperphysics.phy-astr.gsu.edu/hbase/audio/mic.html> (6 March 2003).

SpyChest. Parabolic Microphone DetectEar <http://www. spytechs.com/listen_voice_equip/detect_ear.htm> (6 March 2003).

Tan, P. Multimedia Bluffer's Guides. "Microphones" (1996).<http://home1.pacific.net.sg/~firehzrd/audio/ mics.html> (6 March 2003).

UCSC Electronic Music Studios. Technical Essays. <http:// arts.ucsc.edu/ems/music/tech_background/tech_ background.html> (6 March 2003).

The University of Iowa. Multimedia Writing, Radio essays. <http://twist.lib.uiowa.edu/radio/Resources.html> (6 March 2003).

SEE ALSO

Audio Amplifiers
Laser Listening Devices
Parabolic Microphones

Microscopes

The ability to view things that are too small to be seen by the unaided eye is important in espionage and security. For example, the diagnosis of an infection often relies in part on the visual examination of the microorganism. Information about how the microbe reacts to certain staining methods (e.g, the bacterial Gram stain), the shape of the microbe, and the reaction of antibodies to the microbe all provide important clues as to the identity of the organism.

As well, microscopic examination of documents can reveal information that cannot otherwise be seen. The high magnification and analysis of the elements that make up a sample that is possible using specialized techniques of scanning and transmission electron microscopy can reveal the presence of material that is of suspicious origin (i.e., missile casing), or the presence of codes on a surface.

A microscope is the instrument that produces the highly magnified image of an object that is otherwise difficult or impossible to see with the unaided eye. A microscope is able to distinguish two objects from one another that could not be distinguished with the eye. The resolving power of a microscope is greater than that of the eye.

History of the microscope. In ancient and classical civilizations, people recognized the magnifying power of curved pieces of glass. By the year 1300, these early crude lenses were being used as corrective eyeglasses.

In the seventeenth century Robert Hooke published his observations of the microscopic examination of plant and animal tissues. Using a simple two-lens compound microscope, he was able to discern the cells in a thin section of cork. The most famous microbiologist was Antoni van Leeuwenhoek. Using a single-lens microscope that he designed, Leeuwenhoek described microorganisms in environments such as pond water. His were the first descriptions of bacteria and red blood cells.

By the mid-nineteenth century, refinements in lens grinding techniques had improved the design of light microscopes. Still, advancement was mostly by trial and error, rather than by a deliberate crafting of a specific design of lens. It was Ernst Abbe who first applied physical principles to lens design. Abbe combined glasses that bent light beams to different extents into a single lens, reducing the distortion of the image.

The resolution of the light microscope is limited by the wavelength of visible light. To resolve objects that are closer together, the illuminating wavelength needs to be smaller. The adaptation of electrons for use in microscopes provided the increased resolution.

In the mid-1920s, Louis de Broglie suggested that electrons, as well as other particles, should exhibit wavelike properties similar to light. Experiments on electron beams a few years later confirmed this hypothesis. This was exploited in the 1930s in the development of the electron microscope.

Electron microscopy. There are two types of electron microscope. They are the transmission electron microscope (TEM) and the scanning electron microscope (SEM). The TEM transmits electrons through a sample that has been cut so that it is only a few molecules thin. Indeed, the sample is so thin that the electrons have enough energy to pass right through some regions of the sample. In other regions, where metals that were added to the sample have bound to sample molecules, the electrons either do not pass through as easily, or are restricted from passing through altogether. The different behaviors of the electrons are detected on special film that is positioned on the opposite side of the sample from the electron source.

The combination of the resolving power of the electrons, and the image magnification that can be subsequently obtained in the darkroom during the development of the film, produces a total magnification that can be in the millions.

Because TEM uses slices of a sample, it reveals internal details of a sample. In SEM, the electrons do not penetrate the sample. Rather, the sample is coated with gold, which causes the electrons to bounce off of the surface of the sample. The electron beam is scanned in a back and forth motion parallel to the sample surface. A detector captures the electrons that have bounced off the surface, and the pattern of deflection is used to assemble a three dimensional image of the sample surface.

Scanning, tunneling, and other microscopy techniques. In the early 1980s, the technique called scanning tunneling microscopy (STM) was invented. STM does not use visible light or electrons to produce a magnified image. Instead, a small metal tip is held very close to the surface of a sample and a tiny electric current is measured as the tip passes over the atoms on the surface. When a metal tip is brought close to the sample surface, the electrons that surround the atoms on the surface can actually "tunnel through" the air gap and produce a current through the tip. The current of electrons that tunnels through the air gap is dependent on the width of the gap. Thus, the current will rise and fall as the tip encounters different atoms on the surface. This current is then amplified and fed into a computer to produce a three dimensional image of the atoms on the surface.

Without the need for complicated magnetic lenses and electron beams, the STM is far less complex than the electron microscope. The tiny tunneling current can be simply amplified through electronic circuitry much like that used in other equipment, such as a stereo. In addition, the sample preparation is usually less tedious. Many samples can be imaged in air with essentially no preparation. For more sensitive samples that react with air, imaging is done in vacuum. A requirement for the STM is that the samples be electrically conductive.

Scanning tunneling microscopes can be used as tools to physically manipulate atoms on a surface. This holds out the possibility that specific areas of a sample surface can be changed.

Other forces have been adapted for use as magnifying sources. These include acoustic microscopy, which involves the reflection of sound waves off a specimen; x-ray microscopy, which involves the transmission of x rays through the specimen; near field optical microscopy, which involves shining light through an opening smaller than the wavelength of light; and atomic force microscopy, which is similar to scanning tunneling microscopy but can be applied to materials that are not electrically conductive, such as quartz.

■ **FURTHER READING:**

BOOKS:

Aebi, Engel. *Atlas of Microscopy Techniques.* San Diego: Plenum Press, 2002.

Hayat, M. Arif. *Microscopy, Immunohistochemistry, and Antigen Retrieval Methods for Light and Electron Microscopy.* New York: Plenum Publishing, 2002.

Murphy, Douglas, B. *Fundamentals of Light Microscopy and Electronic Imaging.* New York: Wiley-Liss, 2001.

SEE ALSO

Biological Warfare
Chemical and Biological Detection Technologies

Microwave Weaponry, High Power (HPM)

High-power microwave (HPM) weaponry sends out a short, extremely high-voltage burst of electromagnetic energy capable of disrupting computer systems for a fraction of a second. Although the disruption is short, the burst causes computers to reset, and if the computers operate something as sensitive as the control and navigation systems of a jet in mid-flight, the result could be lethal. HPM systems are effective weapons by virtue of the fact that their use is difficult to trace. For technologically sophisticated powers such as the United States, however, HPM weapons are potentially as much of a threat as they are an asset.

HPM capabilities.

If HPM simply shut down computer systems, that might be enough to make them formidable weapons, but their usefulness does not stop there. As anyone who has ever accidentally put a piece of metal in a microwave oven knows, metal in contact with microwaves tends to spark. If the conductive wire harness inside an airplane fuel tank were hit with a microwave near the end of a transoceanic flight, when the concentration of fumes in the tank is heavy, the result could be an explosion.

To further the threatening quality of HPM weaponry, these systems use "ammunition"—electromagnetic energy—that is invisible, travels at the speed of light, and exists in virtually limitless supply. Nor does an HPM beam leave any markings, like the spent round of a traditional weapon, that would connect it to the weapon that fired it.

HPM uses.

Until the 1970s, HPM technology was impractical. Over the next two decades, however, developments in plasma physics, energy storage, and the technology of switching devices made these weapons systems viable around the time the Cold War came to an end. The Soviets invested more research in the field than did the West, a logical choice because HPM weaponry is more useful to the less technologically advanced side. The more sophisticated a nation's weapons systems, and the more reliant on microprocessors, the more vulnerable these potentially are to HPM.

Russian authorities claimed that in 1995, Chechnyan rebels used HPM to subvert a Russian security system and gain entry to a restricted-access area. Four years later, the Russians maintained that United States forces used HPM weapons to disable Yugoslav communications during the North Atlantic Treaty Organization (NATO) campaign in Kosovo.

Carbon-graphite coils capable of generating an electromagnetic pulse used to destroy electronics equipment—especially communications equipment—can be fitted to cruise missiles. Carbon-graphite equipped cruise missiles were used by U.S.-led forces in raids on Baghdad, Iraq, in 1991 and in 2003.

Scientists at Lawrence Livermore National Laboratory also have developed an HPM weapon for the Department of Justice: aimed at a moving vehicle, the HPM could shut off the electronic ignition, thus bringing a high-speed car chase to an abrupt end.

American use of HPM systems carried with it the threat that enemies might gain access to such weapons as well. In view of this danger, the Department of Defense took steps to "harden" the electronic circuitry of weapons to protect them against attacks.

■ FURTHER READING:

PERIODICALS:

Arkin, William M. "'Sci-Fi' Weapons Going to War." *Los Angeles Times.* (December 8, 2002): M1.

Epstein, Edward. "U.S. Has New Weapon Ready." *San Francisco Chronicle.* (February 14, 2003): A1.

Fulghum, David A. "Microwave Weapons May Be Ready for Iraq." *Aviation Week & Space Technology* 157, no. 6 (August 5, 2002): 24.

Kirkpatrick, Melanie. "Weapons with a Moral Dimension." *Wall Street Journal.* (January 14, 2003): A15.

SEE ALSO

E-Bomb
Electronic Countermeasures
Electronic Warfare
Radio Frequency (RF) Weapons

Middle East, Modern U.S. Security Policy and Interventions

■ JUDSON KNIGHT

The Middle East figures heavily in U.S. national and international security policy. Factors include the existence of enormous oil reserves in several countries, U.S. support for Israel, and the proliferation of terrorism on the part of Palestinian, Arab nationalist, and Muslim fundamentalist organizations. Coupled with these three factors, the last of which became particularly significant as Mideast terrorism reached the United States itself in 1993, was a Cold War-era competition with the Soviet Union for influence in the region. This prompted the U.S. government to aid Afghanistan, a country low in natural resources, but high in strategic value. Later, in the war on terrorism, Afghanistan itself would become a venue for U.S. military action. Such realignments of policy have been a regular feature in U.S. policy, which has seen shifts in its approach toward Egypt, Iran, Iraq, and other countries in the Middle East over the years.

Israel and the Rise of Terrorism

The defeat of the Ottoman Empire in World War I ended the last in a series of Turkish, Arab, and Persian empires that had controlled the region for 13 centuries. Beginning in the 1920s, Turkey rapidly modernized under the leadership of Mustafa Kemal, also known as Atatürk. While maintaining its Muslim faith, Turkey eschewed traditions such as the denial of equal rights for women, and in the eyes of Westerners, served as a model for the region. After World War II, Turkey became a strategic ally and a member of the North Atlantic Treaty Organization (NATO).

In the decade after the end of World War II, new nations emerged from what had formerly been colonies and protectorates controlled by the United Kingdom, France, and other European powers. Some of these new nations, such as Iraq, formed from three Ottoman provinces, were a product of modern agreements, with little historical identity as a national unit. Such conditions created tension between the military, hereditary monarchs, and religious and ethnic groups.

The Arab-Israeli Wars

Nowhere was the tension of the new Middle East more apparent than in the relationship between Israel and its Arab neighbors. A 1947 United Nations (UN) map divided the area today known as Israel almost equally between Israelis and Arabs. Dissatisfied with this proposal, and opposed to the establishment of an Israeli state, Egypt, Iraq, Jordan, and Syria attacked Israel shortly after its establishment as a nation in May 1948. Though outnumbered, the Israelis had a superior military, and defeated the Arab nations. As a result, Israeli territory expanded to encompass an area larger than that allotted in the original UN partition.

Israel attacked Egypt in 1956, as part of the Suez Canal crisis, but was forced back by pressure both from the United States and the Soviet Union. In March 1957, U.S. President Dwight D. Eisenhower proclaimed the Eisenhower Doctrine, whereby "the United States regards as vital to the national interest and world peace the preservation of the independence and integrity of the nations of the Middle East." Up to this point, the Cold War lines in the Middle East were not sharply drawn, but as Egypt's Gamal Abdel Nasser and other Arab leaders entered into agreements with the Soviets, the United States increasingly backed Israel.

In the Six-Day War of June 1967, Israel once again defeated a much larger force, and gained control of the west bank of the Jordan River, which had been Jordanian territory. From that point, the inhabitants of the West Bank gained a political identity not as displaced Jordanians, but as Palestinians. Soon Yasser Arafat and the Palestine Liberation Organization (PLO) would emerge as spokespeople for the Palestinians, but the groups that made up the PLO did not speak with words alone. During the years that followed, Palestinian and other groups

would conduct scores of terrorist attacks that killed hundreds of Israelis, Americans, and others.

The 1973 War and Lebanon. The fourth Arab-Israeli war began with a combined Egyptian and Syrian attack against Israel on October 6, 1973. Other Arab nations eventually sent forces as well. The Arabs were heavily supplied with Soviet arms and equipment, and in retaliation the United States on October 14 began resupplying Israel. On October 18, two days after the Israelis crossed the Suez Canal, the Organization of Petroleum-Exporting Countries (OPEC) announced a cutback in oil production. This raised gasoline prices, causing the first of several energy crises that dealt severe, if temporary, blows to the U.S. economy.

Though Israel would remain at odds with most of its Arab neighbors, events in 1977 and 1978 provided an opportunity for peace with Egypt. Egyptian President Anwar Sadat and Israeli Prime Minister Menachem Begin first conducted talks in late 1977, and in September 1978, President James E. Carter brought both leaders together for talks at Camp David. The Camp David accords provided hope for peace in the Middle East, but incited anger from militants in the Arab world; on October 6, 1981, a member of an Islamic fundamentalist group assassinated Sadat.

In 1978, Israel invaded southern Lebanon, and began a full-scale occupation in 1982. Also overrun by Syria, which sought to exercise control over the country, Lebanon descended into chaos. It was in this context that President Ronald Reagan sent U.S. forces into the capital city of Beirut, where in April and October 1983, two separate terrorist bombings killed a total of 259 Americans, including 242 Marines. Reagan withdrew the troops from Lebanon in 1984.

Islamic Fundamentalism

Although U.S. support for Israel has remained one pretext among many cited by Middle East terrorists as justification for their attacks, the suicide bombers in Beirut were not directly linked with the Palestinian issue. Instead, they were members of a radical Shi'a Muslim group ultimately affiliated with Iran, where Islamic militants had taken control and established a fundamentalist, passionately anti-American theocracy in 1979.

One of the most successful early covert actions of the Central Intelligence Agency (CIA) was Operation AJAX, conducted against the regime of Iranian Prime Minister Mohammad Mossadegh in 1953. Mossadegh had seized control of the Anglo-Iranian Oil Company in 1951, whereupon the British Secret Intelligence Service (MI6) developed a plan for covert action against him. MI6 brought the CIA in on the plan in November 1952, and at the behest of CIA director Allen Dulles, Kermit Roosevelt acted as commander of the operations.

CIA and MI6 support for groups loyal to the deposed monarch, Shah Mohammad Reza Pahlavi, resulted in his restoration to the throne in August 1953. Over the next 25 years, the shah remained a loyal U.S. supporter, and attempted to modernize his country, but accompanied that modernization with acts of repression. His secret police, SAVAK, operated throughout the country, practicing torture and dealing severely with opponents to the shah's rule.

By 1978, popular unrest had reached a boiling point, and the shah fled the country in January of the following year. Shi'ite fundamentalists led by the Ayatollah Ruhollah Khomeini declared Iran the world's first Islamic republic in February 1979. On November 4, militants seized control of the U.S. embassy in Teheran, taking 52 Americans hostage. The Carter administration secretly called on the U.S. military to make a response, and in April 1980, a team composed of personnel from special military units attempted a rescue.

The mission was aborted after a helicopter and transport plane crashed at a remote desert staging area, killing eight men. The incident marked a low point for the U.S. military, which had seen no significant action since the ceasefire in Vietnam seven years earlier, and it proved to be a major contributing factor in Carter's failure to win reelection. Reagan won in part because of promises to build up the military, and on the day of his inauguration in January 1981, Iran released the hostages after 444 days of captivity.

Even as these events were taking place in Iran, neighboring Afghanistan became a Cold War battleground with the Soviet invasion of December 1979. The action called for a U.S. response, but just what that response should be was not immediately clear. Direct U.S. intervention was not considered, and Carter chose economic sanctions, keeping U.S. athletes home from the 1980 Olympics in Moscow. This did little to sway the Soviets, and resulted in the Soviet boycott of the 1984 Games in Los Angeles.

Reagan, on the other hand, chose to supply the resistance, various tribal groups known collectively as the *mujahideen,* or "holy warriors." While Saudi Arabia provided funds, China provided weapons, and Egypt provided training, the United States supplied the group of approximately 100,000 insurgents with sophisticated weaponry. Most notable among these were Stinger antiaircraft missiles, funded as part of a secret October 1985, congressional appropriation of $470 million. The United States also provided a variety of antitank missiles, C-4 explosives, and even Soviet-made equipment such as Kalashnikov rifles, as well as medical supplies, food, and clothing.

Iran-Contra and blowback. U.S. support for the mujahideen was to prove a significant factor in bringing an end to the Soviet occupation of Afghanistan, which in turn helped bring down the entire Soviet empire. Despite this

salutary result, the success in Afghanistan had a number of less positive consequences as well. One of these, the Iran-Contra affair, may not have been so much a by-product as a concurrent event. In both cases, the United States secretly supported Islamic fundamentalists, with whom it had little commonality of aims, in support of objectives dictated by the Cold War.

The most devastating side effect of the Afghanistan war was a phenomenon known to intelligence and security experts as "blowback," or unintended consequences of a highly negative nature. Even after the Soviets began withdrawing in late 1988, Washington continued to send arms to the mujahideen, and did so until a late 1991 agreement with the Soviets to discontinue all activity in Afghanistan. With the Cold War over, Afghanistan lost its strategic importance, and the United States rapidly turned its attention elsewhere.

This left Islamic militants in possession of large weapons caches, and as the world community focused on other issues, various mujahideen factions began fighting amongst themselves. By 1996, moderate groups such as that of the celebrated rebel commander Ahmad Shah Massoud had been defeated by the Taliban, militant fundamentalists with support from neighboring Pakistan. The Taliban provided safe haven for terrorist groups, most notably Osama bin Laden's al-Qaeda network, and supported their activities with heroin sales.

These circumstances would culminate in a number of terrorist attacks by al-Qaeda and other groups with apparent links to training camps in Afghanistan: the 1993 World Trade Center bombing; the June 1996 attack on the U.S. military complex in the Khobar Towers, Dharan, Saudi Arabia (an incident for which several groups have claimed responsibility); al-Qaeda's bombing of two U.S. embassies in Africa in August 1998; the attack on the USS *Cole* in Yemen in October 2000; and eventually the events of September 11, 2001.

State-Sponsored Terror and the Wars with Iraq

In the war on terrorism, much of the U.S. effort would be directed against what the administrations of presidents William J. Clinton and George W. Bush identified as state sponsors of terror. Clinton launched attacks on alleged al-Qaeda facilities in Sudan and Afghanistan in August 1998, while Bush initiated Operation Enduring Freedom in Afghanistan on October 7, 2001, and Operation Iraqi Freedom on March 19, 2003.

Some critics suggested that Saudi Arabia should be considered a terror-sponsoring nations, since bin Laden and most of the September 11 terrorists were Saudi citizens, and the Saudis supported the Taliban and numerous terrorist groups in Palestine. However, the situation with

Saudi Arabia is more complex than almost any other U.S. relationship in the Middle East, including the alliance with Israel.

Because of Saudi Arabia's oil reserves, wealth, and influence in the region, U.S. officials have generally tolerated anti-American statements by Saudi leadership figures. During Operations Desert Shield and Desert Storm, as the United States prepared for and launched military actions against Iraq in 1990 and 1991, Saudi Arabia provided both funds and bases for the operation.

Libya. An example of the degree to which oil wealth contributes to strategic complications in the Middle East is Libya. With its desert location, a population much smaller than New York City, minimal industry, and lack of natural resources other than oil, the North African country would never have been a significant international player had it not been for the discovery of oil in the 1960s. Wealth from oil, however, served to finance a wide array of international adventures on the part of Muammar al-Qaddafi, who seized power in September 1969.

At one point, it was estimated that Qaddafi provided some form of support, ranging from funds to weapons to training facilities, for more than 50 terrorist groups. These included not only Muslim militants, such as those operating in the southern Philippines, but also the Irish Republican Army, the Red Army Faction in Germany, and the Japanese Red Army. The wide geographic and ideological range of Qaddafi's exploits, combined with the seemingly bottomless resources he poured into terrorism, made him a notable foe of Washington in the 1970s.

U.S. planes shot down two Libyan fighter aircraft over the Gulf of Sidra in 1981, and five years later, after receiving credible intelligence of Libyan involvement in a West Berlin discotheque bombing that killed a U.S. soldier, Reagan launched air strikes against Libya. Qaddafi was markedly less active after the April 1986, bombings, but in December 1988, he orchestrated the bombing of Pan American Airlines Flight 103 over Lockerbie, Scotland, which killed 259 people.

During the 1990s, Qaddafi's influence receded as the Libyan economy declined. Eventually, the terrorists associated with the Berlin and Lockerbie bombings were brought to justice, and Qaddafi even made attempts toward a rapprochement with Washington. An Arab nationalist in the Nasser mold, he found himself alienated amid the rise of Muslim fundamentalists such as those of al-Qaeda, and vigorously denounced the September 2001, attacks. On the other hand, in 2003, when the United States attacked the Iraq of Saddam Hussein—another Arab nationalist— he denounced the United States.

Iraq. During the Iran-Iraq war (1980–88), the United States gave most of its support to Iraq, which most of the outside world perceived as the less troublesome of two contentious states. But when Iraq invaded neighboring Kuwait in August 1990, President George H. W. Bush, under the auspices of the United Nations and with international support, retaliated with Operation Desert Storm.

The Persian Gulf War resulted in the Iraqi withdrawal from Kuwait, the imposition of no-fly zones over much of the country, and a requirement that Hussein relinquish all weapons of mass destruction (WMD). But it also left Saddam in power. On April 14, 1993, Iraqi intelligence agents attempted to assassinate Bush (who was no longer president) during a visit to Kuwait. Two months later, the administration of William J. Clinton launched a cruise missile attack on the Iraqi capital of Baghdad.

Saddam Hussein continued to obstruct UN weapons inspection efforts, and eventually forced all inspectors out of the country, claiming that the team included U.S. and Israeli spies. The United States and United Kingdom then launched Operation Desert Fox (December 16–19, 1998), a bombing campaign against strategic sites in Iraq. Saddam allowed the weapons inspectors back in but, in the view of the United States, continued to deceive and evade efforts toward uncovering his WMD.

Some authorities held that Hussein had played a supporting role in the 1993 World Trade Center bombing, and after the 2001 attack, President George W. Bush identified Iraq as a major sponsor of terror, suggesting that the Iraqi leader had directly supported the perpetrators of that attack as well. When Hussein failed to relinquish what Bush maintained were significant caches of weapons of mass destruction, the U.S. launched Operation Iraqi Freedom in March 2003. The campaign proved successful, resulting in Saddam Hussein's removal and sending a powerful message to neighboring Syria and other known supporters of terrorist movements.

■ **FURTHER READING:**

BOOKS:

Lenczowski, George. *American Presidents and the Middle East.* Durham, NC: Duke University Press, 1990.

Lesch, David W. *The Middle East and the United States: A Historical and Political Reassessment.* Boulder, CO: Westview Press, 1990.

Nelson, Jonathan M. *Paths Not Taken: Speculations on American Foreign Policy and Diplomatic History, Interests, Ideals, and Power.* Westport, CT: Praeger, 2000.

Richelson, Jeffrey T. *The U.S. Intelligence Community,* 4th ed. Boulder, CO: Westview Press, 1999.

Rothkopf, David J. *The Price of Peace: Emergency Economic Intervention and U.S. Foreign Policy.* Washington, D.C.: Carnegie Endowment for International Peace, 1998.

Williams, Mary E. *The Middle East: Opposing Viewpoints.* San Diego, CA: Greenhaven Press, 2000.

Military Police, United States

SEE ALSO

ADFGX Cipher
Africa, Modern U.S. Security Policy and Interventions
Bush Administration (1989–1993), United States National Security Policy
Bush Administration (2001–), United States National Security Policy
Carter Adminstration (1977–1981), United States National Security Policy
Clinton Administration (1993–2001), United States National Security Policy
Delta Force
Egypt, Intelligence and Security
Enduring Freedom, Operation
Engulf, Operation
Iran, Intelligence and Security
Iran-Contra Affair
Iranian Nuclear Programs
Iraq, Intelligence and Security Agencies
Iraq War: Prelude to War (The International Debate Over the Use and Effectiveness of Weapons Inspections)
Israel, Counter-terrorism Policy
Iraqi Freedom, Operation (2003 War Against Iraq)
Israel, Intelligence and Security
Jordan, Intelligence and Security
Kenya, Bombing of United States Embassy
Khobar Towers Bombing Incident
Kuwait Oil Fires, Persian Gulf War
Lebanon, Bombing of U.S. Embassy and Marine Barracks
Libya, Intelligence and Security
Libya, U.S. Attack (1986)
Pan Am 103 (Trial of Libyan Intelligence Agents)
Persian Gulf War
Saudi Arabia, Intelligence and Security
Sudan, Intelligence and Security
Suez Canal
Syria, Intelligence and Security
Turkey, Intelligence and Security
USS Cole,
USS Liberty
World Trade Center, 1993 Terrorist Attack
World Trade Center, 2001 Terrorist Attack

Military Police, United States

The U.S. military police are the law enforcement corps within each of the major services. The army has its Military Police Corps, the navy its Shore Patrol, the air force its Air Force Security Police, and the Marine Corps its Military Police. These forces are staffed almost entirely by military personnel, and are responsible for all the ordinary functions of a police force, as well as additional military duties.

Formal organization of military police in the United States dates back to the early twentieth century. Today the largest of the military police corps is, not surprisingly, that of the largest service, the Army, whose provost marshal general sits on the Department of the Army staff. Military police personnel are involved in law enforcement operations ranging from protecting school crossings and writing parking tickets to murder investigations and undercover drug stings.

Personnel at U.S. bases around the country and the world provide temporary confinement of service members charged under the uniform code of military justice (UCMJ). Assuming the individual is found guilty after trial in a military court, where he or she is represented by a member of the judge advocate general (JAG) corps, if the sentence warrants, the convicted will serve time at a federal facility such as Fort Leavenworth in Kansas.

In addition to the regular military police activities, several branches have special undercover contingents—for example, the Army Central Investigation Division (CID)—as well as corrections officers. Military police, known as MPs in the Army and Marines, are trained for combat, and are often involved in second or third waves of an invading force. Once a target area has been subdued, MPs will often undertake the preservation of order, and the MP commander will serve as effective leader of the area until replaced.

■ FURTHER READING:

BOOKS:

Wright, Robert K. *Military Police.* Washington, D.C.: Center of Military History, 1992.

PERIODICALS:

Dominique, Dean J. "Convoy Rat Patrol." *Army Logistician* 34, no. 3 (May/June 2002): 36–37.

Flatter, J. R. "Military Police: A Force of Choice for the 21st Century MEU (SOC)." *Marine Corps Gazette* 81, no. 7 (July 1997): 36.

Warden, John A. III. "The New American Security Force." *Airpower Journal* 13, no. 3 (fall 1999): 75–91.

SEE ALSO

DoD (United States Department of Defense)
Law Enforcement, Responses to Terrorism

MOAB (Massive Ordnance Air Burst Bomb)

In addition to its raw destructive power, the Massive Ordnance Air Burst bomb (MOAB) has became part of a

276

Encyclopedia of Espionage, Intelligence, and Security

A Massive Ordnance Air Blast bomb, or MOAB, the largest conventional bomb in the U.S. weapons arsenal, is prepared for testing at Eglin Air Force Base, Florida, March 11, 2003. AP/WIDE WORLD PHOTOS.

military and intelligence effort to discourage and demoralize enemy forces. Upon detonation, MOAB produces a mushroom cloud similar to a nuclear blast. The MOAB bomb is the most powerful non-nuclear weapon in the U.S. arsenal.

At 21,000 pounds, the MOAB bomb is 6,000 pounds heavier than the next largest conventional bomb, the BLU-82 (nicknamed the "Daisy Cutter") bomb used in Vietnam. Like the BLU-82, the MOAB is a fuel air disbursement bomb. In Vietnam the large blast from the BLU-82 was used to create instant landing zones for helicopters.

Although both the BLU-82 and MOAB are dropped from a B-52 or an MC-130 cargo plane flown by Air Force Special Operations Forces, the MOAB has a GPS based satellite guidance system to enhance accuracy. The BLU-82 has an estimated target error allowance of several hundred feet. In contrast, the MOAB was designed to guide to within one meter of its intended detonation point. This accuracy was important to planners in carefully calculating the radius of the fireball and destructive blast from MOAB.

Fuel air explosives are designed to explode above the ground, disperse aerosolized fuel, and then detonate the highly volatile fuel-air mixture. The concussive detonation produces a violent shock wave.

BLU-82 bombs proved useful in attacking cave complexes in Afghanistan containing Taliban and Al Qaeda terrorists because the violent blast—in addition to its direct destructive force—also deprives those under the blast of oxygen.

The power of the blast is intended not only to kill and destroy—but also to shock and demoralize enemy troops. Discussing the bomb in March of 2003, Defense Secretary Donald H. Rumsfeld acknowledged the Pentagon's plans to use MOAB to shock enemy troops in the impending war with Iraq and asserted, "There is a psychological component to all aspects of warfare." Potential use of MOAB was incorporated by military planners into U.S. "shock and awe" tactical doctrine that calls for swift and intense military attacks to disorient enemy troops.

The United States Air Force conducted a demonstration test of the MOAB at Eglin Air Force Base near Pensacola, Florida, on March 11, 2003. Press coverage was extensive, and within hours of the test the Pentagon released footage of the blast to news services. Pentagon planners hoped that footage would make its way into Iraq and help discourage Iraqi troops from what seemed to be futile resistance against a vastly superior U.S.-led coalition.

■ FURTHER READING:

PERIODICALS:

Shanker, Tom. "Largest Conventional Bomb Dropped in a Test in Florida." *New York Times.* March 12, 2003.

SEE ALSO

Enduring Freedom, Operation
Vietnam War

Molecular Biology: Applications to Espionage, Intelligence, and Security

■ BRIAN HOYLE

Molecular biology involves the use of techniques to determine or rearrange the sequence of the components of deoxyribonucleic acid (DNA).

In the mid-1970s, it became possible, using what came to be called recombinant DNA technology, to splice a specific region of DNA from one organism into the DNA of another to express the protein that the insert coded for.

Molecular biology and "weaponizing"

During the Cold War of the 1950s and 1960s, the consensus in the intelligence community was that the Soviet Union explored the use of recombinant DNA technology to engineer more lethal microorganisms for use as weapons. For example, one project attempted to insert the genetic coding for cobra and scorpion venom into the DNA of a bacteria that could enter the body.

Genetic engineering of bacteria, especially spore-forming types that are resistant to all known antibiotics, is another aspect of molecular biology that has been recognized as a military and national security threat. The infections caused by the engineered bacteria would be virtually impossible to treat. As well, genes that code for toxins could be transferred to spore forming bacteria such as *Bacillus anthracis* or *Clostridium botulinum*. Because the spores can survive for months, even years, in conditions that would kill the actively growing bacteria, the toxins would be more likely to harm an enemy.

To date, however, all indications are that such engineered bacteria do not exist. This may be because, for example, antibiotic resistance is typically not due to the expression of a single gene. Rather, many genes need to be expressed, with their products operating coordinately, to bestow the resistance. Thus, the alteration of one or a few genes is, as of late 2002, unlikely to produce the resistant "superbug." As well, genetically engineered bacteria do not tend to survive well in the environment because there is an energy cost to the bacteria to express the inserted genetic material.

The military use of molecular biology to design biological weapons was banned by the 1972 Biological Warfare Convention. The signatory nations agreed in the 1980 and 1986 reviews of the convention that the ban applies to genetically engineered microorganisms. In the U.S., the Biological Weapons and Anti-Terrorist Act (1989) and the Antiterrorism and Effective Death Penalty Act (1996) prohibit the manufacture of biological weapons and the use of molecular techniques in these processes.

Rogue states and terrorist groups are unaffected by any such agreement. Thus, it has long been viewed as prudent to use molecular biological techniques to devise protective measures against genetically engineered microorganisms, and to conduct basic research on non-engineered, disease-causing microorganisms in order to devise vaccines or other treatments (i.e., rapid detection tests). The U.S. Army has utilized molecular biological techniques to study a variety of harmful bacteria and viruses since 1982 at their Fort Detrick, Maryland, laboratories (the Biological Defense Research Program). Other organizations have research programs as well (i.e., the Unconventional Pathogen Countermeasures Program run by the Defence Advanced Research Projects Agency; DARPA). The studies have involved determining the genetic basis of the infectious capability of microorganisms as well as the involvement of other components of the cell such as surface proteins.

Molecular biology as an identification tool. Since the 1970s, the techniques to extract target DNA (i.e. bacterial DNA) from the background DNA of all the other organisms in a sample has become refined and efficient. The ability to sequence even large segments of DNA can now be accomplished very quickly, largely because of the technology and computational power developed to allow the sequencing of the human genome. Finally, the DNA sequences of microorganisms that are serious health threats and are potential targets of bioterrorists have been determined (e.g., *Bacillus anthracis,* the bacterium that causes anthrax, and variola virus, which causes smallpox).

These developments make it possible to detect DNA sequences from certain bacteria and viruses. The technique known as the polymerase chain reaction (PCR) is critical to this aim. PCR enables a stretch of DNA to be amplified millions of times, to quantities that are detectable on electrophoretic gels or using DNA microchip technology, where the binding of a sequence of DNA that is a mirror image of the target sequence can be visualized.

The molecular approach can be used to distinguish one species of bacteria from another, even closely related species (i.e., *Bacillus anthracis* from *Bacillus subtilis*). A variety of enzymes exist that are capable of recognizing certain nucleotide sequences within the DNA and cutting the DNA apart at the sites where the sequence occurs. The result is fragments of differently sized DNA. The fragments can be separated according to their size using the technique of gel electrophoresis. The pattern of bands for one sample of bacteria that appears in the gel can be compared to the pattern given by another type of bacteria. If the patterns are identical, then the bacteria are the same species.

The enzyme digest technique can be combined with PCR to reveal even very small differences in DNA sequence. This allows sequences that are unique to a given bacterium to be detected. For example, this technique can identify *Bacillus anthracis* and *Yersinia pestis*, the bacterium that causes plague.

Molecular biology allows investigators to probe the cause of a disease outbreak. Learning the identity of the microorganism responsible for the outbreak can provide useful information as to the biological warfare capability of another country. For example, in 1979 an anthrax outbreak in the Soviet Union killed over 60 people. The cause was suspected of being the inhalation of anthrax spores that had been accidentally released from a military research facility. A team from the Los Alamos National Laboratory analyzed the DNA in preserved tissues of victims. At least five different types of *Bacillus anthracis* were found. A natural outbreak typically involves a single strain. The molecular evidence all but ruled out a natural outbreak.

Another area of active research is the development of molecular techniques to detect bacteria that can contaminate food. Naturally occurring bacteria such as *Salmonella typhosa*, *Campylobacter jejuni*, and *Escherichia coli* cause an estimated seven to 30 million cases of foodborne illness and up to 9,000 deaths every year in the United States alone. The economic losses and strain on the health care infrastructure have been identified as national security concerns.

Molecular biology as an intelligence tool.
Molecular biology could potentially be used to encode information in DNA. Scientists have shown that by assigning letters of the alphabet and grammatical symbols to triplets of nucleotide bases, and then constructing a sequence within a DNA molecule, the sequence can yield a message when decoded by the recipient. In one study, DNA containing the coded message was spotted onto a period in a sentence of a letter and then sent through the mail. The recipient, aware of which symbol contained the DNA, extracted the DNA for sequencing, and from the sequence determined the hidden message. Only someone with knowledge of the existence of the DNA spot in the letter could receive the message.

Thus, molecular biology is poised to become an important means of transmitting information.

■ FURTHER READING:

BOOKS:
Alberts, Bruce, Alexander Johnson, Julian Lewis, et al., eds. *Molecular Biology of the Cell.* New York: Garland Publishing, 2002.

PERIODICALS:
Clellenad, C.T., V. Risca, and C. Bancroft. "Hiding messages in DNA microdots." *Nature* no. 399 (1999): 533–534.

ELECTRONIC:
Los Alamos National Laboratory. "Tracing Biothreats with Molecular Signatures." Research Quarterly. Fall 2002. <http://www.damtp.cam.ac.uk/user/gr/public/gal_milky.htm>(December 7, 2002).

SEE ALSO
Biological Weapons, Genetic Identification
DNA Fingerprinting
Forensic Science
Pathogen Genomic Sequencing

Moles

■ JUDSON KNIGHT

A mole is a high-ranking intelligence officer for one agency who covertly feeds information to a rival or enemy agency. In practice, the difference between a mole and an agent-in-place—an employee of one intelligence agency who, of his or her own initiative, offers services to a rival or enemy agency—is a murky one, and seems to involve distinctions of rank. Moles are usually individuals who carry considerable authority within the agencies that employ them, and thus, the information they provide to their secondary employer is likely to be of high caliber.

In order to discuss examples of moles, it is necessary to draw distinctions between these and other categories of spy. Because high rank is usually regarded as a characteristic of a mole, most enlisted military personnel, such as the Marine guards at the U.S. embassy in Moscow during the 1980s, who were literally seduced into spying by attractive female KGB operatives, did not serve as moles, even though the intelligence they provided may have aided the services that used them as agents.

Furthermore, because moles are usually intelligence officers currently employed by the agency against which they are spying, the definition does not encompass all

Michael Raymond, right, is escorted from federal court in 1986 after being sentenced on a weapons charge and served with a Florida murder warrant. Raymond worked as an FBI "mole" uncovering political corruption in Chicago and New York in exchange for leniency. AP/WIDE WORLD PHOTOS.

members of the infamous Walker family spy ring, several of whom had retired from the U.S. Navy before they began spying for the Soviet Union. Most important, a mole is actively engaged in the covert collection and transfer of intelligence, meaning that inactive or sleeper agents, who are simply awaiting instructions before beginning work, do not qualify as moles.

Soviet and Russian Moles

In the superpower conflict between the Soviet Union and the United States during the Cold War, and between the United States and the Russian Federation in the years since, there have been many more known cases of moles employed by the Soviets and Russians than by the Americans. This is most likely not a result of American failure to use moles as extensively; rather, unless they were caught, the identities of moles friendly to the United States are unlikely to be exposed until many years after the fact.

Among the most infamous Soviet moles in the West was the Cambridge spy ring, whose members included Harold (Kim) Philby, Donald Maclean, Guy Burgess, John Cairncross, Anthony Blunt, and others. Recruited at Britain's Cambridge University in the 1930s, these were scions of the privileged classes who had become disillusioned with the system that had fostered them. Beginning with Blunt, they readily provided information against their own nation and its allies, and recruited others to do so.

The members of the Cambridge spy ring for the most part, refused to accept pay for their deeds. This was not only because most of them came from wealthy backgrounds, but also because they genuinely considered that spying for the Soviet Union served an idealistic purpose. Actions of the Cambridge ring cost many lives, either directly or indirectly, and many of those identified by them died in situations involving torture. In the end, several members of the ring, including its leader Kim Philby, crossed the Iron Curtain and spent the remainder of their days under the care of their Soviet sponsors.

Ideology and money. In the ideologically charged atmosphere of the 1930s, and among an elite class such as that of the Cambridge spy ring, it was possible for the Soviets to find agents willing to serve as moles for ideological reasons and not for profit. By the end of World War II and the beginning of the Cold War, however, the pattern had changed: rather than ideology, money had become the principal motivating factor for most moles, who provided mostly technical rather than strategic information to their Soviet handlers.

From the standpoint of the Soviets, this later crop of moles was more reliable than the Cambridge ring and other ideological spies of the 1930s. A spy motivated by ideology fancies himself to be acting on moral principle alone, and thus, free to resist orders that he finds objectionable. By contrast, an individual so driven by greed that he will literally sell human lives for money is not likely to judge any job too dirty if the price is right.

Such was the case with Aldrich Ames of the Central Intelligence Agency (CIA), who provided the Soviets and later the Russians with information for nine years. At the time of his arrest in 1994, he was driving a late model red XJ6 Jaguar, just one of many items he had purchased with the $2.7 million his handlers paid him over the course of the preceding decade. Much the same was the case with Robert Hanssen, a Federal Bureau of Intelligence counterintelligence special agent who served as a mole for the Soviets and Russians prior to his arrest in 2001.

A plethora of moles. The Cambridge ring and the two paid moles of the 1990s are just a few among many examples of Soviet and later Russian infiltration directed against the United States or the West in general. In 1963, it was discovered that French diplomat George Pâques had been collecting intelligence on the North Atlantic Treaty Organization (NATO) and passing it on to the Soviets. Three years later, U.S. authorities arrested William Whelan, an army lieutenant colonel who served as intelligence advisor to the army chief of staff.

During this period, CIA counterespionage chief James Jesus Angleton spent considerable energy and resources on uncovering moles. During the late 1960s and early 1970s, Angleton conducted an aggressive "molehunt" in which more than 120 CIA agents came under suspicion. Quarrels with CIA chief William Colby led to Angleton's dismissal in 1974. Yet, Angleton was not always inaccurate in his judgments; virtually from the moment he met Philby, an officer in British intelligence, he expressed suspicions that Philby was a mole—an assessment borne out by subsequent discoveries.

U.S. and British Moles

The most well known mole for the West was Oleg Penkovsky, a colonel in the KGB. From the late 1940s, Penkovsky served the Soviet regime faithfully, but he became increasingly disillusioned with Communism in general and Premier Nikita Khrushchev in particular. Assigned to set up a KGB network while operating under the cover of a trade delegation, he first attempted to contact U.S. authorities, who initially refused to accept that the high-ranking officer would willingly provide them with secrets. Frustrated, Penkovsky offered his services to British intelligence through businessman Greville Wynne in 1961.

Wynne arranged a meeting with British intelligence in London, and thereafter Penkovsky supplied valuable information to both British and American authorities. Over an 18-month period, he delivered more than 5,000 photographs, as well as other information on Soviet military strength, war plans, missiles, and satellite systems. In the Cuban Missile Crisis of October 1962, President John F. Kennedy would make extensive use of information provided by Penkovsky. Afterward, the Soviets, aware that they had a mole in their midst, conducted a molehunt of their own. Several days after Penkovsky was tried and convicted in a 1963 show trial, he was executed by the KGB.

Another U.S. mole working in the Communist Bloc was Michael Goleniewski, a Polish military intelligence officer who passed secrets to the CIA before defecting to the West in 1960. Less fortunate was the case of Anatoly Filatov, caught in a CIA sex entrapment scheme in Algiers in 1976. Confronted with the threat of compromising revelations, Filatov agreed to provide the CIA with intelligence from the Soviet foreign ministry. Apprehended by the Soviets in 1978, he met the same fate as Penkovsky before him.

■ FURTHER READING:

BOOKS:

Buranelli, Vincent, and Nan Buranelli. *Spy Counterspy: An Encyclopedia of Espionage.* New York: McGraw-Hill, 1982.

Hood, William. *Mole.* New York: Norton, 1982.

Nash, Jay Robert. *Spies: A Narrative Encyclopedia of Dirty Deeds and Double Dealing from Biblical Times to Today.* New York: M. Evans, 1997.

Polmar, Norman, and Thomas B. Allen. *Spy Book: The Encyclopedia of Espionage.* New York: Random House, 1998.

Vise, David A. *The Bureau and the Mole: The Unmasking of Robert Philip Hanssen, the Most Dangerous Double Agent in FBI History.* New York: Atlantic Monthly Press, 2002.

West, Nigel. *Molehunt: Searching for Soviet Spies in British Intelligence.* New York: Berkley, 1991.

Wynne, Greville. *The Man from Moscow: The Story of Wynne and Penkovsky.* London: Hutchinson, 1967.

SEE ALSO

Ames (Aldrich H.) Espionage Case
Cambridge University Spy Ring
Cameras, Miniature
Hanssen (Robert) Espionage Case
Intelligence Agent
Sex-for-Secrets Scandal
United Kingdom, Intelligence and Security
Walker Family Spy Ring

Monroe Doctrine

■ ADRIENNE WILMOTH LERNER

The Monroe Doctrine defined the U.S. position on international affairs involving nations in the Americas and former colonial holdings of European powers. In his seventh annual message to Congress on December 2, 1823, President James Monroe unveiled his plan for United States foreign policy. The United States government acknowledged the sovereignty of independent nations in the Americas, and declared the Americas closed to future colonization. The policy further stated that the United States would not be a party to European conflicts. The policy took decades to come to full fruition, receiving the name "Monroe Doctrine" in 1853. During the nineteenth century, the policy was tested during the Mexican-American and the Spanish-American Wars, though it was only directly invoked in the latter.

The Napoleonic Wars in Europe in the first decades of the nineteenth century stirred nationalist sentiment in both the Old and the New World. As European nations devoted increasing resources to combating Napoleon's invading armies, they politically neglected their colonial holdings abroad. Nationalists in Latin America supported taking up arms against European colonial powers and establishing independent nations. Between 1815 and 1823, Argentina, Venezuela, Mexico, Peru, Colombia, and Chile gained their independence and established republics. These fledgling nations needed, and sought, political recognition from larger, more influential nations. Knowing that they could not rely on the monarchist nations of Europe to support break-away democracies, the new American republics sought recognition from the United States.

In the United States, the European Napoleonic Wars spawned the War of 1812. British troops burned the U.S. capitol, but U.S. forces succeeded in routing British troops long enough to force a cease-fire and peace treaty. This second defeat of British forces more firmly established the United States as a thriving, independent nation, able to compete with European rivals. However, most members of the United States government sought to keep the nation out of European rivalries. When the revolutions in South America yielded new republics, the United States was left in a precarious position, caught between European and American interests.

A rumor circulated in diplomatic circles that the Holy Alliance of Russia, Austria, and Prussia was set to intervene on behalf of Spain in the colonial rebellions. In 1823, France invited Spain to restore the Bourbon monarchy with a promise of further aid against insurgent republics in the Americas. The monarchist alliance angered Great Britain, who was politically torn between the need to defend the principles of monarchist government, and keep the French from regaining strongholds in the Americas and the Caribbean.

British foreign minister George Canning lobbied the United States government to form an Anglo-American alliance to oppose the intervention of France or the Holy Alliance in Latin America. Many in the United States government supported the diplomatic move, but President Monroe and his Secretary of State, John Quincy Adams, were suspicious of the British plan. Adams advocated issuing a unilateral declaration, warning all European powers to refrain from joining colonial wars in which they had no direct involvement.

Monroe heeded Adams counsel. In a yearly speech, Monroe issued a statement proclaiming that any efforts to extend European political power in the Americas would be considered a threat to the security of the United States. Though the doctrine stated that the United States would refrain from participation in European conflicts, it left open the possibility for U.S. involvement in the Americas. Monroe counted on Britain to receive the statement as compromise, and recognize its mutual benefit. Indeed, the doctrine eventually worked largely because of backing from Britain.

The Monroe Doctrine was formally invoked seventy-five years later at the outbreak of the Spanish-American War. The United States cited Spain's continued involvement in Cuba as a threat to U.S. property and interests. The United States won the conflict against Spain, and in the years following the war, the United States acted to prevent European nations from collecting debts from defaulting Latin American nations and former colonial holdings. When the Dominican Republic was bankrupt in 1904, United States President Theodore Roosevelt issued the Roosevelt Corollary to the Monroe Doctrine, stating that the United States could preemptively act to ward off European aggression in the Americas.

■ FURTHER READING:

ELECTRONIC:

The Avalon Project at Yale University. *The Monroe Doctrine, 1823.* <http://www.yale.edu/lawweb/Avalon/Monroe.htm> (April 2003).

Morocco, Intelligence and Security

Morocco gained its independence from France in 1956. The nation, strategically located in western North Africa, close to the Straits of Gibraltar, has long served as the gateway between Africa and Europe. After gaining its independence, Morocco sought to expand its borders and assert its control over various international interests in the region. Morocco was granted control of the internationalized trade city of Tangiers, but a long-standing dispute continues over its occupation of Western Sahara.

Morocco has suffered waves of political turbulence since its founding, but political reforms over the last decade have somewhat stabilized the region. With the recent rise of Islamist extremist groups in North Africa, the Moroccan government has sought to minimize the political impact of such groups in Morocco.

Morocco maintains specially trained military commando and intelligence units that focus on protection of national interests within Morocco, especially in the Western Sahara region. The main government intelligence agency is the *Direction de la Surveillance du Territoire* (DST), or Directorate of Territorial Surveillance. The DST conducts most all of Morocco's intelligence operations, both foreign and domestic. The largest organizational department of the DST is the counter-intelligence unit. Though the DST is known as both an intelligence agency and a secret police force that sometimes carries out political espionage, the agency does conduct joint operations with allied foreign intelligence services.

The Moroccan intelligence community has aided United States and British efforts to stem the spread of the al-Qaeda terrorist network. Surveillance operations carried out by the DST have led to the arrest of several suspects and the seizure of money and weapons destined for terrorist cells in Europe or North Africa. Despite this cooperation with international anti-terrorism efforts and ongoing government reforms Morocco's intelligence and security services remain closely monitored by some organizations. Human rights organizations criticize the Moroccan intelligence community for the arrest, detainment, and torture of political dissidents, especially between 1960 and 1980.

SEE ALSO

Terrorist and Para-State Organizations
Terrorist Organizations, Freezing of Assets

Mossad

■ JUDSON KNIGHT

Israel's principal agency for intelligence collection, counterterrorism, and covert action is the Institute for Intelligence and Special Tasks, best known as Mossad, an abbreviation of its Hebrew name, ha-Mossad le-Modiin ule-Tafkidim Meyuhadim. In a tiny country surrounded by foes, the Mossad has been extremely active ever since its establishment in 1951. Its successes include the capture of former Nazi leaders, most notably Adolf Eichmann, as well as numerous triumphs of intelligence-gathering that contributed to Israeli victory in the 1967 Six-Day War. Mossad also conducted the legendary raid at Entebbe, Uganda, in which it rescued the passengers and crew of a French jetliner hijacked by Palestinian terrorists. Yet, Mossad has often come under criticism for perceived excessive actions against Israel's many enemies.

History

David Ben-Gurion, Israel's first prime minister, established Mossad as ha-Mossad Leteum (the Institute for Coordination) on April 1, 1951. Mossad had a checkered record in its first decade. On the positive side, it was the first intelligence agency to capture a copy of Soviet leader Nikita Khrushchev's February 1956 "Secret Speech," in which he denounced the crimes of Josef Stalin before the 20th Party Congress. Mossad also ran several key operations in Arab lands, with Wolfgang Lotz in Egypt and Eliahu Cohen in Syria.

The Syrians eventually exposed Cohen, however, and hanged him in Damascus Square, while the Egyptians captured, tortured, and imprisoned Lotz in 1964. Meanwhile, another operative in Egypt, David Magen, turned out to be a double agent, and the work of Avraham Dar in Egypt during the mid-1950s ended in a disaster for Israeli intelligence, with numerous agents captured and imprisoned. At least one apparent success of this era turned out

Ephraim Halevy, in the first public address by a head of Mossad, speaks in Herzliya, Israel in 2000. AP/WIDE WORLD PHOTOS.

to be a political failure when Ben-Gurion reversed Mossad efforts to intimidate West German scientists who were assisting the Egyptians. Eager to develop better relations with West Germany, Ben-Gurion dismissed Mossad director Isser Harel (1952–63), who he had once accorded the title *Memuneh,* "the one in charge."

1960s and 1970s. Mossad, which gained its present name as the Institute for Intelligence and Special Tasks in 1963, fared much better in the 1960s. Joint operations with Shin Bet, the internal security force, led to the capture of Eichmann—who had overseen the murder of millions of Jews during the Holocaust—from his hiding place in Argentina. Under the leadership of Meir Amit (1963–68), Mossad focused on intelligence-gathering, which greatly aided Israeli military efforts in 1967. During this period, Mossad also assisted the defection of an Iraqi airman who delivered to Israel a Soviet MiG-21 fighter jet in 1963. In 1968, Mossad successfully captured eight missile boats that Israel had ordered from France, but which President Charles de Gaulle had placed under embargo. That year also saw the capture of nuclear technician Mordechai Vanunu, who had revealed Israeli nuclear secrets to the British press.

Following the massacre of Israeli athletes by the Palestinian terrorist group Black September at the Munich Olympics in 1972, Mossad directed an assassination effort under an action team dubbed "the Wrath of God" (WOG). Over the next two years, WOG tracked down and killed more than a dozen members of Black September, but also accidentally killed a Moroccan waiter who had no affiliation with the terrorist group.

Failure to predict Egyptian actions leading to the Yom Kippur War in 1973 forced the resignation of several top officers, including Mossad director Zvi Zamir (1968–74). Yet, on July 3–4, 1976, Mossad more than recovered its reputation with the daring raid at Entebbe, codenamed Operation Thunderbolt. After intensive intelligence-gathering at the site, the Israelis assaulted the plane, rescuing all but four of its 97 passengers and losing a single officer—along with 20 Ugandan soldiers—in the process.

1980s and 1990s. During the 1980s, Mossad's intelligence-gathering against Arab countries helped pave the way for Israeli airstrikes against Palestine Liberation Organization (PLO) headquarters in Tunisia, and against an Iraqi nuclear reactor. In April 1988, a Mossad assassination team infiltrated the residence of Abu Jihad, deputy to PLO chief Yassir Arafat, and killed him. Two years later, in March 1990, another hit team killed Gerald Bull, a Canadian scientist aiding the Iraqi weapons program, at his apartment in Brussels.

Among the less successful activities of Mossad during the 1980s and 1990s was its involvement in the Iran-Contra affair, when it acted as an intermediary between the United States and Iran. Embarrassment surrounding the failure of Mossad to prevent the assassination of Prime Minister Yitzak Rabin by an Israeli citizen in November 1995 led to the resignation of Mossad director Shabtai Shavit in 1996. Prime Minister Shimon Peres then appointed Major General Danny Yatom, the first Mossad chief ever publicly identified. In 2000, Mossad undertook a recruitment campaign, complete with newspaper advertisements and a Web site that took applications on line.

Organization and Operations

From its headquarters in the Israeli capital of Tel Aviv, Mossad oversees a staff estimated at approximately 1,200 personnel in the mid-1990s. It is assumed to consist of eight departments, of which the largest is Collections, tasked with espionage overseas. Officers in the Collections Department operate under a variety of covers, some diplomatic. The Political Action and Liaison Department is responsible for working both with allied foreign intelligence services, and with nations that have no normal diplomatic relations with Israel.

Among the departments of Mossad is the Special Operations Division or Metsada, which is involved in assassination, paramilitary operations, sabotage, and psychological warfare. Psychological warfare is also a concern of the Lohamah Psichlogit Department, which conducts propaganda and deception activities as well. Additionally, Mossad has a Research Department, tasked

with intelligence production, and a Technology Department concerned with the development of tools for Mossad activities.

■ **FURTHER READING:**

BOOKS:

Eisenberg, Dennis, Uri Dan, and Eli Landau. *The Mossad Inside Stories: Israel's Secret Intelligence Service.* New York: Paddington Press, 1978.

Eshed, Haggai. *Reuven Shiloah: The Man Behind the Mossad: Secret Diplomacy in the Creation of Israel.* Portland, OR: F. Cass, 1997.

Horesh, Joshua. *An Iraqi Jew in the Mossad: Memoir of an Israeli Intelligence Officer.* Jefferson, NC: McFarland & Co., 1997.

Thomas, Gordon. *Gideon's Spies: The Secret History of the Mossad.* New York: St. Martin's Press, 1999.

Westerby, Gerald. *In Hostile Territory: Business Secrets of a Mossad Combatant.* New York: HarperBusiness, 1998.

SEE ALSO

Assassination
Egypt, Intelligence and Security
Eichmann, Adolf: Israeli capture
Israel, Counter-terrorism Policy
Israel, Intelligence and Security
Middle East, Modern U.S. Security Policy and Interventions
Palestinian Authority, Intelligence and Security
Syria, Intelligence and Security

Motion Sensors

■ LARRY GILMAN

In security applications, a motion sensor is a device that detects human presence, usually inside a building or in the immediate vicinity of a building. Not all devices classified as "motion" sensors actually sense motion; for instance, passive infrared systems (PIRs) detect the infrared light (heat radiation) emitted by human beings. "Presence detectors" might be a more accurate term for this class of devices.

The simplest type of motion sensor sets up a circuit or closed electrical path partly composed of a beam of light. This beam is directed across an open space to be monitored to a photoelectric detector, which converts the incident light beam to a voltage signal; any interruption in the beam is detected as an interruption in the voltage signal. This straightforward design, still in use, has the disadvantage of monitoring only the space occupied by the beam itself. This means that several beams must be used to secure a doorway or passageway, and many beams must be used to monitor a large, complex space (e.g., armory).

Further, a beam-circuit system cannot distinguish between intruders of different sizes; a moth can interrupt a beam as effectively as a leg.

PIRs are also commonplace. Low-grade PIRs are often used for automatic lights, while more complex models are used for building security. PIRs do not detect motion, as mentioned above, but relatively rapid changes in the overall amount of infrared light in a scene. Slow, overall changes in the amount of infrared light, such as would occur when the sun goes behind a cloud or a room heats up, should not trigger the sensor; the sudden change caused by a human being entering the sensor's field of view should trigger the sensor. PIR sensors can fail to detect intruder movement that is (a) primarily towards or away from the sensor, rather than across its field of view, or (b) slow.

PIRs are passive because they detect energy that the scene emits of its own accord. Active motion detectors, in contrast, illuminate the scene with laser light, ultrasound (sound waves pitched too high for the human ear to detect), or microwaves (radar). Regardless of the type of energy used to illuminate the scene, there are two basic ways of using reflected energy to detect presence or intrusion: (1) monitor for relatively rapid changes in wave energy reflected from the scene, and (2) monitor for Doppler shifts in wave energy reflected from the scene. A Doppler shift is a change in frequency of a wave that is reflected from or emitted by a moving object or is measured by a moving observer. As in the motion-detection case, the detector is stationary, any frequency shift in waves reflected from the scene must result from the motion of objects in the scene.

Both PIRs and active detectors overcome the inability of the beam-circuit detector to distinguish between a tiny intruder and a large one, as these detector types can be set to trigger a light, door, alarm, or other device only if a certain threshold in signal intensity is crossed. However, there is no one, correct threshold. When designing a system to detect intrusion or presence, one wishes to avoid both a high false-alarm rate (which will over activate lights or doors or, in the case of a security system, eventually cause human operators to ignore the system) and a high likelihood of real presence detection. Yet, these two goals are in opposition; an insensitive detector will fail to detect persons that enter its field of view, but a too-sensitive detector will detect not only intruders, but also insects, vibrations in its mounting bracket, and other causes of minor signal variation. A compromise sensitivity must be chosen for each device type and application.

A more complex but potentially more informative class of motion-detection systems applies computer analysis to video images. By looking for changes from one image frame to the next, a computer can easily detect motion in a scene; the difficulty is to design algorithms that can distinguish between important motion (a man climbing a fence) and unimportant motion (leaves rustling in trees, cloud-shadows moving over the ground, etc.). A reliable video-based motion-detection scheme, therefore, requires the application of artificial intelligence techniques. Such systems are under development, but not yet widely deployed.

■ FURTHER READING:

BOOKS:

Lester, Andrew J., and Clifton L. Smith. "Analyses of Performance of Volumetric Intrusion Detection Technologies." Proceedings, 33rd Annual International Carnahan Conference on Security Technology. Oct. 12–14, 1999: 111–58.

Mount Weather

Mount Weather, Virginia, is one of the United States Continuity of Government (COG) safety sites, though its exact COG functions are undisclosed. In the event of a national disaster that threatens normal government operations in Washington, D.C., facilities in locations such as Mount Weather are used to coordinate vital national operations. The facility is currently managed by the Federal Emergency Management Agency (FEMA) and is the home of the National Emergency Coordinating Center. The center manages FEMA operations after natural disasters and trains emergency management personnel. Though FEMA agents mostly handle more localized natural disasters, such as floods, hurricanes, or tornadoes, personnel are also trained to handle terrorist and massive attack scenarios.

The 434-acre mountain area that became Mount Weather was acquired by the National Weather Bureau (later, National Weather Service) in 1893. The bureau used the site to launch weather balloons and conduct atmospheric research. In the decades preceding World War I, the Weather Bureau monitored a series of kite stations on the site. The Army created an artillery range on the site at the outbreak of war in Europe in 1914. In 1936, the government granted Mount Weather to the Bureau of Mines. A series of tunneling experiments revealed that the mountain had an extremely dense and stable rock composition favorable to extensive tunnel construction. Recognizing the importance of such a site within a short distance of the national capital, the government restricted use of Mount Weather and planned to build a series of underground bunkers. Construction on the site was halted by World War II.

Amidst Cold War tensions, the government took a renewed interest in Mount Weather. In 1954, the Bureau of Mines began construction on the site's network of tunnels and underground rooms. Soon after construction started, security concerns prompted the government to shift control of the project to the military and the Army Corps of

Engineers finished construction of the subterranean facility in 1958. The facility was named "High Point" and was maintained as a shelter for government officials in the event of an attack on Washington, D.C. The underground structure contains offices, sleeping quarters, a hospital, independent water, sewage, and power systems, and radio, television, and computer networks. Estimates on its capacity vary, but Mount Weather is assumed to be able to support over 200 residents for one month.

FEMA was granted control of the premises in 1979, but much of the facility remains classified. FEMA's aboveground facility serves as a command base for its national all-hazards operations. The communication networks located in the underground structure are part of the Emergency Broadcasting System, the national emergency alert system. The Resource Interruption Monitoring System (RIMS) tracks daily function and activity of vital national resources such as power systems and oil reserves. The Contingency Impact Analysis System (CIAS) creates and directs simulations of emergencies for training and readiness assessment purposes.

The largest operational center on the site is the FEMA Mount Weather Assistance Center. The center administers FEMA's aid operations and often processes calls regarding aid requests and claims immediately following a disaster. While regional FEMA offices are equipped to handle most emergencies, the Mount Weather site is frequently active as a reserve operations post for disaster mitigation. Though FEMA continues operations on the site, the Continuity of Government emergency plan and facilities at Mount Weather have only been activated on two occasions. The first full-scale activation occurred during the Northeastern power blackout of November 9, 1965. More recently, some Mount Weather COG measures were set in motion after the September 11, 2001, terrorist attacks.

A government initiated expansion and renovation of many Mount Weather facilities began in 2001.

■ FURTHER READING:

ELECTRONIC:

Federal Emergency Management Agency. Mount Weather Emergency Assistance Center homepage. <http://www.fema.gov/pte/weather.htm>(November 20, 2002).

SEE ALSO

Continuity of Government, United States
Emergency Response Teams

Movies, Espionage and Intelligence Portrayals

■ JUDSON KNIGHT

Although depictions of espionage, intelligence, and related activities in motion pictures have not always tended toward realism, the movies' portrayals of covert operations have to an extent mirrored events in the real world. Through the end of World War II, the activities depicted usually involved Nazis, but by the late 1950s, Hollywood had entered the Cold War espionage genre. Later decades have seen portrayals of terrorism and counterterrorism, as well as intelligence and security operations in futuristic settings. From the 1960s onward, the James Bond movies and other films and television shows have given increasingly whimsical treatments to covert operations. Hence it is ironic that some of what seemed like fanciful spy technology in the Bond movies of another time is now standard equipment, in some cases even within the civilian sector.

From World War I to the Cold War

As early as 1918, with *I Want to Forget* (starring Evelyn Nesbit, whose involvement in a real-life murder drama would be depicted many years later in the book and film *Ragtime*), Hollywood set out to portray spies in film, but most early attempts were less than successful. Pre-World War II films on espionage tended to focus on the romantic and dramatic associations, and offered little in the way of authenticity.

Most authentic among the depictions of espionage in this era were the films of Alfred Hitchcock, whose most well-known espionage thrillers of the prewar era included the first version of *The Man Who Knew Too Much* (1934) and *The 39 Steps* (1935). These films established a theme that would become a fixture of spy movies thenceforth: the non-spy who stumbles into the middle of a conspiracy and is caught up in events he or she does not fully understand. Usually the non-spy ends up providing a key solution or otherwise outsmarting intelligence professionals—a resolution drawn from fantasy rather than real life.

World War II. As World War II began, Hitchcock released *Foreign Correspondent* (1940). The war years featured numerous films depicting Nazi, Japanese, and Allied espionage, and in this era before the establishment of the Central Intelligence Agency (CIA), the spy-hunters were usually special agents in the Federal Bureau of Investigation (FBI).

The era also saw one of the first movies to offer a humorous treatment of espionage: *They Got Me Covered* (1943), in which Bob Hope and Dorothy Lamour teamed

A War Room conference scene from "Dr. Strangelove, or: How I Learned to Stop Worrying and Love the Bomb," a 1964 movie satirizing Cold War tensions among nuclear superpowers. ©THE KOBAL COLLECTION.

up as a pair of amateur spy-hunters chasing Nazis in Washington, D.C. More accurate portrayals of espionage in World War II—e.g., *The Man Who Never Was* (1956) and *Eye of the Needle* (1981, based on a Ken Follett novel of the same title)—had to wait until after the war was over.

A rare exception to the less-than-serious treatment of espionage during the war years actually appeared at the very beginning of the war: Warner Brothers' *Confessions of a Nazi Spy* (1939), starring Edward G. Robinson. As Michael E. Birdwell's 1999 book *Celluloid Soldiers* attested, Jack and Harry Warner were the first major figures in Hollywood to address Nazism, and at a time when the United States remained isolationist, this made *Confessions* a controversial film. According to Birdwell, members of the cast and crew received threats during production, and upon its release, the U.S. Senate called for an investigation of "war-mongering propaganda." Ironically, hearings began in October 1941, just two months before America entered the war against Germany.

The early Cold War period. Espionage movies, like espionage itself, especially flourished in the Cold War era. Such films as *The Iron Curtain* (1948) and *The Third Man* (1949),

with a screenplay by Graham Greene, gave early notice of the high quality of the portrayals. This high quality continued throughout the early Cold War era, with offerings that included *Our Man in Havana* (1959, with a screenplay by Greene adapted from his novel); *The Manchurian Candidate* (1962), based on a Richard Condon novel involving brainwashing in the Korean War; and *The Spy Who Came in from the Cold* (1965), from a John Le Carré novel.

Hitchcock easily made the move to Cold War espionage with works such as his remake of *The Man Who Knew Too Much* (1955), now in a Cold War setting with James Stewart. *North by Northwest* (1959) returned to the theme of the innocent—played in this case by Cary Grant—caught in the middle of a vast international conspiracy. The title of a less well-known, but still critically acclaimed Hitchcock offering from this era, *Torn Curtain* (1966), with Paul Newman and Julie Andrews, refers not to a piece of fabric, but to the iron curtain.

James Bond and the Marriage of Humor, Fantasy, and Espionage

By the late 1950s, depictions of espionage had reached a point at which filmmakers and TV producers could take an entirely different approach. Instead of portraying covert action with the utmost of seriousness, these activities became fodder either for comedy or outlandish fantasy with a comedic twist. No greater example of this trend existed than James Bond, hero of 14 novels by Ian Fleming, himself a British intelligence officer.

Bond, Agent 007 in British intelligence, has a license to kill, and he uses that license—along with the audience's willful suspension of disbelief—to the utmost in his endless operations against the Soviet-style organization known as Smersh. Whereas the Bond of Fleming's books has a cerebral, serious quality, on screen his exploits are so outlandish as to be comical—and intentionally so. As unbelievable as Bond's ability to come away unscathed from every adventure are his seemingly endless seductions of beautiful women, none of whom make any serious emotional demands on him, although several do try to kill him.

For all their apparently unrealistic qualities, the Bond films draw on elements of reality. Smersh was a real Soviet organization, founded by Josef Stalin, and the use of the initial "M" for Bond's boss is a play on the "C" used to designate real-life heads of MI6, the British Secret Intelligence Service. Another figure with an initial for a name, "Q," serves a function not unlike that of the Directorate of Science and Technology at the CIA.

It is Q's job to supply Bond with technologically sophisticated, extremely efficient gadgetry designed to help him meet any challenge. These gadgets are a key feature of the Bond movies, and of other espionage films and TV shows in later years, such as *Mission: Impossible* and *Get Smart*. Many of the devices that seemed otherworldly in the 1960s—wireless telephones, films on silver discs, and computers small enough to fit into the palm of one's hand—are part of everyday life today.

The first Bond book became *Casino Royale* (1953), with David Niven as Bond, but the true Bond film canon begins with *Dr. No* 10 years later. The movie was the first in the series to feature Sean Connery, the actor most widely praised for his portrayals of Bond, and it introduced the first of many beautiful "Bond girls," Ursula Andress. With sexual liberation on the rise, and feminism still lagging behind at that time, subsequent Bond films featured numerous gorgeous sidekicks, seduced by Bond, only to be conveniently eliminated at some point, leaving the hero free to seek further partners in a future adventure.

Connery perfected his Bond persona over the course of four more movies in the 1960s: *From Russia, with Love* (1963), *Goldfinger* (1964), *Thunderball* (1965), and *You Only Live Twice* (1967). Fashion model George Lazenby took over the Bond role in *On Her Majesty's Secret Service* (1969), but proved to be the least critically and popularly successful of all Bonds. Connery played Bond a fifth time in *Diamonds Are Forever* (1971).

The next five Bond movies featured Roger Moore: *Live and Let Die* (1973), *The Man with the Golden Gun* (1974), *The Spy Who Loved Me* (1977), *Moonraker* (1979),

and *For Your Eyes Only*. The last was released in June 1983, four months before Connery reappeared in a low-budget, critically panned final Bond performance, *Never Say Never Again* (1983). After Moore played Bond a sixth and final time in *A View to a Kill* (1985), Timothy Dalton took over in *The Living Daylights* (1987).

At this point, producers had expended all novels, screenplays, and treatments by Fleming, who died in 1964. The first Bond film that did not feature Fleming's work was *Licence to Kill* (1989), also starring Dalton. The franchise went silent for six years, then revived in the mid-1990s with a series of films starring Pierce Brosnan as Bond: *Golden Eye* (1995), *Tomorrow Never Dies* (1997), *The World Is Not Enough* (1999), and *Die Another Day* (2002).

Cold War reality also mingled with humor in the black comedy *Dr. Strangelove; or, How I Learned to Stop Worrying and Love the Bomb* (1964). Peter Sellers impersonated both United States and Soviet leaders in the doomsday film, which culminates in an inadvertent global thermonuclear war.

Television, fantasy, and humor. Simultaneous with the heyday of Bond movies in the 1960s was the advent of television shows with an approach to espionage that was either fantastic, humorous, or both. Among these were the *The Avengers*, which debuted in 1961; *The Man from U.N.C.L.E.* (1964); *Get Smart* (1965), which, like *U.N.C.L.E.* and Bond, was heavy on gadgetry, with another Smersh-like enemy called CHAOS; *The Wild Wild West* (1965), which cleverly backdated modern intrigue and technology, setting them in the old West; *I Spy* (1965), the first television show featuring an African American star, Bill Cosby; *Mission: Impossible* (1966), which sometimes bordered on a serious portrayal of special operations, and which spawned two films starring Tom Cruise in the 1990s; and *The Prisoner* (1967).

The comedic is a recurring element of espionage films of the 1970s and beyond, including *The In-Laws* (1979), which was remade in 2003; *Dead Men Don't Wear Plaid* (1982), with Steve Martin; a number of Leslie Nielsen movies, in which Nielsen plays a bumbling intelligence or law enforcement officer; and *True Lies* (1994), which mixes a semi-serious portrayal of an organization akin to the CIA with comedic touches, courtesy of Tom Arnold and Arnold Schwarzenegger.

Particularly successful have been the film series spawned by two 1997 espionage spoofs. *Austin Powers: International Man of Mystery*, in which Mike Myers plays an unlikely James Bond figure, led to two sequels, and *Men in Black*, starring Tommy Lee Jones and Will Smith, has had one. The latter series plays off of conspiracy theories concerning U.S. intelligence and studies of unidentified flying objects (UFOs) in the late 1940s and beyond, taking as its premise the idea that the UFOs actually were alien spacecraft—a fact that the government has concealed from the populace.

The period from the 1970s onward has seen an ever-expanding variety of films that treat espionage, intelligence, special operations, or terrorism. Notable early examples from this period include *The Day of the Jackal* (1973), *The Conversation* (1974), and *Three Days of the Condor* (1975). Some other critically or popular acclaimed films have included *Another Country* (1984), about the formative years of British turncoat Guy Burgess; *Terminator* (1984) and *Terminator 2* (1991), with Schwarzenegger as an assassin from the future; and *Proof of Life* (2000), in which Russell Crowe plays an undercover operative in the private sector who rescues hostages from terrorist kidnappers.

As time has gone on, the nature of protagonists has evolved from the early emphasis on single white males in the mold of James Bond. *Enter the Dragon* (1973) features an Asian main character, played by Bruce Lee, who spies on a drug cartel while taking part in a martial arts competition. Numerous "blaxploitation" movies of the 1970s feature African American law enforcement or intelligence operatives who usually uncover white perfidy and black collusion. By 2002, *Undercover Brother* spoofed these themes with its portrayal of an all-black intelligence organization called The Brotherhood, which is pitted against white enemies that include White She-Devil and The Man, both of them affiliated with the evil Operation Whitewash.

In *Undercover Blues* (1993), the spy team consists of a married couple (Dennis Quaid and Kathleen Turner) with a six-month-old baby. By then, women protagonists in espionage films were far from unusual. The mid-1980s featured a number of such films with female protagonists, examples being *The Little Drummer Girl* (adapted from a Le Carre novel, 1984), *Jumpin' Jack Flash* (1986), and *Outrageous Fortune* (1987). All of these—starring Diane Keaton, Whoopi Goldberg, and Shelley Long respectively—played on the theme, made famous by Hitchcock, of the innocent caught up in clandestine activities. *Confessions of a Dangerous Mind* (2002) took this "innocent" theme a step further, with its tale of *Gong Show* host Chuck Barris's alleged recruitment by U.S. intelligence.

Drummer Girl and *Jackal* (from a book by Frederick Forsythe) were just two of many book adaptations from the late twentieth and early twenty-first centuries. Particularly notable in this regard were adaptations of Tom Clancy's Jack Ryan books, with Alec Baldwin playing Ryan in *The Hunt for Red October* (1990); Harrison Ford in *Patriot Games* (1992) and *Clear and Present Danger* (1994); and Ben Affleck in *The Sum of All Fears* (2002). Two books published much earlier, *Mother Night* by Kurt Vonnegut and *The Bourne Identity* by Robert Ludlum, were finally adapted for the screen in 1996 and 2002 respectively.

Terrorism. *Patriot Games* was just one of many films about terrorism, and terrorism in Northern Ireland particularly.

The trend began in the 1970s, as terrorism became an increasingly common element of modern life. *Black Sunday* (1977) portrayed fictional events, but many more have, either through drama or documentary, depicted real ones. Examples include *21 Hours at Munich* (1976), *Hijacking of the Achille Lauro* (1989) and *Voyage of Terror: The Achille Lauro Affair* (1990), and *The Tragedy of Flight 103: The Inside Story* (1990). The first World Trade Center bombing was the subject of *Without Warning: Terror in the Towers* (1993), while several documentaries, including *9–11: American Reflections* (2001), *9/11* (2002), and *WTC: The First 24 Hours* (2002), have portrayed the second attack.

Films on the Northern Ireland theme include *Harry's Game* (1982), *The Crying Game* (1992), *In the Name of the Father* (1993), *Michael Collins* (1996), *The Boxer* (1997), *The Devil's Own* (1997), and *The Jackal* (1997), a critically panned remake of *Day of the Jackal* with a change of scenery and characters. Depictions of terrorist-controlled hostage scenarios became popular after the success of *Die Hard* (1988). Many of these have featured airplanes, examples being *Die Hard 2* (1990), *Passenger 57* (1992), *Executive Decision* (1996), and *Air Force One* (1997). The plot of *Barcelona* (1994) includes terrorism of the Cold War era, while *Brazil* (1985) presents a vision of terrorism in the future. After the real-life events of September 2001, the theme has proven less popular in films. As a result of the bombings, Warner Brothers delayed release of its terrorist-related *Collateral Damage* (2002), which starred Schwarzenegger.

■ **FURTHER READING:**

BOOKS:

Birdwell, Michael E. *Celluloid Soldiers: The Warner Bros. Campaign Against Nazism.* New York: New York University Press, 1999.

Gregg, Robert. *International Relations on Film.* Boulder, CO: Lynne Rienner Publishers, 1998.

Lisanti, Tom, and Louis Paul. *Film Fatales: Women in Espionage Films and Television, 1962–1973.* Jefferson, NC: McFarland, 2002.

Mavis, Paul. *The Espionage Filmography: United States Releases, 1898 Through 1999.* Jefferson, NC: McFarland, 2001.

ELECTRONIC:

Internet Movie Database. <http://us.imdb.com> (April 30, 2003).

SEE ALSO

Assassination Weapons, Mechanical
Black Ops
Cameras, Miniature
Drop
Intelligence Literature
Nuclear Regulatory Commission (NRC), United States

Mujahedin-e Khalq Organization (MEK or MKO)

The Mujahedin-e Khalq Organization (MEK or MKO) philosophy mixes Marxism and Islam. Formed in the 1960s, the organization was expelled from Iran after the Islamic Revolution in 1979. Prior to Operation Iraqi Freedom in March 2003, its primary support came from the Iraqi regime of Saddam Hussein. MEK history is studded with anti-Western attacks as well as terrorist attacks on the interests of the clerical regime in Iran and abroad. The MEK now advocates a secular Iranian regime.

The MEK also operates as, or is known as: The National Liberation Army of Iran (NLA, the militant wing of the MEK), the People's Mujahidin of Iran (PMOI), National Council of Resistance (NCR), Muslim Iranian Student's Society (front organization used to garner financial support).

Organization activities. The MEK worldwide campaign against the Iranian government stresses propaganda and occasionally uses terrorist violence. During the 1970s the MEK killed several U.S. military personnel and U.S. civilians working on defense projects in Tehran. It supported the takeover in 1979 of the U.S. Embassy in Tehran. In 1981 the MEK planted bombs in the head office of the Islamic Republic Party and the Premier's office, killing some 70 high-ranking Iranian officials, including Chief Justice Ayatollah Mohammad Beheshti, President Mohammad-Ali Rajaei, and Premier Mohammad-Javad Bahonar. In 1991, it assisted the government of Iraq in suppressing the Shia and Kurdish uprisings in northern and southern Iraq. Until Operation Iraqi Freedom the MEK continued to perform internal security services for Saddam Hussein's government. In April 1992, MEK conducted attacks on Iranian embassies in 13 different countries, demonstrating the group's ability to mount large-scale operations overseas. In recent years the MEK has targeted key military officers and assassinated the deputy chief of the Armed Forces General Staff in April 1999. In April 2000, the MEK attempted to assassinate the commander of the Nasr Headquarters—then the interagency board responsible for coordinating policies on Iraq.

The normal pace of MEK anti-Iranian operations increased during Operation Great Bahman in February 2000, when the group launched a dozen attacks against Iran. In 2000 and 2001, the MEK was involved regularly in mortar attacks and hit-and-run raids on Iranian military and law enforcement units and government buildings near the Iran-Iraq border. Since the end of the Iran-Iraq War the tactics along the border have garnered few military gains and have become commonplace. Prior to Operation Iraqi Freedom, MEK insurgent activities in Tehran constituted the biggest security concern for the Iranian leadership. In February 2000, for example, the MEK attacked the leadership complex in Tehran that houses the offices of the supreme leader and president.

Prior to Operation Iraqi Freedom, several thousand MEK fighters were located on bases scattered throughout Iraq and armed with tanks, infantry fighting vehicles, and artillery. The MEK also had an overseas support structure. Most of the fighters were organized in the MEK's National Liberation Army (NLA). Following Operation Iraqi Freedom and the removal of Saddam Hussein's government in April 2003, the fate of the MEK remains undetermined.

In the 1980s the MEK's leaders were forced by Iranian security forces to flee to France. After resettling in Iraq in 1987, the group conducted internal security operations in support of Saddam Hussein's regime. In the mid-1980s the group did not mount terrorist operations in Iran at a level similar to its activities in the 1970s, but by the 1990s the MEK had claimed credit for an increasing number of operations in Iran. Beyond support from the former Iraqi regime, the MEK used front organizations to solicit contributions from expatriate Iranian communities.

■ FURTHER READING:

ELECTRONIC:

Central Intelligence Agency. World Factbook, 2002. <http://www.cia.gov/cia/publications/factbook/> (April 16, 2003).

Taylor, Francis X. U.S. Department of State. Patterns of Global Terrorism 2001. Annual Report: On the Record Briefing. May 21, 2002 <http://www.state.gov/s/ct/rls/rm/10367.htm> (April 17, 2003).

U.S. Department of State. Annual reports. <http://www.state.gov/www/global/terrorism/annual_reports.html> (April 16, 2003).

SEE ALSO

Terrorism, Philosophical and Ideological Origins
Terrorist and Para-State Organizations
Terrorist Organization List, United States
Terrorist Organizations, Freezing of Assets

Multisensory Grenades.

SEE *Audio Amplifiers.*

Mustard Gas

■ JUDYTH SASSOON

Mustard gas is a substance used in chemical warfare. It is the popular name for the compound with the chemical

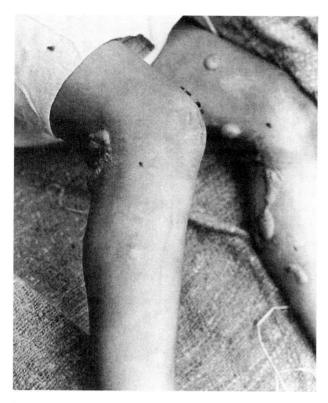

Blisters on the legs of a Chinese soldier after exposure to mustard gas in 1941. ©BETTMANN/CORBIS.

corrosive hydrochloric acid and several other vesicant intermediates, which are able to blister epithelial surfaces.

Despite the ease of hydrolysis, mustard gas may be preserved underground in a solid form for up to ten years. The reason for this is that in an environment where the concentration of water is relatively low, the reaction pathway proceeds to form an intermediate known as thiodiglycol. In a low moisture environment, most of the water available at the solid surface is used in this reaction. Subsequently, another intermediate in the reaction pathway, a sulfonium ion, reacts with the thiodiglycol in the place of water. This reaction then creates stable, non-reactive sulfonium salts, which can act as a protective layer around the bulk of the solid mustard preventing further degradation.

Mustard gas as a chemical weapon is a particularly deadly and debilitating poison and when it was first used in 1917, it could penetrate all the masks and protective materials that were available at that time. In more recent years, urethane was found to be resistant to mustard gas, and also has several other advantages for use in combat; urethane is tough, resistant to cuts and is stable at a wide range of temperatures.

Detoxification procedures from mustard gas are difficult because of its insolubility and also because of the drastic effects it can have on lung epithelial tissue following inhalation. During World War I, physicians had no curative means of treating the victims of mustard gas exposure. The only method of detoxification that was known involved a rather extreme oxidation procedure using superchlorinated bleaches, such as 5% sodium hypochlorite. Today, several novel methods of detoxification have been developed to counter the effects of mustard gas and these include the use of sulphur-amine solutions and magnesium monoperoxyphthalate. The most effective method to date employs peroxy acids, because they are able to react quickly with the mustard gas. Furthermore, the addition of a catalyst can speed up the detoxification reaction even more effectively.

Although mustard gas has been shown to have long-term carcinogenic properties, it can also be used as an agent in the treatment of cancer. In 1919, it was observed that victims of mustard gas attack had a low white blood cell count and bone marrow aplasia (tissue growth failure). More detailed research in the years following 1946 showed that nitrogen mustards, which differ from traditional mustard gas, could reduce tumor growth in experimental mice by cross-linking DNA strands. It had been shown previously that the sensitivity of mouse bone marrow to mustard gas was similar to that of humans and more detailed research eventually led to successful clinical trials. Today, nitrogen mustards are part of the spectrum of substances used in modern anti-cancer chemotherapy. They are primarily used in the treatment of conditions such as Hodgkin's disease and cancers of the lymph glands.

designation 1,1-thiobis(2-chloroethane) (chemical formula: Cl-CH2-CH2-S-CH2-CH2-Cl). Mustard gas has a number of other names by which it has been known over the years, including H, yprite, sulfur mustard and Kampstoff Lost. Because the impure substance is said to have an odor similar to that of mustard, garlic or horseradish, the name mustard gas is most commonly applied. However, in the pure form, mustard gas has neither color nor odor. The gas was used for the first time as an agent of chemical warfare during World War I, when it was distributed with devastating effect near Ypres in Flanders on July 12, 1917.

The synthesis of mustard gas was reported much earlier than its first use as a chemical weapon. In 1860, Frederick Guthrie observed that when ethylene reacted with chlorine a substance was produced which, in small quantities, could produce toxic effects on the skin. Exposure to low concentrations of mustard gas classically causes the reddening and blistering of skin and epithelial tissue. On inhalation, the gas will cause the lining of the lungs to blister and leads to chronic respiratory impairment. Higher concentrations of mustard gas will attack the corneas of the eyes and eventually cause blindness. Exposure to mustard gas can lead to a slow and painful death and any moist area of the body is especially susceptible to its effects. The compound is only slightly soluble in water, but it undergoes a hydrolysis reaction liberating highly

■ FURTHER READING:

PERIODICALS:

Devereaux, A., D. E. Amundson, J. S. Parrish, and A. A. Lazarus. "Vesicants and nerve agents in chemical warfare: Decontamination and treatment strategies for a changed world." *Postgrad. Med.* 1 (2002): 90–96.

Evison, D., D. Hinsley, and P. Rice. "Chemical Weapons." *BMJ* 324 (2002): 332–335.

Jones, G. B. "From mustard gas to medicines: the history of modern cancer chemotherapy" *Chem. Herit.* 15 (1998): 8–9; 40–2.

ELECTRONIC:

United Kingdom National Archives Learning Curve. "Mustard gas." <http://www.spartacus.schoolnet.co.uk/FWWmustard.htm> (February 20, 2003).

SEE ALSO

Nerve Gas

NAILS (National Automated Immigration Lookout System)

NAILS (National Automated Immigration Lookout System) is a centralized database and computing system used by entry inspectors to identify aliens not eligible for admission. NAILS (and the updated version, NAILS II) allows inspectors to quickly retrieve and review biographical or historical case data and was designed to facilitate evaluation of entrant status.

The primary source of data for the NAILS database is gleaned directly from data supplied by potential immigrants on entry and immigration documents. This base of data provides a framework for the addition of information obtained from other federal, state, and foreign agencies.

Following the September 11, 2001, terrorist attacks on the United States, the NAILS system drew criticism because it is essentially a name-based system that can be thwarted by the use of a false name or falsified supporting documents. By relying on names rather than biometrics, NAILS provided gaps through which determined terrorists could slip into the United States.

NAILS is a secure database with access restricted on a "need to know" basis that was, prior to March 2003, operated by the Immigration and Naturalization Service (INS). On March 1, the newly created United States Department of Homeland Security (DHS) absorbed the former Immigration and Naturalization Service (INS). All INS border patrol agents and investigators—along with agents from the U.S. Customs Service and Transportation Security Administration—were placed under the direction of the DHS Directorate of Border and Transportation Security (BTS). Responsibility for U.S. border security and the enforcement of immigration laws was transferred to BTS.

BTS is scheduled to incorporate the United States Customs Service (previously part of the Department of Treasury), and the enforcement division of the Immigration and Naturalization Service (previously part of the Department of Justice). Former INS immigration service functions are scheduled to be placed under the direction of the DHS Bureau of Citizenship and Immigration Services. Under the reorganization the INS formally ceases to exist on the date the last of its functions are transferred.

Although the description of the technologies involved in the NAILS entry security program remain the same as when operated by the INS, in an effort to facilitate border security, BTS envisions higher levels of coordination between formerly separate agencies and databases. As of April 2003, the specific coordination and future of the NAILS program was uncertain with regard to name changes, program administration, and policy changes.

Although the NAILS system is limited as an isolated system, even prior to DHS integration, data contained in the NAILS system, along with data from the Consular Lookout and Support System (CLASS), and the Treasury Enforcement Communications System (TECS II), was available to inspectors through the Interagency Border Inspection System (IBIS) maintained by U.S. Customs Service.

One reason for separate database systems is that it allows easier compartmentalization of data, keeping classified information secure while allowing access to data that may be requested under the Freedom of Information Act (FOIA).

■ FURTHER READING:

ELECTRONIC:

Department of Homeland Security. April 2, 2003. <http://www.dhs.gov/dhspublic/index.jsp> (April 11, 2003).

Department of Homeland Security, Bureau of Citizenship and Immigration Services. Law Enforcement: The National Border Patrol Strategy. <http://www.immigration.gov/graphics/publicaffairs/statements/igstate.htm> (April 12, 2003).

SEE ALSO

APIS (Advance Passenger Information System)
IBIS (Interagency Border Inspection System)
IDENT (Automated Biometric Identification System)
INSPASS (Immigration and Naturalization Service Passenger Accelerated Service System)
PORTPASS (Port Passenger Accelerated Service System)
SENTRI (Secure Electronic Network for Travelers' Rapid Inspection)

Name Recognition Software.

SEE IBIS (Interagency Border Inspection System).

Nanotechnology

K. LEE LERNER

Defense programs in many countries are now concentrating on nanotechnology research that will facilitate advances in such technology used to create secure but small messaging equipment, allow the development of smart weapons, improve stealth capabilities, aid in developing specialized sensors (including bio-inclusive sensors), help to create self-repairing military equipment, and improve the development and delivery mechanisms for medicines and vaccines.

Nanotechnology builds on advances in microelectronics during the last decades of the twentieth century. The miniaturization of electrical components greatly increased the utility and portability of computers, imaging equipment, microphones, and other electronics. Indeed, the production and wide use of such commonplace devices such as personal computers and cell phones was absolutely dependent on advances in microtechnology.

Despite these fundamental advances there remain real physical constraints (e.g., microchip design limitations) to further miniaturization based upon conventional engineering principles. Nanotechnologies intend to revolutionize components and manufacturing techniques to overcome these fundamental limitations. In addition, there are classes of biosensors and feedback control devices that require nanotechnology because—despite advances in microtechnology—present components remain too large or slow.

Advances in Nanotechnology

Nanotechnology advances affect all branches of engineering and science that deal directly with device components ranging in size between 1/10,000,000 (one ten millionth of a millimeter) and 1/10,0000 millimeter. At these scales, even the most sophisticated microtechnology-based instrumentation is useless. Engineers anticipate that advances in nanotechnology will allow the direct manipulation of molecules in biological samples (e.g., proteins or nucleic acids) paving the way for the development of new materials that have a biological component or that can provide a biological interface.

In addition to new tools, nanotechnology programs advance practical understanding of quantum physics. The internalization of quantum concepts is a necessary component of nanotechnology research programs because the laws of classical physics (e.g., classical mechanics or generalized gas laws) do not always apply to the atomic and near-atomic level.

Nanotechnology and quantum physics. Quantum theory and mechanics describe the relationship between energy and matter on the atomic and subatomic scale. At the beginning of the twentieth century, German physicist Maxwell Planck (1858–1947) proposed that atoms absorb or emit electromagnetic radiation in bundles of energy termed quanta. This quantum concept seemed counter-intuitive to well-established Newtonian physics. Advancements associated with quantum mechanics (e.g., the uncertainty principle) also had profound implications with regard to the philosophical scientific arguments regarding the limitations of human knowledge.

Planck's quantum theory, which also asserted that the energy of light (a photon) was directly proportional to its frequency, proved a powerful concept that accounted for a wide range of physical phenomena. Planck's constant relates the energy of a photon with the frequency of light. Along with the constant for the speed of light, Planck's constant ($h = 6.626 \times 10^{-34}$ Joule-second) is a fundamental constant of nature.

Prior to Planck's work, electromagnetic radiation (light) was thought to travel in waves with an infinite number of available frequencies and wavelengths. Planck's work focused on attempting to explain the limited spectrum of light emitted by hot objects. Danish physicist Niels Bohr (1885–1962) studied Planck's quantum theory of radiation and worked in England with physicists J. J. Thomson (1856–1940), and Ernest Rutherford (1871–1937) to improve their classical models of the atom by incorporating quantum theory. During this time, Bohr developed his model of atomic structure. According to the Bohr model, when an electron is excited by energy it jumps from its ground state to an excited state (i.e., a higher energy orbital). The excited atom can then emit energy only in certain (quantized) amounts as its electrons jump back to lower energy orbits located closer to the nucleus. This excess energy is emitted in quanta of electromagnetic radiation (photons of light) that have exactly the same energy as the difference in energy between the orbits jumped by the electron.

The electron quantum leaps between orbits proposed by the Bohr model accounted for Plank's observations that atoms emit or absorb electromagnetic radiation in quanta. Bohr's model also explained many important properties of the photoelectric effect described by Albert Einstein (1879–1955). Einstein assumed that light was transmitted as a stream of particles termed photons. By extending the well-known wave properties of light to include a treatment of light as a stream of photons, Einstein was able to explain the photoelectric effect. Photoelectric properties are key to regulation of many microtechnology and proposed nanotechnology level systems.

Quantum mechanics ultimately replaced electron "orbitals" of earlier atomic models with allowable values for angular momentum (angular velocity multiplied by mass) and depicted electron positions in terms of probability "clouds" and regions.

In the 1920s, the concept of quantization and its application to physical phenomena was further advanced by more mathematically complex models based on the work of the French physicist Louis Victor de Broglie (1892–1987) and Austrian physicist Erwin Schrödinger (1887–1961) that depicted the particle and wave nature of electrons. De Broglie showed that the electron was not merely a particle but a waveform. This proposal led Schrödinger to publish his wave equation in 1926. Schrödinger's work described electrons as a "standing wave" surrounding the nucleus, and his system of quantum mechanics is called wave mechanics. German physicist Max Born (1882–1970) and English physicist P. A. M. Dirac (1902–1984) made further advances in defining the subatomic particles (principally the electron) as a wave rather than as a particle and in reconciling portions of quantum theory with relativity theory.

Working at about the same time, German physicist Werner Heisenberg (1901–1976) formulated the first complete and self-consistent theory of quantum mechanics. Matrix mathematics was well established by the 1920s, and Heisenberg applied this powerful tool to quantum mechanics. In 1926, Heisenberg put forward his uncertainty principle which states that two complementary properties of a system, such as position and momentum, can never both be known exactly. This proposition helped cement the dual nature of particles (e.g., light can be described as having both wave and particle characteristics). Electromagnetic radiation (one region of the spectrum that comprises visible light) is now understood to have both particle and wave like properties.

In 1925, Austrian-born physicist Wolfgang Pauli (1900–1958) published the Pauli exclusion principle states that no two electrons in an atom can simultaneously occupy the same quantum state (i.e., energy state). Pauli's specification of spin ($+\frac{1}{2}$ or $-\frac{1}{2}$) on an electron gave the two electrons in any suborbital differing quantum numbers (a system used to describe the quantum state) and

made completely understandable the structure of the periodic table in terms of electron configurations (i.e., the energy-related arrangement of electrons in energy shells and suborbitals).

In 1931, American chemist Linus Pauling published a paper that used quantum mechanics to explain how two electrons, from two different atoms, are shared to make a covalent bond between the two atoms. Pauling's work provided the connection needed in order to fully apply the new quantum theory to chemical reactions.

Advances in nanotechnology depend upon an understanding and application of these fundamental quantum principles. At the quantum level the smoothness of classical physics disappears and nanotechnologies are predicated on exploiting this quantum roughness.

Applications

The development of devices that are small, light, self-contained, use little energy and that will replace larger microelectronic equipment is one of the first goals of the anticipated nanotechnology revolution. The second phase will be marked by the introduction of materials not feasible at larger than nanotechnology levels. Given the nature of quantum variance, scientists theorize that single molecule sensors can be developed and that sophisticated memory storage and neural-like networks can be achieved with a very small number of molecules.

Traditional engineering concepts undergo radical transformation at the atomic level. For example, nanotechnology motors may drive gears, the cogs of which are composed of the atoms attached to a carbon ring. Nanomotors may themselves be driven by oscillating magnetic fields or high precision oscillating lasers.

Perhaps the greatest promise for nanotechnology lies in potential biotechnology advances. Potential nano-level manipulation of DNA offers the opportunity to radically expand the horizons of genomic medicine and immunology. Tissue-based biosensors may unobtrusively be able to monitor and regulate site-specific medicine delivery or regulate physiological processes. Nanosystems might serve as highly sensitive detectors of toxic substances or used by inspectors to detect traces of biological or chemical weapons.

In electronics and computer science, scientists assert that nanotechnologies will be the next major advance in computing and information processing science. Microelectronic devices rely on recognition and flips in electron gating (e.g. where differential states are ultimately represented by a series of binary numbers ["0" or "1"] that depict voltage states). In contrast, future quantum processing will utilize the identity of quantum states as set forth by quantum numbers. In quantum cryptography systems with the ability to decipher encrypted information will rely on precise knowledge of manipulations used to achieve various atomic states.

Nanoscale devices are constructed using a combination of fabrication steps. In the initial growth stage, layers of semiconductor materials are grown on a dimension limiting substrate. Layer composition can be altered to control electrical and/or optical characteristics. Techniques such as molecular beam epitaxy (MBE) and metallo-organic chemical vapor deposition (MOCVD) are capable of producing layers of a few atoms thickness. The developed pattern is then imposed on successive layers (the pattern transfer stage) to develop desired three dimensional structural characteristics.

Nanotechnology Research

In the United States, expenditures on nanotechnology development tops $500 million per year and is largely coordinated by the National Science Foundation and Department of Defense Advanced Research Projects Agency (DARPA) under the umbrella of the National Nanotechnology Initiative. Other institutions with dedicated funding for nanotechnology include the Department of Energy (DOE) and National Institutes of Health (NIH).

Research interests. Current research interests in nanotechnology include programs to develop and exploit nanotubes for their ability to provide extremely strong bonds. Nanotubes can be flexed and woven into fibers for use in ultrastrong—but also ultralight—bulletproof vests. Nanotubes are also excellent conductors that can be used to develop precise electronic circuitry.

Other interests include the development of nanotechnology-based sensors that allow smarter autonomous weapons capable of a greater range of adaptations enroute to a target; materials that offer stealth characteristics across a broader span of the electromagnetic spectrum; self-repairing structures; and nanotechnology-based weapons to disrupt—but not destroy—electrical system infrastructure.

■ FURTHER READING:

BOOKS:

Mulhall, Douglas. *Our Molecular Future: How Nanotechnology, Robotics, Genetics, and Artificial Intelligence Will Change Our World.* Amherst, NY: Prometheus Books, 2002.

PERIODICALS:

Bennewitz, R., et. al., "Atomic scale memory at a silicon surface." *Nanotechnology* 13 (2000): 499–502.

ELECTRONIC:

National Science and Technology Council. "National Nanotechnology Initiative." <http://www.nano.gov/start.htm> (March 19, 2003).

SEE ALSO
DARPA (Defense Advanced Research Projects Agency)

Napoleonic Wars, Espionage During

■ ALEXANDR IOFFE

The Napoleonic wars pitted France, led by Napoleon Bonaparte, against a number of countries in Europe from 1797 through 1815. At different times during this period, Great Britain, Austria, Russia, Prussia, Denmark, Sweden, and the Neapolitan Kingdom all waged war against France in various coalitions. The main rivals in this struggle were Great Britain and France. During this time, the methods of intelligence gathering, espionage, and counterespionage did not differ so much from modern methods, apart from the differences in technological progress. Compared to other periods, however, espionage was a much more intense activity during the Napoleonic wars. This rise in espionage activity resulted mainly from revolutionary events in France and the following French emigration, which was in turn, used by Britain to achieve their own goals.

France had one unsurpassed master of intrigue in the famous person of Joseph Fouché, who spied rampantly on his social and professional contacts alike. Fouché remained as permanent minister of police during four consecutive regimes: directory, consulate, empire, and the restored monarchy.

During this period, Switzerland became a place of intensive intelligence activity by Britain, mostly against France. In 1794 the new charge d'affaire of Great Britain was the newly arrived William Wickham (1761–1840), for whom his diplomatic work in Bern was a cover. Wickham's main activity was to collect information about France and to lead various royalist organizations, which acted inside France as well as abroad. In particular, Wickham organized invasions of royalist armies into France, one of which was the Quiberon Bay invasion of 1795; the effort failed within one month. Both Wickham's agents and those of the royalist organizations actively participated for almost three years in different conspiracies against France, but in 1797, many of those involved were arrested. Wickham was forced to leave Switzerland in 1798, but the successive charge d'affaire continued the same activity.

British espionage against the Italian Army of France was also well organized. Here, the main figures were Count d'Antreg, one of the organizers of the royalist underground, and the British diplomat Francis Drake. D'Antreg received information from the generals of the French army, such as key information about the Egyptian expedition of Bonaparte. D'Antreg was arrested in 1797 by the French in Venice and was scheduled for extradition to France, but was first granted an audience with Napoleon. After gaining Napoleon's favor, d'Antreg was released on his word of honor. He was then quickly aided in an escape to Switzerland.

British intelligence agents pursued Napoleon and his army during the Egypt expedition, and even attempted to organize the general's assassination. One well-known attempt was organized by one of the top officers of the British intelligence service. A fellow officer named Foure was married to one of Napoleon's mistresses; the plan called for Madame Foure to carry out the assassination during one of her dalliances with Napoleon. Foure eventually refused his mission, and the plan was not executed.

Another attempt to assassinate Napoleon was made on December 24, 1800. The First Consul Napoleon was required to be present at a performance in the Paris Grande Opera. When Napoleon's carriage rushed along Saint Nicolas Street, an explosion resounded. Napoleon did not suffer; his carriage was driving too quickly, but the power of the explosion was such that almost 50 people were killed or wounded and 46 neighboring houses were damaged. The source was a barrel of gunpowder laced with shrapnel that was hidden in a harnessed wagon at the roadside. At first, the Jacobins were accused of the attempt, and some were executed. But those who headed the investigation quickly determined that it was the work of royalists through whom was apparent "the hand of London."

Yet another attempt on Napoleon was undertaken by royalists (again supported from London) in 1803 to 1804, but it was stopped by Fouche's police. Fouche identified the plotters using his "Chouan's Geography," an elementary data base (card-index) compiled in his ministry containing detailed information about 1000 active royalists. The French word *chouan* is associated with royalty, or in this case, royalists.

Britain also actively collected all possible information about France during the Napoleonic period. For this purpose they used (in addition to traditional methods) various royalist organizations (in particular the "Correspondence," which mainly collected intelligence data). Smugglers, and fishers, and the inhabitants of Jersey Island were also actively recruited, especially during the continental blockade, for contact between Britain and the continent, as well as for espionage. One of these Jersey inhabitants, a British agent, was able to make 184 spying trips from Jersey to France before he was eventually captured by the French and executed in 1808.

Led by Fouche, the French used counterespionage and organized the assassinations of unwelcome persons, or at the least, discredited them. One example is the brilliantly executed operation directed against the British diplomat Francis Drake. The French agent Mehde de la

Touch was sent to London, where with great difficulty he was able to gain the confidence of top British authorities. De la Touch was able to persuade them that he represented a Jacobin committee that wanted to overthrow Napoleon. De la Touch was put in contact with Drake, at that time the ambassador in Munich, Bavaria, and using Drake, the phony committee was able to swindle large amounts of money from the British government. After a long period of such activity, the French published this information in the French press, Drake was discredited, and was forced to flee from Munich.

Napoleon himself was also actively interested in espionage. Among Napoleon's secret agents, the most successful was the Alsatian Charles Schulmeister, a trader from Strasbourg. Schulmeister brilliantly infiltrated the Austrian army, including its intelligence service, and by collecting vital information from and disseminating misinformation to the Austrian military commanders, ensured Napoleon's victory in Austria.

The year 1805 marked the beginning of Napoleon's war with Austria and Russia. Schulmeister was sent to Vienna with the mission to discern the character and plans of General Karl von Mack, commander of the Austrian Army on the Danube. Schulmeister gained the confidence of those in the aristocratic circles of Vienna and was soon introduced to General Mack. Schulmeister then persuaded Mack that he represented a royalist opposition, showing him secret data about the French army, given to him according to Napoleon's order, and false documents about his own Hungarian aristocratic origin. Soon Schulmeister was completely trusted by Mack and, incredibly, was designated chief of intelligence in General Mack's army. Schulmeister immediately informed Napoleon about Mack's plans, and Napoleon, in turn, ordered the printing of false newspapers and letters detailing the unrest in the French army. Mack swallowed the bait. He assumed that France was close to an uprising, and believed the information that Napoleon's troops were retreating from the front line on the Rhine River. He began to pursue the French. Most likely Mack was surprised when he collided with the "retreated" corps of French General Ney, and then discovered French troops at his flanks and back. The army of the gullible general was surrounded in Uhlm, and all that was left to do was to surrender. Napoleon then gained one of his most famous victories at the battle of Austerlitz, captured Vienna, and installed Schulmeister as its chief of police.

Napoleon soon required the further services of Schulmeister in Germany, where the operative set up an effective spy cluster that provided Napoleon, for a while, with valuable information from adversaries to the East. Schulmeister was awarded wealth for his efforts, but longed for the Legion of Honor, which Napoleon never bestowed, claiming, "gold is the only suitable reward for spies." After Napoleon's defeat at Waterloo and subsequent exile, Schulmeister was arrested, and bought his freedom with his fortune. Years later and nearly penniless,

Schulmeister sold tobacco at a stand in Strasbourg and regaled customers with stories of espionage during the Napoleonic wars.

■ FURTHER READING:

BOOKS:

Dallas, Gregor. *The Final Act: The Roads to Waterloo.* New York: Henry Holt and Co., 2001.

Durant, Will, and Ariel Durant. *The Age of Napoleon.* New York: Simon and Schuster, 1975.

ELECTRONIC:

Sparrow, Elizabeth. *Secret Service: British Agents in France, 1792–1815.* Woodbridge, UK: Boydell Press, 1999.

Hollins, David. "The Hidden Hand: Espionage and Napoleon." *Osprey Military Journal* Issue 2.2, Osprey Publishing, <http://www.ospreypublishing.com/content4.php/cid=71> (December 30, 2002).

SEE ALSO

France, Intelligence and Security

In a joint research project, the Defense Advanced Research Projects Agency, NASA, and the U.S. Air Force used a Grumman X-29A with a forward-swept wing in fighter research during the 1980's and 1990's. ©MUSEUM OF FLIGHT/CORBIS.

NASA (National Air and Space Administration)

■ MORGAN SIMPSON

The Department of Defense (DOD) and the National Aeronautics and Space Administration (NASA) have to date elevated aerospace technologies to great heights. In a July 31, 1915, interview in *Collier's Weekly,* aviation pioneer Orville Wright (1871–1948) said, "The greatest use of the aeroplane [airplane] to date has been as a tremendously big factor of modern warfare." His statement could also be considered true today, along with the role played by commercial transportation in world's affairs. The victory of the United States in Operation Iraqi Freedom in 2003 illustrated the utilization of air and space to quickly quell an opponent's fighting ability. In this conflict, air and space utilization came in the form of direct air support, air to ground strategic targeting, Global Positioning System (GPS) targeting, and aerospace reconnaissance, both airplane and satellite. This utilization of air and space remains among the most powerful physical tools for ensuring national security.

NASA and DOD joint research has propelled the advances that make air and space important military assets. NASA's part in national security strategy is not as substantial as it was during NASA's first 35 years of existence (during the space race), but it still plays an important role. As a national icon, NASA inspires nationalism in the American people, and its achievements are projected worldwide as an exhibit of America's scientific ability. A superpower nation with a space program was historically perceived as a potential threat to other nations, as seen with the United States reaction to the launching of the Soviet Union's *Sputnik* during the Cold War. The nation's response was the creation of a national civilian air and space agency called NASA.

NASA aeronautical research spurred numerous advances in aviation from which the military benefited; early studies regarding lifting bodies and fly-by-wire aircraft, which used NASA-developed electronics to control the inherently unstable aircraft, are two examples. Many of the aerospace research projects at the Dryden Flight Research Center (DFRC) in California are joint projects that advance aerospace engineering, science, and develop military hardware. Some of the research involves speed of sound (sonic and supersonic) studies, aeroelastic wing research, lifting body studies, unmanned vehicles, and other proprietary research.

Even though DOD and NASA have different space programs, they share numerous resources and have many joint contracts that support both the DOD program and the NASA program. These range from the simple support contracts for routine battery maintenance to expansive operations such as communications and spacecraft tracking. Both organizations share launch pads for expendable launch vehicles. Some of the expendable launch vehicles at the Kennedy Space Center (KSC) at Cape Canaveral, Florida, are the Titan, Atlas, and Delta rockets. Launch and other facilities at KSC are resources shared by NASA, the Navy, and the Air Force.

NASA played a direct role in national security by providing the means to take heavy payloads into orbit. DOD has made its most direct use of NASA equipment in utilizing the Space Shuttle to bring up numerous DOD payloads. The contents of many of these payloads are classified information. There have been ten DOD dedicated shuttle launches. They are STS 51C, 51J, 27, 28, 33, 36, 38, 39, 44, and 53 (STS, which stands for Space Transportation System, also known as the Space Shuttle). Many of these missions remain secret even today, although some general knowledge about national security-based payloads has been disseminated and reported. In *The Space Shuttle Roles, Missions and Accomplishments* space historian David M. Harland stated that the shuttle delivered three new reconnaissance satellites in recent years. One satellite, called Lacrosse, provides all-weather vehicle-tracking capability. Another satellite included an advanced geostationary listening post. The third satellite is considered to house advanced imaging capabilities. It remains a secret as to what other DOD dedicated missions delivered to orbit or accomplished using the shuttle. Classified DOD missions continue to be carried out today, but mainly utilize the expendable launch vehicles. DOD and NASA both frequently have multiple minor payloads in addition to the major payload on a mission (both shuttle and expendable) to save costs. Some of these minor payloads are DOD sponsored payloads.

At one point, the vision of routine Space Shuttle launches was so powerful that the Air Force reluctantly agreed to phase out expendable launch vehicles. The Air Force's acceptance of the shuttle came with imposing requirements on the shuttle to launch heavy payloads of up to 60,000 pounds and to provide a cargo bay of 18 meters. The shuttle's payload mass weight has been downgraded to increase its margin of safety. The failure of the shuttle to run routinely, once a week, and the *Challenger* accident in 1986 motivated the DOD and NASA to change the DOD's main launching platform back to the expendable launch vehicles. Department of Defense then moved to utilizing new heavy lifting expendable launch vehicles to replace the shuttle's heavy lifting capacity. These new heavy-launch expendable launch vehicles can deliver almost 50,000 pounds to low Earth orbit.

Launch vehicles, including the Space Shuttle, utilize hardware that could be used for military applications such as the sophisticated guidance and navigations systems. The loss of the Space Shuttle *Columbia* in 2003 required personnel to retrieve instrumentation from the crash site to secure it to protect the secrecy of the technology.

The most well known NASA personnel are its astronauts. Astronauts have been used to carry out the DOD dedicated Space Shuttle missions. This required the astronauts to receive training on the secret payloads in order to properly execute the mission. The classified information given to the astronauts is usually kept to a minimum of relevant required knowledge. The payloads are normally loaded into the launch vehicle at the latest possible opportunity in order to maintain security. Shuttle astronauts repaired one DOD satellite via EVA (Extra Vehicular Activity), spacewalk, when it failed to start. The majority of astronauts chosen for these missions have a military background, mostly for the flight experience. It is difficult to define to what extent NASA personnel have worked on DOD payloads because of the classified nature and the numerous joint research activities.

The Air Force has had astronaut-like programs, such as the Spaceflight Engineers and the Military-Man-In-Space program. Before the shuttle, spaceflight engineers were recruited to utilize the Gemini spacecraft to go to a planned Manned Orbiting Laboratory. The orbiting laboratory was cancelled with the introduction of automated cameras on satellites. Afterwards, spaceflight engineers were Air Force pilots who would train to be the specialist that would fly on the shuttle to oversee specific DOD payloads. In January, 1985, Gary Payton (a Spaceflight Engineer) flew on the first dedicated DOD shuttle mission, STS 51C, to supervise the deployment of a classified payload. The spaceflight engineers program was later disbanded. The Military-Man-In-Space program was designed to determine the potential for humans to be used for Earth observations. Human vision and intelligence was found to be a valuable asset as remote sensors, because of man's adept ability to distinguish subtle variations in hues more accurately than cameras and film. Remote sensing from space with accurate ground truth can greatly enhance the understanding of large natural systems like forests and ocean dynamics.

NASA's main role for national security is to inspire the youth of today that will populate aerospace professions in the future. This pool of technically minded persons will give the DOD a more intelligent and numerous base from which to recruit a future workforce. High-risk technologies have the potential to provide tremendous benefit for mankind. For aeronautics, NASA research divisions are positioned to study more technologies for their own benefit as well as that of the DOD, and the nation as a whole.

■ FURTHER READING:

BOOKS:

Harland, David M. *The Space Shuttle Roles, Missions and Accomplishments.* New York: John Wiley & Sons Ltd, 1998.

ELECTRONIC:

Dryden Flight Research Center. "Flight Research Milestones." <http://www.dfrc.nasa.gov/Dryden/mistone.html> (May 6, 2003).

SEE ALSO

Geospatial Imagery

Infrared Detection Devices
Near Space Environment
Satellites, Spy
Strategic Defense Initiative and National Missile Defense
USSTRATCOM (United States Strategic Command)

National Archives and Records Administration (NARA), United States

The National Archives and Records Administration (NARA) is an independent government agency that stores and provides public access to historical and significant documents related to the American government and its citizens.

Before NARA was created in the 1930s, government documents were stored randomly, with little thought to preservation. As a result, many important works were destroyed in fires or floods, or lost in the transfer from one storage facility to another. In fact, the Declaration of Independence, a crucial piece of American history, nearly disappeared on one of its journeys. In the mid-1920s, Congress recognized the need for a central facility to house important government documents, and authorized funds for a national archives building. On June 19, 1934, President Franklin D. Roosevelt signed the National Archives Act. R.D.W. Connor became the first official national archivist.

Based in Washington, D.C., NARA's now monumental collection recounts the history of America—and Americans. Housed within its collection are some of the most famous documents in American history, including the Declaration of Independence, the U.S. Constitution, the Bill of Rights, and the historic Nixon audiotapes. NARA's thirty-three facilities hold more than four billion pages of government documents, nearly 300,000 films, fourteen million photographs and posters, and five million maps. In addition, NARA hosts many permanent and temporary exhibits showcasing historical documents, artwork, letters, and photographs, and holds the personal collections of every president from Herbert Hoover to George Bush. Everything within the collection is open to the American public.

Not only does NARA store historically important materials, it cares for them as well. Archivists sift through piles of government documents each year to determine which items deserve a place in its stacks. Conservators work diligently to preserve each document, cleaning, repairing rips, and restoring damaged bindings. Retrieval staff respond to nearly 800,000 public requests for information each year.

Protection of archived national icons, such as the Declaration of Independence and the Constitution, has been identified as a high priority in the national strategy to prevent terrorism, and falls under the responsibility of the Department of Homeland Security.

■ FURTHER READING:

BOOKS:

Rudy Smith, Christina. *The National Archives and Records Administration (Know your Government).* Philadelphia, PA: Chelsea House Publishers, 1989.

United States National Archives and Records Administration. *The National Archives in the Nation's Capital: Information for Researchers.* Washington, D.C.: National Archives and Records Administration, 2001.

ELECTRONIC:

U.S. National Archives & Records Administration. <http:// <http://www.archives.gov/>.

SEE ALSO

FOIA (Freedom of Information Act)
Libraries and Information Science (NCLIS), United States National Commission

National Command Authority

The national command authorities of a nation are the persons or officeholders (or their duly deputized alternates or successors) who have the legal power to direct military activities. In almost all national governments, ultimate national command authority rests in a single office or individual, but there are almost always others involved in carrying out military policy. In the United States, the national command authorities are the president, the secretary of defense, and/or their duly deputized alternates or successors.

One of the hallmarks of the American system, and that of virtually all constitutional democracies, is civilian control over the military. Therefore, ultimate military authority rests in the civilian chain of command, the national command authority. Highest in the chain of command, of course, is the president. However, the chief executive oversees so many aspects of national policy that even in wartime, his duties necessarily force his attention to be directed toward other matters. Therefore, the secretary of defense plays a critical role in the oversight of military action. He or she answers to the president, and in turn guides military action along two lines of authority.

On the one hand are military forces not specifically assigned to combatant commands. These answer to the chiefs of the services, who report to the secretaries of the military departments (Army, Navy, and Air Force). The secretaries are in turn subordinate to the secretary of defense. On the other hand, there are combatant commands, whose commanders answer directly to the secretary of defense. During the Persian Gulf War of 1991, the distinction between these two lines of authority became particularly noticeable in the form of the war's two most prominent military figures: General H. Norman Schwarzkopf, commander of allied forces on the ground, and General Colin Powell, chairman of the Joint Chiefs of Staff.

■ FURTHER READING:

BOOKS:

Gilmour, Robert S., and Alexis A. Halley. *Who Makes Public Policy? The Struggle for Control Between Congress and the Executive.* Chatham, NJ: Chatham House Publishers, 1994.

Richelson, Jeffrey T. *The U.S. Intelligence Community,* 4th ed. Boulder, CO: Westview Press, 1999.

Trask, Roger R., and Alfred Goldberg. *The Department of Defense, 1947–1997: Organization and Leaders.* Washington, D.C.: U.S. Government Printing Office, 1997.

SEE ALSO

DoD (United States Department of Defense)
Joint Chiefs of Staff, United States
Persian Gulf War

National Drug Threat Assessment

The National Drug Threat Assessment (NDTA) is an annual report of the National Drug Intelligence Center that assists in the formation of United States counterdrug policy and strategy by identifying criminal trends. Created by the General Counterdrug Intelligence Plan of 2000, the NDTA gathers intelligence from national, state, and local agencies and indicators to determine the level of danger that marijuana, cocaine, heroin, and methamphetamines pose to American society.

The NDTA obtains information by collecting the National Drug Threat Survey from 2,600 participating local and state law enforcement groups. The national agencies that share information with the NDTA are: Drug Enforcement Administration; Federal Bureau of Investigation; U.S. Coast Guard; U.S. Customs Service; El Paso Intelligence Center; Financial Crimes Enforcement Network; Crime and Narcotics Center; National Institute on Drug Abuse; Substance Abuse and Mental Health Services Administration; and National Institute of Justice. The indicators used by the NDTA are: Arrestee Drug Abuse Monitoring Program, Drug Abuse Warning Network, Monitoring the Future Study, National Household Survey on Drug

Abuse, Parents' Resource Institute on Drug Education Survey, and Treatment Episode Data Set.

While overall demand for illegal drugs has remained stable, NDTA intelligence suggests changing patterns of consumption and trafficking. The increased production of high potency marijuana may lead to greater demand, while the use of methamphetamines is growing. Young adults who are part of the rave culture are taking a combination of MDMA and heroin as well as compound MDMA/methamphetamine tablets. They are increasingly obtaining these drugs from localized groups and individuals, as opposed to the Mexican and Colombian organizations traditionally associated with trafficking. This changing distribution pattern has led to the rising availability of these drugs in suburban and rural areas.

Law enforcement agencies must correctly allocate limited resources to effectively combat illegal drugs. The NDTA will likely remain in production as part of this war on drugs.

■ FURTHER READING:

BOOKS:

National Drug Intelligence Center, United States Department of Justice. *National Drug Threat Assessment 2001: The Domestic Perspective.* Johnstown, PA: National Drug Intelligence Center, October 2000.

ELECTRONIC:

United States Department of Justice. "National Drug Threat Assessment 2002." December 2001 <http://www.usdoj.gov/ndic/pubs/716/> (March 11, 2003).

SEE ALSO

Crime Prevention, Intelligence Agencies
DEA (Drug Enforcement Administration)
FBI (United States Federal Bureau of Investigation)
Intelligence and Law Enforcement Agencies
NDIC (Department of Justice National Drug Intelligence Center)
NIJ (National Institute of Justice)

National Information Infrastructure Protection Act, United States

The national information infrastructure is the collective computer and communication system that facilitates the operation of banks, businesses, schools, media, and the government. This infrastructure is crucial to the national economy and has expanded rapidly during the last decade. Because the network is computer based in the transmission of data, however, it is also vulnerable. In 1995,

Congress passed the National Information Infrastructure Protection Act, a bill providing for increased security of federal and private computers, and Internet server systems.

The National Information Infrastructure Protection Act was created to further expand the protections granted by the Computer Fraud and Abuse Act of 1986. Under the new act, protective measures were extended to computer systems used in foreign and interstate commerce and communication. The bill consolidated several older laws, including standing espionage laws, and labeled new crimes for stealing classified information from government computers.

Privacy was another major concern expressed in the act. It further criminalized the use of government computers to obtain confidential records, such as individual tax or medical records. Violators would be subject to prosecution under federal law, and charged with a separate crime for the use of the computer to hack and disperse sensitive documents. If these documents were obtained and dispersed for personal gain or profit, the crime becomes a felony. Convicted common security hackers were thus sentenced more leniently than those who prosecutors demonstrated acted with malicious intent. In its final provision, the act identified and criminalized the practice of computer blackmail, that is the ransoming of stolen information or the demand for access to an online account.

Not only did the bill cover computer fraud, but it also had implications for copyright law and corporate espionage. A copyright law amendment to the National Information Infrastructure Protection Act sought to grant jurisdiction over certain web contents to individual parties. The bill failed because it would have placed regulations on the Internet. The issue of ownership in cyberspace, however, remains an unclear legal question.

Since the passage of the act, computer crimes continued to rise in number, but not in severity. Incidences of viruses, stolen identities, and computer espionage peaked before the turn of the new millennium.

SEE ALSO

Computer Fraud and Abuse Act of 1986
Computer Hackers
Computer Hardware Security
Information Security (OIS), United States Office of
Internet Surveillance

National Intelligence Estimate

∎ JUDSON KNIGHT

National Intelligence Estimates (NIEs) are reports by the National Intelligence Council (NIC), drawing on estimative views from across the intelligence community. The practice of creating NIEs developed in the late 1940s and early 1950s, as a response to previous intelligence failures.

Background on NIEs

Despite the many advances in military and civilian intelligence that attended the successful completion of World War II and the creation of the Central Intelligence Agency (CIA) two years later, both CIA and military intelligence were taken completely by surprise when North Korean troops invaded South Korea in June 1950. In the months leading up to the invasion, intelligence personnel attached to General Douglas MacArthur's Tokyo headquarters regularly issued reports that downplayed the threat from North Korea and its Chinese allies, whose entrance into the ensuing war in late 1950 would greatly expand the scale of the conflict. Determined to create a framework and mechanism for the production of reliable intelligence estimates, General Walter Bedell Smith, when he became Director of Central Intelligence (DCI) in October 1950, instituted the concept of the NIE.

Today NIEs are the responsibility of the NIC, which serves the entire intelligence community and reports to DCI in his capacity as head of that community. It is the job of the NIC to bring together estimative views, not only from the CIA, but also from the Defense Intelligence Agency, the four military services, the National Security Agency, the Department of State Bureau of Intelligence and Research, and the intelligence units of the Federal Bureau of Investigation, the Department of Energy, and the Treasury Department. The directors of all of these organizations together constitute the National Foreign Intelligence Board, which reviews each NIE and must approve it before it is sent to the president and other national leaders.

Since 1950, numerous NIEs have been produced, and those that relate to matters that are now moot—for example, the conflicts of Cold War era—have been declassified. This has enabled at least some analysis of their accuracy. On the negative side, an NIE in 1962 maintained that Russian president Nikita Khrushchev would not put missiles in Cuba, a prediction proven inaccurate by the Cuban Missile Crisis in October of that year. Likewise, NIEs failed to predict the Yom Kippur War of 1973, or the fall of the Shah of Iran in 1978. Most infamously, in 1989, an NIE showed that Saddam Hussein's Iraq, exhausted by an eight-year war with Iran, would not instigate any significant military actions in the next three years—a prediction proven wrong by the Iraqi invasion of Kuwait in August 1990.

Yet, there were also numerous successes in the NIEs regarding the nation that most clearly threatened U.S. national security in the years from 1950 to 1990: the Soviet Union. As with much else about intelligence work, where NIEs are concerned, it is primarily the failures that attract attention. Successes, on the other hand, either remain hidden entirely from view, or, where the success in question is an accurate estimate or prediction, hindsight makes the wisdom behind it seem self-evident. Yet, as NIC director Joseph S. Nye, Jr., showed in a 1994 piece for *Foreign Affairs,* analysis of declassified materials indicates that NIEs on Soviet capabilities and intentions were usually quite accurate. Furthermore, NIEs on the situation in Vietnam during the 1960s tended to be much more accurate than the prognoses of the White House or the Pentagon: whereas the nation's military and political leaders continued to believe until early 1968 that victory was inevitable, NIEs offered gloomy estimates on the chances of a U.S. military victory in Southeast Asia much earlier.

Nye also noted that NIEs have been faulted for overestimating Soviet military strength, but much of this occurred in the era before reconnaissance satellites, when U.S. intelligence had to rely much more on the Soviets' own, often exaggerated, claims as to their military capabilities. By the late 1960s and early 1970s, when America had satellites in the skies, it was in retreat globally, and NIEs of the time tended to *underestimate* Soviet power. As for the failure of the intelligence community to predict the fall of the Soviet Union—a failure that led Senator Daniel Patrick Moynihan (D-NY) to call for the abolition of the CIA—Nye observed that even Soviet President Mikhail Gorbachev failed to predict that his government would collapse as quickly as it did.

Developments of the 1990s and later.

In an attempt to develop better NIEs, Nye reported in 1994, the NIC had "increased its emphasis on alternative scenarios rather than single-point predictions." On the one hand, NIEs were less likely to predict a specific outcome, and instead tended to offer a variety of possible results contingent on other events—even ones that might be considered unlikely. On the other hand, national intelligence estimates eschewed what Nye described as "vague words like 'possibly' or 'small but significant chance'" in favor of numerical percentages or odds for or against a particular event occurring.

The terrorist attacks of September 11, 2001, present an example of an event that would have seemed preposterous if someone had predicted it even a few days earlier. Yet, in the aftermath, one of the first questions Americans asked themselves was how their national intelligence and security apparatus had failed to see the attacks coming. Later, as President George W. Bush began to call for a war on Iraq as a sponsor of international terrorism, this claim was news to much of the public. Yet, the CIA had in its files such damning information as the fact that Saddam and Osama bin Laden had signed a non-aggression pact as far back as 1993; that al-Qaeda operatives had received training in Baghdad; and that Iraqi intelligence officers had met with bin Laden in Afghanistan and the Sudan.

According to a blistering analysis by Jim Hoagland in the *Washington Post* in October 2002, the reason that this information had not reached the general public was that it simply was not fashionable among policy circles in the 1990s. Under the administration of President William J. Clinton, Hoagland maintained, "the need not to know very much about Iraq and terrorism was very strong." Due to predictive failures in the NIEs, Bush had not been inclined to trust them, but the character of post-September 2001, NIEs reflected a new direction in national intelligence. The threats of North Korean missile attacks, and al-Qaeda computer hackers, both treated as remote possibilities before, were now being taken more seriously in NIEs. In 2002 and 2003, the brinksmanship of North Korean dictator Kim Jong Il, along with the sensitive data found on captured al-Qaeda computers, reinforced the advisability of this change.

■ FURTHER READING:

PERIODICALS:

Donnelly, John. "N. Korean Missile Has U.S. Range." *Boston Globe.* (February 13, 2003): A1.

Gellman, Barton. "Cyber-Attacks by al-Qaeda Feared." *Washington Post.* (June 27, 2002): A1.

Hoagland, Jim. "CIA's New Old Iraq File." *Washington Post.* (October 20, 2002): B7.

"Let's Have Straight Talk on Missile Defenses." *Aviation Week & Space Technology* 145, no. 16 (October 14, 1996): 86.

Nye, Joseph S., Jr. "Peering into the Future." *Foreign Affairs* 73, no. 4 (July/August 1994): 82.

Wall, Robert. "Review of NMD Fallout Underway." *Aviation Week & Space Technology* 152, no. 19 (May 8, 2000): 31–32.

Zelikow, Philip. "The Global Infectious Disease Threat and Its Implications for the United States." *Foreign Affairs* 79, no. 4 (July/August 2000): 154–155.

ELECTRONIC:

National Intelligence Council. <http://www.cia.gov/nic/> (March 17, 2003).

SEE ALSO

DCI (Director of the Central Intelligence Agency)
Intelligence Community
NFIB (United States National Foreign Intelligence Board)
NIC (National Intelligence Council)
Nongovernmental Global Intelligence and Security

National Interagency Civil-Military Institute (NICI), United States

The National Interagency Civil-Military Institute (NICI) is an educational institute—funded by the Department of

Defense (DOD) through the National Guard Bureau—with the mission of improving the efficiency and effectiveness of joint civilian and military initiatives. To this end, it provides education to middle- and upper-level managers from the military, law enforcement agencies, emergency management and public safety organizations, and community groups. Founded in 1989 as the National Interagency Counterdrug Institute, its initial areas of focus involved border security and drug interdiction efforts, but it has expanded its course offerings since that time.

An incident along the Mexican border in October 1988 prompted the founding of NICI during the following year. While conducting a routine patrol for drug smugglers in the California desert, three National Guard soldiers and five deputy sheriffs in a UH-1 helicopter spotted a suspicious-looking parked vehicle with its lights off. As they descended to get a better look at the vehicle, they crashed into a power line, and all eight were killed. Ironically, the vehicle that had caught their attention belonged to the U.S. Border Patrol.

The tragic incident highlighted the need for greater coordination and cooperation among military and law enforcement, and in 1989, Dr. William Jefferds, former deputy adjutant general of the California National Guard, submitted a proposal to the National Guard Bureau for an institute to train individuals and agencies in joint operations. Congress approved the plan for NICI, established at Camp San Luis Obispo in California.

Among the programs NICI has added over the years are counterdrug demand reduction training, included in 1992 and expanded two years later. In 1994, NICI added a course in military support to civil authorities (MSCA), and in the following year held its first international MSCA course, attended by participants from several former Soviet republics. Following several terrorist attacks during the mid-1990s, NICI in 1997 developed antiterrorism courses, as well as blocks of instruction in community response to emergencies. It also conducts force protection level II training under the guidance of the U.S. Military Police School.

■ FURTHER READING:

PERIODICALS:

Haskell, Bob. "A Plan Well-Executed." *Soldiers* 53, no. 5 (May 1998): 38.

"Tuition-Free, Counter-Drug Courses Offered." *National Guard* 54, no. 10 (October 2000): 10.

ELECTRONIC:

National Interagency Civil-Military Institute. <http://www.nici.org/> (March 30, 2003).

SEE ALSO

DOD (United States Department of Defense)
Homeland Security, United States Department

Law Enforcement Training Center (FLETC), United States Federal

National Liberation Army (ELN)–Colombia

The National Liberation Army (ELN) in Colombia is a Marxist insurgent group formed in 1965 by urban intellectuals inspired by Fidel Castro and Che Guevara. ELN began a dialogue with Colombian officials in 1999 following a campaign of mass kidnappings—each involving at least one U.S. citizen—to demonstrate its strength and continuing viability and force the Pastrana administration to negotiate. Peace talks between Bogota and the ELN started in 1999 and continued sporadically through 2001 until Bogota broke them off. Negotiations ultimately resumed in Havana, Cuba, by the end of 2001.

Organization activities. The ELN uses kidnapping, hijacking, bombing, extortion, and guerrilla war. ELN boasts a modest conventional military capability. ELN annually conducts hundreds of kidnappings for ransom, often targeting foreign employees of large corporations, especially in the petroleum industry. ELN attacks frequently target energy infrastructure and the group has inflicted major damage on pipelines and the electric distribution network.

ELN has an estiamted 3,000 to 5,000 armed combatants and an unknown number of active supporters. The ELN is active mostly in rural and mountainous areas of north, northeast, and southwest Colombia, and Venezuela border regions. Cuba provides ELN fighters some medical care and offers political consultation to its leadership.

■ FURTHER READING:

ELECTRONIC:

Central Intelligence Agency. World Factbook, 2002. <http://www.cia.gov/cia/publications/factbook/> (April 16, 2003).

Taylor, Francis X. U.S. Department of State. Patterns of Global Terrorism 2001, Annual Report: On the Record Briefing. May 21, 2002. <http://www.state.gov/s/ct/rls/rm/10367.htm> (April 17, 2003).

U.S. Department of State. Annual Reports. <http://www.state.gov/www/global/terrorism/annual_reports.html> (April 16, 2003).

SEE ALSO

Terrorism, Philosophical and Ideological Origins
Terrorist and Para-State Organizations
Terrorist Organization List, United States
Terrorist Organizations, Freezing of Assets

National Military Joint Intelligence Center

The United States National Military Joint Intelligence Center (NMJIC), sometimes called the National Military Joint Intelligence Alert Center, is the nerve center for defense intelligence activities in support of joint military operations. Located physically and administratively close to the Joint Chiefs of Staff (JCS), NMJIC is also the fullest realization of the joint intelligence center (JIC) principle that developed in the last days of the Cold War.

The Fleet Intelligence Center falls victim to changing views.

One of the most significant agencies absorbed into the then-new NMJIC during the early 1990s was the United States Navy Fleet Intelligence Center (FIC). With precedents dating back to the early days of World War II, the FIC operated on shore and provided United States fleets with intelligence support. Out of these wartime foundations emerged Fleet Intelligence Center Pacific (FICPAC) in 1955, FIC Europe (FICEUR) in 1960, and FIC Atlantic (FICLANT) in 1968.

The last two merged in 1974 to form FIC Europe-Atlantic (FICEURLANT). FICPAC played a critical role in providing intelligence to United States Navy and Marine forces in Vietnam. With more than 500 active-duty personnel by 1991, FICEURLANT was the largest of the FIC units. As it turned out, 1991 also marked the end of FIC, which fell victim to changing times. However, the army and air force counterparts—the Analysis and Control Element and the Air Intelligence Squadron respectively—managed to survive the change.

As for the causes of this change, this emerged in the 1980s, a period that saw the rise in popularity of the unified command principle among United States military circles. According to this principle, unified or area commanders in chief would direct all United States military operations in a given geographic area. For their intelligence needs, they relied on the JIC. The latter served as J-2, or joint intelligence, making it a "one-stop shop" for the intelligence needs of a given combatant command.

The nerve center of joint intelligence.

At the national level, the function of J-2 is performed by the Defense Intelligence Agency (DIA), which oversees NMJIC. The latter in turn supports JCS, serving their needs, as well as those of unified commanders. NMJIC maintains a focus on global indications and warnings (I&W; intelligence that relates to time-sensitive information involving potential threats); operational intelligence (intelligence involved in military planning for a particular theatre or area of operations); national targeting support (prioritizing areas for possible action); production of reports; and database management.

Located alongside the National Military Command Center and the Defense Collection Coordination Center, NMJIC monitors worldwide political and military developments on a 24-hour basis, with an eye toward crises that may require United States intervention. Among the components of NMJIC are an alert center, warning and crisis analysts, targeting specialists, and a network of intelligence personnel, some of whom may deploy in support of war operations. In addition to DIA and those organizations, such as FIC, that have been subordinated to NMJIC, the center also includes representatives of the National Security Agency, Central Intelligence Agency, State Department, Defense Mapping Agency, and other United States military services.

■ FURTHER READING:

BOOKS:

Richelson, Jeffrey T. *The United States Intelligence Community,* 3rd ed. Boulder, CO: Westview Press, 1995.

ELECTRONIC:

Appendix A: Joint and Naval Intelligence Organizations That Support Naval Operations. Navy Warfare Development Command. <http://www.nwdc.navy.mil/Library/Documents/NDPs/ndp2/ndp20007.htm> (January 22, 2003).

SEE ALSO

DIA (Defense Intelligence Agency)
Joint Chiefs of Staff, United States

National Preparedness Strategy, United States

Events of the 1990s, particularly the first World Trade Center bombing in 1993 and the Oklahoma City attack two years later, revealed that the continental United States was far more vulnerable to terrorist attack than Americans had supposed. The federal government's response to these and other situations had been on an *ad hoc* basis, resulting in the establishment of response capabilities under various Cabinet-level departments. The result, in many cases, was disorganization and duplication of services. By 1999, leaders had recognized the need for a national preparedness strategy, and three years later, the General Accounting Office (GAO) established, in broad outlines, what such a strategy should entail.

The 1999 study: a searing critique.

According to the results of a 1999 national vulnerability study, "The country's seeming inability to develop and implement a clear, comprehensive, and truly integrated national preparedness strategy means that the government and citizens was still seen as possibly incapable of responding effectively to a serious terrorist attack." The report came from an 18-member commission, chaired by Virginia governor James S. Gilmore III (R) and composed of retired military leaders, as well as figures from the medical, emergency planning, and intelligence communities.

Much of the commission's 67-page report, delivered to President William J. Clinton on December 15, was a critique of the existing system for terrorism and emergency response. Much of the dissatisfaction noted in the study came from state and local officials, who found that federal plans failed to take appropriate account of community needs. For example, much federal planning focused on the 220 largest cities in the nation, effectively leaving smaller communities to fend for themselves.

The 2002 study: a guide to effective partnership.

Following the September 11, 2001, terrorist attacks, the administration of President George W. Bush commissioned the GAO to report on the needs and challenges associated with the formation of a cohesive national preparedness strategy. Patricia A. Dalton, strategic issues director for the GAO, delivered her report, *Combating Terrorism: Enhancing Partnerships through a National Preparedness Strategy*, on March 28, 2002.

As Dalton noted, the GAO had long called for a national terrorism preparedness strategy that would integrate federal, state, and local response capabilities. Such a strategy, according to GAO, should include definition and clarification of the roles and responsibilities of various entities; establishment of goals and performance measures; and thoughtful decision-making with regard to the tools that would best assist in implementing a national strategy.

An array of legislation and presidential directives addressed the national response to terrorism, including several bills introduced in Congress following the September 2001 attacks. Funding was in place, with $29.3 billion allocated for homeland security in the 2002 budget and $37.7 billion requested for 2003. What was most sorely lacking, Dalton's report indicated, was an overall plan, and with some 40 government agencies devoted to dealing with terrorism, there was bound to be a great deal of redundancy, waste, and inefficiency.

Attempting to deal with these problems, Attorney General Janet Reno had in December, 1998, presented a five-year Interagency Counterterrorism Crime and Technology Plan, but GAO found it lacking in a system for measuring outcomes. Additionally, Reno's plan failed to identify state and local government roles. "The emphasis," Dalton noted, "Needs to be on a national rather than a purely federal plan." Not only had local communities in many cases failed to receive adequate help from the federal government due to a confusion of response capabilities, but even those parts of the federal government officially involved in some aspect of emergency response were sometimes left out of decision-making on relevant matters.

To improve the situation, Dalton recommended the establishment of a one-stop "clearinghouse" for federal assistance to state and local response organizations. In order to develop a comprehensive response capability, her report indicated, it would be necessary to streamline the emergency-response apparatus. Additionally, an effective national preparedness strategy would encourage much greater cooperation among federal agencies, and between agencies at the federal, state, and local levels.

■ FURTHER READING:

BOOKS:

Dalton, Patricia A. *Combating Terrorism: Enhancing Partnerships through a National Preparedness Strategy.* Washington, D.C.: General Accounting Office, 2002.

PERIODICALS:

Melton, R. H. "Panel Criticizes U.S. Anti-Terrorism Preparedness." *Washington Post.* (December 16, 1999): A6.

SEE ALSO

GAO (General Accounting Office, United States)
Radiological Emergency Response Plan, United States Federal
United States, Counter-terrorism Policy
World Trade Center, 1993 Terrorist Attack

National Response Team, United States

The United States National Response Team, an interagency group co-chaired by the Environmental Protection Agency (EPA) and the U.S. Coast Guard (USCG), is charged with emergency response planning and coordination. It does not respond directly to emergency situations, but rather supports incident response forces by distributing information, planning emergency responses in advance, and training personnel to deal with response. In addition to backing federal components of emergency response, it also supports regional response teams (RRTs).

NRT members, in addition to EPA and USCG, include the departments of Defense, Energy, Agriculture, Commerce, Health and Human Services, Interior, Justice, Labor, Transportation, and the Treasury; the Federal Emergency

Management Agency (FEMA); the General Services Administration; and the Nuclear Regulatory Commission. Each has a specific role to play, as coordinated by the NRT: USCG, for example—among its many responsibilities for the team—manages the National Response Center and maintains 46 round-the-clock staffed facilities in major U.S. ports. FEMA advises and assists lead agencies in coordinating relocation assistance.

Even those parts of the NRT whose functions are not normally associated with emergency response have significant roles to play. The Department of Agriculture, for instance, monitors the effect of hazardous substances on natural resources, as does the Department of Interior, through offices such as the Fish and Wildlife Service, Bureau of Mines, Geological Survey, and National Park Service. The Department of Labor conducts health and safety inspections at hazardous waste sites through its Occupational Safety and Health Administration.

Coordinating these efforts is the NRT itself, which ensures that the roles of each agency are clearly outlined in the National Contingency Plan. It supports the training, education, and preparedness of members, both through courses within and outside the NRT, and through member committees that include the Preparedness Committee, the Response Committee, and the Science and Technology Committee. In working with RRTs, the NRT reviews regional or area contingency plans, and monitors RRT effectiveness during an incident.

■ FURTHER READING:

PERIODICALS:

"New Guidelines Offered for Emergency Response Plans." *Environmental Management Today* 7, no. 3 (July/August 1996): 5.

Soltis, Dan. "Integrated Emergency Response Plans Will Save U.S. Industry Millions." *Water Engineering & Management* 144, no. 2 (February 1997): 17.

Steinman, Adam H. "Streamline Your Facility's Emergency Response Plans." *Chemical Engineering* 106, no. 3 (March 1999): 102.

ELECTRONIC:

Emergency Response Program, National Response Team. Environmental Protection Agency. <http://www.epa.gov/superfund/programs/er/nrs/nrsnrt.htm> (March 30, 2003).

U.S. National Response Team. <http://www.nrt.org/> (March 30, 2003).

SEE ALSO

Chemical Safety: Emergency Responses
Coast Guard National Response Center
Emergency Response Teams
EPA (Environmental Protection Agency)
FEMA (United States Federal Emergency Management Agency)
Radiological Emergency Response Plan, United States Federal

National Security Act (1947)

■ ADRIENNE WILMOTH LERNER

In the aftermath of World War II, the United States government undertook a dramatic reorganization of the national military and intelligence community. Departments created for wartime operations, such as cryptology, intelligence, and domestic security, needed restructuring for useful peacetime employment. Congress, and a special council of presidential advisors, reviewed military and government operations. Based on their recommendations, the National Security Act of 1947 outlined the ambitious plan to unify the military departments under the direction of a cabinet-level secretary. The individual responsibilities of the army and navy were more clearly defined, and the air force was created. The National Security Act of 1947 created the National Security Council, a formal foreign policy and military advisory team for the president, and the Central Intelligence Agency (CIA). The act was amended several times between 1945 and 1985, yielding the current government, intelligence, and military structure present in the United States today.

Signed into law on July 26, the National Security Act of 1947 initiated an immediate reorganization of the intelligence community. During the war, the Office of Strategic Services (OSS) performed most intelligence operations and trained a new generation of intelligence personnel. Though the OSS was initially slated for dissolution after the war, advisors close to President Harry S. Truman convinced the president that the organization could be retooled for peacetime operation, especially as Cold War tensions with the Soviet Union mounted. The act thus established a civilian successor agency to the OSS, the Central Intelligence Agency (CIA). The CIA was granted a broader mission to collect foreign intelligence data and conduct strategic surveillance. The position of director of central intelligence was created to administer the new agency and serve as a liaison between the intelligence community and the executive branch. The act assigned the task of domestic intelligence to the Federal Bureau of Investigation (FBI).

To facilitate the sharing of information, the formation of strategic foreign policy, and the protection of national security, the National Security Act of 1947 established the National Security Council (NSC). Comprised of the president, vice president, secretary of state, and the secretary of defense, the council meets to discuss security, intelligence, and strategic issues. The director of central intelligence and the chairman of the Joint Chiefs of Staff serve on the NSC in an advisory capacity. The role of the council was intentionally left somewhat ambiguous in the act so that each president could use the council that best suited his administration and foreign policy agenda. The council mostly convened as an advisory board until the Nixon Administration when the NSC gained the permanence and prominence in foreign and strategic affairs that it has today.

The 1947 act substantially reordered the military, in addition to the intelligence community. The War Department was abolished, and its duties incorporated with those of the former Navy Department into the Department of Defense (DOD). The position of Secretary of Defense was created to govern the new Department of Defense, but the individual branches of military service retained their own Secretaries. The original National Security Act of 1947 has been amended several times to further alter the structure of the DOD. In 1949, the DOD was elevated to a high-level executive department and the secretary of defense gained more power over military department Secretaries. In 1986, the position of the secretary of defense was firmly established in the executive chain of command as part of revisions to national Continuity of Government plans.

The operational duties of the individual military branches were also altered by the adoption of the National Security Act. The organizational structure of the army remained the same, but new emphasis was placed on training and maintaining permanent, professional forces. The act granted the navy the ability to maintain airplane squadrons to conduct any flight operations that it deemed essential to its main sea operations. The navy also remained the governmental custodian of the marines. After the value of aircraft and air defenses were proved on the battlefields of Europe and in the Pacific Theater during World War II, the National Security Act of 1947 recognized the strategic need for a professional and permanent air fleet by creating the air force.

Amendments to the original 1947 act have changed some structural and functional aspects of the military and intelligence communities, but the basic structure remains in place today. The September 11 terrorist attacks on the United States sparked a reexamination of the structure of national intelligence services and the manor in which information is shared by government departments. The recent passage of the Homeland Security Act, and the creation of the Department of Homeland Security, signal the largest reorganization of government security and intelligence agencies since the National Security Act of 1947.

■ FURTHER READING:

BOOKS:

Hogan, Michael H. *A Cross of Iron: Harry S. Truman and the Origins of the National Security State, 1945–1954.* Cambridge University University Press, 1998.

U.S. Department of State. *Foreign Relations of the United States: Department of State, 1945–1950.* Washington, D.C., 1996.

SEE ALSO

CIA (United States Central Intelligence Agency)
CIA, Formation and History
FBI (United States Federal Bureau of Investigation)
National Security Advisor, United States
NSC (National Security Council)
NSC (National Security Council), History

National Security Advisor, United States

Officially known as the Assistant to the President for National Security Affairs, the National Security Advisor—the more commonly used title—has a role defined as much by the chief executive as by law. The position did not exist as such for more than a decade after the establishment of the National Security Council (NSC), nor does that legislation mention the role of the advisor. Yet, as the chief counsel to the president on matters of national security, the advisor holds a role of unquestioned significance.

Beginnings of the NSC and the advisor's role. The enabling legislation for the NSC, the National Security Act of 1947, created the body to serve as advisory board to the president on domestic, foreign, and military matters involving national security, and to facilitate cooperation between agencies on these issues. Intelligence and covert operations were not encompassed in that original mission, not so much because such matters are seldom mentioned in public law, but because at the time of that legislation—which also created the Central Intelligence Agency (CIA)—few guessed the importance these activities would gain in years to come.

The 1947 legislation created the NSC as a small permanent staff whose director would be an executive secretary appointed by the president. Nowhere was it stated that the president required to submit this appointment for Senate confirmation. In future years, this would keep the role of National Security Advisor independent from the inner politics, not only of the legislative branch, but also of the executive branch. Removed from Congress and the bureaucracy of the State and Department of Defense, the Advisor would be the president's own counsel.

Ironically, in 1947, these other centers of power each viewed the new council as advancing their own interests, but none could have guessed the changes that would take place. For example, a 1949 reorganization of the NSC reduced the influence of the Department of Defense by removing the three service secretaries (army, navy, air force) from its membership. And while President Dwight D. Eisenhower created the role of President's Special Assistant for National Security Affairs, the position had little of the significance the National Security Advisor took on under President John F. Kennedy.

National Security Advisors. Starting with President Eisenhower's Special Assistants, U.S. National Security Advisors have included:

■ Robert Cutler (March 1953-April 155)
■ Dillon Anderson (April 1955-September 1956)
■ Robert Cutler (January 1957-June 1958)

U.S. National Security Advisor Condoleezza Rice fields a question during a press briefing at the White House, November 1, 2001. ©REUTERS NEWMEDIA INC./CORBIS.

▮ Gordon Gray (June 1958-January 1961)

Presidents Kennedy and Johnson:

▮ McGeorge Bundy (January 1961-February 1966)
▮ Walt W. Rostow (April 1966-December 1968)

Presidents Nixon and Ford:

▮ Henry A. Kissinger (December 1968-November 1975; served concurrently as Secretary of State from September 1973)
▮ Brent Scowcroft (November 1975-January 1977)

President Carter:

▮ Zbigniew Brzezinski (January 1977-January 1981)

President Reagan:

▮ Richard V. Allen (January 1981-January 1982)
▮ William P. Clark (January 1982-October 1983)
▮ Robert C. McFarlane (October 1983-December 1985)
▮ John M. Poindexter (December 1985-November 1986)
▮ Frank C. Carlucci (November 1986-November 1987)
▮ Colin Powell (November 1987-January 1989)

President George H. W. Bush:

▮ Brent Scowcroft (January 1989-January 1993)

President Clinton:

▮ W. Anthony Lake (January 1993-March 1997)
▮ Samuel R. Berger (March 1997-January 2001)

President George W. Bush:

▮ Condoleeza Rice (January 2001—)

The years from Kennedy onward have seen each president personalize his administration in part through his appointment of the National Security Advisor, and in smaller measures through aspects of the NSC itself. Bundy, under Kennedy and later Lyndon B. Johnson, was the first powerful National Security Advisor, but his influence appears minimal compared to that of the most powerful individual ever to hold the position: Henry Kissinger. Emblematic of Kissinger's role was the fact that for part of his tenure as National Security Advisor to presidents Richard M. Nixon and Gerald R. Ford, he also served as Secretary of State.

From the Nixon era onward, presidents have likewise placed their personal stamp on the NSC through presidential directives, classified orders often drafted with the assistance of the National Security Advisor. These orders became known, in turn, as National Security Decision Memorandums (Nixon and Ford), Presidential Directives (Carter), National Security Decision Directives (Ronald Reagan), National Security Directives (George H. W. Bush),

Presidential Decision Directives (William J. Clinton), and National Security Presidential Directives (George W. Bush).

■ FURTHER READING:

BOOKS:

Best, Richard A. *The National Security Council: An Organizational Assessment.* Huntington, NY: Novinka Books, 2001.

Felix, Antonia. *Condi: The Condoleeza Rice Story.* New York: Newmarket Press, 2002.

Hillen, John. *Future Visions for U.S. Defense Policy: Four Alternatives Presented as Presidential Speeches.* New York: Council on Foreign Relations, 1998.

Kissinger, Henry. *Problems of National Strategy: A Book of Readings.* New York: Praeger, 1965.

Powell, Colin L., and Joseph E. Persico. *My American Journey.* New York: Ballantine Books, 1996.

ELECTRONIC:

Official Intelligence Documents. American Federation of Scientists. <http://fas.org/irp/offdocs/> (March 24, 2003).

SEE ALSO

Executive Orders and Presidential Directives
National Security Act (1947)
NSC (National Security Council)
NSC (National Security Council), History
President of the United States (Executive Command and Control of Intelligence Agencies)

National Security Strategy, United States

The National Security Strategy (NSS), as its name suggests, is a document outlining the blueprint for national security envisioned by the president of the United States. It has been issued, on a more or less annual basis, by each administration since Congress mandated its issuance in 1986, but prior to the September 2002 NSS of George W. Bush, the strategy report was little more than a statement of existing policy. The 2002 NSS, however, was not merely the first statement of its kind by a new administration, it was the first statement of national security strategy in a new era.

Early History of the NSS

From the time of President Richard M. Nixon in the early 1970s, it was routine for chief executives of the United States to issue statements of policy as it related to national security. The issuance of these statements became law in 1986, when Congress passed the Goldwater-Nichols Act. This legislation, which represented the fourth major reorganization of the U.S. Department of Defense since World War II, mandated that the White House present Congress with an annual statement of national security policy.

The Goldwater-Nichols Act was an expression of longstanding congressional frustration with the executive branch when it came to making clear executive policy on national security. Congressional leaders never doubted that a consistent national security strategy existed, as U.S. Military Academy political scientist Don Snider observed in *Foreign Policy*, but by requiring the White House to make its policy explicit, Congress would have an opportunity to exert greater influence on that strategy. The Goldwater-Nichols Act would also have the effect of asserting greater civilian control over the military.

NSSs under Reagan, Bush, and Clinton. Congressional frustration with presidential administrations in the matter of national security strategy was a phenomenon that had little to do with political party lines. Even when the same party controlled both the Oval Office and Congress, as University of Virginia political scientist Larry Sabato noted in *Foreign Policy*, the relationship between the White House and Capitol Hill tended to be more competitive than cooperative. The history of the NSS has tended to reinforce, rather than overturn, that background of competition between the legislative and executive branches of the federal government.

The NSSs submitted by the administrations of presidents Ronald Reagan, George H. W. Bush, and William J. Clinton usually did little more than simply restate policies then in effect. They were often bland, inciting little discussion on Capitol Hill or elsewhere, and some seemed more like promotional brochures on administration policy than carefully reasoned documents of national security. In 1994, an angry Senator Strom Thurmond, one of those involved in passing the Goldwater-Nichols Act, complained that the reports "seldom met . . . expectations."

Thurmond also noted that reports tended to be late, if presidents even bothered to submit them at all. For his first NSS, Clinton and his aides went through 21 drafts before finally submitting it, a year and a half after the due date. George W. Bush failed to submit his NSS on the due date, June 15, 2001, and in any case, events three months later would have rendered that NSS moot. As it was, Bush did not finally submit his first NSS until September 2002—and when he did, its tardiness was the least of its controversial aspects.

The 2002 NSS. Bush's 2002 NSS was an extraordinary document in the fact that it provided the blueprint for the new era that began with the terrorist attacks of September 11, 2001, as well as a framework for U.S. action resulting from those attacks. It is a detailed document outlining an aggressive, but idealistic foreign and military policy. At the time the 2002 NSS was published, it appeared that the United Nations (U.N.) would support Bush's plans to force Saddam Hussein of Iraq to comply with U.N. demands regarding disarmament—a support that evaporated when the moment of truth came—but in any case, Bush's NSS makes little mention of the U.N. or other international organizations. In fact, the preamble lists the U.N. along with other groups of much smaller stature, suggesting that the administration was already beginning to chart a course separate, if necessary, from the U.N.

The 2002 NSS recognizes that the United States carries unique responsibilities as the sole remaining dominant superpower and would guarantee peace, freedom, and prosperity to those who agreed to pursue those aims. In its pages, it outlines an eight-part strategy, in both general and specific terms, for defeating terrorism and tyranny, encouraging global trade as a means to prosperity, fostering freedom and respect for human life, helping to build democratic institutions and free societies, spurring economic and infrastructure development, building cooperation for peace with other nations, and reforming American national security institutions to meet those challenges.

■ FURTHER READING:

PERIODICALS:

Gaddis, John Lewis. "A Grand Strategy for Transformation." *Foreign Policy* no. 133 (November/December 2002): 50–57.

Hirsch, Michael. "Bush and the World." *Foreign Affairs* 81, no. 5 (September/October 2002): 18–44.

Lucia, Christine. "Counterproliferation at Core of New Security Strategy." *Arms Control Today* 32, no. 8 (October 2002): 30.

Rice, Condoleeza. "Anticipatory Defense in the War on Terror." *New Perspectives Quarterly* 19, no. 4 (fall 2002): 5–8.

ELECTRONIC:

The National Security Strategy of the United States of America. <http://www.whitehouse.gov/nsc/nss.html> (March 18, 2003).

SEE ALSO

Bush Administration (1989–1993), United States National Security Policy
Bush Administration (2001–), United States National Security Policy
Clinton Administration (1993–2001), United States National Security Policy
National Preparedness Strategy, United States
NSC (National Security Council)
President of the United States (Executive Command and control of Intelligence Agencies)

Reagan Administration (1981–1989), United States National Security Policy
September 11 Terrorist Attacks on the United States

National Security Telecommunications Advisory Committee

The National Security Telecommunications Advisory Committee (NSTAC) is a presidential advisory board composed of leaders in various key industries. Its membership is made up of thirty chief executives who represent the leading communications, network service, and information technology companies, as well as the most prominent firms in the areas of aerospace technology and finance. Created under Executive Order 12382, signed by President Ronald Reagan in September 1982, NSTAC has advised presidents on issues that include communications, information systems, protection of critical infrastructure, information assurance, and other concerns relating to national security and emergency preparedness (NS/EP).

A subsidiary of the National Communications System (NCS), NSTAC acts as a liaison between government agencies and the private sector. NCS is among the leading government agencies concerned with national security and emergency preparedness, and it works closely with NSTAC in assessing challenges to the communication infrastructure, as well as in implementing solutions. Among projects initiated by NSTAC is the National Coordination Center for Telecommunications (NCC), established in 1984, in which thirteen NSTAC member companies work with NCS to develop, protect, and update national security and emergency preparedness (NS/EP) facilities nationwide.

■ FURTHER READING:

BOOKS:

Fifteen Years of Serving the President, 1982–1997. Washington, D.C.: National Security Telecommunications Advisory Committee, 1997.

ELECTRONIC:

National Security Telecommunications Advisory Committee. <http://www.ncs.gov/NSTAC/nstac.htm> (February 2, 2003).

SEE ALSO

Communications System, United States National

Critical Infrastructure Assurance Office (CIAO), United States

National Telecommunications Information Administration, and Security for the Radio Frequency Spectrum, United States

The Federal Communications Commission (FCC) regulates airwaves in the United States, but in order to make necessary determinations regarding allocation, the FCC turns to the National Telecommunications Information Administration (NTIA). A unit of the Department of Commerce, NTIA works with a number of participants in the increasingly crowded radio spectrum, including the private sector, the Department of Defense (DOD), and various law enforcement and emergency response agencies. Its aim is to meet commercial needs for the radio spectrum while maintaining availability for defense and security communication.

Established in 1978 by Executive Order 12046, NTIA serves as the president's principal advisor on telecommunication policies. On behalf of the President, it manages the radio frequency spectrum, and, in conjunction with the FCC and Department of State, promotes U.S. interests regarding spectrum use at the international level. Among its most important work is management of that portion of the frequency spectrum below 3 GHz. Though this represents about 1 percent of the usable radio spectrum, more than 93 percent of all FCC licenses and federal government frequency authorizations lie within that range.

NTIA supports defense, law enforcement, and public safety in a number of ways. In the emergency conditions following the September 11, 2001, terrorist attacks, it responded by going into 24-hours-a-day, seven-days-a-week mode to process all requests for special frequency allocation, and fulfilled nearly 7,000 such requests from entities that ranged from DOD to the White House to the Red Cross. The relationship between NTIA and DOD is a particularly strong one, since 40 percent of all federal frequency allocations are for defense use. Some 56 percent of these are in support of land, sea, and air mobile operations by the military services. NTIA also works closely with the DOD Joint Spectrum Center.

During the late 1990s and early 2000s, NTIA found itself confronted with two examples of its classic challenge: meeting security needs on the one hand, and fostering commerce on the other. In the case of third-generation

(3G) mobile and satellite-based broadband, as well as that of ultra-wideband (UWB) technology, spectrum space was needed for new, highly significant telecommunications advances. In the case of the UWB allocation, critical government systems used some of the frequencies involved, so in 2000, the FCC began the process of attempting to integrate UWB devices without harming vital communications. To make this possible, NTIA conducted extensive measurements and analysis, including tests using the global positioning satellite (GPS) system.

■ FURTHER READING:

PERIODICALS:

"Commerce Secretary Participates in China/U.S. Telecom Summit." *Communications Today.* (October 6, 1997): 1.

Noguchi, Yuki. "'Star Trek' Tech Gets Limited Approval." *Washington Post.* (February 15, 2002): E1.

Stern, Christopher. "Federal Radio Spectrum up for Bid." *Broadcasting & Cable* 124, no. 7 (February 14, 1994): 46.

ELECTRONIC:

National Telecommunications and Information Administration. <http://www.ntia.doc.gov/> (March 28, 2003).

SEE ALSO

Commerce Department Intelligence and Security Responsibilities, United States
Electromagnetic Spectrum
FCC (United States Federal Communications Commission)
FM Transmitters

NATO (North Atlantic Treaty Organization)

■ CARYN E. NEUMANN

Headquartered in Brussels Belgium, the North Atlantic Treaty Organization (NATO) is a military and diplomatic alliance of countries in Europe and North America that offers security to its members by pooling military resources and sharing intelligence. Formed in 1949 during the initial years of the Cold War as a response to Soviet aggression, the first countries to join the alliance were Belgium, Canada, Denmark, Great Britain, Italy, Luxembourg, Netherlands, Norway, Portugal, United States, France, Spain, and Iceland. Greece and Turkey were added to NATO in 1952 while Germany was admitted in 1955 and Spain entered in 1982. With the collapse of the Soviet Union, former satellite states have begun to join NATO. The Czech Republic, Hungary, and Poland became members in 1999 while Bulgaria, Estonia, Latvia, Lithuania, Romania, Slovakia and Slovenia are expected to complete the membership process in 2004. The northern boundary

Thousands of ethnic Albanians waving Turkish and Albanian flags welcome Turkish NATO peacekeeping soldiers in Prizren, Yugoslavia, in 1999. AP/WIDE WORLD PHOTOS.

of the alliance is established at the North Pole, past the Northwest Territories of Canada, while the southern terminus is located at the Tropic of Cancer, which runs between Florida and Cuba.

The idea for NATO germinated as the Cold War descended. Some democratic nations of Europe feared that they had been so weakened by World War II that they did not have the strength to fend off an attack by an increasingly aggressive Soviet Union without American assistance. Policymakers hoped that future war could be avoided by declaring that an armed attack upon one NATO member constituted an attack upon all members and that the threat of U.S. involvement would act as a particularly powerful deterrent to the Soviets. The treaty establishing NATO was signed in Washington, D.C. on April 4, 1949, and then subsequently ratified by its member countries. The NATO signatories agreed that if such an armed attack occurred, each NATO member would assist the victimized state by taking individually and in concert with each other such actions deemed necessary, including the use of armed force, to restore and maintain international peace and security. The vagueness of the treaty meant that the exact mechanism of the alliance would develop over time. In the initial decade of its existence, NATO planned to deploy nuclear weapons in retaliation for a Soviet military attack. Under influence from U.S. President John F. Kennedy, the doctrine of flexible response replaced massive retaliation and no longer would automatic use of nuclear weapons be NATO policy.

Although the United States has been the dominant member in the past, NATO is governed by a North Atlantic Council that consists of permanent representatives of all member countries, who meet weekly. The council explains NATO decisions to the general public and to nonmember nations. It also bears responsibility for creating subsidiary bodies to foster the political work of NATO. The Supreme Allied Commander of the Supreme Headquarters Allied Powers Europe (SHAPE) handles the military responsibilities of NATO. This command is divided into three parts: Allied Forces North Europe (AFNORTH), Allied Forces South Europe (AFSOUTH), and Other Commands. AFNORTH protects Belgium, Czech Republic, Denmark, Germany, Great Britain, Luxembourg, Netherlands, Norway, Poland, North Sea, Irish Sea, English Channel, and the Baltic Sea. It consists of Allied Air Forces North based in Ramstein, Germany, and Allied Naval Forces North based in Northwood, United Kingdom. AFSOUTH covers Greece, Hungary, Italy, Spain, Turkey, Black Sea, Sea of Azov, the whole of the Mediterranean and the Atlantic approaches to the Strait of Gibraltar east of longitude 7°

23' 48" W, and an area around the Canary Islands and its associated airspace. Headquartered in Naples, Italy, the force is made up of Allied Air Forces South and Allied Naval Forces South. Other Commands included the Maritime Immediate Reaction Forces, which offers continuous naval protection, and the NATO Airborne Early Warning Force, which provides air surveillance.

The collapse of the Soviet Union has challenged NATO by removing its main reason for existence. The organization is struggling to find a new role and has begun to focus on the fight against terrorism. The NATO-Russia Council, established in 2002, is identifying opportunities for joint action in all areas of mutual interest but especially in the use of the military to combat terrorist attacks. The future will probably see increasing cooperation between these former enemies as NATO alters in response to changing transatlantic security needs.

■ FURTHER READING:

BOOKS:

Cook, Don. *Forging the Alliance: The Birth of the NATO Treaty and the Dramatic Transformation of U.S. Foreign Policy Between 1945 and 1950.* New York: Arbor House/William Morrow, 1989.

Kay, Sean. *NATO and the Future of European Security.* Lanham, Maryland: Rowman and Littlefield, 1998.

Park, William. *Defending the West: A History of NATO.* Brighton: Wheatsheaf, 1986.

Schmidt, Gustav, ed. *A History of NATO: The First Fifty Years.* New York: Palgrave, 2001.

ELECTRONIC:

NATO. "North Atlantic Treaty Organisation." January 31, 2003. <http://www.nato.int/> (February 1, 2003).

NATO. "Supreme Headquarters Allied Powers Europe." January 31, 2003. <http://www.nato.int/shape/index.htm.> (February 1, 2003).

SEE ALSO

Cold War (1945–1950): The Start of the Atomic Age
Cold War (1950–1972)
Cold War (1972–1989): The Collapse of the Soviet Union
Kennedy Administration (1961–1963), United States National Security Policy

Natural Resources and National Security

■ WILLIAM C. HANEBERG

The ability of a nation to grow and defend itself is controlled in large part by the availability of natural resources.

Nations that do not possess sufficient mineral, energy, agricultural, and water resources within their boundaries must obtain them on the international market, where prices can be volatile and supplies unreliable. In times of war, all or part of the international market may be inaccessible and critical resources unavailable for import.

Mineral and energy resources have become increasingly important since the advent of mechanized warfare. Even before that, however, other natural resources played an important role in the growth of nations. A seventeenth- or eighteenth-century ship of the line in the British Navy may have required 400,000 board feet of lumber, much of which came from Britain's colonies in North America. A typical suburban home in the United States, in comparison, might require about 2000 board feet of lumber. Timber and, in later years, coal and iron resources helped the British Empire to become a dominant world power in the seventeenth, eighteenth, and nineteenth centuries.

The word resource refers to a naturally occurring concentration of minerals or fuels, whereas the word reserve refers to the portion of a resource that meets minimum criteria related to its extraction and processing. An accumulation of gold, for example, may be a resource but not a reserve if it cannot be mined and refined using existing technology. Resources can become reserves over time as technology improves and the economics of extraction and processing change. Therefore, the distinction is one of economics and engineering rather than geology. Resources are described as being measured, indicated, or inferred depending on the degree of certainty with which they are known. A measured resource is one for which the size has been established by geologic mapping, test drilling, and sampling. An inferred resource is one for which there is a reasonable amount of geologic evidence, but that has not been verified by drilling or sampling. Reserves are similarly described as being proven, probable, or possible.

Energy resources. The ability of a modern nation to defend itself or, should it be aggressive, to expand its territory depends on a reliable source of energy. Until the beginning of the twentieth century, this meant coal. Although coal remains an important energy source that is used to generate most of the electricity used in the United States, it has been joined in strategic importance by petroleum and nuclear fuels. The United States currently imports more than 3 billion barrels of oil per year from countries ranging from neighboring Canada and Mexico to Saudi Arabia, Nigeria, Iraq, and Angola. Although the United States contains significant petroleum reserves, they are not large enough to satisfy the long-term demand. It is, in most cases, also more expensive to produce oil from domestic reservoirs than to import it from countries that have abundant and easily recovered petroleum resources. The federal government maintains a Strategic Petroleum Reserve to help offset the potential effects of an oil embargo or other supply interruption. President George W. Bush ordered the first ever emergency withdrawal from the reserve in an attempt to stabilize world oil prices that were fluctuating in response to the 1991 Iraqi invasion of Kuwait.

Although the United States and Canada contain significant uranium reserves, the currently depressed price of uranium on the international market generally makes it less expensive to import this energy source than produce it domestically.

The worldwide distribution of energy resources such as coal, petroleum, and uranium ore is controlled by geology and is far from uniform. Some nations, therefore, have an abundance of resources whereas others have little or no domestic supply of strategically important materials. A lack of petroleum reserves forced Nazi Germany to embark on an ambitious synthetic fuels program during the 1930s. The raw material for the German synthetic fuel program was coal, of which Germany had abundant supplies and which had satisfied its industrial and military energy needs until the beginning of the 20th century. Two synthetic fuel processes were employed by the Germans. One process produced automobile and aviation fuel and the other produced lubricating oil and diesel fuel. Twenty-one synthetic fuel plants, some of them using forced labor, had been constructed in Germany by the end of World War II.

Other countries, most notably Persian Gulf states such as Saudi Arabia and Kuwait, have petroleum resources that are disproportionately rich in relation to their geographic size and, just as importantly, inexpensive to produce. Some of these countries have been able to form strategic alliances with larger nations that depend on their petroleum. In addition, cartels such as the Organization of Petroleum Exporting Countries (OPEC) can strongly influence prices by increasing or decreasing their production, as was proven by the 1973 oil embargo.

Another potentially important energy resource is hydroelectric power, which requires large rivers as well as the ability to construct technologically sophisticated dams and hydroelectric power plants. The production of both aluminum for aircraft and fissionable plutonium for weapons requires large amounts of electricity. Inexpensive and abundant hydroelectric power was therefore an important strategic asset to the United States during World War II. During that time, dams along the Columbia River provided electricity to aluminum smelters throughout the Columbia River Basin and Manhattan Project facilities at the Hanford Site in Washington.

Mineral resources. Mineral resources include the ores of base metals such as copper, iron, and lead as well as strategic and critical metals such as chromium, titanium, platinum, cobalt, manganese, indium, palladium, and others. The latter are metals that are used in nuclear reactors, jet aircraft engines, missiles, computers, and industrial machinery, but of which the United States has little or no domestic supply. Therefore, they must be imported from countries that include the former Soviet Union, Zaire, and

Zimbabwe. Guerrilla warfare in Zaire during the 1970s caused the worldwide price of cobalt to increase from $6 to $45 per pound, and a United Nations trade boycott of Rhodesia (now Zimbabwe) made it impossible to legally obtain chromium mined in that country.

The importance of critical and strategic metals to the security of modern nations was recognized by the United States during World War I, when tungsten, tin, chromite (chromium ore), optical grade glass, and manila fiber for ropes were all in short supply. The War Department subsequently prepared a list of 28 materials that had been in short supply during World War I, and since then Congress has funded stockpiles of strategic materials that are essential for national security. The United States Geological Survey began its strategic minerals program in 1939, first concentrating on seven strategic metals and then expanding the program to include base metals and petroleum. Even with strategic minerals programs in place and stockpiles established before the war, conservation and recycling were essential during World War II. After the war, the Defense Minerals Administration was formed in 1951 to promote mineral exploration and development in the interest of national security, and its successor agencies were eventually merged into the Geological Survey.

Agricultural land and water. A third class of natural resources that is vital for national security includes agricultural land and water. As is the case for other resources, food or water that cannot be produced within a nation must be imported. Therefore, countries with large amounts of arable land, favorable climates, and fresh water can be less dependent on outside supplies than nations that lack one or more of those resources. In cases where technological solutions do exist, for example desalinization of seawater to produce drinking water in arid coastal areas, they can be too expensive for all but the wealthiest of nations.

■ **FURTHER READING:**

BOOKS:

Deffeys, K. S. *Hubbert's Peak: The Impending World Oil Shortage.* Princeton, New Jersey: Princeton University Press, 2001.

Yergin, Daniel. *The Prize: The Epic Quest for Oil, Money, and Power.* New York: Simon and Schuster, 1991.

Youngquist, W. L. *GeoDestinies.* Portland, Oregon: National Book Company, 1997 .

ELECTRONIC:

Cartwright, M. R. "Mineral Resources/Reserves in Appraisal." March 21, 1999. <http://www.minval.com/reserve_mineral.html> (14 December 2002).

Energy Information Administration. "Imports of Crude Oil into the United States by Country of Origin, 2001." June 18, 2002. <http://www.eia.doe.gov/neic/rankings/crudebycountry.htm> (14 December 2002).

Energy Information Administration. "25th Anniversary of the 1973 Oil Embargo." March 7, 2000. <http://www.eia.doe.gov/emeu/25opec/anniversary.html> (14 December 2002).

Stranges, A. N. "Germany's Synthetic Fuel Industry 1927–45." October 26, 2000. <http://www.caer.uky.edu/fseminar/fsstrang.htm> (14 December 2002).

U.S. Department of Energy. "Profile of the Strategic Petroleum Reserve." <http://www.fe.doe.gov/spr/> (14 December 2002).

SEE ALSO

Bush Administration (1989–1993), United States National Security Policy
DOE (United States Department of Energy)
Energy Technologies
Petroleum Reserves, Determination

Navy Criminal Investigative Service (NCIS)

The Navy Criminal Investigative Service (NCIS) is responsible for providing law enforcement on behalf of United States Navy and Marine Corps personnel and their families. Originally part of the Office of Naval Intelligence (ONI), the organization was staffed primarily by military personnel, whereas today it is a largely civilian organization. NCIS has been involved in murder investigations and drug sweeps, and since September 11, 2001, it has also taken on a homeland security role.

NCIS began as part of ONI, which was deployed during World War II to detect potential spies and saboteurs on the domestic front. Through the end of World War II, the investigative branch of ONI was composed mainly of military personnel. In the postwar era, however, the Secretary of the Navy developed a coterie of civilian agents responsible for conducting criminal investigations, counterintelligence, and security background investigations on naval and marine personnel and civilians associated with the U.S. Navy and Marine Corps.

Only on February 4, 1966, did the Naval Investigative Service (NIS), as NCIS's predecessor was called, gain an identity separate from that of ONI. Nonetheless, it remained a part of the naval intelligence office. In 1972, the newly formed Defense Investigative Service took over responsibility for background checks, leaving NIS free to concentrate on counterintelligence and criminal investigations. During the 1980s, the organization went through a number of name changes until, in December 1992, it gained its present identity.

At the time of its establishment as NCIS, a civilian director, Roy D. Nedrow (formerly with the U.S. Secret Service), assumed leadership. During the following year,

he undertook reorganization in accordance with the broader downscaling of military and security organizations that attended the end of the Cold War. Whereas in 1991, NCIS had 2,281 personnel, including 1,167 civilian special agents operating in more than 200 offices worldwide, a decade later its ranks numbered 1,603, of whom 877 were civilian special agents operating in some 150 offices worldwide. In addition, 51 military agents, most of them from the Marine Corps, were assigned to NCIS. As part of Nedrow's reorganization, NCIS was restructured as a federal law-enforcement agency with 14 field offices.

NCIS at work. NCIS has received numerous accolades for its efficiency, not least for the work of its "cold-case squad," which has reopened scores of previously unsolved homicide cases, and successfully solved dozens. Working with the cold-case squad of the Fairfax County, Virginia, law-enforcement authorities, for instance, NCIS helped solve a homicide case that was extremely "cold" (old)—so much so that the accused had finished high school, had a full career in the Navy, and retired—all in the quarter-century between the murder and his arrest.

The case involved Paul S. Sorensen, who was 16 years old in 1975, when he allegedly stabbed to death a convenience store clerk while robbing a 7-Eleven. Sorensen entered the Navy after graduating high school in 1976, and in 1999, having attained the rank of chief petty officer, retired to Corpus Christi, Texas. Three years later, and five years after NCIS and Fairfax County reopened the cold case, Sorensen—knowing that he would soon be arrested anyway—turned himself in to authorities.

Another example of NCIS at work was the drug sweep that in July 2002 netted 84 marines and sailors at Camp Lejeune, North Carolina. Code-named Operation Xterminator, the sweep took two years and yielded $1.4 million in narcotics. NCIS has also been involved in homeland security since the September 2001 terrorist attacks on the United States. Not only has the agency helped provide security for the naval base at San Diego Bay in California, but NCIS agents have taken part in community education programs designed to teach civilians how to monitor their neighborhoods for suspicious activity.

■ FURTHER READING:

BOOKS:

The Naval Criminal Investigative Service: To Protect and Serve. Washington, D.C.: U.S. Department of the Navy, 1994.

PERIODICALS:

Crawley, James W. "Details of Port Security Are Off-Limits." *San Diego Union-Tribune.* (August 23, 2002): B1.

"Drug Sweep Nets 84 Marines, Sailors." *Commercial Appeal* (Memphis, TN). (July 3, 2002): A4.

Jackman, Tom. "Retiree Surrenders in 1975 Va. Killing." *Washington Post*. (May 22, 2002): B7.

ELECTRONIC:

Naval Criminal Investigative Service. <http://www.ncis.navy.mil> (January 18, 2003).

SEE ALSO

Military Police, United States

NCIX (National Counterintelligence Executive), United States Office of the

Formerly known as the National Counterintelligence Center (NACIC), the U.S. Office of the National Counterintelligence Executive (NCIX) was created early in the twenty-first century. It educates members of government organizations and the private sector on the need to maintain vigilance against espionage, both the political and national forum and in the economic and industrial arena. NCIX conducts regional seminars, issues publications, and produces other materials in support of its mission to provide the federal government with strong policy leadership in the area of counterintelligence education.

Establishment of the NCIX

Just two weeks before leaving office, on January 5, 2001, President William J. Clinton issued Presidential Decision Directive (PDD) 75, "U.S. Counterintelligence Effectiveness—Counterintelligence for the Twenty-first Century." PDD 75 presented specific measures that would enhance the ability of members of the U.S. counterintelligence (CI) community to identify and counteract threats.

First among the provisions of PDD 75 was the establishment of the Counterintelligence Board of Directors, which would be chaired by the director of the Federal Bureau of Investigation (FBI) and composed of the Deputy Secretary of Defense, the Deputy Director of Central Intelligence, and a senior representative of the Department of Justice. The directive also established the position of CI executive, or NCIX, to undertake certain responsibilities on behalf of the Board.

The NCIX, who would serve as a *de facto* director of counterintelligence activities at the national level, would be a federal employee selected by the board with the agreement of the Attorney General, Director of Central Intelligence, and the Secretary of Defense. The NCIX would

work closely with the National Coordinator for Security, Infrastructure Protection, and Counterterrorism. He or she would report to the FBI director, as board chairperson, but would be accountable to all board members, and would have the responsibility of advising them on counterintelligence programs, policies, and challenges.

PDD 75 went on to stipulate that the NCIX would chair the National Counterintelligence Policy Board, whose members would include (at a minimum) senior counterintelligence officials from the departments of State, Defense, Justice, and Energy, as well as from the Joint Chiefs of Staff, Central Intelligence Agency, FBI, and National Security Council (NSC). The NCIX would also oversee the Office of the National Counterintelligence Executive, which would replace the old NACIC.

NACIC background and the change to the Office of the NCIX.
Whereas the new Office of the NCIX was ultimately under the leadership of the FBI, the NACIC had been attached to the NSC. Established by an earlier Presidential Decision Directive, in 1994, NACIC was also responsible for guiding U.S. counterintelligence activities. It was controlled by a National Counterintelligence Policy Board directed by the NSC, and had a number of functions, among them efforts to counter economic or industrial espionage.

In this capacity, the NACIC operated a threat assessment office that compiled information—both from the U.S. Intelligence Community and from open sources in the media and elsewhere—on activities by foreign powers and their intelligence agencies that posed a potential threat to U.S. companies. NACIC also analyzed possible espionage concerning emerging technologies from the United States, as well as threats to U.S. executives or business personnel. It also kept a close watch on the effects of foreign ownership, technology transfers, and joint ownership on U.S. economic concerns.

As would be the case later with the Office of the NCIX, the NACIC made available to the U.S. business community its reports on economic espionage, and sought to strengthen ties between private enterprise and federal agencies for enhanced counterintelligence awareness. PDD 75 ensured that those activities would continue, but under the direction of the FBI. On November 27, 2002, Public Law 107–306 formally established the Office of the National Counterintelligence Executive.

An expanded outreach to the private sector. The new Office of the NCIX expanded the outreach to the private business community undertaken by the NACIC. The latter had already been conducting regional seminars on CI, but due to a lack of private-sector security organizations involved in administering the seminars, their visibility had been limited. The new office, instead of appealing to those few civilian security organizations (examples included the National Classification Management Society, as well as

various Industrial Security Advisory councils), sought to broaden its appeal.

The Office of the NCIX also created, and made available to the private sector, a vast array of products designed to enhance awareness of CI. The office published on the Internet its *Annual Report to Congress on Foreign Economic Collection and Industrial Espionage,* as well as its *Counterintelligence News and Developments (CIND)* newsletter. It also published booklets and brochures such as *Be Alert!,* designed to instruct American travelers abroad as to the ways that they might become targets of foreign intelligence collection activities. At its Web site, the Office of the NCIX also sold videos such as *Insider Betrayal,* regarding FBI and private-sector cooperation to counter economic espionage. It also sold posters, and made available for free various computer screen savers and background screens designed to heighten awareness of counterintelligence.

■ FURTHER READING:

BOOKS:

Survey of the Counterintelligence Needs of Private Industry. Washington, D.C.: National Counterintelligence Center, 1995.

PERIODICALS:

Barth, Steve. "Spy vs. Spy." *World Trade* 11, no. 8 (August 1998): 34–37.

Gottlieb, Daniel W. "Keeping Trade Secrets Secret: Counterspies, Codes Courts." *Purchasing* 126 no. 7 (May 6, 1999): 24–25.

Kaltenhauser, Skip. "Industrial Espionage Is Alive and Well." *World Trade* 10, no. 7 (July 1997): 24–26.

ELECTRONIC:

Office of the National Counterintelligence Executive. <http://www.ncix.gov> (March 17, 2003).

SEE ALSO

Economic Espionage
Economic Intelligence
Intelligence Community

NDIC (Department of Justice National Drug Intelligence Center)

The Department of Justice National Drug Intelligence Center (NDIC) is the lead counterdrug agency within the U.S.

Attorney General John Ashcroft, speaking at a news conference at the National Drug Intelligence Center in Johnstown, Pennsylvania, in August, 2002, said that the technology now being used to combat illicit drugs has also proven useful in tracking the movement of terrorist groups. AP/WIDE WORLD PHOTOS.

intelligence community. Created in 1993, it is responsible for providing national leadership as well as law enforcement officials, with a strategic picture of the traffic in illegal drugs throughout the United States. It offers its client base a number of intelligence products and services, including information provided by its Document Exploitation Division.

NDIC products and services. Principal among NDIC's intelligence products are its threat assessments, of which the most significant is its annual National Drug Threat Assessment. The latter identifies principal drug threats, provides data on changes in consumption patterns, analyzes the availability of drugs by geographic market, and tracks patterns of distribution and trafficking. NDIC also creates drug threat assessments by state, and issues information bulletins in response to drug-related issues as those arise.

The Intelligence Division of NDIC includes six geographic units, as well as four units with specialized tasks. These are the Drug Trends, Organized Crime and Violence, National Drug Threat Assessment, and National Interdiction

Support units. Some information comes to NDIC by means of field program specialists, whose position was created by a January 2001 initiative intended to encourage sharing of information among law-enforcement officials at the federal, state, and local levels. Field representatives are independent contractors, usually with years of experience in drug law enforcement.

NDIC's Document Exploitation Division analyzes information seized in major federal drug raids or investigations. Document Exploitation teams make use of proprietary software known as the Real-time Analytical Intelligence Database, or RAID. RAID allows agents to process massive quantities of information from seized documents and computers. The program collects, collates, and labels large information packets, then subject this data to intensive analysis in a search for hidden information on assets, associates, and other valuable leads.

The center also provides counterdrug analysis training courses for personnel in local, state, and federal law enforcement agencies. This education program is a cooperative effort of NDIC and the Federal Bureau of Investigation, Drug Enforcement Administration, National Guard Bureau, U.S. Customs Service, and Financial Crimes Enforcement Network. In performing its overall mission, NDIC works closely with these agencies, as well as with the U.S. Coast Guard, the Bureau of Alcohol, Tobacco, and Firearms, the Bureau of Prisons, and the Office of National Drug Control Policy.

■ FURTHER READING:

PERIODICALS:

Strong, Ronald L. "The National Drug Intelligence Center: Assessing the Drug Threat." *The Police Chief* 68, no. 5 (May 2001): 55–60.

ELECTRONIC:

National Drug Intelligence Center. <http://www.usdoj.gov/ndic/> (February 23, 2003).

National Drug Intelligence Center. Federation of American Scientists. <http://www.fas.org/irp/agency/doj/ndic/> (February 23, 2003).

SEE ALSO

DEA (Drug Enforcement Administration)
Drug Control Policy, United States Office of National
Justice Department, United States

Near Space Environment

■ CECILIA COLOME

The near-Earth environment is far from empty. In addition to the natural meteoroid material, solar wind plasma, and cosmic rays, the space above Earth's atmosphere contains several hundreds of satellites and thousands of tons of space debris. Space debris orbiting the Earth consists of mostly non-functional man-made objects, many of which are fragments of satellites or rockets and residues from launches. On February 1, 2003, the space shuttle *Columbia* tragically ended its 16-day mission during its re-entry into Earth's atmosphere. One of the first questions that the scientific community investigated was whether *Columbia* had been struck by space debris.

There are about 600 active satellites orbiting the Earth. They are used for communication, remote sensing for weather, land surveys, national security, navigation, and support for scientific missions. These satellites are located in only a few orbital regions, mostly in the semisynchronous orbit, or the low Earth orbit (LEO) and the geosynchronous orbit (GEO). It is also in these regions where most of the space debris is located. The space debris around Earth not only poses risks to active satellites, but also to space missions and astronomical observations. Space debris is a major source of light pollution in wide-field imaging of astronomical objects.

One of the main problems associated with space debris is its duration, or lifetime. In contrast to meteoroids, which either burn in Earth's atmosphere or cross the near-Earth region to continue their travel through the solar system, space debris potentially can remain in orbit for millions of years. There are three issues of crucial importance in regards to space debris, namely how it can be cleaned up, how to avoid debris collisions with active spacecraft, and how to minimize the generation of more debris.

As early as the 1970s NASA began to investigate the feasibility of forcing space junk into the Earth's atmosphere, where remnants not destroyed by re-entry would fall to the ground. The central idea of this project, known as Orion, was to focus a high-powered laser beam into individual debris fragments, causing their outer layers to vaporize, and creating a thrust that would deflect their orbits. The research for the Orion project demonstrated that the clean-up would be extremely expensive, mainly because of the high power required by the laser and the high cost of the adaptive optics necessary to focus energy into small objects at great distances from the ground. This idea still might serve for the future, when technology may be able to equip satellites with the high-powered lasers and enable them to "sweep" space debris into the Earth's atmosphere.

There are two major risks from objects reentering the Earth's atmosphere. First, if they are too large to evaporate completely during re-entry, they could cause damage on the ground. Second, if the falling debris contains radioactive material, the atmosphere or ground could be contaminated. Currently, roughly 50 nuclear devices orbit the Earth, carrying a total of 1,300 kg (1.3 tons) of radioactive material. There have been at least two confirmed nuclear mishaps from space. In 1964, the orbit of an American satellite decayed into the Earth's atmosphere, releasing radioactive radiation over the Indian Ocean, and in 1978, a Soviet satellite lost its orbit and crashed in northern Canada, dispersing more than 30 kg (66.1 pounds) of enriched uranium. Nuclear reactors were very popular in space because they provide large energy sources in very small and lightweight volumes. All theses devices were built and launched prior to 1988, and since then, nuclear reactors have not been incorporated into satellites.

As the density of the Earth's atmosphere decreases with altitude, objects in LEO experience more air friction than objects at higher altitudes. Over time, the orbits of non-functional objects decay to lower altitudes. The re-entry of large objects, with cross-sections of one square meter or more is significant; about one object re-enters daily, and some of them have survived the heat produced by re-entry air friction. Two notorious examples of debris re-entry are from the tanks belonging to a Delta rocket. In 1997, one of the tanks landed near a house, not far from a busy highway in Texas; a second tank from the Delta rocket landed in South Africa near Cape Town in 2000. To this date, there has been only one reported incident of a human being struck by space debris: in 1997, a woman in Tulsa, Oklahoma, was hit on the shoulder by a 6-inch piece of metal, and fortunately, it did not lead to any serious injury.

Both meteoroids and space debris pose a serious hazard to spacecraft and astronauts. The vast majority of meteoroids are small dust particles with typical sizes of tenths of a millimeter. Although they are small, due to their high speeds, up to 70 km/s, they represent a hazard in space. Current satellites are well shielded to withstand meteoroid impacts. Nevertheless, meteoroid collisions on spacecraft can be devastating for their operations. During a collision of a meteoroid, it evaporates partially or completely, and it may cause the evaporation of a small area of the external material on the spacecraft. The result is a plasma of electrons and ions. These particles are capable of inducing high electric currents on spacecraft, interfering with their basic control operations.

The dimensions of space debris cover a wide size range, from tiny dust particles to large non-functional rockets. Some of the main sources of space debris have been explosions of rockets. The collision avoidance with the larger (>10 cm, or >4 in) debris population is performed by tracking methods from the ground, either by radar or by optical measurements. Meteoroids are generally small, too small to be tracked reliably. Their potential collisions with spacecraft are taken into account in the shield design of spacecraft, and because they cannot be tracked, their collisions with active spacecraft can be treated only statistically. Ground-based radars are mostly used to monitor the space debris in LEO, while optical observations are used to track objects in GEO. Both methods have their own advantages and limitations. Radar measurements are not affected by weather nor day-night conditions, but because of their narrow bandwidths they cannot detect small objects at great distances. Optical tracking of space debris through telescopes requires the objects to be illuminated by sunlight against a dark sky. In LEO, objects can be observed for only a few hours, but for objects in GEO, this method can be used during an entire night. Several countries are currently using radar and optical methods for tracking and making catalogues of space debris. Among them are England, France, Germany, Japan, Russia, Spain, and the United States.

The Haystack Auxiliary and Goldstone radars in the United States have provided ample data on the debris population with sizes smaller than 30 cm. The international collective effort has provided almost 9,000 catalogued large (>10 cm, or > 4 in) objects. These catalogues are essential to avoid catastrophic collisions with active spacecraft. Three catalogues are updated regularly, one by the United States Space Command Satellite, one by the Russian Space Surveillance, and the other by the Information System Characterizating Objects in Space of the European Space Agency (ESA).

Explosions of spacecraft are considered to be the main source of large fragments of space debris. Part of the Pegasus rocket exploded in 1996, two years after its launch, creating 700 fragments large enough to be catalogued. The explosion of the Chinese Long March 4 rocket created more than 300 large fragments. At least three reported maneuvers of satellites have been performed in order to avoid collisions with space debris: both the European Remote Sensing Satellite (ERS-1) and the Satellite pour-l'observation de la Terre (SPOT–2) in 1997, and the International Space Station (ISS) in 1999. A severe space accident occurred in 1996 when the French CERISE spacecraft was hit by a catalogued object, thought to be a fragment of the Ariane rocket's upper stage.

In order to gain better data on the space debris population, in 1984 the space shuttle *Challenger* deployed NASA's Long Duration Exposure Facility (LDEF). Its retrieval was scheduled for 1986, but due to the loss of the space shuttle *Challenger* it was postponed until 1990, when it was retrieved by *Columbia*. The LDEF orbited the Earth for almost 6 years, providing data on the near-Earth space environment, and returned to Earth covered by more than 30,000 craters. The LDEF was a large cylinder weighing more than 20,000 lbs, one of the heaviest objects deployed by any space shuttle. It contained 86 trays on its periphery where 57 experiments were carried out. These experiments were designed by NASA, the Department of Defense, universities and private companies, and were aimed for meteoroid and space debris studies, radiation surveys, and infrared video surveys. A major challenge in the study of the trays on LDEF was to distinguish between craters created by meteoroid impacts and those due to collisions with space debris, was accomplished by extensive chemical analysis. The data collected by LDEF had a major impact on the design of spacecraft after 1990. Most of the design changes involved the substitution of materials that deteriorate in space, such as Teflon, Kapton, Dracon, Mylar, and polymeric films. For example, the design of the radiator of the International Space Station was changed from Teflon to a ceramic paint. In general, ceramic materials are better survivors of erosion due to bombardment of atomic oxygen and UV radiation.

One peculiar kind of potential space debris are tethers. Tethers are chains or ropes that connect astronauts to their spacecraft while working in space. They are also used as links between components on spacecraft. Tethers are a potential source of debris if they are discarded from spacecraft, but they also might help in the reduction of space debris. As a tether crosses the Earth's magnetic field lines, it becomes an electric generator. This energy source can be used not only to deploy spacecraft, but also to create the necessary thrust for lowering the altitude of non-functional objects. NASA has developed a unique experiment for future uses of tethers in space, The Propulsive Small Expendable Deployer System (ProSEDS), a thin wire 5 km long connected to a 10 km non-conductive rope. ProSEDS was scheduled for launch in 2003, and remains a high-priority for launch payload.

All effective clean-up procedures of space debris are still in experimental phases, although great advances have been made in slowing the increase of space debris with time. Spacecraft are now covered with longer lasting paints and their protective covers are much less affected by erosion by small meteoroids, particle bombardment, and UV radiation. Newer satellites are becoming increasingly smaller. This also reduces the probability of more generation of space debris, because the smaller the object is, the lower the probability of experiencing collisions.

■ FURTHER READING:

BOOKS:

CETS. *Engineering Challenges to the Long-Term Operation of the International Space Station.* Washington, D.C.: The National Academies Press, 2000.

CPSMA. *Radiation and the International Space Station: Recommendations to Reduce Risk.* Washington, D.C.: The National Academies Press, 2000.

Gehrels, T., ed. *Hazards due to Comets & Asteroids.* Tempe, AZ: The University of Arizona Press, 1995.

Simpson, J. A., ed. *Preservation of Near-Earth Space for Future Generations.* New York: Cambridge University Press, 1994.

Tribble, A. C. *The Space Environment: Implications for Spacecraft Design.* Princeton: Princeton University Press, 1995.

PERIODICALS:

National Aeronautics and Space Agency. *Orbital Debris Quarterly News Letter.* Houston: Johnson Space Flight Center.

Revkin, Andrew C. "Wanted: Traffic Cops for Space." *New York Times.* February 18, 2003.

SEE ALSO

NASA (National Air and Space Administration)
Satellites, Non-Governmental High Resolution
Satellites, Spy

Space Shuttle
Strategic Defense Initiative and National Missile Defense

Nerve Gas

■ JUDYTH SASSOON

Nerve gases, or nerve agents, are mostly odorless compounds belonging to the organophosphate family of chemicals. Nerve gasses are either colorless or yellow-brown liquids under standard conditions. Two examples of nerve gases that have gained some notoriety through their powerful physiological effects are Sarin and VX. Even in small quantities, nerve gases inhibit the enzyme acetylcholinesterase and disrupt the transmission of nerve impulses in the body. Acetylcholinesterase is a serine hydrolase belonging to the esterase enzyme family, which acts on different types of carboxylic esters in higher eukaryotes. Its role in biology is to terminate nerve impulse transmissions at cholinergic synapses. It does this by rapidly hydrolysing the neurotransmitter, acetylcholine, which is released at the nerve synapses. Inhibition of the acetylcholinesterase results in the excessive buildup of acetylcholine in, for example, the parasympathetic nerves leading to a number of important locations in the body: the smooth muscle of the iris, ciliary body, the bronchial tree, gastrointestinal tract, bladder and blood vessels; also the salivary glands and secretory glands of the gastrointestinal tract and respiratory tract; and the cardiac muscle and endings of sympathetic nerves to the sweat glands. An accumulation of acetylcholine at parasympathetic sites gives rise to characteristic muscarinic signs, such as emptying of bowels and bladder, blurring of vision, excessive sweating, profuse salivation and stimulation of smooth muscles. The accumulation of acetylcholine at the endings of motor nerves leading to voluntary muscles ultimately results in paralysis.

Nerve gases are highly toxic, stable, and easily dispersed. They produce rapid physiological effects both when absorbed through the skin or through the respiratory tract. They are also fairly easy to synthesize and the raw materials required for their manufacture are inexpensive and readily available. This means that anyone with a basic laboratory can produce them. Nerve gases are, therefore, a significant concern for authorities as they are an easily available weapon for terrorist groups.

In 1936, the German chemist Gerhard Schrader of the I. G. Farbenindustrie laboratory in Leverkusen first prepared the agent Tabun (ethyl-dimethylphosphoramidocyanidate). At the time, Schrader was leading a program to develop new types of insecticides, working first with fluorine-containing compounds such as acyl fluorides, sulfonyl fluorides, fluoroethanol derivatives and fluoroacetic acid derivatives. Schrader's research eventually led to the synthesis of Tabun as an extremely powerful

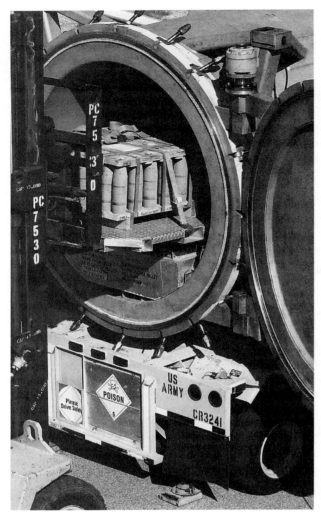

Cold War-era artillery shells containing GB nerve gas are carefully loaded into a steel cask for transport to an incinerator at a chemical depot in Utah in 2001. AP/WIDE WORLD PHOTOS.

agent against insects. Schrader found that as little as 5 parts per million (ppm) of Tabun killed all the leaf lice used in his experiments. Soon after Schrader's experiments, the potential use of this substance as an agent of war was realized.

In 1939, a pilot plant for Tabun production was set up at Munster-Lager, near the German Army training grounds at Raubkammer. In January 1940, Germany began the construction of a full-scale plant, code named Hochwerk, at Dyernfurth-am-Oder (now Brzeg Dolny in Poland). A total of 12,000 tons of Tabun was produced during the ensuing three years (1942–1945) and at the end of WWII, large quantities were seized by the Allied Forces. In addition to Tabun, Schrader and his colleagues produced some 2000 new organophosphates, including Sarin in 1938 and the third of the "classic" nerve agents, Soman, in 1944. These three nerve agents, Tabun, Sarin and Soban,

are known as G-agents. The manufacture of Sarin was never fully developed in Germany and only about 0.5 tons were produced in a pilot plant before the end of WWII in 1945.

After 1945, a great deal of research began to focus on understanding the physiological mechanisms of nerve gas action, so that more effective means of protection could be devised against them. However, these efforts also allowed for the development of new and more powerful agents, closely related to the earlier ones. The first official publications on these compounds appeared in 1955. The authors, British chemists Ranajit Ghosh and J. F. Newman, described Amiton, one of the newly developed nerve agents, as being particularly effective against mites. At this time, researchers were devoting a great deal of energy to studying organophosphate insecticides both in Europe and in the United States. At least three chemical firms independently studied and quantified the intense toxic properties of these compounds during the years 1952–53 and some of them became available on the market as pesticides. By the mid-1950s, following in the wake of the intensive research activity, a new group of highly stable nerve agents had been developed. These were known as the V-agents and were approximately ten-fold more poisonous than Sarin. The V-agents can be numbered among the most toxic substances ever synthesized. VX, a persistent nerve gas, was discovered by Ghosh and was touted as being more toxic than any previously synthesized compound. Since the discovery of VX, there have been only minor advancements in the development of new nerve agents.

A contemporary use of nerve gas occurred during the Iran-Iraq war of 1984–1988. In this conflict, the United Nations confirmed that Iraq used Tabun and other nerve gases against Iran. This incident is a prime example of how the technology of chemical weapons was shared during the Cold War. The Soviets would arm their allies while the U.S. did the same for its allies. Iraq was a benefactor and implemented its chemical stockpiles during this period. Another contemporary incident of nerve gas use occurred in Japan in 1995. Members of the Aum Shinrikyo cult introduced Sarin gas into Tokyo's subway system. This incident gives an example of the possible new roles that nerve gases may play in the future, as tools of terrorism rather than the weapons of powerful nations.

■ FURTHER READING:

BOOKS:

Paxman, J., and R. Harris. *A Higher Form of Killing: The Secret Story of Chemical and Biological Warfare.* New York: Hill and Wang, 1982.

Poolos, J. *Nerve Gas Attack on the Tokyo Subway.* Rosen Publishing Group Inc., 2002.

Stockholm International Peace Research Institute. *The Problem of Chemical and Biological Warfare. A Study of the Historical Technical, Military, Legal, and Political Aspects of CBW and Possible Disarmament Measures.*

Vol. 1. The Rise of CB Weapons. New York: Humanities Press, 1971.

PERIODICALS:

Evison D, D. Hinsley, and P. Rice. "Chemical Weapons." *BMJ* 324 (2002): 332–335.

Yergler, M. "Nerve Gas Attack." *Am. J. Nurs.* 1 (2002): 57–60.

ELECTRONIC:

Lenthall, Joe. University of Oxford. "Molecule of the month, VX gas." <http://www.chem.ox.ac.uk/mom/vx/VX.htm> (February 20, 2003).

SEE ALSO

Chemical and Biological Defense Information Analysis Center (CBIAC)
Chemical and Biological Detection Technologies
Chemical Biological Incident Response Force, United States
Chemical Warfare
Chemistry: Applications in Espionage, Intelligence, and Security Issues
Terrorist Threat Integration Center

NEST Team.

SEE *Nuclear Emergency Support Team, United States.*

Netherlands, Intelligence and Security

The Kingdom of the Netherlands was established following the Napoleonic Wars in 1815. Since its founding, the Netherlands has been influential in international politics, but has long maintained a policy of stated neutrality. Despite their officially neutral position, the Netherlands was invaded and occupied by Nazi forces during World War II. Though the Queen and many government officials fled to Britain before the invasion, the Dutch people formed secret resistance groups and refugee smuggling networks, many led by members of the Dutch intelligence community.

After World War II, the Netherlands reformed several government agencies, including the intelligence and security services. The Dutch government strengthened the intelligence community, and its accountability to government officials. Separate civilian and military intelligence services were created, but were designed to work in cooperation with each other. Today, the Netherlands is a member of the European Union, and hosts the international courts of the United Nations.

The main civilian intelligence agency is the *Algemene Inlichtingen -en Veiligheidsdienst* (AIVD), or the General Intelligence and Security Service. The agency conducts all means of intelligence operations, but focuses on domestic intelligence. The AIVD is charged with the protection of domestic security and assessment of threats to Dutch interests within its national and territorial borders. The agency analyzes all intelligence information, and reports threats and other security issues to government officials.

The Netherlands established their military intelligence service immediately before the outbreak of World War I maintained those services, even operating clandestinely during the World War II Nazi occupation. The current, primary, Dutch military intelligence agency is the *Militaire Inlichtingendienst* (MID), or Military Intelligence Agency. The Ministry of Defense, Ministry of Justice, and the Ministry of Affairs all contribute to the administration of the MID. Though foreign intelligence and external security issues are the primary focus of the MID, the agency also conducts strategic communications, economic, technological, and limited political intelligence operations. The agency maintains a counter-terrorism and counter espionage force, the Counter Intelligence Task Bureau, (CIV). Securing military and government interests and guarding them from espionage are the chief concerns of the CIV.

Dutch intelligence works closely with allies in the European Union and the North Atlantic Treaty Organization (NATO). In addition to supporting international intelligence efforts to halt weapons proliferation and fight global terrorism, the Dutch intelligence and security communities also protect significant United Nations interests in The Hague.

SEE ALSO

European Union
World War II

Neural Network Based Optics.

SEE *Brain-Machine Interfaces.*

New People's Army (NPA)

The New People's Army (NPA) is the military wing of the Communist Party of the Philippines (CPP). A Maoist group formed in March, 1969, its aim includes overthrowing the Philippine government through protracted guerrilla warfare. The chairman of the CPP's Central Committee and the NPA's founder, Jose Maria Sison, directs all CPP and NPA activity from the Netherlands, where he lives in self-imposed exile. Fellow Central Committee member and director of the CPP's National Democratic Front (NDF) Luis

Jalandoni also lives in the Netherlands and has become a Dutch citizen.

Although primarily a rural-based guerrilla group, the NPA has an active urban infrastructure to conduct terrorism and uses city-based assassination squads. The NPA derives most of its funding from contributions of supporters in the Philippines, Europe, and elsewhere, and from so-called "revolutionary taxes" extorted from local businesses.

The NPA primarily targets Philippine security forces, politicians, judges, government informers, former rebels who wish to leave the NPA, and alleged criminals. NPA opposes any U.S. military presence in the Philippines, and before the base closures in 1992 attacked U.S. military installations. Press reports in 1999 and in late 2001 indicated that the NPA is again targeting U.S. troops participating in joint military exercises as well as U.S. Embassy personnel. The NPA claimed responsibility for the assassination of congressmen from Quezon and Cagayan and many other killings. NPA strength is estimated at over 10,000. NPA operates in rural Luzon, Visayas, and parts of Mindanao with cells in Manila and other metropolitan centers.

■ FURTHER READING:

ELECTRONIC:

CDI (Center for Defense Information), Terrorism Project. CDI Fact Sheet: Current List of Designated Foreign Terrorist Organizations. March 27, 2003. <http://www.cdi.org/terrorism/terrorist.cfm> (April 17, 2003).

Central Intelligence Agency. World Factbook, 2002. <http://www.cia.gov/cia/publications/factbook/> (April 16, 2003).

Taylor, Francis X. U.S. Department of State. "Patterns of Global Terrorism 2001," Annual Report: On the Record Briefing. May 21, 2002. <http://www.state.gov/s/ct/rls/rm/10367.htm> (April 17,2003).

U.S. Department of State. Annual Reports. <http://www.state.gov/www/global/terrorism/annual_reports.html> (April 16, 2003).

SEE ALSO

Terrorism, Philosophical and Ideological Origins
Terrorist and Para-State Organizations
Terrorist Organization List, United States
Terrorist Organizations, Freezing of Assets

New Zealand, Intelligence and Security

New Zealand gained its independence from Britain in 1907, but remains a member of the British Commonwealth. A longtime, close ally with Britain, Australia, and the United States, New Zealand retreated from international politics during the last two decades to address ethnic tensions between European-descended New Zealanders and the native Maori people. The New Zealand government strived to recognize past aggression against the Maori community, reforming national government and social policy to address native grievances. As part of these reforms, the New Zealand government declassified information gained from past surveillance of Maori populations.

The Security Intelligence Service (SIS) is New Zealand's primary civilian intelligence agency. Charged with the gathering, processing, and analyzing of foreign and domestic intelligence, the SIS conducts a wide-variety of intelligence operations. The agency maintains a small human intelligence force, choosing to gather information from carefully negotiated liaisons with allied foreign intelligence services, such as those of Britain, the United States, and Australia. The main mission of the SIS is the protection of New Zealand's national, military, economic, technological, and scientific infrastructure.

The Government Communications Security Bureau (GCSB) limits its operations to foreign intelligence and counter-intelligence operations. The bureau supervises the protection of government communications, computer, and information systems. The agency also processes collected foreign intelligence information for dissemination to international intelligence and security agencies.

New Zealand's civilian intelligence community is administered by the Office of the Prime Minister and the Cabinet Strategy Subcommittee on Intelligence and Security (CSSIS). The CSSIS has limited power to mobilize military responses to identified threats against national interests. In most cases, however, the CSSIS relies on the New Zealand Parliament to authorize the use of force.

In addition to civilian intelligence forces, New Zealand also maintains substantial military intelligence forces. Special intelligence units are embedded in the operations divisions of the various branches of service. Since these units focus on strategic intelligence, the military works closely with civilian agencies to gather and analyze intelligence. New Zealand's Naval Intelligence is the largest military intelligence organization, specializing in signals, communications, and remote intelligence operations in the South Pacific.

In 2001, New Zealand's intelligence community pledged to support global anti-terrorist operations. The strategic position of New Zealand in the Austral-Asian South Pacific facilitates remote intelligence and surveillance operations in the region. New Zealand often contributes intelligence regarding the ongoing conflict in Indonesia to the United Nations and other international security agencies.

SEE ALSO

Australia, Intelligence and Security
United Kingdom, Intelligence and Security

NFIB (United States National Foreign Intelligence Board)

The National Foreign Intelligence Board (NFIB) was created by the National Security Act of 1947. The NFIB acts as a communications channel among various national intelligence agencies and facilitates interagency exchange of information. The board also develops policy regarding the protection of intelligence information. In addition to coordinating domestic matters, the board also handles relationships with foreign intelligence agencies that share information with the United States and allocates that information to the appropriate U.S. agencies.

The NFIB is chaired by the Director or Deputy Director of Central Intelligence. In permanent membership, all agencies within the United States intelligence and federal law enforcement community are represented on the committee, as well as the Departments of Energy and Treasury. Other agencies are occasionally represented on the board. Representatives from the Department of the Interior and the Department of Health and Human Services sometimes join the board to discuss counter-terrorism measures, but are not permanent sitting members of the NFIB. The major subsidiary committee of the NFIB is the National Intelligence Council, which coordinates intelligence studies and analyses of various issues, threats, or locations.

While the board was created to address the transfer of information regarding military and political national security threats, the NFIB has become increasingly interested in the role of the intelligence community in the preservation and regulation of international economic interests. The Department of Treasury was added to the NFIB in 1972 to foster links between monetary policy makers, banks, international funds and economic cooperatives and intelligence agencies.

Upon full implementation of the Department of Homeland Security, the NFIB will be restructured to include, be governed by, or be replaced by the new agency. Since the new Homeland Security Department is will perform many of the same functions as the older interagency committee, the future structure and role of the NFIB has yet to be fully determined.

NIC (National Intelligence Council)

The National Intelligence Council (NIC) oversees the estimative process of the United States intelligence community, and produces National Intelligence Estimates (NIEs). The NIC answers directly to the Director of Central Intelligence (DCI) in his capacity as head of the intelligence community. In addition to producing NIEs, NIC generates other reports, and avails itself of knowledge provided by civilian experts through its Global Expertise Reserve Program (GERP).

Mission and organization. NIC is the principal intelligence community center for mid-term and long-term strategic analysis. Among its principal functions are supporting DCI as leader of the intelligence community; providing a tasking office whereby policymakers may present requests for information to members of the intelligence community; drawing on the expertise of non-government authorities in academia and the private sector, so as to broaden the intelligence community's perspective on issues of importance; and leading in the production of NIEs and other informational products.

NIC has several national intelligence officers (NIOs) focused on geographic areas or specific issues regarding national security and intelligence. As of 2003, it had NIOs devoted to Africa, conventional military issues, east Asia, economics and global issues, Europe, Latin America, the Near East and south Asia, Russia and Eurasia, science and technology, strategic and nuclear programs, and warnings. In addition, there was an at-large NIO.

NIOs have the responsibility of advising the DCI, supporting the needs of senior intelligence consumers, producing estimative intelligence, tapping the knowledge and insights of outside experts, helping to assess the capabilities of intelligence community analytic producers, promoting collaboration between producers of analysis within the intelligence community, and articulating priorities to guide future efforts in intelligence collection, evaluation, and procurement.

NIC products and programs. By far the most significant NIC product is the NIE, which dates back to the intelligence failures of the late 1940s—particularly the miscalculations of Chinese and North Korea intentions on the Korean peninsula that led to the surprise invasion of South Korea in 1950. Responding to these failures, General Walter Bedell Smith, upon becoming DCI in October, 1950, created the NIE as a means of drawing upon the expertise of the entire intelligence community. In addition to the NIE, NIC has produced studies and reports such as "Transformations in Defense Markets and Industries," issued in late summer 2001. The report noted two trends in national armament policies: on the one hand, governments were broadening the range of sources from which they purchased weapons, and on the other hand, national defense industries were competing to export arms to other nations. These trends were creating "a world characterized by the routine diffusion of weapons and technology."

In December, 2000, NIC issued an enormous report titled *Global Trends 2015: A Dialogue About the Future with Nongovernment Experts.* The report identified seven key factors that would shape the world over the next 15 years, and made specific predictions, for instance suggesting the strong possibility of international conflict over water rights and access to fresh water. Among the larger trends cited in the report were scientific and technological advances, changes in the nature of military power and conflict, globalization of markets, and increased conflict over oil and other energy sources.

GERP. Many of the NIC's products are a result of GERP, through which it has sought to expand the reach of the intelligence community by fostering dialogue between intelligence analysts and non-government experts. Reservists, as participants in GERP are called, come from academia, the corporate world, and private think tanks. They are typically U.S. citizens who have traveled widely, and who have closely followed a particular topic or geographic area of interest for at least 10 years. As NIC noted on its Web site in 2003, "In the past, topics covered by the Reserve have ranged from stability and conflict in sub-Saharan Africa, to the impact of organized crime in the Caribbean, to economic growth in Iran."

Participation in GERP, as NIC also noted, "is not about being 'James Bond'"; in other words, reservists serve purely in the role of consultants, and are not involved in the collection of intelligence, or in other covert activities. Nor are they called upon to take any action on behalf of the federal government. Rather, their role is simply to participate with NIC as consultants. All reservists are paid for their work, and some are placed on retainer, while others are consulted on a case-by-case basis. They are expected to maintain confidentiality as appropriate, but outside of restrictions relating to national security, they are free to publish.

■ FURTHER READING:

PERIODICALS:

Nye, Joseph S., Jr. "Peering into the Future." *Foreign Affairs* 73, no. 4 (July/August 1994): 82.

Postel, Sandra L., and Aaron T. Wolf. "Dehydrating Conflict." *Foreign Policy* no. 126 (September/October 2001): 60–67.

Wall, Robert. "New Arms Policies Seen Altering Warfare." *Aviation Week & Space Technology* 155, no. 10 (September 3, 2001): 100.

Zelikow, Philip. "The Global Infectious Disease Threat and Its Implications for the United States." *Foreign Affairs* 79, no. 4 (July/August 2000): 154–155.

ELECTRONIC:

Global Trends 2015: A Dialogue About the Future with Nongovernment Experts. Central Intelligence Agency. <http://www.cia.gov/cia/publications/globaltrends2015/> (March 17, 2003).

National Intelligence Council. <http://www.cia.gov/nic/> (March 17, 2003).

SEE ALSO

DCI (Director of the Central Intelligence Agency)
Intelligence Community
Nongovernmental Global Intelligence and Security

Nicaragua, Intelligence and Security

Nicaragua gained independence from Spain in 1821, and became a republic in 1838. Late-twentieth-century politics in the region have been marked by violence and turmoil. A brief civil war in 1979 ushered the Marxist Sandinistas to power. Cold War politics, and Sandinista military aid to other leftist rebel groups in the region, prompted the United States to assist anti-Sandinista, contra forces. By the end of 1989, the Sandinistas had lost control of much of Nicaragua, but not before continued violence, rampant corruption, and the actions of secret police forces had devastated the nation.

Domestic intelligence is the responsibility of the Directorate of Intelligence Affairs (DAI). The DAI does conduct limited foreign intelligence operations and processes most of the information gathered by other Nicaraguan intelligence forces. The chief officers of the DAI, as well as members of the Ministry of the Interior, act as a liaison between the intelligence community and the government executive. The relationship between the intelligence community and the government is somewhat ambiguous, with no formal means of accountability or a standardized oversight process. Even following the recent democratic elections, the DAI has come under increasing scrutiny for political espionage activities.

Nicaragua's main military intelligence agency is the Directorate of Military Intelligence. the agency coordinates military and foreign intelligence operations, but also conducts surveillance of paramilitary and opposition groups in the region. The routine operations of the Directorate of Military Intelligence remain largely unknown, but the organization has close ties to political officials and the civilian intelligence community.

Nicaraguan free elections in 1990, 1996, and 2001 ousted the Sandinistas from power, but economic and political recovery has been difficult. Drug trafficking and corruption remain endemic problems, and years of guerrilla fighting have left many Nicaraguans with a deep distrust of the government, military, and other security forces.

Nicaragua is a member of the United Nations (UN) and several other Central and Latin American defense and economic organizations. The government has joined international efforts to stem drug trafficking, combat illegal arms sales, and fight global terrorism.

■ FURTHER READING:

ELECTRONIC:

Central Intelligence Agency. "Nicaragua." CIA World Factbook. <http://www.cia.gov/cia/publications/factbook/geos/nu.html> (April 8, 2003).

Nigeria, Intelligence and Security

In 1998, Nigeria overthrew its ruling dictatorship, which possessed close ties to the nation's military. The transitional government that gained power attempted to restore the long-suspended Constitution of 1979 and institute democratic reforms. The progress of reform has been slow.

The Nigerian intelligence community was an instrumental part of the former authoritarian regime. Political espionage, surveillance of citizens, and detainment of political dissidents was commonplace, garnering criticism for its brutality from the international community.

Nigeria's intelligence community was radically restructured in 1986. The National Security Organization was dissolved, prompting the formation of three, smaller, more specialized agencies. The National Intelligence Agency (NIA) is Nigeria's main civilian intelligence agency. The main responsibilities of the NIA are counterintelligence and foreign intelligence collection operations. The NIA focuses on external threats to Nigerian national interests. The State Security Service (SSS) manages domestic intelligence, and works closely with the Federal Investigation and Intelligence Bureau (FIIB), the liaison agency between law enforcement and intelligence services.

Nigeria's military intelligence is also coordinated through the executive office of the government. The Defense Intelligence Agency (DIA) is responsible for foreign and domestic military intelligence. The DIA is more secretive in its operations and maintains a larger special action force than the civilian intelligence agencies.

Democratic reforms have progressed slowly in Nigeria. Government corruption remains endemic. Despite changes made to the Nigerian intelligence community, political espionage and abuse of intelligence resources are still reported by Western human rights agencies, which claim that accusations of the rape and torture of citizens along with destruction of private property increased in 2002. Human rights agencies and western intelligence service reports maintain that Nigerian government censorship of media and communications, including the use of intelligence resources for surveillance, persists.

Nigeria is the most populous nation in Africa. The nation's major export is oil, which provides the government with over half of its annual income. In 2002, Nigeria was the fifth largest oil supplier to the United States.

Night Vision Scopes

■ LARRY GILMAN

Night vision scopes are devices that enable machines or people to "see in the dark," that is, to form images when illumination in the visible band of the electromagnetic spectrum is inadequate. Although it is not possible to form images in *absolute* darkness, that is, in the absence of any electromagnetic radiation whatsoever, it is possible to form images from radiation wavelengths to which the human eye is insensitive, or to amplify visible-light levels so low that they appear dark to the human eye.

There are two basic approaches to imaging scenes in which visible light is inadequate for human vision:

(1) Low-level visible light that is naturally present may be amplified and presented directly to the viewer's eye. (Light in the near-infrared part of the electromagnetic spectrum [>.77–1.0 microns], either naturally present or supplied as illumination, may also be amplified and its pattern translated into a visible-light pattern for the viewer's benefit.) This technique is termed image intensification.

(2) Light in the infrared part of the spectrum (>.8 microns) is emitted by all warm objects and may be sensed by electronic devices. A visible-light image can then be produced for the user's benefit on a video screen. This technique is termed thermal imaging.

Image intensification. Image intensification, the method used for the devices termed night-vision scopes, exist in a variety of forms and can be mounted on weapons or vehicles or worn as goggles by an individual. Image-intensification devices have been used by technologically advanced military organizations since the 1950s. In a modern, high-performance light amplifier, light from the scene is collimated—forced to become a mass of parallel rays—by being passed through a thin disk comprised of thousands of short, narrow glass cylinders (optical fibers)

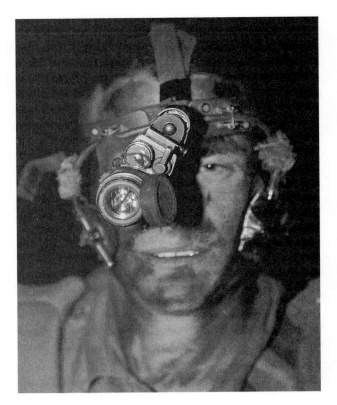

An Israeli soldier checks his night vision equipment at an Israeli army base in the Jewish settlement of Avnei Hefetz in March, 2002. AP/WIDE WORLD PHOTOS.

packed side by side. The parallel rays of light emerging from these optical fibers are directed at a second disk of equal size, the microchannel plate. The microchannel plate is also comprised of thousands of short, narrow cylinders (.0125–mm diameter, about one fourth the diameter of a human hair), but these microchannels are composed of semiconducting crystal rather than optical fiber. A voltage difference is applied between the ends of each microchannel. When a photon (the minimal unit of light, considered as a particle) strikes the end of a microchannel, it knocks electrons free from the atoms in the semiconducting crystal. These are pulled toward the voltage at the far end of the microchannel, knocking more electrons loose as they move through the crystal matrix. Thousands of electrons can be produced in a microchannel by the arrival of a single photon. At the far end of the microchannel, these electrons strike a phosphor screen that is of the same size and shape as the microchannel disk. The phosphor screen contains phosphor compounds that emit photons in the green part of the visible spectrum when struck by electrons; thus, that part of the phosphor disk affected by a single microchannel glows visibly, the brightness of its glow being in proportion to the intensity of the electron output of the microchannel. (Green is chosen because the human eye can distinguish brightness variations in green more efficiently than in any other

color.) The phosphor-disk image is comprised of millions of closely packed dots of light, each corresponding to the electron output of a single microchannel. The light from the phosphor disk is collimated by a second fiber-optic disk and presented to the viewer's eye through a lens. The function of the lens is to allow the user's eye to relax (i.e., focus at infinity), rather than straining to focus on an image only an inch or so away. Alternatively, the phosphor-disk image can be filmed by a camera.

A pair of night-vision goggles may contain two such systems, either one for each eye, or, as in the case of the U.S. Army's AN/PVS-7B night vision goggles, a single image may be split into identical copies and presented to both the user's eyes simultaneously.

A "third generation" image intensifier has been described above; several other image-intensification technologies remain in the field. All, however, operate by using photons to liberate electrons, amplifying the resulting electron current, and using the amplified electron current to liberate visible photons.

Image intensifiers form sharp images with natural contrast patterns. Also, they use very little power and so can run for many hours on, say, a battery mounted in a helmet. Because they are relatively cheap and can provide a mobile individual with the ability to see in most "dark" conditions, hundreds of thousands of night-vision goggles and scopes based on image intensification have been sold to military and police forces worldwide. Criminals have also been using them increasingly, as a number of models are now available on the consumer market. However, night-vision goggles provide poor peripheral vision, which can disorient pilots or drivers. Further, they cannot work in settings where visible and near-infrared light are truly absent (e.g., inside a windowless building). The latter disadvantage can only be partly offset by providing active illumination (e.g., a laser), because such light sources reveal themselves to enemy forces equipped with image intensifiers.

Infrared imaging. Image intensification amplifies radiation *reflected* by objects; infrared imaging works by detecting radiation *emitted* by objects. All objects at non-cryogenic temperatures glow spontaneously in the infrared region of the spectrum. Air is opaque to some of this radiation, but has two wavelength "windows" through which infrared radiation passes freely: the 3–5 micron window and the 8–12 micron window. (One micron is a millionth of a meter.)

Semiconductor devices sensitive to infrared radiation in either of the two atmospheric infrared windows can be built, in large numbers, on the surface of a chip. An infrared image focused on the surface of such an array can be read off electronically as image information, which is then used to construct a visible-light image on a screen.

Infrared imaging systems are bulkier and more expensive than image intensification systems. However, they work even in a complete absence of illumination (since all scenes "glow" in infrared) and can detect otherwise invisible phenomena, such as hot, nonsmoky exhaust plumes or buried landmines, that may be of military or security interest. Infrared imagers are also used for a wide variety of forensic and industrial purposes, as they can reveal chemical compositional differences not evident in visible light.

■ FURTHER READING:

BOOKS:

Schlessinger, Monroe. *Infrared Technology Fundamentals.* New York: Marcel Dekker, Inc., 1995.

PERIODICALS:

Owens, Ken, and Larry Matthies. "Passive Night Vision Sensor Comparison for Unmanned Ground Vehicle Stereo Vision Navigtaion," in proceedings from the *International Conference on Robotics and Automation.* (2000): 122–131.

Thompson, R. J. "New Developments in Night-Vision Equipment and Techniques," in proceedings from the *1995 International Carnahan Conference on Security Technology.* (2000): 144–446.

NIH (National Institutes of Health)

■ BELINDA ROWLAND

The National Institutes of Health (NIH) is a federal agency that serves as the fiscal agent of medical research in the United States. The mission of the NIH is to foster medical and behavioral research on living systems and to use that knowledge to prevent, identify, diagnose, and treat illness and disability.

The NIH originated in 1887 as a one-room bacteriological laboratory on Staten Island that was called The Hygienic Laboratory. The Hygienic Laboratory was established by the Marine Hospital Service (The Public Health Service) to diagnose and study bacterial epidemics. This laboratory marked the beginning of government-supported medical research in the United States. The Laboratory's name was changed to the National Institutes of Health in 1930. In 1938, the NIH moved to its present location in Bethesda, Maryland.

As the primary medical research agency in the United States, NIH conducts research in its own laboratories, allocates research funds for non-federal scientists, trains

research scientists, and promotes the spread of medical information. Funds for the NIH are appropriated from Congress. In 2002, the NIH was appropriated almost $23.4 billion. Research grants for non-federal scientists account for about 84 percent of the appropriation. NIH's in-house research accounts for about 10 percent of the appropriation. The remainder of the budget goes toward research support costs.

NIH is one of the agencies of the Public Health Service, which is a component of the Department of Health and Human Services. NIH is comprised of 27 institutes and centers:

- Center for Information Technology
- Center for Scientific Review
- John E. Fogarty International Center
- National Cancer Institute
- National Center for Complementary and Alternative Medicine
- National Center on Minority Health and Health Disparities
- National Center for Research Resources
- National Eye Institute
- National Heart, Lung, and Blood Institute
- National Human Genome Research Institute
- National Institute on Aging
- National Institute on Alcohol Abuse and Alcoholism
- National Institute of Allergy and Infectious Diseases
- National Institute of Arthritis and Musculoskeletal and Skin Diseases
- National Institute of Biomedical Imaging and Bioengineering
- National Institute of Child Health and Human Development
- National Institute on Deafness and Other Communication Disorders
- National Institute of Dental and Craniofacial Research
- National Institute of Diabetes and Digestive and Kidney Diseases
- National Institute on Drug Abuse
- National Institute of Environmental Health Sciences
- National Institute of General Medical Sciences
- National Institute of Mental Health
- National Institute of Neurological Disorders and Stroke
- National Institute of Nursing Research
- National Library of Medicine
- Warren Grant Magnuson Clinical Center

The role of NIH in a national health crisis. The NIH would play a crucial role in the event of a national health crisis.

The appropriate institutes within NIH would be called upon to conduct and support research that is relevant to the crisis at hand. NIH policy and the planning and management of all NIH activities is the responsibility of the Office of the Director. The Department of Homeland Security integrates many of the government's agencies to protect the American people from potential threats.

United States President George W. Bush is committed to providing a large appropriation to NIH to support biological terrorism research. In the wake of the September 11, 2001 attacks, the National Institute of Allergy and Infectious Diseases (NIAID) and the National Institute of Mental Health (NIMH), which are institutes within NIH, were called into action. NIAID has supported much of the research into the prevention, diagnosis, and treatment of illnesses caused by microorganisms that may be used by bioterrorists. Immediately after the October 2001 bioterrorist attacks, NIAID accelerated the research of bacteria and viruses that the Centers for Disease Control and Prevention (CDC) classifies as "Category A" agents. Category A agents are microorganisms that cause severe illness and high death rates and are easy to spread.

NIMH has provided information and counseling to Americans who were trying to cope with the September 11, 2001 terrorist attacks. They support the survivors, emergency personnel, and millions of others who were directly or indirectly affected by the attacks.

■ FURTHER READING:

BOOKS:

Kondratas, R. *Images from the History of the Public Health Service.* U.S. Department of Health and Human Services, Public Health Service, 1994.

Kurian, G. T., ed. *A Historical Guide to the U.S. Government.* New York: Oxford University Press, 1998.

Mullan, F. *Plagues and Politics: The Story of the United States Public Health Service.* New York: Basic Book, Inc., 1989.

Wilcox, W. *Public Health Sourcebook: Basic Information About Government Health Agencies.* Detroit: Omnigraphics, 1998.

ELECTRONIC:

National Institutes of Health, 9000 Rockville Pike, Bethesda, Maryland 20892. <http://www.nih.gov.> (January 1, 2003).

Office of the Public Health Service Historian, 18–23 Parklawn Building, 5600 Fishers Lane, Rockville, Maryland, 20857. (301) 443–5363. August 21, 2000. <http://lhncbc.nlm.nih.gov/apdb/phsHistory.> (October 19, 2000).

SEE ALSO

Bioterrorism
CDC (United States Centers for Disease Control and Prevention)

Health and Human Services Department, United States
Homeland Security, United States Department of
Microbiology: Applications to Espionage, Intelligence and Security
NIMH (National Institute of Mental Health)
Public Health Service (PHS), United States
September 11 Terrorist Attacks on the United States

NIJ (National Institute of Justice)

The National Institute of Justice (NIJ) serves the United States Department of Justice in the areas of research, development, and evaluation. Established under the authority of the Omnibus Crime Control and Safe Streets Act of 1968, its purpose is to provide independent, evidence-based tools to assist state and local law enforcement. Its programs address a variety of law-enforcement issues, including use of DNA evidence, drug abuse, and domestic violence.

Appointed by the President and confirmed by the Senate, the director of NIJ is responsible for establishing objectives in alignment with Justice Department priorities, as well as the current needs of the field. It works to take account of views from professionals in all areas of criminal justice and related fields in its search for knowledge and tools to guide the policy and practice of law enforcement nationwide. On January 12, 2003, it reorganized, streamlining its structure from three offices to two; the Office of Development and Communications and the Office of Research and Evaluation.

NIJ has set research priorities in a number of fields, including law enforcement and policing; justice systems (sentencing, courts, prosecution, defense); corrections; investigative and forensic sciences (including DNA); counterterrorism and critical incidents; crime prevention/causes of crime; violence and victimization (including violent crimes); drugs, alcohol, and crime; interoperability, spatial information, and automated systems; and program evaluation. Among its programs are the Arrestee Drug Abuse Monitoring Program (ADAM); Community Mapping, Planning, and Analysis for Safety Strategies (COMPASS); National Commission on the Future of DNA Evidence; and the Violence Against Women and Family Violence Research and Evaluation Program.

■ FURTHER READING:

BOOKS:

Connors, Edward F. *Convicted by Juries, Exonerated by Science: Case Studies in the Use of DNA Evidence to Establish Innocence After Trial.* Washington, D.C.: National Institute of Justice, 1996.

Kelling, George L. *Broken Windows and Police Discretion.* Washington, D.C.: National Institute of Justice, 1999.

Riley, Kevin Jack. *Crack, Powder Cocaine, and Heroin: Drug Purchase and Use Patterns in Six U.S. Cities.* Washington, D.C.: National Institute of Justice, 1998.

PERIODICALS:

"Crime Year in Review." *Crime Control Digest* 36, no. 35 (August 30, 2002): 1.

"NIJ Technologies for Public Safety." *Law & Order* 50, no. 8 (August 2002).

Waldron, Ronald J. "National Institute of Justice Helps Facilities Implement Telemedicine Program." *Corrections Today* 64, no. 2 (April 2002): 184.

ELECTRONIC:

National Institute of Justice. <http://www.ojp.usdoj.gov/nij/> (March 28, 2003).

SEE ALSO

DNA Fingerprinting
Justice Department, United States
Law Enforcement, Responses to Terrorism

NIMA (National Imagery and Mapping Agency)

The National Imagery and Mapping Agency (NIMA) was formed in October, 1996, to provide the United States military and intelligence agencies with up-to-date and accurate imaging and geospatial information. NIMA is a Department of Defense agency and is a member of the United States intelligence community. NIMA uses satellite and aerial imaging equipment to produce maps that can be used by both military planners and soldiers in the field.

NIMA assumed the duties of the Defense Mapping Agency, the Central Imagery Office, the Defense Dissemination Program Office, the National Photographic Interpretation Center, and parts of the Defense Intelligence Agency, the National Reconnaissance Office (NRO), Defense Airborne Reconnaissance Office, and the Central Intelligence Agency. NIMA now serves as the sole source for mapping and imaging needs of the U.S. military and intelligence agencies.

NIMA uses satellite photographic, radar, and infrared imaging information to create and analyze a database of cartographic and geodetic images. NIMA can then customize these images to suit the needs of its customers.

NIMA's database allows the creation of two-dimensional and three-dimensional (elevation) models of any part of the world. NIMA also catalogs man-made and natural features, which can be used for navigational or intelligence purposes.

For information gathering, NIMA uses Department of Defense, NRO, and other government owned imaging satellites. NIMA also contracts out for the use of privately owned imaging satellites in a cost-saving effort. NIMA declassifies many of the images obtained from these commercial satellites for use by American allies.

The National Imagery and Mapping Agency contributes to achieving United States foreign policy and national security objectives by providing intelligence agencies and policymakers with current imagery information. Military and civilian intelligence agencies use NIMA's cartographic and geospatial intelligence to monitor the proliferation of nuclear, chemical, and biological weapons, track arms shipments, and ensure that global treaties are being upheld.

NIMA's primary function is to provide accurate geospatial information for combat planning and support. NIMA tailors its products to fit the needs of its target audience. When the United States began military operations in Afghanistan in 2001, American military forces had little information on Afghan geography and topography. NIMA assisted the various U.S. forces involved in this conflict by quickly producing high quality maps for strategists and soldiers. NIMA used its resources to produce different maps for different operations. Maps for Naval aviators included detailed information about targets for the U.S. bombing campaign. Maps for special operations forces noted possible food and water locations, as well as the locations of enemies and non-combatants.

NIMA provided similar logistical support for Operation Iraqi Freedom in 2003. During the planning stages of the war, NIMA provided policymakers and military coordinators with maps that included the locations of enemy forces, suspected chemical and biological weapons depots, and potential government and military targets. Maps also noted strategic locations, including oil wells. During combat, NIMA's technologically advanced imaging systems supplied U.S. forces with near real-time maps that allowed American forces to engage enemy combatants before visually confirming the enemies' presence.

NIMA is currently working on the Shuttle Radar Topography Mission (SRTM), a mission that recorded elevation data for most of the Earth's surface. By accumulating elevation data from a single source, NIMA will be able to produce a uniform elevation map of the Earth.

■ FURTHER READING:

ELECTRONIC:

Department of Defense. "United States National Imagery and Mapping Agency." <http://www.nima.mil> (May 2003).

SEE ALSO

Mapping Technology
NASA (National Air and Space Administration)
DOD (United States Department of Defense)

NIMH (National Institute of Mental Health)

The National Institute of Mental Health (NIMH) falls under the umbrella of the government's medical research agency, the National Institutes of Health (NIH). The NIMH is the branch of the NIH that focuses on the brain, behavior, and mental health.

The creation of the NIMH in the 1940s ushered in a new approach to the diagnosis and treatment of mental illness. Psychologists began to realize that mentally ill patients would benefit more from evaluation and treatment than from institutionalization, and asylums were gradually replaced by well-equipped, well-staffed mental health facilities. In 1946, President Harry S. Truman signed the National Mental Health Act, which redirected the funding and oversight of mental health programs from the state to the federal level. The act also called for the establishment of the NIMH to lead research efforts relating to the brain and psychiatric disorders. The agency was formally established in 1949.

The NIMH became the foremost behavioral science and mental-illness research center in the country and provided funding and training for state mental health facilities. During the 1960s, the institute expanded its offerings by establishing centers for the study of child mental health, crime, urban mental health issues, and suicide. Alcohol and substance abuse were added as separate areas of study in the late 1960s and early 1970s. Thanks to rapid expansion during the 1960s, the NIMH was separated from the NIH and added to the newly established Health Services and Mental Health Administration, but it rejoined the NIH in 1973.

Scientists at the NIMH use a combination of neuroscience, behavioral science, molecular genetics, and brain imaging to delve into the underlying physiological and genetic mechanisms that trigger mental illness. Their aim is to discover ways to prevent and treat mental illnesses through a combination of pharmacological and behavioral therapies. The agency not only conducts its own laboratory research and clinical trials, but also funds research by universities, private companies, and individual scientists. The NIMH also provides educational materials to patients, medical professionals, local governments, and organizations around the country.

In 2003, the NIMH will conduct a study, following over 200,000 people exposed to the ash and dust resulting from the destruction of the World Trade center by terrorists in 2001. In one of the largest studies ever conducted, the NIMH will observe patterns of illness and recovery among the residents and workers of lower Manhattan. The NIMH also maintains divisions that focus on preparing and coping with disasters and emergencies.

■ FURTHER READING:

BOOKS:

Mintzer, Richard. *The National Institutes of Health.* Philadelphia, PA: Chelsea House Publishers, 2002.

PERIODICALS:

Grob, Gerald N. "Creation of the National Institute of Mental Health."*Public Health Reports* no. 4 (July-August 1996):378–381.

ELECTRONIC:

National Institute of Mental Health. <http://www.nimh.nih.gov/> (December 7, 2002).

SEE ALSO

NIH (National Institutes of Health)
Public Health Service (PHS), United States

9–11 Terrorist Attacks.

SEE *September 11 Terrorist Attacks on the United States.*

NIST (National Institute of Standards and Technology), United States

■ JUDSON KNIGHT

The National Institute of Standards and Technology (NIST) is a non-regulatory federal agency under the aegis of the Undersecretary for Technology in the U.S. Department of Commerce. It is concerned with maintaining measurement standards and developing technology in order to improve productivity, promote commerce, and enhance the qualify of life in the United States. It also has a number of security functions, which have come to the forefront in the aftermath of the September 11, 2001, terrorist attacks upon the United States.

Background. Founded in 1901 as the Bureau of Standards, NIST today involves the development and maintenance of standards and measures used in virtually every arena of public and private life. Private industry in the United States uses more than 9,000 NIST standards.

Characterizing the breadth of the NIST mission, Anne C. Mulkern wrote in the *Denver Post,* "When consumers buy beef at the butcher, it's weighed on a scale that's calibrated to a NIST-developed standard. Automobile seat belts all must adhere to a safety standard set by NIST." At its Web site in 2003, the institute itself described the range of areas in which it is involved: "From automated teller machines and atomic clocks to mammograms and semiconductors, innumerable products and services rely in some way on technology, measurement, and standards provided by [NIST]."

Organization. In line with its mission, NIST oversees four major cooperative programs: the NIST Laboratories, which advance the national technology infrastructure; the Baldridge National Quality Program, designed to encourage excellence among U.S. manufacturers, service providers, health-care companies, and educational institutions; the Manufacturing Extension Partnership, a network of local centers that assists small manufacturers; and the Advanced Technology Program, whose function is to promote research and development of new technologies in the private sector.

With a 2003 operating budget of $810 million, NIST employs some 3,000 scientists, engineers, technicians, and support and administrative personnel. Some 1,600 other guest researchers also work with the institute. Additionally, NIST works with some 2,000 manufacturing specialists and support staff at various locations nationwide. It has two offices: a 578-acre (234-hectare) facility in Gaithersburg, Maryland, and a 208-acre (84-hectare) installation at Boulder, Colorado.

Intelligence and security work. In addition to the work of its Computer Security Division and efforts to assist law-enforcement agencies in detecting criminal activity on computers, NIST has played a significant part in the investigation of the September 11 terrorist attacks. Mulkern, writing in January 2002, discussed the greatly enhanced stature of the institute, which at that time was being considered for a lead role in the investigation of the World Trade Center collapse.

NIST scientist Ronald Rehm, according to Mulkern, "goes to work every day and watches the World Trade Center burn, over and over again." His purpose was not to relive a moment of national agony, but to study it the way a coroner does a cadaver—for clues as to the cause of death. One finding he had already turned up, which contradicted the accepted wisdom about the collapse, was that the temperature inside the buildings was not high

enough to melt steel. Instead, the levels of heat had only been enough to bow the steel, and this alone put enough pressure on the walls and floors that the buildings fell. Additionally, the heat of the jet fuel alone did not explain the rapid spread of the fire, according to Rehm, who had determined that the large paper supplies in the offices, along with other combustible materials, greatly abetted the conflagration.

Not only was NIST involved in the investigation of what happened, it was also deeply concerned with efforts to prevent another such tragedy by helping to interdict suspicious persons. Among its tasks in the post-attack security environment was a mandate from the federal government to develop standards for biometric recognition systems, which use face recognition, retina scanning, voiceprints, and other characteristics of an individual's physique to provide identification. NIST has also been tasked to study the use of electromagnetic waves as a means of detecting objects hidden under clothing.

■ FURTHER READING:

PERIODICALS:

Mulkern, Anne C. "Agency Tackles National Security: NIST's Boulder Lab Developing Technologies to Combat Terrorism." *Denver Post.* (January 25, 2002): C1.

Piazza, Peter. "Tools for Digital Sleuths." *Security Management* 46, no. 4 (April 2002): 36.

ELECTRONIC:

National Institute of Standards and Technology. <http://www.nist.gov/> (January 28, 2003).

SEE ALSO

Commerce Department Intelligence and Security Responsibilities, United States
IDENT (Automated Biometric Identification System)
NIST Computer Security Division, United States

NIST Computer Security Division, United States

The Computer Security Division (CSD) is one of eight divisions within the Information Technology Laboratory of the National Institute of Standards and Technology (NIST), itself a bureau of the Chamber of Commerce. CSD is concerned with raising awareness of information technology (IT) risks, vulnerabilities, and protection requirements, especially for new and emerging forms of technology.

In addition to its support and security role with regard to new technologies, CSD is involved in researching IT vulnerabilities, advising federal and state agencies of these, and developing means to provide cost-effective protection. Also, in line with its mission as a part of NIST, it helps develop standards, tests, validation programs, and metrics in computer systems and services with an eye toward security.

NIST involvement in "digital sleuthing," or the use of computers in detective work, often allows the division to team up with a consortium of law-enforcement agencies to develop computer forensics technology. NIST and CSD scientists worked with agents from the Federal Bureau of Investigation, United States Customs Service, and other agencies, along with software vendors, to create the National Software Reference Library (NSRL), which allows easier review of the contents of a computer, especially with regard to material potentially relevant to a criminal investigation. By examining file tag attachments NIST CSD programs can easily identify certain types of files (e.g., picture files that may be hidden in other programs).

Thanks to Presidential Decision Directive 63, signed by President William J. Clinton in 1998, NIST and CSD received $5 million (which was much less than the $50 million Clinton had requested from Congress) to encourage the development of secure information systems for support of the telecommunications, transportation, and government service infrastructures. In the country's heightened security environment after September 11, the work of CSD has become—like that of most agencies either within or at the periphery of the security and intelligence apparatus of the federal government—critical to national defense. Among the areas of focus for CSD are development of cryptographic standards and applications, security testing, and research in the interests of emerging technologies.

■ **FURTHER READING:**

PERIODICALS:

Frank, Diane. "NIST Aims Grants at Systems Security." *Federal Computer Week* 15, no. 11 (April 23, 2001): 12.

Piazza, Peter. "Tools for Digital Sleuths." *Security Management* 46, no. 4 (April 2002): 36.

————. "E-mail and Patching Hints from NIST." *Security Management* 46, no. 7 (July 2002): 44.

ELECTRONIC:

Computer Security Division. National Institute of Standards and Technology. <http://csrc.nist.gov> (January 28, 2003).

SEE ALSO

Commerce Department Intelligence and Security Responsibilities, United States
Computer Hardware Security
Computer Software Security
NIST (United States National Institute of Standards and Technology)

Nixon Administration (1969–1974), United States National Security Policy

■ CARYN E. NEUMANN

Richard Nixon took office in 1969 as the country struggled to deal with the effects of the war in Vietnam. The inability of the United States to quickly win the war forced a review of national security policy. With the resulting Nixon Doctrine, the U.S. adjusted its foreign commitments to more effectively and efficiently utilize its resources. The Nixon administration pursued an honorable exit in Vietnam, sought peace with the Soviet Union, and reduced tensions with communist China by normalizing relations, while declining to pursue idealistic goals peripheral to the balance of military and geopolitical power.

The Nixon administration began with an overhaul of the national security advisory process. Nixon had apparently harbored resentments over perceived snubs delivered by Foreign Service officers when he served as vice-president under Eisenhower. He also preferred a solitary approach to decision-making. As president, he was determined to circumvent and minimize the State Department's traditional role in foreign policy in favor of conducting policy from the White House.

The National Security Council (NSC) under Nixon would function as a rival State Department with only adviser Henry Kissinger participating in the President's important discussions with visiting foreign officials. To further keep the State Department shut out of negotiations with foreign governments, Kissinger relied upon CIA communications for "back channel" messages as he traveled from country to country. The NSC also took control of the process of clearing key policy cables to overseas posts. Secretary of State William P. Rogers, less experienced in foreign affairs, played a minor role in policy formulation. In late 1973, Kissinger replaced Rogers. For the first time, one individual held simultaneously the positions of national security adviser and secretary of state.

The Vietnam War dominated American affairs in the late 1960s and it became the first major dilemma faced by the Nixon administration. To restore American power, Nixon decided to exit Southeast Asia in a way that would preserve the reputation of the U.S. as a country that honored its commitments. The administration elected to pursue a two-pronged approach of a phased withdrawal of ground troops and a modernization of the South Vietnamese military to enable it to assume full responsibility for the fighting. This policy stressed that an allied country must demonstrate the ability to provide for its own security since the U.S. would no longer provide the major defensive effort. The U.S. completed disengagement from Vietnam in 1973.

President Richard M. Nixon (right-center) meets with members of the Security Council on Janurary 21, 1969, his first full day as President of the United States. ©BETTMANN/CORBIS.

While the U.S. had been focused upon Vietnam, the Soviet Union had moved from a position of strategic inferiority to one of strategic parity. The system of mutual deterrence that rested upon the threat of retaliatory annihilation now no longer existed because the Soviets had developed a first-strike capability. Kissinger argued that the Soviets were more likely to be conciliatory if they feared that the U.S. would seek cordial relations with China. Since 1949, when the communists established control on mainland China, the U.S. had preferred to regard the exiled regime on Taiwan as the legitimate Chinese government. However, a Sino-American alliance would create a new balance of power by checking the Soviet superiority in conventional military forces. Accordingly, Nixon visited China in 1972 and drove a wedge between the two chief bastions of communism in the world. The Soviets, now anxious for an easing of tensions (known as détente) signed the Strategic Arms Limitation Talks agreement in May 1972 to limit the number of intercontinental ballistic missiles (ICBMs) and the construction of antiballistic missile systems (ABMs).

The Watergate scandal that forced Nixon's resignation in 1974 overshadowed his foreign policy accomplishments and contributed to a perceived mistrust of national leaders. Despite the enormous impact of Watergate, Nixon's pragmatic approach to international relations continues to influence debates about the proper role of the U.S. in world affairs.

■ FURTHER READING:

BOOKS:

Boll, Michael M. *National Security Planning Roosevelt Through Reagan.* Lexington: University Press of Kentucky, 1988.

Crabb, Cecil V., and Kevin V. Mulcahy. *American National Security: A Presidential Perspective.* Pacific Grove, CA: Brooks/Cole, 1991.

Record, Jeffrey. *Making War, Thinking History: Munich, Vietnam, and Presidential Uses of Force from Korea to Kosovo.* Annapolis, MD: Naval Institute Press, 2002.

ELECTRONIC:

White House. "History of the National Security Council, 1947–1997." <http://www.whitehouse.gov/nsc/history.html> (April 25, 2003).

SEE ALSO

CIA (United States Central Intelligence Agency)
Cold War (1950–1972)
Cold War (1972–1989): The Collapse of the Soviet Union
Department of State, United States

National Security Advisor, United States
National Security Strategy, United States
NSC (National Security Council)
NSC (National Security Council), History

NMIC (National Maritime Intelligence Center)

The National Maritime Intelligence Center (NMIC) brings together several military intelligence operations for the United States: Navy, Marine Corps, and Coast Guard. The first of these, being by far the largest, is the dominant participant in NMIC, whose headquarters in Suitland, Maryland, are home to the Office of Naval Intelligence (ONI). NMIC also houses offices for the Naval Information Warfare Activity (NIWA), as well as the principal intelligence agencies of the two smaller services, the Marine Corps Intelligence Activity (MCIA) and Coast Intelligence Coordination Center (ICC).

NMIC does not represent a single command; indeed, it would be hard for it to do so, given the fact that the navy and marines fall under the Department of Defense, while the Coast Guard, as of March 2003, is under the aegis of Department Homeland Security. Rather, NMIC offers a united source for maritime intelligence at the national level, and provides support to joint warfighters of the three services involved, as well as to the Department of Defense (DOD), and to other national agencies and departments requiring maritime intelligence.

The physical facilities of NMIC are located on the 226-acre (91.5-hectare) Suitland Federal Center in Suitland, Prince George's County, Maryland. Situated on the Metro's Green Line alongside the Census Bureau, Washington National Records Center, and Atmospheric Administration, NMIC itself occupies 42 acres (17 hectares). It is housed in a 603,000 square-foot facility (5.6 hectares; depicted on the NMIC Web site, listed below), which contains the headquarters of ONI, as well as offices for NIWA, MCIA, and ICC.

Historical background. The origins of NMIC lie in the early 1990s, when the United States, had successfully concluded the Cold War following the fall of the Soviet empire. During this era, long before the war on terrorism that commenced with the attacks on the World Trade Center and Pentagon on September 11, 2001, the federal government began to scale down its defense and intelligence operations.

By September 1991, just after the end of the Cold War, the U.S. Navy had seven intelligence organizations: ONI, the Naval Intelligence Command (NIC), Task Force 168, the Naval Technical Intelligence Center (NTIC), the Navy Operational Intelligence Center (NOIC), the Naval Intelligence Activity (NIA), and the Naval Security Group Command. Highest in prestige and authority was ONI, with NIC occupying a second level of authority, while all the others—with the exception of the last named—were subordinate to NIC.

In October 1991, the Navy closed down NTIC, Task Force 168, and NOIC. Formerly, Task Force 168 had been involved in overt collection of data from human sources; NTIC had performed the duties of a scientific and technical intelligence organization, specializing in information on the Soviet navy; and NOIC had used signals intelligence to monitor naval forces worldwide. Thenceforth, these offices would fall under a new Naval Maritime Intelligence Center (NAVMIC).

The consolidation continued in January 1993, when the navy disestablished NAVMIC after less than two years, and placed it, along with NIC and NIA, under ONI. The latter would thus take over the functions of the other organizations, including NIA's responsibility for the provision of automatic data processing support to naval intelligence organizations. ONI then was reorganized into eight major directorates, each with direct access to the Director of Naval Intelligence. In 1994, NMIC was formed as a joint operating center for ONI, NIWA, and the intelligence agencies of the marines and Coast Guard.

Naval components of NMIC. ONI organizes and trains intelligence personnel; provides highly specialized intelligence analysis related to maritime activities; and operates in an oversight capacity with regard to security and intelligence manpower issues for the navy. It serves as a liaison between DOD and non-DOD agencies, and supports foreign liaisons. Additionally, it is engaged in long-term analysis of foreign military (particularly naval) forces and operations, as well as broader scientific, technical, and strategic trade analysis. ONI is also involved in intelligence systems acquisition.

Established in 1882, ONI has the distinction of being the oldest continually operating intelligence agency in the United States. Until the First World War, it was concerned primarily with collection of technical data on foreign governments and their naval forces, and with conducting war games in association with the Naval War College in Newport, Rhode Island. The world war brought with it expanded responsibilities for ONI, which was deployed to provide security at war material plants, conduct security checks of navy personnel, and hunt down spies and saboteurs.

Just as ONI would survive the downscaling of the U.S. armed forces after the end of the Cold War three-quarters of a century later, it weathered the downsizing of the military that occurred during the interwar period. As Japan began mobilizing for war in the 1930s, ONI, in association with the Navy's Office of Communication, maintained a close watch on Japanese diplomatic dispatches. After World War II, it endured another period of downsizing, but thanks to the support of Fleet Admiral Chester W. Nimitz, ONI was strengthened rather than reduced in the postwar era.

As of the early twenty-first century, ONI housed the vast majority of its personnel—some 500 military and 1,000 civilians—at NMIC. Even in the aftermath of September 11, it maintained an appearance of relative openness that, while perhaps illusory, served to welcome intelligent and talented men and women as recruits, particularly recruiting architects, engineers, communications analysts, scientists, and mathematicians.

Much more secretive is NIWA, which, while many of its personnel are housed at NMIC, has its headquarters at Fort Meade, Maryland. It serves as the technical agent for the Chief of Naval Operations in pursuit of technologies useful in information warfare. In particular, NIWA is responsible for threat analysis and assessment of vulnerabilities. It evaluates and assesses new forms of information technology, and other concepts relating to naval defensive information warfare systems.

Marine and Coast Guard components.
MCIA, which also has facilities at Quantico, Virginia, is focused on providing threat assessments and expeditionary intelligence to Marine Corps headquarters. It works with marines in the field, as well as with other services, and with other organizations in the U.S. intelligence community, to provide threat, technical, and terrain analysis tailored to the specific needs of Marine Corps tactical units. It also serves as the primary coordination link with ONI for expeditionary intelligence analysis.

Aside from being much smaller than the "big three"—army, air force, and navy—the Coast Guard and marines could hardly be more different. Whereas the marines are widely perceived as being the most "military" of the military services, the Coast Guard is not even supervised by DOD. And whereas the marines are regularly deployed to far-flung theatres, the Coast Guard's purview is primarily—though not exclusively—along the U.S. coastline.

Formed in 1984, as the war on drugs began to heat up, ICC included some 50 Coast Guard and civilian personnel as of 2003. Though it is the most notable arm of Coast Guard intelligence, its functions are augmented by intelligence staff who work with the Atlantic and Pacific Coast Guard commanders.

Coast Guard intelligence is concerned with everything from drug smuggling to illegal fishing, and the war on terrorism begun after September 11, 2001, has served to greatly expand its importance as a protector of homeland security. In particular, ICC, and the Coast Guard as a whole, has been tasked with monitoring ships destined for the United States as a means of intercepting terrorist operatives. According to a December 2002 report that appeared in the *Seattle Times,* the al-Qaeda terror network

is assumed to control up to15 cargo freighters operating under false papers worldwide.

■ **FURTHER READING:**

BOOKS:

Dorwart, Jeffery M. *The Office of Naval Intelligence: The Birth of America's First Intelligence Agency, 1865–1918.* Annapolis, MD: Naval Institute Press, 1979.

Packard, Wyman H. *A Century of U.S. Naval Intelligence.* Washington, D.C.: Office of Naval Intelligence, 1996.

Richelson, Jeffrey T. *The U.S. Intelligence Community,* 3rd ed. Boulder, CO: Westview Press, 1995.

PERIODICALS:

Brinkley, Joel. "Coast Guard Encounters Big Hurdles in New Effort to Screen Arriving Ships." *New York Times.* (March 16, 2002): A9.

Killian, Michael. "New Defensive Posture for Former Prosecutor: Threat from Sea a Top Priority." *Chicago Tribune.* (February 13, 2002): 7.

Mintz, John. "Fearing Attack by Sea, U.S. Tracking 'Ships of Concern.'" *Seattle Times.* (December 31, 2002): A1.

Thompson, Phillip. "A Crystal Ball for Intelligence Needs." *Sea Power* vol. 44, no. 3 (March 2001): 51–53.

ELECTRONIC:

National Maritime Intelligence Center/Office of Naval Intelligence. <http://www.nmic.navy.mil/nmicpic.htm> (January 17, 2003).

SEE ALSO

Coast Guard (USCG), United States
Homeland Security, United States Department of
Information Warfare

NNSA (United States National Nuclear Security Administration)

■ K. LEE LERNER/JUDSON KNIGHT

Created in 1999 and put into operation the following year, the National Nuclear Security Administration (NNSA) was a response to security concerns with regard to United States nuclear materials and information. In order to better protect these sensitive properties, Congress established NNSA as a separate agency within the Department of Energy (DOE). NNSA operates a variety of programs

The Lightweight Epidemiology Advanced Detection and Emergency Response System, better known as LEADERS and demonstrated in this photo, reaches into hospitals and can send fast, automated alerts by scanning electronic records for clues to a bioterror disease outbreak. AP/WIDE WORLD PHOTOS.

geared toward the security of U.S. nuclear stockpiles, while its Nuclear Nonproliferation Verification Research and Development Program works for security in the broader, more global sense. NNSA also has intelligence and incident preparedness responsibilities.

History

The creation of NNSA was a saga in itself, an outgrowth of concerns over vulnerabilities to Chinese espionage under the administration of President William J. Clinton. Even as political opponents in the Republican Party accused Clinton and Vice-President Al Gore of accepting illegal campaign donations from the Chinese, information surfaced regarding Clinton appointees with close ties to the People's Republic of China. Of most concern were allegations regarding the illegal sale of defense technology to China, as well as evidence of Chinese spying at nuclear labs.

In response to these concerns, Congress in 1999 created NNSA as a "semi-autonomous" agency within DOE. Energy Secretary Bill Richardson, along with other members of DOE leadership, maintained that the new agency would create confusion, obscure the chain of command, and place roadblocks in the way of DOE's environmental and safety oversight roles. Nevertheless,

Clinton signed the legislation, which had been linked to defense appropriations for 2000.

Clinton then authorized Richardson "to perform all duties and responsibilities" of the newly created Undersecretary of Energy for Nuclear Security position, the director of NNSA. In so doing, he effectively circumvented the congressional attempt to pull nuclear materials from direct DOE authority, a move that infuriated congressional Republicans.

Under the threat that Congress would cut the pay of top DOE officials, Richardson met with House leaders. After some discussion, the White House put forward former Air Force General John Gordon, then serving as deputy director of the Central Intelligence Agency (CIA), as the first NNSA director and undersecretary for nuclear security.

Mission and Organization

NNSA, which began operation on March 1, 2000, has the mission of improving national security through defense uses of nuclear energy; maintaining the U.S. nuclear stockpile, and enhancing its safety, reliability, and performance; providing the U.S. Navy with safe, reliable, and effective nuclear propulsion plants; advancing nuclear safety and nonproliferation internationally; reducing the global threat posed by weapons of mass destruction; and supporting America's leading role in the realms of science and technology.

The NNSA administrator oversees all functions of NNSA except those accorded to the deputy administrator for naval reactors by Executive Order 12344 (Naval Nuclear Propulsion, February 1, 1982). The administrator's responsibilities roles include strategic management, policy development and guidance, program management and direction, budgets and other financial matters, resource allocation, safeguards and security, emergency management, environment and health matters, administration of contracts, intelligence, counterintelligence, personnel, procurement, legal matters, legislative affairs, public affairs, and interactions with other DOE offices and other units of federal, state, and local government.

NNSA staff supports the administrator in a number of these functions, particularly counterintelligence, nuclear security, legal affairs, policy planning and assessment, legislative and intergovernmental affairs, public affairs, and matters of the environment, safety, and health. Also reporting to the administrator are deputy administrators for defense programs, nonproliferation, and naval reactors. There are also associate administrators for facilities and operations, and for management and administration.

At the heart of NNSA is the Nonproliferation Verification Research and Development Program, which operates, or has operated, a number of programs. Among these is the International Materials Protection, Control, and Accounting Program, whereby NNSA personnel work with Russia and former Soviet republics to ensure against proliferation, to return to the country of origin all weapons-usable nuclear materials, to convert or dispose of those materials wherever possible, and to develop new safeguards.

The Nonproliferation Verification Research and Development Program is responsible for creating and testing detection systems that will advance America's ability to respond to national threats from nuclear, chemical, or biological weapons. Its three principal elements are the monitoring of nuclear explosions and tests, a function overseen by DOE; proliferation detection; and the Chemical and Biological National Security Program (CBNP).

Nuclear smuggling and threat assessment.
As explained by Linton F. Brooks, NNSA administrator under President George W. Bush, in a statement to the House of Representatives Energy and Commerce Committee on July 9, 2002, the technologies developed in the proliferation detection segment serve functions both of nonproliferation and homeland security. Accordingly, those areas supportive of homeland security that could be separated from NNSA would move to the new Department of Homeland Security (DHS).

Among the key components of the proliferation detection program is the nuclear smuggling component. In this area, NNSA, together with the U.S. National Laboratories, put to use unique insights regarding nuclear proliferation, including the characteristics or "signatures" of particular weapons. Working with such future DHS agencies as U.S. Customs and the U.S. Coast Guard, as well as the departments of Transportation and Justice, NNSA had conducted demonstrations of radiation detection methods at international ports, border rail yards, and airports.

Also scheduled for transfer was the DOE Nuclear Threat Assessment Program. Initiated at Lawrence Livermore National Laboratory in September 1978, the program had been applied in assessing the credibility of more than 60 threats of nuclear extortion, 25 claimed threats to nuclear reactors, 20 non-nuclear extortion threats, and some 650 instances involving the attempted or alleged sale of nuclear materials. As nuclear threats are a federal violation, credibility assessment teams work under Federal Bureau of Investigation direction, in conjunction with representatives of CIA, the Defense Intelligence Agency, Customs, and the State Department. In the aftermath of the September 11, 2001, terrorist attacks, one of the key tasks of the program was the separation of critical from non-critical information as to possible threats.

CBNP.
Also moved to DHS was CBNP. CBNP actually predates NNSA, having been initiated by DOE in 1997 to respond to events such as the Tokyo nerve-gas attack that took place two years earlier. The program develops systems and technologies to protect civilian populations against the threats of the modern battlefield. NNSA and the national laboratories of DOE have undertaken extensive studies in chemistry, biology, materials science, and engineering to develop prototypes, which, if approved, can actually be manufactured by outside bidders.

For example, CBNP, in conjunction with the Centers for Disease Control, conducted research on the biological foundations required to establish signatures of biological agents—that is, DNA profiles of pathogens, such that medical personnel would be able to more quickly treat victims. These signatures would also provide forensic evidence for the prosecution of terrorists. One practical creation of this program may be a palm-sized device, identified by a CBNP project manager in early 2001 as the Chemlab, that will be able to detect and identify biological agents quickly and accurately.

To maintain cost effectiveness, CBNP attempts to use existing technology as much as possible. For example, one area of research is in microchips or cards that could plug into existing palm-size computers to detect dangers ranging from toxins to viruses. CBNP also adapted existing technology for its RSVP, or Rapid Syndrome Validation Program, a software package that makes it possible for doctors to network regarding the symptoms they see in patients—a highly useful tool in the event of a biological attack.

CBNP also conducts or directs exercises, such as the PROTECT subway demonstration, designed to simulate the 1995 Tokyo attacks. In the Nevada desert, at a site where nuclear tests were once conducted, NNSA operates the Weapons of Mass Destruction Terrorism Response Domestic Preparedness Program, a counterterrorism training facility. Up to 100 personnel from law-enforcement and emergency-response departments around the country train there, undergoing rigorous simulations that may involve being woken at 2:00 a.m. with cries of "Terrorists have taken hostages at a nuclear facility!" Among those trained at the site prior to September 11, 2001, were New York City law enforcement personnel who later put their training to use in an all too vivid real-life experience.

■ FURTHER READING:

BOOKS:

Homeland Security: Hearing Before the Committee on Energy and Natural Resources, United States Senate, One Hundred Seventh Congress, Second Session on the Present and Future Roles of the Department of Energy/National Nuclear Security Administration National Laboratories in Protecting Our Homeland Security, July 10, 2002. Washington, D.C.: U.S. Government Printing Office, 2002.

National Nuclear Security Administration: Joint Hearing Before the Committee on Energy and Natural Resources and the Committee on Governmental Affairs, United States Senate, One Hundred Sixth Congress, First Session on the Department of Energy's Implementation of Provisions of the Department of Defense Authorization Act Which Create the National Nuclear Security Administration, October 19, 1999. Washington, D.C.: U.S. Government Printing Office, 2000.

Safety and Security Oversight of the New National Nuclear Security Administration: Joint Hearing Before the Subcommittee on Energy and Power and the Subcommittee on Oversight and Investigations of the Committee on Commerce, House of Representatives, One Hundred Sixth Congress, Second Session, March 14, 2000. Washington, D.C.: U.S. Government Printing Office, 2000.

The Secretary of Energy's Priorities and Plans for Department of Energy National Security Programs: Hearing Before the Committee on Armed Services, United States Senate, One Hundred Seventh Congress, First Session, February 8, 2001. Washington, D.C.: U.S. Government Printing Office, 2002.

PERIODICALS:

Bleek, Philipp C. "New DOE Nuclear Security Organization Begins Work." Arms Control Today 30, no. 3 (April 2000): 29–30.

Dao, James. "Nuclear Study Raises Fears About Weapon." New York Times. (November 17, 2002): section 1, p. 22.

Gorman, Tom. "Rescue Worker Boot Camp." Los Angeles Times. (October 11, 2001): A6.

Johnson, Jeff. "Unclear Future at Weapons Labs." Chemical & Engineering News 78, no. 49 (December 4, 2000): 51–58.

Pincus, Walter. "DOE Plan Riles Senate GOP: Choice of Richardson to Run New Bomb Agency Spurs Pay Threat." Washington Post. (October 19, 1999): A17.

———. "Nuclear Security Gets First Director: Gordon Confirmed as GOP Blasts His Boss, Richardson." Washington Post. (June 15, 2000): A31.

Warchol, Glen. "Beam Us Up, Scotty: 'Tricorder' May Fight Biological Threats." Salt Lake Tribune. (May 7, 2001): D1.

ELECTRONIC:

National Nuclear Security Administration. <http://www.nnsa.doe.gov> (March 7, 2003).

SEE ALSO

Chinese Espionage Against the United States
DOE (United States Department of Energy)
Nonproliferation and National Security, United States
Nuclear Weapons

NOAA (National Oceanic & Atmospheric Administration)

The National Oceanic & Atmospheric Administration (NOAA) monitors environmental, climatic, and weather conditions in the United States and around the world. The administration manages an extensive network of satellites, sensory aircraft, and specialized monitoring equipment to provide information on meteorological events and their impact. The mission of NOAA is to protect persons, property, national security, and United States economic interests. NOAA also works with foreign meteorological services, international search and rescue units, and independent research scientists.

The administration has several operating divisions responsible for various agency responsibilities and research programs. The National Weather Service (NWS) is perhaps the most well known NOAA operational division. The NWS maintains the most extensive satellite network and meteorological research equipment, providing national, regional, and local weather through a variety of media. NOAA Weather Radio, the voice of the National Weather Service, broadcasts constant weather updates and is linked to the Federal Emergency Management Agency's Emergency Broadcast System. Though developed for government use, the radio broadcasts are available to private citizens.

In conjunction with the Department of Defense, NOAA also oversees the Defense Meteorological Satellite Program (DMSP). A key component of aerospace development, the space program, and weapons development, the

DMSP organizes the construction, launch, and maintenance of satellites that monitor atmospheric, oceanographic, and solar-terrestrial environments. The DMSP maintains a large network of satellites 1330 miles (about 850 km) above the earth's surface. Data from the satellites is sent to the Air Force Weather Agency, the National Geophysical Data Center, and the National Center for Atmospheric Research.

Another NOAA division, the National Environmental Satellite, Data, and Information Service (NEDIS) provides information on significant environmental events recovered from satellite imagery and other means of remote sensing. The NEDIS also licenses commercial remote sensing satellites, including global positioning systems (GPS). In conjunction with Russia's Cospas satellite system, the NOAA Cospas-Sarsat system can locate lost or endangered individuals through emergency transmissions. NOAA Geostationary Operational Environmental Satellites (GOES) detect signals from Emergency Position Indicating Radio Beacons on boats, airplanes, and other individual vessels, and send information to search and rescue teams. In 2002, nearly 1,500 people were rescued worldwide, most of them at sea.

NOAA's charting and marine safety programs provide information, products, and services that aid marine traffic, commerce, and private use of domestic and international waterways. NOAA creates and distributes tidal and current tables, conducts hydrographic surveys, works closely with several other government agencies to constantly update marine and terrestrial charts and maps. Recently, NOAA began testing International Electronic Navigational Charts, or "smart charts" for private civilian use. Smart Charts work in conjunction with global positioning systems and weather satellites to aid safe navigation. NOAA also develops aeronautical charts used by government and commercial airplanes.

Aside from its role in security, NOAA also funds and conducts research on the global environment and ocean systems. Via satellite and other sensor mechanisms, the administration monitors conditions such as widespread deforestation, ozone depletion, volcanoes, fires, and water pollution. Special attention is paid to the long-term effects of these processes on atmospheric and marine systems and their potential impact on global environments, flora and fauna, climate, and economic systems.

■ FURTHER READING:

ELECTRONIC:

United States National Oceanic & Atmospheric Administration. <http://www.noaa.gov.> (15 January 2003).

SEE ALSO

Coast Guard (USCG), United States
FEMA (United States Federal Emergency Management Agency)
Remote Sensing

Noise Generators

■ DAVID TULLOCH

Generating noise is a simple, cheap, and versatile method of blocking signals or shielding communication from a range of devices. From the disruption of radio broadcasts to the masking of conversations, noise generators use a simple concept to great effect.

Noise is an unpredictable disturbance that causes errors in the transmission of all types of communication. Background chatter at a party, static on a radio, poor handwriting, a patchy cellphone connection, and 'snow' (electronic interference) on a television screen are all examples of noise.

By flooding a frequency, or band of frequencies, with noise, the original communication signal can be drowned in a sea of static. Noise generation has been used to jam torpedo guidance systems and block battlefield communications. During the Cold War the broadcasts of Radio Free Europe and the Voice of America were often jammed by Soviets using a network of radio transmitters that covered the entire Soviet Union. In the 1970s the British government jammed pirate radio stations in an attempt to maintain control of the airwaves.

However, by far the most widespread use of noise generators is as a countermeasure against listening devices. The monitoring of conversations is not an activity limited to the world of spies. Companies and individuals are often bugged by rivals seeking to gain private information, and government agencies often spy on the activities of suspected individuals, illegal or otherwise. While removing potential bugs is the surest way to avoid being overheard sometimes this is not possible, or there are doubts that all the listening devices have been detected. Acoustic noise generators can stop the monitoring of spoken conversations from microphone and tape recorders, transmitting bugs, carrier current transmitters, through-wall devices, laser bounce listening equipment, and infrared transmitters. Because they can protect against such a wide variety of covert devices, and do not require the bugs to be found, acoustic noise generators are versatile and popular security items.

■ FURTHER READING:

BOOKS:

Johnson, William, with Jack Maguire. *Who's Stealing your Business?: How to Identify and Prevent Business Espionage.* New York, NY: AMACOM, American Management Association, 1998.

Petersen, Julie K., *Understanding Surveillance Technologies: Spy Devices, their Origins & Applications.* Boca Raton, FL : CRC Press, 2001.

SEE ALSO
Bugs (microphones) and Bug Detectors
Laser Listening Devices
Microphones

Nongovernmental Global Intelligence and Security

Global intelligence and security is not purely the province of governmental agencies. An important advisory role is occupied by think tanks, private corporations, university departments, and other groups. Some of these pursue specific ideological or policy goals, while others are avowedly neutral. Some have specific points of focus, for example on weapons or economic issues. Most are not-for-profit, but not all: an important sector of analysis on global intelligence and security involves companies ranging from publishers to insurers.

Governmental and nongovernmental groups compared. In the realm of global security and intelligence, the most visible roles belong to national agencies, particularly those of the world's one superpower, the United States. Also significant are groups such as Interpol and the Financial Action Task Force on Money Laundering, which oversee intelligence and security across national lines.

There are also the military and action forces of international organizations such as the North Atlantic Treaty Alliance (NATO) or the United Nations (U.N.): though neither has its own army, under certain circumstances national armies serve these international organizations. NATO, the U.N., and other groups also have their own policy, oversight, and executive teams that play significant roles, a notable example being the U.N. weapons inspection teams active in Iraq since 1991.

In addition to these agencies and instruments of national governments and multinational quasi-governmental entities, there are also civilian groups that serve in advisory, analysis, and sometimes even action roles. They lack the power to make or enforce laws, of course, but their recommendations are often of value to governments, which in many cases regularly call on their expertise. Included in this broad array of entities are university departments and schools, think tanks and research foundations, study centers, independent evaluation firms, information providers, risk management companies, and others.

Think tanks. The range of groups that provide research, analysis, and policy recommendations to governmental bodies is enormous. A leading example is RAND, a name formed from the contraction of "research and development." Though it is independent, RAND was created in 1946 by the Army Air Forces to evaluate aircraft and other technology. Since that time, RAND's staff has grown to include more than 1,600 persons, most of them involved in research across a variety of disciplines that include not only defense and technology but also public policy.

Another important analysis group is the Center for Strategic and International Studies (CSIS), which at different times has involved such leading public figures as former Senate Armed Services Committee chairman Sam Nunn, former Defense Secretary John J. Hamre, and former National Security Adviser Brent Scowcroft. The mission of CSIS is to advise world leaders on current and emerging global issues by providing strategic insights and policy solutions.

Across the ideological spectrum. RAND and CSIS are both examples of "think tanks," or multidisciplinary research institutions. One of the nation's first think tanks was the Hoover Institution, founded in 1919 by future United States President Herbert Hoover. Its original purpose was to study the causes of World War I, but by the beginning of the twenty-first century it had grown to include more than 60 scholars specializing in areas ranging from international relations to economics. During the cold war, the Hoover Institution's annual reports on communist movements worldwide were a key information source for U.S. policy analysts.

Many think tanks have a particular ideological agenda. For example, on the political right, in addition to the Hoover Institution, there is the Heritage Foundation, whose recommendations typically favor reduction of government spending in most areas other than defense. On the political left, by contrast, is the Brookings Institution, which is dedicated to a model of government as an instrument of their visions of national and international social justice, as well as the Carter Center, established by former President James E. Carter. On the other hand, there are numerous academic policy research groups, departments, and schools—several notable examples are affiliated with Georgetown University in Washington, D.C.—that have no obvious or overt political leaning.

Profit-making enterprises. While most entities involved in global security and intelligence are nonprofit organizations, this is not true of all. One of the most respected sources of information on military equipment of all types, as well as other kinds of security- and intelligence-related information, is the English-based publisher Jane's. A childhood fascination with warships on the part of its founder, Fred T. Jane, led to the publication of the first edition of *Jane's All the World's Fighting Ships* in 1898. By the beginning of the twenty-first century, Jane's published about 200 different products, including *Jane's Defence Weekly*, *Jane's Fighting Ships*, and *Jane's All the World's Aircraft*.

Other examples of for-profit businesses involved in world security and intelligence analysis include companies in the insurance industry and the related field of risk management. In order to calculate the costs of insuring persons and properties in various locales, it is necessary for companies to possess detailed information on the security climate, including threats related to government coups, asset seizure, and terrorist attack. Some insurers may even employ the services of private hostage-rescue companies that effectively function as non-governmental special-operations teams.

■ FURTHER READING:

ELECTRONIC:

Brookings Institution. <http://www.brookings.edu> (February 27, 2003).

Center for Strategic and International Studies. <http://www.csis.org> (February 27, 2003).

Heritage Foundation. <http://www.heritage.org> (February 27, 2003).

Hoover Institution. <http://www-hoover.stanford.edu> (February 27, 2003).

Jane's. <http://www.janes.com> (February 27, 2003).

RAND. <http://www.rand.org> (February 27, 2003).

SEE ALSO

Interpol (International Criminal Police Organization)

Nonlethal Devices.

SEE Less lethal Weapons Technology.

Nonproliferation and National Security, United States

The United States government has long had an interest in nonproliferation as a means of ensuring national security. The logic governing this interest is straightforward: as long as weapons continue to proliferate among foreign and hostile powers, U.S. national security remains under threat. At the same time, weapons buildups in other nations arguably necessitate a corresponding buildup in the United States. This can have a number of undesirable effects, ranging from increased spending to a heightened chance of a confrontation such as the one that occurred during the Cuban Missile Crisis of October 1962.

U.S. interest in nuclear nonproliferation dates to the 1950s, when the United States ceased to be the sole

atomic power, and the Soviet challenge greatly increased the chances of global nuclear war. In 1968, the United States, Soviet Union, and United Kingdom made explicit their desire for limits on proliferation through the Nuclear-Non Proliferation Treaty. This was one of several key turning points in the Cold War, as the United States and Soviet Union for the first time began to establish specific limits on nuclear arsenals and the buildup of weapons. These treaties and talks, which began in the late 1960s and continued in various forms for two decades, served to change the character of the Cold War, greatly reducing the threat of open superpower confrontation and limiting the battle to relatively low-level conflicts.

Since 1992, after the end of the Cold War, the United States has devoted considerable effort to overseeing the destruction of nuclear weapons in the former Soviet Union, and to preventing the proliferation of nuclear, biological, or chemical weapons among other nations such as North Korea, Iran, and Iraq. To this end, President William J. Clinton in September, 1998, created the position of Assistant Secretary of Energy for Nonproliferation and Nuclear Security. Two years later, the newly created National Nuclear Security Administration, a unit of the Energy Department, took over these responsibilities. Additionally, the State Department has its Bureau of Arms Control, established in 1999, while the Director of Central Intelligence (DCI) oversees the DCI Center for Weapons Intelligence, Nonproliferation, and Arms Control.

■ FURTHER READING:

PERIODICALS:

Gallucci, Robert L. "Non-Proliferation and National Security." Arms Control Today 24, no. 3 (April 1994): 13.

Pincus, Walter. "U.S. Agrees to Funds for Russian Scientists." Washington Post. (September 20, 1998): A26.

ELECTRONIC:

Carnegie Endowment for International Peace. <http://www.ceip.org/> (April 5, 2003).

National Nuclear Security Administration. <http://www.nn.doe.gov/> (April 5, 2003).

Nuclear Non-Proliferation, 1945–1990. George Washington University. <http://www.gwu.edu/˜nsarchiv/nsa/publications/nnp/nuclear.html> (April 5, 2003).

SEE ALSO

Arms Control, United States Bureau
Cold War (1972–1989): The Collapse of the Soviet Union
Cuban Missile Crisis
DCI (Director of the Central Intelligence Agency)
International Atomic Energy Agency (IAEA)
Iraq War: Prelude to War (The International Debate Over the Use and Effectiveness of Weapons Inspections.)
NNSA (United States National Nuclear Security Administration)
North Korean Nuclear Weapons Programs
Nuclear Weapons
START I Treaty

START II
Strategic Defense Initiative and National Missile Defense
Weapons of Mass Destruction

NORAD

∎ CARYN E. NEUMANN

The North American Air Defense Agreement, signed on May 12, 1958 by the United States and Canada, created a continental air defense warning and surveillance system in response to Cold War fears of an airborne attack by the Soviet Union. The resulting North American Air/Aerospace Defense Command (NORAD) has since shifted strategies from guarding against long-range bombers to warning of ballistic missile attacks and maintaining space surveillance. While both North American countries provide considerable support for NORAD, the United States, as the dominant partner, makes major policy and leadership decisions.

During the 1950s, the United States aimed to deter any attacks by the Soviet Union on North American soil by threatening massive retaliation. The main Soviet menace in this era came in the form of long-range bombers that would likely fly over Canadian territory to reach American targets. Because any Soviet attack upon the U.S. would involve Canada, it was logical for the U.S. to form an official military alliance with its neighbor to the north. NORAD formalized a cooperative air defense agreement that had existed between the Royal Canadian Air Force and the U.S. Air Force (USAF). It brought the two nations together to develop continental air defense plans; to maintain and operate the land-based radar and communications systems that would warn of an impending attack; and, in the event of an attack, to employ air defense forces to direct a retaliatory strike away from heavily populated areas. In light of the population density of the U.S., the agreement meant that Canada consented to direct any conflict towards its sparsely peopled north.

Although NORAD is a joint military command, Canada is clearly the subordinate partner. The agreement provides for an American Commander-in-Chief (CINC-NORAD) and a Canadian Deputy Commander headquartered in the U.S., at Peterson Air Force Base in Colorado Springs, Colorado. Military and civilian personnel from both countries are assigned to all NORAD elements, but the pilots assigned to intercept threats generally come from the ranks of the USAF. North America is divided into

Large computer screens display maps of the globe inside the main command center for the North American Air/Aerospace Defense Command (NORAD) in Cheyenne Mountain Air Station, 1997. AP/WIDE WORLD PHOTOS.

The "steel city" defense complex of the North American Air/Aerospace Defense Command, NORAD, shown in 1997, was carved out of Cheyenne Mountain in Colorado in the early 1960s. Fifteen steel buildings inside the mountain stand on rows of huge steel springs, designed to negate the earthquake effect of a nuclear blast. AP/WIDE WORLD PHOTOS.

three regions per the NORAD agreement: Alaska, Canada, and the continental U.S., and each of these regions receives information from a surveillance network of ground-based radars augmented by airborne radars, such as those carried by spy planes like the SR-71 and satellites. Federal Air Administration (U.S.) and Transport Canada radars also feed into the network.

In the 1960s, the nuclear-tipped intercontinental ballistic missile and the race for dominance in space began to dominate defense concerns and the emphasis of NORAD was adjusted to respond to these new concerns. The 1966 renewal of the NORAD agreement gave the command responsibility for North American aerospace attack warning and control. Aerospace warning involves the monitoring of man-made objects in space as well as the detection, assessment, and warning of any threat against North America whether by aircraft, missiles, or man-made space vehicles. Aerospace control includes the duties of providing surveillance and control of Canadian and American airspace. In 1974, NORAD began providing surveillance,

warning, and assessment services to command authorities stationed worldwide to assist in deterring attacks upon North American soil.

When the Cold War came to a close in 1989, NORAD struggled to find a role in the absence of an organized military threat. It joined the American War on Drugs in 1989 when Congress requested that the USAF interdict smugglers. Military authorities gave the anti-smuggling duties to NORAD because of its intelligence systems. NORAD received official responsibility for fighting drug trafficking in 1991 and joined the war against terrorism in 1996 when it received a mandate to identify and eliminate a limited missile attack, such as a terrorist launch, an accidental launch, or a launch by a Third World nation.

Despite these activities, NORAD activity began to wind down in the mid-1990s. The Over-the-Horizon Backscatter (OTH-B) radars in the U.S. were shut down. The North Warning System was operating at about 50% of its capacity and needed about three months to be brought back to full activation. The thirty interceptor bases were reduced to thirteen, with pilots now on a one-hour recall instead of a five-minute callback. A Cold War-era concept, NORAD served its purpose and now its mission in the twenty-first century remains uncertain.

■ FURTHER READING:

BOOKS:

Crosby, Ann Denholm. *Dilemmas in Defence Decision-Making: Constructing Canada's Role in NORAD, 1958–96.* New York: St. Martin's Press, 1998.

Lindsey, George R. *The Strategic Defence of North America.* Toronto: The Canadian Institute of Strategic Studies 1986.

Murray, Douglas. "NORAD and U.S. Nuclear Operations," in *Fifty Years of Canada-United States Defense Cooperation: The Road from Ogdensburg.* Edited by Joel J. Sokolsky and Joseph T. Jockel. Lewiston, Maine: Edwin Mellen, 1992.

North American Aerospace Defense Command. *NORAD: Into the 21st Century.* Colorado Springs, Colorado, 1997.

SEE ALSO

Aviation Intelligence, History
Ballistic Missiles
Cold War (1950–1972)
Cold War (1972–1989): The Collapse of the Soviet Union
RADAR
SR-71 Blackbird
Terrorism, Intelligence based Threat and Risk Assessments

North Korea, Intelligence and Security

The nation of North Korea was established on September 9, 1948, during the grab for satellite nations at the beginning of the Cold War. Supported by the Soviet Union, North Korea established a communist regime under dictator Kim Il-sung. The new government gained popularity by nationalizing former Japanese-owned and remnant European colonial industries and economic interests. Cold War politics plunged the region into war between 1950 and 1953. After the Korean War, North Korea distanced itself from the Soviet Union and became more reactionary and isolationist.

North Korea continues to resist reforms, and relies on the cult of personality of its leaders, and an oppressive political espionage and censorship system, to preserve the nation's communist regime. The North Korean intelligence committee is largely a political mechanism, conducting domestic and foreign political espionage. In recent years, North Korea has taken increasing interest in gathering foreign intelligence on weapons and nuclear systems.

The Cabinet General Intelligence Bureau is North Korea's main intelligence and security agency. Concentrating on foreign intelligence, the agency's Liaison Department actively seeks to subvert the governments of Japan and South Korea, and conducts espionage on United States interests in those nations. The Research Department for External Intelligence (RDEI) collects and analyzes all foreign intelligence gathered by North Korean agents and remote listening equipment. The agency shares information with the communist Central Committee and North Korean leaders.

Preservation of internal security is the main mission of the Ministry of Public Security and the State Security Department. However, in North Korea, internal security is defined in wholly political terms. The ruling political party, the Korean Worker's Party, controls the agencies' network of informants and most resources of the intelligence community. The director of the State Security Department was ousted in 1987, and the directorship was likely assumed by North Korean leader, Kim Jong-il. The State Security Department regularly engages in political espionage, surveillance of citizens and government officials, and monitoring of communication systems. The agency also contributes to the pervasive censorship of all means of expression, such as media and personal speech.

In 2003, North Korea reactivated a nuclear reactor earlier ordered closed under international nuclear nonproliferation agreements. North Korea also announced plans to construct a complex for processing nuclear materials. The international community suspects North Korea of possessing weapons of mass destruction, including intercontinental ballistic missile capability. The region remains a geo-political hot spot, despite efforts of the international diplomatic community to disarm North Korea.

■ FURTHER READING:

ELECTRONIC:

Global Security.org. North Korean Intelligence Agencies. <http://www.globalsecurity.org/intell/world/dprk/> (March 26, 2003).

SEE ALSO

Korean War
Non-Proliferation and National Security, United States
North Korean Nuclear Weapons Programs

North Korean Nuclear Weapons Programs

■ K. LEE LERNER

In October 2002, North Korean officials announced that, in violation of an agreement with the United States, North

Korea had a secret program to "enrich uranium for nuclear weapons."

History. With the assistance of the Soviet Union, the Democratic People's Republic of Korea (DPRK, also known as North Korea) constructed a nuclear complex at Yongbyon in the 1960s. In the late 1970s, North Korea expanded these facilities to include an operational 5 MW natural uranium, graphite-moderated reactor. North Korea also constructed an ore processing plant and a fuel rod fabrication plant.

In 1977, North Korea agreed to IAEA mentoring of its Soviet-supplied 2MW research reactor and 0.1MW critical assembly facility located at Yongbyon. In 1985, the DPRK signed the Treaty on the Non-Proliferation of Nuclear Weapons (NPT). Shortly thereafter, however, North Korea started construction on two gas-graphite reactors in Yongbyon and also started the construction of radiochemical and reprocessing facilities. United States intelligence suspected North Korea was attempting to develop a nuclear weapons program.

In 1990, before the fall of the Soviet Union, the Soviet government announced a halt to the exportation of nuclear equipment and fuel to North Korea. North Korea continues to refuse to sign IAEA inspection agreements until "the United States removes nuclear weapons from South Korea." The United States rejects North Korea's demand, in part because of North Korea's larger conventional forces on the Peninsula. The North Korean statement began a series of shifting demands (including demanding a promise from the United States that it never attack North Korea) as preconditions to cooperation. North Korean President Kim Il-sung continually declined attempts at a diplomatic solution to the impasse.

In 1991, South Korean Defense Minister Lee Jong-ku announced that South Korea might use military force to destroy North Korea's nuclear facilities at Yongbyon if North Korea does not agree to inspections and IAEA safeguards. North Korean President Kim Il-sung terms the statement a "virtual declaration of war" but continued to decline attempts at a diplomatic solution to the impasse.

Then International Atomic Energy Agency (IAEA) director, Hans Blix, asked the United Nations Security Council to seek more aggressive inspections of facilities in countries suspected of violating the NPT. North Korea declared United Nations efforts a hostile act but began talks aimed at eventually allowing more detailed inspections. North Korean defector, Ko Young-hwan, subsequently revealed that North Korean leaders never intended to commit to rigorous international inspections and that North Korean diplomatic efforts were aimed at securing a place in the United Nations and to allow North Korean nuclear weapons programs time to advance.

In 1992, under threat of possible United States action, North Korea agreed to an IAEA-monitored NPT Safeguards Agreement. IAEA monitoring and inspections start soon after the U.S. informed North Korea that it would impose sanctions if North Korea does not permit full international inspections of its nuclear facilities.

At the outset of inspections, North Korea admitted in a report to the IAEA and United Nations to having "nuclear material and design information, a fuel rod fabrication plant and storage facility at Yongbyon, a research reactor and critical assembly at the Institute of Nuclear Physics, a sub-critical facility at Kim Il-sung University in Pyongyang, two uranium mines and two centers for uranium concentrate production, a 5 MW nuclear reactor and a radiochemical laboratory under construction at the Institute of Radiochemistry in Yongbyon, a 50 MW nuclear plant under construction in Yongbyon, a 200 MW plant under construction in Taechon, and three planned 635 MW nuclear reactors." North Korea declared that its radiochemical laboratory was intended for uranium separation research and for plutonium waste management. North Korea also announced its intentions to continue nuclear development, including research on a potential fast-breeder reactor, the development of composite nuclear fuel, and completion of the reprocessing facility at Yongbyon.

Once inspections started, IAEA inspectors found discrepancies between the status of DPRK nuclear programs and DPRK claims in its formal declarations to the IAEA. After comparing physical inspection reports with DPRK declarations, IAEA inspectors suspected that North Korea might possess undeclared plutonium stores. North Korean officials refused IAEA requests to conduct additional inspections to clarify the situation. Inspectors were also specifically blocked from inspecting sites that the North Koreans denied existed but which were known to IAEA inspectors because of intelligence (including spy satellite photographs) supplied by the United States. North Korean representatives subsequently claimed the photographs—although derived from multiple imaging locations—were fake.

Despite claims of having nothing to hide, North Korea threatened to withdraw from the NPT if IAEA inspectors continued to demand to inspect suspect facilities shown in United States intelligence photographs.

Special requests for inspections continued to be rejected by North Korea and in April 1993, the IAEA ruled that North Korea was in "non-compliance" with its agreements regarding nuclear inspection and safeguards. The United Nations Security Council insisted that North Korea comply with its prior agreements. As a result, North Korea announced that it would withdraw from the Treaty on the Non-Proliferation of Nuclear Weapons. After two months of tense diplomatic negotiations, in June 1993 North Korea announced that it had "suspended the effectuation" of its withdrawal from the NPT.

The framework agreement. Limited inspections of North Korean nuclear facilities took place for the remainder of 1993 and into 1994. During that time IAEA inspectors concluded that their limited inspections could not provide "meaningful assurance" that North Korea was using its nuclear facilities for peaceful purposes (e.g., only for energy generation or authorized research). United States President William Jefferson Clinton stated that North Korea's offer to allow IAEA inspectors access to a portion of its nuclear sites was "inadequate and unacceptable." In March 1994, North Korea ignored another call by the U.N. Security Council to allow more complete and comprehensive inspections of their nuclear program.

In the summer of 1994, North Korean scientists discharged the fuel from their operational 5 MW reactor. This action effectively prevented IAEA inspectors from employing testing procedures that could have verified North Korea's declared use of the reactor core or whether nuclear materials had ever been diverted from the core. Soon thereafter, North Korea withdrew from its agreements and membership with IAEA. In accord with prior agreements, neither the IAEA or United Nations considered North Korea released from its treaty and safeguard agreements.

To break the impasse, the United States started direct negotiations with North Korea and entered into a Framework Agreement in October 1994. Under the Agreed Framework the United States pledged to provide fuel for electrical generation and aid in the construction of limited use reactors in exchange for a North Korean freeze and eventual dismantlement of reactors capable of producing weapons grade materials (e.g., graphite-moderated reactors and related facilities). As a consequence of the agreement, the Korean Peninsula Energy Development Organization (KEDO) was formed to facilitate fuel shipments to North Korea.

An important and direct consequence of the agreed framework between the United States and North Korea was the return of IAEA inspectors to monitor the freeze. IAEA inspectors returned to Yongbyon and related facilities, including the partially built 50 and 200MW nuclear power plants. Immediately following the return of IAEA monitoring teams, friction developed between inspectors and North Korean authorities. Over a span of six years, nearly 20 technical conferences failed to produce North Korean cooperation in resolving key monitoring issues.

The 2002–2003 crisis.

In 1999, IAEA officials reported to the United Nations Security Council that "critical parts" of the North Korean reactor at Yongbyon had been unaccounted for since 1994. Missing parts included those needed to control nuclear reactions and/or those that would be needed to construct another nuclear reactor.

In 2000, the United Nations Secretariat determined that it would take at least three years to complete verifications that had been pending for nearly a decade. North Korea ignored the United Nations and failed to even discuss a timeframe for resolving outstanding issues at technical meetings in November 2001. The following year, while the United States was preoccupied diplomatically and militarily with a developing crisis in Iraq, North Korean leaders demanded that the United States once again enter into unilateral negotiations regarding nuclear arms proliferations issues. The demand for talks was widely interpreted by news agencies and diplomatic corps personnel in the United States as a signal that North Korea—facing desperate economic conditions and starvation for a significant portion of its population—sought additional concessions, money, and aid from the United States. President George W. Bush's administration declined the offer for unilateral talks and vowed not to succumb to "nuclear blackmail" by North Korea. In October 2002, North Korean officials announced that, in violation of the Framework Agreement with the United States, their government had a secret program to "enrich uranium for nuclear weapons."

Ongoing negotiations between North Korea and South Korea in Pyongyang stalled because of North Korea's nuclear program admissions. United States Secretary of State Colin Powell warned that further aid to North Korea under the 1994 Framework Agreement was in danger. In exchange for North Korea allowing inspections and discontinuing efforts to develop nuclear weapons, the United States (through the KEDO Board) had agreed to supply fuel for conventional electrical generation and to facilitate the construction of two safe lightwater nuclear power reactors (LPRs). Construction of the first LPR had been started in 2000 and was scheduled for completion in 2005. Diplomatic efforts stalled, and in response the United States and KEDO Board announced that they would suspend heavy oil shipments to North Korea.

In December 2002, North Korea informed IAEA inspectors that the freeze on nuclear facility use would be lifted. North Korea also announced their intent to remove IAEA seals and disable surveillance cameras. Removal of those seals and the dismantling of IAEA monitoring equipment began in late December 2002 and on December 27, North Korea ordered IAEA inspectors to leave the country. On January 11, 2003, North Korea announced its withdrawal from the Nuclear Non-Proliferation Treaty. The United States and United Nations continued to insist that North Korea's prior NPT agreement remained binding and enforceable.

Scientists and intelligence experts openly doubted North Korea's claims that its nuclear program was designed solely to produce electricity. Experts cited the fact that the Yongbyon reactor was too small for significant power generation. Experts also argued that by restarting its nuclear program, North Korea could produce enough plutonium for five or six nuclear bombs within a few months. The IAEA issued the following statement: "Restarting this now unsafeguarded nuclear facility will further demonstrate the DPRK's disregard for its nuclear non-proliferation obligations."

Intelligence and political estimates of North Korean capabilities and motives.

The C.I.A. has warned that North Korea

may already have two nuclear weapons—possibly developed before the 1994 nuclear freeze accord. What United States officials more openly fear is that nuclear fuel might be sold by North Korea to terrorist organizations that seek to build nuclear weapons to use against the United States.

In addition, North Korea has started a series of missile tests with the goal of demonstrating that North Korea could build a rocket capable of reaching the western coast of the United States. In 2002 North Korea heightened tensions in the region with a launch of a ballistic missile over Japanese territory.

In February 2003, North Korea announced that its nuclear facilities were fully reactivated. The North Korean program included known sites at Yongbyon (a 5 MW experimental nuclear power reactor and a partially completed plutonium extraction facility), Taechon, Pyongyang, and the LPRs being built at Kumho. The IAEA announced that North Korea was in breach of its agreements and referred the matter to the United Nations Security Council.

The rhetoric and tensions continued to escalate. North Korean dictator Kim Jong-Il warned that any U.S. strike against its nuclear facilities at Yongbyon would trigger "full-scale war." North Korea maintained a standing army of more than one million soldiers. America maintained less than 40,000 troops in South Korea. Some western intelligence sources openly speculated that North Korea possessed one or two operational nuclear weapons, as well as enough spent fuel rods to make additional weapons.

Despite North Korean threats of pre-emptive action and heavy troop commitments to the Middle East in anticipation of having to forcefully disarm a defiant Iraq, the United states sent reinforcements in the form of heavy bombers and naval vessels toward the Korean peninsula.

In early March 2003, four North Korean fighter jets intercepted a United States reconnaissance plane in international air space. The jets followed the reconnaissance plane and locked on with targeting RADAR. (In 1969, a United States reconnaissance plane was shot down under similar circumstances.) Ultimately the U.S. plane returned safely to base.

After ignoring yet another missile firing by North Korea, United States officials insisted that they intended to pursue a policy that would put "maximum pressure" on North Korea to "not just freeze its weapons of mass destruction, but begin to dismantle them." Bush administration officials—in referring to the failed unilateral agreement reached between the U.S. and North Korea in 1994—consistently asserted that North Korea froze its plutonium program, it then began a separate uranium enrichment program. The United States maintained that a solution to the crisis needed to come from pressure and influence applied by the "collective weight of the international community, not just from the United States alone." Secretary of State Colin Powell articulated the American position by stating "We can't fall into that trap again of paying them off to stop what they're doing, only to discover that they're doing it again at a later time."

Tensions also escalated between allies as anti-American demonstrations began taking place in South Korea. Fueled in part by a general global anti-American backlash over the anticipated war against Iraq the demonstrations were mainly fears that America's failure to renounce the option of a military strike against North Korea might escalate into a devastating war in the Korean peninsula. After having secured South Korea's independence at the cost of many American lives and following more than 50 years of commitment to the country's security, the South Korean protests were an affront to the United States and forced administration and defense officials to publicly ponder the possibility of reducing or removing American forces.

The Bush administration continued to downplay the crisis and insisted that it was a regional matter to be solved by joint diplomacy rather than unilateral talks. In late April 2003, the first round of talks on the crisis began as American, North Korean, and Chinese officials met in Beijing.

As of May, 2003, IAEA inspectors asserted that they had never been able to verify the completeness and correctness of even the initial report of North Korea with regard to its NPT Safeguards Agreement. Since 1993, the IAEA has maintained that North Korea was in "non-compliance" with its obligations under NPT and inspection agreements to verify the peaceful use of its nuclear materials.

■ FURTHER READING:

BOOKS:

Michael Mazarr, M. *North Korea and The Bomb: A Case Study in Nonproliferation.* New York: St. Martin's Press, 1995.

Oberdorfer, Don. *The Two Koreas: A Contemporary History.* Reading, MA: Addison-Wesley, 1997.

Sigal, Leon V. *Disarming Strangers: Nuclear Diplomacy with North Korea.* Princeton, NJ: Princeton University Press, 1998.

PERIODICALS:

Gordon, M. R. "U.S. Nuclear Plan Sees New Targets and New Weapons." *New York Times.*, March 10, 2002.

Loeb, Vernon, and Peter Slevin. "Overcoming North Korea's 'Tyranny of Proximity'." *Washington Post.* January 20, 2003.

Sanger, David E. "U.S. Eases Threat On Nuclear Arms For North Korea." *New York Times.* December 30, 2002.

ELECTRONIC:

"Beyond the Agreed Framework: The DPRK's Projected Atomic Bomb Making Capabilities, 2002–09." An Analysis of The Nonproliferation Policy Education Center (NPEC) (December 3, 2002) <http://www.npec-web.org/projects/fissile2.htm>. December 12, 2002.

IAEA News Update on IAEA and North Korea. IAEA (March 10, 2003) <http://www.iaea.org/worldatom/Press/Focus/IaeaDprk/> (March 10, 2003).

"North Korea Nuclear Profile." Center for Nonproliferation Studies. <http://www.nti.org/db/profiles/dprk/nuc/nuc_overview.html> (January 12, 2003).

Pinkston, D., and S. Lieggi. "North Korea's Nuclear Program: Key Concerns." Center for Nonproliferation Studies, <http://cns.miis.edu/research/korea/keycon.htm.> (December 12, 2002).

SEE ALSO

Air Plume and Chemical Analysis
North Korea, Intelligence and Security
Nuclear Detection Devices
Nuclear Reactors
Nuclear Weapons

Norway, Intelligence and Security

During World War I, Norway maintained a stated policy of neutrality in international affairs. When WWII erupted in 1939, the Norwegian government again asserted that the nation would remain neutral in the conflict. However, on April 9, 1940, the German army invaded Norway. The Gestapo and Abwehr established intelligence bases in Norway to monitor radio and wire traffic from Britain, the Soviet Union, and the North Atlantic. Members of the Norwegian government who were able to escape fled to Britain. This group of refugees included members of the Norwegian intelligence services. Many of them aided British Military Intelligence with data collection, cartography, and cryptography operations.

Today, Norway's intelligence service is dominated by the Control Committee for the Intelligence and Security Services. The Control Committee coordinates intelligence operations, collects and analyzes intelligence information, assesses national security threats, and briefs government officials on intelligence matters. Staffed predominantly by civilian government intelligence personnel, the Control Committee also employs military officers to foster cooperation between Norway's main intelligence agencies and smaller, specialized military intelligence units.

The Joint Defense Intelligence Service (FE) is responsible for most Norwegian intelligence operations, including signals, communications, electronic, and human intelligence. Although the stated mission of the FE includes assessing and thwarting both external and internal threats to national security, the FE concentrates mainly on foreign intelligence.

Domestic intelligence, as well as the coordination with law enforcement agencies of protective services for Norwegian diplomats and national interests, is the chief task of the Joint Defense Security Service (FS). The FS often works closely with the Police Intelligence Service (PO) to investigate high crimes, such as money laundering, illegal trafficking, and business corruption. The two agencies also maintain counter-intelligence units.

Norway has since eased its hard-line stance on neutrality. While Norway abstains from membership in the European Union, it did join the North Atlantic Treaty Organization (NATO). Though Norway has participated in several NATO intelligence and military operations, the Norwegian government insists that military bases in the country cannot be used by foreign powers unless Norway is under threat of attack. Norway also maintains restrictions on its territorial waters, even for NATO allies. Norway is also a member of the Organization for Security and Cooperation in Europe (OSCE) and the Council of Baltic Sea States.

Norway pledged intelligence and limited military support for the recent international campaign against terrorism. In 2002, The Norwegian government authorized the deployment of military Special Forces for participation in the United States-led Operation Enduring Freedom in Afghanistan.

SEE ALSO

European Union

NRO (National Reconnaissance Office)

The National Reconnaissance Office (NRO) is a member of the United States' fourteen-member intelligence community. Established in 1960, the existence of the NRO was not declassified until 1992. The NRO collects and analyzes satellite and airplane reconnaissance information for various military and civilian intelligence agencies. As part of this mission, the NRO also researches, designs, and deploys reconnaissance satellites.

Although the NRO is a Department of Defense agency, the Director of Central Intelligence and the Secretary of Defense share control over the agency. Members of the Central Intelligence Agency (CIA) and the Department of Defense staff the NRO. The Under Secretary of the Air Force serves as the Director of the NRO and reports directly to the Secretary of Defense. However, the Secretary of Defense must nominate the Under Secretary of the Air Force in conjunction with the Director of Central Intelligence. The Senate must confirm the nomination. Six Congressional Committees oversee NRO operations.

Although the United States was already developing a space-based reconnaissance program, the Eisenhower administration shook up the organization of this program following the downing of Gary Powers' U-2 spy plane by the Soviet Union in May, 1960. Because of the Powers' incident, the Eisenhower administration quickly formed a committee to examine the continuation of America's high-altitude and space-based intelligence gathering capabilities.

In August, 1960, Secretary of Defense Thomas Gates presented his committee's findings to the National Security Council. Secretary Gates recommended the formation of an agency that would balance the intelligence concerns of both civilian intelligence agencies and the military. Based on the Gates committee findings, the Eisenhower and Kennedy administrations worked with the Department of Defense, the CIA, and the Air Force to develop the NRO.

By 1961, control of the NRO fell to the CIA and the Department of Defense, represented by the Air Force. This power-sharing arrangement has been the source of conflicts, as each agency has advocated its specific agenda. In the early 1960s, budgetary concerns and competing interests led to clashes between the CIA and Air Force for control of the NRO. The Air Force wanted the NRO to assist in military operations and tactics, while the CIA believed that the primary role of the NRO should be to protect national interests.

These conflicts led to the development of several splintered programs in the NRO. Major reorganizations of the NRO in 1989 and 1992 centralized command of the program under the Director of the NRO. Many critics, however, argue that the effectiveness of the NRO still suffers because of these competing interests. With a substantial budget at stake each year, technological advancements tend to focus too heavily on the development of new satellite systems, some critics claim, while advancements in data analysis often suffer.

During the Cold War, the NRO's primary concern was tracking the troop, plane, and missile deployments of the Soviet Union and its satellite states. After its formation, the NRO took over administration of CORONA, the world's first photo reconnaissance satellite. The CORONA program, declassified in 1995, operated from August, 1960 until May 1972. During its twelve years, CORONA took over 800,000 images.

After the Cold War, the NRO shifted its mission to better assist in intelligence gathering in regional conflicts. The NRO provided crucial information to military and civilian intelligence agencies during the coalition efforts in the Gulf War in 1991 and United States and NATO operations in the Balkans. Following the collapse of the Soviet Union, the NRO also focused much of its energy on tracking the smuggling of nuclear weapon components.

Since September, 2001, the NRO has played an increased role in the effort to combat terrorism. NRO satellite information assists the intelligence community in identifying suspected terrorist training camps, tracing arms shipments, and searching for the development of weapons of mass destruction by terrorists and rogue nations. By providing military and civilian intelligence agencies with information on developments in these areas, the NRO's mission is to use satellite reconnaissance to prevent attacks against the United States military, economy, infrastructure, and civilians.

■ FURTHER READING:

ELECTRONIC:

United States National Reconnaissance Office. <http://www.nro.gov> (May 2003).

SEE ALSO

Satellites, Spy

NSA (United States National Security Agency)

■ JUDSON KNIGHT

Legendary for its secrecy, the National Security Agency (NSA) is the leading cryptologic organization in the United States intelligence community. Focused on cryptologic and cryptanalytic missions, it is the nation's leading employer of mathematicians, yet little is known about the inner workings of this secretive agency. Those few details in the public domain have come either through treachery (namely, revelations made public by defectors in the early 1960s) or the tireless efforts of a writer, James Bamford, whose 1982 book *The Puzzle Palace: A Report on America's Most Secret Agency* was the first detailed study of the NSA.

NSA and the Cold War

NSA's creation in 1952 followed years of efforts to coordinate communications intelligence (COMINT) activities by U.S. forces. The creation of the Armed Forces Security Agency (AFSA) in 1949 seemed to solve this problem, but the experience of cryptologic services early in the Korean War revealed that it had not. Instead of replacing the cryptologic operations of the U.S. Army, Navy, and Air Force, AFSA clashed with these, and rather than take the lead, it simply became a fourth military cryptologic operation.

The result was a secret memorandum by President Harry S. Truman, National Security Council Intelligence Directive (NSCID) No. 9, issued on October 24, 1952. Although the bulk of NSCID 9 has never been made public, it is clear that this document established NSA to take the lead position in COMINT operations. The choice of "national" in the organization's title emphasized the fact that it would serve both military and nonmilitary needs, and instead of reporting to the Joint Chiefs of Staff, the head of legitimate scholars writing on ciphers and codes or the organization itself. The first of these was David Kahn, an amateur cryptologist whose 1967 book *The Codebreakers* came so close to revealing NSA cryptologic methodology that the agency tried to stop its publication. When it did finally appear, it was published by a British publishing house. Fifteen years later, Bamford used the access granted by the Freedom of Information Act to write *The Puzzle Palace.* A book whose publication NSA opposed with even greater vigor than it had *The Codebreakers,* Bamford's work was the first full-scale study of NSA, and one of the few that exists even today.

NSA today.

Though today's NSA is far from an open book, several of its actions in the 1990s reveal a much greater degree of openness in the post-Cold War environment. During the mid-1990s, the agency opened both a Center for Cryptologic History and a National Cryptologic Museum, the latter located near its Fort Meade, Maryland, headquarters in a former motel that NSA purchased years before to prevent enemies from using it as a listening post. Kahn and Bamford, once anathema to the agency, had gained new respect: Kahn was given a position as visiting distinguished historian at the Center for Cryptologic History, while Bamford received full cooperation from NSA when writing a second book about the agency.

The title of that book—*Body of Secrets: Anatomy of the Ultra-Secret National Security Agency: from the Cold War Through the Dawn of a New Century* (2001)—might seem a bit incongruous in light of NSA's new openness, but in this case, "openness" is a relative term. NSA remains highly secretive about its operations, and even the most minor of its civilian employees is subject to extensive scrutiny and oversight. Plans to marry a foreign citizen—even if the person marrying is not the employee *but a relative of the employee*—must be announced to supervisors. The same is true of plans for travel overseas, and those who fail to comply are presumably fired, though not before extensive checks determine whether they passed secrets to an enemy. Even the physicians an employee visits must be on an approved list, in case the employee reveals sensitive secrets under anaesthesia.

Some 20,000 people work at the NSA's 650-acre campus at Fort Meade, making this organization the largest employer in Maryland. The Fort Meade facility includes the National Cryptologic School, a vast printing plant, and a massive factory producing computer chips. The chips are used at the heart of NSA operations, the supercomputers at Fort Meade, where codes and ciphers are made and broken. In the mid-1990s, NSA was estimated to have an annual budget of $3.5 billion.

In addition to the 20,000 at Fort Meade, up to an estimated 100,000 other personnel, mostly military, work for NSA in other parts of the world. The director of NSA is a three-star general or admiral experienced at intelligence work. He also serves as head of an agency within the agency, the Central Security Service (CSS), which is even

National Security Agency Director Lt. General Michael Hayden answers questions about what went wrong prior to the September 11, 2001, attacks before the Senate Select Committee on Intelligence, October 17, 2002. ©REUTERS NEWMEDIA INC./CORBIS.

NSA would answer to the Secretary of Defense. The Secretary, in turn, delegated all his COMINT responsibilities to the Director, NSA, as that position was thenceforth known. AFSA, though not officially abolished by NSCID 9, simply faded away.

Revelations.

For years, Americans had almost no idea as to the workings of the NSA. Then, in September 1960, NSA cryptographers William H. Martin and Bernon F. Mitchell held a news conference in Moscow to announce their defection. They proceeded to divulge a number of previously secret details about NSA, including the fact that it monitored communications from and in more than 40 countries, including not only members of the Warsaw Pact, but also putative U.S. allies such as France. Three years later, a third NSA defector, research analyst Victor N. Hamilton, told the Soviet newspaper *Izvestia* that NSA was in the process of breaking numerous countries' diplomatic codes and ciphers. He also revealed that NSA had been intercepting communications to and from specific nations' missions at United Nations headquarters in New York City.

In light of these experiences, occurring as they did against the backdrop of the Cold War at its height, it is perhaps not surprising that NSA reacted with hostility to more secretive than NSA itself. Tasked with providing information security to U.S. communications and cracking the codes of other nations, CSS was established in 1972. Nesting within it, at a still deeper layer of secrecy, is the Special Collections Service, an elite unit devoted to listening in on communications in countries hostile to the United States.

Under the control of NSA is a vast global network of ground stations, ships, aircraft, and satellites that together give it an almost supernatural aura of omniscience. This aura is more than a matter of mere reputation or hype: NSA itself estimates that several times a day, it processes more information than is contained in all the volumes in the Library of Congress. Among the most impressive of its surveillance programs is Echelon, through which NSA, working with other intelligence services in the English-speaking world, monitors communications throughout Europe.

■ FURTHER READING:

BOOKS:

Bamford, James. *The Puzzle Palace: A Report on America's Most Secret Agency.* Boston: Houghton Mifflin, 1982.

———. *Body of Secrets: Anatomy of the Ultra-Secret National Security Agency: From the Cold War through the Dawn of a New Century.* New York: Doubleday, 2001.

Kahn, David. *The Codebreakers.* London: Weidenfeld and Nicholson, 1967.

Richelson, Jeffrey T. *The U.S. Intelligence Community,* 4th ed. Boulder, CO: Westview Press, 1999.

ELECTRONIC:

National Security Agency. <http://www.nsa.gov/> (March 24, 2003).

National Security Agency. Federation of American Scientists. <http://www.fas.org/irp/nsa/index.html> (March 24, 2003).

SEE ALSO

COMINT (Communications Intelligence)
Satellites, Spy
SIGINT (Signals Intelligence)
Special Collection Service, United States

NSC (National Security Council)

■ JUDSON KNIGHT

Established by the National Security Act of 1947, the National Security Council (NSC) was intended to serve as the principal advisory board for the president of the United States on matters of national security and foreign policy. In practice, the importance of the NSC and the National Security Advisor has depended on the degree of power the chief executive accords to it. The NSC consists of four statutory members—president, vice president, and secretaries of State and Defense—along with two statutory advisors, the Chairman of the Joint Chiefs of Staff and the Director of Central Intelligence. Other officials participate as requested.

Presidents and their NSCs

The 1947 National Security Act became Public Law 235–61 Stat. 496; U.S.C. 402. Two years later, Congress passed the National Security Act Amendments of 1949 (63 Stat. 579; 50 U.S.C. 401 et seq.) These amendments led to a reorganization plan whereby the NSC became part of the executive office of the president. Whereas Congress and the departments of State and Defense had each sought to place the new council under their control, thenceforth—assuming it had any role at all—the NSC would be under the leadership of the president.

Harry S. Truman, the first president with an NSC, made little use of the council, but Dwight D. Eisenhower relied heavily on the NSC. John F. Kennedy, on the other hand, placed little emphasis on the NSC as such, but relied heavily on the first of many powerful National Security Advisors, McGeorge Bundy. In subsequent administrations, the emphasis on the NSC itself has shifted, but the president's reliance on the National Security Advisor seems to be a constant.

Democratic presidents, including Lyndon B. Johnson, James E. Carter, and William J. Clinton, have tended to approach the NSC with distrust upon entering office, and to supplant its functions with outside committees thereafter. Nevertheless, each relied heavily on National Security Advisors, including Bundy in Johnson's early years, Zbigniew Brzezinski throughout Carter's term, and Samuel "Sandy" Berger in Clinton's second term.

Republican administrations. Republicans, by contrast, have typically entered office with a positive view of the NSC itself, or at least of the National Security Advisor's role. In the administration of Richard M. Nixon, the NSC itself played little role, but NSC Advisor Henry Kissinger was perhaps second only to Nixon in power during the early 1970s. As Nixon's influence waned due to the Watergate scandal, Kissinger's importance continued into the administration of Gerald R. Ford.

The NSC of Ronald Reagan took an extremely activist role in overseas affairs, to such an extent that this led to another scandal, the Iran-Contra affair. National Security Advisor Robert McFarlane and his successor, Admiral John Poindexter, played key roles in fomenting the scheme to sell arms to the Iranian fundamentalist regime in exchange for the release of hostages, and to direct proceeds from these sales to the anticommunist Contras in Nicaragua.

President Bush sits with his National Security Council during a meeting in the Cabinet Room of the White House, September 12, 2001. From left to right, Secretary of State Colin Powell, President Bush, Vice-President Dick Cheney, and Chairman of the Joint Chiefs of Staff General Henry Shelton. AP/WIDE WORLD PHOTOS.

After Poindexter's departure, Reagan appointed Lieutenant General Colin Powell, who ran a tight, no-nonsense NSC. George H. W. Bush, who made Powell Chairman of the Joint Chiefs of Staff, appointed Brent Scowcroft as National Security Advisor. Scowcroft, who had directed the NSC after Kissinger left the position in 1975, was known for his warm relations with other centers of power around the president—including the National Security Advisor's two traditional rivals for the president's ear, the secretaries of Defense and State. This collegial tradition continued in the administration of George W. Bush, as National Security Advisor Condoleeza Rice worked closely with Secretary of State Powell and Secretary of Defense Donald Rumsfeld in the war on terror.

NSC members. The chairman of the National Security Council is the president, who relies to varying degrees on the National Security Advisor. The position of the latter, whose

official title is Assistant to the President for National Security Affairs, is not mentioned in the original legislation, and in fact the role of National Security Advisor emerged only during the Kennedy administration.

In addition to the four statutory members, the two statutory advisors on military and intelligence affairs, and the National Security Advisor, the Secretary of the Treasury is a regular attendee at NSC meetings. The Chief of Staff to the President, Counsel to the President, and Assistant to the President for Economic Policy are invited to attend any NSC meeting, while the Attorney General and the Director of the Office of Management and Budget are invited to attend those meetings that pertain to their responsibilities.

The directors of other executive departments and agencies, as well as other senior officials, are invited to attend meetings of the NSC when appropriate. Among those holding positions created by latter-day presidents:

the National Economic Advisor, established by Clinton, and the Secretary of Homeland Security, a Cabinet-level post created by George W. Bush in the wake of the September 2001 terrorist attacks. The first of these directs the National Economic Council, which works closely with the NSC and with presidential advisors who report to the National Security Advisor.

■ FURTHER READING:

BOOKS:

Best, Richard A. *The National Security Council: An Organizational Assessment.* Huntington, NY: Novinka Books, 2001.

Crabb, Cecil Van Meter, and Kevin V. Mulcahy. *American National Security: A Presidential Perspective.* Pacific Grove, CA: Brooks/Cole, 1991.

Hillen, John. *Future Visions for U.S. Defense Policy: Four Alternatives Presented as Presidential Speeches.* New York: Council on Foreign Relations, 1998.

Leitzel, Jim. *Economics and National Security.* Boulder, CO: Westview Press, 1993.

Lord, Carnes. *The Presidency and the Management of National Security.* New York: Free Press, 1988.

ELECTRONIC:

National Security Council. <http://www.whitehouse.gov/nsc/> (March 24, 2003).

SEE ALSO

National Security Act (1947)
National Security Advisor, United States
NSC (National Security Council), History
President of the United States (Executive Command and Control of Intelligence Agencies)

NSC (National Security Council), History

■ JUDSON KNIGHT

The history of the United States National Security Council (NSC) lends itself to widely diverging views of the NSC, depending on the presidential administration in question. Held in suspicion by President Harry S. Truman, the organization became a vital part of the Dwight D. Eisenhower administration. Thereafter it remained, for the most part, a significant aspect of subsequent administrations, although in differing manners. For example, four very different chief executives—John F. Kennedy, Richard M. Nixon, James E. Carter, and George W. Bush—relied heavily on powerful National Security Advisors (McGeorge Bundy,

Henry Kissinger, Zbigniew Brzezinski, and Condoleeza Rice, respectively), yet the similarities in organizational style end there.

The Roots of the NSC (1947–53)

Among its many provisions, which collectively reformed the U.S. defense, intelligence, and security apparatus, the National Security Act of July 26, 1947, created the NSC. The latter was to serve as a presidential advisory board on issues of significance to the military, security, intelligence, and foreign policy. Its chairman would the president, and its members would include the secretaries of State, Defense, the Army, Navy, and Air Force, as well as the director of the National Security Resources Board. Other Cabinet-level secretaries and officials with prominent security roles could attend occasionally. The Central Intelligence Agency (CIA), also created by the National Security Act, was to report to the NSC in an advisory role, but the Director of Central Intelligence (DCI) was not an NSC member.

The enabling legislation, designated as Public Law 80–253, made no mention of the National Security Advisor, a figure whose role would become prominent only in the Kennedy years. However, there was a powerful precedent for the idea of trusted White House advisors as guides for national policy; during World War II, President Franklin D. Roosevelt had depended on top White House aides such as Harry Hopkins and Admiral William D. Leahy at least as much as he did on his Cabinet secretaries. Likewise, during the early years of his administration, President Truman enjoyed a similar rapport with Special White House Counsel Clark Clifford.

This relationship with Clifford coexisted with Truman's ambivalence toward the NSC. Wary of a surfeit of advice and advisors that could impair his ability to make executive decisions, Truman largely ignored the NSC until the outbreak of the Korean War, attending only 10 of 55 meetings in those first three years of the body's existence. In 1949, however, Truman signaled a new interest in it when he instructed the Secretary of the Treasury to attend all NSC meetings. Congress also amended the earlier act to remove the three service secretaries, who would be represented thenceforth by the Secretary of Defense. The amendment also added the vice president to the Council, and made the Joint Chiefs of Staff (JCS) permanent advisors on military matters.

Other events of 1949—the formation of the North Atlantic Treaty Organization, Soviet detonation of an atomic bomb, the Communist takeover in China—all signaled a growth in importance for the Council, but the real change came after the outbreak of hostilities in Korea in June 1950. Thereafter, Truman, although he continued to rely on other sources for advice, attended most NSC meetings. Through the Council, he authorized the first of what were to be many covert operations on the part of the U.S. intelligence community.

President Lyndon Johnson (right side, second from right) shown meeting with the National Security Council in 1964 with the prime topic expected to be the North Vietnamese torpedo boat attack on the U.S. destroyer Maddox. ©BETTMANN/CORBIS.

The Eisenhower Years (1953–61)

As a former general, Eisenhower came to the White House with an appreciation for advisory staffs and for the organized system of strategic planning that the NSC concept embodied; therefore, the Council flourished under his administration. So, too, did various study groups, headed by the Operations Coordinating Board (OCB), which included the Undersecretary of State for Political Affairs, the Deputy Secretary of Defense, DCI, and others. Eventually, there would be more than 40 interagency working groups, and critics of the Eisenhower NSC complained that it was bogged down by too many committees and excess reports.

At the heart of the NSC were four full-time statutory members: the president, vice president, and the secretaries of State and Defense. Along with the Director of the Office of Defense Mobilization, these formed the core of the Eisenhower NSC. The Treasury Secretary, JCS Chairman, DCI, and others regularly attended meetings. Eisenhower created the position of Special Assistant for National Security Affairs, forerunner of the modern National Security Advisor, but in the 1950s this job was chiefly that of a staff coordinator, with little independent power.

A hands-on leader, Eisenhower attended the vast majority of NSC meetings—329 out of 366—that took place during his eight years in office. NSC meetings were the single most significant regularly recurring item on his weekly agenda, and through the Council he closely oversaw a burgeoning roster of covert missions, most notably in Iran in 1953 and Guatemala in 1954. His emphasis on the NSC had many detractors, among them Secretary of State John Foster Dulles, who naturally feared that the Council would eclipse his own importance in foreign policy; Senator Henry Jackson, chairman of the Senate Subcommittee on National Policy Machinery (1960–61); and others.

Kennedy and Johnson (1961–69)

The report of Jackson's subcommittee had a strong effect on Kennedy, who, upon assuming leadership in 1961, immediately cut NSC staff from 74 to 49. He also reduced the number of substantive members, and the frequency of their meetings. Therefore, it is ironic that Kennedy would ultimately strengthen the NSC by establishing the position of National Security Advisor, and by appointing Bundy—already a closely trusted associate—to the job.

The apparent contradiction in Kennedy's position on the NSC is explained by the aftermath of the disastrous Bay of Pigs invasion, an abortive April 1961 attempt to wrest control of Cuba from Communist dictator Fidel

Castro. In Kennedy's view, the State Department failed to effectively orchestrate the White House response to the debacle, so he turned to Bundy and the NSC for this assistance.

In 1962, NSC gained a powerful tool, both symbolic and real, for its implementation of policy when the Situation Room was established in the White House basement. The Sit Room, as it was called, connected the President with State, Defense, and the CIA, while providing the National Security Advisor with an opportunity to monitor cables from foreign service posts around the world.

Kennedy remained ambivalent toward the NSC as such, which met only 49 times in his three years as president. Much of its work was replaced by the Standing Group, which consisted of Bundy, DCI, the Deputy Secretary of Defense, and the Undersecretary for Political Affairs, who served as its chair.

As crises developed during the course of Kennedy's tenure in the White House, the President or Bundy established committees to respond to them. This was in sharp contrast to Eisenhower's emphasis on long-range planning, but sometimes these ad hoc groups outlasted their original purposes, and continued to serve in planning for the future.

For example, the Executive Committee of the National Security Council, formed as the Cuban Missile Crisis was heating up in the early fall of 1962, continued to meet until the spring of the following year. During that time, its agenda included a number of items besides Cuba. Kennedy also formed the 5412 Committee to oversee covert operations. Although chaired by Bundy, the committee operated outside the NSC framework.

This reliance on ad hoc committees was one of several practices that would continue under Lyndon B. Johnson when he assumed leadership after Kennedy's assassination in November, 1963. In February, 1965, as the war in Vietnam was reaching its height, Johnson convened the NSC frequently, but after that month, it seldom met. When it did, its role was to simply approve actions decided by the White House rather than to direct policy.

Also like Kennedy, Johnson's antipathy toward the NSC contrasted with his reliance on the National Security Advisor. Bundy remained in that position until February 1966, when he was replaced by Walt Rostow. The National Security Advisor, along with Secretary of State Dean Rusk and a few other key figures, met with the President for lunch almost every Tuesday from February 1964 onward, and this "Tuesday Lunch Group" largely performed the advisory role for which the NSC had been designed.

Nixon, Ford, and the Kissinger Era (1969–77)

Two names from the Nixon era epitomize the emphasis he placed on the role of the National Security Advisor: Henry Kissinger and William Rogers. Kissinger was Nixon's National Security Advisor, while Rogers served as Nixon's first Secretary of State. Nixon went into office intending to direct foreign policy from the White House with the aid of a highly effective National Security Advisor. Therefore, to avoid conflicts with the State Department, he appointed a virtual unknown and inexperienced diplomat to its top position.

Kissinger would replace Rogers as Secretary of State in September 1973, becoming the only person in history to hold that position while remaining National Security Advisor. By then, the power of Kissinger himself, magnified by the eclipse of Nixon in the Watergate scandal, was far greater than the influence formally accorded to any government position. Under Gerald R. Ford, who succeeded Nixon after his resignation in August 1974, Kissinger relinquished his dual role when Lieutenant General Brent Scowcroft became National Security Advisor in November 1975. Kissinger remained the President's chief advisor, however, and Scowcroft deferred to Kissinger as the leading figure in foreign policy.

Kissinger relied on a number of planning and review committees to help him manage an ever-widening array of issues that included Vietnam, rising tensions in the Middle East, efforts toward normalization of relations with China, and the birth of detente with the Soviet Union. This necessitated expansion of the NSC staff from 12 to 34 members, as well as other measures. Through his secretary, Jeanne Davis, he instituted a computerized document-tracking system, a revolutionary move in the 1970s. With the help of the White House Communication Agency, which had special aircraft that operated as communication centers, Kissinger could travel the globe, operating a one-man command post.

So great was his power that his accession to the top position at the State Department in 1973 was more of an annoyance to Kissinger than anything else; as he later recalled in his memoirs, serving in dual roles forced him into the inherently ridiculous position of having to represent the Department of State's interests at the NSC. For this reason alone, aside from more obvious concerns about one person having too much power, it is unlikely that both positions will again be held by the same person at the same time.

The Carter Interregnum (1977–81)

James E. Carter acceded to the presidency in January 1977 with a promise to reform many of the excesses that had darkened Washington. Among these was the virtually unprecedented accumulation of power by Kissinger, which he sought to counteract by returning the NSC to a role of policy coordination and research. Once again, the NSC staff was cut, this time reduced by half. For his National Security Advisor, however, Carter chose another strong personality, Zbigniew Brzezinski.

Carter also allowed the growth of new committees, which replaced those of the Kissinger era. Brzezinski chaired only one of the two principal NSC committees, the Standing Coordinating Committee, and thus Carter hoped to hold the NSC's influence in check. These committee meetings ultimately formed the basis for presidential directives, classified orders from the White House that originated with Nixon.

The NSC as a whole met only 10 times in Carter's four years, a far cry from the 125 meetings of the eight years of Republican administrations that proceeded his. Like his Democratic predecessors, Carter relied instead primarily on informal and ad hoc groups. Whereas Johnson had his Tuesday lunches, Carter had his Friday breakfasts, at which he met with Vice President Walter Mondale, Secretary of State Cyrus Vance, Secretary of Defense Harold Brown, Brzezinski, and others.

Despite Carter's efforts to prevent the rise of another Kissinger, Brzezinski soon emerged as a leading figure of his administration. Differences between Brzezinski and Vance, combined with the lack of strong leadership from the top, helped spawn the series of foreign-policy debacles that would help bring the Carter years to an end. Whereas Brzezinski favored taking a strong, activist stance toward U.S. enemies—the Soviets who had invaded Afghanistan, and the fundamentalists who had seized control of Iran—Vance took a more cautious position. These differences in approach came to a head during the abortive March 1980 attempt to rescue the U.S. hostages from Iran. Conceived by Brzezinski, the move was submitted to so many changes in an effort to ameliorate all sides (a fact symbolized by the multiservice team undertaking the attempted rescue) that it ultimately lacked the clear direction essential to such a bold move. In the wake of the hostage-rescue disaster, Vance resigned, and Carter's fate in the coming election was sealed.

Ronald Reagan and George H. W. Bush (1981–93)

Seeing Carter's failure to resolve the rivalry between NSC and the State Department, as a presidential candidate, Ronald Reagan called for a decrease in the power of the National Security Advisor. On the day of Reagan's inauguration, his Secretary of State, Alexander Haig, drafted a presidential directive placing all foreign-policy planning under his own department. It seemed that the problem had been resolved, but in fact a new one had been created, because other members of the Reagan administration feared that the new direction of foreign policy took too much power away from the president.

Reagan, however, was determined to reduce the power of the NSC, and he directed National Security Advisor Richard Allen to report to presidential advisor Edwin Meese. This marked the first time since the inception of the NSC that the National Security Advisor did not have a direct line of contact with the President. Meese chaired a meeting in February 1981, that revived senior interdepartmental groups (SIGs), first introduced under Johnson. The meeting established three SIGs, on foreign, defense, and intelligence issues, that would be chaired by the secretaries of State and Defense and the DCI, respectively.

Allen resigned in January 1982, and Reagan replaced him with Deputy Secretary of State William Clark, a close friend. Thenceforth the National Security Advisor would again hold a powerful role. There followed a series of presidential directives and other orders clarifying the functions of the advisor and the SIGs, and establishing new SIGs and interagency groups (IGs). Meanwhile, in June 1982, Haig resigned and was replaced by George P. Schultz, signaling a move to a less activist State Department—even as the influence of the NSC continually increased.

Iran-Contra and the fallout. Robert McFarlane, with Admiral John Poindexter as his deputy, replaced Clark as National Security Advisor in October 1983. By then, the ever-growing number of committees had created an NSC bureaucracy that, critics would later charge, made it easy for Lieutenant Colonel Oliver North to carve out his own miniature empire within the NSC. More significant, however, was the fact that the NSC under McFarlane took an increasingly active role in formulating and implementing policy, particularly in the Middle East and Central America.

All these threads came together in the Iran-Contra situation, whereby the NSC (Poindexter replaced McFarlane as advisor in December 1985) sought to purchase the release of hostages held by pro-Iran groups in the Middle East and simultaneously provide funds to the Contras, anticommunist guerrillas in Nicaragua. They would do this by selling arms to the Iranian regime, which they believed they could cultivate as an ally against a common enemy, the Soviets. Arms sales would fund the Contras, to whom a Democrat-dominated Congress had refused support.

Once word of the Iran-Contra operation leaked to the press in late 1986, it sparked a scandal that would darken the remainder of Reagan's administration. In the wake of Iran-Contra, the Presidential Review Board—better known as the Tower Board after its leader, Senator John Tower—made a number of recommendations that collectively limited the size and power of the NSC.

In November 1986, Reagan appointed Frank Carlucci as National Security Advisor, with Lieutenant General Colin Powell as his deputy. Carlucci, whose tenure was marked by continued reforms of the NSC, served for less than a year before succeeding Caspar Weinberger as Secretary of Defense. Reagan replaced him with Powell, who ran an NSC that was tightly controlled, disciplined, efficient, and unobtrusive.

Vice President George Bush, elected to succeed Reagan, assumed office in January 1989, on the brink of momentous changes in the world. The Cold War was coming to an end, and the period that followed would give rise to an increasingly uncertain international situation in which the United States would become involved in conflicts around the globe, including Panama in 1989, Kuwait in 1991, and Somalia in 1993.

In line with these changes, Bush altered the NSC. Colin Powell became Chairman of the JCS, while Scowcroft returned to his old position as National Security Advisor. This time, Scowcroft would hold more power than in the Kissinger years, and he enjoyed a close working relationship with the president. At the same time, Scowcroft helped sow friendly relations between the NSC and its old rival, the Department of State. Instead of constituting competing fiefdoms, the NSC, along with the State and Defense Departments and other key centers of power, more closely followed its original mandate of serving the administration's larger needs.

The Clinton Era (1993-2001)

As had been the practice from Carter's time, William J. Clinton initiated his presidency with a presidential directive. Also like Carter and all presidents since, he created new names for his directives—Clinton's were called Presidential Decision Directives (PDD), for instance, in contrast to the National Security Directives of his predecessor—as well as for other aspects of NSC operations. PDD 1, for instance, issued on his first day in office, established these new names, while PDD 2 on the following day increased the membership of the NSC.

Thenceforth, in addition to the four statutory members (president, vice president, secretaries of State and Defense), members would include the secretary of the Treasury, the U.S. Representative to the United Nations, the Assistant to the President for National Security Affairs (i.e., the National Security Advisor), the Chief of Staff to the President, and the Assistant to the President for National Economic Policy. (The last, head of the newly created National Economic Council, was a creation of the Clinton administration.) DCI and the Chairman of the JCS would retain their statutory roles as advisors, while the Attorney General and others would attend when invited to do so.

George W. Bush and the Post September 11, 2001, World (2001-present)

When George W. Bush assumed the presidency, he appointed Dr. Condoleeza Rice, most recently the provost of Stanford University, as his National Security Advisor. He also scaled back the roster of NSC members to the statutory core, with others invited to participate as needed. Eight months later, Bush's administrative agenda changed, along with the entire fabric of American life, in the aftermath of the September 11, 2001, terrorist attacks.

From at least the time of the 1993 terrorist attack on the World Trade Center towers, the Clinton administration had declared a "war on terror," but until the attacks that brought those towers down eight years later, the "war" was ill-defined. With the launch of an attack against Afghanistan on October 7, 2001, the war became far more than a figure of speech. By that point, Americans had become accustomed to seeing Bush at public appearances surrounded by the other principal leaders in that war: Rice, Secretary of Defense Donald Rumsfeld, and Powell, now serving as Secretary of State.

Others sometimes appeared alongside this core group, among them one who most clearly qualified as a core participant: Vice President Dick Cheney. Like Rumsfeld and Powell, Cheney had served in past Republican administrations—in his case, that of Bush's father—but despite a close relationship, Bush and Cheney appeared together only infrequently to reinforce the idea that if anything happened to one leader, the other would be on hand to run the nation.

One figure identified with the core group was former Pennsylvania Governor Tom Ridge, leader of the newest Cabinet department, Homeland Security. By the late fall of 2001, there was already talk in policy circles about the return of the kind of turf battles that had animated the corridors of the White House decades earlier. Only the players had changed, and this time it was the NSC and the Office of Homeland Security (as it was known prior to March 2003) bickering over control of the White House Situation Room.

Battles of this kind will probably continue in one form of another for as long as the national leadership exists, and to an extent, they play a role in maintaining healthy checks and balances within a constitutional, democratic state possessing multiple centers of power. Conversely, it was emblematic of the post-September 11 America that the Bush team could act as much in concert with one another as they did. In a White House that had seen half a century's worth of struggles between the NSC and the Departments of State and Defense, the sight of Rice, Powell, and Rumsfeld standing shoulder-to-shoulder—not just literally but figuratively—was a testament to the sense of shared duty that animated many Americans in the early twenty-first century.

■ FURTHER READING:

BOOKS:

Best, Richard A. *The National Security Council: An Organizational Assessment.* Huntington, NY: Novinka Books, 2001.

Kissinger, Henry, and Clare Boothe Luce. *White House Years.* Boston: Little, Brown, 1979.

Menges, Constantine Christopher. *Inside the National Security Council: The True Story of the Making and Unmaking of Reagan's Foreign Policy.* New York: Simon and Schuster, 1988.

Prados, John. *Keepers of the Keys: A History of the National Security Council from Truman to Bush.* New York: Morrow, 1991.

Zegart, Amy B. *Flawed by Design: The Evolution of the CIA, JCS, and NSC.* Stanford, CA: Stanford University Press, 1999.

PERIODICALS:

Newman, William W. "Reorganizing for National Security and Homeland Security." *Public Administration Review* 62 (September 2002): 126–137.

ELECTRONIC:

History of the National Security Council. American Federation of Scientists. <http://www.fas.org/irp/offdocs/NSChistory.htm> (March 24, 2003).

SEE ALSO

Bush Administration (1989–1993), United States National Security Policy
Bush Administration (2001–), United States National Security Policy
Carter Adminstration (1977–1981), United States National Security Policy
Clinton Administration (1993–2001), United States National Security Policy
Department of State, United States
Eisenhower Administration (1953–1961), United States National Security Policy
Executive orders and Presidential directives
Ford Administration (1974–1977), United States National Security Policy
Johnson Administration (1963–1969), United States National Security Policy
Kennedy Administration (1961–1963), United States National Security Policy
National Security Act (1947)
National Security Advisor, United States
Nixon Administration (1969–1974), United States National Security Policy
NSC (National Security Council)
Reagan Administration (1981–1989), United States National Security Policy
Truman Administration (1945–1953), United States National Security Policy

NSF (National Science Foundation)

The National Science Foundation (NSF) directs and funds science research. An independent agency in the United States government, the NSF was established May 10, 1950, by passage of the National Science Foundation Act. Subsequent amendments to the act granted the NSF further authority to develop, fund, and oversee research in the government, academic, and industrial sectors.

The stated mission of the National Science Foundation is to promote scientific research that aids national health and prosperity, and protects national security interests. The foundation endeavors to foster communication and cooperation in the national and global science communities. A president-appointed director, deputy director, and eight assistant directors govern the agency. The foundation is further staffed by the twenty-four member National Science Board.

The NSF grants student fellowships for graduate studies in the sciences, medicine, and engineering, and sponsors post-doctoral research opportunities. Research programs backed by the NSF range in scope from disease research to space exploration. The foundation also develops science education programs for school-aged children, and cosponsors symposia, conferences, and seminars for college students and professional researchers. In conjunction with independent researchers, professional organizations, government agencies, and international scholars, the NSF publishes and revises a code of ethical research practices.

The NSF often works in conjunction with the Defense Advanced Research Projects Agency (DARPA), an organization within the Department of Defense, to develop research projects with military, intelligence, and national security interests. In 2001, the two organizations cosponsored research concerning government computer systems and data security. While NSF may aid research with implications on national security and military technology, DARPA is responsible for classified weapons and technology research.

As a response to the September 11, 2001, attacks on the United States, the NSF has increased its backing of scientific research beneficial to counterterrorism. Studying epidemic disease, combating the effects of biological and chemical weapons, water and soil safety, and developing better information protection systems are some of the present science- and engineering-related national security issues addressed by NSF sponsored research.

■ FURTHER READING:

ELECTRONIC:

National Science Foundation. <http://www.nsf.gov> (15 January 2003).

SEE ALSO

DARPA (Defense Advanced Research Projects Agency)

NTSB (National Transportation Safety Board)

The United States National Transportation Safety Board (NTSB) is an independent national agency responsible for investigating transportation accidents within the United States. The agency has custody of all debris and wreckage

Investigators from the National Transportation Safety Board (NTSB) gather around the wreckage of American Airlines flight 1420, which crashed June 1, 1999. ©AFP/CORBIS.

from accidents that it investigates, and thorough investigations sometimes take years to complete. The primary focus of NTSB operations is the investigation of civil aviation accidents, however the agency is also required to report on railroad, pipeline, and significant marine and highway accidents. For the NTSB to be involved in an accident investigation, the accident must involve a national transportation infrastructure, a public vessel, or hazardous materials.

The NTSB was established on April 1, 1967. In its early days, the agency worked closely with the Department of Transportation. Concerned with the NTSB's ties to the nation's transportation regulatory agency and the transportation industry, Congress sought to make the NTSB an independent, and impartial, entity. In 1975, the agency became independent, receiving funding in its own right through the Independent Safety Board Act.

The NTSB is managed by a five-person board. Members are appointed by the President to serve five-year terms. The board directs agency field investigators, and certifies final accident reports.

In addition to accident investigation, the NTSB maintains the government database of civil aviation accidents. The database permits NTSB researchers to search for patterns in accident occurrence, as well as publish safety statistics for carriers and airports. The NTSB conducts regular studies of transportation safety procedures, making improvement suggestions to transportation officials and Congress when necessary. Since its inception in 1967, the NTSB has issued nearly 12,000 recommendations. Though the NTSB does not have the power to act as a regulatory authority, most of its recommendations have been adopted by the national transportation industry.

The NTSB is also an instrument of national transportation law. The board sometimes hears the appeals of pilots, mechanics, and mariners who have been stripped of professional privileges, certificates, or incurred disciplinary fines. For advice on these cases, the NTSB employs legal council. Council is also provided to any witnesses or parties involved in an accident who are questioned by NTSB investigators.

Although the investigative jurisdiction of the NTSB does not extend beyond national borders, the agency provides investigators for international accidents involving United States registered aircraft or maritime vessels. United States NTSB investigators, or foreign NTSB Accredited Representatives, have occasionally been welcomed by foreign governments that do not have their own investigative services to report on accidents.

After the 2001 terrorist attacks on the United States, the NTSB began widespread investigations of the airlines' safety and screening procedures. The newly created Transportation Safety Administration temporarily assumed many of the NTSB safety recommendation duties. The NTSB continues to investigate the actual September 11, 2001, airline crashes associated with the terrorist attacks.

■ FURTHER READING:

ELECTRONIC:

United States National Transportation Safety Board. <http://www.ntsb.gov> (30 April 2003).

SEE ALSO

Airline Security
Aviation Security Screeners, United States
FAA (United States Federal Aviation Administration)
September 11 Terrorist Attacks on the United States

Nuclear Detection Devices

■ LARRY GILMAN

Nuclear detection devices, also termed radiation detectors, are systems designed to detect the presence of radioactive materials. These materials may take the form of gases, particles suspended in air, or solid metals (often alloys of uranium or plutonium). Detection of nuclear materials is needed for safety monitoring of all facilities handling nuclear materials, for the interdiction of nuclear smuggling, and for arms-control monitoring of peaceful nuclear programs to detect any diversions of fissile material to bomb-building programs.

Although radioactive materials can be (and, in the laboratory, often are) detected by direct chemical assay, it is far easier in practice to detect them at second hand by measuring the radiation they emit. Nuclear materials emit two kinds of radiation as the nuclei of their atoms spontaneously break apart: fast particles (i.e., neutrons, electrons, and ions) and electromagnetic radiation (i.e., X rays and gamma rays). Different nuclear materials emit different blends of these radiation types. This radiation, unless blocked by layers of matter (shielding), reveals the presence of the nuclear material. The use of nuclear detection devices or radiation detectors is thus, key to monitoring

for the presence of radioactive substances. The arms-control monitoring programs of the International Atomic Energy Agency, for example, depend heavily on both automated and hand-carried detection devices that seek to measure the telltale radiations emitted by nuclear materials.

Furthermore, radiation can cause illness, injury, or death. A single fast particle, X ray, or gamma ray can damage a DNA molecule so that a healthy cell is converted to a cancer cell, and sufficiently large numbers of particles or rays can disturb enough of a cells' molecules to kill it. Therefore, nuclear detection devices are also used to alert to releases of radioactive material, whether deliberate (e.g., caused by a "dirty bomb") or accidental (e.g., material escaping from a nuclear power plant, waste-storage facility, or fuel-reprocessing plant).

To be detectable, radiation must be partly or wholly absorbed by ordinary matter. Radiation is said to have been absorbed by a mass of material when it has given up most or all of its energy to that material; radiation that is difficult to absorb (e.g., neutrino flow) is correspondingly difficult to detect. There are several different radiation-absorption phenomena, each of which is exploited in the design of a different class of detection devices. The most important form of absorption is ionization, that is, the separation of neutral atoms in the absorbing medium into free electrons (negatively charged) and free ions (positively charged atoms lacking one or more electrons). All forms of radiation mentioned above can cause ionization. Ionization, in turn, can be detected in numerous ways. One way is chemical, as ions, because they lack electrons, readily combine with other atoms to form new molecules. In a photographic film, this recombination appears as the chemical change known as exposure. Film-badge dosimeters measure radiation by accumulating chemical changes in response to ionizing radiation.

A more precise and continuous measure of ionizing radiation is obtained by electronic amplification of individual ionization events. The best known of the tools that measures radiation in this way is the Geiger counter. In a Geiger counter, a voltage is placed across a chamber filled with gas (usually argon or xenon); this causes an electric field to exist between one end of the chamber and the other. When a fast particle or high-energy ray passes through the chamber, it ionizes neutral atoms, that is, splits them up into free electrons and positively-charged ions. Under the influence of the electric field, the electrons accelerate toward one end of the chamber and the ions toward the other. If the electrical field is strong enough, it accelerates them enough so that when they strike other atoms in the gas they ionize them as well. The electrons and ions thus produced may also be accelerated enough to cause ionization, and so on. The resulting brief avalanche of charged particles constitutes a pulse of electrical current that can be detected, amplified, and counted by appropriate circuitry. In the audio output circuit of a Geiger counter, a single ionization event is amplified to produce the device's trademark "click." Although the arrival

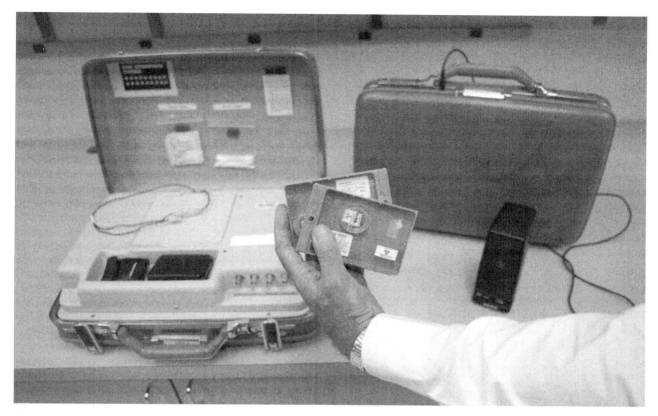

A Nuclear Emergency Search Team (NEST) member shows portable sensing equipment used to detect radioative sources.The briefcase design allows NEST members to carry the sensing device undetected in crowded environments. AP/WIDE WORLD PHOTOS.

of any one ray or particle is a randomly timed event, the average rate of such arrivals, smoothed over time, gives an accurate idea of how much radiation is present.

Another type of radiation-detection device is the scintillation detector. Certain crystals, when struck by a single high-energy photon or particle, produce a scintillation, that is, a flash of light consisting of thousands or tens of thousands of visible photons. In the early twentieth century, one method of measuring radiation was to count scintillation rates under a microscope; modern detectors use electronic circuits for the same purpose.

The interactions of radiation with semiconducting crystals such as silicon can also be measured. Semiconducting radiation detectors have the advantages of small size, high sensitivity, and high accuracy.

■ FURTHER READING:

BOOKS:

Delaney, C. F. G., and E. C. Finch. *Radiation Detectors.* New York: Oxford University Press, 1992.

SEE ALSO

Dosimetry

Nuclear Emergency Support Team, United States

The Nuclear Emergency Support Team (NEST) is part of an emergency response branch of the National Nuclear Security Administration (NNSA), itself a unit of the United States Department of Energy (DOE). Established in the mid-1970s—long before NNSA itself—NEST has analyzed hundreds of cases involving potential nuclear threats. It is one of seven emergency response groups operated by NNSA, and members work in the field alongside the Federal Bureau of Investigation's Domestic Emergency Support Team or the State Department's Foreign Emergency Support Team.

NEST in the NNSA emergency response context. The seven NNSA emergency response teams include the Aerial Measuring System, which detects, measures, and tracks radioactive material; the Atmospheric Release Advisory Capability, which monitors and predicts the release of hazardous materials into the atmosphere; the Accident Response Group, which supports the successful resolution of U.S. nuclear weapons accidents anywhere in the world; the

Nuclear Emergency Search Team members install radiation-sensing equipment into a helicopter at the NEST facility at Nellis Air Force Base in Nevada. AP/WIDE WORLD PHOTOS.

Federal Radiological Monitoring and Assessment Center, which coordinates radiological efforts on the federal, state, and local levels; the Radiological Assistance Program, the usual NNSA first responder in radiological emergencies; the Radiation Emergency Assistance Center/Training Site, which trains respondents and provides medical treatment for injuries resulting from radiation exposure; and NEST, which provides specialized technical expertise in response to nuclear or radiological terrorist incidents.

Established in 1975, NEST has addressed a variety of possible nuclear threats. For example, in its first year of operation, NEST responded to a threat by a group claiming that it would detonate a nuclear device in New York City if it were not given $30 million. Police provided what was purportedly a payment, but actually a lure for the criminals, who failed to materialize—along with their alleged bomb. NEST has analyzed the credibility of some 60 extortion threats involving nuclear materials, 25 reactor threats, and 20 non-nuclear extortion threats. It has also investigated well over 650 reports of illegal sales involving nuclear materials.

NEST at work. As of the early twenty-first century, NEST had some 70 responders and a larger pool of approximately 900 personnel on call. Operational teams of 45 or fewer people, including chemists, physicists, mathematicians, communications specialists, and technicians, are equipped with handheld detectors. In addition to four helicopters and three planes, they have vans fitted with detectors and diagnostic equipment. A support department even supplies fake commercial artwork to disguise NEST vans.

Not surprisingly, NEST's services have been in particularly high demand since September 11, 2001. In January 2002, the administration of President George W. Bush called on NEST to search large U.S. cities for a possible "dirty bomb"—a crude nuclear device—that was a reported tool of the terrorist organization al Qaeda. NEST teams, equipped with gamma and neutron detectors, could blend into crowds by disguising their equipment as briefcases, backpacks, or even beer coolers. In February, 2002, NEST teams also quietly provided support to security efforts at the Winter Olympics in Salt Lake City, Utah.

■ FURTHER READING:

PERIODICALS:

Hall, Mimi. "Preparations Underway for Radiation Attack." *USA Today*. (July 8, 2002): A2.

Waller, Douglas. "The Secret Bomb Squad." *Time*. (March 18, 2002): 23.

ELECTRONIC:

National Nuclear Security Administration. <http://www.nnsa.doe.gov> (March 7, 2003).

Oppenheimer, Andy. Nuclear Incident Response in the U.S. Jane's International Security News. <http://www.janes.com/security/international_security/news/jcbw/jcbw020827_1_n.shtml> (March 26, 2003).

Render Safe, Defusing a Nuclear Emergency. Los Alamos National Laboratory. Fall 2002. <http://www.lanl.gov/quarterly/q_fall02/render_safe.shtml> (March 26, 2003).

SEE ALSO

Atmospheric Release Advisory Capability (ARAC)
Domestic Emergency Support Team, United States
FEST (United States Foreign Emergency Support Team)
NNSA (United States National Nuclear Security Administration)
Radiological Emergency Response Plan, United States Federal

Nuclear Power Plants, Security

■ LARRY GILMAN

Nuclear power plants pose two basic security concerns. First, all nuclear reactors both use and produce radioactive elements (e.g., uranium and plutonium) that can be used to build nuclear weapons. Second, all reactors and nuclear-waste storage facilities contain large amounts of radioactive material. This material might be stolen for later use as a terrorist weapon (e.g., by being combined with conventional explosives to form a radiological dispersal weapon, also termed a "dirty bomb") or, in the case of concentrated fuel, to build nuclear weapons. Alternatively, radioactivity might be released directly to the environment by sabotaging safety systems or blowing up a facility with missiles, planted charges, or hijacked jet aircraft. Thus, nuclear facilities on a nation's own territory threaten its security as a target of enemy action, while nuclear facilities on an enemy's territory threaten security as a possible source of nuclear weapons.

Nuclear proliferation, as the possession of nuclear weapons by ever-greater numbers of nations is termed, has been a recognized global hazard since at least the 1960s. In contrast, the possibility that nuclear facilities on one's own territory might be employed by an enemy as ready-made weapons has been of greatly heightened public concern since the terror attacks of September 11, 2001. Both threats are serious and plausible. Even a relatively small nuclear weapon of the size that destroyed the city of Hiroshima on August 9, 1945, could kill hundreds of thousands of people, and such a bomb requires only

A Pennsylvania State Police officer patrols the entrance of the Three Mile Island nuclear power plant near Harrisburg, Pennsylvania, in July 2002, as security at power plants has been increased since the attacks of September 11, 2001. AP/WIDE WORLD PHOTOS.

about 15 lb (7 kg) of uranium-235 (U^{235}) or a similar quantity of plutonium. Every large (i.e., 100-MW range) nuclear power plant contains hundreds of pounds of both these substances and produces hundreds of additional pounds of plutonium every year. Meanwhile, release of a significant fraction of the radioactive material in any large nuclear reactor, reprocessing plant, or waste-storage facility could cause an unpredictable number of deaths over a continent-sized area and make thousands of square miles of land uninhabitable for time periods ranging from days to centuries.

Reactor fuel and bomb material. Both nuclear reactors and fission-type nuclear weapons exploit the fact that atoms of some elements (e.g., uranium and plutonium) are unstable, that is, their nuclei have a natural tendency to break apart. When a nucleus breaks apart (fissions), it releases smaller nuclei, electrons, high-energy photons, and fast-moving neutrons. If one of these neutrons strikes another unstable nucleus, that nucleus may also fission, releasing still more neutrons, which may trigger still other nuclei, and so on and so on in a self-sustaining chain reaction. This chain reaction is the energy source of both reactors and fission bombs, the main difference being that in a reactor the chain reaction proceeds at approximately constant speed, while in a bomb, it spreads at geometrically increasing speeds.

Reactor fuel—the mixture of radioactive metals used to sustain a chain reaction in the core of a typical electricity-generating reactor—is only 3–5 percent U^{235}, the rest being mostly uranium-238 (U^{238}), a comparatively stable form of uranium. This means that a nuclear bomb cannot be made directly out of ordinary commercial reactor fuel. However, "research" reactors, most of which produce radioisotopes for medical and industrial purposes, run on nearly pure U^{235}, the same material used to destroy Hiroshima. There are about 550 such reactors in the world, several of which—including Israel's reactor at Dimona—have actually been used to produce nuclear weapons clandestinely. Furthermore, during the ordinary process of "burning" reactor fuel some of its U^{238} is changed by neutron bombardment to plutonium-239 (Pu^{239}). This can be extracted from the spent fuel, concentrated, and used either as reactor fuel or to build bombs.

Western intelligence sources assume that India, Israel, Pakistan, South Africa, and (probably) North Korea have built nuclear weapons using U^{235} or Pu^{239} obtained from reactor programs publicly dedicated to research or electrical power generation. Other nations will probably do so in the future.

Security and proliferation.

For many years, as part of the Atoms for Peace program initiated by President Eisenhower in 1953, the United States literally gave away reactors, nuclear materials, and essential nuclear knowledge to many countries. At least 26 reactors fueled by highly-enriched (bomb-grade) uranium were given to countries including Argentina, Brazil, Iran, Israel, South Korea, Pakistan, Spain, and Taiwan. Thousands of scientists from these countries and others were trained in reactor theory, plutonium extraction and enrichment, and other knowledge essential to nuclear bomb manufacture. Thanks to Atoms for Peace (and sales of nuclear technologies by other nuclear powers), preventing the global proliferation of nuclear weapons by restricting nuclear materials, reactors, and reprocessing facilities to a relatively few states ceased to be an option long ago. Nuclear proliferation has occurred and will probably continue. Israel is now believed by most observers to possess more than 200 nuclear weapons, India exploded its first nuclear weapon in 1974, and Pakistan (whose first nuclear reactor was a gift from the U.S.) exploded its first nuclear weapon in 1998.

Systematic efforts, however, have been made to control the proliferation of nuclear weapons worldwide. The International Atomic Energy Agency (IAEA) is an arm of the United Nations charged with the promotion and global monitoring of nuclear power. The IAEA has sought, through inspections programs, to prevent the diversion of nuclear materials from reactors to weapons. Compliance with IAEA inspections is, however, voluntary. Furthermore, diversions below the "measurement noise level" could suffice to build a nuclear weapon. For example, in a nuclear facility where 1,000 1-kilogram units of fissionable material were measured to an accuracy of .001 kilogram each year, up to 1 kilogram (1,000 samples of less than .001 kg each) could be undetectably diverted annually, and enough for a bomb accumulated in a few years. Many observers deem it unlikely that any state seriously desiring to manufacture nuclear weapons has yet been prevented from doing so by IAEA inspections.

Another method for controlling proliferation, so far adopted only by Iran and Israel, is the destruction of nuclear facilities possessed by enemy states. On September 30, 1980, planes bearing Iranian markings destroyed Iraq's Tuwaitha nuclear research center near Baghdad, the capital of Iraq. On June 7, 1981, 16 Israeli aircraft destroyed the Osirak "research" reactor just south of Baghdad. Israel had tried to prevent completion of the French-supplied facility by means of threatening letters, sabotage, and assassination, but had failed. (The June 7 air attack demolished the facility before it was fueled and operational, so no life-threatening release of radiation occurred.) These attacks may have been effective in their goal of preventing Iraq from obtaining nuclear weapons. However, it is not practical to prevent nuclear proliferation by these means on a global scale.

Thus there does not seem to be any long-term, sure-fire method of preventing technically sophisticated countries that possess nuclear reactors from exploiting them to build nuclear weapons if they so desire. If this is true, absolute security from nuclear weapons is a chimerical goal, and the best that can be hoped for is ongoing negotiation for a state of permanent, radical, and global *in*security.

Protecting nuclear facilities.

Many radioactive elements besides Pu^{239} accumulate in reactor fuel as it is irradiated in a reactor core. The fast-moving particles and high-energy photons emitted by these elements can kill living things either directly or by causing genetic damage; spent reactor fuel and materials derived from it are, therefore, dangerous to approach or ingest. Furthermore, they will remain so for periods of time greatly exceeding the duration of human history thus far; Pu^{239}, for example, has a half-life of approximately 24,000 years (i.e., only half the atoms in any sample of Pu^{239} will have fissioned after 24,000 years).

Material radioactive enough to be classified as high-level waste is produced continuously by operating nuclear reactors and by facilities that reprocess spent fuel to extract plutonium. For example, the fuel in a typical electricity-generating reactor (of which 104 are operating in the United States) must be swapped out for fresh fuel every few years. The best long-term hope for disposing of this spent fuel is deep burial in rocks that seem likely to remain stable for hundreds of thousands of years. However, in most of the world, including the United States, no deep-burial program yet exists, so all high-level waste is stored on the surface in containers, usually on the grounds of the nuclear plants that produce it. Release to the environment of the material in even one such repository would be a highly effective act of terrorism.

Persons wishing to attack a nuclear reactor or other nuclear facility have a wide range of options. They may seek to intercept or sabotage shipments of fuel or waste; invade a facility using armed force or deception, then proceed to steal radioactive material, blow up the facility, or (if it is a reactor) cause it to melt down; or seek to breach the containments of reactors or waste-storage facilities using truck bombs, missiles, hijacked aircraft, or other means. All facilities containing significant amounts of radioactive material must therefore be defended from a wide range of possible attacks.

Reactor and waste-storage security has been based for decades on a concept termed "defense in depth." The defense-in-depth method requires that each nuclear facility be surrounded by concentric security barriers. The outermost barrier is invariably a high fence topped with razorwire. The grounds near the fence, inside and out, are monitored by intruder-detection devices, and vehicles can only enter through checkpoints staffed by armed guards. Thirty to 40 guards are on duty at all times at a typical nuclear power plant, and vehicle gates, doors, and the like remain locked.

Defense in depth seeks to provide security against an imaginary scenario termed the Design Basis Threat, which is defined by the U.S. Nuclear Regulatory Commission (NRC). Prior to September 11, 2001, the Design Basis Threat included a truck bomb the size of that used to attack the World Trade Center in 1993, three outside attackers, and one collaborator inside the plant. Also, the NRC stated in its public-relations material that there was no credible security threat to the nation's nuclear facilities. The NRC removed these statements from the Web along with the rest of its website shortly after the September attacks, wishing to "review posted material to make sure there was no sensitive information that could be misused to harm the security of our nation" (http://www.nrc.gov/what-we-do/safeguards/response-911.html).

However, among some scientists, there had long been skepticism about the adequacy of defense in depth and the Design Basis Threat. From the 1970s until 2001, the NRC staged mock attacks (termed Operational Safeguard Response Evaluations) to test plant security. Forty-six percent of plants tested from the 1970s until 1998 failed evaluation; from 1998 to September 11, 2001, 9 out of 11 plants tested failed; no evaluations have been conducted since. Furthermore, doubts linger about the ability of plant personnel to defend against determined attack. Most of the guards who are supposed to be able to repel a determined (perhaps suicidal) paramilitary or terrorist assault are actually hired from private security companies, in some cases paid less than janitors working at the same facilities. In the wake of the September 11, 2001 attacks, state troopers and National Guard troops have been deployed to assist these personnel in guarding nuclear plants against attack; however, in response to NRC orders to increase security, some are now working extraordinarily long hours, and further supplemental plans are under review.

The terrorist attacks of September 2001 have given official credibility to the use of wide-body civilian aircraft as weapons. However, no nuclear facility has been specifically designed to withstand such an attack. The NRC states that "previously...[it] had no reason to perform a detailed engineering analysis of the consequences of a deliberate attack on nuclear facilities by a large airliner," yet the idea of targeting reactors with jumbo jets was being pointed out over twenty years ago by critics who recalled the Christmas Day, 1974, hijacking of a jumbo jet by a man who threatened to crash it into the center of Rome. (The man was overpowered after making his threat.) It is likely that such extreme threats to nuclear-facility security were not considered prior to September 11 not because nobody had thought of them but because (a) they were thought to be highly improbable, and (b) the cost of rendering facilities attack-proof against them (e.g., by building them underground) would have made nuclear power too expensive to develop for civilian markets.

The NRC states that it is now analyzing the consequences of a aerial attack on a nuclear power plant and plans to upgrade its Design Basis Threat to include as many attackers as were involved in the attacks of September 2001. It is not known whether the new NRC standard, when announced, will include provisions for defending plants against jumbo jets used as weapons, either by shooting them down or hardening reactor facilities against massive impact and fire. It is also not known what security precautions the NRC will mandate for in-transit nuclear waste if the federally-owned deep-storage facility at Yucca Mountain, Nevada, begins to receive high-level waste shipments from around the country in 2010 as planned.

As of July 2002, at least 16 states had taken the precaution of requesting stockpiles of potassium iodide pills from the NRC. All persons, especially children, are vulnerable to thyroid cancer caused by even small quantities of radioactive iodine, a substance expected to be a major component of the fallout from any nuclear incident. If ingested in a timely way, potassium iodide saturates the thyroid gland with non-radioactive iodine and prevents it from absorbing lethal levels of radioactive isotopes.

Conclusion. The security of nuclear facilities of all kinds is under more intense scrutiny—both by defenders and by potential attackers—than ever before, and not only in the United States. Old security standards are now admitted to have been inadequate, but enhanced standards have not yet been officially defined and uniformly implemented.

The goal of security—both from nuclear weapons derived from power plants and other "peaceful" facilities, and from takeover of nuclear facilities by groups of well-armed attackers—remains urgent, but elusive. In January 2002, President George W. Bush announced that "diagrams of nuclear power plants" had been found among items captured from terrorist groups in Afghanistan.

■ **FURTHER READING:**

BOOKS:

Lovins, Amory B., and L. Hunter Lovins. *Brittle Power: Energy Strategy for National Security.* Andover, MA: Brick House Publishing, 1982.

———. *Energy/War: Breaking the Nuclear Link.* San Francisco: Friends of the Earth, 1980.

Ramberg, Bennett. *Nuclear Power Plants as Weapons for the Enemy: An Unrecognized Military Peril.* Berkeley, CA: University of California Press, 1984.

PERIODICALS:

Wald, Matthew L. "Guards at Nuclear Plants Say They Feel Swamped by a Deluge of Overtime." *New York Times.* October 20, 2002.

ELECTRONIC:

"States Mull Anti-Cancer Pill in Response to Terrorist Attack." National Council of State Legislatures. July, 2002. <http://www.ncsl.org/programs/health/anticancerpills.htm> (December 11, 2002).

"Nuclear Security—Before and After September 11." U.S. Nuclear Regulatory Commission. September 23, 2002. <http://www.nrc.gov/what-we-do/safeguards/response-911.html> (December 11, 2002).

SEE ALSO

Nuclear Regulatory Commission (NRC), United States Weapon-Grade Plutonium and Uranium, Tracking

Nuclear Proliferation.

SEE *Non-Proliferation and National Security, United States.*

Nuclear Reactors

■ LARRY GILMAN

Nuclear reactors are complex devices in which fissionable elements such as uranium, thorium, or plutonium are made to undergo a sustainable nuclear chain reaction.

Nuclear reactor at the Bhabha Atomic Research Center in Bombay, photographed in 1997, near the site of a unit that extracted plutonuim for use in India's 1974 nuclear tests. AP/WIDE WORLD PHOTOS.

This chain reaction releases energy in the form of radiation that (a) sustains the chain reaction; (b) transmutes (i.e., alters the nuclear characteristics of) nearby atoms, including the nuclear fuel itself; and (c) may be harvested as heat. Transmutation in nuclear reactors of the common but weakly fissionable nuclide uranium-238 (^{238}U) into plutonium-239 (^{239}Pu) is an important source of explosive material for nuclear weapons, and heat from nuclear reactors is used to generate approximately 16 percent of the world's electricity and to propel submarines, aircraft carriers, and some other military vessels. Nuclear reactors have also been used on satellites and proposed as power sources for locomotives, aircraft, and rockets.

How a nuclear reactor works. A nuclear reactor exploits the innate instability of some atoms—in general, those that have a large atomic number or that contain an imbalance of protons and neutrons—which break apart (fission) at random times, releasing photons, neutrons, electrons, and alpha particles. For some nuclides (atomic species having a specific number of protons and neutrons in the nucleus), the average wait until a given atom spontaneously fissions is shorter. When enough atoms of such an unstable isotope are packed close together, the neutrons released by fissioning atoms are more likely to strike the nuclei of nearby unstable atoms. These may fission at once, releasing still more neutrons, which may trigger still other fission events, and so forth. This is the chain reaction on which nuclear reactors and fission-type nuclear bombs depend. In a reactor, however, the fission rate is approximately constant, whereas in a bomb it grows exponentially, consuming most of the fissionable material in a small fraction of a second.

To produce a sustained chain reaction rather than a nuclear explosion, a reactor must not pack its fissionable atoms too closely together. They are therefore mixed with less-fissionable atoms that do not sustain the chain reaction. For example, in a reactor utilizing ^{235}U as its primary fuel, only 3 percent of the fuel is actually ^{235}U; the rest is mostly ^{238}U, a much less fissionable isotope of uranium. The higher the ratio of active fuel atoms to inert atoms in a given fuel mix, the more "enriched" the fuel is said to be; commercial nuclear power plant fuel is enriched only 3 to 5 percent ^{235}U, and so cannot explode. For a fission bomb, 90 percent enrichment would be typical (although bombs could be made with less-enriched uranium). Naval nuclear reactors, discussed further below, have used fuels enriched to between 20 and 93 percent.

Having diluted its active fuel component (e.g., ^{235}U), a typical nuclear reactor must compensate by assuring that the neutrons produced by this diluted fuel can keep the chain reaction going. This is done, in most reactors, by embedding the fuel as small chunks or "fuel elements" in a matrix of a material termed a "moderator." The moderator's function is to slow (moderate) neutrons emitted by fissioning atoms in the fuel. Paradoxically, a slow neutron is more likely to trigger fission in a uranium, plutonium, or thorium nucleus than a fast neutron; a moderator, by slowing most neutrons before allowing them to strike nuclei, thus increases the probability that each neutron will contribute to sustaining the chain reaction. Graphite (a form of pure carbon), water, heavy water (deuterium dioxide or ^{2}H$_2$O), and zirconium hydride can all be used as moderators. Ordinary water is the most commonly used moderator.

If the chain reaction sustained by a nuclear reactor produces enough heat to damage the reactor itself, that heat must be carried off constantly by a gas or liquid as long as the reactor is operating. Once removed from the reactor, this energy may be ejected into the environment as waste heat or used, in part, to generate electricity. (Electricity, if generated, is an intermediate energy form; all the energy generated in a nuclear reactor or other power plant eventually winds up in the environment as heat.) In the case of a nuclear-powered rocket, such as the one the U.S. National Aeronautics and Space Administration (NASA) seeks to develop with its Project Phoenix, heat is removed from the system by ejected propellant. Liquid sodium, pressurized water, boiling water, and helium have all been used as cooling media for nuclear reactors, with pressurized or boiling water being used by commercial nuclear power plants. Typically, heat energy

removed from the reactor is first turned into kinetic energy by using hot gas or water vapor to drive turbines (essentially enclosed, high-speed windmills), then into electrical energy by using the turbines to turn generators.

Nuclear power sources that do not produce enough heat to melt themselves, and which therefore require no circulating coolant, have been used on some space probes and satellites, both U.S. and Russian. Such a power source, termed a radioactive thermoelectric generator or RTG, consists of a mass of highly radioactive material, usually plutonium, that radiates enough heat to allow the generation of a modest but steady flow of electricity via the thermoelectric effect. The efficiency of an RTG is low but its reliability is very high.

Reactor byproducts.
The neutron flow inside a reactor bombards, and by bombarding changes, the nuclei of many atoms in the reactor. The longer a unit of nuclear fuel remains in a reactor, therefore, the more altered nuclei it contains. Most of the new atoms formed are radioactive nuclides such as cesium-144 or ruthenium-106; a significant number are, if ^{238}U is present, isotopes of plutonium, mostly ^{239}Pu. (Absorption of one neutron by a ^{238}U nucleus turns it into a ^{239}Pu nucleus; absorption of one, two, or three neutrons by a ^{239}Pu nucleus turns it into a ^{240}Pu, ^{241}Pu, or ^{242}Pu nucleus.) Plutonium is found in nature only in trace amounts, but is present in all spent nuclear fuel containing ^{238}U. If it is extracted for use as a reactor fuel or a bomb material, it is considered a useful by-product of the nuclear reactor; otherwise, it is a waste product. In either case, plutonium is highly toxic and radioactive, and remains so for tens of thousands of years unless it is further transmuted by particle bombardment, as in a particle accelerator, reactor, or nuclear explosion. Reactors specially designed to turn otherwise inert ^{238}U into ^{239}Pu by neutron bombardment are termed fast breeder reactors, and can produce more nuclear fuel than they consume; however, all nuclear reactors, whether designed to "breed" or not, produce plutonium.

This fact has a basic military consequence: Every nation that possesses a nuclear power plant produces plutonium, which can be used to build atomic bombs. Plutonium sufficiently pure to be used in a bomb is termed bomb-grade or weapons-grade plutonium, and the process of extracting plutonium from irradiated nuclear fuel is termed reprocessing. (The alloy used in sophisticated nuclear weapons is nearly pure plutonium, but the U.S. Department of Energy has estimated that an unwieldy bomb could be made with material that is only 15 to 25 percent plutonium, with less-unwieldy bombs being possible with more-enriched alloys.) Every nation that possesses a nuclear reactor and reprocessing capability thus possesses most of what it needs to build nuclear weapons. Several nations, including India and Pakistan, have in fact built nuclear weapons using plutonium reprocessed from "peaceful" nuclear-reactor programs. A large (100 MW electric) nuclear power plant produces enough plutonium for several dozen bombs a year.

Besides producing plutonium that can, and sometimes is, extracted to produce nuclear weapons, every nuclear reactor has the feature that if bombed, its radioactive contents could be released into the environment, greatly amplifying the destructive effects of a wartime or terrorist attack. Nuclear reactors thus have a two-edged aspect: as producers, potentially, of weapons for use *against* an enemy, and as weapons, if attacked, *for* an enemy.

Naval nuclear reactors. The primary military use of nuclear reactors, apart from the production of material for nuclear weapons, is the propulsion of naval vessels. Nuclear power sources enable naval vessels to remain at sea for long periods without refueling; modern replacement cores for aircraft carriers are designed to last at least 50 years without refueling, while those for submarines are designed to last 30 to 40 years. In the case of submarines, nuclear power also makes it possible to remain submerged for months at a time without having to surface for oxygen. Furthermore, reactors have the general design advantage of high power density, that is, they provide high power output while consuming relatively little shipboard space. A large nuclear-powered vessel may be propelled by more than one reactor; the U.S. aircraft carrier USS *Enterprise*, launched in 1960, is powered by eight reactors. Britain, France, China, and Russia (formerly the Soviet Union) have also built nuclear-powered submarines and other vessels.

Although the design details of the nuclear reactors used on submarines and aircraft carriers are secret, they are known to differ in several ways from the large land-based reactors typically used for generating electricity. The primary difference is that in order to achieve high power density, naval reactors use more-highly-enriched fuel. Older designs used uranium enriched to at least 93 percent ^{235}U; later Western reactors have used uranium enriched to only 20 to 25 percent, while Russian reactors have used fuels enriched to up to 45 percent. Small quantities of ex-Soviet submarine fuel have appeared on the global black market; larger quantities could be used as a bomb material.

The first nuclear-powered vessel, was a U.S. submarine launched in 1955, the USS *Nautilus*. Only three civil vessels (one U.S.-made, one German, and one Japanese) have ever been propelled by nuclear power; all proved too expensive to operate. About 160 nuclear-powered ships, mostly military, are presently at sea; at the peak of the Cold War, there were approximately 250.

■ **FURTHER READING:**

BOOKS:

Glasstone, Samuel, and Alexander Sesonske. *Nuclear Reactor Engineering. Vol. I: Reactor Design Basics.* New York: Chapman & Hall, 1994.

Todreas, Neil E., and Mujid S. Kazimi. *Nuclear Systems I: Thermal Hydraulic Fundamentals.* New York: Hemisphere Publishing Corporation, 1990.

SEE ALSO

Nuclear Detection Devices
Nuclear Emergency Support Team, United States
Nuclear Power Plants, Security
Russian Nuclear Materials, Security Issues

Nuclear Regulatory Commission (NRC), United States

Established by the Energy Reorganization Act of 1974, the Nuclear Regulatory Commission (NRC) is an independent agency of the federal government tasked with regulating civilian use of nuclear materials. It deals with spent nuclear reactors, radioactive waste, and nuclear and source material, including thorium and isotopes of uranium. Among the important events of the NRC's early history was its handling of the Three Mile Island nuclear incident in 1979. Following the September 11, 2001, terrorist attacks, NRC officials were forced to contemplate the scenario of a similar terrorist attack upon a nuclear power plant.

Organization and Responsibilities

The NRC is directed by a five-member commission, one of whose members is designated by the president of the United States as chairman and official spokesperson. The commission formulates policies and regulations regarding the safety of nuclear reactors and materials, issues orders to licensees, and adjudicates legal matters on nuclear power that are brought to its attention.

Answering to the commission is the executive director for operations (EDO), who carries out its policies and decisions, and oversees a number of offices. In addition to bureaus designated according to area of responsibility, the NRC has four regional offices, in the Atlanta, Philadelphia, Chicago, and Dallas areas. These oversee inspection, enforcement, and emergency response programs for licensees within their respective quadrants of the nation.

Among the other NRC offices, which collectively work to ensure the safe commercial use of nuclear power, are the offices of nuclear regulatory research, state and tribal programs, investigation, enforcement, and nuclear security and incident response. The last of these includes divisions for nuclear security, threat assessment, reactor

Workers man the control room of the Davis-Besse Nuclear Station in Oak Harbor, Ohio. The Nuclear Regulatory Commission, after an examination of the facility, concluded that no radiation was released after the plant took a direct blow from a tornado in 1998. AP/WIDE WORLD PHOTOS.

safeguards, materials safeguards, information security, and incident response.

Overseeing plants, materials, and waste.

Two offices are together responsible for the actual oversight of nuclear materials and the plants that produce them. The Office of Nuclear Material Safety and Safeguards oversees nuclear waste and radioactive materials, while the Office of Nuclear Reactor Regulation is concerned with reactors.

Nuclear materials are divided into three types, all of which pose potential health and environmental hazards if not handled properly. Source material includes natural uranium and thorium, as well as depleted uranium. Byproduct material is nuclear material that has been made radioactive in a nuclear reactor, as well as tailings and waste produced by the extraction or concentration of uranium or thorium. A third variety of nuclear material poses an additional hazard, one of security. This category is known as special nuclear material, including uranium-233 and uranium-235, enriched uranium, and plutonium—any of which could be used in a nuclear device.

Regulated waste is also divided into three categories: low-level waste, including radioactively contaminated protective clothing, tools, and other materials; high-level waste, or used nuclear fuel; and uranium mill tailings, or the residues remaining in natural ore after uranium and thorium have been extracted. As with the handling of nuclear materials, the Office of Nuclear Material Safety and Safeguards provides strict guidelines regarding the storage and disposal of these waste products.

Reactors regulated by the Office of Nuclear Reactor Regulation fall into two categories: power reactors, or commercial reactors used to generate electric power, and non-power reactors, or reactors used in research, testing, and training. Among the areas of responsibility for the office are reactor decommissioning, operator licensing, and new reactor licensing.

History of the NRC

Prior to the advent of the NRC, the Atomic Energy Commission (AEC), established by Congress with the Atomic Energy Act of 1946, regulated nuclear energy. The Atomic Energy Act of 1954, which superseded its predecessor, legalized the development of commercial nuclear power for the first time in history. Among the provisions of the act was the assignment to the AEC of various functions relating to nuclear power production, including promotion of nuclear power and regulation of safety.

By the 1960s, the AEC had come under criticism for what many regarded as its failure to exercise sufficient rigor in a number of areas, including reactor safety, environmental protection, and standards for radiation protection. In 1974, Congress abolished the AEC with the Energy Reorganization Act, which in turn replaced it with the Energy Research and Development Administration (established as the Department of Energy in 1977) and the NRC.

Concerns over nuclear power.

As the NRC began operations on January 19, 1975, public sentiment against nuclear power was on the rise. The dissemination to mainstream society of environmentalist and anti-industrial ideas prevalent in the 1960s was a factor, as was lack of public understanding regarding the means by which nuclear power was generated and handled. Real bases for concerns existed, particularly with the dramatic increase in the size and number of nuclear plants that occurred during the late 1960s and early 1970s. Then, on March 28, 1979, an accident at the Three Mile Island plant outside Harrisburg, Pennsylvania caused half the reactor's core to melt.

In 1979, the modern system of around-the-clock news reporting via cable channels still lay many years in the future, yet for a few days in the spring of 1979, America followed the Three Mile Island catastrophe through regular news reports. No one died at Three Mile Island, and thanks in part to the NRC's efforts, the federal government dealt with the situation effectively. In the aftermath of Three Mile Island, the NRC placed a much greater emphasis on training of plant operators, studying plant histories for signs of vulnerability, and guarding against the failure of equipment.

During the 1970s, the rise of international terrorism, as well as the proliferation of nations hostile to the United States, spurred NRC leadership to take measures toward the protection of nuclear materials from theft or sabotage. Yet, in the aftermath of the September 2001, terrorist attacks, many critics maintained that power plants were vulnerable, and that the NRC was not taking appropriate measures to address the problem.

Given the destruction wreaked by the planes that flew into the World Trade Center and Pentagon, the September 11 attacks raised real fears concerning the vulnerability of nuclear plants. Questioned about the likelihood of damage from such an attack, an NRC spokesperson initially stated that these facilities could withstand an attack by a jet, but later admitted that "nuclear power plants were not designed to withstand such crashes."

■ FURTHER READING:

BOOKS:

Walker, J. Samuel, and George T. Mazuzan. *Containing the Atom: Nuclear Regulation in a Changing Environment, 1963–1971.* Berkeley: University of California Press, 1992.

———. *Permissible Dose: A History of Radiation Protection in the Twentieth Century.* Berkeley: University of California Press, 2000.

PERIODICALS:

Hirsch, Daniel. "The NRC: What, Me Worry?" *Bulletin of the Atomic Scientists* 58, no. 1 (January/February 2002): 38–44.

Swanekamp, Robert. "Nuclear Renaissance Converges on Life Extension and Upgrades." *ENR* 247, no. 23 (December 3, 2001): PC54.

ELECTRONIC:

U.S. Nuclear Regulatory Commission. <http://www.nrc.gov/> (April 15, 2003).

SEE ALSO

Chernobyl Nuclear Power Plant Accident, Detection and Monitoring
DOE (United States Department of Energy)
EPA (Environmental Protection Agency)
International Atomic Energy Agency (IAEA)
NNSA (United States National Nuclear Security Administration)
Nuclear Power Plants, Security
Nuclear Reactors

Nuclear Spectroscopy

■ K. LEE LERNER

Nuclear spectroscopy is a powerful tool in the arsenal of scientists and forensic investigators because it allows detailed study of the structure of matter based upon the reactions that take place in excited atomic nuclei. It is a widely used technique to determine the composition of substances because it is more sensitive than other spectroscopic methods and can detect the trace presence of elements in an unknown substance that may only be present on the order of parts per billion. Nuclear spectroscopic analysis techniques provided forensic investigators with evidence that linked several of what were eventually to be known as the Washington area "sniper shootings" in late 2002.

Basic principles.

A number of methods can be used to excite atomic nuclei and then measure their decaying gamma ray emissions as the atoms return to normal energy levels (i.e., their ground state). The emissions are then analyzed and separated into an emission spectrum that is characteristic for each element. Excitation can be accomplished by colliding nuclei, heavy ion beams, and a number of other methods, but the fundamental purpose remains to measure the spectral properties of a sample as a tool to learn something about the quantum structure of the atoms in the sample.

Like other forms of spectroscopy, the fundamental measurements of nuclear spectroscopy involve recording the emission or absorption of photons by atoms. The specific emissions or absorptions reflect the energy levels, spin states, parity, and other properties of an atom's structure (e.g., quantized energy levels). A qualitative analysis identifies the components of a substance or mixture. Quantitative analysis, on the other hand, measures the amounts or proportions of those components. Because each element—and each nuclide (i.e., an atomic nucleus with a unique combination of protons and neutrons)—emits or absorbs only specific frequencies and wavelengths of electromagnetic radiation, nuclear spectroscopy is a qualitative test (i.e., a test designed to identify the components of a substance or mixture) to determine the presence of an element or isotope in an unknown sample.

In addition, the strength of emission and absorption for each element and nuclide can allow for a quantitative measurement of the amount or proportion of the element in an unknown. To perform quantitative tests, that is, to measure amounts of an element present, the measured spectrum needs to be narrowed down to analysis of photons with specific energies (i.e., electromagnetic radiation of a specific wavelength or frequency). Quantitative computation using Beer's Law is then applied to the measured intensities of photon emission or absorption. Many other spectroscopic methods use this technique (e.g., atomic absorption spectroscopy and UV-visible light spectroscopy) to determine the amount of a element present.

Nuclear activation analysis.

One of most widely used methods of nuclear spectroscopy used to determine the elemental composition of substances is Nuclear activation analysis (NAA). In this type of analysis the goal is to determine the composition of an unknown substance by measuring the energies and intensities of the gamma rays emitted after excitation and the subsequent matching of those measurements to the emissions of gamma rays from standardized (known) samples. In this regard, neutron activation analysis is similar to other spectroscopic measurements that utilize other portions of the electromagnetic spectrum. Infrared photons, x-ray florescence, and spectral analysis of visible light are all used to identify elements and compounds. In each of these spectroscopic methods, a measurement of electromagnetic radiation is compared with some known quantum characteristic of an atomic nucleus, atom, or molecule. With NAA, of course, high-energy gamma-ray photons are measured.

Neutron activation analysis involves a comparison of measurements from an unknown sample with values obtained from tests with known samples. Depending on which elements are being tested for, the samples are irradiated with energetic neutrons. The process of radioactivity results in the emission of products of nuclear reactions (in this case, gamma rays) that are measurable by instruments designed for that purpose. After a time (dependent on the duration of radiation) the gamma rays are counted by gamma ray sensitive spectrometers. Because the products of the nuclear reactions are characteristic of the elements present in the sample and a measure of the amounts present, neutron activation analysis is both a qualitative and quantitative tool. Although NAA usually involves the measurement of gamma rays emitted from the radioactive sample, more complex techniques also measure beta and positron emissions.

Nuclear magnetic resonance.

Nuclear magnetic resonance (NMR) is another form of nuclear spectroscopy that is widely used in medicine and in forensic analysis. NMR is based on the fact that a proton in a magnetic field has two quantized spin states. The actual magnetic field experienced by most protons is, however, slightly different from the external applied field because neighboring atoms serve to alter it. As a result, a picture of complex structures of molecules and compounds can be obtained by measuring differences between the expected and measured photons absorbed. NMR spectroscopy is an important tool used to determine the structure of organic molecules.

When a group of nuclei are brought into resonance—that is, when they are absorbing and emitting photons of similar energy (electromagnetic radiation, e.g., radio waves, of similar wavelengths)—and then small changes are made in the photon energy, the resonance must change. How quickly and to what form the resonance changes allows for the non-destructive (because of the use of low-energy photons) determination of complex structures. This form of NMR is used by physicians as the physical and chemical basis of a powerful diagnostic technique termed Magnetic Resonance Imaging (MRI). MRI can also be used for non-invasive examinations for concealed substances or implanted objects.

■ FURTHER READING:

BOOKS:

deGraaf, R. *In Vivo NMR Spectroscopy: Principles and Techniques.* New York: John Wiley & Sons, 1999.

SEE ALSO

Electromagnetic Spectrum
Scanning Technologies

Nuclear Waste.

SEE *Weapon-Grade Plutonium and Uranium, Tracking.*

A Minuteman III intercontinental ballistic missile engine is loaded into a truck in 2000 for transport to another building for refurbishment at Hill Air Force Base in Utah. AP/WIDE WORLD PHOTOS.

Nuclear Weapons

■ LARRY GILMAN/K. LEE LERNER/
DEAN ALLEN HAYCOCK

Nuclear weapons are explosive devices that utilize the processes of fission and fusion to release nuclear energy. An individual nuclear device may have an explosive force equivalent to millions of tons (megatons) of trinitrotoluene (TNT, the chemical explosive traditionally used for such comparisons), more than enough to completely destroy a large city. The destructive power of nuclear weapons derives from the core of the atom, the nucleus. One type of nuclear weapon, the fission bomb, uses the energy released when nuclei of heavy elements, such as plutonium, fission or split apart. A second even more powerful type of nuclear weapon, the fusion or hydrogen bomb, uses the energy released when nuclei of hydrogen are forced to fuse (join together).

Nuclear devices have been fashioned into weapons of many shapes with many purposes. Bombs can be dropped from airplanes; warheads can be delivered by missiles launched from land, air, or sea; artillery shells can be fired from cannons; mines can be placed on the land and in the sea. Some nuclear weapons are small enough to destroy only a portion of a battlefield; others, as already mentioned, are large enough to destroy entire cities and more.

Unlike chemical explosives, nuclear weapons have had no peacetime uses, although in the 1950s the U.S. government briefly considered using them to blast artificial harbors in the Alaskan coastline. They are possessed by a number of nations, including the United States, France, Great Britain, China, India, Israel, Pakistan, and the Russian Federation along with several former Soviet Republics. Iran and North Korea, among other nations, are interested in building them. Since nuclear weapons were invented during World War II, they have been used only twice, both times against cities in Japan by the United States.

Development of nuclear weapons. German physicist Albert Einstein (1879–1955) did not know it at the time, but when he published his Special Theory of Relativity in 1905 he provided the world with the basic information needed to build nuclear weapons. Einstein said that the amount of matter of an object (i.e., its mass) is equivalent to a specific amount of energy. The exact amount of energy in an object equals its mass multiplied by the square of the speed of light. The speed of light is large—186,282 miles per second (300,000 km/sec)—so even a small piece of matter contains a vast amount of energy. A baseball-size sample of uranium-235, for example, can explode with as much energy as 20,000 tons of TNT—and this involves the conversion of only a tiny fraction of the uranium's mass into energy. One pound of explosive material in a fission weapon is approximately 100,000 times as powerful as one pound of TNT.

As World War II approached, two German chemists, Fritz Strassmann (1902–1980) and Otto Hahn (1879–1968), pointed a stream of neutrons at a sample of uranium and succeeded in splitting the nuclei of some of its atoms. This splitting of nuclei is termed nuclear fission. The energy released through nuclear fission was the source of power for the first atomic bomb, which was built in the United States by a large team of scientists led by U.S. physicist J. Oppenheimer (1904–1967). This secret research and development program was termed the Manhattan Project.

The first atomic bomb was detonated in a test at Alamogordo, New Mexico, on July 16, 1945. Three weeks later, on August 6, a bomber named *Enola Gay* dropped a four-ton atomic bomb containing 12 lb (5.4 kg) of uranium-235 on the Japanese city of Hiroshima. Seventy thousand people died as a direct result of the blast. Within two months, nearly twice that many were dead from blast injuries and radiation. Three days later, on August 9, a bomb containing several pounds of plutonium was dropped on Nagasaki. Thirty thousand people died in the seconds following the explosion, and more later. The Japanese surrendered the next day, ending World War II.

These first nuclear weapons were atomic bombs or A-bombs. They depended on the energy produced by nuclear fission for their destructive power. However, scientists like U.S. physicist Edward Teller (1908–) knew even before the first atomic bomb exploded that the fission weapons could be used to create an even more powerful explosive, now called a thermonuclear device, hydrogen bomb, or H-bomb. This weapon gets it power from the energy released when atoms of the hydrogen isotopes deuterium or tritium are forced together, a process called nuclear fusion. Starting a nuclear fusion reaction is even more complicated than setting off a fission atomic bomb; it requires such heat to initiate it that a fission bomb is used as a detonator to explode the fusion bomb. The United States tested the first hydrogen bomb on November 1, 1952. It exploded with the force of 10.4 megatons (millions of tons of TNT equivalent). Three years later, the Soviet Union exploded a similar device.

For the next 40 years, the United States, with its allies, and the former Soviet Union, with its allies, raced to build more nuclear weapons, with each side producing tens of thousands. The end of the cold war and the breakup of the Soviet Union in the early 1990s led to the elimination of a significant number of nuclear weapons; however, the U.S. and Russia still possess many thousands of nuclear weapons.

The physics and mechanics of nuclear weapons.

Conventional, chemical explosives get their power from the rapid rearrangement of chemical bonds, the links between atoms made by sharing electrons. In chemical explosives, atoms dissociate from other atoms and form new associations; this releases energy, but the atoms themselves do not change. Nuclear weapons are based on an entirely different principle. They derive their explosive power from changes in the structure of the atom itself, specifically, in the core of the atom, its nucleus.

Atomic bombs use the energy released when nuclei of heavy elements split apart or fission. Uranium and plutonium are the two elements that can be used as fuel for this type of weapon. When nuclei of these atoms are struck with rapidly moving neutrons, they are broken into two pieces nearly equal in size. They also release more neutrons, which split more nuclei. This is called a chain reaction. If enough atomic nuclei split they will release enough neutrons to ensure that all the nuclei of all the atoms in a sample will be split. Enormous amounts of energy are then released in a fraction of a second. This release of energy is the power behind the atomic bomb.

Uranium and plutonium are termed fissile materials because they can support a fission chain reaction if enough material is concentrated in one place. Too small a sample would not generate enough neutrons to keep the fission process going; for example, a one-pound (.45-kg) sample of uranium-235, a sample about the size of a ping-pong ball, is not large enough to support a chain reaction. The atomic bombs used in World War II proved that 12 or so pounds (about 5.5 kg) of fissile material, larger than a ping-pong ball but still small enough to fit into your hand, is enough to maintain a chain reaction. The smallest amount of material that can support a chain reaction is called the critical mass.

The instant enough bomb material is gathered together into a critical mass, a chain reaction begins. (At higher density, less mass is required.) This means that fissile material cannot be assembled in a critical mass until it is meant to explode. Therefore, the sample of uranium or plutonium in an atomic bomb is separated into several pieces, each of which is below critical mass. To set the bomb off, the separated pieces of bomb material are rammed together to create a critical mass. One design for creating a critical mass involves firing a subcritical "bullet" of fissile material into a subcritical "target" of fissile material. Together, the bullet and the target create a critical mass that starts a chain reaction leading to a nuclear explosion.

A different design was used to detonate the bomb dropped on Nagasaki. Plutonium was stored in one large but subcritical mass. It was compressed to a critical density by means of surrounding chemical explosives. When the chemical explosive detonated, the blast forced the bomb material into a density that reached criticality. In either type of design, once criticality is reached the explosion follows in a millionth of a second.

In order for nuclear fission to occur, a bomb must use heavy atoms for fuel. Heavy atoms have many nucleons—neutrons and protons—in their nuclei. When these heavy nuclei split apart they release energy (and neutrons, which may cause nearby heavy nuclei to split apart also). Another more powerful type of nuclear weapon uses forms of hydrogen as fuel. Hydrogen has few subatomic particles in its nuclei—usually only a proton, but the isotope deuterium has a proton plus a neutron, while the isotope tritium has a proton plus two neutrons. Instead of being split apart, these light atomic nuclei are forced together in high-speed collisions, a process called nuclear fusion. Energy is released when hydrogen nuclei fuse, forming helium. Fusion only occurs at temperatures of millions of degrees, such as exist in the hearts of stars. (The sun and other stars generate their energy primarily by fusing hydrogen into helium.) On Earth only an atomic bomb can raise kilograms of material to such a temperature, which is why atomic bombs are used as detonators for hydrogen fusion bombs.

Because hydrogen is lighter than uranium, more hydrogen atoms fit into a sample of the same weight. Thus, even though one fusion reaction releases less energy than one fission reaction, more hydrogen than uranium atoms can be packed into a nuclear weapon and many more fusion reactions can take place in the weapon than fission reactions can take place in a fission bomb. Fusion weapons, therefore, produce bigger explosions than fission weapons of the same physical bulk.

By 1954, a new feature had been added to the hydrogen bomb to create an even more dangerous weapon. Like earlier hydrogen bombs, this weapon was detonated with the explosion of an atomic or fission weapon. This raised temperatures enough to cause the hydrogen atoms in the bomb to fuse and explode like a regular hydrogen bomb. The designers also enclosed this new bomb in a shell of uranium-238. Neutrons released from the fusion of hydrogen caused the uranium-238 in the surrounding jacket to undergo fission, adding to the power of the blast. This new device was, in effect, a fission-fusion-fission bomb.

The power or "yield" of a nuclear weapon is expressed in terms of how much TNT would be required to equal the weapon's blast. Units of kilotons (thousands of tons) and megatons (millions of tons) of TNT are used to describe nuclear blasts.

Effects of nuclear weapons.
Nuclear weapons produce two important effects that are also produced by conventional, chemical explosives: they release heat and generate shock waves, or pressure fronts of compressed air that smash objects in their paths. The heat released in a nuclear explosion creates a sphere of burning, glowing gas that can range from hundreds of feet to miles in diameter, depending on the power of the bomb. This fireball emits a flash of heat that travels outward from the site of the explosion (ground zero), the area directly under the explosion. This heat can cause second degree burns to bare

human flesh miles away from the blast site if the bomb is large enough. (Although this heat can start fires, it seems that much of the fire damage in Hiroshima and Nagasaki following the nuclear explosions resulted from damaged electrical, fuel, gas, and other systems following physical damage caused by the shock or blast wave that accompanied the explosion.)

The shock wave produced when a nuclear weapon explodes creates a front of moving air more powerful than any produced by a natural storm. Destructive winds follow the front of displaced air, causing more damage to objects in their path. Many nuclear weapons are designed to be detonated high above their targets to take advantage of this shock effect. The more powerful the bomb, the higher in the sky it will be detonated. The fission bombs dropped on Japan (Hiroshima, 13.5 kilotons; Nagasaki, 22 kilotons) exploded between 1,500 and 2,000 feet (458–610 m) above their targets. A bomb with the power of 10 megatons is capable of destroying most houses within a distance of more than 10 miles from the blast site.

Unlike conventional explosives, nuclear devices can also release significant amounts of radioactivity and pulses of electromagnetic energy. Radioactivity is the release of fast particles and high-energy photons from unstable atomic nuclei. Besides the greater explosive power of nuclear weapons, radiation is the primary feature that most clearly distinguishes chemical from nuclear explosions. Radiation can kill outright at high doses and cause illnesses, including cancer, at lower doses. The initial burst of radiation during a nuclear explosion is made up of X rays, gamma rays, and neutrons. The energy of this radiation is so high that it can often penetrate buildings. Radioactive materials then contaminate the explosion site and often enter the atmosphere where they can travel thousands of miles before falling back to earth. This source of radiation is called radioactive fallout. Radioactive fallout can harm living things for years following a nuclear explosion. Fission bombs and fission-fusion-fission bombs produce more fallout than hydrogen bombs because the fusion of hydrogen atoms generates less radioactive byproducts than does fission of uranium or plutonium.

Electromagnetic pulses (EMPs) are also produced by nuclear weapons that are exploded at high altitudes, and are caused by the interaction of radiation from the explosion with electrons in the atmosphere and with the Earth's magnetic field. EMPs are essentially powerful radio waves that can destroy many electronic circuits.

The effects of fires and destruction following a large-scale nuclear war could even change the climate of the planet. In 1983 a group of scientists, including U.S. astronomer Carl Sagan (1934–1996), published the "nuclear winter" theory, which suggested that particles of smoke and dust produced by fires caused by many nuclear explosions would, for a time, block the Sun's rays from reaching the surface of Earth. This, in turn, would reduce temperatures and change wind patterns and ocean currents. These climatic changes, according to the theory, could destroy crops and lead to the death by famine of many more animals and humans than were killed outright by nuclear explosions. Some scientists have challenged these predictions, but others, including some United States government agencies, support them. On the other hand, there is no controversy about whether a large-scale nuclear war could kill hundreds of millions of people and imperil the future of modern civilization, even apart from nuclear winter effects.

Modern nuclear weapons.
Today nuclear weapons are built in many sizes and shapes not available in the 1940s and 1950s, and are designed for use against many different types of military and civilian targets. Some weapons are less powerful than 1,000 tons of TNT, while others have the explosive force of millions of tons of TNT. Small nuclear shells can be fired from cannons. Nuclear warheads mounted on missiles can be launched from land-based silos, ships, submarines, trains, and large wheeled vehicles. Several warheads can be fitted into one missile and directed to different targets in the same geographic area upon reentry into the Earth's atmosphere. These multiple independently-targeted reentry vehicles (MIRVs) can release 10 or so individual nuclear warheads far above their targets, making enemy interception more difficult and increasing the deadliness of each individual missile.

In general, nuclear weapons with "low" yields (in the kiloton, rather than the megaton, range) are termed "tactical," and are designed to be used in battle situations against specific military targets, such as a concentration of enemy troops or tanks, a naval vessel, or the like. These weapons are termed tactical because the word tactics, in military jargon, refers to the relatively small-scale maneuvers undertaken to win particular battles. Larger nuclear weapons are classed as "strategic," because the word strategy, again in military jargon, refers to the large-scale maneuvers undertaken to win whole wars. Strategic nuclear weapons are targeted mostly at cities and at other nuclear weapons, and are generally designed to be dropped by bombers or launched on ballistic missiles; tactical nuclear weapons are delivered by smaller devices over shorter distances. However, one nation's "tactical" warhead may be another's "strategic" warhead: Russia, for example, maintains that U.S. tactical warheads in Western Europe are in fact strategic warheads, because they can strike targets inside Russia itself, while Russian "tactical" warheads in the same arena cannot strike the U.S. heartland.

In the summer of 2002, the George W. Bush administration sought and received permission from Congress to design a new class of nuclear weapons: "mini-nukes" are relatively low-yield tactical nuclear weapons for use against underground bunkers and other small battlefield targets. Also in 2002, the U.S. military—according to a secret Pentagon document leaked to the press—drew up an official set of contingency plans for attacking seven countries with nuclear weapons (China, Russia, Iraq, North Korea, Iran, Libya and Syria). Advocates of these new weapons point to the uniquely powerful, compact "punch" that can be delivered by a nuclear weapon; critics argue

that even a small nuclear weapon may cause many civilian casualties, and, more important, that actual use of a nuclear weapon of any size would break the taboo on such use that has held since the end of World War II, making the use of larger, more destructive nuclear weapons more likely in future conflicts. Some analysts stressed that the Pentagon's explicit willingness to use nuclear weapons in a "first-use" fashion, that is, in response to "unexpected military situations" not involving attack on U.S. forces by nuclear weapons, or to use them on targets (e.g., deep bunkers) resistant to conventional explosives signaled a major shift in United States nuclear use doctrine.

Even the ability of nuclear weapons to release radioactivity has been exploited to create different types of weapons. "Clean bombs" are weapons designed to produce as little radioactive fallout as possible. A hydrogen bomb without a uranium jacket would produce relatively little radioactive contamination, for example. A "dirty bomb" could just as easily be built, using materials that contribute to radioactive fallout. Such weapons could also be detonated near Earth's surface to increase the amount of material that could contribute to radioactive fallout. "Neutron" bombs have been designed to shower battle fields with deadly neutrons that can penetrate buildings and armored vehicles without destroying them. Any people exposed to the neutrons, however, would die. (Neutron bombs also destroy with blast effects, but their deadly radiation zones extend far beyond the site of their explosions).

The United States and Russia signed a Strategic Arms Reduction Treaty in 1993 to eliminate two thirds of their nuclear warheads in 10 years. By 1995, nearly 2,500 nuclear warheads had been removed from bombers and missiles in the two countries, according to U.S. government officials. ("Elimination," in this context, does not necessarily mean dismantlement; many of the weapons that have been "eliminated" by the treaty have been put in storage.) Although thousands of nuclear weapons still remain in the hands of many different governments, especially those of the U.S. and the Russian Federation, recent diplomatic trends have at least helped to lower the number of nuclear weapons in the world. This has caused many people to assume that the danger of nuclear weapons evaporated with the end of the Cold War.

However, the number of nations possessing nuclear weapons continues to increase, and the possibility of nuclear weapons being used against human beings for the first time since World War II may be larger than ever. In May 1995, more than 170 members of the United Nations agreed to permanently extend the Nuclear Non-Proliferation Treaty, first signed in 1960. Under the terms of the treaty, the five major countries with nuclear weapons—the United States, Britain, France, Russia, and China—agreed to commit themselves to eliminating their arsenals as an "ultimate" goal. The other 165 signatory nations agree not to acquire nuclear weapons. Israel, which is believed to possess nuclear weapons (but officially denies doing so), did not sign the treaty. Two other nuclear powers also refused to renounce nuclear weapons: India and Pakistan, each of which probably possess several dozen nuclear weapons, have fought a number of border wars in recent decades, and in 2002 came close, as many observers thought, to fighting a nuclear war. As of 2003, North Korea had reactivated its nuclear-weapons-material production facilities and was engaged in a tense diplomatic standoff with the United States, which insisted that North Korea abandon its nuclear-weapons program.

■ FURTHER READING:

BOOKS:

Rhodes, Richard. *Dark Sun: The Making of the Hydrogen Bomb (Sloan Technology Series).* New York: Simon & Schuster, 1995.

Sagan, Scott D. and Kenneth N. Waltz. *The Spread of Nuclear Weapons: A Debate Renewed,* 2nd ed. W. W. Norton & Co., 2003.

Walmer, Max. *An Illustrated Guide to Strategic Weapons.* New York: Prentice Hall Press, 1988.

ELECTRONIC

"U.S. Has Nuclear Hit List." BBC News. March 2, 2002. <http://news.bbc.co.uk/2/hi/americas/1864173.stm> (Feb. 26, 2003).

SEE ALSO

Arms Control, United States Bureau
Iranian Nuclear Programs
Manhattan Project
North Korean Nuclear Weapons Programs
Nuclear Detection Devices
Russian Nuclear Materials, Security Issues
World War II

Nuclear Winter

■ AGNES GALAMBOSI

Nuclear winter is a meteorological theory estimating the global climatic consequences of a nuclear war—or a natural disaster such as a major asteroid impact—that injects large amounts or dust or water vapor into the atmosphere. Nuclear winter models predict prolonged and worldwide cooling and darkening caused by the blockage of sunlight.

During the Cold War, concern about the use of nuclear weapons initially concentrated on initial blast damage and the dangers of radioactive fallout. Subsequently, researchers began to explore the possible environmental effects of nuclear war. The term nuclear winter was first defined and used by American astronomer Carl Sagan (1934–1996) and his group of colleagues in their 1983 article (later referred to as the TTAPS-article, from the initials of the authors' family names). This article was the first one to take into consideration not only the direct damage, but also the indirect effects of a nuclear war.

During a nuclear war, the exploding nuclear warheads would create huge fires, resulting in smoke and soot from burning cities and forests being emitted into the troposphere in vast amounts. According to nuclear winter theory, this would block the Sun's incoming radiation from reaching the surface of Earth, causing cooling of the surface temperatures. The smoke and soot soon would rise to high altitude because of their high temperature and drift there for weeks without being washed out. Finally, the particles would settle in the Northern Hemisphere mid-latitudes as a black particle cloud belt, blocking sunshine for several weeks.

The ensuing darkness and cold, combined with nuclear fallout radiation, would kill most of Earth's vegetation and animal life, which would lead to starvation and diseases for the human population surviving the nuclear war itself. At the same time, because the smoke would absorb sunlight, the upper troposphere temperatures would rise and create a temperature inversion causing further retention of smog at the lower levels. Another predicted consequence is that nuclear explosions would produce nitrogen oxides that would damage the protective ozone layer in the stratosphere and allow more ultraviolet radiation to reach Earth's surface.

Although the basic findings of the original TTAPS-article have been confirmed by later reports and sophisticated computer modeling, some later studies report a lesser degree of cooling that would last for weeks instead of the initially estimated months. In the extreme, however, depending on the number of nuclear explosions, their spatial distribution, targets, and many other factors, a cloud of soot and dust could remain for many months, reducing sunlight almost entirely and decreasing average temperatures to well below freezing over a majority of the densely inhabited areas of the Northern Hemisphere.

The nuclear winter scenario remains scientifically controversial because the exact level of atmospheric damage, along with the extent and duration of subsequent processes cannot be agreed upon with full confidence. Opponents of the nuclear winter theory argue that there are many problems with the hypothesized scenarios either because of the model's incorrect assumptions (e.g., the results would be right only if exactly the assumed amount of dust would enter the atmosphere, or because the model assumes uniformly distributed, constantly injected particles). Other critics of the nuclear winter scenario point out that the models used often do not include processes and/or feedback mechanisms that may moderate or mitigate the initial effects of nuclear blasts on the atmosphere (e.g., the moderating effects of the oceans). In contrast to nuclear winter models, some climate models actually postulate a "nuclear summer," resulting from a worldwide warming caused by many small contributions to the greenhouse effect from carbon dioxide, water vapor, ozone, and various aerosols entering the troposphere and stratosphere.

What all scenarios and models forecast, however, is that a nuclear war would have a significant effect on the atmosphere and climate of Earth. This in turn would drastically and negatively affect many aspects of life such as food production and energy consumption.

■ FURTHER READING:

BOOKS:

International Seminar on Nuclear War and Planetary Emergencies, 20th Session: The Role of Science in the Third Millennium, Man-Made & Natural Disasters, Post-Berlin-Wall Problems-Nuclear Proliferation in the Multipolar World. Singapore: World Scientific Publishing, 1997.

Weinberger, Casper. "The Potential Effects of Nuclear War on the Climate." *Nuclear Winter, Joint Hearing before the Committee on Science and Technology and the Committee on Interior and Insular Affairs, U.S. House of Representatives.* Washington, D.C.: Government Printing Office, 1985.

PERIODICALS:

Ehrlich, Paul, et al., "Long-Term Biological Consequences of Nuclear War." *Science* 222, 4630 (1983).

Turco, R. P., O. B. Toon, T. P. Ackerman, J. B. Pollack, and Carl Sagan. "Nuclear Winter: Global Consequences of Multiple Nuclear Explosions." *Science* 222, 4630 (1983).

White Paper. "Nuclear Winter: Scientists in the Political Arena." *Physics in Perspective* 3:1 (2001):76–105.

SEE ALSO

Nuclear Detection Devices
Nuclear Emergency Support Team, United States
Radiation, Biological Damage
Radiological Emergency Response Plan, United States Federal

Nucleic Acid Analyzer (HANAA)

■ AGNIESZKA LICHANSKA

HANAA is an acronym for the hand-held advanced nucleic acid analyzer. It was developed by the Lawrence Livermore National Laboratory in 1999 based on a previous model of the nucleic acid analyzer ANAA produced in 1997. HANAA is a real time polymerase chain reaction (PCR) based system for detecting pathogens (disease-causing organisms). It is highly sensitive as it can detect 200 organisms per milliliter. Although a number of rapid real time PCR instruments were constructed, HANAA is the first hand-held device allowing easy testing of samples directly in the field, and was employed by the United Nations inspectors in Iraq during their 2003 searches for biological weapons.

Technology behind HANAA

The instrument takes advantage of real time PCR technology that was developed in recent years. PCR amplification of DNA requires repetitive sample heating (to approximately 95°C (or 203°F) and cooling to a lower temperature specific for the sample (usually 50–72°C, or 122–161°F). Traditional instruments require two to three hours to complete a PCR run and additional time to run the products on a gel to detect positive samples. New real-time PCR instruments have heating and cooling systems allowing a reduction of the running time to less than 30 minutes. The same instruments also allow observation of product formation during the run. This is achieved by incorporation of fluorescent detection methods to visualize product formation.

The main part of the instrument is a sample module containing a miniaturized silicon thermal cycle of high heating and cooling efficiency. These small thermal units are a major breakthrough in technology as they can be efficiently supported by batteries. In comparison, most of the existing real-time systems are comparatively larger and heavier and cannot be operated in the field with ease, despite the similarly good technology for detection or time of analysis. HANAA also has an advantage over its predecessor ANAA, which was as big as a small suitcase. HANAA fits into a palm and weighs just under one kilogram (around two pounds). It can operate 1.4 to 5.5 hours depending on the battery used. A run on the instrument is approximately 7–20 minutes depending on the program used for detection.

The PCR process used by HANAA is based on using TaqMan-type probes, which rely on a short DNA oligonucleotide being labeled by two fluorescent molecules, a quencher and a reporter. When a probe anneals to DNA, there is no signal as the short distance between the quencher and the reporter results in the reporter's fluorescence being quenched. However, during amplification, the reporter molecule is released and an increase in fluorescence is observed.

HANAA has four chambers for analysis and can perform two independent identifications in each chamber, therefore it is able to test for up to eight pathogens at one time. Each of the sample units can be run independently, which makes the instrument highly flexible in use. The unit is operated by a keypad, with all the menu options and results displayed on a LCD (liquid crystal display) screen as text or bar charts. A positive sample is announced by an audible alarm.

The instrument and technology are still dependent on the quality of the sample and lack of any possible PCR inhibitors in the sample. However, sample preparation is relatively simple. A template for PCR is prepared by placing sample in a liquid buffer in a small (0.020 ml) test tube and reagents are added directly to the same tube.

Potential uses for HANAA are in the areas of pathogen detection, military or counter-terrorist applications by army and police, identification of genetically modified organisms (Department of Agriculture), and diagnostic at the first point of contact, especially in a case of bioterrorist attack. The main advantage of the instrument is the ease of operation, coupled with the short training time (just a one-day session is required).

■ FURTHER READING:

ELECTRONIC:

Lawrence Livermore National Laboratories. "Chemical and Biological Detection Technologies." <http://www.llnl.gov/nai/rdiv/chbio.html> (15 January 2003).

Ronald Koopman et al. HANAA: Putting DNA Identification in the Hands of First Responder. <http://coffee.phys.unm.edu/BTR/2001%20Conference/pdf/Koopman_Ronald.pdf> (15 January 2003).

SEE ALSO

Biological Weapons, Genetic Identification
DNA Fingerprinting
DNA Recognition Instruments
DNA Sequences, Unique
Polymerase Chain Reaction (PCR)

O

Oak Ridge National Laboratory (ORNL)

Oak Ridge National Laboratory (ORNL) is a United States National Laboratory managed for the U.S. Department of Energy (DOE) by UT-Battelle, LLC. In addition to basic scientific research, ORNL conducts research projects and isotope production designed to contribute to national security.

The 58-square-mile Oak Ridge facility was originally known as the Clinton Laboratories or Clinton Engineering Works, but in 1943 ORNL was tasked with the separation of plutonium for the Manhattan Project (the U.S program during World War II to develop an atomic bomb). During the war, the Oak Ridge site became one of three major laboratories developed for the Manhattan Project—the others were located at Hanford, Washington, and Los Alamos, New Mexico.

Bomb design work and testing was completed at Los Alamos under the leadership of the physicist J. Robert Oppenheimer, but the critical fuel production problems were solved, and actual fuel production work completed, at the Oak Ridge and Hanford sites. The Oak Ridge site was chosen, in part, because the Tennessee Valley Authority (TVA) was able to supply the large electrical requirements of isotope separation equipment. At the Oak Ridge site, the process of gaseous diffusion was used to extract the U-235 isotope from uranium ore. By early 1945, the Oak Ridge lab was capable of producing uranium-235 purified to weapons grade use.

The modern ORNL staff includes more than 1500 scientists and engineers and more than 200 support and administrative personnel. In addition, ORNL annually hosts approximately 3000 additional visiting scientists and engineers who collaborate on specific projects. To the extent that research complements DOE missions or enhances national security issues, ORNL personnel are allowed to collaborate on research projects for non-DOE sponsors.

The Oak Ridge research program encompasses the Oak Ridge National Laboratory (ORNL), Oak Ridge Institute of Science and Education (ORISE), and Thomas Jefferson National Accelerator Facility (Jefferson Lab). Oversight of ORNL is also coordinated by Oak Ridge Associated Universities, a not-for-profit consortium of 86 colleges and universities.

Environmental remediation and nuclear waste disposal issues are a part of the majority of ORNL programs. I addition to providing global assistance and expertise in remediation matters, ORNL scientists and engineers also use those skills and technologies in clean-up operations at the Oak Ridge Reservation; past research efforts have left portions of the site contaminated with nuclear and chemical waste. The Environmental Protection Agency (EPA) lists Oak Ridge among the nation's clean-up priorities.

The Y-12 National Security Complex houses many of the most secret national security projects, including research on nuclear weapon components and nuclear propulsion systems for the U.S. Navy. Among other ORNL advances is the refinement of a Chemical Biological Mass Spectrometer (CBMS) used in the enhanced detection of chemical and biological agents.

ORNL also produced the Raman Tunable Integrated Sensor (RAMiTS) used by inspectors and first responders to detect chemical agents (including explosive agents). The portable unit weighs only 40 pounds and includes a 12-foot fiber-optic sensing probe that allows inspectors to examine suspected agents from a safer distance.

In conjunction with other national laboratories and DOE Joint Genome Institute (JGI), ORNL researchers are advancing means of rapid DNA sequencing that can be used to identify and characterize specific microbial pathogens.

Other ORNL bioscience projects include research on artificial neural network engineering.

Researchers at the Oak Ridge National Laboratory in Oak Ridge, Tennessee, test a portable chemical and biological agent monitor developed for the army and marines in 2001. AP/WIDE WORLD PHOTOS.

ORNL scientists also form a key component of the Stockpile Stewardship and Management Program (SSMP), operated primarily by the Lawrence Livermore National Laboratory (LLNL). The SSMP program is designed to ensure that U.S. nuclear weapons remain reliable without detonation testing.

■ FURTHER READING:

ELECTRONIC:

Environmental Measurements Laboratory. National Security. <http://www.eml.doe.gov/> (March 16, 2003).

United States Department of Energy, Office of Science. National Laboratories and User Facilities. <http://www.sc.doe.gov/Sub/Organization/Map/national_labs_and_userfacilities.htm> (March 23, 2003).

United States Department of Homeland Security. Research & Technology. <http://www.dhs.gov/dhspublic/display?theme=27&content=374> (March 23, 2003).

SEE ALSO

Argonne National Laboratory
Brookhaven National Laboratory
DOE (United States Department of Energy)
Environmental Measurements Laboratory
Lawrence Livermore National Laboratory (LLNL)
Los Alamos National Laboratory
NNSA (United States National Nuclear Security Administration)
Pacific Northwest National Laboratory
Plum Island Animal Disease Center
Sandia National Laboratories

Official Secrets Act, United Kingdom

■ ADRIENNE WILMOTH LERNER

The Official Secrets Act of the United Kingdom prohibits the transfer of information deemed sensitive to national security interests. The first Official Secrets Act was passed

Former MI5 British secret agent David Shayler leaves London's Charing Cross police station after he was released on bail for charges of breaking the Official Secrets Act in 2000. AP/WIDE WORLD PHOTOS.

in 1889, and criminalized the sharing, disclosure, or publication of government information by employees and former employees of the intelligence and security forces. The act also covered the disclosure of information by journalists. The Intelligence Bureau, under the recommendation of the Committee for Imperial Defense, lobbied Parliament for the legislation. The act also codified the gathering of evidence to try an individual on the crime of treason based on espionage or the purveying of sensitive information. Parliament hurried the bill to passage, but some dissenters noted failings in the act, especially that the act did not grant explicit powers to search someone on suspicion of illegal activity and did not address new advances in technology, such as photography.

As tensions heightened in Europe in the years leading up to World War I, Parliament sought to broaden the Official Secrets Act. The newer act addressed some of the concerns raised in 1889 upon passage of the original legislation. The Official Secrets Act of 1911 included provisions criminalizing the sketching or photographing of restricted places, especially military installations.

While stipulating expanded criteria for illegal information, the 1911 act contained a few sweeping provisions that remained controversial for nearly 80 years. The Official Secrets Act of 1911 broadened the original act to give the government full discretion over what information would be considered illegal to disclose, and placed lifetime orders of silence on civil servants and security personnel regarding their actions and any confidential knowledge gained during their tenure of service.

The government did set forth some guidelines over the classes of information protected by the Official Secrets Act. Information provided by agents of foreign governments and organizations, security and intelligence forces, intercepted communications, and information related to crime and law enforcement was covered by the act. Opponents of the act cited the broadness of these categories, alleging that any government information or news could be construed to fit the designated categories.

Perhaps the largest controversy surrounding the act was that it gave scant consideration to tests for harm. It stipulated that no motive or proof of intent to cause harm is necessary to prosecute, but that both can be inferred from a defendant's conduct, character, or associations. The law furthermore did not permit a defendant to claim that disclosure of information was in the public interest or that such information was already in the public domain. While criticism of the law subsided during wartime, it began to draw sharp criticism in the 1960s and 1970s from journalists who claimed the act allowed the government to cull the press of embarrassing information and prosecute journalists who used government employees as sources. Other opponents claimed it permitted government abuses in the intelligence and security forces to go unchecked, and failed to provide information to the public regarding security and terrorist threats.

In 1989, Parliament revisited the Official Secrets Act and replaced the long controversial Section 2 of the 1911 draft. The definition of secrets and information covered by the act was tightened to include only information deemed vital to national security and intelligence interests. Civil servants and military personnel wishing to report fraud and abuses now appeal to intra-government review boards, but are still prohibited from public disclosure of confidential government information, even if gained second-hand. Despite these revisions, the act remains contentious in Britain, especially among journalists who view the 1989 amendment as a negligible victory for freedom of information in the press.

■ FURTHER READING:

ELECTRONIC:

Parliament of the United Kingdom. Select Committee on Public Administration, Third Report, 1998. <http://www.parliament.the-stationery-office.co.uk/pa/cm199798/cmselect/cmpubadm/398-vol1/39812.htm> (January 2, 2003).

SEE ALSO

United Kingdom, Intelligence and Security

One-Time Pad.

SEE *Cipher Pad.*

OPEC (Organization of Petroleum Exporting Countries)

■ JOSEPH PATTERSON HYDER

The Organization of Petroleum Exporting Countries (OPEC) is a coalition of eleven nations that controls over fifty percent of the world's oil and natural gas exports. OPEC members are Algeria, Indonesia, Iran, Iraq, Kuwait, Libya, Nigeria, Qatar, Saudi Arabia, United Arab Emirates, and Venezuela. OPEC strives to protect the economic interests of participating countries while maintaining a stable petroleum market by establishing production quotas for its member states.

Large Western oil companies controlled and profited from oil production in the Middle East and Africa in the first half of the twentieth century. The oil companies angered the leaders of these oil-rich countries by retaining 65 percent of the profits. OPEC was established in 1960 in order for the oil producing countries to maintain a larger percentage of oil-derived profits.

Although OPEC represented its members in negotiations with the large oil companies, the organization exercised little control over the world oil market until 1973. With inflation spiraling around the world and with increasing oil demands in the United States and Europe, OPEC realized that the stage was set for a major power grab.

Inflation led the Richard M. Nixon administration to place price controls on oil products in March 1973, resulting in increased demand. Faced with oil shortages because of increased demand, Nixon tapped U.S. oil reserves. By autumn 1973, the U.S. had nearly drained its reserves. The United States had become more dependent on oil imports than ever before.

The Yom Kippur War began in October 1973, with the United States and Western Europe supporting Israel over Egyptian and Syrian forces. OPEC, comprised primarily of Middle Eastern countries sympathetic to Egypt and Syria, made a move to seize increased control of the world oil market. OPEC imposed an oil embargo against the United States and increased oil prices in Europe. The price of crude oil doubled in a matter of days, from three U.S. dollars per barrel to over five dollars per barrel. In January 1974, prices reached 11.75 dollars per barrel.

The oil embargo of 1973–1974 inconvenienced frustrated Americans, who had to modify their lifestyles to accommodate the steep increase in oil prices. The White House encouraged Americans to conserve energy by driving less, carpooling, and turning down thermostats. The Nixon administration responded by extending Daylight Savings Time in the United States, encouraging companies to trim work hours, and pushing Congress to approve construction of the Alaskan Pipeline.

The energy crisis that resulted from the OPEC embargo fueled a worldwide recession. The Dow-Jones lost 45 percent over the next two years. Oil shortages led to long lines at gasoline pumps. When OPEC finally lifted the oil embargo against the U.S. in March 1974, it had established itself as one of the most powerful economic forces in the world.

OPEC's strategy backfired, however, when public and political opinion in the United States and Europe was inflamed. The United States increased its oil production with the completion of the Alaskan Pipeline in 1977. Large

American and European oil companies also sought to regain some of their lost influence by increasing oil exploration in non-OPEC countries and offshore. As a result, much of the power that OPEC had wielded over world energy markets was eroding.

For the first several years of the 2000s, OPEC sought a stable oil market by maintaining an average price of $22 to $28 per barrel of crude oil; exerting price controls had become more difficult and less profitable for members. An example of OPEC's increasing ineffectiveness occurred in 2001, when crude oil prices fell by one-third. During the same year, OPEC cut its oil production by over twenty percent.

OPEC has experienced periods of waning effectiveness in the past, but these periods were usually the result of internal disagreements. OPEC's more recent problems stem from the rise of large, non-OPEC oil producing states, such as Russia, Norway, Mexico, Oman, and Angola. In order for OPEC to remain a viable power, it needs the cooperation of these states. Russia, Norway, and Mexico have tended to follow OPEC's lead, but continued support from these states is questionable. Russia has already indicated that it will proceed independently for the foreseeable future.

Many OPEC members have expressed an unwillingness to limit their oil production and profits if non-OPEC countries continue pumping at full capacity and flooding the market with cheap oil. If OPEC cannot hold sway over these emerging oil-producing states, then the primary reason for the existence of OPEC may eventually be in question.

■ FURTHER READING:

ELECTRONIC:

Organization of Petroleum Exporting Countries (OPEC). <http://www.opec.org> (May 2003).

SEE ALSO

Indonesia, Intelligence and Security
Iran, Intelligence and Security
Iraq, Intelligence and Security Agencies
Kuwait Oil Fires, Persian Gulf War
Libya, Intelligence and Security
Nigeria, Intelligence and Security
Saudi Arabia, Intelligence and Security

Operation Liberty Shield

On March 18, 2003, United States Secretary of Homeland Security Tom Ridge announced the implementation of Operation Liberty Shield, a specific set of measures designed to deter attack and protect Americans during periods of heightened risk of terrorism. The operation included a comprehensive and coordinated response among federal, state, and local authorities to an elevated threat level. Liberty Shield was designed to move the nation to a higher terror alert level in anticipation of the war against Iraq, imminent at that time.

Ridge announced that intelligence and law enforcement estimates indicated that terrorist groups and disgruntled individuals would "probably use military action in Iraq as pretext to attack." In raising the terror alert level to "high" (condition color orange), government officials automatically activated plans to disperse critical command and control elements of the government's emergency response forces and to restrict access to command operations. Operation Liberty Shield was specifically designed to augment these measures by staffing all response and recovery teams and to raise public awareness of both increased danger levels and specific protective measures.

As a component of Operation Liberty Shield, individuals seeking asylum for political purposes would be detained until their identity could be properly verified and their reasons for seeking asylum confirmed as legitimate. While all individuals seeking asylum would be temporarily detained, individuals from countries with known terrorist sympathies would receive extra screening and investigation.

Specific Liberty Shield measures included extended deployment of National Guard units and the positioning of those units alongside local law enforcement personnel to guard potential targets. Facilities designated as critical to the national infrastructure such as selected bridges, national landmarks, and medical and research facilities were put on special alert and in many cases, additional protective forces were deployed to those sites.

Liberty Shield operational plans called for heightened security at the nation's borders and additional Coast Guard patrols. Increased inspections were ordered at border crossings, and the Coast Guard stepped up its escorts of ships into harbor. Special security measures and enhanced screening was mandated for transportation facilities, including airport and railroad terminals. Railroads and trucking industries were ordered to increase inspections and protection of cargo.

Flight restrictions or limitations to operations were instituted over many United States cities. Flight restrictions were extended over some petroleum and all nuclear facilities. Additional guards were assigned to petroleum storage facilities, nuclear reactors, and nuclear waste sites.

As a part of Operation Liberty Shield, the FBI and Homeland Security personnel increased monitoring of individuals suspected of contributing to terrorist organizations and organizations suspected of funneling funds to terrorist organizations. Special units of agents and engineers were detailed to monitor Internet support facilities and to respond to possible cyberterrorism. Treasury agents instituted special computer-based checks to monitor and protect the nation's financial transfer systems.

To deter bioterrorism, state and local health departments were asked to be especially alert to and report unusual diseases, suspect symptoms, or suspicious disease patterns. Increased security measures were implemented in the nation's food supply network. Department of Agriculture officials ordered special inspections at feedlots, stockyards, and food distribution sites.

Ridge encouraged Americans to "be informed, stay alert, and report unusual activity." Additional details of emergency preparedness operations were posted at www.ready.gov, a website maintained by the Department of Homeland Security. Ridge stated that during Liberty Shield operations, government officials would place special emphasis on public communications.

■ FURTHER READING:

ELECTRONIC:

Department of Homeland Security. " Ready.gov." March 18, 2002. <http://www.ready.gov/> (March 18, 2003).

SEE ALSO

Terror Alert System, United States

Operation Magic

■ ADRIENNE WILMOTH LERNER

Operation Magic was the cryptonym given to United States efforts to break Japanese military and diplomatic codes during World War II. The United States Army Signals Intelligence Section (SIS) and the Navy Communication Special Unit worked in tandem to monitor, intercept, decode, and translate Japanese messages. Intelligence information gathered from the messages was sent to military command at the Office of Strategic Services (OSS). The ability to decipher and read Japanese communications was one of the key components of the Allied victory in the Pacific.

Even before the outbreak of World War II in Europe in 1939, the United States began its efforts to decode Japanese diplomatic and military communications. In 1923, a United States Navy intelligence officer obtained contraband copy of the World War I era Japanese Imperial Navy Secret Operating Code. Photographs of the codebook were passed on to the cryptologists at the Research Desk, where code was placed in red folders after the additive code keys were fully discovered. The simple additive code became known as "Red," after the folders in which it was stored.

For high-level communications, the Japanese replaced Red with Blue, a more sophisticated code in 1930. However, the new code too closely resembled its predecessor, allowing United States cryptologists to fully break the new cipher in less than two years. At the outbreak of World War II, the Japanese were still using both Red and Blue for various communications. U.S. military intelligence established listening stations throughout the Pacific to monitor ship-to-ship, command-to-fleet, and land-based communications.

After war broke out in Europe, the Japanese received encryption and security help from Nazi Germany. The Germans had discovered that U.S. intelligence was monitoring and decoding Japanese communications as early as 1935, but they did not immediately inform the Japanese. Later, Germany sent a copy of their infamous Enigma encryption machine, with a few modifications, to help secure Japanese communications. As a result, U.S. intelligence could no longer read Japanese intercepts. The painstaking work of U.S. cryptologists began anew.

U.S. cryptanalysts named the new code Purple. Applied to several variations of the initial Enigma code, Purple provided the most significant challenge to both United States and British intelligence during the war.

With the aid of information from Polish and Swedish cryptologists, the British military intelligence cryptanalysis unit at Bletchley Park first broke the German Enigma code. They then developed sophisticated decoding bombes and the first programmable computer to facilitate the deciphering of the complex Enigma code. By 1943, British intelligence was able to utilize almost real-time intelligence information received from translated Enigma intercepts.

In the United States, cryptologists struggled to break the Purple by hand. However, the structure of Japanese messages, always beginning with the same introductory phrase, aided code breakers in determining the sequencing of the multi-rotored Japanese cipher machine. United States code breakers had made significant progress on the Purple code by 1941, gaining the ability to read several lines of intercepts. The process remained slow, and the information gained from Purple was usually outdated by the time it was translated.

Aware of British successes against the German Enigma machine, United States military intelligence asked their ally to share code-breaking information. The British sent top Bletchley Park cryptographers and engineers to the United States to help train code breakers and build decoding bombes. However, they closely guarded, and did not share, the secret of Enigma code breaking efforts (code named Operation Ultra) that involved Colossus, the Bletchley Park decoding computer.

With the aid of the British, United States intelligence made significant progress against Purple in a short time. A replica of the Japanese Purple machine, built in 1939 by

American cryptologist William Friedman, was used to adapt a German Enigma bombe to decode Japanese Purple. Although the settings for each message had to be determined by hand, United States intelligence gained the ability to read Japanese code with greater ease, in a more timely manner, by 1942, six months after the Japanese bombing of Pearl Harbor and the entry of the United States into World War II.

Utilizing their extensive network of listening stations in the Pacific, United States intelligence intercepted and decoded several other types of messages. Diplomatic Purple messages, paired with JN-25 intercepts, another broken Japanese Navy code, gave U.S. military command vital information about Japanese defenses at Midway. Operation Magic intercepts provided useful information during the ensuing Battle of Midway, turning the tide of the war in the Pacific in favor of the allied forces. A year later, Purple intercepts gave the U.S. information about a diplomatic flight on which Japanese General Yamamoto, the mastermind behind the Pearl Harbor attack, was traveling. U.S. planes shot down the Japanese aircraft.

Operation Magic provided critical intelligence information in both the Pacific and European theaters of war. Diplomatic messages between Berlin and Tokyo, encoded with Enigma and Purple, yielded British and United States intelligence information regarding German defenses in France. The information helped commanders plan the D-Day invasion of Normandy in June 1944.

The Japanese government remained unaware that the United States broke the Purple code. Japanese Imperial forces continued to use codes broken by Operation Magic throughout the war and in the weeks following the Japanese surrender in 1945.

■ FURTHER READING:

BOOKS:

Boyd, Carl. *Hitler's Japanese Confidant: General Oshima Hiroshi and MAGIC Intelligence, 1941–1945.* Lawrence, KS: University Press of Kansas, 1993.

Budiansky, Stephen. *Battle of Wits: The Complete Story of Codebreaking in World War II.* New York: Touchstone Books, 2002.

Clark, Ronald William. *The Man Who Broke Purple: The Life of Colonel William F. Friedman, Who Deciphered the Japanese Code in World War II.* Boston: Little Brown, 1977.

Matthews, Tony. *Shadows Dancing: Japanese Espionage Against the West.* New York: St. Martin's Press, 1993.

SEE ALSO

Bletchley Park
Bombe
Purple machine
Red code
Ultra, Operation

World War II
World War II, United States Breaking of Japanese Naval Codes

Operation Mongoose

■ ADRIENNE WILMOTH LERNER

In November 1961, following the disastrous Bay of Pigs invasion, President John F. Kennedy and his advisors launched Operation Mongoose, a covert operation intended to disrupt Cuban government and economic infrastructure. The ultimate goal of the operation was to thoroughly undermine, or even assassinate if necessary, Cuban revolutionary leader Fidel Castro. President Kennedy named his brother, United States Attorney General Robert Kennedy, to oversee Operation Mongoose. Robert Kennedy conducted Operation Mongoose in cooperation with President Kennedy's Foreign Intelligence Advisory Board, a group of civilian experts on foreign relations.

Before Kennedy's election, the CIA clandestinely explored the notion of assassinating Castro. Castro's communist policy and close ties with the Soviet Union unnerved administration officials. The physical proximity of Cuba to the United States added Cold War security risks. Based upon interviews and declassified materials, historians assert that in 1960 several senior CIA officials allegedly began working with members of the mafia. The mafia would give the CIA plausible deniability if the assassination plot were uncovered. The mafia had operatives in Cuba, and a motive for assassinating Castro, who had disrupted casinos, travel, and mafia business interests in Havana.

Although official confirmations and a great deal of evidence remains unavailable to the public, espionage historians assert that these talks reached a loggerhead and eventually dissipated just as the Kennedy Administration assumed control of the White House. One of the first priorities of the new administration was to address the situation of Cuba. To this end, Operation Mongoose was established. Mongoose was, in essence, a continuation of a secret operation against the Cuban regime that began during the Eisenhower Administration. Psychological operations (PsyOps) such as propaganda and staged incidents were part of the plan, but Mongoose also contained provisions for far more ambitious physical threats to Castro and his allies.

In 2001, 400 pages of documents relating to Operation Mongoose were declassified. These declassified documents show that Operation Mongoose had several primary objectives. The Kennedy Administration sought to disable or destroy power plants in Cuba, lay mines to disrupt Cuban shipping, and undermine or destroy Castro's leadership. To achieve these goals, the Operation Mongoose creators proposed placing American intelligence operatives in Cuba.

The second objective of Operation Mongoose was to assassinate Castro. Operation Mongoose explored several possible means by which to carry out the assassination. The Kennedy administration considered poisoning cigars with *botulism* toxin and presenting them to Castro as a gift, poisoning a drink for Castro, and even rigging explosives to seashells on the sea floor to tempt the avid diver.

The final component of Mongoose was psychological warfare. Air Force Brigadier General Edward Lansdale commanded the PsyOps portion of Operation Mongoose. Lansdale created an anti-Castro radio broadcast that covertly aired in Cuba. Leaflets were distributed that depicted Castro as getting fat and wealthy at the expense of citizens. Operatives circulated stories about heroic freedom fighters.

Yet, the main thrust of Lansdale's plans was a series of large scale "dirty tricks" meant to evoke a call to arms against Cuba in the international community. One plan called for a space launch at Cape Canaveral to be sabotaged and blamed on Cuban agents. Operation Bingo called for a staged attack on the U.S. Navy Base at Guantanamo Bay in hopes of creating a mandate for the U.S. military to overthrow Castro.

When the Church Committee investigated the actions of the national intelligence agencies in the wake of the Watergate scandal in 1974, notes on Operation Mongoose surfaced for the first time. The committee commented not only on the assassination plots, but also noted the "dirty tricks" proposed by Lansdale. Little else was revealed about the operation for three more decades.

Ultimately, Operation Mongoose existed on paper more than in practice. While some elements of the initiative were attempted, such as elements of propaganda dissemination, the operation was abandoned by Kennedy's successor, President Johnson.

■ FURTHER READING:

BOOKS:

Chang, Laurence, ed. *Cuban Missile Crisis, 1962: A National Security Archive Documents Reader.* Washington, D.C.: United States Government Press, 1998.

Fursenko, Alexandr and Timothy J. Naftali. *One Hell of a Gamble: Khrushchev, Castro, and Kennedy, 1958–1964.* New York: W.W. Norton and Company, 1998.

SEE ALSO

Church Committee
Cuban Missile Crisis

Kennedy Administration (1961–1963), United States National Security Policy

Operation Shamrock

■ ADRIENNE WILMOTH LERNER

Operation Shamrock was a covert, domestic intelligence gathering operation that monitored telegraph communications. Shamrock began as a military intelligence program during World War II, but continued until the 1970s. The operation sparked controversy when details of Shamrock were leaked to the public after a government investigation in 1975. The government investigative committee claimed that Shamrock intended to monitor only messages that posed a threat to national security, but that it had free access to all wire traffic.

At its outset, Shamrock was a World War II military intelligence program. In the months before war broke out in Europe in 1939, the Army Signal Security Agency asked the three largest wire service companies, ITT World Communications, Western Union International, and RCA Global, for permission to tap their international cables to eavesdrop on foreign coded transmissions. The companies agreed, and Army Intelligence intercepted coded messages. Later, intelligence agents began to intercept all civilian and military wire traffic, both ciphered and plain-text.

Telegraph messages between the frontline and the home front were monitored and censored for sensitive content, such as troop locations and strategic battle plans. Military intelligence agents also sought to root out espionage communications and kept intercepts between political groups and other organizations with Axis sympathies. Thus, Shamrock was initially a wartime censorship program to cull sensitive information from the public domain in the interest of national security.

Shamrock continued, however, for nearly three decades after the end of World War II. At the war's end, Army Intelligence appealed to the major communications companies to continue their monitoring of international wire traffic. Their request was granted. When President Harry S. Truman created the National Security Agency (NSA) in 1952, the agency immediately took control of the ongoing telegraph communications monitoring. The program then acquired the code name Operation Shamrock. NSA authorities continued to monitor incoming and outgoing wire traffic from the monitoring station in New York. However, the transport of voluminous telegraph recording tape became difficult to transport. Technological advancements permitted the recording of the data on magnetic tapes, and to centralize the operation, the NSA created a New York office devoted to Shamrock. The office continued to operate until the mid 1970s, but the nature of monitoring and recording information changed significantly since the program's inception.

After World War II, the focus of Shamrock shifted to follow Cold War policies. Shamrock sought to identify and monitor Soviet sympathizers, radical political organizations, international espionage agencies, and other perceived security threats. When the Vietnam conflict was at its height, Shamrock operatives kept lists of anti-war organizations and monitored communications of some individuals who fled the draft. These lists were code named Minaret, and by 1974 contained information on nearly 70,000 American citizens.

In 1975, the Senate Select Committee to Study Governmental Operations with Respect to Intelligence Activities, otherwise known as the Church Committee after its chairman, Senator Frank Church, conducted a comprehensive investigation of the U.S. intelligence agencies after the Watergate scandal. The Church Committee report concluded that Army intelligence and the NSA did have free access to wire traffic, and did compile information on private citizens. The committee further concluded that Shamrock did not continue past 1974, and that no further action or investigation of the matter was necessary.

■ FURTHER READING:

ELECTRONIC:

United States National Security Agency. <http://www.nsa.gov>(03 January 2003).

SEE ALSO

Church Committee

Operation Z.

SEE *Pearl Harbor, Japanese attack on.*

Orange Volunteers (OV)

Orange Volunteers (OV) is a terrorist group that appeared in the late 1990s and is comprised largely of disgruntled loyalist hardliners who split from groups observing the cease-fire between Ireland and Northern Ireland. OV seeks to prevent a political settlement with Irish nationalists by attacking Catholic civilian interests in Northern Ireland. The group has been linked to pipe-bomb attacks and sporadic assaults on Catholics. Following a successful

security crackdown at the end of 1999, the OV declared a cease-fire in September 2000.

Operating principally in Northern Ireland, OV may have up to 20 dedicated members, some of whom are experienced in terrorist tactics and bombmaking.

■ FURTHER READING:

ELECTRONIC:

CDI (Center for Defense Information), Terrorism Project. CDI Fact Sheet: Current List of Designated Foreign Terrorist Organizations. March 27, 2003. <http://www.cdi.org/terrorism/terrorist.cfm> (April 17, 2003).

Central Intelligence Agency. World Factbook, 2002. <http://www.cia.gov/cia/publications/factbook/> (April 16, 2003).

Taylor, Francis X. U.S. Department of State. "Patterns of Global Terrorism 2001," Annual Report: On the Record Briefing. May 21, 2002 <http://www.state.gov/s/ct/rls/rm/10367.htm> (April 17, 2003).

U.S. Department of State. Annual Reports. <http://www.state.gov/www/global/terrorism/annual_reports.html> (April 16, 2003).

SEE ALSO

Terrorism, Philosophical and Ideological Origins
Terrorist and Para-State Organizations
Terrorist Organization List, United States
Terrorist Organizations, Freezing of Assets

OSS (United States Office of Strategic Services)

■ ADRIENNE WILMOTH LERNER

The Office of Strategic Services (OSS) was the first centralized United States intelligence agency. Created in 1942, the agency spearheaded the United States intelligence community, both civilian and military, during World War II. The mission of the OSS was to collect foreign intelligence and sabotage enemy war efforts. Maintaining espionage, analysis, and research forces, the OSS acted as a clearinghouse for information gathered from human and signals intelligence sources. At its peak, the agency employed 13,000 men and women.

Before World War II and the formation of the OSS, the United States employed only small, select intelligence forces within the military. During the American Civil War, a large espionage and intelligence network flourished, but intelligence services were disbanded following the end of the conflict. The military built up its intelligence services again during the Spanish-American War and World War I. Technological advances in communications, transportation, and weapons in the early twentieth century prompted military commands to continue to operate select intelligence units even during peacetime. The Army maintained its Signals Intelligence Service, a surveillance and cryptanalysis force, and the Navy further developed its intelligence services. Despite the recognition by national leaders that peacetime intelligence was a strategic necessity, the War Department's G-2 Intelligence Division was ill equipped to process, analyze, and disseminate the intelligence information it received from military operations.

The outbreak of World War II in Europe prompted President Franklin D. Roosevelt to press for a more efficient, centralized, and capable national intelligence service. In 1941, with the aid of representatives from the British intelligence community, Roosevelt and his advisors drafted a plan for the creation of new United States intelligence community. William J. Donovan was appointed to act as Coordinator of Information (COI), a civilian office responsible for collating intelligence information and reporting significant discoveries to the President.

When the United States entered the war in 1941, after the bombing of Pearl Harbor, Donovan seized the opportunity to promote the value of the COI and push for an expanded role for his growing intelligence service. The organization was placed under the administration of the Joint Chiefs of Staff, though it remained largely autonomous. The Office of War Information assumed some COI duties, including the government's "white," or attributable, oversees propaganda campaign. Clandestine operations remained in Donovan's control, and his agency was renamed the Office of Strategic Services.

In 1942, the OSS began operations abroad, aiding the Allied war effort in Europe and North Africa. The first major success of the OSS was Operation Torch, a network of agents and informants operating under diplomatic cover in North Africa. Torch operatives reported on German diplomatic relations in the region, as well as troop movements, and strategic battle plans. Torch then contributed key information to Allied command's plans to invade North Africa.

As OSS operations grew more extensive, the agency created specialized operational departments. Though each department conducted independent missions, they worked closely together and had to report at all times to Donovan and other OSS leaders. The most famous of these operational departments was the human intelligence network, the Secret Intelligence Branch (SI). The SI was led by Whitney H. Shepardson and maintained espionage networks in Europe, Asia, and the Middle East.

The mission of the SI created much of the operations doctrine and tradecraft practiced in modern espionage. In 1942, station chief Allen Dulles created one of the most successful units of the SI. Incorporating refugee members of the former French intelligence service who fled the Nazi occupation of France, Dulles established a network of agents, based in Switzerland, who infiltrated Nazi strongholds and government offices throughout Europe. The SI group provided Allied military command with warnings and information about German V-1 and V-2 missile programs, and later aided the failed attempt by leading German Abwehr agents to assassinate Hitler in 1944. In 1945, Dulles's group of agents, in an operation called Sunrise, helped to secretly broker the surrender of German forces in Italy.

The Special Operations Branch (SO) was the special action force of the OSS. Modeled after the British SOE intelligence group with which it worked, the SO trained intelligence and military officers to aid Resistance groups in France. The SO and SOE created specialized infiltration teams to help organize anti-Nazi groups and assist partisans with weapons and communications equipment. The Jedburghs, as the groups of special SO and SOE agents became known, parachuted in behind enemy lines to coordinate Resistance sabotage efforts. Their mission was to strengthen partisan groups, distract Nazi troops, break enemy supply lines, and aid the Allied invasion forces. The Jedburgh groups achieved their goals with notable success. After the Allied invasion of Normandy in 1944, Jedburghs helped train Resistance members with whom they worked to fight alongside the Allied forces.

Although the espionage-based departments of the OSS gained greater notoriety, the agency's Research and Analysis Department (R&A) was a wholly novel contribution to modern espionage. R&A, comprised of leading academic professors, scientists, engineers, and research specialists in various fields, composed reports using available information to aid covert and military operations. R&A's gathered information about Germany's fuel resources, refineries, and distribution structures. The information allowed Allied airplanes to bomb critical oil production and storage targets, crippling the Nazi war effort. Information about German factories, railroads, and financial networks also contributed to Allied military policy.

Despite the successes and valuable contributions of the OSS, the agency was sometimes limited in its effectiveness. Months after the agency's inception, the government denied the OSS access to enemy communications intercepts and banned it from staffing its own cryptologists to decipher enemy radio and telegraph messages. Fleet commanders in the Pacific rarely utilized OSS forces, and the agency's role in the war against Japan was minimal. The FBI and Naval Intelligence blocked the OSS from extensive domestic counterintelligence work, despite the success of the OSS X-2 strategic counterintelligence network that operated oversees. As a result of its limited participation in routine, domestic defense operations, the OSS came to be seen as a wartime office, a significant factor in its ultimate demise.

Following the end of World War II in 1945, the United States government conducted a wide-scale audit of wartime agencies. The review process was followed by a massive government restructuring effort, phasing out wartime offices, and incorporating their duties into new agencies. The OSS was disbanded in 1945. Within two years, amid escalating Cold War tensions, the need for a centralized peacetime intelligence service became apparent. The Central Intelligence Agency (CIA) assumed many of the duties of the former OSS.

■ FURTHER READING:

BOOKS:

Aldrich, Richard J. *Intelligence and the War Against Japan: Britain, America and the Politics of Secret Service.* Cambridge University Press, 2000.

Bank, Aaron. *From OSS to Green Berets: The Birth of Special Forces.* Novato, CA: Presidio Press, 1986.

Katz, Barry M. *Foreign Intelligence: Research and Analysis in the Office of Strategic Services, 1942–1945.* Cambridge, MA: Harvard University Press, 1989.

ELECTRONIC:

Central Intelligence Agency. *The Office of Strategic Services: America's First Intelligence Agency.* <http://www.cia.gov/cia/publications/oss/> (1 March 2003).

SEE ALSO

CIA (United States Central Intelligence Agency)
CIA, Formation and History
Cold War (1945–1950), The start of the atomic age
KGB (Komitet Gosudarstvennoi Bezopasnosti, USSR Committee of State Security)
World War II

P-3 Orion Anti-Submarine Maritime Reconnaissance Aircraft

First used in the early 1960s, the P-3 Orion was the leading aircraft for United States Navy maritime and anti-submarine reconnaissance over the course of nearly four decades. Many of these aircraft were modified for the collection of electronic intelligence, or ELINT. In 1998, an aging P-3 fleet went through renovations, returning to the skies in the form of the EP-3E Aries. The latter would become involved in an infamous incident involving U.S. reconnaissance over China, a task to which the P-3 had once been deployed.

Replacing the P2V Neptune, the P-3, originally designated P3V, was built by Lockheed and based on the design of the L-188 Electra passenger airliner. The only external differences between the Orion and the Electra were the unpressurized weapons bay forward of the wing, the shorter fuselage, and the magnetic anomaly detector or MAD, a security device, on the tail. Excellent at short takeoff and general handling, the P-3 could readily be modified for the purposes of gathering ELINT. In the latter capacity, it was equipped with direction finders, radar signal analyzers, and other systems.

The first operational flight of the P-3 took place during the Cuban Missile Crisis in October 1962, and during the Vietnam War, several squadrons of P-3s monitored North Vietnamese boats as part of Operation Market Time. In 1963, the Central Intelligence Agency (CIA) converted three P-3As into reconnaissance platforms for use against the People's Republic of China, and these were deployed with Republic of China Air Force markings.

During the 1980s, the U.S. Customs Service began using the P-3 to combat drug trafficking. In 1998, the Navy began updating its aging P-3s, and from these efforts emerged the EP-3E, an airborne radar platform. On April 1, 2001, a Navy EP-3E with a crew of 24 (22 navy personnel, as well as an air force officer and a marine) collided with a Chinese fighter jet off the China coast. The Chinese pilot was killed in the crash, and the damaged U.S. plane landed on nearby Hainan Island. The administration of President George W. Bush called for the immediate return of the plane and crew, but the Chinese ended up holding them for 11 days.

■ FURTHER READING:

BOOKS:

Bishop, Chris, ed. *The Encyclopedia of Modern Military Weapons: The Comprehensive Guide to over 1,000 Weapon Systems from 1945 to the Present Day.* New York: Barnes & Noble, 1999.

Bonds, Ray, ed. *The Modern U.S. War Machine: An Encyclopedia of American Military Equipment and Strategy.* New York: Military Press, 1987.

PERIODICALS:

"Hainan Incident Increases Pressure in Sino-U.S. Relations." *Defense Daily International* 1, no. 2 (April 6, 2001): 14.

"Upgrades for P-3s to Begin in 1998." *Aviation Week & Space Technology* 146, no. 13 (March 31, 1997): 33.

SEE ALSO

E-2C
Reconnaissance
Ships Designed for Intelligence Collection
SIGINT (Signals intelligence)
Undersea Espionage: Nuclear vs. Fast Attack Subs

A U.S. Navy aviation systems warfare operator searches for and tracks surface contacts using radar and the Infrared Detection System of his P-3 Orion patrol aircraft during a routine flight in support of Operation Enduring Freedom in October 2001. AP/WIDE WORLD PHOTOS.

Pacific Northwest National Laboratory

Since 1965, the Pacific Northwest National Laboratory (PNNL) has been managed by Battelle corporation. Beginning in the 1980s PNNL has operated as a part of the U.S. Department of Energy's national laboratory system—adding the term "National" to its name in 1995—and Battelle now manages the site for the Department of Energy's Office of Science. PNNL scientists and engineers conduct basic science research, joint research projects with private industry, and specialized research related to national security issues.

Although initially founded to conduct research work related to the Hanford nuclear site in Washington State— including the development of technology to improve safety in fabricating and handling nuclear fuels—research has since expanded to encompass an interdisciplinary approach to environmental, biotechnology, computer science, and national security related projects.

Of historical interest, PNNL scientists assisted NASA scientists in the analysis of materials collected during Apollo lunar exploration missions. PNNL studies included measurements of radionuclides that provided evidence of not only lunar processes, but of solar processes not easily measured in Earth materials. Other PNNL historical achievements include the development of optical digital recording technologies used in preparing compact discs.

In an attempt to address the growing need for finding safer modes of hazardous waste disposal, PNNL scientists developed the process of vitrification (a process that encases hazardous waste in a stable glass matrix that can then be safely stored for thousands of years). Expanding on its history in developing hazardous waste technology, more recent PNNL projects have developed new methodologies to handle nuclear tank waste often stored in deteriorating and vulnerable underground tanks. Clean up and the development of protocols for handling contaminated materials focuses on preventing radionuclide loss or other hazardous material contamination of the surrounding environment. As part of environmental research programs, PNNL scientists have developed sophisticated global climate models that allow researchers to predict the global atmospheric spread of hazardous materials or the movement of hazardous wastes through groundwater systems. PNNL-developed technology assists monitoring of nuclear testing ensures adherence to the Comprehensive (Nuclear) Test Ban Treaty (CTBT).

A senior research engineer at the Pacific Northwest National Laboratory conducts a tour of the napalm canister separation plant located at the Naval Weapons Station Seal Beach Detachment in 2001. After a two-year effort, the Navy disposed of more than 34,000 napalm bombs that sat for more than a quarter of a century on fields surrounding the facility. AP/WIDE WORLD PHOTOS.

PNNL's Chemical and Biological Defense Program is continuing research into detection technologies capable of identifying prohibited chemical and biological agents. PNNL technologies that facilitate pathogen detection include the Matrix-Assisted Laser Desorption/Ionization Mass Spectrometry (MALDI-MS) program that utilizes mass spectrometry to rapidly identify pathogens. Instead of conventional bio-identification procedures that can take days of laboratory analysis time—and thus, delay effective response to acts of bioterrorism—MALDI-MS holds the potential to allow pathogen identification within minutes. For example, the Biodetection Enabling Analyte Delivery System (BEADS) analyzes microbe DNA for pathogen identification. In conjunction with private industry, PNNL projects include the development and evaluation of systems to effectively distribute enzymes and chemicals that decontaminate a structure following chemical or biological agent exposure.

In partnership with U.S. Department of Energy's Hazardous Materials Management and Emergency Response (HAMMER), PNNL staff offers training to law enforcement officers, emergency medical responders, and military personnel in methods of managing responses to potential nuclear, chemical, or biological accidents and deliberate acts of terrorism.

To support inspection efforts—such as those conducted by U.N. weapons inspectors in Iraq prior to the 2003 U.S.-led war against Iraq—PNNL scientists developed acoustic inspection devices that were capable of detecting compartments inside liquid-filled containers.

Other PNNL projects related to national security include a holographic imaging system that enhances noninvasive personal screening for use by the Federal Aviation Administration.

■ FURTHER READING:

ELECTRONIC:

Pacific Northwest National Laboratory. March 2003. <http://www.pnl.gov/> (April 2, 2003).

United States Department of Energy, Office of Science. National Laboratories and User Facilities. <http://www.sc.doe.gov/Sub/Organization/Map/national_labs_and_userfacilities.htm> (March 23, 2003).

United States Department of Homeland Security. Research & Technology. <http://www.dhs.gov/dhspublic/display?theme=27&content=374> (March 23, 2003).

SEE ALSO

Argonne National Laboratory
Brookhaven National Laboratory
DOE (United States Department of Energy)
Environmental Measurements Laboratory
Lawrence Berkeley National Laboratory
Lawrence Livermore National Laboratory (LLNL)
Los Alamos National Laboratory
NNSA (United States National Nuclear Security Administration)
Oak Ridge National Laboratory (ORNL)
Plum Island Animal Disease Center
Sandia National Laboratories

Pakistan, Intelligence and Security

In 1947, the British ended their colonial control of the Indian subcontinent. British India was divided into two sovereign states, predominantly Hindu India and Muslim Pakistan. A war in 1971 further divided the region, creating the nation of Bangladesh. The division sparked endemic strife in the region, especially in the ethnically diverse Kashmir province. Tensions over Kashmir, water rights of the Indus River, and occasional armed conflict continue to plague Pakistan and India.

Conflict in the region escalated in the late 1990s when India began extensive nuclear weapons testing near the Pakistani border. In 1998, Pakistan began a nuclear weapons program. Western nations, including the United States, are concerned not only with the possibility of dueling nuclear powers on the Indian subcontinent, but also with the possible proliferation of nuclear materials and technology to neighboring nations and terrorist organizations. Pakistan's intelligence services are suspected of playing a crucial role in the country's nuclear program, both securing nuclear materials and conducting espionage on other nuclear programs.

Pakistan's intelligence community is divided into three main agencies. The agencies are neither wholly civilian, nor wholly military, and their duties in foreign and domestic intelligence often overlap. Inter-Services Intelligence (ISI) is the premier Pakistani intelligence and security organization. The ISI collects domestic and foreign intelligence, focusing especially on surveillance of foreign diplomats operating within Pakistan. No government or military body oversees the actions of the ISI, which has led to

the agency gaining significant power. The ISI monitors communications, maintains a special, military-trained action group, and conducts political espionage.

Various operational divisions within the ISI attend to different aspects of the organization's mission to protect national security. The Joint Signal Intelligence Bureau coordinates communications and signal surveillance operations. The Joint Counter Intelligence Bureau monitors Pakistani diplomats serving abroad and conducts counterespionage operations. Assessing threats to national security and collating intelligence data is the primary responsibility of the Joint Intelligence X.

The Intelligence Bureau (IB) is Pakistan's main domestic intelligence and espionage agency. The IB conducts political surveillance of politicians, government agents, businesses, and citizen groups. Political surveillance is used to identify and infiltrate groups that the Pakistani government considers hostile or anti-government. Although the agency has no formal arrest powers, suspects are often arrested and detained by law enforcement at the request of IB officials. In 1996, the IB was granted control of government censorship programs, controlling information dissemination via mail, wire, or electronic medium.

The Pakistani government has been dominated by military forces for decades. The election of some moderate leaders in 2000 led to minor demilitarization reforms within the government. In subsequent elections, Islamist hardliners gained seats in Pakistan's parliament, effectively halting impending reforms. A reflection of the government, the Pakistani intelligence community is also a mix of military and civilian forces. Military Intelligence (MI) performs the same duties as its government agency counterpart, conducting political surveillance and protecting national security. While the MI is especially concerned with the security of military installations, weapons facilities, and border control, its routine operations are similar to the ISI and IB.

While some reforms have been made to the Pakistani intelligence community, the national government continues to take criticism from the international community on its lack of support for antiterrorism measures in the region. The United States officially warned Pakistan to cease terrorist operations in India in the late 1990s. Following the September 11, 2001, terrorist attacks on the United States, Pakistan again came under the scrutiny of Western nations for its tolerance of terrorist organizations, such as al-Qaeda, operating within its borders. Although Pakistan's leader, General Pervez Musharraf, eventually pledged and lent support to the United States-led coalition in the war against the Taliban in Afghanistan, some Western analysts initially challenged the commitment and loyalties of the Pakistani intelligence service toward the international war on terrorism. Subsequent actions have signaled Pakistan's overt willingness to become a full and active participant in the international war on terrorism. On March 1, 2003, agents of Pakistan's ISI intelligence agency, in cooperation with U.S. CIA operatives tracked down and arrested Khalid Sheikh Mohammed, the suspected al-Qaeda operations director implicated in a string of terrorist attacks. Pakistan intelligence agents were also instrumental in the prior arrest of another highly placed al-Qaeda terrorist, Abu Zubaida. Both terrorists were turned over to the CIA for interrogation at an undisclosed location.

◼ FURTHER READING:

BOOKS:

Jaffrelot, Christophe. *A History of Pakistan and Its Origins.* Translated by Gillian Beaumont. New York: Anthem Press, 2002.

Jones, Owen Bennett. *Pakistan: Eye of the Storm.* New Haven, CT: Yale University Press, 2002.

Ziring, Lawrence. *Pakistan in the Twentieth Century: A Political History.* Oxford: Oxford University Press, 1998.

PERIODICALS:

Gauhar, Altaf. "How Intelligence Agencies Run Our Politics." *The Nation.* September 1997: 4.

SEE ALSO

India, Intelligence and Security
Nonproliferation and National Security, United States
Weapons of Mass Destruction
Weapons of Mass Destruction, Detection

Palestine Islamic Jihad (PIJ)

The Palestine Islamic Jihad (PIJ) originated among militant Palestinians in the Gaza Strip during the 1970s. The PIJ-Shiqaqi faction, currently led by Ramadan Shallah in Damascus, is most active. Committed to the creation of an Islamic Palestinian state and the destruction of Israel through holy war, PIJ also opposes moderate Arab governments that it believes have been tainted by Western secularism.

Organization activities. PIJ activists have conducted many attacks including large-scale suicide bombings against Israeli civilian and military targets. The group increased its operational activity in 2001 during the Intifadah, claiming numerous attacks against Israeli interests. The group has not targeted U.S. interests and continues to confine its attacks to Israelis inside Israel and the territories.

The actual number PIJ activists is unknown. The PIJ operates primarily in Israel, the West Bank and Gaza Strip, and other parts of the Middle East, including Lebanon and Syria, where the leadership is based. They receive financial assistance from Iran and limited logistical support from Syria.

ELECTRONIC:

Central Intelligence Agency. World Factbook, 2002. <http://www.cia.gov/cia/publications/factbook/> (April 16, 2003).

Taylor, Francis X. U.S. Department of State. Patterns of Global Terrorism 2001. Annual Report: On the Record Briefing. May 21, 2002. <http://www.state.gov/s/ct/rls/rm/10367.htm> (April 17, 2003).

U.S. Department of State. Annual reports. <http://www.state.gov/www/global/terrorism/annual_reports.html> (April 16, 2003).

SEE ALSO

Terrorism, Philosophical and Ideological Origins
Terrorist and Para-State Organizations
Terrorist Organization List, United States
Terrorist Organizations, Freezing of Assets

Palestine Liberation Front (PLF)

The Palestine Liberation Front (PLF) broke away from the Popular Front for the Liberation of Palestine-General Command (PFLP-GC) in the mid-1970s. The PLF later split again into pro-PLO, pro-Syrian, and pro-Libyan factions. The Pro-PLO faction is led by Muhammad Abbas (Abu Abbas), who became a member of the PLO Executive Committee in 1984 but left it in 1991.

Organization activities. The Abu Abbas-led faction is known for aerial attacks against Israel. Abbas's group also was responsible for the attack in 1985 on the cruise ship *Achille Lauro* and the murder of U.S. citizen Leon Klinghoffer. Following a brief standoff, Egypt granted free passage to the hijackers in exchange for the release of the ship and remaining hostages. The plane carrying the hijackers to refuge in Tunisia was intercepted by U.S. Navy jets and diverted to Italy. Although Abbas's coconspirators were rapidly convicted and sentenced to prison, Abbas was freed by the Italian authorities, who claimed they had insufficient evidence to detain him. Abbas was, however, subsequentely convicted in absentia of masterminding the hijacking.

Abu Abbas was found in Baghdad following Operation Iraqi Freedom and as of April 2003, was in U.S. custody. Abbas had been cited by President George W. Bush as an example of terrorists given safe haven by the Saddam Hussein regime. During Operation Iraqi Freedom, U.S. marines found bombmaking equipment, explosives, gas masks, and other weapons at a large PLF training facility east of Baghdad.

The size of the PLF is unknown; the PLO faction was based in Tunisia until the *Achille Lauro* attack, and then in

Iraq until Operation Iraqi Freedom. Prior to the military action in Iraq the PLF received support mainly from Saddam Hussein's regime. The PLF also has received support from Libya.

■ FURTHER READING:

ELECTRONIC:

Central Intelligence Agency. World Factbook, 2002. <http://www.cia.gov/cia/publications/factbook/> (April 16, 2003).

Taylor, Francis X. U.S. Department of State. Patterns of Global Terrorism 2001. Annual Report: On the Record Briefing. May 21, 2002. <http://www.state.gov/s/ct/rls/rm/10367.htm> (April 17, 2003).

U.S. Department of State. Annual reports. <http://www.state.gov/www/global/terrorism/annual_reports.html> (April 16, 2003).

SEE ALSO

Terrorism, Philosophical and Ideological Origins
Terrorist and Para-State Organizations
Terrorist Organization List, United States
Terrorist Organizations, Freezing of Assets

Palestinian Authority, Intelligence and Security

The Israeli-Palestinian struggle has been marked by violence and international diplomatic conflict since the British "Balfour Declaration" opened the predominately Arab territory of Palestine to large-scale Jewish immigration. Tensions escalated in the region, with outbreaks of periodic violence, even before the establishment of the State of Israel in 1947. Israeli territorial expansion in 1948 further angered Palestinians when Jerusalem was declared an Israeli city, violating the original agreement that made the religious seat an international city. The Six Day War in the late 1960s further expanded Israeli control in the region, again sparking violence between the region's factions.

In the 1990s, Israel and the Palestinian Authority began a series of peace talks. However, growing nationalism and radical fundamentalism in both Israel and Palestine undermined the peace process. The Palestinian State claims that Israel continues to occupy Palestinian territory illegally, and Israel says that its military presence is necessary to protect Jewish peripheral settlements. In 2001, a new wave of violence in the region marked the beginning of the second Intifadah. The Palestinian Authority, and its military and intelligence community have been cited by the international community for prolonging the Intifadah and encouraging anti-Israeli and anti-American terrorism.

Little is known about the structure and the daily functions of the Palestinian intelligence and security community. The main intelligence agencies are the National Security Service and General Intelligence. Domestic political intelligence and foreign intelligence (mostly espionage against Israeli defense forces) is carried out by these organizations, which rely on a large network of human intelligence and informants. There is no real distinction between civilian and military intelligence forces, since much of the Palestinian Authority is para-military in nature.

The Palestinian Authority maintains three major security forces. The Presidential Police protect Palestinian officials and provide a special guard to Palestinian leader Yassar Arafat. The Civil Police protect public welfare, and sometimes operate with the military against Israeli forces. The Preventative Security Forces are a quasi-intelligence based, secret police force.

After the terrorist attacks on the United States, Arafat quickly distanced his national forces from those of Al-Qaeda. However, many in the international community remain skeptical, noting Arafat's connection to other Islamist groups. In 2003, the United States government released a "Road Map to Peace," a long-term compromise proposal to halt growing Israeli-Palestinian violence. However, many Palestinians and Israelis disagree on the future prospects of peace in the region, and the nature of any settlement between their two governments, especially in light of the conflict in Iraq. The Palestinian Authority continues its endeavors to gain international support for and recognition of an independent Palestine.

■ FURTHER READING:

ELECTRONIC:

United Nations. *"The Question of Palestine."* <http://www.un.org/Depts/dpa/ngo/history.html> (13 March 2003).

SEE ALSO

Israel, Intelligence and Security
Terrorism, Philosophical and Ideological Origins
Terrorist and Para-State Organizations
United Nations Security Council

PanAm 103, (Trial of Libyan Intelligence Agents)

■ MICHAEL J. O'NEAL

On December 21, 1988, a bomb planted on PanAm Flight 103 en route to New York exploded while the plane was airborne over Lockerbie, Scotland. After an extensive investigation, two men with alleged ties to the intelligence service of Libya were extradited and brought to trial. In

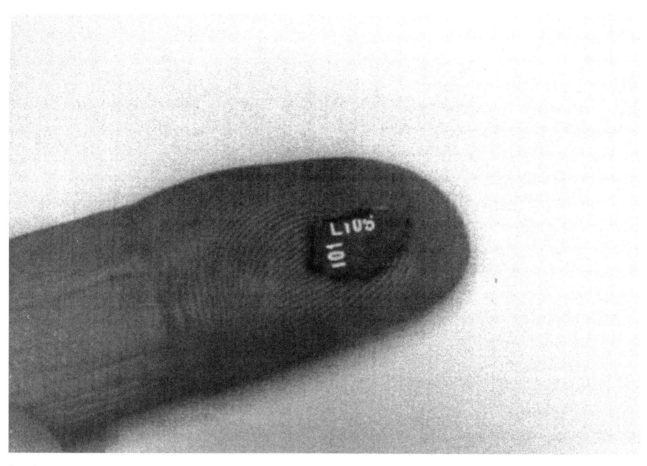

One of two fragments that proved crucial in tracking down the bombers of PanAm Flight 103, which exploded over Lockerbie, Scotland, in 1988, is shown on the tip of a finger. AP/WIDE WORLD PHOTOS.

January 2001, one of the accused was found guilty and sentenced to life in prison; the other was acquitted.

Background.

PanAm Flight 103, which originated in Frankfurt, Germany, took off from London's Heathrow Airport at 6:25 PM on December 21, 1988. The flight path of the plane was to take it over the British Isles and the North Atlantic Ocean on its way to New York City. At 6:56 PM the plane leveled out at 31,000 feet. Seven minutes later, the air traffic controller at Shanwick Oceanic Control transmitted the plane's final oceanic clearance but received no acknowledgment from the aircraft. During the transmission, the plane's radar return disappeared from controller radar screens.

What air traffic controllers and others later learned was that at 7:02 and 50 seconds, the Boeing 747 exploded in midair over Scotland, killing all 259 passengers and crew members aboard. The bulk of the wreckage hit a residential area called Sherwood Crescent at the southern edge of the town of Lockerbie, digging a crater 155 feet wide and 196 feet long, destroying 21 residential buildings, and killing 11 people on the ground. The impact of

the crash was so strong that the British Geological Survey reported what appeared to be an earthquake registering 1.6 on the Richter scale. Other parts of the plane fell into the countryside east of town, but investigators later discovered bits of wreckage as far away as 80 miles. Within hours, journalists flooded the scene and transmitted the first pictures of the smoking wreckage.

The investigation.

Responsibility for determining the cause of the crash fell to the United Kingdom's Air Accident Investigation Branch (AAIB). The AAIB quickly began the task of painstakingly reassembling the nearly four million pieces of wreckage recovered, often having to sift through bags of mud and debris to find them. After reconstructing the plane, the investigators determined that the cause of the catastrophe was an explosion, which in turn was caused by a so-called IED, or "intentional explosive device."

The PanAm 103 investigation focused on a Toshiba radio/cassette recorder that had been packed into a brown suitcase stowed in the cargo hold of the plane. Inside the recorder were the remains of a timing device that detonated the bomb. The central question, of course, was the identity of the person or persons who planted the bomb.

There was no shortage of theories. Families of many of the victims publicly tied the explosion to the government of Iran, claiming that Iranian hard-liners were bent on vengeance for an incident in July 1988 when the U.S. Navy cruiser *Vincennes* accidentally shot down an Iranian plane with 290 passengers aboard. Others pointed a finger at the Palestinians, for the barometric timing device that detonated the bomb matched similar devices found during an October 26, 1988 raid by German police on two apartments occupied by members of the Popular Front for the Liberation of Palestine. There they found a virtual bomb factory complete with timers, barometric devices, explosives, detonators, and Toshiba radio/cassette recorders.

The Libyan connection. In November 1991, after a three-year investigation, Scotland's chief law enforcement officer issued warrants for the arrest of two Libyans. One was Al-Amin Khalifa Fhimah, an alleged member of the Libyan Intelligence Services and the station officer of Libyan Arab Airlines on the Mediterranean island of Malta. The other was Abdel Baset al-Megrahi, alleged to have been a senior officer in the Libyan Intelligence Services and head of Libyan Airlines security.

It was one thing to issue warrants. It was another matter entirely to extricate the suspects from Libya, a north African nation ruled by Colonel Muammar Gaddafy. The United States had long identified Gaddafy's Libya as a "rogue" state, and Gaddafy never attempted to hide his virulent anti-Western sentiments. Tensions between Gaddafy and the United States came to a boil in March 1986, when Libya attacked a fighter aircraft of the U.S. Sixth Fleet, which was on maneuvers in the Mediterranean. The United States retaliated by bombing Libyan radar and missile installations. Then in April, a bomb in a Berlin discotheque killed an American soldier and a Turkish woman. The United States had evidence that Libya was behind the bombing and in retaliation attacked military and civilian targets in the Libyan capital of Tripoli, including Gaddafy's residence.

Against this backdrop, Gaddafy argued for nearly eight years that the suspects could not receive a fair trial in a Scottish court. In spite of sanctions by the United Nations that eventually cost Libya an estimated $33 billion, Gaddafy refused to extradite the suspects until 1998, after UN Secretary General Kofi Annan and South African leader Nelson Mandela intervened, possibly offering assurances that Gaddafy himself would be granted immunity from prosecution for the crime. Authorities agreed to Gaddafy's condition that the trial be conducted in a neutral third country. Accordingly, in 1998 the Netherlands agreed to set aside Camp Zeist, a former air base, as the site of the trial, complete with an $18 million courtroom constructed with bulletproof glass.

The trial attracted worldwide attention because of its international implications. The prosecution argued that the men had acted under the orders of Gaddafy himself, whose motive was revenge for the 1986 bombing raid on Tripoli that killed his daughter. The defense countered that the real perpetrators were an extreme militant faction of the Popular Front for the Liberation of Palestine with help from the governments of Iran and Syria. In its verdict, announced in early 2001, the three-judge panel of Scottish judges did not address these wider issues. Based on over 10,000 pages of testimony from 235 witnesses, the panel found Fhimah not guilty because the prosecution was never able to establish that he was at the airport in Malta when he was alleged to have used his position to get the bomb on a plane bound for Frankfurt.

In convicting al-Megrahi, however, the court focused on a number of pieces of evidence. On December 20, 1988, al-Megrahi had traveled to Malta under a false name. There, according to a Maltese shop owner, he purchased clothes, but he did not seem to be very interested in what clothes he was buying. The clothes and the bomb were placed aboard an Air Malta flight to Frankfurt, where they were transferred to Flight 103. While the shop owner was never able positively to identify al-Megrahi, bits of the clothing he purchased were found with the Toshiba cassette parts recovered in Scotland. Finally, al-Megrahi had a close association with Edwin Bollier, an electronics expert from Zurich, Switzerland, who, prosecutors said, had manufactured the timer for the bomb. With regard to the timer, though, some observers continue to have questions. The timer that prosecutors said detonated the bomb was sophisticated enough that it could have been set to detonate when the plane was over the Atlantic. Doing so would have thwarted investigators in their efforts to recover debris and track down the bombers. Cruder timers, though, could be set for no longer than 45 minutes, within the time frame when the bomb exploded. This led some to wonder whether the Toshiba fragments prosecutors produced in evidence were really parts of the timer that detonated the bomb.

Al-Megrahi's conviction did not settle the case. Some of the victims' families continued to insist that Iran played a role in the bombing. Others continued to call for prosecution of al-Megrahi's superiors, including Gaddafy himself. Civil suits for damages against the Libyan government are likely to continue for years. In 2021, al-Megrahi will be eligible for parole.

■ **FURTHER READING:**

BOOKS:

Cohen, Susan, and Daniel Cohen. *Pan Am 103: The Bombing, the Betrayals, and the Bereaved Families' Search for Justice.* New York: Signet, 2001.

Emerson, Steven, and Brian Duffy. *The Fall of Pan Am 103.* New York: Putnam, 1990.

Gerson, Allan, and Jerry Adler. *The Price of Terror.* New York: HarperPerennial, 2002.

House Committee on Foreign Affairs. *U.S. Policy in the Aftermath of the Bombing of Pan Am 103.* Hearing before the Subcommittees on International Security, International Organizations, and Human Rights. 103rd Cong., 2nd sess., July 28, 1994.

PERIODICALS:

"Case Closed?" *Time International.* February 12, 2001: 16ff.

ELECTRONIC:

Morse, Amanda, and Derek Brown. "The Lockerbie Trial." *The Guardian.* January 31, 1997. <http://www.guardian.co.uk/theissues/article/0,6512,216784,00.html>.

SEE ALSO

Airline Security
Bomb Damage, Forensic Assessment
Libya, Intelligence and Security
Terrorist Organization List, United States

Panama Canal

▌ JUDSON KNIGHT

From the time of its opening in 1914 until 1977, when the United States transferred it to the nation of Panama, the Panama Canal was a symbol of U.S. influence in the Americas and, ultimately, the world. Despite the bitterness that attended the debate over its transfer to Panama, combined with fears of foreign takeover that surfaced when Panama took formal control on December 31, 1999, the Canal lacks the strategic importance it enjoyed in its heyday. Still, it remains one of several important "chokepoints"—areas in which the flow of the world's oil supply traverses a narrow passage vulnerable to attack—and for this reason, the United States remains committed to the Canal's defense.

Early history

From the earliest voyages of discovery in the area of Central America and the Caribbean, it became clear that a canal across one of Central America's narrowest points would greatly shorten travel and transport time between Atlantic and Pacific ports. In 1835, the U.S. Senate passed a resolution in favor of building such a canal, but through Nicaragua. In 1881, a French team under the leadership of Ferdinand de Lesseps, builder of the Suez Canal, attempted to build a canal across the isthmus of Panama, but the project suffered a number of misfortunes, including bankruptcy and outbreaks of disease among workers. The French project was scrapped for good in 1898.

Meanwhile, the idea of a canal remained a topic of debate in the United States, which still favored a route through Nicaragua. After much political wrangling, however, Congress in 1902 passed the Spooner Act, which authorized the United States to purchase the assets of the French company and begin building a canal through Panama. The latter at that time belonged to Colombia, and when treaty negotiations with Colombia stalled, U.S. authorities gave their support to a declaration of independence by Panama in November 1903. Colombia, convulsed by four years of civil war, could do little to stop the act of secession, and the United States completed a treaty with the new nation of Panama. In February 1904, Congress created the Panama Canal Zone.

The building of the Canal took place over a 10-year period beginning in the summer of 1904. Its builders, who numbered as many as 40,000 at any one time, consisted of American and European engineers and technicians, with Latin American and Chinese immigrant labor. Among the challenges they confronted were disease, carried by mosquitoes that lived in the swampy lands along the canal route, and topography. Rather than build at sea level, the engineers finally decided on a plan involving a series of locks and an earthen dam, which created what was then the world's largest artificial lake, Gatun. The Canal—which actually follows a route from the northwest to the southeast, rather than east to west—opened on August 15, 1914.

Rethinking the Canal

Although the Canal was a vital lifeline during the two world wars, by the time of the Korean War, its limitations had begun to show. The Canal could not accommodate very large aircraft carriers, an increasingly critical aspect of U.S. national security. By the mid-1970s, most large oil tankers were also too big for passage.

Coupled with the physical issues were political ones associated with the growth of anti-American sentiment in Panama and elsewhere. On January 9, 1964, American refusal to fly the Panamanian flag over a high school in the Canal Zone sparked riots that left 23 Panamanians and four U.S. Marines dead. Afterward, Panama called for new treaty discussions with the United States.

The treaties. On September 7, 1977, President James E. Carter and Panamanian military dictator Omar Torrijos signed the Panama Canal Treaty, which abolished the Canal Zone, terminated all prior treaties regarding the Canal, and provided for the full transfer of the Canal to Panama on December 31, 1999. A separate Neutrality Treaty guaranteed the neutrality of the Canal in perpetuity.

The Neutrality Treaty and several aspects of the Panama Canal Treaty served to protect U.S. interests—interests that, in the view of many Treaty supporters, were best supported by a voluntary transfer of the Canal. The alternative, supporters maintained, would be a political and public-relations disaster for the United States, and would only serve to bolster Latin American resentment against the wealthy, powerful neighbor to the north.

As ten percent of the world's ships are unable to pass through the strategic Panama Canal waterway, the canal is undergoing its largest expansion since workers carved the 50-mile path through Panama's mountains, linking the Pacific and Atlantic oceans. AP/WIDE WORLD PHOTOS.

Opponents to the Canal agreements, led by future President Ronald Reagan, cited the Treaty as one further sign of America's worldwide retreat, and warned of foreign takeover. Nevertheless, the transfer plan enjoyed support from a number of Republicans, including former President Gerald R. Ford and former Secretary of State Henry Kissinger. In 1978, the Senate ratified both treaties, and in 1979 Congress passed the Panama Canal Act. Among its many provisions, the Act created the Panama Canal Commission, which would act as custodian over the Canal for the next 20 years.

The transfer. Panama has not fared well in the years since the Treaty. The United States deposed another dictator, Manuel Noriega, in 1989, acting partly to protect the Canal from takeover. The country has been run by civilian governments since then, but these have proven inadequate to solve the nation's domestic problems. As the December, 1999, deadline loomed, some Panamanians expressed reservations regarding the transfer of the Canal.

On the one hand, its acquisition would greatly enhance national prestige, but many wondered if any small, poor country could undertake an operation hitherto overseen by the world's leading superpower. Similar concerns in the United States led to a proposal regarding a continued U.S. military presence. However, talks between the two nations ended in September, 1998, without any such agreement.

On the last day of the 1900s, U.S. Army Secretary Louis Caldera led a delegation that officially turned over control of the Canal to Panama, represented by President Mireya Moscoso. Minutes before the hoisting of the Panamanian flag over the Canal administration building, a triumphant Moscoso proclaimed to her people, "The Canal is ours!"

The Canal Today

Subsequent events have not served to reinforce this initial enthusiasm. The Canal has faced several environmental problems, including a lack of rainwater, important to the transport of ships through its 12 locks, caused by droughts resulting from the El Niño weather phenomenon. Political and economic corruption has also shadowed the Canal. Not only did a local land-sale scam involving Canal properties bilk investors, but in November, 2000, it was discovered that millions of dollars in U.S. equipment (including firearms) from the former Canal Zone had disappeared.

Some of the fears raised prior to the transition, however, have proven illusory. One was the question of Chinese control, a powerful issue in Washington due to allegations of widespread Chinese espionage against the United States during the administration of President William J. Clinton. When the Hong Kong conglomerate Hutchison-Whampoa gained a contract to manage ports on the Atlantic and Pacific sides, this raised concerns that the Chinese might use this as an opportunity to seize control of the Canal. Subsequent events, however—or rather, the lack of events in this regard—have served to support the view of those who pointed out that China has never been expansionist beyond Asia.

If the Canal faces a serious foreign threat, it is likely to come from much closer to home, such as from Colombia, which continually teeters on the brink of anarchy as its government battles drug traffickers, revolutionaries, and paramilitary groups. At the beginning of the twenty-first century, many international observers expressed grave concerns that Panama in general, and the Canal in particular, could be drawn into these struggles.

In any case, the Canal lacks the strategic significance it once held, and in 2000 only 1.7 percent of total U.S. petroleum imports passed through it. Though as many as 10,000 vessels navigate the Canal each year, traffic has declined since the peak year, 1970, and today 10 percent of the world's cargo ships are too large to traverse it. Additionally, the Trans-Panama Pipeline, opened in October 1982, could be used to ship oil across the Panamanian isthmus if the Canal were closed. Discussions regarding an enlarged or alternate canal are ongoing, though it is unlikely such a project could undertaken without a wealthy nation or nations to underwrite it.

■ FURTHER READING:

BOOKS:

Collin, Richard H. *Theodore Roosevelt's Caribbean: The Panama Canal, the Monroe Doctrine, and the Latin American Context*. Baton Rouge: Louisiana State University Press, 1990.

Falcoff, Mark. *Panama's Canal: What Happens When the United States Gives a Small Country What It Wants*. Washington, D.C.: AEI Press, 1998.

Leonard, Thomas M. *Panama, the Canal, and the United States: A Guide to Issues and References*. Claremont, CA: Regina Books, 1993.

Major, John. *Prize Possession: The United States and the Panama Canal, 1903–1979*. New York: Cambridge University Press, 1993.

Strong, Robert A. *Working in the World: Jimmy Carter and the Making of American Foreign Policy*. Baton Rouge: Louisiana State University Press, 2000.

SEE ALSO

Americas, Modern U.S. Security Policy and Interventions
Carter Adminstration (1977–1981), United States National Security Policy
Clinton Administration (1993–2001), United States National Security Policy
Suez Canal

Parabolic Microphones

■ LARRY GILMAN

A parabolic microphone is an ordinary microphone mounted inside a sound-reflecting dish having a parabolic cross section. Sound waves passing straight into the parabolic reflector are focused by it on the microphone; sounds entering the reflector dish from other angles impinge directly on the microphone, but are not focused on it by the reflector. Thus, the parabolic microphone is highly directional, that is, more sensitive to sound sources at which it is directly pointed than to other sources. This makes the parabolic microphone useful for recording localized sources of relatively faint sounds, such as conversations or bird calls, at a distance.

A paraboloid reflector is used because of the unique geometrical properties of the parabola. A parabola is an open curve resembling a V with a rounded point. (Mathematically, the two arms of the curve go on forever; in building a parabolic reflector, the arms are cut short.) The "axis" of the parabola is a straight line that passes through it like a vertical line drawn through the center of a V. All rays that enter a parabola parallel to its axis and are reflected from the curve (like light rays from a mirror) pass through a single point inside the parabola, the focus. In a parabolic microphone system, the microphone is placed at this point; sound waves entering the dish parallel to the axis are focused on the microphone and, thus, amplified.

Another type of directional microphone, the shotgun mike, attains directionality by embedding the microphone in a long, narrow, open-ended tube; only sound approaching the mike along the axis of the tube can reach the mike. On one hand, the shotgun design does not *focus* sound on the mike, and so is not as sensitive as the parabolic design; on the other, the shotgun mike is less cumbersome and less open to off-axis sounds.

Parabolic reflectors are also used to create light beams from point sources. All light emanating from a point source placed at the focus of a parabolic reflector will exit the reflector in the direction of the parabola's axis. (The bulbs of car headlights are placed at the foci of parabolic reflectors.)

■ FURTHER READING:

ELECTRONIC:

Weisstein, Eric W. "Parabola." MathWorld (Wolfram Research). <http://mathworld.wolfram.com/Parabola.html> (April 17, 2003).

Pathogen Genomic Sequencing

The Pathogen Genomic Sequencing program initiated by the Defense Advanced Research Project Agency (DARPA) in 2002 focuses on characterizing the genetic components of pathogens in order to develop novel diagnostics, treatments and therapies for the diseases they cause. In particular, the program will collect an inventory of genes and proteins that are specific to pathogens and then look for patterns among these molecules. This information will facilitate the development of tools for identifying pathogens in a variety of vectors. It will also provide a foundation for engineering antibodies to identify pathogens. Initially, one representative strain of the bacteria that cause a variety of diseases (or their close relatives) are being studied for this program: *Brucella suis* (brucellosis), *Burkholderia mallei* (melioidosis), *Clostridium perfringens* (botulism), *Coxiella burnetti* (Q fever), *Franciscella tularensis* (tulareremia), and *Rickettsia typhi* (Rocky Mountain spotted fever).

As part of the Pathogen Genomic Sequencing project, a website focusing on orthopox viruses has been created. Known as the Poxvirus Bioinformatics Resource, this website serves as a repository for genetic sequence data for orthopox viruses. It currently contains sequence data for 35 viral pathogens including the virus that causes smallpox. In addition, the website contains data-mining and sequence analysis software and a poxvirus literature resource. The goals of the Poxvirus Bioinformatics Resource are the development of novel therapies for human diseases caused by orthopox viruses, the ability to detect orthopox viruses in the environment and the development of quick diagnostic tools for detecting pox diseases.

■ FURTHER READING:

ELECTRONIC:

Defense Advanced Research Projects Agency. Defense Sciences Office. "Pathogen Genomic Sequencing." <http://www.darpa.mil/leaving.asp?url=http://www.poxvirus.org.> (April 1, 2003).

Poxvirus Bioinformatics Resource Center. <http://www.poxvirus.org/> (April 1, 2003).

SEE ALSO

DARPA (Defense Advanced Research Projects Agency)
Pathogens

Pathogen Transmission

Pathogens are microorganisms such as viruses, bacteria, protozoa, and fungi that cause disease in humans and other species. Pathogen transmission involves three steps: escape from the host, travel to, and infection of the new host. Pathogen transmission occurs in several ways, usually dependent on the ecology of the organism. For example, respiratory pathogens are usually airborne, while pathogens of the digestive tract tend to occur in food or water. Epidemiologists group pathogen transmission into two general types of contact, direct and indirect, within which there are several mechanisms.

Pathogen transmission by direct contact takes place when an infected host transmits a disease directly to another host. The pathogens that travel this way are extremely sensitive to the environment and cannot be outside of the host for any length of time. For example, pathogens that cause sexually transmitted diseases (STDs) are transmitted via blood, semen, or saliva. Some pathogens responsible for STDs include *Tremonema palidum* (syphilis), *Neisseria gohorrhoeae* (gonorrhea), and the pathogen that causes Acquired Immunodeficiency Syndrome or AIDS, Human Immunodeficiency Virus (HIV). The viruses responsible for hemorrhagic fever, such as Ebola, are also transmitted by direct contact via the blood.

Indirect transmission occurs when an agent is required to transfer the pathogen from an infected host to a susceptible host. The agent may be either animate or inanimate. Animate transmission agents, which are referred to as disease vehicles, include air, water, and food. Inanimate agents also include fomites, which are objects on which the pathogen has been deposited. Examples of fomites are toys, clothes, bedding, or surgical instruments. Animate, or living, agents of disease transmission are most often insects, mites, fleas, and rodents. Living agents of transmission are referred to as vectors. Diseases that are spread via indirect contact in hospitals are specifically referred to as nosocomial infections.

Many respiratory viruses and bacterial spores are light enough to be lifted by the wind. These agents can subsequently be inhaled, where they cause lung infections. A particularly important example of an airborne bacterial pathogen is the spore form of the anthrax-causing bacterium *Bacillus anthraci*. This bacterium forms spores that can spread through the air and cause a severe respiratory disease when inhaled. Biological weapons can be equipped with anthrax spores aimed at infecting populations upon detonation. In 2001, the United States was plagued by a bioterrrorist who placed spores in mail so that the people who handled the envelopes contracted cutaneous or inhalation anthrax.

A common route of indirect pathogen transmission is via water. The ingestion of contaminated water introduces the microbes into the digestive system, where they can attack the gastrointestinal tract. Some pathogenic organisms use the cells that line the digestive tract in order to gain entry to the bloodstream. From there, an infection can become systemic. A common water borne pathogen is *Vibrio cholerae*, the bacterium that causes cholera. The contamination of drinking water by this bacterium still causes cholera epidemics in some areas of the world.

Foodborne pathogens are grouped into two categories: those that produce toxins that poison the host and those that infect the host and then grow there. Food poisoning is most often caused by the bacterium *Staphylococcus aureus*, which produces enterotoxins that result in vomiting and diarrhea. The bacterium *Clostridium botulinum* is responsible for the disease botulism, which is an extremely severe and sometimes fatal food poisoning.

Vectors harbor the microorganisms that cause disease and transfer them to humans via a bite or by other contact. *Coxiella burnetti*, the bacterium that causes Q fever, is transmitted to humans from the handling of animals such as sheep. Insects are common vectors of disease. Mosquitos spread the protozoan *Plasmodium vivax* that causes malaria. Deer ticks are responsible for infection by the spirochete *Borrelia burgdorferi* that causes Lyme disease. The bacterium that causes plague *Yersina pestis* is transmitted by the rat flea.

According to the United States Centers for Disease Control, the pathogens that are most likely to be used as biological weapons use a variety of modes of transmission. Included in this list of pathogens are the airborne bacterium *Bacillus anthracis* and the airborne Variola virus that causes smallpox; the foodborne bacterium *Clostridium botulinum*; *Yersina pestis*, which requires a vector; and the Ebola virus, which requires direct bloodborne transmission.

■ FURTHER READING:

ELECTRONIC:

United States Centers for Disease Control. "Biological Diseases/Agents." <http://www.bt.cdc.gov/Agent/agentlist.asp#categorydescriptions> (February 26, 2003).

SEE ALSO

Anthrax, Terrorist Use as a Biological Weapon
Bioterrorism, Protective Measures
Food Supply, Counter-Terrorism
Infectious Disease, Threats to Security
Vaccines

Pathogens

■ BRIAN HOYLE

Pathogens are organisms, frequently microorganisms, or components of these organisms, that cause disease. Microbial pathogens include various species of bacteria, viruses, and protozoa. Many diseases caused by microbial pathogens, and the frequency of these diseases, are a national security issue.

Pathogens and disease. A disease is any condition caused by the presence of an invading organism or a toxic component that damages the host. In humans, diseases can be caused by the growth of microorganisms such as bacteria, viruses, and protozoa. Bacterial growth, however, is not mandatory to cause disease. For example, some bacterial pathogens cause disease by virtue of a toxic component of the bacterial cell such as lipopolysaccharide. Finally, the damaging symptoms of a disease can be the result of the attempts by the host's immune system to rid the body of the invader. One example is the immune-related damage caused to the lungs of those afflicted with cystic fibrosis, as the body unsuccessfully attempts to eradicate the chronic infections caused by *Pseudomonas aeruginosa*.

Not all pathogens cause diseases that have the same severity of symptoms. For example, an infection with the influenza virus can cause the short term aches and fever that are hallmarks of the flu, or it can cause more dire symptoms, depending on the type of virus that causes the infection. Bacteria also vary in the damage caused. For example, the ingestion of food contaminated with *Salmonella enteritica* causes intestinal upset. But, consumption of *Escherichia coli* O157:H7 causes a severe disease, which can permanently damage the kidneys and which can even be fatal.

Types of bacterial pathogens. There are three categories of bacterial pathogens. Obligate pathogens are those bacteria that must cause disease in order to be transmitted from one host to another. These bacteria must also infect a host in order to survive, in contrast to other bacteria that are capable of survival outside of a host. Examples of obligate bacterial pathogens include *Mycobacterium tuberculosis* and *Treponema pallidum*.

Opportunistic pathogens can be transmitted from one host to another without having to cause disease. However, in a host whose immune system is not functioning properly, the bacteria can cause an infection that leads to a disease. In those cases, the disease can help the bacteria spread to another host. Examples of opportunistic bacterial pathogens include *Vibrio cholerae* and *Pseudomonas aeruginosa*.

Finally, some bacterial pathogens cause disease only accidentally. Indeed, the disease actually limits the spread of the bacteria to another host. Examples of these "accidental' pathogens include *Neisseria meningitides* and *Bacteroides fragilis*.

Spread of pathogens. Pathogens can be spread from person to person in a number of ways. Not all pathogens use all the available routes. For example, the influenza virus is transmitted from person to person through the air, typically via sneezing or coughing. But the virus is not transmitted via water. In contrast, *Escherichia coli* is readily transmitted via water, food, and blood, but is not readily transmitted via air or the bite of an insect.

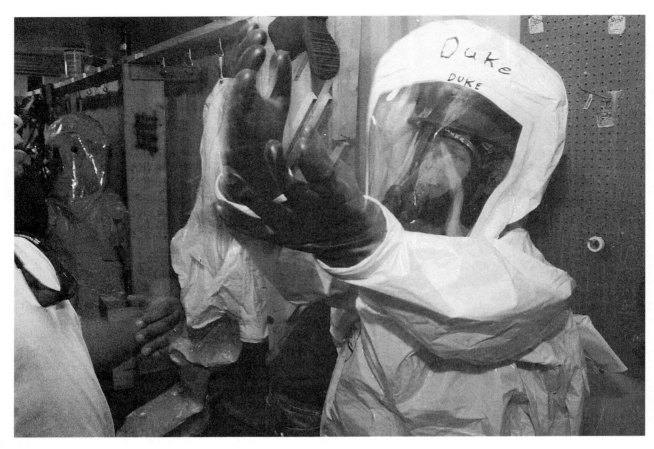

A worker gets into his chemical protection suit before entering an environmentally sealed tent at Area B-11 on the grounds of Ft. Detrick, Maryland, during a chemical cleanup operation. AP/WIDE WORLD PHOTOS.

While routes of transmission vary for different pathogens, a given pathogen will use a given route of transmission. This has been used in the weaponization of pathogens. The best-known example is anthrax. The bacterium that causes anthrax—*Bacillus anthracis*—can form an environmentally hardy form called a spore. The spore is very small and light. It can float on currents of air and can be breathed into the lungs, where the bacteria resume growth and swiftly cause a serious and often fatal form of anthrax. As demonstrated in the United States in the last few months of 2001, anthrax spores are easily sent through the mail to targets. As well, the powdery spores can be released from an aircraft. Over a major urban center, modeling studies have indicated that the resulting casualties could number in the hundreds of thousands.

Contamination of water by pathogens is another insidious route of disease spread. Water can look crystal clear despite the presence of millions of bacteria in each milliliter. Viruses, which are much smaller, can be present in even higher numbers without affecting the appearance of the liquid. Thus, water can be easily laced with enough pathogens to cause illness.

Food-borne pathogens cause millions of cases of disease and hundreds of deaths each year in the United States alone. Frequently the responsible microbes are bacteria, viruses, or protozoa that usually reside in the intestinal tract of humans or other creatures. Examples of such microorganisms include *Escherichia coli* O157:H7, *Campylobacter jejuni*, and rotavirus.

Pathogens can be transmitted to humans through contact with animals, birds, and other living creatures that naturally harbor the microorganism. The agent of anthrax—*Bacillus anthracis*—naturally dwells in sheep. Other examples include *Brucella abortic* (Brucellosis), *Coxiella burnetti* (Q fever), and viruses that cause hemorrhagic fevers such as Ebola and Marburg.

Pathogenic mechanisms. Microorganisms have various strategies to establish an infection in a host. Some microorganisms recognize molecules on the surface of the host cell, and use these as receptors. The binding of bacteria or viruses to receptors brings the microorganism in close contact with the host surface.

The nature of the interaction between the host receptor molecule and the attachment molecule on the surface of the bacteria, virus, or protozoan has in some cases been defined, even to the genetic level. The use of recombinant

DNA technology—where a target section of genetic material is removed from one organism and inserted into a certain region of the genetic material of another organism, in a way that does not affect the expression of the gene—allows the genetic manipulation of a microorganism so as to enhance its ability to cause an infection. Alternatively, inserting a gene that codes for a toxin into a bacterium that is a normal inhabitant of an environment like the intestinal tract could produce a formidable pathogen. This altered bacteria would readily associate with host cells, but would also carry the toxin.

Viruses almost always damage the host cells. Because viruses cannot reproduce on their own, they rely on the replication mechanism of the host cell to make more copies of themselves (i.e., they are obligate pathogens). Then, the new viral particles will exit the cell and search for another cell to infect. This exit is often very physically damaging to the host cell. Thus, viral infections can be detrimental because of the loss of function of host cells.

Some viral pathogens are capable of causing a disease long after they have infected a host. This delayed response occurs because the viral genetic material becomes incorporated into the genetic material of the host. Thereafter, the viral genetic material is replicated along with that of the host, using the replication enzymes and other machinery of the host. But, in response to a number of signals, the viral material can be excised from the host material and form the template for the manufacture and assembly of new virus particles. A prominent example of such a virus is the Human Immunodeficiency Virus, which is acknowledged to be the cause of Acquired Immunodeficiency Syndrome.

Because viruses must infect other cells in order to replicate, they have developed means of escaping (at least for a time) the defensive responses of the host. This efficiency of attack has not escaped the attention of molecular biologists bent on the malicious use of viruses. By inserting gene coding for a toxic compound into a viral genome, particularly into the genome of an infectious virus (i.e., influenza or cold viruses) the virus becomes a bioweapon. For example, scientists in the former Soviet Union attempted to construct an influenza virus that contained the gene coding for cobra toxin.

■ FURTHER READING:

BOOKS:

Fields, Bernard N., Peter M. Howley, and Diane E. Griffin, eds. *Virology*. Philadelphia: Lippincott Williams & Wilkins, 2001.

Shnayerson, Michael, and Mark J. Plotkin. *The Killers Within: The Deadly Rise of Drug Resistant Bacteria*. New York: Little Brown & Company, 2002.

Smith, H., C. J. Dornan, G. Dougan, et al., eds. *The Activities of Bacterial Pathogens In Vivo*. River Edge, NJ: World Scientific, 2001.

ELECTRONIC:

Centers for Disease Control and Prevention. "Disease Information." Special Pathogens Branch. July 26, 2002. <http://www.cdc.gov/ncidod/dvrd/spb/mnpages/disinfo.htm> (28 December 2002).

SEE ALSO

Biocontainment Laboratories
Decontamination Methods
Infectious Disease, Threats to Security

Patriot Act Terrorist Exclusion List

As mandated by the Patriot Act of 2001 (officially the Uniting and Strengthening America by Providing Appropriate Tools Required to Intercept and Obstruct Terrorism Act), the United States Department of State Office of the Coordinator for Counterterrorism, in conjunction with the Attorney General, compiles a Terrorist Exclusion List (TEL) of groups and individuals excluded entry into the United States because of terrorist related activities. Individuals and organizations who commit, incite, or aid in the commission of a terrorist act with the intention to cause death or bodily injury may be placed on the TEL. Acts prior to the commission of a terrorist act, or that aid terrorist organizations also qualify individuals and groups for exclusion. Such preparation or aid can include—but is not limited to—the gathering of intelligence for, or financial support of, terrorist activities.

For purpose of compiling the TEL, the Department of State use the definition of terrorism set forth in United States law and that specifically defines terrorism as "the commission of acts, formulation of plans, or threat to engage in unlawful acts that include—but are not limited to—hijacking, sabotage, the taking of hostages, a violent and deliberate attack on civilians; assassination; the use or transportation of nuclear, chemical, or biological weapons."

TEL designation is intended to disregard supposed political or ideological purposes for terrorist acts while providing a legal framework to exclude or deport aliens associated with TEL-designated organizations. TEL designations are also intended to deter contributions to terrorist groups, to increase public awareness of such groups, and isolate designated organizations.

■ FURTHER READING:

ELECTRONIC:

U.S. Department of State. International Information Programs. Fact Sheet: Terrorist Exclusion List Bolsters Homeland Security. November 15, 2002. <http://usinfo.state.gov/topical/pol/terror/02111803.htm> (April 16, 2003).

SEE ALSO

Coordinator for Counterterrorism, United States Office
Terrorist and Para-State Organizations
Terrorist Organization List, United States
Terrorist Organizations, Freezing of Assets
Terrorist Threat Integration Center

Patriot Act, United States

The Patriot Act, or Uniting and Strengthening America by Providing Appropriate Tools Required to Intercept and Obstruct Terrorism Act, was signed into law on October 26, 2001, in the wake of terrorist attacks on the World Trade Center and Pentagon. The legislation grants law enforcement and intelligence agencies more power to detain and question suspects for longer periods of time, and increases their ability to conduct surveillance operations.

The act further calls on federal agencies to share information regarding terrorist activities with each other, and with foreign intelligence services if necessary. Thus, domestic law enforcement was granted new privileges to deal directly with international agencies. The bill asks, but cannot compel that foreign intelligence services reciprocate and share information with United States authorities.

Some provisions, such as the authority to intercept wire communications that possibly relate to terrorism and the sharing of criminal investigative information, are set to expire in 2005. Some debated provisions, however, will remain indefinitely. The sharing of grand jury information and the ability to search without a warrant in limited cases, for example, do not expire.

The Patriot Act extended the government's surveillance authority under the Foreign Intelligence Surveillance Act (FISA), which was passed by the United States Congress in 1978. New powers included roving wiretap authority (the surveillance of communications related to an individual or organization without regard to particular telephone line, computer station, or other mode of communication to be monitored). Other extensions included a more liberalized use of pen register, trap and trace devices (removing the need to assert that the surveillance target is "an agent of a foreign power"). In May 2002, the Foreign Intelligence Surveillance Court specifically rejected Justice Department attempts at "information screening" and "minimization" procedures intended to allow the use of material gathered under Foreign Intelligence Surveillance Court authorization in criminal proceedings. The Department of Justice appealed the ruling to the Foreign Intelligence Surveillance Court of Review.

Supporters of the Patriot Act say that the legislation is not drastic and that law enforcement and intelligence must not be hampered in their pursuit of suspected terrorists. Opponents assert the law infringes on constitutional protections on legal search, seizure, and detention of property and persons. Some are wary of the implications of the Patriot Act on Internet and computer privacy. Others argue that the measure is acceptable during wartime, or when specifically applied against suspected terrorists, but that broad interpretation and application of the law could be problematic in its constitutionality.

The newness of the law means that it has yet to be both fully implemented and ultimately tested. Thus, a final assessment on its efficacy, intent, application, and legacy will require the perspective of time.

SEE ALSO

Homeland Security, United States Department of
September 11 Terrorist Attacks on the United States

Patriot Missile System

Among the world's most advanced ground-based air defense systems, the Patriot Air and Missile Defense System is in service to the United States and other nations. The missile system, produced jointly by Raytheon and Lockheed Martin Missiles and Fire Control, was a notable feature in the Persian Gulf War of 1991 and Operation Iraqi Freedom in 2003. Since 1991, the U.S. Department of Defense (DOD) has spent more than $3 billion in further improvements. As effective as the Patriot has been, however, its record is not flawless.

Among the most significant aspects of the Patriot missile system are the multifunction phased array radar, the track-via-missile guidance with midcourse correction commands and ground radar downlink, and the human override to its automated operations. The system also includes an engagement control station, electronic power plant vehicle, as many as 16 remote launching stations (each with four Patriots ready to fire), and an antenna mast group for communications.

In the Persian Gulf War, allied forces used the Patriot to stop Iraqi Scud missiles, particularly when Saddam Hussein's military fired on Israel. After the war ended, DOD invested in numerous upgrades such as the development of the Patriot Guidance Enhanced Missile Plus (GEM+), which includes a new fuse and a low-noise front end that increases the sensitivity to low radar targets. With 148 missiles contracted, Raytheon delivered the first GEM+ models in November 2002.

Despite the successes of the Patriot in Operation Desert Storm, there were mishaps, as when a Patriot at Dharan, Saudi Arabia, failed to intercept an incoming Scud on February 25, 1991, resulting in the deaths of 28 Americans. During Operation Iraqi Freedom 12 years later, the Patriot was involved in several unfortunate incidents, including the downing of a British Royal Air Force Tornado

Senator Patrick Leahy (with camera) peers over the shoulder of President Bush during a ceremony for the signing of the Patriot Act in the White House East Room in October 2001. AP/WIDE WORLD PHOTOS.

with two airmen aboard on March 23, 2003. Aside from the United States, nations that possess Patriots include Germany, Japan, Israel, Saudi Arabia, Kuwait, Taiwan, Greece, and the Netherlands. Patriots have also been cleared for sale to Egypt.

■ FURTHER READING:

PERIODICALS:

Kilian, Michael. "Patriot Missile Miscalculations a Cause for U.S. Concern." *Chicago Tribune.* (March 27, 2003): 5.

Marshall, Eliot. "Patriot's Scud Busting Record Is Challenged." *Science* 252, no. 5006 (May 3, 1991): 640–641.

ELECTRONIC:

GAO Report: Patriot Missile Defense. Federation of American Scientists. <http://www.fas.org/spp/starwars/gao/im92026.htm> (April 7, 2003).

Patriot Missile Air Defense System, USA. Army Technology. <http://www.army-technology.com/projects/patriot/> (April 7, 2003).

A Patriot anti-missile missile is launched during a 2001 joint Israeli-American military exercise in the Negev Desert in southern Israel. AP/WIDE WORLD PHOTOS.

SEE ALSO

Ballistic Missile Defense Organization, United States
Ballistic Missiles
Cruise Missile
IFF (Identification Friend or Foe)
Iraqi Freedom, Operation (2003 War Against Iraq)
Persian Gulf War
Strategic Defense Initiative and National Missile Defense

Pearl Harbor, Japanese Attack on

❚ MICHAEL J. O'NEAL

On December 7, 1941, Japanese military forces attacked the United States naval fleet anchored at Pearl Harbor on the Hawaiian island of Oahu. The surprise attack nearly devastated the American Pacific fleet. Three cruisers, three destroyers, and eight battleships along "Battleship Row" were severely damaged, and two battleships, the *Oklahoma* and the *Arizona,* were sunk. Additionally, nearly 350 American warplanes on Oahu were destroyed, virtually all that were on the ground. Over 2,400 U.S. servicemen lost their lives, and nearly 1,200 were wounded. The success of the daring attack severely impaired America's ability to check the expansion of the Japanese empire in the Pacific during the first years of WWII.

Background. As an island nation, Japan had developed a rich and complex social structure. It resisted westernization by sealing itself off from contact with the outside world, particularly Europe and the United States. By the early twentieth century, though, Japan's efforts to achieve self-sufficiency were failing, for the nation lacked its own raw materials and other resources. Some members of the ruling class argued that Japan could grow and prosper only by modernizing and adopting Western technology. Japanese nationalists, though, advocated a different path: the establishment of an empire that would not only elevate Japan's stature in the eyes of the world but also

Three U.S. battleships are hit from the air during the Japanese attack on Pearl Harbor on December 7, 1941. From left are: USS *West Virginia*, severly damaged; USS *Tennessee*, damaged; and USS *Arizona*, sunk. AP/WIDE WORLD PHOTOS.

guarantee access to the resources the nation needed. Moreover, many members of the nation's traditional warrior class—the Samurai—were embittered by the aftermath of World War I. Japan had backed the victorious Allies, but the Samurai believed that in the peace negotiations following the war the United States and Great Britain had treated Japan as a second-class nation. They, too, longed to assert Japan's place in world affairs.

Japan began to flex its muscles in 1931. Japanese forces stationed in Manchuria, northeast of China, to protect a Japanese railway that transported goods and raw materials out of the country suddenly seized control of all of Manchuria. Then in 1937, Japanese forces attacked the eastern provinces of China, seizing China's capital, Nanking, and the old capital, Beijing, in brutal fashion. Observers in the West were horrified by reports of the atrocities against civilians committed by Japanese invaders in the so-called "Rape of Nanking." Under the leadership of Minister of War Hideki Tojo, Japan's objective was to establish a

defensive perimeter—the "Greater East Asia Co-Prosperity Sphere"—in the western Pacific. This perimeter was to extend from the Jurile Islands northeast of Japan, south to the Marianas and Marshall Islands, west through the Solomon Islands, New Guinea, and the East Indies, then northward into the Indian Ocean and southeast Asia. Tojo believed that Japan could thus drive out the Western powers, achieve a position of preeminence in East Asia, and free the nation from its dependence on Western oil, coal, rubber, ore, and other vital resources.

Tojo's strategy, however, was bringing him ever closer to conflict with those powers. The Dutch, for example, controlled the East Indies, France had a presence in Indo-China, the United States controlled the Philippines, and Malaya was a British colony. Concerned about Japanese aggression, Holland, Great Britain, and the United States imposed a trade embargo on Japan on July 26, 1941, cutting off supplies of resources to the increasingly belligerent nation. Tojo, now prime minister, was convinced that the West's goal was to starve Japan into submission.

Events came to a boil in September, 1941. United States Secretary of State Cordell Hull demanded that Japan withdraw its troops from China and Southeast Asia. While many Japanese military leaders quailed at the prospect of going to war with the United States, Tojo convinced them that acceding to American demands would be a humiliating diplomatic defeat. While carrying on protracted—and deceptive—negotiations with the United States, Japan invaded Thailand, Malaya, Burma, and the East Indies. And on November 26, the Japanese navy set sail for Pearl Harbor, where most of the U.S. Pacific fleet was docked.

The attack.

Traveling under strict radio silence and screened from view by a large weather front, the Japanese battle fleet—six aircraft carriers, two battleships, two cruisers, and nine destroyers—remained undetected until it came within two hundred miles of the Hawaiian Islands. On the morning of December 7, 183 torpedo bombers and dive-bombers took off from the aircraft carriers. The Japanese pilots knew exactly where they were going because spies on the islands had given them elaborate and detailed scale models of the base, including Battleship Row. Because it was Sunday morning, most of the U.S. naval personnel were ashore, and most of the antiaircraft defenses were unmanned. At 7:49 AM local time, the attack began—and by 8:12, much of the fleet had been damaged or sunk. A second wave of bombers arrived at nine o'clock to finish what the first wave had started. In a little more than an hour, the United States fleet was severely crippled. Two days later, on December 9, the United States declared war on Japan.

Japanese espionage.

The U.S. Army's Hawaii Department was charged with coastal defenses on the islands in 1941. In a 1955 interview, its chief, Major General Charles D. Herron, stated, "It was a matter of common knowledge that the Japanese Consulate in Honolulu was the hotbed of espionage in Oahu." In large part, the attack on Pearl Harbor was so successful because Japanese spies, under cover of "diplomatic" posts, were able to blend easily with the large Japanese population on the islands and in the process gather valuable intelligence.

One such diplomat, for example, was Takeo Yoshikawa, who openly arrived in Hawaii by ship on March 27, 1941, as Tadashi Morimura. Yoshikawa was a trained spy assigned to the Japanese consulate on Oahu. He took a second-story room that gave him a view of Pearl Harbor and Hickam Field, where the American air fleet was based. In the weeks and months after his arrival, Yoshikawa moved freely about the island. At times he would loiter in a sugar cane field near Pearl Harbor, posing as a fieldworker. At other times he would observe Pearl Harbor from a peninsula at the end of the island or through telescopes

for sightseers at a Japanese-owned restaurant on a hill overlooking the harbor. Little about his work was glamorous. He made notes, took photos, chartered small boats and planes. He even mailed back home postcards with aerial views of Pearl Harbor that helped planners construct mock-ups used to train bomber pilots for the raid. In these endeavors, he was ably supported not only by his superiors in the consular office but even by the taxi driver who frequently drove him around the island. He observed, for example, that there tended to be a large number of ships in port on Saturdays and Sundays, fewer on weekdays. He also observed American air patrols, noticing that they tended rarely to fly to the north. The kinds of details Yoshikawa meticulously noted and passed along to military planners in Japan proved invaluable on December 7, a Sunday, when Japanese planes approached Oahu from the north.

American intelligence.

A question that continues to intrigue historians is how American intelligence could have failed so spectacularly, given the circumstances. The diplomatic situation was tense, and growing tenser. It was known that Germany, a Japanese ally, was pressing Japan to take action to divert American attention away from Europe. As early as January 27, 1941 Joseph Grew, the U.S. ambassador in Japan, reported to Secretary of State Hull that the embassy had learned from Japanese sources that a mass attack on Pearl Harbor was planned in case hostilities broke out. The United States had broken the Japanese diplomatic code (called Purple), so war planners from the president on down knew that spies had been reporting on the fleet deployment in Hawaii. In the weeks and days before the attack, encrypted diplomatic traffic became heavier, and increasingly ominous. On November 19, for example, American codebreakers intercepted a message from Tokyo to diplomatic posts in Washington, D.C., and several West Coast cities. The message instructed these offices to destroy all codes, coding machines, papers, and the like if they heard the words "East Wind Rain" (*Higashi No Kazeame*) in the daily weather forecast. On Thursday, December 4, the United States intercepted the so-called "winds message." Even on the morning of December 7, Army Chief of Staff General George C. Marshall sent an urgent warning to commanders in the Pacific that intercepted Japanese diplomatic messages strongly suggested an attack was imminent. Military signalmen, however, could not raise Pearl Harbor on military channels, so the message was sent by slower commercial cable. By the time it arrived, Japanese planes were in the air over Pearl Harbor.

Given this flood of intelligence, historians and military analysts question why the military failed to take steps to defend Pearl Harbor. One answer might lie in the flood of messages intercepted. Few of the hundreds of intercepted diplomatic messages specifically mentioned Pearl Harbor. Those that did—requests for information on fleet deployment at Pearl, for example—were part of general requests for similar information about numerous American bases in the Pacific. While events proved that Pearl Harbor was Japan's intended target, that seemed less apparent in 1941, when bits of unconnected intelligence arrived on the president's desk on a daily basis and no one was charged with the responsibility of "connecting the dots." Ironically, the only American official who had clear intelligence regarding Pearl Harbor was FBI director J. Edgar Hoover. The information, though, was provided by a Yugoslav double agent named Dusko Popov, who had received clear indications of Japanese intentions while operating in Germany. Hoover, though, hated Slavs, despised Popov, cut his interview with Popov short, and failed to send Popov's vital information on to the president.

Although evidence is lacking or conflicting, some revisionist historians have presented scenarios that may explain U.S. failures to protect the fleet. Some of these scenarios involve a deliberate disregard for intelligence by U.S. and British leaders on the grounds that the attack would likely force America's entrance into WWII. Most historians, however, dismiss these theories as either inconsistent with the greater body of evidence, or simply convoluted and needlessly complex explanations of normal intelligence and communications failures.

∎ FURTHER READING:

BOOKS:

Andrew, Christopher. *For the President's Eyes Only: Secret Intelligence and the American Presidency from Washington to Bush.* New York: HarperCollins, 1995.

Benson, Robert Louis. *A History of U.S. Communications Intelligence During World War II: Policy and Administration.* Washington, D.C.: Center for Cryptologic History, National Security Agency, 1997.

Persico, Joseph E. *Roosevelt's Secret War: FDR and World War II Espionage.* New York: Random House, 2001.

Prange, Gordon W. *At Dawn We Slept: The Untold Story of Pearl Harbor.* New York: McGraw-Hill, 1981.

Winton, John. *Ultra in the Pacific: How Breaking Japanese Codes & Cyphers Affected Naval Operations Against Japan: 1941–45.* London: Leo Cooper, 1993.

ELECTRONIC:

Singh, Simon. "US Codebreakers in World War II." <http://www.vectorsite.net/ttcode7.html> (January 9, 2003).

SEE ALSO

Cipher Machines
Codes and Ciphers
Cryptology, History
Double Agents
Purple Machine
World War II

PEN Register.

SEE *Internet Surveillance.*

Pentagon Terrorist Attack.

SEE *September 11 Terrorist Attacks on the United States.*

People Against Gangsterism and Drugs (PAGAD)

People Against Gangsterism and Drugs (PAGAD) was formed in 1996 as a community anti-crime group fighting drugs and violence in the Cape Flats section of Cape Town, South Africa, but by early 1998 it had also become anti-government and anti-Western. PAGAD and its Islamic ally Qibla view the South African Government as a threat to Islamic values and consequently, promote a greater political voice for South African Muslims. Abdus Salaam Ebrahim currently leads both groups. PAGAD's G-Force (Gun Force) operates in small cells and is believed to be responsible for carrying out acts of terrorism. PAGAD uses several front names, including Muslims Against Global Oppression (MAGO) and Muslims Against Illegitimate Leaders (MAIL), when launching anti-Western protests and campaigns. PAGAD's activities were severely curtailed in 2001 by law enforcement and prosecutorial efforts against leading members of the organization. PAGAD's bombing targets have included South African authorities, moderate Muslims, synagogues, gay nightclubs, tourist attractions, and Western-associated restaurants. PAGAD is believed to have masterminded the bombing in August, 1998, of the Cape Town Planet Hollywood.

Estimated at several hundred members, PAGAD's G-Force probably contains fewer than 50 members. PAGAD operates mainly in the Cape Town area, South Africa's foremost tourist venue.

∎ FURTHER READING:

ELECTRONIC:

CDI (Center for Defense Information), Terrorism Project. CDI Fact Sheet: Current List of Designated Foreign Terrorist Organizations. March 27, 2003. <http://www.cdi.org/terrorism/terrorist.cfm> (April 17, 2003).

Central Intelligence Agency. World Factbook, 2002. <http://www.cia.gov/cia/publications/factbook/> (April 16, 2003).

Taylor, Francis X. U.S. Department of State. "Patterns of Global Terrorism 2001." Annual Report: On the Record Briefing. May 21, 2002. <http://www.state.gov/s/ct/rls/rm/10367.htm> (April 17, 2003).

U.S. Department of State. Annual reports. <http://www.state.gov/www/global/terrorism/annual_reports.html> (April 16, 2003).

SEE ALSO

Terrorism, Philosophical and Ideological Origins
Terrorist and Para-State Organizations
Terrorist Organization List, United States
Terrorist Organizations, Freezing of Assets

Persian Gulf War

▌ JUDSON KNIGHT

The Persian Gulf War, in which a coalition led by the United States drove Iraqi forces out of Kuwait in early 1991, was one of the most successful campaigns in history. At a cost of less than 300 Allied lives, coalition troops, whose military actions were largely funded by Saudi Arabia, drove out Saddam Hussein's forces. Thousands of Iraqi lives were lost in the process, however. In their victory, the coalition depended in large part on advances in military technology by the United States, whose arsenal included tools ranging from the F-117A stealth fighter to the M1A1 Abrams tank, and from the Global Positioning System (GPS) to unmanned drones and Patriot missiles. Less clearly successful was U.S. intelligence, which had failed to predict the war. Equally questionable was the ultimate outcome of the war, whose scores would not fully be settled until 12 years later.

The Persian Gulf War is sometimes called simply the Gulf War or Operation Desert Storm, after the U.S.-led campaign that comprised the bulk of the fighting. It may ultimately come to be known as "Gulf War II," or "Persian Gulf War II," with the 2003 operation in Iraq becoming the third in this series. The first, also known as the Iran-Iraq War, lasted from 1980 to 1988, and pitted the dictatorship of Saddam Hussein against the Islamic theocracy in Iran.

Both regimes had taken power in 1979, but the conflict concerned long standing disputes involving lands on the borders between the two nations. In the ensuing hostilities, most nations—including much of the Arab world, the United States, western Europe, and the Soviet bloc—supported Iraq, generally regarded as the lesser of two evils. (Both the Americans and the Soviets also gave covert support to the Iranians as well.) The war, which cost some 850,000 lives, resulted in a stalemate, and both nations built monuments to their alleged victories.

In the aftermath of the first Gulf War, analysts working for the U.S. Central Intelligence Agency (CIA) prepared a report on the likelihood of Iraqi aggression in the near future. According to the now-infamous study, Saddam had so overextended his resources in the war with Iran that he would not take any major aggressive action for at least three years. In this instance, the CIA underestimated Saddam's penchant for military adventurism.

Invasion and Buildup

On August 2, 1990, without advance warning, Iraqi tanks and troops rolled into neighboring Kuwait. Both nations possessed considerable oil wealth, but Kuwait was by far the richer of the two, and Iraq—particularly under Saddam's regime—had long had designs on Kuwait. Given the importance of oil from the Persian Gulf region, which at that time fueled a great part of the world, neither the United States nor the United Nations (UN) Security Council was inclined to ignore Hussien's aggressive action.

The Security Council on August 3 called for an Iraqi withdrawal, and on August 6 it imposed a worldwide ban on trade with Iraq. On August 5, President George H. W. Bush declared that the invasion "will not stand," and a day later, King Fahd of Saudi Arabia met with U.S. Defense Secretary Richard Cheney to request military assistance. Saudi Arabia, Japan, and other wealthy allies would underwrite most of the $60 billion associated with the resulting military effort. By August 8, U.S. Air Force fighters were in Saudi Arabia.

Numerous countries were involved in the military buildup during late 1990, a program known as Operation Desert Shield. By January 1991, the United States alone had some 540,000 troops, along with another 160,000 from the United Kingdom, France, Egypt, Saudi Arabia, Syria, Kuwait, and other nations. On November 29, 1990, the Security Council authorized use of force against Iraq unless it withdrew its troops by January 15. Saddam's only response was to continue building his troop strength in Kuwait, such that by the time the Allies counterattacked, he had some 300,000 men on the ground.

On January 17, 1991, Operation Desert Shield became Operation Desert Storm, which consisted largely of bombing campaigns against Iraq's command and control, infrastructure, and military assets. In retaliation, Iraq attacked Israel with Scud missiles on January 18. A great portion of the Allied losses occurred in this initial phase, when the Iraqis shot down several low-flying U.S. and British planes.

After thus severing the tail of the invading force, the Allies in February began concentrating on Iraqi positions in Kuwait. Having initially planned an amphibious landing, Allied commander General H. Norman Schwarzkopf instead opted for an armored assault. On February 24, in a campaign phase named Operation Desert Sabre, Allied troops moved northward from Saudi Arabia and into Kuwait. By February 27, they had taken Kuwait City.

At the same time, operations in Iraq itself continued. In the only major bombing run on the capital city of Baghdad, Stealth fighters struck Iraqi intelligence headquarters, while U.S. Army Special Forces teams inserted themselves deep in Iraq. In the southern part of the country, U.S. tanks pounded Iraqi armored reserve forces, while Allied ground forces neutralized Hussien's "elite"

A line of captured Iraqi soldiers are marched through the desert in Kuwait past a group of U.S. Marine vehicles during the 1991 Persian Gulf War. AP/WIDE WORLD PHOTOS.

Republican Guard south of Basra. President Bush declared a cease-fire on February 28.

The war had lasted 42 days, and the principal campaign, the mid-January bombing, took just over 100 hours. Credit for this extraordinary success goes to a number of factors, not least of which was strong leadership. On the military side, there was Schwarzkopf on the ground, and in Washington, General Colin Powell, Chairman of the Joint Chiefs of Staff, who served as the principal military spokesman during the war. In this, the first major U.S. action since the end of fighting in Vietnam nearly two decades earlier, the performance of both leaders and troops showed that military capabilities had improved extraordinarily since then.

Among the civilian leaders were Cheney, Secretary of State James Baker, National Security Advisor Brent Scowcroft, and President Bush. The president, sometimes criticized for a failure to communicate his aims to his subordinates or the public as a whole, was quite clear in his objectives for the Persian Gulf War. On January 15, 1991, Bush sent his principal security advisors a memorandum which outlined four major aims: to force an Iraqi withdrawal from Kuwait, to restore Kuwait's government, to protect American lives, and to promote stability and security in the Gulf region.

Another factor in the success—and another point of comparison with Vietnam—was the near-unanimous support for the action. Whereas American allies and foes alike questioned the value of the action in Vietnam, virtually no one other than Saddam's regime (along with a handful of antiwar protestors at home) opposed the U.S. effort to liberate an invaded nation. This support was helped rather than hurt by an unprecedented level of television coverage. While Vietnam became known as "the first televised war," TV reporting in the 1960s and 1970s was minimal compared to the round-the-clock reportage offered by cable outlets, most notably the Cable News Network (CNN), in 1990 and 1991.

The U.S. arsenal. While human factors deserve a great deal of credit for the success of Allied operations in the Persian Gulf War, the war would not have been won as efficiently without the technological superiority offered by modern weaponry. Among the tools in the U.S. arsenal were a variety of aircraft, including the AH-64 Apache helicopter, the leading anti-armor attack chopper. Introduced in 1984, the Apache could operate in conditions of darkness or low visibility, and was made to sustain heavy pounding from antiaircraft guns.

The E-3 Sentry AWACS (airborne warning and control system) was a masterpiece of modern technology. Packed with electronics, the aircraft—based on the Boeing 707 and introduced in 1977—was made to identify enemy aircraft, jam enemy radar, guide bombers to their targets, and manage the flow of friendly aircraft. Even more cutting-edge were the Pointer and Pioneer drones, or remotely piloted vehicles (RPVs).

Based on Israeli designs and first used by the United States during the war, the RPVs served as airborne spy platforms. The Pioneer, with a range of about 100 miles (161km) and a flight duration of five hours, could take high-definition pictures from 2,000 feet (610 meters) and transmit them to a processing center. In addition to its video cameras, it was equipped with infrared heat sensors, and provided a wealth of intelligence on everything from enemy troop movements to the recommended path for Tomahawk cruise missiles.

Other aircraft included the B-52 Stratofortress bomber, the F-117A Stealth fighter, and the E-8G JSTARS surveillance aircraft. Among the other notable weapons used in the Persian Gulf War were the M1A1 Abrams tank, the Bradley Fighting Vehicle, the MIM-104 Patriot missile defense system, and the Tomahawk cruise missile. High above the ground was the GPS, whose 24 satellites helped soldiers find their bearings in the desert, and assisted artillery in targeting.

Controversies. More controversial than the role of weapons systems was that of intelligence in the Persian Gulf War. The CIA did not inspire a great deal of confidence, either with its initial estimate of Iraqi intentions or from its August 1996 "Final Report on Intelligence Related to Gulf War Illnesses." In the wake of illnesses that broke out among returning personnel, the CIA sought to investigate the connection between these conditions and Iraqi use of chemical or biological agents. The CIA report found no evidence that Iraq had intentionally used such weapons against the United States, even though Saddam used chemical weapons against rebellious Kurds in the north.

More successful was the performance of Defense Department intelligence and related activities, both on the part of the Defense Intelligence Agency (DIA) and various military intelligence and psychological warfare units. DIA began operations in Iraq long before the war, and regularly gathered intelligence reports that proved invaluable to military leadership. The same was true of military intelligence units, while psychological operations had an immeasurable impact by coercing Iraqis to provide the Allies with intelligence on their forces' activities and capabilities.

In addition to controversies over the success of intelligence, there remained questions concerning the success of the war as a whole. This fact was symbolized by the failure of Bush—who, after the war, had the highest poll numbers of any U.S. President since scientific polling began—to gain reelection in 1992. Ironically, Saddam Hussein, who many U.S. leaders had expected to be toppled in the unrest that followed the war, remained in power despite UN sanctions and the imposition of a no-fly zone over the northern and southern portions of the country. Among the factors cited for Bush's sudden loss of popularity from mid-1991 onward (in addition to an economic slowdown and clever campaigning by challenger William J. Clinton) was his failure to remove Saddam Hussein. However, as Bush rightly noted, such action was not within his mandate from the UN.

In 1993, the CIA uncovered evidence that Saddam Hussein had attempted to assassinate Bush, in response for which U.S. warships fired 23 cruise missiles at Iraqi secret service headquarters. The years that followed saw a lengthy process of UN and U.S. attempts to find weapons of mass destruction thought to be hidden in Iraq continually thwarted by Saddam Hussein. When he evicted UN inspectors in 1998, the United States and United Kingdom launched a four-day bombing campaign, Desert Fox, against Iraq.

Although overt evidence was lacking, some in the U.S. intelligence and defense communities suspected Iraqi ties to the 1993 World Trade Center bombing, and after the 2001 destruction of those buildings, President George W. Bush indicated that the attacks had been sponsored or at least abetted by Iraq. In March, 2003, the United States launched Operation Iraqi Freedom, a land invasion of Iraq. Though many putative experts claimed that the campaign would not be as successful as the Persian Gulf War, this one—while much less popular globally—was actually shorter, and achieved something the earlier war did not: the removal of Saddam Hussein from his position of leadership. Assisting the younger Bush were several figures from the Persian Gulf War, including Cheney and Powell, now vice president and secretary of state respectively.

■ **FURTHER READING:**

BOOKS:

Allen, Thomas B., F. Clinton Berry, and Norman Polmar. *War in the Gulf.* Kansas City, MO: Andrews & McMeel, 1991.

Atkinson, Rick. *Crusade: The Untold Story of the Persian Gulf War.* Boston: Houghton Mifflin, 1993.

Clancy, Tom, and Fred Franks. *Into the Storm: A Study of Command.* New York: Putnam, 1997.

Dunnigan, James F., and Austin Bay. *From Shield to Storm: High-Tech Weapons, Military Strategy, and Coalition Warfare in the Persian Gulf.* New York: W. Morrow, 1992.

Freedman, Lawrence, and Efraim Karsh. *The Gulf Conflict, 1990–1991: Diplomacy and War in the New World Order.* Princeton, NJ: Princeton University Press, 1993.

Gordon, Michael R., and Bernard E. Trainor. *The Generals' War: The Inside Story of the Conflict in the Gulf.* Boston: Little, Brown, 1995.

Hawley, T. M. *Against the Fires of Hell: The Environmental Disaster of the Gulf War.* New York: Harcourt Brace Jovanovich, 1992.

MacArthur, John R. *Second Front: Censorship and Propaganda in the Gulf War.* New York: Hill and Wang, 1992.

ELECTRONIC:

Fog of War. WashingtonPost.com. <http://www.washingtonpost.com/wp-svr/inatl/longterm/fogofwar/fogofwar.htm> (April 13, 2003).

Frontline: The Gulf War. Public Broadcasting System. <http://www.pbs.org/wgbh/pages/frontline/gulf/> (April 13, 2003).

SEE ALSO

B-52
Bush Administration (1989–1993), United States National Security Policy
Cruise Missile
F-117A Stealth Fighter
GPS
Information Warfare
Iraqi Freedom, Operation (2003 War Against Iraq)
Iraq, Intelligence and Security Agencies
Iraq War: Prelude to War (The International Debate Over the Use and Effectiveness of Weapons Inspections.)
J-Stars
Kuwait Oil Fires, Persian Gulf War
Patriot Missile System

Peru, Intelligence and Security

Peru is the seat of the ancient Incan Empire, one of the most advanced indigenous civilizations in the Americas. Spanish conquistadors captured the empire in 1533. In 1921, Peru declared its independence.

In the last two decades of the twentieth century, Peru sought a stable government and a means of overcoming endemic economic woes. The 1990 election of Alberto Fujimori ushered in a brief era of prosperity and stability, but increasing accusations of corruption and authoritarianism undermined the legitimacy of the Fujimori government. He was ousted from power in November 2000. Although democratic elections were held in 2001, the Peruvian government continues to weather occasional political turmoil.

Intelligence and security services have existed in Peru since the era of the Incan Empire. In the modern era, Peru's intelligence community resembles that of neighboring nations, and takes an active, cooperative role in addressing regional intelligence and security issues.

The main civilian intelligence agency in Peru is the National Intelligence Service (SIN). The agency was restructured in 1990 to eliminate military influences and abuses. Restructuring in 2002 sought to minimize the organization's ties to political espionage during the Fujimori regime.

Peru's Technical Police (PT) is the primary communications and electronic surveillance force. The agency works closely with the other organizations in the Peruvian intelligence community, but has been accused on several occasions of aiding government-backed political espionage against dissidents.

Peru's military intelligence community is organized within the nation's army and administered by Army Intelligence Directorate (DINTE). The Army Intelligence Service (SIE) focuses on foreign intelligence and the protection of military installations. In addition, individual military units in the Peruvian navy and air force may maintain their own strategic intelligence forces.

The prevalence of drug trafficking networks in the region, as well as a rise in paramilitary organizations connected to organized crime, prompted the development of the National Counter-terrorism Division, or Dincote, as it is more commonly known. Dincote specializes in anti-terrorism intelligence, using both electronic surveillance and human intelligence to infiltrate anti-government groups.

Peru is a member of the United Nations, the Organization of Latin American States, and several other international security organizations. Peruvian intelligence services participate in ongoing international and domestic anti-drug trafficking and anti-terrorism operations.

■ FURTHER READING:

ELECTRONIC:

Central Intelligence Agency. "Peru." CIA World Factbook. <http://www.cia.gov/cia/publications/factbook/geos/pe.html> (April 8, 2003).

PET (Positron Emission Tomography).

SEE *Scanning Technologies.*

Petroleum Reserves, Determination

■ WILLIAM J. ENGLE

Petroleum reserves are the recoverable portion of hydrocarbon accumulations that exist below Earth's surface in traps or reservoirs. The quantification of these reserves is essential to the world's effort to utilize hydrocarbons as a major energy source. The identification of petroleum reserves, both foreign and domestic, is an increasingly important scientific component of national economic and strategic security.

The process of quantifying reserves is governed by a host of scientific, political and economic considerations. Reserve determination is an interpretive process for which there is no finite answer until the end of a reservoir's producing life. Independent reserve estimates for the same asset base can vary significantly even though based on the same source data and with the application of prudent and customary technical methods. For general studies and large scale planning purposes statistical methods may be used to project reserves within an acceptable range of uncertainty, but specific projects beyond the earliest exploratory phase require at least a minimum of physical data. Uncertainty in reserve estimates is inversely proportional to the understanding of the producing characteristics of the accumulation and will remain a concern throughout the life of the project.

Uncertain reserve estimates for a reservoir or an entire project typically decrease over the life of a project as more factual information becomes known and actual production is observed.

Reserve estimates during the pre-drill exploratory phase are often based on known geologic factors from other areas thought to be sufficiently similar to the area under study applied to a reservoir description based on site specific interpretive data. In-place and recoverable reserve factors are applied to volumetric maps derived from seismic data and other geologic studies. The range of uncertainty at this time can be quite large. The actual existence of hydrocarbons has yet to be verified by actual well data and characterized as to their nature, quality, and economic viability. All studies at this point are speculative and highly dependent upon the creditability of the data available.

The first well drilled in the prospect enables project geologists and engineers to begin refining the assumptions used in the initial reservoir characterization efforts. Just how much this initial information improves the reserve estimate depends upon the degree and quality of data obtained. Each additional exploratory well adds more information and further refines the reserve estimates until it becomes possible to make a decision to go forward with project development or not based on an assessment of technical and economic risks. Ideally an actual flow test that includes a brief flow test of reservoir fluids and collection of fluid samples is conducted during this phase. However, this is not always done if confidence in other data more easily obtained is high and correlates well with the expected outcome, as flow testing can be quite expensive.

Each additional well, either as an expendable appraisal or a development well, further refines the data available and improves the interpretive understanding of project potential and further reduces but does not eliminate uncertainty in the reserve estimate. Until actual sustained production is established, the reserve estimate remains a volumetric determination and is highly dependent on the accuracy of the reservoir description. Nonetheless, the decision to make the significant capital investments required for project development is often based on a risked assessment of reserve potential with much yet unknown.

First production is a significant step toward improving the quality of reserve estimates. With continued geologic and engineering study and surveillance of actual reservoir performance the assumptions used to make previous reserve estimates are further refined with greater confidence. The range of uncertainty in the reserve estimate continues to narrow with actual performance.

Considerations that must be taken into account when estimating reserves tend to fall into the four categories of geology, fluid behavior, reservoir mechanics, and economic and political considerations.

Many of the geological factors considered in making the estimate of in-place reserves have to be refined and described in considerably greater detail if their effects upon hydrocarbon recovery are to be understood. These factors include but are not limited to structural geometry, size, shape, rock composition and compressibility, porosity, permeability, and compartmentalization.

The reservoir must be thought of in its three-dimensional configuration (e.g., whether it is in the shape of a box, sphere, dune, or an ancient river channel or a beach; whether it spreads over a massive area or it is intermittently scattered; whether is it flat, tilted, or undulating). Other considerations include analysis of whether the rock is clean sand, a mixture of sand and shale, limestone, or a number of other potential rock types that behave differently. A fundamental question involves whether the rock will compress as reservoir pressure depletes with fluid withdrawal. The degree of rock porosity—and the degree of minute rock particles called "fines" that exist in the pore space—are important considerations in determining whether the well will flow smoothly. Without effective permeability, the reservoir is of limited value. Once these other factors are known, the critical issue of compartmentalization remains (e.g. whether the reservoir is broken into sub-compartments by structural fractures or variations in permeability or whether fractures are sealing so as to prevent fluid flow across them). Obviously the more actual well data in an area, the better able one is to answer these questions. Until such data is available, advanced interpretations of seismic surveys and geologic models will be made and refined as well data is incorporated into the process.

The character of the reservoir fluid itself is a critical factor. Geologists conduct specific tests to determine the in-place gas or liquid phase and to what degree the phase is affected by temperature and pressure changes. A gas phase has low viscosity and high mobility, while liquids may have a viscosity ranging from that of water to that of solid asphalt. In calculating in-place reserves, the pore space saturation of other fluids is considered, most notably water but other potentially existing fluids such as carbon dioxide, nitrogen, hydrogen sulfide, elemental sulfur and others must be accounted for. The analysis of fluid and rock samples is critical.

Recovery is also dependent on which fluid actually wets the rock grain surface and to what extent resulting capillary pressures retain fluids within the rock matrix. These effects may restrict fluid flow through the porous rock media and govern how much of the original fluid saturation in-place can be recovered and how much will remain as residual saturation. Depending upon the lithology of the reservoir rock, residual gas saturation (i.e., the fraction of in-place gas that will remain in the reservoir) can range between 15 percent and 50 percent. For oil, residual saturation may range between 18 and 65 percent.

Reservoir mechanics are a major determining factor in hydrocarbon recovery and represent the energy that causes mobile fluids to flow through reservoir rock, also know as the drive mechanism. In a gravity drainage system, there is little pressure trapped within the bound fluid and the primary moving force is the pull of gravity on the density of the liquid. The resulting recovery is quite low, as may be demonstrated by fully wetting a sponge then lifting it out of the water with out squeezing it to see how much water runs out and how much is retained; then try this experiment with a more viscous fluid.

If reservoir fluids are under pressure, they may expand as pressure is released. This condition is an expansion drive and one in which the expanding fluid effectively flows from high pressure at the reservoir boundary to low pressure in the producing wellbore. Fluid recovery in an expansion drive is better than gravity drainage. The gas phase and recovery will tend to be a function of the real gas law where the relationship between changing pressure, temperature, and volume must be also adjusted for changing gas compressibility. Liquid recovery will be a function of fluid expansion. However, fluid recoveries are limited to their own ability to expand, thus an expansion or pressure depletion drive still leaves a considerable amount of hydrocarbon behind.

The highest yielding unassisted drive mechanism is a water drive system. In this case, the hydrocarbon bearing zone is in contact with a considerably larger body of water that can effectively push the hydrocarbon to the producing well(s) as the water itself expands as in a depletion drive. The strength of a water drive system is dependent on the size of the supply of water, or aquifer, and its relative energy potential or source. The larger the aquifer, the better the water drive. However the manner in which the water or "flood front" moves through the reservoir has great effect on its displacement of hydrocarbons. Irregularities in rock quality can cause channels to occur that may cause the moving water to have a low sweep-efficiency and possibly bypass large quantities of in-place hydrocarbons.

And of course a reservoir may exist in a combination of several drive mechanisms and each may dominate performance at different times in the life of the reservoir. Typically, under primary depletion, gas recoveries can range from as low as 50 percent to close to 90 percent of the original in-place volume. Oil recoveries will range between 5 percent and 35 percent and in some cases a little better. Artificial means of lifting fluids or adding energy to a reservoir with pumps, gas injection, or water injection as secondary recovery projects can increase recoveries to some extent. In less frequent occurrences, tertiary recovery techniques may be applied through several forms of miscible flooding with a fluid that will reduce the residual oil saturation left behind or going as far as starting a fire flood within the reservoir. However the incremental recoveries to be gained from secondary and tertiary recovery can be costly to put in place and have their own inherent uncertainties that must be closely monitored.

Economic and political considerations will also impact recoverable reserves. As a field declines, it will ultimately reach an economic limit beyond which it is impractical to continue producing operations. The economic limit is impacted by declining well productivity, higher maintenance expense late in the life of a field, changing commodity prices, taxation and the cost of employing technology, and complying with changing rules and regulations. Very often the economic limit is one of the most uncertain factors affecting ultimate recovery.

■ FURTHER READING:

BOOKS:

Craft, B. C. *Applied Petroleum Reservoir Engineering,* 2nd ed. Englewood Cliffs, NJ: Prentice Hall, Inc., 1991.

SEE ALSO

DOE (United States Department of Energy)

PFIAB (President's Foreign Intelligence Advisory Board)

■ CARYN E. NEUMANN

The President's Foreign Intelligence Advisory Board (PFIAB) provides unbiased monitoring of the overall intelligence effort of the United States by continually reviewing the activities of agencies and departments engaged in intelligence work. Through briefings and visits to intelligence installations, the sixteen board members seek to identify deficiencies in the collection, analysis, and reporting of intelligence while eliminating duplication. Created by President Dwight D. Eisenhower in 1956 as part of a reorganization of the executive branch, the board languished under President John F. Kennedy until the Bay of Pigs fiasco exposed the need for an objective evaluation of intelligence efforts. The board has served all subsequent presidents.

The PFIAB began when the 1955 Hoover Commission on Organization of the Executive Branch of the Government recommended that the president appoint a committee of knowledgeable private citizens to examine and report to him periodically on American foreign intelligence efforts. Accordingly, on February 6, 1956, Eisenhower issued an executive order establishing the President's Board of Consultants on Foreign Intelligence Activities (PBCFIA). The board focused on the quality of training and personnel, security, progress in research, effectiveness of specific projects, and general competence in carrying out assigned tasks.

Eisenhower left office in 1960 and Kennedy declined to appoint new PBCFIA members. Meanwhile, the new president had inherited a plan, approved by Eisenhower, for the invasion of Cuba. The CIA and most military advisors assured Kennedy that the plan was sound, but the Cubans anticipated the Bay of Pigs attack and defeated the American-backed forces within three days. Amidst widespread international condemnation and a humiliating loss of national prestige, Kennedy reinstituted the board, now named PFIAB, to prevent another embarrassing disaster. Kennedy placed Clark Clifford (1906–98), the man who had written the 1947 legislation establishing the CIA, upon the board and later made him chair. President Jimmy Carter replaced the board in 1977 with the smaller Intelligence Oversight Committee as part of a reevaluation of intelligence gathering. President Ronald Reagan brought the PFIAB back to life in 1982.

The activities and deliberations of the PFIAB have remained classified. However, it is known that the PFIAB expressed particular concern with the internal procedures of the CIA. It also examined the delay in receiving information about the installation of Soviet offensive nuclear missile sites in Cuba. These sites, which precipitated the Cuban Missile Crisis, had been discovered in 1962 by a U-2 spy plane that had been aided in development by the PFIAB. Technical collection programs, like the one that produced the U-2, are heavily monitored by PFIAB as part of its interest in ensuring that intelligence technology reflects the best technical capabilities of the nation. Lastly, it is also known that the board investigated the U.S. government's failure to predict the 1968 Soviet invasion of Czechoslovakia, which had been decided upon at a meeting of Warsaw Pact nations concerned about the threat that proposed Czech reforms posed to the preservation of the communist system. The board has very rarely addressed covert political action.

The PFIAB conducts deliberations every two months for two days. Chairs of the board have included Clifford; retired Army General Maxwell D. Taylor (1901–87), former Chairman of the Joint Chiefs of Staff who succeeded Clifford from 1968–70; retired Admiral George W. Anderson, Jr., Chief of Naval Operations under Kennedy, 1970–76; Anne L. Armstrong, former Ambassador to the United Kingdom, 1982–90; Warren Rudman, former U.S. Senator, 1997–2001, and current chair, retired Air Force Lieutenant General Brent Scowcroft. The history of intelligence disasters and the importance of good information to national security likely guarantees that the PFIAB will continue to monitor intelligence efforts.

■ **FURTHER READING:**

BOOKS:

Congressional Research Service. *The United States Intelligence Community: A Brief Description of Organization and Functions.* Washington, D.C.: Library of Congress, 1975.

Hoxie, R. Gordon. et al. *The Presidency and National Security Policy.* New York: Center for the Study of the Presidency, 1984.

Marchetti, Victor, and John Marks. *The CIA and the Cult of Intelligence.* New York: Alfred A. Knopf, 1974.

ELECTRONIC:

The White House. "President's Foreign Intelligence Advisory Board." <http://www.whitehouse.gov/pfiab/> (March 29, 2003).

SEE ALSO

Air Force Intelligence, United States
Aviation Intelligence, History
Carter Adminstration (1977–1981), United States National Security Policy
CIA (United States Central Intelligence Agency)
CIA, Formation and History
Cuban Missile Crisis
Eisenhower Administration (1953–1961), United States National Security Policy
Executive Orders and Presidential Directives
Johnson Administration (1963–1969), United States National Security Policy
Kennedy Administration (1961–1963), United States National Security Policy
President of the United States (Executive Command and Control of Intelligence Agencies)
Reagan Administration (1981–1989), United States National Security Policy
United States, Intelligence and Security
United States Intelligence, History

Phoenix Program

In an attempt to cripple or eliminate South Vietnamese communist guerilla resistance (the Vietcong) to both United States forces and the U.S.-backed government of South

Vietnam, the Phoenix program was allegedly designed to conduct arrest and assassination operations against suspected Vietcong and Vietcong sympathizers. The Phoenix program was developed and operated by the United States Central Intelligence Agency (CIA), the United States Army, and components of several South Vietnamese intelligence and law enforcement agencies.

U.S. CIA personnel (including those assigned to Intelligence Coordination and Exploitation operations) provided the core of Phoenix leadership. Starting in 1967, the program, which was based in Saigon (then the capital of South Vietnam) used a complex network of informants, a mix of military intelligence, and even trials at computer algorithms to determine appropriate targets for "neutralization." In 1968, CIA officer William Colby (who would become Director of Central Intelligence in 1973) assumed command of the program.

Initially named the Phuong Hoang Operation (named after a mythical Vietnamese bird of prey), the renamed Phoenix program resulted in the arrest, detention, brutal interrogation, and execution of thousands of Vietcong fighters and sympathizers at the hands of South Vietnam police and intelligence agencies. In addition to identifying suspected Vietcong and Vietcong sympathizers, Phoenix intelligence operations also accumulated data that exonerated thousands of suspects. Phoenix operations, and the identification of Vietcong infrastructure became increasingly important after the 1968 Tet Offensive and Phoenix generated intelligence was used to determine military targets.

■ FURTHER READING:

BOOKS:

Colby, William E., and James McCargar. *Lost Victory: A First Hand Account of America's Sixteen-year Involvement in Vietnam.* Chicago, IL: Contemporary Books, 1989.

Moyar, M. *Phoenix and the Birds of Prey: the CIA's Secret Campaign to Destroy the Viet Cong.* Annapolis, MD: Naval Institute Press, 1997.

Photo Alteration

The camera was invented in 1839, and by the next decade, photographers had already begun to manipulate photographic images. Initially, the manipulation was part of the exploration of the artistic potential of the new medium. Soon, the informational power of the photograph became recognized.

The techniques of photo alteration have been exploited to generate images that are different from the actual scene that is photographed for purposes of intelligence gathering or deception. For example, by the 1940s, the Soviet Union was actively manipulating photos in a campaign of misinformation to portray their leaders favorably.

In the intelligence and security communities, photo alteration serves two important purposes. The first purpose is to gather information, most often through magnification of photos. The use of spy satellites reveals facilities and operations that can be crucial to national security. One example is the famous photos of a Soviet rocket installation in Cuba during the presidency of John F. Kennedy. In the modern era, satellite photos purporting to show biological weapons production facilities have increased the resolve of the United States to topple the government of Iraq. The ability to produce photographs that reveal more detail than do traditional photographs, especially at longer distances or using small cameras, has increased the information that can be gathered.

The second purpose of photo alteration is to misinform or deceive. With new technology, the ability to alter a photographic image is easier than ever before. For example, in a traditional photograph, the difference in skin tone between a face and the neck or shadows that point in different directions can be clues that an image has been manipulated. However, these visual discrepancies can be eliminated in the digital image. Thus, the ability to generate false or misleading information has become routine.

Traditional photo alteration. In the days before digital technology, photo alteration was accomplished in the darkroom during the development and printing of the photograph. In a technique called dodging, the light shining through the photographic negative onto light-sensitive paper was obscured. Because less light strikes the paper, that region appears lighter in the developed image. In contrast, the technique of burning allows an increased amount of light to strike the photographic paper. The result of burning is to make the region appear darker in the print.

The traditional techniques of dodging and burning are used to enhance or disguise aspects of the photo. As well, details can be excluded from an image by the use of cropping, where only the selected portion of the image is printed. Photographs can also be enlarged to selectively print portions of the image. Enlarging cannot be done indefinitely, however, since the eventual inability to separate the informational components of the image from one another produces a blurry picture.

A skilled technician can even paint a picture to remove someone, replacing the person with the background. Photographing the altered image produces an image that can often pass for the real thing. A classic example of this manipulation is the picture of Vladimir Lenin addressing a crowd in front of Moscow's Bolshoi Theater in 1920. In

Senator Joseph McCarthy answering charges that the photo, foreground, submitted as an exhibit at Army dispute hearings in 1954, had been altered. AP/WIDE WORLD PHOTOS.

reality, Leon Trotsky was also on the film. In a massive campaign of historical revisionism during the leadership of Joseph Stalin, Trotsky's involvement in this and other photographed events was erased in an attempt to purge the memory of opposition to Stalin's leadership.

Another ploy of photo manipulation is the false captioning of an image. By excluding, exaggerating, or falsifying details of an image, the viewer can misinterpret what is seen. For example, during World War II the United States plowed fields on some South Pacific Islands, then took aerial photos of them. The photos were labeled as representing air bases, creating a deception that the military resources in the area were much more extensive than was actually the case.

Digital photo alteration. The coming of digital photography revolutionized the ability to alter photographs. The laborious darkroom manipulations of preceding times could be accomplished by a few commands in specialized photographic software.

In traditional photography, the reflected light from the subject enters the camera through the lens and is focused onto the surface of a light-sensitive emulsion. The emulsion records the image, which can be beamed onto light-sensitive photographic paper. The paper is subsequently treated with chemicals to make the image appear. It is during this latter printing process that the alteration of the photograph can be accomplished.

In digital photography, the reflected light that enters the camera is focused onto a chip that is known as a charged coupling device (CCD). The surface of the CCD contains an array of light-sensitive photo diodes. Each diode represents a pixel (the basic unit of programmable color in a computer image). Each photo diode is hooked up to a transistor, which sends an electrical signal (whose voltage corresponds to the light intensity that registered on the photo diode) to another chip. The second chip converts the electrical signal to digital information—1s and 0s—that can be interpreted by computerized photo manipulation software programs.

Colors are assigned a code sequence between 0 and 255; 0 is black and 255 reveals the most intense shade of red possible by the software. These coded assignments are in turn converted to sequences of 0s and 1s. Black, for example, is 00000000, while the most intense red is 11111111. Shades in between are combinations of 0s and 1s in the eight-digit sequences.

Digital photo manipulation involves the alteration or elimination of the digital 1s and 0s. Changing an eight-digit sequence is trivial. When the digital information is reconstructed into an electronic image, the result can be an altered color.

In addition to color change, a myriad of effects are possible, including color enhancement, elimination of regions of the image, increased contrast, correction of a blurred image, and the merging of other images with the original image (a photographic version of the "cut and paste" operations in word processing).

As digital photo manipulation software has increased in technical sophistication, and people have become more adept at using the software, the task of detecting manipulated images has become very challenging. Digital photographic manipulation is now so sophisticated that it can sometimes be impossible to discern whether people or objects in a photograph were actually there when the photo was taken. This has spurred efforts, especially in the military and intelligence communities, to establish a system of image verification. In this regard, the United States Air Force Research Laboratory in Rome, New York, has developed a technique called digital watermarking. Akin to the watermarking of paper currency to establish authenticity, digital watermarking embeds an encrypted image over the actual photo image. The encrypted image is invisible to the naked eye, but can be detected by specially designed image scanners. The lack of the digital watermark is evidence of an altered image.

Digital cameras can also be mounted in satellites in orbit hundreds of miles above the Earth. These cameras can provide images that can be manipulated to allow objects that are as close to one another as a meter or two to be visually distinguished from each other. This resolution is a vast improvement from that possible using traditional light-sensitive photographic film. This form of digital photo manipulation has improved the capability of intelligence agencies to spy on other countries or organizations from a long distance.

In the U.S., government scrutiny and interpretation of photographs is the function of the National Imagery and Mapping Agency's National Photographic Interpretation Center (once part of the Central Intelligence Agency's Directorate of Science and Technology).

■ FURTHER READING:

BOOKS:

Beale, Stephen. *Web Tricks and Techniques: Photo Manipulation: Fast Solutions for Hands-On Web Design.* Gloucester, MA: Rockport Publishers, 2002.

Brugioni, Dino A. *Photo Fakery: The History and Techniques of Photographic Deception.* Washington, D.C.: Brassey's, 1999.

SEE ALSO

Computer Modeling
Document Forgery

Photographic Interpretation Center (NPIC), United States National

The Central Intelligence Agency (CIA) established the National Photographic Interpretation Center (NPIC) in the 1950s to provide skilled interpretation of photographic images obtained by low- and high-flying aircraft, and later by satellites. Originally a unit of the CIA Directorate of Intelligence, NPIC in 1973 transferred to the Directorate of Science and Technology (DS&T). In 1996, it was moved to the newly formed National Imagery and Mapping Agency (NIMA).

An intelligence photograph, rather like the sonogram of an unborn baby, seldom yields an abundance of secrets to the untrained eye. An expectant parent is unlikely to guess the sex of the child from a sonogram photo, whereas an experienced practitioner can ascertain such information with a high degree of certainty. Similarly, an aerial image of a military installation may appear, to the layman, as no more than a grid of fuzzy rooftops and curving roads, whereas a specialist skilled at extracting intelligence from photography may see all manner of incriminating details.

Americans became more acquainted with photographic interpretation on February 5, 2003, when Secretary of State Colin Powell presented NIMA/NPIC imagery to the United Nations (UN) Security Council as proof that Iraqi dictator Saddam Hussein was stockpiling chemical weapons in defiance of international bans. Likewise, NPIC played a critical role in a much earlier international situation, that of the Cuban Missile Crisis of October 1962.

The center's analysts had been studying photos taken from U-2s over the Soviet Union since July 1956, and over Cuba since October 1960, but it did not officially come into existence until President Dwight D. Eisenhower signed National Security Council Intelligence Directive No. 8 on January 18, 1961. As the Soviets began sending arms and other supplies to Havana during the early days of John F. Kennedy's administration, NPIC personnel attempted to measure—and, if possible, identify the contents of—each crate unloaded on the docks. Kennedy relied heavily on

NPIC, as well as Defense Department equivalents in the navy and air force. During the crisis, he dispatched emissaries, bearing NPIC photographs as proof, to several U.S. allies before he confronted Soviet premier Nikita Khrushchev with evidence of the buildup in Cuba.

■ FURTHER READING:

PERIODICALS:

Munro, Neil. "Fighting for Intelligence Funds." *Washington Technology* (July 27, 1995): 1.

Pincus, Walter. "CIA, Pentagon Back NIMA 'Concept,' Combining Spy Satellite Photo Units." *Washington Post.* (November 29, 1995): A23.

Seffers, George I. "NIMA 'Inadequate' in Analyzing Spy Data." *Federal Computer Week* 15, no. 3 (February 5, 2001): 55.

ELECTRONIC:

National Photographic Interpretation Center. Fellowship of American Scientists. <http://www.fas.org/irp/overhead/npic.htm> (February 13, 2003).

SEE ALSO

CIA Directorate of Science and Technology (DS&T)
NIMA (National Imagery and Mapping Agency)
Photographic Resolution
Photography, High-Altitude

Photographic Resolution

The term resolution, in the context of photography, refers to the degree to which adjacent objects can be distinguished from one another in a photographic image. Obviously, the higher the degree of resolution—which is a function of the acuity of the photographic equipment used, as well as the abilities of the operator—the better the quality of the photograph. The lower the figure given for the resolution, in metric or English units, the higher the degree of resolution.

For example, the first four satellites of the CORONA project, which remained aloft throughout most of the period from June 1959 to December 1963, had a relatively high resolution of 25 feet (7.6 m), meaning that objects smaller than that size were likely to be indistinguishable from one another. Higher still was the resolution of the fifth satellite in the series, KH-4B (September 1967-May 1972), at 6 feet (1.8 m). Photographs taken by KH-5, a satellite deployed for mapping purposes between February 1961 and August 1964, had a much lower degree of photographic resolution: 460 feet (140 m).

■ FURTHER READING:

BOOKS:

Williams, John B. *Image Clarity: High-Resolution Photography.* Boston: Focal Press, 1990.

ELECTRONIC:

Declassified Intelligence Satellite Photographs. <http://mac.usgs.gov/isb/pubs/factsheets/fs09096.html> (February 13, 2003).

SEE ALSO

Cameras
Photography, High-Altitude

Photography, High-Altitude

The United States conducts, and has conducted, operations in high-altitude photography for a number of purposes. In addition to intelligence-gathering operations such as that of the CORONA program in the 1960s, civilian undertakings such as those of the U.S. Geological Survey (USGS) have an obvious, if unspoken, intelligence application. High-altitude photography, which offers several advantages over ground-based surveillance, has evolved over the years, along with the equipment: from balloons to prop planes, jets, and satellites.

High-Altitude Photography and its Applications

High-altitude photography enables the coverage of large areas—for example, a military installation—in a single photographic frame. For a larger region such as a metropolitan area or state, it may be necessary to form a mosaic of several photographs. The more sophisticated the photographic equipment, the more the area that can be portrayed with a reliable degree of photographic resolution.

The same goes for the technology necessary to keep the camera aloft: a satellite, because it orbits at a considerably greater height than the highest-flying plane, by definition possesses a much better vantage point for breadth of coverage. The July 1976 issue of *National Geographic,* which commemorated the U.S. bicentennial, illustrated this breadth dramatically with a fold-out aerial photograph of the United States patched together from hundreds of satellite photographs.

From balloons to satellites. In the mid-nineteenth century, European and later American armies began using balloons as observation platforms. From this it was a logical step to mount camera equipment on the balloons. The advent of the airplane as an instrument of both combat and surveillance was all but concurrent with the use of photographic equipment for intelligence purposes. By the end of World War I, the use of high-altitude craft for the gathering of photographic intelligence was firmly established.

The use of airplanes in surveillance did not rule out the application of balloons. These included both ordinary balloons, which had made their debut in the late eighteenth century, as well as airships, or guided balloons, pioneered in the last third of the nineteenth century. As late as 1956, the U.S. Air Force was using balloons in Project GENETRIX, a failed effort to conduct surveillance of Eastern Europe, the Soviet Union, and the People's Republic of China.

Yet the age of the jet and the satellite was well under way by then. Already the Central Intelligence Agency (CIA) was putting the finishing touches on its plans to employ the high-speed U-2 aircraft for overflights of the Soviet Union and other countries, and in 1957, the Soviets themselves launched the first artificial satellite, *Sputnik.*

Satellites.

In the years since, the United States has used satellites in a number of information-gathering capacities. Significant among these operations was CORONA, which involved the launch of some 145 satellite flights between 1960 and 1972. CORONA collected some 800,000 images, most of which covered an area about 10 miles (16 km) wide and 120 miles (193 km) long. Resolution was accurate for objects as small as 6.6 feet (2 m).

CORONA operations took place before the era of digital imaging, and therefore images had to be sent back to Earth manually, by means of film capsules attached to parachutes and retrieved by an Air Force C-119. Information gathered by the CORONA systems, which were designated KH-1, KH-2, KH-3, KH-4A, and KH-4B by the intelligence community, was declassified by Executive Order 12958 in 1995. Today USGS controls most of the images.

USGS photographic operations.

A unit of the Department of the Interior, USGS is responsible for measuring and mapping areas of Earth's surface, particularly those in the United States; for managing resources; and for minimizing threats to life and property by identifying hazards. Although USGS is ostensibly outside the security and intelligence component of the federal government, its application in those areas is clear. Among its undertakings is the Military Geology Project, which is primarily concerned with monitoring nuclear tests, and breaches of nuclear treaties, worldwide.

Geologists make extensive use of remote sensing, or the gathering of data without actual contact with the materials or objects being studied. High-altitude photography is among the most significant techniques of remote

sensing, and USGS has used airplanes and satellites for a number of projects.

Among these was the National High Altitude Photography Program (NHAP), launched in 1980 to collect aerial photographic images of the 48 conterminous states every five to seven years. Undertaken in an effort to eliminate duplication of government mapping programs, NHAP in 1987 became the National Aerial Photography Program (NAPP). NHAP acquired photographs at 40,000 feet (12,190 m), and NAPP at half that altitude. Both used a 6-inch focal length lens, which for NHAP obtained black-and-white pictures and for NAPP either color infrared or black-and-white. NHAP also used an 8.25-inch lens to obtain color infrared images.

At a much higher altitude, USGS has also been one of the principal agencies involved in the Landsat satellite program, which began with the launch of Landsat 1 in 1972 and continued in the early twenty-first century with Landsats 5 and 7. Tasked primarily with providing information on environmental hazards and natural disasters, Landsat 7 orbits the planet every 99 minutes. Its photographic equipment, while noted for its high spatial resolution—98 feet (30 m)—in comparison to that of other scientific satellites, is of relatively low resolution compared to that of intelligence satellites such as CORONA three decades earlier.

Overflights.

Even with satellites in space, the United States has continued to employ overflights, or missions by spy planes over enemy countries to collect intelligence via electronic or photographic equipment. The concept of the overflight, which involves the gathering of information on strategic activities in the country rather than the tactical activities of its enemy forces, dates back at least to 1952, when the United States sent B-47 Stratojets over Soviet airspace.

Perhaps the most well known use of overflights was that of the U-2 over the Soviet Union, a fact that came to world attention when pilot Francis Gary Powers was shot down in 1960. Though it made its debut in 1955, the U-2 was still being used in 2003, as part of United Nations weapons inspector's work in Iraq. Even in the early 1960s, the photographic equipment aboard the U-2 was exceptional: its camera had a 944.7-millimeter lens, and was capable of capturing an area measuring some 125 miles (201 km) by 2,174 miles (3,499 km) in 4,000 photographs.

The SR-71 Blackbird made its debut in 1964, when it was presented as a successor to the U-2. In fact the two flew concurrently, and the U-2 remained in the skies during a period from 1990 to 1995, when the SR-71 was mothballed due to its high costs of operation. Much faster and higher-flying than the U-2, the SR-71 has been used to photograph operations in enemy countries ranging from China and North Vietnam to Libya and Iraq to Cuba and the communist Nicaragua of the 1980s. An SR-71 photographed China's first hydrogen bomb explosion in 1967.

■ FURTHER READING:

BOOKS:

Barrett, E. C., and L. F. Curtis. *Introduction to Environmental Remote Sensing.* New York: Chapman & Hall, 1992.

Walker, James W., and Steven Leroy De Vore. *Low Altitude Large-Scale Reconnaissance: A Method of Obtaining High Resolution Vertical Photographs for Small Areas.* Denver, CO: Interagency Archeological Services, National Park Service, 1995.

ELECTRONIC:

Declassified Intelligence Satellite Photographs. <http://mac.usgs.gov/isb/pubs/factsheets/fs09096.html> (February 13, 2003).

United States Geological Survey. <http://www.usgs.gov> (February 13, 2003).

SEE ALSO

Balloon Reconnaissance, History
NIMA (National Imagery and Mapping Agency)
Photographic Interpretation Center (NPIC), United States National
Reconnaissance
Satellites, Non-Governmental High Resolution
Satellites, Spy

M	O	N	A	R
C	H	Y	B	D
E	F	G	I/J	K
L	P	Q	S	T
U	V	W	X	Z

Playfair Cipher

The Playfair cipher is a method of cryptography invented in 1854 by English physicist Sir Charles Wheatstone (1802–1875). The encryption method was named for Wheatstone's friend, Lyon Playfair, who helped popularize the cipher by successfully lobbying for its official adoption by the British government.

All cryptography schemes are designed to conceal a message's meaning and maintain confidentiality in communications. The Playfair is a block cipher that disguises a message by substituting each pair of letters in the plaintext with a secondary pair of letters. Each unit or pair of letters is known as a digraph.

A keyword, usually only known to the sender and recipient, is written into a five-by-five square. Repeated letters are omitted. After the keyword is spelled out, empty blocks are filled with the rest of the letters of the alphabet in alphabetical order. The letters I and J are treated as the same letter and therefore, combined in the same block. The following example is a Playfair cipher decoded by Lord Peter Wimsey in Dorothy L. Sayers's *Have His Carcase.* The keyword is "Monarchy."

Enciphering the phrase, "We are discovered. Save yourself," involves several steps. First, the plaintext is divided into two-letter groups. An X is added when there is an uneven number of letters.

WE AR ED IS CO VE RE DS AV EY OU RS EL FX

Next, locate the position of the two plaintext letters in the box matrix. Letters appearing in different rows and columns are replaced by the letter that is in the same row but in the other column; i.e., to encrypt WE, replace W with U, and E by G.

When a pair appears in the same row, as A and R does above, each letter is encrypted as the next cyclically appearing letter; i.e., AR becomes RM. The same rule of thumb applies when the pair is in the same column. In this example, IS would be encrypted as SX.

The enciphered phrase for Sayers's Playfair becomes:

UG RMK CSXHMUFMKB TOXG CMVATLUIV

In the event a double letter occurs, a bogus letter, such as an X, replaces the repeating letter. In order to decrypt the message, simply reverse the process.

The simplicity and reliability of this primitive code-cracking method made it extremely popular on the battlefield. The British employed the Playfair in the Boer War in addition to World War I. Several militaries relied on the Playfair as a back-up cipher during the Second World War. Lieutenant (and later, President) John F. Kennedy used the Playfair encryption method to send an emergency message after his PT-109 sank in the Solomon Islands in 1943.

■ FURTHER READING:

ELECTRONIC:

University of North Dakota. "The Cipher Exchange and Cipher Standards." <http://www.und.nodak.edu/org/crypto/crypto/.chap08.html#PLAYFA> (December 09, 2002).

Glyphworks. "Classical Cryptography." <http://storm.
prohosting.com/~glyph/crypto/class_sub.shtml> (December 09, 2002).

NOVA Online. "The Playfair Cipher." November 2000.
<http://www.pbs.org/wgbh/nova/decoding/playfair.
html> (December 14, 2002).

SEE ALSO

Cryptology and Number Theory
FISH (German Geheimschreiber *Cipher Machine)*

Plum Island Animal Disease Center

The Plum Island Animal Disease Center (PIADC), located
on a 180-acre site off the northeastern tip of Long Island,
New York, is part of the Department of Homeland Security's efforts to protect the United States food supply.
PIADC works to protect U.S. consumers and safeguard the
integrity of U.S. animal product exports against biologic
agents introduced accidentally or deliberately introduced
by terrorists.

PIADC scientists protect American livestock by developing methods to identify and isolate foreign animal diseases. PIADC scientists have developed testing, containment, and treatment protocols for a range of foreign
animal diseases including foot-and-mouth disease, African swine fever, and African horsesickness. PIADC researchers are specifically responsible for developing a
number of antiviral drugs and vaccines for foreign animal
diseases and for the development of disease-specific nu-
cleic-acid-based probes that serve in diagnostic tests.

For example, PIADC researchers discovered and developed a synthetic DNA copy of the genetic information
contained in the foot-and-mouth disease virus. Further
research into the enzyme biochemistry of the virus responsible for foot-and-mouth disease has allowed vaccines to be designed in such a way to enhance vaccine storage. PIADC research also aims to perfect existing vaccines, for example developing enzyme-linked
immunosorbent assay (ELISA) tests for foot-and-mouth
disease variants that can be used outside the laboratory
(i.e., in field tests) because the test does not contain live
virus. In standard ELISA tests an enzyme or a radioisotope
is covalently linked to the pure antigen or antibody. The
unlabeled component, which most often is the antigen, is
attached to the surface of a plastic well. The labeled
antibody is allowed to bind to the unlabeled antigen. The
plastic well is subsequently washed with plenty of buffer
that will remove any excess non-bound antibody and

The Plum Island Animal Disease Center in Plumb Island, New York, is
shown in an aerial view. Researchers at the facility focus on animal
diseases that can affect the health, security, and economic interests of
the United States, such as the prevention of a foot-and-mouth disease
outbreak introduced into the country by foreign livestock and travelers.
AP/WIDE WORLD PHOTOS.

prevent non-specific binding. Antibody binding is measured as the amount of radioactivity retained by the coated
wells in radioimmunoassay or as fluorescence emitted by
the product of an enzymatic reaction.

PIADC scientists also sequenced (i.e., determined the
specific sequence of nucleic acids) the DNA of the African
Swine Fever virus, which, as of March 2003, was the
largest animal virus ever sequenced. The work at PIADC
allowed researchers to compare the genome of the African Swine Fever virus with the genomes of the human
immunodeficiency virus (HIV) and human herpesvirus 6.
The genomic comparisons provided evidence that the
disease (African Swine Fever) was not causally related to
either HIV or human herpesvirus 6 infections.

PIADC cooperates with industry to produce livestock
vaccines. In addition, PIADC personnel conduct diagnostic
investigations for suspected cases of foreign or emerging
animal diseases and train veterinarians and other animal
health professionals in the diagnosis of foreign animal
diseases.

PIADC facilities operate at or above Biosafety Level 3
(BSL-3) standards, and general safety protocols require
the use of airlocks, HEPA (High Efficiency Particulate Air)

filters, and other specialized vents and filters that remove any virus particles from air leaving the laboratory. Materials leaving laboratories are decontaminated, with waste products incinerated or specially heat-treated to kill viruses. The relative isolation of PIADC's setting and scientific containment facilities allow high confidence in the safety of pathogen storage and testing at PIADC. As of March, 2003, PIADC had never recorded a loss of pathogen containment. PIADC research supports work carried out by the United States Department of Agriculture (USDA) Agricultural Research Service and the USDA Animal and Plant Health Inspection Service.

■ FURTHER READING:

ELECTRONIC:

Plum Island Animal Disease Center. <http://www.ars.usda.gov/plum/index.html> (March 23, 2003).

United States Department of Energy, Office of Science. National Laboratories and User Facilities. <http://www.sc.doe.gov/Sub/Organization/Map/national_labs_and_userfacilities.htm> (March 23, 2003).

United States Department of Homeland Security. Research & Technology. <http://www.dhs.gov/dhspublic/display?theme=27&content=374> (March 23, 2003).

SEE ALSO

Argonne National Laboratory
Brookhaven National Laboratory
DOE (United States Department of Energy)
Environmental Measurements Laboratory
Lawrence Berkeley National Laboratory
Lawrence Livermore National Laboratory (LLNL)
Los Alamos National Laboratory
NNSA (United States National Nuclear Security Administration)
Oak Ridge National Laboratory (ORNL)
Pacific Northwest National Laboratory
Sandia National Laboratories

Plutonium Production.

SEE Nuclear Reactors.

Poland, Intelligence and Security

Germany's invasion of Poland was the catalyst for World War II. During the Nazi occupation, Polish citizens were subject to interrogation and torture at the hands of officers of the Gestapo, the Nazi secret police. Holocaust death camps were located in occupied Poland. After the war, Poland became a Soviet satellite nation. The fall of the Berlin Wall in 1989 opened Poland to the west. The following year, elections swept the labor union based Solidarity party into power. Poland then began the long process of democratizing the government and reforming the economy.

Before World War II, Poland had one of the strongest intelligence forces in Europe. The work of Polish spies and cryptographers broke several key German codes before the outbreak of the war. Fleeing Poland during the invasion, Polish agents successfully smuggled code breaking information and a German Enigma cipher machine to British Military Intelligence. Polish intelligence information directly aided British cryptography efforts at Bletchley Park.

Poland's Ministry of Internal Affairs governs domestic intelligence and security operations that relate to national security issues. In June 2002, the government dissolved the Office of State Protection (UOP). Though the organization was created after the fall of the communist regime, it failed to overcome public fears about its close association with former communist intelligence services and secret police forces. Two new agencies were established, the Domestic Security Office and the Intelligence Service. The Domestic Security Office works with law enforcement to protect diplomats, government officials, and national assets. The Intelligence Service directs most civilian intelligence operations, including counter-intelligence and counter-espionage.

Poland maintains an army, navy, and air defense force. Each military branch of service employs its own specially trained intelligence units. Operations that utilize military forces and government intelligence personnel, however, are supervised by the National Security Council (RBN) or a joint intelligence council. The Ministry of National Defense governs the Military Information Service, the electronic, signals, and communications intelligence agency.

While most of Eastern and Central Europe is still struggling with economic reform, Poland's government-driven rapid revitalization program has yielded the most robust economy in the region. Poland joined the North Atlantic Treaty Organization (NATO) in 1999, and is currently pursuing membership in the European Union (EU).

■ FURTHER READING:

BOOKS:

Snyder, Timothy. The Reconstruction of Nations: Poland, Ukraine, Lithuania, Belarus, 1569–1999. New Haven, CT: Yale University Press, 2003.

SEE ALSO

Bletchley Park
European Union
NATO (North Atlantic Treaty Organization)
Ultra, Operation
World War II

Politics: The Briefings of United States Presidential Candidates

∎ JUDSON KNIGHT

In accordance with a practice established by President Harry S. Truman, presidential nominees of both major political parties receive intelligence briefings at some point between the summer political conventions and the presidential elections every four years. Assuming a candidate is an incumbent president or vice president, he is already accustomed to receiving such briefings, but for a contender who has not served in the inner circles of a previous administration, the briefing is an entirely new experience. The pace of briefings intensifies once a candidate is chosen in the November elections, and continues in the period leading up to inauguration day. Thereafter, the new chief executive will receive intelligence briefings on a regular basis in the form of the presidential daily briefing (PDB).

Who Receives Briefings

Lyndon B. Johnson, Richard M. Nixon, Gerald R. Ford, and George H. W. Bush had all served as vice presidents, and therefore had received intelligence briefings while holding the nation's second-highest office. The same was true of several ultimately unsuccessful candidates for the presidency, including Nixon in 1960, Hubert Humphrey in 1968, Walter Mondale in 1984, and Albert Gore in 2000. Additionally, there had been several instances in which an incumbent ran for reelection and was defeated, meaning that in the period between November of election year and January of the following year, the successful challenger received intelligence briefings even as the sitting president received PDBs. Such was the case with Ford in 1976, James E. Carter in 1980, and Bush in 1992.

The system of intelligence briefings extends only to candidates of major parties. Although H. Ross Perot garnered more than 20 million votes in 1992, no serious consideration was given toward the idea of providing him with highly sensitive materials on national security and intelligence.

Anatomy of the briefing system. The career of George H. W. Bush, which included service as director of the Central Intelligence Agency (CIA), which administers the briefings, and later as vice-president and president, placed him in several interesting circumstances with regard to briefings. In 1976, he personally provided briefings to Carter, and in 1980 helped arrange briefings for Ronald Reagan, who had defeated him in the Republican primaries, and on whose ticket he was now running as vice-president.

In 1992, Bush was running for reelection as president against then-Arkansas governor William J. Clinton. After the latter received the nomination at the Democratic Convention, National Security Adviser Brent Scowcroft contacted Washington attorney Samuel Berger (who would hold Scowcroft's position in the second Clinton administration) to arrange briefings. CIA director Robert Gates traveled to Little Rock to personally brief Clinton and vice-presidential candidate Gore.

Clinton's briefings in 1992. The first briefings, on September 4, 1992, concerned the major national security issues of the moment, including turmoil in the soon-to-be-defunct Soviet Union and escalating conflict in Yugoslavia. Clinton received no further briefings until after the election, at which point a CIA team established a presence in Little Rock. Leading the briefings from that point onward was John L. Helgerson, who latter wrote *Getting to Know the President: CIA Briefings of Presidential Candidates, 1952–1992,* published by CIA's Center for the Study of Intelligence in 1996.

On November 11, Helgerson met with Clinton, Berger, and Nancy Soderberg of the governor's staff. Two days later, he began his briefings with Clinton. As Helgerson explained to the candidate, the PDB goes to the vice-president, national security advisor, chairman of the Joint Chiefs of Staff, White House chief of staff, and secretaries of State and Defense. In view of the growing importance of economic issues, Helgerson suggested that the Secretary of the Treasury also be included. Clinton agreed.

Other than this one suggestion, Helgerson indicated, he was hesitant to guide the president-elect in any way. Helgerson recalled that, in view of what he described as CIA "policy buzz saws" of the 1980s (most notably, the Iran-Contra scandal), he took great pains not to try to influence Clinton's thinking on any issues. Over the period from November 13 to January 16, 1993, Helgerson and others provided the president elect with daily briefings while Bush, now a "lame duck" president, received exactly the same material in his PDB. Beginning January 17, the briefing team moved from Little Rock to Washington, preparing to make the transition to providing Clinton with daily briefings as president.

∎ FURTHER READING:

BOOKS:

Helgerson, John L. *Getting to Know the President: CIA Briefings of Presidential Candidates, 1952–1992.* Washington, D.C.: Central Intelligence Agency, 1996.

PERIODICALS:

Auerbach, Stuart. "Party Nominees to Get Trade Briefing." *Washington Post.* (June 25, 1988): D12.

SEE ALSO

CIA (United States Central Intelligence Agency)
CIA, Legal Restriction
Iran-Contra Affair
PFIAB (President's Foreign Intelligence Advisory Board)
*President of the United States (Executive Command and
    Control of Intelligence Agencies)*

Pollard Espionage Case

Jonathan Jay Pollard, a veteran of U.S. Navy intelligence forces, sold secrets to the Israeli government during the 1980s. Pollard fed Israel intelligence information regarding Israeli rivals in the Middle East and beyond. Pollard claimed that although he did spy for Israel, he did not conduct espionage against the United States, as the two nations are allies. Following his arrest, Pollard's case drew international attention.

Born in 1954, Pollard was instilled with a devotion to Israel at an early age. He majored in political science at Stanford University. Pollard's questionable activities began there, when he falsely told classmates he had dual citizenship in the United States and Israel, and that he was a member of the Mossad, an Israeli secret agency. He longed to emigrate to Israel, imagining himself as a fantastic character of espionage, fighting on Israel's behalf. Instead of moving to Israel, however, he went to Boston and enrolled in a graduate program at Fletcher School of Law and Diplomacy at Tufts University. At Tufts, he provided information on foreign students to the CIA.

Although he already had his foot in the door with the CIA, the agency turned him down when he applied for a job. In 1979, he gained employment with U.S. Naval Intelligence as a civilian intelligence analyst. Working in Washington, Pollard quickly became disillusioned with what he viewed as an anti-Semitic attitude among his co-workers. After attending a 1982 meeting between U.S. Navy and Israeli intelligence officers, Pollard was convinced that Israeli security was threatened because the U.S. was withholding crucial secrets from its ally.

When a friend called to tell Pollard he had met Colonel Aviem Sella, a noted Israeli war hero, Pollard insisted the friend set up a meeting between himself and Sella. Pollard was initially screened by Israeli intelligence, and Sella was cleared by his superiors to meet confidentially with Pollard at the coffee shop of the Washington Hilton Hotel on May 29, 1984. Pollard told Sella his goal was to supply Israel with U.S. secrets to help the country "strengthen its defense capability." The next time the two met, Pollard handed over 48 documents, and the relationship was secured.

Jonathan Pollard, a former U.S. Naval Intelligence clerk, grants an interview at the Federal Correction Institution in Butner, NC, where he is serving a life sentence for passing military secrets to Israel. AP/WIDE WORLD PHOTOS.

Because of his high-level security clearance, Pollard had the authority to check out classified documents and take them home. Israel became hungry for the information, and Pollard was soon smuggling out suitcases full of classified material. The U.S. government claimed Pollard leaked classified information on the Pakistani nuclear-bomb program, Iraqi and Syrian chemical weapons, Libyan air defenses, and the layout of the Palestine Liberation Organization's headquarters in Tunisia, which Israel then bombed. All told, he photocopied and turned over more than 1,000 classified messages and 800 documents to Israel. In exchange for the information, the Israeli government paid Pollard $2,500 per month, in addition to trips to Europe and a $7,000 ring for his wife, who reportedly knew of his espionage activities.

The Federal Bureau of Investigation (FBI) was finally alerted to the quantities of files that Pollard was signing out, but Pollard portrayed himself as a dedicated researcher, working even at home. The FBI did not act immediately, but shadowed Pollard around the clock, suspecting that he might meet with a foreign representative, and give the FBI insight into what he was doing with the material.

In 1985, fearing the increased suspicion of FBI investigators, Pollard and his wife decided to seek asylum and flee to Israel. The two drove to the Israeli Embassy in

Washington, D.C., tailgating a diplomatic limousine through the embassy's front gates. Pollard requested political asylum using his own name, and Danny Cohen, the pseudonym he had been given by the Israeli government, but to no avail. Once turned out by embassy guards, the two were picked up by the FBI.

Pollard was charged with espionage and sentenced to life in prison. According to his supporters, Pollard was the only person in history to spy for an ally and receive a sentence longer than ten years. His wife was charged with collusion and was sentenced to five years in prison.

Although the Israeli government initially denied any involvement with Pollard, they later granted him citizenship. His potential release to return to Israel became a hot-button item. Israel threatened to cease peace talks with the U.S. until the issue was resolved, but failed to gain Pollard's release from prison. Pollard's case was considered by Presidents Reagan, Bush, and Clinton, all of whom denied him clemency.

■ FURTHER READING:

BOOKS:

Nash, Jay Robert. *Spies: A Narrative Encyclopedia of Dirty Deeds and Double Dealing from Biblical Times to Today.* N.p., M. Evans, 1997.

SEE ALSO

CIA (United States Central Intelligence Agency)
Israel, Intelligence and security

Polygraphs

■ JULI BERWALD

A polygraph test is administered to determine whether or not statements made by the subject taking the test are deceptive. During the test, the subject is monitored by a polygraph machine and interrogated by an administrator trained in forensic psychophysiology. The machine measures changes in the subject's blood pressure, heart rate, respiration rate and sweat production. The theory underlying the polygraph test is that a person who is lying exhibits involuntary physiological responses that can be detected by the polygraph instrument. These changes include rapid breathing and heartbeat and increased blood pressure and perspiration.

The Polygraph Instrument

The polygraph instrument usually measures four to six physiological reactions recorded by three different medical instruments that are combined in one machine. Older polygraph machines were equipped with long strips of paper that moved slowly beneath pens that recorded the various physiological responses. Newer equipment uses transducers to convert the information to digital signals that can be stored on computers and analyzed using sophisticated mathematical algorithms.

The three components of the polygraph instrument include the cardio-sphygmograph, the pneumograph, and the galvanograph. Blood pressure and heart rate are measured by the cardio-sphygmograph component of the polygraph, which consists of a blood pressure cuff that is wrapped around the subject's arm. During the questioning the cuff remains inflated. The movement of blood through the subject's veins generates a sound that is transmitted through the air in the cuff to a bellows that amplifies the sound. The magnitude of the sound relates to the blood pressure and the frequency of the changes in the sound relates to the heart rate. The pneumograph component of the polygraph records the subject's respiratory rate. One tube is placed around the subject's chest and a second is placed around his or her abdomen. These tubes are filled with air. When the subject breaths, changes in the air pressure in the tubes are recorded on the polygraph. The galvanograph section records the amount of perspiration produced. It consists of electrical sensors called galvanometers that are attached to the subject's fingertips. The skin of the fingertips contains a high density of sweat glands, making them a good location to measure perspiration. As the amount of sweat touching the galvanometers increases, the resistance of the electrical current measured decreases and these changes are recorded by the polygraph. Most forensic psychophysiologists (FPs) consider the cardio-sphygomgraph and the pneumograph components more informative than the galvanograph.

The Polygraph Test

During the polygraph test, the examiner and the subject are alone in the questioning room. Before the test begins, the examiner spends about an hour talking with the subject. Most forensic psychophisiologists consider this pretest phase an extremely important part of the polygraph. The examiner obtains a baseline read on his or her emotional state and develops the questions that are asked during the actual test. Before the test begins, the examiner goes over each question with the subject so that he or she knows exactly what to expect. When they are ready start, the person administering the polygraph attaches the various components of the polygraph instrument to the examinee.

The polygraph test itself usually consists of about 10 to 12 questions that require yes or no responses. Several methods of composing questions for polygraph tests exist, but all include asking the subject both relevant questions and control questions. Relevant questions relate

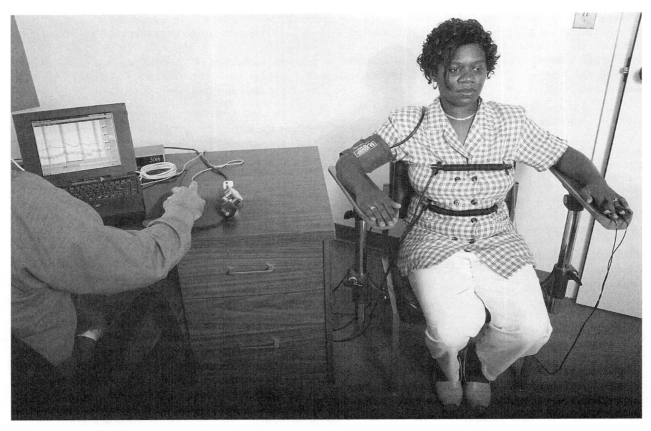

New recruits at the FBI Academy must undergo lie detector tests. ©ANNA CLOPET/CORBIS.

directly to the focus of the polygraph test. Examples of relevant questions are "Did you commit crime X?" or "Did you ever use drug Y?" Control questions vary depending on the type of test administered. The most common type of polygraph test is the Control Question Test (CQT), in which control questions are composed so that the subject can answer them honestly, however, the examiner may make them slightly provocative to evoke an emotional response. Examples of control questions are "Did you ever think of doing crime Y?" or "Were you ever drunk in the last year?" This allows the examiner to understand the subject's physiological responses to challenging questions. In the CQT, greater physiological responses to the relevant questions than to the control questions indicate deceptive behavior.

There are variations to the CQT. In Directed Lie Tests (DLT), the examiner substitutes very broad questions for the control questions and the subject is directed to answer them with lies. An example is "Have you ever told a lie?" to which the subject is directed to respond "No." This response gives an examiner an understanding of the subject's physiological response associated with lying. In Positive Control Tests (PCT), a relevant question itself is used as a control. The subject is instructed to answer truthfully the first time the question is asked and falsely the second time it is asked. The only factor that influences

the response is whether or not the subject is lying. In the Truth Control Test (TCT), the control questions are composed to make the subject think that he or she is being accused of a fictitious crime. This gives the examiner information on how the subject responds to a truthful denial.

During the post-test, the forensic pschophysiologist analyzes the subject's responses to the questions and scores them. Each channel of the polygraph is scored individually. For any channel, if the control response is larger than the relevant response, the score is from +1 to +3, depending on the magnitude of the difference. If the relevant response is larger the score is from −1 to −3. The scores are summed over all channels and all repetitions of the questions to get to the total score. If the final score is sufficiently large and positive, then the subject is considered to have made truthful statements. If the final score is sufficiently large and negative, then the statements are considered deceptive. If the result is close to zero, then the test is inconclusive.

There is much debate as to the accuracy of polygraph tests. Most forensic psychophysiologists agree that the rate of detecting deceptive behavior is greater than the rate of detecting truthful behavior. The American Polygraph Association claims that the accuracy rate for polygraph tests is between 85 and 95 percent. However, reports of false positives have reached as high as 75 percent in research done by the Congressional Office of Technology Assessment.

History and Uses of the Polygraph

Methods for determining whether or not a person is lying have been part of civilization since ancient times. Ancient Hindus required an accused person to chew a mouthful of rice and then spit it out on a leaf from a sacred tree. If the person could spit the rice he or she was declared honest and if the rice stuck in the mouth, dishonest. This test presumptively relies on the physiological response, which makes a person's mouth dry when being deceptive. In the nineteenth century, Italian criminologist Cesare Lombroso developed an early device for measuring and determining the pulse and blood pressure of a person undergoing interrogation, similar to the cardio-sphymograph component of the polygraph. In the early 1900s, Russian psychologist A. R. Luria measured the reaction time and tremors in the fingers of suspected criminals.

A student in experimental psychology at Harvard University, William M. Marston invented the modern polygraph prior to 1921. His treatise *The Lie Detector Test* on understanding physiological responses related to deception was published in 1938. John A. Larson, a police officer in Berkeley, California, modified Marston's polygraph, developing a technique for continuous recording of physiological responses. One of Larson's colleagues, Leonarde Keeler, added the gavanograph component to the polygraph. He joined the faculty of Northwestern University School of Law in Chicago in 1930 and established the Keeler Polygraph Institute of Chicago.

Lawyer, John E. Reid played an important role in the development of questioning techniques used during a polygraph test. In a 1947 paper, he described the use of control questions to evoke emotional responses. In collaboration with Cleve Backster's work, this idea eventually became the Control Question Test (CQT), which is used by the majority of forensic psychophysiologists today.

During the 1960s and 1970s, the polygraph business grew rapidly. Employee screening became a multi-million dollar industry. Polygraph testing began to be used routinely in police work and polygraphers were used as expert witnesses in criminal court trials.

During the late 1970s and early 1980s, the use of the polygraph by the military and security agencies expanded drastically. Between 1973 and 1983, polygraph tests by the federal government tripled. By 1985, the Department of Defense was administering 25,000 tests a year. They used polygraphs to screen employees for classified status, for counterintelligence and for criminal investigations. The FBI, CIA, and National Security Agency used the polygraph to screen job candidates. In 1979, two-thirds of the people rejected for employment from CIA jobs were rejected on the basis of failed polygraph tests.

In the 1980s the scientific validity of polygraphs was brought into question by psychologists. In 1988, the federal Polygraph Protection Act was passed, prohibiting employers from using polygraphs for employment screening. As a result of this legislation, businesses can ask an employee to take a polygraph, but the employee's refusal will not result in any disciplinary treatment. This law does not protect government employees, including people who work in schools, prisons, public agencies, and businesses under contract with the federal government.

The use of polygraphs in court was brought to trial in 1989. In the case of United States v. Piccinonna, a polygraph was deemed admissible as evidence, only if both sides agree to its use or the judge allows it based on criteria set forth in the case. A Supreme Court ruling in 1998 expanded the judge's authority in the use of polygraphs in federal cases. Some states accept this ruling, but not all. On the state level, polygraph use is dependent upon the judge and the case. And, in U.S. v. Schellee (1998), the Supreme Court upheld a personal evidentiary rule against the admissibility of polygraph evidence at military trials.

■ FURTHER READING:

BOOKS:

Harrelson, Leonard. *Lietest: Deception, Truth and the Polygraph.* Ft. Wayne, IN: Jonas Publishing, 1998.

Lykken, David T. *A Tremor in the Blood: Uses and Abuses of the Lie Detector.* Reading, MA: Perseus Books, 1998.

Jussim, Daniel. *Drug Tests and Polygraphs.* New York: Julian Messner, 1987.

ELECTRONIC:

How Stuff Works. "How Lie Detectors Work." <http://science.howstuffworks.com/lie-detector.htm/printable> (April 15, 2003).

American Polygraph Association. <http://www.polygraph.org/> (April 15, 2003).

Polymerase Chain Reaction (PCR)

■ BRYAN R. COBB

The Polymerase Chain Reaction, or PCR, refers to a widely used technique in molecular biology that has become quintessential in many aspects of DNA analysis with broad-based applications in medicine and forensic investigations. PCR is the amplification of specific sequences of genomic DNA, the genetic material found in virtually all living cells. This technology was conceived by the Californian geneticist Kary B. Mullis (1944), who won a Nobel Prize in chemistry in 1993 for developing PCR. It was

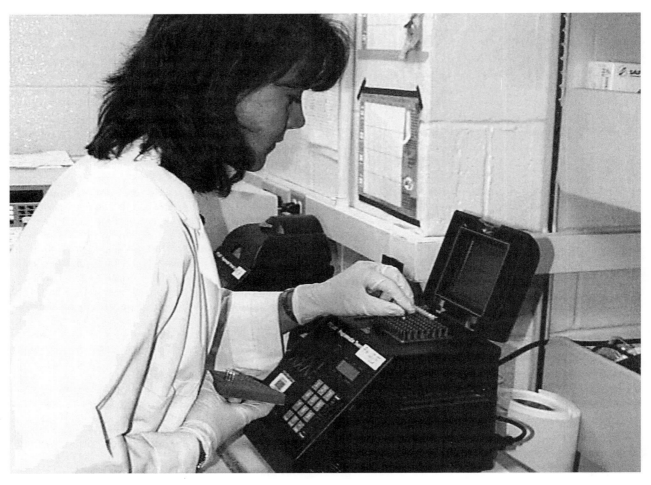

A scientist at the U.S. Army's biodefense laboratory at Ft. Detrick, Maryland, performs PCR analysis on anthrax samples. AP/WIDE WORLD PHOTOS.

first applied to basic science research and later revolutionized modern medicine by improving the diagnosis of human diseases through enhanced genetic testing and medical research. More recently, PCR technology has significantly contributed to both domestic and international forensic sciences as well as applications aimed at improving United States homeland security.

PCR requires specialized equipment that is customized to fluctuate between specifically timed temperature variations. Before PCR is performed, DNA must be isolated from peripheral blood, hair follicles, cheek cells, or tissue samples. Isolated DNA is double stranded, meaning that there are two sequences of letters or nucleotide bases (A or adenine, G or guanine, C or cytosine, and T or thymine). The double stranded DNA is held together by complementary base pairings in that A binds to T, C binds to G and vice versa. Therefore, knowing of the sequence of one strand will reveal the sequence of the complementary strand. Amplification is necessary because there are 3.9 billion bases, and although there is a lot of total DNA, there is not enough to properly analyze specific gene or gene segments. Amplification, therefore, makes it possible to obtain ample quantities of specific sequences of DNA to perform a variety of analyses.

PCR requires "primers," or two sequences about 20–25 bases long with one binding to the beginning sequence of interest and the other binding at the end of the same sequence. In order to get the primers to bind to the targeted sequences in the genome, the PCR machines will undergo several cycles at different temperatures. In the first cycle, the DNA is heated to break apart the two strands. The temperature is then reduced so that the primers can bind or anneal to their complementary base sequence in the DNA. Finally, an enzyme called Taq polymerase adds letters from a pool of bases or letters included in the reaction to the position next to the last base of each the primer. Synthesis of one strand of DNA is in the opposite direction of the other. The result is a double stranded DNA sequence. These cycles are repeated several times and amplification of first the DNA sequence in the genome is copied and this copied DNA is re-copied in the next cycle resulting in exponential growth of the specific sequence. Thirty cycles amplified the target DNA between 100,000- to 10,000,000-fold. However, only DNA sequences of 100 to 2000 bases long are ideally suitable for PCR amplification. In this way, a gene of interest or part of the gene can be amplified to quantities that make genetic studies possible.

PCR, therefore, is rapid, inexpensive, and a relatively easy way of producing a large number of copies of a specific DNA sequence. This is particularly advantageous when there is very little or poor quality DNA. RNA, which is converted from DNA into protein, can also be amplified in the same manner as DNA, however, DNA is much more stable and is easier to isolate. Since each individual inherits sequences of DNA that are different from other individuals, the importance of DNA and PCR technology in identifying an individual is exemplified in the courtroom. DNA analysis can be a powerful tool in criminal investigations, especially those classified as homicides, theft, and sexual assault. Physical evidence left at the scene of any crime can be helpful in reconstructing the sequence of events and potentially reveal the criminal. It can also reveal non-paternity if the pattern of DNA in the offspring does not match the pattern of DNA in the assumed father.

Forensic science relies heavily on PCR technology to amplify specific sequences of DNA that will establish a connection between a specific suspect and a crime scene. Amplification of DNA is critical in cases where the source of DNA is minimal or the integrity is compromised. DNA evidence is also a powerful tool that has been used to ultimately prove the innocence of previously convicted individuals. Additionally, DNA can reveal many characteristics that can help forensic scientists and law enforcement officers identify the perpetrator. This is becoming increasingly applicable to national security as well as international intelligence. PCR has revolutionized law enforcement in this way and will continue to enhance the justice system in the future. For example, using complex algorithms and known sequences of DNA, it is possible to analyze the genetic DNA pattern from an unknown person to predict eye color, gender, and even ethnicity.

In 1985 American geneticist Alec Jeffereys, Ph.D. used PCR technology to amplify regions in the human genome that were highly variable. These DNA fragments were comprised of specific sequences that were repeated. The repeat number was found to be highly variable from individual to individual with the exception of identical twins. These DNA fragments could be amplified using PCR and then studied for variable fragment lengths of repeats. This technology was collectively referred as genetic fingerprinting and became widely used. In a highly publicized case called the Narborough Murder Enquiry, criminal investigators were able to identify the perpetrator using DNA fingerprinting.

One of the more recent applications of PCR technology is for improving national security. After the September 11, 2001 terrorist attacks on the United States, the fear of further attacks involving biological weapons increased. Rapid identification of terrorists and specific biological agents using PCR-based methods represents a plausible approach to gathering critical information about these individuals and weapons.

With the identification, characterization, and genetic engineering of viruses, bacteria, and fungi, the likelihood of strategic, harmful applications involving these organisms is growing. Biological species that represent a serious health risk to humans have been used as weapons for years. These risks can include the U.S. agricultural economy, food supplies, and the environment. To combat bioterrorism, President George W. Bush in February 2002 called for a budget increase to $5.9 billion for Homeland Security directed towards protecting against bioterrorist attacks. The creation of a national database that catalogs pathogens and individuals that are authorized to study these pathogens is also of ongoing concern. A benefit of these databases would be to identify the genetically engineered pathogens used as biological weapons (allowing quick access to specific medical treatment protocols) and to potentially link pathogens to the bioterrorists that developed them.

PCR technology can also be employed to identify the specific disease-causing microorganism. The U.S. Postal Service is working in conjunction with the biotech industry on initiatives to develop intelligent mail. Using PCR to identify anthrax, for example, is one way to quickly ascertain the nature of the contaminated mail or screen high-risk mail. This technology was the government's primary weapon against mail deemed unsuitable for circulation since irradiation provided a limited, unsubstantial solution and often damaged the mail. This high-tech strategy for mail surveillance can be particularly useful by sucking out air samples from the mail and testing for specific molecular signatures using PCR to detect a possible biological contaminant.

Defending against bioterrorism after the September 11 attacks includes developing advances in biological detection instrumentation. In conjunction with the Centers for Disease Control and Prevention (CDC), Lawrence Livermore National Laboratory and its sister laboratory at Los Alamos are currently developing DNA profiles of the most threatening pathogens such as anthrax and the plague using PCR technology. Biodetection instrumentation for genetic profiling has led to the miniaturization and subsequently the portability of DNA analytical devices, particularly for PCR. Forensic scientists and criminologists also benefit from mobile PCR machines by bringing the science to the scene of the crime leading to more rapid crime-solving capabilities.

Security at the 2002 Winter Olympic Games in Salt Lake City was led by The Biological Aerosol Sentry and Information System (BASIS). Miniaturized PCR machines called Smart Cyclers developed by a company called Cepheid were used at the field laboratory operation set up by BASIS. The purpose was to prepare for a bioterrorism threat by having appropriate and rapid biological sample identification to allow for accurate bioterrorist assessment and validation so that the proper responses could be executed.

Recent concerns over genetic engineering of agricultural food products and the potential risks to food safety have prompted studies investigating the molecular signatures of crops using PCR. A study in the scientific journal *Nature* revealed that genetically manipulated DNA from industrial produced maize had been introduced into corn fields in Oaxaca, Mexico. Although the ramifications to health and food safety are unknown and most likely benign, surveillance of crops using PCR is a formidable approach in the implementation of security measures to help protect against harmful pathogenic contaminations that can threaten food safety. As the cost and use of PCR are eased and as the collection of databases with recognizable DNA profiles of various microorganisms is increased, the utility of this technology in human and food safety will be greatly improved.

■ **FURTHER READING:**

BOOKS:

Friedman, J., F. Dill, M. Hayden, and B. McGillivray. *Genetics.* N.P.: Williams & Wilkins, 1996.

Lodish, J., D. Baltimore, A. Berk, S. L. Zipursky, P. Matsudaira, and J. Darnell. *Molecular Cell Biology.* New York: Scientific American Books, 1995.

PERIODICALS:

Jefferys, A. J. "Hypervariable 'minisatellite' regions in human DNA." *Nature* no. 314 (1987): 67–73.

Mullis, K. B., and F. A. Faloona. "Specific synthesis of DNA in vitro via a polymerase catalysed chain reaction." *Methods in Enzymology* no. 155 (1987): 335–350.

Nakamura, Y., M. Leppert, P. O'Connell, et al. "Variable number tandem repeat (VNTR) markers for human gene mapping." *Science* no. 237 (1987): 1616–1622.

Quist, D., and I. H. Chapela. "Transgenic DNA introgressed into traditional maize landraces in Oaxaca, Mexico." *Nature* no. 414 (2001): 541–3.

Wong, Z., V. Wilson, A. J. Jefferys, et al. "Cloning a selected fragment from a human DNA 'fingerprint': isolation of an extremely polymorphic minisatellite." *Nucleic Acids* no. 14 (1986): 4605–616.

Wyman, A. R. and R. White. "A highly polymorphic locus in human DNA." *PNAS* no. 77 (1980): 6754–6758.

ELECTRONIC:

Access Excellence. "Kary B. Mullins." The National Health Museum. March, 2002. <http://www.accessexcellence.org/AB/BC/Kary_B_Mullis.html> (December 13, 2002).

Access Excellence. "PCR Technology." Connie Veilleax. July 8, 2002. <http://www.accessexcellence.org/LC/SS/PS/PCR/PCR_technology.html> (December 16, 2002).

Center for strategic and international solutions. "New Technology Counters Bioterrorism Threat, Policy Issues." CSIS. Fall, 2002. <http://www.csis.org/pubs/prospectus/02fall_bacastow.htm> (December 11, 2002).

Edvotek. "Biotechnology: DNA Fingerprinting for Forensics and Paternity." 2001. <http://www.edvotek.com/experiments/biotech/04/334.html> (December 12, 2002).

Government Security. "Who are you?" Technology solutions in defense of the homeland. July 22, 2002. <http://govtsecurity.securitysolutions.com> (December 15, 2002).

Kari Sable Burns. "Green River Killer." True Crimes. 2002. <http://www.karisable.com/greenriverdnatime.htm> (December 15, 2002).

United States Congress 107th Congress 2nd Session. "Technology assessment in the war on terrorism and homeland security: the role of OTA" Committee Print. April, 2002. <http://www.fas.org/irp/congress/2002_hr/ota.html> (December 15, 2002).

Westburg. "Human Diagnostics: forensics." Cambridge Molecular Diagnostics. 2001. <http://www.westburg.nl/htm/md/hd_forensics.htm> (December 15, 2002).

SEE ALSO

Anthrax
Anthrax, Terrorist Use as a Biological Weapon
Anthrax Vaccine
Anthrax Weaponization
Biochemical Assassination Weapons
Biocontainment Laboratories
Biodetectors
Bio-Engineered Tissue Constructs
Biological and Toxin Weapons Convention
Biological Warfare
Biological Warfare, Advanced Diagnostics
Biological Weapons, Genetic Identification
CDC (United States Centers for Disease Control and Prevention)
Chemical and Biological Defense Information Analysis Center (CBIAC)
Microbiology: Applications to Espionage, Intelligence and Security
Microchip

Popular Front for the Liberation of Palestine (PFLP)

At one time affiliated with the PLO, the Popular Front for the Liberation of Palestine (PFLP) is a Marxist-Leninist group founded in 1967 by George Habash. The PFLP joined the Alliance of Palestinian Forces (APF) to oppose the Declaration of Principles signed in 1993 and suspended participation in the PLO. The PFLP broke away from the APF, along with the DFLP, in 1996 over ideological differences. PFLP officers took part in meetings with Arafat's Fatah party and PLO representatives in 1999 to discuss national unity and the reinvigoration of the PLO but the PFLP continues to oppose current negotiations with Israel.

PFLP committed numerous international terrorist attacks during the 1970s. Since 1978, PFLP has conducted attacks against Israeli or moderate Arab targets, including killing a settler and her son in December 1996. The PFLP increased operational activity in 2001, highlighted by the shooting death of the Israeli tourism minister in alleged retaliation for Israel's killing of a PFLP leader.

The PFLP is estimated to have approximately 800 members, and has operated in Syria, Lebanon, Israel, West Bank, and Gaza. They receive safe haven and logistical assistance from Syria.

■ FURTHER READING:

ELECTRONIC:

Central Intelligence Agency. World Factbook, 2002. <http://www.cia.gov/cia/publications/factbook/> (April 16, 2003).

Taylor, Francis X. U.S. Department of State. Patterns of Global Terrorism 2001. Annual Report: On the Record Briefing. May 21, 2002. <http://www.state.gov/s/ct/rls/rm/10367.htm> (April 17, 2003).

U.S. Department of State. Annual reports. <http://www.state.gov/www/global/terrorism/annual_reports.html> (April 16, 2003).

SEE ALSO

Terrorism, Philosophical and Ideological Origins
Terrorist and Para-State Organizations
Terrorist Organization List, United States
Terrorist Organizations, Freezing of Assets

Popular Front for the Liberation of Palestine-General Command (PFLP-GC)

The Popular Front for the Liberation of Palestine-General Command (PFLP-GC) split from the Popular Front for the Liberation of Palestine (PFLP) in 1968, claiming it wanted to focus more on fighting and less on politics. Opposed to Arafat's Palestine Liberation Army (PLO), the PFLP-GC is led by Ahmad Jabril, a former captain in the Syrian Army. The PFLP-GC maintains close ties to both Syria and Iran.

The PFLP-GC carried out dozens of attacks in Europe and the Middle East during the 1970s-80s. Known for cross-border terrorist attacks into Israel using unusual means, such as hot-air balloons and motorized hang gliders, PFLP-GC's recent primary focus is on guerrilla operations in southern Lebanon, small-scale attacks in Israel, West Bank, and Gaza.

The PFLP-GC has an estimated several hundred adherents, and is headquartered in Damascus with bases in Lebanon. They receive support from Syria and financial support from Iran.

■ FURTHER READING:

ELECTRONIC:

Central Intelligence Agency. World Factbook, 2002. <http://www.cia.gov/cia/publications/factbook/> (April 16, 2003).

Taylor, Francis X. U.S. Department of State. Patterns of Global Terrorism 2001. Annual Report: On the Record Briefing. May 21, 2002. <http://www.state.gov/s/ct/rls/rm/10367.htm> (April 17,2003).

U.S. Department of State. Annual reports. <http://www.state.gov/www/global/terrorism/annual_reports.html> (April 16, 2003).

SEE ALSO

Terrorism, Philosophical and Ideological Origins
Terrorist and Para-State Organizations
Terrorist Organization List, United States
Terrorist Organizations, Freezing of Assets

Port Security

Security of national ports has always been a concern for any great power, but between the War of 1812 and the terrorist attacks of September 11, 2001, Americans tended to take such security for granted. Other than a thwarted German attempt to form an alliance with Mexico against the United States—an effort that brought America into World War I—and limited Axis attempts to infiltrate both coasts in World War II, no foreign power launched a successful attack on the contiguous United States prior to the al Qaeda bombings. Since September, 2001, the federal government has adopted much stricter standards for port security. Key elements in this undertaking are the U.S. Coast Guard (USCG), the U.S. Customs Service, and the two agencies' parent organization, the Department of Homeland Security.

On September 24, 2001, less than two weeks after the terrorist attacks on the World Trade Center in New York, the House Transportation and Infrastructure Committee and the Senate Commerce, Science, and Transportation Committee issued a joint request to Transportation Secretary Norman Mineta for a rapid response team to reduce the vulnerability of American ports to terrorist attack. In accordance with this request, Mineta requested additional funds for his department's leading antiterrorism service, the USCG.

At that time, several statutes already existed providing USCG with extensive enforcement powers. These included Section 89 of Title 14, U.S. Code, which authorized USCG to board any vessel subject to the jurisdiction, or operation of any law, of the United States in order to make inquiries or conduct examinations, inspections, searches, seizures, or arrests. The Ports and Waterway

Safety Act of 1972 gave the Secretary of Transportation broad authority to regulate movements and activities of vessels subject to U.S. jurisdiction, with USCG as Transportation's operational arm in these undertakings.

Additional powers came from the Omnibus Diplomatic Security and Antiterrorism Act of 1986, passed after a U.S. citizen was killed during the terrorist seizure of the passenger vessel *Achille Lauro* in 1985. Title XI of that law became known as the International Maritime and Port Security Act. The latter gave USCG authority to require inspections, patrol ports and harbors, establish security and safety zones, and develop contingency plans and procedures in an effort to combat terrorism.

USCG Responds to 9/11

As Mineta noted before the joint committees, USCG had launched "the largest homeland port security operation since World War II" in the aftermath of September 11. As part of Operation Noble Eagle and Enduring Freedom, first phases of the effort to destroy al Qaeda, USCG deployed 55 cutters (small armed vessels), 42 aircraft, and hundreds of boats to establish port and coastline patrols. It also called up more than 2,800 reservists to support homeland security operations at the country's 361 ports.

At the ports of San Francisco, Los Angeles, and San Diego, USCG developed a pilot armed escort initiative, the Sea Marshals program, whereby it provided armed escort to vessels during their transit through U.S. waters. USCG also established Naval Vessel Protection Zones, the maritime equivalent of no-fly zones, for a distance of 500 yards (457 m) around all U.S. naval vessels in the navigable waters of the United States.

Vital to these operations, and to future efforts to protect U.S. ports, were USCG Port Security Units (PSUs). Staffed primarily with selected reservists, along with a core of active duty personnel, PSUs had a mission of providing waterborne security, along with limited land-based protection, for shipping and critical port facilities both in U.S. waters and in theatres of combat. In the latter capacity, PSUs had been deployed to the Persian Gulf during Operation Desert Storm in 1990, and to Haiti for Operation Uphold Democracy in 1994. In December, 2000, following the terrorist attacks on the USS *Cole* in Yemen, PSU 309 from Port Clinton, Ohio, was deployed to the Middle East to provide vital force protection for Navy assets.

Capable of deploying within 24 hours and establishing operations within 96 hours after initial call-up, PSUs had transportable boats equipped with dual outboard motors, along with support equipment to sustain activities for up to 30 days. Because the specialized training for PSU operations was not available within USCG, reservists assigned to PSUs were required to undergo a two-week basic skills course at the PSU Training Detachment, located on the U.S. Marine base at Camp Lejeune, North Carolina.

The Maritime Security Act

On November 15, 2002, the House passed the Maritime Security Act, approved by the Senate two days earlier. Among other provisions, the new legislation extended USCG powers by giving its units authority to require background checks of some port employees; put in place a new tracking system for commercial ships; require all 361 nationwide ports to establish committees bringing together federal, state, local, and private security officers; establish marine anti-terrorism methods; set new standards to make container seals tamper-proof; and authorize the Sea Marshal program.

Congress appropriated $500 million to dispatch more security operatives to inspect cargo at its point of origin, and for other specific measures that included development of equipment to detect nuclear, biological, and chemical weapons hidden in containers. In securing the nation's 25,000 miles of navigable waterways, USCG called on the help of TRW Systems, to which it awarded a $31-million, five-year contract to assess security measures and assist in developing guidelines, as well as self-assessment methodology.

An example of new container security measures could be found at the busy port of Hampton Roads, Virginia, where U.S. Customs had installed radiation detection equipment to interdict hidden radioactive material. Hampton Roads authorities reported that the alarm sounded two or three times a week, each time for reasons that had nothing to do with terrorism: smoke detectors, for instance, have trace amounts of radioactive materials, as do some medications and plants. These false alarms caused only minor delays, and port security officials gave the $125,000 system high marks.

Likewise, maritime industry representatives attending a public hearing sponsored by USCG in San Pedro, California, in February, 2003, expressed approval of new plans for increased security in the local port. However, they did request federal assistance in raising the estimated $6 billion needed to put the new measures in place.

Funding issues were also a concern for Senator Ernest Hollings (D-SC), former chairman of the Senate Commerce Committee and sponsor of the Maritime Security Act. He had hoped to raise several hundred million more dollars through users' fees on cargo and shipping companies, a move bitterly opposed by the shipping industry. Due to this opposition, Hollings had removed the fee from his original bill, but in March, 2003, his staffers told the *Chicago Tribune* that he intended to keep pursuing the idea.

Continuing concerns. A number of situations in late 2002 and early 2003 highlighted the need for increased port security measures. One of these was a war game staged in the fall of 2002 by some 85 officials representing the Central Intelligence Agency, Federal Bureau of Investigation, Office of Homeland Security (as the new department was called prior to March 2003), and international trade businesses.

The premise was a terrorist plot to deliver weapons of mass destruction to the United States through one of its ports. In order to stop the attack, participants searched ports nationwide, yet they failed to find the "terrorists," who succeeded in smuggling their deadly cargo in a container through a port on the East Coast. Had these been real terrorists, they would have been free to explode a "dirty bomb" (radioactive material packed with explosives) in the middle of downtown Chicago, their target in the exercise.

A contract dispute between dock workers and employers on the West Coast in the fall of 2002 shut down ports for 10 days, causing a $1 billion impact on retailers—thus, illustrating the devastating economic impact a shutdown could have. Participants in the war games exercise calculated that, if U.S. ports had to shut down because of a terrorist incident, the Dow Jones industrial index could rapidly plunge and leave a dent in the economy measured in the tens of millions within a day.

Other real-life incidents and phenomena raised concerns during this period. A boatload of illegal immigrants from Haiti penetrated port security in Miami in early 2003, and periodically stowaways from China managed to get into the ports of the West Coast inside shipping containers. Far more ominous were reports throughout 2002 of al Qaeda "ships of concern," with U.S. intelligence estimating that the terrorist group had anywhere from 12 to 50 rogue vessels plying the world's seas.

■ FURTHER READING:

PERIODICALS:

Brand, Lois. "Helping Coast Guard Enhance Port Security." *National Defense* 87, no. 590 (January 2003): 45.

Haynes, V. Dion. "U.S. Works to Shore up Port Security; War Game Underscores Acute Risk." *Chicago Tribune.* (March 10, 2003): 8.

Mintz, John. "15 Freighters Believed to Be Linked to al Qaeda." *Washington Post.* (December 31, 2002): A1.

Schoch, Deborah. "Port Security Upgrade Welcomed, But Industry Asks Who Will Pay." *Los Angeles Times.* (February 6, 2003): B3.

ELECTRONIC:

Meeks, Brock N. Container, Port Security Seen Lacking. MSNBC News. <http://www.msnbc.com/news/888290. asp?0s=-> (March 29, 2003).

Port Security Units. U.S. Coast Guard. <http://www.uscg. mil/hq/g-cp/comrel/factfile/Factcards/PSUs.html> (March 29, 2003).

The Subcommittee on Coast Guard and Maritime Transportation Hearing on Port Security. House of Representatives. December 6, 2001. <http://www.house.gov/transportation/cgmt/12–06-01/12–06-01memo.html> (March 29, 2003).

SEE ALSO

Coast Guard (USCG), United States

Customs Service, United States
Homeland Security, United States Department of
September 11 Terrorist Attacks on the United States

PORTPASS (Port Passenger Accelerated Service System)

PORTPASS (Port Passenger Accelerated Service System) is a generic term for programs developed to expedite passage through U.S. national entry systems. PORTPASS components include the INSPASS (Immigration and Naturalization Service Passenger Accelerated Service System), SENTRI (Secure Electronic Network for Travelers' Rapid Inspection), OARS (Outlying Area Reporting Station), and RVIS (Remote Video Inspection System) systems. The general goal of PORTPASS programs is to identify pre-approved low-risk international travelers and allow inspectors additional time to focus on high-risk entrants.

As with other automated entry systems, PORTPASS databases utilize a "one-to-one" search protocol to verify identity. Instead of comparing gathered biometrics or vehicle identification data across a broad database, an identification number allows direct comparison with the data assigned to a PORTPASS identification number.

INSPASS is used at selected airports to facilitate passage through entry checkpoints. INSPASS systems utilize hand geometry biometrics that include measurements of hand length, thickness and translucency.

SENTRI is used at selected border crossings to facilitate quick passage through entry inspection checkpoints. SENTRI programs screen participants and their vehicles against information already gathered in the program database. SENTRI utilizes digital license plate readers and camera scans that allow inspectors to validate both the identity of the vehicle and the identity of the occupants of the vehicle against digitized photographs of approved participants in the SENTRI database and other law enforcement databases.

OARS was developed as a counterpart to the Canadian Border Boat Landing Program (I-68 program) that allows registered participants facilitated entry to U.S. waters for recreational purposes through a self-reporting system located at fueling docks, boating marinas, and state parks.

RVIS is a PORTPASS program in use along the U.S. border with Canada. Using video surveillance, inspectors can remotely monitor border crossings. Inspectors can verify registered RVIS participants and alert enforcement authorities in the event of an unauthorized border crossing. Automated systems are also backed with a video inspection system so that, if the identification systems fail to provide a positive match to approved database information, inspectors located offsite can still interview the prospective entrant.

As of March 1, 2003, the newly created United States Department of Homeland Security (DHS) absorbed the former Immigration and Naturalization Service (INS). All INS border patrol agents and investigators—along with agents from the U.S. Customs Service and Transportation Security Administration—were placed under the direction of the DHS Directorate of Border and Transportation Security (BTS). Responsibility for U.S. border security and the enforcement of immigration laws was transferred to BTS.

BTS is also scheduled to incorporate the United States Customs Service (previously part of the Department of Treasury). Former INS immigration service functions are scheduled to be placed under the direction of the DHS Bureau of Citizenship and Immigration Services. Under the reorganization, the INS formally ceases to exist on the date the last of its functions are transferred.

Although the technologies involved in PORTPASS entry security programs remain viable, in an effort to facilitate border security, BTS plans currently envision higher levels of coordination between formerly separate agencies and databases. As of April 2003, the specific coordination and future of PORTPASS programs was uncertain with regard to potential name changes, program administration, and policy changes.

■ FURTHER READING:

ELECTRONIC:

Bureau of Citizenship and Immigration Services. INSPASS. March 1, 2003. <http://www.immigration.gov/graphics/howdoi/inspassloc.htm> (April 14, 2003).

Department of Homeland Security. April 2, 2003. <http://www.dhs.gov/dhspublic/index.jsp> (April 11, 2003).

Department of Homeland Security. Secure Electronic Network For Travelers Rapid Inspection (SENTRI). March 26, 2003.<http://www.immigration.gov/graphics/shared/lawenfor/bmgmt/inspect/sentri.htm> (April 9, 2003).

United States Department of Homeland Security. Bureau of Citizenship and Immigration Services. PORTPASS. March 11, 2003. <http://www.immigration.gov/graphics/howdoi/portpass.htm> (April 9, 2003).

United States Department of Homeland Security. Immigration Information. INSPASS. March 4, 2003. <http://www.immigration.gov/graphics/shared/howdoi/inspass.htm> (April 9, 2003).

SEE ALSO

APIS (Advance Passenger Information System)
IBIS (Interagency Border Inspection System)
IDENT (Automated Biometric Identification System)
INSPASS (Immigration and Naturalization Service Passenger Accelerated Service System)
NAILS (National Automated Immigration Lookout System)
SENTRI (Secure Electronic Network for Travelers' Rapid Inspection)

Portugal, Intelligence and Security

Portugal's tumultuous twentieth-century political history affected public perception of the nation's government and intelligence officials. In the 1940s, António de Oliveira Salazar's dictatorship created a secret police force, the International Police for the Defense of the State (PIDE). The PIDE gained a reputation for domestic and political espionage, and the arrest, detainment, and torture of anti-government dissidents. The secret police operated above the law in Portugal for over three decades, but used especially brutal means of coercion in the nation's African colonies as an attempt to crush independence movements.

After a coup overthrew Salazar's successor, Marcello Caetano, the secret police was abolished. The agency that replaced the PIDE could not overcome the legacy of its predecessor and was quickly dissolved. Public outcry and government apprehension prevented the formation of a new intelligence service in Portugal for over a decade. In the early 1980s, a string of terrorist attacks on Portuguese interests, including the bombing of their embassy in Turkey, prompted the formation of new intelligence and security service. The new Portuguese intelligence service was established by a newly elected progressive government. Constitutional reforms in 1989 guaranteed that the new intelligence services would be regulated by the government and barred from political and domestic espionage.

Today, Portugal maintains both military and civilian intelligence and security forces. The main intelligence agency is the *Sistema de Informacoes da Republica Portuguesa* (SIRP), or the Intelligence System of the Portuguese Republic. The SIRP is charged with the protection of national security by producing and analyzing intelligence information gathered from foreign and domestic sources.

The SIRP is divided into two major operational branches. The Security Information Service (SIS) coordinates military and civilian efforts to protect national military, economic, and government interests. The SIS has both counter-intelligence and anti-terrorism special task forces. While the SIS is controlled by the Ministry of Internal Administration, the Ministry of National Defense operates the other significant SIRP division, the *Serviço de Informações Estratégicas de Defesa e Militares* (SIEDM) or Strategic Defense and Military Intelligence Service. The SIEDM primarily focuses on external intelligence and threats to state property and interests abroad. The agency cooperates closely with the military to conduct defense and anti-terrorism operations.

The Portuguese Armed Forces also maintain their own, individual intelligence units. Operations of all military intelligence forces are classified, but closely monitored by the office of the Prime Minister.

The socialist and democratic socialist parties have continued to vie for power in Portugal's government. Elections held in 2001 yielded a gain of several local offices for the democratic socialists, leading to a turnover in the national government. The current Portuguese government is endeavoring to further the massive constitutional reforms begun in 1986. Portugal is a member of the North Atlantic Treaty Organization (NATO). Part of the European Union (EU), Portugal participates in pan-European intelligence and security organizations as well as the EU currency program.

SEE ALSO

European Union

Postal Security

∎ BELINDA ROWLAND

Postal security refers to the safeguarding of United States Postal Service (USPS) employees and customers from hazardous materials that may be contained in the mail.

In October 2001, pieces of mail containing the anthrax bacterium infected 23 persons, five of whom died. The USPS immediately took measures to insure the safety of its employees and customers. Furthermore, the USPS developed a plan to safeguard the mail system and protect employees and customers without compromising the level of mail service.

FBI agents check the identification of a postal worker seeking to enter the Federal Building in Los Angeles as security measures were tightened coast to coast after the terrorist attacks of September 11, 2001. AP/WIDE WORLD PHOTOS.

USPS Emergency Preparedness Plan

Because of the complexity of the USPS system and volume of mail that is processed, achieving postal security is no small undertaking. The postal service handles nearly 680 million pieces of mail each day. The USPS has about 300 processing and distribution centers that use computer-controlled sorting equipment and data processing systems to distribute mail to its destination.

The Emergency Preparedness Plan was developed to protect USPS employees and customers from future bioterrorism attacks. The Plan is composed of six initiatives: prevention, protection and health-risk reduction, detection and identification, intervention, decontamination, and investigation. Each initiative is a point where actions can be taken to reduce the risk or effects of bioterrorism.

Prevention. The first initiative is to reduce the risk that a person could use the mail as a vehicle for bioterrorism.

The addition of detection, containment, and sterilization technologies to the 350,000 mail collection boxes in use is not yet feasible. The USPS has been investigating the use of intelligent mail in which each piece of mail has a unique identifier. This measure would reduce anonymous mail.

Protection and health-risk reduction. This initiative's objective is to reduce the risk that USPS employees and customers could be exposed to biological weapons and to prevent contaminated mail from contaminating other mail. USPS employees can wear protective equipment. Mail-processing machinery could be cleaned with high-efficiency particulate air (HEPA)-filtered vacuum systems. Enhanced heating, ventilation, and air-conditioning (HVAC) systems could be used to trap or kill bacteria in the air. As of late 2002, the application of HEPA-filtration technologies to the mail system is still being investigated.

Detection and identification. The objective of the third initiative is to detect and identify biological weapons as early in the mail stream as possible. This initiative involves two technologies: triggering and confirmation. Triggering technologies would provide continuous monitoring of the mail and report the presence of a possible threat. Confirmation technologies would detect the presence of specific microorganisms. Application of these technologies to the mail system is still under investigation.

Intervention. Routine decontamination of mail is a precautionary measure. The possible methods for mail decontamination work by exposing mail to radiation (eg. e-beams), high pressure, or gases. Microorganisms, such as the anthrax bacterium or spore, cannot survive these conditions. In 2001, the USPS bought eight e-beam machines and planned to install them in Washington D.C. and the New York and New Jersey area. As of late 2002, irradiation is the only acceptable method for decontaminating mail, and e-beam technology has been used to sterilize incoming federal government mail only.

Decontamination. This initiative refers to the elimination of known biological weapons in the mail, mail processing equipment, and buildings. The decontamination processes described for the intervention initiative can be applied to sterilize mail that is known to be contaminated with dangerous microorganisms. Certain gases have antimicrobial properties and are used for disinfection and sterilization. Chlorine dioxide was used to disinfect an office building that was contaminated with anthrax spores.

Investigation. This initiative aims to enhance criminal investigation methods as related to postal security. Technologies consistent with this initiative include mailpiece tracking and tracing using a Wide Field of View camera, image capture and analysis, and positive product tracking. These technologies would enable the USPS to track contaminated mail and equipment.

■ FURTHER READING:

PERIODICALS:

"Months After Anthrax Scare, Mail-Safety Goals are Unmet." *USA Today.* (August 29, 2002):12a.

Rhodes, Keith A., "USPS Air Filtration Systems Need More Testing and Cost Benefit Analysis Before Implementation." *FDCH Government Account Reports* (August 22, 2002).

ELECTRONIC:

United States Postal Service. <http://www.usps.com/welcome.htm> (January 1, 2003).

SEE ALSO

Anthrax, Terrorist Use as a Biological Weapon

Bioterrorism, Protective Measures
Decontamination Methods
Mail Sanitization
Postal Service (USPS), United States
September 11 Terrorist Attacks on the United States

Postal Service (USPS), United States

The United States Postal Service (USPS) is an independent government agency that collects and disseminates the mail to millions of homes and businesses across the country.

In the early days of America, colonists had to either ferry their own mail or rely on messengers and merchants to carry their letters and packages. The first official postal service emerged in 1639, when Richard Fairbanks' Boston tavern became the repository of all mail sent from abroad. The postal service was initially run by the British, but in 1775, America's Continental Congress voted to establish its own postal system, with Benjamin Franklin as its first postmaster general. By the 1780s, the postal system consisted of seventy-five post offices and about twenty-six post riders. The first postage stamps were introduced in 1847.

Over the next two centuries, the postal service expanded and evolved. Americans' westward expansion gave rise to the Pony Express in the 1860s, a team of horse-riding letter carriers who distributed the mail between Missouri and California. Over the years, letter carriers traded in their horses for faster means of transportation: trains, steamboats, and trucks. With the introduction of the airplane in the early 1900s, the Postal Service could for the first time deliver mail quickly and affordably across the oceans.

The next major overhaul to the postal system occurred on August 12, 1970, when President Richard Nixon signed the Postal Reorganization Act. The Act replaced the old Post Office Department with the U.S. Postal Service. It was designed to make the service run more like a business and less like a government agency. Today, the USPS is directed by an eleven-member Board of Governors, led by a Postmaster General. Postage rates and service fees are decided upon by an independent Postal Rate Commission.

Every day, the USPS handles more than 680 million pieces of mail. The Postal Service relies on the revenue from these deliveries to survive, because it does not receive funding from taxpayer dollars. To protect its customers from mail theft, mail fraud, and other criminal activities involving the mail, the USPS has its own law enforcement agency, called the U.S. Postal Inspection Service. This agency works closely with federal law enforcement officials to ensure that the mail service is safe.

In October 2001, mail security became a matter of national urgency. Following the discovery of anthrax-tainted letters, which ultimately infected twenty-two people and killed five in the northeastern United States, the USPS announced that it was adopting tighter security measures. Many postal facilities were outfitted with state-of-the-art irradiation systems, which sanitize the mail using the same radiation technology that protects the food supply from bacterial contaminants. Also installed were vacuum/filtration cleaning systems to remove hazardous particles from sorting machines.

■ FURTHER READING:

BOOKS:

Bolick, Nancy O'Keefe. *Mail Call!: The History of the U.S. Mail Service.* Danbury, CT: Franklin Watts, Incorporated, 1994.

Kule, Elaine A. *The U.S. Mail (Transportation and Communication Series).* Berkeley Heights, NJ: Enslow Publishers, Inc., 2002.

ELECTRONIC:

The United States Postal Service. <http://www.usps.com/> (December 20, 2002).

SEE ALSO

Anthrax, Terrorist Use as a Biological Weapon
Mail Sanitization
Nixon Administration (1969–1974), United States National Security Policy
Postal Security

Potassium Iodide

Potassium iodide (chemical formula KI) is a salt that is similar in structure and physical character to common table salt (sodium chloride; NaCl). Indeed, potassium iodide is a common commercial additive to table salt, to produce "iodized" salt.

Potassium iodide is noteworthy in security because of its ability to block the uptake of radioactive iodine by the body's thyroid gland. Located in the neck, the sole task of the thyroid gland is the production of a hormone that is one of the body's principle metabolic regulators. Thus, the disruption of the thyroid gland—such as occurs when the uptake of radioactive iodine triggers the development of thyroid cancer—threatens health and can even led to death.

If taken in time following an accidental or deliberate release of radioactive iodine, such as would occur with a leak from a nuclear power plant or the detonation of a bomb containing a radioactive payload, potassium iodide saturates the thyroid with a form of iodine that persists in the gland. The radioactive form of iodine cannot outcompete this stable form of iodine, and so is excreted from the body.

Ingestion of KI has long been a precaution for workers in nuclear power plants and for military personnel engaged in a conflict where the use of nuclear weapons is considered to be a possibility. Much of what is known of the protective effects of potassium iodide has come from the measurements of radiation accumulation in the thyroid glands of hundreds of thousands of people in the weeks following the Chernobyl reactor disaster of April 1986, and the therapeutic effects KI achieved in Poland during that time.

Since the terrorist attacks on the United States in the latter months of 2001, the need for a distribution of KI to civilians has become recognized. This has become especially evident with the exposed vulnerability of nuclear power plants to terrorist attack, and to the conceivable use of "dirty" bombs by terrorists. The latter, essentially a conventional explosive charge that spews out radioactive substances including iodine, could contaminate many people in a crowded urban area.

The protective effects of potassium iodide last about 24 hours from the time it is ingested. Thus, a civilian or military protective strategy requires daily doses of KI. Longer term or more permanent use of the salt is not recommended yet, as prolonged use has been linked to thyroid malfunction, especially in those with Grave's disease or autoimmune inflammation of the thyroid gland.

■ FURTHER READING:

BOOKS:

Harrison, J. R., W. Paile, and K. Baverstock. "Public Health Implications of Iodine Prophylaxis in Radiological Emergencies" in: Thomas, G., A. Karaoglou, and E. D. Williams, eds. *Radiation and Thyroid Cancer.* Singapore: World Scientific, 1999.

PERIODICALS:

Astakhova, L. N., L. R. Anspaugh, G. W. Beebe, et al. "Chernobyl-Related Thyroid Cancer in Children in Belarus." *Radiation Research* no. 150 (1998): 349–356.

Robbins, J., and A. B. Schneider. "Thyroid Cancer following Exposure to Radioactive Iodine." *Reviews in Endocrine and Metabolic Disorders* no. 1 (2000): 197–203.

ELECTRONIC:

U.S. Food and Drug Administration. "Guidance: Potassium Iodide as a Thyroid Blocking Agent in radiation Emergencies." Center for Drug Evaluation and Research. December 10, 2001. <http://www.fda.gov/cder/guidance/4825fnl.htm> (April 9, 2003).

U.S. Nuclear Regulatory Commission. "Frequently Asked Questions About Potassium Iodide." National Research

Council. April 2, 2003. <http://www.nrc.gov/what-we-do/regulatory/emer-resp/emer-prep/ki-faq.html> (April 12, 2003).

SEE ALSO

Atmospheric Release Advisory Capability (ARAC)
Chernobyl Nuclear Power Plant Accident, Detection and Monitoring
Nuclear Weapons

President of the United States (Executive Command and Control of Intelligence Agencies)

∎ JUDSON KNIGHT

As commander in chief, the President of the United States oversees not only all U.S. military forces, but U.S. national security as a whole. In this capacity, the President exercises executive command and control of intelligence agencies, and issues executive orders and presidential directives that shape national security policy. The nation's 14 largest intelligence agencies belong to the Intelligence Community, whose leader, the Director of Central Intelligence (DCI), reports directly to the President. Executive oversight of intelligence also emanates through the National Security Council (NSC) and the President's Foreign Intelligence Advisory Board (PFIAB). The President in turn presents intelligence budgets to the U.S. Congress, which exercises checks and balances on executive power.

Architect of National Security

The modern age of national security began in 1947, with the passage of the National Security Act, which reorganized the Department of Defense (DOD) and established the Central Intelligence Agency (CIA) and NSC. Prior to that time, the President had always exercised control over the armed forces as commander in chief, but now he also supervised a nascent security and intelligence apparatus destined to grow considerably over the years.

The modern President articulates much of his role as director of national security policy through executive orders and, more recently, presidential directives. Executive orders, which originated under the administration of President Theodore Roosevelt and grew considerably in number after World War II, are theoretically subject to congressional override, but in practice amount to executive edicts. Important executive orders from the 1970s and onward

have addressed issues such as the organization of the Intelligence Community and the handling of classified documents.

Whereas executive orders are open to the public, presidential directives are classified, and knowledge of their content only emerges, if at all, after the fact. These directives have guided security and intelligence policy since the administration of President John F. Kennedy, and each administration has sought to place its own stamp on them by giving them specific titles as a class. For example, they were known as national security directives under George H. W. Bush, presidential decision directives under William J. Clinton, and national security presidential directives under George W. Bush.

In 1986, Congress called on presidents to issue an annual National Security Strategy (NSS), a document outlining the blueprint for national security. Prior to the 2002 NSS of George W. Bush, these usually did little more than simply restate policies then in effect. The Bush NSS, on the other hand, outlined an explicit framework for U.S. actions to be taken in the wake of the September 11, 2001, terrorist attacks.

The Advisors

In directing intelligence policy, the President relies on Cabinet-level advisors whose departments have a role in national security. Most notable among these are the secretaries of State, Defense, Homeland Security, Energy, and the Treasury, as well as the Attorney General. Other Cabinet officials, including the secretaries of Agriculture, Commerce, and Transportation, also support some national-security functions, and may be called upon for advice relating to their specific areas.

The role of the Vice-President as advisor varies as a function of his relationship with the President. Kennedy, for instance, worked little with Lyndon B. Johnson, whose inclusion on the winning 1960 ticket had resulted from a marriage of convenience designed to attract conservative Southern Democrats. On the other hand, George W. Bush has relied heavily on Vice-President Dick Cheney, who served in the administration of his father.

The NSC. The Vice President is, along with the secretaries of State and Defense, a statutory member of the NSC, as is the Chairman of the Joint Chiefs of Staff and the DCI. The chairman of the NSC is the President himself. Intended to serve as the principal advisory board on matters of national security and foreign policy, the NSC has in practice functioned to a level of importance determined by the chief executive.

In general, Democratic presidents have tended to take an *ad hoc* approach to the NSC, while Republicans, starting with Dwight D. Eisenhower, have relied more heavily on the NSC, or at least on the National Security Advisor, who played an important role in the administrations of

Richard M. Nixon, George W. Bush, and others. The role of the National Security Advisor, officially titled the Assistant to the President for National Security Affairs, is not mentioned in the National Security Act, and emerged only during the Kennedy administration.

In addition to the four statutory members, the two statutory advisors on military and intelligence affairs, and the National Security Advisor, the Secretary of the Treasury is a regular attendee at NSC meetings. The Chief of Staff to the President, Counsel to the President, and Assistant to the President for Economic Policy are invited to attend any NSC meeting, while the Attorney General and the Director of the Office of Management and Budget (OMB) are invited to attend those meetings that pertain to their responsibilities. The directors of other executive departments and agencies, as well as other senior officials, are called to attend when appropriate. Under the George W. Bush administration, the Director (later Secretary) of Homeland Security has been a regular participant in NSC meetings.

PFIAB. Established by President Eisenhower in 1956, PFIAB is an independent advisory board within the Executive Office of the President. It consists of 16 uncompensated members, selected by the President from outside the ranks of government. PFIAB reviews the activities and performance of all agencies involved in intelligence activities, and advises the President on its assessments of their performance. It also provides the President with input on the objectives, conduct, and coordination of activities by members of the Intelligence Community.

Under the aegis of the PFIAB is the three-member Intelligence Oversight Board (IOB), established by President Gerald Ford in 1976. The IOB is responsible for oversight regarding the legality and propriety of intelligence activities, particularly—according to its charter—those "intelligence activities that the IOB believes may be unlawful or contrary to executive order or presidential directive." Originally an independent body, the IOB became a standing committee of the PFIAB in 1997.

The Intelligence Community, Budgeting, and Congress

In addition to leading the CIA, DCI serves as the President's principal advisor on intelligence matters. He also leads the Intelligence Community, which, along with CIA, includes 13 other agencies within the departments of Defense, State, Energy, Justice, the Treasury, and Homeland Security. Among the members of the Intelligence Community are the Federal Bureau of Investigation, National Security Agency, and Defense Intelligence Agency.

DCI reports to the President both directly and (depending on the operational structure of the administration in question) through the National Security Advisor. As head of the Intelligence Community, DCI presents the President with the annual Intelligence Community budget, known as the National Foreign Intelligence Program (NFIP).

In preparing the budget for intelligence and national security activities in the coming fiscal year, the President also relies on the Secretary of Defense. The latter presents the President with two budgets: the Joint Military Intelligence Program (JMIP) for military intelligence, and Tactical Intelligence and Related Areas (TIARA) for specific tactical intelligence requirements of the military services.

Using the NFIP, JMIP, and TIARA budgets, the President proceeds to establish an overall DOD intelligence budget with the help of the National Security Advisor and the OMB. He then presents these requests to Congress, which, once it approves the request, passes the annual intelligence authorization act. The latter originated in the late 1970s, as a result of congressional distrust toward the executive branch in the fallout from the Watergate scandal.

Intelligence authorization acts, in addition to numerous mechanisms for direct congressional oversight of intelligence, gives Congress influence over intelligence activities. In the case of the intelligence authorization process, Congress may refuse budgeting for certain requested activities, with the result being a tug-of-war between the White House and Capitol Hill. On the other hand, the President himself may veto intelligence authorization acts, which also include other, non-budgetary, provisions.

■ **FURTHER READING:**

BOOKS:

Andrew, Christopher M. *For the President's Eyes Only: Secret Intelligence and the American Presidency from Washington to Bush.* New York: HarperCollins, 1995.

Gore, Albert. *The Intelligence Community: Accompanying Report of the National Performance Review, Office of the Vice President.* Washington, D.C.: U.S. Government Printing Office, 1993.

Helgerson, John L. *Getting to Know the President: CIA Briefings of Presidential Candidates, 1952–1992.* Washington, D.C.: Central Intelligence Agency, 1996.

Mann, Thomas E. *A Question of Balance: The President, Congress.* Washington, D.C.: Brookings Institution, 1990.

Thompson, Kenneth W. *The President, the Bureaucracy, and World Regions in Arms Control.* Lanham, MD: University Press of America, 1998.

SEE ALSO

Executive Orders and Presidential Directives
Intelligence Authorization Acts, United States Congress
Intelligence Community
Intelligence, United States Congressional Oversight
National Security Strategy, United States
NIC (National Intelligence Council)
NSC (National Security Council)
PFIAB (President's Foreign Intelligence Advisory Board)
Politics: The Briefings of United States Presidential Candidates
United States, Intelligence and Security

Pretty Good Privacy (PGP)

■ LEE W. LERNER

PGP, or Pretty Good Privacy, is a security software application used for the encryption and decryption of data. In 1991, Philip R. Zimmermann wrote PGP for the purpose of sending secured data across an insecure network, such as the internet. Individuals, businesses, and governments use strong cryptography programs such as PGP to secure networks, emails, documents, and stored data.

PGP was originally designed as a combination of RSA encryption and a symmetric key cipher known as Bass-O-Matic. RSA is a public key cryptographic algorithm named after its designers Ronald Rivest, Adi Shamir, and Leonard Adleman. The RSA algorithm, developed in 1977 (earlier versions of which were partially developed by intelligence agencies), quickly became a major advancement in cryptology. The RSA algorithm depends upon the difficulty in factoring very large composite numbers and is currently the most commonly used encryption and authentication algorithm in the world. The RSA algorithm forms were used in the development of modern Internet web browsers, spreadsheets, email, and word processing programs.

Bass-O-Matic is a conventional (often referred to as symmetric) key algorithm. Bass-O-Matic was later replaced by another conventional key algorithm known as IDEA, which enabled more powerful encryption technology.

Conventional cryptology is based on the concept that one key is used in both the encryption and decryption process. The major benefit of conventional cryptology is the speed in which the encryption process takes place. Conventional encryption can be up to one thousand times faster than public key encryption. However, secure key distribution is a major problem in this form of cryptology.

In 1975, Whitfield Diffie and Martin Hellman developed public key cryptology to increase the security of exchanging keys. Each user of a public key based system has a public and private key. First, the user publishes the public key to a server or contact. Next, the contact encrypts the message to the user's public key. Finally, the user employs the private key to decrypt the cipher text (encoded message) received. The combination of both public and conventional key cryptology makes PGP a hybrid cryptosystem. This allows for users of PGP to be able to securely exchange keys and still have a speedy transaction of secured data.

PGP follows a simple process when encrypting plaintext into cipher text. PGP first compresses the document desired for encryption. This saves modem transmission time and strengthens the cryptographic security of the plaintext. Next, PGP creates a session key. The key is a number correlating to the random movements of the user's mouse and the keys that are typed. The key then works with a cryptographic algorithm to encrypt the plaintext. A cryptographic algorithm is a mathematical function in which a computable set of steps must be followed to achieve a desired result. The strength of this encryption is dependent on the strength of the algorithm.

After the data has been encrypted into cipher text, PGP encrypts the session key. The session key is encrypted to the recipient's public key. PGP uses digital certificates to prove the identity of a public key. The cipher text and encrypted session key are then transmitted to the recipient. When the recipient receives the data, PGP uses the user's private key to decrypt the session key. When PGP has recovered the session key, it can be used to decrypt the cipher text.

Though the plaintext has been recovered, there is still a question of authentication. PGP uses digital signatures to provide the recipient of an encryption with an origin and identification. Digital signatures are created in the opposite way a public cryptography system works. The sender encrypts a digital signature with their private key and attaches it to the rest of the data transmitted. When the digital signature is received, PGP decrypts it with the sender's public key. Through this process, PGP is able to determine the authenticity of the signature.

Digital signatures produce large amounts of data, slowing transmission and processing speeds. PGP uses a hash function to regulate the amount of data sent. The hash function takes variable amounts of data (the size of the plaintext) and produces a fixed amount called a message digest. PGP then creates a digital signature with the message digest and the user's private key. The hash function also helps to prove the authenticity of the encryption. If the encryption is changed after this process takes place, an entirely new message digest is created. This allows for PGP to detect encryption tampering.

Although PGP encryption has been available to the general public for several years, debate regarding encryption technologies and national security issues, especially in the United States, has ensued. Many government officials argue that strong cryptography programs should not be exported outside the United States. Security algorithms used in PGP type programs were classified as munitions by the United States government. As such, they remained subject to severe export control and restrictions that inhibited their widespread distribution and use. Due to these concerns, there are presently two available PGP applications: PGP and PGPi (international). Any user outside of the United States is currently required to utilize PGPi.

The National Institute of Standards and Technology (NIST), oversees the development of many cryptography standards. One such standard, developed by commercial entities and the United States National Security Agency (NSA) in the 1970s was termed the Data Encryption Standard (DES). In anticipation of increasing security needs, in the late 1990s, NIST began to work toward the implementation of the Advanced Encryption Standard AES to replace DES.

FURTHER READING:

BOOKS:

Kaufman, Charles, et. el. *Network Security: Private Communication in a Public World,* 2nd. ed. Upper Saddle River, NJ: Prentice Hall, 2002.

Stallings, William. *Cryptography and Network Security: Principles and Practice,* 3rd. ed. Upper Saddle River, NJ: Prentice Hall, 2002.

Zimmerman, Phillip. *The Official PGP User's Guide* Cambridge, MA: MIT Press, 1995.

SEE ALSO

Computer and Electronic Data, Destruction
Computer Fraud and Abuse Act of 1986
Computer Hackers
Computer Hardware Security
Computer Security Act (1987)
Computer Software Security
Computer Virus
Cryptology and Number Theory
Cyber Security
Encryption of Data

Privacy: Legal and Ethical Issues

▌ JUDSON KNIGHT

Among the foundational principles of the Western liberal tradition that binds the American political system is the belief that the rights of the individual, wherever possible, must be preserved against the authority of the state. Emanating from that principle is the implication that individuals have a right to privacy, a right implied—as noted by several distinguished Supreme Court justices over time—in the U.S. Constitution. Balancing and sometimes apparently contradicting this right to privacy is the need for security on a national and sometimes a local level. This conflict of needs and aims has given rise to public debate over numerous specific issues, including national security measures undertaken in the wake of the September 11, 2001, terrorist attacks.

Privacy Rights in Tort and Constitutional Law

A wide array of U.S. laws, both tort and constitutional, support the individual's right to privacy. In tort law, persons have a right to seek legal redress for invasions of privacy undertaken for the purposes of material gain, mere curiosity, or intention to defame. These protections extend to all persons under U.S. law, though public figures—a term strictly defined in legal statutes—have somewhat less broad rights of privacy.

Some national constitutions spell out the rights of the individual, with the assumption that all other privileges belong to the government. The U.S. Constitution, by contrast, delineates government authority, with the provision that all other rights belong to individuals. To James Madison and other founders of the republic, these guarantees did not go far enough, and therefore, Congress passed the Bill of Rights, or the first 10 amendments to the Constitution. Among these are several that would later figure heavily in debates over privacy: the First Amendment, with its protection of free speech; the Fourth Amendment, against unlawful search and seizure; and the Fifth Amendment, which provides for due process under law. The Fourteenth Amendment, passed after the Civil War to protect the rights of freed slaves, extends Fifth Amendment provisions to states as well.

Contrary to popular belief, neither the Constitution nor its amendments contain any reference to privacy as a right *per se*. The concept of "The Right to Privacy" comes from an influential 1890 *Harvard Law Review* article by that title, under which Supreme Court Justice Louis Brandeis, writing with Samuel Warren, put forward the proposition that privacy rights extend beyond mere protection against clear-cut intrusions on privacy. Thereafter, a number of landmark decisions in the Supreme Court broadened the concept of privacy as defined in constitutional law. Among these was *Griswold v. Connecticut* (1965), involving a state law that prohibited the use of contraceptives. Writing for the Court, which struck down the law, Justice William O. Douglas held that the "penumbra" of the First, Fourth, and Fifth collectively provides a "zone of privacy".

The Revolution of the 1970s

The 1970s saw a revolution in privacy rights, not only through the Court—whose *Griswold* decision set the stage for the protection of abortion rights in *Roe v. Wade* (1973)—but also in the legislative branch of government. In 1974, Congress passed the Privacy Act, which restricts the authority of government agencies to collect information on individuals or to disclose that information to persons other than the individual. The Privacy Act also requires agencies to furnish the individual with any information on him or her that the agency had in its files.

In 1967, Congress had passed the Freedom of Information Act (FOIA), which limits the ability of U.S. federal government agencies to withhold information from the public by classifying that information as secret, but it greatly expanded FOIA provisions in 1975. Together with the Privacy Act—the two are often referred to collectively as the Freedom of Information-Privacy Acts (FOIPA)—these served to further extend the rights of individuals against government intrusion. Like FOIA, the Federal Wiretapping Act of 1968 had been passed earlier, but it, too, was extended in the 1970s. (Today, all U.S. states have laws against wiretapping and telephone recording.)

Many of these changes occurred as a response, either directly or indirectly, to the Watergate scandal and the subsequent revelations of illegal wiretapping, recording, and surveillance activity conducted by the Nixon White House and other compartments of the federal government. In 1976, Congress passed the Foreign Intelligence Surveillance Act (FISA). FISA, which became law in 1978, placed checks and balances on the authority of government agencies to conduct surveillance on persons accused of conducting espionage—authority that had been misused by Federal Bureau of Investigation director J. Edgar Hoover in some domestic intelligence campaigns during the 1950s and 1960s.

Privacy Issues in the 1990s and Beyond

In September, 1997, Congress passed the Fair Credit Reporting Act (FCRA), which requires potential employers to obtain written authorization from a job candidate or employee before accessing records from a consumer reporting agency. The employer is also required to notify the employee or applicant if any adverse action is taken pursuant to a negative report. Thus federal law extended privacy rights to protect the individual from intrusion by businesses as well as the government.

Many privacy issues at the dawn of the twenty-first century involved new technologies and new developments in the national security environment. In the area of technology, the broadening of access to the Internet brought with it a number of concerns regarding government monitoring of e-mail and other traffic—concerns heightened by the revelation, in the late 1990s, that the National Security Agency and counterparts in other parts of the English-speaking world monitor global communications through the Echelon surveillance system. On the one hand, the Internet has provided new venues for illegal activity such as the dissemination of child pornography; on the other hand, groups such as the American Civil Liberties Union (ACLU) contend that government monitoring of such activities is often used against innocent persons.

The ACLU has been among the most vocal opponents to intensified security measures undertaken in the wake of the September 2001 bombings. In October 2001, Attorney General John Ashcroft presented a proposed antiterrorism bill that would broaden government authority under FISA. Questioning these and other measures, ACLU spokespersons, acknowledging the need for heightened security, stated that the ACLU's goal is to monitor the proposal for increased law enforcement power to ensure that they have maximum effectiveness with a minimal erosion of civil liberties."

■ FURTHER READING:

BOOKS:

Alderman, Ellen, and Caroline Kennedy. *The Right to Privacy.* New York: Knopf, 1995.

Branscomb, Anne W. *Who Owns Information? From Privacy to Public Access.* New York: Basic Books, 1994.

Diffie, Whitfield, and Susan Eva Landau. *Privacy on the Line: The Politics of Wiretapping and Encryption.* Cambridge, MA: MIT Press, 1998.

Harrison, Maureen, and Steve Gilbert. *Landmark Decisions of the United States Supreme Court.* Beverly Hills, CA: Excellent Books, 1991.

Henderson, Harry. *Privacy in the Information Age.* New York: Facts on File, 1999.

Rosen, Jeffrey. *The Unwanted Gaze: The Destruction of Privacy in America.* New York: Random House, 2000.

SEE ALSO

Cameras
Computer Keystroke Recorder
Domestic Intelligence
Echelon
FOIA (Freedom of Information Act)
Foreign Intelligence Surveillance Act
Genetic Information: Ethics, Privacy and Security Issues
Internet Surveillance
Pretty Good Privacy (PGP)
Security Clearance Investigations
Telephone Caller Identification (Caller ID)
Telephone Recording Laws
Telephone Recording System
Telephone Scrambler
Telephone Tap Detector
Watergate

Profiling

■ JUDSON KNIGHT

Profiling is the process of developing descriptions of the traits and characteristics of unknown offenders in specific criminal cases. It is often used in situations for which authorities have no likely suspect. There are two basic varieties of profiling: inductive, which involves the development of a profile based on known psychological typology; and deductive profiling, which reasons exclusively from the details of the victim and crime scene to develop a unique profile. Profiling as a law enforcement tool emerged in the late 1960s, and today, the leading entity engaged in profiling is the National Center for the Analysis of Violent Crime (NCAVC) of the Federal Bureau of Investigation (FBI).

Profiling should not be confused with *racial profiling.* Racial profiling, a topic surrounded with considerable controversy, came to the forefront in the late 1980s and

1990s, when a number of activists and social scientists maintained that law enforcement officials tended to single out African Americans, particularly young males, for arrest and abuse. After the September, 2001, terrorist attacks, random searches and other forms of attention directed toward against Middle Eastern males were also decried in some quarters as racial profiling.

In contrast to the socially explosive topic of racial profiling, criminal profiling—while it may be controversial among law enforcement authorities and forensic scientists, not all of whom agree on its merits or the proper approach to it—is not controversial in society at large. In fact, television programs concerning crime, as well as dramatic portrayals in popular films have raised considerable public interest in profiling. Thanks to this interest, leading profilers are well-known outside the law-enforcement community.

Misconceptions.
Indicative of this popularity was the prominence given to profiling opportunities on a frequently asked questions (FAQ) page in the employment section of the FBI's Web site in 2003. Alone among FBI specialties, profiling was featured with the question "I just want to be an FBI 'profiler.' Where do I begin the application process?" As the bureau noted in its response, "You first need to realize the FBI does not have a job called 'Profiler.'" The answer went on to discuss the NCAVC, located at FBI headquarters in Quantico, Virginia. The FBI also noted on the site that "these FBI Special Agents [involved in profiling] don't get vibes or experience psychic flashes while walking around fresh crime scenes. [Instead, profiling] is an exciting world of investigation and research. . . . "

Two varieties of profiling.
Criminal profiling originated from the work of FBI special agents Howard Teten and Pat Mullany in the late 1960s. It is especially used in cases involving serial killers, who usually are not personally acquainted with their victims. Most murders involve people who know one another, and in most murder investigations, likely suspects can be readily identified. For example, if a married woman is murdered, her husband often quickly becomes the focus of police investigation. If, however, there is nothing to suggest that a victim has been murdered by someone he or she knows, or if the victim's identity is unknown, profiling may be necessary in order to develop a set of leads for investigators.

Criminal profilers make use of two types of reasoning, which, in the view of some profiling experts, constitute two schools of thought. Inductive criminal profiling, like the larger concept of induction in the philosophical discipline of epistemology (which is concerned with the nature of knowledge) develops its portrait of a suspect based on the results gathered from other crime scenes. Inductive criminal profiles draw on formal and informal studies of known criminals, on the experience of the profiler, and on publicly available data sources, to provide guidance.

By contrast, deductive criminal profiling relies purely on information relating to the crime scene, the victim, and the evidence. Instead of drawing on the facts of other crimes, the deductive profile draws only on the information relating to the crime in question. For instance, if a search of the crime scene reveals that the killer had smoked an expensive variety of cigar, this would lead the deductive profiler to posit that the killer was wealthy and probably well educated. The profiler working through pure deduction would not, however, seek to compare this fact with information on other killers in the past who had smoked expensive cigars.

NCAVC and VICAP.
FBI profilers are supervisory special agents with NCAVC. In order to be considered for the program, an individual must have served as an FBI special agent for three years. However, due to high competition for placement in the program, individuals selected usually have eight to 10 years of experience with the bureau. Newly assigned personnel typically undergo a structured training program of more than 500 hours. Alongside these special agents work other, civilian, personnel in positions that include intelligence research specialist, violent crime resource specialist, and crime analyst. It is their job to research violent crime from a law enforcement perspective, and to provide support to NCAVC special agents.

In addition to developing criminal profiles, NCAVC provides major case management advice and threat assessment services to law-enforcement officials around the nation and the world. Special agents may also provide law enforcement officials with strategies for investigation, interviewing, and prosecution. Among the services provided by NCAVC to the law enforcement community at large is VICAP, the Violent Criminal Apprehension Program.

VICAP is a nationwide data information center tasked with collecting, collating, and analyzing information on violent crimes, particularly murder. Cases eligible for VICAP include solved or unsolved homicides or attempts, especially ones involving an abduction; apparently random, motiveless, or sexually oriented homicides; murders that are known or suspected to be part of a series (i.e., serial murder); unresolved missing persons cases, particularly those in which foul play is suspected; and unidentified dead bodies for whom the manner of death is known or suspected to be homicide.

Local law enforcement agencies participating in VICAP are able to draw on its information database in solving crimes. For example, if a murder were committed with a rare variety of handmade pistol, VICAP could be consulted for information on other cases involving such a weapon. Once a case has been entered into the VICAP database, it is compared continually against all other entries on the basis of certain aspects of the crime. VICAP has been used to solve a number of homicides nationwide.

■ FURTHER READING:

BOOKS:

Ainsworth, Peter B. *Offender Profiling and Crime Analysis.* Portland, OR: Willan, 2001.

Evans, Collin. *The Casebook of Forensic Detection: How Science Solved 100 of the World's Most Baffling Crimes.* New York: Wiley, 1996.

Holmes, Ronald M. *Profiling Violent Crimes: An Investigative Tool.* Newbury Park, England: Sage Publications, 1989.

Turvey, Brent E. *Criminal Profiling: An Introduction to Behavioral Evidence Analysis.* San Diego, CA: Academic Press, 1999.

ELECTRONIC:

Federal Bureau of Investigation. <http://www.fbi.gov> (May 4, 2003).

SEE ALSO

FBI (United States Federal Bureau of Investigation)
Forensic Science
Intelligence and Counter-Espionage Careers
Justice Department, United States

Propaganda, Uses and Psychology

■ CARYN E. NEUMANN

Propaganda is a form of communication that attempts to influence the behavior of people by affecting their perceptions, attitudes and opinions. Propaganda can restructure hostile attitudes, reinforce friendly attitudes, or maintain the continued neutrality of those people who are undecided. A characteristic of propaganda is its reliance upon devices designed to discourage reflective thought such as name calling, use of glittering generalities like "freedom" or "injustice," use of prestigious symbols, endorsements from prominent persons, endorsements from regular folk, get-on-the-bandwagon representations, and cardstacking to minimize or maximize events. Propaganda does not always advance an argument and is often aimed instead at advancing an image or general system of ideas that implicitly supports an action or policy.

While propaganda has existed for ages, the advent of twentieth century mass communication enabled it to flourish and it has been employed with increasing sophistication in all major conflicts beginning with World War I.

Unlike other forms of warfare, the success or failure of propaganda cannot be immediately known or measured. It is a continuous process that persuades without seeming to do so. The sources and accuracy of propaganda mark it as being one of three forms: white, black, or gray.

White propaganda comes from a source that is identified correctly and the information in the message tends to be accurate. The Voice of America (VOA) is an example of a white propaganda unit because it presents a positive image of the United States. While the VOA is not connected with the military, armed forces have commonly used radio to destroy the enemy's will to resist with a minimum loss of blood. During the 1991 Persian Gulf War, the U.S. Fourth Psychological Operations Group produced a white propaganda radio program that featured testimonials from happy Iraqi prisoners of war along with prayers from the Koran and the location of U.S. bomb targets for the next day. A great majority of Iraqi defectors said that the broadcasts influenced their decision to surrender. White propaganda attempts to build credibility with the audience by convincing them of the good intentions of the sender.

Black propaganda, from a source that is often well concealed, employs a high number of distortions or outright falsehoods. It is also categorized as disinformation, from the name of a KGB division, *dezinformatsia,* that specialized in such a form of creative deceit. In World War I, Germany made a crude and futile attempt to persuade French soldiers at the front to abandon their units by posting large signs advising them that British men were engaging in sexual relations with the soldiers' wives. By World War II, the same sort of message designed to demoralize troops received more polish through the transmissions of Lord Haw Haw and Tokyo Rose. A similar style of disinformation came in the form of "The New England Broadcasting Station." This station, supposedly run by discontented British subjects, began sending radio transmissions of war news in the weeks prior to the planned invasion of England by Germany. The station was actually an undercover German operation that aimed to reduce the morale of the British people. Black propaganda seeks to destroy the credibility of opposition governments.

Gray propaganda may or may not be correctly identified and the accuracy of the information is uncertain. In the aftermath of the failed 1961 CIA-led Bay of Pigs invasion, the VOA denied any American involvement. While the source of the information was clearly identified as the VOA, the information was false. Sometimes gray propaganda is true and designed to embarrass an enemy. During the Cold War, the Soviet Union used examples of American racism, such as lynchings, to slow U.S. advances throughout Africa, Asia, and Latin America. The damage that this gray propaganda caused to foreign relations ultimately prompted the U.S. government to back domestic civil rights legislation.

By turning enemies into friends or neutrals through the power of persuasion, propaganda offers a relatively

A crowd of people read the displayed information at the Nazi propaganda exhibition in Munich, Germany, in 1937. ©HULTON-DEUTSCH COLLECTION/CORBIS.

inexpensive way of reducing armed conflict and bolstering national security. For this reason, it will most likely remain a popular weapon in government arsenals.

■ FURTHER READING:

BOOKS:

Dudziak, Mary L. *Cold War Civil Rights: Race and the Image of American Democracy.* Princeton: Princeton University Press,2000.

Jowett, Garth S., and Victoria O'Donnell. *Propaganda and Persuasion.* Thousand Oaks, CA: Sage Publications, 1999.

Sproule, J. Michael. *Channels of Propaganda.* Bloomington, IN: EDINFO Press, 1994.

SEE ALSO

Bay of Pigs
Black Ops
CIA (United States Central Intelligence Agency)
Cold War (1945–1950): The start of the atomic age
Cold War (1950–1972)
Disinformation
Information Warfare
KGB (Komitet Gosudarstvennoi Bezopasnosti, USSR Committee of State Security)
Lord Haw-Haw
Persian Gulf War
Tokyo Rose
Voice of America (VOA), United States

Pseudoscience Intelligence Studies

■ JUDSON KNIGHT

During the 1960s, Soviet intelligence services became interested in the possible use of paranormal abilities for "psychic intelligence" or "remote viewing"—the use of telekinetic powers to glimpse or otherwise comprehend objects not immediately available to the senses. Remote viewing, it was claimed, would help intelligence officers gain access to information that could not be seen or heard by ordinary means. U.S. intelligence officials, particularly in the Defense Intelligence Agency (DIA), learned of the Soviet interest, and themselves became fascinated with remote viewing. The result was a $20 million DIA program known as Stargate, which lasted throughout the 1980s. Ultimately red-flagged by CIA, Stargate in its heyday attracted considerable respect within sectors of the U.S. intelligence community.

Soviet Experiments in the 1960s

The catalyst for American interest in pseudoscientific intelligence methods was the publication, in 1970, of *Psychic Discoveries Behind the Iron Curtain.* According to authors Sheila Ostrander and Lynn Schroeder, a number of Soviet scientists were interested in various aspects of the paranormal, including telekinesis, extrasensory perception (ESP), parapsychology, and various other psychic phenomena. These scientists had worked with military and intelligence agencies in their country to explore methods for deployment of paranormal abilities for defense and intelligence-collection purposes.

Among the most intriguing stories included in the book was an account of an experiment involving rabbits. Electrodes were inserted into the brain of a mother rabbit, and baby rabbits—without implanted electrodes—were placed on a submarine that was then taken out to sea and submerged. A baby rabbit was killed, and as the scientists recorded, the brain of the mother, many miles away on shore, reacted at the moment of death. Setting aside all questions of animal cruelty and experimental ethics, the was interpreted to show that ESP existed and served to connect minds.

Early CIA Experiments

Psychic Discoveries elicited considerable interest in the use of the paranormal for intelligence-gathering, but U.S. programs in psychic intelligence seem to have started much earlier, probably sparked by an awareness of Soviet activities in this area. The CIA conducted its own experiments with remote viewing through its Directorate of Science and Technology (DS&T), beginning in the mid-1960s, and continuing for many years thereafter.

During the early part of this period, Carl Duckett, who became CIA Deputy Director for Science and Technology in 1966, funded remote viewing experiments at the Stanford Research Institute (SRI) in California. Remote viewers at SRI attempted to locate targets of interest in the Soviet Union, and in other nations whose nuclear capabilities were a matter of concern to the United States.

Evaluating results. In late 1975, a team at Los Alamos National Laboratory conducted a study of one experiment, in which remote viewer Pat Price evaluated a site under investigation by both the CIA (which called it URDF-3, or Unidentified Research and Development Facility-3) and the Air Force, which referred to it as PNUTS, or Possible Nuclear Underground Test Site. The Los Alamos evaluator compared Price's "findings" with those obtained by satellite photography.

On the positive side, Price had "seen" a gantry crane that was actually there, but he had also discerned nine other objects whose presence the satellite revealed to be fictional. According to the Los Alamos report, from December 1975, "the validity of Price's remote viewing of URDF-3 appears to be a failure." Years later, after the end of the Cold War, American scientists had an opportunity to view the site firsthand, and learned that it was concerned with developing nuclear-powered rockets for space flight.

DIA and Stargate. During the late 1970s, DIA began developing a project codenamed Grillflame, which ultimately became Stargate. The connection between *Psychic Discoveries* and Stargate is not a clear one, but Pentagon officials did examine the book, and Stargate seems to have been a U.S. response to Soviet efforts.

At the time of the book's publication, DIA was a young agency attempting to prove itself within the Intelligence Community. Formed in 1961, it had not fared well during the Vietnam War, when it faced considerable intransigence from the intelligence agencies of the various military services. The idea of using unorthodox means to gain intelligence was seen by some personnel to offer a way of gaining a competitive edge within the Intelligence Community.

Although lacking in scientific evidence, Stargate drew in a number of respectable intelligence organizations—not just DIA, but also the National Security Agency (NSA), which in September, 1979, requested remote viewers' help with regard to Soviet submarine construction projects. One remote viewer produced a surprisingly accurate reading, predicting the launch of a new sub in 100 days. In fact the craft was glimpsed 120 days later, but it had fewer than the 18 to 20 missile launch tubes predicted by the remote viewer. Skeptics of remote viewing point out that "hits" were often based upon clues given to "viewers" and that misses were numerous.

In fairness to Stargate, it should be noted that Joseph McMoneagle, one of the chief remote viewers, later said that all readings by remote viewers were intended merely to augment, not supplant, intelligence gained by more conventional means. Additionally, the NSA, the Joint Chiefs of Staff, the Drug Enforcement Administration, Secret Service, Customs Bureau, and Coast Guard requested readings from Stargate remote viewers. So, too, did the CIA, but in the mid-1990s the agency took over the program, had it evaluated scientifically, then cut off funding.

In 1995, as a result of an executive order by President William J. Clinton authorizing the declassification of certain materials, information on both the SRI program, initiated in 1972, and Stargate became public. Both programs appear to have lasted into the early 1990s, and when this information became public, many observers wondered just how the Intelligence Community could have invested so much money in such fanciful activities.

One explanation was the cultural environment of the United States at the time—an influence to which intelligence officials are not necessarily any less susceptible than ordinary citizens. The 1970s was the heyday of the paranormal, the occult—Satanism made the cover of *Time* magazine in 1972—and what scientists would describe as pseudoscience. Israeli psychic Uri Geller appeared to bend spoons with his mind on television, and popular TV programs such as *In Search of. . .* (hosted by *Star Trek*'s Leonard Nimoy) treated outlandish notions with the utmost of seriousness.

Despite the best efforts of professional skeptics like James Randi to expose the fraud in pseudoscience, the fascination with bizarre programs continued. During the 1970s, bestsellers such as Erik von Daniken's *Chariots of the Gods* promised evidence that extraterrestrial visitors had left countless clues of their ancient journeys to Earth at sites such as the Great Pyramids in Egypt. Interest in Nostradamus's writings swelled, and religious cults flourished. It was an ideal time for experimentation in psychic intelligence-gathering, and thus, it seems to be no accident that the CIA and DIA programs took place during this period.

Additionally, there was the desire, noted earlier, to keep up with the Soviets. Herein lies an irony. Though the United States would attempt to develop its own psychic intelligence programs in competition with the Soviet Union, it appears that the Soviets were only trying to keep up with the Americans in the first place. *Psychic Discoveries* noted that Soviet experiments were sparked by a 1959 report in the French magazine *Constellation* regarding alleged telepathy experiments conducted by the U.S. Navy. The article, "Thought Transmission—Weapon of War," was based on a misreading or misunderstanding of Navy activities. Therefore it is possible to characterize experiments in psychic intelligence on both sides of the iron curtain as, to some degree, a comedy of errors.

■ FURTHER READING:

BOOKS:

Mandelbaum, W. Adam. *The Psychic Battlefield: A History of the Military-Occult Complex.* New York: St. Martin's Press, 2000.

Morehouse, David. *Psychic Warrior: Inside the CIA's Stargate Program: The True Story of a Soldier's Espionage and Awakening.* New York: St. Martin's Press, 1996.

Ostrander, Sheila, and Lynn Schroeder. *Psychic Discoveries Behind the Iron Curtain.* Englewood Cliffs, NJ: Prentice-Hall, 1970.

ELECTRONIC:

Haines, Gerald K. A Die-Hard Issue: CIA's Role in the Study of UFOs, 1947–90. *Studies in Intelligence* 1, No. 1, 1997. Central Intelligence Agency. <http://www.cia.gov/csi/studies/97unclass/ufo.html> (April 28, 2003).

Richelson, Jeffrey T. Science, Technology and the CIA. National Security Archive, George Washington University. <http://www.gwu.edu/~nsarchiv/NSAEBB/NSAEBB54/index2.html> (April 24, 2003).

UFOs. Central Intelligence Agency FOIA. <http://www.foia.cia.gov/ufo.asp> (April 28, 2003).

SEE ALSO

Area 51 (Groom Lake, Nevada)
CIA (United States Central Intelligence Agency)
CIA Directorate of Science and Technology (DS&T)
DIA (Defense Intelligence Agency)

Pseudorandom Number Generators (PNGs).

SEE *Cipher Pad.*

Psychotropic Drugs

■ JUDYTH SASSOON

Psychotropic drugs are a loosely defined grouping of agents that have effects on psychological function and include the antidepressants, hallucinogens, and tranquilizers. They are all compounds that affect the functioning of the mind through pharmacological action on the central nervous system. Psychotropic drugs are ubiquitous in our society and encompass both prescription psychiatric medications and illegal narcotics, as well as many over the counter remedies. Because these compounds affect human behavior, there is much suspicion, misunderstanding, and controversy surrounding their use. Sedative drugs first appeared in the late 1800s. They were followed by barbiturates and amphetamines in the early 1900s. But it was drugs such as chlorpromazine hydrochloride (Thorazine) and lithium, introduced in the 1950s that dramatically affected psychiatric medicine. Medicine essentially recognizes four main psychotropic drug categories: antipsychotics, mood stabilizers, antianxiety agents and antidepressants.

Antipsychotics include chlorpromazine, which was released in 1954 for the treatment of schizophrenia. Originally designated as a major tranquilizer, it was also found to be effective in subduing the hallucinations and delusions of psychotic patients. Since then, other antipsychotics, including haloperidol (Haldol) and clozapine (Clozaril) were developed for the treatment of various kinds of psychosis. Mood stabilizers were first recognized following Australian psychiatrist John F. J. Cade's 1949 discovery of the beneficial effects of lithium on manic-depressive disorder. Patients with schizophrenia, however, did not respond to lithium, leading psychiatrists to a degree of diagnostic precision that was previously not possible. Recently, some antiepileptic medicines—valproic acid (Depakene) and carbamazepine (Epitol, Tegretol) have also been used to treat manic-depressive disorder. Barbiturates were widely prescribed before the 1960s to relieve anxiety, but were found to be highly sedating and addictive and did not always work successfully. Chlordiazepoxide (e.g. Librium) and the other benzodiazepine agents developed from the 1960s to the 1980s rapidly replaced barbiturates. Antidepressants are possibly the most widely used psychotropic drugs in the United States. In any given 6-month period, about 3 percent of adult Americans experience severe depression. For the millions whose depressed mood becomes a clinical syndrome, though, psychotropic therapy is one way to relieve the symptoms. The tricyclic imipramine hydrochloride (Tofranil), developed during the late 1950s and introduced during the early 1960s, was the first of the now-available antidepressants and still is often prescribed. Research has progressed considerably since then and current theories attribute depression to psychological causes (e.g. low self-esteem, important losses in early life, history of abuse) and biological causes (e.g. imbalance of neurotransmitters, including serotonin and dopamine; disruptions in the sleep-wake cycle) as well as experiential and social factors. The various classes of antidepressants, tricyclics, MAOIs, serotonin-specific agents, and individual drugs including nefazodone (Serzone), mirtazapine (Remeron), venlafaxine (Effexor), and bupropion hydrochloride (BuSpar) target the biological causes. At present, the selective serotonin reuptake inhibitors (SSRIs) hold center stage, and fluoxetine hydrochloride (Prozac) is in the spotlight. The result of years of focused research and design, fluoxetine was rapidly accepted and prescribed to millions within a few months after its introduction in December 1987.

Psychotropic drugs and law enforcement. Though much of the research and understanding of psychopharmacology comes from the field of medicine and psychiatry, there are of course, other areas where psychotropic drugs have been used, ranging from illegal recreational use to the possibility of applying them as agents of "mind control." The Central Intelligence Agency (CIA) Crime and Narcotics Center monitors, reviews, and delivers information about international trafficking in illegal drugs and international organized crime to the nation's leaders and law enforcement agencies. Former Director of Central Intelligence William Webster created what became today's DCI Crime

and Narcotics Center in April 1989. The center is staffed by people from the 13 agencies making up the US Intelligence Community, including the CIA, as well as from law enforcement agencies. The Crime and Narcotics Center's staff are responsible for estimating the amount of illegal drugs, mainly coca, opium poppy, and marijuana, produced around the world. They also assist law enforcement agencies to break up drug and organized crime groups and help law enforcement agencies detect and capture illegal drug shipments.

The CIA's interest in psychotropic drugs does not end in law enforcement, however. MK-ULTRA was a CIA "mind-control" project backed during the Cold War years. Because the Soviets were supposedly researching a drug that could be used as a "truth serum," the CIA set out to beat them with heavily-funded research into consciousness altering drugs, and techniques of behavioral control. More recently, following the September 11, 2001, attacks on the World Trade Center in New York by al-Qaeda, there has been some discussion among some CIA and FBI staff, including William Webster, about the use of "truth drugs" to extract information from uncooperative terrorist suspects. United States Secretary of Defense Donald Rumsfeld asserted that narcoanalysis is not used by United States military and intelligence personnel, but suggested that other countries have made use of the technique in the interrogation of suspected terrorists. One such drug is sodium pentothal, which is used as a sedative and anaesthetic during surgery. It depresses the central nervous system, slows the heart rate and lowers blood pressure. Patients on whom the drug is used as an anaesthetic are usually unconscious less than a minute after it enters the veins. Because of its effectiveness as a sedative, it was also one of the first of three drugs to be used by the U.S. prison system during executions. In milder doses, the drug affects people such that they often become more communicative and share their thoughts without hesitation. Despite its name, however, sodium pentothal will not make a person tell the truth against their will; a recipient is only likely to lose inhibitions and therefore, may be more likely to volunteer the truth.

According to conventions set forth by the United Nations, the FBI and other U.S. law enforcement agencies disavow the practice of physically coercing or drugging prisoners, but point to the fact that many other countries around the world utilize drugs in interrogations. U.S. officials prefer to use psychology and investigative knowledge to extract information. Authorities are officially focused on making sure they obtain information without violating a suspect's constitutional rights because they do not want to jeopardize having such evidence ruled inadmissible in court. In attempting to prevent future acts of terrorism, however, authorities are sometimes focused more on obtaining quality information than they are on preparing cases for court, thus, in the present political situation, the FBI may be considering more aggressive methods of interrogation of terrorist suspects that might involve the use of psychoactive drugs.

A recent alleged use of a psychotropic drug by the U.S. was reported in the Russian newspaper, *Komsomolskaya Pravda.* In April 2001, it was reported that U.S. spies used drugged cookies and drinks to break the will of a Russian defense employee and recruit him as an agent. The employee was identified as a 58-year-old worker of a defense ministry facility near Zhukovsky air base, the Russian air force's top flight test center near Moscow. Whether accurate or not, the article illuminates the fact that the U.S. and Russia continue to show interest in spying on each other, despite better relations, and that psychotropic drugs may still play a part in espionage.

■ **FURTHER READING:**

BOOKS:

Maxmen, Jerrold S., and Nicholas G. Ward. *Psychotropic Drugs: Fast Facts,* 2nd ed. N.p., Norton & Company, 1995.

PERIODICALS:

Romanko, J. R. "Truth Extraction." *New York Times Magazine.* (November 19, 2000): 54.

SEE ALSO

Chemistry: Applications in Espionage, Intelligence, and Security Issues
CIA (United States Central Intelligence Agency)
FBI (United States Federal Bureau of Investigation)

Public Health Service (PHS), United States

■ BELINDA ROWLAND

The United States Public Health Service is a federal government agency that promotes the health of the people of the United States and the world. It is a principle component of the Department of Health and Human Services (HHS) and is composed of eight agencies. Among other duties, the Public Health Service is charged with, through its agencies, preparing for and leading the nation's medical response to a threat or disaster, whether naturally occurring or an act of terrorism.

The PHS originated in 1798 through the passage of an act that provided for the care of injured and sick merchant seamen. Politicians of the time assumed that healthy seamen would protect the security and economic well being of the country. A marine hospital fund was created to provide medical services to merchant marines. Monies

for this fund came, in part, from an American seaman tax of 20 cents each month. This became the first program for medical insurance in the United States. Marine hospitals were established along coasts and inland waterways. By 1981, all of the marine hospitals and clinics had closed.

In 1870, the independently controlled network of hospitals was organized into the Marine Hospital Service. The Service was administered by the Supervising Surgeon General, a title that was later changed to Surgeon General. At this time, the Service developed a military organization and approach. The medical officers were called surgeons and had to pass entrance exams and wear uniforms. In 1889, legislation to formalize the uniformed service aspect of the Service created the Commissioned Corps. As a result, medical officers were given military titles and pay.

By the late 1800s, the activities of the Marine Hospital Service extended beyond the care of seamen. In the effort to control infectious disease, the Service was given the power to quarantine and was responsible for the medical examinations of immigrants. As a result of its expanding responsibilities, in 1902 the name of the service was changed to the Public Health and Marine Hospital Service. The name "Public Health Service" was adopted in 1912.

The PHS celebrated its 200th anniversary in 1998. At that time, it employed about 5,700 Commissioned Corps officers and 51,000 civilians. In 1993, the budget of the PHS was 17 billion dollars. The PHS is administered by the Assistant Secretary for Health and the Surgeon General. It is composed of the Office of Public Health and Science, 10 Regional Health Administrators, and eight agencies. The eight agencies within the PHS are:

■ Centers for Disease Control and Prevention (CDC). The mission of the CDC is to promote health through the prevention and control of disease, injury, and disability. The CDC functions on both national and international levels.

■ Agency for Toxic Substances and Disease Registry (ATSDR). The ATSDR mission is to prevent the exposure to and adverse effects of toxic substances in the environment.

■ National Institutes of Health (NIH). The NIH is a medical research center that conducts and funds medical research with the goal of achieving better health for the people of the United States and the world. It is composed of 27 Institutes and Centers and is one of the world's leading medical research centers.

■ Food and Drug Administration (FDA). The FDA assures the safety and effectiveness of drugs, medical devices, and biological products as well as the safety of cosmetics and foods.

■ Substance Abuse and Mental Health Services Administration (SAMHSA). SAMHSA strives to reduce the illness, disability, death, and costs resulting from mental illness and substance abuse.

■ Health Resources and Services Administration (HRSA). The HRSA directs national health programs which assure that the American people have equal access to healthcare.

- Agency for Healthcare Research and Quality (AHRQ). The AHRQ funds research intended to improve the quality and outcome of healthcare, examine medical errors, address patient safety, and expand access to effective healthcare. It provides information to persons so that they can make better healthcare decisions.

- Indian Health Services (IHS). The IHS is the healthcare provider and advocate for Alaska Natives and American Indians.

■ FURTHER READING:

BOOKS:

Kondratas, R. *Images from the History of the Public Health Service.* N.p., U.S. Department of Health and Human Services, Public Health Service, 1994.

Kurian, G. T., ed. *A Historical Guide to the U.S. Government.* New York: Oxford University Press, 1998.

Mullan, F. *Plagues and Politics: The Story of the United States Public Health Service.* New York: Basic Book, Inc.,1989.

ELECTRONIC:

Kondrates, R. "Images from the History of the Public Health Service." April 27, 1998. <http://www.nlm.nih. gov/exhibition/phs_history/contents.htm> (December 14, 2002).

Office of the Public Health Service Historian, 18–23 Parklawn Building, 5600 Fishers Lane, Rockville, Maryland, 20857. (301) 443–5363. January 15, 2002. <http://lhncbc.nlm. nih.gov/apdb/phsHistory.> (December 14, 2002).

SEE ALSO

CDC (United States Centers for Disease Control and Prevention)
NIH (National Institutes of Health)
Health and Human Services Department, United States

Pueblo Incident

■ ADRIENNE WILMOTH LERNER

The *Pueblo* incident involved the 1968 seizure and hijacking of the USS*Pueblo* by North Korean military forces. The *Pueblo*, a naval intelligence ship, was conducting offshore surveillance of North Korean radar and radio installations when it was overtaken by the North Korean fleet. Following seizure of the ship, diplomatic tensions between the United States and North Korea heightened. North Korean officials claimed that the vessel, and the United States government, had been warned about conducting espionage activities in the region. In contrast, United States officials claimed that the *Pueblo* was seized in international waters, without provocation. The crew of the *Pueblo*

was detained in North Korea for nearly a year before their release was negotiated.

In 1967, the Navy refurbished one of its aging cargo ships, transforming it into a remote intelligence collection vessel. The old hull provided sufficient camouflage for the classified communications and radar locator systems onboard. Because the projected missions for the ship were considered low risk, the *Pueblo* was outfitted with only minimal defensive weapons. The U.S Fifth Air Force stationed in Fuchu, Japan, was designated to aid the *Pueblo* if necessary, but no specific teams were reserved from daily operations or put on alert.

The *Pueblo*, commanded by U.S. Navy Commander Lloyd. M. "Pete" Bucher, was assigned a new, and relatively inexperienced crew. The crew reported to San Diego for training maneuvers, and then departed for Pearl Harbor, Hawaii. Upon its arrival in Pearl Harbor, the *Pueblo* needed significant repairs to its steering engine.

Pueblo's mission CBIAC operations. The ultimate mission of the *Pueblo* crew remained classified until official mission orders were given to the crew after departing Pearl Harbor in late November, 1967. The ship arrived in Yokosuka, Japan, were further adjustments to onboard systems were made, and soon after departed on January 11, 1968.

Bound for international waters off the eastern coastline of North Korea, the *Pueblo's* stated mission was oceanographic research. However, the ship was part of a covert naval intelligence mission code named Operation Clickbeetle. The ship was charged with conducting a detailed survey of increasing North Korean naval activity, including assessing its potential fleet strength. Operation Clickbeetle further used the sophisticated equipment below decks on the *Pueblo* to intercept Soviet-North Korean communications, and locate radar and radio stations inland. Naval intelligence, in conjunction with the National Security Agency and the Naval Security Group Command, devised Operation Clickbeetle as part of a larger Cold War-era monitoring and espionage project intended to garner information about the influence of the Soviet Union on its satellite nations.

The *Pueblo* was assigned three operational areas in which to work, code named Pluto, Venus, and Mars. The first two areas, Pluto and Venus, off the northeast coast of the Korean Peninsula, yielded very little information. The *Pueblo* therefore moved to its final area further south, Mars, ahead of schedule. While in transit, the *Pueblo* crossed paths with a Soviet-made North Korean subchaser vessel. Since the *Pueblo* was instructed to maintain radio silence, it did not report the encounter to its support team in Japan. Furthermore, the *Pueblo* was 30 miles from the coastline, well into established international waters. After arriving in Op Area Mars on January 22, the *Pueblo* was again approached by two North Korean vessels. The two boats, apparent fishing trawlers, circled the *Pueblo* at close range. Sensing the foreign vessels may have been

The USS *Pueblo*, shown underway at sea, was captured in 1968 by North Korean patrol boats with 83 men aboard, who smashed intelligence-gathering equipment and burned sensitive documents just moments before the vessel was boarded by North Koreans. AP/WIDE WORLD PHOTOS.

sent to conduct reconnaissance on the *Pueblo*, Commander Bucher sent a civilian team to the ship's deck to conduct oceanographic research, maintaining the ship's cover. After the North Korean vessels left the area, the communications room aboard the *Pueblo* began intercepting increasing electronic communications between the ships and on shore stations. The *Pueblo* broke communications silence and notified Naval command of the situation.

Naval command received the message sent by the *Pueblo* fourteen hours later. During that time, a special unit of North Korean soldiers, dressed as South Korean military personnel, crossed the internationally established Demilitarized Zone into South Korea. The unit traveled to Seoul on a mission to attack South Korean government buildings and potentially assassinate the South Korean President. The North Korean saboteurs were discovered within miles of the presidential palace, and later executed. The incident brought the two nations again to the brink of war, and heightened tensions between the United States

and the Soviet Union. United States Naval Command decided that the *Pueblo* did not need to be informed about the event, and that the vessel was safe in international waters. They advised the ship merely to relocate an additional five nautical miles from the coastline, a full 15 nautical miles into international waters.

On January 23, a small fleet of North Korean ships approached the *Pueblo*. Commander Bucher and the crew noticed that the vessels were staffed at battle stations. The *Pueblo* intercepted transmissions revealing that the intent of the ships was to board the *Pueblo*, overtake the crew, and pilot the ship to North Korea. The crew was put on alert, and the *Pueblo* made way further into international waters. A North Korean subchaser signaled four nearby torpedo boats, and the fleet encircled the *Pueblo*. A North Korean military boarding party attempted to come aside the *Pueblo*, but the ship took evasive measures. Soon after, one of the North Korean vessels fired upon the *Pueblo*. Commander Bucher ordered all of the classified documents, information, and devices on the ship be destroyed. The ship then radioed Navy Pacific Fleet Command requesting emergency aid from military installations in Japan.

Hijack of the ship and crew.

Another group of North Korean military attempted to board the *Pueblo*, this time sweeping the deck with heavy fire. At this time, fireman Duane Hodges, was killed while fending off the group attempting the board the ship. The United States vessel again attempted evasive maneuvers, but the ship was too slow and heavily out gunned by the surrounding four torpedo boats, two subchasers, and two Soviet-made MiG aircraft. The *Pueblo* stopped in the water and heeded instructions to follow the lead North Korean boat. Commander Bucher ordered the vessel to travel at its slowest speed to give the men time to destroy the classified equipment onboard. The *Pueblo* then steamed full speed and again tried to evade the fleet. The North Korean forces fired explosive shells onto the deck of the ship, injuring several crewmembers. The *Pueblo* again stopped, and the ranking officer of the North Korean vessels ordered the boarding party to seize control of the U.S. ship. A North Korean fisherman, working for the military, then piloted the *Pueblo*, at full speed, into the harbor at Wonsan. The crewmembers of the *Pueblo* were tied up and corralled on the forward well deck, before being transferred to their quarters.

After the arrival of the ship into North Korean port, the crew and command of the *Pueblo* were paraded in front of national media as grand propaganda and then shipped to a series of secret detainment facilities. Their imprisonment began in a sparse, remote prison on January 24, 1968. Over the course of a year, the crew suffered mental and physical torture at the hands of their captors. Severe beatings were routine, and the crew received inadequate food and medical care. While United States diplomatic envoys tried to secure their release, the North Korean government provided staged photographs of the prisoners playing sports and enjoying leisure activities. Several crewmembers displayed their middle finger in the photographs to indicate that the photos were merely staged propaganda. When North Korean officials realized the gesture's meaning, the crew was again beaten.

Official diplomatic negotiations failed to secure the release of the *Pueblo* crew. Only after Commander Bucher and the other officers of the ship capitulated under severe duress to demands to sign a confession of wrongdoing and espionage activities did the North Korean government agree to discuss the release of their American prisoners. Members of the Military Armistice Committee met twenty eight times after the capture of the *Pueblo*. The United States and North Korean diplomats fought over the release of the ship's crew for nearly eleven months before the U.S. diplomatic mission agreed to admit guilt for the incident and sign a statement similar to that signed by the *Pueblo* officers. Before the official signing of the North Korean drafted document, diplomatic representative Major

General Gilbert Woodward issued a statement to the United States government disavowing the admission of culpability and dismissing the North Korean treaty. He further stated that the United States does not officially apologize for any past actions in the incident and that the North Korean document would be signed for no other purpose than to insure the release of the *Pueblo* crew. The command and crew of the *Pueblo* was officially released on December 28, 1968, after nearly a year of captivity.

Although the North Korean government finally capitulated to the release of the crew of *Pueblo*, they refused to return the ship itself. The ship was evaluated and photographed by North Korean military intelligence, as well as Soviet officials. Because much of the classified equipment onboard had been destroyed by the crew during the hijacking, the North Koreans and Soviets gained little information about United States remote intelligence gathering equipment and operations. The *Pueblo* remained in Wonsan harbor for nearly three decades, serving as a propaganda piece and museum. In 1998, the North Korean government relocated the *Pueblo*. The boat was towed to the west coast of North Korea, and remains a propagandistic museum.

The crew of the *Pueblo* received little recognition for their actions in preventing the transfer of classified material onboard the ship to enemy powers, or for their time in captivity. Following their release, crewmembers received the Purple Heart for wounds received in action. The *Pueblo's* officers endured a series of inquiries and hearings regarding their negotiations with their North Korean captors. At one time, naval officials considered court marshal for Commander Bucher and several other officers for signing the North Korean written confession of American wrongdoing. However, no member of the command or crew ever received disciplinary action. The lack of recognition for their service, and the numerous conduct inquiries, drew sharp criticism from the veterans of Operation Clickbeetle and the public. At the end of the Vietnam War, a series of retrospective stories in a national magazine drew attention to the *Pueblo* Incident and the plight of the *Pueblo* crew. The Navy then granted several more awards to various crewmembers, including a posthumous award of the Silver Star to Duane Hodges. In 1990, in accordance with a special act of Congress, the crew and command of the *Pueblo* was finally granted Prisoner of War (POW) status for their time in captivity.

The *Pueblo* was the first United States Navy vessel commandeered since the American Civil War. It was the only ship to surrender to hostile forces, other than those with whom the United States was at war, since the *Chesapeake* in 1807.

■ FURTHER READING:

BOOKS:

Bucher, Loyd M. *My Story*. New York: Doubleday, 1970.

Lerner, Mitchell B. *The Pueblo Incident: A Spy Ship and the Failure of American Foreign Policy.* Lawrence, KS: University Press of Kansas, 2002.

SEE ALSO

Korean War
North Korea, Intelligence and Security
Radio, Direction Finding Equipment
Vietnam War

Purple Machine

▌ ADRIENNE WILMOTH LERNER

The Purple Machine was an Allied codename for one of several Japanese cipher machines used during World War Two. The nickname Purple Machine was derived from the name of the code the machine produced. The first intercepted Japanese code was dubbed "Orange" by American code breakers. As the codes increased in sophistication and difficulty to decipher, cryptologists referred to the various cipher permutations with the names of colors. "Purple" was the most difficult Japanese code to break, and was used to transmit diplomatic messages from 1939 until 1945.

The mechanics of the Purple Machine were similar to other Axis encoding machines, such as the German Enigma cipher. The Purple Machine used the twenty-six-letter Latin alphabet, programmed into a pegboard with corresponding wires that governed cipher wheels, or rotors. The machine itself consisted of a typewriter joined by wires and a circuit board to a series of four rotors that shifted the type in various permutations on a second typewriter to produce coded text. The coded text was sent by wire, preceeded by a series of coded numbers that revealed the permutations used to create the code. With the setting adjusted as specified, the encoded text could

Two intelligence analysts work at Purple code deciphering machines at the headquarters of the U.S. Army cryptanalysis service in Arlington, Virginia, in 1944. AP/WIDE WORLD PHOTOS.

then be deciphered by again running it through the machine.

While many pre-war Japanese codes were broken mathematically with pen and paper, effectively deciphering Purple required constructing an identical cipher machine. American cryptologist William Friedman built a replica of the Purple Machine, based on intelligence information, in 1939. When the machine became operational, American code breakers were able to monitor most Japanese diplomatic messages that used the Purple code.

While breaking Purple gave U.S. intelligence services a great deal of information regarding diplomatic activities and strategies, it seldom yielded specific information regarding naval actions or fleet positions. The Japanese used a separate code for military operations, fleet positions, and troop deployments. In the months prior to the bombing of Pearl Harbor in 1941, Purple Machine intercepts indicated that the Japanese were planning an attack, but the messages did not mention Hawaii, Pearl Harbor, or a date for such an attack. However, the Japanese government did use Purple to deliver their ultimatum the day before the attack. Cryptologists decoded the series of fourteen messages between the Japanese government and their embassy in Washington, D.C., and passed the messages along to the Department of the Navy. A further intercept in the early hours of December 7, 1941, indicated that the Japanese fleet was poised and awaiting the order to attack. No action was taken on the information in the intercepts, and the U.S. Pacific fleet was bombed in port at Pearl Harbor later that day.

After Pearl Harbor, deciphered Purple Machine intercepts yielded substantial intelligence information for the United States. Paired with deciphered Japanese Navy dispatches that used another broken code, Purple Machine intercepts helped the United States to victory at the battle of Midway. In the weeks before the battle, code breakers discovered a series of messages from Tokyo to Japanese diplomats and Navy officers that discussed battle strategy in the Pacific. Some of the communications yielded fleet positions. Decoded Purple messages also allowed Allied planes to track and shoot down a military flight carrying Japanese Admiral Isoroku Yamamoto.

Breaking Purple Machine code even aided the Allied effort on the European front. A long series of dispatches between Japanese diplomats in Germany and the Japanese command in Tokyo discussed meetings with Hitler and revealed information about German defenses in occupied France. This information helped Allied forces prepare for the D-Day invasion of the continent.

The Japanese remained confident throughout the war that the Purple Machine and its code remained unbroken by the Allies, and continued to use the code even in the weeks immediately following their surrender in 1945. In United States hearings regarding intelligence, military, and political oversights in the days prior to Pearl Harbor, the government revealed that it broke the Purple code before the outbreak of the war. It was the first time former Japanese forces heard that the secrecy of the Purple Machine had been long compromised.

■ **FURTHER READING:**

BOOKS:

Clark, Ronald William. *The Man Who Broke Purple: The Life of Colonel William F. Friedman, Who Deciphered the Japanese Code in World War II.* New York: Little & Brown, 1977.

Budiansky, Stephen. *Battle of Wits: The Complete Story of Codebreaking in World War II.* New York: Touchstone Books, 2002.

SEE ALSO

World War II
World War II, United States Breaking of Japanese Naval Codes

Q

Quadratic Sieves.

SEE *Cryptology and Number Theory.*

Quantum Physics: Applications to Espionage, Intelligence, and Security Issues

▌K. LEE LERNER/LARRY GILMAN

Quantum physics, which has been called "the science of the very small," is essential to the design of modern microelectronics. Without quantum physics it would not be possible to design the microscopic structures that make today's digital circuits possible. Such circuits, in turn, are essential to the conduct of all kinds of modern espionage, warfare, and security operations. The further application of quantum physics to computing and communications is at present being systematically researched by many groups, including the U.S. Quantum Information Science and Technology (QuIST) Program of the Defense Advanced Research Projects Agency (DARPA). DARPA has historically funded the development of such fundamental advances in electronics as the microchip.

Limitations of Conventional Electronics

Ordinary circuit components obey the laws of classical physics; that is, their behavior is predictable and single-valued. An integrated-circuit memory cell is either ON or OFF, never both at once. There is no upper limit on how large a device exhibiting such behavior can be; one could build a computer out of stars and planets, if one had the means to move them about. However, the laws of quantum physics place strict limits on how small a device can be and still behave classically. Quantum physics tells chip designers how small they can make their transistors and other circuit components and still obtain classical, causal behavior from them.

However, quantum effects (those physical laws that dominate the behavior of matter at the subatomic level) are not only an obstacle to infinite miniaturization, they can be exploited to produce devices that have no parallel in the macroscopic world, the world of large objects. An early example of such a device is the tunnel diode (invented in 1958), an electronic device that takes advantage of the fact that an individual subatomic particle can appear randomly on the far side of an otherwise insurmountable barrier (i.e., "tunnel" through the barrier). Despite a few oddities such as the tunnel diode, however, quantum phenomena have for decades been perceived by designers of computers and communications systems more as a limiting factor on conventional device size than as an invitation to build novel devices.

Since the 1990s, physicists have realized that quantum phenomena open the door to powerful new techniques in computing and communications. In particular, they are hoping to exploit the phenomenon of quantum "entanglement" to produce superfast computers, unbreakable cryptographic systems, and error-free transmission of information. All of these advances, when they become available in working devices, will have many uses in both the civil and military sectors.

The concepts of quantum entanglement and quantum information are basic to the development of new quantum computing, cryptography, and communications technologies, and are reviewed separately below.

Entanglement

Individual subatomic particles, such as photons, do not exist in single, well-defined states like on-off light switches.

Rather, they exist as a superposition of states. Experiments show, for example, that prior to observation (i.e., definitive interaction with a large-scale system) a photon can actually have more than one polarization at once and be in more than one place at once.

Not only can individual particles exist in superposed or ambiguous states prior to observation, but the superposed states of pairs, triplets, or larger groups of particles can be related to each other by means of entanglement. Entanglement arises because the superposed states of particles that have interacted directly retain a definite, permanent relationship even after the particles have separated. Two entangled photons, for example, may be sent to two different detectors, A and B. Individually the photons do not, while in transit, have definite polarizations. When the polarization of one of the photons is collapsed to a definite value by measurement at detector A, however, photon, bound for detector B, instantly takes on the opposite polarization. There is no delay; the effect is truly instantaneous.

Despite appearances, this does not offer a means of faster-than-light communication (which would contradict the special theory of relativity); there is, in principle, no way to control what polarization detector A observes. The observed value at detector A is random, and the value that is instantly imposed on the photon bound for detector B is also random. There is thus no way for A to signal to B by using the instantaneous relationship between the entangled photons. However, entanglement is still useful. Transmission of an identical string of random bits to two receivers is important in cryptography, and using a stream of entangled photons for transmitting that bitstream has the valuable property that it cannot be eavesdropped upon, as quantum physics declares that any effort to interfere with (i.e., measure) either entangled photon en route will be detectable by the intended receivers. Nonquantum or classical communications links cannot give this absolute privacy guarantee. Transmission of entangled photon pairs over tens of kilometers of optical fiber has recently been demonstrated, bringing quantum cryptography closer to practical realization.

Entangled photons can also be used to achieve what is termed superdense coding or quantum dense coding—the transmission of multiple bits of classical information through the transmission of a smaller number of qubits (entangled photons). Another application of entanglement is quantum teleportation, discussed further below.

Quantum Information and its Implications for Communications and Computing

The quantum phenomena of superposition and entanglement have important implications for computing and communications, even apart from cryptography. In classical information theory, the minimum unit of information is a bit (short for "binary digit," since a bit is usually, though arbitrarily, symbolized as a 1 or 0); in quantum information theory, the minimum unit of information is the quantum bit or qubit (pronounced CUE-bit). One qubit is the amount of quantum information stored by a microscopic system (e.g., photon) that exists in a superposed pair of states. Quantum computation applies logical operations to qubits, much as classical computation applies Boolean logical operations to bits. The advantage of quantum computation arises from the superposition property of quantum systems: L qubits (e.g., isolated atoms) can, through superposition, contain the equivalent of 2^L bits, and quantum-logical operations can be performed simultaneously on all those bits. The result, potentially, is massive parallelism with corresponding speedup of certain calculations. One important class of calculations that would be greatly speeded by a quantum computer is the factorization of a large integer N. Factorization is the discovery, given N, of two numbers x and y such that $x \times y = N$. For large N this is a time-consuming calculation, and it is on this difficulty that many cryptosystems (e.g., public-key cryptography) depend. When quantum computers are built, such cryptosystems will quickly become worthless, for the factorization problem with have become manageable even for very large N.

Many nuts-and-bolts obstacles remain, however, in the construction of a full-scale quantum computer. One challenge is the accurate transmission of quantum information—qubits, held in superposed quantum states—from one place to another within a quantum computer or between one quantum computer and another. Quantum teleportation may provide a practical answer to this problem. Quantum teleportation allows the perfect recreation of a quantum system at the far end of a transmission channel. In this technique, one member of an entangled photon pair is combined at a transmitter with the quantum system to be teleported—a photon, other particle, or even a collection of particles—in such a way that bits of classical information (1s and 0s) are produced that characterize the system to be teleported. Both the entangled photon and the system to be teleported are destroyed by this process; that is, they no longer exist as a superposition of quantum states, but are measured as having definite, unique values. The classical information (bits) derived by the transmitter from its measurements is sent in conjunction with the remaining member of the entangled photon pair to a distant receiver. The receiver can re-create or "resurrect" the original quantum system with all its superpositional ambiguity (qubit content) intact, just as if it had never been measured (destroyed) by the transmitting system. Because quantum physics declares that systems with identical quantum-mechanical descriptions are not only *similar* but are *the same*—have no individuality, cannot be distinguished from each other—the "resurrected" system in effect *is* the original system: that is, the original system has been teleported from the transmitter to the receiver, including whatever quantum information it contains. (Strictly speaking, every quantum system—e.g., photon—contains an infinite amount of information; most of this, however, is in principle unextractable.) Quantum teleportation has already been demonstrated at kilometer distances for single-particle systems, and may eventually be used to communicate quantum information without error from one part of a quantum computer to another. However, it will never be practical to teleport large systems of particles such as human beings; the number of bits to be transmitted would be prohibitively large.

■ FURTHER READING:

PERIODICALS:

Bennett, Charles H., and Peter W. Shor. "Privacy in a Quantum World." *Science* 284 (April 30, 1999):747–748.

Bennett, Charles H., and David P. DiVincenzo. "Quantum information and computation." *Nature* 404 (March 16, 2000): 247–255.

Taubes, Gary. "Quantum Mechanics: To Send Data, Physicists Resort to Quantum Voodoo." *Science* 274 (Oct. 25, 1996): 504–505.

SEE ALSO

Nanotechnology

Quarantine.

SEE *Communicable Diseases, Isolation, and Quarantine.*